Lecture Notes in Computer Science 6313

Commenced Publication in 1973
Founding and Former Series Editors:
Gerhard Goos, Juris Hartmanis, and Jan van Leeuwen

Kostas Daniilidis   Petros Maragos
Nikos Paragios (Eds.)

Computer Vision – ECCV 2010

11th European Conference on Computer Vision
Heraklion, Crete, Greece, September 5-11, 2010
Proceedings, Part III

 Springer

Volume Editors

Kostas Daniilidis
GRASP Laboratory
University of Pennsylvania
3330 Walnut Street, Philadelphia, PA 19104, USA
E-mail: kostas@cis.upenn.edu

Petros Maragos
National Technical University of Athens
School of Electrical and Computer Engineering
15773 Athens, Greece
E-mail: maragos@cs.ntua.gr

Nikos Paragios
Ecole Centrale de Paris
Department of Applied Mathematics
Grande Voie des Vignes, 92295 Chatenay-Malabry, France
E-mail: nikos.paragios@ecp.fr

Library of Congress Control Number: 2010933243

CR Subject Classification (1998): I.2.10, I.3, I.5, I.4, F.2.2, I.3.5

LNCS Sublibrary: SL 6 – Image Processing, Computer Vision, Pattern Recognition,
and Graphics

ISSN   0302-9743

ISBN   978-3-642-15557-4 Springer Berlin Heidelberg New York

springer.com

© Springer-Verlag Berlin Heidelberg 2010

Typesetting: Camera-ready by author, data conversion by Scientific Publishing Services, Chennai, India
Printed on acid-free paper   06/3180

Preface

The 2010 edition of the European Conference on Computer Vision was held in Heraklion, Crete. The call for papers attracted an absolute record of 1,174 submissions. We describe here the selection of the accepted papers:

- Thirty-eight area chairs were selected coming from Europe (18), USA and Canada (16), and Asia (4). Their selection was based on the following criteria: (1) Researchers who had served at least two times as Area Chairs within the past two years at major vision conferences were excluded; (2) Researchers who served as Area Chairs at the 2010 Computer Vision and Pattern Recognition were also excluded (exception: ECCV 2012 Program Chairs); (3) Minimization of overlap introduced by Area Chairs being former student and advisors; (4) 20% of the Area Chairs had never served before in a major conference; (5) The Area Chair selection process made all possible efforts to achieve a reasonable geographic distribution between countries, thematic areas and trends in computer vision.

- Each Area Chair was assigned by the Program Chairs between 28–32 papers. Based on paper content, the Area Chair recommended up to seven potential reviewers per paper. Such assignment was made using all reviewers in the database including the conflicting ones. The Program Chairs manually entered the missing conflict domains of approximately 300 reviewers. Based on the recommendation of the Area Chairs, three reviewers were selected per paper (with at least one being of the top three suggestions), with 99.7% being the recommendations of the Area Chairs. When this was not possible, senior reviewers were assigned to these papers by the Program Chairs, with the consent of the Area Chairs. Upon completion of this process there were 653 active reviewers in the system.

- Each reviewer got a maximum load of eight reviews—in a few cases we had nine papers when re-assignments were made manually because of hidden conflicts. Upon the completion of the reviews deadline, 38 reviews were missing. The Program Chairs proceeded with fast re-assignment of these papers to senior reviewers. Prior to the deadline of submitting the rebuttal by the authors, all papers had three reviews. The distribution of the reviews was the following: 100 papers with an average score of weak accept and higher, 125 papers with an average score toward weak accept, 425 papers with an average score around borderline.

- For papers with strong consensus among reviewers, we introduced a procedure to handle potential overwriting of the recommendation by the Area Chair. In particular for all papers with weak accept and higher or with weak reject and lower, the Area Chair should have sought for an additional reviewer prior to the Area Chair meeting. The decision of the paper could have been changed if the additional reviewer was supporting the recommendation of the Area Chair, and the Area Chair was able to convince his/her group of Area Chairs of that decision.

- The discussion phase between the Area Chair and the reviewers was initiated once the review became available. The Area Chairs had to provide their identity to the reviewers. The discussion remained open until the Area Chair meeting that was held in Paris, June 5–6. Each Area Chair was paired to a buddy and the decisions for all papers were made jointly, or when needed using the opinion of other Area Chairs. The pairing was done considering conflicts, thematic proximity, and when possible geographic diversity. The Area Chairs were responsible for taking decisions on their papers. Prior to the Area Chair meeting, 92% of the consolidation reports and the decision suggestions had been made by the Area Chairs. These recommendations were used as a basis for the final decisions.

- Orals were discussed in groups of Area Chairs. Four groups were formed, with no direct conflict between paper conflicts and the participating Area Chairs. The Area Chair recommending a paper had to present the paper to the whole group and explain why such a contribution is worth being published as an oral. In most of the cases consensus was reached in the group, while in the cases where discrepancies existed between the Area Chairs' views, the decision was taken according to the majority of opinions.

- The final outcome of the Area Chair meeting, was 38 papers accepted for an oral presentation and 284 for poster. The percentage ratios of submissions/acceptance per area are the following:

Thematic area	# submitted	% over submitted	# accepted	% over accepted	% acceptance in area
Object and Scene Recognition	192	16.4%	66	20.3%	34.4%
Segmentation and Grouping	129	11.0%	28	8.6%	21.7%
Face, Gesture, Biometrics	125	10.6%	32	9.8%	25.6%
Motion and Tracking	119	10.1%	27	8.3%	22.7%
Statistical Models and Visual Learning	101	8.6%	30	9.2%	29.7%
Matching, Registration, Alignment	90	7.7%	21	6.5%	23.3%
Computational Imaging	74	6.3%	24	7.4%	32.4%
Multi-view Geometry	67	5.7%	24	7.4%	35.8%
Image Features	66	5.6%	17	5.2%	25.8%
Video and Event Characterization	62	5.3%	14	4.3%	22.6%
Shape Representation and Recognition	48	4.1%	19	5.8%	39.6%
Stereo	38	3.2%	4	1.2%	10.5%
Reflectance, Illumination, Color	37	3.2%	14	4.3%	37.8%
Medical Image Analysis	26	2.2%	5	1.5%	19.2%

- We received 14 complaints/reconsideration requests. All of them were sent to the Area Chairs who handled the papers. Based on the reviewers' arguments and the reaction of the Area Chair, three papers were accepted—as posters—on top of the 322 at the Area Chair meeting, bringing the total number of accepted papers to 325 or **27.6%**. The selection rate for the 38 orals was **3.2%**. The acceptance rate for the papers submitted by the group of Area Chairs was 39%.

- Award nominations were proposed by the Area and Program Chairs based on the reviews and the consolidation report. An external award committee was formed comprising David Fleet, Luc Van Gool, Bernt Schiele, Alan Yuille, Ramin Zabih. Additional reviews were considered for the nominated papers and the decision on the paper awards was made by the award committee. We thank the Area Chairs, Reviewers, Award Committee Members, and the General Chairs for their hard work and we gratefully acknowledge Microsoft Research for accommodating the ECCV needs by generously providing the CMT Conference Management Toolkit. We hope you enjoy the proceedings.

September 2010

Kostas Daniilidis
Petros Maragos
Nikos Paragios

Organization

General Chairs

Argyros, Antonis University of Crete/FORTH, Greece
Trahanias, Panos University of Crete/FORTH, Greece
Tziritas, George University of Crete, Greece

Program Chairs

Daniilidis, Kostas University of Pennsylvania, USA
Maragos, Petros National Technical University of Athens, Greece
Paragios, Nikos Ecole Centrale de Paris/INRIA Saclay île-de-France, France

Workshops Chair

Kutulakos, Kyros University of Toronto, Canada

Tutorials Chair

Lourakis, Manolis FORTH, Greece

Demonstrations Chair

Kakadiaris, Ioannis University of Houston, USA

Industrial Chair

Pavlidis, Ioannis University of Houston, USA

Travel Grants Chair

Komodakis, Nikos University of Crete, Greece

Area Chairs

Bach, Francis	INRIA Paris - Rocquencourt, France
Belongie, Serge	University of California-San Diego, USA
Bischof, Horst	Graz University of Technology, Austria
Black, Michael	Brown University, USA
Boyer, Edmond	INRIA Grenoble - Rhône-Alpes, France
Cootes, Tim	University of Manchester, UK
Dana, Kristin	Rutgers University, USA
Davis, Larry	University of Maryland, USA
Efros, Alyosha	Carnegie Mellon University, USA
Fermuller, Cornelia	University of Maryland, USA
Fitzgibbon, Andrew	Microsoft Research, Cambridge, UK
Jepson, Alan	University of Toronto, Canada
Kahl, Fredrik	Lund University, Sweden
Keriven, Renaud	Ecole des Ponts-ParisTech, France
Kimmel, Ron	Technion Institute of Technology, Ireland
Kolmogorov, Vladimir	University College of London, UK
Lepetit, Vincent	Ecole Polytechnique Federale de Lausanne, Switzerland
Matas, Jiri	Czech Technical University, Prague, Czech Republic
Metaxas, Dimitris	Rutgers University, USA
Navab, Nassir	Technical University of Munich, Germany
Nister, David	Microsoft Research, Redmont, USA
Perez, Patrick	THOMSON Research, France
Perona, Pietro	Caltech University, USA
Ramesh, Visvanathan	Siemens Corporate Research, USA
Raskar, Ramesh	Massachusetts Institute of Technology, USA
Samaras, Dimitris	State University of New York - Stony Brook, USA
Sato, Yoichi	University of Tokyo, Japan
Schmid, Cordelia	INRIA Grenoble - Rhône-Alpes, France
Schnoerr, Christoph	University of Heidelberg, Germany
Sebe, Nicu	University of Trento, Italy
Szeliski, Richard	Microsoft Research, Redmont, USA
Taskar, Ben	University of Pennsylvania, USA
Torr, Phil	Oxford Brookes University, UK
Torralba, Antonio	Massachusetts Institute of Technology, USA
Tuytelaars, Tinne	Katholieke Universiteit Leuven, Belgium
Weickert, Joachim	Saarland University, Germany
Weinshall, Daphna	Hebrew University of Jerusalem, Israel
Weiss, Yair	Hebrew University of Jerusalem, Israel

Conference Board

Reviewers

Caputo, Barbara
Carreira-Perpinan,
   Miguel
Caselles, Vincent
Cavallaro, Andrea
Cham, Tat-Jen
Chandraker, Manmohan
Chandran, Sharat
Chetverikov, Dmitry
Chiu, Han-Pang
Cho, Taeg Sang
Chuang, Yung-Yu
Chung, Albert C. S.
Chung, Moo
Clark, James
Cohen, Isaac
Collins, Robert
Colombo, Carlo
Cord, Matthieu
Corso, Jason
Costen, Nicholas
Cour, Timothee
Crandall, David
Cremers, Daniel
Criminisi, Antonio
Crowley, James
Cui, Jinshi
Cula, Oana
Dalalyan, Arnak
Darbon, Jerome
Davis, James
Davison, Andrew
de Bruijne, Marleen
De la Torre, Fernando
Dedeoglu, Goksel
Delong, Andrew
Demirci, Stefanie
Demirdjian, David
Denzler, Joachim
Deselaers, Thomas
Dhome, Michel
Dick, Anthony
Dickinson, Sven
Divakaran, Ajay
Dollar, Piotr

Domke, Justin
Donoser, Michael
Doretto, Gianfranco
Douze, Matthijs
Draper, Bruce
Drbohlav, Ondrej
Duan, Qi
Duchenne, Olivier
Duric, Zoran
Duygulu-Sahin, Pinar
Eklundh, Jan-Olof
Elder, James
Elgammal, Ahmed
Epshtein, Boris
Eriksson, Anders
Espuny, Ferran
Essa, Irfan
Farhadi, Ali
Farrell, Ryan
Favaro, Paolo
Fehr, Janis
Fei-Fei, Li
Felsberg, Michael
Ferencz, Andras
Fergus, Rob
Feris, Rogerio
Ferrari, Vittorio
Ferryman, James
Fidler, Sanja
Finlayson, Graham
Fisher, Robert
Flach, Boris
Fleet, David
Fletcher, Tom
Florack, Luc
Flynn, Patrick
Foerstner, Wolfgang
Foroosh, Hassan
Forssen, Per-Erik
Fowlkes, Charless
Frahm, Jan-Michael
Fraundorfer, Friedrich
Freeman, William
Frey, Brendan
Fritz, Mario

Fua, Pascal
Fuchs, Martin
Furukawa, Yasutaka
Fusiello, Andrea
Gall, Juergen
Gallagher, Andrew
Gao, Xiang
Gatica-Perez, Daniel
Gee, James
Gehler, Peter
Genc, Yakup
Georgescu, Bogdan
Geusebroek, Jan-Mark
Gevers, Theo
Geyer, Christopher
Ghosh, Abhijeet
Glocker, Ben
Goecke, Roland
Goedeme, Toon
Goldberger, Jacob
Goldenstein, Siome
Goldluecke, Bastian
Gomes, Ryan
Gong, Sean
Gorelick, Lena
Gould, Stephen
Grabner, Helmut
Grady, Leo
Grau, Oliver
Grauman, Kristen
Gross, Ralph
Grossmann, Etienne
Gruber, Amit
Gulshan, Varun
Guo, Guodong
Gupta, Abhinav
Gupta, Mohit
Habbecke, Martin
Hager, Gregory
Hamid, Raffay
Han, Bohyung
Han, Tony
Hanbury, Allan
Hancock, Edwin
Hasinoff, Samuel

Hassner, Tal
Haussecker, Horst
Hays, James
He, Xuming
Heas, Patrick
Hebert, Martial
Heibel, T. Hauke
Heidrich, Wolfgang
Hernandez, Carlos
Hilton, Adrian
Hinterstoisser, Stefan
Hlavac, Vaclav
Hoiem, Derek
Hoogs, Anthony
Hornegger, Joachim
Hua, Gang
Huang, Rui
Huang, Xiaolei
Huber, Daniel
Hudelot, Celine
Hussein, Mohamed
Huttenlocher, Dan
Ihler, Alex
Ilic, Slobodan
Irschara, Arnold
Ishikawa, Hiroshi
Isler, Volkan
Jain, Prateek
Jain, Viren
Jamie Shotton, Jamie
Jegou, Herve
Jenatton, Rodolphe
Jermyn, Ian
Ji, Hui
Ji, Qiang
Jia, Jiaya
Jin, Hailin
Jogan, Matjaz
Johnson, Micah
Joshi, Neel
Juan, Olivier
Jurie, Frederic
Kakadiaris, Ioannis
Kale, Amit

Kamarainen,
   Joni-Kristian
Kamberov, George
Kamberova, Gerda
Kambhamettu, Chandra
Kanatani, Kenichi
Kanaujia, Atul
Kang, Sing Bing
Kappes, Jörg
Kavukcuoglu, Koray
Kawakami, Rei
Ke, Qifa
Kemelmacher, Ira
Khamene, Ali
Khan, Saad
Kikinis, Ron
Kim, Seon Joo
Kimia, Benjamin
Kittler, Josef
Koch, Reinhard
Koeser, Kevin
Kohli, Pushmeet
Kokiopoulou, Efi
Kokkinos, Iasonas
Kolev, Kalin
Komodakis, Nikos
Konolige, Kurt
Koschan, Andreas
Kukelova, Zuzana
Kulis, Brian
Kumar, M. Pawan
Kumar, Sanjiv
Kuthirummal, Sujit
Kutulakos, Kyros
Kweon, In So
Ladicky, Lubor
Lai, Shang-Hong
Lalonde, Jean-Francois
Lampert, Christoph
Landon, George
Langer, Michael
Langs, Georg
Lanman, Douglas
Laptev, Ivan

Larlus, Diane
Latecki, Longin Jan
Lazebnik, Svetlana
Lee, ChanSu
Lee, Honglak
Lee, Kyoung Mu
Lee, Sang-Wook
Leibe, Bastian
Leichter, Ido
Leistner, Christian
Lellmann, Jan
Lempitsky, Victor
Lenzen, Frank
Leonardis, Ales
Leung, Thomas
Levin, Anat
Li, Chunming
Li, Gang
Li, Hongdong
Li, Hongsheng
Li, Li-Jia
Li, Rui
Li, Ruonan
Li, Stan
Li, Yi
Li, Yunpeng
Liefeng, Bo
Lim, Jongwoo
Lin, Stephen
Lin, Zhe
Ling, Haibin
Little, Jim
Liu, Ce
Liu, Jingen
Liu, Qingshan
Liu, Tyng-Luh
Liu, Xiaoming
Liu, Yanxi
Liu, Yazhou
Liu, Zicheng
Lourakis, Manolis
Lovell, Brian
Lu, Le
Lucey, Simon

Luo, Jiebo
Lyu, Siwei
Ma, Xiaoxu
Mairal, Julien
Maire, Michael
Maji, Subhransu
Maki, Atsuto
Makris, Dimitrios
Malisiewicz, Tomasz
Mallick, Satya
Manduchi, Roberto
Manmatha, R.
Marchand, Eric
Marcialis, Gian
Marks, Tim
Marszalek, Marcin
Martinec, Daniel
Martinez, Aleix
Matei, Bogdan
Mateus, Diana
Matsushita, Yasuyuki
Matthews, Iain
Maxwell, Bruce
Maybank, Stephen
Mayer, Helmut
McCloskey, Scott
McKenna, Stephen
Medioni, Gerard
Meer, Peter
Mei, Christopher
Michael, Nicholas
Micusik, Branislav
Minh, Nguyen
Mirmehdi, Majid
Mittal, Anurag
Miyazaki, Daisuke
Monasse, Pascal
Mordohai, Philippos
Moreno-Noguer,
    Francesc
Mori, Greg
Morimoto, Carlos
Morse, Bryan
Moses, Yael
Mueller, Henning

Mukaigawa, Yasuhiro
Mulligan, Jane
Munich, Mario
Murino, Vittorio
Namboodiri, Vinay
Narasimhan, Srinivasa
Narayanan, P.J.
Naroditsky, Oleg
Neumann, Jan
Nevatia, Ram
Nicolls, Fred
Niebles, Juan Carlos
Nielsen, Mads
Nishino, Ko
Nixon, Mark
Nowozin, Sebastian
O'donnell, Thomas
Obozinski, Guillaume
Odobez, Jean-Marc
Odone, Francesca
Ofek, Eyal
Ogale, Abhijit
Okabe, Takahiro
Okatani, Takayuki
Okuma, Kenji
Olson, Clark
Olsson, Carl
Ommer, Bjorn
Osadchy, Margarita
Overgaard, Niels
    Christian
Ozuysal, Mustafa
Pajdla, Tomas
Panagopoulos,
    Alexandros
Pandharkar, Rohit
Pankanti, Sharath
Pantic, Maja
Papadopoulo, Theo
Parameswaran, Vasu
Parikh, Devi
Paris, Sylvain
Patow, Gustavo
Patras, Ioannis
Pavlovic, Vladimir

Peleg, Shmuel
Perera, A.G. Amitha
Perronnin, Florent
Petrou, Maria
Petrovic, Vladimir
Peursum, Patrick
Philbin, James
Piater, Justus
Pietikainen, Matti
Pinz, Axel
Pless, Robert
Pock, Thomas
Poh, Norman
Pollefeys, Marc
Ponce, Jean
Pons, Jean-Philippe
Potetz, Brian
Prabhakar, Salil
Qian, Gang
Quattoni, Ariadna
Radeva, Petia
Radke, Richard
Rakotomamonjy, Alain
Ramanan, Deva
Ramanathan, Narayanan
Ranzato, Marc'Aurelio
Raviv, Dan
Reid, Ian
Reitmayr, Gerhard
Ren, Xiaofeng
Rittscher, Jens
Rogez, Gregory
Rosales, Romer
Rosenberg, Charles
Rosenhahn, Bodo
Rosman, Guy
Ross, Arun
Roth, Peter
Rother, Carsten
Rothganger, Fred
Rougon, Nicolas
Roy, Sebastien
Rueckert, Daniel
Ruether, Matthias
Russell, Bryan

Russell, Christopher
Sahbi, Hichem
Stiefelhagen, Rainer
Saad, Ali
Saffari, Amir
Salgian, Garbis
Salzmann, Mathieu
Sangineto, Enver
Sankaranarayanan,
    Aswin
Sapiro, Guillermo
Sara, Radim
Sato, Imari
Savarese, Silvio
Savchynskyy, Bogdan
Sawhney, Harpreet
Scharr, Hanno
Scharstein, Daniel
Schellewald, Christian
Schiele, Bernt
Schindler, Grant
Schindler, Konrad
Schlesinger, Dmitrij
Schoenemann, Thomas
Schroff, Florian
Schubert, Falk
Schultz, Thomas
Se, Stephen
Seidel, Hans-Peter
Serre, Thomas
Shah, Mubarak
Shakhnarovich, Gregory
Shan, Ying
Shashua, Amnon
Shechtman, Eli
Sheikh, Yaser
Shekhovtsov, Alexander
Shet, Vinay
Shi, Jianbo
Shimshoni, Ilan
Shokoufandeh, Ali
Sigal, Leonid
Simon, Loic
Singaraju, Dheeraj
Singh, Maneesh

Singh, Vikas
Sinha, Sudipta
Sivic, Josef
Slabaugh, Greg
Smeulders, Arnold
Sminchisescu, Cristian
Smith, Kevin
Smith, William
Snavely, Noah
Snoek, Cees
Soatto, Stefano
Sochen, Nir
Sochman, Jan
Sofka, Michal
Sorokin, Alexander
Southall, Ben
Souvenir, Richard
Srivastava, Anuj
Stauffer, Chris
Stein, Gideon
Strecha, Christoph
Sugimoto, Akihiro
Sullivan, Josephine
Sun, Deqing
Sun, Jian
Sun, Min
Sunkavalli, Kalyan
Suter, David
Svoboda, Tomas
Syeda-Mahmood,
    Tanveer
Süsstrunk, Sabine
Tai, Yu-Wing
Takamatsu, Jun
Talbot, Hugues
Tan, Ping
Tan, Robby
Tanaka, Masayuki
Tao, Dacheng
Tappen, Marshall
Taylor, Camillo
Theobalt, Christian
Thonnat, Monique
Tieu, Kinh
Tistarelli, Massimo

Todorovic, Sinisa
Toreyin, Behcet Ugur
Torresani, Lorenzo
Torsello, Andrea
Toshev, Alexander
Trucco, Emanuele
Tschumperle, David
Tsin, Yanghai
Tu, Peter
Tung, Tony
Turek, Matt
Turk, Matthew
Tuzel, Oncel
Tyagi, Ambrish
Urschler, Martin
Urtasun, Raquel
Van de Weijer, Joost
van Gemert, Jan
van den Hengel, Anton
Vasilescu, M. Alex O.
Vedaldi, Andrea
Veeraraghavan, Ashok
Veksler, Olga
Verbeek, Jakob
Vese, Luminita
Vitaladevuni, Shiv
Vogiatzis, George
Vogler, Christian
Wachinger, Christian
Wada, Toshikazu
Wagner, Daniel
Wang, Chaohui
Wang, Hanzi
Wang, Hongcheng
Wang, Jue
Wang, Kai
Wang, Song
Wang, Xiaogang
Wang, Yang
Weese, Juergen
Wei, Yichen
Wein, Wolfgang
Welinder, Peter
Werner, Tomas
Westin, Carl-Fredrik

Wilburn, Bennett
Wildes, Richard
Williams, Oliver
Wills, Josh
Wilson, Kevin
Wojek, Christian
Wolf, Lior
Wright, John
Wu, Tai-Pang
Wu, Ying
Xiao, Jiangjian
Xiao, Jianxiong
Xiao, Jing
Yagi, Yasushi
Yan, Shuicheng
Yang, Fei
Yang, Jie
Yang, Ming-Hsuan

Yang, Peng
Yang, Qingxiong
Yang, Ruigang
Ye, Jieping
Yeung, Dit-Yan
Yezzi, Anthony
Yilmaz, Alper
Yin, Lijun
Yoon, Kuk Jin
Yu, Jingyi
Yu, Kai
Yu, Qian
Yu, Stella
Yuille, Alan
Zach, Christopher
Zaid, Harchaoui
Zelnik-Manor, Lihi
Zeng, Gang

Zhang, Cha
Zhang, Li
Zhang, Sheng
Zhang, Weiwei
Zhang, Wenchao
Zhao, Wenyi
Zheng, Yuanjie
Zhou, Jinghao
Zhou, Kevin
Zhu, Leo
Zhu, Song-Chun
Zhu, Ying
Zickler, Todd
Zikic, Darko
Zisserman, Andrew
Zitnick, Larry
Zivny, Stanislav
Zuffi, Silvia

Sponsoring Institutions

Platinum Sponsor

INSTITUT NATIONAL
DE RECHERCHE
EN INFORMATIQUE
ET EN AUTOMATIQUE

 *INRIA*

Gold Sponsors

Google

Microsoft
Research

 technicolor

Silver Sponsors

 **Adobe**

 **DynaVox**
Mayer-Johnson
Advancing human expression
and learning.

ERCIM
European Research Consortium
for Informatics and Mathematics

 IBM

 Johnson
Controls

 POINT GREY

UNIVERSITY of
HOUSTON

 **SIEMENS**

Table of Contents – Part III

Spotlights and Posters T1

Geometry

Spotlights and Posters T2

Image Features and Motion

Spotlights and Posters W1

Learning a Fine Vocabulary

Andrej Mikulík, Michal Perdoch, Ondřej Chum, and Jiří Matas

CMP, Dept. of Cybernetics, Faculty of EE, Czech Technical University in Prague

Abstract. A novel similarity measure for bag-of-words type large scale image retrieval is presented. The similarity function is learned in an unsupervised manner, requires no extra space over the standard bag-of-words method and is more discriminative than both L2-based soft assignment and Hamming embedding.

We show experimentally that the novel similarity function achieves mean average precision that is superior to any result published in the literature on a number of standard datasets. At the same time, retrieval with the proposed similarity function is faster than the reference method.

1 Introduction

Recently, large collections of images have become readily available [1–3] and image-based search in such collections has attracted significant attention of the computer community [4–8]. Most, if not all, recent state-of-the-art methods build on [4] that represents the image by a histogram of "visual words", *i.e.* discretized SIFT descriptors [9]. The bag-of-words representation possesses many desirable properties required in large scale retrieval. If stored in inverted files, it is compact and supports fast search. It is sufficiently discriminative and yet robust to acquisition "nuisance parameters" like illumination and viewpoint change as well as occlusion[1].

The discretization of the SIFT features is necessary in large scale problems as it is neither possible to compute distances on descriptors efficiently nor feasible to store all the descriptors. Instead, only (the identifier of) the vector quantized prototype for visual word is kept. After quantization, Euclidean distance in a high (128) dimensional space is approximated by a $0-\infty$ metric - features represented by the same visual word are deemed identical, else they are treated as "totally different". The computational convenience of such a crude approximation of the SIFT distance has a detrimental impact on discriminative power of the representation. Recent methods like soft assignment and in particular the Hamming embedding aim at a better space-speed-accuracy trade off.

In this paper, unsupervised learning on a large set of images is exploited to improve on the $0-\infty$ metric. First, an efficient clustering process with spatial verification establishes correspondences within a huge (>5M) image collection. Next, a fine-grained vocabulary is obtained by hierarchical approximate nearest neighbour. The automatically established correspondences are then used to define a similarity measure on the basis of a probabilistic relationships of visual words; we call it the *PR visual word similarity*.

---

[1] We only consider and compare with methods that support queries that cover only a (small) part of the test image. Global methods like GIST [10] achieve a much smaller memory footprint at the cost of allowing whole image queries only.

K. Daniilidis, P. Maragos, N. Paragios (Eds.): ECCV 2010, Part III, LNCS 6313, pp. 1–14, 2010.

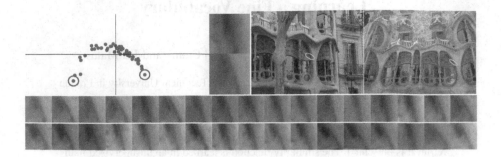

Fig. 1. An example of corresponding patches. A 2D PCA projection of the SIFT descriptors (left); two most distant patches in the SIFT space and the images where they were detected (right); a set of sample patches (bottom). The average SIFT distance within the cluster is 278, the maximum distance is 591.

When combined with a 16 million word vocabulary (one or two orders of magnitude larger than commonly used), the PR similarity has the following desirable properties:

(i) it is more accurate, *i.e.* it is more discriminative, than both standard $0-\infty$ metric and Hamming embedding.
(ii) the memory footprint of the image representation for PR similarity calculation is roughly identical to the standard method and smaller than that of Hamming embedding.
(iii) search with PR similarity is faster than the standard bag-of-words.

As a main contribution of the paper, we present a novel similarity measure that is learned in an unsupervised manner, requires no extra space (only $O(1)$) in comparison with the bag-of-words and is more discriminative than both $0-\infty$ and L2-based soft assignment.

2   Related Work

In this section, approaches to vocabulary construction and soft assignment suitable for large-scale image search are reviewed and compared.

In [4], the 'bag of words' approach to image retrieval was introduced. The vocabulary (the number of visual words $\approx 10^4$) is constructed using a standard k-means algorithm. Adopting methodology from text retrieval applications, the image score is efficiently computed by traversing inverted files related to visual words present in the query. The inverted file related to a visual word W is a list of image ids that contain the visual word W. It follows that the time required for scoring the documents is proportional to the number of different visual words in a query and the average length of an inverted file.

Hierarchical clustering. The hierarchical k-means and scoring of Nistér and Stewenius [5] is the first image retrieval approach that scales up. The vocabulary has a hierarchical

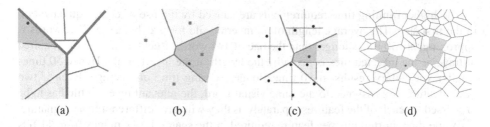

(a)   (b)   (c)   (d)

Fig. 2. Different approaches to the soft assignment (saturation encodes the relevance): (a) hierarchical scoring [5] – the soft assignment is given by the hierarchical structure; (b) soft clustering [11] assigns features to r nearest cluster centers; (c) hamming embedding [12] – each cell is divided into orthants by a number of hyperplanes, the distance of the orthants is measured by the number of separating hyperplanes; (d) the set of alternative words in the proposed PR similarity measure.

structure which allows efficient construction of large and discriminative vocabularies. The quantization effect are alleviated by the so called hierarchical scoring. In such a type of scoring, the scoring visual words are not only located in the leafs of the vocabulary tree. The non-leaf nodes can be thought of as virtual or generic visual words. These virtual words naturally score with lower *idf* weights as more features are assigned to them (all features in their sub-tree). The advantage of the hierarchical scoring approach is that the soft assignment is given by the structure of the tree and no additional information needs to be stored for each feature. On the downside, experiments in [11] show that the quantization artifacts of the hierarchical k-means are not fully removed by hierarchical scoring, the problems are only shifted up a few levels in the hierarchy. An illustrative example of the soft assignment performed by the hierarchical clustering is shown in Fig. 2(a).

Lost in quantization. In [11], an approximate soft assignment is exploited. Each feature is assigned to $n = 3$ (approximately) nearest visual words. Each assignment is weighted by $e^{-\frac{d^2}{2\sigma^2}}$ where d is the distance of the feature descriptor to the cluster center.

The soft assignment is performed on features in the database as well as the query features. This results in n times higher memory requirements and n^2 times longer running time – the average length of the inverted file is n times longer and there are up to n times more visual words associated with the query features. For an illustration of the soft assignment, see Fig. 2(b).

Hamming embedding. Jégou et al. [12] have proposed to combine k-means quantization and binary vector signatures. First, the feature space is divided into relatively small number of Voronoi cells (20K) using k-means. Each cell is then divided by n independent hyper-planes into 2^n subcells. Each subcell is described by a binary vector of length n. Results reported in [12] suggest that the hamming embedding provides good quantization. The good results are traded off with higher running time requirements and high memory requirements.

The higher running time requirements are caused by the use of coarse quantization in the first step. The average length of an inverted file for vocabulary of 20K words is approximately 50 times longer than the one of 1M words. Recall that the time required to traverse the inverted files is given by the length of the inverted file. Hence 50 times smaller vocabulary results in 50 times longer scoring time on average. Even if two query features are assigned to the same visual word, the relevant inverted file has to be processed for each of the features separately as they will have different binary signature.

While the reported bits per feature required in the search index ranges from 11 bits [8] to 18 bits [11], hamming embedding adds another 64 bits. The additional information reduces the number of features that can be stored in the memory by a factor of 6.8.

Summary. All approaches to soft clustering mentioned above are based on the distance (or its approximation) in the descriptor (SIFT) space. It has been observed that the Euclidian distance is not the best performing measure. Learning a global Mahalanobis distance [13, 14] showed that the matching is improved and / or the dimensionality of the descriptor is reduced. However, even in the original work on SIFT descriptor matching [9] it is shown that the similarity of the descriptors is not only dependent on the distance of the descriptors, but also on the location of the features in the feature space. Therefore, learning a global Mahalanobis metric is suboptimal and a local similarity measure is required. For examples of corresponding pathes where SIFT distance does not predict the similarity well, see Figures 1, 3, and 4.

3   The Probabilistic Relation Similarity Measure

Consider a feature in the query image with descriptor $D \in \mathcal{D} \subset R^d$. For most accurate matching, the query feature should be compared to all features in the database. The contribution of the query feature to the matching score should be proportional to the probability of matching the database feature. It is far too slow, *i.e.* practically not feasible, to directly match a query feature to all features in a (large) database. Also, the contribution of features with low probability of matching is negligible.

The success of fast retrieval approaches is based on efficient separation of (potentially) matching features from those that are highly unlikely to match. The elimination is based on a simple idea – the descriptors of matching patches will be close in some appropriate metric (L2 is often used). With an appropriate data structure, enumeration of descriptors in proximity is possible in time sub-linear in the size of the database. All bag-of-words based methods use partitioning $\{W_i\}$ of the descriptor space : $\cup W_i = \mathcal{D}, \quad W_i \cap W_{j \neq i} = \emptyset$. The partitions are then used to separate features that are close (potentially matching) from those that are far (non-matching).

In the case of hard assignment, features are associated with the quantized visual word defined by the closest cluster center. In the scoring that evaluates the query and database image match, only features with the same visual word as the query feature are considered.

We argue that the descriptor distance is a good indicator of patch similarity only up to a limited distance, where the variation in the descriptors is caused mostly the imaging noise. In our approach, we abandon the assumption that the descriptor distance provides a good similarity measure of patches observed under different viewing angles or under different illumination conditions. Instead, we propose to exploit the matching probability between a feature observed in the query image and a database feature. Since our aim is to address retrieval in web-scale databases where storage requirements are critical, we constrained our attention to solution that store no extra information per feature, or more exactly, that have a minimum overhead in comparison with the standard inverted file representation.

The proposed approach. We propose to use a fine partitioning of the descriptor space where the partitions only compensate for imagining noise (or even less). Even though the fine partitioning is learned in a data dependent fashion (as in the other approaches), the fine partitioning unavoidable separates matching features into a number of clusters.

For each partition (visual word) we learn which other partitions (called *alternative visual words*) are likely to contain descriptors of matching features. This step is based on the probability of observing visual word W_j in a matching database image when visual word W_q was observed in the query image

$$P(W_j|W_q). \tag{1}$$

The probability (eqn. 1) is estimated from a large number of matching patches.

A simple generative model, independent for each feature, is adopted. In the model, image features are assumed to be (locally affine) projections of a (locally close to planar) 3D surface patches Z_i. Hence, matching features among different images are those that have the same pre-image Z_i. To estimate the probability $P(W_j|W_q)$ we start with (a large number of) sets of matching features, each set containing different projections of a patch Z_i. Using the fine vocabulary (partitioning) the sets of matching features are converted to sets of matching visual words. We estimate the probability $P(w_j|w_q)$ from the feature tracks as

$$P(W_j|W_q) \approx \sum_{Z_i} P(Z_i|W_q)P(W_j|Z_i). \tag{2}$$

For each visual word W_q, a fixed number of alternative visual words that have the highest conditional probability (eqn. 2) is recorded.

3.1 Learning Stage

The first step of our approach is to obtain a large number of matching image patches. The links between matching patches are consequently used to infer links between quantized descriptors of those patches, *i.e.* between visual words. As a first step towards unsupervised collection of matching image patches, called (feature) tracks, clusters of matching images are discovered. Within each cluster, feature tracks are found by a wide-baseline matching method. This approach is similar to [15], where the feature tracks are used to produce 3D reconstruction. In our case, it is important to find a larger variety of patch appearances rather than precise point locations. Therefore, we adopt a slightly different approach to the choice of image pairs investigated.

Image clusters. We start by analyzing connected components of the image matching graph (graph with images as vertices, edges connect images that can be matched) produced by a large-scale clustering method [16, 17]. Any matching technique is suitable provided it can find clusters of matching images in a very large database. In our case, an image retrieval system was used to produce the clusters of spatially related images. The following structure of image clusters is created. Each cluster of spatially related images is represented as an oriented tree structure (the skeleton of the cluster). The children of each parental node were obtained as results of an image retrieval using the parent image as a query image. Together with the tree structure, an affine transformation (approximately) mapping child image to its parent are recorded. These mappings are later used to guide (speed-up) the matching.

Feature tracks. To avoid any kind of bias (by quantization errors, for example), instead of using vector quantized form of the descriptors, the conventional image matching (based on the full SIFT [9]) has to be used. In principle, one can go back even to the pixel level [18, 19], however such an approach seems to be impractical for large volumes of data.

It is not feasible to match all pairs of images in image clusters, especially not in clusters with a large number of images (say more than 1000). It is also not possible to simply follow the tree structure of image clusters because not all features are detected in all images (in fact, only a relatively small portion of features is actually repeated). The following procedure, that is linear in the number of images in the cluster, is adopted for detection of feature tracks that would exhibit as large variety of patch appearances as possible. For each parental node, a sub-tree of height two is selected. On images in the sub-tree, a $2k$-connected graph called circulant graph [20] is constructed. Algorithm for construction of minimal $2k$-connected graph is summarized in Algorithm 1. Images connected by an edge in such a graph are then matched using standard wide-baseline matching. Since each image in the image cluster participates in at most 3 sub-trees (as father, son and grand-son), the number of edges is limited to $6kN$, where N is the size of the cluster. Instead of using epipolar geometry as a global model, a number of close-to-planar (geometrically consistent) structures is estimated (using affine homography). Unlike the epipolar constraint, such a one-to-one mapping enables to verify the shape of the feature patch. Connected components of matching and geometrically consistent features are called feature tracks.

Tracks that contain two different features from a single image are called inconsistent [15]. These features clearly cannot have a single pre-image under perspective projection and hence cannot be used in the process of 3D reconstruction. Such inconsistent tracks are often caused by repeated patterns. Inconsistent feature tracks are (unlike in [15]) kept as they provide further examples of patch appearance.

Large vocabulary generation. To efficiently generate a large visual vocabulary we employ a hybrid approach - approximate hierarchical k-means. A hierarchy tree of two levels is constructed, each level has 4K nodes. In the assignment stage of k-means, approximate nearest neighbour, FLANN [21], is used for efficiency reasons.

Input: K - requested connectivity, N - number of vertices
Output: V a set of vertices, $E \subset V \times V$ a set of edges of $2K$ connected graph (V,E).

---

1. **if** $2K \geq N - 1$ **then**
   return fully connected graph with N vertices.
   end
2. $S :=$ a random subset of $\{2, \ldots, \lfloor \frac{N-1}{2} \rfloor\}$, $|S| = K - 1$
3. $V := \{v_0, \ldots, v_{N-1}\}$
4. $E := \{(v_i, v_j) \mid v_i, v_j \in V, j = (i + 1) \bmod N\}$
5. **for** $s \in S$
6. $E := E \cup \{(v_i, v_j) \mid v_i, v_j \in V, j = (i + s) \bmod N\}$
7. **end**

Algorithm 1. Construction of the 2K connected graph with a minimal number of edges as a union of circulants

First, a level one approximate k-means is applied to a random sub-sample of 5 million SIFT descriptors. Then, a two pass procedure on 10,713 million SIFTs (from almost 6 million images) is performed. In the first pass, each SIFT descriptor is assigned to the level one vocabulary. For each level one visual word a list of descriptors assigned to it is recorded. In the second pass, approximate k-means on each list of the descriptors is applied. The whole procedure takes about one day on a cluster of 20 computers.

Balancing the tree structure. For the average speed of the retrieval, it is important that the vocabulary is balanced, *i.e.* there is approximately the same number of instances of each visual word in the database.

There are two options how to balance the proposed structure. The level one structure can be balanced so that the branches are of approximately equal weight by constraining the length of the mean vectors (this stems from the fact that SIFT features live approximately on a hyper-sphere). Balancing can be also achieved by un-even splitting at the second level – proportional to the weight of the branch. In our implementation, we have used the former.

The imbalance measure [12] for our vocabulary is 1.17 for the training image set (>5M images) and 1.33 for the Oxford 105k (compared to 1.21 in [12]).

Computing the conditional probability. To compute the conditional probability (eqn. 2) from the feature tracks, an inverted file structure is used. The tracks are represented as forward files (named Z_i), *i.e.* lists of matching SIFT descriptors. The descriptors are assigned their visual word from the large vocabulary. Then, for each visual word w_k, a list of patches Z_i so that $P(Z_i|w_k) > 0$ (the inverted file) is constructed. The sum (eqn. 2) is evaluated by traversing the relevant inverted file.

Statistics. Over 5 million images were clustered into almost 20 thousand clusters covering 750 thousand images. Out of those 733 thousand were successfully matched in the wide-baseline matching stage. Over 111 million feature tracks were established,

Fig. 3. A 2D PCA projection of a feature track of SIFT descriptors (left); the most distant patches and their images (right); sample of feature patches from the track. The distance of the most distant SIFT descriptors is 542 and is caused by an enormous change in the viewpoint.

Fig. 4. A 2D PCA projection of a feature track of SIFT descriptors (left); the most distant patches and their images (right); sample of feature patches from the track. The distance of the most distant SIFT descriptors is 593 and is caused by the viewpoint and scale change.

out of which 12.3 millions are composed of more than 5 features. In total, 564 million features participated in the tracks, 319.5 million features belong to tracks of more than 5 features. Some examples of feature tracks are shown in Figures 5 and 6.

Memory and time efficiency. For the alternative words storage, only constant space is required, equal to the size of the vocabulary times the number of alternative words. The pre-processing consists of image clustering ([16] reports near linear time in the size of the database), intra-cluster matching (linearity enforced by the $2k$-connected circulant matching graph), and of the evaluation of expression eqn. (2) for all visual words. The worst case complexity of the last step is equal to the number of tracks (correspondences) times the size of the vocabulary squared. In practice, due to the sparsity of the representation, the process took less than an hour for the dataset of over 5 million images mentioned above.

3.2 Retrieval Stage

The implementation of the retrieval stage is fairly standard, using inverted files [4] for candidate image selection which is followed by fast spatial verification and query expansion [6]. The modifications listed below are the major differences in our retrieval implementation.

Unique matching. Despite being assigned to more than one visual word, each query feature is a projection of a single physical patch. Thus it can match only at most one feature in each image in the database. We find that applying this uniqueness constraint adds negligible computational cost and improves the mean average precision (mAP) by approximately 1%.

Weights of alternative words. Contribution of each visual word is weighted by the *idf* weight [22]. A number of re-weighting schemes for alternative words have been tried, none of them affecting significantly the results of the retrieval.

4 Experiments

We have evaluated the performance of the PR similarity on a standard retrieval dataset Oxford 105K[2]. The experiments focus on retrieval accuracy and speed. Since both our training set of 6 million images and the Oxford dataset were downloaded from FLICKR, we have explicitly removed all images from the training set that appear (or their scaled duplicate) in the test dataset.

4.1 Retrieval Quality

We follow the protocol of 55 queries (11 landmarks, 5 queries each) defined in [23] and use the mean average precision as a measure of retrieval performance. We start by studying the properties of the PR similarity for a visual vocabulary of 16 million words.

In the first experiment, the quality of the retrieval as a function of the number of alternative words was measured, see Figure 7. The plots show that performance improves monotonically for plain retrieval without query expansion and almost monotonically when it is used for post-processing.

The second experiment studies the effects of the vocabulary size, the number of alternative words and compares the PR similarity with soft assignment. The left-hand part of Table 1 shows results obtained with the 16M vocabulary with three different settings 'std' – standard tf-idf retrieval with hard assignment of visual words; '5L' and '16L' – retrieval using alternative words (4 and 15 respectively). The righthand part presents results of reference state-of-the-art results [8] obtain with a vocabulary of 1M visual words learned on the PARIS dataset[3]. Two version of the reference algorithm are tested, without ("std") and with the query soft assignment to 3 nearest neighbours ("SA 3NN").

The experiments supports the following observations:

(i) For a hard assignment to a single visual word, 1M dictionary outperforms the 16M one. For the 0–∞ metric, the 16M visual word dictionary is too fine.
(ii) Similarity calculation with the learned alternative words increases significantly the accuracy of the retrieval, both with and without query expansion.

---

[2] http://www.robots.ox.ac.uk/~vgg/data/oxbuildings/
[3] http://www.robots.ox.ac.uk/~vgg/data/parisbuildings/

Fig. 5. Three examples of feature tracks of size 50. Five selected images and all 50 patches of the track. Even though the patches are similar, the SIFT distance of some pairs is over 500.

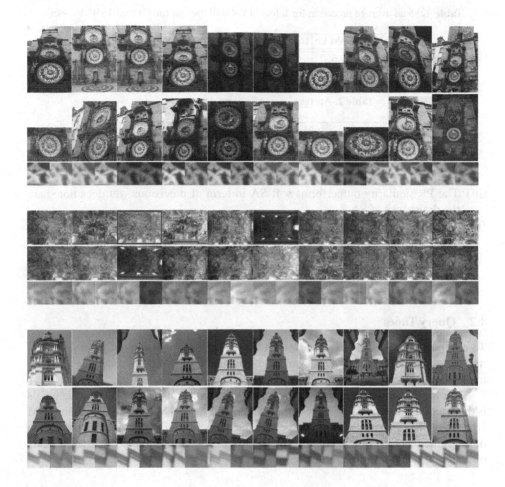

Fig. 6. Three examples of feature tracks of size 20. Images and corresponding patches, note the variation in appearance.

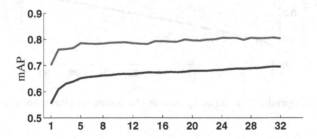

Fig. 7. The quality of the retrieval, expressed as mean average precision (mAP), increases with the number of alternative words. The mAP after (upper curve) and before (lower curve) query expansion is shown.

Table 1. Mean average precision for selected vocabularies on the Oxford 105k data-set

	16M std	16M L5	16M L16	PARIS 1M std	PARIS 1M SA 3NN
plain	0.554	0.650	**0.674**	0.574	0.652
QE	0.695	0.786	**0.795**	0.728	0.772

Table 2. Average execution time per query in sec

	16M std	16M L5	16M L16	PARIS 1M std
Oxford 105K	0.071	0.114	0.195	0.247

(iii) The PR similarity outperforms soft SA in term of precisions, yet does not share the drawbacks of SA.

(iv) The PR similarity outperforms the Hamming embedding approach combined with query expansion, Jegou et al. [12, 24] report the mAP of 0.692 on this dataset.

 (v) The mAP result for 16M L16 is superior to any result published in the literature on the Oxford 105k dataset.

4.2   Query Times

To compare the speed of the retrieval, an average query time over the 55 queries defined on the Oxford 105K data set was measured. Running times recorded for the same methods and parameter settings as above are shown in Table 2.

The plot showing dependence of the query time on the number of alternative words is depicted in Figure 8. The times for the references PARIS 1M std method and the 16M L16 are of the same order. This is expected since the average length of inverted files is of the same order for both methods. The proposed method is about 20% faster, but this might be just an implementation artefact.

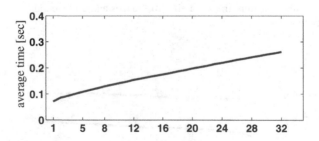

Fig. 8. Dependence of the query time on the number of alternative words

Finally, we looked at the dependence of the speed of the proposed method as a function of the number alternative words. The relationship shown in Fig. 8 is very close to linear plus a fixed overhead. The plot demonstrates that speed-accuracy trade-off is controllable via the number of alternative words.

4.3   Results on Other Datasets

The proposed approach has been tested on a number of standard datasets. These include Oxford, INRIA holidays (with manually corrected orientation of images, where the correct (sky-is-up) orientation is obvious), and Paris datasets. In all cases (Table 3), the use of the alternative visual words improves the results. On all datasets except the INRIA holidays the method achieves the state of the art results.

Table 3. Results (mAP) of the proposed method on a number of publicly available datasets.

Dataset	16M std	16M L16	16M QE	16M L16 QE
Oxford 5k	0.618	0.742	0.740	0.849
Paris	0.625	0.749	0.736	0.824
Paris + Oxford 100k	0.533	0.675	0.659	0.773
INRIA holidays rot	0.742	0.749	0.755	0.758

5   Conclusions

We presented a novel similarity measure for bag-of-words type large scale image retrieval. The similarity function is learned in an unsupervised manner using geometrically verified correspondences obtained with an efficient clustering method on a large image collection.

The similarity measure requires no extra space in comparison with the standard bag-of-words method. We show experimentally, that the novel similarity function achieves mean average precision that is superior to any result published in the literature on a number of standard datasets. At the same time, retrieval with the proposed similarity function is faster than the reference method.

Acknowledgement. The authors are grateful for the support from EC project FP7-ICT-247022 MASH, Czech Government research program MSM6840770038, GAČR project 102/09/P423, and Google.

References

1. http://books.google.com/help/maps/streetview/ (www)
2. http://www.panoramio.com/ (www)
3. http://www.flickr.com/ (www)
4. Sivic, J., Zisserman, A.: Video Google: A text retrieval approach to object matching in videos. In: Proc. of ICCV, pp. 1470–1477 (2003)
5. Nister, D., Stewenius, H.: Scalable recognition with a vocabulary tree. In: Proc. CVPR (2006)
6. Chum, O., Philbin, J., Sivic, J., Isard, M., Zisserman, A.: Total recall: Automatic query expansion with a generative feature model for object retrieval. In: Proc. ICCV (2007)
7. Jegou, H., Douze, M., Schmid, C.: Hamming embedding and weak geometric consistency for large scale image search. In: Forsyth, D., Torr, P., Zisserman, A. (eds.) ECCV 2008, Part I. LNCS, vol. 5302, pp. 304–317. Springer, Heidelberg (2008)

8. Perdoch, M., Chum, O., Matas, J.: Efficient representation of local geometry for large scale object retrieval. In: CVPR (2009)
9. Lowe, D.: Distinctive image features from scale-invariant keypoints. International Journal of Computer Vision 60, 91–110 (2004)
10. Oliva, A., Torralba, A.: Building the gist of a scene: The role of global image features in recognition. Visual Perception, Progress in Brain Research 155 (2006)
11. Philbin, J., Chum, O., Isard, M., Sivic, J., Zisserman, A.: Lost in quantization: Improving particular object retrieval in large scale image databases. In: Proc. CVPR (2008)
12. Jégou, H., Douze, M., Schmid, C.: Improving bag-of-features for large scale image search. IJCV 87, 316–336 (2010)
13. Hua, G., Brown, M., Winder, S.: Discriminant embedding for local image descriptors. In: Proc. ICCV (2007)
14. Mikolajczyk, K., Matas, J.: Improving sift for fast tree matching by optimal linear projection. In: Proc. ICCV (2007)
15. Agarwal, S., Snavely, N., Simon, I., Seitz, S., Szeliski, R.: Building Rome in a day. In: Proc. ICCV (2009)
16. Chum, O., Matas, J.: Large-scale discovery of spatially related images. IEEE PAMI 32, 371–377 (2010)
17. Li, X., Wu, C., Zach, C., Lazebnik, S., Frahm, J.M.: Modeling and recognition of landmark image collections using iconic scene graphs. In: Forsyth, D., Torr, P., Zisserman, A. (eds.) ECCV 2008, Part I. LNCS, vol. 5302, pp. 427–440. Springer, Heidelberg (2008)
18. Ferrari, V., Tuytelaars, T., Van Gool, L.: Simultaneous object recognition and segmentation by image exploration. In: Pajdla, T., Matas, J(G.) (eds.) ECCV 2004. LNCS, vol. 3021, pp. 40–54. Springer, Heidelberg (2004)
19. Cech, J., Matas, J., Perdoch, M.: Efficient sequential correspondence selection by cosegmentation. In: Proc. CVPR (2008)
20. Godsil, C., Royle, G.: Algebraic Graph Theory. Springer, Heidelberg (2001)
21. Muja, M., Lowe, D.G.: Fast approximate nearest neighbors with automatic algorithm configuration. In: VISSAPP (2009)
22. Baeza-Yates, R., Ribeiro-Neto, B.: Modern Information Retrieval. ACM Press, New York (1999) ISBN: 020139829
23. Philbin, J., Chum, O., Isard, M., Sivic, J., Zisserman, A.: Object retrieval with large vocabularies and fast spatial matching. In: Proc. CVPR (2007)
24. Jégou, H., Douze, M., Schmid, C.: On the burstiness of visual elements. In: Proc. CVPR (2009)

Video Synchronization Using Temporal Signals from Epipolar Lines

Dmitry Pundik and Yael Moses

The Interdisciplinary Center Herzliya , Israel
pundik.dmitry@post.idc.ac.il, yael@idc.ac.il

Abstract. Time synchronization of video sequences in a multi-camera system is necessary for successfully analyzing the acquired visual information. Even if synchronization is established, its quality may deteriorate over time due to a variety of reasons, most notably frame dropping. Consequently, synchronization must be actively maintained. This paper presents a method for online synchronization that relies only on the video sequences. We introduce a novel definition of low level temporal signals computed from epipolar lines. The spatial matching of two such temporal signals is given by the fundamental matrix. Thus, no pixel correspondence is required, bypassing the problem of correspondence changes in the presence of motion. The synchronization is determined from registration of the temporal signals. We consider general video data with substantial movement in the scene, for which high level information may be hard to extract from each individual camera (e.g., computing trajectories in crowded scenes). Furthermore, a trivial correspondence between the sequences is not assumed to exist. The method is online and can be used to resynchronize video sequences every few seconds, with only a small delay. Experiments on indoor and outdoor sequences demonstrate the effectiveness of the method.

1 Introduction

Applications of multiple camera systems range from video surveillance of large areas such as airports or shopping centers, to videography and filmmaking. As more and more of these applications utilize the information obtained in the overlapping fields of view of the cameras, precise camera synchronization and its constant maintenance are indispensable. Given enough video time, however, synchronization will be violated because of technical imperfections that cause frame dropping or incorrect timing between sequences. The tendency to use mostly inexpensive components makes such violations a certainty in many video systems. Manual synchronization is out of the question, as it is labor-intensive and cannot be performed constantly; thus, it cannot handle arbitrary frame-dropping. Precise time synchronization via satellite, as in GPS systems, may be too expensive or limited in indoor environments. Using distributed protocols for clock synchronization methods depends on the properties of the communication network

K. Daniilidis, P. Maragos, N. Paragios (Eds.): ECCV 2010, Part III, LNCS 6313, pp. 15–28, 2010.

and is sensitive to communication failures. Obvious alternative sources of time information are the video streams themselves, which often provide sufficient and reliable information for automatic synchronization. In this work we address the problem of computing and maintaining the temporal synchronization between a pair of video streams with the same frame rate, relying only on the video data.

Previous Work

Synchronization can be achieved using visual information by correlating spatio-temporal features or events viewed by two or more cameras. Several synchronization methods considered moving cameras viewing a static scene [10,12] or a scene with relatively little motion [8,6]. Our method considers static cameras acquiring a moving scene. Previous attempts to synchronize such sequences can be classified by the choice of features used for matching. The most straightforward approach is finding both spatial and temporal correspondence between point features at frames taken in all possible time shifts between the two video streams. Such approaches are vulnerable to correspondence ambiguities and require a large search space. A method for reducing the complexity of the search was suggested in [1]. Higher level features that contain temporal information also assist to reduce the matching ambiguity and the search complexity. Motion trajectories of features [9,14,12,2,6,11] or objects [13,3] could be used to this end. The computation of the trajectories and its quality strongly depend on the scene and can often be hard to compute as in the video considered in this paper. Since the motion of the objects may be 3D, matching the observed 2D trajectories in each sequence is ill posed. Several directions were considered for overcoming this problem, for instance, assuming the existence of a homography transformation that aligns the two trajectories [2], or using a three-or-more camera system and 3D tensors [13,6]. Another direction assumed an affine projection and used a linear combination approach in order to avoid exact point correspondence [14,11]. Highly discriminative action recognition features were also proposed for synchronization [4]. Naturally, such high-level features are limited to scenes for which these actions appear and can be detected.

In an effort to avoid complex computations such as tracking and action recognition, an approach based on brightness variation over the entire image was suggested in [2]. However, this method requires spatial alignment of the sequences (e.g., using Homography transformation), that is not necessarily exist between the views. Another approach suggested using statistics over low level space-time interest points in each of the sequences [15]. This concept steers clear of computing point-to-point, trajectory, or action correspondence. However, since the statistics are computed over the entire image, the approach is strongly sensitive to the overlapping regions of the two views and the relative viewing angle. The limitations of these two approaches motivate the solution suggested in this paper.

Proposed Approach

We present a method for obtaining online time synchronization of a pair of video sequences acquired by two static cameras, possibly in a wide-baseline setup. The fundamental matrix between each pair of sequences, which provides epipolar line-to-line correspondence, is assumed to be known. (It can be computed directly from static corresponding features of the videos when there is no motion in the scene.) This is the only spatial correspondence required by our method. We consider sequences of general 3D scenes which contain a large number of moving objects, focusing on sequences for which features or object trajectories may be hard to compute due to occlusions and substantial movement (see Fig. 1). Furthermore, trivial correspondence (e.g., alignment by a homography transformation) between the sequences is not assumed. The temporal misalignment is considered to be only a translation, i.e., the sequences have the same frame rate. Therefore, we do not detect sub-frame time shifts, as we are correcting synchronization errors as frame-drops.

Our method is based on matching temporal signals defined on epipolar lines of each of the sequences. Hence, the spatial matching is given by the fundamental matrix. The temporal matching is performed using a probabilistic optimization framework; independent simultaneous motion occurring on different epipolar lines improve our synchronization. Failure to find such a matching (despite the observed motion in the scene) indicates that the epipolar geometry is incorrect. In a general scene, the correspondence between pixels at different time steps changes due to 3D motion of objects in space. Therefore, the synchronization cannot rely on corresponding pixels. For overcoming this problem, the temporal signal is defined as an integration of the information along an epipolar line, during a sufficient interval of time. A simple background subtraction algorithm is used as an input to the integration. Integrating the information along epipolar lines rather than considering signals at the pixel level not only avoids the search for correspondence but allows the handling of general moving scenes.

The main contribution of this paper is the use of low level temporal events along corresponding epipolar lines for video synchronization. Our method does not require high level computation such as tracking, which may be hard to compute in crowded scenes as the ones considered in our experiments. Furthermore, we bypass the need to compute point-to-point correspondences between pixels [5]. Finally, our method can be used in an *online* framework, because it detects the synchronization errors (e.g., frame drops) in a matter of seconds, as they occur in the video.

2   Method

Given a pair of color (or gray-level) sequences and a fundamental matrix, we achieve synchronization by time registration of temporal signals from the two sequences. We first present our novel definition of temporal signals of a sequence, followed by a probabilistic approach for registering two of them. The summary of the algorithm flow is presented in Algorithm 1 and Algorithm 2.

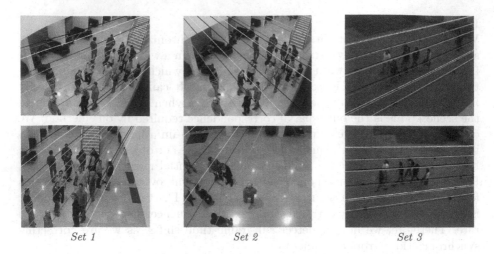

Set 1   Set 2   Set 3

Fig. 1. Example of two frames from each video pairs. The two rows show frames from the first and second view of each pair, respectively; the images contain an exemplary subset of the used epipolar lines, each set of lines for each video pair.

2.1   A Temporal Signal

To define the temporal signals, we make unconventional use of epipolar geometry of a pair of images. Given the fundamental matrix F for a pair of images, a set of epipolar lines $\mathcal{L} = \{\ell_r\}$ and $\mathcal{L}' = \{\ell'_r\}$ and their correspondence, $\ell_r \leftrightarrow \ell'_r$ are computed [5]. The correspondence of a given point $\hat{p} \in \ell_r$ is constrained to lie on the epipolar line $\hat{\ell}'_r = F\hat{p}$ in its synchronized frame (the points and the lines are given in homogeneous coordinates). Traditionally, this property is used for constraining the correspondence search in stereo or motion algorithms. Pixel correspondence is not guaranteed to remain the same over time due to 3D motion. However, two corresponding epipolar lines in both sequences will continue to correspond. (The only possible exception is a major occlusion on one of the views.) Using this observation, we define the signals on the entire epipolar line, avoiding not only the problem caused by the change of pixels correspondence over time but also the general challenge of computing spatial correspondence between frames.

A background subtraction algorithm is used for defining the temporal signal of each sequence. The base of the motion signal is the Euclidean distance between the data frame and the selected background frame for each pixel. For each epipolar line, a motion indicator is taken to be the sum of these distances of the line's pixels. The temporal signal of an epipolar line, the *line signal*, is defined to be the set of motion indicators on an epipolar line as a function of time. Formally, let $I(p, t)$ and $B(p, t)$ be the intensity values of a pixel $p \in \ell_r$, in

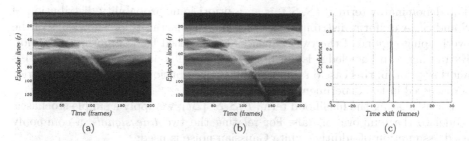

(a)   (b)   (c)

Fig. 2. (a),(b) are examples of temporal signals $\mathbb{S}$ and $\mathbb{S}'$ of two sequences, containing 130 epipolar lines for a time period of 8 seconds (200 frames). Each pixel in the signal is the motion indicator of an epipolar line at a time point. (c) is the matching result for those signals with a high-confidence peak at the correct time shift of $\Delta t = -1$ frames.

some video frame and corresponding background frame[1], respectively. The *line signal* of that epipolar line, $\mathcal{S}_r(t)$, is defined to be the distance between the two vectors:

$$\mathcal{S}_r(t) = \Sigma_{p \in \ell_r} \| I(t, p) - B(t, p) \|. \tag{1}$$

The collection of *line signals* for all the epipolar lines in a video, is the temporal signal of the video sequence. The temporal signals of two considered sequences are represented by matrices $\mathbb{S}$ and $\mathbb{S}'$ (Fig. 2), where each row r of this matrix consists of a *line signal*, $\mathcal{S}_r$. That is, $\mathbb{S}_{r,t}$ is the motion indicator of an epipolar line ℓr at a time step t. Only a few dozen epipolar lines from each frame, a few pixels apart, are considered.

2.2 Signal Registration

In this section we present the time registration of a given pair of temporal signals of the video sequences. For robust results, and in order to combine information from different *line signals*, the matching is determined using a probabilistic framework, utilizing a maximum a posteriori estimation. The time shift is detected by finding a maximum likelihood value for the two signals, with different time shifts applied to the second signal. A sliding window in a predefined range is used to determine Δt.

Let $\mathcal{S}$ and $\mathcal{S}'$ be a pair of *line signals*, extracted from corresponding epipolar lines in two video sequences. At this stage, assume a single consistent time shift between the two sequences and no frame drops in any of them. We begin with considering the probability distribution of a time shift Δt of $\mathcal{S}'$ to match $\mathcal{S}$. Applying Bayes' law we obtain:

$$P(\Delta t \,|\, \mathcal{S}, \mathcal{S}') = \frac{P(\mathcal{S}, \mathcal{S}' \,|\, \Delta t) P(\Delta t)}{P(\mathcal{S}, \mathcal{S}')}. \tag{2}$$

---

[1] $B_r(p, t)$ is a function of t, because in the general case an adaptive background subtraction can be used.

The denominator term, $P(\mathcal{S}, \mathcal{S}')$, is an a priori joint probability distribution of $\mathcal{S}$ and $\mathcal{S}'$. A uniform distribution is assumed. In general, prior knowledge of the overlapping regions of the two sequences can be used for computing this prior. Extracting such knowledge is out of the scope of this paper. The term $P(\Delta t)$ is another prior, in this case on the probability distribution of Δt. Use of this prior is discussed in the experimental part.

For estimating the likelihood term, $P(\mathcal{S}, \mathcal{S}' | \Delta t)$, we apply a simple stochastic model to the temporal signals. For relating the two *line signals*, a commonly used assumption of additive white Gaussian noise is used:

$$S(t) = S'(t + \Delta t) + \mathcal{N}(\mu, \sigma^2), \tag{3}$$

where Δt is the correct time shift between the two signals, and μ is the difference between the averages of both.

In a somewhat simplified representation, different photometric parameters of the camera, as well as the object foreshortening on corresponding epipolar lines, will cause difference of gain and offset between the two *line signals*. By subtracting the average μ from each *line signal*, we eliminate the offset effect. In the rest of the paper each line signal $\mathcal{S}$ is used after this average subtraction. The gain component between the signals is not eliminated, as we assume that it will not affect the search for the optimal shift.

Using this model assumption, the likelihood of two *line signals*, given Δt, is obtained by:

$$L(\mathcal{S}, \mathcal{S}', \Delta t) = \frac{1}{\sigma\sqrt{2\pi}}\, e^{-\sum_t \frac{(S(t) - S'(t + \Delta t))^2}{2\sigma^2}}. \tag{4}$$

This representation has a hidden assumption of independence between the motion indicators in a single *line signal*. In reality, adjacent indicators are expected to be correlated to some degree, because the objects captured in the video have finite speed, relative to the sampling frame rate. Despite these simplifications, the results are satisfying, as demonstrated by our experiments.

The desired time shift Δt is the one maximizing the value of $P(\Delta t | \mathcal{S}, \mathcal{S}')$, which is identical to that maximizing the value of $P(\mathcal{S}, \mathcal{S}' | \Delta t) P(\Delta t)$:

$$\arg\max_{\Delta t} P(\Delta t | \mathcal{S}, \mathcal{S}') = \arg\max_{\Delta t} P(\Delta t)\frac{1}{\sigma\sqrt{2\pi}}\, e^{-\sum_t \frac{(S(t) - S'(t + \Delta t))^2}{2\sigma^2}}. \tag{5}$$

As defined above, each row in $\mathbb{S}$ and $\mathbb{S}'$ represents a *line signal* for an epipolar line $\ell_r \in \mathcal{L}$. We consider those signals to be independent, due to the spatial distance between the selected epipolar lines. Therefore, computing the likelihood can be extended to *sequence signals* $\mathbb{S}$ and $\mathbb{S}'$ by taking the product of the likelihoods of all the *line signals*. Up to this point, this method assumed a single consistent

---

Algorithm 1. Temporal signal update
The algorithm is triggered for every new frame acquired.
Input: two new frames from the video sequences

1. Perform background subtraction
2. For each epipolar line ℓ_r: calculate the motion indicators (Eq. 1).
3. Update the matrices $\mathbb{S}$ and $\mathbb{S}'$.

---

time shift between $\mathbb{S}$ and $\mathbb{S}'$. In order to incorporate it into an online framework, the algorithm must work on a finite time interval at each iteration. Thus, the synchronization at a given time step, t_0, is determined only from a k interval of the *sequence signal*, taken from $t_0 - k$ up to t_0 . Furthermore, the sought for Δt is bounded by some finite range $-c \le \Delta t \le c$. (In our experiments, k corresponds to roughly 4 to 8 seconds and c corresponds to 1 to 3 seconds). Inserting all of the above into Eq. 2 and Eq. 5, we obtain:

$$\arg\max_{\Delta t} P(\Delta t \,|\mathbb{S},\mathbb{S}') = \arg\max_{\Delta t} P(\Delta t) \prod_{\ell_r \in \hat{\mathcal{L}}(t)} P(\Delta t \,|\mathcal{S}_r, \mathcal{S}'_r) \tag{6}$$

$$= \arg\max_{-c \le \Delta t \le c} P(\Delta t) \, e^{\displaystyle -\sum_{r \in \mathcal{L}(t)} \sum_{t=t_0-k}^{t_0} \frac{\left(\mathbb{S}_{r,t} - \mathbb{S}'_{r,t+\Delta t}\right)^2}{2\sigma^2}}$$

where $\hat{\mathcal{L}} \subseteq \mathcal{L}$ is the subset of epipolar lines participating in the computation (defined in 2.3), and S_r and S'_r are signals of corresponding epipolar lines ℓ_r.

The time shift Δt that yields maximal likelihood according to Eq. 6 is the correct time shift for the two given video sequences (Fig. 2(c)). The actual value of the likelihood is used as a confidence level of the resulting Δt. This value is taken after a normalization step, which ensures that the probability distribution of Δt in the range $-c \le \Delta t \le c$ sums up to 1. The higher the probability is, the more robust the answer is. In the online synchronization framework, only the high-confidence results will be taken into account.

2.3   Epipolar Line Filtering

Registration of only a subset of the *line signals* is sufficient for synchronization. Moreover, line signals that contain negligible motion information may insert noise into the registration process, and are therefore removed from the computation. We next define the subset of epipolar lines $\hat{\mathcal{L}} \subseteq \mathcal{L}$, that participate in the computation for a given time step t (see Eq. 6). The signals are removed on the basis of both sequences considered. We test for motion information only at short time interval. We do so by computing the temporal gradient along an epipolar line, taking into consideration some noise estimation of such a gradient. The noise at each image pixel is assumed to be additive white Gaussian noise

---

Algorithm 2. Synchronization iteration

The algorithm is triggered every 0.8 seconds.
Input: two temporal signals $\mathbb{S}$ and $\mathbb{S}'$.

1. Extract the data corresponding to the time interval k from $\mathbb{S}$ and $\mathbb{S}'$.
2. Compute $\hat{\mathcal{L}}$ by filtering $\ell_r \in \mathcal{L}$ for the current time step (Sec. 2.3).
3. For each $\ell_r \in \hat{\mathcal{L}}$ subtract its average μ_r.
4. Compute the likelihood for each $-c \leq \Delta t \leq c$ using Eq. 6.
5. Apply the prior for $P(\Delta t)$.
6. Normalize the distribution of resulting probability such that it sums up to 1.
7. Find the maximal value of the probability.

---

with some variance σ_m^2. Hence, we determine significant motion on the epipolar line r only if the residual information on the time gradient along the epipolar line goes beyond the estimated noise threshold. In case of no real motion, this time gradient yields only noise. Formally, the motion probability at a given time t, for an epipolar line ℓ_r is given by:

$$
P_{motion}(\ell_r, t) = \frac{1}{\sigma_m \sqrt{2\pi}} e^{-\sum_{p \in \ell_r} \frac{(I(t,p) - I(t-1,p))^2}{2\sigma_m^2}} . \tag{7}
$$

The subset $\hat{\mathcal{L}}$ consists only of epipolar lines with motion probability over some threshold. This simple filtering process compensates for the background subtraction algorithms, which are not ideal, and eliminates any wrongly detected residual motion caused by them.

3   Experiments

We conducted a number of experiments to test the effectiveness of our method. The input for each is a pair of video sequences taken with the same frame rate. In addition, a fundamental matrix (computed manually) and a rough synchronization (up to an error of 50 frames) are assumed to be given. The method was implemented in Matlab. The corresponding epipolar lines of each pair of sequences were computed using a standard rectification method. A naive background subtraction was used where the background consists of an empty frame, subtracted from all the other frames in the video stream. The framework triggers the synchronization computation every 0.8 seconds of the video.

Three sequences were taken, as shown in Fig. 1. *Set 1* is an indoor scenario of a dense crowd – around 30 people – walking about. The cameras were placed at an elevation of approximately 6 meters. The cameras' fields of view have a relatively large overlap. *Set 2* is similar to *Set 1*. In addition to the density of the crowd, the challenge in this sequence is in the large difference in the viewing angles and the small overlapping fields of view. Both videos consist of 5000 frames (3.33 minutes) and were recorded at 25 fps, with a frame size of 640 × 480. *Set 3* is an outdoor scenario with only few people walking around. The challenges in this set are the small amount of motion along epipolar lines and the dark illumination. The cameras were located at an elevation of about 6 meters, the videos were recorded at 15 fps, with a frame size of 640×512 pixels. In the indoor video sequences a flicker effect is evident, caused by fluorescent lighting in the scene. In order to avoid distractions to the synchronization algorithm, the flicker was removed by a temporal low-pass filtering of the video. All the results of the experiments, including video clips, are available on the web.

3.1   Basic Results

The presented tests were performed on the three sets. The interval size was taken to be $k = 140$, no prior on $P(\Delta t)$ was used (i.e., uniform distribution is assumed on $P(\Delta t)$). The value of σ for *Set 1* and *Set 2* was set to 1300, and for *Set 3* to 600. (Setting the values of σ is discussed bellow.) The results consist of a set of time shifts between two video streams with a probability (confidence) value for each shift. Each of the time-shifts for *Set 1*, *Set 2*, and *Set 3* are represented by a single dot in Fig. 3(a), Fig. 3(b), and Fig. 4(a), respectively. The x-axis is the computed time shift and the y-axis is the confidence in the computed result. Ideally, we would like the dots to align along the correct time shift, and to have high confidence. The correct time shift, computed by hand, is $\Delta t = -1$ frames for all sets.

To evaluate the percentage of correct results, it is necessary to set a threshold on the confidence value. The threshold 0.7 is considered in the analysis of the three data sets. A result is considered to be correct if it is in the range of ± 1 frames from the correct synchronization.

Using this threshold on *Set 1*, approximately 50% of the obtained results have high levels of confidence, and 95% pecent of them are correct. That is, the system yields, on average, a high-confidence result each 1.6 seconds.

The percentage of the correct high-confidence results obtained for *Set 2* is 100%. However, only 12% of the obtained results had high confidence(> 0.7). It is mostly due to the relatively small overlapping field of view of the two cameras, resulting in a small number of epipolar lines that can participate in the registration. As the working area is small, the algorithm analyses long time periods without motion, which yield low-confidence results.

For *Set 3*, the percentage of correct results is 100% with only 13% of the results having high confidence. In addition, the low confidence results consist of a relatively large amount of errors. This is due to the small number of moving objects in the scene and objects moving along the direction of epipolar lines. Note that a movement along an epipolar line is not expected to produce good synchronization, since it induces ambiguities, as discussed in Sec. 4. The effect of a non-uniform prior on $P(\Delta t)$ when incorporated into this set is discussed in Sec. 3.3.

To summarize, our method constantly and reliably maintains the time synchronization between the two sequences. It is important to note that tracking objects or features in the crowded scene of *Set 1* and *Set 2* from a single camera

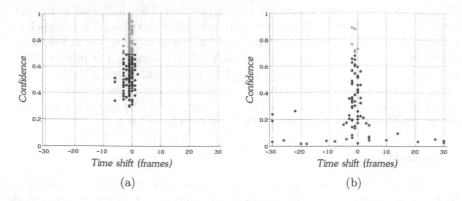

Fig. 3. Each of the 250 computed time-shifts for (a) *Set 1* and (b) *Set 2*, one for each 0.8 seconds, are represented by a single dot. Each dot in the graph represents the computed time shift for a single time step. Low confidence results are marked in blue, correct and incorrect high confidence results are marked by green and red, respectively. The x-axis is the computed time shift and the y-axis is the confidence in the computed result.

is considered to be an extremely difficult task due to substantial movement and a large number of occlusions. Hence, synchronization studies that rely on trajectories detected by each of the cameras (e.g., [3,13]) are not adequate in this case. Furthermore, the scene consists of a genuine 3D structure and the distance between the cameras is non-negligible. Hence, a homography transformation of the pair of sequences cannot be used to match pixels or trajectories (as in [2]).

3.2   Frame Dropping

Frame dropping is expected in a simple commercial system when it operates over a long period of time. The need to detect frame dropping and resynchronize is one of the main motivations for an online synchronization algorithm. To test the robustness of our method in the presence of frame dropping, we applied our algorithm to *Set 1* where 3 frame drops occurred during the video. That is, the correct time shift changed from -1 to 16, then to -8 and finally, back to -1. The rest of the experiment setup was identical to the basic one. The results are presented in Fig. 5(b), where the detected time shift is plotted as a function of time. The result demonstrates that the correct time shift is detected, and the reaction time to the drop is approximately 7-8 seconds. This reaction time is due to the interval of 140 frames, which, in addition to the search range $c = 30$, corresponds to 8 seconds. During this time period the two registered temporal signals contain inconsistent information with a frame drop in it. Hence, the results are incorrect and have low confidence.

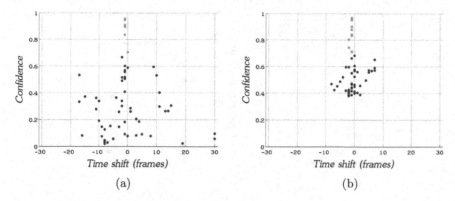

Fig. 4. Each of the 60 computed time-shifts, one for each 0.8 seconds, are represented by a single dot computed fot *Set 3*. (a) without prior and (b) with a prior. The axes description and color codes interpretation are as in Fig. 3.

3.3   Using a Prior on $P(\Delta t)$

In an online framework, a non-uniform probability distribution on Δt can be applied, using the result of the previous synchronization iteration. It is assumed that the time synchronization rarely changes during the video, and the changes are of a few frames only (due to frame dropping). We tested our method using a Gaussian distribution of $P(\Delta t)$ with $\sigma = 2$ and a mean set to the previously detected high-confidence time shift (starting with 0). Comparing the results with (Fig. 4(a)) and without (Fig. 4(b)) use of the prior, shows that the prior reduces the instability of the low-confidence results. We tested the effect of using a prior on *Set 1* (with and without frame dropping) and on *Set 2*. In all these tests the results remain the same. Hence we can conclude that on the one hand the prior can reduce errors for unstable results, and on the other hand it does not impair other results.

3.4   Setting the Parameters

In addition to the confidence threshold, there are two parameters that have to be set. The time interval k controls the number of frames that participate in the signal registration procedure. Longer intervals will lead to more robust results, especially for areas and times with limited motion. According to our tests, in a video pair with a lot of motion, an interval of $k = 20$ frames (0.8 seconds) is sufficient for robust synchronization results. However, for limited and sporadic motion, such an interval yields a somewhat noisy output, therefore $k = 140$ frames was used in all our experiments. The downside of large intervals is the increase in computation time and the slower reaction time in the presence of frame drops. The reaction time to such changes can, in the worst case, be as long as the interval time, as discussed in Sec. 3.2.

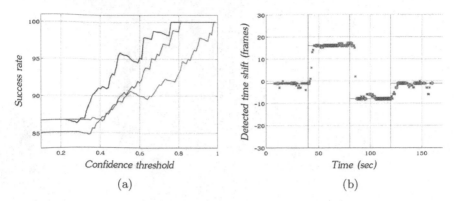

Fig. 5. (a) A graph showing the success rate as a function of the confidence threshold for three different values of σ (see Eq. 6). The blue, red and green lines represent $\sigma =$ 1600, 1300, and 1000, respectively. (b) Frame dropping example, drop reaction time $= 7$ seconds. The green and the red dots represent high and low confidence, respectively. The vertical blue lines indicate the time at which the frame drop occurred. The black line is the correct time shift.

The other parameter is the σ in Eq. 3-6. This value serves as a normalization factor in the probability calculations. In general, it depends on photometric parameters of the used cameras, as well as on their relative location. In the experiments, the value of σ was set empirically. This factor affects the numerical outcome of the confidence for each time shift, as demonstrated in Fig. 5(a). High values of σ suppress the confidence, hence flatten the probability distribution of $P(\Delta t \, | \mathcal{S}, \mathcal{S}')$, causing indecisiveness and noisy output. However, lower values of σ increase the confidence of all the measurements, and as a result, the confidence of incorrect time shifts increases as well. Thus, in order the preserve the correct output of the framework, the final confidence threshold must be selected in accordance to the value of σ. It is left for future study the automatic setting of this parameter.

3.5   Verification of Calibration

The main goal of our method was to compute synchronization between a pair of sequences, while the camera calibration (i.e., the epipolar geometry) is assumed to be given to the system. Incorrect epipolar geometry causes motion indicators on corresponding epipolar lines to be uncorrelated. In particular, the confidence of all the possible synchronization results is expected to be low. An experiment for demonstrating this observation was conducted, simulating a scenario of a small tilt in one of the cameras. The tilt causes calibration failure, as it breaks the correspondence of the epipolar lines. This leads to a total synchronization failure. Consequently, it is impossible to use our method when the system is out of calibration. Yet, this property of our method can be used to verify calibration, i.e., to distinguish between correct and incorrect calibration of the cameras.

Although it cannot be used in a straightforward manner for camera calibration, because the search space for a fundamental matrix is too large, it does serve as an essential first step towards recalibration, following calibration failure.

3.6   Additional Tests

We discussed in the introduction and the method sections why we choose to use epipolar lines signals rather than point signals. Here we challenge our choice to use epipolar line signals rather than a similar signal defined by a motion indicator based on the entire frame (similar to the approach taken by [15]). When the temporal signal is defined on the entire frame, any spatial correspondence between motion indicators is neglected. We modified our method to sum the motion indicators on the entire frame in order to obtain the motion signal. As expected, the obtained result cannot be used for sequence synchronization. Such an approach fails in the presence of complex motion in the scene.

To verify that our method works properly on other video sequences used in the literature, we have performed the synchronization of a pair of short videos used in [2]. The sequences contain a single car moving in a parking lot.[1] The success rate of our method on this sequence is 100% with the parameters: confidence threshold of 0.6, $\sigma = 400$ and $k = 80$.

4   Conclusion

We presented a novel method for synchronizing a pair of sequences using only motion signals of corresponding epipolar lines. Our method is suitable for detecting and correcting frame dropping. Its simplicity is in bypassing the computation of spatial correspondence between features, tracked trajectories or image points, which may be hard to compute in the scenes considered in our experiments. The only spatial correspondence required is between epipolar lines, which are computed directly from the given fundamental matrix of the sequence pairs. The relatively low computational effort will enable our algorithm to be incorporated into real-time systems, after a short optimization cycle. Furthermore, it can detect the synchronization errors (e.g., frame drops) in a matter of seconds, as they occur in the video. Thus, it can be used in an online framework. Finally, the method can be used for detecting calibration failures, as a first step in recalibration.

Our method requires sufficient motion in the overlapping regions of the two sequences in order to compute the correct time shift between the two sequences. However, when the entire motion is strictly along epipolar lines, the temporal matching is expected to yield the same probability for all time shifts. Therefore, no high-confidence result will be obtained and the time-shift will not be computed. This problem can be resolved when a system with more than two cameras is considered, and other pairs of epipolar lines are expected to produce

---

[1] http://www.wisdom.weizmann.ac.il/~vision/VideoAnalysis/Demos/Seq2Seq/
Seq2Seq.html

the required confidence. We intend to study the extension of the proposed approach to handle more than two sequences. Such extension should be natural due to the probabilistic properties of the algorithm. Another case that should be considered is when motion occurs on non-overlapping regions of epipolar lines. In this case, the method may produce an incorrect result if accidental correlation between motion at different times occurs. More likely, such motion reduces the confidence of the correct result. In order to overcome this problem, it is worth exploring a method for detecting overlapping regions of cameras, as in e.g. [7].

Acknowledgment. This work was partially supported by the VULCAN project of the Israeli Ministry of Industry.

References

1. Carceroni, R., Padua, F., Santos, G., Kutulakos, K.: Linear sequence-to-sequence alignment. In: Proc. IEEE Conf. Comp. Vision Patt. Recog., vol. 1 (2004)
2. Caspi, Y., Irani, M.: Spatio-temporal alignment of sequences. IEEE Trans. Patt. Anal. Mach. Intell., 1409–1424 (2002)
3. Caspi, Y., Simakov, D., Irani, M.: Feature-based sequence-to-sequence matching. Int. J. of Comp. Vision 68(1), 53–64 (2006)
4. Dexter, E., Pe'rez, P., Laptev, I.: Multi-view synchronization of human actions and dynamic scenes. In: Proc. British Machine Vision Conference (2009)
5. Hartley, R., Zisserman, A.: Multiple view geometry. Cambridge university press, Cambridge (2000)
6. Lei, C., Yang, Y.: Tri-focal tensor-based multiple video synchronization with sub-frame optimization. IEEE Transactions on Image Processing 15(9) (2006)
7. Mandel, Z., Shimshoni, I., Keren, D.: Multi-camera topology recovery from coherent motion. In: ACM/IEEE International Conference on Distributed Smart Cameras, pp. 243–250 (2007)
8. Serrat, J., Diego, F., Lumbreras, F., Álvarez, J.M.: Synchronization of Video Sequences from Free-Moving Cameras. In: Martí, J., Benedí, J.M., Mendonça, A.M., Serrat, J. (eds.) IbPRIA 2007. LNCS, vol. 4478, p. 627. Springer, Heidelberg (2007)
9. Singh, M., Basu, A., Mandal, M.: Event dynamics based temporal registration. IEEE Transactions on Multimedia 9(5) (2007)
10. Spencer, L., Shah, M.: Temporal synchronization from camera motion. In: Proc. Asian Conf. Comp. Vision (2004)
11. Tresadern, P., Reid, I.: Synchronizing image sequences of non-rigid objects. In: Proc. British Machine Vision Conference, vol. 2, pp. 629–638 (2003)
12. Tuytelaars, T., Van Gool, L.: Synchronizing video sequences. In: Proc. IEEE Conf. Comp. Vision Patt. Recog., vol. 1 (2004)
13. Whitehead, A., Laganiere, R., Bose, P.: Temporal synchronization of video sequences in theory and in practice. In: IEEE Workshop on Motion and Video Computing (2005)
14. Wolf, L., Zomet, A.: Correspondence-free synchronization and reconstruction in a non-rigid scene. In: Proc. Workshop Vision and Modeling of Dynamic Scenes (2002)
15. Yan, J., Pollefeys, M.: Video synchronization via space-time interest point distribution. In: Proc. Advanced Concepts for Intelligent Vision Systems (2004)

The Generalized PatchMatch
Correspondence Algorithm

Connelly Barnes[1], Eli Shechtman[2], Dan B Goldman [2], and Adam Finkelstein [1]

[1] Princeton University
[2] Adobe Systems

Abstract. PatchMatch is a fast algorithm for computing dense approximate nearest neighbor correspondences between patches of two image regions [1]. This paper generalizes PatchMatch in three ways: (1) to find k nearest neighbors, as opposed to just one, (2) to search across scales and rotations, in addition to just translations, and (3) to match using arbitrary descriptors and distances, not just sum-of-squared-differences on patch colors. In addition, we offer new search and parallelization strategies that further accelerate the method, and we show performance improvements over standard kd-tree techniques across a variety of inputs. In contrast to many previous matching algorithms, which for efficiency reasons have restricted matching to sparse interest points, or spatially proximate matches, our algorithm can efficiently find global, dense matches, even while matching across all scales and rotations. This is especially useful for computer vision applications, where our algorithm can be used as an efficient general-purpose component. We explore a variety of vision applications: denoising, finding forgeries by detecting cloned regions, symmetry detection, and object detection.

1 Introduction

Computing correspondences between image regions is a core issue in many computer vision problems, from classical problems like template tracking and optical flow, to low-level image processing such as non-local means denoising and example-based super-resolution, to synthesis tasks such as texture synthesis and image inpainting, to high level image analysis tasks like object detection, image segmentation and classification. Correspondence searches can be classified as either *local*, where a search is performed in a limited spatial window, or *global*, where all possible displacements are considered. Correspondences can also be classified as *sparse*, determined only at a subset of key feature points, or *dense*, determined at every pixel or on a dense grid in the input.

For efficiency, many common algorithms only use local or sparse correspondences. Local search can only identify small displacements, so multi-resolution refinement is often used (e.g., in optical-flow [3]), but large motions of small objects can be missed. Sparse keypoint [4, 5] correspondences are commonly used for alignment, 3D reconstruction, and object detection and recognition. These methods work best on textured scenes at high resolution, but are less effective

K. Daniilidis, P. Maragos, N. Paragios (Eds.): ECCV 2010, Part III, LNCS 6313, pp. 29–43, 2010.

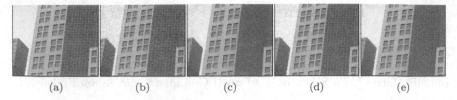

(a)   (b)   (c)   (d)   (e)

Fig. 1. Denoising using Generalized PatchMatch. Ground truth (a) is corrupted by Gaussian noise (b). Buades et al. [2] (c) denoise by averaging similar patches in a small local window: PSNR 28.93. Our method (d) uses PatchMatch for nonlocal search, improving repetitive features, but uniform regions remain noisy, as we use only $k = 16$ nearest neighbors: PSNR 29.11. Weighting matches from both algorithms (e) gives the best overall result: PSNR 30.90.

in other cases. More advanced methods [6, 7] that start with sparse matches and then propagate them densely suffer from similar problems. Thus, such methods could benefit from relaxing the locality and sparseness assumptions. Moreover, many analysis applications [8–11] and synthesis applications [12–15] inherently require dense global correspondences for adequate performance.

The PatchMatch algorithm [1] finds dense, global correspondences an order of magnitude faster than previous approaches, such as dimensionality reduction (e.g. PCA) combined with tree structures like kd-trees, VP-trees, and TSVQ. The algorithm finds an approximate nearest-neighbor in an image for every small (e.g. 7x7) rectangular patch in another image, using a randomized cooperative hill climbing strategy. However, the basic algorithm finds only a single nearest-neighbor, at the same scale and rotation. To apply this algorithm more broadly, the core algorithm must be generalized and extended.

First, for problems such as object detection, denoising, and symmetry detection, one may wish to detect multiple candidate matches for each query patch. Thus we extend the core matching algorithm to find k nearest neighbors (k-NN) instead of only 1-NN. Second, for problems such as super-resolution, object detection, image classification, and tracking (at re-initialization), the inputs may be at different scales and rotations, therefore, we extend the matching algorithm to search across these dimensions. Third, for problems such as object recognition, patches are insufficiently robust to changes in appearance and geometry, so we show that arbitrary image descriptors can be matched instead.

The resulting generalized algorithm is simple and fast despite the high dimensional search space. The difficulty of performing a 4D search across translations, rotations, and scales had previously motivated the use of sparse features that are invariant to some extent to these transformations. Our algorithm efficiently finds dense correspondences despite the increase in dimension, so it offers an alternative to sparse interest point methods. Like the original PatchMatch algorithm, our generalized algorithm is up to an order of magnitude more efficient than kd-tree techniques. We show how performance is further enhanced by two improvements: (1) a new search technique we call "enrichment" that generalizes "coherent" or locally similar matches from spatial neighborhoods to neighborhoods in nearest neighbor space and (2) a parallel tiled algorithm on multi-core machines. Finally, for k-NN and enrichment, there were many possible algorithms, so we performed extensive comparisons to determine which worked best.

In summary, our main contributions are: (1) an extended matching algorithm, providing k nearest neighbors, searching across rotations and scales, and descriptor matching (Section 3.2-Section 3.5); (2) acceleration techniques, including a new search strategy called "enrichment" and a parallel algorithm for multi-core architectures (Section 3.3, Section 3.6) We believe this Generalized PatchMatch algorithm can be employed as a general component in a variety of existing and future computer vision methods, and we demonstrate its applicability for image denoising, finding forgeries in images, symmetry detection, and object detection. .

2   Related Work

When a *dense, global* matching is desired, previous approaches have typically employed tree-based search techniques. In image synthesis (e.g., [16]), one popular technique for searching image patches is dimensionality reduction (using PCA) followed by a search using a kd-tree [17]. In Boiman et al [18], nearest-neighbor image classification is done by sampling descriptors on a dense grid into a kd-tree, and querying this tree. Other tree structures that have been employed for querying patches included TSVQ [19] and vp-trees [20]. Another popular tree structure is the k-means-tree that was successfully used for fast image retrieval [21]. The FLANN method [22] combines multiple different tree structures and automatically chooses which one to use according to the data. Locality-sensitive hashing [23] and other hashing methods can be used as well. Each of these algorithms can be run in either approximate or exact matching mode, and find multiple nearest neighbors. When search across a large range of scales and rotations is required, a dense search is considered impractical due to the high dimensionality of the search space. The common way to deal with this case is via keypoint detectors [4]. These detectors either find an optimal local scale and the principal local orientation for each keypoint or do an affine normalization. These approaches are not always reliable due to image structure ambiguities and noise. The PatchMatch algorithm [1] was shown to find a single nearest neighbor one to two orders of magnitude faster than tree-based techniques, for equivalent errors, with running time on the order of seconds for a VGA input on a single core machine. This paper offers performance improvements and extends it to dense k-NN correspondence across a large range of scales and rotations. The Generalized PatchMatch algorithm can operate on any common image descriptors (e.g., SIFT) and unlike many of the above tree structures, supports any distance function. Even while the algorithm naturally supports dense global matching, it may also be constrained to only accept matches in a local window if desired.

Section 4 investigates several applications in computer vision, and prior work related to those applications is mentioned therein.

3   Algorithm

This section presents four generalizations of the PatchMatch algorithm suitable for a wide array of computer vision problems. After reviewing the original algorithm [1], we present our extensions, including k-nearest neighbors, matching across rotations and scale, and matching descriptors. We finally show how performance can be improved with a new search strategy called "enrichment," and a parallel tiled algorithm suitable for multi-core architectures.

3.1   The PatchMatch Algorithm

Here we review the original PatchMatch algorithm as proposed by Barnes et al. [1]. It is an efficient randomized approach to solving the following problem: for every $p \times p$ patch in image A, find the approximate nearest neighbor patch in image B, minimizing the sum-squared difference between corresponding pixels.

A *nearest-neighbor field* (NNF) is a function $\mathbf{f} : A \mapsto \mathbb{R}^2$, defined over all possible patch coordinates (locations of patch centers) in image A, for some distance function D between two patches. Given patch coordinate $\mathbf{a}$ in image A and its corresponding nearest neighbor $\mathbf{b}$ in image B, $\mathbf{f}(\mathbf{a})$ is simply $\mathbf{b}$.[1] We refer to the values of f as *nearest neighbors*, and they are stored in an array whose dimensions are those of A.

Note that the NNF differs from an optical flow field (OFF). The NNF uses no smoothness constraints and finds the best match independent of neighboring matches. The OFF is defined by ground truth motion and is often computed with smoothness constraints.

The randomized algorithm works by iteratively improving the nearest-neighbor field $\mathbf{f}$ until convergence. Initially, the nearest neighbor field is filled with random coordinates, uniformly sampled across image B. Next, the field is iteratively improved for a fixed number of iterations, or until convergence. The algorithm examines field vectors in scan order, and tries to improve each using two sets of candidates: *propagation*, and *random search*.

The *propagation* trials attempt to improve a nearest neighbor $\mathbf{f}(\mathbf{x})$ using the known nearest neighbors above or to the left. The new candidates for $\mathbf{f}(\mathbf{x})$ are $\mathbf{f}(\mathbf{x} - \boldsymbol{\Delta}_p) + \boldsymbol{\Delta}_p$, where $\boldsymbol{\Delta}_p$ takes on the values of $(1, 0)$ and $(0, 1)$. Propagation takes a downhill step if either candidate provides a smaller patch distance D. (On even iterations, propagation is done in reverse scan order, and candidates below and to the right are examined, so information propagates up and left.) Propagation converges very quickly, but if used alone ends up in a local minimum. So a second set of trials employs *random search*: a sequence of candidates is sampled from an exponential distribution, and $\mathbf{f}(\mathbf{x})$ is improved if any of the candidates has smaller distance D. Let $\mathbf{v_0}$ be the current nearest neighbor $\mathbf{f}(\mathbf{x})$. The candidates $\mathbf{u}_i$ are constructed by sampling around $\mathbf{v_0}$ at an exponentially decreasing distance: $\mathbf{u}_i = \mathbf{v_0} + w\alpha^i \mathbf{R}_i$, where $\mathbf{R}_i$ is a uniform random in $[-1, 1] \times [-1, 1]$, w is the maximum image dimension, and α is a

---

[1] Our notation is in absolute coordinates, vs relative coordinates in Barnes et al. [1]

ratio between window sizes ($\alpha = 1/2$ was used). The index i is increased from $i = 0, 1, 2, ..., n$ until the search radius $w\alpha^i$ is below 1 pixel. For more details, see Barnes et al. [1].

3.2 k-Nearest Neighbors

For problems such as denoising, symmetry detection, and object and clone detection, we wish to compute more than a single nearest neighbor at every (x, y) position. This can be done by collecting k nearest neighbors for each patch. Thus the NNF $\mathbf{f}$ is a multi-valued map, with k values. There are many possible modifications of PatchMatch to compute the k-NN. We have compared the efficiency of several of these against a standard approach: dimensionality reduction with PCA, followed by construction of a kd-tree [17] with all patches of image B projected onto the PCA basis, then an independent ϵ-nearest neighbor lookup in the kd-tree for each patch of image A projected onto the same basis.

Since each of these algorithms can be tuned for either greater accuracy or greater speed, we evaluated each across a range of settings. For PatchMatch, we simply computed additional iterations, and for kd-trees we adjusted the ϵ and PCA dimension parameters. The relative efficiency of these algorithms is plotted in Figure 2. We also compare with FLANN [22], a package that includes kd-tree, k-means tree, a hybrid algorithm, and a large number of parameters that can be tuned for performance.

Heap algorithm. In the most straightforward variant, we associate k nearest neighbors with each patch position. During propagation, we improve the nearest neighbors at the current position by exhaustively testing each of the k nearest neighbors to the left or above (or below or right on even iterations). The new candidates are $\mathbf{f}_i(\mathbf{x}-\boldsymbol{\Delta}_p)+\boldsymbol{\Delta}_p$, where $\boldsymbol{\Delta}_p$ takes on the values $(1, 0)$ and $(0, 1)$, and $i = 1 \ldots k$. If any candidate is closer than the worst candidate currently stored at $\mathbf{x}$, that worst candidate is replaced with the candidate from the adjacent patch. This can be done efficiently with a max-heap, where the heap stores the patch distance D. The random search phase works similarly: n samples are taken around each of the k nearest neighbors, giving nk samples total. The worst element of the heap is evicted if the candidate's distance is better. When examining candidates, we also construct a hash table to quickly identify candidates already in our k list, to prevent duplicate entries.

Details of the additional strategies tested can be found in supplementary material. Briefly, they include variants of the heap algorithm in which fewer than k samples are taken from the neighbor list for propagation and/or search ("P best," "P random", "RS best", "RS random", "P varying", "RS varying"); variants of the heap algorithm where k is changed over time ("Increase k", "Decrease k"); and modifications of the original 1NN algorithm in which no heap is used but the sequence of candidates is retained ("List 1-NN", "Run 1-NN k times"). Some of these algorithms complete single iterations faster than the basic heap algorithm described above, but convergence is slower as they propagate less information within an iteration. In general, the original heap algorithm is a good choice over a wide range of the speed/quality curve.

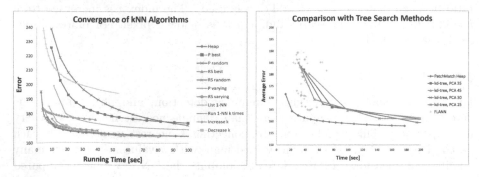

Fig. 2. *Left:* Performance of k-PatchMatch variants, with $k = 16$, averaged over all images in Figure 4, resized to 0.2MP, and matched against themselves. Error is average L^2 patch distance over all k. Points on each curve represent progress after each iteration. *Right:* Comparison with kd-tree and FLANN, at 0.3 MP, averaged over the dataset.

We find the basic heap algorithm outperforms kd-tree over a wide range of k and image sizes: for example, our algorithm is several times faster than kd-tree, for $k = 16$ and input images of 0.1 to 1.0MP. In our comparisons to the kd-tree implementation of Mount and Arya [17] and FLANN [22], we gave the competition the benefit of the doubt by tuning all possible parameters, while adjusting only the number of iterations for our heap algorithm. FLANN offers several algorithms, so we sampled a large range of algorithmic options and parameters, indicated by the + marks in Figure 2. FLANN can also automatically optimize parameters, but we found the resulting performance always lies within the convex hull of our point-sampling. In both cases, this extensive parameter-tuning resulted in performance that approached – but never exceeded – our heap algorithm. Thus, we propose that the general k-PatchMatch heap algorithm is a better choice for a wide class of problems requiring image patch correspondence. With additional optimization of our algorithm, the performance gap might be even greater.

3.3 Enrichment

In this section we propose one such optimization for improving PatchMatch performance further. The propagation step of PatchMatch propagates good matches across the spatial dimensions of the image. However, in special cases we can also consider propagating matches across the space of patches themselves: For example, when matching an image A to itself – as in non-local-means denoising (Section 4.1) – many of a patch's k nearest neighbors will have the original patch and some of the other $k - 1$ patches in their own k-NN list.

We define enrichment as the propagation of good matches from a patch to its k-NN, or vice versa. We call this operation enrichment because it takes a nearest neighbor field and improves it by considering a "richer" set of potentially good candidate matches than propagation or random search alone. From a graph-theoretic viewpoint, we can view ordinary propagation as moving good matches

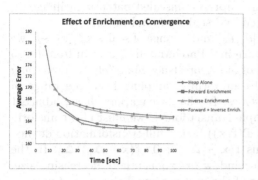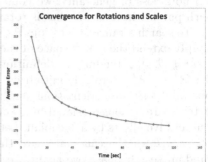

Fig. 3. *Left:* Comparison of the heap algorithm with and without enrichment. As in Figure 2, times and errors are averaged over the dataset of Figure 4 at 0.2 megapixels and $k = 16$ neighbors. *Right:* Searching across all rotations and scales.

along a rectangular lattice whose nodes are patch centers (pixels), whereas enrichment moves good matches along a graph where every node is connected to its k-NN. We introduce two types of enrichment, for the special case of matching patches in A to other patches in A:

Forward enrichment uses compositions of the function $\mathbf{f}$ with itself to produce candidates for improving the nearest neighbor field. The canonical case of forward enrichment is $\mathbf{f}^2$. That is, if $\mathbf{f}$ is a NNF with k neighbors, we construct the NNF $\mathbf{f}^2$ by looking at all of our nearest neighbor's nearest neighbors: there are k^2 of these. The candidates in $\mathbf{f}$ and $\mathbf{f}^2$ are compared and the best k overall are used as an improved NNF $\mathbf{f}'$. If min() denotes taking the top k matches, then we have: $\mathbf{f}' = \min(\mathbf{f}, \mathbf{f}^2)$. See the supplementary material for other variants.

Similarly, **inverse enrichment** walks the nearest-neighbor pointers backwards to produce candidates for improving the NNF. The canonical algorithm here is $\mathbf{f}^{-1}$. That is, compute the multi-valued inverse $\mathbf{f}^{-1}$ of function $\mathbf{f}$. Note that $\mathbf{f}^{-1}(a)$ may have zero values if no patches point to patch a, or more than k values if many patches point to a. We store $\mathbf{f}^{-1}$ by using a list of varying length at each position. Again, to improve the current NNF, we rank our current k best neighbors and all neighbors in $\mathbf{f}^{-1}$, producing an improved NNF $\mathbf{f}''$: $\mathbf{f}'' = \min(\mathbf{f}, \mathbf{f}^{-1})$. Note that in most cases the distance function is symmetric, so patch distances do not need to be computed for $\mathbf{f}^{-1}$. Finally we can concatenate inverse and forward enrichment, and we found that $\mathbf{f}^{-1}$ followed by $\mathbf{f}^2$ is fastest overall. The performance of these algorithms is compared in Figure 3.

In the case of matching different images A and B, inverse enrichment can be trivially done. Forward enrichment can be applied by computing nearest neighbor mappings in both directions; we leave this investigation for future work.

3.4 Rotations and Scale

For some applications, such as object detection, denoising or super-resolution, it may be desirable to match patches across a range of possible rotations or scales.

Without loss of generality, we compare upright unscaled patch a in image A, with patch b in image B that is rotated and scaled around its center.

To search a range of rotations $\theta \in [\theta_1, \theta_2]$ and a range of scales $s \in [s_1, s_2]$, we simply extend the search space of the original PatchMatch algorithm from (x, y) to (x, y, θ, s), extending the definition of our nearest-neighbor field to a mapping $\mathbf{f} : \mathbb{R}^2 \mapsto \mathbb{R}^4$. Here $\mathbf{f}$ is initialized by uniformly sampling from the range of possible positions, orientations and scales. In the propagation phase, adjacent patches are no longer related by a simple translation, so we must also transform the relative offsets by a Jacobian. Let $\mathbf{T}(\mathbf{f}(\mathbf{x}))$ be the full transformation defined by (x, y, θ, s): the candidates are thus $\mathbf{f}(\mathbf{x} - \mathbf{\Delta}_p) + \mathbf{T}'(\mathbf{f}(\mathbf{x} - \mathbf{\Delta}_p))\mathbf{\Delta}_p$. In the random search phase, we again use a window of exponentially decreasing size, only now we contract all 4 dimensions of the search around the current state.

The convergence of this approach is shown in Figure 3. In spite of searching over 4 dimensions instead of just one, the combination of propagation and random search successfully samples the search space and efficiently propagates good matches between patches. In contrast, with a kd-tree, it is nontrivial to search over all scales and rotations. Either all rotations and scales must be added to the tree, or else queried, incurring enormous expenses in time or memory.

3.5   Matching with Arbitrary Descriptors and Distance Metrics

The PatchMatch algorithm was originally implemented using the sum-of-squared differences patch distance, but places no explicit requirements on the distance function. The only implicit assumption is that patches with close spatial proximity should also be more likely to have similar best-nearest-neighbors, so that PatchMatch can be effective at propagating good nearest neighbors and finding new ones. This turns out to be true for a variety of descriptors and distance functions. In fact, the algorithm can converge even more quickly when using large-area feature descriptors than it does with small image patches, because they tend to vary relatively slowly over the image. In general, the "distance function" can actually be any algorithm that supplies a total ordering, and the matching can even be performed between entirely different images — the rate of convergence depends only on the size of coherent matching regions. Thus, our matching is quite flexible.

In this paper we explore several examples. In Section 4.3 we implement symmetry detection with a modified L^2 patch distance that is robust to changes in luminance. In Section 4.4, we perform label transfer by sampling a SIFT descriptor at every pixel. Our matching algorithm performs a global search, so two matched objects can be present in different regions of the image.

3.6   Parallel Tiled Algorithm

Barnes et al. proposed a parallel variant of PatchMatch using "jump flooding" for the propagation phase [1]. This algorithm was intended for GPU usage. However, on the CPU, this approach is less effective than serial propagation and converges more slowly in each iteration.

Fig. 4. Dataset of 36 input images for denoising

On a multi-core architecture, we propose parallelizing PatchMatch by dividing the NNF into horizontal tiles, and handling each tile on a separate core. Because the tiles are handled in parallel, information can propagate vertically the entire length of a tile in a single iteration. To ensure information has a chance to propagate all the way up and down the image, we synchronize using a critical section after each iteration. To prevent resource conflicts due to propagation between abutting tiles, we write back the nearest neighbors in the last row of the tile only after synchronization. Note that both propagation/random search and forward enrichment can be parallelized using this tile scheme.

We observe a nearly linear speed-up, on our 8 core test machine. Our timing values in this paper use only one core unless otherwise indicated. See the supplementary material for details.

4   Vision Applications

This section investigates several possible applications for the generalized PatchMatch algorithm: denoising, clone detection, symmetry detection, and object detection.

4.1   Non-local Means Denoising

For image denoising, Buades et al. [2] showed that high-quality results could be obtained by *non-local means denoising:* finding similar patches within an image and then averaging these. Subsequent work [24, 25] showed that this patch-based method could be extended to obtain state-of-the-art results by performing additional filtering steps. While Buades et al. [2] searched for similar patches only within a limited search window, Brox et al. [26] showed that a tree-based method could be used to obtain better quality for some inputs. However they do increase the distance to far away patches so searching is still limited to some local region.

Our kNN algorithm can be used to find similar patches in an image, so it can be used as a component in these denoising algorithms. We implemented the simple method of Buades et al. [2] using our kNN algorithm. This method works by examining each source patch of an image, performing a local search over all patches within a fixed distance r of the source patch, computing a Gaussian-weighted L^2 distance d between the source and target patch, and computing a weighted mean for the center pixel color with some weight function $f(d)$.

To use our kNN algorithm in this denoising framework, we can simply choose a number of neighbors k, and for each source patch, use its k-NN in the entire image as the list of target patches. To evaluate this algorithm, we chose 36 images as our dataset (Figure 4). We corrupted these images by adding to each RGB channel noise from a Gaussian distribution with $\sigma = 20$ (out of 256 grey levels). If the dataset is denoised with Buades et al (using an 11x11 search window) the average PSNR is 27.8. Using our kNN algorithm gives an average PSNR of 27.4, if the number of neighbors is small ($k = 16$). Counterintuitively, our algorithm gives worse PSNR values because it finds better matches. This occurs because our algorithm can search the entire image for a good match, therefore in uniform regions, the patch's noise pattern simply matches similar noise.

One solution would be to significantly increase our k. However, we found that Buades et al and our algorithm are complementary and both are efficient. Therefore, we simply run both algorithms, and list all target patches found by each, before averaging the patches under a weight function $f(d)$. We train the weight function on a single image and then evaluate on the dataset. This combined algorithm has an average PSNR of 28.4, showing that our kNN matching can improve denoising in the framework of Buades et al. The best results are obtained on images with repeating elements, as in Figure 1.

We also compared our results with the state-of-the-art BM3D algorithm [24]. For our dataset, BM3D produced an average PSNR of 29.9, significantly outperforming our results. However, we intentionally kept our denoising algorithm simple, and hypothesize that more advanced algorithms [24, 25] that are based on local search for speed, could do even better with our kNN algorithm.

4.2   Clone Detection

One technique for digitally forging images is to remove one region of an image by cloning another region. For example, this can be done using Adobe Photoshop's clone brush. Such forgeries have been a concern in the popular press of late, as fake photos have been published in major newspapers.

Methods of detecting such forgeries have been proposed recently [11, 27]. These methods propose breaking the image into either square or irregularly shaped patches, applying PCA or DCT to discard minor variations in the image due to noise or compression, and sorting the resulting blocks to detect duplicates.

We can apply our kNN algorithm for the purposes of detecting cloned regions. Rather than sorting all blocks into a single ordered list, we can consider for each patch, its k-NN as potentially cloned candidates. We identify cloned regions by detecting connected "islands" of patches that all have similar nearest neighbors.

Specifically, we construct a graph and extract connected components from the graph to identify cloned regions. The vertices of the graph are the set of all (x, y) pixel coordinates in the image. For each (x, y) coordinate, we create a horizontal or vertical edge in the graph if its kNN are similar to the neighbors at $(x + 1, y)$ or $(x, y + 1)$, respectively. We call two lists A and B of kNN similar if for any pair of nearest neighbors $(ax, ay) \in A$ and $(bx, by) \in B$, the nearest neighbors are within a threshold distance T of each other, and both have a patch distance less than a maximum distance threshold. Finally, we detect connected

(a) original   (b) forged   (c) detected forgery

Fig. 5. Detecting image regions forged using the clone brush. Shown are (a) the original, untampered image, (b) the forged image, (c) cloned regions detected by our kNN algorithm and connected components. Imagery from [11]

Fig. 6. Symmetry detection using a regular lattice (superimposed white dots)

components in the graph, and consider any component with an area above a minimum cloned region size C (we use $C = 50$) to be a cloned region.

Examples of our clone detection implementation are shown in Figure 5. Note that cloned areas are correctly identified. However, the area of the clone is not exactly that of the removed objects because our prototype is not robust to noise, compression artifacts, or feathering. Nevertheless, we believe it would be easy to adapt the algorithm to better recover the complete mask.

4.3 Symmetry Detection

Detecting symmetric features in images has been of interest recently. A survey of techniques for finding rotational and reflective symmetries is given by Park et al. [28]. Methods have also been developed for finding translational symmetries in the form of regular lattices [8].

Because our kNN algorithm matches repeated features non-locally, it can be used as a component in symmetry detection algorithms. Symmetries have been detected using sparse interest points, such as corner detectors or SIFT or edge interest points [28]. In contrast to sparse methods, our algorithm can match densely sampled descriptors such as patches or SIFT descriptors, and symmetries can be found by examining the produced dense correspondence field. This suggests that our algorithm may be able to find symmetric components even in the case where there are no sparse interest points present.

To illustrate how our method can be used for symmetry detection, we propose a simple algorithm for finding translational symmetries in the form of repeated elements on a non-deformed lattice. First we run our kNN algorithm. The descriptor for our algorithm is 7x7 patches. We calculate patch distance using L^2 between corresponding pixels after correcting for limited changes in lighting

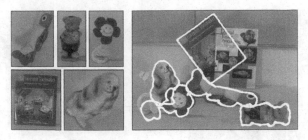

Fig. 7. Detecting objects. Templates, left, are matched to the image, right. Square patches are matched, searching over all rotations and scales, as described in Section 3.4. A similarity transform is fit to the resulting correspondences using RANSAC.

by normalizing the mean and standard deviation in luminance to be equal. We find $k = 16$ nearest neighbors, and then use RANSAC [29] to find the basis vectors $\mathbf{v}_1$ and $\mathbf{v}_2$ that form the lattice. We classify as inliers the coordinates where the distance between the lattice and all of the kNN is small. A result of our symmetry detection is shown in Figure 6.

4.4   Object Detection

Methods for object detection include deformable templates [30], boosted cascades [31], matching of sparse features such as SIFT [5], and others. Our algorithm can match densely sampled features, including upright patches, rotating or scaled patches, or descriptors such as SIFT. These matches are global, so that correspondences can be found even when an object moves across an image, or rotates or scales significantly. Provided that the descriptor is invariant to the change in object appearance, the correct correspondence will be found.

In Figure 7 we show an example of object detection. Similar to the method of Guo and Dyer [32], we break the template into small overlapping patches. We query these patches against the target image, searching over all rotations, and a range of scales, as per Section 3.4. A similarity transform is fit from the template to the target using RANSAC. We calculate patch distance using L^2, after correcting for lighting as we did in symmetry detection. The result is that we can find objects under partial occlusions and at different rotations and scales.

For greater invariance to lighting and appearance changes, a more complex local appearance model is needed. However it is straightforward to incorporate more complex models into our algorithm! For example, suppose we have photographs of two similar objects with different appearance. We might wish to propagate labels from one image to the other for all similar objects and background. The SIFT Flow work [33] shows that this can be done using SIFT features correspondence on a dense grid combined with an optical-flow like smoothness term. The resulting field is solved using a coarse-to-fine approach and global optimization (belief propagation). Like most optical flow methods, SIFT Flow assumes locality and smoothness of the flow and thus can fail to align objects under large displacements. As shown in Figure 8, we can correctly transfer labels even when objects move a large amount. We do this by densely sampling SIFT descriptors and then matching these as described in Section 3.5.

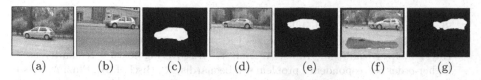

(a)   (b)   (c)   (d)   (e)   (f)   (g)

Fig. 8. Label transfer using our method with SIFT descriptors. (a) car A; (b) car B; (c) labeled A; (d) A warped to match B using SIFT Flow [33] as well as the transferred label mask in (e); (f) A warped to B using our method and the transferred label mask in (g). Our flow is globally less smooth but can handle arbitrarily large motions.

5   Discussion and Future Work

This paper generalizes the PatchMatch algorithm to encompass a broad range of core computer vision applications. We demonstrate several prototype examples, but many more are possible with additional machinery. For example, example-based super-resolution can use PatchMatch, using a single [34] or multiple [12] images. Section 4.4 shows an example of transferring labels using correspondences without a term penalizing discontinuity, but in other settings a neighborhood term is necessary for accurate optical flow [3, 6]. Finally, although we demonstrate object detection, our speed is not competitive with the best sparse tracking methods. It is possible that some variations of this approach using fewer iterations and downsampled images could be used to provide real-time tracking.

Acknowledgements

We thank ECCV reviewers for helpful comments, as well as the support of Adobe and NSF Award 0937139, and Flickr users for Creative Commons imagery: Moogs, Swami Stream, Laurence & Annie, Bill Liao, Badwsky, Cwalker71, Swamibu, Stuck in Customs, Xymox, Christopher S. Penn, Eric Brumble, Kibondo, Mazzaq-Mauro Mazzacurati, Slack12, Thomashawk, Bex in Beijing, Paul Keleher, CarbonNYC, SteveWhis, Arranging Matches, Professor Bop, Whirling Phoenix, Cindy47452.

References

1. Barnes, C., Shechtman, E., Finkelstein, A., Goldman, D.: PatchMatch: a randomized correspondence algorithm for structural image editing. ACM Transactions on Graphics (Proc. SIGGRAPH) 28, 24 (2009)
2. Buades, A., Coll, B., Morel, J.: A non-local algorithm for image denoising. In: Proc. CVPR II, p. 60 (2005)
3. Baker, S., Scharstein, D., Lewis, J., Roth, S., Black, M., Szeliski, R.: A database and evaluation methodology for optical flow. In: Proc. ICCV, vol. 5 (2007)
4. Mikolajczyk, K., Schmid, C.: A performance evaluation of local descriptors. IEEE Transactions on Pattern Analysis and Machine Intelligence, 1615–1630 (2005)
5. Lowe, D.: Distinctive image features from scale-invariant keypoints. International Journal of Computer Vision 60, 91–110 (2004)

6. Brox, T., Malik, J.: Large displacement optical flow. In: CVPR (2009)
7. Simon, I., Seitz, S.: A probabilistic model for object recognition, segmentation, and non-rigid correspondence. In: Proc. CVPR, pp. 1–7 (2007)
8. Hays, J., Leordeanu, M., Efros, A., Liu, Y.: Discovering texture regularity as a higher-order correspondence problem. In: Leonardis, A., Bischof, H., Pinz, A. (eds.) ECCV 2006. LNCS, vol. 3952, p. 522. Springer, Heidelberg (2006)
9. Boiman, O., Irani, M.: Detecting irregularities in images and in video. International Journal of Computer Vision 74, 17–31 (2007)
10. Bagon, S., Boiman, O., Irani, M.: What is a good image segment? A unified approach to segment extraction. In: Forsyth, D., Torr, P., Zisserman, A. (eds.) ECCV 2008, Part IV. LNCS, vol. 5305, p. 44. Springer, Heidelberg (2008)
11. Popescu, A., Farid, H.: Exposing digital forgeries by detecting duplicated image regions. Department of Computer Science, Dartmouth College (2004)
12. Freeman, W., Jones, T., Pasztor, E.: Example-based super-resolution. IEEE Computer Graphics and Applications, 56–65 (2002)
13. Efros, A., Leung, T.: Texture synthesis by non-parametric sampling. In: Proc. ICCV, vol. 2, pp. 1033–1038 (1999)
14. Criminisi, A., Pérez, P., Toyama, K.: Region filling and object removal by exemplar-based image inpainting. IEEE Trans. on Image Processing 13 (2004)
15. Simakov, D., Caspi, Y., Shechtman, E., Irani, M.: Summarizing visual data using bidirectional similarity. In: Proc. CVPR (2008)
16. Hertzmann, A., Jacobs, C., Oliver, N., Curless, B., Salesin, D.: Image analogies. ACM Transactions on Graphics (Proc. SIGGRAPH), 327–340 (2001)
17. Mount, D.M., Arya, S.: ANN: A library for approx. nearest neighbor search (1997)
18. Boiman, O., Shechtman, E., Irani, M.: In defense of nearest-neighbor based image classification. In: Proc. CVPR., vol. 2, p. 6 (2008)
19. Niyogi, S., Freeman, W.: Example-based head tracking. In: Proc. of Conf. on Automatic Face and Gesture Recognition (FG 1996), p. 374 (1996)
20. Kumar, N., Zhang, L., Nayar, S.K.: What is a good nearest neighbors algorithm for finding similar patches in images? In: Forsyth, D., Torr, P., Zisserman, A. (eds.) ECCV 2008, Part II. LNCS, vol. 5303, pp. 364–378. Springer, Heidelberg (2008)
21. Nister, D., Stewenius, H.: Scalable recognition with a vocabulary tree. In: Proc. CVPR, vol. 5 (2006)
22. Muja, M., Lowe, D.: Fast approximate nearest neighbors with automatic algorithm configuration. In: VISAPP (2009)
23. Datar, M., Immorlica, N., Indyk, P., Mirrokni, V.: Locality-sensitive hashing scheme based on p-stable distributions. In: Symp. on Comp. Geom., pp. 253–262 (2004)
24. Dabov, K., Foi, A., Katkovnik, V., Egiazarian, K.: Image denoising by sparse 3-D transform-domain collaborative filtering. IEEE Trans. Image Processing 16 (2007)
25. Mairal, J., Bach, F., Ponce, J., Sapiro, G., Zisserman, A.: Non-local sparse models for image restoration. In: Proc. of ICCV (2009)
26. Brox, T., Kleinschmidt, O., Cremers, D.: Efficient nonlocal means for denoising of textural patterns. IEEE Transactions on Image Processing 17, 1083–1092 (2008)
27. Bayram, S., Sencar, H., Memon, N.: A Survey of Copy-Move Forgery Detection Techniques. In: IEEE Western New York Image Processing Workshop (2008)
28. Park, M., Leey, S., Cheny, P., Kashyap, S., Butty, A., Liuy, Y.: Performance evaluation of state-of-the-art discrete symmetry detection. In: CVPR (2008)
29. Fischler, M., Bolles, R.: Random sample consensus: A paradigm for model fitting with apps. to image analysis and automated cartography. ACM Comm. 24 (1981)

30. Jain, A., Zhong, Y., Dubuisson-Jolly, M.: Deformable template models: A review. Signal Processing 71, 109–129 (1998)
31. Viola, P., Jones, M.: Rapid object detection using a boosted cascade of simple features. In: Proc. CVPR (2001)
32. Guo, G., Dyer, C.: Patch-based image correlation with rapid filtering. In: The 2nd Beyond Patches Workshop, in Conj. with IEEE CVPR 2007 (2007)
33. Liu, C., Yuen, J., Torralba, A., Sivic, J., Freeman, W.T.: SIFT flow: Dense correspondence across different scenes. In: Forsyth, D., Torr, P., Zisserman, A. (eds.) ECCV 2008, Part III. LNCS, vol. 5304, p. 28. Springer, Heidelberg (2008)
34. Glasner, D., Bagon, S., Irani, M.: Super-Resolution from a Single Image. In: Proc. of ICCV (2009)

Automated 3D Reconstruction and Segmentation from Optical Coherence Tomography

Justin A. Eichel[1], Kostadinka K. Bizheva[2],
David A. Clausi[1], and Paul W. Fieguth[1]

[1] Systems Design Engineering, University of Waterloo, Canada
[2] Department of Physics and Astronomy, University of Waterloo, Canada
{jaeichel,kbizheva,dclausi,pfieguth}@uwaterloo.ca

Abstract. Ultra-High Resolution Optical Coherence Tomography is a novel imaging technology that allows non-invasive, high speed, cellular resolution imaging of anatomical structures in the human eye, including the retina and the cornea.

A three-dimensional study of the cornea, for example, requires the segmentation and mutual alignment of a large number of two-dimensional images. Such segmentation has, until now, only been undertaken by hand for individual two-dimensional images; this paper presents a method for automated segmentation, opening substantial opportunities for 3D corneal imaging and analysis, using many hundreds of 2D slices.

Keywords: OCT, UHROCT, cornea, non-invasive imaging, statistical modelling, segmentation, reconstruction.

1 Introduction

Optical Coherence Tomography is an optical imaging technique that allows for non-invasive (non-contact), micrometer-scale imaging of transparent objects and biological tissue. Some of the most advanced medical applications of OCT are in the field of ophthalmology for non-invasive imaging of healthy and diseased human retina and cornea [1–4].

The human cornea, which is the application focus of our research, consists of five distinct layers of variable thickness: Epithelium ($\sim 50 \mu m$), Bowman's membrane ($\sim 15 \mu m$), Stroma ($\sim 500 \mu m$), Descemet's membrane ($\sim 10 \mu m$) and Endothelium ($\sim 5 \mu m$), labeled in Figure 1. Identifying individual corneal layers in OCT tomograms and the precise measurement of their thicknesses is essential in the evaluation of corneal disease, for example to study the progression and treatment of Keratitis, Keratoconus, Fuchs' dystrophy, and Hypoxia [5–8], as these corneal diseases transform the shape and layer thickness of the cornea.

Until now, corneal layer segmentation has only been undertaken by hand for individual 2D images, greatly limiting the types of problems or number of patients who could be studied, and making completely impractical any 3D study based on the segmentation and registration of hundreds of 2D images.

K. Daniilidis, P. Maragos, N. Paragios (Eds.): ECCV 2010, Part III, LNCS 6313, pp. 44–57, 2010.
© Springer-Verlag Berlin Heidelberg 2010

This paper presents a method for automated segmentation, opening substantial opportunities for 3D corneal imaging and analysis. The proposed segmentation method is the first fully automated algorithm, to the author's knowledge, that can segment the five corneal layers based on Optical Coherence Tomography images. Since both boundaries of the Descemet's membrane are less than the imaging resolution, the Descemet's Endothelium complex is represented by a single boundary instead. The data in this paper were acquired with an UltraHigh Resolution Optical Coherence Tomography (UHROCT) system, which allows for non-invasive imaging of a human cornea with $3\mu m$ axial resolution and an acquisition rate of 47,000 2D scans per second [9].

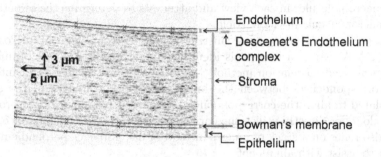

Fig. 1. UHROCT image of the cornea containing labeled layer boundaries

The Background section discusses existing 3D corneal reconstruction techniques and segmentation algorithms. The Reconstruction Method section describes the novel 2D segmentation algorithm, developed in this paper, applied to multiple cornea images, leading to the development of an approach for 3D reconstruction.

2   Background

The proposed method intends to extend existing reconstruction techniques so that a 3D model can be obtained from a series of noisy UHROCT images. The following sections describe existing reconstruction methods and several segmentation methods that can be used to facilitate corneal reconstruction.

2.1   3D Reconstruction

Existing medical imaging techniques can be utilized for imaging large organs, such as the brain using MRI, or imaging small cells using electron microscopy. Depending on the scale of the object, different reconstruction algorithms are applied to the data collected from the imaging process.

When performing gross medical imaging, a series of 2D images might be stacked together if the object motion and the imaging system motion is negligible compared to the overall dimensions of the object. For example, when performing ultra-sound to image large organs, the vibrations of the ultra-sound probe and the small motion of muscles surrounding the organs are insignificant due to the relative scale of the object being imaged [10]. In addition, stacking can be acceptable if a stationary object reference is visible in each frame. When performing a brain MRI, the stationary bone structure of the skull can be used to translate the 2D scans for the registration process [11].

Although on the smaller scale, electron microscopy is used to image cells. In these cases, the vibrations and motions of the cells are significant. However, like in gross medical imaging, electron microscopy can use reference points that are present in multiple 2D images [12]. Single-particle analysis [13, 14] attempts to identify macromolecules in each view and attempts to determine the orientation of each macromolecule in the particle.

Scarpa presents a method to reconstruct a cornea from confocal microscope imaging [15]. A region of interest is identified in each sequential set of images, then a normalized correlation method [16] is applied to the region of interest to find correspondences between the image frames. The images in the stack are translated to align the correspondences in consecutive images. The process, however, does not directly utilize the corneal layer boundaries for reference. The process also relies on a stack of images instead of using images perpendicular to the stack to assist with alignment.

Li applied confocal microscopy through focusing to measure the central layer thickness of the Epithelium, Bowman's layer, and total corneal thickness [17]. Although the approach is limited to manually measuring the central thickness, it was the first technique to obtain measurements for three of the five corneal layers. The proposed algorithm automates the manual process and extends the segmentation to all five corneal layer boundaries.

Currently, corneal OCT images may be aligned using a software package from Amira. Amira provides a suit of tools that can be used to align a stack of OCT images by comparing the direct image intensity and any salient features contained in sequential images [18, 19]. The software also allows the users to manually align the images. Unfortunately, the package does not use the structural properties of the cornea in the reconstruction process, preventing a suitable 3D reconstruction, and the 3D reconstructions generated failed to yield the accuracy necessary for corneal layer thickness research.

The proposed method attempts to automate and extend the 3D reconstruction process by utilizing the corneal layer boundaries and orthogonal UHROCT images to establish accurate point correspondences.

2.2 Segmentation

The proposed 3D reconstruction algorithm requires the segmentation of the corneal layer boundaries within the 2D UHROCT images.

Snakes and active contours are curves designed to surround lines and shapes that may be present in the image [20–24]. The active contour converges when the sum of internal (prior) and external (measurement) forces are minimized, such that the internal forces prefer contour smoothness (or some other prior shape), and the external forces prefer a fit to the given image, normally related to the image gradient.

The concept of intelligent scissors [25] allows the user to semi-manually segment the image. By placing points on the image, the user guides the intelligent scissor algorithm, which snaps to the image gradient as the algorithm fits a curve through the user-defined points. The advantage of this algorithm is that the user can specify a few points on each corneal layer boundary while the algorithm fits a curve to the image gradient that follows the layer boundaries. When applied to a smooth image gradient, the algorithm can fit a curve to the gradient with little user interaction. However, when applied to the UHROCT images, the intelligent scissors fit the noise obscured the otherwise smooth gradient preventing the effective segmentation of the boundaries. Figure 2(b) illustrates the performance of the algorithm despite having the user generate 20 to 30 points for each layer.

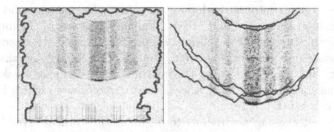

Fig. 2. UHROCT segmentation results for (left) geometric active contour and (right) intelligent scissors. Neither method produces accurate segmentation results.

Fig. 3. Comparison of retinal (left) and corneal (right) UHROCTs. Unlike corneal layers, each retinal layer has a visibly distinct intensity compared to adjacent layers. In contrast, corneal layers contain a visible thin, dark boundary between each layer.

While many well developed retinal OCT imaging techniques exist to identify layer boundaries of the retina, corneal imaging provides different challenges.

Garvin proposes the use of a general graph-based approached that attempts to reconstruct the retinal images into a 3D model and isolate the surfaces that correspond to the retinal layers [26]. In addition, Mishra developed a method using image gradient information and a kernel function to successfully compensate for the speckle noise, present in OCT images, and efficiently segments retinal layers [27]. The major difference between retinal and corneal segmentation is due to composition of the layers. As shown in Figure 3, unlike the cornea, the retinal layers have different mean intensities for each layer. The retinal methods are good at finding the edge between these layers. In contrast, corneal layers have a similar mean intensity, but are separated by low-contrast, discontinuous, thin layer boundaries instead. As a result, retinal methods were able to find the high contrast outer layers, but could not locate the inner layers.

3   Reconstruction Method

A variety of active contours, including parametric, geometric, and edge-free, were implemented and tested on UHROCT images. Not one of the implemented methods was able to segment the cornea; Figure 2(a) illustrates a typical example of the final state of a geometric active contour [28]. In many ways this failure is unsurprising: the images are noisy, the contours have frequent breaks, and the active-contour methods have only a weak prior (smoothness) which knows very little about corneal structure.

The failure of existing algorithms to segment the corneal layer boundaries motivated the development of a method to perform 2D corneal segmentation. The proposed method imposes a corneal model on the data to allow the corneal layer boundaries to be segmented, despite the presence of noise and imaging artefacts.

The reconstruction process consists of two major steps. The 2D UHROCT images are first segmented so that each of the five layer boundaries can be obtained and the layers are subsequently used as markers to for a second step, the 3D reconstruction. These two respective steps are described in the following two sections.

3.1   2D Reconstruction

The 2D reconstruction uses a corneal model to locate the internal layers of the cornea. The starting point is to observe that the upper and lower corneal layers have sufficient contrast, due to the high refractive index at the interface between the cornea and the surrounding fluid, to segment these layers robustly. The model then asserts that all internal layers can be derived using the curvature information from the upper and lower corneal layers.

Let the data acquired from the UHROCT imaging device be a 2D greyscale image $I(x, y)$. During the imaging process, a higher contrast endothelium layer can be obtained by focusing the UHROCT system on the endothelium layer instead of the epithelium layer. Since the epithelium layer boundary is the interface between air and the cornea, the refractive index can produce sufficient contrast for the segmentation algorithm. The focusing emphasizes the contrast of the endothelium layer. However, as a consequence the cornea becomes inverted on the image plane, as seen in Figure 4(a).

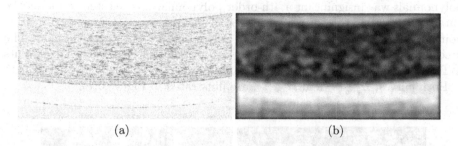

(a)   (b)

Fig. 4. (a) The original UHROCT image obtained from the imaging system. (b) The result of preprocessing applied to the original UHROCT image, to improve contrast to robustly find the upper and lower layers.

The UHROCT layer boundaries appear quite noisy. The boundaries are about one to two pixels thick, have a varying pixel intensity, and are surrounded by what appears to be speckle or correlated noise, actually due to the distribution of cells within the cornea. To improve segmentation accuracy in the presence of noise, image preprocessing is undertaken by applying contrast-limited adaptive histogram equalization [29] to normalize pixel intensities across the image, morphological operators to enhance arc structures, and a Gaussian blur filter to smooth the remaining noise. The resulting preprocessed image, $I_{pre}(x, y)$, shown in Figure 4(b), contains sufficient contrast to clearly separate the cornea from the surrounding fluid.

As a most basic segmentation of cornea from fluid, a Prewitt edge detector is applied to find horizontal edges fragments in $I_{pre}(x, y)$, producing edge map $I_{edge}(x, y)$, containing edges that correspond to the upper and lower boundaries, as shown in Figure 5(a). Candidate endothelium / epithelium pixel locations are determined by locating those edges stronger than some threshold in the upper / lower half of I_{edge}.

Manually-segmented boundaries were available for a limited number of images, making it possible to learn a model and as ground truth in assessing the learned layers. Then an optimization problem is formulated to fit a quadratic curve, $Q_{end}(s)$ over arc-length s, to the upper layer boundary. An initial quadratic polynomial, $Q_{end}(s)$, based on statistics from the manual boundaries, was used to specify an initial curve for the optimization algorithm, as shown in Figure 5(b), where

$$\sum_{\forall p \in P_{end}} \left[\min_s \|p - Q_{end}(s)\|_2 \right] \qquad (1)$$

is minimized, minimizing the Euclidean distance from the curve to all thresholded edge points.

The quadratic is robust, but not a terribly good fit to the anatomy of the cornea. Various polynomials were tested to find the lowest order that could best model the corneal curvature. Since the difference between 5th and 4th-order polynomials was insignificant a 4th-order polynomial was selected to model the data. Having found the optimal quadratic fit, outlier rejection was performed by point trimming and the best 4th-order polynomial fit $Q^*_{end}(s)$ was found. The preceding process was applied, unchanged, to the bottom half of the edge points to find the best-fit curve to the epithelium $Q^*_{epi}(s)$.

Both curves, $\Omega^*_{end}(s)$ and $\Omega^*_{epi}(s)$, are illustrated in Figure 5(c).

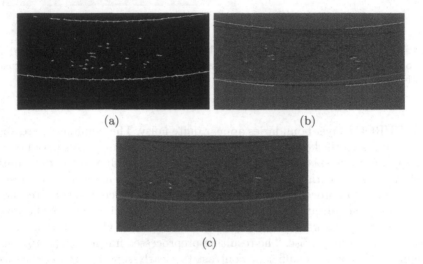

(a)   (b)

(c)

Fig. 5. (a) Edge detection applied to the preprocessed OCT Image. (b) The initial model of the upper and lower curves are independent of UHROCT image. (c) The segmentation of the upper and lower layer boundaries.

The model asserts that a continuous transformation exists that maps the Endothelium to the Epithelium; consequently, the curves representing the three internal layer boundaries are expressed as a low-dimensional parameterized function that uses the upper and lower curves as a basis:

$$\Omega^{\alpha=0}(s) = \Omega^0_{epi}(s - s_0) \qquad \Omega^{\alpha=1}(s) = \Omega^0_{end}(s - s_1) \qquad (2)$$

The parameterized corneal model is illustrated in Figure 6. Any of the five corneal layers can be represented by the parameterized curve $\Omega^\alpha(s)$, where parameter α provides a mechanism to continuously transition between the upper and lower curves:

$$\Omega^\alpha(s) = (1 - \alpha)\Omega^{\alpha=0}(s) + \alpha\Omega^{\alpha=1}(s) \qquad (3)$$

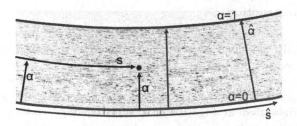

Fig. 6. Corneal model parametrization. s indexes along the arc, whereas α is essentially an interpolation parameter between the bottom ($\alpha = 0$) and top ($\alpha = 1$) curves.

where the parameters s_0 and s_1 are required to establish point correspondences between the upper and lower curves, established by the medial axis transform.

All five corneal layer boundaries are detected using a process essentially based on the generalized Hough transform [30]. The mean pixel intensity, μ_α of the UHROCT image, $I(x, y)$, is sampled along the curve $\Omega^\alpha(s)$ as a function of α:

$$\mu_\alpha = \frac{1}{n} \sum_{i=1}^{n} I\left(\Omega^\alpha\left(\frac{i}{n}\right)_x, \Omega^\alpha\left(\frac{i}{n}\right)_y\right) \tag{4}$$

An example of μ_α for a particular UHROCT is shown in Figure 7. The proposed algorithm applies a peak detector that identifies the peaks with the largest difference between the proximate maximum and minimum. In this example the five most significant peaks occur at $\alpha = [0.0930, 0.0138, 0.1227, 0.9917,$ and $0.9598]$, which correspond to the five corneal layers.

Figure 9 illustrates six examples of segmenting the five layers overlaid onto the original UHROCT image and illustrates the robustness of the algorithm when applied to UHROCT data containing imaging artifacts. It needs to be emphasized that the method is fully automated and that, to this point, no such algorithm has existed which is able to perform such a segmentation. The results are accurate, and robust in the presence of significant imaging artifacts.

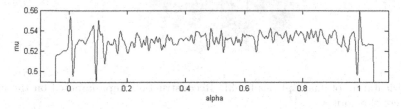

Fig. 7. A plot of the generalized Hough projection μ_α, projecting along corneal arcs, to identify prospective layers

3.2   3D Reconstruction

The novelty and performance of the 2D segmentation from the previous section is already a highly significant step in ophthalmologic research. Our ideal goal, however, is 3D reconstruction.

A 3D reconstruction of the cornea can be obtained from an ensemble of 2D segmented images either imaged in parallel or, preferably, in two orthogonal directions, as illustrated in Figure 8. Parallel imaging requires some sort of model regarding cross-plane behaviour, whereas perpendicular planes can be fused without prior assumptions, by using the intersections of the image planes as reference points for alignment. Since the primary source of alignment error is due to eye motion and camera vibration, it is reasonable to assume that the dominant inter-plane offsets are translational, rather than rotational or changes in scale. The local coordinates $\left| x\ y\ 0\ 1 \right|^{T}_{\parallel}$, for the parallel images, and $\left| x\ y\ 0\ 1 \right|^{T}_{\perp}$ for the perpendicular images are mapped to the global coordinates $\left| X\ Y\ Z\ 1 \right|^{T}$ using the linear transformations

$$
\begin{vmatrix} X \\ Y \\ Z \\ 1 \end{vmatrix} = H^0_{\parallel} \begin{vmatrix} x \\ y \\ 0 \\ 1 \end{vmatrix}_{\parallel} \quad \begin{vmatrix} X \\ Y \\ Z \\ 1 \end{vmatrix} = H^0_{\perp} \begin{vmatrix} x \\ y \\ 0 \\ 1 \end{vmatrix}_{\perp} \tag{5}
$$

where

$$
H^0_{\parallel} = \begin{vmatrix} 1 & 0 & 0 & x_o \\ 0 & 1 & 0 & y_o \\ 0 & 0 & 1 & z_o \\ 0 & 0 & 0 & 1 \end{vmatrix} \quad H^0_{\perp} = \begin{vmatrix} 0 & 0 & 1 & z_o \\ 0 & 1 & 0 & y_o \\ 1 & 0 & 0 & x_o \\ 0 & 0 & 0 & 1 \end{vmatrix} \tag{6}
$$

The framework can be extended to six degrees of freedom by manipulating the homogeneous transformation matrices, where (5) transforms the local coordinates of $\Omega^{\alpha}(s)$ into global coordinates generating 3D coordinates for each layer boundary.

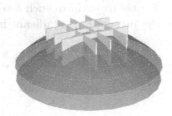

Fig. 8. Orientation of image planes for 3D Reconstruction, superimposed on the notional layers of a cornea

The intersection of the ith parallel plane with the jth perpendicular plane produces a line on both image planes. The intersection of this line with the layer boundaries can produce point correspondences for each image. An optimization problem can be formulated to minimize the total Euclidean distance, in 3D space, between all of the corresponding points. The intersection of two lines can be derived by relating the coordinates the ith parallel plane with the jth perpendicular plane

$$
\begin{vmatrix} x \\ y \\ 0 \\ 1 \end{vmatrix}_j = H_i^j \begin{vmatrix} x \\ y \\ 0 \\ 1 \end{vmatrix}_i = \begin{vmatrix} z_i - x_o^j \\ y_i + y_o^i - y_o^j \\ x_i + x_o^i - z_o^j \\ 1 \end{vmatrix} \tag{7}
$$

using a homogeneous transformation, H_i^j,

$$
H_i^j = \left(H_\perp^0 \right)^{-1} H_\parallel^0 = H_0^\perp H_\parallel^0 = \begin{vmatrix} 0\ 0\ 1 & z_o^i - x_o^j \\ 0\ 1\ 0 & y_o^i - y_o^j \\ 1\ 0\ 0 & x_o^i - z_o^j \\ 0\ 0\ 0 & 1 \end{vmatrix} \tag{8}
$$

The sequence of steps, below, in (9), defines the distance $d_{i,j}$ between the boundary layer defined by α_i on the ith image plane and the corresponding boundary defined by α_j on the jth image plane:

$$
x_i = z_o^j - x_o^i
$$
$$
solve\left(\Omega_i^{\alpha_i}(s_i)_x = x_i, s_i \right)
$$
$$
y_i = \Omega_i^{\alpha_i}(s_i)_y
$$
$$
y_j = y_i + y_o^i - y_o^j
$$

$$
x_j = z_o^i - x_o^j
$$
$$
solve\left(\Omega_j^{\alpha_j}(s_j)_x = x_j, s_j \right)
$$

$$
d_{i,j}^2 = \left(y_j - \Omega_j^{\alpha_j}(s_j)_y \right)^2
$$

$$
\tag{9}
$$

The method is extensible to the general case, including rotations to allow six degrees of freedom, however the intersection line becomes significantly more complicated.

4   Results

The 2D segmentation algorithm has been tested on 2,050 UHROCT images obtained from 12 healthy subjects. The images were also manually segmented to provide ground truth. The proposed algorithm located the Epithelium and Endothelium boundaries to within about 2.5 pixels of the manually segmented images for all of the images, with a standard deviation of about 1.3 and 3.2 pixels, respectively. Table 1 contains the results in pixels and a approximation of μm for the other layers. These results can also be immediately improved by compensating for the segmentation bias. Each boundary is statistically too high in the image by between 0.7 to 3.7 pixels depending on the boundary. The boundaries can be systematically adjusted to reduce the error.

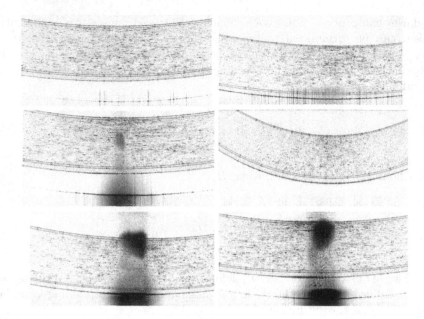

Fig. 9. Six examples of applying 2D corneal segmentation to OCT images. The model accomplishes exact segmentation, despite significant noise and varying corneal layer location within the image. The prominent imaging artifacts result from the high reflectively of the cornea when imaging near the apex.

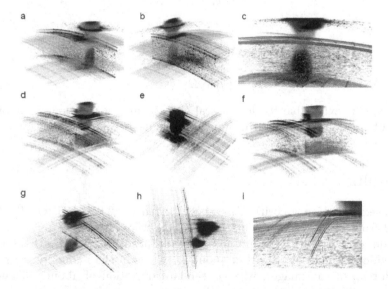

Fig. 10. Nine 3D Corneal reconstructions from the segmentation and mutual alignment of 2D UHROCT images. The images are taken from three subjects, one on each row. The segmentation results are superimposed on the underlying UHROCT data, which can be seen to have significant noise and artifacts.

Table 1. Segmentation Experimental Results

Layer	Error			
	Bias [pixels]	Std.Dev [pixels]	Bias [pixels] [μm]	Std.Dev [μm]
epi	1.32	1.26	3.92	4.38
bow	0.709	10.7	4.59	5.38
str	2.56	5.19	2.86	3.50
des	3.68	4.69	5.94	6.07
end	2.52	3.25	6.52	7.11

The 3D reconstruction algorithm used the results of the 2D segmentation algorithm applied to 3 healthy human subjects. Although four datasets were collected from each human subject, initial problems with the imaging procedure prevented the use of some data because the cornea moved out of the imaging plane as the subjects were being scanned. Figure 10 illustrates the 3D reconstruction obtained from the algorithm. Notice that the reconstruction for subject 2, image panes (d-f), contains sparse data due to the aforementioned imaging problem (since corrected). The figure visually shows how well the 3D reconstruction process aligned all of the layer boundaries, and supplementary material provided with this paper includes video, rotating the results in 3D to better illustrate how well the layers are aligned.

During the study, 442 UHROCT tomograms were successfully segmented for all three subjects. The segmentation process required approximately eight hours using MATLAB on a dual-core 2.5GHz laptop (if these layers were manually segmented, at an average rate of 15 minutes per image, it would take an experienced user about 110 hours). The advantage of the segmentation algorithm is that it is immune to fatigue and, given multiple processors, can segment UHROCT images in parallel. With such segmentation quality and reconstruction rates, the inference and clinical use of 3D corneal layer boundaries becomes quite feasible.

5 Conclusions

The method proposed in this paper is capable of automatically producing two-dimensional segmentations and three-dimensional reconstructions of a human cornea.

The proposed segmentation algorithm was applied to over two-thousand images, segmenting each *automatically*, a performance so far unmatched in any published method.

The three-dimensional corneal reconstruction is based on the simultaneous co-alignment of segmented two-dimensional frames, with each frame permitted translational degrees of freedom, to be optimized. The resulting three-dimensional reconstruction was successfully applied to three test subjects.

The ability to produce large, three-dimensional corneal reconstructions opens significant clinical and research opportunities. Collaborators in science and optometry are eager to continue refining the methodology, to allow future work in revealing details of corneal and retinal anatomy.

Further work can introduce additional degrees of freedom in the perpendicular planes to account for variance in planar orientation. Although perpendicular planes were proposed, there is no inherit requirement in the algorithm prohibiting planes of arbitrary orientation. Perpendicular planes were selected for imaging convenience.

Acknowledgment

The authors would like to thank C. Hyun, S. Hariri, N.Hutchings, T. Simpson assistance with the acquisition of the corneal images and helpful discussions. This research was sponsored by the Natural Sciences and Engineering Research Council (NSERC) of Canada as well as GEOIDE (GEOmatics for Informed Decisions). The 3D visualization was built using components from the Tech Soft 3D, LLC HOOPS 3D Library.

References

1. Povaay, B., Hermann, B., Unterhuber, A., Hofer, B., Sattmann, H., Zeiler, F., Morgan, J.E., Falkner-Radler, C., Glittenberg, C., Blinder, S., Drexler, W.: Three-dimensional optical coherence tomography at 1050 nm versus 800 nm in retinal pathologies: enhanced performance and choroidal penetration in cataract patients. J. Biomed. Opt. 12 (2007)
2. Akiba, M., Maeda, N., Yumikake, K., Soma, T., Nishida, K., Tano, Y., Chan, K.P.: Ultrahigh-resolution imaging of human donor cornea using full-field optical coherence tomography. J. Biomed. Opt. 12 (2007)
3. Jungwirth, J., Baumann, B., Pircher, M., Gtzinger, E., Hitzenberger, C.K.: Extended in vivo anterior eye-segment imaging with full-range complex spectral domain optical coherence tomography. J. Biomed. Opt. 14 (2009)
4. Gora, M., Karnowski, K., Szkulmowski, M., Kaluzny, B.J., Huber, R., Kowalczyk, A., Wojtkowski, M.: Ultra high-speed swept source imaging of the anterior segment of human eye at 200 khz with adjustable imaging range. Opt. Express. 17 (2009)
5. Martn-Navarro, C.M., Lorenzo-Morales, J., Cabrera-Serra, M.G., Rancel, F., Coronado-Alvarez, N., Piero, J., Valladares, B.: The potential pathogenicity of chlorhexidine-sensitive acanthamoeba strains isolated from contact lens cases from asymptomatic individuals in tenerife, canary islands, spain. J. Med. Microbiol. 57, 1399–1404 (2008); PMID: 18927419
6. Smolin, G., Foster, C.S., Azar, D.T., Dohlman, C.H.: Smolin and Thoft's The cornea. Lippincott Williams & Wilkins (2005)
7. Kostadinka, B., Hyun, C., Eichel, J., Hariri, S., Mishra, A., Clausi, D., Fieguth, P., Simpson, T., Hutchings, N., Manns, F., Soderberg, P.G., Ho, A.: Evaluation of hypoxic swelling of human cornea with high speed ultrahigh resolution optical coherence tomography. In: Ophthalmic Technologies XIX, San Jose, CA, USA, vol. 7163, pp. 71631G–71631G-6. SPIE (2009)
8. Snell, R.S., Lemp, M.A.: Clinical anatomy of the eye. Wiley-Blackwell (1998)
9. Drexler, W., Morgner, U., Ghanta, R.K., Kartner, F.X., Schuman, J.S., Fujimoto, J.G.: Ultrahigh-resolution ophthalmic optical coherence tomography. Nat. Med. 7, 502–507 (2001)

10. Colchester, A., Hawkes, D.J.: Information processing in medical imaging. Springer, Heidelberg (1991)
11. Hajnal, J.V., Hawkes, D.J., Hill, D.L.G.: Medical image registration. CRC Press, Boca Raton (2001)
12. Kuo, J.: Electron microscopy. Humana Press, Totowa (2007)
13. Frank, J.: Three-dimensional electron microscopy of macromolecular assemblies. Oxford University Press, US (2006)
14. Gu, J.: Structural bioinformatics, 2nd edn. Wiley-Blackwell, Hoboken (2009)
15. Scarpa, F.: In vivo three-dimensional reconstruction of the cornea from confocal microscopy images. In: Conf. Proc. IEEE Eng. Med. Biol. Soc., pp. 747–750 (2007)
16. Dani, P.: Automated assembling of images: image montage preparation. Pattern Recognition 28, 431 (1995)
17. Li, H.: Epithelial and corneal thickness measurements by in vivo confocal microscopy through focusing (CMTF). Current Eye Research 16, 214 (1997)
18. Reinhard, T., Larkin, D.F.P.: Cornea and external eye disease. Springer, Heidelberg (2006)
19. Stachs, O., Zhivov, A., Kraak, R., Stave, J., Guthoff, R.: In vivo three-dimensional confocal laser scanning microscopy of the epithelial nerve structure in the human cornea. Graefes Arch. Clin. Exp. Ophthalmol. 245, 569–575 (2007)
20. Kass, M., Witkin, A., Terzopoulos, D.: Snakes: Active contour models. Int. J. Comput. Vision 1, 321–331 (1988)
21. Amini, A.A., Weymouth, T.E., Jain, R.C.: Using dynamic programming for solving variational problems in vision. IEEE Transaction on Pattern Analysis and Machine Intelligence 12, 855–867 (1990)
22. Cohen, L.: On active contour models and balloons. Computer Vision Graphics and Image Understanding 53, 211–218 (1991)
23. Kass, M., Witkin, A., Terzopoulos, D.: Snakes: Active contour models. International Journal of Computer Vision 1, 321–331 (1988)
24. Malladi, R., Sethian, J.A., Vemuri, B.C.: Shape modeling with front propagation: A level set approach. IEEE Transaction on Pattern Analysis and Machine Intelligence 17, 158–175 (1995)
25. Mortensen, E.N., Barrett, W.A.: Intelligent scissors for image composition. In: Proc. 22nd Annu. Conf. on Comput. Graphics and Interact. Tech., vol. 22, pp. 191–198. ACM, New York (1995)
26. Garvin, M.K., Abrmoff, M.D., Wu, X., Russell, S.R., Burns, T.L., Sonka, M.: Automated 3-D intraretinal layer segmentation of macular spectral-domain optical coherence tomography images. IEEE Trans. Med. Imaging 28, 1436–1447 (2009); PMID: 19278927
27. Mishra, A., Wong, A., Bizheva, K., Clausi, D.A.: Intra-retinal layer segmentation in optical coherence tomography images. Opt. Express. 17, 23719–23728 (2009)
28. Caselles, V., Catt, F., Coll, T., Dibos, F.: A geometric model for active contours in image processing. Numerische Mathematik 66, 1–31 (1993)
29. Zuiderveld, K.: Contrast limited adaptive histogram equalization. In: Graphics Gems IV, pp. 474–485. Academic Press Professional, Inc., London (1994)
30. Ballard, D.H.: Generalizing the hough transform to detect arbitrary shapes. Pattern Recognition 13, 111–122 (1981)

Combining Geometric and Appearance Priors for Robust Homography Estimation[*]

Eduard Serradell[1], Mustafa Özuysal[2], Vincent Lepetit[2],
Pascal Fua[2], and Francesc Moreno-Noguer[1]

[1] Institut de Robòtica i Informàtica Industrial, CSIC-UPC, Barcelona, Spain
[2] Computer Vision Laboratory, EPFL, Lausanne, Switzerland
eserradell@iri.upc.edu, mustafa.oezuysal@epfl.ch,
vincent.lepetit@epfl.ch, pascal.fua@epfl.ch, fmoreno@iri.upc.edu

Abstract. The homography between pairs of images are typically computed from the correspondence of keypoints, which are established by using image descriptors. When these descriptors are not reliable, either because of repetitive patterns or large amounts of clutter, additional priors need to be considered. The Blind PnP algorithm makes use of geometric priors to guide the search for matches while computing camera pose. Inspired by this, we propose a novel approach for homography estimation that combines geometric priors with appearance priors of ambiguous descriptors. More specifically, for each point we retain its best candidates according to appearance. We then prune the set of potential matches by iteratively shrinking the regions of the image that are consistent with the geometric prior. We can then successfully compute homographies between pairs of images containing highly repetitive patterns and even under oblique viewing conditions.

Keywords: Homography estimation, robust estimation, RANSAC.

1 Introduction

Computing homographies from point correspondences has received much attention because it has many applications, such as stitching multiple images into panoramas [1] or detecting planar objects for Augmented Reality purposes [2,3]. All existing methods assume that the correspondences are given *a priori* and usually rely on an estimation scheme that is robust both to noise and to outright mismatches. As a result, the best ones tolerate significant error rates among the correspondences but break down when the rate becomes too large. Therefore, in cases when the correspondences cannot be established reliably enough such as in the presence of repetitive patterns, they can easily fail. In this paper, we

---

[*] This work has been partially funded by the Spanish Ministry of Science and Innovation under CICYT projects PAU DPI2008-06022 and UbROB DPI2007-61452; by MIPRCV Consolider Ingenio 2010 CSD2007-00018; by the EU project GARNICS FP7-247947 and by the Swiss National Science Foundation.

K. Daniilidis, P. Maragos, N. Paragios (Eds.): ECCV 2010, Part III, LNCS 6313, pp. 58–72, 2010.

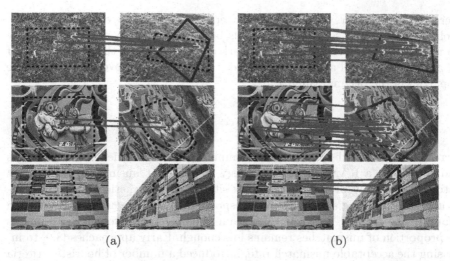

(a)   (b)

Fig. 1. Detecting an oblique planar pattern. **(a)** PROSAC fails due to high number of outliers caused by the extreme camera angle. **(b)** Our approach can reassign correspondences as the homography space is explored and can recover the correct homography.

introduce an estimation scheme that performs well even under such demanding circumstances.

We build upon the so-called *Blind PnP* approach [4] that was designed to simultaneously establish 2D to 3D correspondences and estimate camera pose. To this end, it exploits the fact that, in general, some prior on the camera pose is often available. This prior is modeled as a Gaussian Mixture Model that is progressively refined by hypothesizing new correspondences. Incorporating each new one in a Kalman filter rapidly reduces the number of potential 2D matches for each 3D point and makes it possible to search the pose space sufficiently fast for the method to be practical.

Unfortunately, when going from exploring the 6-dimensional camera-pose space to the 8-dimensional space of homographies, the size of the search space increases to a point where a naive extension of the Blind PnP approach fails to converge. This is in part because this approach is suboptimal in the sense that it does not exploit image-appearance, which can be informative even in ambiguous cases. In general, any given 2D point can be associated to several potentially matching 2D points with progressively decreasing levels of confidence. To exploit this fact without having to depend on *a prori* correspondences, we explicitly use similarity of image appearance to remove both low confidence potential correspondences and pose prior modes that do not result in promising match candidates. We further improve convergence rates by ignoring potential matches that are least likely to reduce the covariances of the Kalman filter.

As a result, our algorithm performs well even in highly oblique views of planar scenes containing repetitive patterns such as the one of Fig. 1. In such scenes, interest point detectors exhibit very poor repeatability and, as a result, even such a reliable algorithm as PROSAC [5] fails because *a priori* correspondences are too undependable. We will use benchmark data to quantify the effectiveness of our approach. We will also show that it can be used to improve the convergence properties of the original Blind PnP.

2   Related Work

Correspondence-based approaches to computing homographies between images tend to rely on a RANSAC-style strategy [7] to reject mismatches that point matchers inevitably produce in complex situations. In practice, this means selecting and validating small sets of correspondences until an acceptable solution is found. The original RANSAC algorithm remains a valid solution, as long as the proportion of mismatches remains low enough. Early approaches [8,9] to increasing the acceptable mismatch rate, introduced a number of heuristic criteria to stop the search, which were only satisfied in very specific and unrealistic situations. Other methods, before selecting candidate matches, consider all possible ones and organize them in data structures that can be efficiently accessed. Indexing methods, such as Hash tables [10,11] and Kd-trees [12], or clusters in the pose space [13,14] have been used for this purpose. Nevertheless, even within fast access data structures, these methods become computationally intractable when there are too many points.

Several more sophisticated versions of the RANSAC algorithm, such as Guided Sampling [15], PROSAC [5], and ARRSAC [16] have been proposed and they address the problem by using image-appearance to speed up the search for consistent matches. However, when the images contain repetitive structure resulting in unreliable keypoints and truly poor matches such as in Fig. 1, even they can fail. In those conditions, simple outlier rejection techniques [25] also fail.

In the context of the so-called *PnP* problem, which involves recovering camera pose from 3D to 2D correspondences, the Softposit algorithm [17] addresses this problem by iteratively solving for pose and correspondences, achieving an efficient solution for sets of about 100 feature points. Yet, this solution is prone to failure when different viewpoints may yield similar projections of the 3D points. This is addressed in the Blind PnP [4] by introducing weak pose priors, that constrain where the camera can look at, and guide the search for correspondences. Although achieving good results, both these solutions are limited to about a hundred feature points, and are therefore impractical in presence of the number of feature points that a standard keypoint detector would find in a high resolution textured image.

In this paper, we show that the response of local image descriptors, even when they are ambiguous and unreliable, may still be used in conjunction with geometric priors to simultaneously solve for homographies and correspondences. This lets us tackle very complex situations with many feature points and repetitive patterns, where current state-of-the-art algorithms fail.

3 Algorithm Overview

We next give a short overview of the algorithm we propose to simultaneously recover the homography that relates two images of a planar scene and point correspondences between them. We achieve this by

- **Introducing a Geometric prior:** We first define the search space for the homography. It can cover the whole homography space or depending on the application can be constrained to cover a smaller space, for example to limit the range of rotations or scales. We generate random homography samples in this search space, as we detail in Section 4. We then fit a Gaussian Mixture Model (GMM) to these samples using the Expectation Maximization (EM) algorithm. The modes of this GMM forms the *geometric prior*.
- **Introducing an Appearance prior:** For each keypoint pair $(\mathbf{x}_i, \mathbf{x}_j)$, we define the *appearance prior* as the similarity score $s_A(\mathbf{x}_i, \mathbf{x}_j)$ given by a local matching algorithm.
- **Iteratively solving for correspondences and homography:** We explore the modes of the geometric prior until enough consistent matches and the corresponding homography are found. Section 5 gives the details, we provide a brief overview here. This prior exploration starts at each prior mode mean with the covariance matrices estimated by EM. Each model point is transfered using the homography, while the projection of its covariance defines a search region for potential matches. We use the appearance prior to limit number of correspondences as explained in Section 4.3. The homography estimate and its covariance are iteratively updated by a Kalman filter that uses the best correspondences as measurements until the covariance becomes negligible.

4 Priors on the Search Space

In this section we give details on how both geometric and appearance priors are built, and on the pruning strategies we define to robustly reduce the number of keypoints and eliminate unnecessary geometric priors. As we will show in Section 6, this lets us to handle highly textured images with a large number of interest points.

4.1 Parameterization of Homographies

To define a search space for the homography, we first need to select a parameterization for the homography. Then we can randomly sample these parameters to obtain homography samples from the search space. A natural choice is to decompose the homography as

$$\mathbf{x}' = \mathbf{A}' \left(\mathbf{R} - \mathbf{t}\mathbf{v}_\pi^T \right) \mathbf{A}^{-1}\mathbf{x} \,,$$

where $\mathbf{A}$ and $\mathbf{A}'$ are the intrinsic parameters of the cameras, $\mathbf{R}$ and $\mathbf{t}$ their extrinsic transformation, $\mathbf{v}_\pi$ is the unit normal to the scene plane, $\mathbf{x}'$ is a point on the target image, and $\mathbf{x}$ is a point on the model image. However this is an over-parameterization and has even more than 8 parameters. Therefore we look for a direct parameterization of the 8 DOF of a homography:

$$\mathbf{x'} = \mathbf{Hx} \,,$$

Once such possibility is to consider its action on a unit square centered around the origin. We can therefore parameterize the homography with the coordinates of the resulting quadrangle as $\mathbf{H}(u_1, v_1, u_2, v_2, u_3, v_3, u_4, v_4)$. Given the 2D correspondences between the four vertices of the quadrangle, we can find the corresponding homography as the solution of the linear system

$$M\hat{\mathbf{H}} = \mathbf{0} \,, \tag{1}$$

where M is a 8×9 matrix made of the vertices coordinates, $\hat{\mathbf{H}}^T = [\mathbf{H_{11}}, \ldots, \mathbf{H_{33}}]^\mathbf{T}$, $\mathbf{H_{ij}}$ are the components of the matrix $\mathbf{H}$, and $\mathbf{0}$ is a vector of zeros. We can also work out its Jacobian evaluated at $(u_1, v_1, u_2, v_2, u_3, v_3, u_4, v_4)$

$$\mathbf{J_H} = \begin{bmatrix} \frac{\delta \mathbf{H_{11}}}{\delta u_1} & \frac{\delta \mathbf{H_{12}}}{\delta u_1} & \cdots & \frac{\delta \mathbf{H_{33}}}{\delta u_1} \\ \vdots & \vdots & & \vdots \\ \frac{\delta \mathbf{H_{11}}}{\delta u_4} & \frac{\delta \mathbf{H_{12}}}{\delta u_4} & \cdots & \frac{\delta \mathbf{H_{33}}}{\delta u_4} \end{bmatrix} \,,$$

which we will need when computing the projection of covariances defining the search space for correspondences. Therefore, we can propagate a covariance assigned to the prior modes to the model image as follows

$$\Sigma_w = \mathbf{J}_{uv} \mathbf{J_H} \Sigma_{us} \mathbf{J_H}^T \mathbf{J}_{uv}^T$$

and $\mathbf{J}_{uv}$ stands for the Jacobian of the homography evaluated for the image point (u', v'). It can be written as

$$\mathbf{J}_{uv} = \delta \mathbf{u'}/\delta \mathbf{h} = \frac{1}{z'} \begin{bmatrix} \mathbf{x}^T & \mathbf{0} & -u'\mathbf{x}^T \\ \mathbf{0} & \mathbf{x}^T & -v'\mathbf{x}^T \end{bmatrix} \,, \tag{2}$$

where $\mathbf{u'} = (u', v')^T = (x'/z', y'/z')^T$ are the inhomogeneous coordinates.

4.2 Geometric Prior

To define the geometric prior, we use a set of homography samples representing the set of all possible deformations of the image plane. If an estimate of the internal parameters is available, it can be parametrized directly by the camera rotation and translation. We apply all deformations obtained in this way to the unit square and obtain a set of sample parameter values corresponding to coordinates of the deformed square. Using EM we fit a GMM to these samples, which yields G Gaussian components with 8-vectors $\{\mathbf{h}_1, \ldots, \mathbf{h}_g\}$ for the means, and 8×8 covariance matrices $\{\mathbf{\Sigma}_1^h, \ldots, \mathbf{\Sigma}_g^h\}$. Note that it is possible to use a larger or smaller set of deformations to define the geometric prior depending on the constraints imposed by the application.

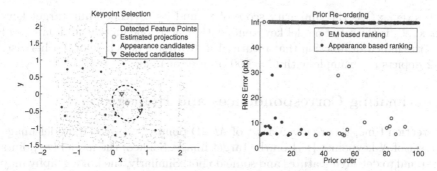

Fig. 2. Pruning based on appearance. **Left:** For the projected model point on the image, a direct adaptation of the *Blind PnP* would select every point within the uncertainty ellipse as a correspondence candidate. Considering appearance, our algorithm only selects a small subset of them. **Right:** We plot the residual re-projection error for each prior mode. Modes with lower indexes have higher rank and are explored first. A residual error of 'Inf' denotes a mode that does not converge to a good homography. A blind approach explores the modes following the EM ranking therefore spending time on ones that eventually do not result in good pose hypotheses. We use appearance to rank the modes and explore a smaller subset without missing out the good ones.

4.3   Appearance Prior

To compute the similarity score between keypoint pairs, we have chosen to work with the Ferns keypoint classifier [18] since it is fast and directly outputs a probability distribution for each keypoint. However, our approach can use other state-of-the-art keypoint descriptors such as SIFT [19] or SURF [20], provided that we can assign a similarity score to each hypothetical correspondence. We exploit the computed score in two ways.

Pruning keypoints. Using appearance, we are able to reduce for each model point, the whole set of potential candidates to a small selection of keypoints. The probability of finding a good match remains unaltered but the computational cost of the algorithm is highly reduced. Fig. 2 shows the effect of pruning keypoints. Note that it significantly reduces the number of potential matches. Additionally, we select only the most promising model keypoints that have a high scoring correspondence given by *Ferns* posterior distributions.

Pruning prior modes. To avoid exploring all modes of the geometric prior, we assign an appearance score to each one and eliminate the ones with lower scores. To compute the appearance score S_A for each mode $\mathbf{h}_g$, we transform the set of model keypoints $\mathbf{x}_i$ only once using the corresponding homography given by the mode, pick the ones that has only one potential candidate, and sum their similarity scores as

$$S_A(\mathbf{h}_g) = \frac{1}{M} \sum_{i=1}^{M} \delta(\mathbf{x}_i \in \mathcal{C}_1) \cdot s_A(\mathbf{x}_i, \mathbf{x}_j), \qquad (3)$$

where $s_A(\mathbf{x}_i, \mathbf{x}_j)$ is the similarity score of $\mathbf{x}_i$ and its corresponding target keypoint $\mathbf{x}_j$, $\mathcal{C}_1$ is the set of model keypoints with exactly one match candidate, and $\delta(.)$ is the indicator function that returns 1 if its argument is true or 0 otherwise. Fig. 2 depicts an example with $G = 100$ pose prior modes.

5   Estimating Correspondences and Homography

At detection time, we are given a set of M 2D points $\{\mathbf{x}_i\}$ on the model image and a set of N keypoints $\{\mathbf{x}_j\}$ on the target image. Some of the model keypoints correspond to detected features and some do not. Similarly, the homography may transfer some of the model points to locations without any nearby keypoints. Our goal is to find both the correct homography $\mathbf{H}$ and as many point-to-point correspondences as possible. Let $\mathcal{M}$ be a set of $(\mathbf{x}_i, \mathbf{x}_j)$ pairs that represents these recovered correspondences and $\mathcal{N}_{nd}$ be the subset of points for which no match can be established. We want to find the correct homography $\mathbf{H}$ and matches $\mathcal{M}$ by minimizing

$$\text{Error}(\mathbf{H}) = \sum_{(\mathbf{x}_i, \mathbf{x}_j) \in \mathcal{M}} ||\mathbf{x}_j - \mathbf{H}\mathbf{x}_i||^2 + \gamma |\mathcal{N}_{nd}|, \tag{4}$$

where γ is a penalty term that penalizes unmatched points.

Pose Space Exploration. We sequentially explore the pose prior modes by picking candidate correspondences $(\mathbf{x}_i, \mathbf{x}_j)$ and by updating the mode mean $\mathbf{h}_g$ and covariance Σ_g using the standard Kalman update equations,

$$\mathbf{h}_g^+ = \mathbf{h}_g + \mathbf{K}(\mathbf{x}_j - \mathbf{H}_g\mathbf{x}_i),$$
$$\Sigma_g^{p+} = (\mathbf{I} - \mathbf{K}\mathbf{J}(\mathbf{x}_i))\Sigma_g^p,$$

where $\mathbf{H}_g$ is the homography corresponding to the mean vector $\mathbf{h}_g$, $\mathbf{K}$ is the Kalman Gain, and $\mathbf{I}$ is the Identity matrix.

Candidate Selection. We use the covariance Σ_g^h to restrict the number of potential of matches between the points of the two images, by transferring the model points $\mathbf{x}_i$ using the homography to target image coordinates $\mathbf{u}_i$ and the projected covariances Σ_i^u. Error propagation yields

$$\Sigma_i^u = \mathbf{J}(\mathbf{x}_i)\Sigma_g^h\mathbf{J}(\mathbf{x}_i)^T, \tag{5}$$

where $\mathbf{J}(\mathbf{x}_i) = \mathbf{J}_{uv}\mathbf{J}_H$ is the Jacobian of the transfer by homography $\mathbf{H}_g\mathbf{x}_i$ that we derived in Section 4. This defines a search region for the point $\mathbf{x}_i$, and we only consider the detected image features $\mathbf{u}_j'$ such that

$$(\mathbf{u}_i - \mathbf{u}_j')^T \Sigma_i^u (\mathbf{u}_i - \mathbf{u}_j') \leq \mathcal{T}^2 \tag{6}$$

as potential matches for $\mathbf{x}_i$ and only if they have a high enough similarity score $s_A(\mathbf{u}_i, \mathbf{u}_j')$. $\mathcal{T}$ is a threshold chosen to achieve a specified degree of confidence, based on the cumulative chi-squared distribution.

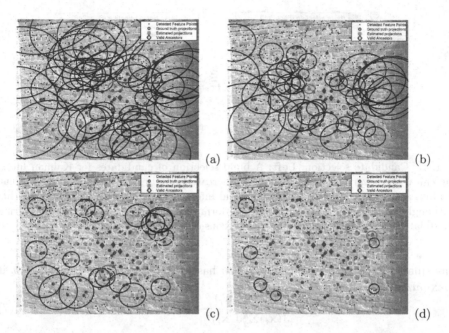

Fig. 3. Pose space exploration. **(a)** Exploration of a prior mode starts by picking correspondences with small projected covariance hence high confidence. **(b)** In the third iteration, covariances are much smaller. Also the selected candidate has larger covariance than the 3 model points indicated with yellow ellipses. Their locations will not be updated and they will not be considered for future Kalman updates. **(c)** The fourth point is picked despite its large uncertainty since the other points close to the center will not help to reduce covariance as much. **(d)** The covariances are very small as four points have already been used to update the homography. We can still use a fifth point to remove the uncertainty close to the borders.

Blind PnP selects the point with minimum number of potential candidates inside the threshold ellipse. When the number of potential candidates is high ($n \approx 5$) this works just fine because it minimizes the number of possible combinations. In our case, taking advantage of the appearance, n becomes very small and most of the points have either zero or one potential candidate. In this case, this blind selection process becomes random and the updates may not converge to a good homography.

Another way to select the point to introduce into the Kalman Filter is the one proposed by [21,22] that selects at each iteration the most informative point, which would make the algorithm converge quickly to the optimal solution. However, this method is sensitive to outliers and the optimal solution may be hard to find if it is found at all.

As none of the preceding methods was suitable, we implemented a new approach for candidate selection. Instead of trying to converge as fast as possible, we choose the point which has the minimum number of correspondences,

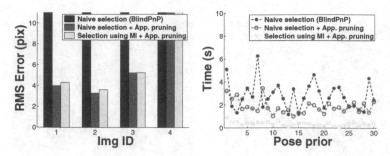

Fig. 4. Candidate selection. **Left:** A blind selection of candidates for Kalman filtering can not recover homographies due to increased number of pose space dimensions. Adding appearance with or without mutual information solves this problem. **Right:** Although it has almost no effect on final performance, using mutual information during candidate selection speeds up convergence considerably.

has small projected covariance and also has a high similarity score so that it maximizes

$$s_{ij} = \frac{dist(\mathbf{u}_i, \mathbf{u}'_j)}{\left|\mathbf{J}(\mathbf{x}_i)\mathbf{\Sigma}^h_g\mathbf{J}(\mathbf{x}_i)^T\right|} \cdot s_A(\mathbf{u}'_j|\mathbf{u}_i). \tag{7}$$

This leads to a small and robust step towards the solution. We then remove all other model points with smaller covariance from the list of potential points to introduce into the Kalman Filter. This is motivated by the observation that they will have even smaller covariance after the update and they can not reduce the uncertainty significantly since a low covariance indicates a low Mutual Information with the pose. As a result, we avoid making unnecessary computations while decreasing the number of iterations. Figure 3 illustrates this selection and pruning of model point projections as we iterate using the Kalman filter. Note that at first low covariance candidates are preferred and during the iterations we select candidates that lie progressively farther away from the plane center that has the least uncertainty. Figure 4 shows that this candidate selection using both mutual information and appearance outperforms the blind selection method or appearance alone. The time values are given for our MATLAB implementation.

Homography Refinement. After performing four updates on a prior mode, the covariance becomes very small, so we can directly transform model keypoints and match them to the closest target keypoint. Finally, the homography needs to be refined using all available information.

We tried directly using DLT [23] with all recovered correspondences to estimate a refined homography but this did not yield satisfactory results as the estimated homography is not always close and the number of correspondences is not large enough. Instead we use a PROSAC [5] algorithm as follows:

– For each model keypoint, we establish potential correspondences without using the similarity scores but only the projected covariances. This significantly increases the number of correct matches that can be recovered.

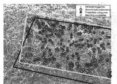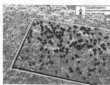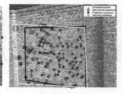

Fig. 5. Pose Refinement. **Left:** The Kalman Filter output refined by DLT using all available correspondences. The result is inaccurate since the appearance scores are too ambiguous leading to a low number of correct matches. **Right:** The correct homography is recovered, using a robust estimator that can re-assign correspondences.

- During PROSAC iterations each model point is considered as an inlier only for one of its potential correspondences.

Since potential matches are obtained using the result of the Kalman Filter, this refinement is constrained enough to let us efficiently re-assign correspondences with ambiguous appearance scores. Fig. 5 shows the results after refinement.

6   Results

We demonstrate the effectiveness of our approach using synthetic experiments, on standard benchmark datasets as well as on a new sequence especially captured to show robustness against repetitive textures. Finally, we show that appropriately using appearance can significantly speed up the original *Blind PnP* approach for camera pose estimation.

6.1   Synthetic Experiments

We used a synthetic scenario to evaluate the algorithm under the effects of *clutter*, *occlusions* and different values for the sensor noise. More specifically, we performed experiments varying the principal parameters such as the percentage of noise in the images, the percentage of clutter points in the detected image, the percentage of detected model points, and the *Depth* of the distribution of the inlier correspondences. The *Depth* parameter represents the position that the match candidate occupies, in a list of candidate points ordered according appearance information. For instance, a model point with $Depth = 5$, means that its true match corresponds to its fifth best candidate according to appearance alone. Note that, the more repetitive patterns contains an scene, the depth values for their features points will be higher, and hence, solving the matching will be a more complex task.

We repeat the experiment 5 times for each set of parameters. We compare the results with PROSAC and we show that our algorithm outperforms it when dealing with *occlusions* while showing a similar robustness against *cluttered* images. Our algorithm is not affected by the degradation in the probability distributions of inlier matches as the experiment shows that depth affects PROSAC only.

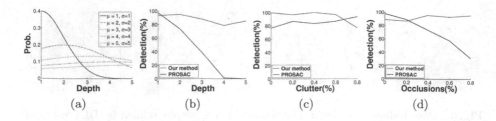

(a)   (b)   (c)   (d)

Fig. 6. a) Probability distribution function used to assign scores to the correspondences. **b)** The experiment shows that our method is correctly estimating the solution when the correct match is between the first 5 correspondences while PROSAC fails. **c)** Algorithm robustness against *clutter* and **d)** occlusions.

The probability distribution functions used to assign appearance scores to the correspondences and the results obtained in the experiments are shown in Fig. 6.

6.2   Homography Estimation

To test the method in real images, we have used images from various sources. First, we tested our algorithm in some of the image datasets presented in [24]. In particular, we present the results obtained by experiencing on marked as *structured* datasets like *Graffiti* (Fig.7) and *textured* datasets like *Wall* (Fig.8). We also have built our own set of images showing a building wall with repetitive texture as the viewpoint changes.

In all the experiments, the number of model points is $M = 200$, while the number of detected keypoints is fixed at $N = 3000$ for the *Graffiti* and *Wall* datasets and to $N = 1500$ for the rest. We considered a depth of correspondence hypothesis below $N' = 10$ in all of the sequences and the number of model points kept has been fixed to $M' = M/3$. For every dataset, $G = 300$ homography prior modes was computed by EM from which we only keep a subset of $G' = 30$ at the end of prior pruning by the appearance score.

From the bottom histograms of Figs. 7, 8, and 9, it can be clearly seen that as the viewpoint goes towards extreme angles, the repeatability of the feature detector decreases, as the percentage of the correct ground truth matches do, and it becomes more and more difficult to extract the correct homography without considering hypotheses at higher *Depth* value. Observe how our algorithm can manage to correctly retrieve the homography in most of experiments, while PROSAC requires a large number of inliers with $Depth = 1$. Obviously it fails when in extreme cases where there are no inliers with a *Depth* value < 10, such as the right-most image in Fig. 8.

6.3   Camera Pose Recovery with an Appearance Prior

The *Blind PnP* approach uses only a geometric prior to recover 2D-to-3D correspondences and also the camera pose with respect to the scene. In a final

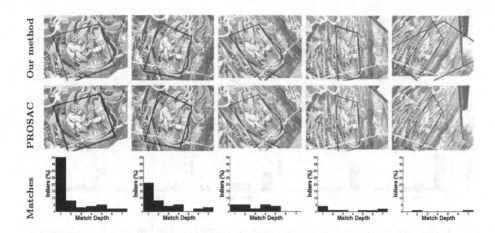

Fig. 7. *Graffiti* sequence. PROSAC fails to extract the homography when the simple keypoint detector we use can not repeatedly detect the most keypoints visible in the frontal view. Since it also relies on the geometric prior our algorithm continues to work.

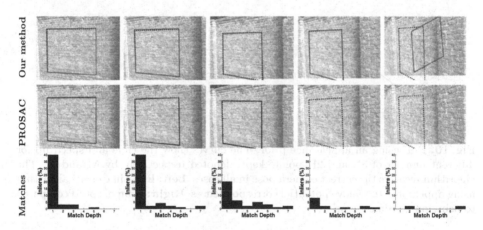

Fig. 8. *Wall* sequence. The highly ambiguous texture on the wall rapidly reduces the matches that can be obtained using only the appearance. Our algorithm can still recover the correct homography even after PROSAC starts to fail.

experiment we used the appearance prior of Section 4.3, to limit the number of 2D-3D correspondences and also to search only priors with high appearance scores given by Eqn. 3. Figure 10 shows that this speeds up the algorithm significantly since the computational complexity of *Blind PnP* is linear in the number of 3D points and prior modes. Again, time values are obtained using our MATLAB implementation.

70   E. Serradell et al.

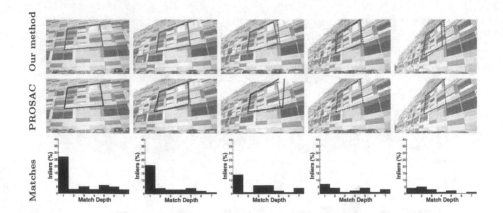

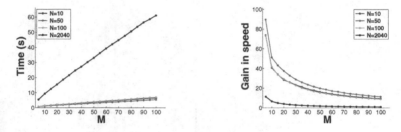

Fig. 9. *Building* sequence. Due to the repeated texture on the building first appearance matches are incorrect even if the keypoint detector responds strongly in the correct location. This is reflected in the distribution of inliers as we consider up to first 7 matches. While PROSAC works only with the first match, our approach is able to utilize correct matches from several levels and recover the correct homography.

Fig. 10. PnP using an appearance prior. The curves show the time and speed up for different number of 3D and 2D points kept, denoted respectively by M and N. The algorithm recovers the correct camera pose in all cases. **Left:** Run-time of the algorithm using appearance to remove potential correspondences. **Right:** Gain in speed compared to using on a geometric prior.

7   Conclusion

We have presented a novel approach to simultaneously estimate homographies and solve for point correspondences by integrating geometric and appearance priors. The combination of both cues within a Kalman filter framework that iteratively guides the matching process, this yields an approach that is robust to high numbers of incorrect matches and low keypoint repeatability. We show this by testing thoroughly in synthetic and real databases of complex images with highly repetitive textures.

The formulation of our approach is fairly general, and allows integrating additional features. As part of future work, we consider exploiting motion coherence and use the method for tracking homographies in real time.

References

1. Szeliski, R.: Image Alignment and Stitching: A Tutorial. Found. Trends. Comput. Graph. Vis. 2, 1–104 (2006)
2. Scherrer, C., Pilet, J., Lepetit, V., Fua, P.: Souvenirs du Monde des Montagnes. Leonardo, special issue on ACM SIGGRAPH, 350–355 (2009)
3. Wagner, D., Reitmayr, G., Mulloni, A., Drummond, T., Schmalstieg, D.: Pose Tracking from Natural Features on Mobile Phones. In: ISMAR (2008)
4. Moreno-Noguer, F., Lepetit, V., Fua, P.: Pose Priors for Simultaneously Solving Alignment and Correspondence. In: Forsyth, D., Torr, P., Zisserman, A. (eds.) ECCV 2008, Part II. LNCS, vol. 5303, pp. 405–418. Springer, Heidelberg (2008)
5. Chum, O., Matas, J.: Matching with PROSAC - Progressive Sample Consensus. In: CVPR, pp. 220–226 (2005)
6. Lowe, D.: Distinctive Image Features From Scale-Invariant Keypoints. IJCV (2004)
7. Fischler, M., Bolles, R.: Random Sample Consensus: A Paradigm for Model Fitting with Applications to Image Analysis and Automated Cartography. ACM Comm., 381–395 (1981)
8. Ayache, N., Faugeras, O.D.: Hyper: A New Approach for the Recognition and Positioning to Two-Dimensional Objects. PAMI, 44–54 (1986)
9. Grimson, W.E.L.: The Combinatorics of Heuristic Search Termination for Object Recognition in Cluttered Environments. PAMI, 920–935 (1991)
10. Lamdan, Y., Wolfson, H.J.: Geometric Hashing: A General and Efficient Model-Based Recognition Scheme. In: ICCV, pp. 238–249 (1988)
11. Burns, J.B., Weiss, R.S., Riseman, E.M.: View Variation of Point-Set and Line-Segment Features. PAMI, 51–68 (1993)
12. Beis, J.S., Lowe, D.G.: Indexing Without Invariants in 3d Object Recognition. PAMI, 1000–1015 (1999)
13. Olson, C.F.: Efficient Pose Clustering Using a Randomized Algorithm. IJCV (1997)
14. Stockman, G.: Object Recognition and Localization Via Pose Clustering. Comput. Vision Graph. Image Process. 40, 361–387 (1987)
15. Tordoff, B., Murray, D.W.: Guided Sampling and Consensus for Motion Estimation. In: Heyden, A., Sparr, G., Nielsen, M., Johansen, P. (eds.) ECCV 2002. LNCS, vol. 2350, pp. 82–98. Springer, Heidelberg (2002)
16. Raguram, R., Frahm, J., Pollefeys, M.: A Comparative Analysis of Ransac Techniques Leading to Adaptive Real-Time Random Sample Consensus. In: Forsyth, D., Torr, P., Zisserman, A. (eds.) ECCV 2008, Part II. LNCS, vol. 5303, pp. 500–513. Springer, Heidelberg (2008)
17. David, P., DeMenthon, D., Duraiswami, R., Samet, H.: Softposit: Simultaneous Pose and Correspondence Determination. IJCV, 259–284 (2004)
18. Ozuysal, M., Calonder, M., Lepetit, V., Fua, P.: Fast Keypoint Recognition Using Random Ferns. PAMI, 448–461 (2010)
19. Lowe, D.: Object Recognition From Local Scale-Invariant Features. In: ICCV, pp. 1150–1157 (1999)
20. Bay, H., Tuytelaars, T., Gool, L.: Surf: Speeded Up Robust Features. In: Leonardis, A., Bischof, H., Pinz, A. (eds.) ECCV 2006. LNCS, vol. 3951, pp. 404–417. Springer, Heidelberg (2006)
21. Davison, A.J.: Active Search for Real-Time Vision. In: ICCV, pp. 66–73 (2005)

22. Chili, M., Davison, A.: Active Matching. In: Forsyth, D., Torr, P., Zisserman, A. (eds.) ECCV 2008, Part I. LNCS, vol. 5302, pp. 72–85. Springer, Heidelberg (2008)
23. Abdel-Aziz, Y.I., Karara, H.M.: Direct Linear Transformation from Comparator Coordinates into Object Space Coordinates in Close-Range Photogrammetry. In: Proc. ASP/UI Symp. Close-Range Photogrammetry, pp. 1–18 (1971)
24. Mikolajczyk, K., Tuytelaars, T., Schmid, C., Zisserman, A., Matas, J., Schaffalitzky, F., Kadir, T., Gool, L.: A Comparison of Affine Region Detectors. IJCV (2005)
25. Stewart, C.: Robust Parameter Estimation in Computer Vision. SIAM Rev (1999)

Real-Time Spherical Mosaicing
Using Whole Image Alignment

Steven Lovegrove and Andrew J. Davison

Imperial College London, London SW7 2AZ, UK
{sl203,ajd}@doc.ic.ac.uk

Abstract. When a purely rotating camera observes a general scene, overlapping views are related by a parallax-free warp which can be estimated by direct image alignment methods that iterate to optimise photoconsistency. However, building globally consistent mosaics from video has usually been tackled as an off-line task, while sequential methods suitable for real-time implementation have often suffered from long-term drift. In this paper we present a high performance real-time video mosaicing algorithm based on parallel image alignment via ESM (Efficient Second-order Minimisation) and global optimisation of a map of keyframes over the whole viewsphere. We present real-time results for drift-free camera rotation tracking and globally consistent spherical mosaicing from a variety of cameras in real scenes, demonstrating high global accuracy and the ability to track very rapid rotation while maintaining solid 30Hz operation. We also show that automatic camera calibration refinement can be straightforwardly built into our framework.

Keywords: Real-time tracking, spherical mosaicing, SLAM, auto-calibration.

1 Introduction

A set of images can be fused into a mosaic if there is no parallax between them, and this is the case either when a generally moving camera browses a plane or when a general 3D scene is observed by a camera which only rotates. There is a great deal of literature on building mosaics from multiple images or video (see the tutorial by Szeliski [1]). The emphasis has been on methods which operate off-line, consisting of pair-wise image registration achieved either with features (e.g. [2] using SIFT matching, or [3]) or whole image alignment (e.g. [4]), and global optimisation. Meanwhile, methods that were able to operate from video in real-time such as [5] achieved accurate local registration but were subject to drift over longer periods due to the lack of explicit global optimisation.

The core issue of mosaicing is to accurately estimate the motion of the camera, and if globally consistent mosaics are to be constructed from video in real-time this motion estimation must be drift-free over arbitrarily long time periods. Like any case of estimating the motion of an outward-looking sensor in a previously unknown environment, mosaicing can be considered as a Simultaneous Localisation and Mapping (SLAM) problem. This is important, because in SLAM

K. Daniilidis, P. Maragos, N. Paragios (Eds.): ECCV 2010, Part III, LNCS 6313, pp. 73–86, 2010.
© Springer-Verlag Berlin Heidelberg 2010

research, originating in the mobile robotics area, there has been great attention paid to developing algorithms which run sequentially in real-time but are also able to generate globally consistent scene models.

The predominant early approaches to SLAM were based on sequential probabilistic filtering algorithms, most importantly the Extended Kalman Filter (EKF), to jointly estimate the positions of both the moving sensor and the features which it observed. This methodology was recently successfully applied to image mosaicing by Civera *et al.* [6], in the first work which was able to demonstrate drift-free mosaicing at frame-rate from a rotating camera. The computational cost of the EKF backbone of this technique, however, scales badly with the number of features kept in the map state, and this meant that only around 10–15 features (matched using 11×11 pixel patches) could be tracked per frame; all but 3% of every image was ignored for the purposes of image alignment, and this sets a limit on the mosaicing quality which can be achieved.

Recently in real-time 3D camera tracking, methods based not on filtering but parallel pose estimation relative to keyframes and global optimisation have enabled large amounts of image correspondence information to be used in all frames. This approach was pioneered by Klein and Murray's Parallel Tracking and Mapping (PTAM) system [7] where hundreds of feature points are tracked per frame and built into a globally consistent 3D model of a workspace. Importantly, PTAM demonstrated that only tracking relative to the nearest keyframe is necessarily required to run at frame-rate to maintain live operation. The global optimisation component of PTAM (bundle adjustment of scene points and keyframes) runs in a parallel thread and repeats only as often as processing resources allow at a fraction of frame-rate.

This decoupling of local motion tracking from building a consistent global world model has become a dominant methodology in more generic SLAM research in robotics, since the pioneering work of Lu and Milios [8] and the first full implementation of a sequential mapping algorithm combining local tracking with interleaved global optimisation by Gutmann and Konolige [9], in this case with 2D laser scan data. With this interleaved approach, one is free to choose raw data alignment methods for the local tracking component, and the SLAM 'map' consists of the historically estimated sensor poses rather than feature locations.

In our work, we adapt this parallel tracking/optimisation approach to live video mosaicing, and make use of a state of the art whole image alignment method both for local rotation tracking and at the heart of a parallel optimisation thread for globally consistent alignment of a set of keyframes spanning the whole viewsphere. We are also able to refine estimates of camera intrinsic parameters in this global optimisation. Whole image alignment, as opposed to feature tracking, densely makes use of all of the texture in the images to permit registration which is as accurate as possible. Further, we show that a hierarchical implementation via an image pyramid permits the tracking to be efficient while maintaining a wide basin of convergence allowing very rapid camera rotation to be tracked.

Still one of the most widely used methods for estimating the warp between images, the Lucas-Kanade [10] method is based on the iterative minimisation of a cost function related to how well one reference image matches that of a warped comparison image. The parameters of the warp define the dimensionality of this space. By computing the derivative of the cost function with respect to the warp parameters, the parameter space gradient can be 'surfed' to a minimum, which may or may not be the global minimum.

Within our system, we make extensive use of the technique proposed by Malis, named Efficient Second-order Minimisation (ESM) [11] which instead finds the second order minimiser of the cost function while using only first order terms. This provides stable convergence in fewer iterations than the Lucas-Kanade method.

2   Method

Our algorithm is split into two tasks which run as parallel threads on a multi-core PC: a) tracking from a known map, and b) global map maintenance and optimisation (see Figure 1), an approach inspired by PTAM [7]. In the first 'tracking' thread, we use the direct, whole image second order optimisation method ESM of Malis [11], with further contributions from Mei *et al.* [12], which we implement on graphics hardware for high-quality real-time tracking relative to our map. In the second parallel thread, we run a global optimisation procedure also based on ESM which adjusts the estimated orientations of all keyframes of our map and camera intrinsics simultaneously. This allows us to produce globally consistent mosaics in real-time. We remove radial distortion from all live frames as they enter our system, and deal only with perspective images from then on. We use a third party tool to establish the distortion parameters. Additionally, we describe an automatic method for relocalisation if tracking should fail, allowing the current mosaic to be re-joined without corruption.

Keyframe Map. Within our system, we store a collection of key historic camera poses with associated image data, which we call keyframes. Keyframes within

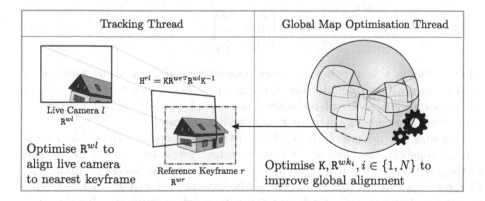

Fig. 1. System overview showing separation of tracking and mapping

our map are related to one another by a 3DOF rotation. We store the current estimate of a keyframe's pose as a rotation matrix R^{wk} relating the camera's local frame of reference, k, to that of the world, w.

Tracking. When tracking commences, we set the first live image to be our first keyframe, k_0 with pose R^{wk_0} set to the identity. For each subsequent live frame, we use the previous live pose to select the closest keyframe from our map. We estimate the current pose by considering the image warp between this keyframe and the current image, which in turn allows us to estimate the relative motion.

Exploration. As tracking continues, we create new keyframes and add them to the map if the overlap between our current image and closest keyframe becomes too small and falls below a threshold. Keyframes which we add inherit the pose of the live camera at that time.

2.1   Local Motion Estimation

For local motion estimation, we update our current pose estimate, R^{wc}, by considering the live image and a reference keyframe r with known pose, R^{wr}.

For two cameras in a general configuration observing a plane, we can describe pixel correspondence within their images by a plane induced homography. Cameras which purely rotate, however, allow us to disregard the scene entirely. Defining H^{ba} as the homography that transfers points imaged in camera a to the equivalent points in camera b, we can write H^{ba} as a function of R^{ba}:

$$H^{ba} = KR^{ba}K^{-1} \ , \tag{1}$$

where K is the 3×3 camera intrinsic calibration matrix:

$$K = \begin{pmatrix} f_u & 0 & u_0 \\ 0 & f_v & v_0 \\ 0 & 0 & 1 \end{pmatrix} . \tag{2}$$

This enables us to generate views from rotated 'virtual' cameras by warping an existing image. Our frame to frame tracking problem is then to find an update to the parameters of the plane induced homography H^{lr} which best reflects the warp between reference keyframe r and our live camera l.

Following the method of Malis [11], we parametrise updates to our pose using the Lie Algebra. The class of 3×3 rotation matrices belong to the Lie Special Orthogonal group SO(3). This group can be minimally parametrised around the identity by a three-vector belonging to the associated Lie Algebra $\mathfrak{so}(3)$. This parametrisation is locally Euclidean about **0**, which is important for the ESM method. An element $x \in \mathfrak{so}(3)$ is related to a member $R(x) \in SO(3)$ through the matrix exponential map, where elements of x form coefficients for the group generators, $A_i, i \in [1, 2, 3]$:

$$R(x) = \exp \left(\sum_{i=1}^{3} x_i A_i \right).$$ (3)

Given a current estimate of the rotation, $\hat{R}^{lr}$, and an update parametrised by $x \in \mathfrak{so}(3)$, $R^{lr}(x)$, we update our estimate using the following rule:

$$\hat{R}^{lr} \longleftarrow \hat{R}^{lr} R^{lr}(x).$$ (4)

We can now define an objective function describing the sum of squared differences between pixels in the live and reference images related by the homography, itself a function of the current rotation estimate $\hat{R}^{lr}$, and the update x:

$$f(x) = \frac{1}{2} \sum_{p_r \in \Omega_r} \left[\mathcal{I}^l \left(H \left(\hat{R}^{lr} R(x)^{lr} \right) p_r \right) - \mathcal{I}^r (p_r) \right]^2.$$ (5)

$\mathcal{I}^r$ and $\mathcal{I}^l$ represent the reference keyframe and live image respectively. The sum is formed from each pixel p_r in the set of pixels Ω_r defined in the reference image.

It can be shown that, up to second order, this function is minimised at x_0 (Equation 6), where $+$ is the pseudo-inverse and J the Jacobian relating change in parameters to changes in the cost function (Equation 7) [12]:

$$x_0 = -J^+ f(0)$$ (6)

$$J = \left(\frac{J_{\mathcal{I}^l} + J_{\mathcal{I}^r}}{2} \right) J_w J_K J_R J_x.$$ (7)

The reader is asked to refer to [11,12,13] for details, including the definition of these Jacobians. The special formulation of these Jacobians taken about the reference and current images and the subsequent minimisation of this objective function is what is referred to as Efficient Second-order Minimisation (ESM).

If we instead write $f(x)$ explicitly as the norm of a residual difference vector $\mathbf{d}$ (Equation 8), where each row corresponds to a pixel in Ω_r (Equation 9), we see that the size of the system can be reduced by solving instead its normal equations (Equation 10):

$$f(x) = \frac{1}{2} \|d(x)\|^2$$ (8)

$$d_{p_r}(x) = \mathcal{I}^l \left(H \left(\hat{R}^{lr} R^{lr}(x) \right) p_r \right) - \mathcal{I}^r (p_r)$$ (9)

$$x_0 = -(J^\mathsf{T} J)^{-1} J^\mathsf{T} f(0).$$ (10)

Since J has dimensions *num pixels* $\times 3$, $J^\mathsf{T} J$ (a 3×3 matrix) is significantly smaller than J, and can be computed by summing the individual outer products of rows of J. We progress by iteratively solving this non-linear least squares system, applying the update $\hat{R}^{lr} = \hat{R}^{lr}R^{lr}(x_0)$ until convergence.

Upon convergence, $\hat{R}^{lr}$ represents the transformation between the live and reference cameras. Applying this to consecutive frames from a video sequence could form the basis for a visual odometry system. Here, instead, we match the current live image against the 'closest' keyframe in our map.

2.2   Global Map Optimisation

Joint global optimisation of all keyframes of the map and camera intrinsics occurs concurrently in a separate thread. We apply the ESM method to a more general objective function. We parametrise updates to pose through the Lie Algebra as before, but formulate updates to the camera intrinsic parameters by a vector, $k \in \mathbb{R}^4$, through exponentiation. Thus, $k = \mathbf{0}$ represents no change to the intrinsics. The update rule becomes:

$$\begin{pmatrix} f_u \\ f_v \\ u_0 \\ v_0 \end{pmatrix} \longleftarrow \begin{pmatrix} f_u e^{k_0} \\ f_v e^{k_1} \\ u_0 e^{k_2} \\ v_0 e^{k_3} \end{pmatrix}.$$ (11)

For N keyframes, our update vector x can be decomposed into rotation parameters, $r_i \in \mathfrak{so}(3)$, and intrinsic parameters: $x = (k, r_1, r_2, ...r_N)$. The objective function which we now wish to minimise includes all pairs of overlapping images:

$$f(x) = \frac{1}{2} \sum_j \sum_i \sum_{p_j \in \Omega_j} \left[\mathcal{I}^i \left(\mathtt{H}^{ij}(x) p_j \right) - \mathcal{I}^j \left(p_j \right) \right]^2.$$ (12)

$$\mathtt{H}^{ij}(x) = \hat{K}K(k)\hat{R}^{ij}R^{ij}(r_i, r_j)(\hat{K}K(k))^{-1}$$ (13)

$$\hat{R}^{ij}R^{ij}(r_i, r_j) = (\hat{R}^{wi}R^{wi}(r_i))^{\mathsf{T}}\hat{R}^{wj}R^{wj}(r_j).$$ (14)

We calculate the incremental minimiser of this function x_0 using exactly the same machinery as before. Iterations of this minimisation take place continuously, helping to improve the map consistency.

Auto-calibration of camera intrinsics is particularly well posed in the case of a camera which only rotates [14]. In our system, the expected performance of calibration refinement is much further enhanced by our ability to match images automatically around full 360° panoramas, giving the potential for accurate calibration even for cameras with a narrow field of view.

2.3   Recovery from Tracking Loss

We have provided our SLAM system with a straightforward relocalisation capability similar in spirit to the 'small blurry image' method of PTAM [7] but which directly takes advantage of the main ESM pose estimate algorithm. If the camera becomes 'lost' then we aim to recover a pose estimate by simply attempting ESM pose estimation from a number of seed locations visible in our current mosaic, starting at the smallest image size in an image pyramid. Of the estimated warp parameters obtained, we refine the most photo-consistent estimate by performing more ESM iterations at higher resolutions in the pyramid. We use the poses of our keyframes as seed locations, but indeed any regular sample would be equally valid.

Computation time for relocalisation is proportional to the number of seed locations. For spherical mosaics, relocalisation need not be costly. When lost (measured using observed photoconsistency between the current keyframe and live camera), we run the relocalisation procedure on one in ten frames. This method operates well in environments with low perceptual aliasing.

3   Implementation

To achieve real-time performance, we make extensive use of commodity graphics hardware and the parallelism that this can afford. Graphics cards usually have a number of very simple, high throughput shaders that are ideal for stream processing tasks; taking quantities of data which are largely independent of each other and transforming this data in some way.

We use the portable graphics language Cg, which can run on the majority of today's PCs and laptops. In this section, we will outline some of the more interesting implementation details of our system.

3.1   Real-Time Hierarchical ESM for Local Tracking

Our local tracking ESM implementation is split into three very simple stages targeting the graphics card, described below.

Hierarchical Construction. After a frame is received from the video camera, it is uploaded as a texture on the GPU. Once in graphics memory, a fragment shader is invoked once for each desired level in a power-of-two reduction pyramid.

The fragment shader, which operates per pixel, simply takes the value of the average of the corresponding 4-block from the level above. This gets rendered back into a different texture of half the size. Typically, we use five levels in our pyramid which correspond to four invocations of this fragment shader. The individual levels of the pyramid are left on the graphics card and never downloaded to the CPU.

By first estimating the warp parameters between images at the smallest resolution in the pyramid, we benefit from a wider parameter-space convergence basin and lower processing costs. By assuming that per-pixel derivatives are meaningful at each of the levels, we are able to reuse our estimated warp parameters in the next highest resolution image and repeat. We can tune for performance/accuracy by setting how many iterations to perform at various levels.

Construction of Least Squares System Elements. For every step in the ESM method, Jacobian terms common to all pixels are computed on the CPU (J_K, J_R, J_x). This leaves the data-centric terms (J_w, $J_{\mathcal{I}^l}$, $J_{\mathcal{I}^r}$) to be computed on the GPU. $J_{\mathcal{I}^l}$ and $J_{\mathcal{I}^r}$ are computed by central difference. The 9×3 matrix $J_K J_R J_x$ is loaded onto the GPU as parameters to a fragment shader in three 3×3 blocks, which are supported as primitives in the Cg language.

Invoking the fragment shader runs a simple Cg function per pixel p^r that enables us to compute the appropriate row of J, J_{p^r} and the residual d_{p^r}. This shader function also computes the outer product $J_{p^r}^T J_{p^r}$ and product $J_{p^r}^T d_{p^r}$. Since $J_{p^r}^T J_{p^r}$ is symmetric, it has 6 unique elements; $J_{p^r}^T d_{p^r}$ has 3. The shader function returns these 9 values as pixel 'colours' across three floating point RGBA textures stored on the GPU. We use OpenGL framebuffers to enable this.

Reduction to Linear System. Given our three textures, where a channel of each image, for every pixel p^r, corresponds to elements of $J_{p^r}^T J_{p^r}$ and $J_{p^r}^T d_{p^r}$, we wish to compute $J^T J$ and $J^T d$. This involves summing the channels of each pixel, which we perform in two stages. The first is a vertical reduction in another Cg fragment shader. This shader is invoked on an output set of images containing a single row. For each pixel, this shader sums the pixels of the input images in the same column.

Finally, we download these three row images to the CPU, where the final horizontal reduction takes place to a single vector, which is unpacked into the appropriate matrix and vector. Here, it is solved using an efficient Cholesky decomposition.

3.2   Rendering

Two common approaches to visualising rotational mosaics are spherical and cylindrical projection. A spherical mosaic is visualised from within the center of a view-sphere, where images are projected to the sphere surface. Cylindrical projections are instead projected on to a cylinder, which we can then unwrap into a single image, visualising all of the mosaic at once.

We again make use of Cg shaders to enable us to visualise the full quality, blended mosaic live, and for correctly sampling from the constituent keyframes.

Spherical Panorama. For rendering a spherical panorama, we treat our virtual (OpenGL) camera much like a keyframe, positioned at the origin and parametrised by the camera to world transform R^{wc}. We can map image space coordinates from our OpenGL viewport to a keyframe k by composing the homography $H^{kc} = K R^{wk^T} R^{wc} K^{-1}$.

We use a shader which we invoke once for each keyframe within the field of view of the virtual camera, passing in as a parameter the homography H^{kc} which enables us to place the keyframe within the viewport. This shader, operating per-pixel, simply adds the keyframe's colour value to the colour already in the frame buffer associated with the viewport. Additionally, it adds 1.0 to the alpha channel for the pixel which serves as a counter.

Finally, we invoke another normalisation shader, which simply divides the Red, Green and Blue channels by the alpha channel. The result is a panorama where each keyframe is displayed blended with equal weight. One of the nice aspects of this method is that image fusion occurs in the space of the viewport. This means that each keyframe, whose pixel data is not sampled to the same 'grid' in viewport space, gets mixed to form an image of higher resolution of the constituent images. Dependent on the quality of image registration, this can enable 'super resolution' images to be displayed at frame rate.

Cylindrical Panorama. To create cylindrical panoramas, we use similar machinery as for spherical panoramas. Within the shader, the u and v viewport coordinates are interpreted as yaw (ψ) and pitch (θ) in the range $[-\pi, +\pi]$ and $[-\frac{\pi}{2}, +\frac{\pi}{2}]$ respectively.

For each keyframe, we invoke the shader, where, for each pixel we then compute the desired image ray described by the unit vector $\hat{\mathbf{r}}$,

$$\hat{\mathbf{r}} = (\cos\theta\cos\psi, \sin\theta, \cos\theta\sin\psi)^{\mathrm{T}}. \tag{15}$$

This is transferred into the frame of reference of the keyframe using the virtual camera to keyframe rotation matrix, $\mathbf{R}^{kc}$, which is uploaded as a parameter to the shader. Finally, the camera intrinsic matrix can be used to map this to keyframe image-space coordinates. Given this correspondence, we proceed as with the spherical panorama.

4   Results

We wish to evaluate our system against two criteria; how accurately local motion is estimated, and how consistently frames are registered into a final mosaic.

In all of the results, as our submitted video also highlights, mosaics were computed incrementally and rendered live at frame rate, a solid 30fps. We cap per frame ESM iterations to 48 at the 5th level of the pyramid, 16 at the 4th, 8 at the 3rd, 4 at the 2nd, and 2 at the 1st. We use any remaining time to perform iterations at the 0th level which corresponds to the original image — this typically is one, two or three iterations. We drop new keyframes when less than 80% of the current keyframe is visible.

4.1   Local Motion Estimation and Dynamics

To test the ability of our method to track dynamic local motion, we have compared the angular velocity output of our method against a solid state gyroscope bolted to the back of the camera, which was mounted on a tripod and oscillated to produce increasingly rapid motion (up to around 5 cycles per second) about each of its axes in turn.

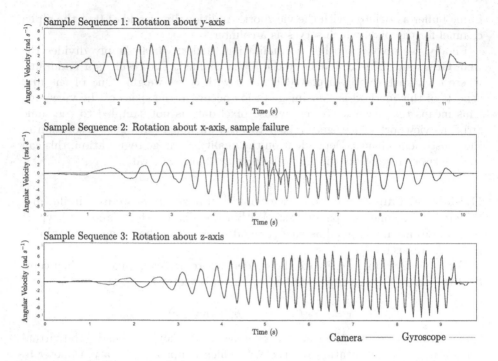

Fig. 2. Graphs illustrating high dynamic tracking performance; the plots show angular velocity estimates from our vision system compared with the output from a gyroscope as the camera was vigorously oscillated about each of the three camera-oriented axes in turn (y axis pan; x elevation, z cyclotorsion)

The characteristics of estimation are somewhat different depending on the axis of rotation, as the plots of Figure 2 illustrate. Angular velocity about the z-axis (cyclotorsion) is estimated very accurately. Note that the truncated peaks of the gyroscope data show that the tracking limits of the device were exceeded while visual tracking still continued accurately — our system was able to maintain fidelity about this axis in excess of $7 \, rads^{-1}$, which is significantly faster than a camera would normally move in a tracking scenario.

Angular velocity about the y-axis, corresponding to camera pan, tracks the gyroscope data closely, with a very slight systematic under-estimation. We suspect that camera calibration may be the predominant cause, or a slight misalignment between the camera and gyroscope frames of reference.

The plot showing rotation about the x-axis, corresponding to camera elevation, demonstrates a failure case of visual tracking caused by extreme motion. The tracking under-shoots, and takes several oscillations to re-acquire correspondence with the keyframe against which it is tracking. If the motion was non-cyclic, it would be harder for the system to recover to an orientation fixed in the global frame without resorting to relocalisation. The system is least stable about this axis. We suggest that this is due to the narrower vertical field of view.

4.2 Global Consistency and Intrinsics Refinement

For evaluation of global registration, we present several cylindrically projected 360° panoramas (Figures 3, 5) captured with two different cameras, and with two different lenses for each camera. They are constructed by blending every keyframe of the map with equal weight, as described in Section 3.2, enabling us to visualise the quality of their alignment.

For areas of the mosaic formed from multiple images, pixel noise is significantly reduced, and the mosaic appears smoother. The different sampling pattern of keyframes and sub-pixel accuracy we achieve in alignment combine to create a super-sampling, or 'super-resolution' image, efficiently rendered in real-time on the graphics card.

Figure 4 demonstrates the importance of our joint estimation of camera intrinsic parameters, even for pre-calibrated cameras. Starting with intrinsics estimated from a third party camera calibration tool, and continuing with no intrinsics optimisation, the first mosaic in this figure appears fuzzy. Upon inspection we can see that the estimated loop length is longer than the actual length (in pixels), causing the images to bunch up (the enlargement of the whiteboard helps to convey this point). This is caused by intrinsic parameters which are wider than the actual camera. The second mosaic in this figure is the result of allowing our algorithm to optimise intrinsics as well as pose parameters (from the starting point of the first mosaic).

The mosaics in Figure 3 were generated from three different lenses, all at 640 × 480 resolution, and initialised with 'Generic' intrinsic calibration (nearest 10° FOV and central principal point). Table 4.2 shows the initial horizontal field of view, which was based on our knowledge of the lens, and the converged field of view estimate after a full loop was completed for these sequences.

Table 1. Calibration Refinement results for Different Cameras and Lenses. Calibration initialised from Quoted Horizontal Field of View (FOV), and refined by mosaicing cylindrical loops from 640 × 480 indoor sequences.

Camera	Lens	Lens Quality	Initial FOV Estimate	Refined FOV
Point Grey Flea2	Wide Angle	Good	70°	69.42°
Point Grey Flea2	TV Lens	Fair	50°	51.43°
Unibrain	Standard	Poor	50°	45.56°

4.3 Convergence to Global Minimum

The results from mosaicing based on poor initial intrinsics (Figure 3) help to motivate that our system has useful convergence properties. By including intrinsics in our optimisation, we help to enable loop closure by increasing the accuracy of our pose estimate when we come to complete a loop. By completing a loop too soon, or too early, we are more likely to fall into local minima — especially if perceptual aliasing in this area is high.

Fig. 3. 360° cylindrically-projected panoramas for three indoor sequences, taken with different lenses. Point Grey Flea2, 70° FOV wide angle (top, close to full sphere including full hemispherical upward coverage, 27 keyframes), 50° FOV TV Lens (middle, single horizontal loop trajectory, 17 keyframes), and Unibrain 45° FOV Standard lens (bottom, single horizontal loop trajectory, 19 keyframes).

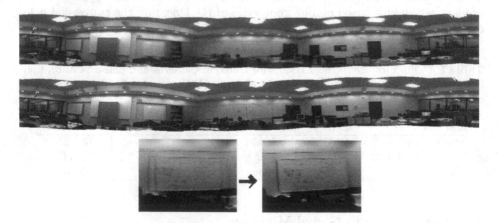

Fig. 4. Mosaicing with fixed intrinsics estimated from a third party calibration tool (top), compared against enabling live intrinsics estimation (middle). An enlargement of the whiteboard from the two mosaics, emphasising improvement in alignment, is shown at the bottom. The whiteboard is representative of several areas of the mosaic.

Figure 5 shows an outdoor mosaic generated from rapid hand-held motion of a Unibrain webcam with a wide angle lens. Note that in this experiment the pure rotation assumption was approximately satisfied without a tripod due to the large distance to the scene. This scene contains high perceptual aliasing in the windows and building pillars, making loop closure difficult. For this sequence, we were unable to converge to a globally consistent mosaic from our generic 80° FOV calibration parameters. Instead, we started from the parameters estimated from a third party calibration tool.

Fig. 5. 360° Tower panorama from 21 keyframes (live hand held Unibrain webcam, 320×240 resolution), shown in horizontally and vertically-oriented cylindrical projection. Note the vertical hole due to poor texture and cloud movement in the sky.

Time to convergence is another important evaluation criterion. Each iteration in our global minimisation is costly — forming the linear system from image data dominates computational time. Actually solving this system is cheap since spherical mosaics require only a relatively small number of keyframes. For this reason, computation time scales linearly with the number of pairs of overlapping pixels. For N keyframes, depending on keyframe alignment, this has a worst case complexity of $O(N^2)$. In practice, our system achieves convergence within time in the order of seconds of completing a loop; often less than one second when a wide angle lens means that the number of keyframes to span a loop is low.

5   Conclusions

We have presented an algorithm based on full image alignment which produces accurate, globally consistent mosaics in real-time. Our key contribution is to show how state of the art image alignment can be used in a robust and accurate real-time mosaicing system which combines the best of a visual gyroscope, with its ability to track rapid motion, with the properties of a visual compass, able to function without long-term drift. We also demonstrate convincing automatic camera calibration refinement, and explain how real-time tracking and rendering can be comfortably achieved using commodity graphics hardware.

The clear extension to our method which we plan to investigate is the capability to track general motion viewing multi-planar scenes, such as building façades and room interiors. We can enforce strong priors in such environments and hope to demonstrate very fast, robust tracking and coarse model construction.

Acknowledgements

This research was supported by an EPSRC DTA studentship to S. Lovegrove and European Research Council Starting Grant 210346. We are very grateful to Richard Newcombe and other colleagues at Imperial College London for many useful discussions.

References

1. Szeliski, R.: Image alignment and stitching: A tutorial. Foundations and Trends in Computer Graphics and Vision 2, 1–104 (2006)
2. Brown, M., Lowe, D.G.: Recognising panoramas. In: Proceedings of the International Conference on Computer Vision (ICCV) (2003)
3. Steedly, D., Pal, C., Szeliski, R.: Efficiently stitching large panoramas from video. In: Proceedings of the International Conference on Computer Vision (ICCV) (2005)
4. Szeliski, R., Shum, H.Y.: Creating full view panoramic image mosaics and environment maps. ACM Transactions on Graphics (SIGGRAPH) (1997)
5. Morimoto, C., Chellappa, R.: Fast 3D stabilization and mosaic construction. In: Proceedings of the IEEE Conference on Computer Vision and Pattern Recognition (CVPR) (1997)
6. Civera, J., Davison, A.J., Magallón, J.A., Montiel, J.M.M.: Drift-free real-time mosaicing. International Journal of Computer Vision (IJCV) 81, 128–137 (2009)
7. Klein, G., Murray, D.W.: Parallel tracking and mapping for small AR workspaces. In: Proceedings of the International Symposium on Mixed and Augmented Reality (ISMAR) (2007)
8. Lu, F., Milios, E.: Globally consistent range scan alignment for environment mapping. Autonomous Robots 4, 333–349 (1997)
9. Gutmann, J.S., Konolige, K.: Incremental mapping of large cyclic environments. In: International Symposium on Computational Intelligence in Robotics and Automation (CIRA) (1999)
10. Lucas, B.D., Kanade, T.: An iterative image registration technique with an application to stereo vision. In: Proceedings of the International Joint Conference on Artificial Intelligence (IJCAI) (1981)
11. Malis, E.: Improving vision-based control using efficient second-order minimization techniques. In: Proceedings of the IEEE International Conference on Robotics and Automation (ICRA) (2004)
12. Mei, C., Benhimane, S., Malis, E., Rives, P.: Efficient homography-based tracking and 3-D reconstruction for single-viewpoint sensors. IEEE Transactions on Robotics (T-RO) 24, 1352–1364 (2008)
13. Silveira, G., Malis, E., Rives, P.: An efficient direct approach to visual SLAM. IEEE Transactions on Robotics (T-RO) 24, 969–979 (2008)
14. Agapito, L., Hayman, E., Reid, I.: Self-calibration of rotating and zooming cameras. International Journal of Computer Vision (IJCV) 45, 107–127 (2001)

Adaptive Metric Registration of 3D Models to Non-rigid Image Trajectories

Alessio Del Bue*

Istituto Italiano di Tecnologia
Via Morego 30, 16163 Genova, Italy
alessio.delbue@iit.it

Abstract. This paper addresses the problem of registering a 3D model, represented as a cloud of points lying over a surface, to a set of 2D deforming image trajectories in the image plane. The proposed approach can adapt to a scenario where the 3D model to register is not an exact description of the measured image data. This results in finding the best 2D–3D registration, given the complexity of having both 2D deforming data and a coarse description of the image observations. The method acts in two distinct phases. First, an affine step computes a factorization for both the 2D image data and the 3D model using a joint subspace decomposition. This initial solution is then upgraded by finding the best projection to the image plane complying with the metric constraints given by a scaled orthographic camera. Both steps are computed efficiently in closed-form with the additional feature of being robust to degenerate motions which may possibly affect the 2D image data (i.e. lack of relevant rigid motion). Moreover, we present an extension of the approach for the case of missing image data. Synthetic and real experiments show the robustness of the method in registration tasks such as pose estimation of a talking face using a single 3D model.

1 Introduction

The analysis of non-rigid motion has great relevance in many life science and engineering tasks. This need arises from the observation that most of the natural shapes are constantly modifying their topology. Such variations may appear smooth and tiny as in the bending of the arm muscles or drastic and violent, as in the reactions taking place at the molecular level. Such degrees of variation have consequently brought new challenges in the Structure from Motion (SfM) [3,12,2,1] and image registration fields [4,8,14]. The problem is made more difficult because the assumption of rigidity is now broken and the classical metric constraints used in rigid SfM [11] are weakened if not irremediably lost. Here specifically, we study the problem of registering a 3D model to a set of 2D trajectories extracted from an image sequence. Our challenge is represented by the fact that the 3D model to register may not be an exact description of the 2D motion shown in the image sequence as exemplified in Figure 1 in a face analysis domain. The aim is to provide a new set of tools which adapt to the new information provided by the image sequence. This problem occurs more often thanks to the rapid

---
* This work was partially supported by FCT, under ISR/IST plurianual funding (POSC program, FEDER) and grant MODI-PTDC/EEA-ACR/72201/2006. Thanks to J. Peyras and J. Xiao for providing the image sequences and tracks.

K. Daniilidis, P. Maragos, N. Paragios (Eds.): ECCV 2010, Part III, LNCS 6313, pp. 87–100, 2010.

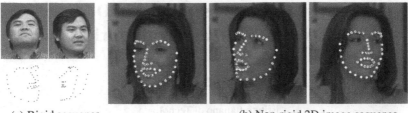

(a) Rigid sequence   (b) Non-rigid 2D image sequence

Fig. 1. The figure shows an example of our problem. In the top row of figure (a), a 3D shape can be recovered from a rigid image sequence with standard SfM algorithms. The model in the bottom row has now to be registered to a new non-rigid image sequence (b) with 2D trajectories extracted from a subject with different somatic traits. We seek the best registration given both 2D and 3D data which satisfy the metric constraints of the shapes. White dots represent the 2D image data and the red circles ○ our algorithm result.

advancements of the modern sensor technologies. Nowadays, it is a more likely occurrence to have available measurements coming from different devices. However, temporally evolving data is mainly restricted to 2D observation (e.g. video from cameras, MRI and ultrasound images) while full 3D information is captured at sparser time instances (e.g. scans given by CT and range sensors). For this reason, a robust 2D-3D registration of data coming from different sources is more often required. Moreover such registration has to adapt to the given observed image motion, since it is likely that the given 3D surface may not be an exact representation of the evolving shape.

This paper proposes a novel registration procedure that adapts the given 3D shape to the 2D data. In order to solve the problem, a general two-step formulation is introduced. First, a compact low-rank description is extracted from both the 2D measurements and the 3D rigid shape. This first decomposition is up to a generic affine transformation. Then, this solution is corrected by finding the best transformation that complies with the metric constraints given the image motion and the shape to register. To the authors knowledge, the closest work to the proposed algorithm is the one by Xiao et al. [14] where the scope of the authors was not only restricted to registration but also to the inference of a full deformable model. Their closed form solution however makes use of the assumption that there exists a set of independent basis shapes and results may vary if this choice is not accurate as noted in [2,12]. Full 3D reconstruction is out of the scope of this paper since our main aim is to find the most appropriate rigid motion describing the non-rigid image trajectories without any assumptions about the model underlying the deformations.

1.1 Contributions and Paper Organization

We first introduce the mathematical framework and a standard solution for the 2D–3D registration problem with rigid models. Such an algorithm however cannot cope properly when the registration is done with inaccurate 3D observations such as the one shown in Figure 1(b). The proposed method instead performs an affine registration

procedure which is derived from the work of Del Bue [5]. The first contribution is a
new set of metric constraints which jointly force the projection constraints for the 2D
data and 3D data. This problem is then formulated by finding a corrective transform
which enforces the given constraints. This optimization can be solved either in closed
form with Least Squares (LS) or by defining the problem with a cost function which is
minimised using convex optimization. In this way, we consequently not only perform a
registration but also the reconstruction of a new rigid shape or deformable model which
adapts automatically to the image measurement and 3D shape geometric constraints.
This solution is particularly robust to degenerate 2D motion given this new set of metric
constraints. The second contribution is an iterative extension of the proposed approach
which deals with the likely event of missing data in the 2D image trajectory.

The paper is structured as follows. Section 2 introduces the problem and a first initial
solution. Section 3 presents the new approach when the 3D shape needs adaptation to
deal with the variations in the 2D data. In the case of missing data, Section 4 provides an
iterative solution to the problem. Section 5 shows synthetic and real data while Section
6 points out the possible improvements and direction for future work.

2   Rigid and Non-rigid 2D–3D Registration

2.1   Rigid Registration with an Exact 3D Model

Consider first the problem of registering a single rigid shape to a set of 2D image trajectories. The 2D image measurements are stored in a single matrix W of size $2F \times P$
with the following structure:

$$W = \begin{bmatrix} w_{11} & \cdots & w_{1P} \\ \vdots & \ddots & \vdots \\ w_{F1} & \cdots & w_{FP} \end{bmatrix} = \begin{bmatrix} W_1 \\ \vdots \\ W_F \end{bmatrix}, \tag{1}$$

where F and P are the total number of frames and the number of points respectively.
The 2-vector $w_{ij} = (u_{ij} \, v_{ij})^T$ stores the image coordinates at each frame i and point j.
Given a known rigid shape B of size $3 \times P$ our aim is then to compute the best projection
that aligns the 3D shape to the 2D data. In this work there are two main assumptions.
The assignments between the image trajectories in W and the 3D points in B are given
and that, initially, W does not contain missing data. However, this last assumption will
be relaxed later in this paper.

The image projection model considered here is a scaled orthographic model denoted
as a 2×3 matrix M_i such that $M_i = c_i R_i$ with the orthogonality constraints given by
$R_i R_i^T = I_2$. The 2D–3D registration problem can be then re-stated as the optimization
of the following cost function:

$$\min_{R_i R_i^T = I_2} \|W - MB\|^2 \tag{2}$$

where M is the matrix obtained by stacking all the sub-blocks M_i for each frame as:

$$M = \begin{bmatrix} M_1 \\ \vdots \\ M_F \end{bmatrix}. \tag{3}$$

A solution to this problem satisfying the exact orthographic constraints can be obtained in two steps. First, by finding an affine Maximum Likelihood (ML) solution using the pseudoinverse of B giving $\tilde{M} = WB^T(BB^T)^{-1}$ and then forcing the orthogonality constraints in $\tilde{M}$. This final step is not performed globally for the collection of the 2×3 sub-blocks $\tilde{M}_i$ as done in the Tomasi-Kanade factorization [11]. Instead, the affine block is projected into the closest scaled orthographic camera matrix $c_i R_i$ as presented by Marques and Costeira [7] in a 3D reconstruction context. Such projection is given by:

$$R_i = UV^T \quad \text{and} \quad c_i = (\sigma_1 + \sigma_2)\backslash 2 \tag{4}$$

where $\tilde{M}_i = UDV^T$ is the SVD of the affine motion matrix and σ_d for $d = 1, 2$ are the singular values stored in D. Such projection is preferred to the global LS solution which may not exactly comply with the scaled orthographic camera matrix constraints. Differently, eq. (4) always gives a matrix R_i that complies with the given constraints as pointed out in [7, Appendix B].

Note that the solution obtained in step 2 of Algorithm 1 is optimal with the assumption of isotropic and zero-mean Gaussian noise affecting the measurements in W. Such assumption is generally valid when accurate 2D measurements are obtained from the image tracks of a rigid object. However, when trajectories are extracted from shapes with consistent directional deformations, such assumption is violated as it was noticed by Xiao et al. [14] in a medical context.

Algorithm 1. Rigid registration with image projections

Require: The 2D image data W and the 3D shape B .
Ensure: A metric 2D–3D registration of the shape to the image measurements.
  1: Compute the image centroid of $t = \frac{1}{P}W1_P$ and register the data as $\bar{W} = W - t1_P^T$
  2: Estimate the affine motion $\tilde{M}$ as $\tilde{M} = \bar{W}B^T(BB^T)^{-1}$.
  3: Project each 2×3 sub-block $\tilde{M}_i$ to the closest scaled orthographic matrix using eq. (4).

2.2 Registration Bias with Inexact Models

Deformation directionality is less noticeable when non-rigid motion is nearly isotropic to the shape centroid or with strong symmetries. Figure 2 shows a case when a 2D image of a cylinder is bending and the actual registration given Algorithm 1 with a rigid 3D shape from the ground truth at rest. As expected, a consistent bias in the 2D–3D registration appears when the shape is bending towards the direction of maximal variation. In such cases, a rigid registration of a single B is unfit since it cannot deal with the deformations. When the data is non-rigid we have at each frame that:

$$W_i = c_i R_i X_i \quad \text{with} \quad X_i \in \Re^{3 \times P} \tag{5}$$

where X_i represents the metric time-varying shape. For the whole set of 3D shapes, the most popular representation used is to parameterize X_i as a set of linear basis shapes [3] giving $X_i = \sum_d l_{id}S_d$. These linear bases are usually sufficient to represent a generic set of deformations however they may require a high number of basis shapes when dealing with non-linear deformations as to the bending cylinder in Figure 2.

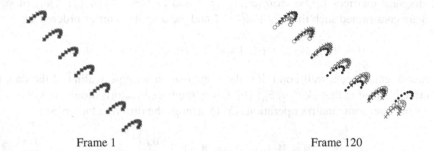

Frame 1   Frame 120

Fig. 2. Black dots • represent the 2D measurements, red circles ○ a half-cylinder 3D shape registered by Algorithm 1 and blue crosses × the results by the proposed Algorithm 2. The image data show the cylinder starting from a rest position in Frame 1 where the registration is perfect. The cylinder is bending at the last 3 semi-circles and the registration at the maximum deformation is strongly biased toward the deformation direction.

3 Adaptive Registration Using Joint Subspaces

Algorithm 1 may perform well when B represents a single instance of the deformations appearing in the image sequence. However such a case is unlikely in many registration scenarios and a method which encompasses some degree of adaptation may strongly reduce the registration error. In the following, the given surface B is not a current observation of the 2D image trajectories (i.e. $X_i \neq B$ for $i = 1 \ldots F$). This will consequently affects the estimated motion parameters in Algorithm 1 giving an additional bias from the unfitness of B. In order to reduce this effect we propose a different approach which first finds an affine joint subspace belonging to the set $\{W, B\}$ and then computes the best solution to registration given the joint metric constraints.

3.1 Affine Joint Subspace Computation

The main idea here is to join the information contained in B with the available measurements in W in order to extract an affine fit which is dependent on both components. In order to do so, we follow the strategy used in [5] for a 3D reconstruction scenario. A *Generalised Singular Value Decomposition* (GSVD) is used to compute a joint row space between the image data and the model to register. In such a way, we decompose both matrices with GSVD as:

$$
\begin{aligned}
W &= U\, D_U\, X^T \\
B &= V\, D_V\, X^T
\end{aligned}
\tag{6}
$$

where X^T is a $P \times P$ matrix which spans the common row space of $\{W, B\}$, U is a $2F \times 2F$ matrix with orthonormal columns ($U^T U = I$) and V is a 3×3 matrix such that $V^T V = I$. The diagonal value matrices D_U and D_V of size $2F \times P$ and $3 \times P$ respectively are given by:

$$
D_U = \begin{bmatrix} \Sigma_U & 0 \\ 0 & I \end{bmatrix} \text{ and } D_V = \begin{bmatrix} \Sigma_V & 0 \end{bmatrix}.
\tag{7}
$$

The diagonal matrices $\Sigma_U = diag(\sigma_1, \ldots, \sigma_3)$ and $\Sigma_V = diag(\mu_1, \ldots, \mu_3)$ of size 3×3 are constrained such that $\Sigma_U^2 + \Sigma_V^2 = I$ and the diagonal entries ordered as:

$$0 \leq \sigma_1 \leq \ldots \leq \sigma_3 \leq 1 \text{ and } 1 \geq \mu_1 \geq \ldots \geq \mu_3 > 0.$$

In order to guarantee a well-conditioned decomposition a single scaling of the data is performed imposing that $\|W\|^2 = \|B\|^2$ [6]. Given the initial factorisation with GSVD, it is possible after some matrix operations [5] to arrange the different factors as:

$$W = \tilde{M}_{2f \times t} \tilde{S}_{t \times p} = [M_J | M_I] \begin{bmatrix} B_J \\ B_I \end{bmatrix}$$

$$B = N_{3 \times 3} B_J$$

(8)

where the J subscript refers to the components obtained from the joint space of B and W while the I refers to the remaining ones. The dimensionality of the joint row space B_J depends directly on the dimension of the model to register. Thus, in the case of rigid registration, the matrix B_J has size $3 \times P$ and the $r = (t - 3)$ dimension of B_I depends on the rank of the independent components. Such value can be estimated by inspecting the singular values of the remaining 2D data and choosing a r which contains most of the energy. Notice that this parameter is not important for the proposed approach since it relies only on the joint components M_J and B_J.

3.2 Joint Metric Upgrade

The next step is to find a corrective transform for both the affine subspaces M_J and N which complies with the metric constraints of the 3D shape to register and the 2D image trajectories. This results in computing a 3×3 transformation matrix Q which enforces the metric constraints such that $M_J Q = M$ and $NQ = Z$ where Z is a rotation matrix with $ZZ^T = I_3$. The following problem is non-linear given the joint set of orthogonality constraints. However, a closed form solution can be computed if we consider the quadratic form $H = QQ^T$ and forming the orthogonality constraints as:

$$m_{ui}^T H m_{ui} - m_{vi}^T H m_{vi} = 0$$
$$m_{ui}^T H m_{vi} = 0$$
$$NHN^T = I_3$$

where m_{ui} and m_{vi} refer to the motion components of the horizontal and vertical image coordinates respectively such that:

$$M_{Ji} = \begin{bmatrix} m_{ui}^T \\ m_{vi}^T \end{bmatrix} \text{ where } M_J = \begin{bmatrix} M_{J1} \\ \vdots \\ M_{JF} \end{bmatrix}.$$

(9)

As follows H is a symmetric matrix which can be computed with LS for the six unique parameters by rearranging eq. (9). Then, if H is positive semidefinite, the matrix Q is given by $H \xrightarrow{eig} Q = U\sqrt{\Delta}$ with U and Δ being the eigenvectors and eigenvalues respectively. On the contrary, if the matrix is not positive semidefinite, we estimate the closest Q by defining:

$$
F = \begin{bmatrix} M_1 \tilde{Q} \\ \vdots \\ M_F \tilde{Q} \end{bmatrix} \quad \text{and} \quad G = \begin{bmatrix} ((M_1 \tilde{Q})^T)^\dagger \\ \vdots \\ ((M_F \tilde{Q})^T)^\dagger \end{bmatrix} \tag{10}
$$

where $\tilde{Q}$ is a SVD approximation of Q using the estimated H (i.e $\tilde{Q} = UD$ if $H = UDV^T$). Then the closest Q given the metric constraints is computed as $Q = \tilde{Q}\sqrt{F\backslash G}$ where $\backslash$ denotes the left matrix division.

Alternatively to this solution, we obtained more accurate results by solving the problem using Semi-Definite Programming (SDP). In this case we can compute explicitly H such that $H \succeq 0$. First we define the cost function by separating the joint motion matrix M_J in its horizontal and vertical image components such that:

$$
M_{Ju} = \begin{bmatrix} \mathbf{m}_{u1}^T \\ \vdots \\ \mathbf{m}_{uf}^T \end{bmatrix} \quad \text{and} \quad M_{Jv} = \begin{bmatrix} \mathbf{m}_{v1}^T \\ \vdots \\ \mathbf{m}_{vf}^T \end{bmatrix} \tag{11}
$$

The problem is then re-formulated as the minimization of the following cost function:

$$
\min_H \left\{ \left\| \mathrm{diag}(M_u H M_v^T) \right\| + \left\| \mathrm{diag}(M_u H M_u^T - M_v H M_v^T) \right\| \right. \tag{12}
$$
$$
\left. + \left\| N H N^T - I_3 \right\| \right\}
$$

such that

$$
H \succeq 0
$$
$$
\mathbf{m}_{u1}^T H \mathbf{m}_{u1}^T = d
$$

where the last constraint $\mathbf{m}_{u1}^T H \mathbf{m}_{u1}^T = d$ imposes an arbitrary value over the first frame to avoid the zero solution. This problem can be solved efficiently with current SDP toolboxes such as SeDuMi [10] since optimization is run over a small 3×3 matrix independently from the size of W and B.

3.3 Registration Algorithm and Discussions

The full approach is finally summarized in Algorithm 2. The idea at the basis of this procedure is to obtain the best possible registration even if the 3D shape to register is not an exact description of the image data. In this sense, given the first initial 3D shape B, we search for a common representation of the set $\{W, B\}$ using GSVD. This representation is then used to find the best metric solution given a joint set of metric constraints. This not only solves for the registration, but also compute a new metric shape $\hat{B}$ given the contribution of both data.

Enforcing the metric constraints for both the 2D measurements and the 3D shape give robustness to degenerate motion in W. This happens often in non-rigid motion analysis whenever a non-rigid shape is not performing enough rigid motion compared to the

---

Algorithm 2. Rigid registration using a joint subspace

Require: The 2D image data W and the 3D shape B .
Ensure: A metric 2D–3D registration of the shape to the non-rigid image measurements.
1: Compute the image centroid of $\mathbf{t} = \frac{1}{P}\mathbf{W1}_P$ and register the data as $\bar{\mathbf{W}} = \mathbf{W} - \mathbf{t1}_P^T$
2: Estimate the joint affine motions $\mathbf{M}_J$ and $\mathbf{N}$ together with the joint shape $\mathbf{B}_J$ as in Section 3.1.
3: Given the affine solution, compute the best metric motion and shape as shown in Section 3.2
   such that:

$$\mathbf{W}_B = \mathbf{M}_J\mathbf{Q} \ \mathbf{Q}^{-1}\mathbf{S}_J = \hat{\mathbf{M}} \ \hat{\mathbf{B}} \tag{13}$$

$$\mathbf{B} = \ \mathbf{NQ} \ \mathbf{Q}^{-1}\mathbf{S}_J = \hat{\mathbf{Z}} \ \hat{\mathbf{B}} \tag{14}$$

4: Project each 2×3 sub-block $\hat{\mathbf{M}}_i$ to the closest scaled orthographic matrix using eq. (4).

---

variations given by the deformations. In such cases, obtaining a reliable estimation of the depth of the shape is rather complex since, without rotation, it is very ambiguous to compute reliable estimates.

4   Registration with Missing Data

If the 2D image trajectories are interrupted due to occlusions or tracking failures, we have to additionally solve for the missing entries in W. In such a task, the cost function to optimise is the following:

$$\min_{\mathbf{R}_i\mathbf{R}_i^T=\mathbf{I}_2} \ \|\mathbf{D} \odot (\mathbf{W} - \mathbf{MB})\|^2 \tag{15}$$

where D is a $2f \times p$ mask matrix with either 1 if the 2D point is present or 0 if it is missing. Given the missing entries, it is not possible to solve for the cost function in closed form. Thus we revert to an iterative approach. Provided an initialisation of the missing entries, the approach first computes an affine solution with GSVD for M given S. After a projection to the correct orthographic camera matrices, missing entries in W are filled given the 3D shape estimated with the joint subspaces provided by the GSVD. The algorithm stops when the updated values have minimal variations from one iteration to the other. Regarding the initialisation, best results were achieved by filling the missing entries at each trajectory with the mean value computed from the known trajectory points in W. Note that in this case we have also to estimate the shape 2D centroid t at each iteration of the algorithm since it depends on the estimated missing data. The algorithm is resumed in the table for Algorithm 3.

5   Experiments

5.1   Synthetic Data

The algorithm performance are evaluated with the following synthetic experimental setup. The 2D data is created from a randomly generated cloud of 20 points S_{mean}

Algorithm 3. Rigid registration with missing data

Require: An initialisation for the 2D image data W and the 3D shape B .
Ensure: A metric 2D–3D registration of the shape to the non-rigid image measurements.
1: Compute the image centroid from the current estimate of W as $\mathbf{t} = \frac{1}{P}W\mathbf{1}_P$.
2: Given $\bar{W} = W - \mathbf{t}\mathbf{1}_P^T$ and B, estimate the joint affine motions M_J and N together with the joint shape B_J as in Section 3.1.
3: Given the affine solution, compute the best metric motion and shape with Algorithm 2.
4: Project each 2×3 sub-block $\hat{M}_i$ to the closest scaled orthographic matrix using eq. (2).
5: Given the metric solution $\hat{M}$ and $\hat{B}$, input the missing entries as $\bar{W} = \hat{M}\,\hat{B}$.
6: Iterate until the update on the 2D missing data points is less then a given threshold.

---

sampled inside a sphere of radius one. Deformations were constructed with a set of K random linear basis $S_1 \ldots S_K$. Each time-varying shape X_i was computed by the linear combination of random linear weights giving $X_i = S_{mean} + \sum_{d=1}^{K} l_{id}S_d$. In order to control the deformation intensity, the *Deformation Power ratio* (DPr) is defined as: $DPr = ||fS_{mean}|| \setminus || \sum_{i=1}^{f} \sum_{d=1}^{K} l_{id}S_d||$. Finally, 50 random orthographic camera matrices R_i and translation $\mathbf{t}_i$ are used to form the 2D measurements onto the image plane. The generation of the shape to register is made by selecting an initial random $X_i = B$. Then, in order to simulate distortion in B, random affine transformation A are applied to B such that: $\tilde{B} = AB$. In more detail, this distortion was computed as $A = I_3 + \aleph$ where $\aleph$ was a 3×3 matrix of Gaussian noise with variance $\sigma_\aleph$. To conclude, zero-mean Gaussian noise with variance of σ_W image pixel was added to the measurements stored in $W_{100 \times 20}$. The 2D data was finally scaled in order to fit into a 320×240 image frame. In the following tests the root mean squared (rms) error was always used to compute the 2D registration error in pixels per point and the rotation misalignment in degrees given the known ground truth.

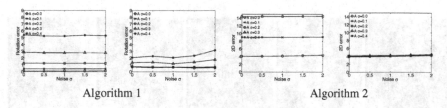

Algorithm 1   Algorithm 2

Fig. 3. Results for a synthetic sequence with $DPr = 0.15$. Top two figures show the result for the rotation error in degrees. The two figures at the bottom present the rms 2D error in image pixel per point.

Figure 3 shows a test result obtained by fixing $DPr = 0.15$ and after running 200 trials for each configuration of noise and affine distortion A (i.e. 25 configurations in total). The results show that both algorithms are relatively robust to the added image Gaussian noise however a difference is noticeable when evaluating the 2D and rotation error at increasing distortions rates for the 3D shape B. An important fact to keep in mind

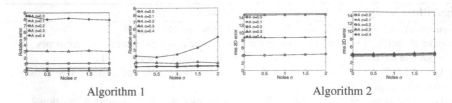

Algorithm 1   Algorithm 2

Fig. 4. Results for a synthetic sequence with $DPr = 0.45$. Top two figures show the result for the rotation error in degrees. The two figures at the bottom present the rms 2D error in image pixel per point.

when evaluating the 2D errors is that we are evaluating a registration of a rigid shape to a non-rigid sequence. Thus there is always a constant residual when plotting the error (bottom plots in Figure 3). In contrast, here we put more emphasis on the worsening of the error with the increase of the affine distortion A. In such case, Algorithm 2 is rather robust for both 2D and rotation error due to the distortions $\aleph$ until the last level of noise where the algorithm starts to perform worse. Algorithm 1 reports a very high 2D error up to 18 pixels rms for the stronger distortion (out of the plot scale). This is expected as the shape is fixed. More interesting is the plot showing the rotational error, indicating slightly better results for tiny distortions in respect to Algorithm 2 but then diverging again up to 5 degrees for higher distortions. Figure 4 shows analogous behaviors for both algorithms but in the case of stronger deformations in the image measurements ($DPr = 0.45$). Algorithm 2 shows decreased the performance as expected but still maintains reasonable values. Differently, Algorithm 1 reaches a misalignment up to 9 degrees.

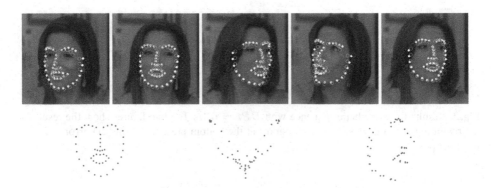

Fig. 5. Real sequence 2D–3D registration with a 3D shape as in Figure 1(b). In the top row, white dots show the 2D tracks extracted from the sequence. Red circles ○ shows the registration with Algorithm 1. Yellow circles show the registration with Algorithm 2 which achieves better reprojection error especially in the eyeborow, mouth and temple areas. Bottom row shows frontal, top and side view of the joint 3D shape $\hat{B}$ obtained from the registration algorithm.

5.2 Real Data

The scenario here considered is the registration of a 3D face model to a set of 2D image trajectories obtained from an AAM tracker [13]. Notice that the 3D model that represents our B of size 3×48 was computed from a subject with different somatic traits as it was shown in Figure 1(a). The model building of B was performed using 2D points obtained from nearly rigid motion of the subject followed by a rigid 3D reconstruction using factorization [11]. The target 2D sequence came from a different video footage as presented in Figure 5. Results for both registration algorithms are shown in Figure 5 with the reprojected image tracks. Algorithm 2 shows its properties of adaptation by registering and computing a joint shape closer to the new subject traits. This can be noticed especially in the different eyebrow shape compared with the registration of the original B obtained by Algorithm 1. Finally for this test, bottom row of Figure 5 shows three views of the reconstructed joint 3D shape $\hat{B}$ which qualitatively describe well the 3D shape of the subject.

A further test presents the performance of the algorithms in the case of a degenerate talking face sequence. This test is especially aimed to show the relevance of the joint metric constraints in this type of image sequences. We used the same rigid shape as the previous example and plotted the registration over the image sequence in Figure 6. Again the subjects presented different physical traits from the reference 3D model B. Figure 6(a) shows a side and top view of the joint shape $\hat{B}$ computed with the joint metric constraints as in Section 3.2. Figure 6(b) instead presents the same computation omitting the cost term $\|NHN^T - I_3\|$ in eq. (12). The resulting 3D shape is geometrically distorted and it is not representing the correct metric characteristics.

Image sequence with registration   (a) Joint metric   (b) 2D metric

Fig. 6. The figure shows the registration results for Algorithm 1 (red circles ∘) and Algorithm 2 (yellow circles). The top three figures show the image sequence of a subject talking and performing minimal rigid motion. Registration is made with the 3D shape as shown in Figure 1(b). Bottom line shows first (a) two views of the shape $\hat{B}$ extracted using the joint metric constraints and figure (b) the distorted shape obtained from the metric constraints of the 2D data alone.

A final experiment shows the algorithm behavior on the IMM database [9] which contains a set of 240 manually annotated face images. The dataset is divided in 6 different poses for 40 subjects. Among those six poses, 2 of them are showing non-rigid motion. Each face is manually annotated with 58 points as shown in Figure 7. A global mean 3D shape is reconstructed from all the subjects by running a rigid Tomasi and Kanade [11] factorization on the first, third and fourth pose of each subject. These frames were showing predominant rigid motion thus they were appropriate for the task. Figure 7 shows as well three views of the 3D rigid reconstruction.

This mean shape was then registered to every image in the database using Algorithm 1 and Algorithm 2 as presented in the paper. Note that in this case we have 40 sequences for each subject composed by six frames. Figure 8 shows the results on 2 subjects. White dots show the 2D tracks manually extracted from each short sequence. Red circles ∘ shows the registration with Algorithm 1. Yellow circles   show the registration with Algorithm 2. Again the proposed algorithm shows its adaptation capabilities when dealing with a large set of people with different somatic traits.

Fig. 7. a) A subject from the database. The white dots represent the manually annotated 2D points. b) Front, top and side views of the mean 3D shape reconstructed from the database.

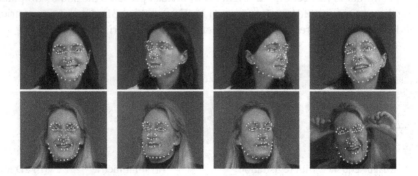

Fig. 8. Four selected frames from subject ♯22 and ♯35 in the IMM database

5.3   Evaluation with Missing Data

The performance of Algorithm 3 was initially tested with synthetic data as showed in the previous setup. Given the same amount of points and image frames, The affine distortion was fixed to $\sigma_\aleph = .20$ and $DPr = 0.25$. The evaluation included 25 tests for each configuration of missing data and noise level (225 tests in total) Experiments were made with increasing percentages of missing data and showed a robustness of the approach until 40% ratio as shown in Figure 9. The maximum number of iterations was fixed to 50 and a stop criteria was fixed at 10^{-6} on the update of the reprojection error of the missing 2D points. Note here that, even if the reprojection error is minimised

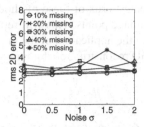
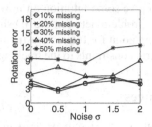

Fig. 9. Results for a synthetic sequence with $DPr = 0.25$ using Algorithm 3 and randomly generated noise and missing data

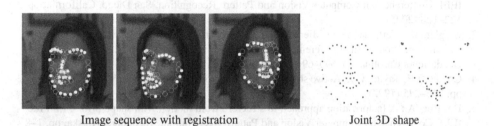

Image sequence with registration   Joint 3D shape

Fig. 10. The figures on the top show the image sequence together with the registration given by Algorithm 3 with 30% of missing data. White dots show the available 2D data while the yellow circles represent the estimated registration. The three images on the bottom present front, top and side view of the joint 3D shape.

for the case of 50% missing data, the error in degrees is around 10 units thus we can consider the registration compromised. For higher levels of missing data, the algorithm fails to obtain a reliable registration and thus results are not presented in the plots.

The real test shown in Figure 10 presents the results on the sequence in Figure 5 where occlusions were randomly created up to a 30% ratio. The algorithm converged after 74 iterations with a threshold on the 2D points update of 10^{-6}. The registration quality is barely degraded still showing a reasonable estimate of face side and frontal profiles. We realised that most of the misalignment were present when the shape was turning on the side. It is possible to notice that now there is less symmetry in the reconstructed 3D shape with a wider gap in the side view corresponding to points lying on the upper jaw. Still most of the depth of the shape was estimated reliably.

6   Conclusions

This paper presented a new approach to the 2D–3D registration problem in the case of non-rigid 2D image trajectories and a shape represented as a set of 3D points. The method is designed for the case when the shape is not an exact description of the 2D trajectories and it can deal with degeneracies in the 2D motion. This solution is targeted for the face analysis and medical registration scenario where often single 3D observations have to be fit to a set of 2D trajectories. The formulation, given the joint subspace may also give some intuition on how to solve the greatest crux of these methods; the matching problem between the 3D shape and the 2D image points. This will represent the starting point for future investigations together with the application of the proposed joint metric constraints to the tracking and non-rigid 3D reconstruction domains.

References

1. Bartoli, A., Gay-Bellile, V., Castellani, U., Peyras, J., Olsen, S., Sayd, P.: Coarse-to-Fine Low-Rank Structure-from-Motion. In: Proc. IEEE Conference on Computer Vision and Pattern Recognition, Anchorage, Alaska, pp. 1–8 (2008)
2. Brand, M.: A direct method for 3D factorization of nonrigid motion observed in 2D. In: Proc. IEEE Conference on Computer Vision and Pattern Recognition, San Diego, California, pp. 122–128 (2005)
3. Bregler, C., Hertzmann, A., Biermann, H.: Recovering non-rigid 3D shape from image streams. In: Proc. IEEE Conference on Computer Vision and Pattern Recognition, Hilton Head, South Carolina, pp. 690–696 (June 2000)
4. Cootes, T.F., Taylor, C.J.: Active shape models. In: Proc. British Machine Vision Conference, pp. 265–275 (1992)
5. Del Bue, A.: A factorization approach to structure from motion with shape priors. In: Proc. IEEE Conference on Computer Vision and Pattern Recognition, Anchorage, Alaska, pp. 1–8 (2008)
6. Hansen, P.: Rank-Deficient and Discrete Ill-Posed Problems: Numerical Aspects of Linear Inversion. Society for Industrial Mathematics (1998)
7. Marques, M., Costeira, J.P.: Estimating 3D shape from degenerate sequences with missing data. Computer Vision and Image Understanding (2008)
8. Shen, D., Davatzikos, C.: An adaptive-focus deformable model using statistical and geometricinformation. IEEE Transactions on Pattern Analysis and Machine Intelligence 22(8), 906–913 (2000)
9. Stegmann, M.B., Ersbøll, B.K., Larsen, R.: FAME – a flexible appearance modelling environment. IEEE Trans. on Medical Imaging 22(10), 1319–1331 (2003)
10. Sturm, J.: Using SeDuMi 1.02, A Matlab toolbox for optimization over symmetric cones. Optimization Methods and Software 11(1), 625–653 (1999)
11. Tomasi, C., Kanade, T.: Shape and motion from image streams under orthography: A factorization approach. International Journal of Computer Vision 9(2), 137–154 (1992)
12. Torresani, L., Hertzmann, A., Bregler., C.: Non-rigid structure-from-motion: Estimating shape and motion with hierarchical priors. IEEE Transactions on Pattern Analysis and Machine Intelligence, 878–892 (2008)
13. Xiao, J., Baker, S., Matthews, I., Kanade, T.: Real-time combined 2d+3d active appearance models. In: Proc. IEEE Conference on Computer Vision and Pattern Recognition, Washington D.C., vol. 2, pp. 535–542 (June 2004)
14. Xiao, J., Georgescu, B., Zhou, X., Comaniciu, D., Kanade, T.: Simultaneous Registration and Modeling of Deformable Shapes. In: Proc. IEEE Conference on Computer Vision and Pattern Recognition, New York, NY, pp. 2429–2436 (2006)

Local Occlusion Detection under Deformations Using Topological Invariants*

Edgar Lobaton[1], Ram Vasudevan[2], Ruzena Bajcsy[2], and Ron Alterovitz[1]

[1] Department of Computer Science
University of North Carolina at Chapel Hill, NC 27599
{lobaton,ron}@cs.unc.edu
[2] Department of Electrical Engineering and Computer Sciences
University of California, Berkeley, CA 94720
{ramv,bajcsy}@eecs.berkeley.edu

Abstract. Occlusions provide critical cues about the 3D structure of man-made and natural scenes. We present a mathematical framework and algorithm to detect and localize occlusions in image sequences of scenes that include deforming objects. Our occlusion detector works under far weaker assumptions than other detectors. We prove that occlusions in deforming scenes occur when certain well-defined local topological invariants are not preserved. Our framework employs these invariants to detect occlusions with a zero false positive rate under assumptions of bounded deformations and color variation. The novelty and strength of this methodology is that it does not rely on spatio-temporal derivatives or matching, which can be problematic in scenes including deforming objects, but is instead based on a mathematical representation of the underlying cause of occlusions in a deforming 3D scene. We demonstrate the effectiveness of the occlusion detector using image sequences of natural scenes, including deforming cloth and hand motions.

1 Introduction

Inherent in the exhaustive work done on edge detection is the belief that discontinuities in image intensity provide valuable clues about scene structure. Edges resulting from occlusions are of special interest since they correspond to locations in an image where one surface is closer to the camera than another, which can provide critical cues about the 3D structure of a scene. Occlusion detection is used in numerous applications including shape extraction, figure-ground separation, and motion segmentation, e.g. [1–6]. The purpose of this paper is to present a completely local, bottom-up approach to detect and localize occlusions in order to provide this powerful low-level information to higher-level reasoning methods. Our approach is applicable to image sequences including deforming objects, which can present difficulties to classical methods.

* This material is based upon work supported by the National Science Foundation under Grant # 0937060 to the Computing Research Association for the CIFellows Project and under Grant # IIS-0905344.

K. Daniilidis, P. Maragos, N. Paragios (Eds.): ECCV 2010, Part III, LNCS 6313, pp. 101–114, 2010.
© Springer-Verlag Berlin Heidelberg 2010

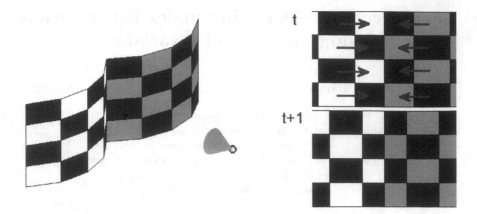

Fig. 1. The figure illustrates the inability of motion flow inconsistency to correctly identify occlusions in scenes with deforming objects. Consider two images (right column) obtained at times t and $t + 1$ after a paper in 3D is folded along a crease (left). Observe that this transformation is in fact not rigid and that there is no occlusion in either image. Assuming perfect motion estimation from the images on the right we would find that the gray colored checkerboard portion is moving to the left and the white colored checkerboard portion is moving to the right, which would seem to indicate the presence of a non-existent occlusion.

Traditional occlusion detectors rely almost entirely on spatiotemporal derivatives or matching to detect the artifacts of occlusions. These artifacts fall into two categories: motion flow inconsistency across an edge and the T-junction. Unfortunately, both methods are effective only under restrictive assumptions about the scene. The motion flow inconsistency approach implicitly assumes that only rigid transformations take place, such as a foreground and background layer moving in distinct directions. Due to this implicit assumption, motion inconsistencies do not necessarily imply an occlusion, as illustrated in Figure 1. Numerous methods are available to find T-junctions, but they all make assumptions about the orientations of the occluding contour. Moreover, even after a T-junction has been detected, an occlusion may not be present. Our method to detect occlusions works under far weaker assumptions than other methods. In particular, we only assume a weak bound on the magnitude of deformation on objects viewed by a camera and a bound on the color variations between frames.

In contrast to prior methods, we model the cause of occlusion, under a local deformation model, and show that the proper measurement of certain topological invariants serves as a definitive indicator to the presence of an occlusion. Prior approaches do not give any analytical guarantee on the validity of their detections, only experimental results. Our approach, in contrast to existing methods, is proven to yield a zero false positive rate as long as the required motion and color variation bounds are satisfied. The strength of our framework is that it is able to operate at different scales providing information that may otherwise be unavailable while not relying on noisy derivatives, not making strict assumptions

Fig. 2. The results of the occlusion detector presented in this paper applied to a sequence of images that depict a piece of cloth being folded. Observe the existence of a self-occlusion. Frames of a sequence are shown (first three columns) and the corresponding occlusion detections centered at time t_1 (right).

about the orientation of occluding contours, not building complex appearance models, and not performing any matching. In Figure 2, we apply our method to an image sequence of a cloth deforming in 3D, creating a self occlusion. Our method successfully detects the occlusion while producing no false positives. Note that these local detections can be fed into a global process such as graph cut in order to segment objects as is done in [2].

The contributions of this work are three-fold. First, in Section 3, we prove that under a deformation model occlusions occur when there does not exist homeomorphisms between pairs of images in an image sequences. Second, in Section 4, we define local topological invariants to detect an occlusion within an image. Finally, in Section 5, we demonstrate the applicability of our occlusion detector including some preliminary results on foreground/background segmentation.

2   Related Work

As described earlier, traditional approaches to occlusion detection can be divided into two categories: those that attempt to detect motion inconsistencies and those that detect T-junctions. Detecting motion inconsistencies is inspired by the classic work of Horn and Schunck [7] and the observation that the motion between the two sides of an occluding edge are generally dissimilar. This argument implicitly assumes that the objects being imaged undergo rigid transformations. This argument is inapplicable if the projection is instead allowed to transform in a more general fashion, as illustrated in Figure 1, and can result in false positives. The algorithms in this domain can be classified by the varying level of assumptions used in order to make the motion estimate robust. The presence of T-junctions in a contour has been shown to be a strong local cue for occlusion [8]. Unfortunately, not all T-junctions are occlusions, which can introduce false positives. Most algorithms in the T-junction domain can be classified according to the methodology they employ to detect and classify them.

At one extreme of motion estimation is the class of layered motion segmentation algorithms which employ a parametric model that is restricted to near-planar, rigidly-moving regions for each layer to segment regions based on the consistency of motion [9–12]. Incorporating a variety of techniques to estimate these models, these algorithms assume a fixed number of layers in the scene, which does not scale well as the number of layers increases. Instead of relying on this requirement, we argue that the low-level reasoning done by an occlusion detector with a deformation model provides appropriate cues to high-level reasoning algorithms like those performing layered motion segmentation.

At the other extreme of motion estimators are those that make the motion estimate robust by smoothing the velocity field spatially or temporally [13, 14]. Regrettably, this has the unintended consequence of making the motion estimate inaccurate at boundaries where occlusions occur. An alternative to this smoothing approach is the use of an implicit model, either learned from local motion cues estimated from training data or based on some fixed model of the distribution of motion cues in the vicinity of occluding boundaries [15–18]. Though these approaches are appealing because they rely on well-defined statistical models, they remain sensitive to deviations of the actual data from the trained model.

T-junction detection has a rich history. Until recently, there have been two predominant approaches to T-junction detection: gradient or filter-based approaches [19–22] and model-based template matching [23]. These approaches work singularly to detect the T-junctions rather than distinguish an occluding T-junction from a non-occluding T-junction. More recently, others define what they call a proper T-junction as a T-junction at which an occlusion takes place [3]. They detect these proper T-junctions by exploiting a rank constraint on a data matrix of feature tracks that would normally be classified as outliers in a multiple-view geometry problem. Although mathematically correct, the method can be overly sensitive to even slight deviations from the given rank condition. Inspired by this work, other alternatives have exploited a discriminative framework to classify these proper T-junctions [1, 2]. Unfortunately, these methods utilize 2D spatiotemporal slices instead of volumes which mean that detections can only be made in fixed orientations.

In contrast to prior work, we prove that, under a deformation model, occlusions occur when pairs of images are not equivalent via deformation. We construct local topological invariants which exploit this result to localize occlusions in an image. Our method applies under weaker assumptions than the aforementioned detectors.

3   Modeling Scenes and Images

In this section, we describe our scene model. We let objects in $\mathbb{R}^3$ correspond to sets in the space. Each point on the surface of an object at a given time is assigned a color. We initially assume that the color at a given point on the surface of an object does not change over time, but we allow the object to deform via a homeomorphism. For simplicity, this model ignores lighting, shadows, and specularities while extensions to account for such effects are discussed in Section 4.2.

The motion of an object is determined via a continuous family of homeomorphisms: $F(x, t) : \mathbb{R}^3 \times \mathbb{R} \to \mathbb{R}^3$, where $F(\cdot, t)$ is a homeomorphism from $\mathbb{R}^3$ to

$\mathbb{R}^3$ for each t. The camera is located at the origin of our coordinate system. The **image domain**, Ω, is defined to be a sphere of radius 1 centered at the origin, $\mathbb{S}^2$. We employ an omni-directional camera model in order to avoid occlusions at the boundaries of the field of view. We consider the effect of boundaries and the case of directional cameras in the next section. Throughout our analysis, we assume for convenience that the camera is static and the world is moving. Fortunately, our analysis applies to situations where the camera and the environment are moving and changing simultaneously. We also assume objects in the scene remain outside the unit sphere at all times.

A **color image**, $\mathcal{I} : \Omega \rightarrow \mathbb{R}$, and **depth image**, $\mathcal{D} : \Omega \rightarrow \mathbb{R}^3$, are defined for every point $s \in \Omega$ via a ray drawn from the origin passing through s. We consider 1D color images (i.e. grayscale) for simplicity. The depth value assigned to s is obtained by finding the point in $\mathbb{R}^3$ at which the ray beginning at the origin through s first intersects. The color value at s is defined similarly. The set of **occluding contours** in an image is the set of points at which the depth image is discontinuous. The following result connects the homeomorphisms in $\mathbb{R}^3$ to homeomorphisms in Ω.

Proposition 1. *If there are no occluding contours for an ordered set of depth images indexed by t in $[0,1]$, then $\mathcal{D}_t(s)$ provides a homeomorphism between Ω and $\mathcal{D}_t(\Omega) \subset \mathbb{R}^3$ which implies that $f(s,t) := \mathcal{D}_t^{-1}(F(\mathcal{D}_t(s),t))$ is a continuous family of image homeomorphisms for which $\mathcal{I}_{t_1}(f(s,t_1)) = \mathcal{I}_{t_2}(f(s,t_2))$ for all t_1 and $t_2 \in [0,1]$.*

We refer to the existence of a family of continuous image homeomorphisms for which $\mathcal{I}_{t1}(f(s,t_1)) = \mathcal{I}_{t2}(f(s,t_2))$ as the **Image Homeomorphism Criterion**. If this criterion is violated, then using the previous theorem we conclude that an occluding contour exists. Though this argument guarantees the existence of an occlusion, it does not help us localize the occluding contour either temporally or spatially. The reader may wonder if the converse of Proposition 1 is valid. The following observation provides an important partial converse to the proposition:

Proposition 2. *If the Image Homeomorphism Criterion is satisfied by a set of color images, then there exists a realization of an object in $\mathbb{R}^3$ that generates the same color images with no occluding contours.*

One such realization corresponds to forming a sphere of radius 2 centered at the origin and coloring the sphere according to the color image. The motion homeomorphism $F(x,t)$ for $\mathbb{R}^3$ is then just the extension of the color image homeomorphism $f(s,t)$. This result verifies that the Image Homeomorphism Criterion is in fact the best achievable result to guarantee the existence of occlusions without making additional assumptions.

4   Localizing Occlusions

In this section, we introduce an approach to locally detect occlusions in image sequences over discrete time by extending the ideas in Section 3. This is done by introducing an additional constraint on the size of deformations in $\mathbb{R}^3$. Then, we generalize the concepts for image sequences in which color information also varies. Finally, we focus on the case in which the image homeomorphisms can be decomposed into a translational and deformation component.

4.1   Local Detections without Color Variation

To begin, we introduce a constraint on the size of deformations in $\mathbb{R}^3$:

Definition 1. *A family of homeomorphisms $F(x,t) : \mathbb{R}^3 \times \mathbb{R} \to \mathbb{R}^3$ is said to be* **Lipschitz** *if for all $x \in \mathbb{R}^3$, t_1 and $t_2 \in \mathbb{R}$*

$$||F(x,t_1) - F(x,t_2)|| \leq K|t_1 - t_2|$$

for some constant K that is independent of x, t_1 and t_2. The smallest such K is called the **Lipschitz constant**.

From now on, we require that the continuous family of homeomorphisms, F, that $\mathbb{R}^3$ transforms under be Lipschitz, and the Lipschitz constant, K, gives an upper bound on the size of these deformations. In practice, this requirement demands bounding the speed of objects in $\mathbb{R}^3$ based on the rate at which the camera captures images. If no occluding contours are present, then the induced image homeomorphism is also Lipschitz with the same constant, K, since all objects are required to remain outside of $\mathbb{S}^2$.

In order to verify if the Image Homeomorphism Criterion has been violated, we study changes to topological invariants of the set $\mathcal{I}^{-1}([a,b])$, where $[a,b] \subset \mathbb{R}$. In particular, we focus on the number of connected components. To illustrate the problem with naïvely comparing the number of connected components to detect local occlusions, consider the sets in Figure 3(a) and corresponding neighborhoods drawn in the rest of the figure. The first neighborhood, E_r, is a square with a side of length $2r$ drawn in Figure 3(b). The second neighborhood E_{r+K} has a side of length $2(r + K)$ drawn in Figure 3(c). E_r has 6 connected components while E_{r+K} has 5 connected components suggesting that some set has

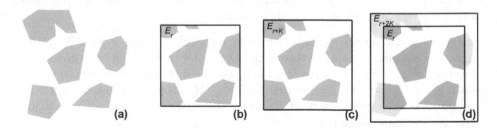

Fig. 3. Illustration of how to count connected components for neighborhoods E_r and E_{r+K}. (a) The original image before any window is applied. Counts of connected components: (b) 6 in E_r; (c) 5 in E_{r+K}; and (d) 5 in E_r after identification using E_{r+2K}. Without identification we would erroneously conclude that the Image Homeomorphism Criterion is violated and that there is an occlusion.

disappeared and that the Image Homeomorphism Criterion has been violated. However, there are no occlusions in this instance. The problem arises because we count the same set twice in the smaller neighborhood. We remedy this problem by identifying sets in E_r that correspond to the same connected component in E_{r+2K}. This solution inspires the construction of a sort of local topological invariant.

Definition 2. *Given a color image $\mathcal{I}$ over the image domain Ω, two collection of intervals, $\mathcal{B} = \{[a_k, b_k]\}_{k=1}^{N_B}$ and $\mathcal{B}' = \{[a'_k, b'_k]\}_{k=1}^{N_B}$, the* **histogram of connected components in a neighborhood** $E \subset \Omega$ **given the bins** $\mathcal{B}$ *is defined as the vector* $\alpha_E(\mathcal{I}|\mathcal{B}) = (\alpha_k)_{k=1}^{N_B}$, *where*

$$\alpha_k = cc\left(\mathcal{I}^{-1}([a_k, b_k]) \cap E\right),$$

and $cc(A)$ is the number of connected components in the set A. Under the assumption that $E \subset E'$ and $[a_k, b_k] \subset [a'_k, b'_k]$ for all k, the **histogram of connected components in E identified with the neighborhood E' given the bins** $\mathcal{B}$ *and $\mathcal{B}'$, denoted $\alpha_{E|E'}(\mathcal{I}|\mathcal{B}, \mathcal{B}')$, is computed in the same way except the connected components in $\mathcal{I}^{-1}([a_k, b_k]) \cap E$ are identified (i.e. treated as the same connected component) if they correspond to the same component in $\mathcal{I}^{-1}[a'_k, b'_k]) \cap E'$.*

Definition 3. *The* **color support in a neighborhood** E **given the bins** $\mathcal{B}$ *is the vector $\sigma_E(\mathcal{I}|\mathcal{B}) = (\sigma_k)_{k=1}^{N_B}$, where σ_k is 0 if $\mathcal{I}^{-1}([a_k, b_k]) \cap E = \emptyset$ and 1 otherwise.*

Employing this new method to calculate connected components, guarantees that under Lipschitz image homeomorphisms, the histogram of connected components in a neighborhood E_r identified with the neighborhood E_{r+2K} is always less than the histogram of connected components in a neighborhood E_{r+K}. If we apply this procedure to the example in Figure 3 and compare the number of connected components, we find that the Image Homeomorphism Criterion is not violated (the number of connected components in E_r after identification is 5 which is the number of components in E_{r+K}). The following result proves that this argument can be used to identify local violations of the Image Homeomorphism Criterion, which allows us to define a local occlusion detector.

Theorem 1. *Given bins $\mathcal{B}$, neighborhoods E_r, E_{r+K}, and E_{r+2K} centered around a common point s, and color images $\mathcal{I}_{t_1}$ and $\mathcal{I}_{t_2}$ where $|t_1 - t_2| = 1$, if either*

$$\alpha_{E_r|E_{r+2K}}(\mathcal{I}_{t1}|\mathcal{B}, \mathcal{B}) \leq \alpha_{E_{r+K}}(\mathcal{I}_{t2}|\mathcal{B}) \tag{1}$$

or

$$\sigma_{E_{r+K}}(\mathcal{I}_{t2}|\mathcal{B}) \leq \sigma_{E_{r+2K}}(\mathcal{I}_{t1}|\mathcal{B}) \tag{2}$$

is violated, where the inequality is checked element wise, then the Image Homeomorphism Criterion is not satisfied between $\mathcal{I}_{t1} \cap E_r$ and $\mathcal{I}_{t2} \cap E_{r+K}$.

The argument for the proof proceeds as follows: For a scene deforming under a Lipschitz homeomorphism, if a set is in the interior of the neighborhood E_r, then it is in the interior of E_{r+K}. If two sets in E_r are connected in E_{r+K} then the path connecting them is in E_{r+2K} which explains why identification using E_{r+2K} guarantees the condition in Equation 1. The second condition just specifies that the colors observed in E_{r+K} are present in E_{r+2K}.

At this point, we make two additional remarks. First, the previous theorem allows us to consider occlusion detection in the case of directional cameras in a straightforward manner. Second, observe that Theorem 1 works both forward and backward in time so that appearance and disappearance events, which are each just types of occlusions, can be identified locally.

4.2   Generalizing to Color Variation

In this section, we generalize our model to include color variations in the images. These variations may include soft shadows and slow lighting variations. However, we do not claim to solve the problem for strong shadows and specularities which are a challenge for all occlusion detection algorithms. In order to quantify the amount of uncertainty allowed, we consider color variations that are Lipschitz over time with constant K_c. That is, if $f(s, t)$ is a family of image homeomorphisms, we must have

$$|\mathcal{I}_{t1}(f(s, t_1)) - \mathcal{I}_{t2}(f(s, t_2))| \leq K_c|t_1 - t_2|$$

instead of $\mathcal{I}(f(s, t_1)) = \mathcal{I}(f(s, t_2))$ (i.e. $K_c = 0$) as was assumed in the previous section. From now on, we require that the color variations be Lipschitz with constant K_c.

We generalize the results of Theorem 1 to incorporate color variations.

Theorem 2. *Assume the same setup as in Theorem 1 with Lipschitz color images with Lipschitz constant K_c. Define $\mathcal{B}^c := \{[a_k - c, b_k + c]\}_{k=1}^{N_B}$ for $c > 0$. If either*

$$\alpha_{E_r|E_{r+2K}}(\mathcal{I}_{t1}|\mathcal{B}, \mathcal{B}^{2K_c}) \leq \alpha_{E_{r+K}}(\mathcal{I}_{t2}|\mathcal{B}^{K_c}) \tag{3}$$

or

$$\sigma_{E_{r+K}}(\mathcal{I}_{t2}|\mathcal{B}^{K_c}) \leq \sigma_{E_{r+2K}}(\mathcal{I}_{t1}|\mathcal{B}^{2K_c}) \tag{4}$$

is violated, then the Image Homeomorphism Criterion under color variation is not satisfied between $\mathcal{I}_{t1} \cap E_r$ and $\mathcal{I}_{t2} \cap E_{r+K}$.

Figure 4 illustrates this process where an object is moved behind a book resulting in an occlusion detection. The sets $\mathcal{I}_{t1}^{-1}([a_k, b_k]) \cap E_r$ are shown in white on the middle row for increasing k from left to right, the sets $\mathcal{I}_{t1}^{-1}([a_k - 2K_c, b_k + 2K_c]) \cap E_{r+2K}$ are also shown in gray on the middle row, and the sets $\mathcal{I}_{t2}^{-1}([a_k - K_c, b_k + K_c]) \cap E_{r+K}$ are shown on the bottom row. The images in this example are of size 240×240, $\mathcal{B} = \{[40(k-1), 40k]\}_{k=1}^7$, $r = 40$, $K = 10$, and $K_c = 5$. The outcome for this example is

$$\alpha_{E_r|E_{r+2K}}(\mathcal{I}_{t1}|\mathcal{B}, \mathcal{B}^{2K_c}) = [1\,0\,1\,2\,0\,0\,0]^\top$$

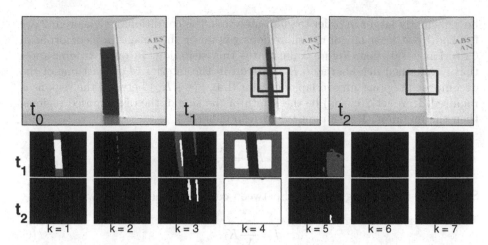

Fig. 4. Demonstration of our local topological occlusion detector. Three images corresponding to an object moving behind a book (top). The sets $\mathcal{I}_{t1}^{-1}([a_k, b_k]) \cap E_r$ and $\mathcal{I}_{t1}^{-1}([a_k - 2K_c, b_k + 2K_c]) \cap E_{r+2K}$ are shown in white and gray respectively (middle). The sets $\mathcal{I}_{t2}^{-1}([a_k - K_c, b_k + K_c]) \cap E_{r+K}$ are shown on the bottom row. Our framework detects an occlusion since the condition in Equation 3 is violated.

and

$$\alpha_{E_{r+K}}(\mathcal{I}_{t2}|\mathcal{B}^{K_c}) = [0\ 0\ 2\ 1\ 1\ 0\ 0]^{\top}.$$

Since the condition in Equation 3 is not satisfied, we conclude that an occlusion has occurred.

4.3   Estimating Translational Component

Theorem 2 gives a mechanism to detect occlusions in situations in which the motions and deformations of objects in 3D are unknown. In certain situations, it may be convenient to take advantage of this structure and decompose the homeomorphism into a translational and pure deformation component.

In this section, we assume that the image homeomorphism can be locally decomposed as follows:

$$f(s, t) = f_t(s, t) + f_d(s, t),$$

where f_t is a translation and f_d is a deformation with Lipschitz constants K_t and K_d, respectively. Using the framework developed in the previous section, we would need to compare the connected components in E_r and $E_{r+K_t+K_d}$. If $K_t >> K_d$ then $E_{r+K_t+K_d}$ would be a large set which would decrease the utility of our algorithm to detect occlusions.

In order to take advantage of our knowledge about the translation components of the homeomorphism, we would like to split $E_{r+K_t+K_d}$ into N_t^2 evenly spaced regions that cover $E_{r+K_t+K_d}$. The diameter of the decomposed regions needs to be sufficiently larger in order to guarantee that the conditions in Theorem 2 are fulfilled by at least one of the subregions whenever the Image Homeomorphism Criterion is satisfied. Figure 5 illustrates this situation. In order to guarantee that a deformed neighborhood E_r is found in the interior of at least one of the decomposed regions, an overlap of greater than $2(r + K_d)$ between the regions is required. If we let $2(r + D)$ be the length of the side of the decomposed regions, then the minimum length required corresponds to:

$$D = K_d + \frac{K_t}{N_t}. \tag{5}$$

Solving for the spacing d required between centers of the regions, we obtain

$$d = \frac{2}{N_t} K_t. \tag{6}$$

Hence, given that we have decomposed the neighborhood $E_{r+K_t+K_d}$ into N_t^2 regions of length $2(r + D)$ with centers spaced d units away, then the Image Homeomorphims Criterion between regions E_r at time t_1 and $E_{r+K_d+K_t}$ at time t_2 is violated if the conditions in Equations 3 and 4 are not satisfied by any of decomposed regions. This result is used in Section 5 to identify occlusions between objects with large translational components. Note that this decomposition approach can be used to estimate motion flow between regions without direct tracking or differential operators applied to the images.

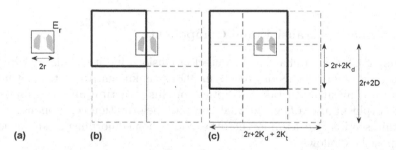

Fig. 5. Choosing an appropriate length for the coveraging sets of $E_{r+K_t+K_d}$ with $N_t = 2$. (a) Given a region E_r, and bounds K_t and K_d, our objective is to obtain a cover that guarantees that E_r can be found within one of the covering sets. (b) A coverage in which E_r is not contained within any of the covering sets since the coverage does not have enough overlap. The dark square corresponds to one of the regions in the coverage. (c) Given that the overlap between the region is greater than $2r + 2K_d$ then the neighborhood E_r can be found in at least one of the covering sets. The length of the sets needed to guarantee this fact are labeled $2r + 2D$.

5   Experiments

In this section, we present experimental results for occlusion detection applying Theorem 2 to make local detections. We also briefly consider how to utilize these results to perform foreground segmentation.

5.1   Implementation

The implementation of our approach takes the following image deformation parameters: the Lipschitz constants K_c, K_t and K_d. It also requires the following algorithmic parameters: the radius for the base regions r, the color bins $\mathcal{B}$, and the number of subsections N_t in which each local neighborhood is decomposed. For simplicity we take N_t to be odd. Note that any choice of the algorithmic parameters is appropriate (e.g. different choices of radius r may yield different detections, but still no false positives). The algorithm takes a base image $\mathcal{I}_{t1}$ and marks detections against image $\mathcal{I}_{t2}$.

We define a grid of points evenly spaced by a distance d (as defined by Equation 6). For each of the points in $\mathcal{I}_{t1}$ we compute $\alpha_{E_r|E_{r+2D}}(\mathcal{I}_{t1}|\mathcal{B}, \mathcal{B}^{2K_c})$ and $\sigma_{E_{r+2D}}(\mathcal{I}_{t1}|\mathcal{B}^{2K_c})$, where D is given by Equation 5. For each of the points in $\mathcal{I}_{t2}$ we compute $\alpha_{E_{r+D}}(\mathcal{I}_{t2}|\mathcal{B}^{K_c})$ and $\sigma_{E_{r+D}}(\mathcal{I}_{t2}|\mathcal{B}^{K_c})$.

For a fixed location x in the grid, let E_r be the neighborhood centered at x in image $\mathcal{I}_{t1}$ and let $E_{r+K_t+K_d}$ be the neighborhood centered at x in image $\mathcal{I}_{t2}$. We test the conditions in Theorem 2 by comparing the histogram of connected components of E_r against each of the histograms from the resulting N_t^2 regions in which $E_{r+K_t+K_d}$ is decomposed. If the conditions are not satisfied by any of the regions then position x at time t_1 is marked as an occluded location.

5.2   Detecting Occluding Contours

To begin, we consider results on real images. Figures 2 and 6 illustrate the results of applying our algorithm on a variety of image sequences: a deforming cloth, a walking person, a closing hand, and a folding colored Macbeth board. The first three columns correspond to frames from the sequence and the last column is the detection results corresponding to the frame at time t_1. Animations of the image sequences and the detected occlusions can be found at: http://www.cs.unc.edu/~ron/research/ECCV2010/.

See the supplementary materials for animations of the image sequences and the detected occlusions. Our method successfully detected occlusions without introducing any false positives. Note that several occluding contours were not highlighted in our detections due to our unconstrained assumptions about the scene (i.e. we made no prior assumptions about the environment and allowed for any type of deformations). To illustrate this point, consider the image sequence with the closing hand (second row in Figure 6). Though there are occluding contours along the edges near the palm of the hand, the hand's movement does not reveal the existence of any local occlusions here which means that the Image Homeomorphism

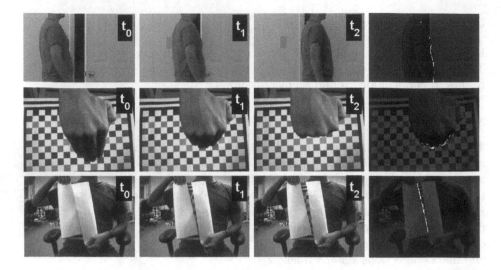

Fig. 6. Detection results for image sequences of a walking person, a closing hand, and a folding colored Macbeth board. Sample frames are displayed (first three columns) and the occluding contours corresponding to the frames at time t_1 (right column).

Criterion is never violated. Proposition 2 implies that there exists a 3D realization of each image in this sequence around this edge that does not contain an occlusion. By applying more global reasoning, one could hope to recover these type of detections, which is the focus of future research.

The method presented in this paper is not directly comparable to other approaches in the literature since our goal is to obtain local detections in unconstrained deforming scenes, an area that has not previously been explored. In future work, we plan to integrate local detections into consistent occluding contours for deforming scenes, which requires a new dataset of deforming scenes for evaluation and comparison of approaches.

5.3   Foreground/Background Segmentation

In this section, we briefly consider how one can employ the presented occlusion detector to do foreground versus background segmentation. We assume that there are two objects each with distinguishable color distributions, one performing the occluding (the foreground) and the other being occluded (the background). When an occlusion occurs, the neighborhood E_r contains samples of a set that becomes occluded and the neighborhood E_{r+K} contains samples of the set that perform the occlusion. We can use this elementary information to learn the color distribution of the foreground and background. After this distribution has been learned, we can test to which segment a given pixel belongs. Figure 7 illustrates this approach applied to a synthetic (top row) and real (bottom row) image sequences.

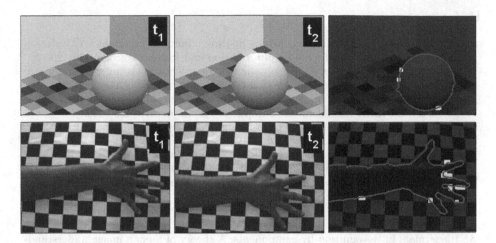

Fig. 7. Foreground/background segmentation results for a synthetic sequence of a ball moving through a room with multicolored tiles (top) and a real sequence of a hand moving in front of a checkerboard (bottom). Sample frames from the sequences (first two columns). Occlusion detections in white and segmentation by learning color distribution in red (right column) centered at time t_1.

6 Conclusion

In this paper, we present a mathematical framework to detect and localize occlusions in image sequences of scenes that can include deforming objects. The method works by measuring changes in a local topological invariant, which guarantees a zero false positive rate when certain motion and color variation bounds are satisfied. Our occlusion detector works under far weaker assumptions than other detectors. If the 3D scene transforms in a more restrictive fashion, the method presented in this paper can be viewed as complementary to traditional detectors. We also presented preliminary results on extending the detections to perform figure-ground separation when the model undergoes Lipschitz deformations. Most current such algorithms employ a fixed statistical model for the variation allowed in the background, but the framework presented here is more general and can work in tandem with a statistical model.

As future research, we plan to study how to integrate this local information in order to come up with global solutions to problems such as segmentation and matching. The descriptors that we used for identifying occlusions can also be thought of as topological features which are robust to deformations. Integrating the information from these local descriptors could lead to the development of new matching and recognition techniques.

The generality of our framework can benefit applications such as tracking in medical applications which involve soft, deformable tissues. For example, knowledge of occlusions could help in the reconstruction of surgical scenes and in performing foreground/background segmentation in scenes with soft tissue.

References

1. Apostoloff, N., Fitzgibbon, A.: Learning Spatiotemporal T-Junctions for Occlusion Detection. In: IEEE Conf. on Computer Vision and Pattern Recognition (2005)
2. Apostoloff, N., Fitzgibbon, A.: Automatic video segmentation using spatiotemporal T-junctions. In: British Machine Vision Conf., vol. 3, p. 1089 (2006)
3. Favaro, P., Duci, A., Ma, Y., Soatto, S.: On exploiting occlusions in multiple-view geometry. In: IEEE Intl. Conf. on Computer Vision, pp. 479–486 (2003)
4. Irani, M., Rousso, B., Peleg, S.: Computing occluding and transparent motions. Intl. J. of Computer Vision 12, 5–16 (1994)
5. Niyogi, S., Adelson, E.: Analyzing and recognizing walking figures in XYT. In: IEEE Conf. on Computer Vision and Pattern Recognition, pp. 469–474 (1994)
6. Stein, A., Hebert, M.: Local detection of occlusion boundaries in video. Image and Vision Computing (2008)
7. Horn, B., Schunck, B.: Determining Optical Flow. Artificial Intelligence 17, 185–203 (1981)
8. Biederman, I.: Recognition-by-components: A theory of human image understanding. Psychological Review 94, 115–147 (1987)
9. Ogale, A., Fermuller, C., Aloimonos, Y.: Motion segmentation using occlusions. IEEE Trans. on Pattern Analysis and Machine Intelligence 27, 988–992 (2005)
10. Smith, P., Drummond, T., Cipolla, R.: Layered motion segmentation and depth ordering by tracking edges. IEEE Trans. on Pattern Analysis and Machine Intelligence 26, 479–494 (2004)
11. Xiao, J., Shah, M.: Accurate motion layer segmentation and matting. In: IEEE Conf. on Computer Vision and Pattern Recognition, vol. 2 (2005)
12. Yin, P., Criminisi, A., Winn, J., Essa, I.: Tree-based classifiers for bilayer video segmentation. In: IEEE Conf. on Computer Vision and Pattern Recognition (2007)
13. Anandan, P.: A computational framework and an algorithm for the measurement of visual motion. Intl. J. of Computer Vision 2, 283–310 (1989)
14. Black, M., Anandan, P.: Robust dynamic motion estimation over time. In: IEEE Conf. on Computer Vision and Pattern Recognition, pp. 296–302 (1991)
15. Black, M., Fleet, D.: Probabilistic detection and tracking of motion discontinuities. Intl. J. of Computer Vision 38, 231–245 (2000)
16. Fleet, D., Black, M., Nestares, O.: Bayesian inference of visual motion boundaries. Morgan Kaufmann Publishers Inc., San Francisco (2003)
17. Nestares, O., Fleet, D.: Probabilistic tracking of motion boundaries with spatiotemporal predictions. In: IEEE Conf. on Computer Vision and and Pattern Recognition, vol. 2, pp. 358–365 (2001)
18. Stein, A., Hoiem, D., Hebert, M.: Learning to Find Object Boundaries Using Motion Cues. In: IEEE Intl. Conf. on Computer Vision, pp. 1–8 (2007)
19. Beymer, D.: Finding Junctions Using the Image Gradient. Massachusetts Institute of Technology, Artificial Intelligence Laboratory (1991)
20. Freeman, W., Adelson, E.: The design and use of steerable filters. IEEE Trans. on Pattern Analysis and Machine Intelligence 13, 891–906 (1991)
21. Li, D., Sullivan, G., Baker, K.: Edge detection at junctions. In: Alvey Vision Conf., vol. 2 (1989)
22. Perona, P.: Steerable-Scalable Kernels for Edge Detection and Junction Analysis. In: Sandini, G. (ed.) ECCV 1992. LNCS, vol. 588, pp. 3–18. Springer, Heidelberg (1992)
23. Parida, L., Geiger, D., Hummel, R.: Junctions: detection, classification, and reconstruction. IEEE Trans. on Pattern Analysis and Machine Intelligence 20, 687–698 (1998)

2.5D Dual Contouring: A Robust Approach to Creating Building Models from Aerial LiDAR Point Clouds

Qian-Yi Zhou and Ulrich Neumann*

University of Southern California

Abstract. We present a robust approach to creating 2.5D building models from aerial LiDAR point clouds. The method is guaranteed to produce crack-free models composed of complex roofs and vertical walls connecting them. By extending classic dual contouring into a 2.5D method, we achieve a simultaneous optimization over the three dimensional surfaces and the two dimensional boundaries of roof layers. Thus, our method can generate building models with arbitrarily shaped roofs while keeping the verticality of connecting walls. An adaptive grid is introduced to simplify model geometry in an accurate manner. Sharp features are detected and preserved by a novel and efficient algorithm.

1 Introduction

Three dimensional building models are very useful in various applications such as urban planning, virtual city tourism, surveillance, and computer games. The advance of acquisition techniques has made aerial LiDAR (light detection and ranging) data a powerful 3D representation of urban areas, while recent research work (*e.g.*,[10,15]) has introduced a successful pipeline to extract individual building point clouds from city-scale LiDAR data.

The aerial LiDAR point clouds are 2.5D data, *i.e.*, the LiDAR sensor captures the details of roof surfaces, but collects few points on building walls connecting roof boundaries. In addition, manually created building models (Figure 2) also show a 2.5D characteristic. Nearly all of them consist of complex roofs (green faces) connected by vertical walls (white faces). Thus, we desire a 2.5D modeling method with the following properties:

- **Accuracy:** The method should produce simple polygonal models fitting the input point clouds in a precise manner.
- **Robustness:** Regardless of the diversity and complexity of building roof shapes, the method should always generate crack-free models, even with the existence of undesired elements such as residual sensor noise and small roof features.

---

* The authors would like to thank Airborne 1 Corp. for providing data sets. The authors acknowledge Mark Pritt of Lockheed Martin for his support. The authors thank Tao Ju, Suya You, and anonymous reviewers for their valuable comments.

K. Daniilidis, P. Maragos, N. Paragios (Eds.): ECCV 2010, Part III, LNCS 6313, pp. 115–128, 2010.
© Springer-Verlag Berlin Heidelberg 2010

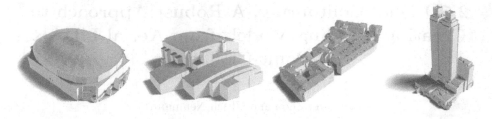

Fig. 1. Various kinds of building models are created using 2.5D dual contouring

Fig. 2. Manually created models [3] show the 2.5D nature of building structures

– **2.5D characteristic:** The method should create 2.5D polygonal models composed of detailed roofs and vertical walls connecting roof layers.

Most of the previous research work is based on the detection of some pre-defined roof patterns, such as planar shapes [8,10,11,15] or a small set of user-given primitives [5,12,13,14]. These methods work well for buildings composed of pre-defined shapes, but lose accuracy and robustness when dealing with arbitrary roof shapes such as those shown in Figure 1. Another way to attack this problem is with traditional data-driven approaches. Polygonal models are first generated directly from input data using rasterization or delaunay triangulation, then simplified with general mesh simplification algorithms. The latter step significantly reduces triangle number while preserving a low fitting error. However, since the general simplification algorithms are usually 'blind' to the 2.5D nature of the problem, they can hardly produce models satisfying our 2.5D requirement.

We propose a novel, data-driven approach to solve this problem, named *2.5D dual contouring*. Like the classic dual contouring [4], we use an adaptive grid as the supporting data structure, and reconstruct geometry in each grid node by minimizing the quadratic error functions known as QEFs. Model simplification is easily achieved by merging grid nodes and combining QEFs.

In order to represent the detailed roof surfaces, our approach works in a 3D space. However, unlike the classic 3D dual contouring, we use a 2D grid as our supporting data structure. We generate a *hyper-point* in each grid cell, which contains a set of 3D points having the same x-y coordinates, but different z values. They can be regarded as a set of points intersected by a vertical line and multiple roof layers. Hence, the consistency between boundary footprints of different roof layers is guaranteed, and vertical walls are produced by connecting neighboring hyper-points together.

Given that our method is built on some of previous work, we explicitly state our original contributions as follows:

1. We propose a new robust method to create 2.5D building models from aerial point clouds. We demonstrate how to simplify geometry in a topology-safe manner and construct polygons within a 2.5D framework. Our results are guaranteed to be accurate watertight models, even for buildings with arbitrarily shaped roofs.
2. We propose an algorithm to detect sharp roof features by analyzing the QEF matrices generated in 2.5D dual contouring. The analysis result is then used to preserve such features in polygon triangulation.
3. Benefiting from a post-refinement step, our algorithm has the ability to produce building models aligning with principal directions, as defined in [14].

2 Related Work

We review the related work on two aspects: building reconstruction methods and volumetric modeling approaches.

2.1 Building Reconstruction from Aerial LiDAR

Many research efforts have addressed the complex problem of modeling cities from aerial LiDAR data. Recent work (*e.g.*, [8,10,11,14,15]) introduced an automatic pipeline with the following characteristics: trees and noises are removed via a classification algorithm, and a segmentation module splits the remaining points into individual building patches and ground points. The building patches are then turned into mesh models by a modeling algorithm.

In the last step, these methods first apply a plane fitting algorithm to extract planar building roofs, then employ different heuristics to guide the modeling process. For example, Matei *et al.*[8] regularize roof outlines by estimating building orientations. Poullis and You [10] create simple 3D models by simplifying boundaries of fitted planes. Verma *et al.*[11] employ a graph-based method to explore the topology relationships between planar roof pieces. Zhou and Neumann [14] learn a set of principal directions to align roof boundaries and this principal direction learning procedure is further extended to city-scale data sets in [15].

To alleviate the problem that only planar shapes can be handled well, primitive-based methods are developed to reconstruct complex building roofs. Lafarge *et al.*[5] propose a two-stages method to find the optimal combination of parametric models based on a RJMCMC sampler. You *et al.*[12] and Zhou and Neumann [14] show the usage of primitives with the help of user-interaction. Zebedin *et al.*[13] detect planes and surfaces of revolution. However, as mentioned previously, all of these methods are limited by the user-defined primitive libraries, thus lose accuracy and robustness when dealing with arbitrary roof shapes.

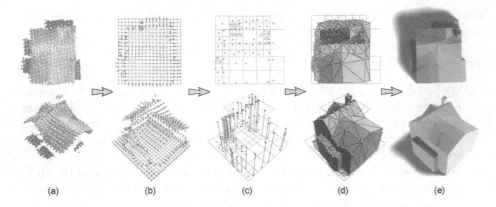

Fig. 3. Robust building modeling pipeline: (a) the input point cloud; (b) a 2D grid with surface Hermite data (gold arrows) and boundary Hermite data (red arrows) attached; (c) hyper-points (turquoise balls connected by red lines) generated by minimizing QEFs; (d) mesh model reconstructed via 2.5D dual contouring; and (e) final model with boundaries snapped to principal directions

2.2 Volumetric Modeling Approaches

Volumetric methods [1,4,7] have proved to be a robust way of generating crack-free models: input points are first scan-converted into a regularized grid; then geometry and topology are created respectively. For example, the dual contouring method [4] creates one mesh vertex in each minimal grid node by optimizing a quadratic error function, and constructs polygons during a traversal over the adaptive grid. Based on this work, Fiocco et al.[2] develop a modeling method combining aerial and ground-based LiDAR.

Nevertheless, these volumetric approaches all work for regular 2D or 3D grids. None of them have the same 2.5D characteristic as our approach.

3   Pipeline Overview

Given a building point cloud as input, our modeling process executes four steps as illustrated in Figure 3:

1. **Scan conversion:** We embed the point cloud in a uniform 2D grid. *Surface Hermite data* samples (gold arrows) are generated at grid points and *boundary Hermite data* samples (red arrows) are estimated on grid edges connecting different roof layers (Figure 3(b)). This 2D grid is also regarded as the finest level of our supporting quadtree.
2. **Adaptive creation of geometry:** In each quadtree cell, we compute a *hyper-point* by minimizing a 2.5D QEF. Geometry simplification is achieved in an adaptive manner by collapsing subtrees and adding QEFs associated with leaf cells (Figure 3(c)).

3. **Polygon generation:** We reconstruct a watertight mesh model by connecting hyper-points with *surface polygons* (turquoise triangles) and *boundary polygons* (purple triangles), which form building roofs and vertical walls, respectively (Figure 3(d)).
4. **Principal direction snapping:** The roof boundaries are refined to follow the principal directions defined in [14] (Figure 3(e)).

4   Scan Conversion

The first step of our modeling algorithm converts the input point cloud into a volumetric form, by sampling Hermite data (in the form of point-normal pairs) over a 2D supporting grid. With elements being considered as their infinite extensions along the vertical direction, this 2D grid has a 3D volumetric connotation. *E.g.*, a grid cell represents an infinite three dimensional volume, while a grid point corresponds to a vertical line containing it.

4.1   Surface Hermite Data

Given a 2.5D point cloud as input, we first segment it into multiple roof layers using a local distance-based region growing algorithm[1], as shown in Figure 4(a). Ideally, each vertical line passing through a grid point intersects with one and only one roof layer. The intersection point is taken as a *surface Hermite data* sample, and estimated by averaging the heights and normals[2] of its k-nearest input points within the same roof layer, illustrated as points marked with blue or purple outlines (taking $k = 4$) in Figure 4(a).

The only difficulty in this process is to robustly detect the right roof layer crossing the vertical line. Intuitively, we say a roof layer L *covers* a grid point g *iff* each of g's four neighboring cells contains at least one input point p belonging to L or a higher cluster L'. *E.g.*, in Figure 4(a), point A is covered by no roof layers, and thus is assigned as ground; point B is only covered by and assigned to the dark-grey layer; covered by both the dark-grey layer and the light-grey layer, point C is assigned to the highest covering layer, *i.e.*, the light-grey layer.

4.2   Boundary Hermite Data

While surface Hermite data captures the surface geometry of building roofs, the shapes of roof boundaries are represented by the *boundary Hermite data*.

Considering a grid edge e connecting two grid points with surface Hermite data samples $\{s_0, s_1\}$ on different roof layers $s_0 \in L_0, s_1 \in L_1$,[3] the vertical

---

[1] The roof layers are always segmented in a local area, as global segmentation may erase local features such as those shown in Figure 8(c). Specifically, the segmentation for grid point g is applied to all the input points in g's four neighboring cells.

[2] Point normals are pre-computed using covariance analysis [14].

[3] To avoid ambiguity, roof layers are determined again by a local segmentation over $\{s_0, s_1\} \cup P$, where P is the input point set within e's two adjacent cells.

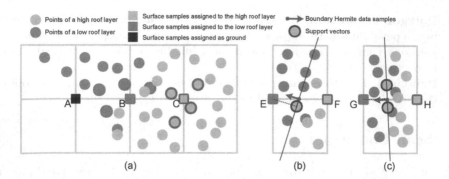

Fig. 4. Generating (a) surface Hermite data samples on grid points: the sample is assigned to the highest roof layer which *covers* the grid point; (b,c) boundary Hermite data samples on grid edges: we find the maximum margin line (thin black lines) to divide the lower surface Hermite data sample from the higher roof layer

wall connecting L_0 and L_1 should split their projection images on the x-y plane. Inspired by the 2D support vector machine algorithm, we find the maximum-margin line l which separates L_0 and L_1 on the x-y plane, and estimate the boundary sample by intersecting line l and edge e.

In practice, with the existence of residual sensor noise, the projections of different roof layers may overlap on the x-y plane. Since our data is collected from a top view, we give more saliency to the higher roof layer L_1 (assuming $height(L_0) < height(L_1)$), and thus take the maximum-margin line l which separates $\{s_0\}$ and L_1 while maximizing $distance(s_0, l)$, shown as the thin black lines in Figure 4(b,c). Empirically, we find this method more robust than other methods including that using a maximum-soft-margin line dividing L_0 and L_1.

5   Adaptive Creation of Geometry

Given a quadtree cell c (not necessarily being a finest-level leaf cell), we denote the set of surface Hermite data samples on the grid points in c as S, and the set of boundary Hermite data samples on atomic grid edges in c as B. The roof layers in c are then determined by segmenting S into k clusters $S = S_1 \cup \cdots \cup S_k$. Intuitively, if an atomic grid edge in c has no boundary sample attached, it connects two surface samples of the same roof layer. Thus, we use an agglomerative clustering algorithm via repeatedly combining surface sample sets connected by edges without boundary samples.

Now our task is to generate k vertices for the k roof layers, denoted as a *hyperpoint* $\chi = \{x_1, \ldots, x_k\}$. To maintain the consistency of roof layer boundaries, we require these k vertices to have the same projection onto the x-y plane, *i.e.*, they should have the same x-y coordinates, but different z values. Thus χ can be expressed as a $k+2$ dimensional vector $\chi = (x, y, z_1, \ldots, z_k)$. We let $x_0 = (x, y, 0)$ for convenience in following discussions.

5.1   2.5D QEF

The hyper-point χ is optimized by minimizing a 2.5D QEF defined as the linear combination of 2D boundary quadratic errors and 3D surface quadratic errors:

$$E(\chi) = \sum_{(p,n)\in B} (\omega n \cdot (x_0 - p))^2 + \sum_{i=1,\ldots,k} \sum_{(p,n)\in S_i} (n \cdot (x_i - p))^2 \tag{1}$$

where ω is a user-given weight balancing between boundary samples and surface samples. Empirically, a weight between $1 \sim 4$ satisfies most of our experiments.

Due to the horizontality of boundary sample normals, the third coordinates of p and x_0 do not affect the 2D error term. However, we choose to write all these variables uniformly in 3D, in order to express the energy function in a matrix product form:

$$E(\chi) = (A\chi - b)^T (A\chi - b) \tag{2}$$

where A is a matrix whose rows come from normals in $B, S_1, \ldots, S_k$, with those in B multiplied by ω. The x-y values of each normal are placed in the first two columns, while the z values of normals in S_i are placed in the $(i+2)$-th column. The remaining entries in A are padded with zeros. b is a vector composed of corresponding inner products $n \cdot p$ with the first $|B|$ entries multiplied by ω.

We employ the QR decomposition proposed in [4] to improve numerical stability during QEF optimization, i.e.,

$$(A \quad b) = Q \begin{pmatrix} \hat{A} & \hat{b} \\ 0 & r \\ 0 & 0 \\ \ldots \ldots \end{pmatrix} \tag{3}$$

where Q is an orthogonal matrix and Equation 2 can be rewritten as:

$$E(\chi) = (A\chi - b)^T Q Q^T (A\chi - b) = (\hat{A}\chi - \hat{b})^T (\hat{A}\chi - \hat{b}) + r^2. \tag{4}$$

Thus, $E(\chi)$ is minimized by solving $\hat{A}\chi - \hat{b} = 0$. To handle the possible singularity of $\hat{A}$, we follow the solutions in previous methods [4,6] by applying an SVD decomposition:

$$\hat{A} = U\Sigma V^T, \tag{5}$$

truncating small singular values in Σ with a magnitude of less than 0.1, and using the pseudo-inverse Σ^+ to compute the hyper-point χ as:

$$\chi = \bar{\chi} + V\Sigma^+ U^T (\hat{b} - \hat{A}\bar{\chi}) \tag{6}$$

where $\bar{\chi}$ is a guessed solution whose first two coordinates come from the centroid of B, and the $(i+2)$-th coordinate is the mean height of samples in S_i. If B is empty, the first two coordinates equal to those of the centroid of S.

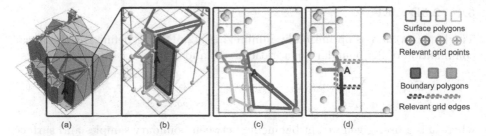

Fig. 5. (a,b) Creating surface polygons (colored hollow polygons) and boundary polygons (colored semitransparent polygons) around hyper-point A. Viewing from top, (c) surface polygons are generated at grid points, while (d) boundary polygons are produced for grid edges which exhibit a roof layer gap.

5.2   Quadtree Simplification with QEFs

Taking a quadtree with QEF matrices pre-computed for all the finest-level cells, we simplify the geometry by collapsing leaf cells into parent cells and combining QEFs in a bottom-up manner. A user-given tolerance δ controls the simplification level by denying sub-tree collapse when the residual is greater than δ.

Combining four regular 3D QEFs can be simply achieved by merging the rows of their upper triangular matrices to form a 16×4 matrix [4]. We follow this method to combine our 2.5D QEF matrices, yet with the consideration of association between matrix columns and roof layers: as roof layers in leaf cells merge into one roof layer in the parent cell, corresponding matrix columns are placed in the same column of the combined matrix. Specifically, we redo the roof layer segmentation in the parent cell before merging matrices. Assuming the i-th roof layer in a leaf cell belongs to the j-th roof layer in the parent cell, we put the $(i + 2)$-th column of the leaf cell matrix into the $(j + 2)$-th column of the combined matrix. 0-columns are used to pad the leaf cell matrices where no roof layers belong to certain roof layers in the parent cell.

Once again, the merged matrix is brought to the upper triangular form via a QR decomposition. Due to the orthogonality of involved transformation matrices, it represents the 2.5D QEF in the parent cell.

6   Polygon Generation

Given the simplified quadtree with hyper-points estimated in each leaf cell, our next task is to create polygons connecting these hyper-points into a mesh. In particular, we generate two kinds of polygons to satisfy our 2.5D characteristic.

1. **Surface polygons:** At each grid point p, we generate a surface polygon by connecting vertices in the hyper-points on the same roof layer as p in its neighboring cells.
2. **Boundary polygons:** At each minimal quadtree edge e, we create a boundary polygon connecting two hyper-point segments in the adjacent cells.

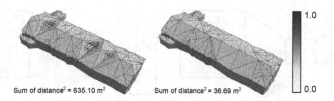

Fig. 6. Triangulation without (left) and with (right) our sharp feature preserving algorithm. The colors of input points represent the squared distances from the mesh.

Figure 5 shows an example of polygon generation around a hyper-point A. The surface polygons and boundary polygons are highlighted with colored outlines and colored semitransparent polygons respectively. To avoid cracks generated within a hyper-point, we make a boundary polygon sequentially pass through the vertices in hyper-point segment in height ascending or descending order. *E.g.*, the dark-blue boundary polygon in Figure 5 goes through all the three vertices in hyper-point A, from the top vertex to the bottom vertex.

Our method is guaranteed to produce crack-free models, which can be derived from the fact that except for the border edges created around the entire grid, the other mesh edges are contained by an even number of polygons. Proof is straightforward: a non-vertical mesh edge is either contained by two surface polygons, or by one surface polygon and one boundary polygon. As for the vertical mesh edges created within a hyper-point, we consider all the boundary polygons around this hyper-point (*e.g.*, the colored semitransparent polygons shown in Figure 5(a,b)). They go up and down though this hyper-point and finally return to the start vertex, forming up a closed edge loop. Thus, each vertical mesh edge in this hyper-point appears even times.

6.1   Sharp Feature Preserving Triangulation

By minimizing QEFs, 2.5D dual contouring has the ability to produce vertices lying on sharp features, which are a common pattern in building roofs. However, we find that a poor triangulation of surface polygons can spoil this advantage, as shown in Figure 6 left. To solve this problem, we propose an efficient sharp feature detection algorithm and preserve these features once detected.

In a grid cell c containing only one roof layer, we apply covariance analysis over the normals of all surface samples, *i.e.*, to get the eigenvalues of matrix:

$$C = \frac{1}{N}\sum_i n_i \cdot n_i^T, \tag{7}$$

and use Equation 3 and 5 to simplify it since c has no boundary samples:

$$C = \frac{1}{N}A^T A = \frac{1}{N}\hat{A}^T \hat{A} = \frac{1}{N}V\Sigma^T \Sigma V^T. \tag{8}$$

Thus, the diagonal of matrix $\frac{1}{N}\Sigma^T \Sigma$ gives the eigenvalues of C, while the columns of V are corresponding eigenvectors. As Pauly [9] suggests, the smallest

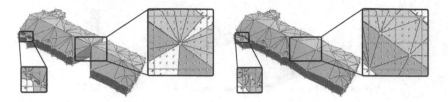

Fig. 7. Comparison between topology-unsafe simplification (left) and topology-safe simplification (right). Undesired features can be created by merging leaf cells in a topology-unsafe manner.

eigenvalue λ_0 and the middle eigenvalue λ_1 estimate the minimal and maximal curvatures, as the corresponding eigenvectors v_0, v_1 point to the curvature directions. Therefore, we find ridges and valleys by detecting vertices with small λ_0 and fairly large λ_1, and use v_0 as the feature direction. Since the involved matrices have all been computed in previous steps, the additional overhead of this algorithm is trivial.

Specifically, for each diagonal e of a surface quad, we calculate:

$$\sum_{p \in e \text{ and } \lambda_0(p) < \tau} \lambda_1(p) \cdot |v_0(p) \cdot e| \tag{9}$$

and choose the diagonal e^* which maximizes this value to split the quad into two triangles. Here τ is a user given threshold. Our experiments take $\tau = 0.01$.

7   Topology-Safe Simplification

So far the quadtree simplification is completely built on QEFs, and the topology of output models may change during this process. Undesired features can be generated as shown in Figure 7 left. To solve this problem, we insert an additional topology test right before sub-tree collapse happens; and reject collapse if the test reveals a danger of topology change. Regarding multiple roof layers as multiple materials, we use the topology test algorithm in [4], with an additional test (step 3) which prevents different roof layers in one leaf cell (top-left cell in Figure 8(a)) from merging into a same roof layer in the coarse cell (Figure 8(b)). This situation may cause removal of small vertical wall features (*e.g.*, Figure 8(c)).

1. Test whether each leaf cell creates a manifold; if not, stop.
2. Test whether the coarse cell creates a manifold; if not, stop.
3. Test whether any two roof layers in a same leaf cell belong to two different roof layers in the coarse cell; if not, stop.
4. Test whether the topology of the dual contour is preserved using following criteria; if not, stop; otherwise, collapse.
   (a) Test whether the roof layer on the middle point of each coarse edge agrees with the roof layer on at least one of the two edge endpoints.
   (b) Test whether the roof layer on the middle point of the coarse cell agrees with the roof layer on at least one of the four cell corners.

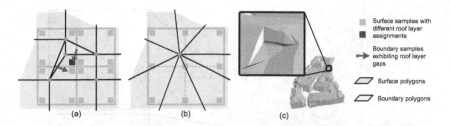

Surface samples with different roof layer assignments

Boundary samples exhibiting roof layer gaps

Surface polygons

Boundary polygons

(a)   (b)   (c)

Fig. 8. An unsafe simplification case denied by the topology safety test step 3. Since the center grid point has different roof layer assignments in these leaf cells, two different layers in the top-left leaf cell (a) belong to the same roof layer in the coarse cell (b). Unsafe merging may erase wall features such as the one shown in (c).

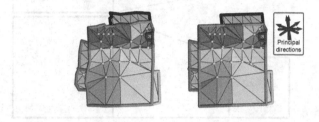

Principal directions

Fig. 9. Roof layer boundaries (thick colored lines) are snapped to principal directions

8 Principal Direction Snapping

Our algorithm is completely data-driven, *i.e.*, no pre-assumptions about the roof shapes have been made. Thus our algorithm can handle complex roofs in a robust manner. On the other hand, in some cases, prior knowledge of the urban area is given and it is a desire to have building models concurring with such knowledge. In this section, we show a post-processing refinement to our results using the prior knowledge of principal directions, which are defined as the roof edge direction preference in a local urban area [14].

The idea is straightforward: once the boundaries of individual roof layers are extracted, we snap them to the principal directions as much as possible without exceeding a small error tolerance. In order to maintain the consistency between boundaries of different layers, the boundaries are handled one by one in height-descending order. *I.e.*, when a roof layer boundary has been processed, the x-y coordinates of the touched hyper-points are fixed, which are then considered as constraints during the subsequent processing of lower roof layers. Figure 9 shows clean and simple roof boundaries generated by the principal direction refinement.

9 Experiment Results

Figure 10 shows an urban area of Los Angeles reconstructed from 26M LiDAR points with 7 samples/sq.m. resolution. We employ the reconstruction pipeline

Fig. 10. Building reconstruction for a 2KM-by-2.5KM urban area of Los Angeles

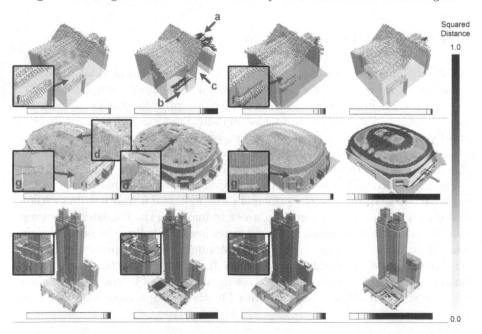

Fig. 11. Building models created using different approaches (from left to right): 2.5D dual contouring, plane-based method proposed in [14], general mesh simplification over a rasterized DEM, and manual creation. Color bars under the models show the ratio of points at different squared distance level.

Table 1. Quantitative evaluation of experiments shown in Figure 11

Models in Figure 11		2.5D dual contouring	Plane-based method [14]	DEM simpli-fication	Manual creation [3]
First row (4679 points)	Triangle number	214	76	198	78
	Average distance^2	0.016	0.599	0.061	0.058
	Outlier ratio	0.06%	12.37%	0.53%	0.83%
Second row (684907 points)	Triangle number	8009	6262	8000	1227
	Average distance^2	0.037	0.465	0.035	7.780
	Outlier ratio	0.44%	7.93%	0.87%	70.38%
Third row (198551 points)	Triangle number	12688	1619	12999	1558
	Average distance^2	0.203	1.610	0.264	16.220
	Outlier ratio	2.03%	21.15%	3.08%	68.28%

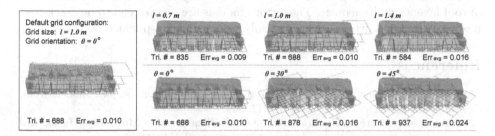

Fig. 12. Models of similar quality are generated with the same point cloud embedded into grids of different sizes or different orientations

proposed in [15] to remove irrelevant parts such as noises, trees, vehicles and even ground. We then test our 2.5D dual contouring on point clouds of individual buildings to create 2.5D models with complex roofs. Our algorithm successfully creates 1879 building models consisting of 857K triangles within 6 minutes on a consumer-level laptop (Intel Core 2 1.8GHz CPU with 2GB memory).

To further demonstrate the ability of handling various kinds of building models, we test our method on a set of buildings from Atlanta, as illustrated in Figure 1. Figure 11 shows a comparison between our method and previous methods. In particular, we compare the average squared distance from input point sets to the generated models, and the ratio of points with squared distances greater than 1sq.m. In Figure 11, point colors denote the squared distances, and the colored bars show the percentage of points at different squared distance levels. As the quantitative results in Table 1 illustrate, our method (first column) is the most accurate algorithm to produce 2.5D models. Plane-based approaches such as [14] (second column) are unable to handle non-flat roofs (a,d) and small roof features (b,e). Cracks often exist when fitting is unsuccessful (c,d). A general mesh simplification over the DEM (third column) is competitive in the sense of fitting quality. However, it cannot produce 2.5D models composed of roofs and vertical walls. In addition, the fitting quality on roof boundaries is unsatisfactory (f,g,h). The last column demonstrates point clouds aligning with manually created models. Designed without knowledge from real-world data, they often lack of accuracy even after registration to the input points.

We finally demonstrate the influence of grid configuration in Figure 12. As an adaptive approach, our method is insensitive to the grid size (top row). In addition, 2.5D dual contouring has the ability to place vertices at optimal positions, thus grid orientation affects the results insignificantly (bottom row).

10 Conclusion

We present a robust method to automatically creating building models from aerial LiDAR point clouds. Our results are 2.5D models composed of complex building roofs connected by vertical walls. By extending dual contouring into a 2.5D method, our algorithm optimizes the surface geometry and the boundaries of roof layers simultaneously. The output models are guaranteed to be crack-free meshes with small fitting error, faithfully preserving sharp features.

References

1. Curless, B., Levoy, M.: A volumetric method for building complex models from range images. In: ACM SIGGRAPH (1996)
2. Fiocco, M., Boström, G., Gonçalves, J.G.M., Sequeira, V.: Multisensor fusion for volumetric reconstruction of large outdoor areas. 3DIM (2005)
3. Google: Google 3d warehouse, http://sketchup.google.com/3dwarehouse/
4. Ju, T., Losasso, F., Schaefer, S., Warren, J.: Dual contouring on hermite data. In: ACM SIGGRAPH (2002)
5. Lafarge, F., Descombes, X., Zerubia, J., Pierrot-Deseilligny, M.: Building reconstruction from a single dem. In: CVPR (2008)
6. Lindstrom, P.: Out-of-core simplification of large polygonal models. In: ACM SIGGRAPH (2000)
7. Lorensen, W., Cline, H.: Marching cubes: A high resolution 3d surface construction algorithm. In: ACM SIGGRAPH (1987)
8. Matei, B., Sawhney, H., Samarasekera, S., Kim, J., Kumar, R.: Building segmentation for densely built urban regions using aerial lidar data. In: CVPR (2008)
9. Pauly, M.: Point primitives for interactive modeling and processing of 3d geometry. PhD thesis, ETH Zurich (2003)
10. Poullis, C., You, S.: Automatic reconstruction of cities from remote sensor data. In: CVPR (2009)
11. Verma, V., Kumar, R., Hsu, S.: 3d building detection and modeling from aerial lidar data. In: CVPR (2006)
12. You, S., Hu, J., Neumann, U., Fox, P.: Urban site modeling from lidar. In: Kumar, V., Gavrilova, M.L., Tan, C.J.K., L'Ecuyer, P. (eds.) ICCSA 2003. LNCS, vol. 2669, pp. 579–588. Springer, Heidelberg (2003)
13. Zebedin, L., Bauer, J., Karner, K., Bischof, H.: Fusion of feature- and area-based information for urban buildings modeling from aerial imagery. In: Forsyth, D., Torr, P., Zisserman, A. (eds.) ECCV 2008, Part IV. LNCS, vol. 5305, pp. 873–886. Springer, Heidelberg (2008)
14. Zhou, Q.Y., Neumann, U.: Fast and extensible building modeling from airborne lidar data. In: ACM GIS (2008)
15. Zhou, Q.Y., Neumann, U.: A streaming framework for seamless building reconstruction from large-scale aerial lidar data. In: CVPR (2009)

Analytical Forward Projection for Axial Non-central Dioptric and Catadioptric Cameras

Amit Agrawal, Yuichi Taguchi, and Srikumar Ramalingam

Mitsubishi Electric Research Labs (MERL), Cambridge, MA, USA

Abstract. We present a technique for modeling non-central catadioptric cameras consisting of a perspective camera and a rotationally symmetric conic reflector. While previous approaches use a central approximation and/or iterative methods for forward projection, we present an analytical solution. This allows computation of the optical path from a given 3D point to the given viewpoint by solving a 6th degree forward projection equation for general conic mirrors. For a spherical mirror, the forward projection reduces to a 4th degree equation, resulting in a closed form solution. We also derive the forward projection equation for imaging through a refractive sphere (non-central dioptric camera) and show that it is a 10th degree equation. While central catadioptric cameras lead to conic epipolar curves, we show the existence of a quartic epipolar curve for catadioptric systems using a spherical mirror. The analytical forward projection leads to accurate and fast 3D reconstruction via bundle adjustment. Simulations and real results on single image sparse 3D reconstruction are presented. We demonstrate ~ 100 times speed up using the analytical solution over iterative forward projection for 3D reconstruction using spherical mirrors.

1 Introduction

Catadioptric cameras allow large field of view 3D reconstruction and stable ego-motion estimation from few images. As analyzed in [1], there are only a few configurations that allow an effective single-viewpoint (central) catadioptric system. Simple mirrors such as sphere as well as configurations when the camera is not placed on the foci of hyperbolic/elliptical mirrors lead to a non-central system. To handle such configurations, it is important to accurately model a non-cental catadioptric camera. Approximations using a central model could lead to inaccuracies such as skewed 3D estimation [2].

The projection of a scene point onto the image plane (Forward Projection) requires computing the light path from the scene point to the perspective camera's center of projection (COP). Thus, the reflection point on the mirror needs to be determined. This is considered to be hard problem and iterative solutions are usually employed assuming there are no closed form solutions. In this paper, we present an analytical solution to compute the forward projection (FP) for conic catadioptric systems, where the mirror is obtained by revolving a conic section around the axis of symmetry and the camera's COP is placed on the

K. Daniilidis, P. Maragos, N. Paragios (Eds.): ECCV 2010, Part III, LNCS 6313, pp. 129–143, 2010.

mirror axis. We show that for a given 3D point, the mirror reflection point can be obtained by solving a 6th degree equation for a general conic mirror. Interestingly, it reduces to solving a 4th degree equation for a spherical mirror, resulting in a closed form solution. We show how to use these analytical solutions for fast 3D reconstruction using bundle adjustment, achieving a two order of magnitude speed up over previous approach [2].

Forward projection for imaging through a refractive sphere (non-central dioptric camera) is even more challenging due to two refractions. We show that the optical path from a given 3D point to a given viewpoint via a refractive sphere can be obtained by solving a 10th degree equation. Thus, similar to mirrors, refractive spheres can also be used for 3D reconstruction by plugging its forward projection equation in a bundle adjustment algorithm. We believe that ours is the first paper to analyze this problem and derive a practical solution.

The epipolar geometry for central catadioptric systems (CCS) and for several non-central cameras (pushbroom, cross-slit, etc.) has been extensively studied. However, analyzing the epipolar geometry for non-central catadioptric cameras is difficult due to non-linear forward projection. We show the existence of a *quartic* epipolar curve for catadioptric systems employing spherical mirror.

Contributions: Our paper makes the following contributions:

- We analyze forward projection for axial non-central dioptric/catadioptric cameras with conic reflectors and refractive spheres, and show that analytical solutions exist.
- We demonstrate that the back-projection for a spherical mirror can be formulated as a matrix-vector product and that the corresponding epipolar curves are quartic.
- We utilize the forward projection equations for fast sparse 3D reconstruction.

1.1   Related Work

Back-Projection and Epipolar Geometry: Baker and Nayar [1] presented the complete class of central catadioptric systems. Svoboda et al. [3, 4] studied the epipolar geometry for CCS and showed that the epipolar curves are conics. Geyer and Daniilidis [5] showed the existence of fundamental matrix for para-catadioptric cameras. A unified imaging model for all CCS was proposed by Geyer and Daniilidis [6]. Using this model for forward/back-projection with second order *lifted image coordinates*, Strum and Barreto [7] formulated the fundamental matrix for all CCS. For non-central cameras, Pless [8] introduced essential matrix for the calibrated case. Rademacher and Bishop [9] described epipolar curves for arbitrary non-central images. The epipolar geometry of cone-shaped mirrors, when restricted to planar motions was derived by Yagi and Kawato [10]. Spacek [11] described the epipolar geometry for two cameras mounted one on top of the other with aligned mirror axes.

Representing back-projection as a matrix-vector product for general mirrors is typically difficult. Several non-central cameras can be modeled by back-projection matrices operating on second order lifted image coordinates, resulting in conic epipolar curves. These include linear pushbroom cameras [12], linear oblique cameras [13], para-catadioptric cameras [14], and all general linear cameras (GLC) [15]. For the one-coefficient classical radial distortion model, the epipolar curves are cubic [16]. We show that for spherical mirror, back-projection can be described as matrix-vector product using *fourth order* lifted image coordinates, and thus the epipolar curves are quartic.

Forward projection for a non-central catadioptric camera is a hard problem, since the point on the mirror where the reflection happens need to be determined. In general, there is no closed-form solution for this problem, so non-linear optimization have been proposed (as in [2, 17]). Gonçalves and Nogueira [18] investigated quadric-shaped mirrors and reduced the problem to an optimization in a single variable. Baker and Nayar [1] were unable to find a closed form solution while analyzing mirror defocus blur and used numerical solutions. Their analysis was in 3D, since the finite camera aperture requires considering viewpoints not on the mirror axis. Vandeportaele [19] also analyzed forward projection for axial case, but in 3D using intersection of quadrics. In contrast, we derive a much simpler solution for the axial case in 2D with lower degree equation compared to [19].

Spherical mirrors have been used for visual servoing and wide-angle 3D reconstruction [2, 17, 20–23]. Both [22] and [2] state that computing forward projection does not have a closed-form solution. In [22], a GLC approximation is used by tessellating the captured multi-perspective image into triangles and associating a GLC with each of them. In [2], an iterative method for forward projection is used. Interestingly, for spherical mirror, forward projection corresponds to the classical Alhazen's problem with four solutions [24]. We show that our FP equation for general quadric mirror reduces to a 4th order equation for spherical mirror. Garg and Nayar [25] used a refractive sphere model for rain drops for generating near-perspective images (environment at infinity). However, they did not solve for the forward projection from a 3D point to compute the optical path, which we describe.

2   Forward Projection: Conic Reflectors

We first derive the forward projection equation for conic catadioptric systems. Let z axis be the mirror axis. A pinhole camera is placed at a distance d from the origin on the mirror axis. Let $P = [X, Y, Z]^T$ be a 3D scene point. Since the mirror is rotationally symmetric, the mirror reflection of P can be analyzed in the plane π containing the mirror axis and P (Figure 1 (left)). Let $(\mathbf{z}_1, \mathbf{z}_2)$ be the local coordinate system of π. In this plane, P has coordinates $\mathbf{p} = [u, v]^T$ given by $u = S \sin \theta$ and $v = Z$, where $S = \sqrt{X^2 + Y^2 + Z^2}$ is the distance of P from the origin and $\theta = \cos^{-1}(Z/S)$ is the angle between the mirror axis and the line joining the origin and the 3D point.

In plane π, the mirror is parameterized as a 2D conic $A z_2^2 + z_1^2 + B z_2 = C$. This parametrization is used in [26] to handle spherical mirror along with other mirrors for computing the caustics. Let $\mathbf{m} = [x, y]^T$ be the reflection point on the

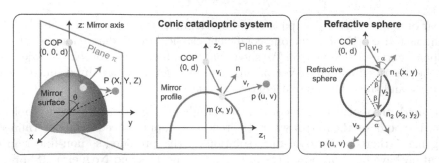

Fig. 1. (Left) Reflection for conic catadioptric systems can be analyzed in the plane π containing the mirror axis and the 3D scene point. (Right) Imaging through a refractive sphere can also be analyzed similarly.

mirror. Then $x = \pm\sqrt{C - By - Ay^2}$. The incident ray vector $\mathbf{v}_i$ and the normal vector $\mathbf{n}$ at $\mathbf{m}$ are given by $\mathbf{v}_i = [x, y - d]^T$ and $\mathbf{n} = [x, B/2 + Ay]^T$. Using the law of reflection, the reflected ray vector $\mathbf{v}_r = \mathbf{v}_i - 2\mathbf{n}(\mathbf{n}^T\mathbf{v}_i)/(\mathbf{n}^T\mathbf{n})$. Since the reflected ray should pass through P, $\mathbf{v}_r \times (\mathbf{p} - \mathbf{m}) = 0$, where $\times$ denotes the cross product. Solving using Matlab symbolic toolbox[1], we obtain a 6th order **forward projection (FP) equation** in y

$$u^2 K_1^2(y) + K_2^2(y)(Ay^2 + By - C) = 0, \tag{1}$$

where $K_1(y)$ and $K_2(y)$ are polynomials in y defined as

$$K_1(y) = K_{11}y^3 + K_{12}y^2 + K_{13}y + K_{14}, \quad K_2(y) = K_{21}y^2 + K_{22}y + K_{23}, \tag{2}$$

and the individual terms are given by

$K_{11} = 4A(1 - A), \quad K_{12} = 4B - 4A(d + Ad + 2B)$
$K_{13} = 8AC - 4Bd - 3B^2 - 4C - 4ABd, \quad K_{14} = -dB^2 + 4CB + 4Cd$
$K_{21} = 4(A - 1)(A(d + v) + B), \quad K_{22} = 8C + 2B^2 + 4A(-2C + B(d + v) + 2dv)$
$K_{23} = B^2(d + v) + 4B(-C + dv) - 4C(v + d).$

For a given P, solving (1) results in six solutions for y. The correct solution can be found by checking the law of reflection for each real solution. Note that for the correct solution $\mathbf{v}_r^T\mathbf{n} = -\mathbf{v}_i^T\mathbf{n}$. Using $x = \text{sign}(u)\sqrt{C - By - Ay^2}$, the 3D mirror reflection point can be obtained as $x\mathbf{z}_1/\|\mathbf{z}_1\| + y\mathbf{z}_2/\|\mathbf{z}_2\|$.

Spherical Mirror: Substituting $A = 1, B = 0, C = r^2$, where r is the mirror radius, results in a 4th order forward projection equation

$$u^2(r^2(d + y) - 2dy^2)^2 - (r^2 - y^2)(r^2(d + v) - 2dvy)^2 = 0. \tag{3}$$

Thus, a close form solution for y can be obtained. Notice that for a spherical mirror, the pinhole location is not restricted. For any pinhole location, a new axis

---

[1] Matlab code and intermediate steps are provided in the supplementary materials.

Table 1. Degree of forward projection equation for central and non-central catadioptric systems using conic reflectors

Mirror Shape	Pinhole Placement	Parameters	Central System	Degree
General	On axis	A,B,C	No	6
Sphere	Any	$A = 1, B = 0, C > 0$	No	4
Elliptic	On axis, At Foci	$B = 0$	Yes	2
Elliptic	On axis, Not at Foci	$B = 0$	No	6
Hyperbolic	On axis, At Foci	$A < 0, C < 0$	Yes	2
Hyperbolic	On axis, Not at Foci	$A < 0, C < 0$	No	6
Parabolic	On axis, $d = \infty$	$A = 0, C = 0$	Yes	2
Parabolic	On axis, Finite d	$A = 0, C = 0$	No	5

joining the pinhole and the sphere center can be defined. In all other cases, the pinhole needs to be on the mirror axis. Table 1 shows the degree of FP equation for spherical ($A = 1, B = 0, C > 0$), elliptical ($B = 0$), hyperbolic ($A < 0, C < 0$) and parabolic ($A = 0, C = 0$) mirrors. Note that when the catadioptric system is central, the degree of FP is two. This is intuitive, since the reflection point can be obtained by intersecting the mirror with the ray joining the 3D point and the effective projection center.

3   Back-Projection and Epipolar Curve for Spherical Mirror

Now we show that back-projection equations for a non-central catadioptric system using a spherical mirror can be written in matrix-vector form. By intersecting the back-projected ray with a general 3D ray, we show the existence of a quartic epipolar curve. Then we verify that the projection of points on the same 3D line onto the image plane using the FP equation results in the same curve.

Let $\mathbf{C}_p = [0, 0, -d]^T$ be the COP and let the spherical mirror of radius r be located at the origin (Figure 2 (left)). For an image point $\mathbf{q}$, let $\mathbf{s} = K^{-1}\mathbf{q}$ be the ray direction, where $K_{3\times3}$ is the internal camera calibration matrix. The intersection points $\mathbf{b}$ with the mirror are given by

$$\mathbf{b} = \mathbf{C}_p + \mathbf{s}\frac{ds_3 \pm \sqrt{d^2 s_3^2 - (d^2 - r^2)(\mathbf{s}^T\mathbf{s})}}{\mathbf{s}^T\mathbf{s}}, \qquad (4)$$

where s_3 is the third element of $\mathbf{s}$. Note that $\mathbf{b}^T\mathbf{b} = r^2$ and the normal at $\mathbf{b}$ is $\mathbf{b}/r$. Since $\mathbf{v}_i = \mathbf{b} - \mathbf{C}_p$, the reflected vector $\mathbf{v}_r$ is given by

$$\mathbf{v}_r = (\mathbf{b} - \mathbf{C}_p) - 2\mathbf{b}(\mathbf{b}^T(\mathbf{b} - \mathbf{C}_p))/r^2 = -\mathbf{b} - \mathbf{C}_p + 2\mathbf{b}(\mathbf{b}^T\mathbf{C}_p)/r^2, \qquad (5)$$

which intersects the mirror axis at $\mathbf{m} = [0, 0, k]^T$, where $k = dr^2/(2db_3 + r^2)$. Thus, the Plücker coordinates of the reflected 3D ray are given by $\mathbf{L} = (\mathbf{b}^T - \mathbf{m}^T, (\mathbf{b} \times \mathbf{m})^T)^T$, where $\times$ denotes the cross product. Similar to [7], we use $\mathbf{L}_+$

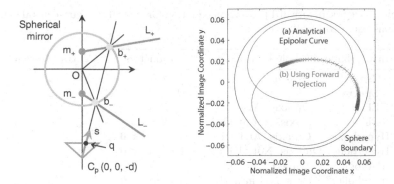

Fig. 2. (Left) Depicting back-projection. (Right) Epipolar curves, analytically computed by Equation (8) (a) and numerically computed by using the FP equation (b) for a known 3D line match.

and $\mathbf{L}_-$ to represent the reflected rays corresponding to the two intersections of $\mathbf{v}_i$ with the sphere ($\mathbf{b}_+$ and $\mathbf{b}_-$). We represent the two lines with a second-order line complex $\mathbf{C}$, described as a symmetric 6×6 matrix

$$\mathbf{C} \sim W(\mathbf{L}_+\mathbf{L}_-^T + \mathbf{L}_-\mathbf{L}_+^T)W, \quad W = \begin{pmatrix} 0 & I \\ I & 0 \end{pmatrix}, \tag{6}$$

where $\sim$ denotes the equality of matrices up to a scale factor. By substituting $\mathbf{b}$ and $\mathbf{m}$, we obtain a line complex $\mathbf{C}$ that includes *quartic* monomials of $\mathbf{s}$. As in [7], let $\mathbf{v}_{sym}(\mathbf{C})$ be the column-wise vectorization of the upper-right triangular part of $\mathbf{C}$ (21-vector) and $\hat{\hat{\mathbf{s}}}$ denote *double lifted* coordinates of $\mathbf{s}$ in the lexicographic order (15-vector). Then we obtain the back-projection equation in a matrix-vector form:

$$\mathbf{v}_{sym}(\mathbf{C}) \sim B_{r,d}\hat{\hat{\mathbf{s}}} = B_{r,d}\hat{\hat{K}}^{-1}\hat{\hat{\mathbf{q}}}, \tag{7}$$

where $B_{r,d}$ is a sparse 21×15 matrix depending only on r and d, as shown in the supplementary materials.

Note that the difference between [7] and ours is that $\mathbf{m} = [0, 0, 0]$ in [7], since the reflected ray passes through the *center* of an imaginary sphere that models all central catadioptric systems [6]. For a non-central catadioptric system, $\mathbf{m}$ becomes dependent on the image pixel $\mathbf{q}$. Note that when the pinhole is on the mirror axis, one can always find the intersection point $\mathbf{m}$ as $[0, 0, k]$ for some k.

Epipolar Curve: Consider a 3D ray defined in the sphere-centered coordinate system and represented with Plücker coordinates as $\mathbf{L}_0$. This ray intersects the line complex $\mathbf{C}$ *iff*

$$\mathbf{L}_0^T\mathbf{C}\mathbf{L}_0 = 0. \tag{8}$$

Since $\mathbf{C}$ includes quartic monomials of $\mathbf{s}$ (thus $\mathbf{q}$), the constraint results in a 4th order curve. The projection of $\mathbf{L}_0$ therefore appears as a quartic curve in the image of spherical mirror, which means that spherical-mirror based catadioptric systems yield quartic epipolar curves. Our FP equation allows us to validate the degree and shape of epipolar curves. Figure 2 (right) compares the epipolar curve analytically computed from (8) with the curve obtained by projecting 3D points on $\mathbf{L}_0$ using the FP equation. We can observe that the shape of curves agree and the numerical curve (using FP) is a continuous section of the analytical quartic curve. Note that the image point converges as the 3D point goes to $\pm\infty$ on $\mathbf{L}_0$.

Similar to perspective cameras, the quartic epipolar curve can be used to restrict the search space for dense stereo matching. Typically, approximations such as epsilon-stereo constraint [22] are used, which assumes that the corresponding match will lie approximately along a line. However, our analysis provides the analytical 2D epipolar curve for non-central spherical mirror cameras. Note that the FP equation for general conic mirrors simplifies the correspondence search for other non-central conic catadioptric systems as well.

4 Sparse 3D Reconstruction Using Spherical Mirrors

We demonstrate the applicability of analytical forward projection (AFP) for sparse 3D reconstruction using well-known bundle adjustment algorithm, and compare it with iterative forward projection (IFP) method [2]. We choose a simpler setup of a single perspective camera imaging multiple spherical mirrors as shown in Figure 4. We assume that the internal camera calibration is done separately (off-line) and the sphere radius is known (we used high sphericity stainless steel balls as spherical mirrors for real experiments). Thus, our optimization involves estimating the sphere centers and the 3D points in the camera coordinate system. Note that the FP equation can be easily applied to more general calibration/3D reconstruction involving rotationally symmetric setups with parabolic/hyperbolic mirrors [2]. For moving camera+mirror system, one may require a central approximation to get the initial estimate of the relative camera motion. However, AFP can replace IFP in subsequent bundle adjustment. In addition, since AFP leads to a fast algorithm, we demonstrate in Section 4.3 that a central approximation is not required for iterative outlier removal.

4.1 Bundle Adjustment for Spherical Mirror Using AFP

Let $\mathbf{C}(i) = \left[C_x(i), C_y(i), C_z(i) \right]^T, i = 1 \ldots M$ be the sphere centers and $\mathbf{P}(j) = \left[P_x(j), P_y(j), P_z(j) \right]^T, j = 1 \ldots N$ be the 3D points in the camera coordinate system, when the pinhole camera is placed at the origin. First we rewrite the FP equation (3) in terms of 3D quantities. For a given 3D point $\mathbf{P}(j)$ and mirror center $\mathbf{C}(i)$, the orthogonal vectors $\mathbf{z}_1$ and $\mathbf{z}_2$ defining plane π are given by $\mathbf{z}_2 = -\mathbf{C}(i)$ and $\mathbf{z}_1 = \mathbf{P}(j) - \mathbf{C}(i)\frac{\mathbf{C}(i)^T\mathbf{P}(j)}{\|\mathbf{C}(i)\|^2}$. Further, $d = \|\mathbf{z}_2\|$, $u = \|\mathbf{z}_1\|$, and $v = -\mathbf{C}(i)^T(\mathbf{P}(j) - \mathbf{C}(i))/\|\mathbf{C}(i)\|$. By substituting d, u and v in (3), the FP equation can be re-written as

$$c_1 y^4 + c_2 y^3 + c_3 y^2 + c_4 y + c_5 = 0, \tag{9}$$

where each coefficient c_i becomes a function of $\mathbf{P}(j)$ and $\mathbf{C}(i)$ only. In general, when the scene point is outside the sphere and is visible through mirror reflection, there are four real solutions. The single correct solution is found by checking the law of reflection for each of them.

Using the solution, the 3D reflection point on the sphere is obtained as

$$\mathbf{R}_m(i,j) = [X_m(i,j), Y_m(i,j), Z_m(i,j)]^T = \mathbf{C}(i) + \sqrt{r^2 - y^2}\frac{\mathbf{z}_1}{\|\mathbf{z}_1\|} + y\frac{\mathbf{z}_2}{\|\mathbf{z}_2\|}. \quad (10)$$

Finally, the 2D image projection pixel is obtained as $p(i,j) = \frac{f_x X_m(i,j)}{Z_m(i,j)} + c_x$, $q(i,j) = \frac{f_y Y_m(i,j)}{Z_m(i,j)} + c_y$, where (f_x, f_y) and (c_x, c_y) are the focal length and the principal point of the camera, respectively.

Let $[\hat{p}(i,j), \hat{q}(i,j)]^T$ be the image projection of the jth 3D point for the ith sphere and $[p(i,j), q(i,j)]^T$ denote their current estimates, computed from the current estimates of sphere centers and 3D scene points. Each pair (i,j) gives a 2-vector error function $F(i,j) = [p(i,j) - \hat{p}(i,j), q(i,j) - \hat{q}(i,j)]^T$, and the average reprojection error is given by $E = \frac{1}{NM}\sum_{j=1}^{N}\sum_{i=1}^{M}\|F(i,j)\|^2$. We perform bundle adjustment by minimizing E (using Matlab function lsqnonlin), starting from an initial solution. The initial 3D points are obtained as the center of the shortest transversal of the respective back-projection rays. The initial sphere centers are perturbed from their true positions (simulations) and obtained using the captured photo (real experiments).

Jacobian Computation: AFP also enables the analytical Jacobian computation, which speeds up bundle adjustment. Let t denote an unknown. Then

$$\frac{\partial F(i,j)}{\partial t} = \begin{bmatrix} \frac{\partial p(i,j)}{\partial t} \\ \frac{\partial q(i,j)}{\partial t} \end{bmatrix} = \begin{bmatrix} f_x\left(\frac{1}{Z_m(i,j)}\frac{\partial X_m(i,j)}{\partial t} - \frac{X_m(i,j)}{Z_m(i,j)^2}\frac{\partial Z_m(i,j)}{\partial t}\right) \\ f_y\left(\frac{1}{Z_m(i,j)}\frac{\partial Y_m(i,j)}{\partial t} - \frac{Y_m(i,j)}{Z_m(i,j)^2}\frac{\partial Z_m(i,j)}{\partial t}\right) \end{bmatrix}. \quad (11)$$

Since X_m, Y_m, Z_m depend on y, the above derivatives depend on $\frac{\partial y}{\partial t}$. Typically, one would assume that a closed form expression for y is required to compute $\frac{\partial y}{\partial t}$. However, it can be avoided by taking the derivative of the FP equation (9) as

$$\frac{\partial y}{\partial t} = -\frac{y^4\frac{\partial c_1}{\partial t} + y^3\frac{\partial c_2}{\partial t} + y^2\frac{\partial c_3}{\partial t} + y\frac{\partial c_4}{\partial t} + \frac{\partial c_5}{\partial t}}{4c_1y^3 + 3c_2y^2 + 2c_3y + c_4}. \quad (12)$$

For a given 3D point $\mathbf{P}(j)$ and sphere center $\mathbf{C}(i)$, y can be computed by solving the FP equation and thus can be substituted in above to obtain $\frac{\partial y}{\partial t}$. The gradient of the reprojection error with respect to each unknown can be obtained using Equations (10),(11), and (12). Thus, we showed that the analytical FP equation can be used to compute the Jacobian of the reprojection error, *without* obtaining a closed-form solution for the mirror reflection point.

4.2   Simulations

We place a pinhole camera at the center of the coordinate system and $M = 4$ spheres (radius $r = 0.5$") at a distance of 200 mm. $N = 100$ 3D points were randomly distributed in a hemisphere of radius 1000 mm surrounding the spheres

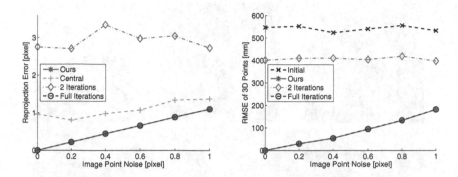

Fig. 3. Bundle adjustment simulations using $M = 4$ spherical mirrors and $N = 100$ 3D points for different image noise levels. (Left) Reprojection error. (Right) RMSE of reconstructed 3D points. The IFP curve matches the AFP curve when sufficient iterations are used.

Table 2. Comparison of bundle adjustment run time (in seconds) using IFP [2] and our AFP for N 3D points and $M = 4$ spherical mirrors. The run times were obtained by repeating bundle adjustment 20 times and averaging.

Run Time	Iterative FP	AFP (Without Jacobian)	AFP (With Jacobian)
$N = 100$	470	6.6	4.0
$N = 1000$	4200	68	48

and their true image projections were computed using the FP equation. Gaussian noise was added both to sphere centers ($\sigma = 0.5$ mm) and true image projections ($\sigma = [0 - 1]$ pixels). We compare the reconstruction error using (a) AFP, (b) central approximation (the projection center was fixed at $0.64r$ mm from the sphere center as in [2]), and (c) IFP [2]. IFP first computes the initial image projection of a 3D point using the central approximation and then performs non-linear optimization to minimize the distance between the 3D point and the back-projected ray. It required ~ 5 iterations to converge in the simulations.

Figure 3 compares the reprojection error and the root mean square error (RMSE) in 3D points for different image noise levels. Note that only when sufficient iterations are performed for IFP (referred to as 'full iterations'), its error reduces to that of AFP (same curve). The central approximation or smaller number of iterations for IFP lead to larger errors. In Figure 3 (right), the error due to central approximation is too large (1.5×10^4 mm) to be shown in the graph.

Run time for projecting 10^5 3D points with a single sphere was 1120 seconds for IFP (full iterations) and 13.8 seconds for AFP (~ 80 times faster). Table 2 compares the bundle adjustment run time, which shows that AFP along with analytical Jacobian computation achieves a speed up of ~ 100. While the number of iterations in bundle adjustment was almost the same for IFP and AFP, IFP takes much longer time due to iterative optical path computation for each 3D point and mirror pair. Similar speed-ups were obtained for elliptic, hyperbolic,

Fig. 4. Input images (left) and zoom-in of sphere images (middle and right) superimposed with extracted SIFT features. Red dots and green crosses respectively represent inliers and outliers determined in the iterative bundle adjustment process. Top shows rendered image using POV-Ray and bottom shows real photo captured using a camera.

and parabolic mirrors as well (projecting 10^5 3D points took 1600–1800 seconds for IFP and 22 seconds for AFP).

4.3   POV-Ray Simulations and Real Results Using Feature Matching

In practice, the corresponding image points are estimated using a feature matching algorithm such as SIFT, and invariably contain outliers and false matches. We first show results using SIFT on sphere images rendered using POV-Ray, which allows performance evaluation using available ground truth data.

Figure 4 (top) shows a rendered image (resolution 2000×2000) of four spherical mirrors, placed at the center of a cube 1000mm on each side. The walls of the cube consist of textured planes. We extract SIFT features and select corresponding points that are consistent among the four sphere images. For initial sphere centers, we add Gaussian noise ($\sigma = 0.3$mm) to their ground truth locations. Since the SIFT matches contains outliers, we perform robust reconstruction by *iterating* bundle adjustment with outlier removal. After each bundle adjustment step, we remove all 3D points whose reprojection error is greater than twice the average reprojection error. Figure 5 shows that by iterating bundle adjustment and outlier removal, the reprojection error and RMSE of 3D points reduces significantly for all planes (from ~ 460 mm to 6 mm). Figure 5 also shows the number of inliers after each bundle adjustment step. Note that since AFP significantly reduces bundle adjustment time, this simple procedure can be repeated multiple times and is effective in handling outliers.

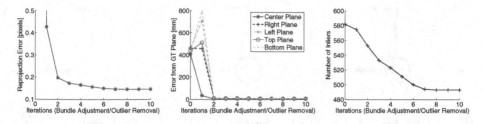

Fig. 5. 3D reconstruction results for the POV-Ray data. (Left) Reprojection error. (Middle) Average distance of reconstructed 3D points from the ground-truth (GT) planes. (Right) Number of inliers after each bundle adjustment/outlier removal step.

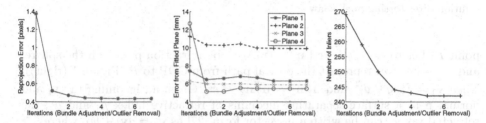

Fig. 6. 3D reconstruction results for the real data. (Left) Reprojection error. (Middle) Average distance of reconstructed 3D points from their fitted planes. (Right) Number of inliers after each bundle adjustment/outlier removal step.

Real Results: We used four spherical mirrors (radius 0.75") placed with an interval of 3", and captured a single photo using a Mamiya 645AFD camera, as shown in Figure 4 (bottom). Each sphere image in the captured photo has 1300×1300 resolution. To determine initial sphere centers, we mark several points on each sphere boundary, corresponding to the rays tangential to the sphere. We find the central ray that makes the same angle α with all the tangential rays. The sphere center is then at a distance of $\frac{r}{\sin \alpha}$ along the central ray. Figure 6 shows the reconstruction results. Since the ground truth is not available, we fit planes to the set of 3D points corresponding to each plane in the scene (Planes 1–4 in Figure 4) and measure the average distance error of the 3D points from the plane. Note that this error measure includes a bias, but validates that the reconstructed 3D points are aligned on a plane with small errors (Figure 6 (middle)).

5   Forward Projection for Refractive Sphere

Now we derive the forward projection equation for imaging through a refractive sphere, which results in a non-central dioptric system. The key idea is to use the vector equation of the refracted ray [27], instead of directly applying Snell's law.

Let a refractive sphere of radius r and constant refractive index μ be placed at the origin of the coordinate system. Let the COP be at distance d from the origin. As before, we consider the plane containing the optical axis and the scene

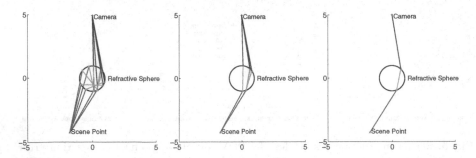

Fig. 7. Solving the FP equation for a refractive sphere with $r = 1$, $\mu = 1.5$ and $d = 5$. (Left) 8 real solutions. (Middle) 4 solutions after constraining $y \geq r^2/d$. (Right) Correct solution after testing Snell's law.

point P. Let $\mathbf{n}_1 = [x, y]^T$ and $\mathbf{n}_2 = [x_2, y_2]^T$ be refraction points on the sphere, and $v_1 \to v_2 \to v_3$ represent the optical path from COP to P (Figure 1 (right)). Then $\mathbf{v}_1 = [x, y - d]^T$ and $\mathbf{n}_1^T \mathbf{n}_1 = \mathbf{n}_2^T \mathbf{n}_2 = r^2$. Given an incoming ray $\mathbf{v}_i$ and normal $\mathbf{n}$ at a surface separating mediums of refractive index μ_1 and μ_2, the refracted ray $\mathbf{v}_r$ can be written in vector form [27] as $\mathbf{v}_r = a\mathbf{v}_i + b\mathbf{n}$, where

$$a = \frac{\mu_1}{\mu_2}, \quad b = \frac{-\mu_1 \mathbf{v}_i^T \mathbf{n} \pm \sqrt{\mu_1^2 (\mathbf{v}_i^T \mathbf{n})^2 - (\mu_1^2 - \mu_2^2)(\mathbf{v}_i^T \mathbf{v}_i)(\mathbf{n}^T \mathbf{n})}}{\mu_2 (\mathbf{n}^T \mathbf{n})}. \quad (13)$$

This gives $\mathbf{v}_r^T \mathbf{n} \propto \pm\sqrt{\mu_1^2(\mathbf{v}_i^T \mathbf{n})^2 - (\mu_1^2 - \mu_2^2)(\mathbf{v}_i^T \mathbf{v}_i)(\mathbf{n}^T \mathbf{n})}$. The correct sign is obtained by using the constraint that the signs of $\mathbf{v}_r^T \mathbf{n}$ and $\mathbf{v}_i^T \mathbf{n}$ should be the same. Since the tangent ray from COP to the sphere occurs at $y = r^2/d$, $y \geq r^2/d$ for valid refraction point. This gives $\mathbf{v}_1^T \mathbf{n}_1 = r^2 - dy \leq 0$. Thus,

$$\mathbf{v}_2 = \frac{1}{\mu}\mathbf{v}_1 + \mathbf{n}_1 \frac{-\mathbf{v}_1^T \mathbf{n}_1 - \sqrt{(\mathbf{v}_1^T \mathbf{n}_1)^2 - r^2(1 - \mu^2)(\mathbf{v}_1^T \mathbf{v}_1)}}{\mu r^2}. \quad (14)$$

The second refraction point $\mathbf{n}_2$ can be written as $\mathbf{n}_1 + \lambda \mathbf{v}_2$ for some constant λ, which can be obtained as follows.

$$r^2 = \mathbf{n}_2^T \mathbf{n}_2 = r^2 + \lambda^2 \mathbf{v}_2^T \mathbf{v}_2 + 2\lambda \mathbf{v}_2^T \mathbf{n}_1, \quad \Rightarrow \lambda = -2\mathbf{v}_2^T \mathbf{n}_1 / \mathbf{v}_2^T \mathbf{v}_2. \quad (15)$$

The outgoing refracted ray is given by $\mathbf{v}_3 = \mu \mathbf{v}_2 + b_3 \mathbf{n}_2$, for some b_3. Note that the symmetry of sphere results in $\mathbf{v}_3^T \mathbf{n}_2 = -\mathbf{v}_1^T \mathbf{n}_1$ and $\mathbf{v}_2^T \mathbf{n}_2 = -\mathbf{v}_2^T \mathbf{n}_1$. Using these constraints, b_3 is obtained as $b_3 = (-\mathbf{v}_1^T \mathbf{n}_1 - \mu \mathbf{v}_2^T \mathbf{n}_1)/r^2$. Finally, the outgoing refracted ray $\mathbf{v}_3$ should pass through the scene point $\mathbf{p} = [u, v]^T$. Thus, $\mathbf{v}_3 \times (\mathbf{p} - \mathbf{n}_2) = 0$. By substituting all the terms, we get

$$0 = \mathbf{v}_3 \times (\mathbf{p} - \mathbf{n}_2) \quad \Rightarrow 0 = K_1(x, y) + K_2(x, y)\sqrt{A} + K_3(x, y)A^{3/2}, \quad (16)$$

where $A = d^2 \mu^2 r^2 - d^2 x^2 - 2d\mu^2 r^2 y + \mu^2 r^4$, and K_1, K_2 and K_3 are polynomials in x and y (provided in the supplementary materials with Matlab code). After

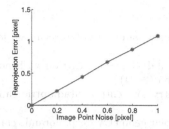 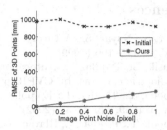

Fig. 8. Bundle adjustment simulations using $M = 4$ refractive spheres and $N = 100$ 3D points for different image noise levels. (Left) Reprojection error. (Right) RMSE of reconstructed 3D points.

removing the square root terms, substituting $x^2 = r^2 - y^2$ and simplifying, we finally obtain a 10th degree equation in y.

Figure 7 shows an example of solving the FP equation for refractive sphere. In general, when the 3D point is not on the axis, only 8 out of 10 solutions are real. Constraining $y \geq r^2/d$ further reduces to 4 solutions and the correct solution is found by testing the Snell's law for each of them. Figure 8 demonstrates that the FP equation can be used in a bundle adjustment algorithm for sparse 3D reconstruction using refractive spheres, similar to catadioptric systems.

6   Discussions and Conclusions

We believe that our paper advances the field of catadioptric imaging both theoretically and practically. Theoretically, we have derived analytical equations of forward projection for a broad class of non-central catadioptric cameras and have shown existence of quartic epipolar curves for spherical-mirror based catadioptric systems. We hope that our work will lead to further geometric analysis of non-central catadioptric cameras for mirror defocus, epipolar geometry, and wide-angle sparse as well as dense 3D reconstruction. Practically, the analytical FP and Jacobian computation significantly reduce the bundle adjustment run time. Thus, the computational complexity of using a non-central model becomes similar to that of a central approximation. The FP equation may be useful for reducing the search space in dense stereo matching and for auto-calibration via projection of scene features such as lines. We have also shown sparse 3D reconstruction using a dioptric non-central camera with refractive spheres, by deriving its forward projection equation. Unlike a catadioptric system, the camera is not visible in the captured image for a refractive setup. This could be a benefit in certain wide-angle applications, replacing expensive fish-eye lenses.

Acknowledgments. We thank the anonymous reviewers for their feedback and Peter Sturm for referring us to [19]. We also thank Jay Thornton, Keisuke Kojima, John Barnwell, and Haruhisa Okuda, Mitsubishi Electric, Japan, for their help and support.

References

1. Baker, S., Nayar, S.: A theory of single-viewpoint catadioptric image formation. IJCV 35, 175–196 (1999)
2. Micusik, B., Pajdla, T.: Autocalibration and 3D reconstruction with non-central catadioptric cameras. In: CVPR, pp. 58–65 (2004)
3. Svoboda, T., Pajdla, T.: Epipolar geometry for central catadioptric cameras. In: IJCV, vol. 49, pp. 23–37 (2002)
4. Svoboda, T., Pajdla, T., Hlavac, V.: Epipolar geometry for panoramic cameras. In: Burkhardt, H.-J., Neumann, B. (eds.) ECCV 1998. LNCS, vol. 1406, pp. 218–231. Springer, Heidelberg (1998)
5. Geyer, C., Daniilidis, K.: Properties of the catadioptric fundamental matrix. In: Heyden, A., Sparr, G., Nielsen, M., Johansen, P. (eds.) ECCV 2002. LNCS, vol. 2351, pp. 140–154. Springer, Heidelberg (2002)
6. Geyer, C., Daniilidis, K.: A unifying theory of central panoramic systems and practical implications. In: Vernon, D. (ed.) ECCV 2000. LNCS, vol. 1843, pp. 159–179. Springer, Heidelberg (2000)
7. Sturm, P., Barreto, J.P.: General imaging geometry for central catadioptric cameras. In: Forsyth, D., Torr, P., Zisserman, A. (eds.) ECCV 2008, Part IV. LNCS, vol. 5305, pp. 609–622. Springer, Heidelberg (2008)
8. Pless, R.: Using many cameras as one. In: CVPR, pp. 587–594 (2003)
9. Rademacher, P., Bishop, G.: Multiple-center-of-projection images. In: SIGGRAPH, pp. 199–206 (1998)
10. Yagi, Y., Kawato, S.: Panoramic scene analysis with conic projection. In: Proc. IEEE Int'l Workshop on Intelligent Robots and Systems, pp. 181–187 (1990)
11. Spacek, L.: Coaxial omnidirectional stereopsis. In: Pajdla, T., Matas, J(G.) (eds.) ECCV 2004. LNCS, vol. 3024, pp. 354–365. Springer, Heidelberg (2004)
12. Gupta, R., Hartley, R.: Linear pushbroom cameras. PAMI 19, 963–975 (1997)
13. Pajdla, T.: Stereo with oblique cameras. IJCV 47, 161–170 (2002)
14. Geyer, C., Daniilidis, K.: Paracatadioptric camera calibration. PAMI 24, 687–695 (2002)
15. Yu, J., McMillan, L.: General linear cameras. In: Pajdla, T., Matas, J(G.) (eds.) ECCV 2004. LNCS, vol. 3022, pp. 14–27. Springer, Heidelberg (2004)
16. Zhang, Z.: On the epipolar geometry between two images with lens distortion. In: ICPR, vol. 1, pp. 407–411 (1996)
17. Micusik, B., Pajdla, T.: Structure from motion with wide circular field of view cameras. PAMI 28, 1135–1149 (2006)
18. Gonçalvez, N., Nogueira, A.C.: Projection through quadric mirrors made faster. In: OMNIVIS (2009)
19. Vandeportaele, B.: Contributions à la vision omnidirectionnelle: Étude, Conception et Étalonnage de capteurs pour lacquisition dimages et la modélisation 3D. PhD thesis, Institut National Polytechnique de Toulouse, France, in french (2006)
20. Hong, J., Tan, X., Pinette, B., Weiss, R., Riseman, E.: Image-based homing. In: ICRA, pp. 620–625 (1991)
21. Lanman, D., Crispell, D., Wachs, M., Taubin, G.: Spherical catadioptric arrays: Construction, multi-view geometry, and calibration. In: 3DPVT, pp. 81–88 (2006)
22. Ding, Y., Yu, J., Sturm, P.: Multi-perspective stereo matching and volumetric reconstruction. In: ICCV (2009)
23. Kojima, Y., Sagawa, R., Echigo, T., Yagi, Y.: Calibration and performance evaluation of omnidirectional sensor with compound spherical mirrors. In: OMNIVIS (2005)

24. Glaeser, G.: Reflections on spheres and cylinders of revolution. J. Geometry and Graphics 3, 121–139 (1999)
25. Garg, K., Nayar, S.K.: Vision and rain. IJCV 75, 3–27 (2007)
26. Swaminathan, R., Grossberg, M., Nayar, S.: Non-single viewpoint catadioptric cameras: Geometry and analysis. IJCV 66, 211–229 (2006)
27. Glassner, A.S. (ed.): An introduction to ray tracing. Academic Press Ltd, London (1989)

5D Motion Subspaces for Planar Motions

Roland Angst and Marc Pollefeys

Computer Vision and Geometry Lab, Department of Computer Science
ETH Zürich, Universitätstrasse 6, 8092 Zürich, Switzerland
{rangst,marc.pollefeys}@inf.ethz.ch
http://www.cvg.ethz.ch/

Abstract. In practice, rigid objects often move on a plane. The object
then rotates around a fixed axis and translates in a plane orthogonal
to this axis. For a concrete example, think of a car moving on a street.
Given multiple static affine cameras which observe such a rigidly moving object and track feature points located on this object, what can be
said about the resulting feature point trajectories in the camera views?
Are there any useful algebraic constraints hidden in the data? Is a 3D
reconstruction of the scene possible even if there are no feature point
correspondences between the different cameras? And if so, how many
points are sufficient? Does a closed-form solution to this shape from motion reconstruction problem exist?

This paper addresses these questions and thereby introduces the concept of 5 dimensional planar motion subspaces: the trajectory of a feature
point seen by any camera is restricted to lie in a 5D subspace. The constraints provided by these motion subspaces enable a closed-form solution for the reconstruction. The solution is based on multilinear analysis,
matrix and tensor factorizations. As a key insight, the paper shows that
already two points are sufficient to derive a closed-form solution. Hence,
even two cameras where each of them is just tracking one single point
can be handled. Promising results of a real data sequence act as a proof
of concept of the presented insights.

Keywords: 3D reconstruction, shape from motion, matrix and tensor factorizations, feature point trajectories, affine cameras, planar rigid motion.

1 Introduction and Related Work

Setting and Objective: Assume a rigid object is moving on a plane. The
object is therefore rotating around a fixed axis orthogonal to this plane and
translations are restricted to shifts inside that plane. Multiple stationary affine
cameras observe the moving object and track feature points located on this object. Computing correspondences across a wide baseline is a difficult problem in
itself and sometimes even impossible to solve (think of two cameras which point
at two completely different sides of the rigid object). In our setting, each camera
therefore tracks its own set of feature points. There are no feature point correspondences between the different cameras. The only available correspondence

K. Daniilidis, P. Maragos, N. Paragios (Eds.): ECCV 2010, Part III, LNCS 6313, pp. 144–157, 2010.

between the cameras is the *motion correspondence*: all the cameras observe the same planar motion. This paper presents a thorough analysis of the geometric and algebraic structure contained in 2D feature point trajectories in the camera image planes. A closed-form solution for the reconstruction problem based on the motion correspondence is derived.

Motivation: The reasons why an analysis of planar motions is important are at least three-fold. Firstly, rigid planar motions are an important special case of rigid motions. Vehicles moving on the street, traffic surveillance and analysis represent prominent examples. Even data from a camera rig mounted on a moving car behaves according to the above described setting: the camera rig can be considered as stationary and the whole surrounding world as a moving rigid object. Because the car is moving on the ground plane, the motion is restricted to a planar motion. Secondly, in a fully practical system, we have to deal with missing data, i.e. lost feature tracks. It is unreasonable to assume in a practical scenario having feature tracks over a long temporal sequence. Thus in practice, we are limited to trajectories over a short period of time. However, continuous motions over a short period can often be well approximated by a rotation and translation in a plane. The third reason is theoretical curiosity. What can be gained by using an affine rather than a projective camera model? What multiple-view insights are hidden in $2D$ feature trajectories obtained under the given setting? The elegance of a theoretical exact derivation of a closed-form solution under the given assumptions should not be despised either.

Main Contributions: A thorough theoretical analysis of the important special case of planar rigid motions observed by multiple stationary affine cameras is presented. Specifically, any feature point trajectory seen by any camera is restricted to a 5 dimensional subspace which is common amongst all the cameras. A general framework for planar motions is proposed. This framework together with the theoretical insights enables a reconstruction algorithm which provides a closed-form solution as long as the total number of tracked points is larger or equal than two. Hence, the two minimal cases of one single camera tracking two points or two cameras where each of them is tracking only one point can be handled by the algorithm. No correspondences between different camera views are required. Moreover, the algorithm fuses the data of all the cameras in order to compute a robust reconstruction.

Related Work: There is a long history in computer vision about factorizations for the structure from motion problem under affine cameras. Due to lack of space, the interested reader is also referred to references contained in the mentioned related work. The initial work by Tomasi and Kanade [1] about monocular rigid factorizations initiated many variations and extensions, such as deformable [2] and articulated objects [3,4]. The concept of motion subspaces has also widely been used for feature trajectory motion segmentation [5]. Factorization based approaches with a projective camera model have been proposed in [6]. Some methods have been suggested to handle missing data in the feature trajectories due to occlusions or outliers [7,8]. The monocular structure from planar motion problem has previously attracted some interest [9,10]. However, these approaches either resort to iterative solutions or require additional information, like e.g. the relative position of the plane of rotation w.r.t. the camera.

Extensions of the factorization approach to the case of multiple cameras observing the same scene have also been proposed, even though less numerous. Most of them [11,12] require feature point correspondences between the cameras to be known. Methods which deal with non-overlapping camera views are generally not based on factorization approaches (e.g. hand-eye-calibration [13]). However, a separate reconstruction for each camera is usually computed and thus strong assumption about the captured data are implicitly assumed. The classical factorization approach [1] has recently been extended to the multi-camera case [14]. This extensions considers the same setting, except the rigid object is assumed to move fully general in 3D space whereas we assume the object to move on a plane. This minor distinction has far reaching consequences. For example, we will see in Sec. 2 that this requires the object to rotate around at least 6 different axes of rotation, otherwise the 13 dimensional motion space is only spanned partially. The 13 dimensional factorization will thus fail miserably if applied to planar motions.

2   Rigid Planar Motions as Vectors in 5D Subspaces

This section presents how rigid planar motions can be embedded in linear subspaces. The general case of non-planar rigid motions has already been investigated [14]. In contrast to that work, where 13-dimensional subspaces were required, planar motions only ask for 5D subspaces.

Some notational conventions have to be defined first. The orthogonal projection matrix onto the column space of a matrix $\mathbf{A}$ is denoted as $\mathbb{P}_{\mathbf{A}}$. The projection matrix onto the orthogonal complement of the columns space of $\mathbf{A}$ is $\mathbb{P}_{\mathbf{A}}^{\perp} = \mathbf{I} - \mathbb{P}_{\mathbf{A}}$. A matrix whose columns span the orthogonal complement of the columns of matrix $\mathbf{A}$ is denoted as $\mathbf{A}_{\perp}$. Concatenation of multiple matrices indexed with a sub- or superscript i is represented with arrows. For example, $[\Downarrow_i \mathbf{A}_i]$ concatenates all the matrices $\mathbf{A}_i$ below each other, implicitly assuming that each of them consists of the same number of columns. The Matlab® standard indexing notation is used for the slicing operation (cutting out certain rows and columns of a matrix). Multiplication of a tensor $\mathcal{T}$ along its i-th mode with the matrix $\mathbf{A}$ is denoted as $\mathcal{T} \times_i \mathbf{A}$. The matrix which results by flattening a tensor along mode i is written as $\mathcal{T}_{(i)}$. We refer to [15] for an introductory text on multilinear algebra, tensor operations and decomposition.

The rotation around an axis $\mathbf{a}$ by an angle α can be expressed as a rotation matrix $\mathbf{R}_{\mathbf{a},\alpha} = \cos\alpha \mathbf{I}_3 + (1 - \cos\alpha)\mathbf{a}\mathbf{a}^T + \sin\alpha [\mathbf{a}]_{\times}$, where $[\mathbf{a}]_{\times}$ denotes the skew-symmetric cross-product matrix. Rotation matrices $\mathbf{R}_{\mathbf{a},\alpha}$ around a fixed axis $\mathbf{a}$ are thus restricted to a three dimensional subspace in nine dimensional Euclidean ambient space $\text{vec}(\mathbf{R}) = [\text{vec}(\mathbf{I}_3) \ \text{vec}(\mathbf{a}\mathbf{a}^T) \ \text{vec}([\mathbf{a}]_{\times})] (\cos\alpha \ 1 - \cos\alpha \ \sin\alpha)^T$ where $\text{vec}()$ vectorizes a matrix by stacking its columns below each other in a column vector. Let the columns of $\mathbf{V} \in \mathbb{R}^{3\times 2}$ denote an orthonormal basis for the orthogonal complement of the rotation axis $\mathbf{a}$, i.e. these columns span the plane orthogonal to the rotation axis. A rigid motion in this plane (i.e. the rotation is around the plane normal and the translations are restricted to shifts inside the plane) is then given by

$$
\begin{bmatrix} \mathbf{R}_{\mathbf{a},\alpha} & \mathbf{Vt} \\ \mathbf{0}_{1\times 3} & 1 \end{bmatrix} \Leftrightarrow \begin{pmatrix} \mathrm{vec}\,(\mathbf{R}_{\mathbf{a},\alpha}) \\ \mathrm{vec}\,(\mathbf{Vt}) \\ 1 \end{pmatrix} = \begin{bmatrix} \mathrm{vec}\,(\mathbf{I}_3) & \mathrm{vec}\,(\mathbf{aa}^T) & \mathrm{vec}\left([\mathbf{a}]_\times\right) & \mathbf{0}_{9\times 2} \\ \mathbf{0}_{3\times 1} & \mathbf{0}_{3\times 1} & \mathbf{0}_{3\times 1} & \mathbf{V} \\ 1 & 1 & 0 & \mathbf{0}_{1\times 2} \end{bmatrix} \begin{pmatrix} \cos\alpha \\ 1 - \cos\alpha \\ \sin\alpha \\ \mathbf{t} \end{pmatrix}, \quad (1)
$$

which shows that *any* rigid motion in this plane is restricted to a five dimensional subspace of 13-dimensional (or 16 if zero-entries are not disregarded) Euclidean space. Interestingly, by noting that the space of symmetric rank-1 matrices $\mathrm{vec}\,(\mathbf{aa}^T)$ considered as a linear space is 6 dimensional, we see that rotations around at least *six different axes of rotation* are required to span the full 13-dimensional space (the vector space of skew-symmetric matrices $[\mathbf{a}]_\times$ is 3 dimensional and thus rotations around 3 different axes already span this space).

3   Tensor Notation

Feature trajectories of points undergoing a planar rigid motion seen by different cameras can be arranged as a 3rd-order tensor. Such a representation clearly reveals the interplay between the three involved subspaces, namely the subspace of the cameras, the points, and the planar rigid motion. The structure (homogeneous coordinates of the N feature points) is given by $\mathbf{S} \in \mathbb{R}^{4\times N}$, the K affine cameras (each of them consisting of two camera axes) are described by $\mathbf{P} \in \mathbb{R}^{2K\times 4}$ and the motion over F frames will be described by the motion matrix $\mathbf{M} \in \mathbb{R}^{F\times 5}$. The projection matrix of camera k is denoted as $\mathbf{P}^k \in \mathbb{R}^{2\times 4}$, the points tracked by this camera as $\mathbf{S}^k \in \mathbb{R}^{4\times N_k}$. The combined camera matrix is thus $\mathbf{P} = [\Downarrow_k \mathbf{P}^k]$, and the combined point matrix $\mathbf{S} = [\Rightarrow_k \mathbf{S}^k]$. The axis of rotation is denoted with the unit vector $\mathbf{a}$ and the two columns of $\mathbf{V} \in \mathbb{R}^{3\times 2}$ are an orthonormal basis for the space orthogonal to the rotation axis. The image coordinate $\mathcal{W}_{[k,f,n]}$ of feature point n, at frame f, seen by camera axis k is thus

$$
\mathcal{W}_{[k,f,n]} = \mathbf{P}_{[k,:]} \begin{bmatrix} \mathbf{R}_{\mathbf{a},\alpha_f} & \mathbf{Vt}_f \\ \mathbf{0}_{1\times 3} & 1 \end{bmatrix} \mathbf{S}_{[:,n]} = \mathrm{vec}\left(\begin{bmatrix} \mathbf{R}_{\mathbf{a},\alpha_f} & \mathbf{Vt}_f \\ \mathbf{0}_{1\times 3} & 1 \end{bmatrix} \right)^T \left[\mathbf{S}_{[:,n]}^T \otimes \mathbf{P}_{[k,:]}\right]^T, \quad (2)
$$

where the Kronecker product property $\mathrm{vec}\,(\mathbf{AXB}) = \left[\mathbf{B}^T \otimes \mathbf{A}\right]\mathrm{vec}\,(\mathbf{X})$ has been used in the second step. The values $\mathcal{W}_{[k,f,n]}$ are interpreted as a third order tensor. In contrast to [14], planar rigid motions are restricted to a five rather than a 13-dimensional space (as we have seen in Sec. 2). Thus, the core tensor $\mathcal{C} \in \mathbb{R}^{5\times 4\times 4}$, which captures the interactions between the three subspaces, becomes in its flattened representation along the temporal mode

$$
\mathcal{C}_{(f)} = \begin{bmatrix} \mathrm{vec}\,(\mathbf{I}_3)^T & \mathbf{0}_{1\times 3} & 1 \\ \mathrm{vec}\,(\mathbf{aa}^T)^T & \mathbf{0}_{1\times 3} & 1 \\ \mathrm{vec}\,([\mathbf{a}]_\times)^T & \mathbf{0}_{1\times 3} & 0 \\ \mathbf{0}_{2\times 9} & \mathbf{V}^T & \mathbf{0}_{2\times 1} \end{bmatrix} \begin{bmatrix} \mathbf{I}_3 \otimes [\mathbf{I}_3\ \mathbf{0}_{3\times 1}] & \mathbf{0}_{9\times 4} \\ \mathbf{0}_{4\times 12} & \mathbf{I}_4 \end{bmatrix} \in \mathbb{R}^{5\times 16} \quad (3)
$$

and the data tensor is described as a Tucker tensor [15] decomposition[1] $\mathcal{W} = \mathcal{C} \times_k \mathbf{P} \times_f \mathbf{M} \times_n \mathbf{S}^T \in \mathbb{R}^{F \times 2K \times N}$. These equations can be derived by arranging the values of Eq. (2) in matrix form $\mathbf{W} = [\Downarrow_f \Rightarrow_{k,n} \mathcal{W}_{[f,k,n]}]$, plugging in Eq. (1) for the planar rigid motions, using Eq. (3) to properly combine the rigid motion matrix with the Kronecker product of the points and camera matrices, and defining the motion matrix as

$$\mathbf{M} = [\Downarrow_f (\cos \alpha_f, (1 - \cos \alpha_f), \sin \alpha_f, \mathbf{t}_f^T)]. \tag{4}$$

The resulting matrix is exactly the same as the data tensor flattened along the temporal mode $\mathbf{W} = \mathcal{W}_{(f)} = \mathbf{M}\mathcal{C}_{(f)} [\mathbf{S} \otimes \mathbf{P}^T]$. The interested reader is referred to related work [14,15] for more details on tensorial representations.

4   Ambiguities

Let $\mathbf{Q}_P = \begin{bmatrix} \mathbf{R}_P & \mathbf{t}_P \\ \mathbf{0}_{1 \times 3} & 1 \end{bmatrix}$ and $\mathbf{Q}_S = \begin{bmatrix} \mathbf{R}_S & \mathbf{t}_S \\ \mathbf{0}_{1 \times 3} & 1 \end{bmatrix}$ denote two affine transformations of the global camera reference frame and the global point reference frame, respectively. The factorization is obviously ambiguous

$$\mathcal{W}_{[k,f,n]} = \mathbf{P}_{[k,:]} \mathbf{Q}_P^{-1} \mathbf{Q}_P \begin{bmatrix} \mathbf{R}_{\mathbf{a}, \alpha_f} & \mathbf{V} \mathbf{t}_f \\ \mathbf{0}_{1 \times 3} & 1 \end{bmatrix} \mathbf{Q}_S \mathbf{Q}_S^{-1} \mathbf{S}_{[:,n]}. \tag{5}$$

In tensor notation, this equation looks like

$$\mathcal{W} = \left(\mathcal{C} \times_k \mathbf{Q}_P \times_f \mathbf{Q}_M \times_n \mathbf{Q}_S^T \right) \times_k \mathbf{P} \mathbf{Q}_P^{-1} \times_f \mathbf{M} \mathbf{Q}_M^{-1} \times_n \left(\mathbf{S}^T \mathbf{Q}_S^{-T} \right), \tag{6}$$

where transformations $\mathbf{Q}_P$ and $\mathbf{Q}_S$ which are restricted to similarity transformations inside the plane of motion can be compensated by a corresponding transformation $\mathbf{Q}_M$ of the reference frame of the motion. In mathematical terms, the overconstrained system $\mathcal{C} \times_k \mathbf{Q}_P \times_f \mathbf{Q}_M \times_n \mathbf{Q}_S^T = \mathcal{C}$ can be solved exactly for $\mathbf{Q}_M$, i.e. $\mathbf{Q}_M = \mathcal{C}_{(f)} [\mathbf{Q}_S^{-1} \otimes \mathbf{Q}_P^{-T}] \mathcal{C}_{(f)}^*$ where $\mathbf{A}^*$ denotes the Moore-Penrose pseudo-inverse. Since the first three columns of $\mathbf{M}\mathbf{Q}_M^{-1}$ should still lead to proper rotations, the scaling factor of the similarity transformations of the cameras and points must cancel each other. A reconstruction inside the plane of rotation is thus unique up to two similarity transformations with reciprocal scaling (one for the cameras and one for the points). Similarity transformations with reciprocal scalings seem to be the only transformations which allow a solution to $\mathcal{C} \times_k \mathbf{Q}_P \times_f \mathbf{Q}_M \times_n \mathbf{Q}_S^T = \mathcal{C}$. This fact will be important later on in our algorithm: Given a reconstruction inside the plane of rotation with proper algebraic structure, we are guaranteed that such a reconstruction is unique up to a similarity transformation.

Transformations of the points or cameras outside the plane of rotation can not be compensated by a transformation of the motion. A out-of-plane transformation of the cameras has to be compensated directly by a suitable transformation

---

[1] $\times_k$, $\times_f$, and $\times_n$ indicate the mode-i product along the mode corresponding to the camera matrix, the motion matrix, and the point matrix, respectively.

of the points. Let $\mathbf{Z}_{\mathbf{a},\lambda} = \begin{bmatrix} \mathbf{V} & \mathbf{a} \end{bmatrix} \mathrm{diag}\,(\mathbf{I}_2, \lambda) \begin{bmatrix} \mathbf{V} & \mathbf{a} \end{bmatrix}^T$ be a scaling along the rotation axis, $\mathbf{R}$ an arbitrary rotation matrix, and $\mathbf{t}_{\|} = \mathbf{a}\beta$ a translation along the rotation axis. With the camera and point transformations

$$\mathbf{Q}_P = \begin{bmatrix} \mathbf{R}\mathbf{Z}_{\mathbf{a},\lambda} & -\mathbf{R}\mathbf{Z}_{\mathbf{a},\lambda}\mathbf{t}_{\|} \\ \mathbf{0}_{1\times 3} & 1 \end{bmatrix} \quad \text{and} \quad \mathbf{Q}_S = \begin{bmatrix} \mathbf{Z}_{\mathbf{a},\lambda}^{-1}\mathbf{R}^T & \mathbf{t}_{\|} \\ \mathbf{0}_{1\times 3} & 1 \end{bmatrix} \tag{7}$$

it can be shown that $\mathcal{C}_{\mathbf{a},\mathbf{V}} \times_k \mathbf{Q}_P \times_n \mathbf{Q}^T = \mathcal{C}_{\mathbf{Ra},\mathbf{RV}}$ where $\mathcal{C}_{\mathbf{a},\mathbf{V}}$ denotes the core tensor with rotation axis $\mathbf{a}$ and orthogonal complement $\mathbf{V}$. Note that neither the scaling nor the translation along the rotation axis influences the core tensor or the motion matrix. Hence, there is a scaling and translation ambiguity along the axis of rotation.

In the problem we are targeting, there are no point correspondences between different cameras. In this situation there is a *per camera* scale and translation ambiguity along the rotation axis. There is still only one global out-of-plane rotation ambiguity: the transformation of the rotation plane is still linked to the other cameras through the commonly observed planar motion, even in the presence of missing correspondences. Fortunately, as we will see later, the scale ambiguity along the rotation axis can be resolved by using orthogonality and equality of norm constraints on the camera axes. The translation ambiguities along the rotation axis however can not be resolved without correspondences between different camera views. Nevertheless, by registering the centroids of the points observed by each camera to the same height along the rotation axis, a solution close to the ground truth can usually be recovered.

5   Closed-Form Solution

In contrast to a rank-13 motion subspace, one camera is sufficient in order to span the complete 5 dimensional motion subspace of a planar motion. This leads to the following idea: Intuitively, a separate reconstruction can be made for each camera. These separate reconstructions are unique up to the ambiguities mentioned previously. This especially means that the reconstruction of each camera restricted to (or projected onto) the plane of rotation is a *valid* similarity reconstruction, i.e. the individual reconstructions are expressed in varying coordinate reference frames which, however, only differ from each other by similarity transformations. Using knowledge from the 5D-motion subspace, these reconstructions can then be aligned in a consistent world reference frame. If the additional assumption is made that the two camera axes of each camera are orthogonal and have equal norm (the norm can vary between different cameras) then the coordinate frame of the reconstruction can be upgraded to a similarity frame in all three dimensions. We thus end up with a consistent 3D-reconstruction.

There is a major drawback of the above algorithmic sketch. The fact that all the cameras observe the very same rigid motion is only used in the final step to align all the individual reconstructions. It is a desirable property that the information from all the cameras should be fused right at the first stage of the algorithm in order to get a more robust reconstruction. Furthermore, in order to

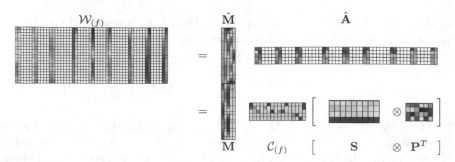

Fig. 1. Visual representation of the rank-5 factorization. Missing data entries due to missing correspondences between different cameras are depicted transparently.

compute the initial reconstruction of a camera, this camera needs to track at least two points. If the camera tracks only one feature point, a reconstruction based solely on this camera is *not* possible: at least two points are necessary to span the 5D-motion subspace. The algorithm which is presented in the upcoming sections on the other hand does not suffer from these shortcomings. The algorithm fuses the information from all the cameras right at the first stage and works even when each camera tracks only one single point. Last but not least, the algorithm provides a closed-form solution.

5.1 Rank-5 Factorization

In a similar spirit to [14], we can fuse the data from all the cameras in order to compute a consistent estimate of the motion matrix. The data tensor $\mathcal{W}^k \in \mathbb{R}^{F \times 2 \times N_k}$ of each camera is flattened along the temporal mode and the resulting matrices $\mathbf{W}^k = \mathcal{W}^k_{(f)} = \mathbf{M}\mathcal{C}_{(f)}\mathbf{S}^k \otimes \mathbf{P}^{k^T}$ are concatenated column-wise in a combined data matrix $\mathbf{W} = [\Rightarrow_k \mathbf{W}^k]$. A rank-5 factorization (e.g. with singular value decomposition) of this combined data matrix reveals the correct column span $\text{span}(\mathbf{M}) = \text{span}(\hat{\mathbf{M}})$ of the motion matrix

$$\mathbf{W} = \hat{\mathbf{M}}\hat{\mathbf{A}} = \underbrace{[\Downarrow_f \cos\alpha_f \ 1 - \cos\alpha_f \ \sin\alpha_f \ t_{f,1} \ t_{f,2}]}_{=\hat{\mathbf{M}}\mathbf{Q}} \mathcal{C}_{(f)} \underbrace{[\Rightarrow_k \mathbf{S}^k \otimes \mathbf{P}^{k^T}]}_{=\mathbf{Q}^{-1}\hat{\mathbf{A}}}, \quad (8)$$

where we have introduced the corrective transformation $\mathbf{Q} \in \mathbb{R}^{5 \times 5}$ in order to establish the correct algebraic structure. This factorization separates the temporally varying component (the motion) from temporally static component (the points and the cameras). The factorization is possible since all the cameras share the same temporally varying component as all of them observe the same rigid motion. If all the cameras only track two points in total, the combined data matrix $\mathbf{W}$ will then only consist of four columns and thus a rank-5 factorization is obviously impossible. Luckily, we know that the first two columns of the motion matrix in Eq. (4) should sum to the constant one vector. Hence, only a rank 4 factorization of the data matrix $\mathbf{W}$ is performed, the resulting motion matrix is augmented with the constant one vector $\hat{\mathbf{M}} \leftarrow [\hat{\mathbf{M}}, \mathbf{1}_{F \times 1}]$ and the second factor is adapted correspondingly $\hat{\mathbf{A}} \leftarrow [\hat{\mathbf{A}}^T, \mathbf{0}_{2N \times 1}]^T$. The rest of the algorithm remains the same.

The corrective transformation is computed in a piecewise (or stratified) way. Specifically, the corrective transformation is split into three separate transformations $\mathbf{Q} = \mathbf{Q}_{trig} \mathbf{Q}_{orient}^{-1} \mathbf{Q}_{transl}^{-1}$ where the transformation $\mathbf{Q}_{trig}$ establishes the correct trigonometric structure on the first three columns of the motion matrix, $\mathbf{Q}_{orient}$ aligns the orientations of the cameras in a consistent similarity reference frame, and $\mathbf{Q}_{transl}$ is related to correctly translate the reconstruction. The individual steps are described in detail in the next sections.

5.2   Trigonometric Structure

The first three columns of $\mathbf{Q} = [\mathbf{q}_1, \mathbf{q}_2, \mathbf{q}_3, \mathbf{q}_4, \mathbf{q}_5]$ can be solved for in the following way: since $\hat{\mathbf{M}}_{[f,:]} \mathbf{q}_i \mathbf{q}_i^T \hat{\mathbf{M}}_{[f,:]}^T = \mathbf{M}_{[f,i]}{}^2$ we have

$$\hat{\mathbf{M}}_{[f,:]}((\mathbf{q}_1 + \mathbf{q}_2)(\mathbf{q}_1 + \mathbf{q}_2)^T)\hat{\mathbf{M}}_{[f,:]}^T = (\cos \alpha_f + (1 - \cos \alpha_f))^2 = 1 \qquad (9)$$

$$\hat{\mathbf{M}}_{[f,:]}(\mathbf{q}_1 \mathbf{q}_1^T + \mathbf{q}_3 \mathbf{q}_3^T)\hat{\mathbf{M}}_{[f,:]}^T = \cos^2 \alpha_f + \sin^2 \alpha_f = 1. \qquad (10)$$

These observations lead to F constraints on symmetric rank-2 matrix $\mathbf{q}_1 \mathbf{q}_1^T + \mathbf{q}_3 \mathbf{q}_3^T$, symmetric rank-1 matrix $(\mathbf{q}_1 + \mathbf{q}_2)(\mathbf{q}_1 + \mathbf{q}_2)^T$, or symmetric rank-3 matrix $b(\mathbf{q}_1 \mathbf{q}_1^T + \mathbf{q}_3 \mathbf{q}_3^T) + (1 - b)(\mathbf{q}_1 + \mathbf{q}_2)(\mathbf{q}_1 + \mathbf{q}_2)^T$ with $b \in \mathbb{R}$:

$$1 = \hat{\mathbf{M}}_{[f,:]}((\mathbf{q}_1 + \mathbf{q}_2)(\mathbf{q}_1 + \mathbf{q}_2)^T)\hat{\mathbf{M}}_{[f,:]}^T = \hat{\mathbf{M}}_{[f,:]}(\mathbf{q}_1 \mathbf{q}_1^T + \mathbf{q}_3 \mathbf{q}_3^T)\hat{\mathbf{M}}_{[f,:]}^T \qquad (11)$$

$$= \hat{\mathbf{M}}_{[f,:]}(b(\mathbf{q}_1 \mathbf{q}_1^T + \mathbf{q}_3 \mathbf{q}_3^T) + (1 - b)(\mathbf{q}_1 \mathbf{q}_1^T + \mathbf{q}_2 \mathbf{q}_2^T))\hat{\mathbf{M}}_{[f,:]}^T \qquad (12)$$

These F equations are linear in the unknown symmetric matrices and result in a one dimensional solution space (since there is a valid solution for any $b \in \mathbb{R}$). [16] shows how to extract the solution vectors $\mathbf{q}_1$, $\mathbf{q}_2$, and $\mathbf{q}_3$ from this one dimensional solution space. Once this is done, the corrective transformation $\mathbf{Q}_{trig} = [\mathbf{q}_1 \ \mathbf{q}_2 \ \mathbf{q}_3 \ [\mathbf{q}_1 \ \mathbf{q}_2 \ \mathbf{q}_3]_\perp]$ is applied to the first factor $\hat{\mathbf{M}} \mathbf{Q}_{trig}$ which establishes the correct trigonometric structure in the first three columns. The inverse of this transformation is applied to the second factor $\tilde{\mathbf{A}} = \mathbf{Q}_{trig}^{-1} \hat{\mathbf{A}}$. Note that the structure of the first three columns of the motion matrix should not get modified anymore and hence any further corrective transformation must have upper block-diagonal structure with an identity matrix of dimension 3 in the upper left corner. The inverse of such an upper block-diagonal matrix has exactly the same non-zero pattern, i.e.

$$\mathbf{Q}_{transl} \mathbf{Q}_{orient} = \begin{bmatrix} \mathbf{I}_3 & \mathbf{Q}_{3 \times 2} \\ \mathbf{0}_{2 \times 3} & \mathbf{I}_2 \end{bmatrix} \begin{bmatrix} \mathbf{I}_3 & \mathbf{0}_{3 \times 2} \\ \mathbf{0}_{2 \times 3} & \mathbf{Q}_{2 \times 2} \end{bmatrix} = \begin{bmatrix} \mathbf{I}_3 & \mathbf{Q}_{3 \times 2} \\ \mathbf{0}_{2 \times 3} & \mathbf{Q}_{2 \times 2} \end{bmatrix}. \qquad (13)$$

5.3   Euclidean Camera Reference Frame

No more information can be extracted from the motion matrix and thus, we turn our attention to the second factor $\tilde{\mathbf{A}}$ which after applying a proper transformation should have the following algebraic form

$$\mathbf{A} = \begin{bmatrix} \mathbf{I}_3 & \mathbf{Q}_{3\times 2} \\ \mathbf{0}_{2\times 3} & \mathbf{Q}_{2\times 2} \end{bmatrix} \tilde{\mathbf{A}} = \mathcal{C}_{(f)} \left[\Rightarrow_k \mathbf{S}^k \otimes \mathbf{P}^{k^T} \right]. \tag{14}$$

This is a particularly tricky instance of a bilinear system of equations in $\mathbf{Q}_{3\times 2}$, $\mathbf{Q}_{2\times 2}$, $\mathbf{S}^k$, and $\mathbf{P}^k$. Based on our experiences, even algebraic computer software does not succeed in finding a closed-form solution. Nevertheless, we succeeded in deriving manually a solution using geometric intuition and reasoning.

Projection onto Plane of Rotation. Eq. (14) together with the known matrix $\mathcal{C}_{(f)}$ in Eq. (3) tells that $\tilde{\mathbf{A}}_{[4:5,:]} = \left[\Rightarrow_k \mathbf{1}_{1\times N_k} \otimes \left(\mathbf{P}^k_{[:,1:3]} \mathbf{V} \mathbf{Q}_{2\times 2}^{-T} \right)^T \right]$, which means that the columns of $\tilde{\mathbf{A}}_{[4:5,:]}$ contain the coordinates (w.r.t. the basis $\mathbf{V}$) of the projection of the rows of the camera matrices onto the plane of rotation. These coordinates however have been distorted with a common, but unknown transformation $\mathbf{Q}_{2\times 2}$. This observation motivates the fact to restrict the reconstruction first to the plane of rotation. Such a step requires a projection of the available data onto the plane of rotation. [16] shows that this can be done by subtracting the second from the first row and keeping the third row of Eq. (14).

$$\begin{bmatrix} 1 & -1 & 0 \\ 0 & 0 & 1 \end{bmatrix} \tilde{\mathbf{A}}_{[1:3,:]} + \underbrace{\begin{bmatrix} 1 & -1 & 0 \\ 0 & 0 & 1 \end{bmatrix} \mathbf{Q}_{3\times 2}}_{=\mathbf{T}_{2\times 2}} \tilde{\mathbf{A}}_{[4:5,:]} \tag{15}$$

$$= \begin{bmatrix} \mathrm{vec}\,(\mathbb{P}_{\mathbf{V}})^T \\ \mathrm{vec}\,([\mathbf{a}]_\times)^T \end{bmatrix} \left[\Rightarrow_k \left(\mathbb{P}_{\mathbf{V}} \mathbf{S}^k_{[1:3,:]} \right) \otimes \left(\mathbb{P}_{\mathbf{V}} \mathbf{P}^k_{[:,1:3]}{}^T \right) \right] \tag{16}$$

$$= \begin{bmatrix} \mathrm{vec}\,(\mathbb{P}_{\mathbf{V}})^T \\ \mathrm{vec}\,([\mathbf{a}]_\times)^T \end{bmatrix} \left[\Rightarrow_k \left(\mathbb{P}_{\mathbf{V}} \mathbf{S}^k_{[1:3,:]} \right) \otimes (\mathbf{V} \mathbf{Q}_{2\times 2}) \left(\mathbf{Q}_{2\times 2}^{-1} \mathbf{V}^T \mathbf{P}^k_{[:,1:3]}{}^T \right) \right]. \tag{17}$$

In the last step we have used $\mathbb{P}_{\mathbf{V}} = \mathbf{V} \mathbf{Q}_{2\times 2} \mathbf{Q}_{2\times 2}^{-1} \mathbf{V}^T$ and the parenthesis in the last term should stress out that for for all the cameras the term $\mathbf{Q}_{2\times 2}^{-1} \mathbf{V}^T \mathbf{P}^k_{[:,1:3]}{}^T$ can be read off from $\tilde{\mathbf{A}}_{[4:5,:]}$. The unknowns of this bilinear equation are the points and the 2-by-2 transformations $\mathbf{T}_{2\times 2}$ and $\mathbf{Q}_{2\times 2}$.

Per-Camera Reconstruction in the Plane of Rotation. Eq. (17) describes a reconstruction problem in a plane which is still bilinear. As with any rigid reconstruction, there are several gauge freedoms. Specifically, the origin and the orientation of the reference frame can be chosen arbitrarily[2]. In the planar case,

---

[2] The first three columns of the motion matrix have already been fixed and the translation of the cameras has been lost by the projection step. Thus, there is only one planar similarity transformation left from the two mentioned in Sec. 4.

this means a 2D offset and the orientation of one 2D vector can be chosen freely. In the following we will make use of the gauge freedoms in order to render this bilinear problem in multiple sequential linear problems. The reconstruction procedure described in the upcoming paragraphs could be applied to one single camera. This would provide $\mathbf{T}_{2\times2}$ and $\mathbf{Q}_{2\times2}$ which could then be used to solve for the points in the remaining cameras. However, increased robustness can be achieved by solving the sequential linear problems for each camera separately and aligning the results in a final step in a consistent coordinate frame. For each camera, the gauge freedoms will be fixed in a different way which enables the computation of a reconstruction for each camera. The reference frames of the reconstructions then differ only by similarity transformations. This fact will be used in the next section in order to register all the reconstructions in a globally consistent reference frame.

In single camera rigid factorizations, the translational gauge freedoms are usually chosen such that the centroid of the points matches the origin of the coordinate system, i.e. $\frac{1}{N}\mathbf{S}\mathbf{1}_{N\times1} = \mathbf{0}$. We will make the same choice $\frac{1}{N_k}\mathbf{S}^k\mathbf{1}_{N_k\times1} = \mathbf{0}$ on a per-camera basis. Let $\tilde{\mathbf{A}}^k$ denote the columns of $\tilde{\mathbf{A}}$ corresponding to camera k. By closer inspection of Eq. (17) and with the Kronecker product property $[\mathbf{AB}] \otimes [\mathbf{CD}] = [\mathbf{A} \otimes \mathbf{C}][\mathbf{B} \otimes \mathbf{D}]$ we get

$$\left[\begin{bmatrix}1 & -1 & 0 \\ 0 & 0 & 1\end{bmatrix}\tilde{\mathbf{A}}^k_{[1:3,:]} + \mathbf{T}_{2\times2}\tilde{\mathbf{A}}^k_{[4:5,:]}\right]\left[\frac{1}{N_k}\mathbf{1}_{N_k\times1} \otimes \mathbf{I}_2\right]$$

$$= \begin{bmatrix}\text{vec}\,(\mathbb{P}_{\mathbf{V}})^T \\ \text{vec}\,([\mathbf{a}]_\times)^T\end{bmatrix}\left(\mathbb{P}_{\mathbf{V}}\mathbf{S}^k_{[1:3,:]}\frac{1}{N_k}\mathbf{1}_{N_k\times1}\right) \otimes \left(\mathbb{P}_{\mathbf{V}}\mathbf{P}^k_{[:,1:3]}{}^T\right) = \mathbf{0}_{2\times2}. \quad (18)$$

The last equation followed since the centroid has been chosen as the origin. The above linear system consists of four linearly independent equations which can readily be solved for the four unknowns in $\mathbf{T}_{2\times2}$.

The remaining two gauge freedoms are due to the arbitrary choice of the orientation of the coordinate frame inside the plane of rotation. These gauge freedoms can be chosen s.t. the first row $(1\ 0)\,\mathbf{P}^k_{[:,1:3]}\mathbf{V}$ of the kth camera matrix equals the known row $(1\ 0)\,\mathbf{P}^k_{[:,1:3]}\mathbf{V}\mathbf{Q}^{-T}_{2\times2}$. Such a choice poses two constraints on $\mathbf{Q}_{2\times2}$

$$(1\ 0)\,\mathbf{P}^k_{[:,1:3]}\mathbf{V} = (1\ 0)\left(\mathbf{P}^k_{[:,1:3]}\mathbf{V}\mathbf{Q}^{-T}_{2\times2}\right) = (1\ 0)\left(\mathbf{P}^k_{[:,1:3]}\mathbf{V}\mathbf{Q}^{-T}_{2\times2}\right)\mathbf{Q}^T_{2\times2}. \quad (19)$$

Knowing $\mathbf{T}_{2\times2}$ as well as the first row of $\mathbf{P}^k_{[:,1:3]}\mathbf{V}$ implies that the remaining unknowns in every second column of $\tilde{\mathbf{A}}^k$ (i.e. the columns which depend on the first row) are only the points. This results in $2N_k$ linear equations in the $2N_k$ unknowns of the projected point coordinates $\mathbb{P}_{\mathbf{V}}\mathbf{S}^k_{[1:3,:]}$. After solving this system, only the entries of $\mathbf{Q}_{2\times2}$ are not yet known. The two linear constraints of Eq. (19) enable a reparameterization with only two parameters $\mathbf{Q}_{2\times2} = \mathbf{Q}_0 + \lambda_1\mathbf{Q}_1 + \lambda_2\mathbf{Q}_2$. Inserting this parameterization into Eq. (17) and considering only every other second column (i.e. the columns corresponding to the second row of the camera) leads to a linear system in λ_1 and λ_2 with $2N_k$ linear equations. The linear least squares solution provides the values for λ_1 and λ_2.

The above procedure works fine as long as every camera tracks at least two points. Otherwise the computation of λ_1 and λ_2 in the final step will fail because of our choice to set the mean to the origin. The coordinates of the single point are then equal to the zero vector and hence, this single point does not provide any constraints on the two unknowns. In order to avoid this problem we use the following trick: instead of choosing the origin as the mean of the points which are tracked by the camera currently under investigation, the origin is rather fixed at the mean of the points of *another* camera. Such a choice is perfectly fine as the origin can be chosen arbitrarily. The computation of $\mathbf{T}_{2\times2}$ for camera k is therefore based on the data of another camera $k' \neq k$. This clever trick allows to compute a reconstruction even for cameras which only track one single point.

Registration in a Common Frame Inside the Plane of Motion. After the previous per-camera reconstruction a camera matrix is known for each camera. Let $\tilde{\mathbf{P}}^k$ denotes its first three columns whose projection onto the plane of rotation is correct up to a registration with a 2-by-2 scaled rotation matrix $\lambda_k \mathbf{R}_k$. On the other hand, we also know the projections $\mathbf{P}^k_{[:,1:3]}\mathbf{V}\mathbf{Q}_{2\times2}^{-T}$ of the camera matrices onto the plane of rotation up to an unknown distortion transformation $\mathbf{Q}_{2\times2}$ which is the same for all the cameras. This implies $\tilde{\mathbf{P}}^k\mathbf{V}\mathbf{R}_k\lambda_k = \mathbf{P}^k_{[:,1:3]}\mathbf{V}$ and thus

$$\tilde{\mathbf{P}}^k\mathbf{V}\mathbf{V}^T\tilde{\mathbf{P}}^{k,T}\lambda_k^2 = \left(\mathbf{P}^k_{[:,1:3]}\mathbf{V}\mathbf{Q}_{2\times2}^{-T}\right)\mathbf{Q}_{2\times2}^T\mathbf{Q}_{2\times2}\left(\mathbf{Q}_{2\times2}^{-1}\mathbf{V}^T\mathbf{P}^k_{[:,1:3]}^T\right). \quad (20)$$

This is a linear system in the three unknowns of symmetric $\mathbf{Q}_{2\times2}^T\mathbf{Q}_{2\times2}$ and K scale factors λ_k^2 which is again solved in the least squares sense. Doing so provides a least squares estimate of the three unknowns of $\mathbf{Q}_{2\times2}^T\mathbf{Q}_{2\times2}$. An eigenvalue decomposition $\mathbf{E}\mathbf{\Lambda}\mathbf{E}^T = \mathbf{Q}_{2\times2}^T\mathbf{Q}_{2\times2}$ provides a mean to recover $\mathbf{Q}_{2\times2} = \mathbf{E}^T\mathbf{\Lambda}^{\frac{1}{2}}$ which allows to express the projections of the camera matrices $\mathbf{P}^k_{[:,1:3]}\mathbb{P}_{\mathbf{V}} = \left(\mathbf{P}^k_{[:,1:3]}\mathbf{V}\mathbf{Q}_{2\times2}^{-T}\right)\mathbf{Q}_{2\times2}^T\mathbf{V}^T$ onto the plane in one single similarity frame.

Orthogonality and Equality of Norm Constraints. As has been previously mentioned, the correct scaling along the rotation axis can only be recovered by using additional constraints, like the orthogonality and equal norm constraints on the two camera axes of a camera. These constraints will be used in the following to compute the remaining projection of the camera matrix onto the axis of rotation. Due to $\mathbf{P}^k_{[:,1:3]} = \mathbf{P}^k_{[:,1:3]}(\mathbb{P}_{\mathbf{V}} + \mathbb{P}_{\mathbf{a}})$ and $\mathbb{P}_{\mathbf{V}}\mathbb{P}_{\mathbf{a}} = 0$ we get $\lambda_k^2\mathbf{I}_2 = \mathbf{P}^k_{[:,1:3]}\mathbf{P}^k_{[:,1:3]}^T = \mathbf{P}^k_{[:,1:3]}\mathbb{P}_{\mathbf{V}}\mathbf{P}^k_{[:,1:3]}^T + \mathbf{P}^k_{[:,1:3]}\mathbb{P}_{\mathbf{a}}\mathbf{P}^k_{[:,1:3]}^T$.

Thanks to the previous registration step, the projections $\mathbf{P}^k_{[:,1:3]}\mathbb{P}_{\mathbf{V}}$ are known for all cameras. As $\mathbf{P}^k_{[:,1:3]}\mathbb{P}_{\mathbf{a}}\mathbf{P}^k_{[:,1:3]}^T = \mathbf{P}^k_{[:,1:3]}\mathbf{a}\mathbf{a}^T\mathbf{P}^k_{[:,1:3]}^T$ and replacing $\mathbf{P}^k_{[:,1:3]}\mathbf{a}$ by $\mathbf{w}^k$, the unknowns of the above equation become λ_k and the two components of the vector $\mathbf{w}^k$. This results in K independent 2nd-order polynomial system of equations with 3 independent equations in the three unknowns $\mathbf{w}^k$ and λ_k. Straight-forward algebraic manipulation will reveal the closed-form solution to this system (see [16] for details). Once $\mathbf{w}^k$ is recovered, the camera matrix is given by solving the linear system $\mathbf{P}^k_{[:,1:3]} [\mathbb{P}_{\mathbf{V}}, \mathbf{a}] = \left[\mathbf{P}^k_{[:,1:3]} \mathbb{P}_{\mathbf{V}}, \mathbf{w}^k \right]$. The solution of the polynomial equation is unique up to the sign. This means that there is a per-camera sign ambiguity along the axis of rotation. Note that this is not a shortcoming of our algorithm, but this ambiguity is rather inherent due to the planar motion setting. However, the qualitative orientations of the cameras w.r.t. the rotation axis are often known. For example, the cameras might be known to observe a motion on the ground plane. Then the axis of rotation should point upwards in the camera images, otherwise the camera is mounted upside-down. Using this additional assumption, the sign ambiguity can be resolved.

Using the orthogonality and equality of norm constraints, it is tempting to omit the registration step in the plane of rotation and to directly set up the system of equations

$$\lambda_k^2 \mathbf{I}_2 = \mathbf{P}^k_{[:,1:3]} \mathbf{P}^k_{[:,1:3]}{}^T = \mathbf{P}^k_{[:,1:3]} \mathbb{P}_{\mathbf{V}} \mathbf{P}^k_{[:,1:3]}{}^T + \mathbf{P}^k_{[:,1:3]} \mathbb{P}_{\mathbf{a}} \mathbf{P}^k_{[:,1:3]}{}^T \tag{21}$$

$$= \left(\mathbf{P}^k_{[:,1:3]} \mathbf{V} \mathbf{Q}_{2\times2}^{-T} \right) \mathbf{Q}_{2\times2}^T \mathbf{Q}_{2\times2} \left(\mathbf{Q}_{2\times2}^{-1} \mathbf{V}^T \mathbf{P}^k_{[:,1:3]}{}^T \right) + \mathbf{w}^k \mathbf{w}^{k^T} \tag{22}$$

in the three unknowns of $\mathbf{Q}_{2\times2}^T \mathbf{Q}_{2\times2}$, the $2K$ unknowns of $\mathbf{w}^k$, and the K unknowns λ_k^2. Interestingly, these constraints on the camera axes are insufficient to compute a valid matrix $\mathbf{Q}_{2\times2}$ and valid vectors $\mathbf{w}^k$, even using non-linear local optimization methods (there are solutions with residuum 0 which however turn out to be invalid solutions). Moreover, experiments showed that this nonlinear formulation suffers from many local minima. This observation justifies the need for the registration step in the plane of motion.

Final Step. Once the first three columns of the camera matrices are known in an Euclidean reference frame, the first three rows in Eq. (14) become linear in the unknowns $\mathbf{Q}_{3\times2}$, $\mathbf{S}$, and the camera translations. A least squares approach again provides the solutions to the unknowns of this overdetermined linear system. The linear system has a $4 + K$-dimensional nullspace in the noisefree case: 4 degrees of freedom due to the planar translational ambiguities (planar translation of the points or the cameras can be compensated by the planar motion) and K degrees of freedom for the per-camera translation ambiguities along the axis of rotation.

6   Results

If synthetic data is generated with affine cameras and without noise, the algorithm expectedly finds the exact solution in closed-form, even for the case of only two cameras each of them tracking one single point. Based on our experience with synthetic data according to a more realistic setting (i.e. projective camera models with realistic internal parameters, some noise and plausible planar motions) we concluded that the robustness of the algorithm strongly depends

Fig. 2. Reconstruction of a planarly moving box: The right image shows a close-up view of the reconstructed structure (tags tracked by one specific camera share the same color)

on the observed motion. This is actually an expected behavior. If the motion clearly spans the 5D motion subspace, the algorithm works robustly. However, if a dimension of this subspace is not explored sufficiently, noise will overrule this dimension and the reconstruction will deteriorate.

As a proof of concept the algorithm has been applied to a real data sequence. Fig. 2 shows the results of a real sequence with four cameras observing the planar motion of a rigid box. The translation ambiguity along the rotation axis has been resolved s.t. the centroids of the front-facing tags share the same coordinate along the axis of rotation. A template based tracker [17] has been used to generate the feature trajectories. Each camera tracked between 10 to 20 points. Even though some cameras actually tracked the very same points, the algorithm was purposely not aware of these correspondences. Such hidden correspondences allow to evaluate the accuracy of the reconstruction. Based on the overlapping area of the 3D model of the tracked feature tags, we conclude that the algorithm succeeds in computing an accurate reconstruction given the fact that the reconstruction is based on the approximate affine camera model and the solution is given in a non-iterative closed-form. The reprojection error of the closed-form solution is $\frac{1}{\sqrt{F \sum_k N_k}} \| \mathbf{W} - \mathbf{M} \mathcal{C}_{(f)} \left[\Rightarrow_k \mathbf{S}_k \otimes \mathbf{P}_k^T \right] \|_F = 8.95$ pixels (the resolution of the cameras is 1920×1080). A successive nonlinear refinement step still based on the affine camera model did not improve the reprojection error. This provides evidence that most of the error is due to the discrepancy between the employed affine camera approximation and the real projective cameras and not due to the sub-optimal sequential steps of the closed-form solution.

7   Conclusions and Future Work

This paper presented an analysis of a planarly moving rigid object observed by multiple static affine cameras. The theoretical insights gained thereby enabled the development of an algorithm, which provides a closed-form solution to the shape from motion reconstruction problem where no feature point correspondences between the different camera views exist. The motion correspondence, namely that all the cameras observe the same planar motion, was captured by a

5D motion subspace. As future work, we plan to adapt the planar motion subspace constraint to a formulation with projective camera models. This probably asks for iterative solutions for which the closed-form algorithm might provide a good initialization. We also consider trying whether the rank-5 constraint could be used as a means to temporally synchronize multiple camera streams.

Acknowledgments. We gratefully acknowledge the support of the 4DVideo ERC Starting Grant Nr. 210806 and a Packard Foundation Fellowship.

References

1. Tomasi, C., Kanade, T.: Shape and motion from image streams under orthography: a factorization method. International Journal of Computer Vision 9, 137–154 (1992)
2. Torresani, L., Hertzmann, A., Bregler, C.: Nonrigid structure-from-motion: Estimating shape and motion with hierarchical priors. IEEE Trans. Pattern Anal. Mach. Intell. 30, 878–892 (2008)
3. Tresadern, P.A., Reid, I.D.: Articulated structure from motion by factorization. In: CVPR (2), pp. 1110–1115. IEEE Computer Society, Los Alamitos (2005)
4. Yan, J., Pollefeys, M.: A factorization-based approach for articulated nonrigid shape, motion and kinematic chain recovery from video. IEEE Trans. Pattern Anal. Mach. Intell. 30, 865–877 (2008)
5. Tron, R., Vidal, R.: A benchmark for the comparison of 3-d motion segmentation algorithms. In: CVPR, IEEE Computer Society, Los Alamitos (2007)
6. Sturm, P.F., Triggs, B.: A factorization based algorithm for multi-image projective structure and motion. In: Buxton, B.F., Cipolla, R. (eds.) ECCV 1996. LNCS, vol. 1065, pp. 709–720. Springer, Heidelberg (1996)
7. Hartley, R., Schaffalitzky, F.: PowerFactorization: 3D reconstruction with missing or uncertain data. In: Japan-Australia Workshop on Computer Vision (2004)
8. Chen, P.: Optimization algorithms on subspaces: Revisiting missing data problem in low-rank matrix. International Journal of Computer Vision 80, 125–142 (2008)
9. Li, J., Chellappa, R.: A factorization method for structure from planar motion. In: WACV/MOTION, pp. 154–159. IEEE Computer Society, Los Alamitos (2005)
10. Vidal, R., Oliensis, J.: Structure from planar motions with small baselines. In: Heyden, A., Sparr, G., Nielsen, M., Johansen, P. (eds.) ECCV 2002. LNCS, vol. 2351, pp. 383–398. Springer, Heidelberg (2002)
11. Bue, A.D., de Agapito, L.: Non-rigid stereo factorization. International Journal of Computer Vision 66, 193–207 (2006)
12. Svoboda, T., Martinec, D., Pajdla, T.: A convenient multicamera self-calibration for virtual environments. Presence 14, 407–422 (2005)
13. Daniilidis, K.: Hand-eye calibration using dual quaternions. I. J. Robotic Res. 18, 286–298 (1999)
14. Angst, R., Pollefeys, M.: Static Multi-Camera Factorization Using Rigid Motion. In: Proc. of ICCV 2009, Washington, DC, USA, IEEE Computer Society Press, Los Alamitos (2009)
15. Kolda, T.G., Bader, B.W.: Tensor Decompositions and Applications. SIAM Review 51, 455–500 (2009)
16. Angst, R., Pollefeys, M.: 5d motion subspaces for planar motions: Supplemental material (2010), http://www.cvg.ethz.ch/people/phdstudents/rangst/Publications
17. Wagner, D., Schmalstieg, D.: Artoolkitplus for pose tracking on mobile devices. In: Proc. of 12th Computer Vision Winter Workshop (2007)

3D Reconstruction of a Moving Point from a Series of 2D Projections

Hyun Soo Park[1], Takaaki Shiratori[1,2], Iain Matthews[2], and Yaser Sheikh[1]

[1] Carnegie Mellon University, 5000 Forbes Ave., Pittsburgh, PA, USA, 15213
[2] Disney Research, Pittsburgh, 4615 Forbes Ave., Pittsburgh, PA, USA, 15213
{hyunsoop,siratori,yaser}@cs.cmu.edu, iainm@disneyresearch.com

Abstract. This paper presents a linear solution for reconstructing the 3D trajectory of a moving point from its correspondence in a collection of 2D perspective images, given the 3D spatial pose and time of capture of the cameras that produced each image. Triangulation-based solutions do not apply, as multiple views of the point may not exist at each instant in time. A geometric analysis of the problem is presented and a criterion, called reconstructibility, is defined to precisely characterize the cases when reconstruction is possible, and how accurate it can be. We apply the linear reconstruction algorithm to reconstruct the time evolving 3D structure of several real-world scenes, given a collection of non-coincidental 2D images.

Keywords: Multiple view geometry, Non-rigid structure from motion, Trajectory basis, and Reconstructibility.

1 Introduction

Without making *a priori* assumptions about scene structure, it is impossible to reconstruct a 3D scene from a monocular image. Binocular stereoscopy is a solution used both by biological and artificial systems to localize the position of a point in 3D via correspondences in two views. Classic triangulation used in stereo reconstruction is geometrically well-posed as shown in Figure 1(a). The rays connecting each image location to its corresponding camera center intersect at the true 3D location of the point — this process is called triangulation as the two rays map out a triangle with the baseline that connects the two camera centers. The triangulation constraint does not apply when the point moves in the duration between image capture, as shown in Figure 1(b). This case abounds as most artificial vision systems are monocular and most real scenes contain moving elements.

The 3D reconstruction of a trajectory is directly analogous to monocular image reconstruction: it is impossible to reconstruct a moving point without making some assumptions about the way it moves. In this paper, we represent the 3D trajectory of a moving point as a compact linear combination of a trajectory

K. Daniilidis, P. Maragos, N. Paragios (Eds.): ECCV 2010, Part III, LNCS 6313, pp. 158–171, 2010.

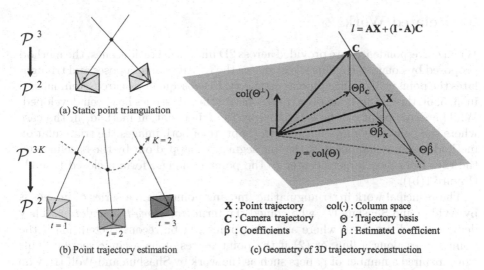

(a) Static point triangulation

(b) Point trajectory estimation

(c) Geometry of 3D trajectory reconstruction

X : Point trajectory   col(·) : Column space
C : Camera trajectory Θ : Trajectory basis
β : Coefficients $\hat{\beta}$: Estimated coefficient

Fig. 1. (a) A point in projective space, $\mathcal{P}^3$, is mapped to $\mathcal{P}^2$. From two views, the 3D point can be triangulated. (b) From a series of images, a point trajectory, $\mathcal{P}^{3K}$, also imaged to $\mathcal{P}^2$. To estimate the trajectory, at least three projections are required when the number of parameters describing the trajectory is 6 (2 for each coordinate, x, y, and z). (c) Geometric illustration of the least squares solution of Equation (4). The estimated trajectory $\Theta\hat{\beta}$ is placed on the intersection between l containing the camera trajectory space and the point trajectory, and the p space spanned by the column space of the trajectory basis matrix, col(Θ).

basis and demonstrate that, under this model, we can recover the 3D motion of the point linearly, and can handle missing data. By posing the problem in this way, we generalize the problem of triangulation, which is a mapping from $\mathcal{P}^3 \to \mathcal{P}^2$, to 3D *trajectory* reconstruction, as a mapping $\mathcal{P}^{3K} \to \mathcal{P}^2$, where $3K$ is the number of the trajectory basis required to represent the 3D point trajectory[1].

The stability of classic triangulation is known to depend on the baseline between camera centers [3]. In this paper, we characterize an instability encountered when interference occurs between the trajectory of the point and the trajectory mapped out by successive cameras centers. We demonstrate that the accuracy of 3D trajectory reconstruction is fundamentally limited by the correlation between the trajectory of the point and the trajectory of successive camera centers. A measure called reconstructibility is defined which can determine the accuracy of reconstruction, given a particular trajectory basis, 3D point trajectory, and 3D camera center trajectory. The linear reconstruction algorithm, in conjunction with this analysis, is used to propose a practical algorithm for the reconstruction of multiple 3D trajectories from a collection of non-coincidental images.

---

[1] Related observations have been made in [1, 2].

2   Related Work

When correspondences are provided across 2D images in static scenes, the method proposed by Longuet-Higgins [4] estimates the relative camera poses and triangulates the point in 3D using epipolar geometry. In subsequent research, summarized in [3, 5, 6], the geometry involved in reconstructing 3D scenes has been developed. While a static point can be estimated by the triangulation method, in the case where the point may move between the capture of both images the triangulation method becomes inapplicable: the line segments mapped out by the baseline and the rays from each camera center to the point no longer form a closed triangle (Figure 1(b)).

The principal work in 'triangulating' moving points from a series of images is by Avidan and Shashua [7], who coined the term *trajectory-triangulation*. They demonstrated two cases where a moving point can be reconstructed: (1) if the point moves along a line, or (2) if the point moves along a conic section. This work inspired a number of papers such as the work by Shashua and Wolf [1], who demonstrated reconstruction for points moving along planes, and the work by Kaminski and Teicher [8] who extended to a general trajectory using the polynomial representation. Wolf and Shashua [9] classified different manifestations of related problems, analyzing them as projections from $\mathcal{P}^N$ to $\mathcal{P}^2$.

In this paper, we investigate the reconstruction of the 3D trajectory of a moving point where the motion of the point can be described as a compact combination of a linear trajectory basis. This generalization allows far more natural motions to be linearly reconstructed. We demonstrate its application in reconstructing dynamic motion of objects from a series of image projections where no two image projections necessarily occur at the same time instant.

The reconstruction of dynamic motion from monocular sequences, or nonrigid structure from motion, is one such domain. The seminal work of Bregler *et al.* [10] introduced linear shape models as a representation for nonrigid 3D structures, and demonstrated their applicability within the factorization-based reconstruction paradigm of Tomasi and Kanade [11]. Subsequently, numerous constraints and techniques have been proposed to specify shape priors depending on models such as facial expressions and articulated body motions [12–16]. In contrast to these methods which represent the instantaneous shape of an object as a linear combination of basis shapes, Akhter *et al.* [17] proposed analyzing each trajectory as a linear combination of basis trajectories. They proposed the use of the Discrete Cosine Transform as a basis, and applied factorization techniques to estimate nonrigid structure. The primary limitation of these factorization-based methods is: (1) the assumption of an orthographic camera, and (2) their inability to handle missing information. Several papers have relaxed the constraint of orthography, such as Hartley and Vidal [2] and Vidal and Abretske [18], and the work by Torresani *et al.* [15] can handle missing data. However, these algorithms remain unstable and have been demonstrated to work only for constrained data like faces or motion capture; studies of this instability have been pursued by Xiao *et al.* [12] and Akhter *et al.* [19].

Unlike previously proposed methods, we do not pursue a factorization based solution. Instead we propose a linear solution to reconstruct a moving point from a series of its image projections inspired by the Direct Linear Transform algorithm [3]. In conjunction with rigid structure from motion estimation, and the trajectory based representation of points, this facilitates the first practical algorithm for dynamic structure reconstruction. It is able to handle problems like missing data (due to occlusion and matching failure) and estimation instability. An analysis is presented which geometrically describes the reconstruction problem as fundamentally restricted by the correlation between the motion of the camera center and the motion of a scene point trajectory. This analysis is leveraged to estimate an optimized trajectory basis to represent scene point motion, given an estimated camera center trajectory. We will assume that scene point correspondences have been provided, and that the relative locations of the view-points have been estimated, and that the basis describing the trajectory are pre-defined: these are reasonable assumptions that will be justified presently.

3   Linear Reconstruction of a 3D Point Trajectory

For a static point in 3D projective space, correspondences across a pair of images enable us to triangulate as shown in Figure 1(a). Traditional triangulation solves for a 3D point from an overconstrained system because there are three unknowns while the number of equations is $2F$, where F is the number of images. For a 3D point trajectory, if it can be represented by K parameters per coordinate, the projection is $\mathcal{P}^{3K} \rightarrow \mathcal{P}^2$ as shown in Figure 1(b). As was the case with static point projection, if $2F \geq 3K$, solving for a 3D trajectory becomes an overconstrained problem. Using this observation, we develop a linear solution for reconstructing a point trajectory given the relative poses of the cameras and the time instances the images were captured.

For a given ith camera projection matrix, $\mathbf{P}_i \in \Re^{3 \times 4}$, let a point in 3D, $\mathbf{X}_i = \begin{bmatrix} X_i\, Y_i\, Z_i \end{bmatrix}^\mathsf{T}$, be imaged as $\mathbf{x}_i = \begin{bmatrix} x_i\, y_i \end{bmatrix}^\mathsf{T}$. The index i used in this paper represents the ith time sample. This projection is defined up to scale,

$$\begin{bmatrix} \mathbf{x}_i \\ 1 \end{bmatrix} \simeq \mathbf{P}_i \begin{bmatrix} \mathbf{X}_i \\ 1 \end{bmatrix}, \quad \text{or} \quad \begin{bmatrix} \mathbf{x}_i \\ 1 \end{bmatrix}_\times \mathbf{P}_i \begin{bmatrix} \mathbf{X}_i \\ 1 \end{bmatrix} = \mathbf{0}, \tag{1}$$

where $[\cdot]_\times$ is the skew symmetric representation of the cross product [3]. This can be rewritten as an inhomogeneous equation,

$$\begin{bmatrix} \mathbf{x}_i \\ 1 \end{bmatrix}_\times \mathbf{P}_{i,1:3}\mathbf{X}_i = -\begin{bmatrix} \mathbf{x}_i \\ 1 \end{bmatrix}_\times \mathbf{P}_{i,4} ,$$

where $\mathbf{P}_{i,1:3}$ and $\mathbf{P}_{i,4}$ are the matrices made of the first three columns and the last column of $\mathbf{P}_i$, respectively, or simply as $\mathbf{Q}_i\mathbf{X}_i = \mathbf{q}_i$, where,

$$\mathbf{Q}_i = \left(\begin{bmatrix} \mathbf{x}_i \\ 1 \end{bmatrix}_\times \mathbf{P}_{i,1:3} \right)_{1:2}, \quad \mathbf{q}_i = \left(\begin{bmatrix} \mathbf{x}_i \\ 1 \end{bmatrix}_\times \mathbf{P}_{i,4} \right)_{1:2},$$

and $(\cdot)_{1:2}$ is the matrix made of two rows from $(\cdot)$. By taking into account all time instants, a closed form for the 3D point trajectory, $\mathbf{X}$, can be formulated as,

$$
\begin{bmatrix} \mathbf{Q}_1 & & \\ & \ddots & \\ & & \mathbf{Q}_F \end{bmatrix} \begin{bmatrix} \mathbf{X}_1 \\ \vdots \\ \mathbf{X}_F \end{bmatrix} = \begin{bmatrix} \mathbf{q}_1 \\ \vdots \\ \mathbf{q}_F \end{bmatrix}, \quad \text{or } \mathbf{Q}\mathbf{X} = \mathbf{q}, \tag{2}
$$

where F is the number of time samples in the trajectory. Since Equation (2) is an underconstrained system (i.e. $\mathbf{Q} \in \Re^{2F \times 3F}$), there are an infinite number of solutions for a given set of measurements (2D projections). There are many ways to constrain the solution space in which $\mathbf{X}$ lies. One way is approximating the point trajectory using a linear combination of any trajectory basis that can describe it as,

$$
\mathbf{X} = \begin{bmatrix} \mathbf{X}_1^\mathsf{T} & \cdots & \mathbf{X}_F^\mathsf{T} \end{bmatrix}^\mathsf{T} \approx \Theta_1 \beta_1 + \ldots + \Theta_{3K} \beta_{3K} = \Theta\beta, \tag{3}
$$

where $\Theta_j \in \Re^{3F}$ is a trajectory basis vector, $\Theta = \begin{bmatrix} \Theta_1 \ldots \Theta_{3K} \end{bmatrix} \in \Re^{3F \times 3K}$ is the trajectory basis matrix, $\beta = \begin{bmatrix} \beta_1 \ldots \beta_{3K} \end{bmatrix}^\mathsf{T} \in \Re^{3K}$ are the parameters or coefficients of a point trajectory, and K is the number of bases per coordinate.

If the trajectory basis are known a priori [17], this linear map between the point trajectory and basis enables us to formulate a linear solution. By plugging Equation (3) into Equation (2), we can derive an overconstrained system by choosing K such that $2F \geq 3K$,

$$
\mathbf{Q}\Theta\beta = \mathbf{q}. \tag{4}
$$

Equation (4) is a linear least squares system for reconstructing a point trajectory, β, which provides an efficient, numerically stable, and globally optimal solution. β is the coefficient of the trajectory based on measurements and known camera poses embedded in $\mathbf{Q}$ and $\mathbf{q}$ and known trajectory basis, Θ.

4   Geometric Analysis of 3D Trajectory Reconstruction

Empirically, the point trajectory reconstruction approaches the ground truth point trajectory when the camera motion is fast or random. On the other hand, if the camera moves slowly or smoothly, the solution tends to deviate highly from the ground truth. To explain these observations, we decompose the process of solving the linear least squares system into two steps: solving Equation (2) and solving Equation (3).

4.1   Geometry of Point and Camera Trajectories

Let $\mathbf{X}$ and $\widehat{\mathbf{X}}$ be a ground truth trajectory and an estimated point trajectory, respectively. The camera matrix can always be normalized by intrinsic and rotation matrices, $\mathbf{K}$ and $\mathbf{R}$, respectively, because they can be factored out without loss of generality (as all camera matrices are known), i.e. $\mathbf{R}_i^T \mathbf{K}_i^{-1} \mathbf{P}_i = [\mathbf{I}_3|-\mathbf{C}_i]$, where $\mathbf{P}_i = \mathbf{K}_i \mathbf{R}_i [\mathbf{I}_3|-\mathbf{C}_i]$, $\mathbf{C}_i$ is the camera center, and $\mathbf{I}_3$ is a 3×3 identity matrix. This follows from the fact that triangulation and 3D trajectory reconstruction are both geometrically unaffected by the rotation of the camera about its center. All $\mathbf{P}_i$ subsequently used in this analysis are normalized camera matrices, i.e. $\mathbf{P}_i = [\mathbf{I}_3|-\mathbf{C}_i]$. Then, a measurement is a projection of $\mathbf{X}$ onto the image plane from Equation (1). Since Equation (1) is defined up to scale, the measurement, $\mathbf{x}$, can be replaced as follows,

$$\left[\mathbf{P}_i \begin{bmatrix} \mathbf{X}_i \\ 1 \end{bmatrix} \right]_\times \mathbf{P}_i \begin{bmatrix} \widehat{\mathbf{X}}_i \\ 1 \end{bmatrix} = 0. \tag{5}$$

Plugging in $\mathbf{P}_i = [\mathbf{I}_3|-\mathbf{C}_i]$ results in, $[\mathbf{X}_i - \mathbf{C}_i]_\times \left(\widehat{\mathbf{X}}_i - \mathbf{C}_i \right) = 0$, or equivalently,

$$[\mathbf{X}_i - \mathbf{C}_i]_\times \widehat{\mathbf{X}}_i = [\mathbf{X}_i]_\times \mathbf{C}_i. \tag{6}$$

The solution of Equation (6) is

$$\widehat{\mathbf{X}}_i = a_i \mathbf{X}_i + (1 - a_i)\mathbf{C}_i, \tag{7}$$

where a_i is an arbitrary scalar. Geometrically, Equation (7) is the constraint for the perspective camera model due to the fact that it enforces the solution to lie on the ray joining the camera center and the point in 3D. From Equation (3), Equation (7) can be rewritten as $\mathbf{\Theta}_i \widehat{\beta} \approx a_i \mathbf{X}_i + (1 - a_i)\mathbf{C}_i$ where $\widehat{\beta}$ is the estimated parameter and $\mathbf{\Theta}_i$ is the matrix from $\mathbf{\Theta}_{(3(i-1)+1):3i}$.

Figure 1(c) illustrates the geometry of the solution of Equation (4). Let the subspace, p, be the space spanned by the column space of the trajectory basis matrix, $\text{col}(\mathbf{\Theta})$. The solution $\mathbf{\Theta}\widehat{\beta}$, has to simultaneously lie on the hyperplane l, which contains the camera trajectory and the point trajectory, and must lie in $\text{col}(\mathbf{\Theta})$. Thus, $\mathbf{\Theta}\widehat{\beta}$ is the intersection of the hyperplane l and the subspace p where $\mathbf{A} = \mathbf{D} \otimes \mathbf{I}_3$.[2] In the figure, note that the line and the plane are a conceptual 3D vector space representation for the $3F$-dimensional space. The camera center trajectory, $\mathbf{C} = [\mathbf{C}_1^T \ldots \mathbf{C}_F^T]^T$, and the point trajectory, $\mathbf{X}$, are projected onto $\text{col}(\mathbf{\Theta})$ as $\mathbf{\Theta}\beta_{\mathbf{C}}$ and $\mathbf{\Theta}\beta_{\mathbf{X}}$, respectively. From this point of view, we want $\mathbf{\Theta}\widehat{\beta}$ to be as close as possible to $\mathbf{\Theta}\beta_{\mathbf{X}}$.

4.2 Reconstructibility

When a point trajectory is identical to the camera trajectory, it is not possible to estimate the point trajectory because a series of 2D projections is stationary. This intuition results in the following theorem.

Theorem 1. *Trajectory reconstruction using any linear trajectory basis is impossible if* $\text{corr}(\mathbf{X}, \mathbf{C}) = \pm 1$.[3]

---

[2] $\otimes$ is the Kronecker product and $\mathbf{D}$ is a diagonal matrix which consists of $\{a_1, \cdots, a_F\}$.

[3] $\text{corr}(X, Y) = \frac{E[(X - \mu_X)(Y - \mu_Y)]}{\sigma_X \sigma_Y}$ where $E[\cdot]$ is the expected value operator and μ and σ are the mean and standard deviation, respectively.

Proof. When $corr(\mathbf{X}, \mathbf{C}) = \pm 1$, or $\mathbf{X} = c\mathbf{C} + \mathbf{d}$ where c is arbitrary scalar and $\mathbf{d}$ is arbitrary constant vector, we can transform $\mathbf{X}$ and $\mathbf{C}$ to $\tilde{\mathbf{X}}$ and $\tilde{\mathbf{C}}$ such that $\tilde{\mathbf{X}} = c\tilde{\mathbf{C}}$ without loss of generality. This linearity causes the RHS of Equation (6) to be zero and the solution $\hat{\mathbf{X}}_i$ to be the same as $\tilde{\mathbf{C}}_i$ up to scale. This results in the scale ambiguity of $\hat{\mathbf{X}}_i$.   □

While Theorem 1 shows the reconstruction limitation due to the correlation between the point trajectory and the camera trajectory, solving Equation (3) with respect to β provides a measure of the reconstruction accuracy for a given trajectory basis. Solving the least squares, $\hat{\mathbf{X}} = \Theta\hat{\beta}$ minimizes the residual error,

$$\underset{\hat{\beta}, \mathbf{A}}{\operatorname{argmin}} \left\| \Theta\hat{\beta} - \mathbf{AX} - (\mathbf{I} - \mathbf{A}) \mathbf{C} \right\|. \tag{8}$$

Let us decompose the point trajectory and the camera trajectory into the column space of Θ and that of the null space, $\Theta^\perp$ as follows, $\mathbf{X} = \Theta\beta_{\mathbf{X}} + \Theta^\perp \beta_{\mathbf{X}}^\perp$, $\mathbf{C} = \Theta\beta_{\mathbf{C}} + \Theta^\perp \beta_{\mathbf{C}}^\perp$, where $\beta^\perp$ is the coefficient for the null space. Let us also define a measure of *reconstructibility*, η, of the 3D point trajectory reconstruction,

$$\eta = \frac{\left\| \Theta^\perp \beta_{\mathbf{C}}^\perp \right\|}{\left\| \Theta^\perp \beta_{\mathbf{X}}^\perp \right\|}. \tag{9}$$

Theorem 2. *As η approaches infinity, $\hat{\beta}$ approaches $\beta_{\mathbf{X}}$.*

Proof. From the triangle inequality, the objective function of Equation (8) is bounded by,

$$\left\| \Theta\hat{\beta} - \mathbf{A}\Theta\beta_{\mathbf{X}} - (\mathbf{I} - \mathbf{A}) \Theta\beta_{\mathbf{C}} - \mathbf{A}\Theta^\perp \beta_{\mathbf{X}}^\perp - (\mathbf{I} - \mathbf{A}) \Theta^\perp \beta_{\mathbf{C}}^\perp \right\| \tag{10}$$

$$\leq \left\| \Theta\hat{\beta} - \mathbf{A}\Theta\beta_{\mathbf{X}} - (\mathbf{I} - \mathbf{A}) \Theta\beta_{\mathbf{C}} \right\| + \left\| \mathbf{A}\Theta^\perp \beta_{\mathbf{X}}^\perp \right\| + \left\| (\mathbf{I} - \mathbf{A}) \Theta^\perp \beta_{\mathbf{C}}^\perp \right\|$$

$$\leq \left\| \Theta^\perp \beta_{\mathbf{C}}^\perp \right\| \left(\frac{\left\| \Theta\hat{\beta} - \mathbf{A}\Theta\beta_{\mathbf{X}} - (\mathbf{I} - \mathbf{A}) \Theta\beta_{\mathbf{C}} \right\|}{\left\| \Theta^\perp \beta_{\mathbf{C}}^\perp \right\|} + \frac{\|\mathbf{A}\|}{\eta} + \|\mathbf{I} - \mathbf{A}\| \right). \tag{11}$$

As η approaches infinity, $\|\mathbf{A}\|/\eta$ in Equation (11) becomes zero. In order to minimize Equation (11), $\mathbf{A} = \mathbf{I}$ because it leaves the last term zero and $\hat{\beta} = \beta_{\mathbf{X}}$ because it also cancels the first term. This leads the minimum of Equation (11) to be zero, which bounds the minimum of Equation (10). Thus, as η approaches infinity, $\hat{\beta}$ approaches $\beta_{\mathbf{X}}$.   □

Figure 2(a) shows how reconstructibility is related to the accuracy of the 3D reconstruction error. In each reconstruction, the residual error (null components) of the point trajectory, $e_{\mathbf{X}} = \left\| \Theta^\perp \beta_{\mathbf{X}}^\perp \right\|$, and the camera trajectory, $e_{\mathbf{C}} = \left\| \Theta^\perp \beta_{\mathbf{C}}^\perp \right\|$, are measured. Increasing $e_{\mathbf{C}}$ for a given point trajectory enhances the accuracy of the 3D reconstruction, while increasing $e_{\mathbf{X}}$ lowers accuracy. Even though we cannot directly measure the reconstructibility (we never

know the true point trajectory in a real example), it is useful to demonstrate
the direct relation with 3D reconstruction accuracy. Figure 2(b) illustrates that
the reconstructibility is inversely proportional to the 3D reconstruction error.

In practice, the infinite reconstructibility criterion is difficult to satisfy because the actual $\mathbf{X}$ is unknown. To enhance reconstructibility we can maximize
e_C with constant $e_\mathbf{X}$. Thus, the best camera trajectory for a given trajectory
basis matrix is the one that lives in the null space, $\text{col}(\Theta^\perp)$. This explains our
observation about slow and fast camera motion described at the beginning of
this section. When the camera motion is slow, the camera trajectory is likely
to be represented well by the DCT basis, which results in low reconstructibility
and vice versa. However, for a given camera trajectory, there is no deterministic
way to define a trajectory basis matrix because it is coupled with both the camera trajectory and the point trajectory. If one simply finds an orthogonal space
to the camera trajectory, in general, it is likely to nullify space that also spans
the point trajectory space. Geometrically, simply changing the surface of p in
Figure 1(c) may result in a greater deviation between $\Theta\beta_\mathbf{X}$ and $\Theta\hat{\beta}$. Yet, if we
have prior information of a point trajectory, we can enhance the reconstructibil-
ity. For example, if one is shooting video while walking, the frequency of the
camera trajectory will be concentrated at a certain frequency, say the walking
frequency, whereas that of a point trajectory is somewhere else. In such a case,
if we find a trajectory basis space that is orthogonal to the walking frequency
basis, the point trajectory can be estimated well, as long as it does not contain
that frequency. This process allows us to eliminate interference from the camera
trajectory.

5   Results

In this section, we evaluate 3D trajectory reconstruction on both synthetic and
real data. In all cases, the trajectory bases are the first K discrete cosine transform (DCT) basis in order of increasing frequency. The DCT basis has been
demonstrated to accurately and compactly model 1D point trajectories [17]. If a
3D trajectory is continuous and smooth, DCT basis can represent it accurately
with relatively few low frequency components. We make the assumption that
each point trajectory is continuous and smooth and use the DCT basis as the
trajectory basis, Θ. We choose the value of K based on the number of visible
points on a trajectory such that the system is overconstrained and $2F \geq 3K$.
We consider two choices of DCT bases: the *original DCT* basis set, and the
specialized DCT basis set. The specialized DCT is a projection of the original
DCT onto the null space of the camera trajectory. The idea here is to limit how
well the specialized DCT reconstructs the camera trajectory and improve the
reconstructibility.

5.1   Simulation

To quantitatively evaluate our method, we generate synthetic 2D images from
3D motion capture data and test it in three perspectives: reconstructibility,

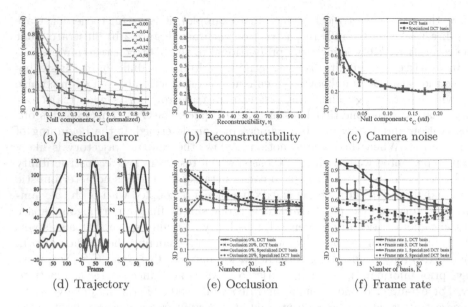

Fig. 2. (a) As the null component of the camera trajectory, e_C, decreases, the closed form solution of Equation (4) deviates from the real solution. (b) Reconstructibility, η, provides the degree of interference between the camera trajectory and the point trajectory. (c) Comparisons of reconstruction accuracy of trajectories reconstructed with the specialized and original DCT basis under various camera trajectories, and (d) trajectories between the ground truth and the original and specialized DCT basis under smooth camera trajectory. Black: the ground truth of the point trajectory, green: the camera trajectory, and blue and red: reconstructed trajectory of the motion capture marker from the original and specialized DCT basis, respectively. Comparisons of robustness between the original and specialized DCT basis with regard to (e) occlusion and (f) frame rate.

robustness, and accuracy. For reconstructibility, we compare reconstruction from the original DCT basis with the specialized DCT basis by increasing the null component, e_C, of the camera trajectory. Reconstruction error from the original DCT basis is higher when there is small e_C. For robustness, we test with missing data and lowered frame rates and we show that the specialized DCT basis performs better. Finally, for accuracy, we compare our algorithm with state-of-the-art algorithms by varying the perspectivity of projection. The results show our method outperforms others, particularly under perspective projection.

Reconstructibility: Earlier, we defined the reconstructibility of a 3D trajectory as the trade off between the ability of the chosen trajectory basis to accurately reconstruct the point trajectory vs. its ability to reconstruct the camera trajectory. To evaluate this effect empirically we generate camera trajectories by varying e_C and measure the error in point trajectory reconstruction in Figure 2(c). Each trajectory is normalized to have zero mean and unit variance so that errors can be compared across different sequences. When e_C is low, there

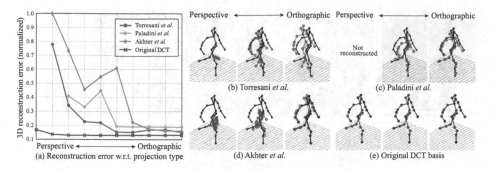

Fig. 3. (a) Quantitative comparisons of reconstruction accuracy with previous methods regarding projection types, and qualitative comparisons of reconstruction errors using the original DCT basis (blue) and the methods by Torresani *et al.* [15](dark green), Paladini *et al.* [16](light green) and Akhter *et al.* [17](orange). (b-e): Qualitative comparison between the ground truth (black) and reconstructed trajectories (red) for each method.

is an advantage in using the *specialized* DCT basis. This is expected as the original DCT basis is able to reconstruct both camera and point trajectories well, and the reconstructibility is lower. As e_C increases, this becomes less of an issue, and both original and specialized DCT perform approximately the same. Figure 2(d) shows the comparison of point trajectories reconstructed using the original and specialized DCT basis compared to the ground truth. For this example the reconstructibility using the specialized DCT is 2.45, and for the original DCT basis it is 0.08.

Robustness: In this experiment, we evaluate the robustness of trajectory reconstruction for smooth camera trajectories with missing 2D point samples. Missing samples occur in practice due to occlusion, self-occlusion, or measurement failure. Figure 2(e) shows the normalized trajectory reconstruction error for varying amounts of occlusion (0% and 20% of the sequence) and different numbers of DCT basis. A walking motion capture sequence was used and each experiment was repeated 10 times with random occlusion. As long as the visibility of a point in a sequence is sufficient to overconstrain the linear system of equations, the closed form solution is robust to moderate occlusion. Figure 2(f) evaluates robustness to the frequency of input samples, i.e. varying the effective frame rate of the input sequence. Visibility of the moving points is important to avoid an ill-posed condition of the closed form solution, and intuitively more frequent visibility results in better reconstruction. The results confirm this observation. In both robustness experiment, the specialized DCT basis perform better than the original DCT basis for reduced number of bases. This is due to the (worst case) smooth synthesized camera trajectories. This effect is reduced as the number of DCT basis increases and the reconstructibility of the sequence increases accordingly.

Accuracy: We compare the accuracy of reconstructed trajectories against methods using shape basis reconstruction by Torresani *et al.* [15] and Paladini *et al.* [16]

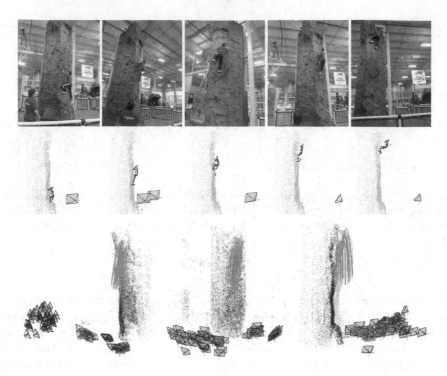

Fig. 4. Results of the rock climbing scene. Top row: sampled image input, second row: five snap shots of 3D reconstruction in different views, and bottom row: reconstructed trajectories (blue line) in different views.

and the method using trajectory basis reconstruction Akhter *et al.* [17]. To validate that our closed form solution is independent of the camera projection model, we parameterize camera projection as the distance between image plane and the camera center and evaluate across a range that moves progressively from projective at one end to orthographic at the other. Note that we are given all camera poses for the closed form trajectory solution, while the previous methods reconstruct both camera poses and point trajectories simultaneously. We set K to 10 for all methods and use the original DCT basis. Figure 3 compares the normalized reconstruction accuracy for the walking scene under a random camera trajectory. The other methods assume orthographic camera projection and are unable to accurately reconstruct trajectories in the perspective case.

5.2   Experiments with Real Data

The theory of reconstructibility states that it is possible to reconstruct 3D point trajectories using DCT basis precisely if a camera trajectory is random. An interesting real world example of this case occurs when many independent photographers take asynchronous images of the same event from different locations. A collection of asynchronous photos can be interpreted as the random motion

Fig. 5. Results of the handshake scene. Top row: sampled image input, second and third row: five snap shots of 3D reconstruction in different views.

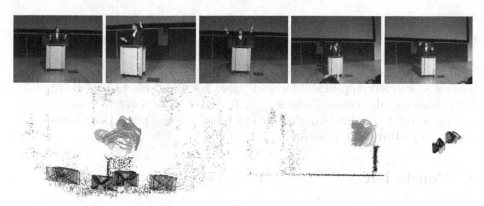

Fig. 6. Results of the speech scene. Top row: sampled image input, and bottom row: reconstructed trajectories (blue line) in different views.

Table 1. Parameters of real data sequences

	F (sec)	# of photos	# of photographers	K
Rock climbing	39	107	5	12
Handshake	10	32	3	6
Speech	24	67	4	14
Greeting	24	66	4	10

of a camera center. Using multiple photographers, we collected data in several 'media event' scenarios: a person *rock climbing*, a photo-op *hand shake*, public *speech*, and *greeting*. The static scene reconstruction is based on the structure from motion algorithm described in [20]. We also extracted timing information

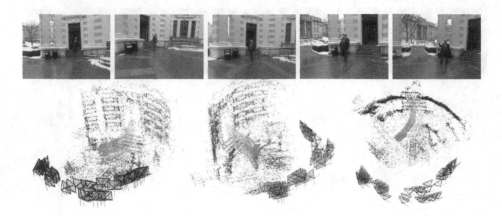

Fig. 7. Results of the greeting scene. Top row: sampled image input, and bottom row: reconstructed trajectories (blue line) in different views.

from image EXIF tags. Correspondences of moving points across images were obtained manually.

The parameters for each scenario are summarized in Table 1. The number of bases was selected empirically for each case. We were able to use the original DCT basis for all scenes. Figures 4, 5, 6, and 7 show some of input images and reconstructed point trajectories. The reconstructed point trajectories look similar to postures of the person.

6 Conclusion

In this paper, we analyze the geometry of 3D trajectory reconstruction and define a measure called reconstructibility to determine the accuracy of 3D trajectory reconstruction. We demonstrate that 3D trajectory reconstruction is fundamentally limited by the correlation between the 3D trajectory of a point and the 3D trajectory of the camera centers. Using this analysis, we propose an algorithm to reconstruct the 3D trajectory of a moving point from perspective images. By constraining the solution space using a linear trajectory basis, the dimensionality of the solution space can be reduced so that an overconstrained linear least squares system can be formulated. The linear algorithm takes as input the camera pose at each time instant, and a predefined trajectory basis. These requirements are met in our practical application, where we reconstruct dynamic scene from collections of images captured by a number of photographers. We estimate the relative camera pose by applying robust structure from motion to the static points in the scene. The Discrete Cosine Transform is used as a predefined basis. As the effective camera trajectory is quite discontinuous, we are able to obtain accurate 3D reconstructions of the dynamic scenes.

Acknowledgements

The authors wish to thank Natasha Kholgade, Ijaz Akhter, and the anonymous reviewers for their invaluable comments. This work was supported by NSF grant IIS-0916272.

References

1. Shashua, A., Wolf, L.: Homography tensors: On algebraic entities that represent three views of static or moving planar points. In: Vernon, D. (ed.) ECCV 2000. LNCS, vol. 1842, pp. 507–521. Springer, Heidelberg (2000)
2. Hartley, R., Vidal, R.: Perspective nonrigid shape and motion recovery. In: Forsyth, D., Torr, P., Zisserman, A. (eds.) ECCV 2008, Part I. LNCS, vol. 5302, pp. 276–289. Springer, Heidelberg (2008)
3. Hartley, R., Zisserman, A.: Multiple View Geometry in Computer Vision. Cambridge University Press, Cambridge (2004)
4. Longuet-Higgins, H.: A computer algorithm for reconstructing a scene from two projections. Nature (1981)
5. Faugeras, O., Luong, Q.T.: The geometry of multiple images. MIT Press, Cambridge (2001)
6. Ma, Y., Soatto, S., Kosecka, J., Sastry, S.S.: An invitation to 3-D vision: From images to Geometric Models. Springer, Heidelberg (2001)
7. Avidan, S., Shashua, A.: Trajectory triangulation: 3D reconstruction of moving points from a monocular image sequence. TPAMI 22, 348–357 (2000)
8. Kaminski, J.Y., Teicher, M.: A general framework for trajectory triangulation. J. Math. Imaging Vis. 21, 27–41 (2004)
9. Wolf, L., Shashua, A.: On projection matrices $\mathcal{P}^k \to \mathcal{P}^2, k = 3, \cdots, 6$, and their applications in computer vision. In: ICCV (2002)
10. Bregler, C., Hertzmann, A., Biermann, H.: Recovering non-rigid 3D shape from image streams. In: CVPR (2000)
11. Tomasi, C., Kanade, T.: Shape and motion from image streams under orthography: a factorization method. IJCV 9, 137–154 (1992)
12. Xiao, J., Kanade, T.: Non-rigid shape and motion recovery: Degenerate deformations. In: CVPR (2004)
13. Bue, A.D.: A factorization approach to structure from motion with shape priors. In: CVPR (2008)
14. Bartoli, A., Gay-Bellile, V., Castellani, U., Peyras, J., Olsen, S., Sayd, P.: Coarse-to-fine low-rank structure-from-motion. In: CVPR (2008)
15. Torresani, L., Hertzmann, A., Bregler, C.: Nonrigid structure-from-motion: Estimating shape and motion with hierarchical priors. TPAMI 30, 878–892 (2008)
16. Paladini, M., Del Bue, A., Stošić, M., Dodig, M., Xavier, J., Agapito, L.: Factorization for non-rigid and articulated structure using metric projections. In: CVPR (2009)
17. Akhter, I., Sheikh, Y., Khan, S., Kanade, T.: Nonrigid structure from motion in trajectory space. In: NIPS (2008)
18. Vidal, R., Abretske, D.: Nonrigid shape and motion from multiple perspective views. In: Leonardis, A., Bischof, H., Pinz, A. (eds.) ECCV 2006. LNCS, vol. 3952, pp. 205–218. Springer, Heidelberg (2006)
19. Akhter, I., Sheikh, Y., Khan, S.: In defense of orthonormality constraints for nonrigid structure from motion. In: CVPR (2009)
20. Snavely, N., Seitz, S.M., Szeliski, R.: Photo tourism: Exploring photo collections in 3D. SIGGRAPH 25, 835–845 (2006)

Manifold Learning for Object Tracking with Multiple Motion Dynamics

Jacinto C. Nascimento and Jorge G. Silva

Instituto de Sistemas e Robótica - Instituto Superior Técnico
Dept. of Electrical and Computer Engineering - Duke University*

Abstract. This paper presents a novel manifold learning approach for high dimensional data, with emphasis on the problem of motion tracking in video sequences. In this problem, the samples are time-ordered, providing additional information that most current methods do not take advantage of. Additionally, most methods assume that the manifold topology admits a single chart, which is overly restrictive. Instead, the algorithm can deal with arbitrary manifold topology by decomposing the manifold into multiple local models that are combined in a probabilistic fashion using Gaussian process regression. Thus, the algorithm is termed herein as *Gaussian Process Multiple Local Models* (GP–MLM).

Additionally, the paper describes a multiple filter architecture where standard filtering techniques, *e.g.* particle and Kalman filtering, are combined with the output of GP–MLM in a principled way. The performance of this approach is illustrated with experimental results using real video sequences. A comparison with GP–LVM [29] is also provided. Our algorithm achieves competitive state-of-the-art results on a public database concerning the left ventricle (LV) ultrasound (US) and lips images.

1 Introduction

There has been long standing interest in learning non-linear models to approximate high-dimensional data, and specifically in reducing the dimensionality of the data, while preserving relevant information. The scope of application is vast, including, *e.g.*, modeling dynamic textures in natural images, surface reconstruction from 3-D point clouds, image retrieval and browsing, and discovering patterns in gene expression data.

Consider the example of an image sequence. In the absence of features such as contour points or wavelet coefficients, each image is a point in a space of dimension equal to the number of image pixels. When facing an observation space of possibly tens or hundreds of thousands of dimensions, it is often reasonable to assume that the data is not dense in such a space and that many of the measured variables must be dependent with only a few free parameters that are embedded in the observed variables, frequently in a nonlinear way. Assuming that the number of free parameters remains the same throughout the observations, and also assuming spatially smooth variation of the parameters, we have geometric restrictions which can be well modeled as a manifold. Learning this

---

* This work was supported by project the FCT (ISR/IST plurianual funding) through the PID-DAC Program funds and by project "HEARTRACK" PTDC/EEA-CRO/098550/2008.

K. Daniilidis, P. Maragos, N. Paragios (Eds.): ECCV 2010, Part III, LNCS 6313, pp. 172–185, 2010.

manifold is a natural approach to the problem of modeling the data, with the advantage of allowing *nonlinear* dimensionality reduction.

This paper proposes a new algorithm, named *Gaussian Process with Multiple Local Models* (GP–MLM), that applies manifold learning ideas to the problem of motion tracking, *e.g.*, in video sequences. The emphasis in motion tracking means that, unlike most manifold learning methods, the observations are assumed to be time-ordered. The proposed methodology addresses the problem of estimating unknown dynamics on an unknown manifold, from noisy observations. This leads to the simultaneous estimation of a nonlinear observation model and a nonlinear dynamical system - a nonlinear system identification type of problem, which has received some attention ([11,29,23]), but seldom in the context of manifolds, with a few recent exceptions [24]. While this problem is ill-posed (see *e.g.* [11]), it can be advantageous to exploit information that is common to both subproblems: the velocity vectors. Moreover, purely from a manifold learning point of view, GP–MLM addresses some limitations of existing methods, namely: (i) it is not limited to a simple coordinate chart - it can deal with arbitrary manifold topology through multiple local models; (ii) it provides a computationally efficient way to partition the manifold into multiple regions and compute the corresponding local parameterizations; (iii) it offers a principled way of combining the estimates from the multiple local models by using Gaussian process regression to compute the corresponding likelihoods. From a tracking perspective, it will be shown that GP–MLM can retrieve the contours with remarkable fidelity.

2 Background

Key concepts: A *manifold* [4] $\mathcal{M}$ is a set contained in $\mathbb{R}^m$, associated with a collection of p one-to-one continuous and invertible functions $\mathbf{g}_i : \mathcal{P}_i \rightarrow \mathcal{U}_i$, indexed by $i = 1, \ldots, p$ with overlapping domains $\mathcal{P}_i \subset \mathcal{M}$ such that $\mathcal{M}$ is covered by the union of the $\mathcal{P}_i$ and where each $\mathcal{U}_i \subset \mathbb{R}^n$. For points $\mathbf{y} \in \mathcal{P}_i \cap \mathcal{P}_j$ in the overlap between patches i and j, with images $\mathbf{x}_i$ and $\mathbf{x}_j$, it is possible to define a *transition function* $\Psi_{ij} : \mathbf{g}_i(\mathcal{P}_i \cap \mathcal{P}_j) \longrightarrow \mathbf{g}_j(\mathcal{P}_i \cap \mathcal{P}_j)$ which converts between the two local coordinate systems. See Fig. 1 for an illustration. Locally, $\mathcal{M}$ is "like" $\mathbb{R}^n$ and its *intrinsic dimension* is n. The $\mathbf{g}_i$ are called *charts*. It is assumed that $\mathcal{M}$ is *compact*, i.e., it can be covered with $p < \infty$ charts. The inverse mappings $\mathbf{h}_i = \mathbf{g}_i^{-1}$ are *parameterizations* of the manifold.

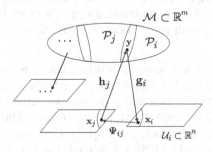

Fig. 1. A manifold and its charts

The $\mathcal{U}_i$ are *parametric domains* and the $\mathcal{P}_i$ are *patches*. Two charts $\mathbf{g}_i$ and $\mathbf{g}_j$ defined in the overlapping region $\mathcal{P}_i \cap \mathcal{P}_j$ should be compatible, that is, $\mathbf{g}_j^{-1}(\Psi_{ij}(\mathbf{g}_i(\mathbf{y}))) = \mathbf{y}$. For manifolds with arbitrary topology, there must be, in general, more than one chart and, therefore, more than one patch in order to maintain the one-to-one property.

The *tangent bundle* [4] of an n-dimensional manifold $\mathcal{M}$ is another manifold, $T(\mathcal{M})$, whose intrinsic dimension is $2n$ and whose members are the points of $\mathcal{M}$ and their tangent vectors. That is, $T(\mathcal{M}) = \{(\mathbf{y}, \mathbf{v}) : \mathbf{y} \in \mathcal{M}, \mathbf{v} \in T_{\mathbf{y}}(\mathcal{M})\}$ where $T_{\mathbf{y}}(\mathcal{M})$ is the tangent space of $\mathcal{M}$ at $\mathbf{y}$. It is readily apparent that $T_{\mathbf{y}}(\mathcal{M})$ is the set of possible velocity vectors of trajectories in $\mathcal{M}$ through $\mathbf{y}$. Therefore, any dynamic system defined in $\mathcal{M}$ must induce trajectories where both the velocities and their points of application belong to $T(\mathcal{M})$.

A *Gaussian process* [22] is a real-valued stochastic process $\{Y_{\mathbf{x}}\}_{\mathbf{x} \in \mathcal{X}}$, over an index set $\mathcal{X}$, where the joint probability density function for any finite set of indices $\{\mathbf{x}_1, \ldots, \mathbf{x}_N\}$ is Gaussian, with mean $\boldsymbol{\mu} \in \mathbb{R}^N$ and covariance $\mathbf{K} \in \mathbb{R}^{N \times N}$. Note that, in order to be a valid covariance matrix, $\mathbf{K}$ must be symmetric and positive semidefinite. This means that it can also be thought of as a valid *Mercer kernel* matrix. An attractive feature of Gaussian processes is that they allow the computation, in closed form, of probability densities in observation space.

Problem statement: Let $\mathbf{y}_{0:T-1} \equiv \{\mathbf{y}_t, t = 0, \ldots, T-1\}$, with discrete t and $\mathbf{y}_t \in \mathbb{R}^m$, be a trajectory. Let $\mathcal{Y} \equiv \{\mathbf{y}_{0:T_l-1}, l = 1, \ldots, L\}$ be a set of L such trajectories. It is assumed that the trajectories in $\mathcal{Y}$ lie close to an unknown manifold $\mathcal{M}$ of intrinsic dimension n (also unknown) embedded in $\mathbb{R}^m$, with $n < m$. Therefore, one or more lower dimensional representations $\mathcal{X}_i$ of the original set $\mathcal{Y}$ can be found, where each $\mathcal{X}_i \equiv \{\mathbf{x}_{0:T_l-1,i}, l = 1, \ldots, L\}$ represents all the trajectories in i-local coordinates, with $\mathbf{x}_{t,i} \in \mathbb{R}^n$. Being assumed compact, $\mathcal{M}$ can be charted by p charts, where p is unknown, and each $\mathcal{X}_i$ corresponds to one of the charts. It is intended to estimate $\mathcal{M}$ and identify the dynamics in the lower dimensional coordinates given by the charts of $\mathcal{M}$, assuming that the trajectories are generated by one or more discrete state space models of the form:

$$\mathbf{x}_{t,i} = \mathbf{f}_i(\mathbf{x}_{t-1,i}) + \boldsymbol{\omega}_{t,i} \tag{1}$$

$$\mathbf{y}_{t,i} = \mathbf{h}_i(\mathbf{x}_{t,i}) + \boldsymbol{\nu}_{t,i} \tag{2}$$

where $\boldsymbol{\omega}_{t,i}$ and $\boldsymbol{\nu}_{t,i}$ are noise variables. $\mathbf{h}_i$ is the ith parametrization being used around $\mathbf{y}_t$, and $\mathbf{f}_i$ defines the dynamics. In summary, given $\mathcal{Y}$, we wish to learn the state model (2) and (1), thus capturing both geometrical and dynamical information about the trajectories.

Prior work: Several manifold learning algorithms have emerged in recent years. Recent advances include, on one hand, probabilistic methods such as the Generative Topographic Mapping (GTM) [2], Gaussian process related algorithms, such as Gaussian Process Latent Variable Models (GP-LVM) [18] and Gaussian Process Dynamical Models (GPDM) [29]; on the other hand, graph spectral methods such as ISOMAP [27], Locally Linear Embedding (LLE) [25], Laplacian [1] and Hessian Eigenmaps [10], as well as Semi-Definite Embedding [31,30].

Most methods assume that the manifold can be modeled using a single coordinate patch, an assumption that fails for manifolds with topologies as simple as a sphere. Also, spectral methods usually do not provide out-of-sample extension. Only a few methods, such as [5,19], attempt to deal with multiple charts without assuming p known somehow.

Estimating the intrinsic dimension n remains a challenge. The most common method [13] for estimating n is based on local Principal Component Analysis (PCA), relying on a threshold to select the n most significant eigenvalues of local covariance matrices. Other approaches can be found in [20,15] and the references therein. With either type of algorithms, the estimate often suffers from high variance and bias, as well as dependence on the unknown scale parameters for neighborhood analysis, as pointed out in [15]. Hence, dimensionality estimation continues to be a challenging problem, although some promising advances have recently been made using multiscale approaches [16].

Finally, while simultaneous dimensionality reduction and dynamical learning has received some attention [23,11,14], many of these approaches are not formulated in terms of manifolds. Some techniques that do explicitly use the manifold assumption are [24,21,12]. In [24], the manifold is modeled as a mixture of local linear hyperplanes (*i.e.*, factor analyzers), while we use instead a mixture of nonlinear GP regressors. In [21], a mapping from high-dimensional observations to latent states is estimated, both not the inverse. In [12] a manifold tracking method is used for learning nonlinear motion manifolds in the recovery of 3D body pose, but does not address the case when significant dynamics changes are observed in the video sequence (*i.e.*, multiple dynamics). Other methods that, like ours, are based on Gaussian Processes include [29,28]. However, [29] assumes one single chart and a priori fixed latent dimensionality, while [28] encourages certain topologies in a top-down manner, based on prior knowledge. Our approach also somewhat resembles, in spirit, the Spatial GPCA method [3], although Spatial GPCA operates at the pixel level rather than extracting contours and requires downsampling for computational reasons. Our main advantage resides in the fact that we perform dimensionality reduction, avoiding the need to downsample. In summary, our proposed method explicitly utilizes the manifold assumption, avoids the need to perform alignment of multiple local coordinate systems and maintains topological flexibility. To summarize, the following main differences should be considered: we consider arbitrary topologies with multiple nonlinear charts and multiple nonlinear dynamics, while existing methods consider either: (i) single nonlinear charts/dynamics [29]; (ii) multiple linear charts/dynamics [24]; or (iii) predefined topologies [28]. Besides, we do not marginalize over parameters and therefore can more easily perform out-of-sample prediction, as well as sequential state estimation, while GPDM [29] and [28] use batch inference.

3   GP–MLM Algorithm

The GP–MLM algorithm comprises the following steps: (i) estimation of intrinsic dimensionality and tangent subspaces; (ii) a nonparametric, nonlinear regression procedure for partitioning the manifold and learning the charts. Each of the steps is described here.

Intrinsic dimension: In the spirit of [13], GP–MLM addresses the problem of dimensionality estimation by automatically finding the "knee" of the eigenvalues $\lambda_1, \ldots, \lambda_m$ of the local covariance $\mathbf{S}_{\mathbf{y}_j} = \frac{1}{|\mathcal{B}_{\mathbf{y}_j,\epsilon}|-1} \sum_{\mathbf{y}_k \in \mathcal{B}_{\mathbf{y}_j,\epsilon}} (\mathbf{y}_k - \mu_{\mathcal{B}_{\mathbf{y}_j,\epsilon}})(\mathbf{y}_k - \mu_{\mathcal{B}_{\mathbf{y}_j,\epsilon}})^T$, using local PCA, but in GP–MLM this is done for *all* ϵ-local neighborhoods $\mathcal{B}_{\mathbf{y}_j,\epsilon}$ around each data point $\mathbf{y}_j$. For each neighborhood, the eigenvalue immediately before the greatest drop in value should correspond to the intrinsic dimension, estimated by $\widehat{n}_j \equiv \arg\max_{i=1,\ldots,m-1} |\lambda_{i+1} - \lambda_i|$. The global estimate is $\widehat{n} = \text{median}_{j=1,\ldots,N}(\widehat{n}_j)$, which is more robust than the mean. The advantage of this approach is that it takes advantage of the potentially large number of local PCA neighborhoods.

Temporal information is also used to improve the estimates of the tangent subspaces. We use the first differences $\Delta_{\mathbf{y}_t} = \mathbf{y}_t - \mathbf{y}_{t-1}$, together with the observations $\mathbf{y}_t$ for performing local PCA, by augmenting $\mathcal{B}_{\mathbf{y}_j,\epsilon}$ with $\mu_{\mathcal{B}_{\mathbf{y}_j,\epsilon}} + \Delta_{\mathbf{y}_k}$, for $k = 1, \ldots, |\mathcal{B}_{\mathbf{y}_j,\epsilon}|$, with the neighborhood centers $\mu_{\mathcal{B}_{\mathbf{y}_j,\epsilon}}$ given by the sample means $\mu_{\mathcal{B}_{\mathbf{y}_j,\epsilon}} = \frac{1}{|\mathcal{B}_{\mathbf{y}_j,\epsilon}|} \sum_{\mathbf{y}_k \in \mathcal{B}_{\mathbf{y}_j,\epsilon}} \mathbf{y}_k$. Note that the velocities (of which the $\Delta_{\mathbf{y}_t}$ are rough estimates), applied at the neighborhood centers, must live on the corresponding tangent subspaces. This leads to an effective increase in the number of available points at each neighborhood, from $|\mathcal{B}_{\mathbf{y}_j,\epsilon}|$ points to $2|\mathcal{B}_{\mathbf{y}_j,\epsilon}|$ (or $2|\mathcal{B}_{\mathbf{y}_j,\epsilon}| - 1$ if either the first or last $\Delta_{\mathbf{y}_t}$ can not be computed).

Charts: At this stage, an estimate $\widehat{n}$ of the intrinsic dimension is available. The tangent bundle $T_{\mathcal{M}}$ can, if approximated by some finite set of $\widehat{n}$-dimensional tangent linear hyperplanes, form a convenient collection of local parametric domains upon which to map the manifold points. We partition $\mathcal{M}$ into overlapping patches $\mathcal{P}_1, \ldots, \mathcal{P}_p$, find p corresponding tangent hyperplanes, and estimate mappings back and forth between the patches and the hyperplanes. It is important to find a partition which facilitates subsequent estimation of the mappings. We follow the Tangent Bundle Approximation (TBA) approach proposed in [26] which is based on *principal angles*, a generalization of the concept of angle to linear subspaces.

The idea is not to allow the maximum principal angle between the tangent subspaces – spanned by matrices $\mathbf{V}_i$ and $\mathbf{V}_j$ of column eigenvectors found by local PCA on neighborhoods i and j – to vary more than a set threshold τ. The exact value of τ is not critical, as long as it is below $\frac{\pi}{2}$.

Patches are found by an agglomerative clustering procedure, *i.e.*, region growing. Each patch grows by appending all neighboring (within an ϵ radius) points where the tangent subspace does not deviate, in maximum principal angle, more than a set threshold from the tangent subspace at the initial seed. Any specific point may belong to more than one patch. The final result is a covering of $\mathcal{M}$ by a finite number, p, of overlapping patches. Within each patch, the curvature is controlled through τ, and the distance test ensures that each patch is a connected set. Subsequently, we find the best fitting hyperplane for each patch using PCA, providing local coordinate systems for different manifold regions. The collection of hyperplanes approximates the tangent bundle. Thus, PCA must be performed twice: first with local scope, in tight neighborhoods $\mathcal{B}_{\mathbf{x},\epsilon}$ around each point, so that the principal angles can be controlled *within the patch* during the partitioning procedure; and second, for all patch members, in order to find an overall hyperplane for charting and the corresponding coordinate system. If $\mathbf{S}_{\mathcal{P}_i}$ is the covariance of the points in $\mathcal{P}_i$, i.e. $\mathbf{S}_{\mathcal{P}_i} = \frac{1}{|\mathcal{P}_i|-1} \sum_{\mathbf{y}_k \in \mathcal{P}_i} (\mathbf{y}_k - \boldsymbol{\mu}_{\mathcal{P}_i})(\mathbf{y}_k - \boldsymbol{\mu}_{\mathcal{P}_i})^T$, then, by performing the eigendecomposition $\mathbf{S}_{\mathcal{P}_i} = \mathbf{V}_{\mathcal{P}_i} \mathbf{D}_{\mathcal{P}_i} \mathbf{V}_{\mathcal{P}_i}^T$, where $\mathbf{V}_{\mathcal{P}_i}$ is the matrix whose columns are the eigenvectors of $\mathbf{S}_{\mathcal{P}_i}$ and $\mathbf{D}_{\mathcal{P}_i} = \mathrm{diag}(\lambda_1, \ldots, \lambda_m)$, an orthonormal basis is found in the columns of $\mathbf{V}_{\mathcal{P}_i}$. Note that the patch mean $\boldsymbol{\mu}_{\mathcal{P}_i}$ does not, in general, coincide with the patch seed. The added computational burden of patch-wide PCA is negligible, compared to that of local PCA.

An important note is that GP–MLM (like TBA) does not guarantee that the number of patches is minimal - in fact, the followed approach usually leads to an overestimation of the number of patches needed to cover a manifold. On the other hand, it should also be noted that, since the principal angles only need to be computed between the data and the seeds, and not between all pairs of data points, the overall complexity of the partitioning algorithm is *not* quadratic in N, but rather it is $O(Np)$.

Gaussian process regression: Using the coordinate systems found above, and since there are no folds in any patch (thanks to the angular restriction), the regression problem associated with the charts is significantly simplified. From the previously obtained partition of the dataset into patches $\mathcal{P}_i$, with $i = 1, \ldots, p$, it is now intended to estimate the charts $\mathbf{g}_i(\mathbf{y})$. Let a particular training point $\mathbf{y}$, belonging to patch $\mathcal{P}_i$, be denoted $\mathbf{y} = [y_1 \ldots y_m]^T$, where $y_j, j = 1, \ldots, m$ refers to the jth coordinate. Projecting $\mathbf{y}$ onto the subspace spanned by $\mathbf{V}_{\mathcal{P}_i}$ yields the ith local representation $\mathbf{x}_i$. This can be done according to $\tilde{\mathbf{x}}_i = \mathbf{V}_{\mathcal{P}_i}^T (\mathbf{y} - \boldsymbol{\mu}_{\mathcal{P}_i})$ in which the intermediate quantity $\tilde{\mathbf{x}}_i$ simply corresponds to $\mathbf{y}$ in a new coordinate system with origin at $\boldsymbol{\mu}_{\mathcal{P}_i}$ and versors given by the columns of $\mathbf{V}_{\mathcal{P}_i}$; the following step is

$$\mathbf{x}_i = [\tilde{x}_{i,1} \ldots \tilde{x}_{i,n}]^T = \mathbf{g}_i(\mathbf{y}) \tag{3}$$

where $\mathbf{x}_i$ denotes a truncated version of $\tilde{\mathbf{x}}_i$ using only the first n components. This is the chart. The inverse mapping, that is, the parametrization $\mathbf{h}_i(\mathbf{x}_i)$ follows the expression

$$\mathbf{h}_i(\mathbf{x}_i) = \mathbf{V}_{\mathcal{P}_i} \left[\mathbf{x}_i \quad \tilde{\mathbf{h}}_i(\mathbf{x}_i) \right]^T + \boldsymbol{\mu}_i \tag{4}$$

in which $\tilde{\mathbf{h}}_i$ must be estimated. The remaining $m - n$ components of $\tilde{\mathbf{x}}_i$ are approximated by $\tilde{\mathbf{h}}_i(\mathbf{x}_i)$, and thus the nonlinear character of the manifold is preserved. In the ith local coordinates, the parametrization is $\mathbf{x}_i \to [\mathbf{x}_i \quad \tilde{\mathbf{h}}_i(\mathbf{x}_i)]^T$.

It is now necessary to estimate $\tilde{\mathbf{h}}$. For a particular $m - n$-dimensional vector $\tilde{\mathbf{x}}_i$, consider an independent Gaussian process for each scalar component $\tilde{x}_j$, dropping the j subscript of the jth coordinate for conciseness – the exposition will proceed, without loss of generality, as if $m - n = 1$. The regression problem is that of estimating $\tilde{\mathbf{h}}_i$, from the set of available data $\tilde{\mathcal{X}}_{\mathcal{P}_i} = \{\tilde{x}_{k,i}\}_{k=1:|\mathcal{P}_i|}$ and the corresponding set of $|\mathcal{P}_i|$ local projections $\mathcal{X}_{\mathcal{P}_i} = \{\mathbf{x}_{k,i}\}_{k=1:|\mathcal{P}_i|}$, all collected in $\tilde{\mathbf{x}} \in \mathbb{R}^{|\mathcal{P}_i|}$ and $\mathbf{X} \in \mathbb{R}^{n \times |\mathcal{P}_i|}$ respectively. The estimate should be the one that best matches the model $\tilde{x}_k = h_i(\mathbf{x}_{k,i}) + \omega_{k,i}$ with noise $\omega_{k,i} \sim \mathcal{N}(0, \sigma_i^2)$, $\forall k$. It is assumed that the joint pdf of $\tilde{x}$ is Gaussian, with zero mean (the data can be mean-subtracted) and with known covariance matrix $\mathbf{K} \in \mathbb{R}^{|\mathcal{P}_i| \times |\mathcal{P}_i|}$. With this assumption, it is possible to derive the conditional density $p(\tilde{x}|\mathbf{X})$. Furthermore, for any new set of inputs $\mathbf{X}^*$ outside of the training set, the conditional density $p(\tilde{x}^*|\mathbf{X}^*, \mathbf{X}, \tilde{x})$ is given [22] by

$$p(y^*|\mathbf{X}^*, \mathbf{X}, \mathbf{y}) = \mathcal{N}(\mathbf{K}(\mathbf{X}^*, \mathbf{X})\mathbf{K}(\mathbf{X}, \mathbf{X})^{-1}\mathbf{y}, \tag{5}$$
$$\mathbf{K}(\mathbf{X}^*, \mathbf{X}^*) - \mathbf{K}(\mathbf{X}^*, \mathbf{X})\mathbf{K}(\mathbf{X}, \mathbf{X})^{-1}\mathbf{K}(\mathbf{X}, \mathbf{X}^*)).$$

For constructing $\mathbf{K}$, we choose the RBF covariance function

$$k(\mathbf{x}_i, \mathbf{x}_j) = \theta_1 \exp(-\frac{1}{2\theta_2}\|\mathbf{x}_i - \mathbf{x}_j\|^2) + \delta_{ij}\theta_3 \tag{6}$$

and optimize the hyperparameters by maximizing the marginal likelihood, as proposed in [22].

4 Dynamical Learning Using the Manifold Model

We now extend GP–MLM to deal with the simultaneous estimation of the data manifold and dynamics. The idea is to start from the state model in (1), (2), assuming that, in the observation equation, $\mathbf{h}$ is given by the manifold model found by the GP–MLM and therefore fixed. We then tackle the following two subproblems: (i) Identification of the dynamics $\mathbf{f}$, given h; (ii) Estimation of the state at time t, given all information up to time t. The first subproblem is called system identification and is solved offline, as explained next.

System identification: We assume that the training trajectories have been mapped to low dimensional points $\mathbf{x}_{t,i}$ in patch $\mathcal{P}_i$, at instant t. For each i, we form training pairs $(\mathbf{x}_{t-1}, \mathbf{x}_t)$. The subscript i has been dropped for conciseness, since it will be assumed that the trajectory segment remains on patch i. This is no loss of generality, since in the case when the original high dimensional $\{\mathbf{y}_t\}_{t=0:T-1}$ crosses patches i and j (or more), this simply results in multiple trajectory segments, $\{\mathbf{x}_{t,i}\}_{t=0:T_i-1}$ and $\{\mathbf{x}_{t,j}\}_{t=0:T_j-1}$, which can be treated separately and which count towards the dynamics in patch $\mathcal{P}_i$ and $\mathcal{P}_j$ respectively.

The regression procedure aims at finding the best $\mathbf{f}_i$ that maps $\mathbf{x}_{t-1}$ to $\mathbf{x}_t$ in patch $\mathcal{P}_i$, given the corresponding set $\mathcal{X}_i$ of trajectory segments pertaining to $\mathcal{P}_i$. The generative model is

$$\mathbf{x}_{t,i} = \mathbf{f}_i(\mathbf{x}_{t-1,i}) + \boldsymbol{\omega}_{t,i}. \tag{7}$$

In the case when the dynamics are linear, and dropping the i subscript, (7) turns into $\mathbf{x}_t = \mathbf{A}\mathbf{x}_{t-1} + \boldsymbol{\omega}_t$, with $\mathbf{A}$ a $n \times n$ matrix. When, additionally, the $\boldsymbol{\omega}_t$ are iid and Gaussian, then this is a thoroughly studied case; identification consists of estimating $\mathbf{A}$ from the pairs $(\mathbf{x}_{t-1}, \mathbf{x}_t)$, which can be done by the Least Mean Squares method.

When $\mathbf{f}$ is not a linear function of $\mathbf{x}$, then we propose a nonparametric approach, again based on Gaussian process regression using the RBF kernel (6).

As in the geometrical step, but now with training pairs $(\mathbf{x}_{t-1}, \mathbf{x}_t)$ arranged in matrices $\boldsymbol{\Xi}, \mathbf{X}$ defined as $\mathbf{X} = [\mathbf{x}_1, \dots, \mathbf{x}_{T-1}]$, $\boldsymbol{\Xi} = [\mathbf{x}_0, \dots, \mathbf{x}_{T-2}]$, the regression procedure yields, for any new $\mathbf{x}_{t-1}^*$, Gaussian conditional densities $p(\hat{x}_t^{(i)} | \mathbf{x}_{t-1}^*, \boldsymbol{\Xi}, \boldsymbol{\xi}^{(i)}) = \mathcal{N}(\mu_{x_t^{(i)}}, \sigma_{x_t^{(i)}}^2)$, for all $i = 1, \dots, n$ components of $\hat{\mathbf{x}}_t$ and with $\boldsymbol{\xi}^{(i)} \in \mathbb{R}^{(T-1)}$ equal to the i-th column of $\mathbf{X}^T$.

Filtering: The second subproblem is one of *filtering*. It is not desirable in general to use one single observation to obtain the state, because simply inverting the observation equation (2) ignores the temporal dependence between successive data points. The

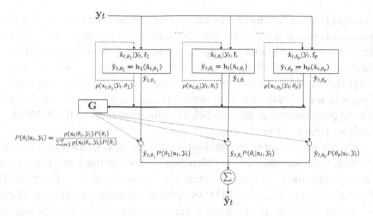

Fig. 2. Block diagram of the mixture architecture for combining the local dynamic models

correct procedure is to estimate the state, at each instant t using information about the whole trajectory up to time t. This can be done online by a variety of filtering methods.

Note that GP–MLM is a multiple-model framework; thus, we employ one filter for each patch, using different dynamics, observation models and coordinate systems. This means that a procedure for combining the local estimates is required. Fig. 2 illustrates how this is performed. Essentially, we make use of the predictive variance from each local GP in order to compute patch posterior probabilities (mixture weights) inexpensively, *i.e.*, we set

$$P(\theta_i|\mathbf{x}, \mathcal{Y}_t) \propto p(\mathbf{x}|\theta_i, \mathcal{Y}_t). \tag{8}$$

The mixture weights provided by block **G** take the different dynamics into account. Different strategies are possible: a "winner-take-all" rule, where only the output of the model with the highest posterior probability is used, or a "blending" rule, where the weighted average using all models is computed. In this paper we present results using Kalman and particle filtering with the above mentioned rules.

5 Experimental Results

This section presents an experimental evaluation of GP–MLM in several data sequences. The evaluation is done in two main situations: first, two ultrasound sequences of the left ventricle (LV) of the heart, aiming at estimating the endocardium boundary. In both, the object of interest undergoes changing motion dynamics. For all experiments, three identification strategies are compared: (i) linear first order; (ii) linear second order and (iii) Gaussian process (GP) first order. In the second experiment, lip sequences are considered. Two situations are presented: (i) speaking, and (ii), singing, where in the latter the lips boundary exhibits a higher deformation. An objective evaluation is conducted for all the experiments using several metrics proposed in the literature.

Heart tracking: This example consists of two ultrasound (US) images sequence. Each US image displays a cross section of the left ventricle (LV) in the long-axis. The length of the sequences is: 490 frames (26 cardiac cycles) and 470 frames (19 cardiac cycles).

The heart motion is described by two dynamics: an expansion motion that occurs in diastole phase, and a contraction motion that characterizes the systole phase. To represent the boundary of the LV, 21 contour points are used, which would require thousands of manual clicks, if we were to obtain ground-truth by hand. Instead, an automatic procedure is used [17]. The MMDA (*Multiple Model Data Association*) tracker is robust with respect to outliers and capable of coping with different, abrupt motion dynamics. Thus, we measure the performance of the GP–MLM with the respect to the MMDA tracking output, which we treat as ground truth.

In this study, we go further in the attempt to find the best technique (*i.e.* Kalman vs particle filtering; "winner-take-all" vs "blending" rules); at the same time we hope to demonstrate the superiority of the non-linear GP 1st order model. To attain this goal an objective evaluation between the MMDA contour estimates (taken as gold contours) and the GP–MLM estimates is provided; several metrics proposed in the literature for contours comparison are used. To accomplish this, a comparison between the contour estimates provided by MMDA tracker (*i.e.* the ground-truth) and the GP–MLM estimate is conducted. Five metrics are used in these tests: Hammoude distance (HMD) [6]; average distance (AV); Hausdorff distance (HDF); Mean sum of Square Distances (MSSD); Mean Absolute Distance (MAD) (as in used in [9]); and the DICE metric. Next, we briefly describe them.

Let $\mathcal{X} = \{\mathbf{x}_1, \mathbf{x}_2, \dots, \mathbf{x}_{N_x}\}$, and $\mathcal{Y} = \{\mathbf{y}_1, \mathbf{y}_2, \dots, \mathbf{y}_{N_y}\}$, be two sets of points obtained by sampling the estimated contour and the reference contour. The smallest distance from a point $\mathbf{x}_i$ to the curve $\mathcal{Y}$ is

$$d(\mathbf{x}_i, \mathcal{Y}) = \min_j \|\mathbf{y}_j - \mathbf{x}_i\| \tag{9}$$

This is known as the distance to the closest point (DCP). The average distance between the sets $\mathcal{X}$, $\mathcal{Y}$ is

$$d_{\text{AV}} = \frac{1}{N_x} \sum_{i=1}^{N_x} d(\mathbf{x}_i, \mathcal{Y}) \tag{10}$$

where N_x is the length of the $\mathcal{X}$ The Hausdorff distance between both sets is defined as the maximum of the DCP's between the two curves

$$d_{\text{HDF}}(\mathcal{X}, \mathcal{Y}) = \max\left(\max_i\{d(\mathbf{x}_i, \mathcal{Y})\}, \max_j\{d(\mathbf{y}_j, \mathcal{X})\}\right) \tag{11}$$

The Hammoude distance is defined as follows [6]

$$d_{\text{HMD}}(\mathcal{X}, \mathcal{Y}) = \frac{\#((R_\mathcal{X} \cup R_\mathcal{Y}) - (R_\mathcal{X} \cap R_\mathcal{Y}))}{\#(R_\mathcal{X} \cup R_\mathcal{Y})} \tag{12}$$

where $R_\mathcal{X}$ represents the image region delimited by the contour $\mathcal{X}$, similarly for $R_\mathcal{Y}$.

To define MSSD [7] and MAD [8] distances, let us consider the tracked sequence S_i with m contours $\{c_1, c_2, \dots, c_m\}$, where each jth contour c_j has n points $\{(x_{j,1}, y_{j,1}), (x_{j,2}, y_{j,2}), \dots, (x_{j,n}, y_{j,n})\}$, the distances of sequence S_i from other version of the sequence S_i^r (which is the ground truth) are

$$d_{\text{MSSD}_i} = \frac{1}{m} \sum_{j=1}^m \frac{1}{n} \sum_{k=1}^n ((x_{j,k} - x_{j,k}^r)^2 + (y_{j,k} - y_{j,k}^r)^2) \tag{13}$$

$$d_{\text{MAD}_i} = \frac{1}{m} \sum_{j=1}^m \frac{1}{n} \sum_{k=1}^n \sqrt{(x_{j,k} - x_{j,k}^r)^2 + (y_{j,k} - y_{j,k}^r)^2} \tag{14}$$

The overall performance measure for a particular method is the averaged distance on the whole test set of L sequences:

$$d_{\text{MSSD}} = \tfrac{1}{L} \sum_{i=1}^{L} d_{\text{MSSD}_i}, \qquad d_{\text{MAD}} = \tfrac{1}{L} \sum_{i=1}^{L} d_{\text{MAD}_i}$$

The DICE metric is also used, which is the mean perpendicular distance between estimated contour and the ground-truth contour. We compute the average metric distance for all points in the curve as follows

$$d_{\text{DICE}} = \tfrac{1}{N} \sum_{i=1}^{N} \|\mathbf{x}_i - \mathbf{y}_i\| \mathbf{n}_i \qquad (15)$$

where $\mathbf{n}_i$ defines the normal vector at point i.

Table 1 left, lists the MSE for the three identification strategies for each path found by GP–MLM. In both sequences the GP consistently provide the best results comparing with the remaining strategies. In these experiments, the data was split in two disjoint training/test sets (50% for training and testing).

Objective evaluation: Table 1 shows the fidelity in the representation of the LV contour obtained in the two US sequences. These values correspond to the mean values of the metrics. From this table and in both sequences and for the majority of the measures, the best values are obtained when ones used particle filtering with the "blending" rule. Although, the particle filtering with the "blending" rule provides the best results, what is important to stress is that any tracking method can be incorporated in the framework and the manifold is always well estimated.

In this study we carried out an additional experiment, we varied the number of frames used in training-testing sets for both sequences, more specifically, we varied the number of training images from 25%, 50% and 75%. Table 2 shows the Hammoude distance using the particle filter with the blending rule (similar behavior is observed of the other tracking versions). From the Table 2, what it is interesting to note is that changing the number of training-test images, the manifold is always well estimated for both sequences, where a slight and negligible increase of this metric is shown.

Table 1. MSE for the three identification strategies obtained in both US sequences: linear $1st$ and $2nd$ order models and a non-linear GP model (left); objective evaluation considering five metrics. The mean values are shown for the two US sequences(right).

Patch #	Sequence # 1 MSE		
	Linear 1st order	Linear 2nd order	GP 1st order
1	4.7826	6.9604	**1.1440**
2	2.5327	1.7007	**0.4164**
3	4.8318	4.4788	**0.4199**
4	7.1060	1.7813	**0.3520**
5	2.0454	4.2491	**0.4662**

Patch #	Sequence # 2 MSE		
	Linear 1st order	Linear 2nd order	GP 1st order
1	5.8521	5.3898	**0.5788**
2	5.9573	3.6770	**0.1379**
3	4.8241	4.5712	**0.4720**
4	6.0968	4.9661	**2.6763**

		d_{HMD}	d_{AV}	d_{HDF}	d_{MSSD}	d_{MAD}	d_{DICE}
Seq. 1	KF - WTA	0.14	3.08	5.48	13.23	3.09	2.52
	KF - BLD	0.14	3.08	5.47	13.20	3.09	2.53
	PF - WTA	**0.09**	2.12	3.86	7.42	2.17	1.79
	PF - BLD	**0.09**	**2.02**	**3.63**	**6.22**	**2.04**	**1.70**
Seq. 2	KF - WTA	0.11	2.73	4.80	10.66	2.79	2.00
	KF - BLD	0.11	2.81	4.89	11.33	2.89	2.04
	PF - WTA	**0.08**	1.76	3.70	4.92	1.78	**1.59**
	PF - BLD	**0.08**	**1.74**	**3.64**	**4.81**	**1.75**	**1.59**

Table 2. Hammoude metric for two US sequences, varying the number of training images

d_{HMD}	25%	50%	75%
Seq. 1	0.063	0.088	0.093
Seq. 2	0.077	0.081	0.090

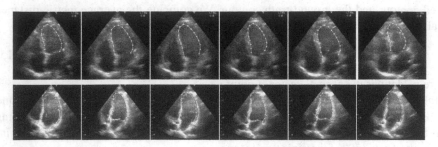

Fig. 3. GP–MLM tracking estimates (yellow line), superimposed with MMDA tracker (red line) taken as gold contours. First sequence (top row), and second sequence (bottom row).

Fig. 3 shows some snapshots for both LV sequences. The manifold results are shown in yellow solid lines, and the ground truth is (output of the MMDA tracker).

Lip tracking: The second example consists of lip tracking in two different situations: speaking and singing. We show results in seven speaking sequences and three singing sequences. In the speaking sequences, each one has about 80 images, while in the singing case the sequence are a bit longer (100 images). Comparing to the previous example, the nonrigid object (lip boundary) exhibits an higher variability in the shape, specially when a person is singing.

From this point on, and due to the lack of space we present the results using particle filtering with the blending rule (other alternatives are, of course, possible to use as previously illustrated).

In the following, the training and testing mechanism follows a leave-one-out strategy (this can be also used in the case of the LV tracking, but there was no need to do this due to the large extension of the LV sequences).

Table 3 (left) shows the results obtained for the speaking case. It can be seen that the framework proposed herein maintain comparable results as in the previous case. Recall that the Hammoude metric (XOR pixel wise operation between the ground truth and the manifold estimates) is always below 15%. Comparing to the results obtained for the singing sequences (see right of the Table 3), we see that a small decrease on this distance, and the small increase of the metrics which penalizes maximum local distances. This is somehow expected, since in this case, a large and sudden changes in the lips boundary may be obtained in consecutive frames. For instance, in Fig. 5 (top row) the $2nd$, $3rd$ and $7th$, $8th$ frames are consecutive in the video frame. These correspond to difficult situations where the GP–MLM is able to produce good results.

We also compare the GP-MLM approach with the *Gaussian Process Latent Variable Model* GPLVM.[1] To perform the comparison, we first used the reconstruction parameters

---

[1] The code is available from the authors at http://www.cs.man.ac.uk/~neill/gplvm/

Table 3. Average distances and metrics obtained using the GP–MLM, for speaking sequences (left) and singing sequences (right)

	Speaking Sequences					
	d_{HMD}	d_{AV}	d_{HDF}	d_{MSSD}	d_{MAD}	d_{DICE}
Seq1	0.08	2.89	5.80	12.58	3.06	2.14
Seq2	0.11	3.68	7.33	22.44	4.07	3.29
Seq3	0.15	4.62	10.29	48.78	5.69	4.26
Seq4	0.09	3.74	7.93	39.99	4.18	3.04
Seq5	0.14	4.36	8.62	35.19	4.71	3.91
Seq6	0.08	3.23	6.86	15.31	3.33	2.53
Seq7	0.10	3.67	8.08	23.65	3.93	3.02

	Singing Sequences					
	d_{HMD}	d_{AV}	d_{HDF}	d_{MSSD}	d_{MAD}	d_{DICE}
Seq1	0.16	5.19	10.82	68.62	6.60	4.52
Seq2	0.14	4.31	9.07	71.53	5.24	4.19
Seq3	0.14	4.95	10.07	54.79	5.48	4.33

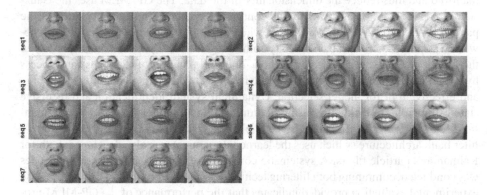

Fig. 4. GP–MLM tracking estimates for seven speaking sequences shown in red dots

of the GPLVM (see [18] for details). We then applied the GPLVM (as we do for the GP-MLM) using the particle filtering with the blending rule for contour tracking. We illustrate the results by showing the Hammoude distance provided by both methods. As previously, this metric is computed between the GP-MLM contour estimates with the output of the MMDA (taken as the ground-truth); and the GPLVM estimates with the MMDA. From the Table 4, we can see that comparable results are achieved. Recall that, for sequences having a higher deformation (see the results in the singing sequences) the GP-MLM exhibits good results.

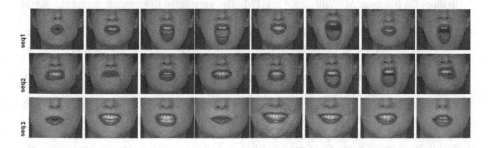

Fig. 5. GP–MLM tracking estimates for three singing sequences shown in red dots

Table 4. Comparison between the tracked contours provided by GP-MLM and the GPLVM in terms of the Hammoude distance. The mean values of the distance are shown for each sequence.

	Left Ventricle		Speaking							Singing		
GP-MLM	**0.088**	**0.081**	0.104	**0.079**	0.142	**0.092**	0.150	**0.084**	**0.113**	**0.157**	**0.141**	**0.145**
GPLVM	0.091	0.088	**0.091**	0.081	**0.112**	0.095	**0.140**	**0.084**	0.127	0.177	0.151	0.156

6 Conclusions

A novel method for manifold learning has been proposed in this paper. This framework employs a local and probabilistic approach to learn a geometrical model of the manifold and thus reduce the dimensionality of the data. The GP-MLM uses the Gaussian process regression as a way to find continuous patches. The decomposition of the patches renders GP-MLM more flexible when dealing to arbitrary topology. A framework was proposed for probabilistically combining the local patch estimates, based on the output of Gaussian process regression. The optimization of the Gaussian process hyperparameters is accomplished via standard gradient descent, which offers a suitable and effective tool for model selection. Dynamical system identification and recursive state estimation are tackled by using the multiple local models returned by the manifold learning step. Identification is accomplished via Gaussian process regression. A filter bank architecture (which uses the learned dynamics) was also developed, both for Kalman and particle filters. A systematic comparative evaluation in several sequences was conducted, combining both filtering techniques with different gating strategies. The experimental evaluation provided indicates that the performance of the GP-MLM provides good results and it is competitive with the GPLVM approach.

Issues for future research include reducing the number of patches, as well as a way to compute the scale parameter ϵ. Reliable estimation of the intrinsic manifold dimension also remains a difficult challenge, on its own right. Robust statistics may be a fruitful direction of research for this problem.

References

1. Belkin, M., Niyogi, P.: Laplacian eigenmaps for dimensionality reduction and data representation. Neural Computation 15, 1373–1396 (2003)
2. Bishop, C., Svensen, M., Williams, C.: GTM: The generative topographic mapping. Neural Computation 10, 215 (1998)
3. Ravichandran, A., Vidal, R., Halperin, H.: Segmenting a Beating Heart Using PolySegment and patial GPCA. In: IEEE International Symposium on Biomedical Imaging, pp. 634–637 (2006)
4. Boothby, W.M.: An Introduction to Differential Manifolds and Riemannian Geometry. Academic Press, London (2003)
5. Brand, M.: Charting a manifold. In: NIPS, p. 15 (2002)
6. Hammoude, A.: Computer-assited endocardial border identification from a sequence of two-dimensional echocardiographic images, PhD (1988)
7. Akgul, Y., Kambhamettu, C.: A coarse-to-fine deformable contour optimization framework. IEEE Trans. PAMI. 25(2), 174–186 (2003)

8. Mikić, I., Krucinki, S., Thomas, J.D.: Segmentation and tracking in echocardiographic sequences: Active contours guided by optical flow estimates. IEEE Trans. Med. Imag. 17(2), 274–284 (1998)
9. Comaniciu, D., Zhou, X., Krishnan, S.: Robust real-time tracking of myocardial border:an information fusion approach. IEEE Trans. Med. Imag. 23(7), 849–860 (2004)
10. Donoho, D.L., Grimes, C.: Hessian eigenmaps: new locally linear embedding techniques for high-dimensional data. Tech. Report TR-2003-08 (2003)
11. Doretto, G., Chiuso, A., Wu, Y., Soatto, S.: Dynamic textures. IJCV (2003)
12. Elgammal, A., Lee, C.-S.: Nonlinear manifold learning for dynamic shape and dynamic appearance. CVIU 106, 31–46 (2007)
13. Fukunaga, K., Olsen, D.R.: An algorithm for finding intrinsic dimensionality of data. In: IEEE Trans. on Computers (1971)
14. Julosky, A., Weiland, S., Heemels, M.: A Bayesian approach to identifications of hybrid systems. IEEE Trans. on Automatic Control 10, 1520–1533 (2005)
15. Levina, E., Bickel, P.J.: Maximum likelihood estimation of intrinsic dimension. In: NIPS (2004)
16. Little, A., Jung, Y.-M., Maggioni, M.: Multiscale Estimation of Intrinsic Dimensionality of Data Dets. AAAI, Menlo Park (2009)
17. Nascimento, J.C., Marques, J.S.: Robust shape tracking with multiple models in ultrasound images. IEEE Trans. on Image Proc. 17(3), 392–406 (2008)
18. Neil, L.: Probabilistic non-linear principal component analysis with gaussian process latent variable models. J. of Machine Learning Research 7, 455–491 (2005)
19. Raginsky, M.: A complexity-regularized quantization approach to nonlinear dimensionality reduction. In: IEEE Int. Symp. on Info. Theory (2005)
20. Raginsky, M., Lazebnik, S.: Estimation of intrinsic dimensionality using high-rate vector quantization. In: NIPS, vol. 18 (2005)
21. Rahimi, A., Recht, B.: Unsupervised regression with applications to nonlinear system identification. In: NIPS, vol. 19 (2007)
22. Rasmussen, C., Williams, C.: Gaussian Processes for Machine Learning. MIT Press, Cambridge (2005)
23. Roweis, S.T., Ghahramani, Z.: An EM algorithm for identification of nonlinear dynamical systems. Kalman Filtering and Neural Networks (2000)
24. Li, R., Tian, T.-P., Sclaroff, S.: Simultaneous Learning of Nonlinear Manifold and Dynamical Models for High-dimensional Time Series. In: ICCV (2007)
25. Roweis, S.T., Saul, L.K.: Nonlinear dimensionality reduction by locally linear embedding. Science 290, 2323–2326 (2000)
26. Silva, J., Marques, J., Lemos, J.M.: Non-linear dimension reduction with Tangent Bundle Approximation. In: ICASSP (2005)
27. Tenenbaum, J.B., de Silva, V., Langford, J.C.: A global geometric framework for nonlinear dimensionality reduction. Science 290, 2319–2323 (2000)
28. Urtasun, R., Fleet, D.J., Geiger, A., Popovic, J., Darrell, T., Lawrence, N.: Topologically-Constrained Latent Variable Models. In: ICML (2008)
29. Wang, J.M., Fleet, D.J., Hertzmann, A.: Gaussian process dynamical models. In: NIPS, pp. 1441–1448. MIT Press, Cambridge (2005)
30. Weinberger, K., Saul, L.: Unsupervised learning of image manifolds by semidefinite programming. IJCV 70(1), 77–90 (2006)
31. Weinberger, K., Sha, F., Saul, L.: Learning a kernel matrix for nonlinear dimensionality reduction. In: ICML, pp. 839–846 (2004)

Detection and Tracking of Large Number of Targets in Wide Area Surveillance

Vladimir Reilly, Haroon Idrees, and Mubarak Shah

Computer Vision Lab, University of Central Florida, Orlando, USA
vsreilly@eecs.ucf.edu, haroon.idrees@knights.ucf.edu,
shah@eecs.ucf.edu
http://www.cs.ucf.edu/~vision

Abstract. In this paper, we tackle the problem of object detection and tracking in a new and challenging domain of wide area surveillance. This problem poses several challenges: large camera motion, strong parallax, large number of moving objects, small number of pixels on target, single channel data and low framerate of video. We propose a method that overcomes these challenges and evaluate it on CLIF dataset. We use median background modeling which requires few frames to obtain a workable model. We remove false detections due to parallax and registration errors using gradient information of the background image. In order to keep complexity of the tracking problem manageable, we divide the scene into grid cells, solve the tracking problem optimally within each cell using bipartite graph matching and then link tracks across cells. Besides tractability, grid cells allow us to define a set of local scene constraints such as road orientation and object context. We use these constraints as part of cost function to solve the tracking problem which allows us to track fast-moving objects in low framerate videos. In addition to that, we manually generated groundtruth for four sequences and performed quantitative evaluation of the proposed algorithm.

Keywords: Tracking, Columbus Large Image Format, CLIF, Wide Area Surveillance.

1 Introduction

Recently a new sensor platform has appeared on the scene, allowing for persistent monitoring of very large areas. The dataset examined in this paper is Columbus Large Image Format or CLIF dataset. In CLIF, the sensor consists of six cameras with partially overlapping fields of view, mounted on an aerial platform flying at 7000 feet. All six cameras simultaneously capture 4016x2672 intensity images at 2 frames per second. See Figure 1(a) for an example of global camera mosaic.

CLIF dataset belongs to the domain of Wide Area Surveillance (WAS), which could be used to monitor large urban environments, as an aid in disaster relief, as well as traffic and accident management. Monitoring such a large amount of data with a human operator is not feasible, which calls for an automated method of processing the data. An initial step for such a system would be the detection

K. Daniilidis, P. Maragos, N. Paragios (Eds.): ECCV 2010, Part III, LNCS 6313, pp. 186–199, 2010.
© Springer-Verlag Berlin Heidelberg 2010

(a)   (b)

Fig. 1. (a) CLIF data - all six cameras. (b) top shows two consecutive frames overlayed in two different color channels: red is frame t, green is frame $t + 1$. (b) bottom shows how far vehicles move between consecutive frames. Red boxes show vehicle positions in previous frame and blue boxes show vehicle positions in next frame.

and tracking of moving objects such as vehicles moving on highways, streets and parking lots.

Data obtained from such a sensor is quite different from the standard aerial and ground surveillance datasets, such as VIVID and NGSIM, which have been used in [1,2], as well as aerial surveillance scenario [3,4,5]. First, objects in WAS data are much smaller, with vehicle sizes ranging from 4 to 70 pixels in grayscale imagery, compared to over 1500 pixels in color imagery in the VIVID dataset. Second, the data is sampled only at 2 Hz which when compared against more common framerates of 15-30 Hz is rather low. Third, the traffic is very dense comprising thousands of objects in a scene compared to no more than 10 objects in VIVID and no more than 100 in NGSIM.

The first issue makes object detection difficult, but more importantly it disallows the use of shape and appearance models for objects during tracking as in [3,1,5,6] and necessitates an accurate velocity model. However, issues two and three make initialization of a velocity model extremely difficult. High speed of vehicles on highway combined with low sampling rate of the imagery results in large displacement of objects between frames. This displacement is larger than spacing between objects, making proximity based initial assignment produce incorrect labeling which results in incorrect velocity model.

Highspeed 60Hz cameras have been used to address this problem in dense scenarios [7,8], where the high sampling rate makes initial proximity based assignment meaningful. Instead, we leverage structured nature of the scene to obtain a set of constraints and use them in our tracking function. Specifically, we derive road orientation and traffic context constraints to help with initial assignment. We cannot define context based on appearance of neighboring objects

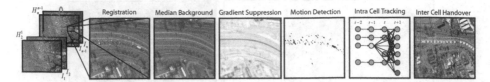

Fig. 2. This figure shows different stages of our pipeline. First, we remove global camera motion using point based registration, then we model the background using a 10 frame median image, perform background subtraction and suppress false positives due to parallax and registration errors. We track objects within individual grid cells, then perform handover of tracks between grid cells.

and background as has been done in [9], instead, we define a descriptor for the geometric relationship of objects with their respective neighbors.

2   Method

Our proposed method consists of the following modules (see figure 2 for reference). First, we register images using a point correspondence based alignment algorithm. Then we perform motion detection via a median image background model. We perform gradient suppression of the background difference image to remove motion detection errors due to parallax and registration. Once we have moving object blobs, we divide the scene into a number of grid cells and optimally track objects within each grid cell using Hungarian algorithm. The use of overlapping cells is a novel idea which makes possible the use of $O(n^3)$ Hungarian algorithm in a scene containing thousands of objects and provides a way to define a set of structured scene constraints to disambiguate initialization of the algorithm. The contribution of our paper is a method for performing object detection and tracking in a new and challenging Wide Area Surveillance dataset characterized by low framerate, fast camera motion and a very large number of fast moving objects. In rest of the paper, we describe how we address all of the challenges and provide details for the individual modules.

2.1   Registration

Prior to motion detection in aerial video, we remove global camera motion. The structured man-made environment in these scenes and large amount of detail yields itself nicely to a point-matching based registration algorithm. It is also much faster than direct registration method. We detect Harris corners in frames at time t as well as at time $t + 1$. Then we compute SIFT descriptor around each point and match the points in frame t to points in frame $t + 1$ using the descriptors. Finally, we robustly fit a homography H_t^{t+1} using RANSAC, that describes the transformation between top 200 matches. Once homographies between individual frames have been computed, we warp all the images to a common reference frame by concatenating the frame to frame homographies.

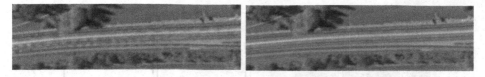

Fig. 3. Left shows a background model obtained using mean which has many ghosting artifacts from moving objects. Right shows background model obtained using median with almost no ghosting artifacts.

2.2   Detection

After removing global camera motion, we detect local motion generated by objects moving in the scene.

To perform motion detection, we first need to model background, then moving objects can be considered as outliers with respect to the background. Probabilistic modeling of the background as in [10] has been popular for surveillance videos. However, we found these methods to be inapplicable to this data. In the parametric family of models, each pixel is modeled as either a single or a mixture of Gaussians. First, there is problem with initialization of background model. Since it is always that objects are moving in the scene, we do not have the luxury of object-free initialization period, not even a single frame. Additionally, since the cameras move, we need to build the background model in as few frames as possible, otherwise our active area becomes severely limited. Furthermore, high density of moving objects in the scene combined with low sampling rate makes the objects appear as outliers. These outliers can be seen as ghosting artifacts as shown in figure 3. In the case of single Gaussian model, besides affecting the mean, the large number of outliers make the standard deviation high, allowing more outliers to become part of the model, which means many moving objects become part of the background model and are not detected.

A mixture of Gaussians makes background modeling even more complex by allowing each pixel to have multiple backgrounds. This is useful when background changes, such as in the case of a moving tree branch in surveillance video. This feature, however, does not alleviate any of the problems we highlighted above.

Therefore, we avoid probabilistic models in favor of simple median image filtering, which learns a background model with less artifacts using fewer frames (figure 3). We found that 10 frame median image has fewer ghosting artifacts than mean image. To obtain a comparable mean image, it has to be computed over at least four times the number of frames which results in smaller field of view and makes false motion detections due to parallax and registration errors more prominent.

We perform motion detection in the following manner. For every 10 frames we compute a median background image B, next we obtain difference image i.e. $I_d = |I - B|$. Prior to thresholding the difference image, we perform gradient suppression. This is necessary to remove false motion detections due to parallax and registration errors. Since we fit a homography to describe the transformation between each pair of frames, we are essentially assuming a planar scene. This

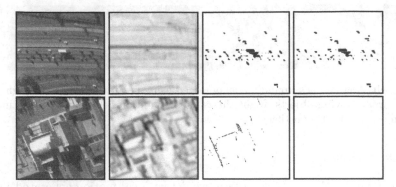

Fig. 4. Left to right: Section of original image, gradient of the median image, motion blobs prior to gradient suppression, motion blobs after gradient suppression. Bottom row shows an area of image that has false motion detections due to parallax and registration errors, top row shows a planar area of the image.

assumption does not hold for portions of the image that contain out of plane objects such as tall buildings. Pixels belonging to these objects are not aligned correctly between frames and hence appear to move even in aligned frames. Additionally due to large camera motion, there may be occasional errors in the alignment between the frames. An example of this is bottom row of figure 4 where we show a small portion of an image containing a tall building (left). Due to parallax error, the building produces false motion detections along its edges (third image from the left). We suppress these by subtracting gradient of the median image ∇B (second column) from the difference image i.e. $I_d^r = I_d - \nabla B$. The top row shows a planar section of the scene and contains moving objects. As evident from figure 4, this procedure successfully suppresses false motion detections due to parallax error without removing genuine moving objects. Also, the method has the advantage of suppressing false motion detections due to registration errors, since they too manifest along gradients. Note that above method works under an assumption that areas containing moving objects will not have parallax error which is valid for roads and highways.

2.3   Tracking

After detecting moving objects, we track them across frames using bipartite graph matching between a set of *label* nodes (circled in blue) and a set of *observation* nodes (circled in magenta). The assignment is solved optimally using the Hungarian algorithm which has complexity $O(n^3)$ where n is the number of nodes. When we have thousands of objects in the scene, an optimal solution for the entire scene is intractable. To overcome this problem, we break up the scene into a set of overlapping grid cells (see figure 8). We solve the correspondence problem within each grid cell independently and then link tracks across grid cells. The use of grid has an additional advantage of allowing us to exploit

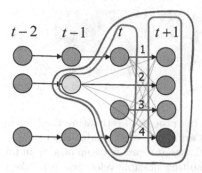

Fig. 5. The figure shows an example of the bipartite graph that we solve at every frame. Four different types of edges are marked with numbers.

local structured-scene constraints for objects within the grid cell, which will be discussed later.

For each grid cell in every pair of frames we construct the following graph. Figure 5 shows an example graph constructed for assigning labels between frames t and $t+1$. We add a set of nodes for objects visible at t to the set of *label* nodes. A set of nodes for objects visible at $t + 1$ are added to the set of *observation* nodes, both types are shown in green. Since objects can exit the scene, or become occluded, we add a set of occlusion nodes to our *observation* nodes, shown in red. To deal with the case of reappearing objects, we also add *label* nodes for objects visible in the set of frames between $t - 1$ and $t - p$, shown in yellow. We fully connect the *label* set of nodes to the *observation* set of nodes, using four types of edges.

1. Edge between label in frame t and an observation in frame $t + 1$.
2. Edge between label in frame $t - p$ and an observation in frame $t + 1$.
3. Edge between a new track label in frame t and an observation in frame $t+1$.
4. Edge between a label and an occlusion node.

We define edge weights in the following manner. Weight for edge of type 3 is simply a constant δ. Weights for edges of type 1 and 2 contain velocity orientation and spatial proximity components. Spatial proximity component C_p is given by

$$C_p = 1 - \frac{\|x^{t-k} + v^{t-k}(k+1) - x^{t+1}\|}{\sqrt{S_x^2 + S_y^2}}, \tag{1}$$

where x is the position of the object, S_x and S_y are the dimensions of the window within which we search for a new object and k is the time past since last observation of the object.

Velocity orientation component C_v is given by

$$C_v = \frac{1}{2} + \frac{v^t \cdot v^{t+1}}{2\|v^t\|\|v^{t+1}\|}, \tag{2}$$

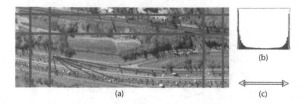

Fig. 6. This figure shows the process of estimating road orientation within a grid cell. Objects tracked in frame t are shown in red, objects detected in frame $t+1$ are shown in blue. (a) Obtain all possible assignments between objects in frame t and frame $t+1$. (b) Obtain a histogram of resulting possible velocities. (c) Take mean of velocities which contributed to the histogram peak.

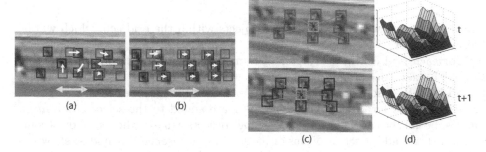

Fig. 7. Vehicles tracked at time t are shown in red while vehicles detected in frame $t+1$ are shown in blue. White arrows indicate the assignment of labels to objects based on proximity only and correspond to resulting velocities of objects. Yellow arrows indicate the road orientation estimate for this particular grid cell. (a) shows a case where road orientation estimate can be used to disambiguate the assignment of labels and (b) shows where it is not useful. To handle cases such as (b), we introduce a new constraint for context of each vehicle, shown in (c). At frames t and $t+1$ we compute vectors between vehicle of interest (green) and its neighbors (orange). We then compute a 2D histogram of orientations and magnitudes of the vectors shown in (c).

where v^t is the last observed velocity of an object, v^{t+1} is the difference between x^{t+1}, the position of observation in current frame, and x^{t-k}, the last observed position of object at frame $t - k$.

We define the weight for edges of type 1 and 2 as follows

$$w = \alpha C_v + (1 - \alpha)C_p. \tag{3}$$

We found these to be sufficient when object's velocity is available. If on the other hand, velocity of the object is unavailable as in initial two frames or when new objects appear in the scene, we use structured scene constraints to compute weights for edges.

Assigning labels based simply on proximity between object centroids is not meaningful in wide area scenario. Due to low sampling rate (2 Hz), high scene density and high speed of objects, proximity based assignment is usually incorrect (see figure 7). Therefore we use road orientation estimate and object context as constraints from the structured scene.

Road orientaion estimate g is computed for each grid cell in the following manner (see figure 6). First, we obtain all possible assignments between objects in frame t and $t+1$. This gives us a set of all possible velocities between objects at frames t and $t+1$. Next, we obtain a histogram of orientations of these velocities and take the mean of orientations that contributed to peak of the histogram. See **Algorithm 1** for a formal description.

Algorithm 1. Algorithm to compute global velocity for each cell in grid of size $m \times n$ using detections D_t and D_{t+1}.

```
 1: procedure COMPUTEGLOBALVELOCITY
 2:     for i ← 1, m do
 3:         for j ← 1, n do
 4:
 5:             for all d ∈ D_t^{i,j} do
 6:                 for all d' ∈ D_{t+1}^{i,j} do
 7:                     θ = tan^{-1} (d' − d)
 8:                     Store θ in Θ
 9:                 end for
10:             end for
11:
12:             h = histogram(Θ)
13:             Find bin ψ s.t. mode(h) ∈ ψ
14:             θ' = mean(θ|θ ∈ ψ)
15:             g⃗(i, j) = [cos(θ')  sin(θ')]
16:
17:         end for
18:     end for
19: end procedure
```

Algorithm 2. Algorithm to compute context $\Phi(O_t^a)$ for object a at frame t.

```
 1: procedure COMPUTECONTEXT
 2:     for all c do
 3:
 4:         if ‖O_t^c − O_t^a‖_2 < r then
 5:             θ = tan^{-1} (O_t^c − O_t^a)
 6:             d = ‖O_t^c − O_t^a‖_2
 7:             Φ = Φ + 𝒩(μ, Σ)
 8:                              ▷ 𝒩 centered on (d, θ)
 9:         end if
10:
11:     end for
12: end procedure
```

Note that orientation of g essentially gives us orientation of the road along which vehicles travel, it does not give us the direction along that road. However, even without the direction, this information is oftentimes sufficient to disambiguate label assignment as shown in figure 7(a). When vehicles travel along the road in a checkerboard pattern, proximity based assignment will result in velocities which are perpendicular to g. That is not the case when a number of vehicles are traveling in a linear formation as in Figure 7(b). Therefore, we introduce an additional formation context constraint (see figures 7(c) and 7(d)). If we are trying to match an object O_a in frame t (or $t-k$) to an observation in frame $t+1$, we compute object context as a 2 dimensional histogram of vector orientations and magnitudes between an object and its neighbors.

In order to account for small intra-formation changes, when computing the context histograms Φ_a and Φ_b, we add a 2D Gaussian kernel centered on the bin to which a particular vector belongs. Furthermore, since $0°$ and $360°$ are equivalent, we make the kernel wrap around to other side of orientation portion of the histogram.

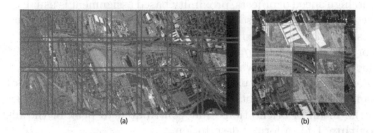

(a)   (b)

Fig. 8. (a) This figure shows an example frame with grid overlayed onto an image. (b) shows the grid cell search procedure for handing over tracks. The bold colored lines correspond to OLLeft, OLBottom, and OLRight, in counterclockwise direction. Only colored grid cells are searched, white cells are ignored.

The road orientation constraint component is defined as

$$C_g = \frac{1}{2} + \frac{|g \cdot v^{t+1}|}{2\|g\|\|v^{t+1}\|} \tag{4}$$

The purpose of this constraint is to prevent tracks from travelling across the road. The context constraint is the histogram intersection between histograms Φ_a and Φ_b:

$$C_c = \sum_p^{Nbins} \sum_q^{Mbins} min(\Phi_a^{p,q}, \Phi_b^{p,q}) \tag{5}$$

Finally, weight for edge of type 3 is computed as follows,

$$w = \alpha_1 C_g + \alpha_2 C_p + (1 - \alpha_1 - \alpha_2)C_c \tag{6}$$

We solve the resulting bipartite graph using Hungarian algorithm. We track all objects within each grid cell by performing the above procedure for all frames. Next, we find and link tracks that have crossed the cell boundaries, using **Algorithm 3** utilizing the overlapping regions of the neighboring grid cells. (see figure 8 for reference).

2.4   Handling Multiple Cameras

There can be several possible frameworks for tracking objects across overlapping cameras which employ inter-camera transformations. One possible way is to establish correspondences at the track level where objects are detected and tracked in each camera independently, and afterwards, tracks belonging to the same object are linked. But, this approach has a serious issue which arises from the fact that background for a particular frame of a camera can only be modeled on overlapping region of all frames used for background. This reduces the area of region where objects can be detected. When objects are detected in cameras separately, reduction in detection regions results in the loss of overlap between

---

Algorithm 3. Algorithm for object handover across grid cells. The size of grid is m x n. $S(i,j)$ represents all tracks for the sequence in the cell at i^{th} row and j^{th} column in grid.

```
 1: procedure INTERCELLHANDOVER
 2:    for i ← 1, m do
 3:       for j ← 1, n do
 4:          Calculate OLLeft, OLRight and OLBottom              ▷ See figure 8
 5:          for all s^{i,j} ∈ S(i,j) do
 6:
 7:             if ∃ k | s_k^{i,j} > OLRight then
 8:                completeTrack(s^{i,j}, S(i + 1, j))
 9:             else if ∃ k | s_k^{i,j} > OLRight ∧ ∃ k | s_k^{i,j} > OLBottom then
10:                completeTrack(s^{i,j}, S(i + 1, j + 1))
11:             else if ∃ k | s_k^{i,j} > OLBottom then
12:                completeTrack(s^{i,j}, S(i, j + 1))
13:             else if ∃ k | s_k^{i,j} < OLLeft ∧ ∃ k | s_k^{i,j} > OLBottom then
14:                completeTrack(s^{i,j}, S(i - 1, j + 1))
15:             end if
16:
17:          end for
18:       end for
19:    end for
20: end procedure

 1: procedure COMPLETETRACK(s, S)        ▷ s=track to complete, S=tracks in neighboring cell
 2:    for all s' ∈ S do
 3:       if ∃ (l,m) | s_l.detectionID = s'_m.detectionID ∧ s_l.t = s'_m.t then
 4:          assign s and s' unique label
 5:       end if
 6:    end for
 7: end procedure
```

---

two cameras. While methods for matching objects across non-overlapping cameras exist [1,11,12,6], low resolution and single channel data disallow the use of appearance models for object hand over, and reacquisition based on motion alone is ambiguous. The increased gap between cameras arising from detection adds further challenge to a data already characterized by high density of objects and low sampling rate of video.

In order to avoid above problems, we perform detection and tracking in global coordinates. We first build concurrent mosaics from images of different cameras at a particular time instant using the Registration method in §2.1 and then register the mosaics treating each concurrent mosaic as a single image.

One problem with this approach, however, is that cameras can have different Camera Response Functions or CRFs. This affects the median background, since intensity values for each pixel now come from multiple cameras causing performance of the detection method to deteriorate. To overcome this issue, we adjust the intensity of each camera with respect to a reference camera using the gamma function [13] i.e.

$$I'_C(x,y) = \beta I_C(x,y)^\gamma, \tag{7}$$

where $I_C(x,y)$ is the intensity of the original image at location (x,y). We find β, γ by minimizing the following cost function:

$$\underset{\beta,\gamma}{\operatorname{argmin}} \sum_{(x,y)\in I_{C1}\cap I_{C2}} (I_{C1}(x,y) - I'_{C2}(x,y))^2, \tag{8}$$

Fig. 9. This figure shows the result of multi-camera intensity equalization. Notice the seam in image on left which in not visible in equalized image on right.

where $I_{C1} \cap I_{C2}$ is the overlap between the two cameras. The cost function is minimized using a trust region method for nonlinear minimization. The approximate Jacobian matrix is calculated by using finite difference derivatives of the cost function. Transformation in equation 7 is then applied to each frame of the camera before generating concurrent mosaics. Results for this procedure are shown in figure 9.

3   Results

We validated our method on four sequences from CLIF 2006 dataset. Sequences 1 to 3 are single camera sequences while sequence 4 has multiple cameras. The average number of objects in these sequences are approximately 2400, 1000, 1200 and 1100 respectively. Objects in sequence 2 and 3 undergo merging more often than objects in the other two sequences. This is primarily due to oblique angle between highway and camera in these sequences as opposed to top view in sequences 1 and 4. Figure 10 shows some of the tracks from these sequences.

For quantitative evaluation, we manually generated ground truth for the four sequences. Due the sheer number of objects, smaller size and similar appearance, generating ground truth for each object is a daunting task. We selected one region from sequence 1,3 and 4 and two regions from sequence 2 for ground truth. Objects were randomly selected and most of them undergo merging and splitting. The number of objects for which ground truth was generated are 34 for sequence 1, 47 and 60 for sequence 2 and 50 each for sequences 3 and 4.

Our method for evaluation is similar to [2] and measures performance of both detection and tracking. We compute the following distance measure between generated tracks and ground truth tracks:

$$D(T_a, G_b) = \frac{1}{|\Omega(T_a, G_b)|^2} \sum_{t \in \Omega(T_a, G_b)} \|\mathbf{x}_t^a - \mathbf{x}_t^b\|^2, \tag{9}$$

where $\Omega(T_a, G_b)$ denotes the temporal overlap between T_a and G_b, $|.|$ denotes cardinality while $\|.\|$ is the Euclidean norm. A set of pairs are associated i.e. $(a, b) \in A$ iff T_a and G_a have an overlap. The optimal association,

$$A^* = \operatorname*{argmin}_{A} \sum_{(a,b) \in A} D(T_a, G_b) \text{ subject to } \Omega(T_a, T_c) = \emptyset \quad \forall (a, b), (c, b) \in A \tag{10}$$

is used to calculate the performance metrics. Abusing notation, we define

$$A(G_b) = \{T_a | (a, b) \in A\}. \tag{11}$$

The first metric *Object Detection Rate*, measures the quality of detections prior to any association:

$$ODR = \frac{\# \text{ correct detections}}{\# \text{ total detections in all frames}}. \tag{12}$$

We cannot compute ODR for each track and then average, because that would bias the metric towards short tracks as they are more likely to have all detections correct. Further notice that, it is not possible to detect false positives as the number of ground truth tracks is less than number of objects. A related metric, *Track Completeness Factor*,

$$TCF = \frac{\sum\limits_{a} \sum\limits_{T_b \in A(G_a)} |\Omega(T_b, G_a)|}{\sum_a |G_a|}, \tag{13}$$

measures how well we detect an object after association. TCF will always be less than or equal to ODR. The difference between ODR and TCF is the percentage of detections that were not included in tracks. Finally, *Track Fragmentation* measures how well we maintain identity of the track,

$$TF = \frac{\sum\limits_{a} |A(G_a)|}{|\{G_a | A(G_a) \neq \emptyset\}|}. \tag{14}$$

Weighing the number of fragments in a track with length, we get *Normalized Track Fragmentation*,

$$NTF = \frac{\sum\limits_{a} |G_a| \cdot |A(G_a)|}{\sum\limits_{a | A(G_a) \neq \emptyset} |G_a|}. \tag{15}$$

which gives more weight to longer tracks as it is more difficult to maintain identity for long tracks than short ones.

We compare our method with the standard bipartite matching using greedy nearest-neighbor initialization. Initial assignment is done based on proximity while linear velocity model is used for prediction. Standard gating technique is used to eliminate unlikely candidates outside a certain radius. The same registration and detection methods were used for all experiments. The values of parameters for our tracking method were $\alpha = 0.5$ (eq. 3) and $\alpha_1 = \alpha_2 = 0.33$ (eq. 6). Table 1 shows the comparison between both methods:

As can be seen from table 1, our method achieved better TCF and TF because unique characteristics of WAS demand the use of scene-based constraints which were not leveraged by the standard bipartite matching. We derived road orientation estimate and object context using only the image data, which allowed for better initialization and tracking performance.

Table 1. Quantitative Comparison

	ODR	Our Method			GreedyBIP		
		TCF	TF	NTF	TCF	TF	NTF
Seq1	0.975	0.716	2.471	2.506	0.361	13.06	13.11
Seq2	0.948	0.714	2.894	2.895	0.489	12.55	12.55
Seq3	0.972	0.727	2.76	2.759	0.583	8.527	8.53
Seq4	0.984	0.824	1.477	1.48	0.638	6.444	6.443

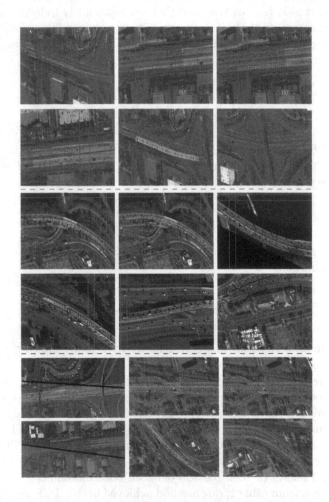

Fig. 10. This figure shows a number of results for different sequences. Top group is for sequence 1, second group is for sequence 2. In the bottom group, first column is from multiple camera sequence (camera boundary is shown in black), next two columns are from sequence 4.

4   Conclusion

We analyzed the challenges of a new aerial surveillance domain called Wide Area Surveillance, and proposed a method for detecting and tracking objects in this data. Our method specifically deals with difficulties associated with this new type of data: unavailability of object appearance, large number of objects and low frame rate. We evaluated proposed method and provided both quantitative and qualitative results. These preliminary steps pave way for more in-depth exploitation of this data such as scene modeling and abnormal event detection.

Acknowledgments. This work was funded by Harris Corporation.

References

1. Javed, O., Shafique, K., Shah, M.: Appearance modeling for tracking in multiple non-overlapping cameras. In: CVPR (2005)
2. Perera, A., Srinivas, C., Hoogs, A., Brooksby, G., Hu, W.: Multi-object tracking through simultaneous long occlusions and split-merge conditions. In: CVPR (2006)
3. Ali, S., Shah, M.: Cocoa: tracking in aerial imagery. In: SPIE, vol. 6209 (2006)
4. Xiao, J., Cheng, H., Han, F., Sawhney, H.: Geo-spatial aerial video processing for scene understanding and object tracking. In: CVPR (2008)
5. Kang, J., Cohen, I., Yuan, C.: Detection and tracking of moving objects from a moving platform in presence of strong parallax. In: ICCV (2005)
6. Arth, C., Leistner, C., Bischof, H.: Object reacquisition and tracking in large-scale smart camera networks. In: ICDSC (2007)
7. Betke, M., Hirsh, D.E., Bagchi, A., Hristov, N.I., Makris, N.C., Kunz, T.H.: Tracking large variable numbers of objects in clutter. In: CVPR (2007)
8. Wu, Z., Hristov, N.I., Hedrick, T.L., Kunz, T.H., Betke, M.: Tracking a large number of objects from multiple views. In: ICCV (2009)
9. Nguyen, H.T., Ji, Q., Smeulders, A.W.M.: Spatio-temporal context for robust multitarget tracking. IEEE PAMI (2007)
10. Stauffer, C., Grimson, W.: Adaptive background mixture models for real-time tracking. In: CVPR (1999)
11. Pflugfelder, R., Bischof, H.: Tracking across non-overlapping views via geometry. In: ICPR (2008)
12. Kaucic, R., Perera, A., Brooksby, G., Kaufhold, J., Hoogs, A.: A unified framework for tracking through occlusions and across sensor gaps. In: CVPR (2005)
13. Farid, H.: Blind inverse gamma correction. IEEE Trans. Image Processing (2001)

Discriminative Tracking by Metric Learning

Xiaoyu Wang[1], Gang Hua[2], and Tony X. Han[1]

[1] Dept. of ECE, University of Missouri
[2] Nokia Research Center, Hollywood
xw9x9@mail.missouri.edu, ganghua@gmail.com, hantx@missouri.edu

Abstract. We present a discriminative model that casts appearance modeling and visual matching into a single objective for visual tracking. Most previous discriminative models for visual tracking are formulated as supervised learning of binary classifiers. The continuous output of the classification function is then utilized as the cost function for visual tracking. This may be less desirable since the function is optimized for making binary decision. Such a learning objective may make it not to be able to well capture the manifold structure of the discriminative appearances. In contrast, our unified formulation is based on a principled metric learning framework, which seeks for a discriminative embedding for appearance modeling. In our formulation, both appearance modeling and visual matching are performed online by efficient gradient based optimization. Our formulation is also able to deal with multiple targets, where the exclusive principle is naturally reinforced to handle occlusions. Its efficacy is validated in a wide variety of challenging videos. It is shown that our algorithm achieves more persistent results, when compared with previous appearance model based tracking algorithms.

1 Introduction

Appearance based visual tracking has been an active research topic for decades [1, 2, 3, 4, 5, 6, 7, 8]. There are two essential tasks: the *modeling* task builds an appearance model for the visual target; then the *matching* task matches the model with the source visual data to recover the motion of the target objects. Appearance models can roughly be put into two categories: *generative* models [2, 3, 4, 6] and *discriminative* models [7, 9, 8, 5].

Generative models seek a compact model to account for as much visual variations of the appearances as possible. Most often a set of training examples is leveraged either to obtain a subspace model [6, 2, 3] using embedding methods such as principle component analysis (PCA) [6, 3] or Gram-Schmidt decomposition [2], or to learn a Gaussian mixture model [1] using the Expectation-Maximization (EM) algorithm [10].

Discriminative models aim at differentiating the appearances of the visual targets from the background. Most previous works proposed to learn a binary classifier to differentiate the visual target from the background by using, for example, support vector machine (SVM) [7], Boosting [8], linear discriminant analysis [9], and multiple instance Boosting [5]. Compared to generative models, discriminative models may be more desirable for tracking due to the discrimination of foreground and background.

K. Daniilidis, P. Maragos, N. Paragios (Eds.): ECCV 2010, Part III, LNCS 6313, pp. 200–214, 2010.
© Springer-Verlag Berlin Heidelberg 2010

After the classifier is learnt, most previous works utilize the continuous output of the classification function as the objective for visual matching and tracking. This may be less desirable since the classification functions are trained to be good mainly for making binary decision. In other words, they may not be able to well capture the manifold structure of the discriminative appearances, a vital factor for robust visual tracking.

Given the visual appearance model, different tracking algorithms [11, 12, 13, 14, 15, 16] come with different optimization paradigm for matching. They can largely be classified into two. The first class [11,12] takes a hypothesis generation and observation verification approach by probabilistic information fusion. Seminal works include Kalman filter, probabilistic data association filter (PDAF) [11], and particle filter [12].

However, both Kalman filter and PDAF [11] make the assumption that the visual observations of the target can be obtained in certain ways, which may not be satisfied in many cases. Although particle filter [12] eliminates this assumption by taking a direct verification approach, it needs sufficient number of particle hypotheses, and hence a lot of computation resources for good performance. It is even worse when dealing with high dimensional motions [17, 18]. This is why partitioned sampling [17] and importance sampling [18] are needed to effeciently utilize the limited particle budget.

The second class takes a direct optimization approach, where iterative gradient based search [13,15] is performed, or a linear program [14,16] is solved to obtain the tracking results. Compared to the first class of tracking algorithms, direct optimization [14, 13] usually does not make any additional assumptions about image observations, and the gradient based optimization can be performed efficiently with modern nonlinear program [19]. This renders them to be more applicable when certain assumptions do not hold or the computational resource is constrained.

We propose a unified discriminative visual tracking framework for both appearance modeling and visual matching. It is cast under a discriminative metric learning algorithm proposed by Globerson and Roweis [20]. In our formulation, appearance modeling is to identify a discriminative embedding, and visual matching performs an exemplar based regression on such a manifold w.r.t. the motion parameters. Both steps optimize the same objective function and are performed alternatively by efficient gradient search. Therefore, we achieve two tasks in an unified formulation.

Without requiring any additional efforts, our formulation can naturally deal with the discriminative modeling and visual matching of multiple targets. Due to the mutual discrimination of the multiple appearances, and the joint optimization of multiple motions in our model, our tracking algorithm naturally reinforces the *exclusive principle* [21]. Exclusive principle states that no two visual targets shall account for the same image observations, which is vital to handle cross occlusions, as manifested in [21].

Our unified formulation presents three benefits to previous works: firstly, it presents a unified discriminative formulation where appearances modeling and matching are optimizing the same objective function. Secondly, the unified discriminative formulation gracefully handles visual modeling and tracking of multiple targets where an exclusive principle is naturally reinforced. This makes it to be robust to occlusions occurring among the different visual targets. Thirdly, a principled criterion is derived from it to select the optimal set of visual examples for online learning and matching.

2 Discriminative Appearance and Motion Model

2.1 A Unified Formulation

We take a unified formulation for joint discriminative appearances modeling and visual matching. More formally, suppose we have a set of labeled training examples $\mathcal{X}_0 = \{\mathbf{x}_i \in \mathbb{R}^N, y_i\}_{i=1}^n$, where $y_i = 1$ means $\mathbf{x}_i$ is among the n_1 foreground samples, and $y_i = 0$ implies that $\mathbf{x}_i$ is one of the $n_0 + 1$ background samples, such that $n_1 + n_0 + 1 = n$. In our experiments, each $\mathbf{x}_i$ is usually a $w \times h$ image patch and $N = w \times h$.

We further denote $\mathbf{I}(\mathbf{m})$ to be the visual target we would like to track where $\mathbf{m} \in \mathbb{R}^L$ is the motion parameters we want to recover. Obviously, the label y of $\mathbf{I}(\mathbf{m})$ is 1, since it represents the visual target. For ease of notation, we denote $\mathbf{x}_0 = \mathbf{I}(\mathbf{m})$. Therefore, our final labeled data set $\mathcal{X} = \mathcal{X}_0 \cup \{(\mathbf{x}_0, y_0 = 1)\}$. Following Globerson and Roweis [20], we propose to learn a Mahalanobis form metric, i.e.,

$$d_{\mathbf{A}}(\mathbf{x}_i, \mathbf{x}_j) = (\mathbf{x}_i - \mathbf{x}_j)^T \mathbf{A}(\mathbf{x}_i - \mathbf{x}_j). \tag{1}$$

where $\mathbf{A}$ is a positive semi-definite (PSD) matrix to be learnt. For each $\mathbf{x}_i \in \mathcal{X}$, define

$$p_{\mathbf{A}}(\mathbf{x}_j | \mathbf{x}_i) = \frac{1}{Z_i} e^{-d_{\mathbf{A}}(\mathbf{x}_i, \mathbf{x}_j)} = \frac{e^{-d_{\mathbf{A}}(\mathbf{x}_i, \mathbf{x}_j)}}{\sum_{k \neq i} e^{-d_{\mathbf{A}}(\mathbf{x}_i, \mathbf{x}_k)}}. \tag{2}$$

The ideal distribution of the optimal $\mathbf{A}$ shall collapse samples from the same class to be a single point. Specifically, the ideal distribution shall take the following form,

$$p_0(\mathbf{x}_j | \mathbf{x}_i) = \begin{cases} \frac{1}{n_l} & y_i = y_j = l \\ 0 & y_i \neq y_j \end{cases}. \tag{3}$$

where $l \in \{0, 1\}$. Recall that $\mathbf{x}_0 = \mathbf{I}(\mathbf{m})$, we define

$$f(\mathbf{A}, \mathbf{m}) = \sum_{i=0}^n KL\left(p_0(\mathbf{x}_j | \mathbf{x}_i) \| p_{\mathbf{A}}(\mathbf{x}_j | \mathbf{x}_i)\right) = C + \sum_{y_i = y_j = l} \frac{1}{n_l} \left(d_{\mathbf{A}}(\mathbf{x}_i, \mathbf{x}_j) + \log Z_i\right) \tag{4}$$

where $C = \sum_{y_i = y_j = l} \frac{1}{n_l} \log \frac{1}{n_l}$ is a constant. To have $p_{\mathbf{A}}(\mathbf{x}_j | \mathbf{x}_i)$ to be as close to $p_0(\mathbf{x}_j | \mathbf{x}_i)$ as possible, we only need to proceed to minimize $f(\mathbf{A}, \mathbf{m})$, i.e.,

$$\min f(\mathbf{A}, \mathbf{m}) \tag{5}$$

$$s.t. \ \forall \mathbf{a} \in \mathbb{R}^N, \mathbf{a}^T \mathbf{A} \mathbf{a} \geq 0. \tag{6}$$

where the constraint in Eq. 6 confines $\mathbf{A}$ to be PSD. Solving the above optimization problem would allow us to jointly obtain the optimal discriminative appearance model defined by $\mathbf{A}$, and track the motion of the target visual object, which is defined by $\mathbf{m}$. We solve both by efficient gradient based search, as presented in the following sections.

We shall emphasize here that we present our formulation and optimization in this section with a single visual target for ease of presentation. We will extend the discussion to present more details on how to deal with multiple objects tracking in Sec. 4.

2.2 Appearance Model Estimation

In our unified formulation, discriminative appearance modeling refers to identifying the optimal $\mathbf{A}$, which defines the discriminative metric, and thus a discriminative embedding. Assume that the motion parameter $\mathbf{m}$ is fixed, following [20], it is easy to figure out that $f(\mathbf{A}, \mathbf{m})$ is a convex function of $\mathbf{A}$. Taking the derivative of $f(\mathbf{A}, \mathbf{m})$ with respect to $\mathbf{A}$, we have

$$\frac{\partial f(\mathbf{A}, \mathbf{m})}{\partial \mathbf{A}} = \sum_{i,j=0}^{n} (p_0(\mathbf{x}_j | \mathbf{x}_i) - p_{\mathbf{A}}(\mathbf{x}_j | \mathbf{x}_i))(\mathbf{x}_j - \mathbf{x}_i)(\mathbf{x}_j - \mathbf{x}_i)^T. \tag{7}$$

Similar to [20], we take a gradient projection algorithm [22] to obtain the optimal $\mathbf{A}$. Specifically the following two steps are performed:

1. GRADIENT DESCENT: $\mathbf{A} = \mathbf{A} - \epsilon \frac{\partial f(\mathbf{A}, \mathbf{m})}{\partial \mathbf{A}}$, where ϵ determines the step length for gradient descent.
2. PSD PROJECTION: Compute the eigen-value decomposition of $\mathbf{A}$, i.e., $\{\lambda_k, \mathbf{u}_k\}_{k=1}^{N}$ such that $\mathbf{A} = \sum_{k=1}^{N} \lambda_k \mathbf{u}_k \mathbf{u}_k^T$, set $\mathbf{A} = \sum_{k=1}^{N} \max(\lambda_k, 0) \mathbf{u}_k \mathbf{u}_k^T$.

The first step above performs gradient descent, and the second step reinforces the constraint to make $\mathbf{A}$ to be a positive semi-definite matrix. These two steps are iterated until convergence. Since $f(\mathbf{A}, \mathbf{m})$ is a convex function of $\mathbf{A}$ given $\mathbf{m}$. The iteration of these two steps is guaranteed to find the optimal solution to $\mathbf{A}$.

2.3 Motion Parameter Optimization

In this subsection, we fix the discriminative appearance model $\mathbf{A}$, and develop the gradient descent search for the motion parameters $\mathbf{m}$. Not losing any generality, we assume that $\mathbf{m}$ is a linear motion model, i.e.,

$$\begin{bmatrix} x \\ y \end{bmatrix} = \begin{bmatrix} a & b \\ c & d \end{bmatrix} \begin{bmatrix} x' \\ y' \end{bmatrix} + \begin{bmatrix} e \\ f \end{bmatrix} \tag{8}$$

where $[x', y']^T$ is the canonical coordinates for the labeled examples, and $[x, y]^T$ is the coordinates in the target video frame. This linear motion model covers a wide variety of motions such as translation, scaling, similarity, as well as full affine motion. We proceed to derive the gradient based search for the full affine motion model.

Recall that $\mathbf{x}_0 = \mathbf{I}(\mathbf{m})$ is the only term that involves the motion parameter $\mathbf{m}$, according to chain rule, we have

$$\frac{\partial f(\mathbf{A}, \mathbf{m})}{\partial \mathbf{m}} = \frac{\partial f(\mathbf{A}, \mathbf{m})}{\partial \mathbf{x}_0} \frac{\partial \mathbf{x}_0}{\partial \mathbf{m}}. \tag{9}$$

With some mathematical manipulation, it can be shown that

$$f(\mathbf{A}, \mathbf{m}) = \frac{1}{n_1} \sum_{y_j=1, j \neq 0} 2d_{\mathbf{A}}(\mathbf{x}_0, \mathbf{x}_j) + \sum_{j=0}^{n} \log Z_j + C(\mathbf{A}) \tag{10}$$

where $C(\mathbf{A})$ is a term which is independent of $\mathbf{x}_0$ and thus independent of $\mathbf{m}$. Therefore, with some more mathematical manipulations, we have

$$\frac{\partial f(\mathbf{A}, \mathbf{m})}{\partial \mathbf{x}_0} = \frac{4}{n_1} \sum_{y_j = 1, j \neq 0} \mathbf{A}(\mathbf{x}_0 - \mathbf{x}_j) - 2 \sum_{j=1}^{n} (p_{\mathbf{A}}(\mathbf{x}_j | \mathbf{x}_0) + p_{\mathbf{A}}(\mathbf{x}_0 | \mathbf{x}_j)) \mathbf{A}(\mathbf{x}_0 - \mathbf{x}_j).$$

(11)

For any parameter $\xi \in \mathbf{m}$, again, applying chain rule, we have

$$\frac{\partial \mathbf{x}_0}{\xi} = \frac{\partial \mathbf{I}(\mathbf{m})}{\partial \xi} = \frac{\partial \mathbf{I}(\mathbf{m})}{x} \frac{\partial x}{\partial \xi} + \frac{\partial \mathbf{I}(\mathbf{m})}{y} \frac{\partial y}{\partial \xi},$$

(12)

where $\frac{\partial \mathbf{I}(\mathbf{m})}{x}$ and $\frac{\partial \mathbf{I}(\mathbf{m})}{y}$ represents the image gradient in the target frame in horizontal and vertical directions, respectively. For ease of notation, we denote them as $\mathbf{I}_x$ and $\mathbf{I}_y$ respectively. Following Eq. 12, we have

$$\frac{\partial \mathbf{x}_0}{\partial a} = \mathbf{I}_x x', \quad \frac{\partial \mathbf{x}_0}{\partial b} = \mathbf{I}_x y', \quad \frac{\partial \mathbf{x}_0}{\partial c} = \mathbf{I}_y x', \quad \frac{\partial \mathbf{x}_0}{\partial d} = \mathbf{I}_y y', \quad \frac{\partial \mathbf{x}_0}{\partial e} = \mathbf{I}_x, \quad \frac{\partial \mathbf{x}_0}{\partial f} = \mathbf{I}_y \quad (13)$$

Therefore, we may easily calculate the gradient of $f(\mathbf{A}, \mathbf{m})$ with respect to $\mathbf{m}$ by applying Eq. 9 to Eq. 13. Then we can take a gradient descent step to recover the optimal motion parameter $\mathbf{m}$, i.e.,

$$\mathbf{m} = \mathbf{m} - \eta \frac{\partial f(\mathbf{A}, \mathbf{m})}{\partial \mathbf{m}}$$

(14)

where the step length η could be estimated, for example, by a quasi-Newton method such as L-BFGS [19].

3   Online Matching and Model Estimation

One of the main challenges in appearance model based visual tracking is to robustly adapt the model to the visual environment. This adaptation may be indispensable for robust tracking since the target objects may go through drastic visual changes from environmental conditions such as extreme lighting, occlusions, casting shadows, and pose and view changes. The unified formulation we proposed in Eq. 5 enables us to naturally fulfill this task. We proceed to present it in a more formal way.

Extended from the notation of Sec. 2, let $\mathcal{X}^{(t)}$ be the set of n labeled examples we maintain at time instance t. We also let $\mathbf{A}_t$ be the current discriminative appearance model, and $\mathbf{m}_t$ be the motion parameters we need to recover. Hence we have $\mathbf{x}_0^{(t)} = \mathbf{I}^{(t)}(\mathbf{m}_t)$. At each time instant t, given $\mathcal{X}^{(t)}$ and $\mathbf{A}_t$, we run the gradient descent optimization algorithm outlined in Sec. 2.3 to obtain the optimal motion parameter $\mathbf{m}_t^\star$. This fulfills our visual matching and tracking task. Then we perturb $\mathbf{m}_t^\star$ to generate a set of α negative samples $\mathcal{X}_-^{(t+1)}$ to replace the oldest α negative sample subset $\mathcal{X}_-^{(t)}$ in $\mathcal{X}^{(t)}$. This results in the new labeled examples $\mathcal{X}^{(t+1)}$, i.e.,

$$\mathcal{X}^{(t+1)} = (\mathcal{X}_0^{(t)} \setminus \mathcal{X}_-^{(t)}) \cup \mathcal{X}_-^{(t+1)}.$$

(15)

Since $\mathbf{m}_t$ has been recovered, for ease of presentation, we abuse the notation to temporally define $\mathbf{x}_0^{(t+1)} = \mathbf{I}^t(\mathbf{m}_t)$. With $\mathcal{X}^{(t+1)}$ We can then run the gradient projection optimization algorithms outlined in Sec. 2.2 to obtain the optimal $\mathbf{A}_{t+1}$. To proceed with the next matching step to identify the optimal $\mathbf{I}^{t+1}(\mathbf{m}_{t+1})$, with a fixed memory budget, we need to retire one positive examples in the current $\mathcal{X}^{(t+1)}$, we propose a least consistent criterion based on the contribution of each positive examples to the unified cost function $f(\mathbf{A}_{t+1}, \mathbf{m}_t)$. Indeed, fixing $\mathbf{A}_{t+1}$ and $\mathbf{m}_t$, $f(\mathbf{A}_{t+1}, \mathbf{m}_t)$ is a function of $\mathcal{X}^{(t+1)}$, i.e., $f(\mathbf{A}_{t+1}, \mathbf{m}_t) = g(\mathcal{X}^{(t+1)})$. We can similarly define a $g(\cdot)$ function for any subset of $\mathcal{X}^{(t+1)}$ based on Eq. 4. Therefore, for each $\mathbf{x} \in \mathcal{X}^{(t+1)}$, a consistent criterion can be defined as

$$c(\mathbf{x}) = g\left(\mathcal{X}^{(t+1)}\right) - g\left(\mathcal{X}^{(t+1)} \setminus \{\mathbf{x}\}\right). \tag{16}$$

It is easy to understand that the larger $c(\mathbf{x})$ is, the more contribution $\mathbf{x}$ has made to $f(\mathbf{A}_{t+1}, \mathbf{m}_t)$. If the label $y(x) = 1$, a larger $c(\mathbf{x})$ indicates that $\mathbf{x}$ is not very compatible to the rest of the positive samples, and hence should be retired from the sample set. More formally, we select

$$\mathbf{x}^\star = \arg\max_{\mathbf{x} \in \mathcal{X}^{(t+1)}, y(\mathbf{x})=1} c(\mathbf{x}) \tag{17}$$

to retire from $\mathcal{X}^{(t+1)}$. In real operation, we only need to change the numbering of $\mathbf{x}_0^{(t+1)} = \mathbf{I}^t(\mathbf{m}_t)$ to the numbering of $\mathbf{x}^\star$, then we reset $\mathbf{x}_0^{(t+1)} = \mathbf{I}^{t+1}(\mathbf{m}_{t+1})$ which is unknown now to kick off the matching process for the optimal motion parameter $\mathbf{m}_{t+1}$.

The above steps will be repeated from time instant t to time instant $t + 1$. Therefore we track the visual target and estimate the discriminative visual appearance model simultaneously in an online fashion, which are all based on efficient gradient based optimization. Most previous approaches resort to heuristics or the oldness of visual samples to select the optimal set of online training examples. While our proposed selection criterion for positive examples in Eq. 17 is derived directly from our unified cost function in a principled fashion, an obvious benefit of our unified formulation.

To initialize the tracking algorithm, we can run an object detector if it applies, such as a face detector [23] or a human detector [24], if we are tracking a face or a person. Or we can request the users to manually specify a tracking rectangle in the first frame. Then the initialized tracking rectangle, either from a detector or manually specified, is perturbed to form the initial set of labeled examples $\mathcal{X}^{(1)}$. More specifically, perturbed rectangles with sufficient overlap with the initial rectangle are regarded as positive examples, while those perturbed rectangles which are deviated too much from the initial rectangles are deemed as negative examples. This bootstraps learning for the optimal discriminative appearance model $\mathbf{A}_2$, which is then adopted to obtain the optimal motion parameter $\mathbf{m}_2$. This processes will be repeated as described above.

Last but not least, when maintaining the labeled example set $\mathcal{X}^{(t)}$, we fix a small set of β negative and β positive examples extracted from the initialization frame in the set, i.e., we never replace them with new examples. This treatment is very important to keep some invariance to our discriminative appearance model and avoid it to be drifted too drastically in the visual tracking process, a trick which has been adopted also in previous work, such as [8].

4   Modeling and Tracking Multiple Objects

Our unified formulation is natural to handle the tracking of multiple targets. To see this, we assume $y_i = 0$ indicates background, and $y_i = 1, \ldots, K$ indicates each of the K visual targets we are intending to track. Let $\mathcal{S}_0 = \{(\mathbf{x}_{0j}, y_{0j} = 0)\}_{j=0}^{n_0}$, and also let $\mathcal{S}_i = \{(\mathbf{x}_{ij}, y_{ij} = i)\}_{j=0}^{n_i}$ for any $i = 1, \ldots, K$, where $\forall i > 0$, $\mathbf{x}_{i0} = \mathbf{I}(\mathbf{m}_i)$ indicates each of the visual targets we want to track in the current frame, where $\mathbf{m}_i$ is represented by $\{a_i, b_i, c_i, d_i, e_i, f_i\}$, as defined in Eq. 8. Following similar steps as we have derived Eq. 4, denote $\mathcal{M} = \{\mathbf{m}_1, \mathbf{m}_2, \ldots, \mathbf{m}_K\}$, and $\mathbf{X} = \{\mathbf{x}_{i0}\}_{i=1}^{K}$ we have

$$f(\mathbf{A}, \mathcal{M}) = C + \sum_{i=0}^{K} \sum_{j \neq k=1}^{n_i} \frac{1}{n_i} \left(d_{\mathbf{A}}(\mathbf{x}_{ij}, \mathbf{x}_{ik}) + \log Z_{ij} \right). \tag{18}$$

where Z_{ij} and $d_{\mathbf{A}}(\cdot, \cdot)$ are all defined similar to the corresponding terms defined in Sec. 2.1. Here $\mathbf{A}$ captures the discriminative appearances information for all the K visual targets, and $\mathbf{m}_i$ represents the motion for the ith visual target which, in our experiments, are again the affine motion parameters defined in Eq. 8.

Following similar derivations as in Sec. 2.2 and Sec. 2.3, we can compute

$$\frac{\partial f(\mathbf{A}, \mathcal{M})}{\partial \mathbf{A}} = \sum_{i=0}^{K} \sum_{j=0}^{n_i} \sum_{k=0}^{K} \sum_{l=0}^{n_k} \omega_{ij}(kl)(\mathbf{x}_{kl} - \mathbf{x}_{ij})(\mathbf{x}_{kl} - \mathbf{x}_{ij})^T \tag{19}$$

where

$$\omega_{ij}(kl) = p_0(\mathbf{x}_{kl}|\mathbf{x}_{ij}) - p_{\mathbf{A}}(\mathbf{x}_{kl}|\mathbf{x}_{ij}). \tag{20}$$

With this formula to compute the gradient, we can utilize similar Gradient projection steps outlined in Sec. 2.2 to obtain the optimal $\mathbf{A}$. Notice that here $\mathbf{A}$ captures both the discriminative appearances among all the visual targets, as well as the discriminative information between the visual targets and background. Similarly, we obtain that

$$\frac{\partial f(\mathbf{A}, \mathcal{M})}{\partial \mathbf{x}_{i0}} = \frac{4}{n_i} \sum_{j=1}^{n_i} \mathbf{A}(\mathbf{x}_{i0} - \mathbf{x}_{ij}) - 2 \sum_{k=1}^{K} \sum_{l=0}^{n_k} \beta_{i0}(kl) \mathbf{A}(\mathbf{x}_{i0} - \mathbf{x}_{kl}). \tag{21}$$

where

$$\beta_{i0}(kl) = p_{\mathbf{A}}(\mathbf{x}_{kl}|\mathbf{x}_{i0}) + p_{\mathbf{A}}(\mathbf{x}_{i0}|\mathbf{x}_{kl}) \tag{22}$$

Following Eq. 13, we also have

$$\frac{\partial \mathbf{x}_{i0}}{\partial a_i} = \mathbf{I}_x x_i', \ \frac{\partial \mathbf{x}_{i0}}{\partial b_i} = \mathbf{I}_x y_i', \ \frac{\partial \mathbf{x}_{i0}}{\partial c_i} = \mathbf{I}_y x_i', \ \frac{\partial \mathbf{x}_{i0}}{\partial d_i} = \mathbf{I}_y y_i', \ \frac{\partial \mathbf{x}_{i0}}{\partial e_i} = \mathbf{I}_x, \ \frac{\partial \mathbf{x}_{i0}}{\partial f_i} = \mathbf{I}_y. \tag{23}$$

Following chain rules and with Eq. 23, we can easily calculate

$$\frac{\partial f(\mathbf{A}, \mathbf{m}_i)}{\mathbf{m}_i} = \frac{\partial f(\mathbf{A}, \mathcal{M})}{\partial \mathbf{x}_{i0}} \frac{\partial \mathbf{x}_{i0}}{\mathbf{m}_i} \tag{24}$$

With Eq. 24, again, we use L-BFGS [19] to solve the nonlinear optimization problem to obtain each set of motion parameters $\mathbf{m}_i$ for the ith visual target. Based on the above two gradient based optimization schemes for $\mathbf{A}$ and each $\mathbf{m}_i$, respectively, following similar ideas as outlined in Sec. 3, we can further develop online appearances modeling and updating algorithms and visual matching algorithms for robust visual tracking of multiple objects. We shall not verbose on it since it follows quite similar steps as those outlined in Sec 3.

4.1 Discriminant Exclusive Principle

We argue that the proposed joint formulation for multiple object tracking naturally incorporates an exclusive principle [17] in the matching process. Therefore it is robust to handle occlusions among the different visual objects. The exclusive principle states that no two visual tracker shall occupy the same image observation. Our proposed algorithm naturally achieves it because of the joint discriminative appearance model $\mathbf{A}$, which reinforces the mutual discrimination of the appearances between two visual targets $\mathbf{I}(\mathbf{m}_i)$ and $\mathbf{I}(\mathbf{m}_j)$. To see this more clearly, given an optimal $\mathbf{A}$, if $\mathbf{I}(\mathbf{m}_i)$ and $\mathbf{I}(\mathbf{m}_j)$ occupy similar image regions (a.k.a, $\mathbf{m}_j \doteq \mathbf{m}_i$), and thus have similar appearance, the mutual discriminative information encoded in $\mathbf{A}$ would incur a large value for $f(\mathbf{A}, \mathcal{M})$. Therefore, $\mathbf{m}_j \doteq \mathbf{m}_i$ is not an optimal solution to $\mathcal{M}$. In other words, the optimal motion parameter $\mathcal{M}$ is more likely to occur when $\forall 1 \le i < j \le K, \mathbf{m}_j \neq \mathbf{m}_i$. Therefore, the exclusive principle among the different visual targets is naturally reinforced.

5   Experiments

We dub the name *TUDAMM* to the Tracker with Unified Discriminative Appearance Modeling and Matching (TUDAMM). Comparing with the results of other state-of-the-art trackers [2, 13], we evaluate our TUDAMM using several challenging video sequences including video clips from CAVIAR dataset [25], and other real-world video sequences downloaded from Internet.

5.1   Evaluation Criteria

Enlightened by the simplicity and the elegance of the Average Precision (AP) criterion used in the PASCAL grand challenge [26] for object detection evaluation, we define a simple measure for tracker evaluation, namely Average Tracking Precision (ATP). More formally, for each tracking task, a ground truth mask for the object of interest is labeled in each frame j. The mask is represented as a point set $\mathcal{G}_j$. The tracking result is represented as a point set $\mathcal{T}_j$ at frame j. $(x_i, y_i) \in \mathcal{G}_j$ or $\mathcal{T}_j$ indicates that the pixel at (x_i, y_i) is inside them. For an ideal tracker, $\forall i, \mathcal{G}_j = \mathcal{T}_j$.

For each frame j, the tracking precision r_j is defined as: $r_j = |\mathcal{G}_j \cap \mathcal{T}_j| / |\mathcal{G}_j \cup \mathcal{T}_j|$. Noticing that $r_j \in [0, 1]$, the ATP for a tracker of an object in a video clip is defined as:

$$ATP = \frac{1}{N} \sum_{j=1}^{N} r_j = \frac{1}{N} \sum_{j=1}^{N} \frac{|\mathcal{G}_j \cap \mathcal{T}_j|}{|\mathcal{G}_j \cup \mathcal{T}_j|}, \tag{25}$$

where N is the running length of the video clips in frame number. For an ideal tracker, $ATP \equiv 1$. We use it as the exclusive quantitative measure to compare the performance of the TUDAMM with other state-of-the-art trackers.

Fig. 1. The sample key frames of the tracking results for CAVIAR dataset. Key frame NO. 443, 455, 467, 488, 501, 772 are shown from left to right. First row: TUDAMM. Second Row: Meanshift [13]. Third row: Incremental Learning Tracker (ILT) [3].

5.2   Visual Tracking of Single/Multiple Target(s)

We firstly present the tracking results of TUDAMM for single target on a video sequence from the CAVIAR dataset[1], where three persons are walking in the corridor of a shopping mall in Portugal. We call this video sequence "ThreePerson". We run the proposed tracking algorithm to track one of the three persons individually. The tracking task is challenging in several aspects: 1) the scales of the visual targets change drastically; 2) the three persons walked across each other and thus induced occlusion; 3) some other crossing person occluded the target person.

As shown in the first row of Fig. 1, the TUDAMM tracker successfully tracked the target person from beginning of the sequence to the end of the sequence without any problem, which is more robust than both the mean-shift tracker [13] (second row) and the incremental PCA tracker [3] (third row). Both of these algorithms failed to track the target after the person with red cloth occluded the target person, as displayed in the second and third row of Fig. 1. The robustness of our TUDAMM tracker attributes to our unified discriminative formulation, which makes it more robust to background clutter. For detailed video results, please check out our video demo file "http://vision.ece.missouri.edu/demo/ECCV2010Tracking.avi".

Quantitative comparisons to other work. Since the ThreePerson video in the CAVIAR dataset has ground-truth labels of the bounding boxes of the walking persons in the video sequence, we use the ATP criterion presented in Sec. 5.1 to quantitatively evaluate the performances of the proposed TUDAMM tracker, the mean-shift tracker (Meanshift) [13], and the incremental PCA tracker (ILT) [3]. We present two such evaluation results for tracking two different persons in the video in Fig. 2(a) and Fig. 2(b), respectively. It is clear TUDAMM consistently presents more accurate tracking results than

---

[1] Data set from EC Funded CAVIAR project/IST 2001 37540, downloaded at URL: http://homepages.inf.ed.ac.uk/rbf/CAVIAR/.

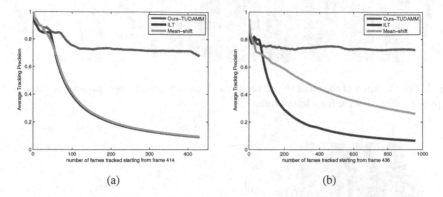

(a)   (b)

Fig. 2. (a) The performance comparison for the person tracked in figure 1. (b) The performance comparison for tracking the black person at right to the red person at the starting frame.

Fig. 3. The top 12 eigenvectors (with the descent order from left to right) for the discriminative matrix A

the other algorithms, which achieves an average tracking ATP of 75%. This demonstrates the good performance of the gradient based matching algorithm to recover the motion parameters.

Visualizing the appearance model A. As a matter of fact, the appearance model A defines a discriminative embedding to differentiate the visual object from the background. Each eigenvector of A is corresponding to one basis vector of the embedding. To have a better understanding of how the appearance model A functions, in Fig. 3, we visualize the top 12 eigenvectors of an optimal A estimated at frame 436 when tracking the person in red in the ThreePerson sequence. As we can clearly observe, these eigenvectors focusing on extracting the contour and thus encode the shape information of the target person. They also tend to focus more on features inside the human contour while suppress features outside the human contour. This indicates that our metric learning framework really picks up the discriminative information for tracking.

Visualizing the gradient optimization processes. To gain a good understanding of the gradient optimization process of both the discriminative appearance estimation as well as the gradient based optimization process for visual matching, we visualize the evolution of both optimization processes in frame 532 of the ThreePerson sequence, as shown in Fig. 4 and Fig. 5, respectively. The tracking target is the rightmost person in this frame. Fig. 4 visualizes how the tenth eigen-vector of the discriminative model

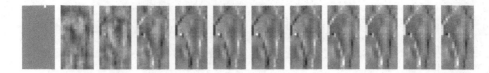

Fig. 4. The evolution of the tenth Eigen vector of **A** during gradient optimization in the first 11 steps of gradient descent from left to right

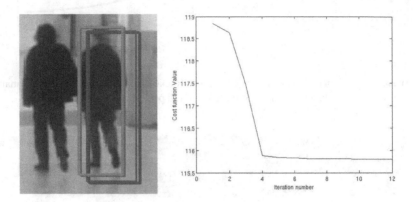

Fig. 5. The gradient optimization of objective function w.r.t. the motion parameters in frame 532 in the CAVIAR sequence. The tracking is initialized as the tracking result in frame 512 for better visualization. Red rectangle in the left image is the final converged matching results. The figure on the right displays how the objective function is minimized by gradient descent.

A evolves in the first 11 iterations. We start the optimization by initializing **A** as an identity matrix, so the initialization of the tenth eigen-vector is a unit vector with the tenth element to be one and all the other elements are zero, as shown in the first image in Fig. 4. As we can clearly observe, only after 8 steps of gradient descent the eigen-vector has already been stabilized. From Fig. 5, we can clearly observe the effectiveness of the gradient optimization process in the visual matching step. In only 4 steps of gradient descent, the matching result is already converged. These figures demonstrate the efficiency of the proposed gradient optimization process.

Tracking under various visual variations. We have also extensively tested the TU-DAMM with other challenging videos used in previous works or downloaded from YouTube with various challenging aspects. We highly recommend to check our demo video for more details of all the tracking results.

More specifically, in Fig. 6, we present the tracking results of a human face from the TUDAMM, the ILT [3], and the Meanshift trackers [13], respectively. The ILT tracker [3] firstly reported results in this video, which is subject to drastic illumination changes and casting shadows. As we can clearly observe in Fig. 6, the TUDAMM

Fig. 6. The sample key frames of the tracking results on the challenging face moving under shadow with big illumination change video . Key frame NO. 201, 210, 220, 230, 240, 260 are shown from left to right. First row: TUDAMM. Second Row: Meanshift. Third row: ILT.

Fig. 7. The sample key frames of the CrazyCarChasing tracking results of TUDAMM with large scale zooming and camera motion.

robustly tracked the human face despite the dramatic shadows and illumination changes. While both the ILT tracker and the Meanshift tracker failed with the drastic visual variations. The results video contains 71 frames.

In Fig. 7, we report the tracking results of TUDAMM on a car chasing video downloaded from YouTube. The video is subject to large scale change and drastic camera motion since it was taken from a helicopter. Our tracking algorithm successfully tracked the motion of the target car without any problem. The results video contains 578 frames. In Fig. 8, we present the tracking results of a rabbit which underwent a lot of non-rigid motions. TUDAMM successfully tracked the rabbit across the video, which contains 156 frames.

Tracking multiple targets with cross occlusion. To demonstrate the ability of TU-DAMM in dealing with occlusions in multiple object tracking, we report results in two video sequences, one is the ThreePerson video from the CAVIAR dataset, and the other is a horse racing video downloaded from YouTube. Tracking results in sample video frames are displayed in Fig 9 and Fig 10, respectively. Three people are tracked in the CAVIAR video, while five horse racers are tracked in the horse racing video. As we can clearly observe, despite severe cross occlusion among the different visual targets, our TUDAMM tracked all of them without any problem. This is attributed to the discriminative appearance model induced from our unified discriminative formulation.

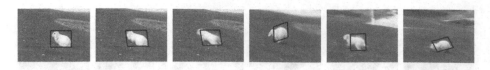

Fig. 8. The sample key frames of the tracking results by TUDAMM on the RabbitRun video with nonrigid motion

Fig. 9. The sample key frames of the tracking results by multiple target TUDAMM on the CAVIAR dataset

Tracking speed. Last but not least, with a PC of 2.3-GHz CPU in Windows XP, without any code optimization in our C++ implementation, our tracker runs at 2 frames per second for tracking a single target. It runs at 0.5 frames per second for tracking the three people and 0.2 frames per second for tracking the 5 horses. We expect to have 10 times speed up with reasonable efforts on code optimization.

Fig. 10. Multiple Tracking results for a horse racing video. The order of the video frame is presented from top-left to bottom-right.

6   Conclusion and Future Work

In this paper, we present a unified discriminative framework based on metric learning for robust tracking of either single or multiple targets, where both the appearance modeling and visual matching are optimizing a single objective with efficient gradient based search. Our experimental results validate the efficacy of the proposed tracking algorithm. When tracking multiple targets, our unified formulation encodes an exclusive principle which naturally deals with cross occlusions among the multiple targets. This has also been manifested in our experiments. Future research includes exploring means of integrating our multiple target tracker with state-of-the-art surveillance systems to handle the appearance of new targets and disappearance of old targets.

References

1. Jepson, A.D., Fleet, D.J., El-Maraghi, T.F.: Robust online appearance models for visual tracking. In: CVPR, vol. 1, pp. 415–422 (2001)
2. Ho, J., Lee, K.C., Yang, M.H., Kriegman, D.: Visual tracking using learned subspaces. In: CVPR, vol. 1, pp. 782–789 (2004)
3. Lim, J., Ross, D., Lin, R.S., Yang, M.H.: Incremental learning for visual tracking. In: NIPS, pp. 801–808 (2005)
4. Yang, M., Wu, Y.: Tracking non-stationary appearances and dynamic feature selection. In: CVPR (2005)
5. Babenko, B., Yang, M.H., Belongie, S.: Visual tracking with online multiple instance learning. In: CVPR (2009)
6. Cootes, T., Edwards, G., Taylor, C.: Active appearance models. In: Burkhardt, H., Neumann, B. (eds.) ECCV 1998. LNCS, vol. 1407, pp. 484–498. Springer, Heidelberg (1998)
7. Avidan, S.: Support vector tracking. In: CVPR (2001)
8. Avidan, S.: Ensemble tracking. In: CVPR (2005)
9. Collins, R.T., Liu, Y.: On-line selection of discriminative tracking features. In: ICCV, vol. 1, pp. 346–352 (2003)
10. Dempster, A., Laird, N., Rubin, D.: Maximum likelihood from incomplete data via the em algorithm. Journal of the Royal Statistical Society Series B 39, 1–38 (1977)
11. Bar-Shalom, Y.: Tracking and data association. Academic Press Professional, Inc., San Diego (1987)
12. Isard, M., Blake, A.: Contour tracking by stochastic propagation of conditional density. In: Buxton, B.F., Cipolla, R. (eds.) ECCV 1996. LNCS, vol. 1065, pp. 343–356. Springer, Heidelberg (1996)
13. Comaniciu, D., Ramesh, V., Meer, P.: Real-time tracking of non-rigid objects using mean shift. In: CVPR, vol. 2, pp. 142–149 (2000)
14. Hager, G.D., Dewan, M., Stewart, C.V.: Multiple kernel tracking with ssd. In: CVPR, vol. 1, pp. 790–797 (2004)
15. Zhao, Q., Brennan, S., Tao, H.: Differential emd tracking. In: ICCV (2007)
16. Wu, Y., Fan, J.: Contextual flow. In: CVPR (2009)
17. MacCormick, J., Isard, M.: Partitioned sampling, articulated objects, and interface-quality hand tracking. In: Vernon, D. (ed.) ECCV 2000. LNCS, vol. 1843, pp. 3–19. Springer, Heidelberg (2000)
18. Wu, Y., Hua, G., Yu, T.: Tracking articulated body by dynamic markov network. In: ICCV, p. 1094 (2003)
19. Zhu, C., Byrd, R.H., Lu, P., Nocedal, J.: Algorithm 778: L-bfgs-b: Fortran subroutines for large-scale bound-constrained optimization. ACM Transaction Mathematical Software 23, 550–560 (1997)
20. Globerson, A., Roweis, S.T.: Metric learning by collapsing classes. In: NIPS (2005)
21. MacCormick, J., Blake, A.: A probabilistic exclusion principle for tracking multiple objects. In: ICCV, pp. 572–587 (1999)
22. Rosen, J.B.: The gradient projection method for nonlinear programming. part i. linear constraints. Journal of the Society for Industrial and Applied Mathematics 8, 181–217 (1960)
23. Viola, P., Jones, M.J.: Robust real-time face detection. Int. J. Comput. Vision 57, 137–154 (2004)
24. Wang, X., Han, T.X., Yan, S.: An hog-lbp human detector with partial occlusion handling. In: ICCV (2009)

25. Ribeiro, H.N., Hall, D., et al.: Comparison of target detection algorithms using adaptive background models. In: Proc. 2nd Joint IEEE Int. Workshop on Visual Surveillance, pp. 113–120 (2005)
26. Everingham, M., Van Gool, L., Williams, C.K.I., Winn, J., Zisserman, A.: The PASCAL Visual Object Classes Challenge 2009 (VOC 2009) Results (2009), http://pascallin.ecs.soton.ac.uk/challenges/VOC/voc2009/

Memory-Based Particle Filter
for Tracking Objects
with Large Variation in Pose and Appearance

Dan Mikami, Kazuhiro Otsuka, and Junji Yamato

NTT Communication and Science Laboratories

Abstract. A novel memory-based particle filter is proposed to achieve robust visual tracking of a target's pose even with large variations in target's position and rotation, i.e. large appearance changes. The memory-based particle filter (M-PF) is a recent extension of the particle filter, and incorporates a memory-based mechanism to predict prior distribution using past memory of target state sequence; it offers robust target tracking against complex motion. This paper extends the M-PF to a unified probabilistic framework for joint estimation of the target's pose and appearance based on memory-based joint prior prediction using stored past pose and appearance sequences. We call it the Memory-based Particle Filter with Appearance Prediction (M-PFAP). A memory-based approach enables generating the joint prior distribution of pose and appearance without explicit modeling of the complex relationship between them. M-PFAP can robustly handle the large changes in appearance caused by large pose variation, in addition to abrupt changes in moving direction; it allows robust tracking under self and mutual occlusion. Experiments confirm that M-PFAP successfully tracks human faces from frontal view to profile view; it greatly eases the limitations of M-PF.

1 Introduction

Visual object tracking, one of the most important techniques in computer vision [1], is required for a wide range of applications such as automatic surveillance, man-machine interfaces [2,3], and communication scene analysis [4]. Target tracking has still been acknowledged as a challenging problem because the target's appearance changes greatly due to pose variation, occlusion, illumination change, etc. For example, when an object rotates, its visible surface gradually becomes invisible, i.e. self-occlusion, and hidden surfaces becomes visible. Mutual occlusion, the interjection of another object between the target and the camera, makes the target's visible surface invisible. Also, the target tracker needs to handle complex motion, such as when the moving direction abruptly reverses, which can occur with occlusions in real world situations.

Bayesian filter-based trackers have been acknowledged as a promising approach; they represent a unified probabilistic framework for sequentially estimating the target state from an observed data stream [5]. At each time step, the Bayesian filter computes the posterior distribution of the target state by using

K. Daniilidis, P. Maragos, N. Paragios (Eds.): ECCV 2010, Part III, LNCS 6313, pp. 215–228, 2010.

observation likelihood and the prior distribution. One variant, the particle filter, has been widely used for target tracking. It represents probability distributions of the target state by a set of samples, called particles. Particle filter can potentially handle non-Gaussian distribution and nonlinear dynamics/observation processes; this contributes to robust tracking. For object tracking, an example of target state is the position and orientation of the target.

We proposed the memory-based particle filter (M-PF) as an extension of the particle filter [6]. M-PF eases the Markov assumption of PF and predicts the prior distribution based on target's long-term dynamics using past history of the target's states. M-PF realized robustness against abrupt object movements and quick recovery from tracking failure without explicit modeling of target's dynamics. However, M-PF employs the same observation process as the traditional PF. The visual tracker in [6] uses a single template representing frontal face, which is built at tracker initialization. Therefore, the M-PF-based tracker can handle face rotation only so long as the initial frontal face remains visible; [6] suggests that the horizontal limit is 50 degrees.

This paper extends M-PF to a unified probabilistic framework for joint estimation of target's position/pose and its appearance based on memory-based joint prior distribution prediction using stored past pose-appearance pairs. We call it the Memory-based Particle Filter with Appearance Prediction (M-PFAP). The appearance of an object varies with its pose. By predicting appearance from pose, M-PFAP enables robust tracking against changes in appearance. A memory-based approach is proposed to generate the joint prior distribution of pose and appearance; the complex relationship between them is not explicitly modeled. M-PFAP can robustly handle the large changes in appearance caused by large pose variation, in addition to abrupt changes in moving direction; it allows robust tracking under self and mutual occlusion. To the best of our knowledge, M-PFAP is the first pose tracker that handles pose-appearance relationship as a probabilistic distribution and that simultaneously predicts future pose and appearance in a memory-based approach. As the tracking target, this paper focuses on the face and we implement the M-PFAP-based face pose tracker. Experiments confirm that M-PFAP successfully tracks human faces from frontal view up to profile view, i.e. 90 degrees horizontally; it far exceeds the limits of M-PF.

This paper is organized as follows. Section 2 overviews related works, Sect. 3 proposes M-PFAP, and Sect. 4 describes face pose tracking based on M-PFAP, experiments, and results. Finally, Sect. 5 gives our conclusions.

2   Related Works

2.1   Template Matching-Based Tracking and Template Update

Template matching has been widely employed for visual target tracking; the template represents the target's appearance from the camera's view. The target position is the best-matched position of the template on the input image. To cope with appearance change, the template is updated repeatedly over time [7,8]. However, error in the estimates of position/pose yields erroneous templates and error accumulates, which results in tracking failure. It is called "drift". To suppress drift, two approaches have been proposed.

The first approach uses pose-invariant features extracted from the target. The tracker of Matthews et al. [9] employs a set of invariant features from multiple views of the target object; the tracker can keep track of the target even when its pose changes. Jepson et al. [10] proposed a WSL model which uses separate models for Stable, Wandering, and Lost situations; these models are mixed to predict the target appearance by using the EM algorithm. Zelniker et al. [11] combined multiple features according to e.g. illumination condition. These methods can be used only for position estimation, not for pose estimation.

The second approach is template updating through adaptive criteria. Morency et al. [12,13] and Ross et al. [14] proposed methods that use an initial template as a supplement to avoid error accumulation; both the initial template and updated template are used for matching. However, the use of the initial template limits the pose range possible. In the example of [13], a frontal face is used as the initial template, and the horizontal rotation angle in their experiment was up to 50 degrees. Lefèvre et al. [15] used view-based templates obtained online. Their approach is to generate templates from not only frontal views but also from profile views. This allows an appearance model to be generated by interpolation, not by extrapolation. However, the trackable angle range is restricted by the profile views.

M-PFAP provides a new approach to handling the large appearance changes caused by pose change. It handles pose-appearance relationship as a probabilistic distribution, and estimates pose and appearance simultaneously in the Bayesian filter framework by using the memory-based approach.

2.2 Memory-Based Particle Filter (M-PF)

M-PF [6] realized robust target tracking without explicit modeling of target's dynamics even when a target moves quickly.

Fig.1 outlines M-PF. M-PF keeps temporal sequence of past state estimates $\hat{\mathbf{x}}_{1:T} = \{\hat{\mathbf{x}}_1, \cdots, \hat{\mathbf{x}}_T\}$ in memory. Here, $\hat{\mathbf{x}}_{1:T}$ denotes a sequence of state estimates from time 1 to time T, and $\hat{\mathbf{x}}_t$ denotes a pose estimate at time t. M-PF assumes that the subsequent parts of past similar states provide the good estimates of the current future.

M-PF introduced Temporal Recurrent Probability (TRP), which is a probability distribution defined in the temporal domain and indicates the possibility that a past state will reappear in the future. To predict the prior distribution, M-PF starts with TRP modeling. It then conducts temporal sampling based on TRP. The sampled histories are denoted by blue dots in Fig.1. It retrieves the corresponding past state estimates for each sampled time step, which are denoted by pink dots in Fig.1. After that, considering the uncertainty in the state estimates, each referred past state is convoluted with kernel distributions (light green dist. in Fig.1), and they are mixed together to generate the prior distribution (green dist. in Fig.1). Finally, a set of particles is generated according to the prior distribution (black dots in Fig.1). M-PF-based face pose tracker

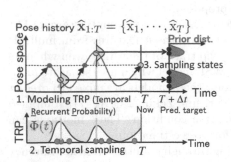

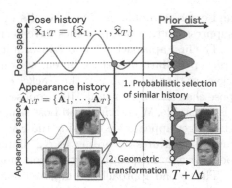

Fig. 1. M-PF employs past state sequences to predict a future state. First, it calculates the reoccurrence possibility of past state estimates (TRP). Past time steps are then sampled based on TRP. Past state estimates corresponding to the sampled time steps are combined to predict prior distribution. M-PF enables the implicit modeling of complex dynamics.

Fig. 2. M-PFAP extends M-PF [6] to realize robustness against large changes in pose. We focus on the fact that the pose-appearance relationship is not one-to-one but stochastic. The key extension from M-PF is prediction of joint prior distribution of pose and appearance.

in [6] estimates the position and rotation at each time step. M-PF uses the same observation process as traditional PF, which uses a single template built at initialization. This yields the 50 degree face rotation limit noted in [6].

M-PFAP extends M-PF. It adds appearance prior distribution prediction to M-PF for enabling handling of large appearance changes while keeping the merits of M-PF; robustness against abrupt movements and recoverability from tracking failure.

3 Memory-Based Particle Filter with Appearance Prediction (M-PFAP)

3.1 Formulation of M-PFAP

In this section, we define M-PFAP by extending the Bayesian filter formulation. The Bayesian filter consists of two processes, *update* and *prediction*, as

$$p(\mathbf{x}_t|\mathbf{z}_{1:t}) = k_t \cdot p(\mathbf{z}_t|\mathbf{x}_t) \cdot p(\mathbf{x}_t|\mathbf{z}_{1:t-1}), \tag{1}$$

$$p(\mathbf{x}_{t+1}|\mathbf{z}_{1:t}) = \int p(\mathbf{x}_{t+1}|\mathbf{x}_{1:t})p(\mathbf{x}_{1:t}|\mathbf{z}_{1:t})d\mathbf{x}_{1:t}, \tag{2}$$

where k_t is a normalization term, $\mathbf{z}_{1:t} = \{\mathbf{z}_1, \cdots, \mathbf{z}_t\}$ and $\mathbf{x}_{1:t} = \{\mathbf{x}_1, \cdots, \mathbf{x}_t\}$ denote a sequence of observation vectors and that of state vectors from time 1 to t, respectively. Equation (1) corresponds to the update process that computes the posterior distribution of the target state, and (2) corresponds to the prediction process, which calculates the prior distribution for the next time step.

M-PF replaced the prediction process in (2) with memory-based prior prediction as written in (3).

$$p(\mathbf{x}_{t+\Delta t}|\mathbf{z}_{1:t}) := \pi(\mathbf{x}_{t+\Delta t}|\widehat{\mathbf{x}}_{1:t}, \Delta t). \tag{3}$$

M-PF obtains the prior distribution at time $t + \Delta t$ from the history of state estimates $\widehat{\mathbf{x}}_{1:t}$ and the lead time Δt.

M-PFAP adds appearance as the state vector in addition to position and rotation. Hereafter, $\mathbf{X}_t = (\mathbf{x}_t, A_t)$ denotes state vector at time t, where $\mathbf{x}_t$ and A_t denote the position/rotation and the appearance at time t, respectively. Examples of appearance include a set of feature points and corresponding gray levels. The posterior distribution and the prior distribution of M-PFAP are defined below.

$$p(\mathbf{X}_t|\mathbf{z}_{1:t}) = k_t \cdot p(\mathbf{z}_t|\mathbf{x}_t, A_t) \cdot p(\mathbf{x}_t, A_t|\mathbf{z}_{1:t-1}), \tag{4}$$

$$p(\mathbf{X}_{t+\Delta t}|\mathbf{z}_{1:t}) = \pi(\mathbf{X}_{t+\Delta t}|\widehat{\mathbf{X}}_{1:t}, \Delta t) = \pi(\mathbf{x}_{t+\Delta t}, A_{t+\Delta t}|\widehat{\mathbf{x}}_{1:t}, \widehat{A}_{1:t}, \Delta t), \tag{5}$$

where $\widehat{\mathbf{X}}_{1:t} = \{(\widehat{\mathbf{x}}_1, \widehat{A}_1), \cdots, (\widehat{\mathbf{x}}_t, \widehat{A}_t)\}$ denotes the sequence of pairs of estimated pose $\widehat{\mathbf{x}}_t$ and appearance $\widehat{A}_t$ at time t. $\widehat{A}_{1:t} = \{\widehat{A}_1, \cdots, \widehat{A}_t\}$ denotes the sequence of appearances from time 1 to time t. We define the joint prior distribution of pose and appearance described in (5) as follows, by introducing a conditional probability of a future appearance given a future pose $\pi(A_{T+\Delta t}|\mathbf{x}_{t+\Delta t}, \widehat{\mathbf{x}}_{1:t}, \widehat{A}_{1:t})$ and a past history of appearance and pose $(\widehat{\mathbf{x}}_{1:t}, \widehat{A}_{1:t})$.

$$\text{Equation (5)} = \pi(\mathbf{x}_{t+\Delta t}|\widehat{\mathbf{x}}_{1:t}, \widehat{A}_{1:t}, \Delta t) \cdot \pi(A_{t+\Delta t}|\mathbf{x}_{t+\Delta t}, \widehat{\mathbf{x}}_{1:t}, \widehat{A}_{1:t}, \Delta t), \tag{6}$$

$$:= \pi(\mathbf{x}_{t+\Delta t}|\widehat{\mathbf{x}}_{1:t}, \Delta t) \cdot \pi(A_{t+\Delta t}|\mathbf{x}_{t+\Delta t}, \widehat{\mathbf{x}}_{1:t}, \widehat{A}_{1:t}). \tag{7}$$

The first part of (7) corresponds to prior distribution of pose $\mathbf{x}_{t+\Delta t}$. It assumes that the pose at Δt time in the future $\mathbf{x}_{t+\Delta t}$ is independent of the past history of appearance $\widehat{A}_{1:t}$, in other words, the dynamics of object movement are independent of the past appearance history. The last part of (7) corresponds to the conditional probability for a given pose, $\mathbf{x}_{t+\Delta t}$; it assumes that the appearance at Δt time in the future $A_{t+\Delta t}$ depends on the pose at time $T + \Delta t$, $\mathbf{x}_{T+\Delta t}$, and is independent of lead time Δt. The first part of (7) is prior distribution of pose; i.e. it equals the prior distribution of M-PF.

To define the conditional probability for a given pose, M-PFAP assumes that the main determinant of appearance is pose. Note that there is no deterministic one-to-one correspondence between them, i.e. significant uncertainty exists in the relationship. This assumption is based on the following observations. First, when the object rotates, its visible surface gradually becomes invisible and vice versa. However, appearance is also influenced by various factors such as illumination change and non-rigid deformation. Moreover, the explicit modeling of the appearance changes caused by pose is difficult, because appearance exhibits complex dynamics of high dimensionality.

Based on the above assumption, M-PFAP represents the relationship between pose and appearance as a probability distribution, like in Fig.3. In Fig.3, the

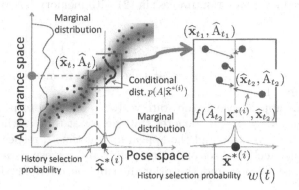

Fig. 3. An illustration of pose-appearance relationship; what we want to compute here is the conditional prior distribution, $p(A|\mathbf{x}^{*(i)})$, for given the pose $\mathbf{x}^{*(i)}$. We approximately represent the conditional distribution using past pose-appearance pairs. Each selected past pair is geometrically transformed, $f(\cdot)$, to compensate the difference between desired pose and selected pose.

horizontal axis and vertical axis denote pose space and appearance space, respectively. As seen in Fig.3, for a given pose, there is a distribution of possible appearances and vise versa. M-PFAP handles such uncertainty within the M-PF framework. It exploits the long-term history of the target state to predict complex prior distribution. This paper proposes a memory-based algorithm that jointly predicts appearance and pose.

3.2   Algorithm of the M-PFAP

M-PFAP sequentially estimates the target position and pose by repeating the posterior distribution estimation in (4) and the prior distribution prediction in (7). In the prior prediction step, M-PFAP predicts a joint prior distribution of pose and appearance. In the posterior prediction step, the observation likelihood of each particle is calculated by using the appearance estimated in the prior prediction step. Then, point estimates of pose and appearance are obtained from their joint posterior distribution. Next, the pair of pose and appearance is added to the history. Prior distribution prediction, posterior distribution estimation, and accumulation of history are described below.

Prior distribution prediction in M-PFAP
M-PFAP generates a set of particles, $\{(\mathbf{x}^{*(1)}, A^{*(1)}), \cdots, (\mathbf{x}^{*(N)}, A^{*(N)})\}$, which represents a joint prior distribution of pose and appearance, by using a memory-based mechanism and the stored history of them.

We focus on the fact that the joint distribution of pose and appearance defined by (7) is the product of the prior distribution of pose and the conditional probability of appearance (conditioned by pose). Therefore, we employ two step solutions. In Step-1, a set of particles that represents a prior distribution of pose is created by the previous M-PF, which is described in Fig.1 and Sect.2.2. In Step-2, the appearance that corresponds to each particle is generated. The process is shown in Fig.2 and Fig.3. In Fig.2, the current time is denoted by T, and prediction target is Δt time future state. Here, we assume we already have the history of pose $\widehat{\mathbf{x}}_{1:T}$ and appearance $\widehat{A}_{1:T}$. Each step is detailed below.

Step-1. Generating pose prior samples

Step-1 generates a set of particles $\{\mathbf{x}^{*(1)}, \cdots, \mathbf{x}^{*(N)}\}$ that represents the prior distribution of pose at time $T + \Delta t$ in the same manner as M-PF. This step corresponds to the first part of (7), $\pi(\mathbf{x}_{T+\Delta t}|\widehat{\mathbf{x}}_{1:T}, \Delta t)$.

Step-2. Prediction of appearance prior

Step-2 uses random sampleing according to $\pi(A_{T+\Delta t}|\mathbf{x}_{T+\Delta t}, \widehat{\mathbf{x}}_{1:T}, \widehat{A}_{1:T})$, which is the last part of (7), to generate a set of appearance samples. It generates appearances $\{A^{*(1)}, \cdots, A^{*(N)}\}$ corresponding to particles $\{\mathbf{x}^{*(1)}, \cdots, \mathbf{x}^{*(N)}\}$, that are obtained from Step-1. Here, what we want to compute is the conditional prior distribution $p(A|\mathbf{x}^{*(i)})$ for given the pose $\mathbf{x}^{*(i)}$. The basic idea is that the appearance distribution can be obtained as a mixture of past appearances whose associated poses are similar to pose condition $\mathbf{x}^{*(i)}$. Based on the idea, first, past pose-appearance pairs are sampled (Step-2-1), and then the past sampled appearances are geometrically transformed to fill in the gap between the desired pose $\mathbf{x}^{*(i)}$ and past sampled pose $\widehat{\mathbf{x}}_t$ (Step-2-2). We define the conditional appearance distribution as

$$p(A|\mathbf{x}^{*(i)}) := \frac{1}{\alpha} \sum_{t=1}^{T} w(t) \cdot \delta(A - f(\widehat{A}_t|\mathbf{x}^{*(i)}, \widehat{\mathbf{x}}_t)), \qquad (8)$$

where $f(\cdot)$ denotes the geometric transformation, $\delta(\cdot)$ denotes the delta function, $w(t)$ denotes the weight which is determined by the difference between $\mathbf{x}^{*(i)}$ and $\widehat{\mathbf{x}}_t$, and α is the normalization factor to make $\int p(A|\mathbf{x}^{*(i)})dA = 1$. Random sampling with weight $w(t)$ based on (8) generates the appearance prior distribution. We name weight $w(t)$ the history selection probability. This is defined in the temporal domain based on pose similarity; the higher the similarity between a pose in the history $\widehat{\mathbf{x}}_t$ and that of the target particle, $\mathbf{x}^{*(i)}$, becomes, the higher the history selection probability becomes. The uncertainty that exists in the appearance-pose relationship can be represented as random sampling from the past history. We expect that the mixture of past appearances well reflects the uncertainty in the appearance-pose relationship. This approach is simple but effective; it does not need explicit modeling or stochastic learning

Step-2-1. Sampling history

This step samples a past history of pose that is similar to the particle $\mathbf{x}^{*(i)}$, denoted by a black dot in the upper part of Fig.2 and in Fig.3 on the horizontal line. More specifically, this paper samples one past pose history, $\widehat{\mathbf{x}}_t, t \sim w(t)$, this is because we use enough samples, $\mathbf{x}^{*(i)}, (i = 1, \cdots, N)$, to create sufficient diversity in the appearance distribution. The sampled history is denoted by a blue dot in the upper part of Fig.2 and Fig.3. As the history selection probability, this paper employs function $w(t)$; this makes the probability proportional to the inverse of the Euclidian distance between the pose of target particle $\mathbf{x}^{*(i)}$ and that of history entry $\widehat{\mathbf{x}}_t$, $(t < T)$.

$$w(t) = \beta / \sqrt{(\widehat{\mathbf{x}}_t - \mathbf{x}^{*(i)})^T \cdot (\widehat{\mathbf{x}}_t - \mathbf{x}^{*(i)})}, \tag{9}$$

where, β is a normalization factor to realize $\sum_{t=1}^{T} w(t) = 1$.

Step-2-2. Appearance prediction

Considering the gap between the pose of sampled $\widehat{\mathbf{x}}_t$ and the target pose $\mathbf{x}^{*(i)}$, Step-2-2 predicts the appearance $A^{*(i)}$ by geometrically transforming $\widehat{A}_t$ based on the pose difference as written in

$$A^{*(i)} = f(\widehat{A}_t | \mathbf{x}^{*(i)}, \widehat{\mathbf{x}}_t). \tag{10}$$

Here, we assume that the local appearance difference caused by the small difference in pose can be well predicted by local geometric transformation. See Sect. 4 for more details.

Posterior distribution estimation

As in (4), posterior distribution is defined by multiplying the prior distribution by the likelihood function for the observation at time step t. In the PF approach, the posterior distribution is represented by weighted particles. The weight is calculated by using a likelihood function for given input image. This function is calculated based on the matching error between the appearance and input images.

In contrast to M-PF, which uses a fixed appearance model, M-PFAP uses predicted appearance in the prior distribution for each particle.

Accumulation of history

At each time T, M-PFAP stores pose-appearance pairs $\widehat{\mathbf{X}}_T = (\widehat{\mathbf{x}}_T, \widehat{A}_T)$. From the particle set that represents the joint posterior distribution of appearance and pose, the point estimates of pose and appearance are calculated. For pose, weight averaging is used, and appearance estimates are obtained from the latest input image by using the target's pose estimates and rough shape model on the current image frame. See Sect.4 for more details.

4   Implementation of Face Pose Tracker

We create a variant of the Sparse Template Condensation Tracker (STCTracker) [16], by using M-PFAP to implement particle filtering. Figure 4 shows the flowchart of the implemented face pose tracker. This section describes some details.

Pose parameter

Target position and pose are described by a vector of seven dimensions, $\mathbf{x} = (m_x, m_y, s, r_r, r_p, r_y, l)$; 2-DOF translation, scale, 3-DOF rotation, and an illumination coefficient.

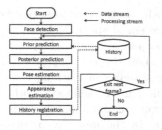

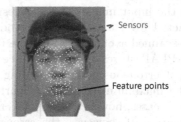

Fig. 4. Flowchart of face pose tracking by using M-PFAP

Fig. 5. Interest points deployed for initial face

Sparse template representation of an appearance

M-PFAP employs sparse template matching, which uses a sparse template as the appearance model, as same as [16]. The sparse template consists of a sparse set of pixels within the target region. Here, appearance A is denoted by $\{(u_{x(1)}, u_{y(1)}, u_{z(1)}, b_{(1)}), \cdots, (u_{x(M)}, u_{y(M)}, u_{z(M)}, b_{(M)})\}$, where M denotes the number of interest points, $(u_{x(i)}, u_{y(i)}, u_{z(i)})$ denotes the 3-D position of an interest point, and $b_{(i)}$ denotes its gray level. The matching error is calculated as the sum of differences between the gray levels of the interest points and those of the corresponding points in the input image. Figure 5 shows the 250 interest points selected in the initialization step. These points are selected from edge sides and from minimum or maximum points among 8 neighbor pixels.

Geometric transform for predicting appearance

As written in Step-2-2, M-PFAP uses geometric transformation to bridge the gap between the sampled pose $\widehat{\mathbf{x}}_t$ and the target pose $\mathbf{x}^{*(i)}$. As the geometric transformation, M-PFAP uses 3-DOF rotation. It transforms interest point's corrdinate $[\widehat{u}_x, \widehat{u}_y, \widehat{u}_z]^T$ into desired pose, $[u_x^{*(i)}, u_y^{*(i)}, u_z^{*(i)}]^T$, as in (11).

$$\left[u_x^{*(i)} \ u_y^{*(i)} \ u_z^{*(i)} \right]^T = R(\mathbf{x}^{*(i)})R'(\widehat{\mathbf{x}}_k)\left[\widehat{u}_x \ \widehat{u}_y \ \widehat{u}_z \right]^T, \tag{11}$$

where $R(\cdot)$ and $R'(\cdot)$ denotes rotation matrix and inverse matrix of $R(\cdot)$, respectively. Additionally, illumination change is assumed by uniform changes in gray levels of a set of interest points. The gray level $b^{*(i)}$ corresponding to interest point $[u_x^{*(i)}, u_y^{*(i)}, u_z^{*(i)}]^T$, is obtained by $b^{*(i)} = v \cdot \widehat{b}$, where $v \sim N(1, \sigma^2)$. $N(1, \sigma^2)$ denotes normal distribution with mean 1 variance σ^2.

Adding pose and appearance into history

At each time step, M-PFAP stores a pose-appearance pair. The pose estimate $\widehat{\mathbf{x}}_T$ is obtained as the point estimate of marginal posterior distribution of pose. Appearance $\widehat{A}_T$, which is a set of three dimensional interest points and corresponding gray levels in this paper, is obtained from the point estimate of the pose and the latest input image.

M-PFAP employs two steps to obtain a new appearance $\widehat{A}_T$; interest point detection and depth information extraction. First, interest points are detected from the input image. Then, corresponding depth values of interest points are extracted from a rough shape model. As the rough shape model, we used a laser-scanned averaged head shape (not a tracked person's model).

M-PFAP stores pose-appearance pairs only when the tracking is stable to prevent erroneous pairs from being stored. The stability of tracking is judged by the maximum likelihood of particles. The maximum likelihood works well in most cases, however, it is not perfect, and erroneous pairs may become held in memory. If, however, the erroneous pairs are in the minority in memory, the stochastic sampling from all past memory yields few erroneous samples and the majority of samples are valid. This condition ensures that M-PFAP does not suffer explosive error growth, which is a serious weakness of the traditional template update scheme.

Additionally, to suppress memory usage and retrieval time, M-PFAP employs the data structuring process. It stores a new pose-appearance pair only when there are no pairs whose pose are very similar to the new pose.

5   Experiments and Results

Experiments in this paper targets face pose. This section describes the experimental environment, the details of the experiments, and the results.

5.1   Experimental Environment

We used PointGreyResearch's FLEA, a digital color camera, to capture 1024 × 768 pixel-size images at 30 frames per second. The tracking processes use only gray images converted from color images. A magnetic-based sensor, Polhemus FASTRAK was used to obtain quantitative ground truth data. The rotation angles, pitch, roll, and yaw roughly correspond to shaking, nodding, and tilting actions, respectively. As shown in Fig.5, two sensors were attached to both temples of the subject. The number of particles was set to 2000.

Table 1 summarizes the proposed method and baseline methods. We employed three baseline methods, all based on M-PF; the first one is the original M-PF, it uses only one template without updating; the second one (LT) updates the template and uses the latest template; the last one (NN) updates the template and uses the template nearest to the target pose.

Table 1. Comparison between proposed method and comparative methods

	template updating	selection criterion of templates
Proposed[M-PFAP]	accumulating history	Probabilistic selection
M-PF	No	initial template
LT	Yes	latest template
NN	Yes	nearest template

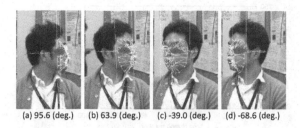

(a) 95.6 (deg.)   (b) 63.9 (deg.)   (c) -39.0 (deg.)   (d) -68.6 (deg.)

Fig. 6. An example of face tracking; the proposed method can track against large appearance changes

5.2   The Effective Tracking by the M-PFAP

To verify the effectiveness of M-PFAP, we used a test video sequence that included a head that rotated from frontal view to profile view (=90 deg. in horizontal direction). The target video includes profile faces. Figure 6 shows the result of M-PFAP. The snapshots in Fig.6 are listed in time order from left to right. In Fig.6, the white mesh represents the estimated position and rotation, and the dots located around center of the face denote the prior distribution of face pose, which only represent positions. The initial template surface is almost invisible in profile view as in Fig.6 (a) and (d) ; old trackers that use only frontal view template cannot track the face anymore. In contrast, M-PFAP successfully tracked the face in profile view.

5.3   Quantitative Evaluation of Tracking Accuracy

Three types of video were employed for this quantitative evaluation. Video-1 included a wide range of moderate rotations. This video was used for evaluating basic performance. Video-2 included abrupt movements, such as abrupt reverse of moving direction and abrupt shaking of the head. This video is used to verify that M-PFAP mirrors the robustness against such abrupt motion of M-PF. Video-3 included occlusions such as the rotating head being hidden by a moving arm. Occlusion recovery is another merit of M-PFAP inherited from M-PF.

Fig.7 shows the tracking results of Video-1. The horizontal axis denotes time and the vertical axis denotes horizontal rotation angle. Figure 7 shows that the M-PFAP output closely followed the ground truth. M-PF, on the other hand, became unstable when the rotation angle exceeds about 60 degrees. NN and LT could not track correctly; they had worse performance than M-PF. We consider that the updated template included errors and so the tracking drifted.

Fig.8 shows snapshots during tracking of the target face moved from left to right abruptly (Video-2). The snapshots are listed from left to right in time order. It was tracked correctly. Absolute average errors of face pose tracking against Video-1 and Video-2 and variances are shown in Table 2. The proposed method yielded improved tracking performance in both videos.

Fig. 7. Head rotation angle in horizontal direction

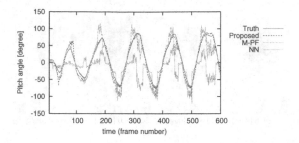

(a) Frame = 750   (b) Frame = 753   (c) Frame = 756   (d) Frame = 759

Fig. 8. Snapshots of tracking the abrupt movements

Video-3 included occlusions. Snapshots of Video-3 during tracking are shown in Fig. 9. In this scene, the face turns from right to left, at the same time, an arm moves from top to bottom causing an occlusion; the face turns and shifts during the occlusion; so the face poses before and after occlusion are completely different. Additionally, the profile face appears immediately after the occlusion; it can not be tracked by the initial template. M-PFAP could recover tracking even in this severe situation.

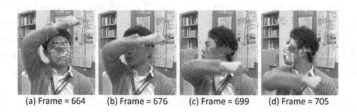

(a) Frame = 664   (b) Frame = 676   (c) Frame = 699   (d) Frame = 705

Fig. 9. Snapshots of occlusion recovery

5.4 Past Appearance Used for Appearance Prediction

Fig.10(b) shows the history entries that were selected to estimate the pose prior distribution of Fig.10(a). It can be observed that many entries were used for appearance prediction. Each entry includes error to some extent. By using a number of entries to estimate appearance, M-PFAP prevents the tracking from accumulating errors and from drifting.

Table 2. Absolute average errors [degree] in horizontal rotation; values in blacket show corresponding variances

	Proposed	M-PF	NN	LT
Video-1	7.1 (35.0)	15.9 (182.7)	35.0 (1316.5)	38.7 (1448.1)
Video-2	8.5 (108.8)	14.3 (117.0)	16.7 (684.7)	31.2 (698.0)

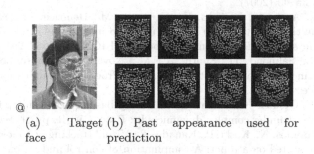

(a) Target face   (b) Past appearance used for prediction

Fig. 10. Pose estimation target and past appearance used for the appearance prior prediction

6 Summary and Future Works

This paper proposed M-PFAP; it offers robust visual tracking of the target's position and pose. M-PFAP is an extension of M-PF and represents a unified probabilistic framework for the joint estimation of target position/pose and its appearance based on memory-based joint prior prediction using stored past pose and appearance sequences. Quantitative evaluations confirmed that M-PFAP successfully tracks human faces in frontal view up to profile view, i.e. 90 degree horizontal rotation; it thus completely overcomes the limitation of M-PF.

Future works include the following two points. First, we consider how to handle appearance change due to illumination change. Among the various illumination changes, the current implementation of M-PFAP realizes robustness against uniform illumination change since the state vector employs an illumination coefficient. Also, M-PFAP potentially can handle non-uniform illumination change by accumulating pose-appearance pairs under gradual changes in illumination. We are going to evaluate the limits of robustness against various illumination conditions and achieve further robustness.

Second, we will tackle GPU implementation. Our current CPU-based M-PFAP does not work in real-time. We consider that M-PFAP suits GPU acceleration, because it is an extension of M-PF and supports parallel processing as does M-PF. M-PF processing was made 10 times faster by GPU implementation. For the GPU implementation, more effective way of storing memory to save memory usage and to save retrieval time should be considered.

References

1. Comaniciu, D., Ramesh, V., Meer, P.: Kernel-based object tracking. IEEE Trans. PAMI 25, 564–577 (2003)
2. Bradski, G.R.: Computer vision face tracking for use in a perceptual user interface. In: Proc. IEEE Workshop Applications of Computer Vision, pp. 214–219 (1998)
3. Tua, J., Taob, H., Huang, T.: Face as mouse through visual face tracking. CVIU 108, 35–40 (2007)
4. Otsuka, K., Araki, S., Ishizuka, K., Fujimoto, M., Heinrich, M., Yamato, J.: A realtime multimodal system for analyzing group meeting by combining face pose tracking and speaker diarization. In: Proc. ACM ICMI, pp. 257–264 (2008)
5. Gordon, N., Salmond, D., Smith, A.F.M.: Novel approach to non-linear and non-Gaussian Bayesian state estimeation. IEE Proc.F:Communications Rader and Signal Processing 140, 107–113 (1993)
6. Mikami, D., Otsuka, K., Yamato, J.: Memory-based particle filter for face pose tracking robust under complex dynamics. In: Proc. CVPR, pp. 999–1006 (2009)
7. Papanikolopoulos, N., Kosla, P., Kanade, T.: Visual tracking of a moving target by a camera mounted on a robot: A combination of control and vision. IEEE Trans. Robot. Autom. 9, 14–35 (1993)
8. Black, M., Yacoob, Y.: Recognizing facial expressions in image sequence using local parameterized models of image motion. IJCV 25, 23–48 (1997)
9. Matthews, I., Ishikawa, T., Baker, S.: The template update problem. IEEE Trans. PAMI 26, 810–815 (2004)
10. Jepson, A.D., Fleet, J.D., El-Margaghi, T.F.: Robust online appearance models for visual tracking. IEEE Trans. PAMI 25, 1296–1311 (2003)
11. Zelniker, E.E., Hospedales, T.M., Gong, S., Xiang, T.: A unified bayesian framework for adaptive visual tracking. In: Proc. BMVC, pp. 100–200 (2009)
12. Morency, L.P., Rahimi, A., Darrell, T.: Adaptive view-based appearance models. In: Proc. CVPR, pp. 803–810 (2003)
13. Morency, L.P., Whitehill, J., Movellan, J.: Monocular head pose estimation using generalized adaptive view-based appearance model. Image and Vision Computing (2009), doi:10.1016/j.imavis.2009.08.004
14. Ross, D., Lim, J., Lin, R.-S., Yang, M.-H.: Incremental learning for robust visual tracking. IJCV 77(1-3), 125–141 (2008), doi:10.1007/s11263-007-0075-7
15. Lefèvre, S., Odobez, J.: View-based appearance model online learning for 3d deformable face tracking. In: Proc. VISAPP (2010)
16. Lozano, O.M., Otsuka, K.: Real-time visual tracker by stream processing. Journal of VLSI Signal Processing Systems (2008), doi:10.1007/s11265-008-0250-2

3D Deformable Face Tracking with a Commodity Depth Camera

Qin Cai[1], David Gallup[2], Cha Zhang[1], and Zhengyou Zhang[1]

[1] Communication and Collaboration Systems Group, Microsoft Research
One Microsoft Way, Redmond, WA 98052 USA
[2] Dept. of Computer Science, UNC at Chapel Hill
Sitterson Hall, UNC-Chapel Hill, Chapel Hill, NC 27599 USA

Abstract. Recently, there has been an increasing number of depth cameras available at commodity prices. These cameras can usually capture both color and depth images in real-time, with limited resolution and accuracy. In this paper, we study the problem of 3D deformable face tracking with such commodity depth cameras. A regularized maximum likelihood deformable model fitting (DMF) algorithm is developed, with special emphasis on handling the noisy input depth data. In particular, we present a maximum likelihood solution that can accommodate sensor noise represented by an arbitrary covariance matrix, which allows more elaborate modeling of the sensor's accuracy. Furthermore, an ℓ_1 regularization scheme is proposed based on the semantics of the deformable face model, which is shown to be very effective in improving the tracking results. To track facial movement in subsequent frames, feature points in the texture images are matched across frames and integrated into the DMF framework seamlessly. The effectiveness of the proposed method is demonstrated with multiple sequences with ground truth information.

1 Introduction

Tracking non-rigid objects, in particular human faces, is an active research area for many applications in human computer interaction, performance-driven facial animation, and face recognition. The problem is still largely unsolved, as usually for 3D deformable face models there are dozens of parameters that need to be estimated from the limited input data.

A number of works in the literature have focused on 3D deformable face tracking based only on videos. There are mainly two categories of algorithms: (1) appearance based, which uses generative linear face appearance models such as active appearance models (AAMs) [1] and 3D morphable models [2] to capture the shape and texture variations of faces, and (2) feature based, which uses active shape models [3] or other features [4] for tracking. Appearance based algorithms may suffer from insufficient generalizability of AAMs due to lighting and texture variations, while feature based algorithms may lose tracking due to the lack of semantic features, the occlusions of profile poses, etc.

Another large body of works considered fitting morphable models to 3D scans of faces [5,6,7,8,9]. These 3D scans are usually obtained by laser scanners or

K. Daniilidis, P. Maragos, N. Paragios (Eds.): ECCV 2010, Part III, LNCS 6313, pp. 229–242, 2010.
© Springer-Verlag Berlin Heidelberg 2010

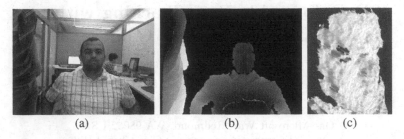

(a)   (b)   (c)

Fig. 1. Data captured by a commodity depth camera. (a) Texture image; (b) depth image; (c) enlarged face region rendered from another viewpoint.

structured light systems, which have very high quality. Fitting these high quality range data with a morphable face model usually involves the well-known iterative closest point (ICP) algorithm [10] and its variants [11], and the results are generally very good. The downside, however, is that these capturing systems are usually very expensive to acquire or operate.

Recently, depth cameras based on time-of-flight or other principles became available at commodity prices, such as 3DV systems and Canesta. Fig. 1 shows some captured data from our test depth camera, which derives depth information from infrared light patterns and triangulation. The camera is capable of recording both texture and depth images with 640×480 pixels resolution at 30 frames per second (fps). In general the depth information is very accurate, though a closer look at the face region (Fig. 1(c)) shows that it is still much noisier than laser scanned results.

In this paper, we propose a regularized maximum likelihood deformable model fitting (DMF) algorithm for 3D face tracking with a commodity depth camera. Compared with existing approaches, this paper has two major contributions. First, unlike most previous works on DMF, we do not assume an identity covariance matrix for the depth sensor noise. This leads to a more general maximum likelihood solution with arbitrary noise covariance matrices, which is shown to be effective for our noisy depth data. Second, the noisy depth data also require regularization in the ICP framework. We propose a novel ℓ_1 regularization scheme inspired by the semantics of our deformable face model, which improves the tracking performance significantly.

2   Related Work

There is a large amount of literature in facial modeling and tracking. We refer the reader to the survey by Murphy-Chutorian and Trivedi [12] for an overview.

Many models have been explored for face animation and tracking. Parametric models use a set of parameters to describe the articulation of the jaw, eyebrow position, opening of the mouth, and other features that comprise the state of the face [13]. Physics-based models seek to simulate the facial muscle and tissue [14]. Blanz and Vetter [2] discovered that the manifold of facial expression and appearance can be effectively modeled as a linear combination of exemplar faces. This morphable model is computed from a large database of registered laser scans, and this approach has proven useful for face synthesis [2], expression transfer [8], recognition [5], and tracking [15]. For tracking, a subject-specific morphable model can be constructed [9], which requires each subject to undergo an extensive training phase before tracking can be performed. In contrast, we use a generic morphable model constructed by an artist, which is first fit to the subject during initialization. Only a few frames with neutral faces are required to automatically compute the subject-specific appearance parameters before tracking.

Several approaches have used range data for face modeling and tracking. Zhu and Fujimura [6] used range data as an additional image channel in optical flow-based tracking. Methods that rely solely on visual appearance will be sensitive to lighting conditions and changes, whereas many ranging techniques are unaffected by lighting conditions. Many methods, such as that of Zhang et al. [7], used structured light or other active ranging techniques. The structured light systems in [7,8,9] required a camera, a projector, and in some cases synchronization circuitry. This hardware is not uncommon, but still expensive to acquire and operate. This paper will study deformable face tracking with a commodity depth camera, which is projected to cost under $100 in the next few years, and has lower resolution and less accuracy than structured light systems. A key part of our method is thus to model the sensor noise and add regularization to improve the tracking performance. Note uncertainty on measurements has been considered in other contexts such as motion analysis for mobile robot navigation [16], though we are not aware of similar work in the context of deformable face tracking.

Iterative closest point (ICP) is a common approach for aligning shapes, such as range images of faces. Besl et al. [10] proposed the ICP algorithm for rigid shape alignment, and variants have been proposed for nonrigid alignment [11]. Lu and Jian [17] used ICP for face matching, and applied ICP in deformable model fitting as an intermediate step assuming the deformation is fixed. ICP has also been used in face recognition [18] and real-time tracking [9]. Note in model fitting and tracking applications, regularization is a common technique to stabilize the final results [11,9]. However, the ℓ_1 regularization that will be introduced in Section 4.5 has not be used in previous works, and its performance improvement is rather significant.

3   Linear Deformable Model

We use a linear deformable model constructed by an artist to represent possible variations of a human face [19], which could also be constructed semi-automatically [2]. The head model is defined as a set of K vertices $\mathcal{P}$ and a set of facets $\mathcal{F}$. Each vertex $\mathbf{p}_k \in \mathcal{P}$ is a point in $\mathbb{R}^3$, and each facet $f \in \mathcal{F}$ is a set of three or more vertices from the set $\mathcal{P}$. In our head model, all facets have exactly 3 vertices. In addition, the head model is augmented with two artist-defined deformation matrices: the static deformation matrix $\mathbf{B}$ and the action

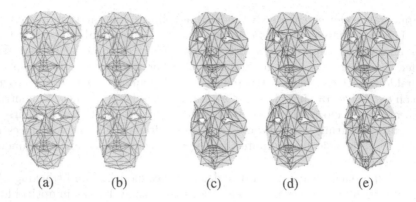

(a)   (b)   (c)   (d)   (e)

Fig. 2. Example deformations of our 3D face model. (a)(b) Static deformations; (c)(d)(e) action deformations.

deformation matrix $\mathbf{A}$. According to weighting vectors $\mathbf{s}$ and $\mathbf{r}$, they transform the mesh linearly into a target head model $\mathcal{Q}$ as follows:

$$\begin{bmatrix} \mathbf{q}_1 \\ \vdots \\ \mathbf{q}_K \end{bmatrix} = \begin{bmatrix} \mathbf{p}_1 \\ \vdots \\ \mathbf{p}_K \end{bmatrix} + \mathbf{A} \begin{bmatrix} r_1 \\ \vdots \\ r_N \end{bmatrix} + \mathbf{B} \begin{bmatrix} s_1 \\ \vdots \\ s_M \end{bmatrix}, \tag{1}$$

where M and N are the number of deformations in $\mathbf{B}$ and $\mathbf{A}$, $\alpha_m \leq s_m \leq \beta_m, m = 1, \cdots, M$, and $\theta_n \leq r_n \leq \phi_n, n = 1, \cdots, N$ are ranges specified by the artist. The static deformations in $\mathbf{B}$ are characteristic to a particular face, such as enlarging the distance between eyes, or extending the chin. The action deformations include opening the mouth, raising eyebrows, etc. Some example deformations of our model are shown in Fig. 2.

4   Regularized Maximum Likelihood DMF

4.1   Problem Formulation

Let $\mathcal{P}$ represent the vertices of our head model, and $\mathcal{G}$ represent the 3D points acquired from the depth camera. We want to compute the rotation $\mathbf{R}$ and translation $\mathbf{t}$ between the head model and the depth camera, as well as the deformation parameters $\mathbf{r}$ and $\mathbf{s}$. We formulate the problem as below.

Following the procedure of ICP [10], let us assume that in a certain iteration, a set of point correspondences between the deformable model and the depth image is available. For each correspondence $(\mathbf{p}_k, \mathbf{g}_k)$, $\mathbf{g}_k \in \mathcal{G}$, we have the equation:

$$\mathbf{R}(\mathbf{p}_k + \mathbf{A}_k \mathbf{r} + \mathbf{B}_k \mathbf{s}) + \mathbf{t} = \mathbf{g}_k + \mathbf{x}_k \tag{2}$$

where $\mathbf{A}_k$ and $\mathbf{B}_k$ represent the three rows of $\mathbf{A}$ and $\mathbf{B}$ that correspond to vertex k. $\mathbf{x}_k$ is the depth sensor noise, which can be assumed to follow a zero mean Gaussian distribution $\mathcal{N}(0, \Sigma_{\mathbf{x}_k})$. The maximum likelihood solution of the unknowns $\mathbf{R}, \mathbf{t}, \mathbf{r}$ and $\mathbf{s}$ can be derived by minimizing:

$$J_1(\mathbf{R}, \mathbf{t}, \mathbf{r}, \mathbf{s}) = \frac{1}{K} \sum_{k=1}^{K} \mathbf{x}_k^T \Sigma_{\mathbf{x}_k}^{-1} \mathbf{x}_k, \tag{3}$$

where $\mathbf{x}_k = \mathbf{R}(\mathbf{p}_k + \mathbf{A}_k \mathbf{r} + \mathbf{B}_k \mathbf{s}) + \mathbf{t} - \mathbf{g}_k$. $\mathbf{r}$ and $\mathbf{s}$ are subject to inequality constraints, namely, $\alpha_m \leq s_m \leq \beta_m, m = 1, \cdots, M$, and $\theta_n \leq r_n \leq \phi_n, n = 1, \cdots, N$. Additional regularization terms may be added to the above optimization problem, which will be discussed further in Section 4.5.

A useful variation is to substitute the point-to-point distance with point-to-plane distance [20]. The point-to-plane distance allows the model to slide tangentially to the surface, which speeds up convergence and makes it less likely to get stuck in local minima. Distance to the plane can be computed using the surface normal, which can be computed from the head model based on the current iteration's head pose. Let the surface normal of point $\mathbf{p}_k$ in the head model coordinate be $\mathbf{n}_k$. The point-to-plane distance can be computed as:

$$y_k = (\mathbf{R}\mathbf{n}_k)^T \mathbf{x}_k, \tag{4}$$

The maximum likelihood solution is thus obtained by minimizing:

$$J_2(\mathbf{R}, \mathbf{t}, \mathbf{r}, \mathbf{s}) = \frac{1}{K} \sum_{k-1}^{K} \frac{y_k^2}{\sigma_{y_k}^2}, \tag{5}$$

where $\sigma_{y_k}^2 = (\mathbf{R}\mathbf{n}_k)^T \Sigma_{\mathbf{x}_k} (\mathbf{R}\mathbf{n}_k)$, and $\alpha_m \leq s_m \leq \beta_m, m = 1, \cdots, M$, and $\theta_n \leq r_n \leq \phi_n, n = 1, \cdots, N$.

Given the correspondence pairs $(\mathbf{p}_k, \mathbf{g}_k)$, since both the point-to-point and the point-to-plane distances are nonlinear, we resort to a solution that solves for $\mathbf{r}, \mathbf{s}$ and $\mathbf{R}, \mathbf{t}$ in an iterative fashion. For ease of understanding, we present the solution for identity noise covariance matrix in Section 4.2 first, and extend it to arbitrary covariance matrix in Section 4.3.

4.2   Iterative Solution for Identity Noise Covariance Matrix

We first assume the depth sensor noise covariance matrix is a scaled identity matrix, i.e., $\Sigma_{\mathbf{x}_k} = \sigma^2 \mathbf{I}_3$, where $\mathbf{I}_3$ is a 3×3 identity matrix. Further, let $\tilde{\mathbf{R}} = \mathbf{R}^{-1}, \tilde{\mathbf{t}} = \tilde{\mathbf{R}}\mathbf{t}$, and

$$\mathbf{y}_k = \tilde{\mathbf{R}}\mathbf{x}_k = \mathbf{p}_k + \mathbf{A}_k \mathbf{r} + \mathbf{B}_k \mathbf{s} + \tilde{\mathbf{t}} - \tilde{\mathbf{R}}\mathbf{g}_k. \tag{6}$$

Since $\mathbf{x}_k^T \mathbf{x}_k = (\mathbf{R}\mathbf{y}_k)^T (\mathbf{R}\mathbf{y}_k) = \mathbf{y}_k^T \mathbf{y}_k$, the likelihood function can be written as:

$$J_1(\mathbf{R}, \mathbf{t}, \mathbf{r}, \mathbf{s}) = \frac{1}{K\sigma^2} \sum_{k=1}^{K} \mathbf{x}_k^T \mathbf{x}_k = \frac{1}{K\sigma^2} \sum_{k=1}^{K} \mathbf{y}_k^T \mathbf{y}_k. \tag{7}$$

Similarly, for point-to-plane distance, since $y_k = (\mathbf{R}\mathbf{n}_k)^T \mathbf{x}_k = \mathbf{n}_k^T \mathbf{R}^T \mathbf{R} \mathbf{y}_k = \mathbf{n}_k^T \mathbf{y}_k$, and $\sigma_{y_k}^2 = (\mathbf{R}\mathbf{n}_k)^T \mathbf{\Sigma}_{\mathbf{x}_k} (\mathbf{R}\mathbf{n}_k) = \sigma^2$, we have:

$$J_2(\mathbf{R}, \mathbf{t}, \mathbf{r}, \mathbf{s}) = \frac{1}{K\sigma^2} \sum_{k=1}^{K} \mathbf{y}_k^T \mathbf{N}_k \mathbf{y}_k, \tag{8}$$

where $\mathbf{N}_k = \mathbf{n}_k \mathbf{n}_k^T$.

We may decompose the rotation matrix $\tilde{\mathbf{R}}$ into an initial rotation matrix $\tilde{\mathbf{R}}_0$ and an incremental rotation matrix $\Delta\tilde{\mathbf{R}}$, where the initial rotation matrix can be the rotation matrix of the head in the previous frame, or an estimation of $\tilde{\mathbf{R}}$ obtained in another algorithm. In other words, let $\tilde{\mathbf{R}} = \Delta\tilde{\mathbf{R}}\tilde{\mathbf{R}}_0$. Since the rotation angle of the incremental rotation matrix is small, we may linearize it as:

$$\Delta\tilde{\mathbf{R}} \approx \begin{bmatrix} 1 & -\omega_3 & \omega_2 \\ \omega_3 & 1 & -\omega_1 \\ -\omega_2 & \omega_1 & 1 \end{bmatrix}, \tag{9}$$

where $\omega = [\omega_1, \omega_2, \omega_3]^T$ is the corresponding small rotation vector. Further, let $\mathbf{q}_k = \tilde{\mathbf{R}}_0 \mathbf{g}_k = [q_{k1}, q_{k2}, q_{k3}]^T$, we can write the variable $\mathbf{y}_k$ in the form of unknowns $\mathbf{r}$, $\mathbf{s}$, $\tilde{\mathbf{t}}$ and ω as:

$$\mathbf{y}_k = \mathbf{p}_k + \mathbf{A}_k \mathbf{r} + \mathbf{B}_k \mathbf{s} + \tilde{\mathbf{t}} - \Delta\tilde{\mathbf{R}}\mathbf{q}_k \approx (\mathbf{p}_k - \mathbf{q}_k) + [\mathbf{A}_k, \mathbf{B}_k, \mathbf{I}_3, [\mathbf{q}_k]_\times] \begin{bmatrix} \mathbf{r} \\ \mathbf{s} \\ \mathbf{t} \\ \omega \end{bmatrix} \tag{10}$$

where $[\mathbf{q}_k]_\times$ is the skew-symmetric matrix of $\mathbf{q}_k$:

$$[\mathbf{q}_k]_\times = \begin{bmatrix} 0 & -q_{k3} & q_{k2} \\ q_{k3} & 0 & -q_{k1} \\ -q_{k2} & q_{k1} & 0 \end{bmatrix}. \tag{11}$$

Let $\mathbf{H}_k = [\mathbf{A}_k, \mathbf{B}_k, \mathbf{I}_3, [\mathbf{q}_k]_\times]$, $\mathbf{u}_k = \mathbf{p}_k - \mathbf{q}_k$, and $\mathbf{z} = [\mathbf{r}^T, \mathbf{s}^T, \tilde{\mathbf{t}}^T, \omega^T]^T$, we have:

$$\mathbf{y}_k = \mathbf{u}_k + \mathbf{H}_k \mathbf{z}. \tag{12}$$

Hence,

$$J_1 = \frac{1}{K\sigma^2} \sum_{k=1}^{K} \mathbf{y}_k^T \mathbf{y}_k = \frac{1}{K\sigma^2} \sum_{k=1}^{K} (\mathbf{u}_k + \mathbf{H}_k \mathbf{z})^T (\mathbf{u}_k + \mathbf{H}_k \mathbf{z}) \tag{13}$$

$$J_2 = \frac{1}{K\sigma^2} \sum_{k=1}^{K} \mathbf{y}_k^T \mathbf{N}_k \mathbf{y}_k = \frac{1}{K\sigma^2} \sum_{k=1}^{K} (\mathbf{u}_k + \mathbf{H}_k \mathbf{z})^T \mathbf{N}_k (\mathbf{u}_k + \mathbf{H}_k \mathbf{z}) \tag{14}$$

Both likelihood functions are quadratic with respect to $\mathbf{z}$. Since there are linear constraints on the range of values for $\mathbf{r}$ and $\mathbf{s}$, the minimization problem can be solved with quadratic programming [21].

The rotation vector ω is an approximation of the actual incremental rotation matrix. One can simply insert $\Delta\tilde{\mathbf{R}}\tilde{\mathbf{R}}_0$ to the position of $\tilde{\mathbf{R}}_0$ and repeat the above optimization process until it converges.

4.3 Solution for Arbitrary Noise Covariance Matrix

When the sensor noise covariance matrix is arbitrary, again we resort to an iterative solution. Note since $\mathbf{y}_k = \tilde{\mathbf{R}}\mathbf{x}_k$, we have $\boldsymbol{\Sigma}_{\mathbf{y}_k} = \tilde{\mathbf{R}}\boldsymbol{\Sigma}_{\mathbf{x}_k}\tilde{\mathbf{R}}^T$. A feasible solution can be obtained if we replace $\tilde{\mathbf{R}}$ with its estimation $\tilde{\mathbf{R}}_0$, i.e.,

$$\boldsymbol{\Sigma}_{\mathbf{y}_k} \approx \tilde{\mathbf{R}}_0\boldsymbol{\Sigma}_{\mathbf{x}_k}\tilde{\mathbf{R}}_0^T, \tag{15}$$

which is known for the current iteration. Subsequently,

$$J_1 = \frac{1}{K}\sum_{k=1}^{K}\mathbf{y}_k^T\boldsymbol{\Sigma}_{\mathbf{y}_k}^{-1}\mathbf{y}_k = \frac{1}{K}\sum_{k=1}^{K}(\mathbf{u}_k + \mathbf{H}_k\mathbf{z})^T\boldsymbol{\Sigma}_{\mathbf{y}_k}^{-1}(\mathbf{u}_k + \mathbf{H}_k\mathbf{z}) \tag{16}$$

$$J_2 = \frac{1}{K}\sum_{k=1}^{K}\frac{\mathbf{y}_k^T\mathbf{N}_k\mathbf{y}_k}{\mathbf{n}_k^T\boldsymbol{\Sigma}_{\mathbf{y}_k}\mathbf{n}_k} = \frac{1}{K}\sum_{k=1}^{K}\frac{(\mathbf{u}_k + \mathbf{H}_k\mathbf{z})^T\mathbf{N}_k(\mathbf{u}_k + \mathbf{H}_k\mathbf{z})}{\mathbf{n}_k^T\boldsymbol{\Sigma}_{\mathbf{y}_k}\mathbf{n}_k} \tag{17}$$

We still have quadratic likelihood functions with respect to $\mathbf{z}$, which can be solved via quadratic programming. Again, the minimization will be repeated until convergence by inserting $\Delta\tilde{\mathbf{R}}\tilde{\mathbf{R}}_0$ to the position of $\tilde{\mathbf{R}}_0$ in each iteration.

4.4 Multi-frame DMF for Model Initialization

In our tracking system, the above maximum likelihood DMF framework is applied differently in two stages. During the initialization stage, the goal is to fit the generic deformable model to an arbitrary person. We assume that a set of L ($L \leq 10$ in the current implementation) neutral face frames are available. The action deformation vector $\mathbf{r}$ is assumed to be zero. We jointly solve the static deformation vector $\mathbf{s}$ and the face rotations and translations as follows.

Denote the correspondences as $(\mathbf{p}_{lk}, \mathbf{g}_{lk})$, where $l = 1, \cdots, L$ represents the frame index. Assume in the previous iteration, $\tilde{\mathbf{R}}_{l0}$ is the rotation matrix for frame l. Let $\mathbf{q}_{lk} = \tilde{\mathbf{R}}_{l0}\mathbf{g}_{lk}$; $\mathbf{H}_{lk} = [\mathbf{B}_k, \mathbf{0}, \mathbf{0}, \cdots, \mathbf{I}_3, [\mathbf{q}_{lk}]_\times, \cdots, \mathbf{0}, \mathbf{0}]$, where $\mathbf{0}$ represents a 3×3 zero matrix. Let $\mathbf{u}_{lk} = \mathbf{p}_{lk} - \mathbf{q}_{lk}$, and the unknown vector $\mathbf{z} = [\mathbf{s}^T, \tilde{\mathbf{t}}_1^T, \boldsymbol{\omega}_1^T, \cdots, \tilde{\mathbf{t}}_L^T, \boldsymbol{\omega}_L^T]^T$. Following Eq. (16) and (17), we may rewrite the overall likelihood function as:

$$J_{\text{init1}} = \frac{1}{KL}\sum_{l=1}^{L}\sum_{k=1}^{K}(\mathbf{u}_{lk} + \mathbf{H}_{lk}\mathbf{z})^T\boldsymbol{\Sigma}_{\mathbf{y}_{lk}}^{-1}(\mathbf{u}_{lk} + \mathbf{H}_{lk}\mathbf{z}) \tag{18}$$

$$J_{\text{init2}} = \frac{1}{KL}\sum_{l=1}^{L}\sum_{k=1}^{K}\frac{(\mathbf{u}_{lk} + \mathbf{H}_{lk}\mathbf{z})^T\mathbf{N}_{lk}(\mathbf{u}_{lk} + \mathbf{H}_{lk}\mathbf{z})}{\mathbf{n}_{lk}^T\boldsymbol{\Sigma}_{\mathbf{y}_{lk}}\mathbf{n}_{lk}}, \tag{19}$$

where $\mathbf{n}_{lk}$ is the surface normal vector for point $\mathbf{p}_{lk}$, $\mathbf{N}_{lk} = \mathbf{n}_{lk}\mathbf{n}_{lk}^T$, and $\boldsymbol{\Sigma}_{\mathbf{y}_{lk}} \approx \tilde{\mathbf{R}}_{l0}\boldsymbol{\Sigma}_{\mathbf{x}_{lk}}\tilde{\mathbf{R}}_{l0}^T$. $\mathbf{x}_{lk}$ is the sensor noise for depth input $\mathbf{g}_{lk}$.

The point-to-point and point-to-plane likelihood functions are used jointly in our current implementation. A selected set of point correspondences is used for $J_{\text{init}1}$ and another selected set is used for $J_{\text{init}2}$ (see Section 5.1 for more details). The overall target function is a linear combination:

$$J_{\text{init}} = \lambda_1 J_{\text{init}1} + \lambda_2 J_{\text{init}2}, \qquad (20)$$

where λ_1 and λ_2 are the weights between the two functions. The optimization is conducted through quadratic programming.

4.5   Regularization for Tracking

After the static deformation vector s has been initialized, we track the face frame by frame, estimating the action deformation vector r and face rotation and translation R and t, while keeping s fixed. Although our maximum likelihood solution above can incorporate arbitrary sensor noise covariance matrices, we found the expression tracking results are still very unstable. Therefore, we propose to add additional regularization terms in the target function to further improve the results.

A natural assumption is that the expression change between the current frame and the previous frame is small. In our case, let the previous frame's face action vector be r^{t-1}, we can add an ℓ_2 regularization term as:

$$J_{\text{track}} = \lambda_1 J_1 + \lambda_2 J_2 + \lambda_3 ||r - r^{t-1}||_2^2, \qquad (21)$$

where J_1 and J_2 follow Eq. (16) and (17). Similar to the initialization process, J_1 and J_2 use different sets of feature points (see Section 5.2 for more details); $||r - r^{t-1}||_2^2 = (r - r^{t-1})^T (r - r^{t-1})$ is the squared ℓ_2 norm of the difference between the two vectors.

The ℓ_2 regularization term works to some extent, though the effect is insignificant. Note as shown in Fig. 2, each dimension of the r vector represents a particular action a face can perform. Since it is hard for a face to perform all actions simultaneously, we believe in general that the r vector shall be sparse. This inspires us to impose an additional ℓ_1 regularization term as:

$$J_{\text{track}} = \lambda_1 J_1 + \lambda_2 J_2 + \lambda_3 ||r - r^{t-1}||_2^2 + \lambda_4 ||r||_1, \qquad (22)$$

where $||r||_1 = \sum_{n=1}^{N} |r_n|$ is the ℓ_1 norm. This regularized target function is now in the form of an ℓ_1-regularized least squares problem, which can be reformulated as a convex quadratic program with linear inequality constraints [21], which can again be solved with quadratic programming methods.

Note for PCA-based deformable face models, the ℓ_1 regularization term may not be applied directly. One can identify a few dominant facial expression modes, and still assume sparsity when projecting the PCA coefficients to these modes.

5   Implementation Details

5.1   Deformable Model Initialization

As described in Section 4.4, we use multiple neutral face frames for model initialization, as shown in Fig. 3. Note the likelihood function J_{init} contains both

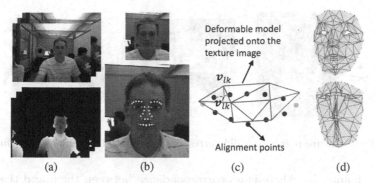

Fig. 3. The process of multi-frame deformable model initialization. (a) Multiple slightly rotated frames with neutral faces as input; (b) face detection (top) and alignment (bottom); (c) define correspondences for edge points around eyebrows, lips etc; (d) DMF with both point-to-point and point-to-plane terms (top) and DMF with point-to-plane term only (bottom).

point-to-point and point-to-plane terms (Eq. (20)). For the point-to-plane term J_{init2}, the corresponding point pairs are derived by the standard procedure of finding the closest point on the depth map from the vertices on the deformable model [20]. However, the point-to-plane term alone is not sufficient, because our depth images are very noisy and the vertices of the deformable model can drift tangentially, leading to unnatural faces (Fig. 3(d)). In the following we discuss how to define the point-to-point term J_{init1}.

For each initialization frame, we first perform face detection and alignment on the texture image. The results are shown in Fig. 3(b). The alignment algorithm provides 83 landmark points of the face, which are assumed to be consistent across all the frames. These landmark points are separated into four categories. The first category contains the green points in Fig. 3(b), such as eye corners, mouth corners, etc. These points have clear correspondences $\mathbf{p}_{lk}$ in the linear deformable face model. Given the calibration information between the depth camera and the texture camera, we simply project these landmark points to the depth image to find the corresponding 3D world coordinate $\mathbf{g}_{lk}$.

The second category contains the blue points on eyebrows and upper/lower lips. The deformable face model has a few vertices that define eyebrows and lips, but they do not all correspond to the 2D feature points provided by the alignment algorithm. In order to define correspondences, we use the following steps illustrated in Fig. 3(c):

1. Use the previous iteration's head rotation $\mathbf{R}_0$ and translation $\mathbf{t}_0$ to project the face model vertices $\mathbf{p}_{lk}$ of eyebrows/lips to the texture image, $\mathbf{v}_{lk}$;
2. Find the closest point on the curve defined by the alignment results to $\mathbf{v}_{lk}$, let it be $\mathbf{v}'_{lk}$;
3. Back project $\mathbf{v}'_{lk}$ to the depth image to find its 3D world coordinate $\mathbf{g}_{lk}$.

The third category contains the red points surrounding the face, which we refer as silhouette points. The deformable model also has vertices that define these

$\hat{p}_{k_1}^{t-1}$
v_k^{t-1}
$\hat{p}_{k_2}^{t-1}$
$\hat{p}_{k_3}^{t-1}$

Texture image at time t-1   Texture image at time t

Fig. 4. Track feature points to build correspondences for the point-to-point function

boundary points, but there is no correspondence between them and the alignment results. Moreover, when back projecting the silhouette points to the 3D world coordinate, they may easily hit a background pixel in the depth image. For these points, we follow a similar procedure as the second category points, but ignore the depth axis when computing the distance between $\mathbf{p}_{lk}$ and $\mathbf{g}_{lk}$.

The fourth category includes all the white points in Fig. 3(b), which are not used in the current implementation.

5.2   Tracking

During tracking, we again use both point-to-point and point-to-plane likelihood terms, with additional regularization as in Eq. (22). The point-to-plane term is computed similarly as during model initialization. To reliably track face expressions, the point-to-point term is still crucial. We rely on feature points detected and tracked from the texture images to define these point correspondences, as shown in Fig. 4. Similar schemes have been adopted in deformable surface tracking applications such as [22].

The feature points are detected in the texture image of the previous frame using the Harris corner detector. These points are then tracked to the current frame by matching patches surrounding the points using cross correlation. One issue with such detected and tracked feature pairs is that they may not correspond to any vertices in the deformable face model. Given the previous frame's tracking result, we first represent the feature points with their barycentric coordinates. Namely, as shown in Fig. 4, for 2D feature point pair v_k^{t-1} and v_k^t, we obtain parameter η_1, η_2 and η_3, such that:

$$v_k^{t-1} = \eta_1 \hat{\mathbf{p}}_{k_1}^{t-1} + \eta_2 \hat{\mathbf{p}}_{k_2}^{t-1} + \eta_3 \hat{\mathbf{p}}_{k_3}^{t-1}, \tag{23}$$

where $\eta_1 + \eta_2 + \eta_3 = 1$, and $\hat{\mathbf{p}}_{k_1}^{t-1}$, $\hat{\mathbf{p}}_{k_2}^{t-1}$ and $\hat{\mathbf{p}}_{k_3}^{t-1}$ are the 2D projections of the deformable model vertices $\mathbf{p}_{k_1}$, $\mathbf{p}_{k_2}$ and $\mathbf{p}_{k_3}$ onto the previous frame. Similar to Eq. (2), we can have the following equation:

$$\mathbf{R} \sum_{i=1}^{3} \eta_i \left(\mathbf{p}_{k_i} + \mathbf{A}_{k_i} \mathbf{r} + \mathbf{B}_{k_i} \mathbf{s} \right) + \mathbf{t} = \mathbf{g}_k + \mathbf{x}_k, \tag{24}$$

where $\mathbf{g}_k$ is the back projected 3D word coordinate of 2D feature point v_k^t. Let $\bar{\mathbf{p}}_k = \sum_{i=1}^{3} \eta_i \mathbf{p}_{k_i}$, $\bar{\mathbf{A}}_k = \sum_{i=1}^{3} \eta_i \mathbf{A}_{k_i}$, and $\bar{\mathbf{B}}_k = \sum_{i=1}^{3} \eta_i \mathbf{B}_{k_i}$. Eq. (24) will be in identical form as Eq. (2), thus tracking is still solved with Eq. (22). Results on the tracking algorithm will be reported in Section 6.

5.3   Noise Modeling

Due to the strong noise in the depth sensor, we find it is generally beneficial to model the actual sensor noise with the correct $\Sigma_{\mathbf{x}_k}$ instead of using an identity matrix for approximation. The uncertainty of 3D point $\mathbf{g}_k$ has two major sources: the uncertainty in the depth image intensity, which translates to uncertainty along the depth axis, and the uncertainty in feature point detection/matching in the texture image, which translates to uncertainty along the imaging plane.

Assuming a pinhole, no-skew projection model for the depth camera, we have:

$$z_k \begin{bmatrix} u_k \\ v_k \\ 1 \end{bmatrix} = \mathbf{K}\mathbf{g}_k = \begin{bmatrix} f_x & 0 & u_0 \\ 0 & f_y & v_0 \\ 0 & 0 & 1 \end{bmatrix} \begin{bmatrix} x_k \\ y_k \\ z_k \end{bmatrix} \tag{25}$$

where $\mathbf{v}_k = [u_k, v_k]^T$ is the 2D image coordinate of the feature point k in the depth image, and $\mathbf{g}_k = [x_k, y_k, z_k]^T$ is the 3D world coordinate of the feature point. $\mathbf{K}$ is the intrinsic matrix, where f_x and f_y are the focal lengths, and u_0 and v_0 are the center biases.

For the depth camera, the uncertainty of u_k and v_k is generally caused by feature point uncertainties in the texture image, and the uncertainty in z_k is due to the depth derivation scheme. These two uncertainties can be considered as independent to each other. Let $\mathbf{c}_k = [u_k, v_k, z_k]^T$, we have:

$$\Sigma_{\mathbf{c}_k} = \begin{bmatrix} \Sigma_{\mathbf{v}_k} & \mathbf{0} \\ \mathbf{0}^T & \sigma_{z_k}^2 \end{bmatrix}. \tag{26}$$

It is easy to find that:

$$\mathbf{G}_k \triangleq \frac{\partial \mathbf{g}_k}{\partial \mathbf{c}_k} = \begin{bmatrix} \frac{z_k}{f_x} & 0 & \frac{u_k - u_0}{f_x} \\ 0 & \frac{z_k}{f_y} & \frac{v_k - v_0}{f_y} \\ 0 & 0 & 1 \end{bmatrix}. \tag{27}$$

Hence as an approximation, the sensor's noise covariance matrix shall be:

$$\Sigma_{\mathbf{x}_k} \approx \mathbf{G}_k \Sigma_{\mathbf{c}_k} \mathbf{G}_k^T. \tag{28}$$

In our current implementation, to compute $\Sigma_{\mathbf{c}_k}$ from Eq. (26), we assume $\Sigma_{\mathbf{v}_k}$ is diagonal, i.e., $\Sigma_{\mathbf{v}_k} = \sigma^2 \mathbf{I}_2$, where $\mathbf{I}_2$ is a 2×2 identity matrix, and $\sigma = 1.0$ pixels in the current implementation. Knowing that our depth sensor derives depth based on triangulation, following [23], the depth image noise covariance $\sigma_{z_k}^2$ is modeled as:

$$\sigma_{z_k}^2 = \frac{\sigma_0^2 z_k^4}{f_d^2 B^2}, \tag{29}$$

where $f_d = \frac{f_x + f_y}{2}$ is the depth camera's average focal length, $\sigma_0 = 0.059$ pixels and $B = 52.3875$ millimeters based on calibration. Note since σ_{z_k} depends on z_k, its value depends on each pixel's depth value and cannot be pre-determined.

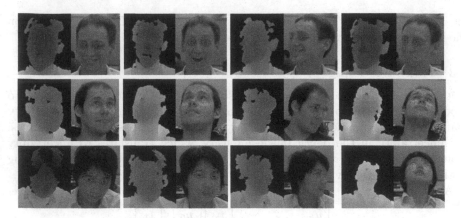

Fig. 5. Example tracking results using the proposed algorithm. From top to bottom are sequence #1 (810 total frames), #2 (681 total frames) and #3 (300 total frames), respectively.

6   Experimental Results

We tested the proposed algorithm with three sequences captured by our depth camera. Both the color and the depth images are at 640×480 pixels resolution and 30 fps. In each sequence the user sat about 3 ft from the depth camera, and moved around with varying expressions. The head sizes in the images are about 100×100 pixels. Throughout the experiments, we set the weights of different terms in J_{init} and J_{track} to be $\lambda_1 = \lambda_2 = 1$, $\lambda_3 = 10^{-6}$ and $\lambda_4 = 10$. All sequences are initialized fully automatically and accurately with the multi-frame DMF algorithm presented in Section 4.4 and 5.1. Initialization from 10 input frames takes about 20 iterations and 6.7 seconds on an Intel 2.66 GHz computer, while tracking usually converges in 2 iterations and can be done at about 10-12 fps without much code optimization.

We first show a few example tracking results using the proposed algorithm in Fig. 5, which demonstrate the robustness of the proposed algorithm despite large face pose and expression variations.

To provide some quantitative results, we manually labeled 12 feature points around the eye and mouth regions of each face in every 3-5 frames of the three sequences, as shown in Fig. 6(a). We then computed the average Euclidian distance from the 2D projections of their corresponding deformable model vertices to the labeled positions. We compared various combinations of algorithms with and without noise modeling, with and without the ℓ_2 regularization, and with and without the ℓ_1 regularization. The results are summarized in Table 1. Note because some combinations could not track the whole sequence successfully, we reported the *median* average error of all the labeled frames in Table 1. It can be seen that all three components improved the tracking performance. More specifically, compared with the traditional scheme that adopts an identity co-variance matrix for sensor noises and ℓ_2 regularization (ID+ℓ_2), the proposed scheme (NM+ℓ_2+ℓ_1) reduced the median average error by 25.3% for sequence

Table 1. Comparison of median tracking error (in pixels) for various algorithms. The suffix "L" indicates that the tracking algorithm lost the face and never recovered. "ID" stands for using the identity covariance matrix for sensor noises, and "NM" stands for using the proposed noise modeling scheme.

	$ID+\ell_2$	$ID+\ell_1$	$ID+\ell_2+\ell_1$	$NM+\ell_2$	$NM+\ell_1$	$NM+\ell_2+\ell_1$
Seq#1 (164 labeled frames)	3.56	2.88	2.78	2.85	2.69	2.66
Seq#2 (164 labeled frames)	4.48	3.78	3.71	4.30	3.64	3.55
Seq#3 (74 labeled frames)	3.98L	3.91	3.91	3.92L	3.91	3.50

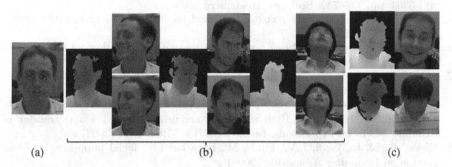

    (a)   (b)   (c)

Fig. 6. (a) Face labeled with 12 ground truth feature points; (b)a few successfully tracked frames with $NM+\ell_2+\ell_1$ (top) which were failed using the traditional approach $ID+\ell_2$ (bottom); (c) two failure examples for the proposed algorithm.

#1 and by 20.8% for sequence #2. The traditional $ID+\ell_2$ scheme lost tracking for sequence #3 after about 100 frames, while the proposed scheme successfully tracked the whole sequence.

Fig. 6(b) shows a few examples where the proposed algorithm tracked the face successfully, while the traditional scheme failed. Nonetheless, our algorithm may also fail, as shown in Fig. 6(c). In the top frame, the head moved very fast and the color image was blurry. In addition, the proposed algorithm is an iterative scheme, and fast motion can cause poor initialization of the estimated parameters. In the bottom frame, the face turned downward, which caused problems in tracking facial features in the color image. Currently we have not built any recovery mechanism in the system such as adding key frames or occasional re-initialization, which will be part of our future work.

7 Conclusions and Future Work

In this paper, we presented a regularized maximum likelihood DMF algorithm that can be used to track faces with noisy input depth data from commodity depth cameras. The algorithm modeled the depth sensor noise with an arbitrary covariance matrix, and applied a new ℓ_1 regularization term that is semantically meaningful and effective. In future work we plan to work on 3D face alignment that can re-initialize the tracking process at arbitrary face poses, thus further improving the performance of the overall system.

References

1. Xiao, J., Baker, S., Matthews, I., Kanade, T.: Real-time combined 2d+3d active appearance models. In: CVPR (2004)
2. Blanz, V., Vetter, T.: A morphable model for the synthesis of 3D faces. In: SIG-GRAPH (1999)
3. Vogler, C., Li, Z., Kanaujia, A., Goldenstein, S., Metaxas, D.: The best of both worlds: Combining 3d deformable models with active shape models. In: ICCV (2007)
4. Zhang, W., Wang, Q., Tang, X.: Real time feature based 3-D deformable face tracking. In: Forsyth, D., Torr, P., Zisserman, A. (eds.) ECCV 2008, Part II. LNCS, vol. 5303, pp. 720–732. Springer, Heidelberg (2008)
5. Blanz, V., Vetter, T.: Face recognition based on fitting a 3d morphable model. IEEE Trans. on PAMI (2003)
6. Zhu, Y., Fujimura, K.: 3d head pose estimation with optical flow and depth constraints. In: 3DIM (2003)
7. Zhang, L., Snavely, N., Curless, B., Seitz, S.M.: Spacetime faces: high-resolution capture for modeling and animation. In: SIGGRAPH 2004 (2004)
8. Wang, Y., Huang, X., Lee, C.S., Zhang, S., Li, Z., Samaras, D., Metaxas, D., Elgammal, A., Huang, P.: High resolution acquisition, learning and transfer of dynamic 3-D facial expressions. In: EUROGRAPHICS 2004 (2004)
9. Weise, T., Li, H., Gool, L.V., Pauly, M.: Face/off: Live facial puppetry. In: Symposium on Computer Animation (2009)
10. Besl, P.J., McKay, N.D.: A method for registration of 3-D shapes. IEEE Trans. on PAMI 14, 239–256 (1992)
11. Amberg, B., Romdhani, S., Vetter, T.: Optimal step nonrigid ICP algorithms for surface registration. In: CVPR (2007)
12. Murphy-Chutorian, E., Trivedi, M.M.: Head pose estimation in computer vision: A survey. IEEE Trans. on PAMI (2009)
13. Cohen, M.M., Massaro, D.W.: Modeling coarticulation in synthetic visual speech. In: Models and Techniques in Computer Animation (1993)
14. Sifakis, E., Selle, A., Robinson-Mosher, A., Fedkiw, R.: Simulating speech with a physics-based facial muscle model. In: Proc. of SCA 2006 (2006)
15. Munoz, E., Buenaposada, J.M., Baumela, L.: A direct approach for efficiently tracking with 3D morphable models. In: ICCV (2009)
16. Zhang, Z., Faugeras, O.D.: Determining motion from 3d line segment matches: a comparative study. Image and Vision Computing 9, 10–19 (1991)
17. Lu, X., Jain, A.K.: Deformation modeling for robust 3D face matching. IEEE Trans. on PAMI 30, 1346–1357 (2008)
18. Bowyer, K.W., Chang, K., Flynn, P.: A survey of approaches and challenges in 3D and multi-modal 3D+2D face recognition. CVIU (2006)
19. Zhang, Z., Liu, Z., Adler, D., Cohen, M.F., Hanson, E., Shan, Y.: Robust and rapid generation of animated faces from video images: A model-based modeling approach. IJCV 58, 93–119 (2004)
20. Chen, Y., Medioni, G.: Object modelling by registration of multiple range images. Image and Vision Computing 10, 145–155 (1992)
21. Boyd, S., Vandenberghe, L.: Convex Optimization. Cambridge Univ. Press, Cambridge (2004)
22. Salzmann, M., Pilet, J., Ilic, S., Fua, P.: Surface deformation models for nonrigid 3d shape recovery. IEEE Trans. on PAMI 29, 1481–1487 (2007)
23. Gallup, D., Frahm, J.M., Mordohai, P., Pollefeys, M.: Variable baseline/resolution stereo. In: CVPR (2008)

Human Attributes from 3D Pose Tracking

Leonid Sigal[1,3], David J. Fleet[1], Nikolaus F. Troje[2], and Micha Livne[1]

[1] Department of Computer Science, University of Toronto
[2] Department of Psychology and School of Computing, Queen's University
[3] Disney Research, Pittsburgh

Abstract. We show that, from the output of a simple 3D human pose tracker one can infer physical attributes (*e.g.*, gender and weight) and aspects of mental state (*e.g.*, happiness or sadness). This task is useful for man-machine communication, and it provides a natural benchmark for evaluating the performance of 3D pose tracking methods (*vs.* conventional Euclidean joint error metrics). Based on an extensive corpus of motion capture data, with physical and perceptual ground truth, we analyze the inference of subtle biologically-inspired attributes from cyclic gait data. It is shown that inference is also possible with partial observations of the body, and with motions as short as a single gait cycle. Learning models from small amounts of noisy video pose data is, however, prone to over-fitting. To mitigate this we formulate learning in terms of domain adaptation, for which mocap data is uses to regularize models for inference from video-based data.

1 Introduction

The fidelity with which one needs to estimate 3D human pose varies from task to task. One might be able to classify some gestures based on relatively coarse pose estimates, but the communication of many biological and socially relevant attributes, such as gender, age, mental state and personality traits, necessitates the recovery of more subtle cues. It is generally thought that current human pose tracking techniques are insufficient for this task. As a consequence, most previous work on action recognition, gesture analysis, and the extraction of biometrics, has focused on 2D image properties, or holistic spatiotemporal representations. On the contrary, we posit that it is possible to infer subtle human attributes from video-based 3D articulated pose estimates. Further, we advocate the inference of human attributes as a natural, meaningful way to assess the performance of 3D pose tracking techniques.

In this paper, we consider the inference of gender, age, weight and mood from video-based pose estimates. One key problem is the lack of suitable training data comprising labeled image sequences with 3D pose estimates. To deal with this issue, our models are bootstrapped from a substantial corpus of human motion capture data, and then adapted using a simple form of inductive transfer learning. In particular, the adaptation accounts for differences between the distributions of features derived from mocap and the video-based pose tracking data. Ground truth gender, age and weight are provided with the mocap and some video-based pose tracking data. We also consider models trained on *perceived* attributes gathered from human perception experiments over the internet. For various aspects of mental state, like mood (happiness), human perception is, at present, our principal source of (ground truth) training data.

K. Daniilidis, P. Maragos, N. Paragios (Eds.): ECCV 2010, Part III, LNCS 6313, pp. 243–257, 2010.

The inference of human attributes has myriad potential uses, ranging from human-computer interaction to surveillance to clinical diagnostics. E.g., biometrics are of interest in security, and retails stores are interested in shopper demographics. The range of potential applications increases further as one considers a wider range of attributes, including, for example, the degree of clinical depression [17], or levels of anxiety.

The goal of this paper is to demonstrate a simple proof-of-concept model for attribute inference. We restrict our attention to walking motions, a generic 3D pose tracker, the extraction of simple motion features, and a very basic set of attributes. Pose tracking from two views is accomplished with an Annealed Particle Filter [8,29], with a likelihood derived from background subtraction and 2D point tracks. We avoid the use of sophisticated activity-specific prior models (*e.g.*, [18,30]) that are prone to over-fitting, thereby biasing pose estimates and masking useful information. Following [23,28,31,33] our motion features are derived from a low-dimensional representation of joint trajectories in a body-centric coordinate frame. We then use a regularized form of logistic regression for classification. The experimental results show that one can infer attributes from video pose estimates (at 60–90% accuracy depending on the attribute). We are confident these results can be improved with advances in 3D pose tracking.

2   Background and Related Work

Perception of Biological Motion: Almost 40 years ago, Johansson [12] showed that a simple display with a small number of dots, moving as if attached to major joints of the human body, elicits a compelling percept of a human figure in motion. Not only can we detect people quickly and reliably from such displays, we can also retrieve details about their specific nature. Biological motion cues enable the recognition of familiar people [6,32], and the inference of attributes such as gender, age, mental state, actions and intentions, even for unfamiliar people [3,20,31].

Humans reliably classify gender from point-light walkers with a hit rate (correct classification rate) of 65 to 75%; frontal views are classified best [20,25,31]. Studies have focused on cues that mediate gender classification, such as the shoulder-hip ratio [7] or the lateral sway of the upper body that is more pronounced in men [20]. Interestingly, depriving observers of kinematics degrades gender classification rates. When in conflict, information conveyed by dynamic features dominates that of static anthropometrics [20,31]. Using PCA and linear discriminants Troje [31] modeled such aspects of human perception. Similar models have even been shown to convey information about weight and mood and the degree of depression in clinical populations [17].

Biometrics: Gait analysis is closely related to our task here. There is a growing literature on gait recognition, and on gender discrimination from gait (see [4] for a good overview), and a substantial benchmark datasets exist for gait recognition ([27]). However, such datasets are not well suited for 3D model-based pose tracking as they lack camera calibration and resolution is often poor. Indeed, most approaches to gait recognition rely mainly on background subtraction and properties of 2D silhouettes. Very few approaches exploit articulated models, either in 2D or 3D (although see [33,35]).

Like gait recognition, gender classification from gait is usually formulated in terms of 2D silhouettes, often from sagittal views where the shape of the upper body, rather than motion, is the primary cue (*e.g.*, [16,19]). With multiple views some form of voting is often used to merge 2D cues [10]. The use of articulated models for gender discrimination has been limited to 2D partial-body models. Yoo *et al.*, [34] used a set of 19 features, including 2D joint angles, dynamics of hip angles, the correlation between left and right leg angles, and the centre coordinates of the hip-knee cyclogram, with linear and RBF SVMs, and a 3-layer feed-forward neural net for gender classification. Samangooei and Nixon [26] consider video retrieval with physical attributes that include gender, age and weight. But they assume 2D sagittal views and a green screen to simplify the extraction of silhouette-based gait signatures.

Unlike the gait recognition problem, inferring attributes of unfamiliar people does not presuppose that test subjects exist in the training data. Further, by using 3D articulated tracking we avoid the need for view-based models and constrained domains (*cf.* [10,26,34]). The video sequences we use were collected in an indoor environment with different (calibrated) camera locations, most of which did not include a proper sagittal view. Finally, here we infer physical attributes as well as aspects of mental state, like the mood of the subject. To our knowledge this is the first paper that attempts to address recovery of such attributes collectively from video-based 3D pose estimates.

Action Recognition: Like biometrics, most work on action recognition has focused on holistic space-time features, local interest points or space-time shapes (*e.g.*, [9,14,21]), in the image domain rather than with 3D pose in a body-centric or world frame. It is widely believed that 3D pose estimation is sufficiently noisy that estimator bias and variance will outweigh the benefits of such compelling representations. Nevertheless, some recent methods have successfully demonstrated that this may not be the case (*e.g.*, [22]). Unlike such work focused on classifying very different motion patterns, we tackle the more subtle problem of inferring meaningful percepts from locomotion.

3D Pose Tracking: The primary benchmark for evaluating techniques for pose tracking, HUMANEVA [29], uses the 3D Euclidean distance between estimated and ground truth (mocap) joint positions. Errors in joint positions and joint angles are easy to measure, but it is not clear how they relate to task requirements. Will RMSE (root-mean-squared error) of 70mm be sufficient to determine gender or mood, or for gesture recognition? Some trackers with errors of 70mm might preserve the relevant information while others may not. As such, task-specific measures, like attribute inference, complement conventional RMSE measures. In particular, attribute inference is relatively complex as it depends on subtle pose and motion information. Furthermore, unlike many activity recognition tasks, which depend on motion and scene context (*e.g.*, [15]), attribute inference is mainly a function of information intrinsic to the agent or the perception of the agent's motion. Human attributes are of clear social significance, and may be directly relevant to applications. That said, an extensive comparison of different pose trackers based on attribute inference is beyond the scope of this paper.

3   Human Motion and Attribute Data

Models for different attributes are learned from a combination of partially labeled video and motion capture data. Unfortunately, since we had video data from only 20 subjects,

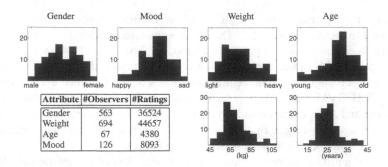

Fig. 1. Web Attribute Data: The top row shows histograms of average ratings from observers for four attributes. The bottom row histograms show ground truth distributions of weight (kg) and age (yrs). The numbers of observers and walkers rated for each attribute are given in the table.

models trained on video-based tracking data are prone to over-fitting. On the other hand, models learned from mocap should not be applied blindly to tracking data because many of the discriminative features in mocap data cannot be reliably estimated during pose tracking. Therefore, as discussed below (Sec. 4), we train from a combination of mocap and tracking data using a simple formulation of transfer learning.

3.1   Motion Capture Data: $\mathcal{D}_{mocap}$

Our source mocap data comprises walking motions from 115 individuals. From 41 physical markers we estimate 15 3D "virtual markers" at major joints of the body, *i.e.*, at shoulder joints, elbows, wrists, hip joints, knees, and ankles, and at the centers of the pelvis, clavicles, and head. Each participant walked for several minutes within the capture volume at their preferred speed, after which we began to record up to 4 trials of walking. The data are also labelled with gender, age and weight (see Fig. 1).

Human Subject Ratings: In addition to physical attributes we also consider perceived attributes, *i.e.*, what people perceive when viewing point-light displays of walking people. With this data one can begin to explore biological cues that convey gender, age and weight. More importantly, this provides us with labels about apparent mental state, such as mood (happiness or sadness).

In a web-based experiment observers were asked to rate walkers using attributes of their choosing. Each observer specified an attribute, and then rated up to 100 walkers (in random order) on a scale of 1 to 6. They were also asked to enter two phrases to indicate what ratings of 1 and 6 represent.[1] From ratings of over 4000 observers, each of whom rated at least 20 walkers, we selected sessions for which the named attribute was one of "gender", "age" or "weight", and the labels for ratings 1 and 6 were meaningful. For "gender" we accepted "male-female" or "masculine-feminine", for "age" they had to contain "young" and "old" (or "elderly"), and for "weight", "light" and "heavy". We accepted any of "mood", "emotion", "happy", or "happiness" for the mood attribute, and ratings 1 and 6 had to include the words "happy" and "sad". The resulting numbers

---
[1] http://www.biomotionlab.ca/Demos/BMLrating.html

Fig. 2. Video Pose Tracking: The APF tracker uses a background model and 2D tracked points from two views (top row). Tracking output for three subjects are shown in the bottom three rows, with average error in 3D joint locations of 63.7 (mm), 59.9 (mm), and 82.3 (mm) respectively. Notice the differences in camera orientations and the background.

of subjects and trials are given in Fig. 1. For each of the 100 walkers displayed, we computed the average rating, over all observers. Fig. 1 shows the distributions. Although data from experiments like this are noisier than those collected under more controlled conditions, they do reveal consistent perceptual interpretations.

3.2 Video Pose Tracking Data: $\mathcal{D}_{video}$

In addition to the mocap above, we also have synchronized binocular video (30Hz) and mocap (120hz). We captured 2-3 sequences for each of 20 subjects (10 male, 10 female) walking, with different camera configurations, but usually with views that were within $30°$ of frontal and sagittal. Each sequence was approximately two gait cycles in length.

The 3D pose tracker was a modified version of an Annealed Particle Filter (APF) [8,29]. The likelihood used a combination of a probabilistic background model with shadow suppression, and 2D point tracks [11] (see Fig. 2 (top)). Point tracks were only used for body parts that remain visible, the likelihood for which was formulated as a truncated Gaussian (for robustness). The same likelihood was used for all subjects. We used a 15-part body model comprising truncated cylinders, with 34 joint angles plus global pose [29] (40 DOFs in total). The prior motion model was a smooth first-order

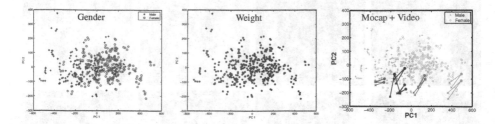

Fig. 3. Subspace Visualization: The distribution of motions in $\mathcal{D}_{mocap}$ in the first 2 principal dimensions is shown. (Left) Males (blue +) and females (red o). (Middle) Weight is depicted with blended colors: Heavy (red) and light (blue). (Right) Video pose tracks and mocap from 5 subjects in $\mathcal{D}_{video}$ are shown in 2 subspace dimensions: (color coded); circles indicate two video trials, crosses corresponding tracks; (cyan – $\mathcal{D}_{mocap}$ males, yellow – $\mathcal{D}_{mocap}$ females).

Markov model, with weak joint limits and inter-penetration constraints. The lack of an activity-specific prior motion model was motivated by the desire to avoid biasing the pose estimates towards a particular population. All experiments used the same APF setup (200 particles/layer, 5 layers), requiring roughly 2 minutes/frame (Matlab). We believe it is possible to estimate partial anthropometrics online while tracking [2], but for simplicity we assumed known anthropometrics.

The tracker performed well except when the legs were close; in rare cases the leg identities were switched. In these cases we did not filter the results in any way. In fact we report performance on all tracks obtained. We ran the tracker twice on every test sequence (yielding 80 pose trajectories). Sample tracking results for three subjects are shown in Fig. 2; in terms of the average Euclidean joint errors, the results are comparable to state-of-the-art [29]. The average Euclidean error in 3D joint locations over the 80 runs had a mean of 73mm and a standard deviation of 19mm.

Finally, note that pose data in $\mathcal{D}_{video}$ and $\mathcal{D}_{mocap}$ have structural differences. To facilitate video tracking the body model in $\mathcal{D}_{video}$ had fewer degrees of freedom. Also the mocap protocol used to estimate joint positions differed in $\mathcal{D}_{video}$ and $\mathcal{D}_{mocap}$.

3.3 Motion Representation

Following [28,31] we represent each motion as a pose trajectory, *i.e.*, a vector comprising the 15 3D joint positions at each time step.[2] We exploit the periodic nature of locomotion, expressing each motion as a Fourier series [23,31]; two harmonics are sufficient for walking [31]. To represent each pose trajectory, we encode the mean (DC) pose, along with the Fourier coefficients at the fundamental frequency and its second harmonic. This yields a 225-D vector for each motion (*i.e.*, 5 real-valued Fourier coefficients for each of 15, 3D markers). This encoding is somewhat robust to the noise in

---

[2] Initially all the walkers are aligned. The world frame is oriented so subjects are walking along the X-axis. We remove slow trends in the forward and lateral directions, based on the motion of the COM (*i.e.*, the average of all 15 joint markers) the XY plane.

the 3D poses within a trajectory, allowing us to better deal with the poor SNR of the video-based pose data.

Let the Fourier-based representation of these N motions be $\{\mathbf{m}_j\}_{j=1}^N$, where $\mathbf{m}_j \in \mathbb{R}^{225}$. Not surprisingly we find that the dimension of the representation can be reduced significantly with PCA. Since the SNR of the mocap data is much higher than the tracking data, we compute the subspace basis from the mocap data (from the 115 subjects described above in Sec. 3.1). Well more than 90% of the data variance is captured in 16 dimensions; in practice, using more than 16 dimensions does not improve the accuracy of attribute prediction appreciably.

Let $\mathbf{B} \equiv [\mathbf{b}_1, ..., \mathbf{b}_K]$ denote the subspace basis, where K is usually 16 or below. Further, let $\mathbf{c}_j$ denote the subspace coefficients for $\mathbf{m}_j$; *i.e.*, $\mathbf{c}_j = \mathbf{B}^T(\mathbf{m}_j - \bar{\mathbf{m}})$ where $\bar{\mathbf{m}}$ is sample mean of the motion data $\{\mathbf{m}_j\}$. Fig. 3 depicts the distribution of gender and weight in the first two principal directions. While not linearly separable, the attribute structure is clearly evident.

Of course there are other possible motion features. For example, Yoo *et al.* [34] use features of an articulated model extracted from a sagittal view of walking people, from which they acheive good gender classification with SVMs. Based on their paper, our implementation of their features with several different classifiers produces no better than 75% correct gender classification on our mocap dataset $\mathcal{D}_{mocap}$, compared to hit rates of 80%-90% obtained here (cf. Fig. 5).

4   Learning

$\mathcal{D}_{mocap}$ provides a significant corpus of labeled mocap, *but* the subspace motion features from $\mathcal{D}_{mocap}$ and $\mathcal{D}_{video}$ have different distributions. First, the pose data in $\mathcal{D}_{video}$ is based on a different joint parameterization (more suitable for video-based pose tracking). More importantly, the video tracking data has a lower SNR and is often biased because certain parts of the body (*e.g.*, the feet) are not tracked well. Indeed, some features that are highly discriminative in $\mathcal{D}_{mocap}$ will be uninformative in $\mathcal{D}_{video}$. Conversely, learning models from the small corpus of noisy video data in $\mathcal{D}_{video}$ is prone to over-fitting.

To mitigate these problems we formulate the learning problem as a form of transfer learning, called *domain adaptation*. It is applicable when the source ($\mathcal{D}_{mocap}$) and target ($\mathcal{D}_{video}$) domains share the same features, but have significantly different feature distributions (*e.g.*, see [24]). Intuitively, we learn source models from the mocap training data. The source models are then adapted to the video-feature domain through the minimization of a loss function on the target data that is biased toward the source model (*e.g.*, [1,5]). The resulting models generalize much better than those learned from the video-based pose data directly, and they produce much better results than the direct application of models learned from $\mathcal{D}_{mocap}$.

In more detail, we use logistic classifiers for the inference of binary attributes and for predicting human ratings. A logistic model expresses the posterior probability of an attribute, $g \in \{0, 1\}$, as a sigmoidal function $\sigma(\cdot)$ of distance from a planar decision boundary, defined by parameters $\theta \equiv (\mathbf{w}, b)$; *i.e.*,

$$p(g = 1 \mid \mathbf{c}, \theta) = \frac{1}{1 + \exp(-\mathbf{c}^T \mathbf{w} - b)} \equiv \sigma(\mathbf{c}^T \mathbf{w} + b) . \tag{1}$$

The weights that define the decision hyperplane are found by ML optimization. That is, given source mocap data, $\{\mathbf{c}_j^s, g_j^s\}_{j=1}^{N_s}$, the optimized parameters are found by minimizing the negative log likelihood of the data with respect to the weight vector $\mathbf{w}$ and the bias offset b, i.e., $\theta^s = (\mathbf{w}^s, b^s) = \arg\min \mathcal{L}_s$, where

$$\mathcal{L}_s(\mathbf{w}, b) = -\log \prod_{j=1}^{N_s} \sigma(\mathbf{c}_j^s; \mathbf{w}, b)^{g_j^s} (1 - \sigma(\mathbf{c}_j^s; \mathbf{w}, b))^{1 - g_j^s} . \tag{2}$$

To adapt the model learned from $\mathcal{D}_{mocap}$ to the target data $\mathcal{D}_{video}$, following [5], we learn a logistic model on the target training data with a Gaussian prior centered at the source model. That is, we minimize a loss function that is a combination of the negative log likelihood of the video training data, $\{\mathbf{c}_j^t, g_j^t\}_{j=1}^{N_t}$, $N_t \ll N_s$, and a quadratic regularizer:

$$\mathcal{L}_t(\mathbf{w}, b) = -\log \prod_{j=1}^{N_t} \sigma(\mathbf{c}_j^t; \mathbf{w}, b)^{g_j^t} (1 - \sigma(\mathbf{c}_j^t; \mathbf{w}, b))^{1 - g_j^t} + \lambda \|\mathbf{w} - \mathbf{w}^s\|^2 . \tag{3}$$

While this formulation assumes an isotropic prior, with variance $1/\lambda$, the loss function is easily generalized to an anisotropic prior that allows some weights to drift more than others. The covariance for an anisotopic prior might be set according to the ratio of variances in the subspace projections of $\mathcal{D}_{mocap}$ and $\mathcal{D}_{video}$ respectively. Nevertheless the experiments reported below are based on an isotropic prior.

Cross-validation is used to determine λ. Also, note that we do not regularize the bias offset since it is often convenient to allow b to vary freely to account for any bias in the tracking data. Minimization of $\mathcal{L}_t$ is accomplished with Newton iterations to solve for critical points, i.e.,

$$\frac{\partial \mathcal{L}_t}{\partial \mathbf{w}, b} = \sum_{j=1}^{N_t} (\sigma(\mathbf{c}_j^t; \mathbf{w}, b) - g_j^t) \begin{pmatrix} \mathbf{c}_j^t \\ 1 \end{pmatrix} + \lambda \begin{pmatrix} \mathbf{w} - \mathbf{w}^s \\ 0 \end{pmatrix} = \mathbf{0} . \tag{4}$$

One can generalize the approach to model the ratings data by replacing the ground truth g in (3) with the average rating (scaled to $(0, 1)$). Treating the average rating as the expected value of g over different observers, (3) can be interpreted as the expected likelihood. Also, while the approach formulated here presupposes labelled target data, it is also possible to extend the technique to the semi-supervised case where the target video data is not labeled (e.g., [1]).

In addition to simple classifiers for binary attributes, we also consider domain-adapted least-squares (LS) regressors for real-valued attributes, such as age and weight. For example, the adapted LS predictor for real-valued attribute a minimizes

$$\mathcal{L}_c(\mathbf{w}, b) = \sum_{j=1}^{N_t} [(\mathbf{w}^T \mathbf{c}_j^t + b) - a_j^t]^2 + \lambda \|\mathbf{w} - \mathbf{w}_{LS}^s\|^2 . \tag{5}$$

where $\mathbf{w}_{LS}^s$ is the LS optimal weight vector learned from the mocap data in $\mathcal{D}_{mocap}$.

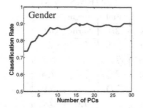 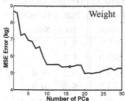 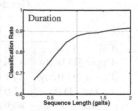

Fig. 4. Effect of Subspace Dimension and Sequence Length: Leave-one-out cross validation is used to asses the effect of subspace dimension on the correct-classification rate for the ground truth gender classification (left) and the RMSE of the real-valued weight regressor (middle). The right plot shows the dependence of gender classification on the duration (in gait cycles) of mocap sequences (based again on leave-one-out cross-validation).

5 Models and Analysis of Source Data: $\mathcal{D}_{mocap}$

We first learn models for the inference of different attributes using the labelled mocap corpus, $\mathcal{D}_{mocap}$. We tried learning with several different loss functions, including Gaussian class-conditional models and linear/RBF SVMs, but none generalized significantly better than logistic or linear LS regression. In all cases we characterize the expected performance of the classifier/regressor using leave-one-out cross-validation.

Figure 4 (left) shows how gender classification depends on the subspace dimension of the motion representation. With fewer than 16 dimensions important information is lost. Classification performance with more than 20 dimensions yields marginal gains; with a 16D subspace the correct classification rate for gender is 90%. Fig. 4 (middle) shows the behaviour of a LS predictor for weight. The weights of our 115 walking subjects ranged from 50 to 100 kg, while the RMSE of predictions (16D features and leave-one-out cross-validation) is 5.4 kg. Fig. 4 (right) shows that gender can be classified with as little as one gait cycle (consistent with human perception [13]).

Normalized Models: To infer attributes from video pose estimates, we may not have access to full 3D pose. For example, with monocular tracking one might be able estimate 3D pose only up to the overall scale of the subject. Many 3D pose trackers simply assume the subject is average height (*e.g.*, [2]). In extreme cases a pose tracker may have no anthropometric knowledge whatsoever. To explore these cases we computed two further subspace representations of the data in $\mathcal{D}_{mocap}$. First all walkers were normalized to be the same height, and second, all anthropometrics are removed (by computing joint angles and then using the mean anthropometrics to reconstruct the motions).

The first row of results in Fig. 5 gives the gender hit rate (*i.e.*, correct classification rate) and the RMSE of linear LS predictors for weight and age, all based on leave-one-out (LOO) testing. One can see that the two normalized models are less informative than using the full 3D data. Predictions from the height-normalized models are somewhat better than the anthropometric-normalized models as expected. Also note that while predictions of gender and weight are quite good, age is poorly predicted. The walking subjects in this dataset ranged in age from roughly 18 to 35 years, while the RMSE for age prediction is 6.9 years.

	Gender (% correct)			Weight (RMSE kg)			Age (RMSE yrs)		
	Full 3D	Height Norm.	Motion Only	Full 3D	Height Norm.	Motion Only	Full 3D	Height Norm.	Motion Only
Full 3D Pose	89.6	86.1	81.7	5.4	9.7	10.9	6.9	6.9	6.4
Upper 3D Body	87.8	86.1	80.9	5.9	9.9	11.0	7.0	7.1	6.3
Lower 3D Body	84.4	80.0	73.9	6.2	9.4	12.2	7.2	7.2	7.3
Frontal 2D Pose	87.0	80.0	76.5	5.5	9.6	10.8	7.0	7.1	6.9
Sagittal 2D Pose	80.9	83.5	79.1	9.9	11.5	12.2	7.1	7.0	6.7

Fig. 5. Inference with $\mathcal{D}_{mocap}$ Models: To assess performance, with and without missing data, we build 3 models: **Full 3D** uses known anthropometrics and kinematics; **Height Normalized** is learned from mocap that is height normalized; and **Motion Only** uses only kinematic information (all walkers have the same limb lengths). The lack of anthropometrics degrades performance, but the inference of gender and weight are above chance in all models. We also report how performance varies with different subsets of markers (*e.g.*, upper/lower body) or 2D projections. Again, despite degradation in performance, the models continue to predict attributes well.

	Gender	Weight	Age	Mood
Full 3D	94	93	88	94
Height Normalized	93	93	86	93
Motion Only	93	94	86	93

Fig. 6. Inference of Perceived Attributes: We report the accuracy of predictions of human ratings for gender, weight, age and mood, all from the source mocap dataset $\mathcal{D}_{mocap}$. Perceived attributes are quantized to one bit based on the average rating for each subject, and the output of the logistic regressor is thresholded at 0.5. The table shows the fraction of subjects for which the classifier matches the quantized rating. Notice that perceived attributes are generally better predicted by the learned models than are ground truth attributes (*cf.* age in Fig. 5).

Incomplete Data: To infer attributes from video-based pose estimates, we must be able to cope with missing data, since parts of the body may be partially or entirely occluded. Let $\mathbf{m} \in \mathbb{R}^{225}$ be a *complete* measurement vector (*i.e.*, the Fourier coefficients for each joint). Let the observed measurements be $\mathbf{m}_0 = P\mathbf{m}$, where the matrix P comprises only those rows of the identity matrix that correspond to the observed joints. It then follows from the generative subspace model, *i.e.*, $\mathbf{m} = \mathbf{Bc} + \bar{\mathbf{m}}$, that a LS pseudo-inverse can be used to estimate the subspace coefficients $\mathbf{c}_0$ from $\mathbf{m}_0$, *i.e.*,

$$\mathbf{c}_0 = (\mathbf{B}^T P^T P\mathbf{B})^{-1}\mathbf{B}^T P^T (\mathbf{m}_0 - P\bar{\mathbf{m}}) . \qquad (6)$$

The columns in Fig. 5 report model performance when data from model joints of the upper body, or from the lower body, are used. Also reported are results when one uses 2D data under orthographic projection from frontal or sagittal views. Interestingly, the observation that frontal views are more informative than sagittal views is consistent with studies of human perception [31].

Predicting Human Ratings: It is also interesting to consider how well one can predict *perceived attributes*. This is a scientific curiosity for physical attributes like gender, age and weight. For mood, however, we have no physical ground truth. Rather, the perceived mood is our only labelled data source. For all attributes, because our perceptual rating data are noisy, we quantize ratings of each attribute to one bit; *i.e.*, each walker is (perceived to be) (1) male or female, (2) heavy or light, (3) young or old, and (4) happy or sad. Then, the average attribute rating for a given training subject (scaled to $(0, 1)$) is taken to be the corresponding probability of being male, heavy, old, and happy, respectively. We use logistic regression to predict these probabilities, with leave-one-out measures of performance given in Fig. 6.

It is striking that, in all cases, we can do a better job predicting human ratings than ground truth. Human observers are, purportly using the available visual cues in a consistent manner, even if it is inconsistent with the ground truth. In particular, while true age is very hard to predict, perceived age is predicted well; *it's not how old you are, it's how old you look*. While interesting, this also shows clearly that perceived attributes may be biased, and therefore require qualification.

6   Attribute Inference from $\mathcal{D}_{video}$

Given the source models learned from $\mathcal{D}_{mocap}$, we use domain adaptation to learn models for the test pose data in $\mathcal{D}_{video}$. Not only is this useful in generating models for the video pose tracking data, it is also useful in building a classifier from the test mocap in $\mathcal{D}_{video}$. The reason is that the pose data in $\mathcal{D}_{video}$ is noisier and is parameterized differently from that in $\mathcal{D}_{mocap}$. The mocap in $\mathcal{D}_{mocap}$ allows for variable joint locations, while the parameterization of the tracker used in $\mathcal{D}_{video}$ has fixed joints. The tracker also has a fewer DOFs. Hence there are structural differences even between the mocap in $\mathcal{D}_{mocap}$ and that in $\mathcal{D}_{video}$.

Domain Adaptation: Figure 7 (left) show the leave-one-out hit rates for gender classifiers learned from $\mathcal{D}_{video}$ with domain adaptation from $\mathcal{D}_{mocap}$. The curves show how performance depends on adaptation from the source model, as a function of λ (see (3) in Sec. 4). The highest hit rates occur with λ between 10^3 and 10^4. For comparison, the crosses (x) depict the hit rate when there is no domain adaptation (i.e., with $\mathbf{w}^s = \mathbf{0}$ in (3)). The circles (o) depict the hit rate when the classifiers are trained solely on the source data $\mathcal{D}_{mocap}$ (with no domain adaptation) and then tested on the mocap in $\mathcal{D}_{video}$. Remember that the body model in $\mathcal{D}_{video}$ has fewer degrees of freedom and was estimated using a different mocap protocol from that in the original mocap in $\mathcal{D}_{mocap}$. Hence even the mocap motion features in $\mathcal{D}_{mocap}$ and $\mathcal{D}_{video}$ are distributed differently, and hence the value of domain adaptation.

Pose Tracking Data: Figure 7 (middle) shows leave-one-out hit rates for gender from video-based 3D pose tracking data (two trials of the APF, for each of 2 walking sequences for each of 20 subjects). As above, the curves show the dependence on the strength of the prior from the source model. The crosses (x) depict hit rates with no domain adaptation (from pose tracking data alone), and the circles (o) depict the hit rates from classifiers trained solely on the source mocap data $\mathcal{D}_{mocap}$. It is not clear why the full 3D model with pose tracking data is much worse than that with mocap input.

Figure 7 (right) shows how predictions of weight from video-based 3D pose data depends on domain adaptation. As above, the crosses (x) and the circles (o) show that predictions are poor when based solely on the data in $\mathcal{D}_{mocap}$ or in $\mathcal{D}_{video}$. With domain adaptation the results improve significantly. The standard deviation of the weight among

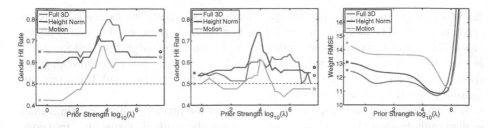

Fig. 7. Domain Adaptation: (a) Gender classification from the *mocap* in $\mathcal{D}_{video}$ for 20 test subjects (from leave-one-out performance), as a function of the strength of the prior λ, for each of 3 models (full 3D, height normalized, motion only). (b) Gender classification from the video-based *pose tracking data* for 20 test subjects (leave-one-out performance). (c) RMSE of weight estimates from *pose tracking data*, for 20 test subjects, as a function of the strength of the prior.

	Gender - mocap			Gender - tracking			Weight - mocap			Weight - tracking		
	(% correct, $\lambda = 10^4$)			(% correct, $\lambda = 10^4$)			(RMSE kg, $\lambda = 10^{1.5}$)			(RMSE kg, $\lambda = 10^5$)		
	Full 3D	Height Norm.	Motion Only	Full 3D	Height Norm.	Motion Only	Full 3D	Height Norm.	Motion Only	Full 3D	Height Norm.	Motion Only
C_{mocap}	75.0	65.0	62.5	53.8	57.5	47.5	5.7	10.9	6.6	51.4	42.1	42.7
C_{track}	65.0	57.5	42.5	55.0	55.0	50.0	4.0	7.3	6.9	12.5	13.1	14.5
$C_{trackTL}$	**77.5**	**70.0**	**67.5**	**61.3**	**73.8**	**61.3**	**3.6**	**7.6**	**6.0**	**10.6**	**10.9**	**12.4**

Fig. 8. Attributes from Mocap and Pose Tracking Data: The tables reports leave-one-out performance on gender classification and weight prediction from test mocap and pose tracking data in the target dataset $\mathcal{D}_{video}$ of 20 subjects. There are 40 mocap sequences (2 walks/subject), and 80 pose trajectories from video tracking (2 tracking trials per sequence). Results from 3 models are reported: C_{mocap} is learned from the source mocap $\mathcal{D}_{mocap}$; C_{track} is learned solely from test data $\mathcal{D}_{video}$; $C_{trackTL}$ is learned with $\mathcal{D}_{video}$ and domain adaptation from $\mathcal{D}_{mocap}$.

the test subjects is approximately 12kg. With domain adaptation, with $\lambda = 10^5$, the RMSE decreases to approximately 10.6. These results with tracking data are worse than those based on training mocap data in Fig. 5, but we find them encouraging nonetheless.

Figure 8 gives numerical results for gender classification and weight prediction, from both test mocap and test pose tracking data (like the plots in Fig. 7). As above, we show results from three models: C_{mocap} is learned solely from the source mocap $\mathcal{D}_{mocap}$; C_{track} is learned solely from test data $\mathcal{D}_{video}$; $C_{trackTL}$ is learned with $\mathcal{D}_{video}$ and domain adaptation from $\mathcal{D}_{mocap}$. Not surprisingly, the predictions of gender and weight from on video tracking data are not as reliable as those from the mocap. They are, however, encouraging. While not shown in the figure, we also note that errors in gender classification are reasonably consistent between the test mocap and the test tracking data. Approximately 85% of the motions classified from the pose tracking data are concistent with classification from the corresponding mocap. Thus, while some of the errors in Fig. 8 are due to noise in the pose tracking data, some are due to the fact that indeed some females consistently walk like males and vice versa.

	Gender	Weight	Age	Mood
$C_{trackTL}$ (Full 3D)	83	79	93	86
$C_{trackTL}$ (Height Normalized)	74	79	90	85

Fig. 9. Classification of Perceived Attributes with Respect to MoCap: The table reports consistency of leave-one-out performance on *perceived* gender, weight, age and mood (happiness) between test mocap and pose tracking data in the target dataset $\mathcal{D}_{video}$ of 20 test subjects. We use predicted attribute values for test mocap as targets to train $C_{trackTL}$ binary classifiers (learned with $\mathcal{D}_{video}$ and domain adaptation from $\mathcal{D}_{mocap}$, all with $\lambda = 10^4$).

Inference of Perceived Attributes: Figure 9 reports leave-one-out hit rates in the prediction of the *perceived* attributes. Like the above experiment in Fig. 6 we quantize perceptual ratings to one bit and use logistic regression for classification (*e.g.*, happy vs. sad). For the purposes of this experiment we also consider the perceptual data as the *ground truth* (indeed for perceived mental state, *e.g.*, mood, that is our only source of data label) and look at the consistency of predictions between the leave-one-out model trained with mocap and with video tracking results from $\mathcal{D}_{video}$.

The consistency between the mocap and pose tracking is very good, with consistent classification rates between 74% to 93%. It is interesting to note that we can recover the mental state – mood (happiness), with 85% to 86% accuracy. Like the results reported in Fig. 6 the perceived age is predicted well when compared to our models for predicting true age.

7 Discussion

This paper demonstrates that one can, from the output of a video-based, 3D human pose tracker, infer physical attributes (*e.g.*, gender and weight) and aspects of mental state (*e.g.*. happiness). The models are used to infer binary attributes (gender) and real-valued attributes (weight). We also consider the prediction of perceived attributes based on human perceptual experiments. This is useful for infering attributes such as mood where human judgements are our source of ground truth. Learning is accomplished using datasets comprising labelled mocap and video-based 3D pose estimates. These sources of training data are combined with a simple for of domain adaptation.

To our knowledge, this is the first paper in the literature that attempted to infer such perceptually and biologically meaningful attributes from 3D video-based pose estimates. In the future we hope to collect large datasets and explore stronger tracking prior models trained from large collections of mocap data. We also hope to be able to test the inference of attributes with monocular pose tracking methods. While the results reported here are interesting in their own right, we also suggest that tasks like this provide a natural way to assess the fidelity with which people trackers estimate 3D pose.

Acknowledgements. This work was financially supported in part by NSERC Canada and the Canadian Institute for Advanced Research.

References

1. Arnold, A., Nallapati, R., Cohen, W.: A comparative study of methods for transductive transfer learning. In: ICDM Workshop on Mining and Management of Biological Data (2007)
2. Balan, A., Sigal, L., Black, M., Davis, J., Haussecker, H.: Detailed human shape and pose from images. In: Proc. IEEE CVPR (2007)
3. Blakemore, S., Decety, J.: From the perception of action to the understanding of intention. Nature Reviews Neuroscience 2(8), 561–567 (2001)
4. Boyd, J., Little, J.: Biometric gait recognition. Advanced Studies in Biometrics: Summer School on Biometrics (2003)
5. Chelba, C., Acero, A.: Adaptation of maximum entropy capitalizer: Little data can help a lot. In: Conf. on Empirical Methods in Natural Language Processing (2004)
6. Cutting, J.E., Kozlowski, L.T.: Recognizing friends by their walk: Gait perception without familiarity cues. Bulletin of the Psychonomic Society 9(5), 353–356 (1977)
7. Cutting, J.E., Proffitt, D.R., Kozlowski, L.T.: A biomechanical invariant of gait perception. J. Exp. Psych.: Human Perception and Performance 4, 357–372 (1978)
8. Deutscher, J., Reid, I.: Articulated body motion capture by stochastic search. IJCV 61(2), 185–205 (2005)
9. Gorelick, L., Blank, M., Shechtman, E., Irani, M., Basri, R.: Actions as space-time shapes. IEEE Trans. PAMI 29(12), 2247–2253 (2007)
10. Huang, G., Wang, Y.: Gender classification based on fusion of multi-view gait sequences. In: Yagi, Y., Kang, S.B., Kweon, I.S., Zha, H. (eds.) ACCV 2007, Part I. LNCS, vol. 4843, pp. 462–471. Springer, Heidelberg (2007)
11. Jepson, A., Fleet, D., El-MAraghi, T.: Robust online appearance models for vision tracking. IEEE Trans. PAMI 25(10), 1296–1311 (2003)
12. Johansson, G.: Visual perception of biological motion and a model for its analysis. Perception & Psychophysics 14(2), 201–211 (1973)
13. Johansson, G.: Spatio-temporal differentiation and integration in visual motion perception. Psychological Research 38, 379–393 (1976)
14. Ke, Y., Sukthankar, R., Hebert, M.: Event detection in crowded videos. In: ICCV (2007)
15. Laptev, I., Marszalek, M., Schmid, C., Rozenfeld, B.: Learning realistic human actions from movies. In: IEEE Conf. CVPR (2008)
16. Lee, L., Grimson, E.: Gait analysis for recognition and classification. In: Proc. IEEE Int. Conf. Auto. Face and Gesture Recog. (2002)
17. Lemke, M., Wendorff, T., Mieth, B., Buhl, K., Linnemann, M.: Spatiotemporal gait patterns during over ground locomotion in major depression compared with never depressed controls. J. Psychiatr. Res. 34, 277–283 (2000)
18. Li, R., Tian, T.P., Sclaroff, S.: Simultaneous learning of non-linear manifold and dynamical models for high-dimensional time series. In: IEEE ICCV (2007)
19. Li, X., Maybank, S., Yan, S., Tao, D., Xu, S.: Gait components and their applications to gender recognition. IEEE Trans. SMC, Part C 38(2) (2008)
20. Mather, G., Murdoch, L.: Gender discrimination in biological motion displays based on dynamic cues. Proceedings of the Royal Society of London Series B 258, 273–279 (1994)
21. Niebles, J., Wang, H., Fei-Fei, L.: Unsupervised learning of human action categories using spatial-temporal words. IJCV 79(3), 299–318 (2008)
22. Ning, H., Xu, W., Gong, Y., Huang, T.: Latent pose estimator for continuous action recognition. In: Forsyth, D., Torr, P., Zisserman, A. (eds.) ECCV 2008, Part II. LNCS, vol. 5303, pp. 419–433. Springer, Heidelberg (2008)
23. Ormoneit, D., Sidenbladh, H., Black, M., Hastie, T., Fleet, D.: Learning and tracking human motion using functional analysis. In: Work. Human Modeling, Anal. & Syn. (2000)

24. Pan, S., Yang, Q.: A survey on transfer learning. IEEE Trans. KDE 12 (2009)
25. Pollick, F., Kay, J., Heim, K., Stringer, R.: Gender recognition from point-light walkers. J. Exp. Psych.: Human Perception and Performance 31(6), 1247–1265 (2005)
26. Samangooei, S., Nixon, M.: Performing content-based retrieval of humans using gait biometrics. Multimedia Tools and Applications (October 2009)
27. Sarkar, S., Phillips, J., Liu, Z., Robledo, I., Grother, P., Bowyer, K.: The human id gait challenge problem: Data sets, performance, and analysis. IEEE TPAMI 27, 162–177 (2005)
28. Sidenbladh, H., Black, M., Fleet, D.: Stochastic tracking of 3d human figures using 2d image motion. In: Vernon, D. (ed.) ECCV 2000. LNCS, vol. 1843, pp. 702–718. Springer, Heidelberg (2000)
29. Sigal, L., Balan, A., Black, M.: Humaneva: Synchronized video and motion capture dataset and baseline algorithm for evaluation of articulated human motion. IJCV (2010)
30. Sminchisescu, C., Jepson, A.: Generative modeling for continuous non-linearly embedded visual inference. In: Int. Conf. Machine Learning, pp. 759–766 (2004)
31. Troje, N.: Decomposing biological motion: A framework for analysis and synthesis of human gait patterns. J. Vision 2(5), 371–387 (2002)
32. Troje, N., Westhoff, C., Lavrov, M.: Person identification from biological motion: effects of structural and kinematic cues. Percept Psychophys 67(4), 667–675 (2005)
33. Urtasun, R., Fleet, D., Fua, P.: Motion models for 3D people tracking. CVIU 104(2-3), 157–177 (2006)
34. Yoo, J.H., Hwang, D., Nixon, M.: Gender classification in human gait using support vector machine. Advances Concepts for Intelligent Vision Systems (2006)
35. Zhang, R., Vogler, C., Metaxas, D.: Human gait recognition. In: IEEE Workshop on Articulated and Nonrigid Motion (2004)

Discriminative Nonorthogonal Binary Subspace Tracking

Ang Li[1], Feng Tang[2], Yanwen Guo[1,3], and Hai Tao[4]

[1] National Key Lab for Novel Software Technology, Nanjing University, China
[2] Multimedia Interaction and Understanding Lab, HP Labs Palo Alto, USA
[3] Jiangyin Institute of Information Technology of Nanjing University, China
[4] University of California, Santa Cruz, USA

Abstract. Visual tracking is one of the central problems in computer vision. A crucial problem of tracking is how to represent the object. Traditional appearance-based trackers are using increasingly more complex features in order to be robust. However, complex representations typically will not only require more computation for feature extraction, but also make the state inference complicated. In this paper, we show that with a careful feature selection scheme, extremely simple yet discriminative features can be used for robust object tracking. The central component of the proposed method is a succinct and discriminative representation of image template using discriminative non-orthogonal binary subspace spanned by Haar-like features. These Haar-like bases are selected from the over-complete dictionary using a variation of the OOMP (optimized orthogonal matching pursuit). Such a representation inherits the merits of original NBS in that it can be used to efficiently describe the object. It also incorporates the discriminative information to distinguish the foreground and background. We apply the discriminative NBS to object tracking through SSD-based template matching. An update scheme of the discriminative NBS is devised in order to accommodate object appearance changes. We validate the effectiveness of our method through extensive experiments on challenging videos and demonstrate its capability to track objects in clutter and moving background.

1   Introduction

Visual object tracking in video sequences is an active research topic in computer vision, due to its wide applications in video surveillance, intelligent user interface, content-based video retrieval and object-based video compression. Over the past two decades, a great variety of tracking methods have been brought forward. Some of them include template/appearance based methods [1,2,3,4,5], layer based methods [6,7], image statistics based methods [8,9,10], feature based methods [11,12], contour based methods [13], and discriminative feature based methods [14,15]. One of the most popular category of method is appearance based approaches, these trackers represent the object to be tracked using an appearance model and it is matched to each new frame to determine the object state. In order to handle appearance variations, an appearance update scheme

K. Daniilidis, P. Maragos, N. Paragios (Eds.): ECCV 2010, Part III, LNCS 6313, pp. 258–271, 2010.
© Springer-Verlag Berlin Heidelberg 2010

is usually employed to adapt the object representation over time. Appearance based trackers have shown to be very successful in many scenarios. However they may not be robust to background clutter where the object is very similar to the background. In order to handle this problem, more and more complicated object representations that take into account color, gradients, texture are used. However, extraction of the complicated features usually incurs more computation which slows down the tracker. Moreover, complex representation will make the inference much more complicated. One natural question to ask is how complicated feature is really needed to track an object? In this paper, we show that with a careful feature selection scheme, extremely simple object representations can be used to robustly track objects.

Essentially, object tracking boils down to the image representation problem - what type of feature should be used to represent the object. Effective and efficient image representation not only makes the feature extraction process fast but also reduces the computation for object state inference. Traditional object representations for example raw pixels, color histograms are generative in natural, they are usually designed to describe the appearance of the object being tracked while completely ignoring the background. Trackers using this representation may fail when the object appearance is very similar to the background. It is worth noting that some appearance based trackers model both foreground and background, for example in the layer tracker [7] the per-pixel layer ownership is inferred by competing the foreground and background likelihoods.

Recently, discriminative methods have opened a promising new direction in the tracking literature by posing tracking as a classification problem. Instead of trying to build an appearance model to describe the object, discriminative trackers seek a decision boundary that can best separate the object and background. The support vector tracker [16] (denoted as SVT afterwards) uses an offline-learned support vector machine as the classifier and embeds it into an optical flow based tracker. Collins et al. [14] were perhaps the first to treat tracking as a binary classification problem. A classifier is learnt in each frame to be used to locate object in the next frame. A feature selection scheme using variance ratio to select the most discriminative features is used to measure feature discriminability and select the best feature for tracking. Avidan's ensemble tracker [15] combines an ensemble of online learned weak classifiers using AdaBoost to label pixels in the next frame. After the data is labeled, the peak of the classification score map is detected to be the object. To handle the object appearance changes and maintain temporal coherence, in each frame some classifiers that do not perform well or have existed longer than a fixed number of frames get removed or pruned from the tracker, and new classifiers are trained to replace them. In co-tracking [17], two semi-supervised support vector machines are built for color and gradient features. A co-training framework is used to update the classifiers.

Previous discriminative trackers generally have two major problems. First, the tracker only relies on the classifier which can well separate the foreground and background and does not have any information what the object is like. This makes it hard to recover once the tracker makes a mistake. Second, discriminative trackers generally have a fixed image representation for all objects to be tracked and this representation is not updated any more. However, adaptive objective representation is more desirable in most cases because it can capture the characteristics of particular object being tracked.

In this paper, we propose an extremely simple object representation using Haar-like features that combines the advantage of generative trackers and discriminative trackers. The representation is generative in nature in that it finds the features that can best reconstruct the foreground object. It is also discriminative because only those features that make the foreground representation different from background are selected. Our representation is based on the nonorthogonal binary subspace(NBS) method in [18]. The original NBS tries to select from an over-complete dictionary a set of Haar-like features that can best represent the image. We extend the NBS method to incorporate discriminative information by adding a discriminative background term. The new representation is called discriminative non-orthogonal binary subspace. The discriminative nonorthogonal binary subspace is a compact representation of an image which is spanned by Haar-like rectangle base vectors. By approximating image patches with discriminative NBS, the inner product between templates could be obtained very fast using integral image trick. We show in this paper that such extremely simple features can be used for effective object tracking even when the object is similar to background.

The rest of this paper is organized as follows. In section 2, we briefly review Haar-like features and the non-orthogonal binary subspace approach. The discriminative nonorthogonal binary subspace is proposed in section 3. In section 4, the application of discriminative NBS to tracking is described. Afterwards, we provide both qualitative and quantitative experimental results in section 5. The paper is concluded in section 6.

2   Background: Nonorthogonal Binary Subspace

The original NBS [18] tries to find a subset of Haar-like features from an over-complete dictionary to span a subspace that can be used to reconstruct the original image.

The Haar-like box function ϕ for NBS is defined as,

$$\phi(u,v) = \begin{cases} 1, & \begin{aligned} u_0 \leq u \leq u_0 + w' - 1 \\ v_0 \leq v \leq v_0 + h' - 1 \end{aligned} \\ 0, & \text{otherwise}, \end{cases} \tag{1}$$

where w' and h' represent the width and height of the box in the template. (u_0, v_0) is its top-left pixel. The advantage of such box functions is that the inner product of the Haar-like base with any same-sized image template can be computed with only 4 additions, by pre-computing the integral image of the template.

Suppose that for a given image template $\mathbf{x} \in R^{WH}$ of size $W \times H$ and the selected binary box features are $\{c_i, \phi_i\}(1 \leq i \leq K)$. c_i is the coefficient of box function ϕ_i. The NBS approximation is expressed as $\mathbf{x} = \sum_{i=1}^{K} c_i \phi_i + \varepsilon$, where ε denotes the reconstruction error. We define $\boldsymbol{\Phi}_K = \{\phi_1, \phi_2, \ldots, \phi_K\}$ as a base matrix, each column of which is a chosen binary base vector. Note that, this base set is non-orthogonal in general, hence the reconstruction vector of template $\mathbf{x}$ is calculated as

$$R_{\boldsymbol{\Phi}_K}(\mathbf{x}) = \boldsymbol{\Phi}_K (\boldsymbol{\Phi}_K^T \boldsymbol{\Phi}_K)^{-1} \boldsymbol{\Phi}_K^T \mathbf{x} . \tag{2}$$

The number of Haar-like box functions is $W(W + 1)H(H + 1)/4$, thus the dictionary of base vectors is highly redundant. In previous work, the NBS is used to approximate the image template. Thus, a specific small number of features are chosen from the over-complete dictionary to optimize the function

$$\arg \min_{\boldsymbol{\Phi}_K} \| \mathbf{x} - R_{\boldsymbol{\Phi}_K}(\mathbf{x}) \| . \tag{3}$$

Since the dictionary is highly redundant, the optimal solution to Eq.(3) is NP-hard. It is shown in [18,19] that a sub-optimal solution can be produced by a greedy algorithm named the optimized orthogonal matching pursuit (OOMP).

3   Discriminative Nonorthogonal Binary Subspace

The NBS method has been successfully used for fast template matching and face recognition [18]. However, it only considers the information embodied in the object image itself without any information about the rest of the image. In the applications such as video object tracking, which is essentially a classification problem, the background content should be taken into account in addition to the object template. To account for this, we propose a discriminative NBS (D-NBS) image representation that considers both foreground object and background. The discriminative NBS method inherits the merits of the original NBS in that it can well describe the object appearance, and at the same time, it captures the discriminant information that can best separate the object from background.

3.1   Formulation

The objective of discriminative NBS is to construct an object representation that can separate object from background. This will facilitate vision tasks such as object tracking. In contrast to the original NBS, we formulate the discriminative NBS by finding the bases such that the foreground can be well separated with background for SSD based template matching.

The main idea behind discriminative NBS is that we want to select features so that the reconstruction error for foreground is small while it is large for background. Different from the original NBS formulation Eq.(3) in which only the foreground reconstruction is considered, in discriminative NBS formulation, the objective function has foreground and background reconstruction terms.

Let $\boldsymbol{\Phi}_K$ be the discriminative NBS based vectors with K bases and $R_{\boldsymbol{\Phi}_K}(\mathbf{X})$ be the reconstruction of $\mathbf{X}$ via $\boldsymbol{\Phi}_K$ using Eq.(2). Note that $\mathbf{F} = \begin{bmatrix} \mathbf{f}_1, \mathbf{f}_2, \ldots, \mathbf{f}_{N_f} \end{bmatrix}$

is a matrix of N_f recent foreground samples. $\mathbf{B} = [\mathbf{b}_1, \mathbf{b}_2, \ldots, \mathbf{b}_{N_b}]$ is a matrix of N_b sampled background vectors. The objective function for Φ_K is

$$\arg\min_{\Phi_K} \left\{ \frac{1}{N_f} \parallel \mathbf{F} - R_{\Phi_K}(\mathbf{F}) \parallel_F^2 - \frac{\lambda}{N_b} \parallel \mathbf{B} - R_{\Phi_K}(\mathbf{B}) \parallel_F^2 \right\}, \tag{4}$$

where $\parallel \cdot \parallel_F$ represents the Frobenius norm. The first term in the equation is to make the foreground better approximated while the second one is to make the representation far away from background. This formulation is a hybrid approach in which the generative and discriminative items are balanced by λ.

To make it more clear, Eq.(4) can be transformed to

$$\arg\min_{\Phi_K} \left\{ \frac{1}{N_f} \sum_{i=1}^{N_f} \parallel \mathbf{f}_i - R_{\Phi_K}(\mathbf{f}_i) \parallel^2 - \frac{\lambda}{N_b} \sum_{i=1}^{N_b} \parallel \mathbf{b}_i - R_{\Phi_K}(\mathbf{b}_i) \parallel^2 \right\}. \tag{5}$$

It can be further simplified to

$$\arg\max_{\Phi_K} \left\{ \frac{1}{N_f} \sum_{i=1}^{N_f} \langle \mathbf{f}_i, R_{\Phi_K}(\mathbf{f}_i) \rangle - \frac{\lambda}{N_b} \sum_{i=1}^{N_b} \langle \mathbf{b}_i, R_{\Phi_K}(\mathbf{b}_i) \rangle \right\}. \tag{6}$$

3.2 Solution

It can be proved that Eq.(4) is a NP hard problem, even verification of a solution is difficult. To optimize the objective function, we propose an extension of OOMP(Optimized Orthogonal Matching Pursuit) [18] called discriminative OOMP. Similar to OOMP, discriminative OOMP is a greedy algorithm to compute adaptive signal representation by iterative selection of base vectors from a dictionary.

We assume that totally K base vectors are to be chosen from the base set $\Psi = \{\psi_1, \psi_2, \ldots, \psi_{N_\psi}\}$. N_ψ is the total number of base vectors in the dictionary. Suppose $k-1$ bases $\Phi_{k-1} = \{\phi_1, \phi_2, \ldots, \phi_{k-1}\}$ have been selected, the k-th base is chosen according to

$$\arg\max_{\psi_i} \left\{ \frac{1}{N_f} \sum_{j=1}^{N_f} \frac{|\langle \gamma_i^{(k)}, \varepsilon_{k-1}(\mathbf{f}_j) \rangle|^2}{\parallel \gamma_i^{(k)} \parallel^2} - \frac{\lambda}{N_b} \sum_{j=1}^{N_b} \frac{|\langle \gamma_i^{(k)}, \varepsilon_{k-1}(\mathbf{b}_j) \rangle|^2}{\parallel \gamma_i^{(k)} \parallel^2} \right\}, \tag{7}$$

where $\gamma_i^{(k)} = \psi_i - R_{\Phi_{k-1}}(\psi_i)$ is the component of base vector ψ_i that is orthogonal to the subspace spanned by Φ_{k-1}. $\varepsilon_{k-1}(\mathbf{x}) = \mathbf{x} - R_{\Phi_{k-1}}(\mathbf{x})$ denotes the reconstruction error using Φ_{k-1}.

In each iteration of the base selection, the algorithm needs to search all the dictionary ψ_i to compute $\gamma_i^{(k)}$. Since the number of bases in dictionary is quadratic to the number of pixels in image, this process may be slow for large templates. We further analyze the above equation for simplification,

$$\langle \gamma_i^{(k)}, \varepsilon_{k-1}(\mathbf{x}) \rangle = \langle \psi_i - R_{\Phi_{k-1}}(\psi_i), \mathbf{x} - R_{\Phi_{k-1}}(\mathbf{x}) \rangle = \langle \psi_i, \mathbf{x} - R_{\Phi_{k-1}}(\mathbf{x}) \rangle. \tag{8}$$

Since ψ_i is a box base, the inner product can be computed in $O(1)$ time with pre-computation of $\mathbf{x} - R_{\Phi_{k-1}}(\mathbf{x})$ using integral image. Because

$$R_{\Phi_k}(\mathbf{x}) = R_{\Phi_{k-1}}(\mathbf{x}) + \frac{\varphi_k \langle \varphi_k, \mathbf{x} \rangle}{\| \varphi_k \|^2} , \qquad (9)$$

where $\varphi_k = \phi_k - R_{\Phi_{k-1}}(\phi_k)$ denotes the component of ϕ_k that is orthogonal to the subspace spanned by Φ_{k-1}, we therefore have

$$\| \gamma_i^{(k)} \|^2 = \| \psi_i - R_{\Phi_{k-2}}(\psi_i) - \frac{\varphi_{k-1}\langle \varphi_{k-1}, \psi_i \rangle}{\| \varphi_{k-1} \|^2} \|^2 = \| \gamma_i^{(k-1)} \|^2 - \frac{|\langle \varphi_{k-1}, \psi_i \rangle|^2}{\| \varphi_{k-1} \|^2}. \tag{10}$$

The denominator for each base vector $\| \gamma_i^{(k)} \|^2$ can be easily updated in each iteration, because the inner product $\langle \varphi_k, \psi_i \rangle$ can be quickly computed.

Note that the reconstruction for any $\mathbf{x}$ (i.e. $R_{\Phi_k}(\mathbf{x})$) can be efficiently computed by pre-storing $\Phi_k(\Phi_k^T \Phi_k)^{-1}$. The calculation of $\Phi_k^T \mathbf{x}$ is the inner products between $\mathbf{x}$ and the base vectors, which can be accomplished in $O(k)$ time. Thus, computing the reconstruction simply costs $O(kWH)$ time, where W, H are respectively the width and height of the base template. As $\langle \varphi_k, \mathbf{x} \rangle$ and $\| \mathbf{x} - R_{\Phi_{k-1}}(\mathbf{x}) \|^2$ can be pre-computed, the total computational complexity is $O(N_\psi K(N_f + N_b))$ with N_ψ the number of features in dictionary.

3.3   Fast Search Using Coherence

As aforementioned, computation of the above algorithm is mainly spent on repetitive searching in the dictionary. Since, in the NBS framework, the size of base dictionary is proportional to $W^2 \cdot H^2$, the computational cost may increase dramatically as the template size increases. A natural way to accelerate it is to reduce the number of bases to be searched in each iteration. We propose to achieve this through basis filtering using coherence.

A μ-coherent dictionary Ψ has coherence μ for $0 \leq \mu \leq 1$, if $| \langle \psi_i, \psi_j \rangle | \leq \mu$ for all distinct $\psi_i, \psi_j \in \Psi$. A 0-coherent base set is orthogonal. In general, bases with high coherence are likely to be redundant in representing the vector space. Coherence is used to reduce dictionary redundancy hence reducing the computation. Using coherence our algorithm can be accelerated by pruning all the base vectors with μ-coherent (μ is a given parameter) after each iteration of base selection.

An example image and the selected Haar-like features using discriminative NBS are shown in the left image of Figure 1. It is compared with the results selected using original NBS in the right image. Figure 2 shows the number of remaining bases for each coherence μ after selection of the largest Haar base. The template size is 50×50.

4   Tracking Using Discriminative NBS

With the discriminative NBS object representation, we locate object position in the current frame through sum of squared difference (SSD)-based matching.

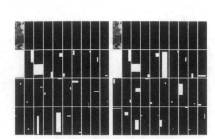 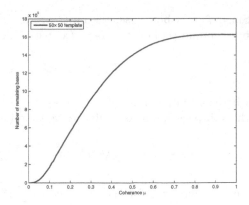

Fig. 1. Top 30 features selected using discriminative NBS (left) and the original NBS (right) for an image

Fig. 2. The number of remaining bases after selecting the largest base

Using discriminative NBS, the object is first compared with the possible locations in an region around the object position detected in the previous frame. The one with the minimum SSD value is the target object location. In order to account for object appearance changes, the foreground and discriminative NBS are automatically updated every few frames.

4.1 Object Localization

The tracker starts from the predicted object position in the previous frame and searches the best matched template in an extended area around it. We use SSD to match the template, due to its high efficiency of matching under the discriminative NBS representation. In each frame t, we specify a rectangular region surrounding the object position with a margin as the search window, in which the templates are sequentially compared with the referenced foreground $\mathbf{x} = R_{\mathbf{\Phi}_K^{(t)}}(\mathbf{f}_{\text{ref}}^{(t)})$.

Suppose that $\mathbf{x}$ is the object and $\mathbf{y}$ is a possible candidate object in the search window. The SSD between them is,

$$\text{SSD}(\mathbf{x}, \mathbf{y}) = \parallel \mathbf{x} - \mathbf{y} \parallel^2 = \parallel \mathbf{x} \parallel^2 + \parallel \mathbf{y} \parallel^2 - 2\langle \mathbf{x}, \mathbf{y} \rangle , \qquad (11)$$

where $\parallel \cdot \parallel$ represents the L^2-norm and $\langle \cdot, \cdot \rangle$ denotes the inner product. $\mathbf{x}$ is approximated by the discriminative NBS $\mathbf{\Phi}_K$ (i.e. $R_{\mathbf{\Phi}_K^{(t)}}(\mathbf{f}_{\text{ref}}^{(t)}) = \sum_{i=1}^{K} c_i^{(t)} \phi_i^{(t)}$), built using the approach in Section 3. Eq.(11) is then transformed to

$$\text{SSD}(\sum_{i=1}^{K} c_i^{(t)} \phi_i^{(t)}, \mathbf{y}) = \parallel \sum_{i=1}^{K} c_i^{(t)} \phi_i^{(t)} \parallel^2 + \parallel \mathbf{y} \parallel^2 - 2\sum_{i=1}^{K} c_i^{(t)} \langle \phi_i^{(t)}, \mathbf{y} \rangle . \qquad (12)$$

The first term is the same for all the candidate locations in the current frame. While the second and third ones can be computed rapidly with using integral image. The online computational complexity of Eq.(12) is only $O(K)$, where K is the number of selected bases.

4.2 Subspace Update

Due to appearance changes of the object, the discriminative NBS built in the previous frame might be unsuitable for the current frame. A strategy to dynamically update the subspace is necessary. Here we update the subspace every 5 frames. Once a new subspace needs to be computed, we first use the updated template and background samples from the current frame to compute the discriminative NBS again as Eq.(4).

Template Update. The object template is also updated constantly to incorporate appearance changes, which serves as the new positive samples. As Eq.(4), NBS is constructed to better represent for a set of foreground templates. Intuitively, these sampled foregrounds should recently appear, in order to more precisely describe the current status of the object. Many previous efforts have been devoted to template update (see [20]). One natural way is to choose the recent N_f referenced foregrounds. Another solution is to update the reference template in each frame, but this may incur considerable error accumulation. Simply keeping it unchanged is also problematic due to object appearance changes. A feasible way is to update the foreground by combining the frames using time-decayed coefficients. Here, we propose to update the foreground reference for every N_u frames,

$$
\mathbf{f}_{\text{ref}}^{(t)} = \begin{cases} \mathbf{f}_0 & t = 0 \\ \gamma \mathbf{f}_{\text{ref}}^{(\lfloor (t-1)/N_u \rfloor N_u)} + (1-\gamma)\mathbf{f}_t & \text{otherwise}, \end{cases} \tag{13}
$$

where $\mathbf{f}_0$ is the foreground specified in the first frame and $\mathbf{f}_t$ is the matched template at frame t. γ is the tradeoff, which is empirically set to 0.5 in our experiments. $\lfloor (t-1)/N_u \rfloor N_u$ is the frame at which the current subspace was updated. $\mathbf{f}_{\text{ref}}^{(\lfloor (t-1)/N_u \rfloor N_u)}$ is the object template at that frame. This means we are updating the template periodically instead of at each frame, which is more robust to tracking errors. This template updating scheme is compared with other methods and results are shown in the experiments section.

Background Sampling. The background samples which closely resemble the reference foreground often interfere with the stability and accuracy of tracker. We sample the background templates which are similar to the current reference object and take them as the negative data in solving the discriminative NBS. We compute a distance map in a region around the object and those locations that are very similar to the object are selected as the negative samples. Note this process can be done very efficiently because the SSD distance map can be computed very efficiently using Haar-like features and the integral image. Once the distance map is computed, locations which are local minima together with a non-minimal suppression are used to select negative samples.

5   Experiments

We first discuss in this section several key parameters used in constructing the discriminative NBS. Then we show qualitative tracking results of our approach on challenging sequences with significant background clutter and camera motion. To demonstrate the advantages of our approach, our tracking results are compared with three kinds of trackers: (1) a standard SSD tracker which uses direct patch matching, (2) an NBS tracker which applies the original NBS for object representation, and (3) a discriminative feature tracker proposed by Collins et al. in [14].

5.1   Parameter Selection

Several parameters are used in the discriminative NBS. Parameters with different settings will influence the accuracy of foreground reconstruction and tracking. We discuss here the justification of selecting them.

The formulation of the discriminative NBS balances the influence of the foreground and background reconstruction terms with a coefficient λ. Intuitively, it should be set to a small value to ensure the accuracy of foreground representation. To find the best value, we use several image sequences (mostly from PETS 2001 data set) with ground-truths to quantitatively evaluate how the parameter changes the tracking result. The tracking performance is evaluated as the mean distance error between the tracked location and the groundtruth object center. The discriminative NBS-based tracker with varying λ from 0 to 1 is applied to this sequence. The curve plotted in Fig. 3 shows the correlation of λ and centroid tracking error averaged over the whole sequence. Obviously, the centroid error is relatively more stable and smaller when λ is set to 0.25.

Another parameter for discriminative NBS is the number of bases K used. The selection of this parameter depends on image content. In general, the more features, the more accurate tracking, but it will also incur more computation. As a tradeoff, we set $K = 30$. Some other parameters we set empirically include: the number of foreground template N_f to 1 and background ones N_b to 3. These parameters are fixed for all the experiments in this paper.

We also conducted experiments to show the effectiveness of our template updating scheme. Here, we review several template updating methods mentioned above by comparing their tracking error of video sequence *browse*. These updating methods include: 1) updating the current template with the previous one, 2) updating the current template with an average of previous 5 frames and our updating method. All of the methods are initialized with the same bounding box at the first frame and the error of object center is computed according to the ground truth. Figure 4 shows that the time-decaying approach is more robust and stable.

5.2   Tracking Results

Qualitative Results. We apply our tracker to several challenging sequences to show its effectiveness. We show some qualitative results on pedestrian videos

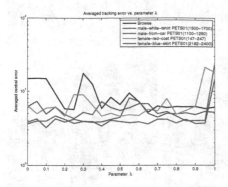 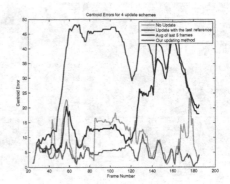

Fig. 3. The influence of λ on tracking errors. The y-axis is logarithmically scaled.

Fig. 4. Comparison for 4 template updating approaches

here to show that our tracker can handle background clutter, camera motion, and object appearance variations. In the following figures, red boxes indicate tracked object while blue boxes indicate the negative samples selected if there is a subspace update in that frame. The subspace is updated every 5 frames and if there is no update of subspace, no blue boxes (background samples) will be showed.

Sequence *Crosswalk* (Figure 5) has totally 140 frames, with two pedestrians walking together along a crowded street with an extremely cluttered background. The tracking result demonstrates the discriminative power of our algorithm. In this sequence the hand-held camera is extremely unstable. The shaky nature of the sequence makes it all the more difficult to accurately track the pedestrians. Despite this, our algorithm is able to track the pedestrians throughout the entire 140 frames of the sequence. Shai Avidan mentions in [15] that the Ensemble Tracker is able to track for the first 80 frames of the sequence but does not mention the performance for the remaining 60 frames.

Sequence *Browse* (Figure 6) is a video clip of frames 24-185 in *Browse1.avi* derived from CAVIAR people (ECCV-PETS 2004)Dataset [21]. This sequence is obtained by a distorted camera. Each frame is 384×288 pixels and the object is bounded by a 44×35 box. With significant distortion, the object can still be tracked.

Sequence *Courtyard* (Figure 7) is a video clip from 134th to 267th frame which records a person walking in the yard. The frame size is 720×480 and the object is manually bounded at frame 134 with a 41×101 red box. With moving background and variation of the object, our tracker can stably track the person.

Sequence *Crowd* (Figure 8) is a video clip (250th to 338th frames) selected from PETS 2007 Data set. In this sequence the background is very cluttered with many distracters. As can be observed the object can still be well tracked. The frame size is 720×576 and the object is initialized with a 26×136 bounding box.

Fig. 5. *Crosswalk* sequence: The frames 0, 16, 50, 74, 105 and 139 are shown. The red boxes are the tracked objects and the blue boxes at $5k$ frame are the sampled backgrounds.

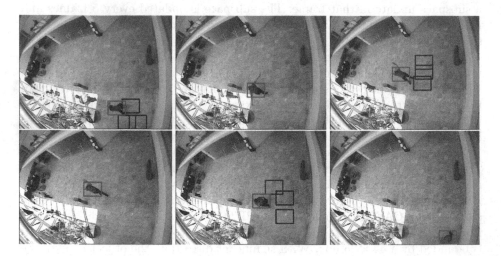

Fig. 6. *Browse* sequence: The frames 24, 45, 74, 115, 139, 185 are shown. The red boxes are the tracked objects and the blue boxes at $5k + 4$ frame are the sampled backgrounds.

Comparative result between our DNBS tracker and another discriminative tracker [14] is showed in Fig. 9. Sequence *Female* is a video clip in PETS 2007 data set. It starts from frame 826 to 870, each of which has 720×576 pixels. The object is initialized at the 826th frame of size 26×106. Collins' tracker drifts away at frame 841, while our method still keeps track all along.

Fig. 7. *Courtyard* sequence: The frames 134, 153, 189, 205, 234, and 267 are shown. The red boxes are the tracked objects and the blue boxes at $5k + 4$ frame are the sampled backgrounds.

Fig. 8. *Crowd* sequence: The frames 250, 267, 295, 306, 325, and 338 are shown. The red boxes are the tracked objects and the blue boxes at $5k$ frame are the sampled backgrounds.

Quantitative Evaluation. In order to quantitatively evaluate the performance of our approach, we compare our results with the ground truth of the above two sequences (*Crosswalk* and *Browse*). The error is measured as the distance between the tracked object center location and the groundtruth object location in pixels. Figure 10 shows the results for three methods: (blue) SSD method, (green) NBS method, (red) Discriminative NBS method, and (light blue) a discriminative feature tracker proposed by Collins et al. [14]. The objects are initialized at the same position at the first frames and the reference templates are updated in

Fig. 9. *Female* sequence: The frames 826, 840, 854 and 870 are shown. The upper row shows results for DNBS tracker and the second row shows results for Collins' tracker.

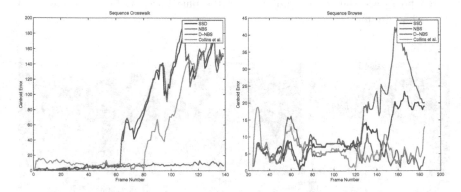

Fig. 10. Quantitative results for the *Crosswalk* and *Browse* sequence. The horizontal axis is the frame number and the vertical axis is the tracking error between the tracked object location and groundtruth.

the same way (with $N_u = 5$ and $\gamma = 0.5$) as mentioned in this paper. As can be observed, our approach is consistently better than these two methods.

6   Conclusions

We have proposed the discriminative NBS, a simple yet informative object representation that can be solved using a variant of OOMP. Such a representation incorporates the discriminate image information to distinguish the foreground and background, making it suitable to be used in object tracking. We use SSD matching built upon the discriminative NBS to efficiently locate object in video frames. Our experiments on challenging video sequences show that the discriminative NBS-based tracker can stably track the dynamic object. We intend to explore the application of discriminative NBS on other vision and multimedia tasks such as image copy detection in future.

Acknowledgments. This work was supported in part by the National Science Foundation of China under Grants 60703084, 60723003, 60721002, the National Fundamental Research Program of China (2010CB327903), and the Jiangsu Science Foundation (BK2009081).

References

1. Hager, G., Dewan, M., Stewart, C.: Multiple kernel tracking with ssd. In: Proc. CVPR, pp. I: 790–797 (2004)
2. Han, B., Davis, L.: On-line density-based appearance modeling for object tracking. In: Proc. ICCV, vol. II, pp. 1492–1499 (2005)
3. Matthews, I., Ishikawa, T., Baker, S.: The template update problem. IEEE Trans. on PAMI 26, 810–815 (2004)
4. Black, M.J., Jepson, A.: Eigentracking: Robust matching and tracking of articulated objects using a view-based representation. In: Buxton, B.F., Cipolla, R. (eds.) ECCV 1996. LNCS, vol. 1065, pp. 329–342. Springer, Heidelberg (1996)
5. Cootes, T., Edwards, G., Taylor, C.: Active appearance models. IEEE Trans. on PAMI 23, 681–685 (2001)
6. Jepson, A., Fleet, D., El-Maraghi, T.: Robust online appearance models for visual tracking. IEEE Trans. on PAMI 25, 1296–1311 (2003)
7. Tao, H., Sawhney, H., Kumar, R.: Object tracking with bayesian estimation of dynamic layer representations. IEEE Trans. on PAMI 24, 75–89 (2002)
8. Comaniciu, D.: Kernel-based object tracking. IEEE Trans. on PAMI 25, 564–577 (2003)
9. Fan, Z., Wu, Y.: Multiple collaborative kernel tracking. In: Proc. CVPR, vol. II, pp. 502–509 (2005)
10. Birchfield, S., Sriram, R.: Spatiograms versus histograms for region-based tracking. In: Proc. CVPR, vol. II, pp. 1158–1163 (2005)
11. Shi, J., Tomasi, C.: Good features to track. In: Proc. CVPR, pp. 593–600 (1994)
12. Tang, F., Tao, H.: Object tracking with dynamic feature graphs. In: Workshop on VS-PETS, pp. 25–32 (2005)
13. Chen, Y., Rui, Y., Huang, T.: Jpdaf based hmm for real-time contour tracking. In: Proc. CVPR, vol. I, pp. 543–550 (2001)
14. Collins, R., Liu, Y., Leordeanu, M.: On-line selection of discriminative tracking features. IEEE Trans. on PAMI 27, 1631–1643 (2005)
15. Avidan, S.: Ensemble tracking. IEEE Trans. on PAMI 29, 261–271 (2007)
16. Avidan, S.: Support vector tracking. IEEE Trans. on PAMI, 184–191 (2001)
17. Tang, F., Brennan, S., Zhao, Q., Tao, H.: Co-tracking using semi-supervised support vector machines. In: Proc. ICCV, pp. 1–8 (2007)
18. Tang, F., Crabb, R., Tao, H.: Representing images using nonorthogonal haar-like bases. IEEE Trans. on PAMI 29, 2120–2134 (2007)
19. Rebollo-Neira, L., Lowe, D.: Optimized orthogonal matching pursuit approach. IEEE Signal Processing Letters 9, 137–140 (2002)
20. Jepson, A.D., Fleet, D.J., El-Maraghi, T.F.: Robust online appearance models for visual tracking. IEEE Trans. on PAMI 25, 1296–1311 (2003)
21. EC Funded CAVIAR project, http://homepages.inf.ed.ac.uk/rbf/CAVIAR/

TriangleFlow: Optical Flow with Triangulation-Based Higher-Order Likelihoods

Ben Glocker[1], T. Hauke Heibel[1], Nassir Navab[1],
Pushmeet Kohli[2], and Carsten Rother[2]

[1] Computer Aided Medical Procedures (CAMP),
Technische Universität München, Germany
{glocker,heibel,navab}@in.tum.de
[2] Microsoft Research, Cambridge, UK
{pkohli,carrot}@microsoft.com

Abstract. We use a simple yet powerful higher-order conditional random field (CRF) to model optical flow. It consists of a standard photo-consistency cost and a prior on affine motions both modeled in terms of higher-order potential functions. Reasoning jointly over a large set of unknown variables provides more reliable motion estimates and a robust matching criterion. One of the main contributions is that unlike previous region-based methods, we omit the assumption of constant flow. Instead, we consider local affine warps whose likelihood energy can be computed exactly without approximations. This results in a tractable, so-called, higher-order likelihood function. We realize this idea by employing triangulation meshes which immensely reduce the complexity of the problem. Optimization is performed by hierarchical fusion moves and an adaptive mesh refinement strategy. Experiments show that we achieve high-quality motion fields on several data sets including the Middlebury optical flow database.

1 Introduction

Currently most methods for optical flow estimation can be roughly divided into two groups: (i) variational methods based on the pioneering work of Horn and Schunck [1], and (ii) discrete methods utilizing combinatorial optimization such as graph-cuts [2]. Both approaches have their advantages and disadvantages. While variational methods often yield very high accuracy, these methods depend on rather local image properties and may also suffer from local minima during optimization of the cost function. Combinatorial optimization is often able to recover strong minima but only with respect to a rather sparse discretization of the search space. Recently, methods have been proposed [3,4] which successfully combine both worlds towards discrete-continuous optimization which is able to avoid local minima and obtain highly accurate (continuous) flow estimates at the same time. A rather comprehensive overview and comparison of latest optical flow methods can be found in [5] and on the website of the Middlebury optical flow database[1].

---

[1] http://vision.middlebury.edu/flow/

K. Daniilidis, P. Maragos, N. Paragios (Eds.): ECCV 2010, Part III, LNCS 6313, pp. 272–285, 2010.

Still, a major limitation of existing algorithms is in the definition of the likelihood (or data) term within the energy formulation. Often, a matching criterion is defined pixel-wise for instance using squared differences on the intensities. In general, such a formulation yields an ill-posed problem since two-dimensional flow vectors have to be recovered from a one-dimensional signal (aperture problem). Ambiguities may arise for matching individual pixels independently. Here, regularization plays an important role to render the problem well-posed such that the optimization yields meaningful solutions.

In contrast, region-based approaches [6,7] use local image patches to estimate point correspondences. Here, a matching criterion such as the correlation coefficient (CC) is evaluated on the whole patch centered at a point for which the motion is to be determined. The distribution of such points can be dense or sparse (by employing a parameterization of the motion field) [8]. Region-based approaches yield a more robust definition of the likelihood compared to pixel-wise methods [9], but often introduce a rough approximation. In fact, in most approaches it is assumed that all pixels within the patch move with constant flow. However, except for pure translation within the patch, the assumption of constant flow does not hold.

One may claim that an optimal definition of the likelihood should be (i) *robust and reliable*, by considering a larger set of unknown variables simultaneously and (ii) *precise and tractable* by modeling the various motions for the set of variables beyond the assumption of constant flow. This leads us to our main contribution in this paper, which we call *higher-order likelihoods*. In the following, we will introduce the concept of higher-order likelihoods and their corresponding energy in a conditional random field (CRF). We demonstrate how triangulation meshes perfectly support our concept. The effectiveness of our approach is evaluated on several datasets including the Middlebury optical flow database. We also revisit the concept of motion layers [10] which, when integrated in our framework, enables us to handle occlusions in a natural way in form of overlapping meshes. We conclude our paper by a discussion on future work.

1.1 Related Work

Conditional random fields are ubiquitous in computer vision. Their success can be certainly attributed in large parts to the existence of powerful optimization methods which have been developed in the last decade. The most commonly used models in low-level vision applications are first-order CRFs[2], which contain cliques of size up to two. Here, the *unary potentials* play the role of the likelihood term evaluating how well a certain label fits to a variable w.r.t. to the observation, independently of all other variables. The *pairwise potentials* are then used to enforce smoothness by penalizing deviations of labelings between two neighboring variables. These models are quite intuitive due to their natural relationship to the image grid itself. Additionally, first-order models are attractive due to efficient optimization methods, which often guarantee to find the global optimum.

---

[2] Note that an n-th order CRF contains cliques of size up to $n + 1$.

Despite the popularity of first-order models, their modeling capabilities are very limited. As already mentioned, a likelihood term based on unaries is either not very reliable or rough approximations have to be used as in previous region-based methods. In some works (e.g. in [11,12,13]), the pairwise terms are considered for the likelihood in order to model a conditional data-dependency on a pair of variables which yields a more appropriate model for the problem at hand.

Recent advances in CRF optimization allow the use of higher-order potentials in an efficient and principled manner [14,15,16]. A combination of fusion moves [17,18], reduction techniques [19], and the QPBO algorithm [20,21] allows to use a second-order model in stereo [22], while a similar model is used for motion in [23] employing belief propagation. Both works use a second-order prior defined on triple-cliques to enforce smoothness based on second derivatives of the disparity/motion field. Still, only unary terms are used for the likelihood.

Recently, many techniques have been developed for larger cliques of up to several hundred variables, e.g. [15,24] just to mention a few. In order to deal with such large cliques in a tractable way , they must exhibit some internal structure. For instance in [15] it is assumed that only a few (important) label-configurations have a low energy and all remaining configurations a constant (high) cost.

In the following, we will introduce our concept of higher-order likelihoods for the task of optical flow. We will derive a likelihood term based on triple-cliques which models the costs of local affine motions exactly without approximations. Additionally, we propose two novel regularization terms, the first one being also based on triple-cliques, and the second one based on quadruple-cliques.

2   Concept of Higher-Order Likelihoods

Consider a set V of variables $i, ..., N$. In optical flow, the variables correspond to pixels and we seek for optimal assignments d_i[3] corresponding to two-dimensional flow vectors. Additionally, we introduce the power set C containing all possible cliques (subsets) c of variables. We define the cost for a *labeling* $\mathbf{d}$ (i.e. every variable is assigned a value d_i) in terms of a general CRF energy as

$$E(\mathbf{d}|\theta) = \sum_{c \in C} \psi_c(\mathbf{d}_c|\theta) \ . \tag{1}$$

The clique potential functions ψ_c evaluate the cost for assigning a sub-labeling $\mathbf{d}_c$ to a clique c conditioned on the observation θ (the image data). In first-order models, the energy would then be simply the sum of unary potentials $\psi_i(x_i|\theta)$ plus the sum of pairwise potentials $\psi_{ij}(d_i, d_j|\theta)$. For simplicity, in the following we will neglect θ in the potential functions.

---

[3] Depending on the context we will treat $i, j, ...$ as random variables and as 2D coordinates. Similarly, we treat labels $d_i, d_j, ...$ also as 2D motion vectors.

Theoretically, reasoning jointly over all variables would be the best approach for finding an optimal labeling. The energy would simply consist of one higher-order potential for a clique containing all variables. Obviously, even for a small number of variables this approach is doomed in practice regarding the computational complexity. A compromise has to be found between the clique size and the tractability of the problem.

Let us concentrate on the problem of optical flow. Determining the flow vector of individual pixels is clearly not well defined due to the aperture problem mentioned earlier. In contrast, solving for the flow for a group of pixels might be more reliable. Assume we are seeking for the optimal flow vectors within a discretized search space L (a set of labels). Then, for a clique of K pixels the solution space for the labeling problem has the cardinality $|L|^K$. Evaluating all of the potential labelings is infeasible. We discuss two alternative solutions to this dilemma. We realize one of these solutions in our practical system, which we discuss in detail in Sec. 2.1.

Let us first consider the alternative solution, which we only discuss theoretically. It is based on the recent work [15], where higher-order cliques are modeled by sparse higher-order representations. Only a few labelings have assigned the correct higher-order cost and all other remaining labelings are assigned a constant (high) cost, which approximates their true cost. The key question is now which labelings should be modeled? Note that there is actually only one labeling, i.e. the *maximum a posteriori* (MAP) labeling $\hat{d}$, which has to be modeled. This is the labeling which corresponds to the global optimum of the CRF energy, which is obviously unknown. One approach is to design a data-driven prediction function which has the observation as input and possible labelings as output. Also, an iterative optimization procedure can be envisioned, where the higher-order terms, which only approximate the current MAP labeling by a constant cost, are redefined and thus improve the modeling of the MAP labeling in the next iteration. However, such an approach might be computationally very expensive. In this paper, we present a simple yet powerful model overcoming this limitation by exploiting inherent properties of optical flow.

2.1   Reduction of Complexity Using Triangulations

Optical flow estimation consists of recovering the apparent motion from two dimensional images capturing a scene of three dimensional objects moving over time. We make two observations: (i) often the scene contains mainly solid objects, which might translate, rotate, and/or scale from one image to another, (ii) the motion of non-solid objects (such as textiles) can be sufficiently represented by several local affine motions. These observations are consistent with other approaches previously proposed for optical flow [25,26,27].

If we restrict the set of labelings to the ones representing affine motions only, we already achieve an immense reduction of complexity. An affine motion in 2D is fully defined by three two-dimensional points (i.e. six degrees of freedom). So, estimating an affine motion from $K(>3)$ pixels is an over-determined problem which allows further simplifications. Additional reduction of complexity can be

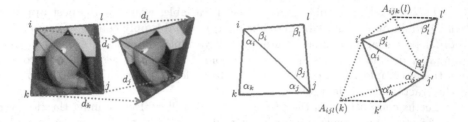

Fig. 1. Left: the triangles (ijk) and (ijl) represent higher-order likelihoods and define local affine warps when labels (d_i, d_j, d_k, d_l) are assigned to the triangle points. Right: illustration of the two different regularization terms. The ADP penalizes changes between initial angles (α, β) and angles (α', β'). The NAMP determines how well the warp of one triangle describes the warp of the other one by computing the (normalized) distance between the warped points k', l' and their locations $A_{ijl}(k), A_{ijk}(l)$ if warped by the neighboring triangle.

achieved by a parameterization of the cliques motion using a simple geometrical transformation model in terms of triangulation. A triangle in 2D space defines an affine warp. We propose to represent a clique of pixels by a single triangle. Then, the task becomes to find the optimal displacements of the triangle points, instead of seeking for individual displacements for each pixel. Let us now derive the energy for this model.

2.2 Likelihood Term

First, we need to define a matching criterion. In this work, we consider the correlation coefficient (CC). For two sets of measurements X and Y, the CC is defined as

$$\mathrm{CC}(X, Y) = \frac{\sum (x_i - \bar{x})(y_i - \bar{y})}{\sqrt{\sum (x_i - \bar{x})^2} \sqrt{\sum (y_i - \bar{y})^2}} = \frac{\mathrm{cov}(X, Y)}{\sigma_x \sigma_y} \quad, \tag{2}$$

where $\bar{x}$ and $\bar{y}$ are the two means and σ_x and σ_y the standard deviations. The CC takes values from $[-1, 1]$, where 1 indicates a perfect linear relationship, 0 indicates no linear relationship, and -1 an inverse linear relationship. In order to use the CC score within an energy minimization, we modify the original term into $\mathrm{CC}' = (1 - \mathrm{CC})$ taking values from $[0, 2]$.

Second, we formalize the local affine motion model based on a triangulation mesh. Assume that a set of triangles covering the image domain is given. We can define a *local affine warp* T_{ijk} of a point $p = (x, y)^\top$ lying in a triangle (ijk) as the sum of the products of the barycentric coordinates $(\omega_i, \omega_j, \omega_k)$ of p and the three displacement vectors (d_i, d_j, d_k) as

$$T_{ijk}(p) = p + \omega_i d_i + \omega_j d_j + \omega_k d_k \quad. \tag{3}$$

This is a simple linear triangle interpolation. The warping is illustrated in Fig. 1(left). Note that instead of expressing the local warp as a linear combination of the three displacements, we can equivalently define an affine transformation matrix A_{ijk} as

$$A_{ijk} = \begin{bmatrix} a_x & b_x & c_x \\ a_y & b_y & c_y \\ 0 & 0 & 1 \end{bmatrix}, \tag{4}$$

which maps (homogeneous) image points to their new locations. The matrix can be determined by solving a simple linear system of equations.

From A_{ijk} we can extract two linear functions $P_{ijk}^x(p) = a_x\, x + b_x\, y + c_x$ and $P_{ijk}^y(p) = a_y\, x + b_y\, y + c_y$, together defining the movement of point p. These definitions are later used in one of our regularization terms.

For convenience, we define some further notation used in the following equations. Given an image I, then I' denotes the warped image $I \circ T$. Additionally, I_{ijk} denotes the triangular sub-image containing only the pixels lying within the triangle (ijk).

Based on the above matching criterion and the triangle motion model, and given two images I and J (i.e. the two adjacent frames in an optical flow sequence), we can now define the higher-order likelihood in terms of triple-clique potential functions

$$\psi_{ijk}(d_i, d_j, d_k) = CC'\left(I'_{ijk}, J_{ijk}\right) = 1 - \frac{\mathrm{cov}(I'_{ijk}, J_{ijk})}{\sigma_{I'_{ijk}}\sigma_{J_{ijk}}}. \tag{5}$$

In fact, any labeling (d_i, d_j, d_k) yields a potential affine warp and the resulting matching cost is evaluated exactly (without approximations) for the set of pixels within the triangular sub-image. One problem remains, which is that the space of affine transformations also includes reflections. This type of transformations should not be considered in case of optical flow. We can enforce this by a simple modification on the likelihood term

$$\psi_{ijk}(d_i, d_j, d_k) = \begin{cases} CC'\left(I'_{ijk}, J_{ijk}\right) & \text{if } O(i, j, k) = O(i', j', k') \\ 2 & \text{otherwise} \end{cases}, \tag{6}$$

where $O(i, j, k)$ determines the orientation (i.e. clockwise or counter-clockwise) of a triangle. Note that this is a very simple and efficient geometrical operation to check whether a triangle warp constitutes a reflection. The assignment of the maximum cost of 2 for reflections avoids such unwanted warps.

An energy based on the sum of such triple-clique potentials could be sufficient for estimating the flow. It imposes some implicit regularization on the transformation since the cliques overlap at the common edge of neighboring triangles. However, texture-less regions and small triangles might benefit from an explicit regularization.

2.3 Regularization Term

Triangles covering homogeneous regions might lead to unreliable estimates. Regularization is needed such that discriminative triangles with reliable motion drive the less reliable triangles towards a good solution. There are several ways for employing a regularization on the mesh of triangles. Here, we propose two different terms. Which of these two terms should be used depends on the application and the motion we expect to be present in the image sequence. We evaluate the performance of both terms later in our experiments.

The first regularization term is based on triple-clique potential functions and we call it the *angle deviation penalty* (ADP). The ADP is defined as

$$\psi_{ijk}(d_i, d_j, d_k) = \|(\alpha_i, \alpha_j, \alpha_k) - (\alpha'_i, \alpha'_j, \alpha'_k)\| \ . \tag{7}$$

The term penalizes the change between the initial angles $(\alpha_i, \alpha_j, \alpha_k)$ and the angles of the warped triangle $(\alpha'_i, \alpha'_j, \alpha'_k)$ (see also Fig. 1(right)). The ADP is invariant to similarity transformations (i.e. all transformations containing only translation, rotation, and isotropic scaling).

The second term is more general and defined on quadruple-cliques. It regularizes the motion between neighboring triangles (ijk) and (ijl). We call this term *non-affine motion penalty* (NAMP) and define it as

$$\psi_{ijkl}(d_i, d_j, d_k, d_l) = \left\| \begin{matrix} \theta_k \\ \theta_l \end{matrix} \right\| \ , \tag{8}$$

with

$$\theta_k = \left\| \begin{matrix} \delta(P^x_{ijl}, k, k'_x) \\ \delta(P^y_{ijl}, k, k'_y) \end{matrix} \right\| \quad \theta_l = \left\| \begin{matrix} \delta(P^x_{ijk}, l, l'_x) \\ \delta(P^y_{ijk}, l, l'_y) \end{matrix} \right\| \quad \delta(P, p, v) = \frac{|P(p) - v|}{\sqrt{a^2 + b^2 + 1}} \ . \tag{9}$$

Intuitively, the term determines how well the warp of one triangle, represented by the linear functions P^x and P^y, describes the motion of the other one. If the two local warps A_{ijk} and A_{ijl} constitute an affine motion on the rectangle $(ijkl)$, then the penalty term evaluates to zero. A geometrical interpretation is illustrated in Fig. 1. We adopted the NAMP from the closely related *distances from planes* measure proposed in [28]. The NAMP can be seen as the multivariate extension.

The final energy of our higher-order CRF is then the weighted sum of the likelihood energy and the regularization energy

$$E(\mathbf{d}) = E_{\text{likelihood}}(\mathbf{d}) + \lambda \, E_{\text{regularization}}(\mathbf{d}) \ , \tag{10}$$

where λ controls the influence of the regularization term.

3   Triangulation

So far, we have defined an energy model which enables us to use any triangulation for estimating optical flow. Since there are various ways for obtaining such triangulations, which might be more or less suitable for optical flow, we would like to discuss some of them in the following, which are all based on the popular Delaunay triangulation [29].

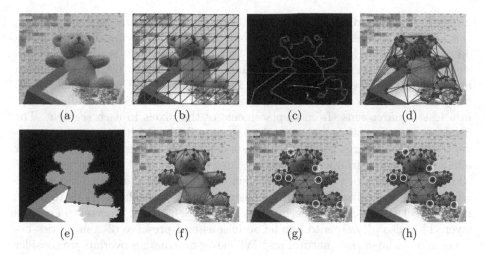

Fig. 2. Illustration of different approaches for obtaining triangulations (cf. Sec. 3) for an input image (a). Triangulation based on a regular mesh in (b), based on Canny edges in (c,d), and based on segmentation in (e,f). Mesh refinement with and without merging step in (g) and (h) (cf. Sec. 3.2).

The simplest way of defining a mesh of triangles is through a uniform distribution of nodes along the image domain (cf. Fig. 2(b)). Such regular meshes have been previously used for optical flow [8], and they can be represented by a small number of parameters (e.g. number of nodes or node spacing). While they have the advantage of simplicity, regular meshes have the drawback of a missing relation to the underlying image data. Triangles might cover different objects and thus probably different layers of motion. Here, data-dependent triangulation (DDT) seems to provide more suitable triangulations. Low-level data-dependence (e.g. using Canny edges as shown in Fig. 2(c)) would allow to place triangle edges along image edges (cf. Fig. 2(d)). However, image edges do not necessarily follow motion boundaries. In [30], a method is proposed which extracts occlusion boundaries from a single image. These boundaries might follow the real motion boundaries more closely. Another approach could be based on object segmentation. In Fig. 2(e), we utilize a mean-shift color segmentation[4] to extract the shape of the teddybear. We perform a Delaunay triangulation for boundary nodes and discard triangles outside the segmentation (cf. Fig. 2(f)). In all these examples, the nodes can be obtained with the Douglas-Peucker algorithm for line simplification [31] from any given boundary or edge image.

3.1   Layered Representation

An elegant and promising approach for motion estimation is based on a multi-layer representation, starting with the work of Wang and Adelson [10] and

---

[4] http://www.caip.rutgers.edu/riul/research/code/EDISON/

numerous ongoing developments, e.g. [32,33,12] just to name a few. However, this approach has fallen a little bit into oblivion when reviewing the list of methods in the popular Middlebury optical flow ranking. In this work, we revisit a simple but effective method for determining motion layers. We follow a similar approach as described in [33]. Initially, we use a mean-shift color segmentation on the first frame to obtain an over-segmentation. Then we estimate affine warps in a least-squares sense from displacements of the pixels in each segment. The displacements are taken from an initial motion field, which we compute in advance using our energy model and a regular mesh. Next, segments with similar affine motions are grouped by spectral clustering. For that purpose we use the end-point distance of warped image boundary points as a distance measure on affine warps and a fixed value of 15 clusters. This approach allows us to define independent meshes, one for each cluster, where each cluster represents a motion layer. This also allows us to handle occlusions and preserve discontinuities between motion layers in a natural way. Whenever two meshes overlap, we consider the mesh with a higher CC score in the overlap area to be in front of the other.

3.2 Mesh Refinement and Area Importance

As discussed earlier, larger triangles are in general more robust in providing reliable flow estimates due to the larger set of pixels considered simultaneously. Now, imagining two neighboring triangles where one of them is significantly larger than the other one, we would trust more in the motion corresponding to the energy minimum of the larger one. However, the actual energy value is independent of the size of the triangles. To this end, we propose to add an area weighting factor. The modified likelihood term becomes

$$\psi_{ijk}(d_i, d_j, d_k) = \begin{cases} \Delta_{ijk} \, \text{CC}' \left(I'_{ijk}, J_{ijk} \right) & \text{if } O(i, j, k) = O(i', j', k') \\ 2 \, \Delta_{ijk} & \text{otherwise} \end{cases} \quad , \quad (11)$$

where Δ_{ijk} is the area of the triangle (ijk). Similarly, we add a weighting factor to the ADP regularization term[5].

Still, smaller triangles are more suitable for recovering local flow, in particular for areas undergoing non-rigid motion. To this end, we propose a hierarchical mesh refinement. Starting with an initial triangulation containing larger triangles which will drive the estimation in the beginning, we subsequently refine the mesh by inserting a node at the center of each edge and recompute the triangulation. Each triangle will be separated into four smaller triangles all having the same size. On this refined mesh we continue the optical flow estimation.

We demonstrate the effectiveness of this refinement strategy in a small experiment on the RubberWhale sequence, for which the ground truth flow field is available. In four different runs, we distribute triangles of same sizes – with different initial sizes in each run – over the whole image domain. We run our energy minimization over four to five levels of refinement (depending on the

---

[5] The NAMP already has an inherent bias towards larger triangles.

initial size), where in each level the motion of the triangles is initialized with the motion from the previous level. The motion of inserted nodes is linearly interpolated. We compute the average angular error for the estimated flow of each level. In Fig. 3 we plot the progress of the error versus the triangle size. The error decreases along with the level of refinement until a certain point where the error increases in all four runs. There seems to be a critical point where the triangle sizes are becoming too small to provide reliable motion estimates.

We conclude that a refinement of triangles improves the result, while a certain size should be preserved. This is exactly the range, where all four runs have their minimum error. In order to preserve these sizes, while still refining triangles above this range, we add a threshold on the edge length in the refinement. Nodes are only inserted on edges having at least a length of 15 pixels which results in minimum triangles of sizes between 100 and 25px^2.

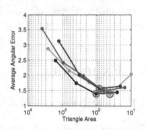

Fig. 3. Error versus Area. Colors show different runs.

In some cases the node insertion can lead to nodes lying very closely next to each other. To this end, after each mesh refinement we identify nodes whose initial position is located at almost the same position and replace the nodes by one averaged node and compute its motion as the average motion of the replaced ones. The refinement with and without this merging step is illustrated in Fig. 2(g) and 2(h).

4   Optimization

In order to optimize our CRF energy, we employ a discrete optimization over hierarchical sets of displacement vectors. We generate a search space for each optimization sweep by defining a maximum range and a sub-sampling of this range by a fixed number of displacements along the eight main directions in 2D (i.e. positive and negative horizontal, vertical, and diagonal direction). A similar quantization strategy has been previously used in [13]. The energy minimization is performed by subsequent sweeps using the QPBO-I algorithm [34], iteratively over the set of displacements. Higher-order potential functions are transformed into pairwise terms based on the reduction techniques for triple-cliques [19], and quadruple-cliques [16]. After an optimization sweep, the displacement set and thus the search range is re-scaled by a user defined factor. This procedure is repeated for a fixed number of sweeps, before we initiate a mesh refinement and rerun the optimization on the refined mesh. Throughout this work, we use fixed setting. We set the initial maximum range to 10 pixels and the number of sub-sampling steps to 5 yielding 41 displacements (including the zero-displacement). We perform 5 sweeps on one mesh level, and after each run we refine the displacements by a factor of 0.66 while we use a total of 4 mesh levels.

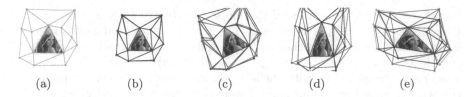

(a)   (b)   (c)   (d)   (e)

Fig. 4. Experiment on regularization behavior of ADP and NAMP for different types of transformations (cf. Sec. 5.1). We show the initial triangulation in (a), and in (b-e) the warp applied on (a) in green and the results for ADP in red and for NAMP in blue.

5   Experiments

5.1   ADP versus NAMP

The purpose of this experiment is to investigate the behavior of the two different regularization terms in a fully controlled setting. Remember, that ADP is invariant to similarity transformations, while NAMP is invariant to affine transformations. We define a triangulation on a test image (cf. Fig. 4(a)) where only one triangle is covering a textured part of the image. The likelihood of this triangle will be the driving force for the alignment to four different warped images. The warped images are generated by applying warps to the initial image and triangulation, i.e. an isotropic scaling, a rotation, an anisotropic scaling, and a shearing (cf. Fig. 4(b) to 4(e)). Except for the one triangle in the middle, the motion of the other triangles will result only from the regularization term. We find that both terms yield very good alignments for the outer triangles in case of similarity transformations. For pure rotation, ADP performs even slightly better, most probably due to the higher invariance of NAMP. In contrast, NAMP yields accurate alignments in case of the two affine transformations, while here ADP prevents a proper alignment of the outer triangles. We conclude that ADP should be used, when mostly similarity transformations are expected. It is also much more efficient w.r.t. to computational time than NAMP. Beyond this experiment, we experienced that NAMP based on quadruple-cliques is currently impracticable for triangulations with several thousands of triangles due to its computational demands. In the following experiment, we will again use both terms and measure the performance w.r.t. to computational time.

5.2   Giraffe

In this experiment, we perform a motion estimation on two frames of the Giraffe sequence (180×144 pixels), where the Giraffe deforms considerably. Segmentations of the giraffe are available, so we can define two motion layers, one for the giraffe and one for the background. We run the estimation with both regularization terms, and each run with three levels of mesh refinement (≈ 800 triangles on the finest level). We find a large difference in the running time. While using ADP, the optimization takes less than one minute, using NAMP takes almost

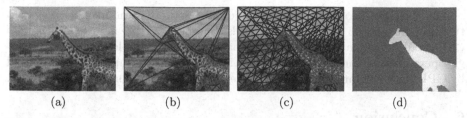

(a)   (b)   (c)   (d)

Fig. 5. Experiment on Giraffe sequence. Target frame in (a), initial and final mesh in (b) and (c), and the resulting flow field in (d) (cf. Sec. 5.2).

Fig. 6. Flow fields for the Army and Teddy sequence for the single-layer approach using a regular mesh on the left, and results for the multi-layer approach on the right (cf. Sec. 5.3). Please note the sharp transitions at motion boundaries in case of the multi-layer approach.

ten minutes until convergence. We show the images, the initial and final meshes, and the color-encoded flow field using ADP in Fig. 5. The NAMP yields a similar result. Despite its more restrictive nature, we are able to obtain a high-accurate flow field using ADP even for the giraffe layer with highly non-rigid motion.

5.3   Middlebury

Finally, we perform an evaluation on the datasets of the Middlebury database. We compare two approaches for defining the triangulation. The first one is based on a single regular mesh, and the second one is based on the layered representation described in Sec. 3.1. Here, the resulting flow fields of the first approach are used for the affine motion clustering yielding the different motion layers. Throughout the experiments we use the ADP regularization with $\lambda = 0.3$. The remaining optimization parameters correspond to those described in Sec. 4. The initial node distance for the regular mesh is set to 60 pixels and subsequently refined to 30, 15, and 7.5. The initial motions of the multi-layer meshes are interpolated from the single-layer result.

The single-layer approach yields already quite reasonable results ranked in the midfield of the database. The multi-layer approach results in high-quality, discontinuity preserving motion fields which are competing with the best methods currently listed in the ranking, including advanced variational methods. In Fig. 6 we show some visual results. The detailed quantitative evaluation can be found online on the Middlebury website and in the supplementary material.

The computationally expensive part of our method is the likelihood evaluation, in particular on the finer mesh levels containing a large number of triangles ($> 10,000$). Since the computations are based on rather simple geometrical triangle operations and linear interpolation, a tremendous speed-up might be achieved by GPU implementation providing efficient, hardware-supported functionalities.

6   Conclusion

We propose a novel CRF model with higher-order likelihoods for the application of optical flow beyond the assumption of constant flow. Likelihood terms are defined on local pixel regions whose motions are constrained to local affine warps through triangle-based parameterization. The energies are defined as triple-cliques for the likelihood as well as the similarity invariant regularization term, while non-affine motions can be penalized through quadruple-clique energies. To our best knowledge, this is the first time that higher-order CRF likelihoods are modeled in such a way. Here, the main advantage of our approach is that the energies are evaluated exactly without approximations yielding a robust and reliable matching process. An interesting direction would be to integrate the whole process of triangulation and motion layer definition into the optimization. A prior on the maximum number of layers, as well as a flow-dependent mesh-refinement could further improve the the results. A step beyond our current approach could allow for the definition of higher-order likelihoods with arbitrary shapes and without restrictions through the parametrization. We believe our model can be seen as a building block for new directions in CRF modeling in computer vision, which directly benefit from future advances in CRF optimization.

References

1. Horn, B., Schunck, B.: Determining optical flow. Artificial Intelligence 17 (1981)
2. Boykov, Y., Veksler, O., Zabih, R.: Fast approximate energy minimization via graph cuts. PAMI 23 (2001)
3. Lempitsky, V., Roth, S., Rother, C.: Fusionflow: Discrete-continuous optimization for optical flow estimation. In: CVPR (2008)
4. Trobin, W., Pock, T., Cremers, D., Bischof, H.: Continuous energy minimization via repeated binary fusion. In: Forsyth, D., Torr, P., Zisserman, A. (eds.) ECCV 2008, Part IV. LNCS, vol. 5305, pp. 677–690. Springer, Heidelberg (2008)
5. Baker, S., Scharstein, D., Lewis, J., Roth, S., Black, M.J., Szeliski, R.: A database and evaluation methodology for optical flow. In: Microsoft Research Technical Report MSR-TR-2009-179 (2009)
6. Lucas, B., Kanade, T.: An iterative image registration technique with an application to stereo vision. In: IJCAI (1981)
7. Veksler, O.: Fast variable window for stereo correspondence using integral images. In: CVPR (2003)
8. Glocker, B., Paragios, N., Komodakis, N., Tziritas, G., Navab, N.: Optical flow estimation with uncertainties through dynamic mrfs. In: CVPR (2008)
9. Hirschmuller, H., Scharstein, D.: Evaluation of stereo matching costs on images with radiometric differences. PAMI 31 (2009)

10. Wang, J.Y.A., Adelson, E.H.: Representing moving images with layers. IEEE Image Processing 3 (1994)
11. Rother, C., Kolmogorov, V., Blake, A.: grabcut: Interactive foreground extraction using iterated graph cuts. ACM SIGGRAPH 23 (2004)
12. Kumar, M.P., Torr, P., Zisserman, A.: Learning layered motion segmentations of video. IJCV 76 (2008)
13. Heibel, T.H., Glocker, B., Groher, M., Paragios, N., Komodakis, N., Navab, N.: Discrete tracking of parametrized curves. In: CVPR (2009)
14. Komodakis, N., Paragios, N.: Beyond pairwise energies: Efficient optimization for higher-order mrfs. In: CVPR (2009)
15. Rother, C., Kohli, P., Feng, W., Jia, J.: Minimizing sparse higher order energy functions of discrete variables. In: CVPR (2009)
16. Ishikawa, H.: Higher-order clique reduction in binary graph cut. In: CVPR (2009)
17. Lempitsky, V., Rother, C., Blake, A.: Logcut - efficient graph cut optimization for markov random fields. In: ICCV (2007)
18. Lempitsky, V., Rother, C., Roth, S., Blake, A.: Fusion moves for markov random field optimization. PAMI 32 (2010)
19. Kolmogorov, V., Zabih, R.: What energy functions can be minimized via graph cuts? PAMI 26 (2004)
20. Hammer, P.L., Hansen, P., Simeone, B.: Roof duality, complementation and persistency in quadratic 0-1 optimization. Mathematical Programming 28 (1984)
21. Kolmogorov, V., Rother, C.: Minimizing nonsubmodular functions with graph cuts-a review. PAMI 29 (2007)
22. Woodford, O.J., Torr, P.H.S., Reid, I.D., Fitzgibbon, A.W.: Global stereo reconstruction under second order smoothness priors. In: CVPR (2008)
23. Kwon, D., Lee, K.J., Yun, I.D., Lee, S.U.: Nonrigid image registration using dynamic higher-order mrf model. In: Forsyth, D., Torr, P., Zisserman, A. (eds.) ECCV 2008, Part I. LNCS, vol. 5302, pp. 373–386. Springer, Heidelberg (2008)
24. Kohli, P., Ladicky, L., Torr, P.H.: Robust higher order potentials for enforcing label consistency. IJCV 82 (2009)
25. Ju, S.X., Black, M.J., Jepson, A.D.: Skin and bones: Multi-layer, locally affine, optical flow and regularization with transparency. In: CVPR (1996)
26. Béréziat, D.: Object based optical flow estimation with an affine prior model. In: ICPR (2000)
27. Nir, T., Bruckstein, A.M., Kimmel, R.: Over-parameterized variational optical flow. IJCV 76 (2008)
28. Dyn, N., Levin, D., Rippa, S.: Data dependent triangulations for piecewise linear interpolation. IMA Journal of Numerical Analysis 10 (1990)
29. Chew, L.P.: Constrained delaunay triangulations. In: Annual Symposium on Computational Geometry (SCG). ACM, New York (1987)
30. Hoiem, D., Stein, A.N., Efros, A.A., Hebert, M.: Recovering occlusion boundaries from a single image. In: ICCV (2007)
31. Douglas, D., Peucker, T.: Algorithms for the reduction of the number of points required to represent a digitized line or its caricature. The Canadian Cartographer 10 (1973)
32. Cremers, D., Soatto, S.: Motion competition: A variational approach to piecewise parametric motion segmentation. IJCV 62 (2005)
33. Min, C., Medioni, G.: Motion segmentation by spatiotemporal smoothness using 5d tensor voting. In: CVPR Workshop (2006)
34. Rother, C., Kolmogorov, V., Lempitsky, V., Szummer, M.: Optimizing binary mrfs via extended roof duality. In: CVPR (2007)

Articulation-Invariant Representation of Non-planar Shapes

Raghuraman Gopalan, Pavan Turaga, and Rama Chellappa

Dept. of ECE, University of Maryland, College Park, MD 20742 USA
{raghuram,pturaga,rama}@umiacs.umd.edu

Abstract. *Given a set of points corresponding to a 2D projection of a non-planar shape, we would like to obtain a representation invariant to articulations (under no self-occlusions). It is a challenging problem since we need to account for the changes in 2D shape due to 3D articulations, viewpoint variations, as well as the varying effects of imaging process on different regions of the shape due to its non-planarity. By modeling an articulating shape as a combination of approximate convex parts connected by non-convex junctions, we propose to preserve distances between a pair of points by (i) estimating the parts of the shape through approximate convex decomposition, by introducing a robust measure of convexity and (ii) performing part-wise affine normalization by assuming a weak perspective camera model, and then relating the points using the inner distance which is insensitive to planar articulations. We demonstrate the effectiveness of our representation on a dataset with non-planar articulations, and on standard shape retrieval datasets like MPEG-7.*

Keywords: Shape representation, articulations, convex decomposition.

1 Introduction

Understanding objects undergoing articulations is of fundamental importance in computer vision. For instance, human actions and hand movements are some common articulations we encounter in daily life, and it is henceforth interesting to know how different 'points' or 'regions' of such objects transform under these conditions. This is also useful for vision applications like, inferring the pose of an object, effective modeling of activities using the transformation of parts, and for human computer interaction in general.

Representation and matching of articulating shapes is a well-studied problem, and the existing approaches can be classified into two main categories namely, those based on appearance-related cues of the object (eg. [1]), and those using shape information which can be contours or silhouettes or voxel-sets (eg. [2–4]). Our work corresponds to the latter category, wherein we represent an object by a set of points constituting its silhouette. Although there are lots of work ([5–7]) on deformation invariant 'matching' of shapes, there is relatively less work on 'representing' a shape invariant to articulations, eg. [2, 8, 9]. Among the above-mentioned efforts only [2] deals with 2D shapes and their representation

K. Daniilidis, P. Maragos, N. Paragios (Eds.): ECCV 2010, Part III, LNCS 6313, pp. 286–299, 2010.

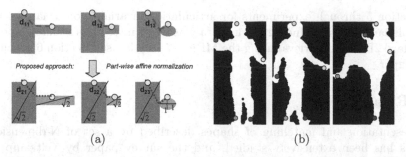

(a)   (b)

Fig. 1. (a): Comparing distances across 2D projections of non-planar articulating shapes. (L-R) Shape 1 and 2 belong to the same 3D object, whereas shape 3 is from a different one. For a pair of points with same spatial configuration (yellow dots), Top: Inner distance [2] yields $\|d_{11} - d_{12}\|_2 > \|d_{12} - d_{13}\|_2$, whereas our method (bottom) gives $\|d_{21} - d_{22}\|_2 < \|d_{22} - d_{23}\|_2$. (b) Keypoints with similar shape description obtained from our method. Points were picked in the first frame, and their 'nearest neighbors' are displayed in other two frames. No holistic shape matching was done, emphasizing the importance of a shape representation. *(All figures are best viewed in color).*

mainly addresses planar articulations. However, most articulating shapes, such as a human, are non-planar in nature and there has been very little effort focusing on this problem. This leads us to the question we are addressing in this work.

Given a set of points corresponding to a 2D projection of an articulating shape, how to derive a representation that is invariant/insensitive to articulations, when there is no self-occlusion? An example where this question is relevant is shown in Figure 1, along with results from our proposed shape representation. Such situations also arise when multiple cameras are observing a scene containing non-planar objects, where the projection of a particular 'region' of an object will depend on its relative orientation with the cameras. Accommodating for such variations, in addition to articulations (for which, each object can have different degrees of freedom) makes this a very hard problem.

Contributions: Under the assumption that a 3D articulating object can be expressed as a combination of rigid convex parts connected by non-rigid junctions that are highly non-convex, and there exists a set of viewpoints producing 2D shapes with all parts of the object visible; given one such instance of the 2D shape, we are interested in obtaining an invariant representation across articulations and view changes. We address this problem by,

1. Finding the parts of a 2D articulating shape through approximate convex decomposition, by introducing a robust area-based measure of convexity.
2. Performing part-wise affine normalization to compensate for imaging effects, under a weak perspective camera model, and relating the points using inner distance to achieve articulation invariance (upto a data-dependent error).

After reviewing the prior work in Section 2, we formally define the problem in Section 3. We then present our proposed method in Section 4 by providing detailed analysis on the model assumptions. We evaluate our shape descriptor in Section 5 through experiments for articulation invariance on a dataset with non-planar shapes, including both intra-class and inter-class studies, and for standard 2D shape retrieval using the MPEG-7 [10] dataset. Section 6 concludes the paper.

2   Related Work

Representation and matching of shapes described by a set of N-dimensional points has been extensively studied, and the survey paper by Veltkamp and Hagedoorn [11] provides a good overview of the early approaches. More recently, there have been advances in matching two non-rigid shapes across deformations. For instance, Felzenszwalb and Schwartz [6] used a hierarchical representation of the shape boundary in an elastic matching framework for comparing a pair of shapes. Yang et al [12] used a locally constrained diffusion process to relate the influence of other shapes in measuring similarity between a pair of shapes. Registering non-rigidly deforming shapes has also been addressed by [7] and [13]. Mateus et al [4] studied the problem of articulation invariant matching of shapes represented as voxel-sets, by reducing the problem into a maximal subgraph isomorphism. There are also efforts, for instance by Bronstein et al [14], on explaining partial similarity between the shapes.

Though there has been considerable progress in defining shape similarity metrics and matching algorithms, finding representations invariant to a class of nonrigid transformations has not been addressed extensively. This is critical for shape analysis because, rather than spending more efforts in matching, we stand to gain if the representation by itself has certain desirable properties. Some works towards this end are as follows. Elad and Kimmel [8] construct a bending invariant signature for isometric surfaces by forming an embedding of the surface that approximates geodesic distances by Euclidean distances. Rustamov [9] came up with a deformation invariant representation of surfaces by using eigenfunctions of the Laplace-Beltrami operator. However in this work, we are specifically interested in articulation insensitive representation of 3D shapes with the knowledge of its 2D projection alone. A key paper that addresses this particular problem is that of Ling and Jacobs [2]. They propose the inner distance, which is the length of the shortest path between a pair of points interior to the shape boundary, as an invariant descriptor of articulations when restricted to a set of translations and rotations of object parts. But such an assumption is applicable only for planar shapes, or when the shape is viewed using an ideal orthographic camera. Since neither of these two settings hold true in most real world scenarios, representing a 2D projection of a 3D non-planar shape invariant to articulations becomes an important problem, which we formalize in the following section.

3   Problem Formulation

An articulating shape $X \subset \mathbb{R}^3$ containing n parts, $\{P_i\}_{i=1}^n$, together with a set of Q junctions, can be written as $X = \{\bigcup_{i=1}^n P_i\} \bigcup \{\bigcup_{i \neq j, \ 1 \leq i,j \leq n} Q_{ij}\}$, where

1. $\forall i, 1 \leq i \leq n$, $P_i \subset \mathbb{R}^3$ is connected and closed, and $P_i \bigcap P_j = \phi, \forall i \neq j, 1 \leq i, j \leq n$
2. $\forall i \neq j, 1 \leq i, j \leq n, Q_{ij} \subset \mathbb{R}^3$, connected and closed, is the junction between P_i and P_j. If there is no junction between P_i and P_j, then $Q_{ij} = \phi$. Otherwise, $Q_{ij} \bigcap P_i \neq \phi$, $Q_{ij} \bigcap P_j \neq \phi$. Further, the volume of Q_{ij} is assumed to be small when compared to that of $P_i{}^1$.

Let $A(.)$ be the set of articulations of X, wherein $A(P_i) \in E(3)$ belong to the rigid 3D Euclidean group, and $A(Q_{ij})$ belong to any non-rigid deformation. Further, let V be the set of viewpoints, and $M \subset (A \times V)$ denote the set of conditions such that the 2D projection of X, say $S \subset \mathbb{R}^2$, has all parts visible; i.e. $S_k = \{\bigcup_{i=1}^{n} p_{ik}\} \bigcup \{\bigcup_{i \neq j, \ 1 \leq i, j \leq n} q_{ijk}\}, \forall k = 1 \ to \ M$, where $p_{ik} \subset \mathbb{R}^2$ and $q_{ijk} \subset \mathbb{R}^2$ are the corresponding 2D projections of P_i and Q_{ij} respectively. The problem we are interested now is, given an instance of S, say S_1, how to obtain a representation $\tilde{R}(.)$ such that,

$$\tilde{R}(S_1) = \tilde{R}(S_k), \ \forall k = 1 \ to \ M \tag{1}$$

4   Proposed Method

In pursuit of (1), we make the following assumptions. (i) X has approximate convex parts P_i that are piece-wise planar, and (ii) X is imaged using a weak-perspective (scaled orthographic) camera to produce $\{S_k\}_{k=1}^{M}$. Let each S_k be represented by a set of t points $\{u_{lk}\}_{l=1}^{t}$. Given two such points $u_{1k}, u_{2k} \in S_k$, we would now like to obtain a distance D such that

$$D(u_{1k}, u_{2k}) = c, \forall k = 1 \ to \ M \tag{2}$$

where c is a constant, using which a representation $\tilde{R}(.)$ satisfying (1) can be obtained. Now to preserve distances D across non-planar articulations, we need to account for (atleast) two sources of variations. First, we compensate for changes in the 2D shape S due to changes in viewpoint V and due to the varying effect of imaging process on different regions of a non-planar X, by performing separate affine normalization to each part $p_{ik} \in S_k$. Let T denote the transformation that maps each part p_{ik} to p'_{ik}. Inherently, every point $u_{lk} \in S_k$ gets transformed as $T(u_{lk}) \rightarrow u'_{lk}$, where the transformation parameters depend on the part to which each point belongs. Next, to account for changes in S_k due to articulations A, we relate the two points $u'_{1k}, u'_{2k} \in S_k$ using the inner distance ID [2] which is unchanged under planar articulations. Essentially, we can write (2) as

$$D(u_{1k}, u_{2k}) = ID(u'_{1k}, u'_{2k}), \forall k = 1 \ to \ M \tag{3}$$

which, ideally, can be used to construct $\tilde{R}$ (1). But, in general,

$$D(u_{1k}, u_{2k}) = c + \epsilon_k, \forall k = 1 \ to \ M \tag{4}$$

---

[1] A glossary of symbols used in this paper is given in the supplementary material.

where,

$$\epsilon_k = \epsilon_{P_k} + \epsilon_{D_k} + \epsilon_{S_k}, \forall k = 1 \ to \ M \tag{5}$$

is an error that depends on the data S_k. ϵ_{P_k} arises due to the weak perspective approximation of a real-world full-perspective camera. ϵ_{D_k} denotes the error in the inner distance when the path between two points, u_{1k} and u_{2k}, crosses the junctions $q_{ijk} \in S_k$; this happens because the shape change of q_{ijk}, caused by an arbitrary deformation of the 3D junction Q_{ij}, can not be approximated by an affine normalization. But this error is generally negligible since the junctions q_{ijk} are smaller than the parts p_{ik}. ϵ_{S_k} is caused due to changes in the shape of a part p_{ik}, while imaging its original piece-wise planar 3D part P_i that has different shapes across its planes. An illustration is given in Figure 2(a).

Under these assumptions, we propose the following method to solve for (1). By modeling an articulating shape $S \subset \mathbb{R}^2$ as a combination of approximate convex parts p_i connected by non-convex junctions q_{ij}, we

1. Determine the parts of the shape by performing approximate convex decomposition with a robust measure of convexity.
2. Affine normalize the parts, and relate the points in the shape using inner distance to build a shape context descriptor.

We provide the details in the following sub-sections.

4.1   Approximate Convex Decomposition

Convexity has been used as a natural cue to identify 'parts' of an object [15]. An illustration is given in Figure 2(b), where the object consists of two approximate convex parts p_1 and p_2, connected by a non-convex junction q_{12}. Since exact convex decomposition is NP-hard for shapes with holes [16], there are many approximate solutions proposed in the literature (eg. [17]). An important component of this problem is a well-defined measure of convexity for which there are two broad categories of approaches namely, contour-based and area-based. Each has its own merits and limitations, and there are works addressing such issues (eg. [18–20]). But the fundamental problems, that of the intolerance of contour-based measures to small boundary deformations, and the insensitivity of area-based measures to deep (but thin) protrusions of the boundary, have not been addressed satisfactorily.

4.1.1   A New Area-Based Measure of Convexity

In this work, we focus on the problem with existing area-based measures. We start from the basic definition of convexity. Given t points constituting an N-dimensional shape S', the shape is said to be convex if the set of lines connecting all pairs of points lie completely within S'. This definition, in itself, has been used for convex decompositions with considerable success (eg. [21, 22]). What we are interested here is to see if a robust measure of convexity can be built upon it.

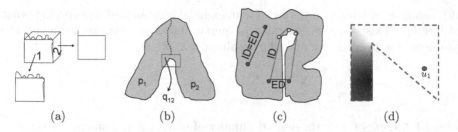

(a)   (b)   (c)   (d)

Fig. 2. (a): Error ϵ_{S_k} (5) illustrated by 2D projections, p_{ik}, with the camera parallel to planes 1 and 2. (b): Our model of an articulating object with two approximate convex parts p_1 and p_2, connected by a non-convex junction q_{12}. (c): Variation between ID and ED for a pair of points (green dots). $ID - ED$ is large for non-convex points, with the yellow dots indicating junction regions. (d): Information conveyed by (6) on the potential convex neighbors of u_l. The shape is enclosed by dashed red line. Color of other points u_m is given by $\frac{ED(u_l, u_m)}{ID(u_l, u_m)}$, with value 1 (white) for convex neighbors and tending towards 0 (black) for non-convex neighbors.

We make the following observation. Given two points $u_1, u_2 \in S'$, let $ID(u_1, u_2)$ denote the inner distance between them, and $ED(u_1, u_2)$ denote their Euclidean distance. For a convex S', $ID = ED$ for any given pair of points, whereas for a non-convex S' this is not the case, as shown in Figure 2(c). We can see that, unlike the Euclidean distance, the inner distance inherently captures the shape's boundary and hence is sensitive to deep protrusions along it. Whereas, the difference between ID and ED is not much for minor boundary deformations. Using this property, which significantly alleviates the core issue of the existing area-based convexity measures, we propose a new measure of convexity as follows

$$1 - \frac{1}{(t^2 - t)} \sum_{u_l \in S'} \sum_{u_m \in S', m \neq l} \left(1 - \frac{ED(u_l, u_m)}{ID(u_l, u_m)}\right) \tag{6}$$

where t is the number of points in S', and $1 \leq l, m \leq t$. For a perfectly convex object, this measure will have a value one. We evaluate the robustness of this measure in Section 5.3, and discuss how it conforms to the properties that a convexity measure should satisfy in the supplementary material.

4.1.2   An Algorithm to Obtain Approximate Convex Segments
We now use (6) to segment an articulating shape S into approximate convex regions p_i. We first study if $\frac{ED(u_1, u_2)}{ID(u_1, u_2)}$, in addition to saying whether points u_1 and u_2 belong to a convex region, can shed more information on the potential 'convex neighbors' of a particular point u_1. We proceed by considering a 2D shape S'_1 having two convex regions, shown in Figure 2(d), and measure how $\frac{ED(u_1, .)}{ID(u_1, .)}$ from u_1 to all other $t - 1$ points in S'_1 vary. We observe that for those points lying in the same convex region as u_1 this term has a value one, whereas its value decreases for points that lie deeper into the other convex region. Hence

(6) also gives a sense of ordering of convex neighbors around any specific point of interest. This is a very desirable property. Based on this, we formulate the problem of segmenting an articulating shape $S \subset \mathbb{R}^2$ as,

$$\min_{n, p_i} \sum_{i=1}^{n} \sum_{u_l \in p_i} \sum_{u_m \in p_i, u_l \neq u_m} \left(1 - \frac{ED(u_l, u_m)}{ID(u_l, u_m)}\right) \tag{7}$$

where $1 \leq l, m \leq t$, n is the desired number of convex parts, and p_i are the corresponding convex regions. We then obtain approximate convex decomposition of S by posing this problem in a Normalized cuts framework [23] and relating all points belonging to S using the information conveyed by (6). The details are provided in Algorithm 1, which is applicable for any N-dimensional shape S'.

Given a set of points t corresponding to an N-dimensional articulating shape S' (which can be a contour or silhouette or voxel-sets, for instance), an estimate $n(> 0)$ of the number of convex parts, and the desired convexity (a number between 0 and 1) for the parts,

(i) Connect every pair of points $(u_l, u_m) \in S'$ with the following edge weight

$$w_{u_l u_m} = exp^{-(\#junctions(u_l, u_m))} * exp^{\dfrac{-\|1 - \frac{ED(u_l, u_m)}{ID(u_l, u_m)}\|_2^2}{\sigma_1^2}} *$$

$$\begin{cases} exp^{\dfrac{-\|ID(u_l, u_m)\|_2^2}{\sigma_X^2}} & if \| ID(u_l, u_m) - ED(u_l, u_m) \|_2 \leq T_2 \\ 0 \ otherwise \end{cases} \tag{8}$$

(ii) Do: Number of segments from $n - \eta$ to $n + \eta$ (to account for possible errors in junction estimates, see Figure 3(a) for example)
(iii) Perform segmentation using Normalized cuts [23]
(iv) Until: The resulting segments satisfy the desired convexity (6).

Algorithm 1. Algorithm for segmenting an N-dimensional shape into approximate convex parts

Estimate of the Number of Parts: We automatically determine the potential number of parts n using the information contained in (6). We do this by identifying junctions $q_{ij}, i \neq j, 1 \leq i, j \leq n$, which are the regions of high non-convexity. For those pair of points with $ID \neq ED$, we analyze the shortest path SP using which their inner distance is computed. This SP is a collection of line segments, and its intermediate vertice(s) represent points, which by the definition of inner distance [2], bridge two potentially non-convex regions. This is illustrated in Figure 2(c) (see the yellow dots). We then spatially cluster all such points using a sliding window along the contour, since there can be many points around the same junction. Let the total number of detected junctions be n_j. The initial estimate of the number of parts n is then obtained by $n = n_j + 1$, since a junction should connect at least two parts.

With this knowledge, we define the edge weight between a pair of points in (8) where the first two terms collectively convey how possibly can two points lie in the same convex region, and the third term denotes their spatial proximity. T_2, σ_I and σ_X are thresholds chosen experimentally. T_2 governs when two nodes need to be connected, and is picked as the mean of $ID(u_l, u_m) - ED(u_l, u_m)$, $1 \leq l, m \leq t$. σ_I and σ_X are both set a value of 5. We chose $\eta = 2$ and desired convexity of 0.85 in all our experiments. Sample segmentation results of our algorithm on silhouettes and voxel data are given in Figure 3.

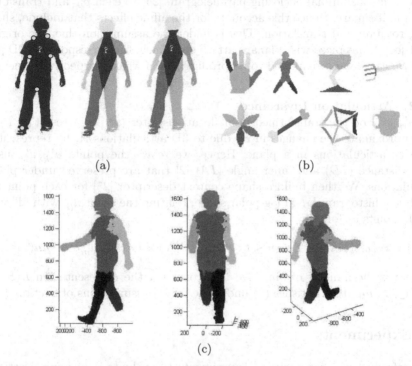

Fig. 3. (a): Result of the segmentation algorithm (Section 4.1.2) on a 2D shape. Junction detection (yellow dots), initial segmentation, followed by the refined segmentation using the desired convexity (=0.85 here) as the user input. (b) Results on shapes from Brown [5] (Top row) and MPEG-7 [10] (Bottom row) datasets. (c): Segmenting a shape represented by voxel-sets using the same algorithm

4.2 Shape Representation Invariant to Non-planar Articulations

We now have an approximate convex decomposition of the articulating shape $S \subset \mathbb{R}^2$, i.e. $S = \{\bigcup_{i=1}^{n} p_i\} \bigcup \{\bigcup_{i \neq j, \ 1 \leq i, j \leq n} q_{ij}\}$. Given a set of M 2D projections of the 3D articulating shape X, $\{S_k\}_{k=1}^{M}$ with all n parts visible, we want to find a representation $\tilde{R}$ that satisfies (1). As before, let $\{u_{lk}\}_{l=1}^{t}$ be the number of points constituting each S_k. Let $u_{1k}, u_{2k} \in S_k$, be two such points. We now compute a distance $D(u_{1k}, u_{2k})$ satisfying (2) using a two step process,

4.2.1 Affine Normalization

To compensate for the change in shape of S_k due to the varying effect of the imaging process on different parts of the non-planar X and due to the changes in viewpoint V, we first perform part-wise affine normalization. This essentially amounts to finding a transformation T such that,

$$T(p_{ik}) \rightarrow p'_{ik} \tag{9}$$

where T fits a minimal enclosing parallelogram [24] to each p_{ik} and transforms it to a unit square. Hence this accounts for the affine effects that include, shear, scale, rotation and translation. This is under the assumption that the original 3D object X has piece-wise planar parts P_i for which, the corresponding 2D part $p_{ik} \in S_k$ can be approximated to be produced by a weak perspective camera.

4.2.2 Articulation Invariance

Let u'_{1k}, u'_{2k} be the transformed point locations after (9). As a result of T, we can approximate the changes in S_k due to 3D articulations A, by representing them as articulations in a plane. Hence, we relate the points u'_{1k}, u'_{2k} using inner distance (ID) and inner angle (IA) [2] that are preserved under planar articulations. We then build a shape context descriptor [25] for each point u'_{lk}, which is a histogram h_{lk} in log-polar space, relating the point u'_{lk} with all other $(t-1)$ points as follows

$$h_{lk}(z) = \#\{u'_{mk}, m \neq l, 1 \leq m \leq t : ID(u'_{lk}, u'_{mk}) \times IA(u'_{lk}, u'_{mk}) \in bin(z)\} \tag{10}$$

where z is the number of bins. We now construct the representation $\tilde{R}(S_k) = [h_{1k} \ h_{2k} \ . . \ h_{tk}]$ that satisfies (1) under the model assumptions of Section 4.

5   Experiments

We performed two categories of experiments to evaluate our shape descriptor (10). The first category measures its insensitivity to articulations of non-planar shapes on an internally collected dataset[2], since there is no standard dataset for this problem. Whereas, the next category evaluates its performance on 2D shape retrieval tasks on the benchmark MPEG-7 [10] dataset. We then validated the robustness of our convexity measure (6) on the dataset of Rahtu et al [20].

For all these experiments, given a shape $S \subset \mathbb{R}^2$, we model it as $S = \{\bigcup_{i=1}^{n} p_i\} \bigcup \{\bigcup_{i \neq j, \ 1 \leq i,j \leq n} q_{ij}\}$. We then sample 100 points along its contour, by enforcing equal number of points to be sampled uniformly from each affine normalized part p'_i. Then to compute the histogram (10), we used 12 distance bins and 5 angular bins, thereby resulting in total number of bins $z = 60$. The whole process, for a single shape, takes about 5 seconds on a standard 2GHz processor.

---

[2] The dataset is available at
www.umiacs.umd.edu/~raghuram/Datasets/NonPlanarArt.zip

5.1   Non-planar Articulations

We did two experiments, one to measure the variations in (10) across intra-class articulations, and the other to recognize five different articulating objects.

5.1.1   Intra-class Articulations

We collected data of an articulating human, observed from four cameras, with the hands undergoing significant out-of-plane motion. The silhouettes, shown in Figure 4, were obtained by performing background subtraction, where the parts p_i of the shape (from Section 4.1) along with some points having similar representation (10) are identified by color-codes.

(a)   (b)

Fig. 4. Dataset with non-planar articulations: Intra-class variations of an articulating human. (a): A set of actions observed from a single camera. (b): A same action observed from 4 cameras. The regions obtained from segmentation (Section 4.1) along with the points having similar shape representation (Section 4.2), are color-coded

We divided the dataset of around 1000 silhouettes, into an unoccluded part of about 150 silhouettes (where there is no self-occlusion of the human) and an occluded part, and compared our representation (10) with the inner distance shape context (IDSC) [2] that is insensitive to articulations when the shape is planar. We chose to compare with this method since, it addresses articulation invariance in 2D shapes from the 'representation' aspect rather than matching. We used dynamic programming to obtain point correspondences between two shapes. Given in Table 1 are the mean and standard deviations of the difference (in L_2 sense) of the descriptions (10) of the matched points. We do this for every pair of shapes in our dataset, with and without occlusion.

It can be seen that the matching cost for our descriptor is significantly less for the unoccluded pair of shapes, and is noticeably lower than [2] for the occluded pair too. This, in a way, signifies that our model assumptions (Section 4) is a good approximation to the problem of representing a shape invariant to non-planar articulations (Section 3).

5.1.2   Inter-class Variations

We now analyze how our representation (10) can be used for recognition across the 2D shapes produced by different 3D non-planar articulating objects. We collected silhouettes of five different objects, a human and four robots, performing articulations observed from different viewpoints. There were ten instances per

Table 1. Shape matching costs on the dataset with an articulating human. The cost for our descriptor is around one-tenth of that of [2].

Method	Matching cost (mean ± standard deviation)	
	Without occlusion	With occlusion
IDSC [2]	0.48 ± 0.21	3.45 ± 1.63
Ours	0.025 ± 0.0012	0.46 ± 0.11

subject, with significant occlusion, leading to fifty shapes in total as shown in Figure 5. We compared our algorithm with IDSC in both a leave-one-out recognition setting by computing the Top-1 recognition rate, and also in a validation setting using the Bulls-eye test that counts how many of the 10 possible correct matches are present in the top 20 nearest shapes (for each of the 50 shapes). We report the results in Table 2. It can be seen that our descriptor, in addition to handling non-planar articulations, can distinguish different shapes. This validates the main motivation behind our work (Figure 1). The errors in recognition are mostly due to occlusions, which our model can not account for. It is an interesting future work to see how to relax our assumptions to address the more general problem stated in Section 3.

Fig. 5. Dataset of non-planar articulations of different subjects. Four robots and human, with a total of 50 shapes.

Table 2. Recognition across inter-class non-planar articulations

Method	Top-1 Recognition rate (in %)	BullsEye score (in %)
IDSC [2]	58	39.4
Ours	80	63.8

5.2   Shape Retrieval

We then evaluated our descriptor for 2D shape retrieval[3] tasks to study its ability in handling general shape deformations, in addition to pure articulations. We used the benchmark MPEG-7 dataset [10], which contains 70 different shape classes with 20 instances per class. This is a challenging dataset with significant intra-class shape deformations. Some example shapes are given in Figure 3(b). The recognition rate is calculated using the Bulls-Eye test by finding the top 40 closest matches for each test shape, and computing how many of the twenty possible correct matches are present in it. The retrieval rates are given in Table 3, and we compare with the most recent and other representative methods.

Almost all shapes in this dataset are planar. So the least we would expect is to perform as well as [2], since but for handling non-planar articulations our representation resembles IDSC. The improvement using our representation is mainly due to cases where the shapes have distinct part structure, and when the variations in the parts are different. A part-driven, holistic shape descriptor can capture such variations better. It is interesting to see that we perform better than methods like [12, 26] that use sophisticated matching methods by seeing how different shapes in the dataset influence the matching cost of a pair of shapes. Hence through this study, we would like to highlight the importance of a good underlying shape representation.

Table 3. Retrieval results on MPEG-7 dataset [10]

Algorithm	BullsEye score (in %)
SC+TPS [25]	76.51
Generative models [27]	80.03
IDSC [2]	85.40
Shape-tree [6]	87.70
Label Propagation [26]	91.00
Locally constrained diffusion [12]	93.32
Ours	93.67

5.3   Experiment on the Convexity Measure

Finally, we performed an experiment to evaluate our convexity measure (6) by comparing it with the recent work by Rahtu et al [20]. Since there is no standard dataset for this task, we provide results on their dataset in Figure 6. We make two observations. 1) For similar shapes (text in red and blue), the variation in our convexity measure is much smaller than that of [20]. This reinforces the insensitivity of our measure to intra-class variations of the shape, which is very desirable. 2) It can also been seen that our convexity measure is very sensitive to lengthy disconnected parts (text in green). This is mainly because, we compute pair-wise variations in ID and ED for all points in the shape, which will be high in such cases. These results, intuitively, are more meaningful than that of [20].

---

[3] Evaluations on the Brown dataset [5] and some illustrations on incorrect retrievals are provided in the supplementary material.

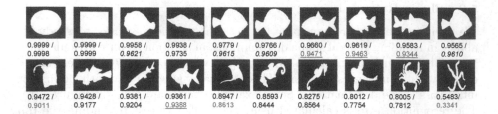

Fig. 6. Performance of our convexity measure on the dataset of [20]. Given at bottom of each shape are the convexity measures of [20] followed by ours (6). Our measure is insensitive to intra-class shape variations (text in red and *blue*), and is more sensitive when a part of the shape is disconnected from other parts (text in **green**).

6   Conclusion

We proposed a method to represent a 2D projection of a non-planar shape invariant to articulations, when there is no occlusion. By assuming a weak perspective camera model, we showed that a part-wise affine normalization can help preserve distances between points, upto a data-dependent error. We then studied its utility through experiments for recognition across non-planar articulations, and for general shape retrieval. It is interesting to see how our assumptions can be relaxed to address this problem in a more general setting.

Acknowledgements. This work was supported by a MURI Grant N00014-08-1-0638 from the Office of Naval Research. R.G. would like to thank Dr. Ashok Veeraraghavan for motivating the problem, and Kaushik Mitra for helpful discussions.

References

1. Zhang, J., Collins, R., Liu, Y.: Representation and Matching of Articulated Shapes. In: CVPR, pp. 342–349 (2004)
2. Ling, H., Jacobs, D.: Shape classification using the inner-distance. IEEE TPAMI 29, 286–299 (2007)
3. Bronstein, A.M., Bronstein, M.M., Bruckstein, A.M., Kimmel, R.: Matching two-dimensional articulated shapes using generalized multidimensional scaling. In: AMDO, pp. 48–57 (2006)
4. Mateus, D., Horaud, R.P., Knossow, D., Cuzzolin, F., Boyer, E.: Articulated shape matching using Laplacian eigenfunctions and unsupervised point registration. In: CVPR, pp. 1–8 (2008)
5. Sebastian, T.B., Klein, P.N., Kimia, B.B.: Recognition of Shapes by Editing Their Shock Graphs. IEEE TPAMI 26, 550–571 (2004)
6. Felzenszwalb, P.F., Schwartz, J.D.: Hierarchical matching of deformable shapes. In: CVPR, pp. 1–8 (2007)
7. Schoenemann, T., Cremers, D.: Matching non-rigidly deformable shapes across images: A globally optimal solution. In: CVPR, pp. 1–6 (2008)

8. Elad, A., Kimmel, R.: On bending invariant signatures for surfaces. IEEE TPAMI 25, 1285–1295 (2003)
9. Rustamov, R.M.: Laplace-Beltrami eigenfunctions for deformation invariant shape representation. In: Eurographics Symposium on Geometry Processing, pp. 225–233 (2007)
10. Latecki, L.J., Lakämper, R., Eckhardt, T.: Shape descriptors for non-rigid shapes with a single closed contour. In: CVPR, pp. 424–429 (2000)
11. Veltkamp, R.C., Hagedoorn, M.: State of the Art in Shape Matching. In: Principles of Visual Information Retrieval, pp. 87–119 (2001)
12. Yang, X., Köknar-Tezel, S., Latecki, L.J.: Locally constrained diffusion process on locally densified distance spaces with applications to shape retrieval. In: CVPR, pp. 357–364 (2009)
13. Wang, J., Chan, K.L.: Shape evolution for rigid and nonrigid shape registration and recovery. In: CVPR, pp. 164–171 (2009)
14. Bronstein, A.M., Bronstein, M.M., Bruckstein, A.M., Kimmel, R.: Partial similarity of objects, or how to compare a centaur to a horse. IJCV 84, 163–183 (2009)
15. Hoffman, D.D., Richards, W.: Parts of recognition. Cognition 18, 65–96 (1984)
16. Lingas, A.: The power of non-rectilinear holes. In: Colloquim on Automata, Languages and Programming, pp. 369–383 (1982)
17. Lien, J.M., Amato, N.M.: Approximate convex decomposition of polygons. In: Computational Geometry: Theory and Applications, vol. 35, pp. 100–123 (2006)
18. Rosin, P.L.: Shape partitioning by convexity. IEEE Transactions on Systems, Man, and Cybernetics, Part A 30, 202–210 (2000)
19. Zunic, J., Rosin, P.L.: A new convexity measure for polygons. IEEE TPAMI 26, 923–934 (2004)
20. Rahtu, E., Salo, M., Heikkila, J.: A new convexity measure based on a probabilistic interpretation of images. IEEE TPAMI 28, 1501–1512 (2006)
21. Shapiro, L.G., Haralick, R.M.: Decomposition of two-dimensional shapes by graph-theoretic clustering. IEEE TPAMI 1, 10–20 (1979)
22. Walker, L.L., Malik, J.: Can convexity explain how humans segment objects into parts? Journal of Vision 3, 503 (2003)
23. Shi, J., Malik, J.: Normalized cuts and image segmentation. IEEE TPAMI 22, 888–905 (2000)
24. Schwarz, C., Teich, J., Vainshtein, A., Welzl, E., Evans, B.L.: Minimal enclosing parallelogram with application. In: Symposium on Computational Geometry, pp. 434–435 (1995)
25. Belongie, S., Malik, J., Puzicha, J.: Shape matching and object recognition using shape contexts. IEEE TPAMI 24, 509–522 (2002)
26. Yang, X., Bai, X., Latecki, L.J., Tu, Z.: Improving shape retrieval by learning graph transduction. In: Forsyth, D., Torr, P., Zisserman, A. (eds.) ECCV 2008, Part IV. LNCS, vol. 5305, pp. 788–801. Springer, Heidelberg (2008)
27. Tu, Z., Yuille, A.L.: Shape matching and recognition-using generative models and informative features. In: Pajdla, T., Matas, J(G.) (eds.) ECCV 2004. LNCS, vol. 3023, pp. 195–209. Springer, Heidelberg (2004)

Inferring 3D Shapes and Deformations from Single Views

Yu Chen, Tae-Kyun Kim, and Roberto Cipolla

Department of Engineering, University of Cambridge
Trumpington Street, Cambridge CB2 1PZ, United Kingdom
{yc301,tkk22,rc10001}@cam.ac.uk

Abstract. In this paper we propose a probabilistic framework that models shape variations and infers dense and detailed 3D shapes from a single silhouette. We model two types of shape variations, the object phenotype variation and its pose variation using two independent Gaussian Process Latent Variable Models (GPLVMs) respectively. The proposed shape variation models are learnt from 3D samples without prior knowledge about object class, e.g. object parts and skeletons, and are combined to fully span the 3D shape space. A novel probabilistic inference algorithm for 3D shape estimation is proposed by maximum likelihood estimates of the GPLVM latent variables and the camera parameters that best fit generated 3D shapes to given silhouettes. The proposed inference involves a small number of latent variables and it is computationally efficient. Experiments on both human body and shark data demonstrate the efficacy of our new approach.

1 Introduction

3D shape estimation from a single image has wide applications for graphics, surveillance, HCI and 3D object recognition. Single view reconstruction is a highly under-constrained problem and requires prior knowledge on 3D shapes of an object class. Various approaches have been investigated with different constraints. While previous methods for general scenes/object categories find it typically hard to capture complex 3D topology of objects, much of recent study has tackled estimating detailed 3D shapes of specific categories, e.g., human faces [11] and body shapes [12,13,14,15]. In this work, we propose an approach for both synthesizing and reconstructing dense 3D shapes of general object categories under articulations or deformations given a single image.

1.1 Literature Review

Below we give a brief overview of related work for general scenes/object categories and work designed specifically for human body.

Methods for general scene reconstruction have relied on primitive geometrical constraints such as symmetry and yielded a coarse pop-up reconstruction: e.g., Criminisi et al. [17] have used vanishing points and projective geometry

K. Daniilidis, P. Maragos, N. Paragios (Eds.): ECCV 2010, Part III, LNCS 6313, pp. 300–313, 2010.
© Springer-Verlag Berlin Heidelberg 2010

constraints and Hoiem et al. [2] assumed planar/ground-vertical scenes. Prasad et al. [1] have tackled reconstruction of curved objects, requiring user interactions to reduce down complexity of 3D object topology. Saxena et al. [18] have investigated to recover rough depth estimate from image features. Hassner and Basri [19] have similarly inferred depth from image appearance. 3D geometries having similar image appearance to that of a query object from a database served as the shape prior. These view based methods require an exhaustive number of samples. Some efforts have been made for 3D shape reconstruction from 2D sketches or line drawings [20], where man-made objects are represented by transparent edge-vertex graphs. Bayesian reconstruction of Han et al's [3] is limited to polyhedral objects, tree or grass only. An unified method to segment, infer 3D shapes and recognise object categories proposed in [4] is based on a voxel representation for the shape prior model and applied to object categories such as a cup, mug, plate etc, all rather simple and *rigid* objects. Torresani et al.'s [21] have attempted to recover non-rigid 3D object shape as in our work but only up to sparse reconstruction using 2D point tracks. Their work falls into a different topic, structure-from-motion.

More related study to ours is the work for estimation of detailed human body shape [13,14,15]. Human body is an articulated object with a number of joint angles. A fixed or deformable crude model based on skeleton, e.g. a cylinder model has been widely exploited for human body pose estimation and tracking. By fitting the model to images, joint angles and a rough 3D shape estimation are obtained, e.g. [6]. Finer body models, e.g. using volumetric representations [7] or generic deformable models [8] have been used to capture more subtle shape variations. These models, however, consider body parts independently and decouple pose from shape variations, therefore not representing shape variations around joints and pose-dependent shape deformations. Recently, a more detailed human model called SCAPE (Shape Completion and Animation for PEople) has been proposed [12]. SCAPE models 3D shape variations among different human bodies in a canonical pose by Principal Component Analysis (PCA), and different poses, i.e. articulation, by joint angles. The shape transfer from a source body to target bodies is obtained by rigid rotations of the 13 body parts manually defined and the pose-dependent deformations for subtle muscular deformation around joints. Balan et al. [13] have adopted this model for the detailed human body shape estimation from silhouettes and formulated the problem as an optimisation over the SCAPE model parameters. However, the optimisation of the SCAPE model is difficult due to uniform priors placed on a number of parameters (joint angles and eigen-coefficients). Stochastic search in [13] is computationally expensive and has initialisation problems. Sigal et al. [14] have used a regression technique to help in initialising the SCAPE model parameters prior to stochastic search and Guan et al. [15] have incorporated more visual cues, the shading cues and internal edges as well as silhouettes to facilitate fitting the SCAPE model to images. Although these methods have shown detailed shape recovery from a few silhouettes, using strong priors on a human body model, i.e.

Fig. 1. 3D shape recovery (blue meshes) of a human body (left) and a shark (right) under pose change and their shapes in the canonical pose (gray meshes)

manually defined skeleton and body parts, makes it difficult to extend to other, especially, free-form object categories without redesigning the representation.

1.2 Proposed Approach

In this work, we propose a probabilistic generative model for both learning and inferring dense and detailed 3D shapes of a class of nonrigid objects from a single silhouette. In contrast to prior-arts, we learn shape priors under a challenging setting including pose variations and camera viewpoint changes, and we infer more complex and general deformable 3D shapes from a single image (see Fig. 1).

In our probabilistic framework the shape variations of objects are modeled by two separate Gaussian Process Latent Variable Models (GPLVMs) [22], named the *shape* generator and the *pose* generator. The former captures the *phenotype* variation, which refers to the shape variation between objects: tall vs short, fat vs thin, etc, while the latter captures the *pose* variation, which includes articulation or other nonrigid self-deformation. They are learnt directly from 3D samples without prior knowledge about object class. The GPLVM has been successfully applied for human pose estimation by mapping a high-dimensional parameter space, i.e., a number of joint angles, to a low dimensional manifold [9]. In our work, it nonlinearly maps the complex 3D shape data into a low-dimensional manifold, expressing detailed shape variations only by a few latent variables. With both generators, arbitrary 3D shapes can be synthesized through shape transfer [5], as shown in Fig. 2.

We also propose a novel probabilistic inference algorithm for 3D shape estimation from silhouettes. The shape estimate is obtained by maximum-likelihood estimation of the latent variables of the shape and pose generators and camera parameters that best match generated shapes to input silhouettes. Compared to stochastic optimisation over a large parametric space, i.e. joint angles in [7,13,14,15], the proposed inference is computationally efficient as the latent space has a very low dimension. Experiments on articulated human bodies and sharks demonstrate efficacy of the proposed method for reconstructing detailed shapes of general deformable object categories.

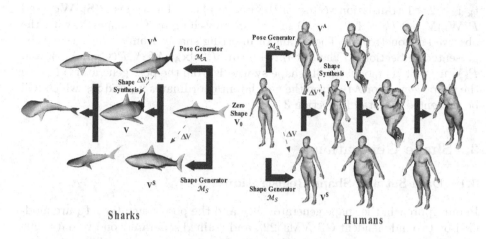

Fig. 2. Synthesizing sharks (left) and human bodies (right) by shape transfer

The rest of this paper is structured as follows. Section 2 presents the proposed probabilistic model; Section 3 explains learning the shape and pose generator and synthesizing new shapes by the shape transfer; Section 4 presents probabilistic inference algorithm; experimental results are shown in Section 5, and discussions conclusions are drawn in Section 6 and 7 respectively.

2   Probabilistic Model for 3D Shape Estimation

The proposed shape estimation is done by: first, synthesizing 3D shapes from a shape generator $\mathcal{M}_\mathcal{S}$ that spans the phenotype variation, and a pose generator $\mathcal{M}_\mathcal{A}$ that spans the pose variation; and then, matching the generated shapes with the input silhouette(s). The proposed graphical model is shown in Fig. 3(a). In the formulation, we consider a more general k-views setting. Let $\mathbf{S_k}$ $(k = 1, 2, \cdots, K)$ be the observed silhouettes in K distinct views, which are given in the form of 2D point sets; $\mathbf{V} = [\mathbf{V_1}, \mathbf{V_2}, \cdots, \mathbf{V_N}]$ is a $3N$-D vector which represents the 3D shape with N sampling points on its surface; and $\mathbf{W_k}$ $(k = 1, 2, \cdots, K)$ is the silhouette of $\mathbf{V}$ in the k-th view. The joint distribution can be written as:

$$P(\{\mathbf{S_k}, \mathbf{W_k}\}_{k=1}^K, \mathbf{V}, \mathbf{u}, \mathbf{v} | \{\gamma_k\}_{k=1}^K, \mathbf{x_A}, \mathbf{x_S}, \mathcal{M}_\mathcal{A}, \mathcal{M}_\mathcal{S})$$

$$= \left(\prod_{k=1}^K P(\mathbf{S_k}|\mathbf{W_k})P(\mathbf{W_k}|\mathbf{V}, \gamma_k) \right) P(\mathbf{u}|\mathbf{x_A}, \mathcal{M}_\mathcal{A})P(\mathbf{v}|\mathbf{x_S}, \mathcal{M}_\mathcal{S})P(\mathbf{V}|\mathbf{u}, \mathbf{v}). \quad (1)$$

In (1), $\mathbf{x_A}$ and $\mathbf{x_S}$ are the latent coordinates of the corresponding models; $\mathbf{u}$ and $\mathbf{v}$ are the respective latent feature vectors generated by $\mathcal{M}_\mathcal{A}$ and $\mathcal{M}_\mathcal{S}$ at $\mathbf{x_A}$ and $\mathbf{x_S}$; $\gamma_k = \{\mathbf{P_k}, \mathbf{t_k}\}$ $(k = 1, 2, \cdots, K)$ are the camera parameters of K views. Here, we assume an affine camera model, $\mathbf{P_k}$ is a 3×2 projection matrix and

$\mathbf{t_k}$ is a 2×1 translation vector on the image plane. The terms $P(\mathbf{S_k}|\mathbf{W_k})$ and $P(\mathbf{W_k}|\mathbf{V}, \gamma_\mathbf{k})$ $(k = 1, 2, \cdots, K)$ model the matching of 3D shapes $\mathbf{V}$ with the observed silhouettes S_k. The details of inferring shapes from silhouettes will be presented in Section 4. The last three terms $P(\mathbf{u}|\mathbf{x_A}, \mathcal{M}_\mathcal{A})$, $P(\mathbf{v}|\mathbf{x_S}, \mathcal{M}_\mathcal{S})$, and $P(\mathbf{V}|\mathbf{u}, \mathbf{v})$ of (1) model the 3D shape synthesis from the pose generator $\mathcal{M}_\mathcal{A}$ and the shape generator $\mathcal{M}_\mathcal{S}$ given the new latent coordinates $\mathbf{x_A}$ and $\mathbf{x_S}$, which will be presented in detail in Section 3.

3 Shape Generation

3.1 Data Set and Shape Registration

In our approach, the shape generator $\mathcal{M}_\mathcal{S}$ and the pose generator $\mathcal{M}_\mathcal{A}$ are modeled by two independent GPLVMs [22], and trained separately on two data sets, named *shape data set* and *pose data set*. The former contains different shape instances in the canonical pose, while the latter is comprised of various poses of a particular shape instance called *zero shape.*

In order to train the generators, we must build up vertex-wise correspondences among training instances so that we can encode the phenotype variation and pose variation in a vectorized form. For the pose data set, the correspondences are straightforward as all the pose data are generated by animating the same 3D instance in our experiment. Such correspondences are, however, not given for the shape data set and shape registration is required.

In our implementation, every instance in the shape data set is registered with the zero shape in the canonical pose. Firstly, we compute hybrid distances as weighted averages of the spatial distance [24] and the χ^2 distance of the 3D shape contexts [23] between every paired sample points of two shapes, and then use Hungarian algorithm to find the minimal cost matching. Secondly, we use the thin-plate spline (TPS) model to recover point-wise displacements between the pair of shapes using the correspondences established. After this, Principal Component Analysis (PCA) is applied to reduce the dimension of input data before training the pose and shape generators. We use the first $m = 30$ principal components as the pose feature $\mathbf{u}$ and shape features $\mathbf{v}$ for training the GPLVMs.

3.2 Synthesizing New Shapes and Poses from GP

Given the new latent coordinates $\mathbf{x_A}$ and $\mathbf{x_S}$, generating the pose vector $\mathbf{u}$ of the zero shape and the shape vector $\mathbf{v}$ of the canonical pose from $\mathcal{M}_\mathcal{A}$ and $\mathcal{M}_\mathcal{S}$ can be formulated as the following Gaussian predictive likelihoods:

$$P(\mathbf{u}|\mathbf{x_A}, \mathcal{M}_\mathcal{A}) = \mathcal{N}\left(\mathbf{u}; \mathbf{k}_\mathbf{U}^\mathbf{T}(\mathbf{x_A})\mathbf{K}_\mathbf{U}^{-1}\mathbf{Y_A}, (k_U(\mathbf{x_A}, \mathbf{x_A}) - \mathbf{k}_\mathbf{U}^\mathbf{T}(\mathbf{x_A})\mathbf{K}_\mathbf{U}^{-1}\mathbf{k_U}(\mathbf{x_A}))\mathbf{I}\right)$$
$$= N\left(\mathbf{u}; \bar{\mathbf{u}}(\mathbf{x_A}), \sigma_A^2(\mathbf{x_A})\mathbf{I}\right) \tag{2}$$

$$P(\mathbf{v}|\mathbf{x_S}, \mathcal{M}_\mathcal{S}) = \mathcal{N}\left(\mathbf{v}; \mathbf{k}_\mathbf{V}^\mathbf{T}(\mathbf{x_S})\mathbf{K}_\mathbf{V}^{-1}\mathbf{Y_S}, (k_V(\mathbf{x_S}, \mathbf{x_S}) - \mathbf{k}_\mathbf{V}^\mathbf{T}(\mathbf{x_S})\mathbf{K}_\mathbf{V}^{-1}\mathbf{k_V}(\mathbf{x_S}))\mathbf{I}\right)$$
$$= N\left(\mathbf{v}; \bar{\mathbf{v}}(\mathbf{x_S}), \sigma_S^2(\mathbf{x_S})\mathbf{I}\right). \tag{3}$$

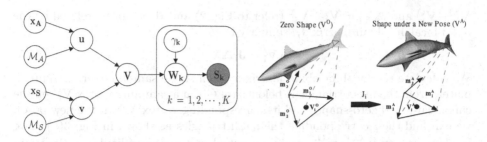

Fig. 3. (a) The graphical model for the 3D shape inference. (b) Transforming local triangle meshes during pose change.

In (2) and (3), $\mathbf{Y_A} = [\mathbf{u_i}]_{i=1}^{N_A}$ and $\mathbf{Y_S} = [\mathbf{v_i}]_{i=1}^{N_S}$ are matrices which contain N_A and N_S training instances in columns for learning $\mathcal{M_A}$ and $\mathcal{M_S}$, respectively; $\mathbf{K_U} = [k_U(\mathbf{x_{A,i}}, \mathbf{x_{A,j}})]_{1 \le i \le N_A, 1 \le j \le N_A}$, $\mathbf{K_V} = [k_V(\mathbf{x_{S,i}}, \mathbf{x_{S,j}})]_{1 \le i \le N_S, 1 \le j \le N_S}$, $\mathbf{k_U}(\mathbf{x_A}) = [k_U(\mathbf{x_A}, \mathbf{x_{A,i}})]_{1 \le i \le N_A}$, $\mathbf{k_V}(\mathbf{x_S}) = [k_V(\mathbf{x_S}, \mathbf{x_{S,i}})]_{1 \le i \le N_S}$ are the corresponding non-linear kernel matrices/vectors. In this paper, k_U and k_V are defined as the RBF+linear kernels [9].

3.3   Shape Transfer Using Jacobian Matrices

$\mathcal{M_A}$ or $\mathcal{M_S}$ only models the shape variation along one of two axes in the shape space. To fully span the shape space, we present a shape synthesis method based on shape transfer in this section.

For the convenience of formulation, we introduce two auxiliary variables $\mathbf{V^A}$ and $\mathbf{V^S}$ to represent the shapes with only the pose variation/phenotype variation imposed, respectively. See Fig. 2. Both of them are $3N$-D vectors, which contain the 3D spatial positions of N sampling vertices of the shape. $\mathbf{V^A}$ and $\mathbf{V^S}$ are recovered from the m-D features $\mathbf{u}$ and $\mathbf{v}$ through linear combinations of the PCA eigen-vectors as: $\mathbf{V^A} = \mathbf{G^A} + \mathbf{A^A}\mathbf{u}$ and $\mathbf{V^S} = \mathbf{G^S} + \mathbf{A^S}\mathbf{v}$, where $\mathbf{G^A}$ and $\mathbf{G^S}$ are the mean vectors, and $\mathbf{A^A}$ and $\mathbf{A^S}$ are $3N \times m$ matrices containing the first m eigen-vectors of the pose and shape data set, respectively; $\mathbf{V^O}$ denotes the zero-shape in the canonical pose.

The concept of transferring deformation from a source object to target objects has been investigated in the previous work [5]. In our problem, an arbitrary shape $\mathbf{V}$ is synthesized by applying the phenotype variation on the posed zero-shape $\mathbf{V^A}$ locally as follows:

$$\mathbf{V} = \mathbf{V^A} + \mathbf{\Delta V'} + \mathbf{n_V}, \tag{4}$$

where $\mathbf{\Delta V'} = [\mathbf{\Delta V_i'}]_{i=1}^N$ is a $3N$-D concatenating displacement vector that represents the pose-dependent local shape variation from $\mathbf{V^A}$, and $\mathbf{n_V}$ is an additional random variable modeled by the white Gaussian noise subjected to $\mathcal{N}(0, \sigma_n^2 \mathbf{I_{3N \times 3N}})$. We assume that the vertex-wise phenotype variations $\mathbf{\Delta V_i}$ and $\mathbf{\Delta V_i'}$ before and after the pose change are locally linear transforms as $\mathbf{\Delta V_i} =$

$V_i^S - V_i^O$ and $\Delta V_i' = V_i - V_i^A$ (refer to Fig. 2) and they can be related by the 3×3 local Jacobian matrix J_i, similarly to [5]:

$$\Delta V_i' = J_i \Delta V_i. \tag{5}$$

We calculate the local Jacobian matrix at each single sampling vertex approximately from the mesh triangle it belongs to. Given a sampling vertex V_i^O on the canonical-posed zero-shape (and its corresponding vertex V_i^A in the new pose), we can find their corresponding the mesh triangles as shown in Fig. 3(b). Two in-plane vectors $m_i^{O,1}, m_i^{O,2}$ and one normal vector perpendicular to the triangle plane $m_i^{O,3}$ are computed for the mesh in the canonical pose and the same $m_i^{A,1}, m_i^{A,2}, m_i^{A,3}$ for the mesh in the new pose. The local Jacobian matrix J_i can then be computed as:

$$J_i = [m_i^{A,1}, m_i^{A,2}, m_i^{A,3}][m_i^{O,1}, m_i^{O,2}, m_i^{O,3}]^{-1}. \tag{6}$$

In the training stage, we compute the Jacobian matrix at every sampling point for all the instances of the data set using the method described above. A weighted average filtering over 8 nearest-neighbor sampling points is applied to Jacobian matrices for smoothness. Finally, these matrices are vectorized and used to learn the pose generator $\mathcal{M}_A$ in junction with the vertex displacements. In the prediction, the elements of Jacobian matrices can thus also be recovered from the pose feature u using PCA mean G^J and eigen-vectors A^J as

$$vec(J) = G^J + A^J u, \tag{7}$$

where $9N$-D vector $vec(J) = [vec(J_1), vec(J_2), \cdots, vec(J_N)]$ is the vectorized-form of matrix J.

3.4   A Probabilistic Model for the Shape Synthesis

The last term $P(V|u, v)$ of (1) models the synthesis of new 3D shapes from the pose feature u and shape feature v, which are generated by GPLVMs in Section 3.2. By combining (4), (5), and (7) the shape synthesis can therefore be formulated as the following equation:

$$\begin{aligned} V &= V^A + J \cdot (V^S - V^O) + n_V \\ &= G^A + A^A u + mat(G^J + A^J u) \cdot (G^S + A^S v - V^O) + n_V, \end{aligned} \tag{8}$$

where $J = diag(J_1, J_2, \cdots, J_N)$ is a $3N \times 3N$ matrix, and $mat(\cdot)$ is an operator which reshapes the $9N \times 1$ vector into a $3N \times 3N$ block diagonal matrix.

We hope to formulate the posterior distribution of the synthesized shape V explicitly given the latent coordinates x_A and x_S of the pose and shape generators $\mathcal{M}_A$ and $\mathcal{M}_S$. From the previous subsection, we know that the distributions of V^A, V^S, and $vec(J)$ have Gaussian form, since they are linearly generated from Gaussian-Process predictions u and v.

$$V^A | x_A, \mathcal{M}_A \sim \mathcal{N}(V^A; \mu_{V^A}(x_A), \Sigma_{V^A}(x_A)), \tag{9}$$

$$V^S | x_S, \mathcal{M}_S \sim \mathcal{N}(V^S; \mu_{V^S}(x_S), \Sigma_{V^S}(x_S)), \tag{10}$$

$$vec(J) | x_A, \mathcal{M}_A \sim \mathcal{N}(vec(J); \mu_J(x_A), \Sigma_J(x_A)). \tag{11}$$

where

$$\mu_{\mathbf{V^A}}(\mathbf{x_A}) = \mathbf{G^A} + \mathbf{A^A}\mu_{\mathbf{u}}, \quad \mu_{\mathbf{V^S}}(\mathbf{x_S}) = \mathbf{G^S} + \mathbf{A^S}\mu_{\mathbf{v}}, \quad \mu_{\mathbf{J}}(\mathbf{x_A}) = \mathbf{G^J} + \mathbf{A^J}\mu_{\mathbf{u}},$$

$$\Sigma_{\mathbf{V^A}}(\mathbf{x_A}) = \sigma_u^2 \mathbf{A^A}\mathbf{A^A}^T, \quad \Sigma_{\mathbf{V^S}}(\mathbf{x_S}) = \sigma_v^2 \mathbf{A^S}\mathbf{A^S}^T, \quad \Sigma_{\mathbf{J}}(\mathbf{x_A}) = \sigma_u^2 \mathbf{A^J}\mathbf{A^J}^T.$$

According to (8), the synthesized shape $\mathbf{V}$ is the product of multi-variate Gaussian $\mathbf{V^S}$ and $\mathbf{J}$, and it is non-Gaussian. However, we find its Gaussian projection $\hat{\mathbf{V}}$ with the same mean and covariance is very good approximation to the true distribution of $\mathbf{V}$, and this projection greatly helps the computation.

$$P(\hat{\mathbf{V}}|\mathbf{x_A}, \mathbf{x_S}, \mathcal{M_A}\mathcal{M_S}) \approx \mathcal{N}(\hat{\mathbf{V}}; \mu_{\mathbf{V}}(\mathbf{x_A}, \mathbf{x_S}), \Sigma_{\mathbf{V}}(\mathbf{x_A}, \mathbf{x_S})), \tag{12}$$

where

$$\mu_{\mathbf{V}} = \mu_{\mathbf{V^A}} + \hat{\mu}_{\mathbf{J}}(\mu_{\mathbf{V^S}} - \mathbf{V^O})$$

$$\Sigma_{\mathbf{V}} = \sigma_n^2 \mathbf{I} + \Sigma_{\mathbf{V^A}} + \hat{\mu}_{\mathbf{J}}\Sigma_{\mathbf{V^S}}\hat{\mu}_{\mathbf{J}}^{\mathbf{T}} + \left[[Tr(\Sigma_{\mathbf{J}mn}^{ij}\mathbf{S}_{ij})]_{m,n=0,1,2} \right]_{i,j=0,1,\cdots,N-1}$$

where $\hat{\mu}_{\mathbf{J}} = \mathbf{mat}(\mu_{\mathbf{J}})$ represents $3N \times 3N$ matrix shape of $\mu_{\mathbf{J}}{}^1$; $\mathbf{S_{ij}} = \mathbf{S}(3i+1 : 3i+3, 3j+1 : 3j+3)$ is the 3×3 sub-matrix of the $3N \times 3N$ matrix $\mathbf{S} = \Sigma_{\mathbf{V^S}} + (\mu_{\mathbf{V^S}} - \mathbf{V^O})(\mu_{\mathbf{V^S}} - \mathbf{V^O})^T$; and $\Sigma_{\mathbf{J}mn}^{ij} = \Sigma_{\mathbf{J}(9i+3m+1:9i+3m+3,9j+3n+1:9j+3n+3)}$ is the 3×3 sub-matrix of the $9N \times 9N$ matrix $\Sigma_{\mathbf{J}}$.

4 Inferring 3D Shapes from Silhouettes

The matching between the synthesized 3D shapes and input silhouettes is formulated as a two-stage process in our approach. The first stage is the projection stage, which models the procedure of projecting the 3D shape $\mathbf{V}$ into a silhouette $\mathbf{W_k}$ in the k-th view, as shown in (13).

$$P(\mathbf{W_k}|\mathbf{V}, \gamma_k) = \mathcal{N}(\mathbf{W_k}; \tilde{\mathbf{P}}_{\mathbf{k}}\mathbf{V} + \tilde{\mathbf{t}}_k, \sigma_w^2 \mathbf{I}), \tag{13}$$

where $\tilde{\mathbf{P}}_{\mathbf{k}} = \mathbf{P_k} \otimes \mathbf{M_k}$ and $\tilde{\mathbf{t}}_k = \mathbf{t}_k \otimes \mathbf{1_{N'}}$ are the expanded version of projection matrix and the offset vector in the k-th view, respectively. Here, $\mathbf{M_k} = [m_{k,ij}]_{1 \le i \le N', 1 \le j \leq N}$ is a $N' \times N$ binary masking matrix with element $m_{k,ij} = 1$ if the projection of the i-th 3D sample points is on the boundary and $m_{k,ij} = 0$ otherwise. $\mathbf{M_k}$ selects the N' silhouette points of the projection in the k-th view and it is fully determined by $\mathbf{P_k}$.

The second stage is the matching stage, which models how well the input silhouette $\mathbf{S_k}$ fits the corresponding boundary projection $\mathbf{W_k}$ of the generated shape in the k-th view. The observation likelihood is defined on the basis of Chamfer matching, which provides more robustness to errors and outliers in the input silhouettes as

$$P(\mathbf{S_k}|\mathbf{W_k}) = \frac{1}{Z}\exp\left(-\frac{1}{2\sigma_s^2}DT_{\mathbf{S_k}}^2(\mathbf{W_k})\right), \tag{14}$$

---

[1] For the convenience of notation, we sometimes omit the parameters of the mean and covariance in the formulation. E.g., $\mu_{\mathbf{J}} = \mu_{\mathbf{J}}(\mathbf{x_A})$.

where $DT_{\mathbf{S}}^2(\cdot)$ refers to the squared L2-distance transform of the silhouette $\mathbf{S} = \{\mathbf{s}_i\}_{i=1}^{|\mathbf{S}|}$. For an arbitrary point set $\mathbf{W} = \{\mathbf{w}_i\}_{i=1}^{|\mathbf{W}|}$, it is defined as $DT_{\mathbf{S}}^2(\mathbf{W}) = \frac{1}{2|\mathbf{W}|}\sum_{i=1}^{|\mathbf{W}|} \min_{\mathbf{s}_i \in S} \|\mathbf{w}_i - \mathbf{s}_i\|^2 + \frac{1}{2|\mathbf{S}|}\sum_{j=1}^{|\mathbf{S}|} \min_{\mathbf{w}_j \in \mathbf{W}} \|\mathbf{w}_j - \mathbf{s}_j\|^2$. To simplify the computation, the normalization factor Z is approximated by a constant here.

As stated in the previous section, generating the 3D shapes $\mathbf{V}$ from $\mathcal{M}_{\mathcal{S}}$ and $\mathcal{M}_{\mathcal{A}}$ can be approximately formulated as a Gaussian Process (12). It follows that the silhouette likelihood $P(\mathbf{W}_{\mathbf{k}}|\mathbf{x}_{\mathbf{A}}, \mathbf{x}_{\mathbf{S}}, \mathcal{M}_{\mathcal{A}}, \mathcal{M}_{\mathcal{S}}, \gamma_{\mathbf{k}})$ also has the Gaussian form by combining (12) with (13):

$$P(\mathbf{W}_{\mathbf{k}}|\mathbf{x}_{\mathbf{A}}, \mathbf{x}_{\mathbf{S}}, \mathcal{M}_{\mathcal{A}}, \mathcal{M}_{\mathcal{S}}, \gamma_{\mathbf{k}}) = \mathcal{N}\big(\mathbf{W}_{\mathbf{k}}; \mu_{\mathbf{W}_{\mathbf{k}}}(\mathbf{x}_{\mathbf{A}}, \mathbf{x}_{\mathbf{S}}, \gamma_{\mathbf{k}}), \Sigma_{\mathbf{W}_{\mathbf{k}}}(\mathbf{x}_{\mathbf{A}}, \mathbf{x}_{\mathbf{S}}, \gamma_{\mathbf{k}})\big) \quad (15)$$

where $\mu_{\mathbf{W}_{\mathbf{k}}} = \tilde{\mathbf{P}}_{\mathbf{k}}\mu_{\mathbf{V}} + \tilde{\mathbf{t}}_{\mathbf{k}}$ and $\Sigma_{\mathbf{W}_{\mathbf{k}}} = \tilde{\mathbf{P}}_{\mathbf{k}}\Sigma_{\mathbf{V}}\tilde{\mathbf{P}}_{\mathbf{k}}^{\mathbf{T}} + \sigma_w^2\mathbf{I}$.

Our target is to find the 3D shape which best fits all the image evidences $\mathbf{S}_{\mathbf{k}}$ $(k = 1, 2, \cdots, K)$ in K views, or equivalently, to find such latent positions $\mathbf{x}_{\mathbf{A}}$, $\mathbf{x}_{\mathbf{S}}$ and the parameters $\gamma_{\mathbf{k}}$ of K cameras. This can be done by finding the maximum of the overall likelihood $P(\{S_k\}_{k=1}^{K}|\mathbf{x}_{\mathbf{A}}, \mathbf{x}_{\mathbf{S}}, \mathcal{M}_{\mathcal{A}}, \mathcal{M}_{\mathcal{S}}, \{\gamma_k\}_{k=1}^{K})$ $(k = 1, 2, \cdots, K)$. The likelihood has no closed form since the direct integral over the terms with distance transform is not tractable, but it can be efficiently optimised by the closed-form lower bound Q [16]:

$$P(\{\mathbf{S}_{\mathbf{k}}\}_{k=1}^{K}|\mathbf{x}_{\mathbf{A}}, \mathbf{x}_{\mathbf{S}}, \mathcal{M}_{\mathcal{A}}, \mathcal{M}_{\mathcal{S}}, \{\gamma_k\}_{k=1}^{K}) \geq Q(\mathbf{x}_{\mathbf{A}}, \mathbf{x}_{\mathbf{S}}, \{\gamma_k\}_{k=1}^{K})$$

$$= \prod_{k=1}^{K} \frac{1}{Z_k\sqrt{\det\big(\mathbf{I} + \frac{1}{\sigma_s^2}\Sigma_{\mathbf{W}_{\mathbf{k}}}\big)}} \exp\big(-\frac{1}{2\sigma_s^2}DT_{\mathbf{S}_{\mathbf{k}}}^2(\mu_{\mathbf{W}_{\mathbf{k}}})\big). \quad (16)$$

Maximizing the lower bound Q, or equivalently, minimizing $-\log Q$, gives a good approximated maximum-likelihood estimate of the latent coordinate $\mathbf{x}_{\mathbf{A}}^{\mathbf{ML}}$, $\mathbf{x}_{\mathbf{S}}^{\mathbf{ML}}$, and camera parameters $\gamma_{\mathbf{k}}^{\mathbf{ML}}$ $(k = 1, 2, \cdots, K)$:

$$(\mathbf{x}_{\mathbf{A}}^{\mathbf{ML}}, \mathbf{x}_{\mathbf{S}}^{\mathbf{ML}}, \{\gamma_{\mathbf{k}}^{\mathbf{ML}}\}_{k=1}^{K}) \approx \arg\min_{\mathbf{x}_{\mathbf{A}}, \mathbf{x}_{\mathbf{S}}, \{\gamma_{\mathbf{k}}\}_{k=1}^{K}} -\log Q(\mathbf{x}_{\mathbf{A}}, \mathbf{x}_{\mathbf{S}}, \{\gamma_{\mathbf{k}}\}_{k=1}^{K}). \quad (17)$$

In our implementation, we minimize $-\log Q$ by adaptive-scale line search and use multiple initializations to avoid local minima. The optimization alternates between finding the latent coordinate $(\mathbf{x}_{\mathbf{A}}, \mathbf{x}_{\mathbf{S}})$ and correcting the camera parameters $\{\gamma_{\mathbf{k}}\}_{k=1}^{K}$ (and hence the masking matrices $\{\mathbf{M}_{\mathbf{k}}\}_{k=1}^{K}$). The convergence usually comes fast, as the latent dimensions of GPLVMs are low. Consequently, the corresponding maximum likelihood estimate of the 3D shape can be approximately given as:

$$P(\mathbf{V}^{\mathbf{ML}}|\mathbf{x}_{\mathbf{A}}^{\mathbf{ML}}, \mathbf{x}_{\mathbf{S}}^{\mathbf{ML}}, \mathcal{M}_{\mathcal{A}}\mathcal{M}_{\mathcal{S}}) \approx \mathcal{N}\big(\mathbf{V}^{\mathbf{ML}}; \mu_{\hat{\mathbf{V}}}(\mathbf{x}_{\mathbf{A}}^{\mathbf{ML}}, \mathbf{x}_{\mathbf{S}}^{\mathbf{ML}}), \Sigma_{\hat{\mathbf{V}}}(\mathbf{x}_{\mathbf{A}}^{\mathbf{ML}}, \mathbf{x}_{\mathbf{S}}^{\mathbf{ML}})\big) \quad (18)$$

which gives the mean shape $\mu_{\hat{\mathbf{V}}}$ and the uncertainty measurement $\Sigma_{\hat{\mathbf{V}}}$.

5   Experimental Results

We have investigated two shape categories in the experiments: human bodies and sharks. For the human data, we used Civilian American and European

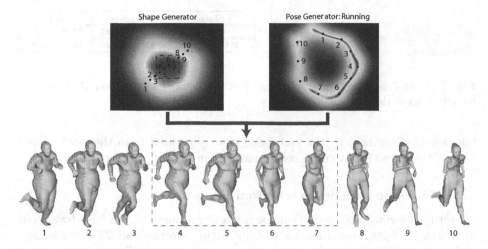

Fig. 4. Generation of new human body shapes in running pose. The shape and pose latent spaces are shown in their first two dimensions. Shapes are spanned by the paired coordinates.

Surface Anthropometry Resource (CAESAR) database as the shape data set, which contains over 2000 different body shapes of North American and European adults in the canonical pose. The pose data set was obtained by synthesizing animations of different 3D poses, e.g, running (150 frames), walking (150 frames), arm stretching and torso movements (250 frames), etc., using the 3D female human model Sydney in Poser 7. For the shark data, the shape data set contains eleven 3D shark models of different shark species available from Internet [19]. For the pose data set, we used an animatable 3D MEX shark model to generate an 11-frame sequence of shark tail-waving motion. The mesh resolution of the zero-shapes are: 3678 vertices/7356 faces for the human data, and 1840 vertices/3676 faces for shark data, respectively. To train $\mathcal{M}_A$ and $\mathcal{M}_S$, we empirically set the latent space dimension $d_S = 6$ for the human shape generator, $d_S = 3$ for the shark shape generator, and $d_A = 2$ for the pose generator for both data sets.

5.1 Shape Synthesis

A direct and important application of our framework is to synthesize a variety of shapes in the category from the shape generator and the pose generator. We visualize the process of synthesizing human shapes in running pose for the latent coordinates of the pose and shape generators in Fig. 4. To examine the synthesis quality, we sampled 10 positions in both the shape and pose latent spaces along the trajectories shown by numbers, and generated the human shapes by pairing up the corresponding shape and pose coordinates. As shown in Fig. 4, a wide-range of body shapes and different stages in the running pose were synthesized. We have also observed that the predictive variances (low variance indicated by red in Fig. 4) imply the quality of shape synthesis. The higher-quality shapes

Data	Precision	Recall
22 sharks	0.8996 ± 0.0481	0.9308 ± 0.0380
20 human bodies	0.7801 ± 0.0689	0.8952 ± 0.0995

Fig. 5. (a) An example of variance estimates of the shark reconstruction; (b) Precision-Recall ratios of the predicted shapes

(shapes $4 - 7$ marked by the rectangle) were generated from the low variance area of the shape latent space, where more training samples were presented.

5.2 3D Shape Reconstruction from Images

To verify the efficacy of our 3D shape inference framework, we have tested our approach over 20 human images in tight-fitting clothes and 22 shark images which were collected from Internet. These images involve different camera poses and various object motions, including human running, walking, arm stretching, and shark tail movement. We adopted GrabCut [25] to roughly segment the foreground and extract the corresponding silhouettes. The goal is to infer the reasonable 3D shapes implied by the pictures given the foreground region.

It is worth mentioning that the single-view reconstruction problem is inherently ambiguous. The single silhouette often corresponds to multiple possible 3D shapes mainly due to symmetry and viewpoint changes. Our software generates multiple shape candidates to the silhouette and provides estimate variances for each prediction (Fig 5(a)). For each image, the running time to predict 10 candidates was about 10 - 15 minutes by our unoptimized c++ codes in 2.8GHz PC. In the implementation, we randomly initialised the latent positions of the shape and pose generators. However, we find it helpful to roughly initialise the camera viewpoint. This will speed up the algorithm and greatly increase the possibility of obtaining desired results.

We have evaluated the performance of the approach qualitatively (see Fig. 6 and 7), and quantitatively by the Precision-Recall (P-R) ratios as given in Fig 5(b). Here, the precision and recall are defined as: $Precision = \frac{|S_F \cup S_R|}{S_R}$, and $Recall = \frac{|S_F \cup S_R|}{S_F}$, where S_F denotes the ground-truth foreground and S_R represents the projection of our prediction. All the 3D results provided in Fig. 6 and 7 correspond to the highest likelihood values given the input silhouettes and the shape priors. It shows that our approach captures both phenotype and pose variations and gives accurate estimates on the camera viewpoint. Also, P-R ratios on human data are of reasonable accuracy in comparison with those generated by the human specific model [13], although it is not straightforward to compare quantitatively due to different data sets and number of silhouettes. The reconstructed human bodies are comparatively worse in both visual quality and the P-R ratios than those of sharks because the more complex articulation structure makes exact pose fitting difficult. For example, the pose generator fails to explicitly model the closing hands in the first example of Fig. 7, although the arm and torso poses are well fit (see Section 6 for more discussions).

Fig. 6. The qualitative results on shark images. Column 1, 4: input images; Column 2 and 5: the reconstructed shapes in contrast with the input silhouettes; Column 3 and 6: the reconstructed shapes at another viewpoint.

6   Discussion

Compared to previous parametric models [12,13], the proposed method has both advantages and disadvantages. The benefits include: 1) requiring no strong class-specific priors (parts and skeletons), which facilitates modeling general categories, 2) estimating a much smaller number of model parameters and thus being more efficient, and 3) providing a probabilistic intuition on the uncertainty of shape generation and inference. However, the second benefit could be the drawback at the same time. E.g. whereas the SCAPE allows all possible body configurations by joint angles, our method generates poses similar to those in the pose data set. When training instances are insufficient, the pose generator can be limited in descriptive power (see the first example of Fig. 7). However, the pose generator is easily extendable by more pose data sets and is able to span sufficient local pose variations (the same advocated for pose estimation in [9]).

It is interesting to compare the shape transfer stage in our approach with that in parametric models. In the SCAPE, part-wise rigid rotations matrices and pose-dependent deformation matrices together serve similar functions as Jacobian matrices in our method do but incorporate joint angles. The shape transfer in our method can also benefit when structure priors are available, e.g. Jacobian matrices can be more reliably computed by enforcing part-wise smoothness constraints.

Although our method exploits only silhouettes in the experiments, more visual cues such as shading and internal edges could be used to improve matching accuracy [15]. More direct mapping from silhouettes to shapes could be learnt by regression techniques [14] from the new shapes of new poses synthesized by the proposed model. This would help initialising the proposed inference.

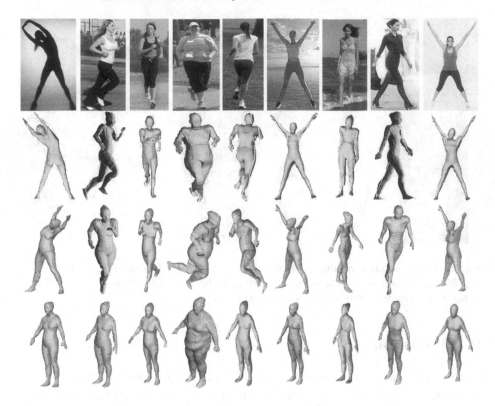

Fig. 7. The qualitative results on human images: Row 1: input images; Row 2: the reconstructed shapes in contrast with the input silhouettes; Row 3: the reconstructed shapes at another viewpoint; Row 4: the body shapes in the canonical pose.

7   Conclusions

In this paper, we have proposed a probabilistic generative method that models 3D deformable shape variations and infers 3D shapes from a single silhouette. The inference in the proposed framework is computationally efficient as it involves a small number of latent variables to estimate. The method is easy to extend to general object categories. It learns and recovers dense and detailed 3D shapes as well as camera parameters from a single image with a little interaction for segmentation. The proposed method can also serve as a good substitution or approximation of a detailed parametric model especially when physical structure of a category is not available.

As future work we shall perform experiments using multiple silhouette inputs for higher precision and extend the framework to incorporate dynamic models for inferring shapes from video sequences. Also, 3D object recognition or action recognition can also be done by the pose-free 3D shape or shape-free pose recovered by the proposed method respectively.

References

1. Prasad, M., Zisserman, A., Fitzgibbon, A.: Single view reconstruction of curved surfaces. In: CVPR, pp. 1345–1354 (2006)
2. Hoiem, D., Efros, A., Hebert, M.: Automatic photo pop-up. In: SIGGRAPH (2005)
3. Han, F., Zhu, S.: Bayesian reconstruction of 3D shapes and scenes from a single image. In: Proc. IEEE Int. Workshop on Higher-Level Knowledge (2003)
4. Rother, D., Sapiro, G.: Seeing 3D objects in a single 2D image. In: ICCV (2009)
5. Sumner, R., Popovic, J.: Deformation Transfer for Triangle Meshes. In: SIG-GRAPH, pp. 399–405 (2004)
6. Deutscher, J., Reid, I.: Articulated body motion capture by stochastic search. IJCV 61(2), 185–205 (2004)
7. Corazza, S., Mundermann, L., Chaudhari, A., Demattio, T., Cobelli, C., Andri-acchi, T.: A markerless motion capture system to study musculoskeletal biome-chanics: Visual hull and simulated annealing approach. Annals Biomed. Eng. 34(6) (2006)
8. Kakadiaris, I., Metaxas, D.: 3D human model acquisition from multiple views. IJCV 30(3), 191–218 (1998)
9. Navaratnam, R., Fitzgibbon, A., Cipolla, R.: Semi-supervised Joint Manifold Learning for Multi-valued Regression. In: ICCV (2007)
10. Salzmann, M., Urtasun, R., Fua, P.: Local deformation models for monocular 3D shape recovery. In: CVPR (2008)
11. Blanz, V., Vetter, T.: A Morphable model for the synthesis of 3D faces. In: SIG-GRAPH, pp. 187–194 (1999)
12. Anguelov, D., Srinivasan, P., Koller, D., Thrun, S., Rodgers, J.: Shape completion and animation of people. In: SIGGRAPH, pp. 408–416 (2005)
13. Balan, A., Sigal, L., Black, M., Davis, J., Haussecker, H.: Detailed Human Shape and Pose from Images. In: CVPR (2007)
14. Sigal, L., Balan, A., Black, M.: Combined discriminative and generative articulated pose and non-rigid shape estimation. In: NIPS (2007)
15. Guan, P., Weiss, A., Balan, A., Black, M.: Estimating human shape and pose from a single image. In: ICCV (2009)
16. Chen, Y., Kim, T.-K., Cipolla, R.: Inferring 3D Shapes and Deformations from Single Views, Technical Report, CUED/F-INFENG/TR.654 (2010)
17. Criminisi, A., Reid, I., Zisserman, A.: Single view metrology. IJCV 40(2), 123–148 (2000)
18. Saxena, A., Chung, S., Ng, A.: 3-D depth reconstruction from a single still image. IJCV 76(1), 53–69 (2008)
19. Hassner, T., Basri, R.: Example based 3D reconstruction from single 2D images. In: Beyond Patches Workshop at CVPR, p. 15 (2006)
20. Liu, J., Cao, L., Li, Z., Tang, X.: Plane-based optimization for 3D object recon-struction from single line drawings. IEEE Trans. PAMI 30(2), 315–327 (2008)
21. Torresani, L., Hertzmann, A., Bregier, C.: Nonrigid structure-from-motion, Esti-mating shape and motion with hierachical priors. IEEE Trans. PAMI 30(5) (2008)
22. Lawrence, N.: Gaussian process latent variable models for visualisation of high dimensional data. In: NIPS, vol. 16, pp. 329–336 (2004)
23. Belongie, S., Malik, J., Puzicha, J.: Shape matching and object recognition using shape contexts. IEEE Trans. PAMI 24(24), 509–522 (2002)
24. Besl, P., Mckey, N.: A method for registration of 3-D shapes. IEEE Trans. PAMI 14(2), 239–256 (1992)
25. Rother, C., Kolmogorov, V., Blake, A.: GrabCut – interactive foreground extrac-tion using iterated graph cuts. In: SIGGRAPH, pp. 309–314 (2004)

Efficient Inference with Multiple Heterogeneous Part Detectors for Human Pose Estimation

Vivek Kumar Singh, Ram Nevatia, and Chang Huang

University of Southern California, Los Angeles, USA
{viveksin,nevatia,huangcha}@usc.edu

Abstract. We address the problem of estimating human pose in a single image using a part based approach. Pose accuracy is directly affected by the accuracy of the part detectors but more accurate detectors are likely to be also more computationally expensive. We propose to use multiple, heterogeneous part detectors with varying accuracy and computation requirements, ordered in a hierarchy, to achieve more accurate and efficient pose estimation. For inference, we propose an algorithm to localize articulated objects by exploiting an ordered hierarchy of detectors with increasing accuracy. The inference uses branch and bound method to search for each part and use kinematics from neighboring parts to guide the branching behavior and compute bounds on the best part estimate. We demonstrate our approach on a publicly available People dataset and outperform the state-of-art methods. Our inference is 3 times faster than one based on using a single, highly accurate detector.

Keywords: Human pose estimation, part based models, branch and bound, message passing.

1 Introduction

We consider the problem of localizing 3-D articulated objects such as humans in their 2-D images; the projected shape varies with the viewpoint and articulations, we choose to model these variations as deformations. An intuitive and widely accepted approach to model an articulated object is to decompose the object into smaller objects (parts) and model the deformability by loose spatial relationships between the parts. [1], [2], [3], [4], [5] used such part based representations to detect and localize objects with large variations. The localization accuracy increases with better part detectors but it comes at the cost of increased computation. We enhance the part based model with multiple heterogeneous features for better detection accuracy, and propose a novel progressive search based method for efficient inference.

A common model for part based object representation is that of *pictorial structures*, which is a tree-structured graphical model that represents the kinematic relationships between the parts; pose is inferred by enforcing kinematics constraints on part hypotheses that are obtained by applying part detectors. Such part based approaches can be *dense* or *sparse* based on how parts are sampled from the image. *Dense sampling* methods [1], [6], [7], [8] apply each part

K. Daniilidis, P. Maragos, N. Paragios (Eds.): ECCV 2010, Part III, LNCS 6313, pp. 314–327, 2010.

detector over all possible locations, orientations and scales; [1] presents exact and efficient inference on densely sampled parts, however for better efficiency, these methods tend to use part detectors that are generally weak. [7] shows that better part detectors can significantly improve the performance accuracy; however better part detectors are often more complex and computationally expensive. The *sparse sampling* methods approximate the part likelihood using few hypotheses and infer the pose from these hypotheses [9], [10], [2], [11]. To avoid applying the part detector over the entire space, these approaches obtain part hypotheses from bottom up feature responses such as by using parallel line segments [10], [2]. For inference, [9] uses non parametric belief propagation which is slow due to its stochastic nature; [10], [11] use integer programming methods to infer pose, but the size of the program grows rapidly with increase in the number of candidate part hypotheses.

An alternate representation is to use hierarchical model in which multiple levels represent the object at varying granularity [3], [12], [5]; parts need not correspond to the natural object parts (such as limbs for human). [13] presented a generic AND/OR graphical model for deformable objects, where the leaf nodes are points on the boundary and the intermediate nodes represent different object parts. [14], [15], [16] use 2-level hierarchical models to find humans with a whole object representation at higher level and subsequent parts at the lower level. [16] used Poselets (tightly coupled local part configurations) at the lower level to achieve more accurate detection. However, these methods use pose-restrictive assumptions such as upright human where torso is above the legs.

We use a densely part sampled approach in this work and propose to use multiple heterogeneous detectors for each part to achieve a higher detection accuracy. More precisely, we use a linearly weighted combination of multiple detectors for a part, and order the detectors by their discriminability and efficiency. The combination weights are learnt in a discriminative framework using *Voted Perceptron* [17], so that the combined detector has better accuracy than the individual detectors. Further, the ordering of the detectors is selected such that as we go up the order, the part detectors become more accurate and precise, but also computationally more expensive.

For efficient inference over the graphical model with ordered heterogeneous features, we propose a novel *collaborative branch and bound algorithm*. The key idea is to use branch and bound search for each part, where the bounds on the best part estimate are obtained by enforcing kinematic consistency between the search branches of neighboring parts; thus, the kinematic constraints form a collaboration model between part search branches. At each step, search space is reduced by applying a more accurate detector for each part and pruning out the subsets that are less likely to contain the best part estimate. The best part estimate refers to the estimate otherwise obtained by dense sampling parts using all the detectors, which is highly inefficient. We demonstrate our approach on a commonly used dataset of complex human poses in cluttered backgrounds [6]. Our algorithm gives better than the state-or-art accuracy on the dataset and inference is ~ 3 times faster than one using a single, highly accurate detector.

In the rest of the paper, we first discuss the pictorial structure with multiple part detectors in section 2 and the collaborative branch and bound algorithm in section 3. Next, we present the parameter learning in section 4, followed by the experiments in section 5 and conclusion in section 6.

2   Pictorial Structure with Multiple Part Detectors

We use pictorial structures [1] to model humans. Instead of part detectors with one type of feature descriptor such as shape context [7] or Haar-like [6], we use detectors with multiple heterogeneous features for each part. We impose a hierarchical ordering on these detectors such that the model becomes more precise as we go up the hierarchy. Thus, different levels in the hierarchy represent part detectors with different descriptors. Figure 1 shows the pictorial structure for full body and a 3-part model with n detectors for each part.

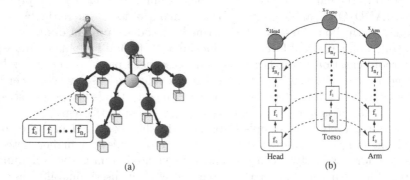

(a)   (b)

Fig. 1. Pose Model: (a) Tree structured human model, with one of the observation nodes showing multiple detectors (b) A 3 part model showing detectors in a hierarchical order. Note that the dotted arrows are not graphical model links but are shown to indicate the relationship between the different detectors.

[Representation Details]
We assume that the output of different detectors of a part are independent of each other and that the part likelihood distributions are conditionally independent given the full object $\mathbf{x}$. Under these assumptions, the posterior log-likelihood of the object $\mathbf{x}$ obtained by applying detectors at level k is given by,

$$\mathcal{F}^k(\mathbf{x}, I) = \sum_{i \in V} \phi_i^k(I|x_i) + \sum_{ij \in E} \psi_{ij}^k(x_i, x_j) \tag{1}$$

where (V, E) is the graphical model, I is the image observation, ϕ_i^k is the likelihood for part i using detector f_k; we refer to ϕ_i^k as the *part support* for i using f_k. The log-likelihood in equation 1 is same as log-likelihood function of a pictorial structure. Note for simplicity we assume that the kinematic models are same at all the levels *i.e.* $\psi_{ij}^k = \psi_{ij}$ for all k, and are assumed to be Gaussian.

Given the part supports ϕ_i^ks obtained by applying all the detectors for part i, we combine them to obtain the part likelihood distribution. Since the accuracy of detectors for each part may vary with parts, we associate a weight with all the detectors for every part. We then define the optimal pose configuration $\mathbf{x}^*$ by

$$\mathbf{x}^* = arg \max_{\mathbf{x} \in \mathbf{X}} \left(\sum_{i \in V} \sum_{k=1}^{n_f} w_i^k \phi_i^k(I|x_i) + \sum_{ij \in E} \psi_{ij}(x_i, x_j) \right) \qquad (2)$$

where, w_i^k is the weight associated detector f_k for part i. Our part representation with hierarchical feature model (eqn 2) can be interpreted as a combination of n_f tree pictorial structures, each with part detectors with different features.

[Model Constraints]
For selection of part detectors that are useful for efficient and more accurate inference, we impose the following constraints on the set of detectors used for each part,
▷ For the ground truth pose $\mathbf{x}^{gt}$, $\mathcal{F}^{k+1}(\mathbf{x}^{gt}, I) > \mathcal{F}^k(\mathbf{x}^{gt}, I)$, where $\mathcal{F}^k(\mathbf{x}, I)$ is the log-likelihood obtained using features at level k (see eqn 1). This ensures that the detectors at level $k + 1$ have better localization accuracy than the detectors at a lower level.
▷ For each part i, $time(\phi_i^{k+1}) > time(\phi_i^k)$ i.e. the detectors at higher level are less efficient than the detectors at lower level.

3   Inference

Next we describe our collaborative search approach for efficient inference over the pictorial structures with hierarchical feature ordering. [1] proposed efficient algorithms for inference on pictorial structures using sum-product/message passing algorithm. However, the proposed method uses a dense search for each object part and hence becomes inefficient with complex (more discriminative) part detectors. [18] proposed an efficient algorithm for localization using complex features by defining quality functions that bound the probability of finding the object within a window. In this work, we use the branch and bound algorithm to iteratively search for the object part using coarse-to-fine features. However in order to quickly concentrate the search in high likelihood regions, we make inter-branch inferences between the active search branches. In other words, the branching algorithm depends on the estimated likelihood of the neighboring parts in the current iteration.

We proceed by briefly describing the message passing algorithm, and then introduce our inference algorithm.

[Belief Propagation on Pictorial Structures] [19]
Pictorial structures infers the object position by maximizing joint distribution of the parts (see eqn 1). [1] presented efficient algorithms for inference using

belief propagation [19]. The algorithm simultaneously computes the posterior distribution of all parts by locally exchanging *messages* between connected parts. The message from part i to part j is the distribution of the joint connecting parts i and j, based on the observation at part i. This distribution is efficiently obtained by transforming the part distribution into the coordinate system of the connecting joint (using eqn 3) and applying a zero mean Gaussian whose variance determines the stiffness between the parts.

$$T_{ij}(x_i) = \begin{pmatrix} px_i + s_i\mu_x^{ji}cos\theta_i - s_i\mu_y^{ji}sin\theta_i \\ py_i + s_i\mu_x^{ji}sin\theta_i + s_i\mu_y^{ji}cos\theta_i \\ \theta_i + \mu_\theta^{ji} \\ s_i \end{pmatrix} \tag{3}$$

where, $x_i = (px_i, py_i, \theta_i, s_i)$ is position, orientation and scale of x_i, (μ_x^{ji}, μ_y^{ji}) is the mean relative position of the joint between i and j, and μ_θ^{ji} is the relative angle of part j in the coordinate frame of part i.

3.1   Collaborative Branch and Bound Algorithm

Now we describe the collaborative search algorithm for a tree-structured pictorial structures with hierarchical part features. We introduce the following terms and notations for our algorithm. The *configuration space* of part i is denoted with D_i; the response function for each part detector is assumed to be of the form $\phi_i : R^d \rightarrow R$. Instead of working over the entire configuration space for each part, the algorithm maintains subsets that are most likely to contain a true part response. We refer to these subsets as *active*. As the subsets are obtained by branching, each active subset is associated with a unique *active branch*, and for each part i, the current set of active branches is denoted by $\mathcal{R}_i$. The subset spanned by a branch t_i is denoted as $S(t_i)$.

[**Initialization**]: Initiate the search for each part i over the entire domain space D_i. Thus the initial set of *active branches* $\mathcal{R}_i = D_i$.

[**Iterative Step**]: Given sets of active branches for all parts **R** at the current iteration k, apply the next detector f_k over all branches $\in$ **R**. Note that as the new detector is applied, the part support at each part location gets accumulated *i.e.* value at location l after applying k^{th} detector f_k is $\sum_k w_k\phi^k(l)$.

Branching: For each branch t_i, uniformly partition the space $S(t_i)$ into non-overlapping subsets $\{S(t_{i,c})\}$ such that $S(t_i) = \bigcup_c S(t_{i,c})$, and initialize new branches $t_{i,c}$ over each partition $S(t_{i,c})$ and add them to active branch set $\mathcal{R}_i$. For simplicity, each space is partitioned uniformly along the all dimensions and thus all the subsets are blocks (hypercuboids). For each active branch including the new branches, say t_i, compute the *max*, *min* and *average* of the detection responses over the subset spanned by the branch $S(t_{i,c})$, denoted by $max(t_i)$, $min(t_i)$ and $avg(t_i)$ respectively. We refer to these values as *branch statistics*.

Inter-branch Message Passing: We use inter branch message passing to compute the quality $q(t_i)$ of each branch t_i. For inter-branch message passing, we define the joint likelihood between a pair of branches from connected parts using eqn 4,

$$\psi(t_i|t_j) = -logN(\delta(T^{ji}(t_i), T^{ij}(t_j)); \mu^{ji}, \Sigma^{ji})$$ (4)

Here, $T^{ji}(t_i)$ is the transformed subset of t_i in the coordinate system of the joint between parts i and j (given by eqn 3), and $\delta(t_i, t_j)$ is the minimum displacement vector between the subsets spanned by t_i and t_j i.e. $S(t_i)$ and $S(t_j)$. More precisely,

$$\delta(t_i, t_j) = l_i - l_j \quad where \quad (l_i, l_j) = \arg\min_{l_i \in S(t_i), l_j \in S(t_j)} ||l_i - l_j||^2$$

Note that since each subset is a block, the minimum displacement vector can be computed very efficiently, and is independent of the size of the subset.

We now define the quality $q(t_i)$ of a thread t_i as the joint posterior of average branch statistic of t_i and max statistic of all threads $t \neq t_i$.

$$q(t_i) = avg(t_i) + \max_{t_i \cup (\mathbf{R} \backslash \mathcal{R}_i)} \left(\sum_{j \in V, j \neq i} max(t_j) + \sum_{(j,k) \in E} \psi(t_j|t_k) \right)$$ (5)

This definition of the branch quality roughly captures the idea that higher branch quality implies greater likelihood of the best part hypothesis to belong to the subset spanned by that branch. Note however that since quality is defined on average statistic, there is no guarantee that the highest quality thread will always have the best part hypothesis.

Compute the bounds on the branch quality $q(t_i)$ using inter-branch message passing over with max and min branch statistic of t_i. More precisely, to obtain an upper bound on $q(t_i)$, say $q^U(t_i)$, compute the joint posterior of max branch statistic of t_i and all threads $t \neq t_i$. Similarly, compute the lower bound $q^L(t_i)$ as the joint posterior of min branch statistic of t_i and min statistic of all threads $t \neq t_i$. Note that equation for $q^U(t_i)$ and $q^L(t_i)$ can be written by replacing the first term in eqn 5 by $max(t_i)$ and $min(t_i)$ respectively.

Pruning: Clearly, the quality of branch $q(t_i)$ belongs to $[q^L(t_i), q^U(t_i)]$. More importantly, notice that $q^L(t_i)$ and $q^U(t_i)$ are upper and lower bounds of the best part estimates for all $x_i \in S(t_i)$ (best part estimate is referred to best hypothesis obtained by belief propagation over entire part space). After these bounds are computed for all the active branches in $\mathcal{R}$, prune the branches in $t_i \in R_i$ when $q^U(t_i)$ is lower than the lower bound of another branch $\hat{t}_i \in R_i$ i.e. $q^U(t_i) < q^L(\hat{t}_i)$. Note that since we are pruning based on the accumulated part support upto level k, the pruning is not guaranteed to retain the best hypothesis for each part. However, in our experiments, we did not observe any loss in accuracy. For greater efficiency, we also prune the branches with a very low quality.

After pruning we then apply the next detector and repeat until all the detectors have been applied.

[**Selecting the Best Pose**]: After we have applied all the features by progressively reducing the search space, we still need to estimate the best pose over the current set of active subsets. One may continue to use branch and bound to reduce the search space, however as branches increase the computational overhead for computing the branch bounds increases. So we use belief propagation over the active subsets to obtain the part posterior distribution, and best pose is obtained by assembling the MAP for each part.

The search algorithm is summarized in Algorithm 1.

Algorithm 1. Collaborative Branch and Bound Algorithm

Initialize each $\mathcal{R}_i$ with a single thread over D_i
for $k \leftarrow 1$ to $|\mathcal{F}|$ do
   ▷ For each branch $t \in \mathbf{R}$, apply the next detector f^k over the entire subset $S(t)$
   Branching
   for each part i do
      ▷ $\mathcal{R}_i \leftarrow partition(\mathcal{R}_i)$
      ▷ Compute *max, min, average* statistic for each branch $t \in \mathcal{R}_i$
   end for
   Inter-thread Message Passing {compute the quality of each active thread}
   ▷ Compute quality $q(t)$ for each branch $t \in \mathbf{R}$ using equation 5
   ▷ Compute quality bounds $q^L(t)$ and $q^U(t)$ for each branch $t \in \mathbf{R}$
   Pruning
   for each part i do
      ▷ Remove branch t if there exists $t_k \in \mathcal{R}_\rangle$ $q^U(t) < q^L(t_k)$
   end for
end for
▷ Compute joint posterior distribution of the parts over the active search space
▷ Obtain the best pose by collecting MAP estimate of each part

---

[**Accuracy vs Efficiency Tradeoff**]: The key aspect of our inference is that the branching and pruning step depends not on the detection responses but also on the kinematic constraints. This allows the algorithm to quickly focus on the subsets that are most likely to contain the best hypothesis. The efficiency of the algorithm depends on branching factor. When branching factor is too high, the inter-branch message passing becomes computationally expensive since the overhead of computing bounds becomes significant. When the branching factor is small, higher level detectors will be applied over a large space, thereby slowing down the inference. Since optimal branching factor for highest efficiency depends on the accuracy of detectors on the input image itself, we empirically select the branching factor based on the performance of our algorithm on the training data.

4   Parameter Learning

Model parameters include the kinematic functions ψ_{ij}s and model weights $\{w_i^k\}$.

[**Kinematic Prior**]: The kinematic function is modeled with Gaussians, *i.e.* position of the connecting joint in a coordinate system of both parts (m^{ij}, σ^{ij}) and

(m^{ji}, σ^{ji}) and the relative angles of the parts at the connected joint $(m_\theta^{ij}, \sigma_\theta^{ij})$. Given the joint annotations that is available from the training data, we learn the Gaussian parameters with a Maximum Likelihood Estimator [1], [7].

[**Feature Weight Vector**]: Since the joint likelihood function is log-linear (eqn 2), we learn the model weights using the *Voted Perceptron algorithm* [17]. The algorithm computes the prediction error given the current set of weights and update the weights based on the error between the true and predicted positions (see Algorithm 2). The algorithm doesn't converge to a zero error but rather gets close a certain value and oscillates around it. Thus as in [17], we use the weights obtained by averaging weights obtained over many runs.

Algorithm 2. Model Weight Learning using Structured Perceptron

Randomly set the initial weights $\overline{w}$
for $t = 1$ to T, $j = 1$ to N do
$\quad \triangleright$ Compute MAP pose $\mathbf{x}^o$ on training image $\mathcal{I}^j$ using current weights $\overline{w}$.
$\quad$ for $p = 1$ to n do
$\quad\quad$ if $x_p^o \neq x_p^{gt}$ then
$\quad\quad\quad \triangleright$ Collect the feature error vector, $\Delta_p^k = \Delta_p^k + \phi_p^k(\mathcal{I}^j|\mathbf{x}^{gt}) - \phi_p^k(\mathcal{I}^j|\mathbf{x}^o)$
$\quad\quad\quad \triangleright$ Update the weight vector, $w_p^k = w_p^k + \frac{\Delta_p^k}{||\Delta_p||_{L1}}$
$\quad\quad$ end if
$\quad$ end for
end for

---

5 Experiments

For evaluation, we use the People dataset [6] which contains 305 images, each with highly articulated human poses in a cluttered background. The images are resized such that the human in these images are about 100 pixels high. The first 100 images were used for training and rest 205 images used for testing, as in other reported experiments on this dataset [6], [7].

5.1 Part Detectors

We use 3 detectors in a hierarchy for each part - minimum edge density (fast but low accuracy), boundary and region templates (slower but more accurate) and boosted cascades (slowest but high accuracy). Figure 2 shows the features and templates used in part detectors.

[**Edge Density Filters**]: We learn edge density filters for each body part from the training set. Edge density filters (EDF) find the potential candidate regions for each part based on the density of edges within a window. This involves computing a Sobel edge map, followed by thresholding applied at each location based on the density of edges within the window. For each part, a square window of

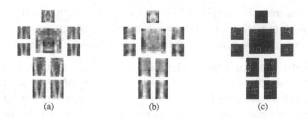

(a)   (b)   (c)

Fig. 2. Templates and features used in part detectors: (a) Boundary templates (b) Region Templates, dark areas correspond to low probability of edge, and bright areas correspond to a high probability; (c) Selected JRoGs, each granule-pair used to compute the feature is indicated by the same color. For clarity, only the first few pairs are shown for each part;

size equal to the length of the part was considered, and integral images were used for efficiency. Note that this filtering process mainly helps in removing obvious regions where the density of edges is low.

[**Boundary and Region Templates**]: We used the boundary and region templates trained by Ramanan et al [6] for localizing human pose (see 2(a, b)). Each template is a weighted sum of the oriented bar filters where the weights are obtained by maximizing the conditional joint likelihood (refer [4] for details on training). The likelihood of a part is obtained by convolving the part boundary template with the Sobel edge map, and the part region template with part's appearance likelihood map. Since the appearance of parts is not known at the start, part estimates inferred using boundary templates are used to build the part appearance models. For each part, an RGB histogram of the part h_{fg} and its background h_{bg} is learnt; the appearance likelihood map for the part is then simply given by the binary map $p(H_{fg}|c) > p(H_{bg}|c)$. For more details, please refer to [6].

[**Boosted JRoG Cascades**]: We trained discriminative part detectors using the JRoG (Joint Ranking of Granules) proposed in [20]. A JRoG captures region dissimilarity between a pair of image blocks due to the difference in grayscale value or the average gradient, and is more accurate and efficient on pedestrian detection tasks [20] than other popular features such as HOG [21] and Edgelets [22]. The likelihood of a part hypothesis is given by the sum of the fraction of layers passed (in the cascade) and detection confidence obtained by the final layer (if all layers are passed). We trained each part cascade detector using boosting with 5000 positive training examples for each part and a million negative examples from the images obtained from the Internet. The positive samples were obtained by the 100 part annotations, their flipped versions and small affine perturbations (rotation, scale and translation). Figure 2(c) shows the first selected JRoG features.

5.2 Human Pose Inference

We used the following hierarchy of detectors: edge-density filters, boundary templates, boosted JRoG cascades and region templates. The joint posterior distribution of parts was efficiently computed using the proposed collaborative branch and bound algorithm. We used RGB histograms discretized into $16 \times 16 \times 16$ bins to model appearance of each part. Part appearance models were learnt using the joint part posterior of the boundary templates and the boosted JRoG cascades. Note that unlike [6], we learn part appearance models and apply the region templates only over the active search space (after applying the JRoG detector) which is much smaller than entire part space.

5.3 Evaluation

We compute the pose accuracy of the entire dataset by computing the average correctness of each body part over all the images (total of 2050 parts). An estimated body part is considered correct if its segment endpoints lie within 50% of the length of the ground-truth segment from their annotated location, as in earlier reported results [7].

[Part Detectors]: We compare the performance of the part detectors used in this work over the entire test set. Each part detector was applied at every pixel in 24 orientations. Both accuracy and timing of the part detectors trained with different features are shown in Table 2. We observed that even though the person in each image has been scaled to approximately 100 pixels, the variance in part sizes is still significant (e.g. lower leg has a standard deviation of ~ 10 pixels over the entire dataset). So we applied the detectors over 5 scales - $\{0.8, 0.9, 1.0, 1.1, 1.2\}$. While applying template detectors over multiple scales did not improve the detection accuracy, the boosted JRoG part detectors applied over multiple scales was much more accurate than for a single scale (shown in Table 1). Thus, in our experiments we apply the template detector over a single scale and the JRoG detectors over all 5 scales. Also notice that the appearance models obtained from more accurate detection responses, improve the accuracy of the region templates [6]. Thus, we use the region templates at the top of our hierarchy.

The times reported in Table 2 are the total time taken by densely applying all the detectors to process a 276×213 image. Timing is computed on a state-of-art machine with 3GHz Dual-Quad Core CPU. Since the part detectors are independent of each other, we apply part detectors in parallel using OpenMP programming. This speeds up the detectors by about ~ 5 times. Template detectors were applied using the fast convolution method in the Intel Image Processing Primitives library.

[Pose Estimation]: We evaluate the performance of our system at various levels in the hierarchy with different combination of part detectors.

Accuracy: Table 2 shows the pose estimation accuracy averaged over all parts (total of 2050 parts). Notice that the detection accuracy increases with the use of

Table 1. Comparison of Part Detector accuracy. Arm and leg numbers are average of left and right parts. The appearance models for region detectors in row 3 and 4 are obtained by using responses from boundary templates and JRoG detectors (shown in parentheses).

Method	Accuracy							Time
	Torso	U-Leg	L-Leg	U-Arm	L-Arm	Head	Total	(in secs)
Edge Density Filters	-	-	-	-	-	-	-	0.12s
Boundary Templates	3.9	6.3	9.7	2.4	5.6	3.9	5.61	2.032s
Region (wBoundary)	18.0	13.4	10.0	1.9	1.7	0.0	7.22	2.047s
Region (wBoundary+JRoG)	30.7	26.6	14.8	3.9	1.7	1.9	12.68	2.047s
JRoG	28.8	16.5	5.8	3.4	1.0	32.4	11.48	2.640s
JRoG (5 scales)	34.1	23.1	13.2	5.1	5.8	42.4	17.13	13.843s

more heterogeneous detectors for each part. Also note that our selection of part detector ordering clearly satisfies the model constraints (increasing accuracy and computation time with increase in level) given in Section 2.2. Learning of feature weights increases the performance accuracy by about $\sim 2\%$. Figure 3(a) shows the variation in the number of poses with number of detected parts per pose; notice that with increase in number of detectors, the number of poses with fewer detected parts decreases while the number of poses with higher detected parts increases.

Timing: The speed up factor using our algorithm depends on the amount of pruning achieved by the faster part detectors. Hence in images with significant background clutter the speed up factor is smaller. Table 2 shows the time taken to process a $\sim 200 \times 180$ image averaged over 50 images from the People dataset. Our inference is about 3.6 times faster than Pictorial Structures' dense search [1]. Over the entire dataset, the speed up factor varied between 3 to 5 with an average factor of ~ 3.7. When the detectors were applied sequentially (without parallel programming), the average speed up factor increased to ~ 4. Figure 3(b) illustrates the progressive search space reduction at various levels in the hierarchy over the entire dataset.

Table 2. Pose Estimation accuracy with different part detector combinations. Time reported is averaged over 50 images of size $\sim 200 \times 180$.

	Accuracy	Time (in secs)	
		Dense Parsing [1]	Collaborative BnB
EDF + Edge Templates	33.95	1.785s	1.487s
EDF + Edge + Region Templates	43.90	3.711s	2.987s
EDF + Boosted JRoG Cascades	51.95	8.727s	6.807s
EDF + Edge + JRoG	54.78	9.832s	3.096s
EDF + Edge + JRoG + Region	**60.88**	11.76s	3.27s

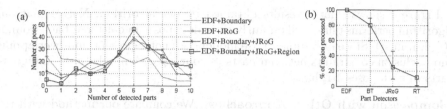

Fig. 3. (a) Number of poses vs number of detected parts per pose (b) the percentage of configuration space processed by detectors at different levels in hierarchy

Table 3. Comparison of Pose Estimation Results with other approaches: Iterative Image Parsing (IIP) [6], Boosted Shape Context with Pictorial Structures (PS) [7].

Method	Torso	Upper leg	Lower leg	Upper arm	Forearm	Head	Total
Boundary-PS [6]	39.5	21.4	20	23.9	17.5	13.6	11.7	12.1	11.2	21.4	19.2
Boundary+Color-IIP [6]	52.1	30.2	31.7	27.8	30.2	17	18	14.6	12.6	37.5	27.2
ShapeContext-PS [7]	81.4	67.3	59	63.9	46.3	47.3	47.8	31.2	32.1	75.6	55.2
MultiPart-CBnB	91.2	69.3	73.7	61.0	68.8	50.2	49.8	34.6	33.7	76.6	**60.88**

Fig. 4. Results on the People Dataset. For each image, the inferred parts (overlaid in red) and the joint likelihood distribution of parts obtained by our algorithm are shown. The image pairs (a-l) are the initial few entries from the dataset (also shown by [7]); (r-u) show some failure cases (see text for description).

Figure 4 shows sample results obtained by our algorithm. Notice that our algorithm performs quite well on fairly articulate poses in cluttered backgrounds 4(d, i, l, m, q). Since our human pose model does not represent non-overlapping and occlusion constraints between parts [8], our algorithm fails to disambiguate parts in such poses 4(f, h, s-u).

[**Comparison with Other Approaches**]: We compare our method with the closely related iterative parsing approach [6] that uses boundary and region templates also used in this work, and pictorial structures with part detectors with boosted shape context features [7]. Table 3 shows the localization accuracy on the People dataset obtained using our approach and those reported by [6], [7]. As Table 3 clearly shows, our method significantly outperforms both methods. A direct speed comparison is difficult as [6], [7] do not report run time numbers.

6   Conclusion

In this paper we proposed a part based model with heterogeneous part features for object pose estimation and demonstrated that the use of multiple detectors for each part improves the accuracy. For efficient inference over these models, we created a hierarchical ordering over the different detectors for each part based on accuracy and efficiency and proposed a collaborative branch and bound algorithm which progressively reduces the search space for each part by imposing kinematic constraints from the neighboring parts. We applied our approach to estimate human pose in a single image and outperformed the state-of-art approaches, and showed that our inference is 3 times faster than dense sampling methods using a single, highly accurate detector and 3.7 times faster than those using multiple detectors.

Acknowledgements. This research was supported, in part, by the Office of Naval Research under grants #N00014-06-1-0470 and #N00014-10-1-0517. The authors would also like to thank Deva Ramanan for providing the edge and region templates and the People dataset.

References

1. Felzenszwalb, P.F., Huttenlocher, D.P.: Pictorial structures for object recognition. IJCV 61, 55–79 (2005)
2. Hua, G., Yang, M.H., Wu, Y.: Learning to estimate human pose with data driven belief propagation. In: CVPR, vol. 2, pp. 747–754 (2005)
3. Zhang, J., Luo, J., Collins, R., Liu, Y.: Body localization in still images using hierarchical models and hybrid search. In: CVPR, pp. 1536–1543 (2006)
4. Ramanan, D., Sminchisescu, C.: Training deformable models for localization. In: CVPR, vol. 1, pp. 206–213 (2006)
5. Felzenszwalb, P., Mcallester, D., Ramanan, D.: A discriminatively trained, multi-scale, deformable part model. In: CVPR (2008)

6. Ramanan, D.: Learning to parse images of articulated bodies. In: NIPS, vol. 19, pp. 1129–1136 (2007)
7. Andriluka, M., Roth, S., Schiele, B.: Pictorial structures revisited: People detection and articulated pose estimation. In: CVPR (2009)
8. Wang, Y., Mori, G.: Multiple tree models for occlusion and spatial constraints in human pose estimation. In: Forsyth, D., Torr, P., Zisserman, A. (eds.) ECCV 2008, Part III. LNCS, vol. 5304, pp. 710–724. Springer, Heidelberg (2008)
9. Sigal, L., Roth, S., Black, M.J., Isard, M.: Tracking loose-limbed people. In: CVPR, pp. 421–428 (2004)
10. Ren, X., Berg, A.C., Malik, J.: Recovering human body configurations using pairwise constraints between parts. In: ICCV, pp. 824–831 (2005)
11. Jiang, H., Martin, D.: Global pose estimation using non-tree models. In: CVPR (2008)
12. Zhu, L., Chen, Y., Lu, Y., Lin, C., Yuille, A.: Max margin and/or graph learning for parsing the human body. In: CVPR (2008)
13. Chen, Y., Zhu, L., Lin, C., Yuille, A., Zhang, H.: Rapid inference on a novel and/or graph for object detection, segmentation and parsing. In: Advances in Neural Information Processing Systems 2008, pp. 289–296 (2008)
14. Lee, M., Nevatia, R.: Human pose tracking using multi-level structured models. In: Leonardis, A., Bischof, H., Pinz, A. (eds.) ECCV 2006. LNCS, vol. 3953, pp. 368–381. Springer, Heidelberg (2006)
15. Ferrari, V., Marin-Jimenez, M., Zisserman, A.: Progressive search space reduction for human pose estimation. In: CVPR (2008)
16. Bourdev, L., Malik, J.: Poselets: Body part detectors trained using 3d human pose annotations. In: ICCV (2009)
17. Collins, M.: Discriminative training methods for hidden markov models: theory and experiments with perceptron algorithms. In: EMNLP (2002)
18. Lampert, C., Blaschko, M., Hofmann, T.: Beyond sliding windows: Object localization by efficient subwindow search. In: CVPR (2008)
19. Kschischang, F., Frey, B., Loeliger, H.A.: Factor graphs and the sum-product algorithm. IEEE Transactions on Information Theory 47, 498–519 (2001)
20. Huang, C., Nevatia, R.: High performance object detection by collaborative learning of joint ranking of granule features. In: CVPR (2010)
21. Dalal, N., Triggs, B.: Histogram of oriented gradients for human detection. In: CVPR, pp. 886–893 (2005)
22. Wu, B., Nevatia, R.: Detection of multiple, partially occluded humans in a single image by bayesian combination of edgelet part detectors. In: ICCV, pp. 90–97 (2005)

Co-transduction for Shape Retrieval

Xiang Bai[1], Bo Wang[1], Xinggang Wang[1], Wenyu Liu[1], and Zhuowen Tu[2]

[1] Department of Electronics and Information Engineering,
Huazhong University of Science and Technology, China
{xbai,liuwy}@hust.edu.cn, {wangbo.yunze,wxghust}@gmail.com
[2] Lab of Neuro Imaging, University of California, Los Angeles
ztu@loni.ucla.edu

Abstract. In this paper, we propose a new shape/object retrieval algorithm, *co-transduction*. The performance of a retrieval system is critically decided by the accuracy of adopted similarity measures (distances or metrics). Different types of measures may focus on different aspects of the objects: e.g. measures computed based on contours and skeletons are often complementary to each other. Our goal is to develop an algorithm to fuse different similarity measures for robust shape retrieval through a semi-supervised learning framework. We name our method co-transduction which is inspired by the co-training algorithm [1]. Given two similarity measures and a query shape, the algorithm iteratively retrieves the most similar shapes using one measure and assigns them to a pool for the other measure to do a re-ranking, and vice-versa. Using co-transduction, we achieved a significantly improved result of 97.72% on the MPEG-7 dataset [2] over the state-of-the-art performances (91% in [3], 93.4% in [4]). Our algorithm is general and it works directly on any given similarity measures/metrics; it is not limited to object shape retrieval and can be applied to other tasks for ranking/retrieval.

1 Introduction

Shape-based object retrieval is an important task in computer vision. Given a query object, the most similar objects are retrieved from a database based on a certain similarity/distance measure, whose choice largely decides the performance of a retrieval system. Therefore, it is critically important to have a faithful similarity measure to account for the large intra-class and instance-level variation in configuration, non-rigid transformation, and part change. Designing such a measure is a very difficult task. Fig. (1) gives an illustration where a horse might have a smaller distance to a dog (based on their contours) than another horse, whereas our human vision systems can still identify them correctly.

In this paper, we refer to shape as the contour of an object silhouette. Our algorithm, however, is general and not limited to any particular similarity measure or representation. Building correspondences is often the first step in computing shape difference but it is challenging: two shapes may not have the direct correspondences in representation, regardless if they are represented by sparse points, closed contours, or parametric functions. For example, two shapes with the same

K. Daniilidis, P. Maragos, N. Paragios (Eds.): ECCV 2010, Part III, LNCS 6313, pp. 328–341, 2010.
© Springer-Verlag Berlin Heidelberg 2010

horse   dog   horse
(a)   (b)   (c)

Fig. 1. A horse in (a) may look more similar to a dog in (b) than another horse in (c)

contour but different starting points typically are considered as the same one. Therefore, measuring the similarity between two shapes often can be done in two ways: (1) computing direct difference in features extracted from shape contours, which are invariant to the choice of starting points and robust to certain degree of deformation, such as moments and Fourier descriptors; (2) performing matching to find the detailed point-wise correspondences to compute the differences [5,6]. The latter recently becomes dominate due to their ability of capturing intrinsic properties, and thus leading to more accurate similarity measures. Recently, Yang et al. [3] explored the group contextual information of different shapes to improve the efficiency of shape retrieval on several standard datasets [2,7]. The basic idea was to use shapes as each others' contexts in propagation to reduce the distances between intra-class objects. The implementation was done by a graph-based transduction approach [8]. Later, several other graph-based transduction methods were suggested for shape retrieval [4,9]. Different similarity measures have different emphasis: for example, similarities computed on matching the skeletons of two objects may be robust against non-rigid transformation, but are hard to capture the rich variability in part change; similarities computed on matching the contour parts can capture subtle change but may not be robust against articulation. It would be natural to think to fuse/combine different complementary metrics together to achieve better performance. A straight-forward way is to linearly combine a few measures together. However, this often requires certain level of supervision or manual tuning and will not necessarily produce the best results (we will see a comparison in the experiments).

This paper provides a different way of fusing similarity/distance measures through a semi-supervised learning framework, *co-transduction*. The user input is a query shape and our system returns the most similar shapes by effectively integrating two distance metrics computed by different algorithms, e.g. Shape Contexts [5] and Inner-Distance [6]. Our approach is inspired by the co-training algorithm [1]. The difference though is that, in co-training, it requires having two conditionally independent views of the data samples. In our problem, each data only has one view but different algorithms report measures by exploring different aspects of the data. Therefore, they may lead to different retrieval results for the same query, which can be helpful to each other. For example, as shown in Fig. (2), the retrieval results of Shape Contexts (SC) [5] in the first row and Inner-Distance Shape Contexts (IDSC) [6] in the second row are very different as their different shape representation, even they can gain the comparable Bull-eyes retrieval rate (SC: 86.8%[1], IDSC: 85.4%) in MPEG-7 Shape dataset [2].

Fig. (3) shows another example for illustrating the motivation of the proposed method: In Fig. 3(1), the SC distances between query shape A and B/C are not small due to articulation. However, in Fig. 3(2), IDSC reports different result as it is more stable than SC for articulation changes (it uses the inner distance to replace the Euclidean distance in SC's representation). As shown in Fig. 3, the SC distance between B and C is small as they have the same pose. Even though C is thicker than B, the SC distance still finds a good match between C and B. We use IDSC to retrieval B out firstly, and then put B and query A together as labeled data; a new classifier based on SC distance trained by A and B will give high confidence to C as shown in Fig. 3(4). Our algorithm is

Fig. 2. The first column shows the query shape. The remaining 10 columns show the most similar shapes retrieved from the MPEG-7 data set. The 1st-4th rows are the retrieval results of SC [5], IDSC [6], SC+LP [3], IDSC+LP [3], respectively. The 5th row is the result of the proposed method by integrating two distance metrics computed by SC and IDSC.

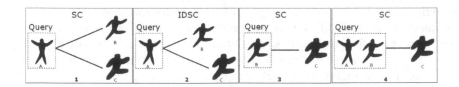

Fig. 3. The motivation of the proposed method

---

[1] Here we use Dynamic Programming (DP) to replace thin plate spline (TPS) as Belongie et al. did in [5] for the matching process and achieve 86.8% on MEPG-7 dataset. The new distance measure by DP based on SC descriptor is used as the input for our retrieval framework.

inspired by co-training [1]. However, unlike co-training in which two independent views (sets of features) are assumed, our algorithm deals with single-view but multiple classifiers; each transduction algorithm on a given similarity measure is a classifier and they help each other by sending most similar results to the others. Co-Transduction is also related to [10] but with the difference: (1) [10] tackles a regression problem; (2) kNN was used in [10]; (3) we focus on fusing different metrics for object retrieval.

2   Co-transduction Algorithm

We first briefly review the graph-based transduction algorithm (label propagation) [8] applied in shape retrieval [3]. Given a set of objects $X = \{x_1, ..., x_n\}$ and a similarity function $sim: X \times X \rightarrow R^+$ that assigns a positive similarity value to each pair of objects. Assume that x_1 is a query object (eg., a query shape), $\{x_2, ..., x_n\}$ is a set of known database objects(or a training set). Then by sorting the values $sim(x_1, x_i)$ in decreasing order for $i = 2, ..., n$ we can obtain a ranking for database objects according to their similarity to the query. A critical issue is then to learn a faithful sim. Yang et al. [3] applied label propagation (diffusion map) to learn a new similarity function sim_T that drastically improves the retrieval results of sim for the given query x_1. They let $w_{i,j} = sim(x_i, x_j)$, for $i, j = 1, ..., n$, be a similarity matrix, then obtain a $n \times n$ probabilistic transition matrix P as a row-wise normalized matrix w.

$$P_{ij} = \frac{w_{ij}}{\sum_{k=1}^{n} w_{ik}} \tag{1}$$

where P_{ij} is the probability of transit from node i to node j.

A a new similarity measure s is computed based on P. Since s is defined as similarity of other elements to query x_1, we denote $f(x_i) = s(x_1, x_i)$ for $i = 1, ..., n$. A key function is f and it satisfies

$$f(x_i) = \sum_{j=1}^{n} P_{ij} \, f(x_j) \tag{2}$$

Thus, the similarity of x_i to the query x_1, expressed as $f(x_i)$, is a weighted average over all other database objects, where the weights sum to one and are proportional to the similarity of the other database objects to x_i. In other words a function $f : X \rightarrow [0, 1]$ such that $f(x_i)$ is a weighted average of $f(x_j)$, where the weights are based on the original similarities $w_{i,j} = sim(x_i, x_j)$.

Note that LP is not limited to only one query object, which also can be used for 2 or more queries as it's a classification method (see the case in Fig. 3(4), there are two query objects A and B). Assume that $\{x_1, ..., x_l\}$ is a group of query objects, and $\{x_{l+1}, ..., x_n\}$ is a set of known database objects. Then the LP algorithm for computing the new similarity can be shown in Fig. 4.

In a general situation, graph-based transduction can be viewed as performing manifold regularization [11]. $f^* = \arg\min_{f \in \mathcal{H}_K} \sum_{i=j}^{l} V(x_j, y_j, f) + \lambda_1 \|f\|_{\mathcal{H}_K}^2 +$

Input: The $n \times n$ row-wise normalized similarity matrix P with the query $\{x_1 ..., x_l\}$, $f_1(x_i) = 1$ for $i = 1, ..., l$, and $f_1(x_i) = 0$ for $i = l+1, ..., n$.
while: $t < T$.
  for $i = l+1, ..., n$,
    $f_{t+1}(x_i) = \sum_{j=1}^{n} P_{ij} \, f_t(x_j)$
  end
  $f_{t+1}(x_i) = 1$ for $i = 1, ..., l$.
end
Output: The learned new similarity values to the query $\{x_1, ...x_l\}$: f_T.

Fig. 4. The pseudo-code of LP algorithm when the query includes a group of objects

$\lambda_2 \mathbf{f}^T L$ which is an approximation to the continuous function space of f based on the labeled (query objects in our case) and unlabeled data (database objects). L is the Laplacian map computed from the similarity measures P. $V(x_j, y_j, f)$ measures classification error of f on the supervised data and $||f||^2_{\mathcal{H}_K}$ is a regularize of f. Now we view LP as a tool to improve an input similarity function by taking the contextual information between objects. *The key problem we want to address in this paper is how to build a robust retrieval system, if there are two (even more) input similarity measures.* A straight-forward solution is to linearly combine different measures and use LP to gain further improvement. We will later show that this yields less encouraging results than the proposed algorithm, co-transduction.

Input: the labeled training set L
      the unlabeled training set U
Process:
    Create a pool U' of examples by choosing u examples at random from U
    Loop for k iterations:
        Use L to train a classifier h_1 that considers only the x_1 portion of x
        Use L to train a classifier h_2 that considers only the x_2 portion of x
        Allow h_1 to label p positive and n negative examples from U'
        Allow h_2 to label p positive and n negative examples from U'
        Add these self-labeled examples to L
        Randomly choose $2p + 2n$ examples from U to replenish U'

Fig. 5. Co-training Algorithm by Blum and Mitchell [1]

Fig. (5) and Fig. (6) give the pseudo-code for co-training [1] and the proposed co-transduction algorithm respectively. Same as in Yang et al. [3], a query object x_1 and database objects $\{x_2, .., x_n\}$ are respectively considered as labeled and unlabeled data for graph transduction. In spirit, co-transduction is in the co-training family; unlike the original co-training algorithm, co-transduction emphasizes single view but different metrics (in a way classifiers). It uses one metric to pull out confident data for the other metric to refine the performance. In implementation, the nearest neighbors of the query object are added to labeled data set for graph transduction in the next iteration based on the other shape similarity. The final similarity sim_F of co-transduction is the average of all the similarities: $sim_F = \frac{1}{2}(sim_1^m + sim_2^m)$.

Input: a query object x_1 (a labeled data)
　　　　the database objects $X = \{x_2, ...x_n\}$ (unlabeled data)
Process:
　　　　Create a $n \times n$ probabilistic transition matrix P_1 based on one type of shape similarity (eg. SC)
　　　　Create a $n \times n$ probabilistic transition matrix P_2 based on another type of shape similarity (eg. IDSC)
　　　　Create two sets Y_1, Y_2 such that $Y_1 = Y_2 = \{x_1\}$
　　　　Create two sets X_1, X_2 such that $X_1 = X_2 = X$
Loop for m iterations:
　　　　Use P_1 to learn a new similarity sim_1^j by graph transduction when Y_1 is used as the query objects ($j = 1, ..., m$ is the iteration index)
　　　　Use P_2 to learn a new similarity sim_2^j by graph transduction when Y_2 is used as the query objects
　　　　　Add the p nearest neighbors from X_1 to Y_1 based on the similarity sim_1^j to Y_2
　　　　　Add the p nearest neighbors from X_2 to Y_2 based on the similarity sim_2^j to Y_1
　　　　　$X_1 = X_1 - Y_1$
　　　　　$X_2 = X_2 - Y_2$
　　　　　(Then X_1, X_2 will be unlabeled data for graph transduction in the next iteration)

Fig. 6. Co-transduction algorithm

When the database of known objects is large, computing all the n objects becomes impractical; in practice, we construct similarity matrix w using the first $M << n$ most similar objects to the query x_1 according to the original similarity, which is similar to Yang et al. [3]. Let S denote the first M similar objects to the query x_1. As different shape similarity often have different S, we use S_1 and S_2 to represent the first M similar objects to x_1 according to two kinds of shape similarity respectively. Then the Pseudo code of an efficient version of Co-Transduction algorithm is shown in Fig. 7, which is used in all our experiments. In our experiments, M is always setting as 300.

Theoretical justification
Next, we provide a brief theoretical discussion of our algorithm. We borrow the analysis from [12], which mostly follows the PAC (probably approximately correct) learning theory. Let H_1^0 and H_2^0 be two classifiers (the two transduction algorithms on different metrics in our case) at round 0. They are respectively bounded by generalization errors $a_0 < 0.5$ and $b_0 < 0.5$ with high probability, $1 - \delta$, in PAC. Then H_1^0 selects u number of unlabeled data samples (database objects) and put them into σ_2 for training H_2^1 using transduction. Let l be the number of labeled data and $G = u \times a_0$. If $l \times b_0 \le e \sqrt[G]{G!} - G$, then

$$Pr[d(H_2^1, H^*) \ge b_1] \le \delta,$$

Input: a query object x_1 (a labeled data)
        the database objects $X = \{x_2, ...x_n\}$ (unlabeled data)
Process:
        Create a $M \times M$ probabilistic transition matrix P_1 based on one
type of shape similarity with the data from S_1
            Create a $M \times M$ probabilistic transition matrix P_2 based on
another type of shape similarity with the data from S_2
        Create two sets Y_1, Y_2 such that $Y_1 = Y_2 = \{x_1\}$
        Create two sets X_1, X_2 such that $X_1 = X_2 = X$
        Loop for m iterations:
            Use P_1 to learn a new similarity sim_1^j by graph transduction
when Y_1 is used as the query objects ($j = 1, ..., m$ is the iteration index)
            Use P_2 to learn a new similarity sim_2^j by graph transduction
when Y_2 is used as the query objects
            Add $N_1 \cap S_2$ (N_1 denotes the p nearest neighbors from X_1 to
Y_1 based on the similarity sim_1^j) to Y_2
            Add $N_2 \cap S_1$ (N_2 denotes the p nearest neighbors from X_2 to
Y_2 based on the similarity sim_2^j) to Y_1
            $X_1 = X_1 - Y_1$
            $X_2 = X_2 - Y_2$
            (Then X_1, X_2 will be unlabeled data for graph transduction
            in the next iteration)

Fig. 7. Co-transduction algorithm for a large database

where H^* is the ideal classifier to retrieve all the correct answers, and $d(H_2^1, H^*)$ measures the difference between learned H_2^1 and H^*. The new error is then

$$b_1 = \max[\frac{l \times b_0 + u \times a_0 - u \times d(H_1^0, H_2^1)}{l}, 0].$$

As we can see, the general guidance to achieve a small b_1 is to: (1) reduce the errors of the original learners (good input metrics); (2) increase the complementariness of the metrics. Our algorithm does not necessarily improve the overall performance if the input metrics are not so good at the first place and they are not so different from each other.

From a different perspective, different measures explore different aspects about similarity; the top M most similar objects w.r.t each measure are often not all correct; however, the most similar one (nearest neighbor) is likely be the case; pulling out the best match by one measure to the other helps to further retrieve similar ones by the other complementary measures. This intuition explains why co-transduction works. Our work is also related to the diffusion map [13] which obtains improved similarity measures for clustering by performing Markov random walks. Our transductive learning component improves similarity measures, just like the diffusion map algorithm, and the fusion of different metrics gives further improvement. By exchanging the improved similarity measures of two transductive learning algorithms, we gradually achieve a fused similarity by letting two originally different measures to meet with each other, which realizes a fusion process. A more detailed theoretical analysis will be left in a longer version.

3   Experimental Results

In this section, we show results on three datasets: MPEG-7 shape dataset [2], Tari's shape dataset [14], and Wei's trademark dataset [15]. In addition, we show our algorithm has a potential to bag-of-feature image search.

3.1   Results on Shape Datasets

The MPEG-7 shape dataset consists of 1400 silhouette images grouped into 70 classes with class having 20 different shapes. Usually the retrieval rate for this dataset is measure by "Bull's eyes test". Every shape in the database is compared to all other shapes, and the number of shapes from the same class among the 40 most similar shapes is reported. The bulls eye retrieval rate is the ratio of the total number of shapes from the same class to the possible number (which is 20×1400). We use the similarities computed by SC [5] and IDSC [6] as the original distance measures. The new similarity obtained by co-transduction resulted in 97.72% on Bull's eyes test, which outperforms existing state-of-the-art algorithms; to further illustrate that our algorithm is independent of specific algorithms, we also use the similarity computed by data-driven general model (DDGM) [16] proposed by Tu and Yuille together with SC or IDSC as the distance measures for co-transduction; we achieve scores 97.45% and 97.31% respectively. These improvements show that the performance gain of our method is general, and not tied to any specific similarity measures. Our results and the scores by several other recent methods on the MPEG-7 dataset are shown in Table 3.1. We observe that co-transduction significantly outperform the alternatives. This demonstrates that integrating different shape similarities is an important direction for shape recognition.

In order to visualize the gain in retrieval rates by our method compared to SC or IDSC , we plot the percentage of correct results among the first k most similar shapes in Fig. 8(a). For example, we plot the percentage of the shapes from the same class among the first k-nearest neighbors for $k = 1, ..., 40$. Recall that each class has 20 shapes and this is the reason for curve $k > 20$. We observe that not only does the proposed method increase the bull's eye score, but also the ranking of the shapes for all $k = 1, ..., 40$ gets improved. In Fig. 8(a), we also plot the curves of retrieval rates for SC/IDSC with graph transduction [3] (eg. SC + LP and IDSC + LP).

Tari's dataset [14] consists of $1,000$ silhouette images grouped into 50 classes with 20 images per class. Tari's dataset has more articulation changes within each class than MPEG-7 dataset as shown in Fig. 9, and consequently IDSC achieved better results than SC on this dataset (see Table 3.1). The retrieval

Table 1. Bull's eyes scores on MPEG-7 dataset [2] and Tari's dataset [14]

Algorithm	MPEG-7 dataset	Tari's dataset
SC [5] (DP)	86.8%	94.17%
IDSC [6]	85.4%	95.33%
DDGM [16]	80.03%	
Planar Graph Cuts [17]	85%	
Shape-tree [18]	87.7%	
Contour Flexibility [19]	89.31%	
IDSC + LP [3]	91%	99.35%
SC + LP [3]	92.91%	97.79%
IDSC + LCDP[9]	93.32%	99.7%
SC + GM + Meta [20]	92.51%	
IDSC + Mutual Graph [4]	93.40%	
SC + IDSC + Co-Transduction	**97.72%**	**99.995%**
IDSC + DDGM + Co-Transduction	**97.31%**	
SC + DDGM + Co-Transduction	**97.45%**	

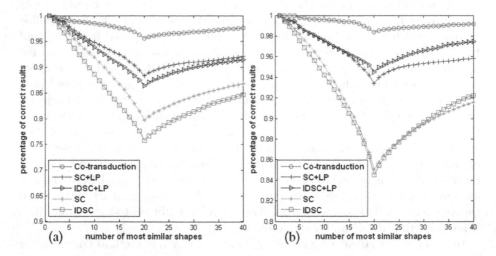

Fig. 8. The curves of retrieval rates for SC, IDSC, SC+LP, IDSC+LP, and Co-Transduction on MPEG-7 shape dataset (a) and Tari's dataset (b)

Fig. 9. Sample images in Tari dataset

performance on this dataset is also measured by "Bull's eyes test". Only one error was made when retrieving all the shapes from the dataset, which means we achieve nearly perfect retrieval rate: 99.995%. Table 3.1 also lists several results of Tari's dataset in comparison with other approaches; we observe that the second highest result by IDSC+LCDP [9] is 99.7% with 60 errors. Same as in Fig. 8(a), the retrieval curves in Fig. 8(b) are plotted to clearly show the performance gain by co-transduction algorithm.

3.2   Results on Trademark Images

We also tested our method on a trademark dataset [15] consisting of 14 different classes with 1,003 trademark images in all. Fig. 10 shows typical some examples from the trademark dataset. To evaluate the performance of trademark retrieval, we use the precision-recall curves. The x-axis and y-axis represent recall and precision rates, respectively. Precision is the ratio of the number of relevant images retrieved to the total number of images retrieved while recall is the number of relevant images to the total number of relevant images stored in the database. For each query image input to the system, the system returns 11 pages of hits with descending similarity rankings, each page containing nine trademark images. This allows the performance of our system to be evaluated on a page-wise manner. Since there are only five classes containing more than 99 images, we only report the precision-recall graph on these five classes. Each curve consists of 11 data points, with the ith point from the left corresponding to the performance when the first i pages of hits are taken into consideration. A precision-recall line stretching longer horizontally and staying high in the graph indicates that the corresponding algorithm performs relatively better. Here, we use two distance measures: moment invariants [21], Zernike [22], which are two kinds of region-based shape features. Then we use our method on these two distance measures. In Fig. 11, the data points shown on the curve for co-transduction are the average precisions and recalls over the five classes. The curves shows that our method can improve the performance of trademark retrieval significantly, which also prove that co-transduction algorithm is good fit for trademark images and different shape distance measures.

Fig. 10. Sample images in Wei's trademark dataset

3.3   Improving Bag-of-Features Image Search with Co-transduction

In this section we show that co-transduction can improve the accuracy of image search. Bag-of-features image representation [23,24] is usually suggested for image search problem. Recently, Jegou et al. [25] proposed a distance learning method called contextual dissimilarity measure (CDM), which can significantly

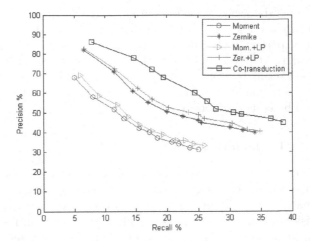

Fig. 11. The precision/recall curves for trademark images

Fig. 12. Sample images of N-S dataset [26]

improve the similarity computed by bag-of-features. We compare our method with CDM on the Nistér and Stewénius (N-S) dataset [26]. The N-S dataset consists of $2,550$ objects or scenes, each of which is imaged from 4 different viewpoints. Hence the dataset has $10,200$ images in total. A few example images from N-S dataset are shown in Fig. 12.

We adopt the method in [25] to compute the similarity for image search. The image descriptor is a combination of Hessian-Affine region detector [27] and SIFT descriptor [28]. A visual vocabulary is obtained using the k-means algorithm on the sub-sampled image descriptors. As co-transduction requires two kind of similarity measures, we proposed a new similarity named **reverse similarity** based on the one by [25]. Let $w_{i,j}$ denote the similarity between objects i and j computed by [25], the reverse similarity $w_{i,j}^r = \frac{1}{d^\beta}$, where d is the ranking number of i when using j as a query for the dataset, and β is a weight factor setting with a constant 10. Reverse similarity is motivated the phenomenon pointed out by [25]: a good ranking is usually not symmetrical in image search, which tells us two objects can be very likely from the same category when they both obtain a good ranking position when using each other as a query. With w and w^r, we can apply co-transduction to image search on N-S dataset, and the measure score is the average number of correct images among

Table 2. The results on N-S dataset

number of distinct visual vocab.	vocab. size	original N-S score	N-S score with CDM	N-S score with co-transduction
1	30000	3.26	3.57	3.66

the four first images returned. Table 3.3 lists the results on N-S dataset. We can observe that co-transduction significantly increases the score from 3.26 to 3.66, which is also better than CDM's result when the number visual vocabulary is 1 and vocabulary size is 30000. Our result demonstrates that co-transduction is also able to improve the performance of image search problem.

3.4 The Parameter Setting and Discussion

As introduced in [29], there are two key parameters for label propagation: α and K. Beside α and K, there are two additional parameters for co-transduction: the iteration number m and the number of nearest neighbors p. For the MPEG-7 and Tari's dataset, we use the following parameter settings: $\alpha = 0.25$, $K = 14$, (which are consistent with the setting in [29]), $m = 4$, and $p = 3$. For the trademark dataset, since the input distance measures are different from the ones for MEPG-7 dataset, the parameter setting is $\alpha = 8$, $K = 8$, $m = 2$, and $p = 2$. For the N-S dataset, the parameters are $\alpha = 0.25$, $K = 10$, $m = 3$, and $p = 1$. Since [29] has introduced a supervised learning method for determining the parameters α and K in details, we no longer review it here. We only need to focus on m and p. As both m and p are integer, the values of them are very easily to set. Table 3.4 shows the scores on MPEG-7 dataset when setting m, p with the integers from 1 to 5. We observe that all these scores are around 97%, which demonstrates the insensitiveness of co-transduction to parameter tuning.

Now we want to discuss why co-transduction is essential. We iteratively run LP on MPEG-7 dataset based on only one type of similarity with the same parameter setting for co-transduction (the p most similar objects will be added into the query set for the next iteration), and we get the bull's eyes scores 92.68% and 91.79% based on SC and IDSC respectively. Compared to the LP's results in Table 3.1, there is not so much change. Let sim'_{SC} and sim'_{IDSC} denote the similarities obtained in the above experiments. We obtain a new similarity sim'_c by linearly combining sim'_{SC} and sim'_{IDSC} as follows: $sim'_c =$

Table 3. The bull's eyes scores on MEPG-7 dataset with different parameter setting

	$m = 1$	$m = 2$	$m = 3$	$m = 4$	$m = 5$
$p = 1$	96.89%	97.05%	97.30%	97.32%	97.34%
$p = 2$	97.06%	97.24%	97.36%	97.45%	97.36%
$p = 3$	97.20%	97.54%	97.63%	97.72%	97.67%
$p = 4$	97.13%	97.30%	97.42%	97.37%	97.32%
$p = 5$	97.24%	97.55%	97.58%	97.20%	96.92%

$\lambda sim'_{SC} + (1-\lambda)sim'_{IDSC}$, where λ is a weight factor. We tuned λ, and the highest score based on sim'_c is 92.0% when λ is 0.9. These results are much lower than the ones by co-transduction, and this illustrates that the performance achieved by co-transduction can not be reached by simply combining the similarities.

4 Conclusion

We have proposed a shape retrieval framework named co-transduction which combines two (our algorithm is actually not limited to just two) different distance metrics. The significant performance improvement on four large datasets has demonstrated the effectiveness of co-transduction for shape/object retrieval.Our future work includes the extension to other problems and providing deeper understanding of the approach.

Acknowledgement

We thank Herve Jegou for the help on the experiments on N-S dataset. This work was jointly supported by NSFC 60903096, NSFC 60873127, ONR N000140910099, NSF CAREER award IIS-0844566, and China 863 2008AA01Z126.

References

1. Blum, A., Mitchell, T.: Combining labeled and unlabeled data with co-training. In: Proc. of COLT, pp. 92–100 (1998)
2. Latecki, L., Lakámper, R., Eckhardt, U.: Shape descriptors for non-rigid shapes with a single closed contour. In: Proc. of CVPR, pp. 424–429 (2000)
3. Yang, X., Bai, X., Latecki, L., Tu, Z.: Improving shape retrieval by learning graph transduction. In: Forsyth, D., Torr, P., Zisserman, A. (eds.) ECCV 2008, Part IV. LNCS, vol. 5305, pp. 788–801. Springer, Heidelberg (2008)
4. Kontschieder, P., Donoser, M., Bischof, H.: Beyond pairwise shape similarity analysis. In: Zha, H., Taniguchi, R.-i., Maybank, S. (eds.) Computer Vision – ACCV 2009. LNCS, vol. 5996. Springer, Heidelberg (2010)
5. Belongie, S., Malik, J., Puzicha, J.: Shape matching and object recognition using shape contexts. IEEE Trans. PAMI 24, 522–705 (2002)
6. Ling, H., Jacobs, D.: Shape classification using the inner-distance. IEEE Trans. PAMI 29, 286–299 (2007)
7. Sebastian, T.B., Klein, P.N., Kimia, B.B.: Recognition of shapes by editing their shock graphs. IEEE Trans. PAMI 25, 116–125 (2004)
8. Zhu, X.: Semi-supervised learning with graphs. In: Doctoral Dissertation, Carnegie Mellon University, CMU–LTI–05–192 (2005)
9. Yang, X., Koknar-Tezel, S., Latecki, L.: Locally constrained diffusion process on locally densified distance spaces with applications to shape retrieval. In: Proc. of CVPR (2009)
10. Zhou, Z.H., Li, M.: Semi-supervised regression with co-training. In: Proc. of IJCAI (2004)

11. Belkin, M., Niyogi, P., Sindhwani, V.: Manifold regularization: A geometric framework for learning from labeled and unlabeled examples. J. of Machine Learning Research 7, 2399–2434 (2006)
12. Wang, W., Zhou, Z.H.: Analyzing co-training style algorithms. In: Kok, J.N., et al. (eds.) ECML 2007. LNCS (LNAI), vol. 4701, pp. 454–465. Springer, Heidelberg (2007)
13. Coifman, R., Lafon, S.: Diffusion maps. Applied and Comp. Harmonic Ana. (2006)
14. Aslan, C., Erdem, A., Erdem, E., Tari, S.: Disconnected skeleton: Shape at its absolute scale. IEEE Trans. PAMI 30, 2188–2201 (2008)
15. Wei, C.H., Li, Y., Chau, W.Y., Li, C.T.: Trademark image retrieval using synthetic features for describing global shape and interior structure. Pattern Recognition 42, 386–394 (2009)
16. Tu, Z., Yuille, A.L.: Shape matching and recognition - using generative models and informative features. In: Pajdla, T., Matas, J(G.) (eds.) ECCV 2004. LNCS, vol. 3023, pp. 195–209. Springer, Heidelberg (2004)
17. Schmidt, F.R., Toeppe, E., Cremers, D.: Efficient planar graph cuts with applications in computer vision. In: Proc. of CVPR (2009)
18. Felzenszwalb, P.F., Schwartz, J.: Hierarchical matching of deformable shapes. In: CVPR (2007)
19. Xu, C., Liu, J., Tang, X.: 2d shape matching by contour flexibility. IEEE Trans. PAMI 31, 180–186 (2009)
20. Egozi, A., Keller, Y., Guterman, H.: Improving shape retrieval by spectral matching and meta similarity. IEEE Trans. Image Processing 19, 1319–1327 (2010)
21. Gonzalez, R., Woods, R., Eddins, S.: Digital image processing using matlab. Prentice-Hall, EnglewoodCliffs (2004)
22. Kim, Y.S., Kim, W.Y.: Content-based trademark retrieval system using a visually salient feature. Image and Vision Computing 16, 931–939 (1998)
23. Nistér, D., Stewénius, H.: Scalable recognition with a vocabulary tree. In: Proc. CVPR, pp. 2161–2168 (2006)
24. Sivic, J., Zisserman, A.: Video google: A text retrieval approach to object matching in videos. In: Proc. ICCV, pp. 1470–1477 (2003)
25. Jegou, H., Schmid, C., Harzallah, H., Verbeek, J.: Accurate image search using the contextual dissimilarity measure. IEEE Trans. PAMI 32, 2–11 (2010)
26. Stewénius, H., Nistér, D.: Object recognition benchmark,
    http://vis.uky.edu/%7Estewe/ukbench/
27. Mikolajczyk, K., Schmid, C.: Scale and affine invariant interest point detectors. IJCV 60, 63–86 (2004)
28. Lowe, D.: Distinctive image features from scale-invariant key points. IJCV 60, 91–110 (2004)
29. Bai, X., Yang, X., Latecki, L., Liu, W., Tu, Z.: Learning context sensitive shape similarity by graph transduction. IEEE Trans. PAMI 32, 861–874 (2010)

Learning Shape Detector by Quantizing Curve Segments with Multiple Distance Metrics

Ping Luo[1,2], Liang Lin[1,2,*], and Hongyang Chao[1]

[1] School of Software, Sun Yat-Sen University, Guangzhou 510275, P.R. China
[2] Lotus Hill Research Institute, P.R. China
pluo.lhi@gmail.com, linliang@ieee.org, isschhy@mail.sysu.edu.cn

Abstract. In this paper, we propose a very efficient method to learn shape models using local curve segments with multiple types of distance metrics. Our learning approach includes two key steps: feature generation and model pursuit. In the first step, for each category, we first extract a massive number of local "prototype" curve segments from a few roughly aligned shape instances. Then we quantize these curve segments with three types of distance metrics corresponding to different shape deformations. In each metric space, the quantized curve segments are further grown (spanned) into a large number of ball-like manifolds, and each of them represents an equivalence class of shape variance. In the second step of shape model pursuit, using these manifolds as features, we propose a fast greedy learning algorithm based on the information projection principle. The algorithm is guided by a generative model, and stepwise selects the features that have maximum information gain. The advantage of the proposed method is identified on several public datasets and summarized as follows. (1) Our models consisting of local curve segments with multiple distance metrics are robust to the various shape deformations, and thus enable us to perform robust shape classification and detect shapes against background clutter. (2) The auto-generated curve-based features are very general and convenient, rather than designing specific features for each category.

1 Introduction

Although many shape descriptors have been proposed for distortion and deformation measurement, learning shape detector incorporating with multiple types of distance metrics has been rarely addressed in previous work. This paper presents a novel learning-based shape detector for detecting and matching shapes from cluttered edge maps.

In the following, we briefly review the previous work for (i) shape descriptors (or similarity measurements) and (ii) learning shape models.

(i) Many shape matching problems are posed as minimizing the distance measures of deformation and bending by searching corresponding points between two shapes. Most of these distance measures are mainly defined on the spaced landmarks of shape boundaries and designed to account for various shape transformation. For example, the procrustes distance [9] is very robust to the rigid affine transformation; the inner distance [13] and shock graph distance [21] capture the articulation transformation very well. Recently, to deal with more complex non-rigid shape deformations

---

* Corresponding author.

K. Daniilidis, P. Maragos, N. Paragios (Eds.): ECCV 2010, Part III, LNCS 6313, pp. 342–355, 2010.

and configurations, the context and hierarchy of shapes have been the theme of recent work [1, 7, 17, 16]. Despite of the acknowledged success of these methods, it is still an open problem to adaptively select the proper shape distances corresponding to different shape categories.

(ii) Early work on learning shape models include learning contour groups with perception organization [19, 26] and learning global modes of variation with the Active Shape Models [3]. In the research of object detection, contour-based features were widely adopted due to their large invariance against lighting conditions and variations in object color and texture [22, 8]. However, in the context of noisy edge maps and background clutter, shape contours are often considered as been less discriminative. Some recent hierarchical or part-based object models [10, 23] prefer region (or appearance) features.

In this paper, we argue that automatic object recognition was indeed achievable by employing only shape contour information. Incorporating with multiple types of distance metrics, the proposed shape detectors are robust to capture various shape deformations, and thus enable us to perform stable shape classification and detect shapes against background clutter. Our approach includes two key steps: (i) automatic feature generation and (ii) generative shape model pursuit.

In the first step, for each category, we first extract a massive number of local "prototype" curve segments from roughly aligned shape instances and quantize each of them with three types of different descriptors, i.e. procrustes distance [18], articulation distance and geodesic distance [12]. This is inspired by the classical work of shape analysis [6], which shows that the arbitrary deformation of a shape curve (or contour) can be decomposed into three types: the rigid (affine) transformation, articulation transformation, and distortion (twist). The three distances we employed are proven to accordingly capture the three typical transformations very well. In the rest of this paper, we call these "prototype" curve segments as proto-curves for simplification.

In the perspective of mathematics, each proto-curve quantized by a descriptor can be viewed as a point in the metric space, where this point can be further spanned into a manifold by introducing a statistical fluctuation ϵ. As illustrated in Fig.1 (a), we visually define the manifold centering at a proto-curve as an "ϵ-ball", in the sense that the ball-like manifold is essentially an equivalence class of the proto-curve in the metric space. Moreover, each ϵ-ball encodes the relative location (i.e. global spatial configuration) of the proto-curve with respect to the center of the shape that we extracted the proto-curve from, inspired by the Implicit Shape Model [14]. Therefore, given an input shape, each ϵ-ball can be further defined as a "visual feature" or classifier that decides whether the testing shape has the similar local deformation corresponding to the ϵ-ball.

In the second step of shape model pursuit, we propose a fast greedy feature selection algorithm based on the information projection principle [4]. For each shape category, the training set consists of a small number of positive samples and a certain amount of reference samples chosen over all categories. The algorithm is guided by a generative shape model based on the Pietra's representation [20], in that each feature (ϵ-ball) captures the shape variance explicitly and generatively. In our learning algorithm, different types of features, (i.e. proto-curves quantized by different metrics), are made comparable to each other by an information gain criterion; the shape model pursuit is formulated

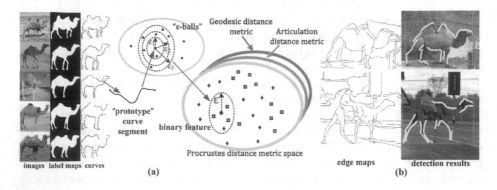

Fig. 1. (a) Illustrates that we extract "prototype" curve segments from the roughly aligned shapes and quantize each of them with three metrics. Each quantized proto-curve is spanned to a few manifolds. We name each manifold "ϵ-ball" and define it as binary feature. Here the circle, square and diamond denote the proto-curve, positive sample and reference (negative) sample respectively. (b) shows two significant clutter edge maps and their corresponding detection results. The detected curves and shape bounding box are plotted in yellow and green respectively.

as the procedure of maximizing the log-likelihood ratio of positive samples against the reference samples, with stepwise feature selection. By pruning the correlated features within the feature selection, we assume that the likelihood ratio can be factorized into individual likelihood ratios of the features. As a result, the shape model is in the form of the weighted sum of a small number of ϵ-balls. In the testing stage, given a learned shape model, we adopt the sliding window approach to fast localize and match shapes from clutter edge maps, as shown in Fig.1 (b).

The key contribution of this paper is summarized as follows. (1) We propose a general approach to produce shape features by growing manifolds from curve segments in different distance metrics. (2) We present a simple algorithm to learn generative shape models consisting of multiple types of features by an information gain criterion. (3) Our approach is tested on two challenging datasets, such as the ETHZ shape dataset [8] and a 40 categories image dataset chosen from LHI database [24], and shows the-state-of-the-art performance.

The remainder of this paper is arranged as follows. We first introduce our curve-based features in sec.2, including three distance metrics and feature generation. The algorithm for pursuing shape models and a shape matching algorithm are proposed in sec.3. The experimental evaluations are presented in sec.4. The paper concludes with a summary in sec.5.

2   Feature Generation via ϵ-Balls

In this section, we will introduce the procedure of curve-based feature generation with three types of shape distances.

In our method, a shape **S** is represented by a batch of curve segments {**c**}. As illustrated in Fig.2, a curve segment c from the shape **S** is described as a two tuple

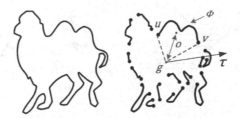

Fig. 2. A shape **S** is represented by a batch of curve segments. We encode the relative position of the curve segment with respect to the shape. u, v denote two end points of the curve, the mass center of the shape is g and the orientation of a shape is τ.

$\{\Phi, \Gamma = (\theta_u, \theta_v, o)\}$, where Φ is the set of interpolated landmarks along c. $\Gamma = (\theta_u, \theta_v, o)$ indicates the relative position of the curve segment c with respect to the shape **S**. Supposing u, v denote two end points of c, the mass center of the shape is g and the orientation of the shape is τ, θ_u denotes the relative angle between gu and τ, and θ_v is defined similarly at end point v. o is the offset of the curve centroid related to g. Note that the orientation of a shape can be calculated by the PCA method.

At the first step of feature generation, we extract a number of curve segments, namely, proto-curve, from the shape instances in the training set. We denote this proto-curve as boldface letter **c**. Then we quantize each curve segment with three different distances corresponding to various shape deformation. In the three metric spaces, each quantized proto-curve **c** is further spanned into a number of ball-like manifold, called "ϵ-ball", as follows,

$$\Omega^w(\mathbf{c}) = \{c : \mathcal{D}^w(c, \mathbf{c}) < \epsilon\}, \tag{1}$$

where $w \in \{'p','a','g'\}$ indicates the type of distance metrics, i.e. procrustes distance, articulation distance and geodesic distance. We will introduce three distance metrics later on. Each ϵ-ball can be viewed as an equivalent class bounded by residual ϵ, in which each element c may share the same statistical characteristics with respect to **c**.

Furthermore, an ϵ-ball can be naturally transformed to a binary feature (weak classifier), $h_i = \Omega^w(\mathbf{c}), i = 1, \ldots M$, ($M$ indicates the size of the feature set), and given a testing shape **S**, its response is defined as,

$$r_i(\mathbf{S}) = \begin{cases} 1, & \mathcal{D}^w(c', \mathbf{c}) < \epsilon, \exists c' \in \mathbf{S} \ s.t. \ \Gamma_{c'} \approx \Gamma_{\mathbf{c}}, \\ 0, & otherwise, \end{cases} \tag{2}$$

where $\Gamma_{c'} \approx \Gamma_{\mathbf{c}}$ indicates that two curve segment c' and **c** have the similar relative position with respect to the shape. Intuitively, one shape **S** is predicted as positive by the feature h is equivalent to existing a curve c' in **S** that has the almost the same relative position as well as the same similarity the distance metric similar deformation compared to the proto-curve **c**. Unlike the discriminative boundaries in many previous work [8], the proposed manifold features "keep silence" (equal to 0) to a shape **S** not falling into them.

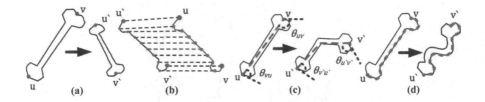

Fig. 3. (a) Shows the rigid transformation between two bones and (b) shows bijection correspondence between two curve segments using procrustes analysis. (c) and (d) illustrate the articulated transformation and distortion (twist) between two shapes respectively.

2.1   Quantizing Curve Segments

For each proto-curve **c**, we map it into three different metric space, in that the proto-curves are transformed as a quantized point. It worth mentioning that though the various distance metrics are not entirely uncorrelated, they capture different characteristics of the shape.

Procrustes distance metric: $\varOmega^p(\mathbf{c})$. We adopt the squared Procrustes distance [6] to measure the goodness of match between a pair of curve segments. By writing the co-ordinates of $x_i = (\xi_i, \eta_i)$ in c and $y_i = (\xi_i', \eta_i')$ in **c** in complex form, namely, X and Y, respectively, we have

$$\mathcal{D}^p(c, \mathbf{c}) = 1 - \frac{|Y^* \cdot X|^2}{Y^* \cdot Y \cdot X^* \cdot X}, \tag{3}$$

where X^* and Y^* are the conjugate forms of X and Y. One exemplar of this metric is illustrated in Fig.3 (a), which shows the rigid transformation between two bones. Fig.3 (b) exhibits bijection correspondence of curves computed by procrustes analysis [9].

Articulation distance metric: $\varOmega^a(\mathbf{c})$. In order to capture articulation invariance shown in Fig.3 (c) between a pair of curve segments, we design articulation distance metric by employing three geometrical shape descriptors as,

$$\mathcal{D}^a(c, \mathbf{c}) = \min | \varUpsilon(c) - \varUpsilon(\mathbf{c}) |, \tag{4}$$

where $\varUpsilon(\cdot)$ denotes a six dimensional vector of the curve segment, (ID,A1,A2,S1,S2,S3), that combines the following three shape descriptors together.

● *Inner-distance between the ends (ID):* The traditional computing process of the inner distance [13] which refers to the shortest path between a pair of points within the whole shape silhouette is suitable for label maps during the learning procedure, but suffers pain when dealing with clutter edge maps in the testing stage, since there is no information about the inner and the outer parts (Fig.1 (b)). Thus we improve it by finding two shortest pathes between u, v following (i) respectively building two weighted undirected-graphs with the landmarks as their nodes on both sides of the curve, and (ii) individually applying the shortest route algorithm (e.g. Bellman-Ford) over these graphical structures.

• *Relative angles (A1, A2):* As shown in Fig.3 (c), we achieve the angles $A1 = \theta_{uv}$, $A2 = \theta_{vu}$ between the path uv and the tangents at u and v respectively.

• *Articulated-invariant curve signature (S1, S2, S3):* Let d^{in} be the inner distance matrix of a curve segment calculated between each pair of landmarks. While mapping d^{in} into Euclidean distance space d^{eu} by multidimensional scaling (MDS), the landmark point set Φ will be transformed into a new one Φ', which can be computed by minimizing the following equation,

$$\Phi'^* = \arg\min_{\Phi'} \sum_i^{|\Phi|} \sum_j^{|\Phi|} \frac{(d^{in}(i, j; \Phi) - d^{eu}(i, j; \Phi'))^2}{d^{in}(i, j; \Phi)^2}. \tag{5}$$

And the articulated-invariant curve signature is defined to be a triple (S1, S2, S3), that it is the l_2-norm between $< u', v' >$, $< u', v'_{cen} >$ and $< v'_{cen}, v' >$ respectively, where $u', v' \in \Phi'$ and v'_{cen} is the center point of the mapped curve segment.

Geodesic distance metric: $\Omega^g(\mathbf{c})$. The geodesic distance between each pair of points on a 3D shape keeps stationary even though the shape is distorted. And this would be the same case if two 2D shapes to be matched have approximately identical view. Thus, we use the contour distance as an analogue to model distortive transformation (Fig.3 (d)). And $\mathcal{D}^g(c, \mathbf{c})$ indicates the Euclidean distance between the contour length of c and the length of the proto-curve. Due to different lengths of the curve segments, $\Omega^g(\mathbf{c})$ has been proved a discriminative distance metric in practice (see sec.4).

2.2 Feature Evolution

We conduct a procedure called "feature evolution" to calculate the residual ϵ for each manifold feature $\Omega^w(\mathbf{c})$. In practice, we generate three ϵ-balls for each proto-curve $\mathbf{c}$ in each metric space.

Recall that the all proto-curves are quantized points in the metric space. Intuitively, for each $\mathbf{c}$, we grow the ϵ starting from an initial small number, and the more neighboring proto-curves will fall into the growing ball when the ϵ increases. The specific value of ϵ relies on the number of neighboring proto-curves in the ϵ-ball. In our implementation, the discretized value of ϵ is computed by the ball containing 0.1%, 0.3% and 0.5% amount of total proto-curves.

We ensure feature independence by pruning those redundant ϵ-balls with high relevance, i.e. having the same similarity and relative position. We thus calculate the mutual correlation between arbitrary two features following the theory of Pearsonian Correlation Coefficient in Statistics,

$$corr(h_i \mid h_j) = \frac{\sum_k r_i(\mathbf{c}_k) \cdot r_j(\mathbf{c}_k)}{\sum_k r_j(\mathbf{c}_k)}. \tag{6}$$

Note the correlation is non-symmetric measured. For example, if a feature h_i is totally covered by h_j, then $corr(h_i \mid h_j) < 1$ and $corr(h_j \mid h_i) = 1$.

3 Learning Shape Models via Information Projection

With a large amount of "ϵ-balls" as features, we introduce a novel learning algorithm based on information projection [4], embedded with a loop named "MaxMin-KL", to pursue the generative shape models that implicitly form the quantized curve segments based deformable templates.

3.1 Learning Procedure

We pursue the generative shape model on a given training set $\{(S_1, l_1), ..., (S_N, l_N)\}$, where $l \in \{1, 0\}$ denotes the label of each sample.

Let $f(S)$ be the target distribution of a shape category. To learn a generative model with a few positive examples, we gradually pursue a series of models $p_1(S), p_2(S), ...,$ $p_t(S)$ to approach $f(S)$ from a background model $q(S)$ (reference samples) by step-wise selecting the most informative features, which lead to the fastest decreasing of the information gain. Since any shape S is projected into the feature spaces, we can redefine our problem that $p_t(r_1, r_2, ..., r_t)$ must agree upon dimensions $(r_1, r_2, ..., r_t)$ with the target distribution $f(r_1, r_2, ..., r_t)$, where r_t is the response of the selected feature h_t. Therefore, in each step, we choose a feature h_t to maximize KL divergence $\mathcal{KL}(p_t(r_t) \parallel p_{t-1}(r_t))$. Since the overlapping features have been roughly pruned, we may assume that $p_{t-1}(r_t) \approx q(r_t)$ (i.e. feature independence). With this independence assumption, the likelihood ratio of $f(r_t)$ and $q(r_t)$ can be factorized into individual likelihood ratios for the features. Thus, our shape model has the following form,

$$p_T(S) = q(S) \prod_{t=1}^{T} \frac{1}{Z_t} \exp\{\lambda_t r_t(S)\}, \tag{7}$$

where $Z_t = E_q[\exp\{\lambda_t r_t(S)\}]$ is the normalized term and each λ_t is found by $E_f[r_t] = E_{p_t}[r_t]$. And the following log-linear equation would provide a matching score against background for a given shape,

$$H(S) = \log \frac{p_T(S)}{q(S)} = \sum_{t=1}^{T} (\lambda_t r_t(S) - \log Z_t), \tag{8}$$

which can be combined with a threshold γ ($\gamma = 0$ in our implementation) for object classification.

We repeat two steps called "MaxMin-KL" for pursuing the shape model, that is se-lecting feature h_t and calculating the parameters λ_t and Z_t in Eq.(8). During the t-th pursuit iteration, we perform:

1) a max-step to argumentatively maximize the $\mathcal{KL}(p_t(r_t) \parallel q(r_t))$ for choosing a most distinct feature h_t.

Proposition 1: *Let $f_i^{obs} = E_f[r_i]$ and $q_i^{ref} = E_q[r_i]$ be the expectations of any feature h_i responding to positives and reference samples respectively. We select a most distinct feature by maximizing KL-divergence in iteration t as*

$$h_t^* = \arg\max(f_t^{obs} - q_t^{ref})^2. \tag{9}$$

Proof: Let $r_t = E_{p_t}[r_t]$ be a variable, we establish a function $\Psi(r_t) = \mathcal{KL}(p_t(r_t) \parallel q(r_t)) = \lambda_t r_t - \log Z_t$. Perform Taylor expansion of $\Psi(r_t)$ at point $E_{p_{t-1}}[r_t]$,

$$\Psi(r_t) \approx \underbrace{\Psi(E_{p_{t-1}}[r_t])}_{=0} + \underbrace{\frac{\partial \Psi(E_{p_{t-1}}[r_t])}{\partial r_t}}_{=0}(r_t - E_{p_{t-1}}[r_t])$$

$$+ \underbrace{\frac{\partial^2 \Psi(\frac{r_t + E_{p_{t-1}}[r_t]}{2})}{2\partial r_t^2}(r_t - E_{p_{t-1}}[r_t])^2}_{\approx (r_t - E_{p_{t-1}}[r_t])^2} + \ldots$$

$$\approx (r_t - E_{p_{t-1}}[r_t])^2 = (E_{p_t}[r_t] - E_q[r_t])^2 \qquad (10)$$

from which we can choose Eq.(9) as an approximation.

Intuitively, after selecting h_t, we can simply update f_i^{obs} and q_i^{ref} for each feature h_i as,

$$f_i^{obs} = E_{p_t}[r_i] \cong \frac{1}{N^+}(1 - corr(h_t \mid h_i)) \sum_{j=1}^{N^+} r_i(\mathbf{S}_j), \qquad (11)$$

$$q_i^{ref} = E_q[r_i] \cong \frac{1}{N^-}(1 - corr(h_t \mid h_i)) \sum_{j=1}^{N^-} r_i(\mathbf{S}_j),$$

where N^+, N^- stand for the number of positives and reference examples respectively and $corr(h_t \mid h_i)$ is defined in Eq.(6), which guides to perform the sparse feature set. In each iteration, the features that have their correlations with the selected feature h_t exceed a threshold δ will be directly excluded ($\delta = 0.2$ in our implementation).

2) a min-step to compute λ_t, Z_t for the selected h_t in order to meet the constraint $E_f[r_t] = E_{p_t}[r_t]$.

Proposition II: *Given the selected feature h_t, the parameters λ_t and Z_t of the current model is,*

$$\lambda_t = \log \frac{f_t^{obs}(1 - q_t^{ref})}{(1 - f_t^{obs})q_t^{ref}} \quad \text{and} \quad Z_t = e^{\lambda_t}q_t^{ref} + 1 - q_t^{ref}. \qquad (12)$$

Proof: *As discussed above, $Z_t = E_q[\exp\{\lambda_t r_t(\mathbf{S})\}] = \sum_{\mathcal{D}^{w_t}} q(r_t)\exp\{\lambda_t r_t(\mathbf{S})\}$, which can be partitioned by $\mathcal{D}^{w_t}$ as*

$$Z_t = \sum_{\mathcal{D}^{w_t} < \epsilon_t} q(r_t)\exp\{\lambda_t\} + \sum_{\mathcal{D}^{w_t} \geq \epsilon_t} q(r_t) \qquad (13)$$

$$= e^{\lambda_t} E_q[r_t] + 1 - E_q[r_t] = e^{\lambda_t}q_t^{ref} + 1 - q_t^{ref}.$$

Similarly, the analytical solution of λ_t can be easily proved in the same way.

The stepwise learning algorithm is summarized in Alg.1.

3.2   Shape Matching from Clutter Background

While the learned shape model in sec.3.1 consists a sparse feature set incorporated with different distance metrics, the corresponding proto-curves of features are directly used

---

Algorithm 1. Features pursuit

Input: A small set of positive shapes (i.e. we name it the "proto set") for extracting
proto-curves and a training set, which contains a small number of positive samples
and a certain amount of reference samples. The positive examples and the shapes
of the proto set have no intersection, and have been normalized to the same scale.

Initialization: determining ϵ for each "ϵ-ball" to generate shape features by feature
evolution (sec.2.2); computing correlation between each pair of features by Eq.(6).

Loop t=1 to T

   max-step: select a distinct feature h_t^* by Eq.(9); update f_i^{obs}, q_i^{ref} for any feature h_i by
Eq.(11) and prune correlated features with δ.

   min-step: calculate λ_t, Z_t for h_t^* by Eq.(12).

   ⋆ *until information gain is smaller than a threshold (say 0.05) then stop.*

Output: A generative model (i.e. a strong classifier with a threshold $\gamma = 0$) for a
shape category,

$$H(\mathbf{S}) = \sum_{t=1}^{T}(\lambda_t r_t(\mathbf{S}) - \log Z_t).$$

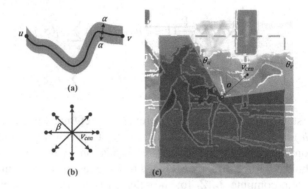

Fig. 4. (a) Shows a proto-curve as in the left of Fig.1 (a). We detect object contours from the edge
map inside a ribbon of each proto-curve. (b) illustrates the idea of moving the ribbon around its
eight neighborhood. (c) shows that each ribbon is used as the deformable template.

as deformable templates to match shape from clutter background in this section. We
adopt a coarse-to-fine sliding window approach [5] and normalize the points inside each
detection window to the same scale as the training step (Alg.1). Our goal is to sample
curves and calculate response of the feature by Eq.(2). Since the object boundaries in
clutter edge map are usually broken and surrounded by noise, it is natural to sample
curves by scanning specific regions according to the spatial configuration of the proto-
curve.

A template is defined as a four tuple $\{\mathbf{c}, v_{cen}, \alpha, \beta\}$, where v_{cen} indicates the center
point of the proto-curve $\mathbf{c}$ and α, β are two radii acting on each landmark of $\mathbf{c}$ and v_{cen}
respectively. Each template is working as follows. (i) We detect object boundary inside
a ribbon of $\mathbf{c}$, that is obtaining by marching each landmark off its normal direction with
a small distance α as illustrated in Fig.4 (a). (ii) A partial scan strategy is proposed
to sample curves from clutter edge map. we first place this ribbon inside the detection
window referring to the position of v_{cen}, which can be accurately calculated by its end

directions and center offset (Fig.4 (c)), and then move it around with a small radius β as shown in Fig.4 (b). (iii) Finally we compute the minimum distance of the sampled curves and the proto-curve using the related distance metric.

The above method is inspired by the part-based detection work [2], which uses single shape contour as template and gradients of each point as feature. The experimental results in sec.4 demonstrate that our promotion is successful. Combining with multiple metrics, the pursued shape model is robust and flexible to account for various deformation, occlusion and noise.

4   Experiments

We evaluate the proposed shape detectors with the following three experiments.

• **Experiment I. Shape detection from cluttered edge maps.** We select four classes (e.g. Bottles, Giraffes, Mugs and Swans) from the ETHZ image dataset [8] for this experiment. For each category, we partition the images into two half for training and testing respectively. Due to too few amount of this dataset, we use another 30 shapes LHI database [24] for extracting proto-curves. It worth mentioning that there are no any overlapped data between the two datasets. In this experiment, our method takes only about 2 minutes to learn four shape models.

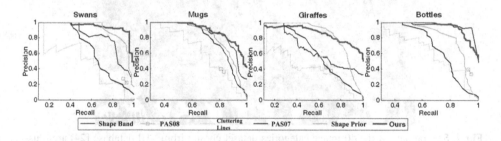

Fig. 5. Comparison of precision vs recall (PR) curves for four classes on ETHZ

Table 1. The precisions are compared to [11, 2, 19, 8] at the same recall rates

	Bottles	Giraffes	Swans	Mugs
Our precision/recall	83.9%/92.7%	83.4%/70.3%	**88.5%/93.9%**	**84.4%/83.4%**
Shape Prior CVPR09 [11]	39.6%/92.7%	**88.7%/70.3%**	60.4%/93.9%	69.9%/83.4%
Shape Band CVPR09 [2]	**95.0%/92.7%**	56.0%/70.3%	44.1%/93.9%	83.3%/83.4%
Cluttering Lines ICCV09 [19]	41.3%/92.7%	37.5%/70.3%	19.8%/93.9%	40.1%/83.4%
Ferrari 2008 [8]	33.3%/92.7%	43.9%/70.3%	23.3%/93.9%	40.9%/83.4%

Detecting results: the results of our algorithm are summarized in Fig.5. We compare with the results by [11, 2, 19, 8] using precision vs recall (PR) curves, where the advantage of our method is clearly identified. We also compared our approach to those

Fig. 6. Some selected results on ETHZ dataset [8] with the detected bounding boxes and contours plotted in green and yellow respectively

Fig. 7. Several data of the 40 image categories dataset chosen from LHI database [24] are illustrated. The last row shows some corresponding label maps.

methods at the same recall rates in Tab.1. Fig.6 shows some representative results on this dataset with the detected boxes (in green color) and localized curves by our system.

• **Experiment II. Shape-based categorization from images.** We further evaluate our method on a 40 categories image dataset selected from LHI database [24]. It contains about 3600 images and each with its corresponding edge map and label map. Our task is to detect and classify shapes from the edge maps. Due to the the heavy occlusion, shading, and surrounding clutter, this task is more complex. For example, the animal faces in Fig.7 are hardly distinguished. In the training stage, for each category, we separate the images into three equal parts: one for extracting proto-curves, one for learning models and the other for testing.

Results: we obtain an overall classification rate approaching 87.3%, which is better than the 81.4% reported in [15], and Fig.8 shows several selected results on this dataset.

Fig. 8. We show some selected results on LHI dataset [24] and demonstrate that the shape detectors are robust to various deformations, background clutter and occlusion

Additional details of Experiment I and II are summarized here: the label maps used during the training stage are roughly annotated and aligned manually. Each of them is normalized to 256×256 with the aspect ratio preserved, and vectorized to 200 landmark points. For each shape in the proto set, we extract about one hundred prototype curves that represented by 30~120 spaced landmarks. There are thus more than 10^4 features in total. The maximum iteration number T in Alg.1 is set to be 500. In the testing stage, we obtain edge maps of the images by canny detector and also normalize each detection window to 256×256. The radius α of each ribbon is set as 15 and the radius β is 10 (see sec.3.2).

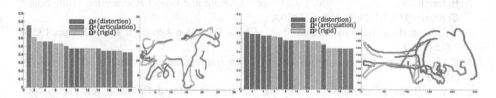

Fig. 9. Top 20 most informative features of horse (left) and mouse (right) are both plotted and visualized . Different colors indicate three distance metrics. From these results, we conclude that horses are more likely to perform articulation and mice are usually distorted, which matches our intuition very well. Moreover, we find that articulation mostly occurs on four limbs while distortion happens more often on the back and tail of animals. The shape models consisting of ϵ-balls can be viewed as the implicit deformable templates that includes different local shape variance.

- **Experiment III. Evaluating for feature selection.** It is an interesting experiment to reveal which types of features, corresponding to different deformation metrics, are effective for different shape categories. We use two categories, horse and mouse, from the data in the Experiment II. As shown in Fig.9, top 20 informative features (i.e. first selected by our algorithm) are plotted and visualized respectively. Features with different distance metrics are denoted by different colors (green for procrustes metric Ω^p, orange for articulation metric Ω^a and purple for geodesic metric Ω^g). The results show that horses are more likely to perform articulation and mice are usually distorted, which matches our intuitive observation very well. Moreover, from these results we find that articulation mostly occurs on the limbs while distortion happens more often on the back and tail of animals. The shape models consisting of ϵ-balls can be viewed as the implicit deformable templates that includes different local shape variance.

5   Conclusion

In this paper, we learn shape models using local curve segments with multiple types of distance metrics. These shape models consisting of quantized curve segments can be viewed as the implicit deformable templates that incorporate different local shape variance. We show that our method significantly improves the shape classification and detection results on two public datasets. In the future work, we will implement a sophisticated design for further modeling distinct shape transformations and supporting wide range of shape descriptors more generally.

Acknowledgements. The work at LHI was supported by NSF China grants 90920009 and 60970156, and China 863 programs 2008AA01Z126 and 2009AA01Z331. The authors are thankful to Dr.Song-Chun Zhu and Dr. Yingnian Wu at UCLA for their insightful discussions and helpful comments.

References

1. Belongie, S., Malik, J., Puzicha, J.: Shape Matching and Object Recognition Using Shape Contexts. TPAMI 24(4), 509–522 (2002)
2. Bai, X., et al.: Shape Band: A Deformable Object Detection Approach. In: CVPR, pp. 1335–1342 (2009)
3. Cootes, T.F., et al.: Active Shape Models - their training and application. CVIU 61, 38–59 (1995)
4. Csiszar, I., et al.: Information Theory and Statistics: A Tutorial. Commun. Inf. Theory 1(4), 417–528 (2004)
5. Dalal, N., et al.: Histograms of Oriented Gradients for Human Detection. In: CVPR, vol. 1(1), pp. 886–893 (2005)
6. Dryden, I.L., Mardia, K.V.: Statistical Shape Analysis. John Wiley and Son, Chichester (1998)
7. Felzenszwalb, P.F., Schwartz, J.D.: Hierarchical Matching of Deformable Shapes. In: CVPR (2007)
8. Ferrari, V., Jurie, F., Schmid, C.: From Images to Shape models for Object Detection. Intern'l Jour. of Computer Vision (2009)
9. Goodall, C.: Procrustes Methods in the Statistical Analysis of Shape. Jour. Royal Statistical Society 53, 285–339 (1991)

10. Gu, C., Lim, J.J., Arbelaez, P., Malik, J.: Recognition using Regions. In: CVPR (2009)
11. Jiang, T., Jurie, F., Schmid, C.: Learning Shape Prior Models for Object Matching. In: CVPR, pp. 848–855 (2009)
12. Klassen, E., Srivastava, A., Mio, W., Joshi, S.: Analysis of Planar Shapes Using Geodesic Paths on Shape Spaces. IEEE Trans. PAMI 26(3), 372–383 (2004)
13. Ling, H., Jacobs, D.W.: Shape Classification Using the Inner-distance. TPAMI 29(2), 286–299 (2007)
14. Leibe, B., et al.: Combined Object Categorization and Segmentation With An Implicit Shape Model. In: ECCV Workshop, pp. 17–32 (2004)
15. Lin, L., et al.: An Empirical Study of Object Category Recognition: Sequential Testing with Generalized Samples. In: ICCV, vol. 1, pp. 419–426 (2007)
16. Lin, L., Wu, T., Xu, Z., Porway, J.: A Stochastic Graph Grammar for Compositional Object Representation and Recognition. Pattern Recognition 42(7), 1297–1307 (2009)
17. Lin, L., Liu, X., Zhu, S.C.: Layered Graph Matching with Composite Cluster Sampling. IEEE Trans. PAMI (2010)
18. McNeill, G., et al.: Hierarchical Procrustes Matching for Shape Retrieval. In: CVPR, vol. 1, pp. 885–894 (2006)
19. Ommer, B., et al.: Multi-Scale Object Detection by Clustering Lines. In: ICCV (2009)
20. Pietra, V.D., et al.: Inducing Features of Random Fields. TPAMI 19, 380–393 (1997)
21. Siddiqi, K., et al.: Shock Graphs and Shape Matching. IJCV 35(1), 13–32 (1999)
22. Shotton, J., Blake, A., Cipolla, R.: Multi-Scale Categorical Object Recognition Using Contour Fragments. IEEE Tran. PAMI (2008)
23. Todorovic, S., Ahuja, N.: Unsupervised Category Modeling, Recognition, and Segmentation in Images. IEEE Tran. PAMI (2008)
24. Yao, B., Yang, X., Lin, L., Lee, M.W., Zhu, S.C.: I2T: Image Parsing to Text Description. Proceedings of IEEE (2010) (to appear)
25. Yu, X., Yi, L., Fermuller, C., Doermann, D.: Object Detection Using Shape Codebook. In: BMVC (2007)
26. Zhu, Q., et al.: Contour Context Selection for Object Detection: A set-to-set contour matching approach. In: Forsyth, D., Torr, P., Zisserman, A. (eds.) ECCV 2008, Part II. LNCS, vol. 5303, pp. 774–787. Springer, Heidelberg (2008)

Unique Signatures of Histograms for Local Surface Description

Federico Tombari, Samuele Salti, and Luigi Di Stefano

CVLab - DEIS, University of Bologna,
Viale Risorgimento, 2 - 40135 Bologna, Italy
{federico.tombari,samuele.salti,luigi.distefano}@unibo.it
http://www.vision.deis.unibo.it

Abstract. This paper deals with local 3D descriptors for surface matching. First, we categorize existing methods into two classes: *Signatures* and *Histograms*. Then, by discussion and experiments alike, we point out the key issues of uniqueness and repeatability of the local reference frame. Based on these observations, we formulate a novel comprehensive proposal for surface representation, which encompasses a new unique and repeatable local reference frame as well as a new 3D descriptor. The latter lays at the intersection between Signatures and Histograms, so as to possibly achieve a better balance between descriptiveness and robustness. Experiments on publicly available datasets as well as on range scans obtained with *Spacetime Stereo* provide a thorough validation of our proposal.

1 Introduction and Previous Work

The ability of computing similarities between 3D surfaces, sometimes referred to as *surface matching* [1], is a key for computer vision tasks such as 3D object recognition and surface alignment. These tasks find numerous applications in fields such as robotics, automation, biometric systems, reverse engineering, search in 3D object databases [1] [2] [3].

There has been strong research interest in surface matching since the 1980's. Early works were based on fitting 3D data with global parametric surfaces such as *geons* [4] or *superquadrics* [5]. For the last 15 years though, the most popular trend for surface matching exploits a compact local representation of the input data, known as *descriptor*, and shares basic motivations with the successful approaches for matching 2D images that rely on local invariant features. Local correspondences established by matching 3D descriptors (Fig. 1) can then be used to solve higher level tasks such as 3D object recognition. This approach allows for dealing effectively with issues such as occlusion, clutter and changes of viewpoint. As a result, a variety of proposals for 3D descriptors can be found in recent literature.

In Table 1 we propose a categorization of the main proposals in the field. As shown in the second column, we divide proposals for 3D descriptors into two main categories, namely *Signature* and *Histogram*. The first category, that includes earliest works on the subject, describes the 3D surface neighborhood of a given point (hereinafter *support*) by defining an invariant local Reference Frame (RF) and encoding, according to the local coordinates, one or more geometric measurements computed individually on each

K. Daniilidis, P. Maragos, N. Paragios (Eds.): ECCV 2010, Part III, LNCS 6313, pp. 356–369, 2010.

Fig. 1. Example of matching local descriptors in an 3D object recognition scenario. Green lines identify correct matches, whereas red ones represent wrong correspondences.

point of a subset of the support. On the other hand, Histogram-based methods describe the support by accumulating local geometrical or topological measurements (e.g. point counts, mesh triangle areas) into histograms according to a specific quantized domain (e.g. point coordinates, curvatures) which requires the definition of either a Reference Axis (RA) or a local RF. In broad terms, signatures are potentially highly descriptive thanks to the use of spatially well localized information, whereas histograms trade-off descriptive power for robustness by compressing geometric structure into bins.

As far as Signature-based methods are concerned, one of the first proposals is *Structural Indexing* [6], which builds up a representation based on either a *3D curve* or a *Splash* depending on the characteristics of the 3D support. The former encodes the angles between consecutive segments of the polygonal approximation of edges (corresponding to depth or orientation discontinuities) on the surface. The latter encodes as a 3D curve the local distribution of surface orientations along a geodesic circle centered on the point. In *Point Signatures* [7] the signature is given by the signed height of the 3D curve obtained by intersecting a sphere centered in the point with the surface. *3D Point Fingerprint* [8] encodes the normal angle variations and the contour radius variations along different geodesic circles projected on the tangent plane. Recently, *Exponential Mapping* [9] proposed a descriptor that encodes the components of the normals within the support by deploying a 2D parametrization of the local surface.

As for Histogram-based methods, those relying on the definition of just a RA are typically based on the feature point normal. For example, *Spin Images* [1], arguably the most popular method for 3D mesh description, computes 2D histograms of points falling within a cylindrical volume by means of a plane that "spins" around the normal. Within the same subclass, *Local Surface Patches* [10] computes histograms of normals and *shape indexes* [11] of the points belonging to the support. As for methods relying on the definition of a full local RF, *3D Shape Context* [12] modifies the basic idea of Spin Images by accumulating 3D histograms of points within a sphere centered at the feature point. *Intrinsic Shape Signatures* [13] proposed an improvement of [12] based on a different partitioning of the 3D local volume as well as on a different definition of the local RF. Finally, Mian et al. [2] accumulate 3D histograms (*Tensors*) of mesh triangle areas within a cubic support.

As pointed out in Tab. 1, all proposals rely on the definition of a local RF or, at least, a repeatable RA. However, we believe that the importance of the choice of the local reference for a 3D descriptor is underrated in literature, with efforts mainly focused on the development of discriminative descriptors. As a consequence, approaches for the choice of the local reference are ambiguous, or not unique, or too sensitive to noise and also lack specific experimental validation. Instead, as we will show in the remainder of the paper, the repeatability of the local RF (or, analogously, of the RA) is mandatory to achieve effective local surface description.

Table 1. Taxonomy of 3D descriptors

Method	Category	Local RF Unique	Unambig.
StInd [6]	Signature	No	Yes
PS [7]	Signature	No	Yes
3DPF [8]	Signature	No	Yes
EM [9]	Signature	Yes	No
SI [1]	Histogram	RA	
LSP [10]	Histogram	RA	
3DSC [12]	Histogram	No	Yes
ISS [13]	Histogram	Yes	No
Tensor [2]	Histogram	No	Yes
SHOT	**Both**	**Yes**	**Yes**

Therefore, the first contribution of this paper is a specific study upon local RFs. We carry out an analysis of repeatability and robustness on proposed local RFs, and provide experiments that demonstrate the strong impact of the choice of the RF on the performance of a 3D descriptor (Sec. 2). Given the impact of such a choice, the second contribution of this paper is a robust local RF that, unlike all other proposals, is unique and unambiguous(Sec. 3).

As for the descriptor, based on the nature of existing approaches highlighted by the proposed categorization, it is our belief that an effective and robust solution to the problem of 3D shape description can be found as a proper combination of *Signatures* and *Histograms*. Hence, the third contribution of the paper is a novel 3D descriptor aware of the proposed categorization (Sec. 4). Its design, inspired by an analysis of the successful choices performed in the related field of 2D descriptors, has been explicitly conceived to achieve computational efficiency, descriptive power and robustness. Finally, we provide a thorough experimental validation of our proposals (Sec. 5). We compare them to three state-of-the-art methods in surface matching experiments run on publicly available datasets as well as on range scans acquired in our lab.

2   On the Traits and Importance of the Local RF

The definition of a local RF, invariant to translations and rotations and robust to noise and clutter, has been the preferred option to endow a 3D descriptor with invariance to the same sources of variations, similarly to the way rotation and/or scale invariance is injected into 2D descriptors. On the other hand, the definition of such an invariant frame is challenging. Furthermore, although almost every new proposal for local shape description is equipped with its own local RF, experimental validation has always been focused on the results obtained by the joint used of an RF and a descriptor, whilst the impact of the selected local RF on the descriptor performance has not been investigated in literature.

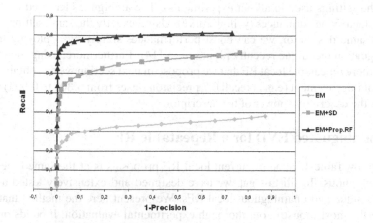

Fig. 2. Impact of the local RF on a descriptor performance

In Table 1 we have reported for each proposal the properties of uniqueness and unambiguity of their local RF. As highlighted in the third column, the majority of proposals are based on RFs that are not *unique* [6] [7] [8] [12] [2], i.e. to obtain an invariant description they require multiple descriptors to be computed at each feature point. This is usually handled by describing a "model" point using multiple descriptors, each based on a different local RFs, and a "scene" point with just one of them. This approach causes additional ambiguity to the correspondence problem since it shifts the intrinsic non-uniqueness of the local RF to the matching stage, thus increasing potential mismatches, computational requirements and sometimes also memory footprint. Another disadvantage brought in by the use of multiple local RFs is that the proposed matching stage is so tailored on the descriptor that it prevents the use of off-the-shelf efficient solutions for matching and indexing, that in principle could be advantageously performed orthogonally with respect to the description. This may result in a severe loss of computational efficiency.

In addition to multiple RFs, another limit of current proposals consists in the intrinsic ambiguity of the sign of the local RF axes. For example, in [9] and [13], normals and principal curvature directions are used. The main problem with this choice is that principal directions are not vectors, i.e. their sign is not defined. From a practical point of view, principal directions are computed using Singular Value Decomposition (SVD) or Eigenvalue Decomposition (EVD) of the covariance matrix of the point coordinates within the support. Of course, the output of the algorithm is a vector with a sign. Nevertheless, this sign is simply a numerical accident and, thus, is not repeatable on different (e.g. rotated) instances of the same mesh, even though the same SVD/EVD algorithm is used, as clearly discussed in [14]. Therefore, such an approach to the definition of the local RF is inherently ambiguous and thus not repeatable. [13] resorts to multiple RFs to overcome this limitation, while [9] does not deal with it explicitly.

To highlight the impact of the local RF on a descriptor performance, we show in Fig. 2 the performance of the EM descriptor [9] with different local RFs. Results are reported as *Recall vs 1-Precision* curves (see Sec. 5 for a discussion about this choice and for the settings used in all our experiments). The ambiguous RF used in [9] leads to unsatisfactory performances (yellow curve). Using exactly the same settings and exactly the same descriptor, we can boost performances simply by deploying the Sign Disambiguation technique recently proposed in [14]. Furthermore, using the more robust and more repeatable local RF that we propose in next section we can obtain another significant improvement (e.g. at recall 0.7 precision raises from 0.308 to 0.994) without changing the descriptive power of the descriptor.

3   Disambiguated EVD for a Repeatable RF

As shown by Table 1, none of current local RF proposals is at the same time unique and unambiguous. To fill this gap we have designed and extensively tested a variety of novel unique and unambiguous local RFs. We present here the method that turned out to be the most robust in our thorough experimental evaluation. It builds on a well known technique presented in [15] and [16], where the problem of normal estimation in presence of noise is specifically addressed. A Total Least Squares (TLS) estimation of the normal direction is obtained in [15] and [16] by EVD of the covariance matrix M of the $k-$nearest neighbors p_i of the point, defined by

$$\mathbf{M} = \frac{1}{k} \sum_{i=0}^{k} (\mathbf{p}_i - \hat{\mathbf{p}})(\mathbf{p}_i - \hat{\mathbf{p}})^T, \ \hat{\mathbf{p}} = \frac{1}{k} \sum_{i=0}^{k} \mathbf{p}_i \ . \tag{1}$$

In particular, the TLS estimation of the normal direction is given by the eigenvector corresponding to the smallest eigenvalue of M. Finally, they perform the sign disambiguation of the normals *globally* by means of sign consistency, i.e. propagating the sign from a seed chosen heuristically.

While this has proven to be a robust and effective technique for surface reconstruction of a single object, it cannot work for local surface description since in the latter case signs must be repeatable across any possible object pose as well as in scenes with multiple objects, so that a *local* rather than global sign disambiguation method is mandatory. Moreover, Hoppe's sign disambiguation concerns the normal only, hence it leaves ambiguous the signs of the remaining two axes.

In our proposal, we start by modifying (1) so as to assign distant points smaller weights, in order to increase repeatability in presence of clutter. Then, to improve robustness, all points laying within the spherical support (of radius R) which are used to compute the descriptor are used also to calculate M. For the sake of efficiency, we also neglect the centroid computation, replacing it with the feature point p. Therefore, we compute M as a weighted linear combination,

$$\mathbf{M} = \frac{1}{\sum\limits_{i:d_i \leq R} (R-d_i)} \sum_{i:d_i \leq R} (R - d_i)(\mathbf{p}_i - \mathbf{p})(\mathbf{p}_i - \mathbf{p})^T \tag{2}$$

where $d_i = \|\mathbf{p}_i - \mathbf{p}\|_2$. Our experimental evaluation indicates that the eigenvectors of M define repeatable, orthogonal directions in presence of noise and clutter. It is worth pointing out that, compared to [15] and [16], in our proposal the third eigenvector no longer represents the TLS estimation of the normal direction and sometimes it notably differs from it. However, this does not affect performance, since in the case of local surface description what matters is a highly repeatable and robust triplet of orthogonal directions, and not its geometrical or topological meaning.

Hence, eigenvectors of (2) represent a good starting point, but they need to be disambiguated to yield a repeatable local RF. The problem of sign disambiguation for EVD and SVD has been recently addressed in [14]. Their proposal basically reorients the sign of each singular or eigenvector so that its sign is coherent with the majority of the vectors it is representing. We determine the sign on the local x and z axes according to this principle. In the following we refer to the three eigenvectors in decreasing eigenvalue order as the $\mathbf{x}^+$, $\mathbf{y}^+$ and $\mathbf{z}^+$ axis, respectively. With $\mathbf{x}^-$, $\mathbf{y}^-$ and $\mathbf{z}^-$, we denote instead the opposite vectors. Hence, the final disambiguated x axis is defined as

$$S_x^+ \doteq \left\{ i : d_i \leq R \wedge (\mathbf{p}_i - \mathbf{p}) \cdot \mathbf{x}^+ \geq 0 \right\} \tag{3}$$

$$S_x^- \doteq \left\{ i : d_i \leq R \wedge (\mathbf{p}_i - \mathbf{p}) \cdot \mathbf{x}^- > 0 \right\} \tag{4}$$

$$\mathbf{x} = \begin{cases} \mathbf{x}^+, & |S_x^+| \geq |S_x^-| \\ \mathbf{x}^-, & \text{otherwise} \end{cases} \tag{5}$$

The same procedure is used to disambiguate the z axis. Finally, the y axis is obtained as $\mathbf{z} \times \mathbf{x}$.

We compare the repeatability of our proposal against two representative RFs: that of PS and that of EM, respectively a not-unique solution and an ambiguous one. To prevent these shortcomings from invalidating the comparison we consider only the global maximum of the height [7] for PS and we add the sign disambiguation of [14] to EM (EM+SD), thereby obtaining two unique and unambiguous RFs. We also consider the original EM approach to show the effectiveness of sign disambiguation. Using again the settings detailed in Sec. 5, in Fig. 3 we plot, for 5 increasing noise levels, the mean cosine between corresponding axes of the local RFs computed on two instances of the same mesh, i.e. the original one and a rotated and noisy instance. On one hand, ambiguity is clearly the most serious nuisance, as the low performances of the original EM proposal demonstrate. On the other hand, the use of a higher number of points to compute the local RF (i.e. the whole surface contained in the spherical support, as done by EM, instead of the 3D curve resulting by the intersection of the spherical support with the surface, as done by PS) yields better robustness, as shown by the relative drop of EM with respect to PS when noise increases. The disambiguation introduced in EM+SD dramatically enhances repeatability. However, both EM and EM+SD subordinate computation of the directions on the tangent plane to the normal estimation (i.e. , the repeatable directions they compute are then projected onto the tangent plane to create an orthogonal basis). This choice sums noise on the normal to the noise inevitably affecting the other directions, thereby leading to increased sensitivity of the estimation of the axes on the tangent plane and finally to poor repeatability. Our proposal, instead, estimates all axes simultaneously and turns out to be the most effective, thanks to the combination of its noise and clutter-aware definition, the effectiveness of the proposed disambiguation and the inherent uniqueness deriving from its theoretical formulation.

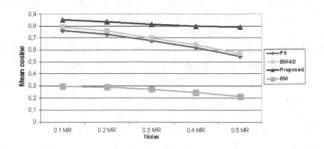

Fig. 3. Comparison between local RFs

4   Description by Signatures of Histograms

In Sec. 1 we have classified 3D descriptors as based on either histograms or signatures. We have designed our proposal following this intuition and aiming at a local representation that is efficient, descriptive, robust to noise and clutter as well as to point density variation. The point density issue is specific to the 3D scenario, where the same 3D volume of the real world may be represented with different amounts of vertexes in its mesh approximation, e.g. due to the use of different 3D sensors (stereo, ToF cameras, LIDARs, etc...) or different acquisition distances.

Beside our taxonomy, another source of inspiration has been the related field of 2D feature descriptors, which has reached a remarkable maturity during the last years. By analyzing SIFT [17], arguably the most successful and widespread proposal among 2D descriptors, we have singled out what we believe are among the major reasons behind its effectiveness. First of all, the use of histograms is spread throughout the algorithm, from the definition of the local orientation to the descriptor itself, this accounting for its robustness. Since a single global histogram computed on the whole patch would be not descriptive enough, SIFT relies on a set of local histograms, that are computed on specific subsets of pixels defined by a regular grid superimposed on the patch. The use of this coarse geometric information creates what we identify as a signature-like structure. Moreover, the elements of these local histograms are based on first order derivatives describing the signal of interest, i.e. intensity gradients. Although it has been argued that building a descriptor based on differential entities may result in poor robustness to noise [7], they hold high descriptive power, as the effectiveness of SIFT clearly demonstrates. Therefore, we believe they can provide a more effective solution for a descriptor than point coordinates [1] [12]. Yet, to account for robustness to noise, differential entities have to be filtered, and not deployed directly, e.g. as done in [9].

Based on these considerations, we propose a 3D descriptor that encodes histograms of basic first-order differential entities (i.e. the normals of the points within the support), which are more representative of the local structure of the surface compared to plain 3D coordinates. The use of histograms brings in the filtering effect required to achieve robustness to noise. Having defined an unique and robust 3D local RF (see Sec. 3), it is possible to enhance the discriminative power of the descriptor by introducing geometric information concerning the location of the points within the support, thereby mimicking a signature. This is done by first computing a set of local histograms over the 3D volumes defined by a 3D grid superimposed on the support and then grouping together all local histograms to form

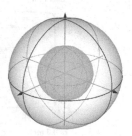

Fig. 4. Signature structure for SHOT

the actual descriptor. Hence, our descriptor lays at the intersection between Histograms and Signatures: we dub it Signature of Histograms of OrienTations (SHOT).

For each of the local histograms, we accumulate point counts into bins according to a function of the angle, θ_i, between the normal at each point within the corresponding part of the grid, $\mathbf{n}_{v_i}$, and the normal at the feature point, $\mathbf{n}_u$. This function is $cos\theta_i$, the reason being twofold: it can be computed fast, since $cos\theta_i = \mathbf{n}_u \cdot \mathbf{n}_{v_i}$; an equally spaced binning on $cos\theta_i$ is equivalent to a spatially varying binning on θ_i, whereby a coarser binning is created for directions close to the reference normal direction and a finer one for orthogonal directions. In this way, small differences in orthogonal directions to the normal, i.e. presumably the most informative ones, cause a point to be accumulated in different bins leading to different histograms. Moreover, in presence of quasi-planar regions (i.e. not very descriptive ones) this choice limits histogram differences due to noise by concentrating counts in a fewer number of bins.

As for the structure of the signature, we use an isotropic spherical grid that encompasses partitions along the radial, azimuth and elevation axes, as sketched in Fig. 4. Since each volume of the grid encodes a very descriptive entity represented by the local histogram, we can use a coarse partitioning of the spatial grid and hence a small cardinality of the descriptor. In particular, our experimentations indicate that 32 is a proper number of spatial bins, resulting from 8 azimuth divisions, 2 elevation divisions and 2 radial divisions (though, for clarity, only 4 azimuth divisions are shown in Fig. 4).

Since our descriptor is based upon local histograms, it is important to avoid boundary effects, as pointed out e.g. in [1] [17]. Furthermore, due to the spatial subdivision of the support, boundary effects might arise also in presence of perturbations of the local RF. Therefore, for each point being accumulated into a specific local histogram bin, we perform quadrilinear interpolation with its neighbors, i.e. the neighboring bins in the local histogram and the bins having the same index in the local histograms corresponding to the neighboring volumes of the grid. In particular, each count is multiplied by a weight of $1 - d$ for each dimension. As for the local histogram, d is the distance of the current entry from the central value of the bin. As for elevation and azimuth, d is the angular distance of the entry from the central value of the volume. Along the radial dimension, d is the Euclidean distance of the entry from the central value of the volume.

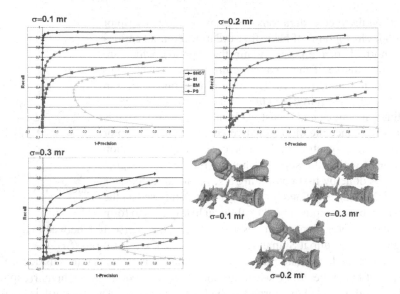

Fig. 5. Exp. 1: Precision-Recall curves on Stanford dataset and a scene at the 3 noise levels

Along each dimension, d is measured in units of the histogram or grid spacing, i.e. it is normalized by the distance between two neighbor bins or volumes.

To achieve robustness to variations of the point density, we normalize the whole descriptor to sum up to 1. This is preferable to the solution proposed in [12], i.e. normalizing each bin with the inverse of the point density and bin volume. In fact, while [12] implicitly assumes that the sampling density may vary independently in every bin, and thus discards as not informative the differences in point density among bins, we assume global (or at least regional) variations of the density and keep the local differences as a source of discriminative information.

5   Experimental Results

In this section we provide experimental validation of our proposals, i.e. the unique local RF together with the SHOT descriptor. To this purpose, we carry out a quantitative comparison against three state-of-the-art approaches in a typical surface matching scenario, where correspondences have to be established between a set of features extracted from a scene and those extracted from a number of models. The considered approaches are: *Spin Images* (SI), as representative of Histogram-based methods due to its vast popularity in the addressed scenario; *Exponential Mapping* (EM) and *Point Signatures* (PS) as representatives of Signature-based methods, the former since it is a very recent approach, the latter given its importance in literature. All methods were implemented in C++ and are made publicly available together with the datasets (www.vision.deis.unibo.it/SHOT).

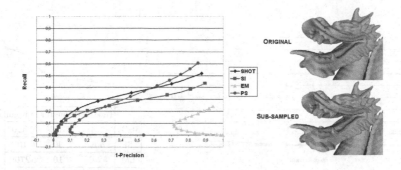

Fig. 6. Exp. 2: Precision-Recall curves on subsampled dataset and a detail from one scene

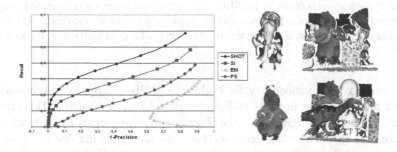

Fig. 7. Exp. 3: Results on Spacetime Stereo dataset and two models (middle) and scenes (right)

For a fair comparison, we use the same feature detector for all algorithms: in particular, we randomly extract a set of feature points from each model, then we extract their corresponding points from the scene, so that performance of the descriptors is not affected by errors of the detector. Analogously, for what concerns the matching stage, we adopt the same matching measure for all algorithms, i.e. , as proposed in [1], the Euclidean distance. We could also have evaluated the synergistic effect of description and matching for those methods that explicitly include a proposal for the latter, e.g. the tolerance band for PS. In turn, we did experiments on the whole dataset with the original EM and PS matching schemes, obtaining slightly worse performance for both. This, and the attempt to be as fair as possible, leaned us to use the same measure for all algorithms. However, we did not discard the characteristics of the descriptors that required a specific treatment during matching: in particular, since EM is a sparse descriptor, we compute the Euclidean distance only on the overlapping subset of EM descriptor pairs, as proposed by the authors; and for PS we use the matching scheme proposed by the authors to disambiguate its not-unique local RF [7]. For each scene and model, we match each scene feature against all model features and we compute the ratio between the nearest neighbor and the second best (as in [17]): if the ratio is below a threshold a correspondence is established between the scene feature and its closest model feature.

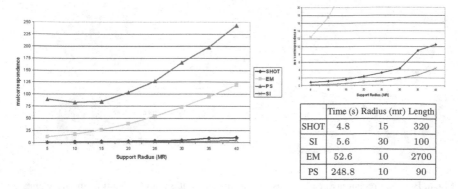

	Time (s)	Radius (mr)	Length
SHOT	4.8	15	320
SI	5.6	30	100
EM	52.6	10	2700
PS	248.8	10	90

Fig. 8. Charts: ms/correspondence vs. support radius (in the smaller chart the time axis is zoomed in for better comparison between SI and SHOT). Table: measured execution times (in Experiment 1) and tuned parameter values. Radius values are reported in mesh resolution units. As for SI, the support radius is the product of the bin size by the number of bins in each side of the spin image

According to the methodology for evaluation of 2D descriptors recommended in [18], we provide results in terms of *Recall* versus *1-Precision* curves. This choice is preferable compared to ROC curves (i.e. *True Positive Rate* versus *False Positive rate*) when comparing descriptors or detectors due to the ambiguity in calculating the *False Positive Rate* [19]. We present three different experiments. Experiment 1 deals with 6 models ("Armadillo", "Asian Dragon", "Thai Statue", "Bunny", "Happy Buddha", "Dragon") taken from the *Stanford 3D Scanning Repository* [1]. We build up 45 scenes by randomly rotating and translating different subsets of the model set so to create clutter[2]; then, similarly to [20], we add Gaussian random noise with increasing standard deviation, namely σ_1, σ_2 and σ_3 at respectively 10%, 20% and 30% of the average mesh resolution (computed on all models). In Experiment 2 we consider the same models and scenes as in Experiment 1, add noise (i.e. σ_1) and resample the 3D meshes down to 1/8 of their original point density. For a fair comparison in this experiment, our implementation of SI -used throughout all the evaluation- normalizes each descriptor to the unit vector to make it more robust to density variations [3]. Finally, in Experiment 3 the dataset consists of scenes and models acquired in our lab by means of a 3D sensing technique known as *Spacetime Stereo* [21], [22]. In particular, we compare 8 object models against 15 scenes characterized by clutter and occlusions, each scene containing two models. Fig. 7 shows two scenes together with the models appearing in them. In each of the three experiments, 1000 feature points were extracted from each model. As for the scenes, in Exp. 1 and 2 we extract $n * 1000$ features per scene (n being the number of models in the scene) whereas in Exp. 3 we extract 3000 features per scene.

Throughout all the three experiments we used the same values for the parameters of considered methods. In particular, we tuned the two parameters of each descriptor (*support radius* and *length of the descriptor*) based on a tuning scene corrupted

---

[1] http://graphics.stanford.edu/data/3Dscanrep

[2] 3 sets of 15 scenes each, containing respectively 3, 4 and 5 models.

with noise level σ_1 and built rotating and translating three Stanford models ("Bunny", "Happy Buddha", "Dragon"). The values resulting from the tuning process are reported in the last two columns of the Table in Fig. 8. It is worth noting that our tuning yielded comparable values of the support radius among the various methods, and that, for SI and PS, the resulting parameter values are coherent, as far as the order of magnitude is concerned, with those originally proposed by their authors (no indication about EM parameters is given in [9]). Yet, we used the finely tuned values instead of those originally proposed by the authors since the former yield higher performance in these experiments.

Results for the three Experiments are reported in Figure 5, 6 and 7, respectively. Experiment 1 focuses on robustness to noise. Given the reported results, it is clear that SHOT performs better than the other methods at all different noise levels on the Stanford dataset. We can observe that, comparing the two Signature methods, PS exhibits a higher robustness than EM. We address this mainly to the higher robustness of its local RF, as shown in Fig. 3. As for SI, it appears to be highly susceptible to noise, its performance notably deteriorating as the noise level increases. This is due to the fact that this descriptor is highly sensitive to small variations in the normal estimation (i.e. SI Reference Axis), that here we compute as proposed in [1]. This is also consistent with the results reported in [12]. As for Experiment 2, it is clear that the point density variation is the most challenging nuisance among those accounted for, causing a severe performance loss of all methods. SHOT, PS and SI obtain comparable performance, nevertheless for high values of precision, that are typical working points for real applications, SHOT obtains the highest levels of Recall. Experiment 3 shows that under real working conditions SHOT outperforms the other methods. It is worth noting that this experiment is especially focused on the descriptiveness of evaluated approaches, since the much smoother shapes of the objects surfaces compared to those of the Stanford models make the former harder to discriminate. Hence, results demonstrate the higher descriptiveness embedded in SHOT with respect to the other proposals.

In addition, we have compared the methods in terms of their computational efficiency and memory requirements. Since, as discussed in Sec. 2, descriptors based on multiple RFs, like PS, can not deploy efficient indexing to speed-up the matching stage, we use a full search strategy for all methods. Results are reported in Fig. 8. The two charts in the Figure, showing the number of milliseconds per correspondence needed by the various methods using different support sizes, demonstrate the notable differences in computational efficiency between the algorithms. In particular, SI and SHOT run one order of magnitude faster than EM and almost two orders of magnitude faster than PS, with SI turning out consistently slightly faster than SHOT at each support size. As for EM, efficiency is mainly affected by the re-parametrization of the support needed to describe each feature point and to the large memory footprint (see next). With regards to PS, as discussed in Sec. (2) the use of multiple local RFs dramatically slows down the matching stage. These results are confirmed by the Table in the Figure (first column), which reports the measured times required to match the scene to the models in Experiment 1 (i.e. 3000 scene features and 3000 models features) using the tuned parameter values. Here, the larger support needed by SI allows SHOT to run slightly faster. As for memory requirements, the reported descriptor length (third column) highlights the much higher memory footprint required by EM compared to other methods.

Finally, as a practical application in a challenging and active research area, we demonstrate the use of SHOT correspondences to perform fully automatic 3D Reconstruction from Spacetime Stereo data. We merge 18 views covering a 360° field of view of one of the smooth objects used in Experiment 3. We follow a 2 steps procedure: 1) we obtain a coarse registration by estimating the 3D transformations between every pair of views and retaining only those maximizing the global area of overlap; 2) we use the coarse registration as initial guess for a final global registration carried out using a standard external tool (*Scanalyze*). In the first step, correspondences among views are established by computing and matching SHOT descriptors on 1000 randomly selected feature points. 3D transformations are estimated by applying a well known Absolute Orientation algorithm [23] on such correspondences and filtering outliers with RANSAC. Maximization of the area of overlap is achieved through the Maximum Spanning Tree approach described in [9]. As shown in Fig. 9, without any assumptions about the initial poses, SHOT correspondences allows for attaining a coarse alignment which is an accurate enough initial guess to successfully reconstruct the 3D shape of the object without any manual intervention. To the best of our knowledge, fully automatic 3D reconstruction from multiple Spacetime Stereo views has not been demonstrated yet.

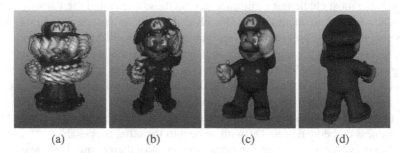

(a)   (b)   (c)   (d)

Fig. 9. 3D Reconstruction from Spacetime Stereo views: (a) initial set of views (b) coarse registration (c) global registration frontal view (d) global registration rear view

6   Conclusion and Future Work

Overall, our proposals compare favorably with the considered methods. The results validate the proposed categorization as well as the intuition that the synergy between the design of a repeatable local RF and the embedding of an hybrid signature/histogram nature into SHOT allows for achieving at the same time state-of-the-art robustness and descriptiveness. Remarkably, our proposal delivers such notable performances with high computational efficiency. As for future work, we plan to investigate on how to improve robustness to point density variations. Comparing our proposal with other relevant methods and on a larger dataset is another main direction of our research.

Acknowledgments. The authors would like to deeply thank Alioscia Petrelli and Alessandro Franchi, of the Computer Vision Lab of the University of Bologna, who helped implementing all the proposals used in our experiments.

References

1. Johnson, A., Hebert, M.: Using spin images for efficient object recognition in cluttered 3D scenes. PAMI 21, 433–449 (1999)
2. Mian, A., Bennamoun, M., Owens, R.: A novel representation and feature matching algorithm for automatic pairwise registration of range images. IJCV 66, 19–40 (2006)
3. Conde, C., Rodríguez-Aragón, L.J., Cabello, E.: Automatic 3D face feature points extraction with spin images. In: Campilho, A., Kamel, M.S. (eds.) ICIAR 2006. LNCS, vol. 4142, pp. 317–328. Springer, Heidelberg (2006)
4. Wu, K., Levine, M.: Recovering parametrics geons from multiview range data. In: CVPR, pp. 159–166 (1994)
5. Solina, F., Bajcsy, R.: Recovery of parametric models from range images: the case for superquadrics with global deformations. PAMI 12, 131–147 (1990)
6. Stein, F., Medioni, G.: Structural indexing: Efficient 3-D object recognition. PAMI 14, 125–145 (1992)
7. Chua, C.S., Jarvis, R.: Point signatures: A new representation for 3D object recognition. IJCV 25, 63–85 (1997)
8. Sun, Y., Abidi, M.A.: Surface matching by 3D point's fingerprint. ICCV 2, 263–269 (2001)
9. Novatnack, J., Nishino, K.: Scale-dependent/invariant local 3D shape descriptors for fully automatic registration of multiple sets of range images. In: Forsyth, D., Torr, P., Zisserman, A. (eds.) ECCV 2008, Part III. LNCS, vol. 5304, pp. 440–453. Springer, Heidelberg (2008)
10. Chen, H., Bhanu, B.: 3D free-form object recognition in range images using local surface patches. Patt. Rec. Letters 28, 1252–1262 (2007)
11. Koenderink, J., Doorn, A.: Surface shape and curvature scales. Image Vision Computing 8, 557–565 (1992)
12. Frome, A., Huber, D., Kolluri, R., Bülow, T., Malik, J.: Recognizing objects in range data using regional point descriptors. In: Pajdla, T., Matas, J(G.) (eds.) ECCV 2004. LNCS, vol. 3023, pp. 224–237. Springer, Heidelberg (2004)
13. Zhong, Y.: Intrinsic shape signatures: A shape descriptor for 3D object recognition. In: ICCV-WS: 3DRR (2009)
14. Bro, R., Acar, E., Kolda, T.: Resolving the sign ambiguity in the singular value decomposition. J. Chemometrics 22, 135–140 (2008)
15. Hoppe, H., DeRose, T., Duchamp, T., McDonald, J., Stuetzle, W.: Surface reconstruction from unorganized points. In: SIGGRAPH, pp. 71–78 (1992)
16. Mitra, N.J., Nguyen, A., Guibas, L.: Estimating surface normals in noisy point cloud data. Int. J. of Computational Geometry and Applications 14, 261–276 (2004)
17. Lowe, D.G.: Distinctive image features from scale-invariant keypoints. IJCV 60, 91–110 (2004)
18. Mikolajczyk, K., Schmid, C.: A performance evaluation of local descriptors. PAMI 27, 1615–1630 (2005)
19. Ke, Y., Sukthankar, R.: PCA-SIFT: A more distinctive representation for local image descriptors. In: CVPR (2004)
20. Unnikrishnan, R., Hebert, M.: Multi-scale interest regions from unorganized point clouds. In: CVPR-WS: S3D (2008)
21. Davis, J., Nehab, D., Ramamoothi, R., Rusinkiewicz, S.: Spacetime stereo: A unifying framework for depth from triangulation. PAMI 27, 1615–1630 (2005)
22. Zhang, L., Curless, B., Seitz, S.: Spacetime stereo: Shape recovery for dynamic scenes. In: CVPR (2003)
23. Horn, B.K.P.: Closed-form solution of absolute orientation using unit quaternions. J. of the Optical Society of America A 4, 629–642 (1987)

Exploring Ambiguities for Monocular Non-rigid Shape Estimation*

Francesc Moreno-Noguer[1], Josep M. Porta[1], and Pascal Fua[2]

[1] Institut de Robòtica i Informàtica Industrial, CSIC-UPC, Barcelona, Spain
[2] Computer Vision Laboratory, EPFL, Lausanne, Switzerland
fmoreno@iri.upc.edu, porta@iri.upc.edu, pascal.fua@epfl.ch

Abstract. Recovering the 3D shape of deformable surfaces from single images is difficult because many different shapes have very similar projections. This is commonly addressed by restricting the set of possible shapes to linear combinations of deformation modes and by imposing additional geometric constraints. Unfortunately, because image measurements are noisy, such constraints do not always guarantee that the correct shape will be recovered. To overcome this limitation, we introduce an efficient approach to exploring the set of solutions of an objective function based on point-correspondences and to proposing a small set of candidate 3D shapes. This allows the use of additional image information to choose the best one. As a proof of concept, we use either motion or shading cues to this end and show that we can handle a complex objective function without having to solve a difficult non-linear minimization problem.

Keywords: 3D shape recovery, deformation model, nonrigid surfaces.

1 Introduction

It has been shown that the 3D shape of deformable surfaces can be recovered from even single images provided that enough correspondences can be established between that image and one in which the surface's shape is already known [1–3]. While effective, these techniques return one single reconstruction without accounting for the fact that several plausible shapes could produce virtually the same projection and therefore be indistinguishable on the basis of correspondences and geometry alone. In practice, as shown in Fig. 1 disambiguation is only possible using additional image information.

In this paper, we introduce an efficient way to sample the space of all plausible solutions. We achieve this by representing shape deformations in terms of a weighted sum of deformation modes and relating uncertainties on the location of point correspondences to uncertainties on the mode weights. This lets us

---

* This work has been partially funded by the Spanish Ministry of Science and Innovation under project DPI2008-06022; by Consolider Ingenio 2010 CSD2007-00018; by the EU project FP7-247947 and by the Swiss National Science Foundation.

K. Daniilidis, P. Maragos, N. Paragios (Eds.): ECCV 2010, Part III, LNCS 6313, pp. 370–383, 2010.

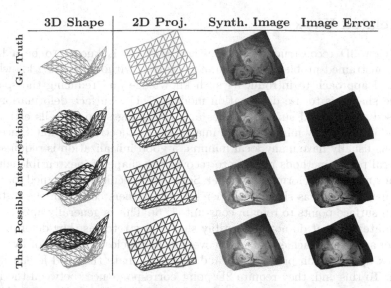

Fig. 1. Handling 3D shape ambiguities. **First Row.** Image of a surface lit by a nearby light source and the corresponding ground truth surface. **Three other Rows.** In each one, a different candidate surface proposed by our algorithm is shown in black. The corresponding projection and synthesized image given automatically estimated lighting parameters are shown in the middle columns. As can be seen, its projection is very similar, even though its shape may be very different from the original one. However, when comparing the true and synthesized images, it becomes clear that the correct shape is the one at the second row.

explore the space of modes and select a very small number of likely ones, which correspond to 3D shapes such as those shown in the left column of Fig. 1.

In this paper, as a proof of concept, we use either shading or motion information to select the best 3D shape among the candidates generated in this manner. When using shading, we show that we can exploit it both when the light sources are distant and when they are nearby. The latter is particularly significant because exploiting nearby light sources would involve solving a difficult non linear minimization problem if we did not have a reliable way to generate 3D shape hypotheses. In our examples, this is all the more true since the lighting parameters are initially unknown and must be estimated from the images. Alternatively, when a video is available, we can exploit three-frame sequences to pick the set of candidate 3D shapes that provides the most temporally consistent motion. We show that both these approaches outperform state-of-the-art methods [4, 5].

Summarizing, our contribution is an approach to avoiding being trapped in the local minima of a potentially complicated objective function by efficiently exploring the solution space of a simpler one. As a result, we only need to evaluate the full objective function for a few selected shapes, which implies we could use a very discriminating and expensive one if necessary.

2   Related Work

Single-view 3D reconstruction of non-rigid surfaces is known to be a highly
under-constrained problem that cannot be solved without *a priori* knowledge.
A typical approach to introducing such knowledge and reducing the space of
possible shapes is to use deformation models [7–11]. Surface deformations are
expressed as weighted sums of modes and retrieving shape entails estimating
the modal weights by minimizing an image-based objective function. Since such
functions usually have many local minima, a good initialization is required.

Several recent methods propose to recover the shape of inextensible surfaces
without an explicit deformation model. Some are specifically designed for applicable surfaces, such as sheets of paper [12, 13]. Others constrain the distances
between surface points to remain constant [1, 6]. This is generally applicable to
many materials that do not perceptibly shrink or stretch as they deform.

Other approaches achieve shape-recovery either in closed form [4] or by solving
a convex optimization problem [2], and thus, eliminate the need for an initialization. To this end, they require 2D point correspondences between the image
in which one wishes to compute the shape and one in which it is already known.
However, as will be shown in the results section, small inaccuracies in the correspondences can result in erroneous reconstructions.

The method proposed in this paper builds on the formalism introduced in [4]
to return not a single solution but a representative set of *all* possible solutions
and then uses additional information to decide which one is best. In this paper,
we use shading or motion but any image cue could have been used instead.

Of course, many methods, such as [14, 15], have been proposed to merge geometric and shading cues into a common framework. However, these techniques,
unlike ours, involve multiple iterative processes that require good initial estimates. An exception is the algorithm of [5] that solves for shape in closed form
but is only applicable for Lambertian surfaces lit by a distant point light source.

3   Exploring the Space of Potential 3D Shapes

Let us assume that we are given a *reference image* in which the shape of a 3D
deformable surface represented by a triangulated mesh is known and a set of
2D point correspondences between this reference image and an *input image* in
which the shape is unknown. In [4], it was shown that this unknown 3D shape
could be computed in closed form by representing the surface deformations in
terms of a weighted sum of modes and picking the weights that minimize the
reprojection errors while preserving the length of the mesh edges. However, the
resulting shape is not always the right one, as shown in Table 1. This is because
the correspondences are not infinitely accurate and the algorithm can trade a
small amount of reprojection error against similarly small violations of the length
constraints. As it turns out, this is enough to result in large changes in 3D shape
since, as discussed earlier, very different shapes can have very similar projections.

To avoid this problem, we also represent the shape as a weighted sum of modes.
But, instead of picking the best set of weights according to a geometric criterion,

Table 1. Mean reconstruction, reprojection and inextensibility errors for the candidate shapes of Fig.1. Note that, although shape#1 violates edge-length constraints slightly more than shape#3, it still is the reconstruction closest to the ground truth by far.

	Shape # 1	Shape # 2	Shape # 3
Reconst. Error (mm)	0.82	4.25	5.35
Reproj. Error (pix)	1.92	1.87	1.93
Inextens. Error (mm)	4.00	4.27	3.97

we fit a Gaussian distribution to those that correspond to acceptable projections. This lets us exhaustively sample the sets of weights that also preserve the length of the mesh edges. This typically results in approximately one hundred candidate shapes per image, among which the best can be picked using additional sources of shape information. In Section 4, we show that either shading or motion cues can be used for this purpose.

3.1 Problem Formulation

We represent our surface as a triangulated 3D mesh with n_v vertices $\mathbf{v}_i$ concatenated in a vector $\mathbf{x}=[\mathbf{v}_1^\top,\ldots,\mathbf{v}_{n_v}^\top]^\top$. We model surface deformations as weighted sums of n_m deformation modes $\mathbf{Q} = [\mathbf{q}_1,\ldots,\mathbf{q}_{n_m}]$, obtained by applying Principal Component Analysis over a set of training meshes. We write

$$\mathbf{x} = \mathbf{x}_0 + \sum_{i=1}^{n_m} \alpha_i \mathbf{q}_i = \mathbf{x}_0 + \mathbf{Q}\boldsymbol{\alpha} \, , \tag{1}$$

where $\mathbf{x}_0$ is a mean shape and $\boldsymbol{\alpha} = [\alpha_1,\ldots,\alpha_{n_m}]^\top$ are unknown weights that define the current surface shape.

As in [4, 5], we treat a correspondence between a 2D point $\mathbf{r}_i$ in the reference image and a 2D point $\mathbf{u}_i$ in the input image as a 2D-to-3D correspondence between $\mathbf{u}_i$ and $\mathbf{p}_i$, the 3D point on the mesh in its reference configuration that projects at $\mathbf{r}_i$. We express the coordinates of $\mathbf{p}_i$ in terms of the barycentric coordinates of the face to which belongs as $\mathbf{p}_i = \sum_{j=1}^3 a_{ij}\mathbf{v}_j^{[i]}$, where the a_{ij} are the barycentric coordinates and the $\mathbf{v}_j^{[i]}$ are the vertices.

Assuming the matrix $\mathbf{A}$ of internal camera parameters to be known and that the 3D points are expressed in the camera referencial, the fact that $\mathbf{p}_i$ projects at $\mathbf{u}_i$ implies that

$$w_i \begin{bmatrix} \mathbf{u}_i \\ 1 \end{bmatrix} = \mathbf{A}\mathbf{p}_i = \begin{bmatrix} \mathbf{A}_{2\times 3} \\ \mathbf{a}_3^\top \end{bmatrix} \mathbf{p}_i \, , \tag{2}$$

where w_i is a scalar, $\mathbf{A}_{2\times 3}$ are the first two rows of $\mathbf{A}$ and $\mathbf{a}_3^\top$ the last one. Since $w_i = \mathbf{a}_3^\top \mathbf{p}_i$, we can write $\left(\mathbf{u}_i\mathbf{a}_3^\top - \mathbf{A}_{2\times 3}\right) \mathbf{p}_i = \mathbf{0}$. By representing $\mathbf{p}_i$ with its barycentric coordinates, we then have

$$\sum_{j=1}^3 a_{ij} \left(\mathbf{u}_i\mathbf{a}_3^\top - \mathbf{A}_{2\times 3}\right) \mathbf{v}_j^{[i]} = \mathbf{0} \, . \tag{3}$$

In short, for each 3D-to-2D correspondence, Eq. 3 provides 2 linear constraints on $\mathbf{x}$. n_c such correspondences yield $2n_c$ constraints which can be written as a linear system $\mathbf{Mx} = \mathbf{0}$, where $\mathbf{M}$ is a $2n_c \times 3n_v$ matrix obtained from the known values a_{ij}, $\mathbf{u}_i$ and $\mathbf{A}$. Injecting the modal description of Eq. 1 then yields

$$\mathbf{MQ}\boldsymbol{\alpha} + \mathbf{Mx}_0 = \mathbf{0} \ , \tag{4}$$

such that any set of weights $\boldsymbol{\alpha}$ that is a solution of it corresponds to a surface that projects at the right place.

3.2 Proposing Candidate Shapes

Since correspondences $\{\mathbf{p}_i, \mathbf{u}_i\}$ are potentially noisy, the simplest way to solve Eq. 4 is in the least-squares sense. This, however, may not be satisfactory because $\mathbf{MQ}$ is an ill-conditioned matrix with several small eigenvalues [4, 5]. As a result, even when there are many correspondences, small changes in the exact correspondence locations, and therefore in the coefficients of $\mathbf{M}$, can result in very large changes of the resulting $\boldsymbol{\alpha}$ values. In other words, many different sets of $\boldsymbol{\alpha}$ weights can result in virtually the same projection. In [4], this is addressed by choosing the weights that best preserve the lengths of the mesh edges. However, as shown by Table 1, this does not necessarily yield the best answer.

In this paper, instead of choosing the best set of weights based on geometric considerations alone we have devised a way to quickly propose a restricted set of candidate solutions among which the best can be chosen using additional sources of image information, as will be done in Sections 4.1 and 4.2. To this end, we first derive an analytical expression of the solution space as a function of the 2D input data statistics. We then efficiently sample this space and keep the best samples in terms of both minimizing reprojection errors and preserving edge lengths.

Gaussian Representation of the Solution Space. The $\boldsymbol{\alpha}$ weights we seek can be computed as the least-squares solution of Eq. 4:

$$\boldsymbol{\alpha} = (\mathbf{B}^\top\mathbf{B})^{-1}\mathbf{B}^\top\mathbf{b} \ , \tag{5}$$

where $\mathbf{B}=\mathbf{MQ}$ is a $2n_c \times n_m$ matrix, and $\mathbf{b}=-\mathbf{Mx}_0$ is a $2n_c$ vector. The components of $\mathbf{B}$ and $\mathbf{b}$ are linear functions of the known parameters a_{ij}, $\mathbf{u}_i$, $\mathbf{Q}$ and $\mathbf{A}$. We have seen that this solution may not, in fact, be the right one because $\mathbf{B}$ is ill-conditioned and solving the system in the least-squares sense magnifies small inaccuracies in the correspondences. We can nevertheless exploit the expression of Eq. 5 to model where to look for other potential solutions as follows.

Let us assume that the estimated correspondence locations are normally distributed around their true locations. Injecting the corresponding $2n_c \times 2n_c$ diagonal covariance matrix $\boldsymbol{\Sigma}_\mathbf{u}$ into Eq. 5 means that the $n_m \times n_m$ covariance matrix for the $\boldsymbol{\alpha}$ weights can be written as $\boldsymbol{\Sigma}_\alpha = \mathbf{J}_\beta \boldsymbol{\Sigma}_\mathbf{u} \mathbf{J}_\beta^\top$, where $\mathbf{J}_\beta$ is the $n_m \times 2n_c$ Jacobian of $(\mathbf{B}^\top\mathbf{B})^{-1}\mathbf{B}^\top\mathbf{b}$ with respect to the 2D correspondence coordinates:

$$\mathbf{J}_\beta = \frac{\partial(\mathbf{B}^\top\mathbf{B})^{-1}}{\partial\mathbf{u}}\mathbf{B}^\top\mathbf{b} + (\mathbf{B}^\top\mathbf{B})^{-1}\frac{\partial\mathbf{B}^\top\mathbf{b}}{\partial\mathbf{u}} \ . \tag{6}$$

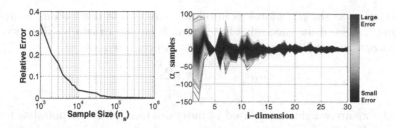

Fig. 2. Efficient exploration of the solution space. **Left:** Number of samples n_s needed to correctly approximate $\mathcal{R}_\alpha$. We plot $\frac{\det(\tilde{\Sigma}_\alpha) - \det(\mathcal{M}^2\Sigma_\alpha)}{\det(\mathcal{M}^2\Sigma_\alpha)}$, an estimate of the distance between the theoretical covariance matrix and its empirical estimate from the samples. It diminishes quickly and becomes negligible for $n_s = 10^5$. **Right:** We represent each set of 30-dimensional α weights by a line whose color encodes the value of the error of Eq. 9, according to the color-code at the right. The black line represents the ground truth. Note how well distributed the samples are around it.

We can therefore represent the family of 3D surfaces whose projections are close to the one that minimizes the reprojection error as being normally distributed around μ_α, the least squares solution of Eq. 4, with covariance Σ_α. Note that, because μ_α is the solution of an ill-conditioned system, it is an unreliable estimate of the distribution's center. We could have improved the system's conditioning by adding a damping term, but this would have amounted to arbitrarily constraining the norm of μ_α. Instead, as discussed in the next section, we use a sampling mechanism to explore different possible values of μ_α.

Efficiently Exploring the Solution Space. To create a set of plausible 3D shapes whose projection are acceptably close to the correct one, we first define a search region $\mathcal{R}_\alpha$ in n_m-dimensional space. We then sample it using a standard numerical technique and progressively apply more stringent constrains to an ever decreasing number of samples.

Given the normal distribution $\mathcal{N}(\mu_\alpha, \Sigma_\alpha)$ introduced above, we take $\mathcal{R}_\alpha$ to be made of the α_i such that

$$(\alpha_i - \mu_\alpha)^\top \Sigma_\alpha^{-1}(\alpha_i - \mu_\alpha) \leq \mathcal{M}^2 \ , \tag{7}$$

where $\mathcal{M}$ is a threshold chosen to achieve a specified degree of confidence. To compute its value we use the cumulative chi-squared distribution, which depends on the dimensionality of the problem . In our experiments, we use $n_m = 30$ modes and $\mathcal{M} = 7$ yields a 98% level of confidence.

To sample $\mathcal{R}_\alpha$, we draw n_s random samples $\{\tilde{\alpha}_i\}_{i=1}^{n_s}$ from the distribution $\mathcal{N}(\mu_\alpha, \mathcal{M}^2\Sigma_\alpha)$. Let $\tilde{\mu}_\alpha$ and $\tilde{\Sigma}_\alpha$ be the mean and covariance matrix of these samples. The technique we use guarantees that $\tilde{\mu}_\alpha = \mu_\alpha$ and that the difference between $\tilde{\Sigma}_\alpha$ and $\mathcal{M}^2\Sigma_\alpha$ approaches zero as n_s increases [16].

In practice, as the μ_α we use is unreliable, we do not draw all n_s samples at once. Instead, we draw successive batches and, having drawn batch k, we draw the next one by sampling from the distribution centered around

$$\mu_\alpha^k = \frac{\sum_{i=1}^{n_s^k} \pi_i^k \tilde{\alpha}_i^k}{\sum_{i=1}^{n_s^k} \pi_i^k} \ , \tag{8}$$

where the π_i^k are weights associated to individual samples, computed as follows.

Let $\tilde{x} = [\tilde{v}_1^\top, \ldots, \tilde{v}_{n_v}^\top]^\top$ be the mesh computed using sample $\tilde{\alpha}$, and let $\{\tilde{u}_i\}_{i=1}^{n_c}$ be the 2D projections of the 3D points for which correspondences u_i are available. $\tilde{\alpha}$ is assigned the weight π such that

$$1/\pi \sim \lambda_1 \sum_i^{n_c} \|\tilde{u}_i - u_i\| + \lambda_2 \sum_{\{i,j\}\in\mathcal{N}} \|\tilde{l}_{ij} - l_{ij}^{ref}\| \ , \tag{9}$$

where the two terms account for the reprojection and inextensibility errors, respectively. Since these errors are expressed in different units of measurement, we use λ_1 and λ_2 to give them similar orders of magnitude. In addition, $\tilde{l}_{ij}$ is the distance between two neighboring vertices $\tilde{v}_i$ and $\tilde{v}_j$, l_{ij}^{ref} is the distance between the same vertices in the reference configuration, and $\mathcal{N}$ represents the indices of neighboring vertices.

In our experiments we used $n_s = 10^5$ random samples, which as shown in Fig. 2(Left), approximate $\mathcal{R}_\alpha$ with an error below 0.5%. These samples were drawn in 10 consecutive batches of 10^4 samples each. As depicted by Fig. 2(Right) the samples generated in this way densely cover a large region of the solution space around the true one. To reduce their number and speed up further processing, we only keep the 10% of the samples with highest weight.

By construction, all these samples represent shapes that yield similar projections and only small violations of the length constraints. Furthermore, many of them yield almost undistiguinshable 3D shapes. To further reduce their number, we therefore run a Gaussian-means clustering algorithm over all the remaining samples in the space of the 3D coordinates [17]. This is a variant of the k-means algorithm that automatically identifies the optimal number of clusters based on statistical tests designed to check whether all the clusters follow a Gaussian distribution. These tests are controlled by means of a significance level parameter which we set to a very low value to favor over-segmentation, that is, to produce more clusters than absolutely necessary to avoid grouping shapes whose difference is statistically significant.

Finally, we take our candidates set of shapes to be the cluster centers. This whole process typically reduces the initial 10^5 samples to about one hundred.

4   Using Additional Cues to Select the Best Candidate

Given correspondences between the reference image and the input image, the algorithm discussed in the previous section returns about 100 candidate 3D meshes that all project correctly in the input image and whose edges have retained their original length. In this section, we show how to use either lighting or motion cues to disambiguate and pick the best one.

4.1 Shading Cues

We consider two different cases. First, we assume the surface is lit by a *distant light source*, which is the situation envisioned in earlier works on monocular deformable surface reconstruction that use shading clues [5, 14, 15]. Second, we address the situation in which the surface is lit by a *nearby light source*. This is more difficult because the inverse of the changing distance to the light source has to be taken into account, which rules out approaches based on simple linear or quadratic constraints. In both cases, we do not assume the lighting parameters known *a priori* and estimate them from the candidate 3D shapes. As shown in Fig. 1, this lets us render the image we would see for any candidate shape, compare it to the real one, and select the best. To perform the rendering, we use ray-tracing and take into account visibility effects and shadows cast by the object on itself. Such non-local and non-linear phenomena are rarely taken into account by continuous optimization-based schemes because they result in highly complex energy landscapes and poor convergence. We now turn to the estimation of the lighting parameters in these two cases.

Light Source at Infinity. Recall from Section 3.1, that we start from a set of correspondences between 3D surface points $\mathbf{p}_i$ and 2D image points $\mathbf{u}_i$ in the input image with intensity I_i. For each i, we also know that $\mathbf{p}_i$ projects at $\mathbf{r}_i$ in the reference image and has intensity I_i^{ref}. In practice, we acquire the reference image under diffuse lighting so that, assuming the surface to be Lambertian, we can take the albedo ρ_i of $\mathbf{p}_i$ to be I_i^{ref}. In the remainder of this Section, let $\mathbf{p}_i$ denote the 3D coordinates of the 3D surface points in the candidate shapes. For each candidate shape, these $\mathbf{p}_i$ are recomputed using the barycentric coordinates, which are the same for all candidates, to average the 3D vertex coordinates of the facets they belong to.

Assuming a distant light source parameterized by its unit direction $\mathbf{l}$ and power L, we can write $I_i = \rho_i L(\mathbf{l} \cdot \mathbf{n}_i)$, where $\mathbf{n}_i$ is the surface normal at $\mathbf{p}_i$, which may be estimated from the $\mathbf{v}_i$ vertex coordinates. Grouping these equations for all n_c correspondences yields

$$\mathbf{I}_\rho = \mathbf{NL} , \qquad (10)$$

where $\mathbf{I}_\rho = [I_1/\rho_1, \ldots, I_{n_c}/\rho_{n_c}]^\top$, $\mathbf{N} = [\mathbf{n}_1, \ldots, \mathbf{n}_{n_c}]^\top$, and $\mathbf{L} = L \cdot \mathbf{l}$. Solving this system in the least-squares sense yields an estimation of $\mathbf{L}$, from which the light intensity and direction can be taken to be $L = \|\mathbf{L}\|$ and $\mathbf{l} = \mathbf{L}/L$.

Nearby Light Source. When considering light sources that are not located at infinity, the fact that the radiosity due to individual light sources decreases with the square of the distance must be taken into account. The image irradiance at $\mathbf{p}_i$ therefore becomes

$$I_i = \rho_i L \frac{\mathbf{l}_i \cdot \mathbf{n}_i}{\|\mathbf{p}_i - \mathbf{s}\|^2} \qquad (11)$$

where $\mathbf{s}$ is the position of the light source and $\mathbf{l}_i = \frac{1}{\|\mathbf{p}_i - \mathbf{s}\|}(\mathbf{p}_i - \mathbf{s})$. $\mathbf{s}$ and L are estimated by minimizing

$$\sum_{i=1}^{n_c} \left| I_i - \rho_i L \frac{\mathbf{l}_i \cdot \mathbf{n}_i}{\|\mathbf{p}_i - \mathbf{s}\|^2} \right| \ , \tag{12}$$

with respect to L and $\mathbf{s}$ using the nonlinear least-squares matlab routine lsqnonlin. To avoid local minima, we define a sparse set of light positions $\{\tilde{\mathbf{s}}_j\}_{j=1}^{n_l}$ and use each one in turn to initialize the optimization. In our experiments, we used $n_l = 125$ light positions uniformly distributed within a hemisphere on top of the reference mesh. Its radius was taken to be sufficiently large to include all distances for which the nearby light assumption holds.

Note that what makes this approach computationally feasible is the fact that we are only attempting to recover the lighting parameters, while fixing the shape parameters. Otherwise, the problem would be massively underconstrained. This should also allow the use of more sophisticated lighting models [18] to relax the single light and Lambertian assumptions.

4.2   Motion Cues

When video sequences are available, we can rely on temporal consistency between consecutive shapes to select the most likely ones. Let us assume that a second order autoregressive model [19] has been learned from training data. Given such a model, the shape at time t, $\mathbf{x}^t$, can be expressed as function of the shapes at times $t - 1$ and $t - 2$ as

$$\mathbf{x}^t = \hat{\mathbf{A}}_2 \mathbf{x}^{t-2} + \hat{\mathbf{A}}_1 \mathbf{x}^{t-1} + \hat{\mathbf{B}} \mathbf{w}^t \ , \tag{13}$$

where $\hat{\mathbf{A}}_2$, $\hat{\mathbf{A}}_1$ and $\hat{\mathbf{B}}$ are $3n_v \times 3n_v$ matrices learned offline, and $\mathbf{w}^t$ is an n_v Gaussian noise vector.

For any three consecutive images and the corresponding shape samples, the most plausible shape in the third one can be found by considering all $\{\tilde{\mathbf{x}}_i^{t-2}, \tilde{\mathbf{x}}_j^{t-1}, \tilde{\mathbf{x}}_k^t\}$ triplets and picking the $\tilde{\mathbf{x}}_k^t$ belonging to the one that best satisfies Eq. 13. Since this is done independently at each time step t, we are not imposing temporal consistency beyond our three consecutive frames windows.

5   Results

We compare the performance of our approach on synthetic and real sequences against that of two state-of-the-art techniques [4, 5], which we refer to as *Salzm08* and *Moreno09*, respectively. As discussed in Section 2, the first essentially returns the approximate solution of Eq. 4 that minimizes the variations in edge-length from the reference shape while the second returns the solution that best fits a shading model involving a point light source at infinity. Note that all three methods compute the 3D shape from either individual images or consecutive triplets, without enforcing temporal consistency across the sequence. We can therefore treat their results as independent and compute their statistics.

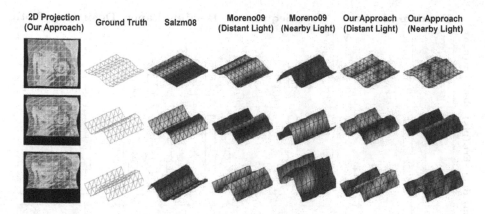

Fig. 3. Results for the synthetic wave sequence. They are best viewed in color as deviations from the ground truth are encoded according the color-code of Fig. 2. Errors of more than 75% of the maximum amplitude of the ground truth shape appear in red.

5.1   Synthetic Experiments

We created two synthetic data sets by deforming an initially planar 9×9 mesh of 30×30 cm. In the first case, we created 500 meshes such as the one of Fig. 1 by randomly changing the angles between neighboring facets. In the second case, we built 250 meshes by giving the surface a wave-like shape, as shown in Fig. 3. In both cases, the virtual camera was placed approximately 75 cm above the mesh and we used a real image as a texture-map. We synthesized a shaded image by selecting a random light-source direction in the hemisphere above the mesh. The light was located either infinitely far or within 30cm of the mesh center. We then produced 100 random 3D-to-2D correspondences between the reference configuration and individual deformed meshes and added a 2-pixel standard deviation Gaussian noise to the 2D coordinates. To compare the sensitivity of Moreno09 and of our approach to lighting conditions, for each synthetic shape we computed two different estimates, one using the image rendered using the distant light and the other using the nearby light.

Fig. 3 depicts results on the synthetic wave sequence using Salzm08, Moreno09, and our own approach in conjunction with either the distant or the nearby lighting. In Fig. 4, we use boxplots[1] to summarize them. We also include the output of an hypothetical algorithm that would be able to select the best candidate shape among all the samples produced by the sampling mechanism of Section 3, which represents the theoretical optimum an algorithm like ours could achieve by using the image information as effectively as possible. Our method consistently returns a lower 3D reconstruction error. This is true even though the reprojection and inextensibility errors are very similar for all three methods,

---

[1] Box denoting the first $Q1$ and third $Q3$ quartiles, a horizontal line indicating the median, and a dashed vertical line representing the data extent taken to be $Q3 + 1.5(Q3 - Q1)$. The red crosses denote points lying outside of this range.

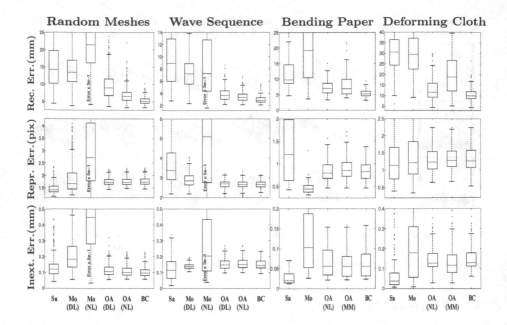

Fig. 4. In each column, reconstruction, reprojection, and inextensibility errors for each of the two synthetic and the two real sequences. Sa: Salzmann08. Mo: Moreno09. OA: Our Approach. BC: An hypothetical algorithm that would always choose the Best Candidate. DL: Distant Light. NL: Nearby Light. MM: Motion Model.

which confirms that minimizing these is not sufficient by itself to retrieve the correct 3D shape. Both Moreno09 and our approach address this issue by taking advantage of shading cues. Since we explicitly model a nearby light, we clearly outperform Moreno09 in that case.

Another measure of success is the *Percentage of correct solutions* of Table 2. Given the ground truth solution, a 3D sample mesh is considered to be correct if at least 75% of its vertices have a reconstruction error smaller than 0.5×Height, where *Height* refers to the maximum amplitude of the ground truth shape. Again, our approach clearly yields the best numbers. The specific ratios –75% and 0.5×Height– are of course *ad hoc* and have been chosen so that 3D meshes that are deemed incorrect produce disturbing effects when viewed in sequence. To provide the reader with an intuitive understanding of what this measure actually represents, in Fig. 3 facets with reconstruction errors of more than 75% are color-coded in red.

Finally, the table at the top of Fig. 5 depicts the accuracy of the estimated lighting parameters. Note that we estimate the position and direction of a light source that was allowed to move freely within a 30 cm radius hemisphere with an accuracy of less than a 1 cm and 10 degrees.

Table 2. Percentages of correct solutions for all four set of experiments. DL: Distant Light. NL: Nearby Light. MM: Motion Model.

	Salzm08	Moreno09 DL	Moreno09 NL	Our Method DL	Our Method NL	Our Method MM	Best Cand.
Random Meshes	84	81	15	91	99	–	100
Wave Sequence	78	95	31	100	100	–	100
Bending Paper	80	–	43	–	99	96	100
Deforming Cloth	59	–	57	–	97	81	99

	Distant Light Direction Err(deg)	Distant Light Power Err(%)	Nearby Light Position Err(mm)	Nearby Light Power Err(%)
Random Meshes	6.9 ± 4.3	5.2 ± 2.1	7.4 ± 6.1	6.8 ± 3.3
Wave Sequence	2.1 ± 0.9	2.2 ± 0.8	3.2 ± 0.8	2.8 ± 1.0

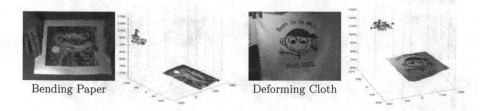

Bending Paper   Deforming Cloth

Fig. 5. Estimated lighting parameters. Upper table: Mean error and standard deviation of the lighting parameters–direction, position and power– estimated independently in each frame of the synthetic sequences. Bottom figures: Light source positions estimated independently in all frames of the real sequences. Note how well clustered they are.

5.2   Real Images

We tested our approach on a 120-frames sequence of bending paper and a 150-frame sequence of a deforming T-shirt, both acquired with a Pointgrey Bum-Blebee stereo rig. The surfaces were lit by a dim ambient lighting and a light source located about 30 cm from the surface. We used the stereo pairs to estimate the ground truth shape and then ran our algorithms using the output of a single camera. We used SIFT [20] to establish correspondences between the reference and input images. In both experiments we used the algorithm described in Sect. 3 to initially produce a set of candidate 3D shapes in each individual frame. We then chose the best using either shading or motion information.

Using Shading to Disambiguate. When using shading, the reconstruction errors depicted in the two right-most boxplots of Fig. 4 exhibit the same patterns as those obtained for the synthetic sequences, which confirms that our method outperforms the other two. As shown in Table 2, we obtain 97% of correct solutions, which represents a 30% increase in performance, using the same definition of "correct" as before. In the bottom of Fig. 5, we plot the estimated

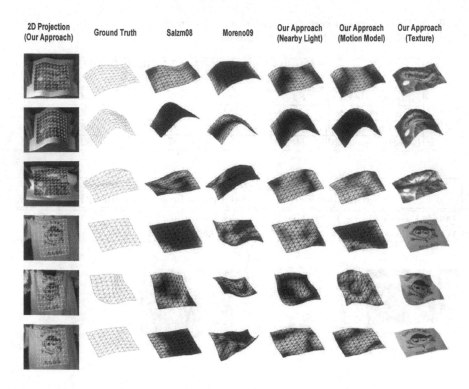

Fig. 6. Results for the two real sequences. Top three rows: Paper. Bottom three rows: Cloth. The reconstruction errors are again color-coded.

light source positions in each frame. Although we did not measure the exact light source locations, the fact that the estimates are tightly clustered is an indication that they are probably correct, given that they all were obtained independently.

Using Motion to Disambiguate. To learn the autoregressive model of Sect. 4.2, we used additional sequences, obtained ground truth data using our stereo rig, and learned the model parameters by probabilistic fitting [19]. In the case of the sheet of paper, as shown in the third column of Fig. 4 and in Table 2, using the motion model yields results similar to those obtained using shading. The performance degrades slightly in the case of cloth because our second order motion model is not accurate enough to perfectly capture the sharp cloth deformations. Nevertheless, our method still outperforms both Salzm08 and Moreno09.

6   Conclusion

For the purpose of single view 3D non-rigid reconstruction, approaches that rely on purely geometric constraints can return incorrect answers because several different shapes that obey, or nearly obey these constraints, often yield very similar projections. To overcome this problem given that the input data is noisy, we use error propagation techniques to derive an analytical expression of the space of potential candidate shapes and to propose a small but representative number of samples. The best among them can then be chosen based on additional image cues, such as shading or motion, which significantly improves results with respect to state-of-the-art methods.

References

1. Perriollat, M., Hartley, R., Bartoli, A.: Monocular template-based reconstruction of inextensible surfaces. In: BMVC (2008)
2. Salzmann, M., Fua, P.: Reconstructing sharply folding surfaces: A convex formulation. In: CVPR (2009)
3. Zhu, J., Hoi, S., Xu, Z., Lyu, M.: An effective approach to 3d deformable surface tracking. In: Forsyth, D., Torr, P., Zisserman, A. (eds.) ECCV 2008, Part III. LNCS, vol. 5304, pp. 766–779. Springer, Heidelberg (2008)
4. Salzmann, M., Moreno-Noguer, F., Lepetit, V., Fua, P.: Closed-form solution to non-rigid 3d surface registration. In: Forsyth, D., Torr, P., Zisserman, A. (eds.) ECCV 2008, Part IV. LNCS, vol. 5305, pp. 581–594. Springer, Heidelberg (2008)
5. Moreno-Noguer, F., Salzmann, M., Lepetit, V., Fua, P.: Capturing 3d stretchable surfaces from single images in closed form. In: CVPR (2009)
6. Ecker, A., Jepson, A.D., Kutulakos, K.N.: Semidefinite programming heuristics for surface reconstruction ambiguities. In: Forsyth, D., Torr, P., Zisserman, A. (eds.) ECCV 2008, Part I. LNCS, vol. 5302, pp. 127–140. Springer, Heidelberg (2008)
7. Cohen, L., Cohen, I.: Finite-element methods for active contour models and balloons for 2-d and 3-d images. PAMI 15 (1993)
8. McInerney, T., Terzopoulos, D.: A finite element model for 3d shape reconstruction and nonrigid motion tracking. In: ICCV (1993)
9. Metaxas, D., Terzopoulos, D.: Constrained deformable superquadrics and nonrigid motion tracking. PAMI 15 (1993)
10. Blanz, V., Vetter, T.: A morphable model for the synthesis of 3-d faces. In: SIGGRAPH (1999)
11. Cootes, T., Edwards, G., Taylor, C.: Active appearance models. In: Burkhardt, H., Neumann, B. (eds.) ECCV 1998. LNCS, vol. 1407, p. 484. Springer, Heidelberg (1998)
12. Gumerov, N., Zandifar, A., Duraiswami, R., Davis, L.: Structure of applicable surfaces from single views. In: Pajdla, T., Matas, J(G.) (eds.) ECCV 2004. LNCS, vol. 3023, pp. 482–496. Springer, Heidelberg (2004)
13. Liang, J., DeMenthon, D., Doermann, D.: Flattening curved documents in images. In: CVPR (2005)
14. Wang, Y., Liu, Z., Hua, G., Wen, Z., Zhang, Z., Samaras, D.: Face re-lighting from a single image under harsh lighting conditions. In: CVPR (2007)
15. White, R., Forsyth, D.: Combining cues: Shape from shading and texture. In: CVPR (2006)
16. Ruanaidh, J., Fitzgerald, W.: Numerical Bayesian Methods Applied to Signal Processing. Springer, Heidelberg (1996)
17. Hamerly, G., Elkan, C.: Learning the k in k-means. In: NIPS (2003)
18. Hara, K., Nishino, K., Ikeuchi, K.: Light source position and reflectance estimation from a single view without the distant illumination assumption. PAMI (2005)
19. Blake, A., Isard, M.: Active contours. Springer, Heidelberg (1998)
20. Lowe, D.G.: Distinctive image features from scale-invariant keypoints. IJCV (2004)

Efficient Computation of Scale-Space Features for Deformable Shape Correspondences

Tingbo Hou and Hong Qin

Department of Computer Science, Stony Brook University
Stony Brook, New York, 11794, USA
{thou,qin}@cs.sunysb.edu

Abstract. With the rapid development of fast data acquisition techniques, 3D scans that record the geometric and photometric information of deformable objects are routinely acquired nowadays. To track surfaces in temporal domain or stitch partially-overlapping scans to form a complete model in spatial domain, robust and efficient feature detection for deformable shape correspondences, as an enabling method, becomes fundamentally critical with pressing needs. In this paper, we propose an efficient method to extract local features in scale spaces of both texture and geometry for deformable shape correspondences. We first build a hierarchical scale space on surface geometry based on geodesic metric, and the pyramid representation of surface geometry naturally engenders the rapid computation of scale-space features. Analogous to the SIFT, our features are found as local extrema in the scale space. We then propose a new feature descriptor for deformable surfaces, which is a gradient histogram within a local region computed by a local parameterization. Both the detector and the descriptor are invariant to isometric deformation, which makes our method a powerful tool for deformable shape correspondences. The performance of the proposed method is evaluated by feature matching on a sequence of deforming surfaces with ground truth correspondences.

Keywords: Shape feature, Scale space, Deformable shape, SIFT.

1   Introduction

In recent years, the rapid development of data acquisition techniques naturally gives rise to a massive collection of 3D scans of the geometric and photometric information of deformable objects. Comparing with 2D images that are generally perspective projections of the scenes, 3D scans capture the shape and the photograph of objects. Feature extraction is an enabling method to organize/index partial 3D scans of an object and track its temporal variations. Strongly motivated by scientific evidences from both physics and biological vision, scale-space features that can appear in multiple scales, are much more desirable with many attractive properties. This paper aims to compute scale-space features directly on deformable surfaces, with a unique application of matching and tracking surfaces undergoing deformation.

K. Daniilidis, P. Maragos, N. Paragios (Eds.): ECCV 2010, Part III, LNCS 6313, pp. 384–397, 2010.

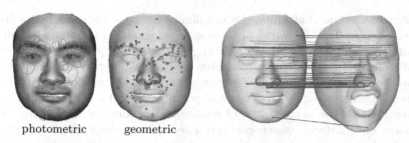

photometric   geometric

Fig. 1. Photometric (green) and geometric (red) features for deformable shape correspondences (right). Oriented circles indicate the scales and orientations of the features. The geometric information here is the Gaussian curvature map.

Different from 2D images, 3D scans acquired by active scanner, stereo vision, multi-view silhouette, or a mixture of them, are commonly represented as triangular meshes, with specific challenges:

- Deformation: Besides shape geometry, consecutive scans recording deformation frequently have unpredictable changes of topology and boundary.
- Irregular grid: The triangulation of scans is typically irregular, with no restriction on the valence (number of connected edges) of a vertex.
- Metric: On curved surfaces, the metric is often referred to the geodesic distance rather than the Euclidean distance.
- Local access: In a triangular mesh, the global index does not reflect its connectivity, and thus the data can only be accessed locally.

Such challenges create many difficulties towards developing algorithms to compute scale-space features on deformable surfaces, with the purpose of shape correspondence. The state of the art therefore is struggling in finding efficient and robust algorithms for local feature extraction and representation on deformable surfaces. For metric choices, some used the Euclidean metric [1–3] that is not preserved under deformation. Some other [4] employed the geodesic metric that is invariant to isometric deformation. Besides, there are also methods converting surfaces to some intrinsic domains to address deformations, e.g., the parametric domain [5–8] and the frequency domain [9, 10]. Parameterization-based methods are usually accompanied by model cutting, and can be easily affected by topological changes. Frequency-based methods decompose the surface into its globally defined Laplace-Beltrami eigenfunctions (LBE), and thus are not applicable for local features. Moreover, most existing methods only focus on geometric characteristics (e.g., normal, curvature, spectrum, etc.). We are interested in the concept of scalar fields on surfaces [3], which neatly combines geometric and photometric characteristics.

In this paper, we develop an efficient method to compute scale-space features using geodesic metric for deformable shape correspondences. Specifically, the contributions of this paper are as follows:

- We present a hierarchical scale space using the pyramid representation, together with geodesic metric. It downsamples the surface when the scale increases, while controlling the sampling rate by a constant factor in the scale space. This hierarchical scale space elegantly integrates photometric and geometric characteristics, and engenders the computation efficiency.

- We propose a new feature descriptor for deformable surfaces enabled by a local parameterization. This descriptor is a gradient histogram on a local region parameterized by geodesics and polar angles in the local tangent plane.
- We evaluate the performance of feature descriptors via a matching experiment on a dataset, which contains a sequence of deforming surfaces with ground truth correspondences.

An example of photometric (green) and geometric (red) features extracted by our method is shown in Fig. 1(left), where the deformable shape correspondences based on these features are shown on the right. The geometric information used here is the Gaussian curvature map.

2   Previous Work

Extracting distinctive local features for 2D images is a fundamental and long-lasting task in computer vision. Perhaps the most influential method with great impact is the scale invariant feature transformation (SIFT) proposed by Lowe [11]. The success of SIFT primarily lies in its effective strategies including pyramid representation, extremum detection in scale space, orientation assignment, histogram of gradients, etc. According to a performance evaluation of local feature descriptors [12], SIFT-based descriptor could reach the best performance. With continuously-increasing interest, extensions have been made to improve the SIFT in recent years. Ke and Sukthankar [13] applied principal components analysis (PCA) to the normalized gradient patch instead of weighted histograms in SIFT. The PCA-SIFT representation with top eigenvectors is more compact than the gradient image, whereas it requires pre-computation over large amount of training data. Mikolajczyk and Schmid [12] proposed the gradient location-orientation histogram (GLOH) descriptor, which extends the rectangular sampling grid of SIFT to a log-polar sampling grid that is more meaningful under rotation. Tola et al. [14] introduced the descriptor "DAISY" replacing the weighted sums of gradient norms in SIFT by convolutions with several oriented derivatives of Gaussian filters, which can be computed even faster without degrading the performance.

Strongly inspired by the prior success of SIFT-like methods on images, some recent work has been dedicated to compute multi-scale features for surfaces. An intuitive idea is to "flatten" surfaces to 2D images via parameterization, and then compute SIFT features of geometric attributes such as normal [6, 7] and curvatures [8]. The parameterization itself, however, suffers from unpredictable changes of topology and boundary, accompanied by domain cutting and shape distortion. In [2], texture was projected to the tangent plane to locally flatten the surface. This method, however, was designed for surfaces with simple geometric shape such as walls. Purely derived from geometry, some other work constructed scale space directly on the 3D surfaces evolving the scale domain information. In [15], a scale space was formulated via surface variation on point-sampled

surfaces. Line-type features were extracted by a multi-scale classification operator that smoothes the surface at different scales. In [16], an intrinsic geometric
scale space (IGSS) of 3D surfaces was proposed for extracting scale-dependent
saliency. Using Ricci Flow, the surface gradually changes its curvature via shape
diffusion. This scale space, therefore, is invariant to conformal deformation. For
scale space on surfaces, Lee et al. [1] adopted 3D Gaussian convolution of curvature maps to compute mesh saliency. The 3D Gaussian scale space is easy to
compute, nevertheless, it is based on Euclidean distance and only feasible for
rigid objects. To improve this, a geodesic scale space (GSS) [4] was introduced
using geodesic-based Gaussian convolution. The cost of computing geodesics,
however, is extremely high as the scale increases. Recently, the concept of scalar
fields defined on 3D surface has been proposed [3], which nicely combines the
photometric and geometric characteristics together. They proposed a 3D feature
detector (MeshDoG) and a descriptor (MeshHoG). The MeshDoG, however, was
computed by 3D Gaussian convolution in 1-ring neighborhood, which is computationally redundant in scale space and may vary subject to shape deformation.

Among descriptors of local features on surfaces, the spin-images [17] is perhaps
the most widely adopted. It maps a local surface patch to a 2D image by the
radial distance and the axial distance. However, its widespread use has been
limited only for rigid objects. The 3D shape context [18] has also been proved to
be a successful shape descriptor. In [19], a statistical approach was proposed to
describe surface features, where the neighbors of a feature were organized by a
spiral pathway, and modeled by a Hidden Markov Model. Others, like the LBE-
based shape signatures [9, 10], are defined globally and dedicated to describe
geometric characteristics only.

3   Hierarchical Scale Space on Deformable Surfaces

3.1   Gaussian Scale Space Using Geodesic Metric

Let S be a surface, a 2D (topological) manifold embedded in $\mathbb{R}^3$, and let $T(V, E, F)$
be an irregular triangular mesh of S with vertex subset V, edge subset E and face
subset F. Irregular meshes have no restriction on the valences of vertices, engen-
dering more flexibility for complex geometric features and topology changes. A
scalar field $L(v)$ where $v \in V$, has attributes defined on all vertices, e.g., texture,
curvature, normal, heat, density, etc.

We build a scale space of the scalar field on the surface using the Gaussian
kernel, given by

$$L(v, \sigma) = G(v, \sigma) * L_0(v), \tag{1}$$

where $L_0(v) = L(v, 0)$ is the initial scalar field, and the scale space $L(v, \sigma)$ varies
according to the scale σ. The Gaussian kernel on surface is defined as

$$G(v, \sigma) = \frac{1}{2\pi\sigma^2} \exp(-\frac{g(v)^2}{2\sigma^2}), \tag{2}$$

where σ is the standard deviation, and $g(v)$ is the geodesic from vertex v to the
Gaussian center. This is a convolution of a family of isometric embeddings that

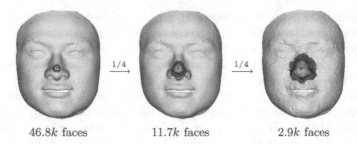

$$46.8k \text{ faces} \qquad 11.7k \text{ faces} \qquad 2.9k \text{ faces}$$

Fig. 2. A pyramid consists of 3 octaves with geodesic neighborhoods of the same radii on different units. It is faster to access large neighbors in higher octave of the pyramid.

preserve geodesic distances from valid neighboring vertices to the center. The discrete Gaussian convolution is then computed in a local region of any v (set as the center)

$$L(v, \sigma) = \frac{\sum_{g(u)<C\sigma} G(u, \sigma) L_0(u)}{\sum_{g(u)<C\sigma} G(u, \sigma)}, \qquad (3)$$

where $C\sigma$ is a sufficiently large cut-off (e.g., $C = 2$ in our implementation) and the unit is the average edge length $\bar{e}$.

3.2   Pyramid Representation

We propose a hierarchical scale space using geodesic metric. The geodesics on arbitrary triangular meshes can be computed by the fast marching method [20]. It solves the Eikonal equation

$$|\nabla T(x)| = F(x), \qquad (4)$$

where the solution $T(x)$ is the shortest time needed to travel from the source to x with $F(x)$ being the time cost. This algorithm has $O(m \log m)$ time complexity for one-source geodesics, where m is the number of traversed vertices. In the discrete Gaussian convolution in Eq. (3), m is related to the area of the neighborhood with radius $C\sigma$, which yields $O(m) = O(\sigma^2)$. Hence, the complexity of computing geodesics for all vertices is $O(n\sigma^2 \log \sigma)$, which is linear w.r.t. the number of vertices n, but quadratic-logarithmic to the scale σ. It implies that the computation cost could be incredibly high when the scale increases.

   To address this problem, we introduce a hierarchical scale space using a pyramid representation, which has demonstrated its efficiency in images [11]. A level of the pyramid, or an octave, is obtained by subsampling the previous octave of the pyramid. For triangular meshes, the subsampling can be accomplished by mesh simplification. There is a large amount of literature on mesh simplification using various error metrics. Here we favor approximately uniform sampling during mesh simplification. Therefore, general approaches such as Progressive mesh [21] and QSlim [22] suffice for this purpose. To make sure that the input mesh is approximately uniformly sampled, we investigate the edge lengths,

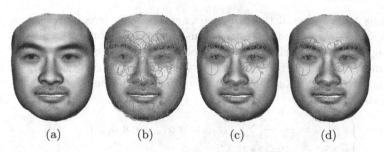

    (a)   (b)   (c)   (d)

Fig. 3. Stages of feature detection: (a) the input scalar field, (b) the initial (494) extrema, (c) selected (150) keypoints by discarding weak responses, and (d) the final (116) keypoints by further removing unstable (i.e., edge, boundary) responses

and insert vertices on edges with length larger than twice of the $\bar{e}$ using linear interpolation.

The pyramid consists of consecutive octaves $[T_0, T_1, ..., T_O]$, where O is the number of octaves, and T_0 is the original mesh. An octave T_i is subsampled from the lower octave T_{i-1} such that the number of faces $n(F_i)$ is one fourth of $n(F_{i-1})$. The unit of the i-th octave is the average edge length $\bar{e}_i \approx \frac{1}{2}\bar{e}_{i-1}$. Fig. 2 shows a pyramid of 3 octaves. It is faster to access large geodesic neighborhoods in higher octave of the pyramid. Therefore, this computation approach is very efficient. Though the geometry in higher octave is coarser, the lost details are not significant for large scales. Each octave contains S scales. The sampling in the scale space is consistent for all octaves by a constant factor $k = 2^{1/S}$. Besides, the pyramid and geodesics can be computed in the pre-processing stage that may be accomplished by the procedure of triangulation.

4 Feature Detector and Descriptor

4.1 Feature Detector

The entire pipeline of feature detection is highlighted in Fig. 3, with specific processes presented as follows.

Local Extrema. Features are detected by finding extrema in the differences of the scales:

$$D(v, \sigma) = L(v, k\sigma) - L(v, \sigma)$$
$$= (G(v, k\sigma) - G(v, \sigma)) * L_0(v), \qquad (5)$$

where $k = 2^{1/S}$ is the factor in scale domain. Assuming the valence of vertex v is n_v, the local extremum of $D(v, \sigma)$ are detected in $(n_v + 1) \times (n_v + 1) \times (n_v + 1)$ neighborhoods of samples. Weak features with small values in $D(v, \sigma)$ are discarded.

Unstable responses. Candidate keypoints with unstable responses (boundaries, edges) are further removed. In regular domain, the edge responses are defined as large ratios of the principal curvatures. In irregular meshes, we can also apply this strategy using algorithms in [23] that compute curvatures in 1-ring neighborhood. Specifically, we project the 1-ring neighbors $N_1(v)$ of v to its local tangent plane, and use the scalar value as the third dimension to build a new mesh structure. The mean curvature κ_H and Gaussian curvature κ_G on the new mesh are given by

$$\begin{cases} \kappa_H(v) = \frac{1}{4A_{mix}} \left| \sum_{u \in N_1(v)} (\cot \alpha_{vu} + \cot \beta_{vu})(v - u) \right| \\ \kappa_G(v) = \frac{1}{A_{mix}} (2\pi - \sum_{j=1}^{n_v} \theta_j) \end{cases}, \qquad (6)$$

where A_{mix} is the area of the generalized Voronoi region for arbitrary meshes, $\cot \alpha_{vu}$ and $\cot \beta_{vu}$ are the well-known "cot" coefficients (please refer to [23] for more details), and θ_j is the angle of the j-th face at the vertex v. The two principal curvatures are then given by

$$\begin{cases} \kappa_1(v) = \kappa_H + \sqrt{\Delta(v)} \\ \kappa_2(v) = \kappa_H - \sqrt{\Delta(v)} \end{cases}, \qquad (7)$$

with $\Delta(v) = \kappa_H^2(v) - \kappa_G(v)$.

Refinement. The detected extremum leads to a local region that contains the location of the feature. Thus, the refinement of feature localization is performed to locate the accurate position. To prevent the localization from leaving the surface, we use projected 1-ring neighbors with scalars in the previous stage. A quadratic function on samples of $D(v, \sigma)$ is fitted over spatial and scale domain in the local coordinate system

$$D(x, y, \sigma) = a_0 x^2 + a_1 y^2 + a_2 \sigma^2 + a_3 xy + a_4 x\sigma +$$
$$a_5 y\sigma + a_6 x + a_7 y + a_8 \sigma + a_9, \qquad (8)$$

where $[a_0, a_1, ..., a_9]$ are a group of coefficients that can be estimated by least-square fitting. The localization $x = [x, y, \sigma]^T$ is updated using

$$\hat{x} = x - \frac{\partial^2 D(x)}{\partial x^2}^{-1} \frac{\partial D(x)}{\partial x}. \qquad (9)$$

4.2   Feature Descriptor

Estimation of Vertex Gradient. For irregular meshes, the gradient of scalar filed $L(v)$ at vertex v, defined as a vector in its local tangent plane, is usually estimated by solving an optimization problem using the finite element method (FEM) [24]. Specifically, let $N_1(v)$ be the 1-ring neighbor of vertex v. The gradient $\nabla L(v)$ can be estimated by minimizing the following error

$$\nabla L(v) = \arg \min_{\nabla L(v)} \sum_{u \in N_1(v)} \left| \nabla L(v)^T P(\overrightarrow{vu}) - \frac{L(u) - L(v)}{g(u)} \right|^2, \qquad (10)$$

where $P(\overrightarrow{vu})$ is the projected unit vector of $\overrightarrow{vu}$ in the local tangent plane $T_v \mathcal{S}$.

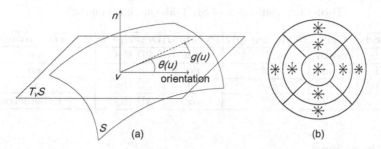

Fig. 4. Local parameterization (a) and descriptor (b). Neighboring vertices are assigned to 9 bins according to their geodesics and polar angles in the local tangent plane T_vS. The histogram of gradients w.r.t. their directions is computed in each bin.

Orientation Assignment. The orientation of the feature is assigned by the dominating direction of gradients in its neighborhood. This assignment makes the detected feature invariant to rotation, which has been a common strategy [3, 11] in computer vision. We divide the local tangent plane into 36 bins, and compute weighed magnitudes of gradients falling into the corresponding bins within a 1.5σ geodesic region. The orientation of the bin with greatest magnitude is assigned as the feature, and a second orientation may also be assigned if there exists a second maximum that is no less than 80% of the highest peak.

Local Parameterization. Previous feature descriptors for curved surfaces (e.g., Spin-images[17], MeshHoG[3]) are typically statistical characteristics distributed in 3D. We propose a new descriptor for deformable surfaces based on a local bivariate parameterization enabled by geodesics and polar angles. Intuitively speaking, any given vertex in a 2D manifold has a neighborhood which is homeomorphic to an open set of a 2D plane. Thus, we parameterize the local region of the vertex v by a polar coordinate system $[g(u), \theta(u)]$ on the surface, where $g(u)$ is the geodesic from vertex v to u, and $\theta(u)$ is the projected polar angle of u from the orientation of v in the local tangent plane T_vS. As shown in Fig. 4(a), this parameterization is completely local, which encodes the geodesic of the destination on the surface and the direction projected in the local tangent plane. Comparing with other local parameterization [25], our method preserves geodesic distances from all neighbors to the origin, and is easy to compute.

Descriptor. A possible drawback of this local parameterization is that the projected polar angles may change subject to severe deformations. To reduce the dependence on the polar angle θ, we quarter the angles in the tangent plane as shown in Fig. 4(b), which affords our shape descriptor to be invariant to most isometric deformations. We use polar grid to cluster vertices into 9 bins, and use tri-linear interpolations to reduce boundary effects. The histogram of gradients w.r.t. eight directions is computed in each bin. The radii of three circles are subject to the ratio of $1 : \sqrt{5} : 3$ with unit σ, so each bin has the same area. The magnitudes of gradients are smoothed by a Gaussian function with 3σ. This descriptor converts histograms of gradients in 2D to a 1D vector that is normalized for matching purpose.

Table 1. Comparison of SIFT-like methods on surfaces

Methods	Grid	Scale Sample	Pyramid	Descriptor	Deform. Invariance
SIFT	regular	$\sigma_0 2^{o+s/S}$	yes	2D HoG	no
GSS	irregular	$\sigma_0 k^n$	no	Spin-images	no
MeshDoG	regular	$\sigma\sqrt{n}$	no	3D HoG	no
ours	irregular	$\sigma_0 2^{o+s/S}$	yes	2D HoG	yes (isometric)

4.3 Discussion

Most recent multi-scale methods of feature detection on surfaces are inspired by the SIFT on images. It is therefore valuable and illustrative to compare them to clarify their differences, as shown in Table 1. Our method is the most similar one in spirit to the SIFT, and is invariant to isometric deformation. Although all of these methods can produce multi-scale representation of scalar inputs, we found that the tight coupling of samplings in scale and spatial domain is critical to scale-dependent features. The SIFT, which has been shown effective, samples by a constant factor $k = 2^{1/S}$ in the scale space: $\sigma_0 2^{o+s/S}$, where σ_0 is the initial value, S is the number of scales per octave, o and s are the order of octave and scale in the pyramid, respectively. By using the pyramid representation, SIFT increases the sampling intervals by a factor 2 in the spatial domain, which allows us to find extrema in larger neighborhoods for greater scales. The GSS method also samples by a constant factor k in the scale space, while the sampling interval in spatial domain remains unchanged for all scales. The MeshDoG method, which builds the scale space by repeatedly convolving the kernel with the same scale σ, samples in the scale domain as $\sigma\sqrt{n}$. The sampling rate gets smaller when the scale increases, so it generate many more redundant samples, while the sampling rate in spatial domain remains unchanged. Our method has similar sampling strategy to that of SIFT, which makes itself both effective and robust.

5 Experimental Results

In this section, experiments are conducted to evaluate the efficiency and reliability of different methods. The deformable surface data being used are 3D scans from [26] acquired by real-time scanners using structured light, and spacetime faces [27] captured by synchronized video cameras and structured light projectors. Previous methods such as the GSS [4] and the MeshDoG/MeshHoG [3] that fall into the same category as our method are used for the comparison purpose.

5.1 Efficiency Evaluation

We run the three methods on three kinds of data with different resolutions and geometric characteristics: complete model, spacetime face, and 3D scan, and show their results in Fig. 5. We use Gaussian curvature maps for scalar fields (a) of data 1 and 2, and photograph for data 3. The scales of detected features

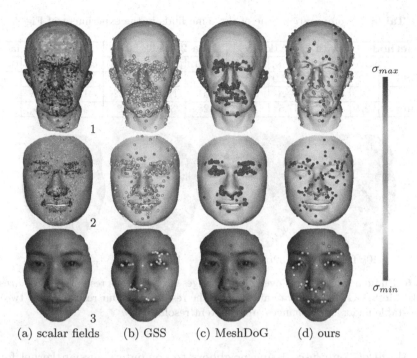

σ_{max}

σ_{min}

(a) scalar fields   (b) GSS   (c) MeshDoG   (d) ours

Fig. 5. Scale-space features on three kinds of data: (a) input scalar fields; (b) results by the GSS; (c) results by the MeshDoG; and (d) our results in this paper. We use Gaussian curvature maps for data 1 and 2, and photograph for data 3. Different colors of detected features represent their scales (better viewed in color).

are represented by their colors: blue for large scale, red for small scale. The GSS method (b) contains 32 scales, and the most features detected belong to small and medium scales. We compute 80 scales in the MeshDoG method (c), while the features only show up in the very small scales. For the data used in our experiments, the two methods have redundant samples in spatial domain and scale domain, indicated by the dense spheres and their intensively distributed colors respectively. Our method (d) has 4 octaves (12 scales) for data 1 and data 2, and has 3 octaves (9 scales) for data 3. The detected features by our method appear to be more intuitive in the sense of scale. We also noticed that the geometric features are related to the resolutions of data. It tends to find more large-scale features for coarse meshes (e.g., data 1), and more small-scale features for fine meshes (e.g., data 2). This fact results from the discrete computation of Gaussian curvatures.

The computation time for the three methods in this experiment are shown in Table 2, obtained from a PC with Quad 2.66GHz CPU and 4GB RAM. In the pre-process (pre), we compute geodesics for the GSS, and geodesics and pyramids for our method. And in the running-process (run) we compute feature detectors and descriptors for all three methods. Compared with the GSS that also uses geodesic metric, our method significantly reduces the pre-process time.

Table 2. Computation time of three methods in the experiment of Fig. 5

Methods	scale	Data 1 (47.1k faces)			Data 2 (46.9k faces)			Data 3 (10k faces)		
		feature	pre-(s)	run-(s)	feature	pre-(s)	run-(s)	feature	pre-(s)	run-(s)
GSS	32	1127	5893.9	11.7	478	6252.0	5.7	38	970.9	1.2
MeshDoG	80	540	N/A	31.8	451	N/A	22.2	15	N/A	1.9
ours	12/9	274	47.5	1.8	128	33.7	0.8	36	6.3	0.2

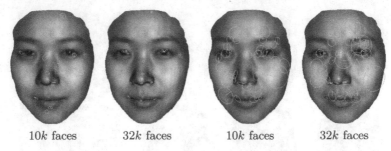

$10k$ faces $32k$ faces $10k$ faces $32k$ faces

Fig. 6. Photometric features over mesh changes and different resolutions. The results by the MeshDoG (left two) are affected by the resolutions. Our results (right two) are more stable under mesh changes and different resolutions.

The MeshDoG only uses 1-ring neighbors to compute Gaussian kernel for all scales, which is actually a bad practice though it saves the pre-process time. In terms of running-process time, our method is still much faster. In fact, for rigid models we can use Euclidean distances to replace geodesics, this will reduce computation time in the pre-process (e.g., about 10 seconds pre-process time for data 1, and the total computation time is about 1/3 of that in the MeshDoG).

Another experiment is conducted to examine the scales of photometric features over mesh changes and different resolutions, with the results shown in Fig. 6. The original scan from [26] has high resolution ($170k$ faces) and moderate accuracy. We downsample them into scans with different resolutions ($10k$ faces and $32k$ faces). The MeshDoG (left) only finds features in the small scales, and thus the results are unstable under resolution changes. Our method (right) is more stable under mesh changes and different resolutions.

5.2   Reliability Evaluation via Feature Matching

The reliability of features for matching purpose can be evaluated by feature matching with ground truth, as in [12, 13]. Thus, we use the spacetime faces which have ground truth correspondences to evaluate the feature descriptors via feature matching. In this experiment, we use the photometric scalar fields, and evaluate two descriptors: MeshHoG and ours. Since the descriptor employed in the GSS is the Spin-images for geometric features on rigid models only, it is not appropriate for our purpose. The matching strategy is a basic nearest neighbor algorithm with cross validation as in [3]. A pair of candidate matches $\{f_i^1, f_j^2\}$ from $\mathcal{S}^1$ and $\mathcal{S}^2$ is identified if they are the nearest neighbor to each other in the

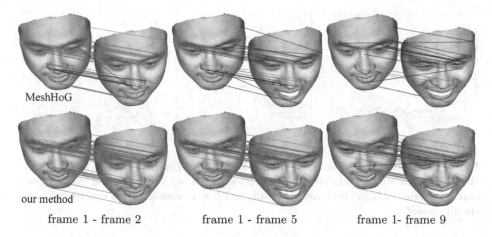

MeshHoG

our method

frame 1 - frame 2   frame 1 - frame 5   frame 1- frame 9

Fig. 7. Selected frames from our evaluation of the MeshHoG (first row) and our method (second row). We match frame 1 to all other frames. Green lines represent correct matches, while black lines represent false matches.

Euclidean space of descriptor. And only matches that are discriminative (i.e., the distance of the closest neighbor is γ or less to that of the second-closest neighbor) can be finally accepted.

The spacetime face data has a sequence of a deforming face, where 34 frames are selected for evaluation which last about 5 seconds. We fix thresholds for the two methods respectively, which maintain about (120 ~ 160) features detected for each frame. Then we match features in the first frame to the ones in other frames to evaluate the reliability of feature descriptors under deformation. The parameter for matching algorithm is set as $\gamma = 0.9$ for both methods. Some selected frames are shown in Fig. 7, where green lines represent correct matches while black lines represent false matches. The complete result (up to 50 frames) can be found in the supplementary material (in the interest of space). Three criteria are employed: effectiveness, recall, and 1-precision. The effectiveness is defined as the ratio between the number of correct matches and the number of detected features, which reflects how effective for the method to find correct matches. The correct matches are identified if the matched feature is within one unit of $\bar{e}$ of the ground truth. The recall and 1-precision are defined conventionally as that in [13]. The number of positives is determined for the detected features using the same way as correct matches. The evaluation results are shown in Fig. 8. The MeshHoG performs well for the first two frames with small deformation, and its performance severely deteriorates for large frame indices (i.e., large deformation) in our experiment. This is primarily because the detected features by the MeshDoG are not distinctive, and the MeshHoG is not deformation-invariant. Our method is more reliable in terms of high effectiveness, recall, and low 1-precision, and is stable even for large deformations.

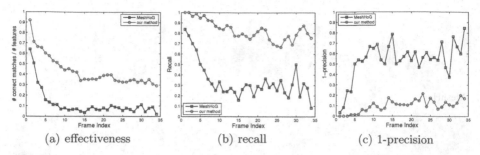

      (a) effectiveness   (b) recall   (c) 1-precision

Fig. 8. Evaluation results on reliability of descriptors. The performance of the Mesh-HoG (blue) severely deteriorates for large deformation, while our method (red) is more stable in terms of high effectiveness, recall, and low 1-precision both consistently and simultaneously.

6 Conclusion

In this paper we have detailed an efficient method to compute scale dependent features on surfaces for deformable shape correspondences, which is a natural generalization of the SIFT. The proposed feature detector and descriptor are invariant to isometric deformation. Unlike previous methods on rigid surfaces, our method takes the 3D scans as scalar fields on deformable manifolds using geodesic metric. By employing a hierarchical scale space and a pyramid shape representation, our method is both efficient and stable, as shown in the experimental results. We have also conducted the comprehensive evaluation of the reliabilities of descriptors via matching features on a sequence of deforming surfaces with ground truth correspondences. Compared with existing work, our method is much more robust and effective under natural deformations. Our on-going research efforts will continue to center on the comprehensive studies on shape matching and registration of deformable surfaces, with new research directions including shape completion in both temporal and spatial domains.

Acknowledgments. This research has been supported in part by NSF grants IIS-0949467 and IIS-0710819. We also wish to thank the University of Washington Graphics and Imaging Laboratory to provide the "spacetime faces" data.

References

1. Lee, C.H., Varshney, A., Jacobs, D.W.: Mesh saliency. ACM Trans. Graph. (TOG) 24, 659–666 (2005)
2. Wu, C., Clipp, B., Li, X., Frahm, J.M., Pollefeys, M.: 3d model matching with viewpoint-invariant patches (vip). In: CVPR (2008)
3. Zaharescu, A., Boyer, E., Varanasi, K., Horaud, R.: Surface feature detection and description with applications to mesh matching. In: CVPR (2009)
4. Zou, G., Hua, J., Dong, M., Qin, H.: Surface matching with salient keypoints in geodesic scale space. Computer Animation and Virtual Worlds 19, 399–410 (2008)

5. Elad, A., Kimmel, R.: On bending invariant signatures for surfaces. TPAMI 25, 1285–1295 (2003)
6. Novatnack, J., Nishino, K.: Scale-dependent 3d geometric features. In: ICCV (2007)
7. Novatnack, J., Nishino, K.: Scale-dependent/invariant local 3d shape descriptors for fully automatic registration of multiple sets of range images. In: Forsyth, D., Torr, P., Zisserman, A. (eds.) ECCV 2008, Part III. LNCS, vol. 5304, pp. 440–453. Springer, Heidelberg (2008)
8. Hua, J., Lai, Z., Dong, M., Gu, X., Qin, H.: Geodesic distance-weighted shape vector image diffusion. TVCG 14, 1643–1650 (2008)
9. Reuter, M., Wolter, F.E., Peinecke, N.: Laplace-beltrami spectra as "shape-dna" of surfaces and solids. Computer-Aided Design (CAD) 38, 342–366 (2006)
10. Rustamov, R.: Laplacebeltrami eigenfunctions for deformation invariant shape representation. In: Symposium of Geometry Processing, SGP (2007)
11. Lowe, D.: Distinctive image features from scale-invariant keypoints. IJCV 60, 91–110 (2004)
12. Mikolajczyk, K., Schmid, C.: A performance evaluation of local descriptors. TPAMI 27, 1615–1630 (2005)
13. Ke, Y., Sukthankar, R.: Pca-sift: A more distinctive representation for local image descriptors. In: CVPR (2004)
14. Tola, E., Lepetit, V., Fua, P.: A fast local descriptor for dense matching. In: CVPR (2008)
15. Pauly, M., Keiser, R., Gross, M.: Multi-scale feature extraction on point-sampled surfaces. Comput. Graph. Forum (CGF) 22, 281–289 (2003)
16. Zou, G., Hua, J., Lai, Z., Gu, X., Dong, M.: Intrinsic geometric scale space by shape diffusion. TVCG 15, 1193–1200 (2009)
17. Johnson, A.: Spin-images: A representation for 3-d surface matching. PhD thesis, Carnegie Mellon University (1997)
18. Frome, A., Huber, D., Kolluri, R., Bülow, T., Malik, J.: Recognizing objects in range data using regional point descriptors. In: Pajdla, T., Matas, J(G.) (eds.) ECCV 2004. LNCS, vol. 3023, pp. 224–237. Springer, Heidelberg (2004)
19. Castellani, U., Cristani, M., Fantoni, S., Murino, V.: Sparse points matching by combining 3d mesh saliency with statistical descriptors. In: Eurographics (2008)
20. Kimmel, R., Sethian, J.A.: Computing geodesic paths on manifolds. In: Proceedings of National Academy of Science USA (PNAS), pp. 8431–8435 (1998)
21. Hoppe, H.: Progressive meshes. In: SIGGRAPH, pp. 99–108 (1996)
22. Garland, M., Heckbert, P.S.: Surface simplification using quadric error metrics. In: SIGGRAPH, pp. 209–216 (1997)
23. Meyer, M., Desbrun, M., Schröder, P., Barr, A.H.: Discrete differential-geometry operators for triangulated 2-manifolds. VisMath (2002)
24. Meyer, T.H., Eriksson, M., Maggio, R.C.: Gradient estimation from irregularly spaced data sets. Mathematical Geology 23, 693–717 (2004)
25. Shapira, L., Shamir, A.: Local geodesic parametrization: An ants perspective. In: Mathematical Foundations of Scientific Visualization, Computer Graphics, and Massive Data Exploration, pp. 127–137. Springer, Heidelberg (2009)
26. Wang, S., Gu, X., Qin, H.: Automatic non-rigid registration of 3d dynamic data for facial expression synthesis and transfer. In: CVPR (2008)
27. Zhang, L., Snavely, N., Curless, B., Seitz, S.: Spacetime faces: High-resolution capture for modeling and animation. In: SIGGRAPH (2004)

Intrinsic Regularity Detection in 3D Geometry

Niloy J. Mitra[1], Alex Bronstein[2], and Michael Bronstein[3]

[1] Indian Institute of Technology, Delhi
[2] Tel Aviv University
[3] Technion

Abstract. Automatic detection of symmetries, regularity, and repetitive structures in 3D geometry is a fundamental problem in shape analysis and pattern recognition with applications in computer vision and graphics. Especially challenging is to detect *intrinsic* regularity, where the repetitions are on an intrinsic grid, without any apparent Euclidean pattern to describe the shape, but rising out of (near) isometric deformation of the underlying surface. In this paper, we employ multidimensional scaling to reduce the problem of intrinsic structure detection to a simpler problem of 2D grid detection. Potential 2D grids are then identified using an autocorrelation analysis, refined using local fitting, validated, and finally projected back to the spatial domain. We test the detection algorithm on a variety of scanned plaster models in presence of imperfections like missing data, noise and outliers. We also present a range of applications including scan completion, shape editing, super-resolution, and structural correspondence.

1 Introduction

Symmetries and regular structures are ubiquitous in nature and in man-made objects, often being closely related to form, function, aesthetics, and manufacturing ease of geometrically complex but procedurally simple shapes. While humans are extremely skilled at perceiving and identifying such patterns, even under a cursory inspection [1], automatic detection of such regularity remains challenging. One of the main difficulties is the fact that neither the parts that are being repeated nor their repetition pattern is known *a priori*. Additionally, the surfaces are often warped in practice, making pattern detection challenging (see Figure 1). Such distortions have been widely studied in computer vision, specially work on shape-from-texture [2], and in the context of pose and articulation invariant shape representation and matching [3–7].

State-of-the-art methods [8–10] can detect structured repetitions in 3D geometry if the Euclidean transformations between repeated patches exhibit group-like behavior. In case of non-rigid and deformable shapes, however, the problem is challenging since no apparent structure is visible to simple Euclidean probes in the absence of repetitive Euclidean transformations to describe the shape (see Figure 4).

In this paper, we address the problem of identifying regularity and repeating structure on an *intrinsic* grid on the shape, i.e., regularity detection on (near) developable surfaces. The Euclidean structure of such a grid depends on the embedding of the shape in the ambient space. Yet, using an intrinsic notion of distance, the grid becomes deformation-invariant, and is simpler to identify and extract. To the best of our knowledge, this is the first attempt to detect grid-regularities invariant under isometric deformations. We demonstrate our algorithm on a variety of scanned plaster models of

K. Daniilidis, P. Maragos, N. Paragios (Eds.): ECCV 2010, Part III, LNCS 6313, pp. 398–410, 2010.

Fig. 1. (Left) A cylindrical seal, (middle) impression left by a cylindrical seal on a (near) developable surface, and (right) near-intrinsic regular marking created by a car tyre on soft ground

stamped surfaces, with missing parts, and varying degree of noise. Such footprints are common among stenciled concrete, industrial patterns, impressions of cylindrical seals, and vehicle tire tracks just to mention a few.

Related work. Symmetry and structure detection in images and shapes is a well-researched topic in the computer vision and graphics communities (see e.g. [10–19]) with applications including segmentation [20], scan completion [9], pose invariant representation [21], image de-fencing [22], shape retrieval [12], and editing images with repeated elements [23].

Local structure and repetition detection for 3D geometry was addressed by Pauly et al. [8] where self-similarity is represented as a collection of local Euclidean transformations, parameterized in a suitably designed 7D transformation space. The paper observes that repeating self-similar structures correspond to regular grids in special slices of the transformation space, and presents an algorithm for detecting such grid and, subsequently, the repeating elements. However, this approach is limited to handle only regular Euclidean lattices. More recently, Park et al. [24] presented a computational framework using a fourth-degree Markov random fields and mean shift belief propagation, interleaved with thin plate spline warping, for detecting deformed lattices or 2D wallpaper patterns in images. To the best of our knowledge, there are no known extensions to handle intrinsic regularity in 3D geometry.

Raviv et al. [25] introduced *intrinsic symmetries* as a natural extension of the notion of symmetry to non-rigid objects, based on a model of shapes as metric spaces [3, 26,

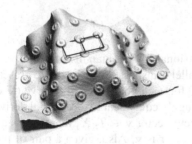
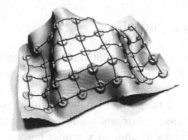

Fig. 2. Embedded intrinsic regularity on a shape as detected, shown in black, by Euclidean transformation analysis [8] (left) and by our algorithm (right)

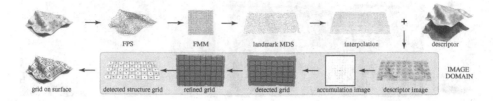

Fig. 3. Stages of the proposed algorithm for intrinsic structure detection: Flattening using MDS, computation of descriptor image, accumulation image, detection of grid generators by autocorrelation analysis, local grid refinement, validation and final detected structure (see Section 3)

27]. In a separate attempt, Ovsjanikov et al. [28] presented a method for symmetry detection based on the properties of eigenfunctions of the Laplace-Beltrami operator of the shape. Since the operator is invariant under isometric deformations, the resultant symmetry detection also detects intrinsic symmetry of objects. Recently, Xu et al. [29] introduced an algorithm to obtain intrinsic reflection symmetry axis (IRSA) transform of objects, followed by an iterative refinement to extract dominant IRSA curves. These efforts, however, are targeted towards detection of pairwise intrinsic symmetry, and not for extracting patterns among the detected symmetries.

Although, intrinsic distances has been employed in computer vision in various contexts like texture mapping [30], face animation and morphing [31], articulation invariant shape matching [3, 4], their use for repetition or regular structure detection has been largely unexplored.

Contribution. We extend the notion of regular structure detection in 3D geometry to handle isometric deformations. The detected structure grids are robust and invariant to bending and articulations of the shapes. State-of-the-art algorithm [8] in regularity detection under Euclidean transformations fails to identify such intrinsic structures in non-rigid shapes since their embedding distorts the Euclidean structures (see Figure 2, left). By using *multidimensional scaling* (MDS), the intrinsic geometry of the surface is mapped into a Euclidean one, thus reducing the problem to the case of Euclidean regularities. Such a planar embedding, however, reduces the problem to a simpler instance of regular grid detection in the plane, instead of intrinsic grid detection on the surface. The use of MDS removes the necessity to detect deformed lattices as proposed by Park et al. [24], leading to a simple, robust, and computationally-efficient algorithm.

2   Background

Let X be a surface modeled as a two-dimensional Riemannian manifold. A parametric curve $\gamma(t)$ on X is called a *geodesic* if parallel transport along the curve preserves the tangent vector $\dot{\gamma}$ to the curve, i.e., $\nabla_{\dot{\gamma}}\dot{\gamma} = 0$ for each point along the curve (∇ denotes the *covariant derivative* on the manifold, roughly equivalent to directional derivative in a vector space). For any point $\mathbf{x}$ and a tangent vector $\mathbf{v} \in T_{\mathbf{x}}X$, there exists a unique geodesic passing though $\mathbf{x}$ whose tangent vector is $\mathbf{v}$. Also, given a pair of points on the manifold, the geodesic curve γ is the (locally) shortest path between the points. We denote by $d_X : X \times X \to \mathbb{R}$ the *geodesic metric* measuring the length of the shortest paths between points on X.

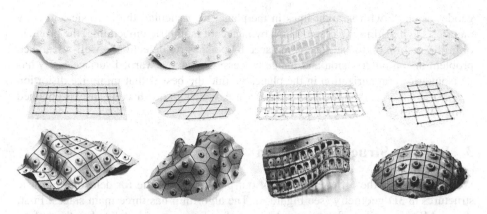

Fig. 4. Photographs of the plasticine imprints scanned in our experiments (top row), the detected grids in the parametrization domain obtained using MDS along with the locally refined grids (middle row), and the corresponding intrinsic structure depicted on the scanned models (last row). Parts of the shape that do not belong to any detected intrinsic regularities are in blue

Recent works [3, 26, 27] have considered non-rigid surfaces as metric spaces of the form (X, d_X) that are deformation-invariant. Raviv et al. [25] defined *intrinsic symmetry* as self-isometry with respect to the metric d_X: surface X is intrinsically symmetric if there exists a non-trivial bijection $\phi : X \to X'$ such that $d_X = d_{X'} \circ (\phi \times \phi)$.

Given a point $\mathbf{x}$ and a tangent vector $\mathbf{v} \in T_{\mathbf{x}}X$, we define translation $\mathbf{t}$ by a fixed length in the direction $\mathbf{v}$ using parallel transport on the manifold along the geodesic passing through point $\mathbf{x}$ in the direction $\mathbf{v}$. Rotation $\mathbf{R}$ is defined as rotation of the tangent vector $\mathbf{v}$ in the tangent plane. With these two operations, we can define an *intrinsic grid* as a collection of points or nodes $G \subset X$ obtained by successive applications of translation and rotation operations. For example, an orthogonal intrinsic grid is defined by setting an origin $\mathbf{x}$ and a vector $\mathbf{v}$, having $\mathbf{R}$ defined as a rotation by $\pi/2$ and $\mathbf{t}$ as a translation by fixed length (Figure 5).

The goal of intrinsic structure detection is to explain the surface using local self-similarity on an intrinsic grid, i.e., finding the largest grid G that for any pair of points $\mathbf{x}_i, \mathbf{x}_j \in G$ the surface is locally self-similar at $\mathbf{x}_i, \mathbf{x}_j$. The main idea of our approach is as follows: Let X (or its subset) has an isometric embedding into the plane, i.e., there exists a bijection $\psi : (X, d_X) \to (\mathbb{R}^2, d_{\mathbb{R}^2})$ satisfying $d_X = d_{\mathbb{R}^2} \circ (\psi \times \psi)$. Here ψ can be thought of as a flattening or parametrization of the surface that replaces

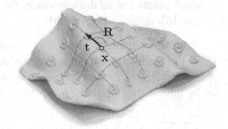

Fig. 5. Example of geodesic grid embedded on the surface

geodesics on X with straight lines in the plane. In particular, the intrinsic regularity manifests as a grid in the plane. Thus, by means of isometric embedding, the problem of grid detection on the surface is replaced by planar grid detection, a well-researched problem in computer vision and image processing. Since a warped surface rarely has an isometric parametrization in the plane, we find the best ψ that minimize distortion $\|d_X - d_{\mathbb{R}^2} \circ (\psi \times \psi)\|$ in the least squares sense, which, in the discrete case, is obtained using MDS [32].

3   Intrinsic Structure Detection

We now describe the different stages of our proposed pipeline for detecting intrinsic structures in 3D geometry (see Figure 3). The algorithm has three main stages: First, we use MDS for surface flattening, which transfers intrinsic grids defined on the surface onto the plane. Second, local shape structure is represented using intrinsic descriptors, and their repeating patterns detected in the plane. Finally, the detected planar grid is refined, validated, and mapped back to the surface.

In the following, we assume that the shape X is presented as a *triangular mesh* built upon a set of vertices $V \equiv \{\mathbf{x}_1, ..., \mathbf{x}_n\}$. Let E denote the set of edges with $(i, j) \in E$ if vertices $\mathbf{x}_i, \mathbf{x}_j$ are connected by an edge. In our experiments, n is typically 50K–100K.

3.1   Shape Flattening

Distance computation. The geodesic metric on the triangular mesh is approximated using *fast marching* (FMM) [33], a numerical solver to the Eikonal equation that computes distance map from a point to the rest of the mesh vertices by simulating wavefront propagation. To reduce the computational cost of the MDS stage, we use a landmark-based approach [34]. The mesh is sampled at $m \ll n$ *landmark points* (denoted, without loss of generality, by $\mathbf{x}_1, ..., \mathbf{x}_m$) using the *farthest point sampling* (FPS) procedure [35], performed as follows: Start with some vertex, say $\mathbf{x}_1$, selected at random. The k-th point is selected from V to be the most distant point from the current selection of $k - 1$ points, i.e.,

$$\mathbf{x}_k = \arg\max_{\mathbf{x} \in V} d_X(\{\mathbf{x}_1, .., \mathbf{x}_{k-1}\}, \mathbf{x}) = \arg\max_{\mathbf{x} \in V} \min_{i=1,..,k-1} d_X(\mathbf{x}_i, \mathbf{x}). \tag{1}$$

FPS produces a subsampling with m approximately equidistant points. Then FMM is employed to compute the $m \times n$ matrix of geodesic distances $d_X(\mathbf{x}_i, \mathbf{x}_j), i = 1, .., m;$ $j = 1, .., n$ between the landmark points and all the vertices of the mesh. In our experiments, we set the sample size m to a default value of 500.

Flattening. The minimum-distortion parametrization ψ is computed using a variant of *landmark MDS* [34]. First, the landmark points are embedded into the plane. We denote by $\mathbf{u}_i = \psi(\mathbf{x}_i)$ for $i = 1, .., m$ their parametrization coordinates in the plane, i.e., $\mathbf{u}_i \in \mathbb{R}^2$, that are found by minimizing the *stress function*

$$\min_{\mathbf{u}_1,...,\mathbf{u}_m} \sum_{i=1}^{m} \sum_{j=i+1}^{m} (d_X(\mathbf{x}_i, \mathbf{x}_j) - \|\mathbf{u}_i - \mathbf{u}_j\|)^2. \tag{2}$$

Fig. 6. Robustness of our method to missing and corrupt data: occlusions due to imperfect acquisition and synthetic holes (left), simulated Gaussian noise (center), and shot noise (right). Regions not explained by detected intrinsic structure are in blue.

The minimizer of the stress function is the minimum-distortion parametrization of the surface in the least squares sense. We use SMACOF iterations [32]

$$U^{(k+1)} = \frac{1}{m} B(U^{(k)}) U^{(k)}, \qquad (3)$$

repeated until convergence, to solve the LS-MDS problem (2) iteratively[1]. Here, U is a $m \times 2$ matrix of landmark point parametrization coordinates with

$$b_{ij}(U) = \begin{cases} \frac{d_X(\mathbf{x}_i, \mathbf{x}_j)}{\|\mathbf{u}_i - \mathbf{u}_j\|} & i \neq j \text{ and } \|\mathbf{u}_i - \mathbf{u}_j\| \neq 0, \\ 0 & i \neq j \text{ and } \|\mathbf{u}_i - \mathbf{u}_j\| = 0, \\ -\sum_{k \neq i} b_{ik} & i = j. \end{cases}$$

We initialize the LS-MDS solver using classical scaling based on a globally-convergent algebraic MDS method minimizing the Frobenius norm of the distance distortion. SMACOF iterations are guaranteed to produce a monotonically decreasing sequence of stress values [37].

Interpolation. The obtained landmark parametrization coordinates are employed to interpolate the parametrization coordinates for the remaining mesh vertices using a distance-based interpolation proposed in [34]. The interpolated coordinates are inferred from the landmark coordinates using

$$\mathbf{u}_j = -\frac{1}{2} U^\dagger (\delta_j - \bar{\delta}),$$

---

[1] SMACOF iteration is equivalent to a weighted gradient descent and generally does not guarantee global convergence. However, using a sufficiently good initialization or multiscale optimization, reasonable convergence is obtained [36].

for $j = m + 1, .., n$, where $U^\dagger$ denotes the pseudoinverse of the matrix of landmark point parametrization coordinates, $\delta_j = (d_X^2(\mathbf{x}_j, \mathbf{x}_1), .., d_X^2(\mathbf{x}_j, \mathbf{x}_m))^{\mathrm{T}}$ is the $m \times 1$ vector of squared distances from $\mathbf{x}_j$ to the landmark points, and

$$\bar{\delta} = \frac{1}{m} \sum_{i=1}^{m} (d_X^2(\mathbf{x}_i, \mathbf{x}_1), .., d_X^2(\mathbf{x}_i, \mathbf{x}_m))^{\mathrm{T}}$$

is the average squared distance between the landmark points. Thus, for every vertex $\mathbf{x} \in V$ on the mesh, we get a mapping to a corresponding point $\mathbf{u} = \psi(\mathbf{x})$ in the plane.

3.2 Grid Detection

Descriptor. We now compute a simple scalar descriptor at each point to facilitate repetition detection in the next stage. The input mesh is smoothed using a discrete Laplacian,

$$(\Delta\mathbf{x})_i = \frac{1}{v(i)} \sum_{j:(i,j)\in E} \mathbf{x}_j, \tag{4}$$

producing a smoothed version $X_p = \Delta X$. Here, $v(i)$ denotes the valence of the vertex $\mathbf{x}_i$, i.e., the number of vertices adjacent to it. We define a scalar descriptor at each vertex of the mesh as $c \equiv \langle \mathbf{x} - \mathbf{x}_p, \mathbf{n} \rangle$, where $\mathbf{x}$ and $\mathbf{x}_p$ are the original and smoothed shape coordinates, respectively, and $\mathbf{n}$ is the normal vector to the smoothed mesh at that point. Such a descriptor captures the high-frequency geometric details or the *coating* of the surface, and is insensitive to low-frequency bending and non-rigid deformations. Mapping the descriptor to the plane using the parametrization ψ results in a *descriptor image* $c \circ \psi^{-1}$, which contains regular Euclidean 2D patterns. In our experiments, we sampled the descriptor image on a regular planar Cartesian grid with the largest dimension of 128.

Accumulation. The 3D surface of the height-field descriptor image contains regular structures in the Euclidean sense. While one can detect the repetitions on this derived surface using the method proposed by Pauly et al. [8], given the nature of the repetitions in the MDS domain, a much simpler approach is to directly detect the grids on the descriptor image. An *accumulation image* representing the repeating patterns in the descriptor image is constructed as

$$A(\mathbf{w}) = \sum_{\mathbf{z}} \exp(-\langle P(\mathbf{z}), P(\mathbf{z} + \mathbf{w}) \rangle / 2\sigma^2) \tag{5}$$

where $P(\mathbf{z})$ and $P(\mathbf{z} + \mathbf{w})$ are normalized descriptor image patches, and the inner product between them is weighted by a Gaussian window with kernel width σ. Thus, if the descriptor image contains many patches that are similar up to a displacement by a vector $\mathbf{w}$, the accumulation image will exhibit a peak at $\mathbf{w}$. In our experiments, by default, the accumulation image was of size 257×257, the patch size was 21×21, and $\sigma = 0.075$ was used.

Autocorrelation. The autocorrelation of the accumulation image allows to find the grid generators, i.e., the vectors that define the grid in the parametrization domain. Autocorrelation is computed as the similarity of the accumulation image to its version shifted by a vector **u**, represented in polar coordinates. Two peaks are detected in the polar autocorrelation image, representing the grid generators. Often, there might exist more than one pair of generators explaining the same grid, as visualized in Figure 10. In such cases, we give preference to shorter ones resulting in a denser grid.

Phase selection. The detected grid is inherently ambiguous to *phase*, i.e., shift along the grid generator vectors (Figure 10). While there is no theoretical preference to a specific phase of the detected grid, some phases produce semantically and visually more meaningful results. We perform phase selection by shifting the grid to maximize the local variation of the descriptor at the grid nodes. This way, the grid locks onto *interesting* geometric features.

3.3   Refinement and Validation

Refinement. Peaks of the autocorrelation function of the accumulation image provide good generators for grids in the MDS domain. However, because of them being only approximate, we locally refine the grid point locations as well as remove grid points and connections that do not correspond to any structural element (see Figure 3). This local correlation and refinement is performed using descriptor images with twice the resolution used in the previous stage. We used images with maximum dimension of 256 pixels as default.

Validation. The input mesh and the corresponding MDS descriptor image do not solely constitute of regular structures. Hence we explicitly identify and extract the structural elements around each grid point using a greedy growth with validation (see Figure 10). Finally, we project back the detected structural elements to the surface. In, Figure 4 the unstructured parts are indicated in blue.

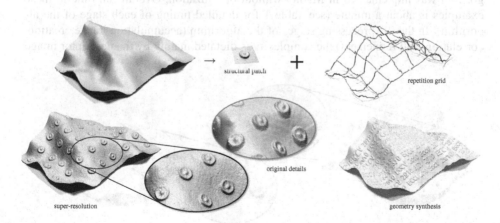

Fig. 7. Square-shape (see Figure 4) is decomposed into a smooth base and a detail layer consisting of a structural patch and a repetition grid (top). This enables geometry processing like super-resolution and synthesis of a shape with the same structural layout but different with geometric details (bottom).

Table 1. Mesh sizes and run times (in seconds) for different stages of the algorithm. Performance measured on a 2 GHz Core Duo Pentium CPU with 3GB of RAM.

	square	oblique	Colosseum	ball
# vertices	54,880	54,817	57,563	40,601
FMM + MDS	5	5	6	4
interpolation	11	10	12	5
descriptor	3	4	4	4
accumulation	23	34	17	54
correlation	31	41	28	59
refinement	13	16	12	18

4   Results and Applications

For the experiments in this paper, we used scans of objects sculpted and stamped using plasticine depicted in Figure 4 (first row). The objects were designed to contain intrinsically repeating structure, which is hard to perceive if considered in a Euclidean way. Four objects were used: deformed surfaces with square and oblique grids, a detail of a curved architectural shape (non-rigid Colosseum), and part of a ball with square grid structure. Each of the objects presents a different challenge in structure recovery. Thus, in the Colosseum shape, the structural elements are holes (windows), and the ball has a non-developable geometry. The objects were scanned using a coded light range camera, producing triangular meshes that were cleaned up and resampled to about 50K vertices. Data and code are available for academic use from the project webpage. Our algorithm is robust to a range of parameter settings, and all the reported results are with a default set of values.

Figure 4 shows the intrinsic grids detected using the proposed algorithm. The algorithm was implemented in Matlab without optimization. Overall run time in these examples is about a minute (see Table 1 for detailed timing of each stage of the algorithm). In the 2D processing stages of the algorithm (accumulation image creation, correlation, and refinement) the complexity is dictated mainly by the descriptor image

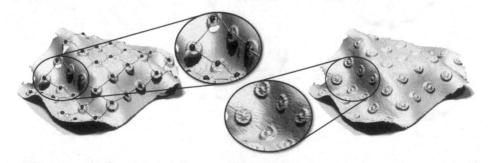

Fig. 8. Intrinsic structures can be detected on scans with missing data (left). The detected structure is used to propagate structural elements from *healthy* regions to conceal the damaged or missing areas (right).

Fig. 9. Structural correspondence, up to phase ambiguity, between two geometrically different shapes having similar repeating structures, established using the detected correspondence between the respective intrinsic grids. Combinatorially similar respective grids are shown at the top right and top left, respectively. High-frequency texture mapping was used to visualize the accuracy of local correspondence.

size, which, in turn, depends on the way MDS embedding maps the surface into the plane. For comparison, Figure 2 (left) shows the results produced by Euclidean structure detection of Pauly et al. [8]. Only a small part of the grid (four points located in the flat part of the shape) is recovered. The behavior is similar for the other scans.

Robustness. The proposed algorithm is insensitive to noise and can work even when large parts of the grid are missing. Figure 6 (left) shows examples of grid detection is shapes suffering from missing details (resulting from real occlusion artifacts in 3D acquisition and synthetic removal of parts of the shape). Despite large portions of the shape missing (up to 35% in Figure 6, middle), most of the grid structure is correctly detected. Figure 6 (middle) shows a shape contaminated by random Gaussian noise with standard deviation of about 70% of the average feature elevation, while Figure 6 (right) shows corruption by shot noise appearing as spikes. Besides a few missing grid nodes, the repeating structure is detected correctly in these cases as well.

Geometry substitution. A shape can be decomposed into a low-frequency base governing the embedding in $\mathbb{R}^3$, and the high-frequency detail admitting the intrinsic repeating pattern. Replacing the detail allows to synthesize new shapes sharing with the original one the 3D layout, while retaining the repeating structure. An example of such a substitution is presented in Figure 7. The low-frequency surface was obtained by solving the Laplace equation for the surface coordinates with the grid lines serving as the boundary conditions. The new detail was mapped onto the low-frequency base using a normal displacement map. Detail substitution can be used to conceal irregularities of a regular shape due to manufacturing or acquisition imperfections. In this case, the structural element from a "healthy" region of the shape is transferred to a damaged one as shown in Figure 8. While MDS mapping by itself can be influenced by topological errors, the grid detection and refinement phases make the pipeline robust to small holes and perforations (see also the Colosseum example). Use of topologically-consistent weighted MDS [38] can increase the stability of the system. In this example, we first closed the holes using smooth interpolation; the interpolated regions were healed by detail transfer from healthy regions resulting in a nearly perfectly regular shape. Substituting the detail with its higher resolution version (obtained, for example, from a

Fig. 10. Ambiguities inherent to intrinsic grid detection: phase (left), shape of the structural element (middle), and different generators explaining the same grid (right). All such results provide plausible explanations to the intrinsic structure of the oblique-shape. For reference, results from Figure 4 are overlaid as blue curves/spheres.

close-up scan or a CAD model) produces *super-resolution* of the original shape, allowing to overcome the classical field-of-view versus resolution tradeoff or combine different acquisition modalities (see Figure 7 for an example).

Structural correspondence. The knowledge of intrinsic structure allows us to establish correspondence between objects significantly different geometrically and topologically, yet resembling in their self-similarity structure. This concept has been recently explored in image analysis applications for comparison of images depicting similar concept in visually different ways [5]. Given two shapes with similar intrinsic structures, we first extract the intrinsic grids and then find the correspondence between these grids. The structural elements and the extrinsic geometry of the shapes can be wildly different, as exemplified in Figure 9. Such a great difference in geometry and topology is an obstacle that most state-of-the-art non-rigid correspondence methods find very challenging to overcome.

5   Conclusions

We presented an approach for intrinsic local self-similarity detection in 3D shapes. Unlike previous approaches limited to Euclidean self-similarity, our approach is able to detect warped and curved grids. By using MDS, we reduce the problem of intrinsic grid detection on the surface to regular grid detection in the plane. We demonstrated the efficiency and robustness of the method on various scanned (stamped) models with different geometries, topologies, and structures, as well as real and simulated artifacts. Examples of applications to scan completion, detail substitution, super-resolution, and correspondence between structurally similar yet geometrically and topologically different shapes were presented.

Limitations and extensions. The current limitation of our approach is that the use of planar parametrization implies a tacit assumption that the topology of the surface is coarsely similar to that of the plane. While this is true in many cases of shapes acquired by means of a range scanner and represented as geometry images, a generic shape may have more complicated topology, e.g. of a sphere. Trying to embed such shapes into the plane would result in large distortions such that intrinsic grids would be no more mapped into planar regular grids. A possible way to handle complex topologies is by applying MDS in a local manner, to disk-like regions on the shape, and then stitch together the detected grids, which we leave to future work.

Other limitations, inherent to regular structure detection in general, are the ambiguities in phase and non-uniqueness of the grid generators and the structural elements (see Figure 10). Optimization over these parameters with the goal to achieve optimal packing of full structural elements over the shape can be a way to resolve such ambiguities.

Acknowledgement

We thank Helmut Pottmann and the anonymous reviewers for their comments and helpful suggestions. Niloy Mitra was partially supported by a Microsoft outstanding young faculty fellowship.

References

1. Leyton, M.: Shape as memory. Springer, Heidelberg (2006)
2. White, R., Forsyth, D.A.: Combining cues: Shape from shading and texture. In: IEEE CVPR, vol. II, pp. 1809–1816 (2006)
3. Elad, A., Kimmel, R.: Bending invariant representations for surfaces. In: CVPR, pp. 168–174 (2001)
4. Ling, H., Jacobs, D.W.: Deformation invariant image matching. In: IEEE ICCV, Washington, DC, USA, pp. 1466–1473. IEEE Computer Society, Los Alamitos (2005)
5. Shechtman, E., Irani, M.: Matching local self-similarities across images and videos. In: CVPR, pp. 511–518 (2007)
6. Zaharescu, A., Boyer, E., Varanasi, K., Horaud, R.: Surface feature detection and description with applications to mesh matching. In: IEEE CVPR, pp. 373–380 (2009)
7. Mitra, N.J., Flory, S., Ovsjanikov, M., Gelfand, N., Guibas, L., Pottmann, H.: Dynamic geometry registration. In: Symposium on Geometry Processing, pp. 173–182 (2007)
8. Pauly, M., Mitra, N.J., Wallner, J., Pottmann, H., Guibas, L.: Discovering structural regularity in 3D geometry. ACM ToG (Proc. SIGGRAPH) 27, #43, 1–11 (2008)
9. Thrun, S., Wegbreit, B.: Shape from symmetry. In: IEEE ICCV, pp. 1824–1831 (2005)
10. Mitra, N.J., Guibas, L., Pauly, M.: Partial and approximate symmetry detection for 3d geometry. ACM ToG (Proc. SIGGRAPH) 25, 560–568 (2006)
11. Zabrodsky, H., Peleg, S., Avnir, D.: Symmetry as a continuous feature. IEEE Trans. Pattern Anal. Mach. Intell. 17, 1154–1166 (1995)
12. Kazhdan, M., Funkhouser, T., Rusinkiewicz, S.: Symmetry descriptors and 3D shape matching. In: Proc. of Symp. of Geometry Processing (2004)
13. Liu, Y., Collins, R.T., Tsin, Y.: A computational model for periodic pattern perception based on frieze and wallpaper groups. IEEE Trans. Pattern Anal. Mach. Intell. 26, 354–371 (2004)
14. Martinet, A., Soler, C., Holzschuch, N., Sillion, F.: Accurate detection of symmetries in 3d shapes. ACM ToG 25, 439–464 (2006)
15. Podolak, J., Shilane, P., Golovinskiy, A., Rusinkiewicz, S., Funkhouser, T.: A planar-reflective symmetry transform for 3D shapes. ACM ToG (Proc. SIGGRAPH) 25 (2006)
16. Loy, G., Eklundh, J.O.: Detecting symmetry and symmetric constellations of features. In: Leonardis, A., Bischof, H., Pinz, A. (eds.) ECCV 2006. LNCS, vol. 3952, pp. 508–521. Springer, Heidelberg (2006)

17. Bokeloh, M., Berner, A., Wand, M., Seidel, H.P., Schilling, A.: Symmetry detection using line features. Computer Graphics Forum (Proc. EUROGRAPHICS) 28, 697–706 (2009)
18. Park, M., Lee, S., Chen, P.C., Kashyap, S., Butt, A.A., Liu, Y.: Performance evaluation of state-of-the-art discrete symmetry detection algorithms. In: IEEE CVPR, pp. 1–8 (2008)
19. Gong, Y., Wang, Q., Yang, C., Gao, Y., Li, C.: Symmetry detection for multi-object using local polar coordinate. In: Jiang, X., Petkov, N. (eds.) Computer Analysis of Images and Patterns. LNCS, vol. 5702, pp. 277–284. Springer, Heidelberg (2009)
20. Simari, P., Kalogerakis, E., Singh, K.: Folding meshes: hierarchical mesh segmentation based on planar symmetry. In: Proc. of Symp. of Geometry Processing, pp. 111–119 (2006)
21. Mitra, N.J., Guibas, L.J., Pauly, M.: Symmetrization. ACM ToG (Proc. SIGGRAPH) 26, #63, 1–8 (2007)
22. Liu, Y., Belkina, T., Hays, J.H., Lublinerman, R.: Image de-fencing. In: IEEE CVPR (2008)
23. Cheng, M.M., Zhang, F.L., Mitra, N.J., Huang, X., Hu, S.M.: Repfinder: Finding approximately repeated scene elements for image editing. ACM ToG (Proc. SIGGRAPH) 29 (2010) (to appear)
24. Park, M., Collins, R., Liu, Y.: Deformed lattice detection via mean-shift belief propagation. In: Forsyth, D., Torr, P., Zisserman, A. (eds.) ECCV 2008, Part II. LNCS, vol. 5303, pp. 474–485. Springer, Heidelberg (2008)
25. Raviv, D., Bronstein, A.M., Bronstein, M.M., Kimmel, R.: Full and partial symmetries of non-rigid shapes. IJCV (preprint)
26. Mémoli, F., Sapiro, G.: A theoretical and computational framework for isometry invariant recognition of point cloud data. Foundations of Comp. Mathematics 5, 313–346 (2005)
27. Bronstein, A.M., Bronstein, M.M., Kimmel, R.: Generalized multidimensional scaling: a framework for isometry-invariant partial surface matching. PNAS 103, 1168–1172 (2006)
28. Ovsjanikov, M., Sun, J., Guibas, L.J.: Global intrinsic symmetries of shapes. Comput. Graph. Forum (Proc. SGP) 27, 1341–1348 (2008)
29. Xu, K., Zhang, H., Tagliasacchi, A., Liu, L., Li, G., Meng, M., Xiong, Y.: Partial intrinsic reflectional symmetry of 3D shapes. ACM ToG (Proc. SIGGRAPH Asia) 28 (2009)
30. Zigelman, G., Kimmel, R., Kiryati, N.: Texture mapping using surface flattening via multi-dimensional scaling. IEEE Trans. on Vis. and Comp. Graphics 9, 198–207 (2002)
31. Bronstein, A.M., Bronstein, M.M., Kimmel, R.: Calculus of non-rigid surfaces for geometry and texture manipulation. IEEE Trans. on Vis. and Comp. Graphics (2008)
32. Borg, I., Groenen, P.: Modern multidimensional scaling - theory and apps. Springer, Heidelberg (1997)
33. Kimmel, R., Sethian, J.A.: Computing geodesic paths on manifolds. PNAS, 8431–8435 (1998)
34. De Silva, V., Tenenbaum, J.: Global versus local methods in nonlinear dimensionality reduction. In: NIPS, pp. 721–728 (2003)
35. Hochbaum, D., Shmoys, D.: A best possible heuristic for the k-center problem. Mathematics of Operations Research 10, 180–184 (1985)
36. Bronstein, M.M., Bronstein, A.M., Kimmel, R., Yavneh, I.: Multigrid multidimensional scaling. Numerical Linear Algebra with Applications 13, 149–171 (2006)
37. Borg, I., Groenen, P.: Modern multidimensional scaling: Theory and applications (2005)
38. Rosman, G., Bronstein, A., Bronstein, M., Kimmel, R.: Topologically constrained isometric embedding. Human Motion: Understanding, Modelling, Capture, and Animation (2008)

Balancing Deformability and Discriminability for Shape Matching

Haibin Ling, Xingwei Yang, and Longin Jan Latecki

Center for Information Science and Technology, Dept. of Computer and Information Science
Temple University, Philadelphia, 19122, USA
{hbling,xingwei.yang,latecki}@temple.edu

Abstract. We propose a novel framework, *aspect space*, to balance deformability and discriminability, which are often two competing factors in shape and image representations. In this framework, an object is embedded as a surface in a higher dimensional space with a parameter named *aspect weight*, which controls the importance of intensity in the embedding. We show that this framework naturally unifies existing important shape and image representations by adjusting the aspect weight and the embedding. More importantly, we find that the aspect weight implicitly controls the degree to which a representation handles deformation. Based on this idea, we present the *aspect shape context*, which extends shape context-based descriptors and adaptively selects the "best" aspect weight for shape comparison. Another observation we have is the proposed descriptor nicely fits context-sensitive shape retrieval. The proposed methods are evaluated on two public datasets, MPEG7-CE-Shape-1 and Tari 1000, in comparison to state-of-the-art solutions. In the standard shape retrieval experiment using the MPEG7 CE Shape 1 database, the new descriptor with context information achieves a bull's eye score of 95.96%, which surpassed all previous results. In the Tari 1000 dataset, our methods significantly outperform previous tested methods as well.

1 Introduction

To understand and analyze object deformation is one of the most important goals in pattern recognition. The study of object shapes dates back to at least a century ago in D'Arcy Thompson's seminal work [35]. Recently, great successes have been achieved in robust image and shape representation for many computer vision tasks [24,25,18,27,9,21,14,5,36,33,13]. Many approaches gain the robustness by using representations that are invariant (or insensitive) to certain groups of deformations. For example, the popular scale invariant feature transform (SIFT) [24] selects scale invariant blob regions [20] for reliable key point matching. Some further works push this frontier to more general deformations such as affine invariant [27], projection invariant [37], or general deformation invariant [25,21]. Similar progress has been made in shape analysis as well. Moment invariants [12] are well known to be robust to similarity transformations. Bending invariants [10,6,7] for 2D and 3D shapes can be achieved by using geodesic distances. Articulation insensitivity is gained similarly by using the inner-distance [22]. Topology invariants [8,30] have been applied for both 2D and 3D shape analysis. Invariant representations are also used in texture analysis [18,39].

K. Daniilidis, P. Maragos, N. Paragios (Eds.): ECCV 2010, Part III, LNCS 6313, pp. 411–424, 2010.
© Springer-Verlag Berlin Heidelberg 2010

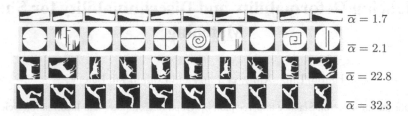

Fig. 1. Four shape classes from the MPEG7 dataset and their discriminative deformabilities $\bar{\alpha}$ (§ 3.3)

On the other hand, invariants to larger groups of deformation often come at a price of reduced discriminability [37,21] and sometimes introduce vulnerability to imaging nuisances such as noises and illumination variations. In fact, as observed in category classification tasks [42], the best local features are often a trade off between descriptive abilities and robustness to deformations.

In Fig. 1, we see that objects often undergo different degrees of deformation and a trade off between deformation robustness and discriminability is desired. For example, simple Euclidean distance based approaches (e.g., shape context [5]) can work well for rigid objects like bottles (first row in Fig. 1) while the articulation invariant representations (e.g., inner-distance shape context [22]) handles articulated shapes like human body (fourth row of Fig. 1) successfully. However, for complicated shapes like the pie-shaped devices in Fig. 1 (second row), articulation invariance becomes an over-killing that easily confuses a query shape with other shapes through articulation. This fact is illustrated in the first row of Fig. 2.

Motivated by the above work and especially by [21,20], we propose a new framework called *aspect space*[1] to balance the deformation and discriminability for object representation. The basic idea is to embed a 2D image or a shape (or a 3D volume) as a surface in a 3D space (or a 4D space) with a parameter named *aspect weight*, which controls the importance of intensity in the embedding. The embedded surfaces with different aspect weights then form an aspect space, such that the aspect weight naturally correlates to the degree of object deformation. By converting silhouettes to binary images, we show that the aspect space provides a unified framework for several popular shape descriptors including the shape context [5], the inner-distance shape context [22], and the bending invariant shape signature [10].

We apply the aspect space framework for shape retrieval tasks that is an important problem in computer vision. Taking advantage of the aspect weight's ability of controlling the degree of deformation, we propose a new shape descriptor named *aspect shape context* (ASC), which extends the inner-distance shape context (IDSC) [22] by replacing the inner-distance with geodesic distances in the aspect space. In fact, both the shape context (SC) [5] and inner-distance shape context are special cases of ASC, corresponding to a zero aspect value and a sufficiently large aspect value, respectively.

---

[1] The "aspect" in our work comes from "aspect ratio", which should not be confused with that used in the "aspect" graph.

Fig. 2. The top 10 nearest neighbors obtained by IDSC (the first row) and ASC (the second row) for the query of a pie-shaped device

When comparing two shapes, the distance between them is chosen as the minimum distance over different aspect weights. This way, ASC successfully balances the shape deformation and discriminability. We tested the proposed approach on a standard shape retrieval experiment with the MPEG7-CE-1 shape database. ASC demonstrates promising retrieval results and improves the previous approach. For example, in Fig. 2, one comparison between IDSC and ASC is given. The query shape is a pie-shape device. It is obvious that the retrieval results of IDSC are very different from the query shape demonstrating that articulation invariance becomes an over-killing factor. The results of the second row clearly show that ASC can balance between deformation robustness and discriminability.

In summary, we make three main contributions in this paper. First, we propose the aspect space framework, which provides a unified image and shape representation that allows controlling the degree of deformation. Second, with the framework, we designed a new shape descriptor that automatically balances the deformation and discriminability for shape matching. The descriptor demonstrates excellent performance for shape matching tasks on two benchmark shape datasets, the MPEG7 shape database [17] and the Tari 100 database [4]. Third, the novel shape descriptor can describe the relation between shapes very well, not only in the same class, but also in different classes. Thus, it provides an excellent input for diffusion based, context-sensitive shape similarity, which reaches the best ever bull's eye score of 95.96% on the MPEG7 shape database. This increases by 20% the best bull's eye scores on this dataset [17] published first time in CVPR 2000, which clearly demonstrates the progress in the field achieved in the last 10 years.

The rest of the paper is organized as follow. § 2 describes the aspect space framework and its relation to existing object and shape representations. Then, we describe the new shape descriptor, aspect shape context, in § 3. To compute a context-sensitive shape distance, we utilize the locally constrained dissuasion process described in § 4. Experimental results are reported and analyzed in § 5. Finally, § 6 concludes the paper.

2   Aspect Space

2.1   Aspect Space and Geodesics

Given an image $I : \Lambda \to [0, 1]$, where $\Lambda \subset \mathbb{R}^2$ is the image domain, we define its induced *aspect space* $\mathcal{A}(I; \alpha)$ of I as

$$\mathcal{A}(I; \alpha) = (x, y, \alpha I(x, y)), \ (x, y) \in \Lambda, \alpha \in [0, \infty) . \tag{1}$$

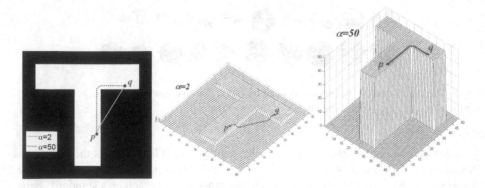

Fig. 3. Aspect spaces and geodesics on embedding surfaces. Left: a "T" shape and two geodesics between points p, q for $\alpha = 2$ and 50 respectively. Middle: the aspect space and the geodesic for $\alpha = 2$. Right: the aspect space and the geodesic for $\alpha = 50$.

Note that the embedding is equivalent to the one used in [21], i.e.,

$$(1 - \alpha)x, (1 - \alpha)y, \alpha I(x, y), \ \alpha \in [0, 1],$$

but the new definition is practically more convenient and numerically stabler. Also note that the embedding and the following derivations are not restricted to 2D.

A natural way to study the embedding in $\mathcal{A}(I; \alpha)$ is to investigate the curves especially geodesics on it. Following [21], for a given parameterized curve

$$\gamma(t) = (x(t), y(t), \alpha I(x, y)), \ t \in [0, 1]$$

on $\mathcal{A}(I; \alpha)$ with a fixed α, its curve length is $l(\gamma) = \int_0^1 \left(\frac{\partial x}{\partial t}^2 + \frac{\partial y}{\partial t}^2 + \alpha^2 \frac{\partial I}{\partial t}^2 \right)^{1/2} dt$. Fig. 3 shows an example of embedding a "T" shape and the geodesics between two points p, q on the embedded surfaces.

It has been shown in [21] that geodesic distances become invariant to general deformation (i.e., homeomorphism) when α approaches ∞, in which case the intensity term dominates $l(\gamma)$. On the other extreme, when α equals to zero, geodesic distances degenerate to the Euclidean distances that are invariant to only rigid deformations. This brings a connection between the *geodesic intensity histogram* [21] and the *spin image* [18]. Motivated by this observation, we will use the aspect space framework for designing robust and discriminative shape descriptor (§ 3).

2.2 Relations to Robust Shape Descriptors

We now show how the aspect space relates to several popular shape descriptors including the shape context (SC) [5], inner-distance shape context (IDSC) [22], and the bending invariant signature [10].

The shape context [5] uses the joint distance-orientation distributions of landmarks for shape description. It has been shown to be very effective in many shape comparison tasks. The inner-distance shape context [22], IDSC extends SC to achieve articulation invariant by using the so called inner-distance, which is defined as the length of shortest paths between landmark points when the paths are restricted within a shape boundary. To relate them in the aspect space framework, we treat a given shape $S : \Lambda \rightarrow [0, 1]$ as a binary mask, i.e.,

$$S(x, y) = \begin{cases} 1 & \text{if } (x, y) \in \text{shape interior} \\ 0 & \text{otherwise} \end{cases} . \tag{2}$$

Consequently, the aspect space of S is defined as

$$\mathcal{A}(S; \alpha) = (x, y, \alpha S(x, y)) . \tag{3}$$

Given two points p, q on shape S, it can be shown that the geodesic distance between them on $\mathcal{A}(S; \alpha)$ is equivalent to the inner-distance between them, for a large enough α. An example is shown in Fig. 3 for $\alpha = 50$. The reason is, when α is large enough, the geodesic path from p to q along the surface will remain on the plateau formed by the object. This means that the geodesic path, which is also a shortest path, is restricted within the shape boundary. Therefore, it reduces to the inner-distance used in IDSC.

On the other hand, when $\alpha=0$, the geodesic distance on the surface degenerates to the Euclidean distance, as illustrated for $\alpha=2$ in Fig. 3. This is the distance used in SC.

The bending invariant signature uses geodesic distances along object surfaces. Let a 3D volume $V : \Lambda' \subset \mathbb{R}^3 \rightarrow [0, 1]$ has boundary $\partial(V)$, we first build a 3D volume mask as following

$$V(\mathbf{x}) = \begin{cases} 1 & \text{if } \mathbf{x} \in \partial(V) \\ 0 & \text{otherwise} \end{cases} . \tag{4}$$

Then, with a large enough aspect weight, the geodesic path on $\mathcal{A}(V; \alpha)$ is restricted on the object boundary $\partial(V)$, which is used for building the bending invariant signatures [10].

It is also worth mentioning that our work is related the work on shape analysis using the diffusion distances [8,30] and the Gromov-Hausdorff framework [7,6].

2.3 Relations to Other Image Representations

Aside from the above representations, the aspect space also closely relates to many other image representations or statistics. For example, when $\alpha \rightarrow \infty$, aspect space relates to the *total variation* (TV) [29] in that only intensity values are taken into account. In this case, the geodesic distance along between points becomes, up to a constant ratio, the total variation of the geodesic path connecting them.

Another important motivation to our work is the Beltrami flow framework [34], where an image is embedded as a surface in 3D space and differential properties of the surface are used for low-level image processing. We expect future works along similar directions in the aspect space.

3 Balancing Deformability and Discriminability for Shape Comparison

3.1 Aspect Shape Context

We propose to use the aspect space framework for shape analysis. As shown in § 2, for a given shape S as defined in equation (2), the geodesic distances between landmark points of S on $\mathcal{A}(S; \alpha)$ varies from the Euclidean distance to the inner-distance when α increases from 0 to a large positive value. This property provides a natural way to unify the shape descriptors taking advantages of both distances, namely the *shape context* (SC) [5] and the *inner-distance shape context* (IDSC) [22]. Motivated by this observation, we present the *aspect shape context* (ASC) as below:

Definition: Let $\{p_i\}_{i=1}^{n}$ be n silhouette landmark points of S, its *aspect shape context* (ASC) is defined as a set of n histograms on its aspect space $\mathcal{A}(S; \alpha)$ as

$$ASC(S, \alpha) = \{H_i(S, \alpha)\}_{i=1}^{n} , \tag{5}$$

where $H_i(S, \alpha) \in \mathbb{R}^{n_g \times n_o}$ is a $n_g \times n_o$ histogram measuring the joint geodesic distance-orientation distribution of landmarks w.r.t. point p_i, such that the geodesic distances and orientations are all computed w.r.t. $\mathcal{A}(S; \alpha)$. Specifically, $H_i(S, \alpha)$ captures the joint distribution of geodesic distances and orientations of all other points with respect to point p_i. In ASC, for the orientation, we use the angle between boundary tangent direction and the direction of the geodesic projected to the 2D image domain, which is an extension of the *inner-angle* defined in [22]. The geodesic distance in our implementation is through the fast marching algorithm [32].

3.2 Comparing Aspect Shape Context

How should we compare two shapes S_1, S_2 given their ASCs? The basic idea is to compare two shapes by adaptively choosing the "best" aspect weight α. We expect that a small α (such that ASC works like SC) will be used for rigid shapes while a large α (such that ASC works like IDSC) for non-rigid ones.

We define the *co-aspect* $\hat{\alpha}$ as the one that produces minimum shape distances between S_1 and S_2[2].

$$\hat{\alpha}(S_1, S_2) = \arg \min_{\alpha} d_H(ASC(S_1, \alpha), ASC(S_2, \alpha)) , \tag{6}$$

where $d_H(.,.)$ computes a distance between two sets of shape context histograms at a fixed α (e.g., the "shape context" distance used in [5,22]). Consequently, the distance between S_1, S_2 is defined as the histogram distance that minimizes (6), i.e.,

$$d_{ASC}(S_1, S_2) = d_H \left(ASC(S_1, \hat{\alpha}(S_1, S_2)), ASC(S_2, \hat{\alpha}(S_1, S_2)) \right) . \tag{7}$$

Another choice is to integrate the distances over α,

$$d'_{ASC}(S_1, S_2) = \int d_H(ASC(S_1, \alpha), ASC(S_2, \alpha)) d\alpha . \tag{8}$$

---

[2] If such α is not unique, the smallest one is chosen.

However, we observed that this definition is less effective than that in (7), since the "smoothing" over all α may wash out the information provided by the right α.

Here we clarify a potential confusion. For two topologically equivalent shapes S_1, S_2, one may guess that $d_{ASC}(S_1, S_2) = 0$ with a very large (theoretically infinite) co-aspect, since they are the same up to a *homeomorphic transformation*. This is fortunately not true, except when S_1, S_2 are related by an articulation. This observation is very important, because it shows that ASC is not biased toward arbitrary deformations while being able to handle articulation.

3.3 Discriminative Deformability

To further understand the relation between aspect weights to shape deformation and discriminability, we define the *discriminative deformability* for a set of shapes $\mathbb{S}=\{S_i\}_{i=1}^{|\mathbb{S}|}$ coming from the same class. The discriminative deformability of $\mathbb{S}$, denoted as $\overline{\alpha}(\mathbb{S})$, is

$$\overline{\alpha}(\mathbb{S}) = \frac{1}{|\mathbb{S}|(|\mathbb{S}| - 1)} \sum_{1 \leq i < j \leq |\mathbb{S}|} \widehat{\alpha}(S_i, S_j) . \tag{9}$$

Roughly speaking, the deformability of a class of object is defined as the average aspect that minimizes the distances between image pairs from the class. Such a deformability naturally takes into account the discriminative information. For example, in Fig. 1, we have shown the discriminative deformabilities of four classes of images. For the pie-shaped devices (e.g., the second row of Fig. 1), each single shape seems to have complex structures that can easily lead to articulation. However, by checking objects in the class, we find no articulation at all and the global shapes of these devices remain fairly rigid. Consequently, it has a relatively small discriminative deformability.

4 Beyond Pairwise Shape Similarity

Recent work clearly demonstrated that adding context information to direct pairwise shape similarity can substantially improver shape retrieval [40,15,41]. Under context of a given shape we understand here its first K nearest neighbors. However, these methods [40,15,41] mainly focus on improving the transduction algorithms. We demonstrate that a 'better' original distance matrix is also very crucial for the shape retrieval with context information. The word 'better' does not necessarily mean a better bull's eye score. Instead, it means the algorithm can balance the deformation and discriminability, so that the retrieval results should have really similar view to the query. In other words, even if the retrieved results are not from the same shape class, they have perceptual resemblance to the query. Otherwise, totally different objects in the top retrieval results may ruin the graph structure constructed by the shapes, which makes negative impact for the graph transduction or diffusion processes to learn the shape manifold structure. In order to show that ASC is suitable for context information based shape retrieval, we use the Locally Constrained Diffusion Process (LCDP) introduced in [41] to learn the sub-manifold structure for shapes.

In LCDP, a fully connected graph is constructed. The vertices are the data points (shapes) and each edge is labeled with the strength of the connection $P(i, j) = k(x_i, x_j)$, where k is a kernel function that is symmetric and positivity preserving. In this paper, given two shapes x_i and x_j, $k(x_i, x_j)$ is defined by applying a Gaussian to $d_{ASC}(x_i, x_j)$. We then normalize row wise the matrix $(P(x_i, x_j))_{i,j}$ so that the sum of each row is one. We obtain a stochastic matrix $(P(x_i, x_j))_{i,j}$, which we denote with the same symbol. Then, the original graph G is replaced by a K nearest neighbor (KNNs) graph G_K that has the edge weights defined as follows: $P_K(i, j) = k(x_i, x_j)$ if x_j belongs to the KNNs of x_i and $P_K(i, j) = 0$ otherwise. We also row wise normalize $(P_K(x_i, x_j))_{i,j}$ to a stochastic matrix. It represents one-step transition probabilities $P_K(x_i, x_j)$ from x_i to x_j.

LCDP only considers the paths between the KNNs of x_i and the KNNs of x_j, which can be viewed as a soft measure of their KNNs' compatibility. The probability of transition from node x_i to x_j is high if all the the paths between points in KNNs(x_i) and in KNNs(x_j) contain high strength. This restriction make the diffusion focus on more meaningful paths, as KNNs have higher probability to be the same class. This helps to remove the negative impact from far away noises. To reach this goal, LCDP defines an iterative method to update probability of transition P_{KK}

$$P_{KK}^{t+1} = P_K \, P_{KK}^t \, (P_K)^T. \tag{10}$$

where t controls the degree of diffusion, $P_{KK}^1 = P$ and $(P_K)^T$ is the transpose of P_K. After several iterations updating, P_{KK} can describe the manifold structure of the shapes well and it is used as the final distances for retrieval. LCDP has been proved to be able to learn the sub-manifold structure of shapes very well and obtain excellent retrieval results [41]. With the help of LCDP, bull's eye score on MPEG-7 data set can reach the highest ever 95.24%, which is discussed in details below.

5   Experiments

5.1   Shape Classification Using MPEG7 Dataset

The proposed framework and shape descriptor is tested for shape classification on a commonly used MPEG7 CE-Shape-1 part B database [17]. The database contains 1400 silhouette images from 70 classes, where each class has 20 different shapes (some examples are shown in Fig. 4). The performance of different solutions is measured by the so called bull's eye score: every shape in the database is submitted as a query and the number of shapes from the same class in the top 40 is counted. The bull's eye score is then defined as the ratio of the number of correct hits to the best possible number of hits (which is 20×1400).

We tested on the MPEG7 dataset using the distance d_{ASC} defined in (7), with $\alpha = 0, 10, \ldots, 60, \infty$, where ∞ indicates the IDSC. We used 300 sample point son each shape and 8×12 distance-orientation bins. Table 1 lists the performance along with previous reported results. It is clear that the proposed ASC descriptor achieves excellent classification rate that is comparable to the state-of-the-art. Example retrieval results by ASC and IDSC are shown in Fig. 2.

Table 2 shows a combined result of LCDP and ASC and compares it to other context-sensitive methods. The proposed method can reach the best ever result 95.96% on MPEG7 data set. For using LCDP, we set $K = 7$ and number of iteration $t = 19$.

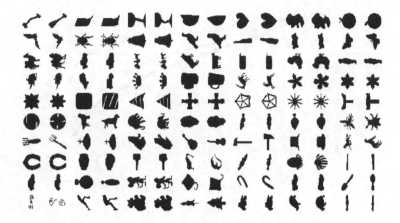

Fig. 4. Typical shape images from the MPEG7 CE-Shape-1, two images from each class

Table 1. Retrieval rates (bull's eye) of different methods on the MPEG-7 data set

Alg.	CSS [28]	Vis. Parts [16]	Shape Context [5]	Multiscale Rep. [1]	IDSC [22]	Hier. Procrustes [26]
Score	75.44%	76.45%	76.51%	84.93%	85.40%	86.35%
Alg.	IDSC+ EMD-L$_1$ [23]	Triangle Area [2]	Shape Tree [11]	ASC (proposed)	Layered Graph [19]	Contour Flexibility [38]
Score	86.56%	87.23%	87.70%	88.30%	88.75%	89.31%

Table 2. Retrieval rates (bull's eye) of different context shape retrieval methods on the MPEG-7 data set

Alg.	IDSC + LP [40]	IDSC + LCDP [41]	IDSC + LCDP+gp [41]	IDSC + Mutual graph [15]	proposed approach + LCDP
Score	91.00%	92.36%	93.32%	93.40%	95.96%

We also show the precision/recall curves of IDSC, the proposed ASC, and ASC with LCDP in Fig. 5. We follow [4] for the precision/recall curves. Precision can be seen as a measure of exactness or fidelity, whereas recall is a measure of completeness, which is more informative for retrieval task. It is clear that ASC has better performance than IDSC not only in the bull's eye score, but also in the precision/recall curve. Moreover, the LCDP improves the performance a lot, which demonstrates ASC provides a very good input to context-sensitive shape retrieval.

In order to further demonstrate the reason why the proposed approach with context information can obtain much better results, we show the bull's eye score increment for each class after LCDP in Fig. 6(a). Compared to Fig. 6(b), which is taken from [41], none of the class bull's eye score has obvious drop after LCDP. This demonstrates the advantage of ASC compared to IDSC. The class which has the most obvious drop in [41] is the class spoon. In Fig. 7, we compare the retrieval results on an example from

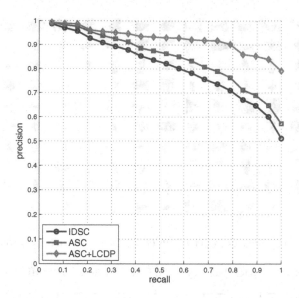

Fig. 5. Precision/Recall curves of IDSC, ASC and ASC+LCDP on the MPEG7 CE-Shape-1 database

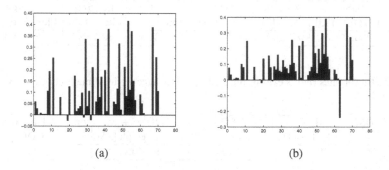

(a)   (b)

Fig. 6. (a) The percent gain in bull's eye retrieval rates for each class by the proposed approach. (b) The percent gain in bull's eye retrieval rates for each class in [41].

class spoon between IDSC+LCDP [41] (the first row) and ASC+LCDP (the second row). The shapes with red rectangles mean wrong retrieval results. They come from the class guitar. It is clear that the ASC+LCDP yields better results than IDSC+LCDP. Only guitars with shape very similar to the query spoon remained.

5.2 Shape Classification Using Tari 1000 Dataset

In order to demonstrate the proposed approach can handle articulated shapes, we also test it on recently constructed Tari 1000 data set [4] (see Figure 8), which is designed to have large intra-class shape deformation. It is formed by extending the 180 data set

Fig. 7. The retrievals of IDSC+LCDP [41] (the first row) and ASC+LCDP (the second row). The shapes with red rectangle are the wrong results.

Fig. 8. Typical shape images from the Tari 1000 dataset, two images from each class

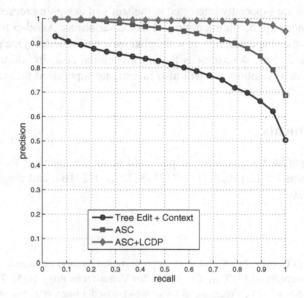

Fig. 9. Precision/Recall curves on Tari 1000 dataset. The result of "Tree Edit+Context" is from [4].

in [3] with shapes collected from various sources including [16,31]. It consists of 1000 shapes with 50 class, each class contains 20 shapes. Many of the shapes are articulated and have large deformation. On this dataset, Baseski et al. [4] have demonstrated an effective shape matching algorithm based on using skeletal trees.

For the experiments on Tari 1000, we use exactly the same parameters as on MPEG7 dataset. For evaluation, however, the authors in [4] did not report the bull's eye score for the whole data set. Instead, they provided the precision/recall curve. We report both of them. ASC can reach 95.44%, and with the help of LCDP, the bull's eye can go to nearly perfect 99.79%. For using LCDP, we set $K = 10$ and number of iteration $t = 3$. The precision/recall curves are shown in Fig. 9.

6   Conclusion and Future Work

In this paper we introduce a general framework, aspect space, to simultaneously address the deformation and discriminatingly problem. The framework naturally models the degree of deformation that is allowed in a representation by adjusting a embedding parameter named aspect weight. In this framework, we designed a new shape descriptor named aspect shape context, which improves the original shape context and inner-distance shape context in a standard shape retrieval benchmark testing, using the MPEG7 CE-Shape-1 database. It also provides a very good input for context-sensitive shape retrieval.

We also show that the framework is closely related to many existing image and shape representations. These attractive properties indicate its potential for many interesting future works. We are especially interested in the study of designing representations that address simultaneously the illumination and shape variations. Another topic we would like to pursue is the shape descriptors without knowing silhouettes. One practical issue with the proposed shape descriptor is the computational cost. In addition to seeking faster computational solution, we will also investigate supervised technology to learn properties for each object class.

Acknowledgments

We thank anonymous reviewers for helpful comments. The work is supported in part by the NSF Grants IIS-0916624, IIS-0812118, BCS-0924164, and the AFOSR Grant FA9550-09-1-0207.

References

1. Adamek, T., O'Connor, N.: A multiscale representation method for nonrigid shapes with a single closed contour. IEEE Tran. Cir. & Sys. for Video Technology 14(5), 742–753 (2004)
2. Alajlan, N., Kamel, M., Freeman, G.: Geometry-based image retrieval in binary image databases. IEEE Trans. Pattern Anal. Mach. Intell. 30(6), 1003–1013 (2008)
3. Aslan, C., Erdem, A., Erdem, E., Tari, S.: Disconnected skeleton: Shape at its absolute scale. IEEE Trans. Pattern Anal. Mach. Intell. 30(12), 2188–2203 (2008)
4. Baseski, E., Erdem, A., Tari, S.: Dissimilarity between two skeletal trees in a context. Pattern Recognition 42(3), 370–385 (2009)
5. Belongie, S., Malik, J., Puzicha, J.: Shape matching and object recognition using shape contexts. IEEE Trans. Pattern Anal. Mach. Intell. 24(4), 509–522 (2002)
6. Bronstein, A.M., Bronstein, M.M., Kimmel, R.: Generalized multidimensional scaling: a framework for isometry-invariant partial surface matching. Proc. Nat. Acad. Sci. 103(5), 1168–1172 (2006)
7. Bronstein, A.M., Bronstein, M.M., Bruckstein, A.M., Kimmel, R.: Analysis of two-dimensional non-rigid shapes. Int. Journal of Computer Vision 78(1), 67–88 (2008)

8. Bronstein, A.M., Bronstein, M.M., Kimmel, R.: A Gromov-Hausdorff framework with diffusion geometry for topologically-robust non-rigid shape matching. Int. Journal of Computer Vision 89(2–3), 266–286 (2010)
9. Cheng, H., Liu, Z., Zheng, N., Yang, J.: A deformable local image descriptor. In: CVPR, pp. 1–8 (2008)
10. Elad, A., Kimmel, R.: On bending invariant signatures for surfaces. IEEE Trans. Pattern Anal. Mach. Intell. 25(10), 1285–1295 (2003)
11. Felzenszwalb, P., Schwartz, J.: Hierarchical matching of deformable shapes. In: CVPR, pp. 1–8 (2007)
12. Hu, M.: Visual pattern recognition by moment invariants. IRE Tran. Information Theory 8, 179–187 (1962)
13. Johnson, A.E., Hebert, M.: Using spin images for efficient object recognition in cluttered 3D scenes. IEEE Trans. Pattern Anal. Mach. Intell. 21(5), 433–449 (1999)
14. Kadir, T., Zisserman, A., Brady, M.: An affine invariant salient region detector. In: Pajdla, T., Matas, J(G.) (eds.) ECCV 2004. LNCS, vol. 3021, pp. 228–241. Springer, Heidelberg (2004)
15. Kontschieder, P., Donoser, M., Bischof, H.: Beyond pairwise shape similarity analysis. In: Zha, H., Taniguchi, R.-i., Maybank, S. (eds.) Computer Vision – ACCV 2009. LNCS, vol. 5996, pp. 655–666. Springer, Heidelberg (2009)
16. Latecki, L.J., Lakämper, R.: Shape similarity measure based on correspondence of visual parts. IEEE Trans. Pattern Anal. Mach. Intell. 22(10), 1185–1190 (2000)
17. Latecki, L.J., Lakamper, R., Eckhardt, U.: Shape descriptors for non-rigid shapes with a single closed contour. In: CVPR, vol. 1, pp. 424–429 (2000)
18. Lazebnik, S., Schmid, C., Ponce, J.: A sparse texture representation using affine-invariant regions. IEEE Trans. Pattern Anal. Mach. Intell. 27(8), 1265–1278 (2005)
19. Lin, L., Zeng, K., Liu, X.B., Zhu, S.C.: Layered Graph Matching by Composite Cluster Sampling with Collaborative and Competitive Interactions. In: CVPR (2009)
20. Lindeberg, T.: Feature detection with automatic scale selection. Int. Journal of Computer Vision 30(2), 79–116 (1998)
21. Ling, H., Jacobs, D.W.: Deformation invariant image matching. In: ICCV, pp. 1466–1473 (2005)
22. H. Ling and D. W. Jacobs. Shape classification using the inner-distance. *IEEE Trans. Pattern Anal. Mach. Intell.*, 29(2):286–299, 2007.
23. Ling, H., Okada, K.: EMD-L1: An Efficient and Robust Algorithm for Comparing Histogram-Based Descriptors. In: Leonardis, A., Bischof, H., Pinz, A. (eds.) ECCV 2006. LNCS, vol. 3953, pp. 330–343. Springer, Heidelberg (2006)
24. Lowe, D.G.: Distinctive image features from scale-invariant keypoints. Int. Journal of Computer Vision 60(2), 91–110 (2004)
25. Matas, J., Chum, O., Urban, M., Pajdla, T.: Robust wide baseline stereo from maximally stable extremal regions. In: BMVC (2002)
26. McNeill, G., Vijayakumar, S.: Hierarchical procrustes matching for shape retrieval. In: CVPR, pp. 885–894 (2006)
27. Mikolajczyk, K., Schmid, C.: Scale & affine invariant interest point detectors. Int. Journal of Computer Vision 60(1), 63–86 (2004)
28. Mokhtarian, F., Abbasi, S., Kittler, J.: Efficient and robust retrieval by shape content through curvature scale space. In: Wkshp on Image DataBases and MultiMedia Search (1996)
29. Rudin, L., Osher, S., Fatemi, E.: Nonlinear total variation based noise removal algorithms. Physica D 60(1-4), 259–268 (1992)
30. Rustamov, R., Lipman, Y., Funkhouser, T.: Interior Distance Using Barycentric Coordinates. In: Symposium on Geometry Processing (2009)
31. Sebastian, T.B., Klein, P.N., Kimia, B.B.: Recognition of shapes by editing their shock graphs. IEEE Trans. Pattern Anal. Mach. Intell. 26(5), 550–571 (2004)

32. Sethian, J.A.: A fast marching level set method for monotonically advancing fronts. Proc. Nat. Acad. Sci. 93(4), 1591–1595 (1996)
33. Sivic, J., Zisserman, A.: Video Google: Efficient visual search of videos. In: Ponce, J., Hebert, M., Schmid, C., Zisserman, A. (eds.) Toward Category-Level Object Recognition, pp. 127–144 (2006)
34. Sochen, N., Kimmel, R., Malladi, R.: A general framework for low level vision. IEEE Trans. Image Processing 7(3), 310–318 (1998)
35. Thompson, D.W.: On Growth and Form. Cambridge University Press, Cambridge (1917)
36. Torralba, A., Murphy, K., Freeman, W., Rubin, M.: Context-based vision system for place and object recognition. In: ICCV, pp. 273–280 (2003)
37. Vedaldi, A., Soatto, S.: Features for recognition: Viewpoint invariance for non-planar scenes. In: ICCV, vol. 2, pp. 1474–1481 (2005)
38. Xu, C., Liu, J., Tang, X.: 2d shape matching by contour flexibility. IEEE Trans. Pattern Anal. Mach. Intell. 31(1), 180–186 (2009)
39. Xu, Y., Ji, H., Fermüller, C.: A projective invariant for textures. In: CVPR, pp. 1932–1939 (2006)
40. Yang, X., Bai, X., Latecki, L.J., Tu, Z.: Improving shape retrieval by learning graph transduction. In: Forsyth, D., Torr, P., Zisserman, A. (eds.) ECCV 2008, Part IV. LNCS, vol. 5305, pp. 788–801. Springer, Heidelberg (2008)
41. Yang, X., Köknar-Tezel, S., Latecki, L.J.: Locally constrained diffusion process on locally densified distance spaces with applications to shape retrieval. In: CVPR (2009)
42. Zhang, J., Marszalek, M., Lazebnik, S., Schmid, C.: Local features and kernels for classification of texture and object categories: A comprehensive study. Int. Journal of Computer Vision 73(2), 213–238 (2007)

2D Action Recognition Serves 3D Human Pose Estimation

Juergen Gall[1], Angela Yao[1], and Luc Van Gool[1,2]

[1] Computer Vision Laboratory, ETH Zurich, Switzerland
[2] KU Leuven, Belgium
{gall,yaoa,vangool}@vision.ee.ethz.ch

Abstract. 3D human pose estimation in multi-view settings benefits from embeddings of human actions in low-dimensional manifolds, but the complexity of the embeddings increases with the number of actions. Creating separate, action-specific manifolds seems to be a more practical solution. Using multiple manifolds for pose estimation, however, requires a joint optimization over the set of manifolds and the human pose embedded in the manifolds. In order to solve this problem, we propose a particle-based optimization algorithm that can efficiently estimate human pose even in challenging in-house scenarios. In addition, the algorithm can directly integrate the results of a 2D action recognition system as prior distribution for optimization. In our experiments, we demonstrate that the optimization handles an 84D search space and provides already competitive results on HumanEva with as few as 25 particles.

1 Introduction

3D human pose estimation in multi-view scenarios is an active field of research [14]. While recent approaches [3,6,11,12] report impressive results on benchmarks like HumanEva [23], real-world applications such as in-house monitoring still pose many challenges. For example, background clutter, occlusions, and interactions with objects are all difficulties not encountered in studio recordings.

To maintain robustness in more unconstrained scenarios, the use of priors on human actions and dynamics have become very popular. For instance, the poses of a certain group of actions can be embedded into a low-dimensional manifold [12,15,29]. While 'full-body' motions like walking, jogging, and golf swings can be nicely embedded, learning embeddings for more ambiguous actions like 'carrying an object', particularly from sparse and noisy data, is a much more difficult task. Furthermore, the complexity increases with the number of actions and many dimensionality reduction techniques struggle to establish useful embeddings for a high number of actions. Instead of embedding all actions into a single manifold, creating separate, action-specific manifolds is an easier task to solve. Moreover, this allows for the incremental addition of new actions, which is an important property to have in practice. Using multiple manifolds, however, leads to an unsolved problem: how can we estimate the pose from a set of manifolds? An approach would be to learn the transitions between each manifold,

K. Daniilidis, P. Maragos, N. Paragios (Eds.): ECCV 2010, Part III, LNCS 6313, pp. 425–438, 2010.

using techniques like motion graphs [10] or switching models [4], but this does not scale with the number of actions.

Here, we propose a new algorithm for optimizing over a set of manifolds that can efficiently estimate human pose even in challenging scenarios like the TUM kitchen dataset [27]. We have adapted a particle-based annealing optimization scheme [7] to jointly optimize over the action-specific manifolds and the human poses embedded in the manifolds. The approach scales in the worst case linearly with the number of manifolds, under the assumption that each manifold can be optimized with the same amount of time, i.e. they have the same dimensionality, which is more efficient than modeling transitions between the manifolds. Since a linear scaling is not optimal for a high number of action classes, we also propose a prior on the distribution of the actions obtained by a 2D action recognition system. In our experiments, we demonstrate that the action prior improves the tracking performance and that the optimization provides already competitive results with as few as 25 particles. The action recognition and tracking performance are evaluated on two state-of-the-art benchmarks, the HumanEva dataset [23] and the TUM Kitchen dataset [27].

2   Related Work

Using priors learned from motion capture databases is now very popular for robust tracking in difficult scenarios [22,30]. By learning a mapping between the image space and the pose space, the pose can be recovered directly from silhouettes and image features [1,3,8,11,24]. In [15,28,29], Gaussian process dynamical models were used for embedding motion in a low-dimensional latent space, while in [12] locally linear coordination is proposed for dimensionality reduction. Retrieved motions from databases have also been used [2] to refine tracked poses.

Action recognition is a rich sub-field of computer vision research in itself; we refer the reader to the recent review [18] and limit our discussion to multi-camera methods. Most work in multi-view action recognition has been focused on achieving view-invariant recognition. One line of approach has been to model the changes with respect to view, either of the location of feature points, using linear basis functions [21] or of the action's appearance, using low-dimensional manifolds [25]. A second line of approach has been to construct templates in either 3D [13,31,32] (2D space and time) or 4D [17] (3D space and time) and then projecting them back to a lower dimension from an arbitrary view, for matching either silhouettes or visual hulls.

Little work, however, has been done in coupling action recognition with pose estimation, as much of the previous work in pose estimation has been focused on sequences of single action classes rather than multi-actioned longer sequences. An exception is the switching Gaussian process dynamic model [4], in which the action is modelled as a hidden switching state. We follow a different approach since we do not model pose estimation as a filtering problem over time but as an optimization problem over the manifolds for each frame. Hence, we do not need to observe transitions between actions for training.

(a) Silhouette   *(b)* Action Recognition   *(c)* Pose Distribution   *(d)* Final Pose

Fig. 1. System Overview. *(a)* Silhouettes are extracted by background subtraction. *(b)* Tracks are built over the entire sequence and classified by a 2D action recognition system. *(c)* Confidences of each action are used to distribute the particles over the action-specific manifolds. *(d)* Final pose is obtained by optimizing over the manifolds.

3   Framework

The multi-view system can be decomposed into action recognition on the 2D images and 3D pose estimation, with the action-specific manifolds acting as a link between the two. First, silhouettes are used to establish a track of the person over the sequence; the action recognition system then assigns labels for the track over time (Section 4). The confidence measure of the action labels are then used to distribute the particles in the particle-based optimization scheme over the action-specific manifolds (Section 5.1). Finally, the pose is estimated by an optimization over the entire set of manifolds (Section 5.3).

4   2D Action Recognition

For 2D action recognition, a separate classifier is trained for each of the cameras in the multi-view setup; results from the individual classifiers are then combined with standard classifier ensemble methods. Motivation for fusing the single views is based on the assumption that actions which are ambiguous in one view, e.g. due to self-occlusion, is more distinguishable from another view.

2D action recognition is performed according to the Hough-transform voting method presented in [33]. It breaks down the action recognition problem into an initial localization stage, which generates tracks of the individual performing the action, and a subsequent classification stage, which assigns action labels to the tracks. In scenarios where the cameras are fixed, it is not necessary to build the tracks with a tracking-by-detection technique as presented in [33]. Instead, background subtraction is used to generate silhouettes of the person performing the action (Fig. 1). Bounding boxes are then extrapolated around the silhouette and the trajectory of the bounding boxes is smoothed to build the track.

The output of the classification stage is a confidence score of each action class over time, normalized such that the confidences over all classes at any time point sum up to 1. A classifier combination strategy such as the max-rule is then used to combine the outputs from the multiple cameras [9].

5   Optimizing over a Set of Manifolds

Having a skeleton and a surface model of the human, the human pose is represented by a vector in a bounded, high-dimensional state space $\mathbb{E} \subset \mathbb{R}^{D+6}$. While $\Theta = \theta_1, \cdots, \theta_D \in \mathbb{E}_\Theta$ denotes the joint angles, the global orientation and position are encoded by the 6D vector (r, t). An element of the search space is given by $x = (r, t, \Theta)$. We formulate pose estimation as an optimization problem over $\mathbb{E}$ for a given positive energy function V, i.e. $\min_{x \in \mathbb{E}} V(x)$. The energy function measures the consistency between the images of all camera views and the projections of the model's surface for a given pose x. As consistency measure, we use edges and silhouettes [20]. Although these features are not optimal for human pose estimation, since edges are sensitive to background clutter and silhouettes are sensitive to occlusions and background changes, the associated energy function is fast to compute and fixed for all our experiments. As a baseline, we implemented the particle-based annealing optimization scheme ISA over $\mathbb{E}$, which has been used in the multi-layer framework [6]. The optimization scheme, based on the theory of Feynman-Kac models [16], iterates over a selection and mutation step, and is also the underlying principle of the annealed particle filter [5].

We modify the baseline algorithm to optimize over a set of manifolds instead of a single state space. To this end, we consider a set of action classes $\mathcal{A} = \{a_1, \cdots, a_{|\mathcal{A}|}\}$, where we learn for each class an action-specific low-dimensional manifold $\mathbb{M}_a \subset \mathbb{R}^{d_a}$ with $d_a \ll D$. We assume that the following mappings are available:

$$f_a : \mathbb{E}_\Theta \mapsto \mathbb{M}_a, \quad g_a : \mathbb{M}_a \mapsto \mathbb{E}_\Theta, \quad h_a : \mathbb{M}_a \mapsto \mathbb{M}_a, \tag{1}$$

where f_a denotes the mapping from the state space to the low-dimensional manifolds, g_a the projection back to the state space, and h_a the prediction within an action-specific manifold. Since the manifolds encode only the space of joint angles, a low-dimensional representation of the full pose is denoted by $y_a = (r, t, \Theta_a)$ with $\Theta_a = f_a(\Theta)$. A particle $s^i = (y_a^i, a^i)$ stores the corresponding manifold label a^i in addition to the vector $y_a^i = (r^i, t^i, \Theta_a^i)$ and the set of particles is denoted by $\mathcal{S}$. Our algorithm operates both in the state space as well as in the manifolds. An overview of the algorithm is given in Fig. 2.

5.1   Action-Specific Manifolds

Each of the action-specific low-dimensional manifolds, $\mathbb{M}_a$, are learned from the joint angles Θ in motion capture data using Isomap [26], a non-linear dimensionality reduction technique. As Isomap does not provide mappings between the high- and low-dimensional pose spaces, we learn two separate Gaussian Process (GP) regressions [19], f_a and g_a (2), to map from the high-dimensional space to the low-dimensional space and back, respectively, where $m(\cdot)$ and $k(\cdot)$ denote the mean and covariance functions.

$$y = f_a(x) \sim \mathcal{GP}(m(x), k(x, x\prime)); \quad x = g_a(y) \sim \mathcal{GP}(m(y), k(y, y\prime)). \tag{2}$$

In addition, a third GP regression, h_a, is learned to model temporal transitions between successive poses within each action-specific manifold:

$$y_t = h_a\left(y_{t-1}\right) \sim \mathcal{GP}\left(m\left(y_{t-1}\right)\right), k\left(y_{t-1}, y'_{t-1}\right)). \tag{3}$$

5.2   Theoretical Discussion

As mentioned in Section 5, one seeks the solution of the minimization problem $\min_{x \in \mathbb{E}} V(x)$. When optimizing over a set of manifolds the problem becomes

$$\min_{a \in \mathcal{A}} \left(\min_{y \in \mathbb{M}_a} V(g_a(y)) \right). \tag{4}$$

Minimizing the problem this way, i.e. searching the global minimum in all manifolds $\mathbb{M}_a$ and then taking the best solution mapped back to the state space, does not scale well with the number of manifolds. Hence, we propose to optimize over all manifolds jointly. Before outlining the optimization procedure in Section 5.3, we briefly discuss the existence and the uniqueness of the solution. Since g_a and f_a are not direct inverses of each other, i.e. $(g_a \circ f_a)$ does not equal the identity function, the optimization over the manifolds (4) does not provide the same solution as the original optimization problem over the state space. Indeed, this is the case only if the following is satisfied:

$$\exists a \in \mathcal{A}, \exists y \in \mathbb{M}_a : \min_{x \in \mathbb{E}} V(x) = V(g_a(y)). \tag{5}$$

The uniqueness of the solution for the manifold and thus of the action a is interesting from the point of action recognition. It is given if and only if

$$\forall a_1, a_2 \in \mathcal{A} \quad \text{with} \quad a_1 \neq a_2 : \min_{y \in \mathbb{M}_{a_1}} V(g_{a_1}(y)) \neq \min_{y' \in \mathbb{M}_{a_2}} V(g_{a_2}(y')). \tag{6}$$

In most cases, optimization of the pose propagates the particles into the "right" manifold, i.e. the correct action, as plotted in Fig. 3. However, there is usually an overlap of poses between the manifolds such that Eq. (6) is not satisfied. Note that in comparison to the action recognition, which takes a sequence of frames into account (Section 4), the pose is optimized only for the current frame.

To cope with the problem defined in (5), we introduce two optimization steps

$$(\hat{y}, \hat{a}) = \operatorname*{argmin}_{a \in \mathcal{A}, y \in \mathbb{M}_a} V(g_a(y)) \quad \text{and} \tag{7}$$

$$\hat{x} = \operatorname*{argmin}_{x \in \mathbb{E}} V(x), \quad \text{with} \quad x_0 = g_{\hat{a}}(\hat{y}) \tag{8}$$

as the initialization. In other words, we first search for the nearest approximation by optimizing over the manifolds and then use this result to initialize the optimization over the state space. With this procedure, we can design an optimization that converges to the global minimum in the state space, see Fig. 2.

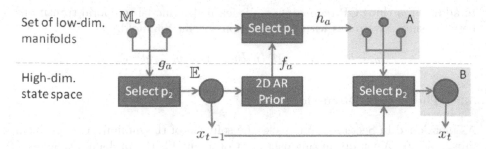

Fig. 2. For each action class a, we learn an embedding in a low-dimensional manifold $\mathbb{M}_a$. The manifolds are indicated by the small circles and the high-dimensional state space $\mathbb{E}$ is indicated by the large circle. Having estimated the pose x_{t-1}, a set of particles is selected from the previous particle sets (*Select p_1*). To this end, the particles in $\mathbb{E}$ are mapped by f_a to $\mathbb{M}_a$ where each particle is associated to one of the manifolds. This process is steered by a prior distribution on the actions obtained by a 2D action recognition system. Since the manifolds are action-specific, the pose for the next frame can be predicted by the function h_a. The first optimization step, *Optimization A*, optimizes jointly over the manifolds and the human poses embedded in the manifolds. Since our manifolds do not cover transitions between actions, we run a second optimization step, *Optimization B*, over the particles mapped back to the state space $\mathbb{E}$ by g_a. Before the optimization, the particle set is augmented by making use of the embedding error of the previous pose x_{t-1} (*Select p_2*).

5.3   Algorithm

Optimization A: Since ISA [7] is not directly applicable for optimizing over a set of manifolds, we have to modify the algorithm. For the weighting, the particles are mapped back to the full space in order to evaluate the energy function V:

$$w^i = \exp\left(-\beta_k \cdot V\left(r^i, t^i, g_{a^i}(\Theta_a^i)\right)\right), \qquad (9)$$

where k is the iteration parameter of the optimization. The weights of all particles are normalized such that $\sum_{s^i} w^i = 1$. Note that the normalization does not take the label of the manifold a^i into account. As result, particles in a certain manifold might have higher weights than particles in another manifold since their poses fit the image data better. Since particles with higher weights are more likely to be selected, the distribution of the particles among the manifolds $\mathbb{M}_a$ changes after the selection step. This is desirable since the particles should migrate to the most likely manifold to get a better estimate within this manifold. While the selection is performed as in [7][1], the mutation step needs to be adapted since the particles are spread in different spaces. To this end, we use $|\mathcal{A}|$ mutation kernels K_a, one for each manifold, and an additional kernel K_0 for the global position and orientation. In our implementation, we use Gaussian kernels with covariance matrices Σ_a proportional to the sample covariance within a manifold,

---

[1] Using the selection kernel $\epsilon_k(\eta) = \frac{1}{\inf\{y\,:\,\eta(\{x \in E\,:\,\exp(-\beta_k\,V(x))>y\})=0\}}$.

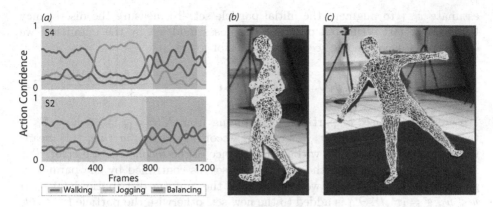

Fig. 3. HumanEva. Action recognition prior from camera C1 *(a)*. The curves show the action confidence per frame. Note the smooth transitions between the actions around frame 800 for subject S4. After jogging, the subject walks a few steps before balancing. At the end of the sequence, the person walks away, as recognized by the action recognition system. The distribution of the particles among the action-specific manifolds after *Optimization A* is shown by the area plot. The particles move to the correct manifold for nearly all frames. Pose estimate for jogging *(b)* and balancing *(c)*.

i.e. $\mathcal{S}_a = \{s^i \in \mathcal{S} : a^i = a\}$;

$$\Sigma_a = \frac{\alpha_\Sigma}{|\mathcal{S}_a| - 1} \left(\rho I + \sum_{s^i \in \mathcal{S}_a} (\Theta_a^i - \mu_a)(\Theta_a^i - \mu_a)^T \right), \quad \mu_a - \frac{1}{|\mathcal{S}_a|} \sum_{s^i \in \mathcal{S}_a} \Theta_a^i. \tag{10}$$

The scaling factor $\alpha_\Sigma = 0.4$ and the positive constant $\rho = 0.0001$, which ensures that the covariance does not become singular, are fixed for all kernels. The kernel K_0 for rotation and translation is computed over the full set of particles $\mathcal{S}$:

$$\Sigma_0 = \frac{\alpha_\Sigma}{|\mathcal{S}| - 1} \left(\rho I + \sum_{s^i \in \mathcal{S}} ((r^i, t^i) - \mu)((r^i, t^i) - \mu)^T \right), \quad \mu = \frac{1}{|\mathcal{S}|} \sum_{s^i \in \mathcal{S}} (r^i, t^i). \tag{11}$$

Since we compute the extra kernel K_0 instead of taking (r, t) as additional dimensions for the kernels K_a, the correlation between (r, t) and Θ_a is not taken into account. However, the number of particles per manifold can be very small, such that K_0 computed over all particles provides a better estimate of the correlation between the global pose parameters (r, t).

Select p_2: Before continuing with the optimization in the full state, the set of particles $\mathcal{S}$ needs to be mapped from the manifolds $\mathbb{M}_a$ to $\mathbb{E}$, where the particles build the initial distribution for the next optimization step. However, it can happen that the true pose is not well represented by any of the manifolds. This is typical of transitions from one action to another, which are not modelled in our setting. As we will show in our experiments, it is useful to use the previous estimate $\hat{x}_{t-1}$ to augment the initial particle set. To measure the discrepancy between the last estimated pose and the poses modeled by the manifolds, we compute $\Sigma_{\hat{a}}$ based on the reconstruction error for $\hat{x}_{t-1}$:

$$\hat{a} = \underset{a \in \mathcal{A}}{\operatorname{argmin}} \left\| \hat{\Theta}_{t-1} - g_a(f_a(\hat{\Theta}_{t-1})) \right\|, \quad \sigma_{\hat{a},i} = \frac{|\hat{\Theta}_{t-1} - g_{\hat{a}}(f_{\hat{a}}(\hat{\Theta}_{t-1}))|_i}{3}. \quad (12)$$

We create a new set of particles by sampling from $\mathcal{N}(\hat{\Theta}_{t-1}, \Sigma_{\hat{a}})$, where $\Sigma_{\hat{a}}$ is the diagonal matrix with $\sigma_{\hat{a},i}$ as entries. According to the 3σ rule, this means that nearly all samples are within the distance of the reconstruction error. The selection process between the two particle sets is controlled by the parameter $p_2 \in [0,1]$. For all $s^i \in \mathcal{S}$, we draw u from the uniform distribution $\mathcal{U}[0,1]$. If $u < p_2$, $s^i = (r^i, t^i, \Theta^i)$ is added to the new set; otherwise the particle $(r^i, t^i, \hat{\Theta})$ is added to the set, where $\hat{\Theta}$ is sampled from $\mathcal{N}(\hat{\Theta}_{t-1}, \Sigma_{\hat{a}})$.

Optimization B: The second optimization step eventually runs ISA [7] on the full state space. However, we do not start from the beginning but continue with the optimization, i.e. when It_A is the number of iterations used for *Opt. A*, we continue with β_{It_A+1} instead of β_1.

Select p_1: After *Opt. A*, all the particles may aggregate into one single manifold, so we distribute the particles again amongst the manifolds $\mathbb{M}_a$ when moving to the next frame I_t; otherwise, we get stuck in a single action class. Similar to the previous selection, we make use of two particle sets; the particles $\mathcal{S}^{\mathrm{M}}$ in the manifolds $\mathbb{M}_a$ after *Opt. A* and the particles in the state space $\mathcal{S}^{\mathrm{E}}$ after *Opt. B*. The selection is controlled by the parameter $p_1 \in [0,1]$. For all $s^i \in \mathcal{S}^{\mathrm{M}}$, we draw u from the uniform distribution $\mathcal{U}[0,1]$. If $u < p_1$, s^i is added to the new set; otherwise the particle $(r^i, t^i, \Theta^i) \in \mathcal{S}^{\mathrm{E}}$ is mapped to one of the manifolds and added to the set. The manifold $\mathbb{M}_{a^i}$ is selected according to the probability $p(A = a | T = t, \mathcal{I})$, yielding the mapped particle $(r^i, t^i, f_{a^i}(\Theta^i), a^i)$. In our experiments, we use two choices for $p(A | T = t, \mathcal{I})$:

$$p(A = a \,|\, T = t, \mathcal{I}) \;=\; p(A = a) = \tfrac{1}{|\mathcal{A}|} \qquad \textit{(Uniform Prior)}$$
$$p(A = a \,|\, T = t, \mathcal{I}) \;=\; p(A = a \,|\, I_{t-l} \cdots I_{t+l}) \qquad \textit{(Action Prior)}$$

The *uniform prior* is independent of the current frame and results in a joint optimization over the manifolds $\mathbb{M}_{a \in \mathcal{A}}$ and poses $y \in \mathbb{M}_a$. However, the prior does not scale well with the number of manifolds since the total number of particles is fixed and there must be a sufficient number of particles available for each manifold. The *action prior* distributes the particles to manifolds that are more likely a-priori, meaning that a manifold $\mathbb{M}_a$ cannot be explored when $p(A = a | T = t, \mathcal{I}) = 0$ and $\{s^i \in \mathcal{S}^{\mathrm{M}} : a^i = a\} = \emptyset$. This also motivates the use of the particle set $\mathcal{S}^{\mathrm{M}}$ to increase the robustness to temporary errors in the *action prior* as demonstrated in Fig. 4(a). Note that a zero-probability error for the true manifold over many frames cannot be compensated. In our experiments, $p(A | I_{t-l} \cdots I_{t+l})$ is obtained by an action recognition system which takes a set of frames in the neighborhood of t into account (Section 4).

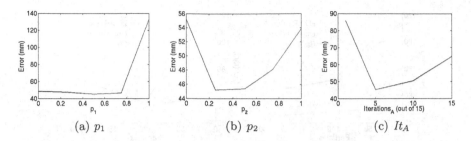

(a) p_1 (b) p_2 (c) It_A

Fig. 4. Evaluation of parameters. *(a) Select p_1*: The best result is obtained by $p_1 = 0.5$, which shows the benefit of taking both particle sets $\mathcal{S}^M$ and $\mathcal{S}^E$ into account. For $p_1 = 1$, the particles $\mathcal{S}^E$ from *Opt. B* are discarded. *(b) Select p_2*: The best results are achieved with $p_2 \in [0.25, 0.5]$. It shows the benefit of taking the reconstruction error for $\hat{x}_{t-1}$ into account. *(c)* Number of iterations for *Opt. A* (It_A) and *Opt. B* (15-It_A). The summed number of iterations was fixed to 15. Without a second optimization step (It_A=15), the error is significantly higher than for the optimal setting (It_A=5).

6   Experiments

HumanEva. The HumanEva-II [23] dataset is the standard benchmark on 3D human pose estimation. It comprises two sequences S2 and S4 with three actions, see Fig. 3. The dataset provides a model for subject S4, which we also use for subject S2 despite differences in body shape. The human pose is represented by 28 parameters. We perform two trials: testing on S2 and training on S4 and vice versa. For learning the action-specific manifolds, we use the tracking results of the multi-layer tracker [6] where we split the data into the three action classes and discard the transitions between the actions. Note that training data from marker-less tracking approaches is in general noisier and less accurate than data from marker-based systems.

In Fig. 4, we plot the impact of the parameters on the tracking accuracy. For evaluation, we use 200 particles, 5 iterations for *Opt. A*, and 10 iterations for *Opt. B* unless otherwise specified. The optimization is run with a polynomial annealing scheme with $b = 0.7$ [7]. The results clearly support our design decisions for the algorithm (Section 5.3).

In Fig. 5, we plot the 3D estimation error of the joints with respect to the number of particles. For comparison, we show the mean and standard deviation for optimizing over the state space $\mathbb{E}$ (*baseline*) and the proposed algorithm with a *uniform prior* and an *action prior*, with the *action prior* computed as described in Section 4. For the baseline, we run *Opt. B* with 15 iterations and without taking the manifolds $\mathbb{M}_a$ into account. Note that according to [6,23], pose estimation requires usually at least 200-250 particles to achieve good results on this dataset. We perform the optimization of the 28 parameters with 200 down to 25 particles. Unsurprisingly, that the error for the *baseline* increases significantly when the number of particles drops below 100. When optimizing over the manifolds and the poses embedded in the manifolds, the error increases gently with a decreasing number of particles. Since the dataset contains only

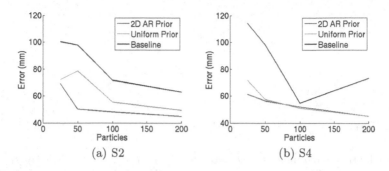

(a) S2   (b) S4

Fig. 5. 3D Estimation error with respect to number of particles. The proposed approach performs significantly better than the direct optimization in the state space $\mathbb{E}$ (baseline), particularly for a small number of particles. The discrepancy between uniform prior and the prior obtained from 2D action recognition is getting larger for very few particles. In this case, the number of particles per manifold becomes very small for a uniform distribution. Note that competitive results are still achieved with only 25 particles. Timings are given in Table 1.

Table 1. Computation time per frame and 3D estimation error of the optimization with respect to number of particles. The 2D action recognition takes additional 0.4 seconds for each frame consisting of 4 images, which is roughly the computation time for 20 particles. *ap: action prior; up: uniform prior; base: baseline.*

	Time (sec.)		S2 Error (mm)			S4 Error (mm)		
n	ap,up	base	ap	up	base	ap	up	base
200	3.89	3.80	44.9 ± 9.5	49.4 ± 19.0	62.9 ± 24.4	45.2 ± 13.4	45.2 ± 11.8	73.1 ± 70.7
100	1.96	1.92	48.2 ± 12.7	55.4 ± 37.8	71.7 ± 25.7	51.9 ± 20.9	51.0 ± 21.3	54.7 ± 25.0
50	0.98	0.96	50.2 ± 13.4	78.7 ± 72.4	98.0 ± 61.1	56.4 ± 19.2	57.6 ± 19.2	98.3 ± 67.4
25	0.5	0.49	69.3 ± 51.1	72.3 ± 51.2	100.5 ± 40.4	61.3 ± 21.2	71.8 ± 29.3	114.3 ± 85.4

3 action classes, the *uniform prior* performs very well. Differences between the two priors become more prominent for very few particles per action class. This indicates that the *action prior* scales better with a large number of classes since this basically limits the number of particles per action class. In general, the *uniform prior* describes the worst case scenario where the action recognition is not better than a random guess. Timings and mean errors are given in Table 1.

Finally, we show the tracking performance with respect to number of camera views in Fig. 6(a); using 200 particles. Again, the proposed approach significantly outperforms the *baseline*. At first glance, the *uniform prior* and the *action prior* seem to perform similarly, due to the scaling of the plot from the large error of the *baseline*, though the *action prior* actually reduces the error on average by 4%. The benefit of the *action prior* is more evident for very few particles per action class as shown in Fig. 5.

TUM Kitchen dataset. A more challenging dataset than HumanEva is the newly released TUM Kitchen dataset [27]. The dataset contains 20 episodes of recordings from 4 views of 4 subjects setting a table. In each episode, a subject moves back and forth between the kitchen and a dining table, each time fetching

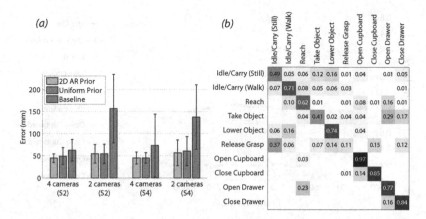

Fig. 6. *(a)* 3D Estimation error with respect to number of views for HumanEva. For the setting with two views, cameras C1 and C2 are taken. The reduced number of views results in more ambiguities. The proposed approach handles these ambiguities better than the direct optimization in the state space $\mathbb{E}$ (baseline). *(b)* Confusion matrix for fused results according to the max-rule for TUM kitchen.

Table 2. Individual camera and fused action recognition performance for subjects 1-4; fused performance is higher than any individual camera view for each subject

	Camera 1	Camera 2	Camera 3	Camera 4	Fused
Subject 1	0.542	0.493	0.569	0.564	0.574
Subject 2	0.532	0.501	0.456	0.560	0.585
Subject 3	0.690	0.718	0.652	0.666	0.740
Subject 4	0.619	0.529	0.610	0.610	0.706
Average	0.596	0.560	0.572	0.600	0.651

objects such as cutlery, plates and cups and then transporting them to the table. The dataset is particularly challenging for both action recognition as well as pose estimation, as the actions are more subtle than those of standard action recognition datasets and parts of the body are often occluded by objects such as drawers, cupboard doors and tables (see Fig. 1). Training was done on episodes *1-0* to *1-5*, all of which are recorded from subject 1 and testing was done on episodes *0-2*, *0-4*, *0-6*, *0-8*, *0-10*, *0-11*, and *1-6*, which are recorded from all 4 subjects. For the action recognition, we use the 9 labels that are annotated for the 'left hand' [27]. Since the labels are determined by the activity of the arms and we would like the manifolds to be representative of the entire body, we further split the idle/carry class according to whether the subject is walking or standing; see Fig. 6*(b)*.

Results of the action recognition for cameras 0 and 2, as well as the fused results are shown in Table 2. For classifier fusion, we use the max-rule that gave the best performance compared to other standard ensemble methods [9], though results were similar for all the methods. Fused results and the confusion matrix are shown in Fig. 7 and Fig. 6*(b)*.

Based on the fused results of the action recognition, we also evaluate the tracking performance. For the dataset, we use the provided models with 84

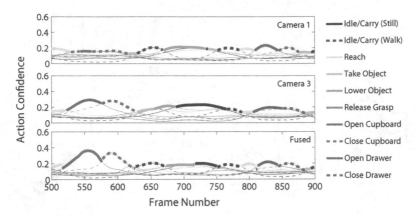

Fig. 7. Normalized action confidences for two camera views as well as fused confidences for frames 500-900 of episode *0-11*

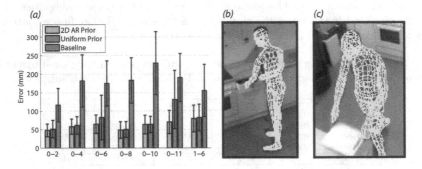

Fig. 8. 3D Error for TUM kitchen dataset *(a)*. The proposed approach performs significantly better than the direct optimization in the state space $\mathbb{E}$ (baseline). The error for the sequences *0-2* and *0-8* are the lowest since the action-specific manifolds were trained on the same subject. Mean and standard deviation are provided in Table 3. Pose estimates for opening drawer *(b)* and lowering object *(c)*.

Table 3. 3D Error for TUM kitchen dataset in mm. *ap: action prior; up: uniform prior; base: baseline.*

(mm)	0-2	0-4	0-6	0-8	0-10	0-11	1-6
ap	48.4 ± 17.1	58.2 ± 20.5	64.7 ± 24.9	49.0 ± 22.5	63.7 ± 25.2	70.5 ± 31.5	79.8 ± 35.9
up	51.6 ± 23.6	61.4 ± 23.9	82.9 ± 60.5	50.5 ± 21.5	64.0 ± 22.0	131.1 ± 78.8	82.5 ± 35.8
base	116.5 ± 45.1	181.9 ± 70.6	174.8 ± 61.2	183.0 ± 61.4	229.4 ± 85.0	190.6 ± 65.0	155.4 ± 70.4

parameters. The large errors for the *baseline* in Fig. 8 show that 200 particles are not enough to optimize over a 84 dimensional search space. Note that we do not make use of any joint limits or geometric information about the kitchen and use only the images as input. The proposed approach estimates the sequences with a comparable accuracy as HumanEva, although the dimensions of the state space increased from 28 to 84, the number of action classes from 3 to 8 (the 'open' and 'close' actions are embedded in one manifold), and the silhouette quality is much worse due to truncations and occlusions. Compared to the *uniform prior*, the *action prior* reduces the error on average by 12%.

7   Conclusion

We have presented an algorithm[2] that efficiently solves the problem of optimizing over a set of manifolds. In the context of 3D pose estimation, we demonstrated that the algorithm handles high-dimensional spaces with very few particles. Since transitions between actions are not explicitly modeled, as in previous work, it is an important step towards pose estimation with many action classes. Furthermore, we have shown that a prior distribution based on action recognition improves the performance. This is interesting since it is expected that the algorithm scales very well with the number of classes when the action recognition system does as well. In this way, 3D human pose estimation can be linked to the progress in the field of action recognition. As there are very few datasets for pose estimation and action recognition available and none contains many action classes, new datasets are required to investigate scalability more in detail.

Acknowledgments. This work has been supported by funding from the Swiss National Foundation NCCR project IM2 as well as the EC project IURO. Angela Yao was also supported by funding from NSERC Canada. We thank Jan Bandouch and Moritz Tenorth for providing the TUM Kitchen dataset and Fabian Nater for helpful discussions.

References

1. Agarwal, A., Triggs, B.: Recovering 3d human pose from monocular images. TPAMI 28(1), 44–58 (2006)
2. Baak, A., Rosenhahn, B., Müller, M., Seidel, H.P.: Stabilizing motion tracking using retrieved motion priors. In: ICCV (2009)
3. Bo, L., Sminchisescu, C.: Twin gaussian processes for structured prediction. IJCV 87, 28–52 (2010)
4. Chen, J., Kim, M., Wang, Y., Ji, Q.: Switching gaussian process dynamic models for simultaneous composite motion tracking and recognition. In: CVPR (2009)
5. Deutscher, J., Reid, I.: Articulated body motion capture by stochastic search. IJCV 61(2), 185–205 (2005)
6. Gall, J., Rosenhahn, B., Brox, T., Seidel, H.P.: Optimization and filtering for human motion capture – a multi-layer framework. IJCV 87, 75–92 (2010)
7. Gall, J., Rosenhahn, B., Seidel, H.P.: An Introduction to Interacting Simulated Annealing. In: Human Motion: Understanding, Modelling, Capture and Animation, pp. 319–343. Springer, Heidelberg (2008)
8. Grauman, K., Shakhnarovich, G., Darrell, T.: Inferring 3d structure with a statistical image-based shape model. In: ICCV, pp. 641–648 (2003)
9. Kittler, J., Society, I.C., Hatef, M., Duin, R.P.W., Matas, J.: On combining classifiers. TPAMI 20, 226–239 (1998)
10. Kovar, L., Gleicher, M., Pighin, F.: Motion graphs. ACM Trans. Graph. 21(3), 473–482 (2002)

---

[2] Source code is available at http://www.vision.ee.ethz.ch/~gallju

11. Lee, C.S., Elgammal, A.: Coupled visual and kinematic manifold models for tracking. IJCV 87, 118–139 (2010)
12. Li, R., Tian, T.P., Sclaroff, S., Yang, M.H.: 3d human motion tracking with a coordinated mixture of factor analyzers. IJCV 87, 170–190 (2010)
13. Lv, F., Nevatia, R.: Single view human action recognition using key pose matching and viterbi path searching. In: CVPR (2007)
14. Moeslund, T., Hilton, A., Krüger, V.: A survey of advances in vision-based human motion capture and analysis. CVIU 104(2), 90–126 (2006)
15. Moon, K., Pavlovic, V.: Impact of dynamics on subspace embedding and tracking of sequences. In: CVPR, pp. 198–205 (2006)
16. Moral, P.D.: Feynman-Kac Formulae. Genealogical and Interacting Particle Systems with Applications. Springer, New York (2004)
17. Pingkun Yan, S.M.K., Shah, M.: Learning 4d action feature models for arbitrary view action recognition. In: CVPR (2008)
18. Poppe, R.: A survey on vision-based human action recognition. Image and Vision Computing (2010)
19. Rasmussen, C.E., Williams, C.K.I.: Gaussian Processes for Machine Learning (Adaptive Computation and Machine Learning). MIT Press, Cambridge (2005)
20. Shaheen, M., Gall, J., Strzodka, R., van Gool, L., Seidel, H.P.: A comparison of 3d model-based tracking approaches for human motion capture in uncontrolled environments. In: IEEE Workshop on Applications of Computer Vision (2009)
21. Sheikh, Y., Sheikh, M., Shah, M.: Exploring the space of a human action. In: ICCV (2005)
22. Sidenbladh, H., Black, M., Sigal, L.: Implicit probabilistic models of human motion for synthesis and tracking. In: Heyden, A., Sparr, G., Nielsen, M., Johansen, P. (eds.) ECCV 2002. LNCS, vol. 2350, pp. 784–800. Springer, Heidelberg (2002)
23. Sigal, L., Balan, A., Black, M.: Humaneva: Synchronized video and motion capture dataset and baseline algorithm for evaluation of articulated human motion. IJCV 87, 4–27 (2010)
24. Sminchisescu, C., Kanaujia, A., Metaxas, D.: Bme: Discriminative density propagation for visual tracking. TPAMI 29(11), 2030–2044 (2007)
25. Souvenir, R., Babbs, J.: Learning the viewpoint manifold for action recognition. In: CVPR (2008)
26. Tenenbaum, J.B., de Silva, V., Langford, J.C.: A Global Geometric Framework for Nonlinear Dimensionality Reduction. Science 290(5500), 2319–2323 (2000)
27. Tenorth, M., Bandouch, J., Beetz, M.: The TUM kitchen data set of everyday manipulation activities for motion tracking and action recognition. In: IEEE Workshop on THEMIS (2009)
28. Ukita, N., Hirai, M., Kidode, M.: Complex volume and pose tracking with probabilistic dynamical model and visual hull constraint. In: ICCV (2009)
29. Urtasun, R., Fleet, D., Fua, P.: 3d people tracking with gaussian process dynamical models. In: CVPR, pp. 238–245 (2006)
30. Urtasun, R., Fua, P.: 3d human body tracking using deterministic temporal motion models. In: Pajdla, T., Matas, J(G.) (eds.) ECCV 2004. LNCS, vol. 3023, pp. 92–106. Springer, Heidelberg (2004)
31. Weinland, D., Boyer, E., Ronfard, R.: Action recognition from arbitrary views using 3d exemplars. In: ICCV, pp. 1–7 (2007)
32. Weinland, D., Ronfard, R., Boyer, E.: Free viewpoint action recognition using motion history volumes. CVIU 104(2-3), 249–257 (2006)
33. Yao, A., Gall, J., van Gool, L.: A hough transform-based voting framework for action recognition. In: CVPR (2010)

A Streakline Representation of Flow in Crowded Scenes

Ramin Mehran[1], Brian E. Moore[2], and Mubarak Shah[1]

[1] Computer Vision Lab
[2] Department of Mathematics
University of Central Florida
ramin@cs.ucf.edu, bmoore@math.ucf.edu, shah@eecs.ucf.edu

Abstract. Based on the Lagrangian framework for fluid dynamics, a streakline representation of flow is presented to solve computer vision problems involving crowd and traffic flow. Streaklines are traced in a fluid flow by injecting color material, such as smoke or dye, which is transported with the flow and used for visualization. In the context of computer vision, streaklines may be used in a similar way to transport information about a scene, and they are obtained by repeatedly initializing a fixed grid of particles at each frame, then moving both current and past particles using optical flow. Streaklines are the locus of points that connect particles which originated from the same initial position. In this paper, a streakline technique is developed to compute several important aspects of a scene, such as flow and potential functions using the Helmholtz decomposition theorem. This leads to a representation of the flow that more accurately recognizes spatial and temporal changes in the scene, compared with other commonly used flow representations. Applications of the technique to segmentation and behavior analysis provide comparison to previously employed techniques, showing that the streakline method outperforms the state-of-the-art in segmentation, and opening a new domain of application for crowd analysis based on potentials.

1 Introduction and Related Work

Behavior analysis in crowded scenes remains an open problem in computer vision due to the inherent complexity and vast diversity found in such scenes. One hurdle, that must be overcome, is finding good ways to identify flow patterns without tracking individual objects, which is both impractical and unnecessary in the context of dense crowds. Another hurdle is finding good ways to understand changes in behavior when the scene context and crowd dynamics can vary over such a wide range.

Several methods based on optical flow have been presented in recent years to handle these hurdles. In computer vision, optical flow is widely used to compute pixel wise instantaneous motion between consecutive frames, and numerous methods are reported to efficiently compute accurate optical flow. However, optical flow does not capture long-range temporal dependencies, since it is based on just two frames, and by itself does not represent spatial and temporal features of a flow that are useful for general applications.

K. Daniilidis, P. Maragos, N. Paragios (Eds.): ECCV 2010, Part III, LNCS 6313, pp. 439–452, 2010.

Recently, based on the Lagrangian framework of fluid dynamics, a notion of *particle flow* was introduced in computer vision. Particle flow is computed by moving a grid of particles with the optical flow through numerical integration, providing trajectories that relate a particles initial position to its position at a later time. Impressive results employing particle flow have been demonstrated on crowd segmentation [1] and abnormal crowd behavior detection [2]. However, in particle flow the spatial changes may be ignored, and it has significant time delays. The main goal of this paper is to introduce a notion of streaklines to computer vision with the intent to remedy these problems, and though our applications are crowd and traffic dynamics, the method of streaklines is applicable to many problems that are approached through optical flow.

Streaklines are well known in flow visualization [3,4] and fluid mechanics [5] as a tool for measurement and analysis of the flow. With regard to flow visualization, streaklines are defined as the traces of a colored material in the flow. To understand streaklines, consider a fluid flow with an ink dye injected at a particular point. If the ink is continuously injected, then a line will be traced out by the ink in the direction of the flow, this is a streakline. If the direction of flow changes, then the streaklines change accordingly.

Streaklines are new to computer vision research. In this context, streaklines may be obtained by repeatedly initializing a grid of particles and moving all particles according to the optical flow, in the spirit of a Lagrangian fluid flow. In other words, place a particle at point p, and move the particle one time step with the flow. In the next time step, the point p is initialized with a new particle, then both particles are moved with the flow. Repeating this process on some time interval T produces particle positions from which we obtain streaklines.

In video scene analysis, which is the scope of this paper, some approaches consider the entire scene as a collection of objects, and methods for scene understanding often involve object trajectory clustering and human action recognition. Examples include the tracking methods of [6] for individuals and [7] for groups of pedestrians, and the more recent work of Pellegrini et al. [8] in tracking based on social force model. Yet, the domain of application for these methods is limited to low density scenes with medium to high pixel resolutions on objects. Our work is concerned with high density scenes and low object resolution.

In other approaches, motion and tracking are represented by a set of modalities such as salient feature points [9,10], spatio-temporal volumes [11]. This promotes occlusion handling while preserving local accuracy. In the related approaches, it is common to represent both crowds and individuals as a set of regions, group of feature points, or sparse flows. In [9], Brostow and Cipolla use low level feature tracking to detect individuals in a dense crowd. Seemann et al. [12] presented a generative model to detect pedestrians as a combination of occupancy distributions.

Other methods of scene understanding involve particle tracking, motion pattern recognition, and segmentation based on dense optical flow [13,14]. These methods are popular due to the intrinsic ability of global approaches to handle occlusion. The framework provides insight to social/group behavior of humans

Table 1. Advantages of Streaklines over Streamlines and Pathlines

Streamlines	Pathlines	Streaklines
Spatial gaps in flow.	Ignores spatial changes.	Fills gaps.
Rough transitions in time.	Time delays.	Captures instant changes.

in crowds, but individual tracking or action recognition is only possible through a top-down framework. Recent works of Ali and Shah [1] on crowd analysis, and [15,16,2] on abnormal behavior detection fall into this category. In addition, the particle video method [17] of Sand and Teller has a potential application in crowded scenes as it was originally introduced to handle occlusions while providing dense motion information.

In this paper, we maintain three major contributions. *First*, we assert a streakline framework as a new tool for analysis of crowd videos. We demonstrate streaklines can be more informative than commonly used flow representations, known as optical flow and particle flow. *Second*, we present an innovative algorithm to compute a fluid like flow of crowds to perform behavior analysis. *Third*, we present potential functions as valuable tools, for behavior analysis, and compliment the streakline framework.

The capabilities of the streakline framework is tested in two applications: crowd segmentation and abnormal behavior detection. The segmentation results demonstrate an improvement for unsteady flows in comparison to state of the art. The behavior detection results show an improvement over base-line optical flow.

2 Streaklines vs. Pathlines and Streamlines

In fluid mechanics there are different vector field representations of the flow [5]:

Streamlines *are tangent to the velocity vectors at every point in the flow.* These correspond to optical flow, and a visual example is given in Figure 1(a).

Pathlines *are trajectories that individual particles in a fluid flow will follow.* These directly correspond to integration of optical flow in time and are illustrated by a set of curves with the spectrum of colors from Blue to Orange in Figure 1(b). Particle flow is the set of pathlines which are computed from time averaged optical flow [1].

Streaklines *represent the locations of all particles at a given time that passed through a particular point.* Figure 1(c) shows streaklines as red curves next to pathlines.

For flows that are steady and unchanging, these three representations are the same, but for flows that are unsteady, so that directions of flow can change with time, they are different. Since we are using a Lagrangian model for fluid flow to exploit the dynamics in crowd videos, where frequent changes in the flow are expected, it is important to know which vector field representation is most appropriate for the given problem. In this work, we provide a juxtaposition of

Table 2. A table of values for x-coordinate particle positions, which are computed from the optical flow. Columns correspond to pathlines and rows correspond to streaklines.

	$L^P(0,T)$	$L^P(1,T)$	$L^P(2,T)$	$\cdots$	$L^P(t,T)$	$\cdots$	$L^P(T,T)$
$S^P(0,0)$	$x_0^P(0)$						
$S^P(0,1)$	$x_0^P(1)$	$x_1^P(1)$					
$S^P(0,2)$	$x_0^P(2)$	$x_1^P(2)$	$x_2^P(2)$				
$\vdots$	$\vdots$	$\vdots$	$\vdots$	$\ddots$			
$S^P(0,t)$	$x_0^P(t)$	$x_1^P(t)$	$x_2^P(t)$	$\cdots$	$x_t^P(t)$		
$\vdots$	$\vdots$	$\vdots$	$\vdots$		$\vdots$	$\ddots$	
$S^P(0,T)$	$x_0^P(T)$	$x_1^P(T)$	$x_2^P(T)$	$\cdots$	$x_t^P(T)$	$\cdots$	$x_T^P(T)$

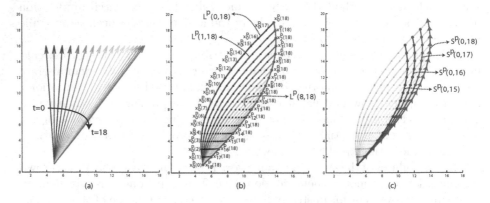

Fig. 1. An illustration of pathlines and streaklines generated using a locally uniform flow field which changes over time. (Labels on points and curves directly correspond to Table 2.) (a) The changes in the flow vectors over time period $t = 0$ to $t = 18$. (b) The pathlines are illustrated as a spectrum of lines. Blue corresponds to the initiating frame of $t = 0$ and orange corresponds to initiating frame of $t = 18$. The red line illustrates the streakline at frame $t = 18$. (c) Streaklines at different frames as red curves to illustrate the evolution of the streaklines through time. The streakline at time $t = 18$ is illustrated along with the initiating motion vector as explained by (2).

streaklines with streamlines and pathlines, which correspond to commonly used methods [16,18] based on optical flow and particle flow, respectively. Our theory and results show that streamlines leave spatial gaps in the flow, as well as choppy transitions between frames. This is because it is produced from instantaneous velocity vectors. Hence, this approach does not produce fluid-like flow for crowd videos [19]. Pathlines overcome this problem by filling the spatial gaps, but do not allow for detection of local spatial changes, and in addition create an artificial time lag. Our streakline approach provides solutions to each of these problems, and Table 1 gives an overview of the advantages.

To explain how streaklines are computed, let $(x_i^p(t), y_i^p(t))$ be a particle position at time t, initialized at point p and frame i for $i, t = 0, 1, 2, \ldots, T$. Repeated initialization at p implies $(x_i^p(i), y_i^p(i)) = (x_0^p(0), y_0^p(0))$. Particle advection is achieved by

$$
\begin{aligned}
x_i^p(t+1) &= x_i^p(t) + u(x_i^p(t), y_i^p(t), t) \\
y_i^p(t+1) &= y_i^p(t) + v(x_i^p(t), y_i^p(t), t) ,
\end{aligned}
\tag{1}
$$

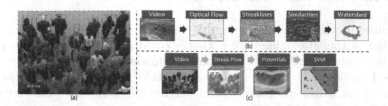

Fig. 2. (a) An illustration of streaklines for a video sequence. (b) The crowd segmentation algorithm. (c) Abnormal behavior detection algorithm.

where u and v represent the velocity field obtained from optical flow. This yields a family of curves, all starting at point p and tracing the path of the flow from that point in frame i. Naturally, for steady flow all these curves lie along the same path, but for unsteady flows the curves vary in direction and shape, characteristic of pedestrian flow.

Particle advection for all $i, t = 0, 1, 2, \ldots, T$ using (1), yields a table of values for $x_i^p(t)$ (shown in Table 2) and similarly for $y_i^p(t)$. The columns of the table show the pathlines $L^p(t, T)$, which are the particle trajectories from time t to T. The rows provide the streaklines $S^p(0, t)$, connecting all particles from t frames that originated at point p. Corresponding to this table, Figure 1 illustrates the set of streaklines and pathlines for an example unsteady flow at time $t = T$. At the start of observation, particles are initiated at every time instant at point p. The spectrum of lines from blue to orange represents the pathlines of particles which have been initiated at time $t = 0$. The solid red color lines depict streaklines. Since the flow is not steady, the streaklines and pathlines are different.

The unsteady flow at a point can be represented by either a set of pathlines or a streakline. However, the streakline provides a speed and memory gain, as a streakline with L particles corresponds to L pathlines with $L \times (L - 1)/2$ particles. There are other interesting, less obvious, properties that streaklines inherit from fluid mechanics. First, in unsteady flows, extra long streaklines may exhibit shapes inconsistent with the actual flow, meaning they can not be allowed to get too long [20]. Second, as invented for visualization purposes, streaklines in fluids transport a color material along the flow, meaning they propagate changes in the flow along their path. Similarly, our setup allows streaklines to propagate velocities, given by the instantaneous optical flow $\Omega = (u, v)^T$ at the time of initialization, along the flow like a material. To this end, we define an *extended particle* i as a set of position and initial velocity

$$P_i = \{x_i(t), y_i(t), u_i, v_i\}, \tag{2}$$

where $u_i = u(x_i^p(i), y_i^p(i), i)$, and $v_i = v(x_i^p(i), y_i^p(i), i)$. In the whole scene, we consider only streaklines comprising extended particles. Figure 2.a depicts streaklines for an example sequence.

3   Computations with Streaklines

Streaklines provide a means to recognize spatial and temporal changes in the flow, that neither streamlines nor pathlines could provide directly. This point is made here using streak flow and potential functions. In essence, streak flow is obtained by time integration of the velocity field, while potential functions are obtained from spatial integration, and each provides useful information concerning the dynamics in the scene.

3.1   Streak Flow

Research in social behavior of pedestrians in crowds reveals that people tend to follow a pathway trailing pedestrians who have similar paths as a group [21]. As a pedestrian passes a point, there is a social expectation that any other pedestrian behind him/her would follow a similar path. Considering this social behavior, the actual, but invisible, flow of pedestrians has no gaps between individuals who are walking similarly. Hence, for crowd motion, gaps in the optical flow should be filled along trajectories with similar motion vectors prior to analysis.

In order to achieve an accurate representation of flow from crowd motion, we use the streaklines to compute a new motion field which we refer to as *streak flow*, denoted $\Omega_s = (u_s, v_s)^T$. To compute streak flow, we compute the streaklines by temporally integrating optical flow, as illustrated in Table 2, and forming the particles as in Equation (2). We describe the computation of u_s; computation of v_s is similar. Given data in the vector.

$U = [u_i]$, where $u_i \in P_i$, $\forall i, p$, we compute the streak flow in the x direction at each pixel.

Based on equations (1), particle positions have sub-pixel accuracy. We compute a triangulation of pixels, which implies that each particle P_i has three neighboring pixels (nearest neighbors). At the sub-pixel level, it is reasonable to consider u_i to be the linear interpolation of the three neighboring pixels. Hence, we define

$$u_i = a_1 u_s(k_1) + a_2 u_s(k_2) + a_3 u_s(k_3) , \tag{3}$$

where k_j is the index of a neighboring pixel, and a_j is the known basis function of the triangulation of the domain for the j-th neighboring pixel. Using a triangular interpolation formula, each $u_s(k_i)$ is computed based on the relative positions of the three pixels and the particle. Using (3) for all the data points in U, we form a linear system of equations

$$Au_s = U , \tag{4}$$

where a_i are entries of the matrix A, and u_s is the least square solution of (4).[1]

Streak flows encapsulate motion information of the flow for a period of time. This resembles the notion of *particle flow* (equivalent to average optical flow) where advection of a grid of particles over a window of time provides information

---

[1] www.mathworks.com/matlabcentral/fileexchange/
8998-surface-fitting-using-gridfit

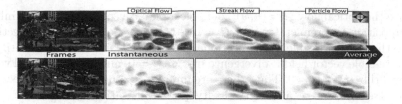

Fig. 3. The comparison of optical flow, particle flow and streak flow for Boston sequence (color coded). The red circle indicates the area to notice.

for segmenting the crowd motion. We argue that streak flows exhibit changes in the flow faster than particle flow, and therefore, they capture crowd motions better in a dynamically changing flow. This can be observed in Figure 3, illustrating sample frames from a video of a traffic intersection, which includes motions from both pedestrians and vehicles. The flow in the scene is unsteady and the different motion patterns appear in the video as the traffic lights change. The figure compares the streak flow to the particle flow and the optical flow in capturing temporal and local changes. For temporal changes the flow is compared at two different times: (1) A the start of the top-down flow of traffic (1st row), and (2) at the ending stage of the up-down traffic flow (2nd row).

Temporal changes: The first row of Figure 3 shows a frame from the sequence a few seconds after the change of a traffic light, so vehicles and pedestrians are now moving in a different direction, from top to bottom. By comparing the area to notice inside the red circle, it is evident that the streak flow is able to capture this change after only a couple of frames, but the particle flow lags in shaping to the new flow, and the optical flow shows choppy flow segments that are difficult to use for further analysis.

Local changes: Both streak flow and particle flow have the ability to fill in the gaps of the non-dense traffic flow. In second row of Figure 3, the optical flow shows the motion of a car making a left turn. The particle flow is unable to capture this change, and the region on the bus and car both show inconsistency compared to instantaneous flow. The figure shows that the streak flow was more accurate in exhibiting immediate flow changes over the car as well as the bus.

3.2 Potential Functions

Building on the fluid dynamics approach to crowd motion, we employ another concept from fluids providing a different point of view. In simplified mathematical models of fluids, it is often assumed that the fluid is imcompressible, and irrotational. These assumptions imply several conservation properties of the fluid, but most importantly, they lead to potential functions, which are scalar functions that characterize the flow in a unique way. For this discourse, potential functions enable accurate classification of behaviors in a scene, which is not possible with streak flow alone. Application of potential functions to abnormal behavior detection is presented in Sections 4 and 5.

Since the optical flow $\Omega = (u, v)^T$ denotes a planar vector field, the Helmholtz decomposition theorem states that $\Omega = \Omega_c + \Omega_r$, where Ω_c and Ω_r respectively denote the incompressible and irrotational parts of the vector field. To clarify, an incompressible vector field is divergence free $\nabla \cdot \Omega = 0$, and an irrotational vector field is curl free $\nabla \times \Omega = 0$. Thus, there are functions ψ and ϕ, known respectively as the stream function and the velocity potential, satisfying $\Omega_c^\perp = \nabla \psi$ and $\Omega_r = \nabla \phi$ (see, for example [5]). Following [22], we use Fourier transforms to decompose incompressible and irrotational parts of the vector field and estimate the potential functions using

$$\phi(x, y) = \phi_0 + \frac{1}{2} \int_0^x \left(u_r(s, y) + u_r(s, 0) \right) ds + \frac{1}{2} \int_0^y \left(v_r(x, s) + v_r(0, s) \right) ds , \quad (5)$$

$$\psi(x, y) = \psi_0 + \frac{1}{2} \int_0^y \left(u_c(x, s) + u_c(0, s) \right) ds - \frac{1}{2} \int_0^x \left(v_c(s, y) + v_c(s, 0) \right) ds . \quad (6)$$

Potential functions are computed in Corpetti et al. [22] and used in a meteorological application to track weather patterns in satellite images. In order to compute valid potential fields, one needs a dense motion field. In that particular application the motion fields are as dense as possible, but in crowd videos the degree of motion density can vary by large amounts. In addition, a potential function computed directly from optical flow is noisy with many valleys and peaks, which quickly disappear and reappear. Streak flows enable us to compute reliable potential functions for crowd flow, incorporating local and temporal changes. In other words, we incorporate streaklines to compute smoothly evolving potential functions, which better reveal the dynamics of the crowd. In a broad view, the stream function ψ provides the information regarding the steady and non-divergent part of the flow, whereas the velocity potential ϕ contains information regarding the local changes in the non-curling motions. Moreover, to have a complete picture of the flow we need information from both potential functions. With this perspective, we illustrate the strength of potentials in discriminating lanes and divergent/convergent regions in five different scenes in Figure 4. In this figure, the velocity potential is accountable for capturing unsteady changes in the flow. For instance, escape to the sides of the scene corresponds to a valley in the center of ϕ and formation of surrounding peaks on the sides. Furthermore, the stream function ψ is incorporated to detect lanes in the steady motion of vehicles. The area between contours of ψ (i.e. streamlines) show the regions of steady and non-divergent motion such as lanes. The algorithm for detection of lane and divergent/convergent regions is explained in Section 4.

4   Applications of Streaklines

Using streak flow and potential functions, we demonstrate the strength of our approach for crowd segmentation and abnormal behavior detection in unsteady flows. In the end, we find that our method performs better than other methods for solving these problems.

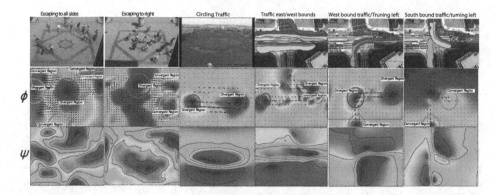

Fig. 4. An illustration of discrimination power of potentials for six manually labelled behaviors. The first two columns, escape panic from UMN Dataset [23], column 3 shows circulating motion of cars in a lane, and column 4 to 6 show traffic forming lanes from NGSIM dataset. Potentials are scaled to maximum value and plotted using jet colormap. (1st row) The lanes are overlaid the frame for the steady motions. (2nd row) divergent regions (red circles) and convergent regions (green circle). (3rd row) Streamlines, which are contours of stream function.

4.1   Crowd Segmentation

In this algorithm, we segment every frame of the video into regions of different motions based on the similarity of the neighboring streaklines. Similar streaklines correspond to similar trajectories of particles passing from neighboring pixels over a period of time. Hence, it captures the affinity of current and previous motions at these pixels. Figure 2.b presents the block diagram of the segmentation algorithm. First, frame by frame optical flow of the video is computed. Using the optical flow, a set of particles are then moved over the frame to construct the streaklines and the streak flow. These quantities are used to compute similarity in a 8-connectivity neighborhood. For every pair of pixels i and j, the similarity is computed in terms of streaklines and streak flow.

Each pixel is associated with a streakline of length l. The streakline similarity is computed using the sum of the normalized projections of internal vectors as $R_s(i,j) = \sum_{m=0}^{l-1} prj(X_m^i, X_m^j)$, where X_m^i and $prj(\cdot, \cdot)$ are defined in Figure 5.a. Streak flow similarity is computed as $R_\Omega(i,j) = |\cos(\angle \Omega_s^i) - \cos(\angle \Omega_s^j)|$, where $\angle \Omega_s^i$ is the angle of the streak flow vector at pixel i. In order to define boundaries of the regions, we compute the similarity map at every pixel using

$$H(i) = \sum_{j \in N(i)} \alpha R_s(i,j) + \beta R_\Omega(i,j) , \qquad (7)$$

where α and β are weights regulating the share of streakline and streak flow similarities in the final segmentation. We use $\alpha = 0.8$ and $\beta = 0.2$ in the experiments. Since similar motions over time build similar streaklines and streak flows, boundaries of different motions form valleys in the similarity map. Using

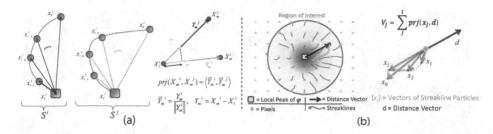

Fig. 5. (a) Streaklines S^i and S^j are sets of vectors $X^i_{1..L}$ and $X^j_{1..L}$. The originating point of streaklines (rectangle), the particles (circles), and the normalized projections of the vectors are used for computing the similarity of streaklines. (b) The computation of divergence factor, V_i, for a region of interest.

the negative of the similarity map, we segment the crowd into regions of similar motion with watershed segmentation. Results are presented in Section 5.1.

Lane detection: In addition to segmenting a frame into regions of consistent motion, we combine information from potentials to detect lanes in each segment. As stated in section 3.2, the area between contours of ψ corresponds to the steady flow, and the rate of the incompressible flow between a pair of contours is equal to the difference between the values of ψ on those contours. Considering this, we detect lanes as parts of a segmented region that fall between two contours of the stream function by a simple intersection operation (see Figure 4).

4.2   Abnormal Behavior Detection

To detect abnormal behavior of crowds, it is necessary to have a global picture of the behavior in a scene, for which we use potential fields. The surfaces ϕ and ψ characterize particle positions and velocities in a global sense, and abnormal behaviors are simply detected as large deviations from the expected. Here, we present an algorithm to detect abnormal behavior in crowds using potential functions for the flow.

Figure 2.c shows the block diagram for the algorithm. For every frame in a video sequence, the Streak flow $\Omega_s = (u_s, v_s)^T$ is computed, and the potential functions of the frame $\{\phi, \psi\}$ are computed using equations (5) and (6). The peaks and valleys of the potential surface convey information regarding the global behavior of the flow (Figure 4). Thus, potentials provide new features to distinguish global behaviors in the crowd in compact form. For every frame, a feature vector V is formed by concatenating the values of ϕ and ψ of that frame. Using feature vector V, we recognize behaviors in each frame by training a support vector machine (SVM) classifier. In Section 5, we provide comparative results of abnormal behavior detection using potentials.

In addition to detecting abnormal behaviors, we incorporate streaklines and the velocity potential ϕ to provide a description of the anomaly based on divergent/convergent regions. The extrema on velocity potentials correspond to

divergent or convergent regions. To robustly detect these regions, we find the major local extrema of ϕ, and then compute the average *divergence factor*, $\bar{V} = \frac{1}{n} \sum_i V_i$, where V_i is defined in Figure 5.b, and n is the number of pixels in the radius r of the extremum point. Simple thresholding of this factor distinguish divergent/convergent regions as $Region\ Type = \begin{cases} Divergent, & \text{if } \bar{V} > T \\ Convergent, & \text{if } \bar{V} < T \end{cases}$.
In the experiments, r is set fixed empirically for each scene and $T = 0$. As it is illustrated in Figure 4 the escape panic scene involves the divergent region in the center and convergent regions on the sides to which the crowd is running. Similarly, a sudden change in the direction of turning vehicles or the entry/exit points form divergent/convergent regions. The circular regions in the second row are the actual output of our algorithm. Obviously, there are some mistakes (20%). For example, in circling traffic, column 3, the region on the right is detected incorrectly.

5   Experimental Results

We present results of algorithms outlined in Section 4, using experiments on two datasets. A stock footage dataset from the web [2] is used for streakline analysis, and a dataset from the University of Minnesota [23], which contains 11 videos of crowd escape panic, is used to evaluate the effectiveness of potentials for abnormal behavior detection.

5.1   Results of Crowd Motion Segmentation

Results of our proposed segmentation algorithm are provided here. We compare with the state of the art [1], considering crowds with dynamic segmentations, such that the motion patterns vary in time exhibiting different states of behavior.

Figure 6 provides segmentation results for two scenes, and video frames are overlaid by colored segmentation regions. In this experiment, the length of streaklines and pathlines is $l = 40$. On the left side of Figure 6, an intersection is shown in Boston, containing three behavioral phases represented by frames 40, 197, and 850. (1) South bound traffic is formed. (2) Traffic lights change and an east/west bound (from/to station) a flow of pedestrians emerges. (3) Traffic lights change again, and a north bound vehicle flow is formed together with an east bound pedestrian flow. On the right side of Figure 6, an intersection is shown in Argentina containing three behavioral phases. (1) East/west bound traffic is formed. (2) After the traffic lights change, a south bound vehicle flow and a north/south pedestrian flow develop. (3) Traffic lights change to the first phase and east/west bound flows resume. Frames 115 and 213 illustrate the start of phases 2 and 3, respectively. The optical flow of this video is particulary noisy as it is based on time-lapse imagery, whereas the Boston sequence is a regular $30 fps$ video. Videos are available in the supplementary material.

Figure 6 demonstrates segmentations based on streaklines are spatially and temporally pronounced and more accurate in dynamic scenes than the state of

Fig. 6. Comparison of segmentation results using streaklines (1st row), and pathlines [1] (2nd row) for scenes with unsteady motions

the art. We highlight the gains in using our method in each frame: (Frame 40) A walking pedestrian and the north bound vehicle motion are segmented correctly. (Frame 197) Pedestrians are distinguished from the south bound cars. (Frame 850) A south bound pedestrian (first row, green) is separated from north bound vehicles. (Frame 115, 4th column) Different pedestrian flows are distinguished (first row, cyan and purple). (Frame 213) West bound vehicle flow (first row, yellow) is segmented earlier, at start of phase 2 of the video.

In Figure 7, the quantitative comparison of the proposed segmentations method and [1] is provided. In this experiment, frame by frame segmentations of both methods are compared as following. The number of objects (human/vehicle) in the each segmented region is counted provided that its direction of motion is no more that 90 degrees apart from the direction motion of the majority of the objects. We refer to this number as the number of correctly segmented objects (see Figure 7.a). To evaluate the methods, this number is counted manually for a subset of frames of Boston and Argentina video sequences. Figure 7 demonstrates that streakline segmentation outperforms the state of the art in number of correctly and incorrectly segmented objects.

5.2   Results of Abnormal Behavior Detection

This section illustrates results for abnormal behavior detection on the UMN dataset [23], containing 11 sequences for 3 scenes. In this dataset, pedestrians initially walk randomly, and exhibit escape panic by running in different directions in the end. Figure 4 shows that potential functions provide rich information about global behavior. Interesting properties of potentials are revealed as we compare ϕ for frames where people escape to all sides to the frames which people run in a single direction (2nd column).

In order to illustrate the strength of potentials in representing the global behavior we compared our method using different features. In *experiment (a)*, we first use frame-based potentials as the input features V for training a SVM with RBF kernels. Second, we use vectorized streak flow $\Omega_s = (u_s, v_s)$ and third, we use average baseline optical flow (pyramidal LK) to perform the same task. Figure 7.e compares the recognition results using any of these three features for a different number of training examples. In order to reduce the computation time, we downsample the features of each frame by factor of $n = 20$. In this experiment,

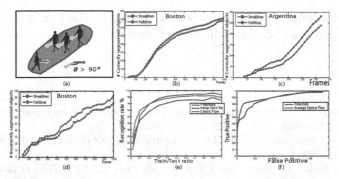

Fig. 7. (a) The criterion for segmentation evaluation, (green) correctly segmented object, (red) incorrectly segmented object. (b), (c), and (d) Quantitative comparison of segmentation results using streaklines (blue), and pathlines [1] (red). (e,f) Abnormal behavior recognition, (e) Variation of the number of training examples. (f) ROC of the cross validation.

the frames from different scenes in the dataset are combined in a single pool and a portion is selected as the train set and the rest is considered as the test set (no overlaps). The figure shows that after increasing the number of examples to merely 20%, the potentials show considerable improvement in performance. In addition, the figure illustrates the strength of streak flows compared to particle flow in providing information for abnormal behavior detection.

In *experiment (b)*, we performed a leave-one-out cross validation on the UMN dataset using downsampled version of potentials and average optical flow. In this experiment, we trained a SVM with RBF kernels on 10 videos and computed the false positive and true positives on one video sequence and repeating this for all the 11 videos. Figure 7.f illustrates the ROC of this experiment which indicates improvement using potentials over baseline optical flow.

6   Conclusion

Based on a Lagrangian particle dynamics framework for fluid flow, we juxtapose three vector field representations of the flow, given by streamlines, pathlines and streaklines. With application to problems in segmentation and abnormal behavior detection for crowd and traffic dynamics, we show that the streakline representation is advantageous. When compared to the other two representations, which are commonly used to solve problems in computer vision, streaklines demonstrated the ability to quickly recognize temporal changes in a sequence, in addition to finding a balance between recognition of local spatial changes and filling spatial gaps in the flow. When used to compute potential functions and to perform segmentation, the streakline approach was superior to using optical flow and comparable to using particle flow, aside from the ability to recognize scene changes. With regard to abnormal behavior detection, the method of streaklines proved superior to both of the other representations, and the introduction of potential functions for this purpose proved valuable.

Acknowledgments. This research was supported by the U.S. Army Research Laboratory and the U.S. Army Research Office under grant number W911NF-09-1-0255.

References

1. Ali, S., Shah, M.: A lagrangian particle dynamics approach for crowd flow segmentation and stability analysis. In: CVPR (2007)
2. Mehran, R., Oyama, A., Shah, M.: Abnormal behavior detection using social force model. In: CVPR (2009)
3. Wijk, V., Jarke, J.: Image based flow visualization. In: SIGGRAPH (2002)
4. Helman, J., Hesselink, L.: Visualizing vector field topology in fluid flows. IEEE Comput. Graph. Appl. 11, 36–46 (1991)
5. Landau, L., Lifshitz, E.: Advanced Mechanics of Fluids (1959)
6. Johnson, N., Hogg, D.: Learning the distribution of object trajectories for event recognition (1995)
7. Marques, J.S., Jorge, P.M., Abrantes, A.J., Lemos, J.M.: Tracking groups of pedestrians in video sequences. In: Proc. CVPRW (2003)
8. Pellegrini, S., Ess, A., Schindler, K., van Gool, L.: You'll never walk alone: Modeling social behavior for multi-target tracking. In: ICCV (2009)
9. Brostow, G., Cipolla, R.: Unsupervised bayesian detection of independent motion in crowds. In: CVPR (2006)
10. Garate, C., Bilinsky, P., Bremond, P.B.: Crowd event recognition using hog tracker (2009)
11. Ke, Y., Sukthankar, R., Hebert, M.: Event detection in crowded videos. In: ICCV (2007)
12. Seemann, E., Fritz, M., Schiele, B.: Towards robust pedestrian detection in crowded image sequences. In: CVPR (2007)
13. Ali, S., Shah, M.: Floor fields for tracking in high density crowd scenes. In: Forsyth, D., Torr, P., Zisserman, A. (eds.) ECCV 2008, Part II. LNCS, vol. 5303, pp. 1–14. Springer, Heidelberg (2008)
14. Saleemi, I., Hartung, L., Shah, M.: Scene understanding by statistical modeling of motion patterns. In: CVPR (2010)
15. Kratz, L., Nishino, K.: Anomaly detection in extremely crowded scenes using spatio-temporal motion pattern models. In: CVPR (2009)
16. Andrade, E.L., Blunsden, S., Fisher, R.B.: Modelling crowd scenes for event detection. In: ICPR (2006)
17. Sand, P., Teller, S.: Particle video: Long-range motion estimation using point trajectories. In: CVPR (2006)
18. Courty, N., Corpetti, T.: Crowd motion capture. Comput. Animat. Virtual Worlds 18, 361–370 (2007)
19. Hughes, R.: The flow of human crowds. Annual Review of Fluid Mechanics 35, 169–182 (2003)
20. Hama, F.R.: Streaklines in a perturbed shear flow. Phys. Fluids 5, 644–650 (1962)
21. Helbing, D., Molnar, P.: Social force model for pedestrian dynamics. Physical Review E 51 (1995)
22. Corpetti, T., Memin, E., Perez, P.: Extraction of singular points from dense motion fields: An analytic approach. Journal of Mathematical Imaging and Vision (2003)
23. University of Minnesota - Crowd Activity Dataset, http://mha.cs.umn.edu/Movies/Crowd-Activity-All.avi

Fast Multi-aspect 2D Human Detection

Tai-Peng Tian and Stan Sclaroff*

Department of Computer Science, Boston University

Abstract. We address the problem of detecting human figures in images, taking into account that the image of the human figure may be taken from a range of viewpoints. We capture the geometric deformations of the 2D human figure using an extension of the Common Factor Model (CFM) of Lan and Huttenlocher. The key contribution of the paper is an improved iterative message passing inference algorithm that runs faster than the original CFM algorithm. This is based on the insight that messages created using the distance transform are shift invariant and therefore messages can be created once and then shifted for subsequent iterations. Since shifting ($O(1)$ complexity) is faster than computing a distance transform ($O(n)$ complexity), a significant speedup is observed in the experiments. We demonstrate the effectiveness of the new model for the human parsing problem using the Iterative Parsing data set and results are competitive with the state of the art detection algorithm of Andriluka, et al.

1 Introduction

We consider the problem of detecting a 2D articulated human figure in a single image. Furthermore, we are interested in recovering the pose of the human figure, where the pose is described by the position and orientation of the legs, arms, torso, and head. This is a difficult problem because the appearance of human figures varies widely due to factors such as clothing, differences in body sizes, articulation of the human body, and viewpoint from which the image is taken. In this paper, we concentrate on modeling the last two factors, i.e., articulation and viewpoint changes.

The prevailing practice is to employ discretization when modeling viewpoint changes and articulations of the human figure. For example, clustering can be used to partition the training data into groups corresponding to different articulation and viewpoint instances [1]. Such an approach is convenient because a simpler single-view or single-configuration model can be used to model the data within each cluster. Unfortunately, there is a price to pay for such a convenience: an additional layer of arbitration logic must be built to coordinate among these models to give an illusion of a multi-aspect and multi-articulation model. This modeling approach is overly complicated and we propose a simpler alternative.

In our approach, we model the geometric deformations of the 2D human figure caused by articulation and viewpoint changes. We separate out these two types of

* This research was funded in part through grant NSF IIS-0713168.

K. Daniilidis, P. Maragos, N. Paragios (Eds.): ECCV 2010, Part III, LNCS 6313, pp. 453–466, 2010.

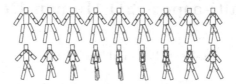

Fig. 1. Fixing the value of the factor for the Common Factor Model (CFM) defines a tree structured Gaussian prior for human poses. Each human pose shown above represents the mean of each distribution for the corresponding value of the factor. In the top row, by varying the factor, the human poses changes from a frontal configuration (leftmost) to a side view (rightmost) configuration. The bottom row depicts the swing of the arms and legs during walking.

deformation into two different modes of variation. These modes can be modeled by a simple extension of the Common Factor Model (CFM) [2] and these modes can be learned using a straightforward training procedure without the need to partition the data into different viewpoints. A concise review of the CFM is given in Sec. 3.

Varying a common factor has the effect of inducing a particular deformation mode in the Pictorial Structure. An intuition for this is given for the human figure model in Fig. 1. If we fix the pose of the human figure and vary the viewpoint by moving along the equator of the view sphere centered on the human figure, then the projected body parts will be translated as the viewpoint changes. Similar observations can be made when a person is walking (viewpoint is kept fixed), which results in rotation and translation of the parts of the Pictorial Structure. This second mode of variation coordinates geometric transformations between body parts; e.g., during a walking cycle the left arm swings forward as the right arm swings backward. Thus, the model of a walking person can be described using a combination of the "walking phase" and "viewpoint" modes. This idea of associating modes of variation with geometric deformations of the Pictorial Structure is general; for example, it is applicable to other types of motion such as a person performing jumping jacks, kicking etc.

Even though CFM inference has linear time complexity, it is still time consuming – especially when the problem size is large, as is the case here. The CFM inference algorithm requires multiple iterations of the min-sum Belief Propagation (BP) algorithm. During each iteration of BP, messages are created from scratch and this is costly because each message contains more than a million entries. Overall, for s iterations of the BP algorithm, there will be $s(n-1)$ messages created for a Pictorial Structure model with n parts.

We propose a new CFM inference algorithm that offers a significant speedup. We reduce the number of messages that need to be created from $s(n-1)$ to $(n-1)$ (a reduction by a factor of s). This speed improvement is significant because the number of BP iterations s scales exponentially in the number of dimensions of the common factor. This speedup relies on two observations: firstly, messages are created using distance transforms and secondly, messages from one iteration of BP to the next differ only by a shift. Since distance transforms are shift invariant (see proof in Sec 4.1), our method replaces costly distance transforms by shifts, thus gaining a speed improvement over the original formulation. Note that shifting an array only requires an $O(1)$ update to the offset of the array while the distance transform is an $O(h)$ operation that requires visiting all the h elements in the array. Details of the algorithm can be found in Sec. 4.

We provide experimental evaluation of our multi-aspect model in Sec. 6. We show experimental results comparing the speed of our new inference algorithm with the original [2] and evaluate the accuracy of our model on the Iterative Parsing data set [3].

Contribution. The contribution of this paper is twofold. Firstly, we provide a method for modeling multiple modes of deformation in a Pictorial Structure model. Secondly, we improve the running time of the original CFM inference algorithm by observing that messages created by distance transforms are shift invariant. Replacing costly $O(h)$ time complexity distance transforms with fast $O(1)$ time complexity shifting yields a significant speed up.

2   Related Work

Our work is related to the use of Pictorial Structures for detecting human figures using tree structured Gaussian graphical models [3–6], as well as loopy graphical model [7–10]. Our work is different from these related work as we focus on modeling geometric deformation of the Pictorial Structures due to factors such as viewpoint changes and phase of the walking cycle.

Our work builds on the Common Factor Model (CFM) [2]. Originally in [2], a 1D latent variable (or factor) is used to model the phase of a walking cycle, and it is used to capture correlations among the upper limbs of the human figure. We provide a new perspective on the CFM by interpreting the dimensions of the factor as modes of geometric deformation in the Pictorial Structure.

Unfortunately, using higher dimensional latent variables increases the CFM inference running time, e.g., if uniformly sampling the 1D factor requires n samples then in 2D it will require n^2 samples. This slows down the CFM inference significantly because multiple distance transforms are required in each iteration of the inference algorithm. We propose a faster CFM inference that only requires a constant number of distance transforms to be computed, i.e., independent of the number of iterations in the CFM inference.

Other multi-aspect modeling works [1, 11, 12] use a discrete set of viewpoints. In contrast, our work uses a continuously parameterized viewpoint.

3   Background: The Common Factor Model

In this section, we review the Common Factor Model (CFM) of [2]. The CFM provides an alternative to high order clique models. Such high order clique models arise in 2D human detection because strong correlations exist among the

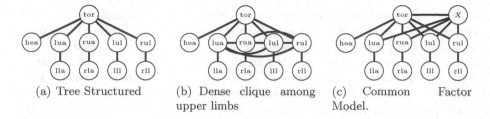

(a) Tree Structured   (b) Dense clique among   (c)   Common   Factor
                              upper limbs   Model.

Fig. 2. Different type of priors used for the ten part human figure. Abbreviations are *tor* : torso, *hea*: head, *lua* : left upper arm, *rll* : right lower leg, etc.

upper arms and upper legs when a person is walking [2]. These dependencies create a large clique among the upper limbs of the graphical model (Fig. 2(b)) and inference over graphical models with large cliques is computationally intensive. The computational difficulty can be ameliorated by breaking up the large clique into smaller cliques. This breaking up is justified by positing that a latent variable X is responsible for the observed correlations among the upper limbs (Fig. 2(c)). More importantly, when the latent variable X is observed, i.e., conditioned on X, then the graphical model becomes a tree again. The latent variable X can be viewed as a hyper parameter and fixing a value for this hyper parameter will produce the tree structured Gaussian prior in Fig. 2(a), but parameters for this tree structured prior will be different for two distinct values of X.

The detection problem is stated as finding the latent variable value X^* and body parts locations L^* that maximize the posterior, i.e.,

$$\langle L^*, X^* \rangle = \arg\max_{L,X} p(L, X|I) = \arg\max_{L,X} p(I|L, X)\, p(L, X), \qquad (1)$$

where I is the image, $L = \{l_i\}$ and i are body part names corresponding to nodes shown in Fig 2(a). Each body part configuration l_i is described by an oriented rectangle comprising the center of the rectangle (u, v) and its orientation θ.

The CFM takes on the following factorization

$$p(I|L, X)p(L, X) = p(I|L, X)p(L|X)p(X)$$

$$\propto \underbrace{\prod_{i \in V} p(I|l_i)}_{\text{likelihood}} \left(\underbrace{\prod_{e_{ij} \in E_X} \phi_{ij}(l_i, l_j, X) \prod_{e_{ij} \in E_T - E_X} \phi_{ij}(l_i, l_j)}_{\text{prior}} \right) p(X),$$

where the likelihood is independent of the latent variable X and the CFM assumes that image appearances among body parts l_i are independent. In the above equation, V is an index set for the body parts of the 2D human model, which corresponds to the set of vertices shown in Fig. 2(a). The set of edges E_T is shown in Fig. 2(a), and E_X is a subset of E_T. Edges from E_X have both end vertices forming a clique with the latent variable X in Fig. 2(c). The prior is factorized according to the graphical model in Fig 2(c), and parameters for the common factor X are learned from data [2]. The compatibility function ϕ_{ij}

between two body parts is defined based on the distance Y_{ij} between the joint locations $T_{ij}(l_i)$ and $T_{ji}(l_j)$, i.e.,

$$Y_{ij} = T_{ij}(l_i) - T_{ji}(l_j). \tag{2}$$

The transformation T_{ij} shifts the body part center to the joint position, i.e.,

$$T_{ij}(l_i) = T_{ij}([u, v, \theta]^T) = [u', v', \theta]^T, \quad \text{where} \quad \begin{bmatrix} u' \\ v' \end{bmatrix} = \begin{bmatrix} u \\ v \end{bmatrix} + R_\theta \begin{bmatrix} u_{ij} \\ v_{ij} \end{bmatrix}. \tag{3}$$

In the above equation, R_θ is the rotation matrix by θ angle, u_{ij} and v_{ij} are connection parameters that are learned from a tree structured prior [5]. The definition for the transformation T_{ji} is similar to T_{ij} and details are given in [5]. For edges that are not involved with the common factor, the compatibility function is given by

$$\phi_{ij}(l_i, l_j) = N(Y_{ij}; 0, \Sigma_{ij}), \tag{4}$$

where Σ_{ij} is a diagonal matrix learned from data [5], and N is the Gaussian function. For edges that are involved with the common factor X, the potential function is given as

$$\phi_{ij}(l_i, l_j, X) = N(Y_{ij} - A_j X; 0, \Psi_j), \tag{5}$$

where A_j is part of the loading matrix A learned from data. Both of these are defined in the next paragraph.

Learning the Loading Matrix A: In order to learn the loading matrix A, the training data for the four body parts $l_{lua}, l_{rua}, l_{lul}, l_{rul}$ are stacked up into a 12 dimensional vector. Suppose there are m training instances, then a $12 \times m$ matrix is formed and Common Factor Analysis is applied on this matrix to recover the loading matrix A and covariance matrix Ψ. If the dimension of the common factor X is two, then the resulting loading matrix A will have dimension 12×2, and the covariance matrix Ψ will be a 12×12 matrix. Therefore, A_{lul} denotes the corresponding 3×2 sub matrix of A whose rows correspond to the stacking order for the body part left upper leg (lul). The covariance sub-matrix Ψ_{lul} will be a 3×3 square matrix that includes the diagonal entries of Ψ whose rows correspond to the stacking order for lul.

3.1 Messages and Dynamic Programming in the CFM

In this section, we review the message passing algorithm applied on the tree structured model generated by the Common Factor Model (CFM). In the CFM inference, the goal is to find the best body part location L^* and common factor X^* that maximize the posterior $p(L, X|I)$. This is equivalent to minimizing the negative log posterior, which is

$$\langle L^*, X^* \rangle = \arg\min_{L,X} c(X) + \sum_{i \in V} m_i(l_i) + \sum_{ij \in E_T - E_X} d_{ij}(l_i, l_j) + \sum_{ij \in E_X} d_{ij}(l_i, l_j, X),$$

$$\tag{6}$$

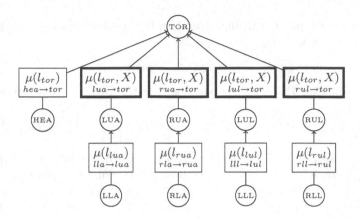

Fig. 3. The boxes show the messages passed during an iteration of the Belief Propagation algorithm for a fixed value of the common factor X. Bold boxes indicate messages parameterized by the common factor X.

where $c(\cdot)$ is the negative log of the prior $p(X)$, $m_i(\cdot)$ is the negative log of the likelihood, and $d_{ij}(\cdot)$ is the negative log of the compatibility function.

Given a fixed value X for the common factor, the resulting graphical model is a tree. Therefore, dynamic programming can be used to find the MAP solution. The dynamic programming proceeds from leaves to the root and intermediate results from the dynamic programming can be interpreted as messages being passed from leaves up to the root. These messages can be efficiently computed via the distance transform [5]. The types of messages passed between a child node j and its parent parent i are

$$
\mu_{j \to i}(l_i) = \begin{cases}
\mathcal{T}_{ij}^{-1} \mathcal{D} \mathcal{T}_{ji}[m_j](l_i), & \text{if } j \text{ is a leaf node,} \\[2mm]
\mathcal{T}_{ij}^{-1} \mathcal{D} \mathcal{T}_{ji} \left[m_j + \sum_{c \in C_j} \mu_{c \to j} \right](l_i), & \text{if } j \text{ is an internal node with children } C_j, \\[2mm]
\mathcal{T}_{ij}^{-1} \mathcal{D} \mathcal{T}_{A_j X} \mathcal{T}_{ji} \left[m_j + \sum_{c \in C_j} \mu_{c \to j} \right](l_i), & \text{if } j \text{ is an internal node with children } C_j \\
& \text{and common factor } X,
\end{cases}
\tag{7}
$$

where $\mathcal{T}_{ij}$ and $\mathcal{T}_{ji}$ are operators that bring the coordinates of body parts into ideal alignment at the joint, $\mathcal{T}_{A_j X}$ is the translation induced by the common factor X, and $\mathcal{D}$ is the distance transform operator. All of these are defined as

$$
\mathcal{T}_{ij}^{-1}[f](l_j) = f(T_{ij}^{-1}(l_j)), \qquad \mathcal{T}_{ji}[f](l_j) = f(T_{ji}(l_i)), \tag{8}
$$
$$
\mathcal{T}_{x_j}[f](l_j) = f(l_j - A_j X_j), \qquad \mathcal{D}[f](l_j) = \min_{l_i \in \mathcal{G}} f(l_i) + \|l_i - l_j\|^2,
$$

where $\mathcal{G}$ represents grid positions on which the function f is sampled. Note the notational difference between $\mathcal{T}_{ij}$ (in calligraphic script) and T_{ij} (in regular font); they are conceptually different as the operator $\mathcal{T}_{ij}$ transforms one function into another, whereas the function T_{ij} transforms coordinates. Lastly, the operators are applied from right to left, i.e., for the chain of operations, $\mathcal{T}_{ij}^{-1}\mathcal{T}_{A_jX}D\mathcal{T}_{ji}[f]$, the operator $\mathcal{T}_{ji}$ is applied first, followed by D, $\mathcal{T}_{A_jX}$ and $\mathcal{T}_{ij}^{-1}$.

These messages are depicted in Fig. 3. At the root node, the messages are combined, and the best configuration for the root is

$$l_{tor}^* = \min_{l_{tor}} \left(m_{tor}(l_{tor}) + \sum_{c \in C_{tor}} \mu_{c \to tor}(l_{tor}) \right). \tag{9}$$

Once the best solution for the root is found, the algorithm backtracks down the tree to recover the corresponding values for other body parts.

4   Faster Inference for the Common Factor Model

We propose a method that speeds up the inference algorithm of Lan and Huttenlocher [2]. First we briefly review the inference algorithm of Lan and Huttenlocher. During inference, values are sampled from the latent variable X and for each sample value, an iteration of dynamic programming (DP) is performed. For each DP iteration, the messages are created from scratch by applying distance transforms [5]. Overall, the number of distance transforms required scales linearly with the sample size of the common factor, i.e., $s(n-1)$ distance transforms are required, where s is the sample size for the common factor X and n is the number of body parts.

We propose a method that reduces the number of distance transforms required. Our method only requires computing $n-1$ distance transforms, i.e., independent of the number of samples size s for X. This is a significant speedup because s scales exponentially in the dimension of the of the common factor X. This speedup is possible because varying the values of X has the effect of shifting the messages, and secondly, distance transforms are shift invariant. Therefore, new messages can be created by simply shifting the previous messages. Computationally, shifting is more efficient than DT because shifting has $O(1)$ time complexity (where we only need to update the offset for the array), compared to $O(h)$ time complexity for DT, where the algorithm has to visit all the h entries in the array (typically, $h \sim 10^6$ for the examples we are testing on).

The next section gives the proof for shift invariance of distance transforms and following that, we describe the inference algorithm.

4.1   Distance Transforms Are Shift Invariant

We prove that the distance transform of a sampled function is shift-invariant under some fairly mild conditions that are usually satisfied in practice. Let $\mathcal{D}$ be the distance transform operator, where

$$\mathcal{D}[f](p) = \min_{q \in \mathcal{G}} f(q) + ||p - q||^2, \tag{10}$$

and p is a position in the grid $\mathcal{G}$ for sampling the function f. The operator $\mathcal{T}_r$ translates a function f by r, that is,

$$\mathcal{T}_r[f](p) = f(p + r). \tag{11}$$

Proposition 1. *Suppose f is a function sampled on the grid $\mathcal{G}$. For any given position $p \in \mathcal{G}$ and a fixed translation r, such that $f(p) = \infty$ if $p \notin \mathcal{G}$, then $\mathcal{DT}_r[f](p) = \mathcal{T}_r\mathcal{D}[f](p)$.*

Proof. Starting from LHS,

$$\mathcal{DT}_r[f](p) = \mathcal{D}[g](p) \qquad (\text{where } g(x) \equiv f(x + r)) \tag{12}$$
$$= \min_{v \in \mathcal{G}} g(v) + ||p - v||^2 \tag{13}$$
$$= \min_{v \in \mathcal{G}} f(v + r) + ||p - v||^2 \tag{14}$$
$$= \min_{(q-r) \in \mathcal{G}} f(q) + ||p + r - q||^2. \qquad (q = v + r) \tag{15}$$

On the RHS,

$$\mathcal{T}_r\mathcal{D}[f](p) = \mathcal{T}_r[h](p) \qquad \text{where } h(p) \equiv \min_{h \in \mathcal{G}} f(q) + ||p - q||^2 \tag{16}$$
$$= h(p + r) \tag{17}$$
$$= \min_{q \in \mathcal{G}} f(q) + ||p + r - q||^2. \tag{18}$$

Therefore, the operator $\mathcal{D}$ commutes with the operator $\mathcal{T}_r$. $\qquad\square$

4.2   Faster Inference

We describe how to exploit the shift invariance property of the distance transform to speed up the inference algorithm. Within different iterations of the inference algorithm, messages originating from the leaves do not change (Fig. 3); only messages affected by the common factor X are recomputed. Those messages affected by the common factor are recomputed using the chain of operators $\mathcal{T}_{ij}^{-1}\mathcal{DT}_{x_j}\mathcal{T}_{ji}$. Notice that the distance transform operator $\mathcal{D}$ is applied *after* the translation operator $\mathcal{T}_{x_j}$; therefore, based on this chain of operations, when the common factor X changes, a distance transform operation is required to compute the new message. Since the distance transform is shift invariant, we can rewrite the messages involving the common factor X as

$$\mu_{j \to i}(l_i) = \mathcal{T}_{ij}^{-1}\mathcal{T}_{x_j}\mathcal{DT}_{ji}[f](l_i), \qquad \text{where } f = m_j + \sum_{c \in C_j} \mu_{c \to j}, \tag{19}$$

where the positions of the operators $\mathcal{D}$ and $\mathcal{T}_{x_j}$ are swapped, i.e., the operator $\mathcal{D}$ has been pushed inwards to the right. Conceptually, this means that we can memoize the result of $\mathcal{DT}_{ji}[f]$ as this does not vary with the common factor X, and for varying X, we only need to apply the operator $\mathcal{T}_{ij}^{-1}\mathcal{T}_{x_j}$ to the memoized

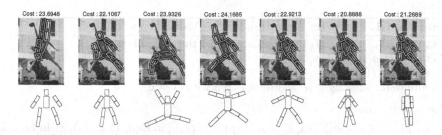

Fig. 4. Human pose prior affects the detection results. **Row 1** shows the optimal pose detected. **Row 2** shows the mean of the tree structured Gaussian prior for the human pose. Notice that the most visually appealing solution (center image) does not correspond to the configuration with the lowest cost.

$\mathcal{DT}_{ji}[f]$. Computationally, this translates to substantial savings because for each new message to be created, we only require the translation operator $\mathcal{T}_{ij}^{-1}\mathcal{T}_{x_j}$. Overall, only $n-1$ distance transformed messages need to be computed, for n body parts, compared to $s(n-1)$ originally, where s is the number of samples for the common factor X.

5   Detection Using the Multi-aspect Model

Computing the the maximum *a posteriori* (MAP) estimate or, equivalently, finding the lowest cost configuration does not necessarily give the most visually correct solution (see the example in Fig. 4). We remedy this problem using a "sample and test" strategy [5, 13]. First, we sample a set of values for the factors of the CFM and recover the corresponding set of detection results. Following that, detection results are re-evaluated using additional constraints. We summarize the detection algorithm in Algorithm. 1. The following constraints are used to re-score the detection results.

1. **Appearance Symmetry:** Humans typically wear clothing that is symmetric and we penalize detection results with dissimilar appearance between the upper arms and upper legs of the Pictorial Structure. Dissimilarity of appearance between two body parts is described using the distance between the two Region Covariance (RC) descriptors [14]. The RC descriptor for a body part is a 5×5 symmetric matrix and involves entries for spatial positions (x, y) and the three color channels of the image (r, g, b). The distance ρ_1 between two RC descriptors C_1 and C_2 is given as

$$\rho_1(C_1, C_2) = \gamma \sqrt{\sum_{i=1}^{5} \lambda_i(C_1, C_2)}, \qquad (20)$$

where $\{\lambda_i(C_1, C_2)\}_{i=1...5}$ are the generalized eigenvalues of C_1 and C_2, and γ is a scaling factor chosen empirically to be 0.1.

Algorithm 1. Detection Algorithm for the Multi-Aspect Model

Let $\mathcal{X} = \{X_1, X_2, \ldots, X_k\}$ be the samples for the common factor.
Let $C = \{lua, rua, lul, rul\}$.
Let $pairs = \{(lua, rua), (lul, rul)\}$
Compute the messages $\underset{j \to i}{\mu}$ shown in Fig. 3 with $X = 0$.

for $k = 1 \ldots s$ **do**

$$\underset{tor}{\mu'}(p) = \underset{hea \to tor}{\mu}(p) + \sum_{i \in C} T_{\mathbf{A_i X_i}} \left[\underset{i \to tor}{\mu} \right](p) \qquad (T_{\mathbf{r}}[\cdot] \text{ in Eqn. 11 and } A_i X_i \text{ in Eqn. 5})$$

$$p^* = \arg \min \underset{tor}{\mu'}(p)$$

$$score(k) = \underset{tor}{\mu'}(p^*) + \sum_{ij \in pairs} \rho_1(l_i, l_j) + \sum_{ij \in pairs} \rho_2(l_i, l_j) \qquad (\rho_1, \rho_2 \text{ Eqn. 20,21})$$

end for

$bestscore = \min score(k)$
To recover the pose with the best score, perform a backtracking on the corresponding messages (similar to backtracking for dynamic programming [5]).

---

2. **Overlapping Bodyparts:** Tree structured Pictorial Structures are prone to the "over counting of evidence" problem, e.g., the legs typically snap onto the same region in the image. We can ameliorate this problem by adding a penalty term

$$\rho_2(l_i, l_j) = \frac{|R(l_i) \cap R(l_j)|}{\min(|R(l_i)|, |R(l_j)|)} \tag{21}$$

for overlapping body parts, where l_i and l_j are the configurations of body parts i and j, $R(\cdot)$ denotes the rectangular region in the image covered by the configuration of a body part and $|\cdot|$ denotes the area. The overlap area is computed by first clipping the rectangle $R(l_i)$ against $R(l_j)$ using the Sutherland Hodgman clipping algorithm and the resulting polygon gives the overlapping region. The overlap area is scaled to the range $[0, 1]$ by dividing it by the smaller body part's area.

6   Experiments

We use the Iterative Parsing (IP) data set [3] for all the experiments. This challenging data set contains a large variety of human figures in difficult poses such as baseball pitchers, sumo wrestlers, etc. The Pictorial Structure parameters are learned from data following [5]. For the body parts detector, we use the code from [4]. All coding is done in Matlab and the computationally intensive functions such as distance transforms are implemented in mex code.

For the common factor, we learned a two-dimensional common factor from the training set in the IP data set. We were able to obtain the viewpoint effect, i.e., varying the first common factor adjusts the joint position between the upper arms / legs to be closer or further apart, giving the effect of a viewpoint change from side view to front view (see Fig. 1). Unfortunately, the training data does not contain sufficient variations in the swing of the arms and legs to learn a

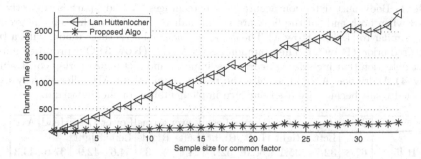

Fig. 5. Comparing the running time for Lan and Huttenlocher's [2] inference algorithm with the proposed algorithm for various sample sizes for the common factor. Both algorithms have linear running time curves but the proposed algorithm is faster, e.g., six times speedup for 10 samples, eight times speedup for 20 samples and nine times speedup for 35 samples. The speedup continues to grow for increasing sample sizes.

common factor for that effect; in contrast, [2] uses primarily walking sequences as training data and is able to capture the arm swing effect in the common factor. As a substitute, the following loading matrix is used in all the the experiments,

$$A = \left[\underset{tor,lua}{A}, \underset{tor,rua}{A} \underset{tor,lul}{A}, \underset{tor,rul}{A} \right]^T,$$ (22)

where

$$\underset{tor,lua}{A} = \begin{bmatrix} 0 & -1 & 0 \\ 0 & 0 & 1 \end{bmatrix}, \underset{tor,rua}{A} = \begin{bmatrix} 0 & 1 & 0 \\ 0 & 0 & -1 \end{bmatrix}, \underset{tor,lul}{A} = \begin{bmatrix} 0 & -1 & 0 \\ 0 & 0 & 0.5 \end{bmatrix}, \underset{tor,rul}{A} = \begin{bmatrix} 0 & 1 & 0 \\ 0 & 0 & -0.5 \end{bmatrix}.$$

For each sub matrix, the three columns are ordered according to (u, v, θ), where (u, v) is the spatial location and θ is the rotation angle. The loading matrices above can be considered as idealized versions of those learned from the IP data set, as well as the the loading matrix published in [2].

Speed Comparison. We compare the running time of the proposed algorithm against [2]. We fix the image (size 454×353) and vary the number of samples for the common factor. The plot of running times versus varying samples for the common factor is shown in Fig. 5. Asymptotically, both algorithms have linear time complexity, but empirically, the proposed algorithm runs significantly faster in practice. For example, when using 10 samples, we observe a six fold speedup (120 seconds vs. 743 seconds). The speed gap between the two algorithms continues to widen as the number of samples is increased, e.g., at 20 samples we observe an eight-fold speedup, and at 35 samples there is a nine-fold speedup. This linear increase in speedup trend is true for increasing number of samples.

Accuracy of Parts Localization. We compare the accuracy of localizing body parts for our algorithm against three state of the art algorithms: the standard PS model [5], the Common Factor Model [2] and the work of Andriluka, et al. [4].

Table 1. Body part detection accuracy in percentages. A body part is correctly localized when both ends of the limb are within half the part's length from the ground truth (similar to [4, 6]). (**Row 1**) The standard pictorial structures model with a tree structured prior. (**Row 2**) The Common Factor Model. (**Row 3**) Our proposed multi-aspect detection that includes appearance symmetry and rectangle overlap constraints. (**Row 4**) Andriluka (AN), et al. [4]. The results obtained for AN differ slightly from published result because we used our own implementation of the algorithm.

	Torso	Upper Arms		Upper Legs		Lower Arms		Lower Legs		Head	Avg
		Left	Right	Left	Right	Left	Right	Left	Right		
FH [5]	67.8	32.7	35.1	58.0	52.7	24.4	27.3	54.6	42.9	37.6	43.3
CFM [2]	78.5	41.0	42.0	63.9	59.5	30.2	28.3	62.4	46.8	53.7	50.6
Our work	**80.0**	41.0	41.0	**65.9**	**62.4**	31.2	30.0	**62.4**	**47.8**	54.1	51.6
AN [4]	79.0	**45.9**	**47.8**	65.4	59.0	**33.7**	**34.1**	61.4	47.3	**57.6**	**53.1**

In the experiments, the Common Factor Model and our multi-aspect model use the same parameter for the prior. Samples are drawn from the 2D common factor X as follows. First, we sample the first dimension (controlling the aspect) while keeping the other dimension fixed and values are sampled in the range $[-22, 15]$ at increments of 1.5 resulting in 26 samples. Next, we sample the other dimension that coordinates the swinging of the arms and legs while keeping the first dimension fixed. Values are sampled in the range $[\frac{-18\pi}{17}, \frac{13\pi}{17}]$ in increments of $\frac{\pi}{17}$ resulting in 26 samples. Overall, there are 52 samples chosen for the common factor X. We have found that uniformly sampling the 2D grid to generate 26^2 samples is excessive for the walking human figure model; e.g., from a front view, deformation of the Pictorial Structure due to walking is small. In contrast, these deformations are more prominent from a side view. Therefore, we concentrate on capturing prominent deformations in our sampling.

The Common Factor Model picks the maximum *a posteriori* solution over these 52 samples, but our multi-aspect model re-scores the solution using the ρ_1 and ρ_2 (Sec. 5), and picks the solution with the minimum cost. The localization results are summarized in Table 1. A part is classified as correctly localized when both endpoints of that body part are within 50% of the length of the body part (similar to [4, 6]).

Our approach (Row 3, Table 1) yields better localization results when compared with the standard Pictorial Structures (Row 1 FH) for all the body parts. The best improvement is in the localization of the left upper leg, which shows an increase in correct detections of 13.9%. This is because the standard Pictorial Structure uses a tree structured Gaussian prior that is biased towards a frontal view, and it is prone to the "over counting of evidence" problem.

When compared against the Common Factor Model (Row 2, Table 1), our results (Row 3, Table 1) show an improvement in correct detection that averages about 2% across all the body parts. The difference between the two algorithms is in the inference step. CFM uses the MAP solution, but we re-score the solutions using additional constraints therefore improvements in the detection results are attributed to the re-scoring step. Qualitative examples are shown in Fig. 6.

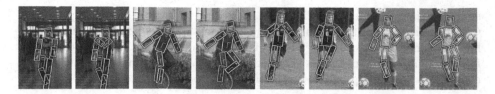

Fig. 6. Examples where incorporating appearance symmetry and rectangle overlap constraints improve detection results. In each pair of image the **left image** shows the detection result using the Common Factor Model [2] and the **right image** shows the detection result obtained using our multi-aspect model. For example, in the first pair of images, the person's left arm is across the chest and this is correctly detected by our method.

Fig. 7. Examples of the "scattered body parts" problem present in Andriluka, et al.'s [4] detection method. In each pair of image the **left image** shows the detection result using Andriluka, et al.'s method and the **right image** shows the detection result obtained using our multi-aspect model.

We have mixed results when comparing with Andriluka (AN), et al. [4] (Row 4, Table 1). AN has better results for localizing upper and lower arms while we have better results for localizing upper and lower legs. We found that AN's approach suffers from the "scattered body parts" problem, which arises because AN's inference algorithm maximizes the marginal posterior and spatial constraints between body parts are not strictly enforced. This results in solutions where body parts are not tightly grouped together. We show more of these examples in Fig. 7. Our detection results do not suffer from this problem.

7 Conclusion

We have presented a multi-aspect model that is capable of capturing the effects of viewpoint changes in Pictorial Structures using an extension of the Common Factor Model (CFM). We also proposed a two stage algorithm that rescores CFM solutions using additional constraints and this method is shown to be effective in the experiments. Furthermore, we demonstrate how to exploit the shift invariance property of distance transforms to provide a speedup for the CFM inference algorithm; consequently, we can sample a larger set of samples for the common factor during CFM inference. Sampling a larger set of samples for the common factor enables testing of more views during inference, which contributes to the improved detection results in our experiments.

References

1. Seemann, E., Leibe, B., Schiele, B.: Multi-aspect detection of articulated objects. In: Proc. CVPR (2006)
2. Lan, X., Huttenlocher, D.P.: Beyond trees: Common-factor models for 2D human pose recovery. In: Proc. ICCV (2005)
3. Ramanan, D.: Learning to parse images of articulated objects. In: Proc. NIPS (2006)
4. Andriluka, M., Roth, S., Schiele, B.: Pictorial structures revisited: People detection and articulated pose estimation. In: Proc. CVPR (2009)
5. Felzenszwalb, P.F., Huttenlocher, D.P.: Pictorial structures for object recognition. IJCV 61, 55–79 (2005)
6. Ferrari, V., Marin-Jimenez, M., Zisserman, A.: Progressive search space reduction for human pose estimation. In: Proc. CVPR (2008)
7. Ren, X., Berg, A.C., Malik, J.: Recovering human body configurations using pairwise constraints between parts. In: Proc. ICCV (2005)
8. Jiang, H., Martin, D.R.: Global pose estimation using non-tree models. In: Proc. CVPR (2008)
9. Crandall, D., Felzenszwalb, P., Huttenlocher, D.: Spatial priors for part-based recognition using statistical models. In: Proc. CVPR (2005)
10. Bergtholdt, M., Kappes, J., Schmidt, S., Schnorr, C.: A study of part-based object class detection using complete graphs. IJCV 28, 416–431 (2009)
11. Kumar, M.P., Koller, D.: Learning a small mixture of trees. In: Proc. NIPS (2009)
12. Lan, X., Huttenlocher, D.: A unified spatio-temporal articulated model for tracking. In: Proc. CVPR (2004)
13. Buehler, P., Everingham, M., Huttenlocher, D.P., Zisserman, A.: Long term arm and hand tracking for continuous sign language TV broadcasts. In: Proc. BMVC (2008)
14. Tuzel, O., Porikli, F., Meer, P.: Region covariance: A fast descriptor for detection and classification. In: Leonardis, A., Bischof, H., Pinz, A. (eds.) ECCV 2006. LNCS, vol. 3952, pp. 589–600. Springer, Heidelberg (2006)

Deterministic 3D Human Pose Estimation Using Rigid Structure

Jack Valmadre[1] and Simon Lucey[2]

[1] University of Queensland, Australia
[2] Commonwealth Scientific and Industrial Research Organisation (CSIRO), Australia
jack.valmadre@gmail.com, simon.lucey@csiro.au

Abstract. This paper explores a method, first proposed by Wei and Chai [1], for estimating 3D human pose from several frames of uncalibrated 2D point correspondences containing projected body joint locations. In their work Wei and Chai boldly claimed that, through the introduction of rigid constraints to the torso and hip, camera scales, bone lengths and absolute depths could be estimated from a finite number of frames (i.e. ≥ 5). In this paper we show this claim to be false, demonstrating in principle one can never estimate these parameters in a finite number of frames. Further, we demonstrate their approach is only valid for rigid sub-structures of the body (e.g. torso). Based on this analysis we propose a novel approach using deterministic structure from motion based on assumptions of rigidity in the body's torso. Our approach provides notably more accurate estimates and is substantially faster than Wei and Chai's approach, and unlike the original, can be solved as a deterministic least-squares problem.

Keywords: Human pose estimation, Structure from motion.

1 Introduction

The task of estimating 3D non-rigid structure from a small number of 2D point correspondences is, in general, an inherently ill posed problem. Recently, Wei and Chai [1] proposed an approach for solving the non-rigid structure from motion problem specifically for bodies. Their approach took advantage of assumed, and empirically validated, rigid constraints in the human body's torso and hip. Their approach is notable in comparison to previous literature [2,3,4,5] in the area as it: (i) makes no assumptions about bone lengths or camera scale, (ii) is not limited/constrained to modeling shapes previously seen in a train set, and (iii) can handle missing body points.

In [1] Wei and Chai claim their approach requires a minimum of five frames with 2D point correspondences (under a weak perspective assumption) for a 17 bone body containing 4 rigid triangles and 7 symmetry constraints, from which they can then estimate bone lengths, camera scale, and articulated pose. Their argument is made elegantly under the assumption that if one wants to reconstruct all unknowns without any ambiguity, one needs at least the same number of constraints. The authors claim that the introduction of rigid constraints

K. Daniilidis, P. Maragos, N. Paragios (Eds.): ECCV 2010, Part III, LNCS 6313, pp. 467–480, 2010.

a finite number of frames (i.e. ≥ 5) balances the number of unknowns with constraints. In this paper we demonstrate that this, rather strong assumption, is false. This dilemma forms the central thesis of our paper. The contributions of our paper are as follows:-

- We demonstrate that Wei and Chai's approach is only valid for rigid substructures of the human body (e.g. torso) rather than the entire body's non-rigid structure. We further demonstrate that the assumption that this approach was valid for non-rigid bodies led to the false claim that camera scales, bone lengths and absolute depths can be solved in minimum of 5 frames for a 17 bone body model. (Section 4)
- A fast and deterministic solution to the problem of estimating camera scale and bone lengths for the body's rigid torso is proposed. This solution differs substantially to the approach employed in [1] which attempted to solve a quartic objective function. Unlike our fast deterministic approach based on canonical rigid structure from motion [6], the method of Wei and Chai requires a slow non-linear optimizer with a number of heuristics needing to be chosen to estimate a satisfactory answer. Our approach also exhibits superior empirical performance to [1]. Further, our approach solves for the full 3D structure of the torso up to a reflection, whereas [1] has inherent ambiguity with respect to the sign of each bone depth. (Section 5)
- A remaining problem now exists, however, with respect to estimating the bone lengths and joint angles of the residual non-rigid structures of the body (e.g, arms, legs, etc.). For this task, we propose an elegant approach based on: (i) making an assumption that all non-rigid bones (taking into account symmetry) will be parallel to the image plane in at least one frame, and (ii) using prior statistics on allowable human joint angles. (Section 6)

The most important contribution, however, of our work is to highlight where assumptions of rigidity help, during 3D human pose estimation, and where they do not. First, our work demonstrates the absolute importance of the accurate labeling of the 4 rigid points on the body's torso. Without these accurate labels it is impossible to estimate camera scale and therefore the lengths of any of the other non-rigid bones. Second, we demonstrate that, with the exception of camera scale, assumptions of rigidity in the body's torso and hip cannot aid in the estimation of bone lengths, or joint angles, in the remaining non-rigid substructures. Further assumptions are required, such as those discussed in Section 6, in order to estimate these additional lengths and angles.

1.1 Background

Factorization approaches, first proposed for recovering rigid structure by Tomasi and Kanade in [6], were extended to handle non-rigidity in the seminal paper by Bregler et al. [5]. In this notable work the authors realized that the only way to make the non-rigid structure from motion problem tractable is to impose some constraint on the object being analyzed (e.g. assuming we are looking at a body). Bregler et al. imposed this constraint as a linear shape basis. A number of approaches that develop the use of shape basis have subsequently been proposed, including [7,8,9]. A fundamental criticism, however, of all these approaches is the specificity, or more critically the poor generalization properties, of the shape basis. For example, the shape basis of a "person walking" will not be the same as that of a "person bending down to pick something up". Akhter et al. [10] recently proposed an approach to non-rigid structure from motion that is shape agnostic, and instead places a constraint on how individual points are allowed to move through space over time. The authors frame this work in a manner similar to Bregler et al. through the introduction of a trajectory basis. A criticism of this approach, however, is that it requires each frame of a video sequence to have 2D point correspondences and cannot handle 2D points of an object sampled at random points in time.

2   The Problem

In this section we will quickly review the problem of establishing 3D human poses from uncalibrated 2D point correspondences. Given a series of F 2D frames of a person in different poses, we seek to establish the 3D weak perspective structure namely, camera scale, bone lengths, and 3D pose. Under weak perspective projection, each camera has a single unknown scale parameter s_f. The length of each bone l_b is constant across all frames. The relative depth across each bone z_{fb} defines the 3D pose.

Let $\mathbf{s}$ and $\boldsymbol{\sigma}$ denote vectors of squared and inverse-squared camera parameters respectively.

$$\mathbf{s} = \begin{bmatrix} s_1{}^2 \\ \vdots \\ s_F{}^2 \end{bmatrix} \quad \boldsymbol{\sigma} = \begin{bmatrix} \sigma_1 \\ \vdots \\ \sigma_F \end{bmatrix} = \begin{bmatrix} s_1{}^{-2} \\ \vdots \\ s_F{}^{-2} \end{bmatrix}$$

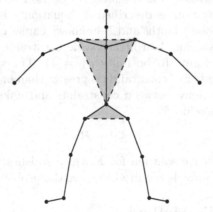

Fig. 1. Human skeleton model with $B = 17$ bones as used by [1]. Wei and Chai propose the introduction of $R = 4$ hidden bones to enforce the rigidity of points on the torso and hip (rigid sub-structures of the body are shaded).

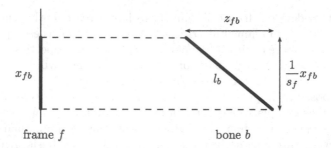

Fig. 2. Weak perspective (or scaled orthographic) projection is a good approximation for perspective projection assuming the length of each bone is small compared to the distance from the camera. In our work we assume each frame f has a single unknown scale parameter s_f, and the length l_b of each bone b is constant across all frames. x_{fb} and z_{fb} are the known projected lengths, and relative depths respectively for each frame and bone.

Let $\mathbf{l}$ be a vector of squared bone lengths. Let $\mathbf{z}_f$ and $\mathbf{x}_f$ be vectors of relative depths and known projected lengths of all bones in frame f respectively; squared.

$$\mathbf{l} = \begin{bmatrix} l_1^{\;2} \\ \vdots \\ l_B^{\;2} \end{bmatrix} \quad \mathbf{z}_f = \begin{bmatrix} z_{f1}^{\;2} \\ \vdots \\ z_{fB}^{\;2} \end{bmatrix} \quad \mathbf{x}_f = \begin{bmatrix} x_{f1}^{\;2} \\ \vdots \\ x_{fB}^{\;2} \end{bmatrix}$$

The problem, generically, can be expressed as minimizing the following objective function,

$$E_p(\mathbf{l}, \mathbf{z}, \boldsymbol{\sigma}) = \sum_{f=1}^{F} \|\mathbf{l} - \sigma_f \mathbf{x}_f - \mathbf{z}_f\|_2^2 \tag{1}$$

The depths for frame f are only estimated up to their absolute value $\{|z_{fi}|\}_{i=1}^{B}$. Estimating the unknown signs is discussed in Section 6, but shall be ignored for the moment. The system as described in Equation 1 has B unknown bone lengths, BF unknown bone depths and F unknown camera scales; with only BF Pythagorean constraints and 1 arbitrary scale constraint (i.e. we can assume the scale on the first frame to be unity $\sigma_1 = 1$). The system will be rank-deficient unless the number of constraints is greater than or equal to the number of unknowns. The difference between constraints and unknowns is $1 - F - B$. The condition on F therefore is,

$$F \leq 1 - B \tag{2}$$

Clearly there is no positive solution for F which satisfies the inequality. Some additional constraints/prior is required to solve the problem in Equation 1.

3   Wei and Chai's Method

In recent work Wei and Chai [1] proposed a novel solution to this under-constrained problem through the introduction of rigid constraints on the torso (3 bones) and the hip (2 bones). The authors demonstrated empirically [1] that the hip and torso can be considered separate rigid structures. In their approach they enforced the rigid constraint through a hidden bone, which closes a pair of bones to form a rigid triangle, resulting in the following rigid constraint function which is quartic (in terms of the squared variables).

$$E_r(\mathbf{e}, \mathbf{z}, \boldsymbol{\sigma}) = \sum_{f=1}^{F} \sum_{i=1}^{R} \left[\left(e_i^2 - x_{fi}^{e\,2} \sigma_f - z_{fj(i)}^2 - z_{fk(i)}^2 \right)^2 - 4 z_{fj(i)}^2 z_{fk(i)}^2 \right]^2 \tag{3}$$

where e_i denotes the length of the i-th hidden bone, x_{fi}^e denotes the corresponding projection length, $j(i)$ and $k(i)$ are indexes to the visible bones that form the rigid triangle with the i-th hidden bone. For R hidden bones, they introduce R extra unknown bone lengths and therefore RF new constraints. Wei and Chai also take advantage of the natural symmetry occurring in human bodies to improve the rank of the system. All visible bones (i, j) in a left-right pair are assumed to be of equal length,

$$l_i^2 - l_j^2 = 0 \tag{4}$$

with this property being encoded into $\mathbf{A}$ resulting in the following symmetric constraint function,

$$E_s(\mathbf{l}) = \|\mathbf{A}\mathbf{l}\|_2^2 \tag{5}$$

Wei and Chai proposed that the objective functions in Equations 1, 3 and 5 can be linearly combined such that the new objective function is,

$$\arg \min_{\mathbf{l}, \mathbf{z}, \boldsymbol{\sigma}, \mathbf{e}} = E_p(\mathbf{l}, \mathbf{z}, \boldsymbol{\sigma}) + \lambda_1 E_s(\mathbf{l}) + \lambda_2 E_r(\mathbf{e}, \mathbf{z}, \boldsymbol{\sigma}) \tag{6}$$

where λ_1 and λ_2 are parameters that are used to control the influence of the two constraint functions $E_s()$ and $E_r()$ respectively. These parameters are tuned through a cross-validation process.

3.1   Constraints versus Variables

At first glance the combination of objective and constraint functions in Equation 6 seems substantially more constrained than the original objective function described in Equation 1. The overall system has $(B+1)F + (B+R)$ unknowns and $(B+R)F + 1$ constraints. Including symmetry adds another M constraints, effectively reducing the number of unknown bone lengths so that the condition on F (assuming $R \geq 2$) is,

$$F \geq 1 + \frac{B - M}{R - 1} \tag{7}$$

It seems for a skeleton with $B = 17$ bones, $M = 7$ symmetry constraints and $R = 4$ rigid bone pairs, it is always possible to find bone lengths, bone depths and camera parameters (up to a constant factor) given point correspondences from 5 distinct frames under weak-perspective projection. In the following section, however, we dissect this claim further showing it to be false.

4   A Toy Problem

Nothing limits the application of Wei and Chai's method to human bodies. More generally, their approach should hold for any connected structure, satisfying Equation 7, containing a subset of rigid points. For convenience we shall continue to refer to the edges connecting points in such structures as bones, even though we are no longer referring to the human body. Figure 3 shows a single free bone attached to a rigid tetrahedron. We define a bone as being *free* if one of its end points is not connected to a rigid structure, implying that the end-point can move non-rigidly with respect to the structure (e.g. bones on the arm or leg of the human body). The shape in Figure 3 according to Wei and Chai's approach can be described as $B = 4$, $R = 3$, and $M = 0$. Applying Equation 7 in this circumstance implies that the lengths and camera scales for the structure can be solved for $F \geq 3$. The absurdity of this claim can be understood if we attempt to solve this problem in an alternative manner using canonical structure from motion [11]. It is widely accepted that the weak-perspective parameters, camera orientations and 3D structure of the tetrahedron can be recovered, given a minimum of 4 non-coplanar points, from $F \geq 3$ frames using the structure from motion theorem [11]. Assuming these variables are known, however, the problem of finding the length of the single free bone remains, in general, fundamentally unsolvable. It is impossible to know the length of a free bone from multiple projections of unknown orientation. It is easy to show through a simple thought experiment, see Figure 4, that no minimum number of images necessarily guarantees that the length of a free bone can be determined. This clearly violates Wei and Chai's conditon on F in Equation 7. This violation occurs due to the misuse of the hidden bones, introduced by Wei and Chai, to enfore rigidity. These rigid constraints only apply to those bones comprising the rigid structure. To understand this further, one can partition the objective function in Equation 6 into separate components describing rigid structures (e.g. the torso and hip) and the residual non-rigid structures. The only variable that is common across these separate partitions is camera scale. Were we to consider the problem under orthography, each free bone would emerge an independent, under-ranked

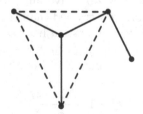

Fig. 3. This figure depicts a tetrahedron with a single free bone (i.e. the end point can move non-rigidly with respect to the rigid points defining the tetrahedron) highlighting the underlying problem in the method of Wei and Chai [1] with regard to non-rigid points. The hidden bones, denoted by a dotted line, enforce rigid structure in the tetrahedron.

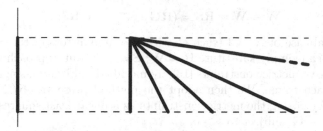

Fig. 4. This figure depicts the inherent ambiguity of a *free* bone projected onto the image plane (assuming parallel projection)

system (or each left-right pair remembering symmetry). It becomes clear that the claim of Wei and Chai is just a mirage, creating the illusion of a solvable system by combining under- (i.e. non-rigid) and over-ranked (i.e. rigid) systems.

5   Estimating Camera Scale from Rigid Sub-structure

From Section 4 it is clear that Wei and Chai's approach cannot be applied to rigid structures with additional free bones. Their approach, however, still holds for the estimation of camera scale, bone lengths and absolute depths for rigid structures. This, unfortunately, involves finding the solution to a quartic objective function, as described in Equation 6, which is susceptible to local minima and requires a slow non-linear, non-deterministic solver. As discussed in Section 4 an alternative method for estimating the camera scale, bone lengths and actual depths of the rigid structure is through the use of canonical structure from motion [11,6]. Canonical structure from motion has a number of advantages over the objective function described in Equation 6 specifically: (i) structure from motion has a deterministic, linear least-squares solution [12], and (ii) the direction of the depth across each bone can be found, not just the magnitude.

Structure from motion, under a weak perspective assumption, involves the resolution of a matrix of 2D projection coordinates $\mathbf{W}$ $(2F \times N)$ into rotation $\mathbf{R}$ $(2F \times 3)$ and structure $\mathbf{S}$ $(3 \times N)$ matrices where $N+1$ is the number of points in the rigid structure [6]. We assemble $\mathbf{W}$ from relative vectors between projected points instead of expressing points relative to their centroid, explaining why $\mathbf{W}$ is $2F \times N$ instead of $2F \times (N+1)$ where,

$$\mathbf{W} = \mathbf{RS} = \begin{bmatrix} s_1 \mathbf{i}_1^T \\ \vdots \\ s_F \mathbf{i}_F^T \\ s_1 \mathbf{j}_1^T \\ \vdots \\ s_F \mathbf{j}_F^T \end{bmatrix} \begin{bmatrix} \mathbf{p}_1 \cdots \mathbf{p}_N \end{bmatrix} \tag{8}$$

Typically, singular value decomposition (SVD) is used to find a rank-3 approximation $\hat{\mathbf{W}} = \hat{\mathbf{R}}\hat{\mathbf{S}}$. The rotation and structure matrices are then determined up to a rotation and constant factor by enforcing metric constraints on $\mathbf{R}$.

$$\mathbf{W} \approx \hat{\mathbf{W}} = \hat{\mathbf{R}}\hat{\mathbf{S}} = (\hat{\mathbf{R}}\mathbf{G})(\mathbf{G}^{-1}\hat{\mathbf{S}}) = \mathbf{R}\mathbf{S} \tag{9}$$

For the special case of $N = 3$ (such as with the human torso), the SVD is not required. We can simply substitute $\hat{\mathbf{R}} = \mathbf{W}$, $\hat{\mathbf{S}} = \mathbf{I}$. In our approach the typical weak perspective metric constraints [13] are modified to obtain a single estimate of scale for each frame. We then adopt the method presented by Morita and Kanade [12] for posing the metric constraints as a linear least squares optimisation to solve for $\mathbf{G}$, subject to $\mathbf{s} > 0$.

5.1   Experiments

Our experiments were carried out on the CMU Motion Capture Database.[1] Experiments were performed using 5 randomly selected frames from each of 128 motion sequences. Each sequence featured one of 20 different actors. For each sequence, the camera parameters and rigid bone lengths on the torso were calculated using our structure from motion approach and variants of Wei and Chai's non-linear optimisation. Histograms of normalized scale and length results are shown in Figures 5 and 6 respectively. Scale and length estimates have all been normalized by their ground-truth values. The more accurate the results, the more they tend towards unity.

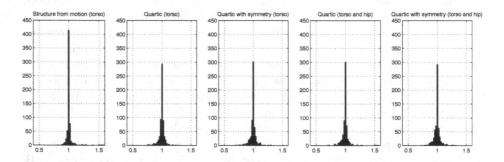

Fig. 5. Histograms of camera scale estimates using our deterministic structure from motion approach compared to Wei and Chai's computationally expensive non-linear optimisation, with and without symmetry and hip bones. All estimates have been normalized by their ground-truth values so that the more accurate the approach the more the scale estimate will tend towards unity.

Experiments were restricted to estimating camera scale, as well as lengths, from just the body's torso not the hip. This is due to the structure from motion theorem [11] which states that you need a minimum of 4 non-coplanar rigid points. Inspecting Figure 1 one can see the torso satisfies this criteria (containing 4 non-coplanar points[2]), but the hip does not (containing only 3 points).

---

[1] http://mocap.cs.cmu.edu/
[2] Care was taken to consistently mark the torso joint at the front of the subject's chest to ensure non-coplanar points.

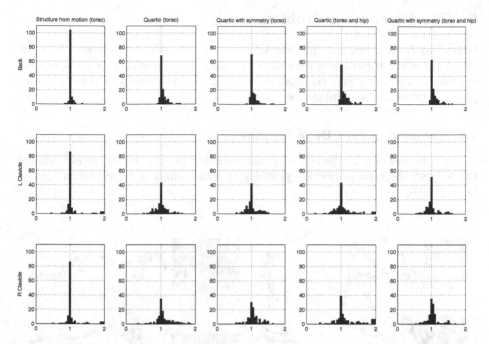

Fig. 6. Histograms of the torso bone lengths; namely the back, left clavicle and right clavicle bones. Length estimates depicted include our deterministic structure from motion approach compared to Wei and Chai's computationally expensive non-linear optimisation, with and without symmetry and hip bones. All estimates have been normalized by their ground-truth values so that the more accurate the approach the more the length estimate will tend towards unity.

Similarly, for Wei and Chai their approach cannot be applied solely to the hip due to there only being $R = 1$ hidden bones enforcing rigidity. Inspecting Equation 7 one can see that there is no F that satisfies the condition for $R = 1$.

Results in Figures 5 and 6 demonstrate that our structure from motion approach consistently outperforms Wei and Chai's for both scale and length estimation (in terms of the estimates tending towards unity). Results did not improve even when the symmetry constraint function (enforcing the left and right clavicle in the torso to be the same length), described in Equation 5, was introduced. Additional results are depicted in Figure 5 to empirically reinforce our claim that the employment of the hip, in conjunction with the torso, does not aid in the estimation of camera scale. All our experiments were conducted in MATLAB. The approach of Wei and Chai, which required the minimization of the quartic objective function described in Equation 6 (using lsqnonlin in MATLAB), empirically took over 300 times as long to compute as our deterministic structure from motion approach.

6   The Remaining Problem

It is clear from Section 5 that we are now able to reliably estimate the rigid structure of the torso along with camera scale using our structure from motion approach. A problem still remains, however, in how to estimate the lengths and joint angles of the remaining free bones.

6.1   Estimating Free Bone Lengths

Given F frames of a free bone in random orientations, as F tends toward infinity the longest observed projection provides an increasingly accurate estimation of bone length,

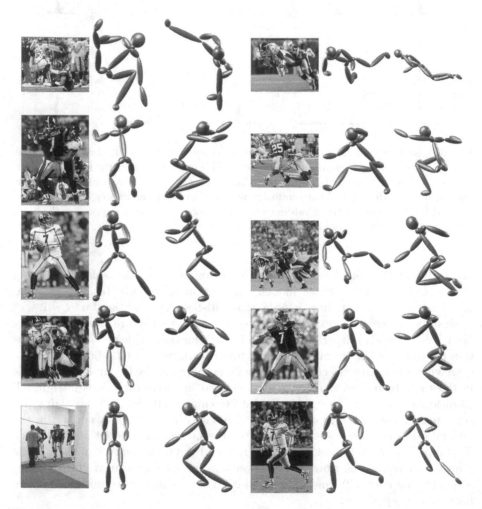

Fig. 7. 3D pose reconstructed from ten manually-labelled images of Steelers quarterback Ben Roethlisberger. Shown from the original front-view and an elevated side-view.

$$l_b^2 \approx \max_{f=1}^{F} \left\{ \frac{1}{s_f^2} x_{fb}^2 \right\} \tag{10}$$

where an estimate of s_f is known from our structure from motion approach. That is, the likelihood of the bone lying parallel to the camera plane in at least one image approaches certainty as F increases. In our approach, instead of requiring a large number of images to find bone lengths, we consider the "human in the loop" responsible for choosing images such that each bone is near-parallel in at least one image. We assume that a finite F well-selected frames will tend towards the true bone length. Symmetry constraints reduce the number of degrees of freedom, but even with symmetry the free bone problem remains under-ranked (by at least one unknown bone length). The key advantage of considering symmetry in free bones is that only one bone in each symmetrical pair need lie parallel to the image plane.

We note from Equation 10 that the accuracy of the solution for free bones depends critically on the accuracy of all scales. If the scale of one image is significantly under-estimated, the length of a free bone could potentially be over-estimated, which affects the 3D pose for all frames. This effect is most obvious for poses where an elbow or knee joint is close to fully extended, but has to be bent in the reconstruction to fit the projection (see the bottom-left image in Figure 7 and the middle image in Figure 9).

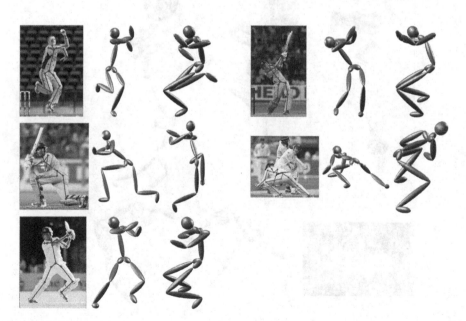

Fig. 8. 3D pose of cricket all-rounder Michael Clarke. Generated from five human-labelled images.

6.2   Estimating Joint Angles

Once we have an estimate of bone length we then also have the absolute bone depth,

$$z_{fb}^2 = l_b^2 - \frac{1}{s_f^2}x_{fb} \tag{11}$$

although we have ambiguities over the sign of z_{fb}. In our approach, we borrow upon Wei and Chai's approach for reducing this ambiguity by enforcing joint angle limit constraints from the biomechanics community. The joint angle limit constraints significantly reduce the ambiguity, but for some poses they are not sufficient to remove all ambiguity. When this happens, we allow the user to specify the sign of z_{fb} for bones that still have ambiguity until we have a solution.

6.3   Experiments on Real Images

We evaluated the effectiveness of our proposed approach using freely available images of four notable athletes, Ben Roethlisberger, Michael Clarke, Yu-Na Kim and Roger Federer, in Figures 7, 8, 9 and 10 respectively.

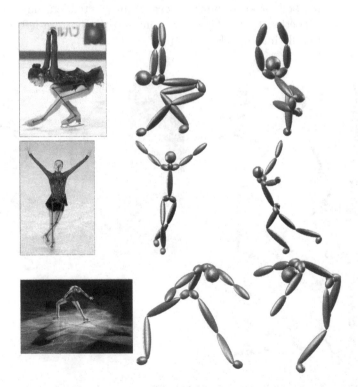

Fig. 9. Korean figure skater Yu-Na Kim, 2010 gold medallist. The 3D poses were reconstructed using only the three images shown. Wei and Chai [1] previously proposed that a minimum of five images were required.

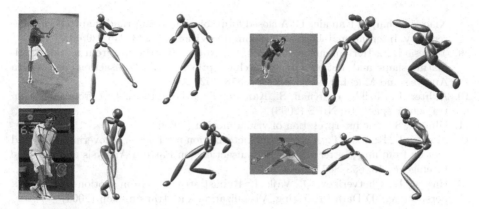

Fig. 10. The 3D pose of Swiss tennis player Roger Federer estimated from four images

7 Discussion and Conclusions

In this paper we present a novel approach for estimating 3D human pose from several frames of uncalibrated 2D point correspondences using a deterministic least-squares approach. Our approach, takes advanatge of rigid constraints in the human body first proposed by Wei and Chai [1]. We have additionally demonstrated that Wei and Chai's approach is only valid for rigid sub-structures of the human body (e.g. torso) rather than the entire body's non-rigid structure. We further demonstrate that the assumption that this approach was valid for non-rigid bodies led to the false claim that camera scales, bone lengths and absolute depths can be solved in minimum of 5 frames for a 17 bone body model.

References

1. Wei, X.K., Chai, J.: Modeling 3D human poses from uncalibrated monocular images. In: IEEE International Conference on Computer Vision (2009)
2. Agarwal, A., Triggs, B.: 3D Human pose from silhouettes by relevance vector regression. In: IEEE Conference on Computer Vision and Pattern Recognition (2004)
3. Taylor, C.J.: Reconstruction of articulated objects from point correspondences in a single uncalibrated image. In: IEEE Conference on Computer Vision and Pattern Recognition, vol. 1, pp. 677–684 (2000)
4. Barron, C., Kakadiaris, I.A.: Estimating anthropometry and pose from a single image. In: IEEE Conference on Computer Vision and Pattern Recognition (2000)
5. Bregler, C., Hertzmann, A., Biermann, H.: Recovering non-rigid 3D shape from image streams. In: IEEE Conference on Computer Vision and Pattern Recognition (2000)
6. Tomasi, C., Kanade, T.: Shape and motion from image streams under orthography: a factorization method. International Journal of Computer Vision 9, 137–154 (1992)
7. Torresani, L., Hertzmann, A., Bregler, C.: Learning non-rigid 3D shape from 2D motion. In: NIPS (2005)

8. Xiao, J., Chai, J., Kanade, T.: A closed form solution to non-rigid shape and motion recovery. International Journal of Computer Vision 67, 233–246 (2006)
9. Torresani, L., Hertzmann, A., Bregler, C.: Non-rigid structure from motion: Estimating shape and motion with hierarchical priors. IEEE Transactions on Pattern Analysis and Machine Intelligence 30, 878–892 (2008)
10. Akhter, I., Sheikh, Y., Khan, S., Kanade, T.: Nonrigid structure from motion in trajectory space. In: NIPS (2008)
11. Ullman, S.: The interpretation of visual motion (1979)
12. Morita, T., Kanade, T.: A sequential factorization method for recovering shape and motion from image streams. IEEE Transactions on Pattern Analysis and Machine Intelligence 18, 858–867 (1996)
13. Hajder, L., Chetverikov, D., Vajk, I.: Robust structure from motion under weak perspective. 3D Data Processing, Visualization and Transmission (2004)

Robust Fusion: Extreme Value Theory for Recognition Score Normalization

Walter Scheirer[1], Anderson Rocha[2], Ross Micheals[3], and Terrance Boult[1,*]

[1] University of Colorado at Colorado Springs & Securics, Inc.
[2] Institute of Computing, University of Campinas
[3] National Institute of Standards and Technology

Abstract. Recognition problems in computer vision often benefit from a fusion of different algorithms and/or sensors, with score level fusion being among the most widely used fusion approaches. Choosing an appropriate score normalization technique before fusion is a fundamentally difficult problem because of the disparate nature of the underlying distributions of scores for different sources of data. Further complications are introduced when one or more fusion inputs outright fail or have adversarial inputs, which we find in the fields of biometrics and forgery detection. Ideally a score normalization should be robust to model assumptions, modeling errors, and parameter estimation errors, as well as robust to algorithm failure. In this paper, we introduce the w-score, a new technique for robust recognition score normalization. We do not assume a match or non-match distribution, but instead suggest that the top scores of a recognition system's non-match scores follow the statistical Extreme Value Theory, and show how to use that to provide consistent robust normalization with a strong statistical basis.

1 Introduction

For many different recognition problems in computer vision, the ability to combine the results of multiple algorithms and/or sensors brings significant improvement in overall recognition performance. While there are many approaches and "levels" of fusion, a widely used approach is score level fusion, where scores from different recognition algorithms are combined. Since score distributions vary as a function of the recognition algorithms, and sometimes the underlying sensors, one must normalize the score data before combining it in score level fusion.

The goal of fusion is to improve recognition accuracy, and hence it is important that the underlying process be robust. Choosing a robust score normalization technique is often a challenge for several reasons. In the literature, the term *robust* has been defined as insensitivity to the presence of outliers (noise) [1] for the estimation of any necessary parameters. While this definition captures one property of good fusion, there are more issues than just the parameter estimation. We

* This work was supported by ONR STTR N00014-07-M-0421, ONR SBIR N00014-09-M-0448, ONR MURI N00014-08-1-0638 and Fapesp Grant 2008/08681-9.

K. Daniilidis, P. Maragos, N. Paragios (Eds.): ECCV 2010, Part III, LNCS 6313, pp. 481–495, 2010.
© Springer-Verlag Berlin Heidelberg 2010

define the term *robust fusion* to be a fusion process (including normalization) that is insensitive to errors in its distributional assumptions on the data, has simple parameter estimation, and a high input failure tolerance. For this work, simple parameter estimation means there is no dependence on a large sample set for modeling the match and non-match distributions for each algorithm, and a very small number of parameters must be estimated experimentally. Failure tolerance means that if one or more recognition algorithms involved in the fusion process is not producing correct matching results, it does not strongly impact the final result of fusion. Ideally, we would like a score normalization that is both robust to failure, and is unencumbered by complicated parameter estimation as score distributions vary. Further, if an algorithm is repeatedly failing, robust fusion should be able to detect this.

Robustness in score level fusion is strongly impacted by normalization in two major ways:

1. The varying nature of the underlying distribution of scores across different recognition algorithms often leads to inconsistency in normalization results. For example, if a normalization technique assumes the algorithms considered for fusion produce scores that follow a Gaussian distribution, and at least one of those distributions is not Gaussian, the results will not be optimal. The distribution of recognition scores is the result of a complex function of both the algorithm and the actual data being processed, and it is dangerous to assume too much about the score distribution.

2. Complications are introduced when one or more sensors or recognition algorithms being considered for fusion fail or are deceived. For recognition problems, failure occurs when an input sample of a class unknown to the system is recognized as being part of a known class, or when an input sample that should be recognized by the system is rejected as being unknown. The scores produced in these failure scenarios become problematic for normalization techniques, especially when they resemble an "expected" (and often estimated) match distribution.

In this paper, we introduce a new score normalization approach for robust fusion based on a probability of confidence that a particular score is not drawn from the non-match distribution. For an overview, we turn to Figure 1. Based on the match scores produced by multiple recognition algorithms applied to a particular object, a post-recognition score analysis [2] [3] is performed to predict the probability of the scores not being from the non-match distribution. For this work, we introduce a statistical Extreme Value Theory normalization that draws these probabilities from the cumulative distribution function of a Weibull distribution (hence "w-score"). The resulting probabilities from the different algorithms are the normalized w-scores, which can then be fused together to produce an overall probability of not being a non-match. In Figure 1, the process is shown for the case of two algorithms, though it applies to any number of inputs.

Traditional normalization techniques change the location and scale parameters of a score distribution in an ad-hoc manner or based on unproven distributional assumption. In contrast, our w-score normalization changes raw scores to probability

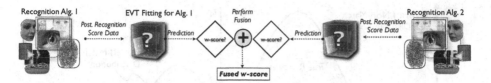

Fig. 1. An overview of the w-score normalization process. Recognition scores are produced by an algorithm for the given input. An Extreme Value Theory statistical model (Weibull) is fit to the tail of the sorted scores. The normalization of all data is done using the cumulative distribution function of the resulting Weibull distribution (hence w-scores). The w-score is an estimate of the probability of a particular score not being from the non-match distribution, and hence an ideal normalization for fusion.

scores based on a strong statistical theory. This is a new paradigm for recognition score normalization supporting robust recognition fusion.

We organize the rest of this paper as follows. In Section 2, we discuss the strengths and weaknesses of common recognition score normalization techniques. In Section 3, we review the post-recognition score analysis based on statistical Extreme Value Theory (pre-requisite to our new normalization technique) and in Section 4, we detail the w-score normalization technique. Finally, we present experimental results for the w-score on a series of biometric recognition algorithms and content-based image retrieval descriptors in Section 5.

2   Recognition Score Normalization

2.1   Recognition Systems

There are multiple formal ways to define what exactly a "recognition" task is. For this work, we consider the general definition of Shakhnarovich et al. [4], where the task of a recognition system is to find the class label c^*, where p_k is an underlying probability rule and p_0 is the input distribution, satisfying

$$c^* = \underset{class\ c}{\operatorname{argmax}} Pr(p_0 = p_c) \tag{1}$$

subject to $Pr(p_0 = p_c^*) \geq 1 - \delta$ for a given confidence threshold δ, or to conclude the lack of such a class (to reject the input). We define *probe* as the input image distribution p_0 submitted to the recognition system in order to find its corresponding class label c^*. Similarly, we define *gallery* to be all the classes c^* known to the recognition system.

Many systems replace the probability in the above definition with a more generic "score," which produces the same answer when the posterior class probability of the identities is monotonic with the score function. In this case, setting the minimal threshold on a score effectively fixes δ. We call this rank-1 recognition, because the recognition is based on the largest score. One can generalize the concept of recognition, as is common in content-based image retrieval some

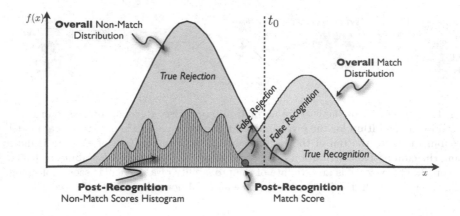

Fig. 2. The match and non-match distributions for the recognition problem. A threshold t_0 applied to the score determines the decision for recognition or rejection. Where the tails of the distributions overlap is where we find *False Rejection* and *False Recognition*. Embedded within the overall distribution is shown a particular set of post-recognition scores, with 1 match (falsely rejected by the threshold t_0) and many non-match samples.

biometrics problems and some object recognition problems, by relaxing the definition of success to having the correct answer in the top K responses. Many researchers use a pseudo-distance measure where smaller scores are better, which is trivially converted to a "larger is better" approach.

For analysis, presuming the ground-truth is known, one can define the overall match and non-match distributions for recognition and the per-instance post-recognition distributions (see Figure 2) . For an operational system, a threshold t_0 on the similarity score s is set to define the boundary between proposed matches and proposed non-matches. The choice of t_0 is often made empirically, based on observed system performance. Where t_0 falls on each tail of each overall distribution establishes where *False Rejection* (Type I error: the probe has a corresponding entry in the gallery, but is rejected) or *False Recognition* (Type II error: the probe does not have a corresponding entry in the gallery, but is incorrectly associated with a gallery entry) will occur. The post-recognition scores in the example yield a False Rejection for the t_0 shown.

2.2   Normalization Techniques

Traditional normalization techniques change the location and scale parameters of a score distribution. Jain et al. [5] define two types of normalizations based on the data requirements for parameter estimation. In *fixed score normalization*, which includes machine learning based approaches, the parameters used for normalization are determined *a priori* using a fixed training set. This means that the training set must accurately reflect the score distribution for each recognition algorithm – any deviation will have an impact on the recognition results. In an approach that is inline with our desire for simple parameter estimation, *adaptive score normalization* estimates parameters based on the scores at hand for a particular recognition instance. As a further consideration, a normalization technique is *robust* if it is insensitive to outliers. In this section, we briefly describe various normalization techniques, including the very popular z-score, which we use for comparison in all of our experiments in Section 5. For each example, a set of match scores $\{s_k\}, k = 1, 2, \ldots, n$ is considered for normalization.

z-scores are adaptive score normalizations that are computed in a straightforward manner. Referring to Equation 2, the normalized score is produced by subtracting the arithmetic mean μ of $\{s_k\}$ from an original score, and dividing this number by the standard deviation σ of $\{s_k\}$. This parameter estimation makes z-score normalization an adaptive score normalization, but it is possible to compute z-score normalization as a fixed score normalization if μ and σ are estimated for the overall distributions of scores produced by different recognition algorithms. z-score normalization is not robust in the traditional sense, and, as we show in this paper, is highly impacted by recognition algorithm failure.

$$s'_k = \frac{s_k - \mu}{\sigma} \tag{2}$$

tanh-estimators [6] are fixed score normalizations that are considered robust to noise, but are far more complicated to compute, compared to the adaptive z-scores. The normalized score is produced by taking the hyperbolic tangent of a z-score-like calculation. The robust nature of tanh-estimators comes from the mean and standard deviation estimates, which are computed from a genuine score distribution that is itself computed from Hampel estimators, making tanh-estimators fixed score normalizations. The Hampel estimators are based on an influence function, which makes the normalization robust to noise by reducing the influence of the scores at the tails of the distribution being considered. The tail points for three different intervals from the median score of the distribution must be defined in an *ad hoc* manner. These parameters can be difficult to determine experimentally, and if chosen incorrectly, limit the effectiveness of tanh-estimators. tanh-estimators are robust to noise, but not parameter estimation. Further, tanh-estimators have been shown to produce good results for noisy data in verification problems [5], but not recognition problems, where the underlying score distributions are different.

Other important work in score normalization has investigated advanced topics in statistical modeling including: the effect of correlation and variance on z-scores [7]; client specific normalization related to classifications made with respect to the Doddington's zoo effect (which includes failure cases) [8]; cost-sensitive performance evaluation of hardware and software failure [9]; and effects related to signal quality [10].

3 Statistical Extreme Value Theory

As we saw in Section 2.1, we can map almost any recognition task into the problem of determining "match" scores between the input data and some class descriptor, and then determining the most likely class [4]. Success in a recognition system occurs when the match is the top score. Failure in a recognition system occurs when the match score is not the top score (or not in the top K, for the more general rank-K recognition). With these two definitions in mind, it is critical to note that the analysis here is done for a single probe at a time, and this assessment is not based on the overall "match/non-match" distributions, such as those in [11] and [12], which include scores over many probes. Rather it is done using a single probe producing at most one match score mixed in with a larger set of non-match scores.

We can formalize our analysis as score-based accuracy prediction for rank-K recognition, determining if the top K scores contain an outlier with respect to the current probe's non-match distribution. In particular, let $\mathcal{F}(p)$ be the distribution of the non-match scores that are generated by the matching probe p, and $m(p)$ to be the match score for that probe. In addition, let $S(K) = s_1 \ldots s_K$ be the top K sorted scores. We can formalize the null hypothesis H_0 of our prediction for rank-K recognition as:

$$H_0(failure) : \forall x \in S(K), x \in \mathcal{F}(p), \tag{3}$$

If we can reject H_0 (failure), then we predict success.

While some researchers have formulated recognition as hypothesis testing given the individual class distributions [4], that approach presumes good models of distributions for each match/class. We cannot model the "match" distribution here effectively, as we only have *one* sample per probe, and so the only way to apply that is to assume a consistent distribution across all probes, which is questionable. That is the key insight; we don't have enough data to model the match distribution, but we have n samples of the non-match distribution — generally enough for a good non-match modeling and outlier detection. If the best score is a match it's an outlier with respect to the rest of the data.

As we seek a more formal approach, the critical question then becomes how to model $\mathcal{F}(p)$, and what hypothesis test to use for the outlier detection. Various researchers have investigated modeling the overall non-match distribution [12], developing a binomial model. Our goal, however, is not to model the whole non-match distribution over the entire population, but rather to model the tail of what exists for a single probe comparison. The binomial models developed by [12] account for the bulk of the data, but have problems in the tails, and are not a good model for a particular probe.

An important observation about the problem we consider here is that the non-match distribution we seek to model is actually a sampling of scores, one or more per "class," each of which is itself a distribution of potential scores for this probe versus the particular class. Since we are looking at the upper tail, the top n scores, there is a strong bias in the samplings that impact the tail modeling; we are interested only in the top similarity scores.

Claiming the tail of a distribution to be an extreme value problem may appear intuitive. Recent work [13] looking at verification score spaces relies on this intuition, but does not explain why extrema value theory applies to the tails of

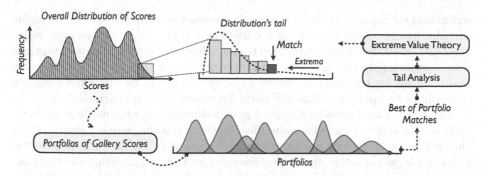

Fig. 3. Why our score analysis is an extreme value problem. One can view this problem as considering a collection of portfolios composed of sub-sets of the gallery, each of which produce scores. One portfolio contains a match-score (red), the rest are non-matching scores (brown). The best of the best of the portfolio scores are those that show up in the tail of the post-recognition score distribution — leaving us with an extreme value problem for the data we consider. The best score in the tail is, if a match, an outlier with respect to the EVT model of the non-match data.

their score distributions. Just being in the tail is not sufficient to make this an extreme value problem, as one can take the top N samples from any particular distribution D, which by definition fit distribution D and not any other distribution. Just considering tails of data is not sufficient justification to invoke the extreme value theorem, just like taking a sample from a distribution does not necessarily invoke the central limit theorem.

We can consider the recognition problem as logically starting with a collection of portfolios, each of which is an independent subset of the gallery or recognition classes. This is shown in Figure 3. From each portfolio, we can compute the "best" matching score in that portfolio. We can then collect the subset where *all* of these scores are maxima (extrema) within their respective portfolios. The tail of the post-match distribution of scores will be the best scores from the best of the portfolios. Looking at it this way we have shown that modeling the non-match data in the tail is an extreme value problem. With this formalized view of recognition, we can invoke the Extreme Value Theorem: [14]:

Extreme Value Theorem 1. *Let $(s_1, s_2, \ldots)$ be a sequence of i.i.d samples. Let $M_n = \max\{s_1, \ldots, s_n\}$. If a sequence of pairs of real numbers (a_n, b_n) exists such that each $a_n > 0$ and*

$$\lim_{x \to \infty} P\left(\frac{M_n - b_n}{a_n} \leq x\right) = F(x) \tag{4}$$

then if F is a non-degenerate distribution function, it belongs to one of three extreme value distributions.

Thus, a particular portfolio is represented as the sampling $(s_1, s_2, \ldots)$, drawn from an overall distribution of scores S. Theorem 1 tells us that a large set of individual maximums M_n from the portfolios must converge to an extreme value distribution. As portfolio maxima fall into the tail of S, they can be most accurately modeled by the appropriate extreme value distribution. The assumptions necessary to apply this for a recognition problem are that we have sufficiently many classes for the portfolio model to be good enough for the approximation in the limit to apply, and that the portfolio samples are approximately $i.i.d.$.

The EVT is analogous to a central-limit theorem, but with minima (or maxima) over the data. Extreme value distributions are the limiting distributions that occur for the maximum (or minimum, depending on the data representation) of a large collection of random observations from an arbitrary distribution. Gumbel [15] showed that for any continuous and invertible initial distribution, only three models are needed, depending on whether you are interested in the maximum or the minimum, and also if the observations are bounded from above or below. Gumbel also proved that if a system/part has multiple failure modes, the failure is best modeled by the Weibull distribution. The resulting three types of extreme value distributions can be unified into a generalized extreme value (GEV) distribution given by

$$GEV(t) = \begin{cases} \frac{1}{\lambda} e^{-v^{-1/k}} v^{-(1/k+1)} & k \neq 0 \\ \frac{1}{\lambda} e^{-(x+e^{-x})} & k = 0 \end{cases} \tag{5}$$

where $x = \frac{t-\tau}{\lambda}, v = (1 + k\frac{t-\tau}{\lambda})$ where k, λ, and τ are the shape, scale, and location parameters respectively. Different values of the shape parameter yield the extreme value type I, II, and III distributions. Specifically, the three cases $k = 0, k > 0$, and $k < 0$ correspond to the Gumbel (I), Frechet (II), and Reversed Weibull (III) distributions. Gumbel and Frechet are for unbounded distributions and Weibull for bounded. Equation 6 gives the CDF of a Weibull.

$$CDF(t) = 1 - e^{-\left(\frac{t}{\lambda}\right)^k} \tag{6}$$

If we presume that match scores are bounded, then the distribution of the minimum (or maximum) reduces to a Weibull (or Reversed Weibull) [16], independent of the choice of model for the individual non-match distribution. For most recognition systems, the distance or similarity scores are bounded from both above and below. If the values are unbounded, the GEV distribution can be used. Most importantly, we don't have to assume a distributional model for overall match or non-match distributions. Rephrasing, no matter what model best fits each non-match distribution, be it a truncated binomial, a truncated mixture of Gaussians, or even a complicated but bounded multi-modal distribution, with enough samples and enough classes *the sampling of the top-n scores always results in a Weibull distribution.*

Given the potential variations that can occur in the class for which the probe image belongs, there is a distribution of scores that can occur for each of the classes in the gallery. Figure 3 depicts the recognition of a given probe image as implicitly sampling from these distributions. Our method takes the tail of these scores, which are likely to have been sampled from the extreme of their

---

Algorithm 1. w-score Normalization Technique

Require: A collection of scores S, of vector length m, from a single recognition
   algorithm j;
1: **Sort** and retain the n largest scores, $s_1, \ldots, s_n \in S$;
2: **Fit** a GEV or Weibull distribution W_S to $s_2, \ldots, s_n$, skipping the hypothesized
   outlier;
3: **while** $k < m$ **do**
4:      $s'_k = \text{CDF}(s_k, W_S)$
5:      $k \leftarrow k + 1$
6: **end while**

---

underlying portfolio, and fits a Weibull distribution to that data. Given the
Weibull fit to the data, we can determine if the top score is an outlier, by
considering the amount of the cumulative distribution function that is to the
right of the top score.

4   Normalization via w-Scores

With the necessary theory covered, we can describe the process for computing
w-scores (Weibull-score, for the statistical fitting that serves as its basis) for
score normalization. The exact process for computing w-score normalization is
given in Algorithm 1. The w-score re-normalizes the data based on its formal
probability of being an outlier in the extreme value "non-match" model, and
hence its chance of being a successful recognition. This is an adaptive score
normalization; we only require the scores from a single recognition instance for
a particular recognition algorithm. w-scores are very robust to noise and failure.

As w-scores are based on the fitting of the Weibull model to the non-match
data of the top scores, an issue that must be addressed is the impact of any
outliers on the fitting. For rank-1 fitting, where the top score is the expected
match data, this bias is easily reduced by excluding the top score and fitting
to the remaining $n - 1$ scores from the top n. If the top score is an outlier
(recognition is correct), then excluding it does not impact the fitting. If the top
score was not a match, including this recognition in the fitting will bias the
distribution to be broader than it should, which will produce lower probability
scores for the correct match and most of the non-matches. In addition, we must
address the choice of n, the tail size to be used in fitting. This tail size represents
the only parameter that must be estimated for w-scores. Including too few scores
might reduce accuracy, including too many items could impact assumptions of
portfolio sampling. However, as we show in Section 5, even very small tail sizes
(3 and 5) produce good normalization. That is consistent with work in other
fields [14], where 3-5 is a very common fitting size range for Weibulls.

Once the fitting has taken place, we have all of the information necessary to
complete the normalization. For every gallery class i, let score $s'_{i,j}$ be its normalized score in the collection of scores S for algorithm j. We use the CDF

defined by the parameters of the fitting W_S to produce the normalized probability score $s'_{i,j}$ (we note that in Algorithm 1, the normalization process follows the sorted list of scores for a single recognition algorithm; $s'_{i,j}$ is a score-index representation for fusion). We then define w-score fusion as

$$f_i = \sum_j s'_{i,j}. \tag{7}$$

Alternatively, similar to Equation 1, one can consider the sum of only those items with a w-score (probability of success) above some given threshold δ, or could consider products or likelihood ratios of the w-scores.

Algorithm 2. w-score Error Detection For Fusion

Require: A collection of w-scores S'_n, where n is the number of algorithms to fuse, and the collection has m different score vectors for each algorithm;
Require: Algorithm FRR/FAR at current settings or ground-truth for each recognition instance;
Require: A significance threshold ϵ and an error percentage threshold $\mathcal{T}$;
1: **while** $i < m$ **do**
2:     **while** $j < n$ **do**
3:         $f_1 \leftarrow f_1 + s'_{i,j,1}$.
4:     **end while**
5:     **if** not a match **then**
6:         **if** $f_1 \geq n \times \epsilon$ **then**
7:             PossibleMatches $\leftarrow$ PossibleMatches $+1$
8:         **end if**
9:     **end if**
10:    $i \leftarrow i + 1$
11: **end while**
12: **if** PossibleMatches $\geq m\mathcal{T}$ **then**
13:     **return** System Error Detected
14: **end if**

The w-score fusion possesses a unique robust property, providing built-in error detection. An inverse Weibull allows us to estimate the "confidence" of particular measurement (refer to the hypothesis test of Section 3). Considering the probabilities for the top score for each algorithm, we can determine if it is highly likely that the final fused score f_1 is not a non-match; if a particular algorithm consistently fails (or the ground-truth shows it is not failing), we have evidence of a possible error, most probably some type of data misalignment. Algorithm 2 describes the process of the error detection. A count of the possible matches is kept, and if it exceeds $\mathcal{T}$ percent, we declare system error.

We have found this error detection property to be useful for indicating three possible errors: (1) the Weibull fitting is inaccurate for valid score data (due to a mis-estimated tail size) (2) invalid score data (from parsing errors) produced a CDF that returns an improbably large number of high w-scores; (3) an error is present in alignment or the ground-truth labeling (off-by-one errors due to bad pre-processing). To our knowledge, no other fusion technique has this property.

5   Experimental Results

In this section, we present experimental results for our w-score method on a series of biometric recognition algorithms and content-based image retrieval descriptors. We compare the w-score approach to the well known *z-score* normalization. *z-score* normalization remains one of the most popular normalization techniques out there (a search for "z-score" using Google scholar returns 102,000 scholarly works), because of its theoretical performance on Gaussian data, and its straightforward parameter estimation. Fixed score normalizations such as tanh-estimators or machine learning based approaches are not considered for the reasons given in Section 2.2.

5.1   Biometric Recognition

For our first set of experiments, we tested a series of biometric recognition algorithms from the NIST BSSR1[17] biometric score set. The data set consists of scores from 2 face recognition algorithms (labeled C & G) and 1 fingerprint recognition algorithm applied to two different fingers (labeled LI & RI). BSSR1's multibiometric subset contains 517 score sets for each of the algorithms, with common subjects between each set. BSSR1 also contains individual score subsets for all algorithms, where the scores do not have common subjects between them. Out of this individual score set data, we created a "Chimera" data set with 3000 score sets and consistent labeling across all algorithms. This was done to address the limited nature of the true multibiometric set, where fusion pushes the recognition rate close to 100% for even weak normalizations.

We performed two different types of experiments on this data. All results are presented as a percentage of error reduction (improvement) compared to z-scores, the most popular type of adaptive score normalization, calculated as

$$\%\text{reduction} = (\%e_z - \%e_w)/\%e_z \qquad (8)$$

where $\%e_z$ is the percentage of incorrect rank-1 results for z-score fusion, and $\%e_w$ is the percentage of incorrect rank-1 results for w-score fusion.

For the first experiment, we fused a variety of face and fingerprint recognition algorithms. We note that in normalization and fusion, performance varies as a function of the data considered. Thus, we only considered the scores equal to a percentage of the total number of classes, expressed as $\%c^*$. This threshold is independent of the Weibull fitting, and is applied to both the w-score and z-score. While we show results for experiments with a consistent percentage of classes for w-scores and z-scores, we note that in our broader experimentation, we were always able to achieve better performance than z-scores when choosing the correct tail size for fitting, and fusing scores within the tail used for fitting. The tail size used for fitting for all biometrics experiments in this paper is 5.

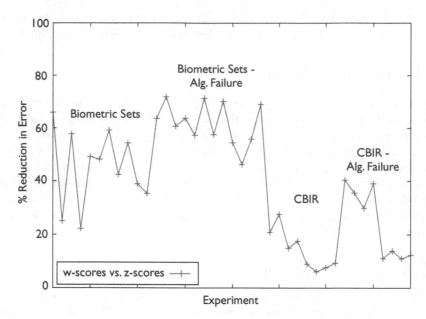

Fig. 4. A graphical summary of all of the results presented in this paper. In all cases, w-scores reduce the margin of error after fusion, when compared to z-scores (baseline), for a variety of biometric recognition algorithms and CBIR descriptors.

The second experiment tests fusion behavior in a failure scenario, where rank-1 recognition for at least one of the algorithms is 0%. For biometrics, this may be thought of as an "impostor" test, where a subject is trying to actively defeat the recognition system (consider the possibility of a facial disguise that causes a face algorithm to fail, but has no effect on a fingerprint recognition algorithm). Results for the BSSR1 multibiometric set and the BSSR1 Chimera set are given in Tables 1 & 2. w-scores have a clear advantage over z-scores for regular fusion, and a significant advantage in cases where a recognition algorithm is failing.

5.2 Content Based Image Retrieval

To show the broader applicability of w-score normalization, we also tested a series of simple CBIR descriptors [18]. Data from the Corel "Relevants" set [19], containing 50 unique classes, and the INRIA "Holidays" set [20], containing 500 unique classes. Using a variety of descriptors, we generated 1624 score sets for Corel Relevants and 1491 score sets for INRIA Holidays. In total, we tested 47 different combinations of descriptors across all experiments, but due to space constraints, we only show four different representative combinations. The experiments are identical to those of the biometric sets in Section 5.1. Results for the Corel Relevants set and the INRIA Holidays set are given in Tables 3 & 4. We note that in all of our fusion experiments with CBIR descriptors, w-scores outperformed z-scores when the appropriate tail size was chosen for Weibull fitting, which is consistent with our biometric results. The tail sized used for fitting for all CBIR experiments is 3.

Table 1. Rank-1 fusion results, expressed as the percentage of error reduction compared to z-scores, for the BSSR1 multibiometric and the BSSR1 "Chimera" data sets

Algorithm	Improve	%c*	Algorithm	Improve	%c*
C & LI	65.9%	2.0%	Chimera C & RI	59.1%	0.2%
C & RI	25.0%	2.0%	Chimera G & LI	42.4%	0.2%
G & LI	57.7%	2.0%	Chimera G & RI	54.3%	0.2%
G & RI	22.2%	2.0%	Chimera C & G & LI	38.9%	0.2%
Chimera C & G	49.1%	0.2%	Chimera C & G & RI	35.3%	0.2%
Chimera C & LI	48.1%	0.2%			

Table 2. Rank-1 fusion results, expressed as the percentage of error reduction compared to z-scores, for the BSSR1 multibiometric and the BSSR1 "Chimera" data sets, fusing with failing algorithms (marked with *). Note the significant reduction in error.

Algorithm	Improve	%c*	Algorithm	Improve	%c*
*C & LI	63.6%	2.0%	Chimera *G & LI	57.5%	0.3%
*C & RI	71.8%	2.0%	Chimera *G & RI	70.1%	0.3%
*G & LI	60.6%	2.0%	Chimera LI & *RI	54.4%	0.3%
*G & RI	63.6%	2.0%	Chimera RI & *LI	46.2%	0.3%
Chimera *C & LI	57.2%	0.3%	Chimera *C & *G & LI	55.8%	0.3%
Chimera *C & RI	71.3%	0.3%	Chimera *C & *G & RI	68.9%	0.3%

Table 3. Rank-1 CBIR fusion results, expressed as the percentage of error reduction compared to z-scores, for the Corel Relevants and INRIA Holidays data sets. We note that fusion performance here is relative to data set difficulty.

CBIR Algorithm	Improve	%c*	CBIR Algorithm	Improve	%c*
Relevants csd & gch	20.8%	6.0%	Holidays csd & gch	8.9%	0.6%
Relevants csd & jac	27.5%	6.0%	Holidays csd & jac	6.1%	0.6%
Relevants cw_{hsv} & cw_{luv}	14.9%	6.0%	Holidays cw_{hsv} & cw_{luv}	7.6%	0.6%
Relevants cw_{hsv} & jac	17.5%	6.0%	Holidays cw_{hsv} & jac	9.3%	0.6%

Table 4. Rank-1 CBIR fusion results, expressed as the percentage of error reduction compared to z-scores, for the Corel Relevants and INRIA Holidays data sets, fusing with failing algorithms (marked with *). Note the significant reduction in error for this experiment, which is consistent with the biometric results presented in Table 2.

CBIR Descriptor	Improve	%c*	CBIR Descriptor	Improve	%c*
Relevants *csd & gch	40.3%	6.0%	Holidays *csd & gch	11.1%	0.6%
Relevants csd & *jac	35.5%	6.0%	Holidays csd & *jac	13.9%	0.6%
Relevants cw_{hsv} & *cw_{luv}	29.8%	6.0%	Holidays cw_{hsv} & *cw_{luv}	11.0%	0.6%
Relevants cw_{hsv} & jac	39.1%	6.0%	Holidays *cw_{hsv} & jac	12.3%	0.6%

6   Conclusion

In this paper, we have introduced a theory of post-recognition score analysis based on statistical Extreme Value Theory, and used this theory to develop our new w-score adaptive score normalization. Through our analysis, we showed that no matter what model best fits each non-match distribution, with enough samples and enough classes, the sampling of the top-n scores always results in a Weibull distribution. With this knowledge, we developed a method that takes the tail of these scores, which are likely to have been sampled from the extreme of their underlying sub-sets from the gallery, and fits a Weibull distribution to that data; the CDF of the resulting distribution allows us to normalize the entire score sequence. In essence, the w-score normalizes scores to a probability score reflecting the confidence of the score not being a non-match. Results on a wide range of biometric and CBIR data show that the w-score is superior to the z-score, the most popular type of adaptive score normalization, especially when one or more recognition algorithms fail or when there are impostor scores.

References

1. Huber, P.: Robust Statistics. Wiley, New York (1981)
2. Li, W., Gao, X., Boult, T.E.: Predicting Biometric System Failure. In: CIHSPS (2005)
3. Wang, P., Ji, Q., Wayman, J.: Modeling and Predicting Face Recognition System Performance Based on Analysis of Similarity Scores. IEEE TPAMI 29, 665–670 (2007)
4. Shakhnarovich, G., Fisher, J., Darrell, T.: Face Recognition From Long-term Observations. In: Heyden, A., Sparr, G., Nielsen, M., Johansen, P. (eds.) ECCV 2002. LNCS, vol. 2352, pp. 851–868. Springer, Heidelberg (2002)
5. Jain, A., Nandakumar, K., Ross, A.: Score Normalization in Multimodal Biometric Systems. Pattern Recognition 38, 2270–2285 (2005)
6. Hampel, F., Rousseeuw, P., Ronchetti, E., Stahel, W.: Robust Statistics: The Approach Based on Influence Functions. Wiley, New York (1986)
7. Poh, N., Bengio, S.: How Do Correlation and Variance of Base Classifiers Affect Fusion in Biometric Authentication Tasks? IEEE. TSP 53, 4384–4396 (2005)
8. Poh, N., Kittler, J.: Incorporating Variation of Model-specific Score Distribution in Speaker Verification Systems. IEEE. TASLP 16, 594–606 (2008)
9. Poh, N., Bourlai, N., Kittler, J.: Benchmarking Quality-Dependent and Cost-Sensitive Score-Level Multimodal Biometric Fusion Algorithms. IEEE. TIFS 4, 849–866 (2009)
10. Poh, N., Bourlai, T., Kittler, J.: A Multimodal Biometric Test Bed for Quality-dependent, Cost-sensitive and Client-specific Score-level Fusion Algorithms. Pattern Recognition 43, 1094–1105 (2010)
11. Shi, Z., Kiefer, F., Schneider, J., Govindaraju, V.: Modeling Biometric Systems Using the General Pareto Dstribution (GPD). In: SPIE, vol. 6944 (2008)
12. Grother, P., Phillips, P.J.: Models of Large Population Recognition Performance. In: IEEE CVPR, pp. 68–75 (2004)
13. Broadwater, J., Chellappa, R.: Adaptive Threshold Estimation Via Extreme Value Theory. IEEE TSP (2009) (to appear)

14. Kotz, S., Nadarajah, S.: Extreme Value Distributions: Theory and Applications, 1st edn. World Scientific, Singapore (2001)
15. Gumbel, E.: Statistical Theory of Extreme Values and Some Practical Applications. In: Number National Bureau of Standards Applied Mathematics in 33, U.S. GPO, Washington, D.C (1954)
16. NIST: NIST/SEMATECH Handbook of Statistical Methods. 33. U.S. GPO (2008)
17. NIST: Biometric Scores Set (2004), www.itl.nist.gov/iad/894.03/biometricscores
18. Datta, R., Joshi, D., Wang, J.: Image retrieval: Ideas, influences, and trends of the new age. ACM CSUR 40, 1–77 (2008)
19. Stehling, R., Nascimento, M., Falcão, A.: A compact and efficient image retrieval approach based on border/interior pixel classification. In: CIKM, pp. 102–109 (2002)
20. Jegou, H., Douze, M., Schmid, C.: Hamming embedding and weak geometry consistency for large scale image search. In: Forsyth, D., Torr, P., Zisserman, A. (eds.) ECCV 2008, Part I. LNCS, vol. 5302, pp. 304–317. Springer, Heidelberg (2008)

Recognizing Partially Occluded Faces from a Single Sample Per Class Using String-Based Matching

Weiping Chen[1] and Yongsheng Gao[1,2]

[1] School of Engineering, Griffith University, Australia
[2] National ICT Australia, Queensland Research Lab
{luke.chen,yongsheng.gao}@griffith.edu.au

Abstract. Automatically recognizing human faces with partial occlusions is one of the most challenging problems in face analysis community. This paper presents a novel string-based face recognition approach to address the partial occlusion problem in face recognition. In this approach, a new face representation, Stringface, is constructed to integrate the relational organization of intermediate-level features (line segments) into a high-level global structure (string). The matching of two faces is done by matching two Stringfaces through a *string*-to-*string* matching scheme, which is able to efficiently find the most discriminative local parts (substrings) for recognition without making any assumption on the distributions of the deformed facial regions. The proposed approach is compared against the state-of-the-art algorithms using both the AR database and FRGC (Face Recognition Grand Challenge) ver2.0 database. Very encouraging experimental results demonstrate, for the first time, the feasibility and effectiveness of a high-level syntactic method in face recognition, showing a new strategy for face representation and recognition.

Keywords: Partial occlusion, Stringface.

1 Introduction

Face recognition has attracted much attention in both academic and industrial communities during the past few decades. A great deal of progress has been made to robustly identifying faces under controlled condition. However, recognizing faces under uncontrolled conditions remains challenging open problems in face recognition community. A face recognition system can be confront occluded faces in real world applications very often due to use of accessories, such as scarf and sunglasses. Hence, the face recognition system has to be robust to occlusion in order to guarantee reliable real-world applications. Recognizing partially occluded face has received considerable attention in recent years [1][11] [14][18].

Penev and Atick [14] proposed a Local Feature Analysis (LFA) technique by modifying PCA to solve the partial occlusion problem. LFA is a derivative of the eigenface method and utilizes specific facial features such as eyes, mouth

K. Daniilidis, P. Maragos, N. Paragios (Eds.): ECCV 2010, Part III, LNCS 6313, pp. 496–509, 2010.
© Springer-Verlag Berlin Heidelberg 2010

and nose for identification instead of the entire representation of the face. These features are used as the basis for representation and comparison. Its performance is dependent on a relatively constant environment and the quality of the image. Bartlett et al. [1] presented an Independent Component Analysis (ICA) architecture to find a spatially local face representation. Conceptually, LFA also finds local basis images for face using the second-order statistics but its kernels are not sensitive to the higher than second-order dependencies in a face image. On the contrast, Independent Component Analysis (ICA) architecture I is sensitive to these high-order statistics. It treats the images as random variables and the pixels as outcomes to find a set of statistically independent basis images. Martinez [11] proposed a probabilistic face recognition approach that could compensate for the imprecise localization, partial occlusion, and extreme expressions with a single training sample. In his method, face images are analyzed locally in order to handle partial face occlusion. The face image is first divided into k local regions and for each region an eigenspace is constructed. If a region is occluded, it is automatically detected. Moreover, weighting of the local regions were also proposed in order to provide robustness against expression variations. Recently, Wright et al. [18] presented a partition Sparse Representation Classification (SRC) method which is inspired by the ideal of compressed sensing. In their method, a face is first partitioned into blocks and compute an independent sparse representation for each block. Then a general classification algorithm and a voting method are used to recognize face images.

In this paper, we propose a novel Stringface representation and matching concept for face recognition with one single model image per person under partial occlusions. Cognitive psychological studies [2][3] indicated that human beings recognize line drawings as quickly and almost as accurately as gray-level images since the line drawings preserve most important feature information. In addition, line segments are less sensitive to illumination changes and local variations as they integrate the inherent local structural characteristics with spatial information of a face image [5]. Based on these findings, we represent a face by an attributed string (Stringface), which groups the relational organization of intermediate-level features (line segments) into a high-level global structure representation. Because the Stringface represents not only the local structural information but also the global structure of a face, it improves upon the local characteristics of feature-based methods [5][7]. Furthermore, the Stringface can be constructed using only a single face image and without training stage involved in this approach. The matching of two frontal faces is done by matching two Stringfaces through a *string*-to-*string* matching scheme. The proposed attributed string matching concept is able to effectively find the most discriminative local parts (substrings) for recognition without making any assumption on the distributions of the deformed facial regions. This substring matching ability is used to address the occlusion problem. This is believed to be the first piece of work on frontal face analysis using a high-level syntactic matching method. The studies and experimental results in this paper are confined to human frontal face recognition. We deal with partial occlusion, but we do not explicitly account for other conditions, such as illumination, expressions and pose. We also assume the detection, cropping and normalization of the face have been performed prior to applying our algorithm.

The paper is organized as follows: Section 2 defines the Stringface representation and matching concept in detail. A feasibility investigation and performance evaluation of the proposed approach is given in Section 3. Finally, the paper concludes in Section 4.

2 Proposed Stringface Recognition Approach

String matching is a syntactic and structural method for similarity measurement between strings or vectors, which has been widely used for pattern search in molecular biology, speech recognition, and file comparison. Strings can be classified into two categories: symbolic strings and attributed strings. The symbolic string matching is widely used for shape recognition, in which shapes are described by string representation and primitives are described by symbols. However, symbols are discrete in nature while most problems of pattern recognition deal with attributes that are basically continuous in nature. It was found inadequate to use symbols as primitives for complex pattern recognition [6]. Hence, the attributed string matching [4][6] were proposed and the attributed string representation makes it easier to handle noise and distortion. One advantage of using variant attributes (location, length and orientation) is that segment merging becomes possible. However, string matching was believed a technique not suitable for frontal face recognition due to its highly ordered global representation and complex nature of a human face. The only most related work [6] is attempted on human face profile. Their method is based on Needleman-Wunsch algorithm [13], which performs a global alignment on two sequences of profile line segments, which fails to work when a face profile has large local shape deformations or occlusions. Obviously, this face representation is not able to describe frontal faces as it only can represent the continuous silhouette of a profile face, ignoring other important but unconnected distinctive features, such as the eyes, eyebrows, mouth and ears. In this study, we propose a novel string representation and matching concept to recognize frontal faces, an unattempted area, to address the challenging problem of face recognition with partial occlusions.

2.1 Stringface Representation

A novel syntactic face representation is proposed here to integrate the structure connectivity information of line segments in a face image. The basic primitives of our syntactic representation are line segments, which are generated by a polygonal line fitting process [9] from a face edge map. Each line segment, L, is represented as $L(l, \theta, x, y)$, where attributes l, θ, x and y are the length, direction and midpoint location of the line, respectively. The line direction θ is defined as the the minimum angle formed between the line segment and the reference line. The line between two eyes is used as the reference line in this study.

Definition 1. *A Stringface (SF) is defined as a syntactic representation of human face, which is viewed as being composed of a set of substrings S_i ($S_i \in SF$). Substrings are connected by null primitives ϕ linking the ith substring S_i and the $(i + 1)$th substring S_{i+1} in SF.*

$$SF = S_1^{SF} \phi S_2^{SF} \phi \cdots \phi S_{n-1}^{SF} \phi S_n^{SF}, \tag{1}$$

where n is the number of substrings. The ith substring S_i^{SF} is given by

$$S_i^{SF} = L_j^{SF} L_{j+1}^{SF} \cdots L_{j+m_i}^{SF}, \tag{2}$$

where L_j^{SF} is the jth primitive in SF as well as the first primitive in substring S_i^{SF} and $(m_i + 1)$ is the number of primitives in S_i^{SF}, $i = 1, \ldots, n$.

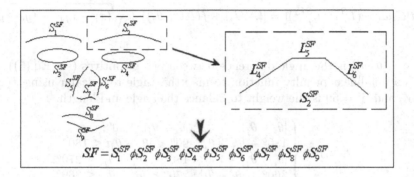

Fig. 1. An example Stringface representation

Fig. 1 illustrates a Stringface representation $SF = S_1^{SF} \phi S_2^{SF} \cdots \phi S_8^{SF} \phi S_9^{SF}$ generated from line segments, where ϕ is a null primitive connecting two substrings and each substring S_i^{SF} is a consecutive run of connected line segments $L_j^{S_i}$ (called primitives), $i = 1, \ldots, 9$. In Fig. 1, S_2^{SF} is composed of three line segments as

$$S_2^{SF} = L_4^{SF} L_5^{SF} L_6^{SF} \tag{3}$$

2.2   Cost Functions

The goal of string matching algorithms is to find a sequence of elementary edit operations which transform one sting into another at a minimal cost. The elementary operations for string matching are deletion, insertion, and substitution.

1. **Substitution (or Change):** to replace a symbol or primitive (e.g. a in $S1$) with the other (e.g. b in $S2$), denoted as $a \to b$.
2. **Insert:** to insert a symbol or primitive (e.g. b) into a string (e.g. $S1$), denoted as $\phi \to b$, where ϕ is a symbol used to denote nothing (called null symbol).
3. **Delete:** to delete a symbol or primitive (e.g. a) from a string (e.g. $S1$), denoted as $a \to \phi$.

A new edit operation, **merge**, is introduced in attributed string matching, which can address the noise and distortion issues. The merge operation is used to combine any number of consecutive primitives in one string and match with those in the other string. An example of merge operation is illustrated in Fig. 2, where primitives $L^{SF}_{i-k+1}, \ldots$ and L^{SF}_i are combined into a new primitive $L^{SF}_{i \to k}$.

We define new cost functions for edit operations of change, insert, delete and merge. Let SF_1 and SF_2 be the input and model Stringfaces, respectively. $L^{SF_1}_i$ and $L^{SF_2}_j$ are the ith and the jth primitives in SF_1 and SF_2 with attributes $(l_i, \theta_i, x_i, y_i)$ and $(l_j, \theta_j, x_j, y_j)$. Let $SF\langle i \to j \rangle$ specify the substring in SF from the ith to the jth primitives, that is $SF\langle i \to j \rangle = L^{SF}_i L^{SF}_{i+1} \cdots L^{SF}_j$. The cost functions of the proposed Stringface matching method are described as follows.

The cost function for change operation from $L^{SF_1}_i$ to $L^{SF_2}_j$ is defined as

$$Cost[Change(L^{SF_1}_i, L^{SF_2}_j)] = |l_i - l_j| + f(\triangle(\theta_i, \theta_j)) + \sqrt{(x_i - x_j)^2 + (y_i - y_j)^2},$$
$$(4)$$

where $\triangle(\theta_i, \theta_j)$ is the angle difference between two primitives (see Eq.(5)), and $f()$ is a non-linear penalty function to map the angle to a scalar using $f(x) = x^2/W$, and $W = 50$ is the weight to balance the angle and length.

$$\triangle(\theta_i, \theta_j) = \begin{cases} |\theta_i - \theta_j| & : |\theta_i - \theta_j| \leq 90°, \\ 180° - |\theta_i - \theta_j| & : 90° < |\theta_i - \theta_j| \leq 180°, \\ |\theta_i - \theta_j| - 180° & : 180° < |\theta_i - \theta_j| \leq 270°, \\ 360° - |\theta_i - \theta_j| & : 270° < |\theta_i - \theta_j| \leq 360°. \end{cases} \quad (5)$$

The costs of delete and insert operations can be derived from the above change cost function by introducing a null primitive ϕ with zero length and indefinite angle and location. The cost functions of these two operations are defined as

$$Cost[delete(L^{SF_1}_i)] = f(K_\theta) + l_i + K_{loc}, \quad (6)$$
$$Cost[insert(L^{SF_2}_j)] = f(K_\theta) + l_j + K_{loc}, \quad (7)$$

where K_θ and K_{loc} are constants to represent the indefinite orientation and location of the line segment. For the purpose of penalization, $90°$ and the diagonal distance of the input image, which are the maximum angle difference and the maximum location difference, are used for K_θ and K_{loc}.

Next, we consider the merge operation. The merge operation is used to combine and match any number of consecutive primitives in one face with those in

Fig. 2. An example of the merge operation

the other. Let $SF\langle i - k + 1 \rightarrow i \rangle = L^{SF}_{i-k+1} L^{SF}_{i-k+2} \cdots L^{SF}_i$ be a substring with k primitives in Stringface SF to be merged, and $L^{SF}_{i \rightarrow k}$ be the merged primitive of these k primitives. An example of merge operation is illustrated in Fig. 2. The merge operation is denoted as $merge(SF\langle i - k + 1 \rightarrow i \rangle, L^{SF}_{i \rightarrow k})$. If $k = 1$, $L^{SF}_{i \rightarrow k} = L^{SF}_i$. This is the case without any merge operation. The merge cost is defined as

$$Cost[merge(SF\langle i - k + 1 \rightarrow i \rangle, L^{SF}_{i \rightarrow k})] = f(\frac{k-1}{l^k} \sum_{p=i-k+1}^{i} \triangle(\theta^k, \theta_p) \times l_p), \quad (8)$$

where k is the number of merged primitives. l^k and θ^k are the length and the line direction of the merged primitive $L^{SF_1}_{i \rightarrow k}$, l_p and θ_p are the length and the line direction of primitive L^{SF}_p in $SF\langle i - k + 1 \rightarrow i \rangle$ before merging. Now, by considering $L^{SF}_{i \rightarrow k}$ as a single primitive, the cost function for a change operation after merge can be rewritten as:

$$Cost[Change(L^{SF_1}_{i \rightarrow k}, L^{SF_2}_{j \rightarrow l})] = |l^k - l^l| + f(\triangle(\theta^k, \theta^l)) + \sqrt{(x^k - x^l)^2 + (y^k - y^l)^2}, \quad (9)$$

which is performed after the k primitives in $SF_1\langle i - k + 1 \rightarrow i \rangle$ are merged as $L^{SF_1}_{i \rightarrow k}$ and the l primitives in $SF_2\langle j - l + 1 \rightarrow j \rangle$ are merged as $L^{SF_2}_{j \rightarrow l}$. If $k = 1$ and $l = 1$, no merge is performed and the above change operation reduces to the conventional one-to-one change operation $Change(L^{SF_1}_i, L^{SF_2}_j)$ (see Eq.4)

2.3   Dynamic Merge Limit Determination

The Stringface is composed of substrings and null primitives. The merge limit $merge\_limit^{SF}_i$ is used to ensure that the merge operation is restricted in the same substring, which means that primitives in substring S^{SF}_i cannot be merged with primitives in its neighboring substrings S^{SF}_{i-1} and S^{SF}_{i+1}. Let SF denote a Stringface:

$$SF = S^{SF}_1 \phi S^{SF}_2 \phi \cdots \phi S^{SF}_n = L^{SF}_1 L^{SF}_2 \cdots L^{SF}_N \quad (10)$$

where L^{SF}_i is the ith line primitive (including ϕ) in SF and S^{SF}_j is the jth substring (curve primitive) in SF, $j = 1, \ldots, n$, $i = 1, \ldots, N$, N and n are the number of line primitives plus the number of null primitives (ϕ) and the number of curve primitives in SF, respectively. Let $|S^{SF}_j|$ be the length of jth substring. For a primitive L^{SF}_i, if $L^{SF}_i \in S^{SF}_j$, then its $merge\_limit$ is defined as

$$merge\_limit^{SF}_i = i - \sum_{t=1}^{j-1} |S^{SF}_t| - j + 1 \quad (11)$$

2.4   Similarity Measure via Dynamic Programming

The similarity between the two faces can be characterized by the edit operation cost using Dynamic Programming (DP) between the two Stringfaces. Let

$SF_1 = L_1^{SF_1} \cdots L_{N_1}^{SF_1}$ and $SF_2 = L_1^{SF_2} \cdots L_{N_2}^{SF_2}$ be string representations of input face and model face, respectively, where N_1 and N_2 are numbers of primitives in SF_1 and SF_2. To find pairs of strings with high degrees of similarity, we set up a similarity matrix S. Let the input Stringface (i.e. SF_1) has N_1 primitives represented by the rows of the similarity matrix S, and let the model Stringface (i.e. SF_2) has N_2 primitives represented by the columns of the similarity matrix S. First we initialize

$$S(i,0) = S(0,j) = 0 \ (0 \le i \le N_1 , \ 0 \le j \le N_2). \tag{12}$$

$S(i,j)$ is the similarity of two strings ending at $L_i^{SF_1}$ and $L_j^{SF_2}$. If $L_i^{SF_1} = \phi$ or $L_j^{SF_2} = \phi$, $S(i,j) = 0$. If $L_i^{SF_1} \ne \phi$ and $L_j^{SF_2} \ne \phi$, $S(i,j)$ is defined as:

$$S(i,j) = \max \begin{cases} 0 \\ S(i,j-1) - Cost[\phi \to L_j^{SF_2}] \\ S(i-1,j) - Cost[L_i^{SF_1} \to \phi] \\ \max_{k,l}\{S(i-k,j-l) \\ \quad +c(SF_1\langle i-k+1 \to i \rangle, \\ \quad SF_2\langle j-l+1 \to j \rangle)\} \end{cases} \tag{13}$$

where $Cost[\phi \to L_j^{SF_2}]$ and $Cost[L_i^{SF_1} \to \phi]$ are costs of insert and delete edit operations, respectively (see Eq.6). ϕ is a null primitive. $c(SF_1\langle i-k+1 \to i \rangle, SF_2\langle j-l+1 \to j \rangle)$ is defined as follows:

$$c(SF_1\langle i-k+1 \to i \rangle, SF_2\langle j-l+1 \to j \rangle)\} = \lambda \\ -Cost[SF_1\langle i-k+1 \to i \rangle, SF_2\langle j-l+1 \to j \rangle], \tag{14}$$

where $Cost[SF_1\langle i-k+1 \to i \rangle, SF_2\langle j-l+1 \to j \rangle]$ is the cost of merge and change edit operations between substring $SF_1\langle i-k+1 \to i \rangle$ and $SF_2\langle j-l+1 \to j \rangle$ (see Eq. 8 and Eq.9). k and l are numbers of the merged primitives. In Eq.14, λ is used to decide the similarity between primitives $SF_1\langle i-k+1 \to i \rangle$ and $SF_2\langle j-l+1 \to j \rangle$. If the cost value $Cost[SF_1\langle i-k+1 \to i \rangle, SF_2\langle j-l+1 \to j \rangle]$ is less than λ, these primitives are considered as similar elements.

For two Stringfaces, SF_1 and SF_2, with primitives $L_i^{SF_1}(i = 1, 2, \ldots, N_1)$ and $L_j^{SF_2}(j = 1, 2, \ldots, N_2)$, we compute all the similarity costs between their primitives and obtain the similarity matrix S and edit operations matrix M:

$$S = \begin{pmatrix} S(0,0) & S(0,1) & \ldots & S(0,N_2) \\ \vdots & \vdots & \vdots & \vdots \\ S(N_1,0) & S(N_1,1) & \ldots & S(N_1,N_2) \end{pmatrix} \tag{15}$$

$$M = \begin{pmatrix} M(0,0) & M(0,1) & \ldots & M(0,N_2) \\ \vdots & \vdots & \vdots & \vdots \\ M(N_1,0) & M(N_1,1) & \ldots & M(N_1,N_2) \end{pmatrix} \tag{16}$$

The pair of substrings with maximum similarity is found by first locating the maximal element in S. The other matrix elements leading to this maximal value are then sequentially determined with a traceback procedure ending with an element of $S(i,j)$ equaling to zero. For example, $S(i_1,j_1) = v_1$ is the maximal element with maximal value v_1 in S. $M(i_1,j_1) = (r_1,c_1)$ is corresponding edit operations with value r_1 and c_1 in M. Then, the next element leading to $S(i_1,j_1)$ is then sequentially determined by r_1 and c_1. If $S(i_1 - r_1, j_1 - c_1) \neq 0$, then $S(i_2,j_2)$ is one of the element in the matched pair of substrings, where $i_2 = i_1 - r_1$ and $j_2 = j_1 - c_1$. The corresponding edit operations of $S(i_2,j_2)$ is $M(i_2,j_2) = (r_2,c_2)$ All elements of can be found using this procedure, until the element $S(i_k - r_k, j_l - c_l) = 0$, where $k \geq 1$ and $l \geq 1$. The pair of segments with the next best similarity is found by applying the traceback procedure to the second largest element in S not associated with the first traceback.

```
S(0,0) := 0
for  i := 1  to  N₁  do  S(i,0) := 0 ;
for  j := 1  to  N₂  do  S(0,j) := 0 ;
for  i := 1  to  N₁
   for  j := 1  to  N₂
      if  L_i^{SF1} = φ  or  L_j^{SF2} = φ
           S(i,j) = 0 ;
   else
      m₁ := S(i, j − 1) − Cost[insert(L_j^{SF2})] ;
      m₂ := S(i − 1, j) − Cost[delete(L_i^{SF1})] ;
      for  k := 1  to  merge_limit_i^{SF1}
         for  l := 1  to  merge_limit_j^{SF2}
            T[k, l] := S(i − k, j − l) + λ
               −{Cost[merge(SF₁(i − k + 1 → i), L_{i→k}^{SF1})]
               + Cost[merge(SF₂(j − l + 1 → i), L_{j→l}^{SF2})]
               + Cost[change(L_{i→k}^{SF1}, L_{j→l}^{SF2})]}
      m₃ := max(T[k, l]) ;
      S(i,j) := max(0, m₁, m₂, m₃) ;
      if  S(i,j) = m₃ ,   M(i,j) = argmax_{k,l}(T(k,l)) ;
      if  S(i,j) = m₁ ,   M(i,j) = (1,0) ;
      if  S(i,j) = m₂ ,   M(i,j) = (0,1) ;
      if  S(i,j) = 0 ,    M(i,j) = (0,0) ;
   end
```

Algorithm 1. Proposed Stringface matching.

String matching is conducted according to Algorithm 1, where $merg\_limit_i^{SF_1}$ and $merg\_limit_j^{SF_2}$ are controlling upper limits on the number of primitives to be merged into a new one in Stringfaces SF_1 and SF_2, respectively (as discussed in Section 2.3). The similarity of associating a group of segments from Stringface SF_1 with a group of segments from Stringface SF_2 is computed as

$$s(SF_1, SF_2) = \xi \times \sum_{i=1}^{f} S_i, \qquad (17)$$

The term S_i is the similarity (the ith maximal element in S matrix table) of the ith best similar substrings between two Stringfaces and f is the number of best similar substrings. ξ is a weight term which emphasizes the importance of matching large parts from both Stringfaces in accordance to the way that humans pay more attention to large shape parts when judging the quality of matching [15]. The proportion of the matched substrings lengths with respect to their total length is used to define ξ:

$$\xi = \frac{length\ of\ matched\ SF_1 + length\ of\ matched\ SF_1}{length\ of\ SF_1 + length\ of\ SF_2} \tag{18}$$

3 Experimental Verification

In this section, we present a system performance investigation on publicly available databases, which covers human face recognition with real and synthetic occlusions.

3.1 Databases and Experimental Settings

In this study, two well-know face databases (AR [12] and FRGC ver2.0 [16]) were tested. The AR database contains faces with different conditions, including partially occluded condition, which can not be found in other latest databases. Hence, AR database is particularly suitable for our evaluation. The FRGC ver2.0 dataset is much larger than the AR database, and is used to test the performance of our proposed method with occlusion variations.

The AR database consists of over 4,000 frontal view images for 126 individuals (70 males and 56 females). Each person has 26 images captured in two different sessions (separated by two-week time interval). Each session contains 13 face images under different light conditions (right light, left light and both lights), different facial expressions (smiling, anger and screaming) and partial occlusions (sunglasses and scarf). Some images were found missing or corrupted for a few subjects. We chose a subset of the data set consisting of 50 male subjects and 50 female subjects for our experiments.

The FRGC ver2.0 dataset consists of 50,000 recordings divided into training and validation partitions. The training partition is designed for training algorithms. The training set consists of 12,776 images from 222 subjects, with 6,388 controlled still images and 6,388 uncontrolled still images and contains from 9 to 16 subject sessions per subject. The validation partition is for assessing performance of an approach in a laboratory setting. The validation set contains images from 466 subjects collected in 4,007 subject sessions. Each subject session consists of four controlled still images, two uncontrolled still images, and one three-dimensional image. The validation partition contains from 1 to 22 subject sessions per subject. In our experiment (Section 3.4), 410 subjects from the validation set with more than 2 subject sessions are used. Hence, The data set used in our experiments consists of 820 FRGC controlled frontal face images with neutral expressions corresponding to 410 subjects, with two images per subject (two sessions).

In all the experiments, the original images were first normalized (in scale and orientation). Then, the facial regions are cropped to the size of 160 x 160. In all experiments, there is only one single image per person used as the model of the person. We quantitatively compare our method to several popular techniques for face recognition in the vision literature. Partitioned SRC [18] (with tuned block size 4 x 2) is one of the latest partially occluded face recognition algorithms and achieved higher recognition rate. LocPb (local probabilistic approach) [11] is a well-known method to recognize partially occluded faces and widely used as a benchmark algorithm in many partial matching methods. ICA I [1], LNMF [10] and PCA [17] are three popular methods used as benchmarks in recent face recognition approaches under occlusions [18]. LEM (Line Edge Maps) method [5] which is one of the best illumination insensitive methods based on facial edges with only one training face image per individual. AWPPZMA (Adaptively Weighted Patch Pseudo Zernike Moment Array) [8] is one of the best moment-based face recognition techniques to address occlusion and illumination when only one exemplar image per person is available.

3.2 Determination of λ

In this section, we examine the parameter (λ) involved in the propose method (see Eq.14). To determine λ, an experimental investigation on recognition accuracy was conducted under controlled condition with different values of λ on AR face database. The neutral faces under controlled/ideal condition taken in the first session were selected as the gallery set and the neutral faces under controlled/ ideal condition taken in the second session were used as the probe set. Fig. 3 shows the curve of recognition rate against the values of λ. The horizontal axis indicates the value of λ used and the vertical axis represents the rate of correct face recognition, which is the rate that the best returned face is from the correct class. The recognition rate increases greatly from $\lambda = 2$ to $\lambda = 8$. Between $\lambda = 8$ and $\lambda = 14$, the rate remains stable. Then it decreases with further increase of λ. In the rest of the experiments, λ is set as 10.

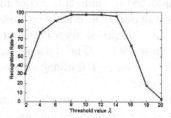

Fig. 3. The effect of λ on the recognition rate under controlled/idea condition

3.3 Face Recognition with Partial Occlusions

In this section, we test the performance of the proposed approach to cope with real partial occlusions using AR face database, which is the only database available that contains real images with disguise accessories. In the experiment, we

Fig. 4. Images of one subject in the AR database with different partial occlusions. (a) is a neutral facial image taken from the first session; (b-e) are images with partial occlusions taken from the first session and the second session, respectively.

Table 1. Performance comparison for sunglasses and scarf occluded faces

Methods	Session-1		Session-2	
	sunglasses	scarf	sunglasses	scarf
Stringface	88.0%	96.0%	76.0%	88.0%
SRC	86.0%	92.0%	64.0%	86.0%
LocPb	80.0%	82.0%	54.0%	48.0%
AWPPZMA	70.0%	72.0%	58.0%	60.0%
ICA I	54.0%	56.0%	38.0%	50.0%
LNMF	33.5%	24.0%	18.5%	9.6%

chose a subset of the data set consisting of 50 male subjects and 50 female subjects from AR face database. The neutral face images of the first session (see Fig. 4) were used as the galley set. Sunglasses and scarf occluded face images of the first and the second sessions (see Fig. 4 (b-e)) were used as the probes. The performance comparisons of the proposed approach with these benchmark methods are tabulated in Table 1, showing that the proposed approach archived the highest accuracies in both experiments.

3.4 Face Recognition with Random Block Occlusions

To further verify the performance of our method against various level of contiguous occlusions, we conducted a simulation experiment on the FRGC ver2.0 database . The data set used in our experiments consists of 820 FRGC controlled frontal face images with neutral expressions corresponding to 410 subjects, with two images per subject (two sessions). The data set is divided into gallery and probe sets. The gallery set consists of 410 images from 410 subjects. The rest of images are used as the probe set.

Occlusions are added to the probe images by using a black square of $s \times s$ with $s \in \{10, 20, \ldots, 100\}$ at a random location, as shown in Fig. 5. Note that

Fig. 5. Examples of FRGC ver2.0 face images with simulated occlusions. (a) images in the database; (b-k) the generated test images with random occluding blocks of sizes (10x10,20x20, ..., 100x100).

the $s \times s$ occlusion masks are randomly added to the images in probe sets. The graph in Fig. 6 shows the recognition rates of all four algorithms under varying degrees of occlusion. As can be seen, the Stringface method again outperformed the three benchmark methods for all levels of occlusion. Although there is only one sample image per person used as a template, SRC [18] still performed excellent as the proposed approach when the occlusion block size is small. The better performance of the Stringface approach against SRC becomes clear as the occlusion block size increases. Because of insufficient training samples, LNMF, ICA and PCA performed poorly in this single sample per class condition.

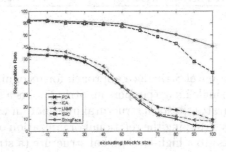

Fig. 6. Recognition under varying level of random occlusion (10x10, 20x20, ..., 100x100 of occluding blocks)

3.5 Preliminary Experiment under Varying Lighting and Expression Conditions

To evaluate the effects of different lighting conditions and facial expressions on the proposed approach, the preliminary experiment was designed using face images taken under different lighting conditions and facial expression from the AR database. In this experiment, we chose a subset of the data set consisting of 50 male subjects and 50 female subjects from AR database. The neutral face images taken in the first session were used as single models of the subjects. The face images under three different light conditions and facial expressions taken in the first session were used as probe images. The proposed approach is compared with the eigenface and LEM methods.

The experimental results on probe images with three lighting conditions and different facial expressions (smiling, angry and screaming) are illustrated in Table 2. In the three experiments under varying lighting conditions, the proposed Stringface method significantly outperformed the eigenface approach and also consistently performed better than the illumination-insensitive LEM approach[5]. The experimental results on faces with smile, anger and scream expressions show that the Stringface method achieved varying results compared to the LEM and eigenface methods.

Table 2. Preliminary results under varying lighting conditions and facial expressing changes

Conditions	Recognition rate(%)				LEM	AWPPZMA	Stringface
	Eigenface						
	k = 20	k = 60	k = 100	k = 100(w/o 1st 3)			
Left Light on	6.25%	9.82%	9.82%	26.79%	92.86%	74.36%	96.43%
Right Light on	4.46%	7.14%	7.14%	49.11%	91.07%	64.96%	95.53%
Both Light on	1.79%	2.68%	2.68%	64.29%	74.11%	42.74%	75.89%
Smiling	87.87%	94.64%	93.97%	82.04%	78.57%	96.58%	87.50%
Angry	78.57%	84.82%	87.50%	73.21%	92.86%	87.18%	87.50%
Screaming	34.82%	41.96%	45.54%	32.14%	31.25%	38.46%	25.89%

4   Conclusions

This paper proposes a novel Stringface approach for recognizing faces with partial occlusions from a single image per person. Stringface is a syntactic face representation, which integrates the local structural information with spatial information of a face image by grouping the relational organization of intermediate-level features (line segments) to a high-level global structure (a string). The proposed approach represents a face image as a string and enables it to define complex discontinuous features in a human frontal face. The matching of two frontal faces is achieved by matching two Stringfaces through a *string-to-string* matching, which was believed a technique not suitable for frontal face recognition due to its highly ordered global representation and complex nature of a human face. The performance of the proposed approach has been evaluated and compared with several state-of-the-art approaches. Experimental results demonstrated the feasibility and effectiveness of a high-level syntactic method in face recognition, showing a new way for face representation and recognition.

References

1. Bartlett, M., Movellan, J., Sejnowski, T.: Face recognition by independent component analysis. IEEE Transactions on Neural Networks 13(6), 1450–1464 (2002)
2. Biederman, I., Ju, G.: Surface versus edge-based determinants of visual recognition. Cognitive Psychology 20, 38–64 (1988)
3. Bruce, V., Hanna, E., Dench, N., Healey, P., Burton, M.: The importance of mass in line drawings of faces. Applied Congnitive Psychology 6(7), 619–628 (1992)
4. Chen, S.W., Tung, S.T., Fang, C.Y., Cheng, S., Jain, A.K.: Extended attributed string matching for shape recognition. Computer Vision and Image Understanding 70(1), 36–50 (1998)
5. Gao, Y., Leung, M.K.: Face recognition using line edge map. IEEE Transactions on Pattern Analysis and Machine Intelligence 24(6), 764–779 (2002)
6. Gao, Y., Leung, M.K.: Human face profile recognition using attributed string. Pattern Recognition 35, 353–360 (2002)
7. Gao, Y., Qi, Y.: Robust visual similarity retrieval in single model face databases. Pattern Recognition 38(7), 1009–1020 (2005)

8. Kanan, H.R., Faez, K., Gao, Y.: Face recognition using adaptively weighted patch pzm array from a single exemplar image per person. Pattern Recognition 41(12), 3799–3812 (2008)
9. Leung, M., Yang, Y.: Dynamic two-strip algorithm in curve fitting. Pattern Recognition 23(1-2), 69–79 (1990)
10. Li, S., Hou, X.W., Zhang, H.J., Cheng, Q.S.: Learning spatially localized, parts-based representation. In: IEEE Computer Society Conference on Computer Vision and Pattern Recognition, vol. 1, pp. I-207–I-212 (2001)
11. Martínez, A.: Recognizing imprecisely localized, partially occluded, and expression variant faces from a single sample per class. IEEE Transactions on Pattern Analysis and Machine Intelligence 24(6), 748–763 (2002)
12. Martínez, A., Benavente, R.: The AR face database. CVC Technical Report 24 (1998)
13. Needleman, S.B., Wunsch, C.D.: A general method applicable to the search for similarities in the amino acid sequence of two proteins. J. Mol. Biol. 48(3), 443–453 (1970)
14. Penev, P.S., Atick, J.J.: Local feature analysis: A general statistical theory for object representation. Network: Computation in Neural Systems 7, 477–500 (1996)
15. Petrakis, E.G., Diplaros, A., Milios, E.: Matching and retrieval of distorted and occluded shapes using dynamic programming. IEEE Transactions on Pattern Analysis and Machine Intelligence 24(11), 1501–1516 (2002)
16. Phillips, P., Flynn, P., Scruggs, T., Bowyer, K., Chang, J., Hoffman, K., Marques, J., Min, J., Worek, W.: Overview of the face recognition grand challenge. In: Proceedings of IEEE Computer Society Conference on Computer Vision and Pattern Recognition, vol. 1, pp. 947–954 (2005)
17. Turk, M., Pentland, A.: Eigenfaces for recognition. Journal of Cognitive Neuroscience 3(1), 71–86 (1991)
18. Wright, J., Yang, A.Y., Ganesh, A., Sastry, S.S., Ma, Y.: Robust face recognition via sparse representation. Pattern Analysis and Machine Intelligence, IEEE Transactions on 31(2), 210–227 (2009)

Real-Time Spatiotemporal Stereo Matching Using the Dual-Cross-Bilateral Grid

Christian Richardt[1], Douglas Orr[1], Ian Davies[1],
Antonio Criminisi[2], and Neil A. Dodgson[1]

[1] University of Cambridge, United Kingdom
[2] Microsoft Research Cambridge, United Kingdom
Christian.Richardt@cl.cam.ac.uk, Douglas.Orr@cantab.net,
Ian.Davies@cl.cam.ac.uk, antcrim@microsoft.com, Neil.Dodgson@cl.cam.ac.uk

Abstract. We introduce a real-time stereo matching technique based on a reformulation of Yoon and Kweon's adaptive support weights algorithm [1]. Our implementation uses the bilateral grid to achieve a speedup of 200× compared to a straightforward full-kernel GPU implementation, making it the fastest technique on the Middlebury website. We introduce a colour component into our greyscale approach to recover precision and increase discriminability. Using our implementation, we speed up spatial-depth superresolution 100×. We further present a spatiotemporal stereo matching approach based on our technique that incorporates temporal evidence in real time (>14 *fps*). Our technique visibly reduces flickering and outperforms per-frame approaches in the presence of image noise. We have created five synthetic stereo videos, with ground truth disparity maps, to quantitatively evaluate depth estimation from stereo video. Source code and datasets are available on our project website[1].

1 Introduction

In contrast to global stereo matching techniques such as graph cuts [2] or belief propagation [3], Yoon and Kweon's adaptive support weights [1] only aggregate evidence over a finite window size. The effectiveness of their technique is due to aggregation of support over large window sizes and weights that adapt according to similarity and proximity to the central pixel in the support window. Results are good, but the algorithm is slow, taking about one minute to process the Tsukuba images on a current generation CPU. This has prompted people to resort to a separable implementation [4] to achieve interactive frame-rates.

We take a different approach. We rewrite their technique (section 2) as a *dual-cross-bilateral filter* with Gaussian weights (section 3). Based on the bilateral grid (section 3.1), we present a real-time GPU-based implementation (section 3.2) and improve its performance using a dichromatic approach (section 3.3). We show how spatial-depth super-resolution can be accelerated using our technique (section 3.4) and we extend our technique to stereo video (section 3.5). We conclude with results (section 4) and discussion of future work (section 5). Key literature is referred to in-line where it is most relevant.

---

[1] http://www.cl.cam.ac.uk/research/rainbow/projects/dcbgrid/

K. Daniilidis, P. Maragos, N. Paragios (Eds.): ECCV 2010, Part III, LNCS 6313, pp. 510–523, 2010.
© Springer-Verlag Berlin Heidelberg 2010

2   Adaptive Support Weights

We start with a brief summary of Yoon and Kweon's technique. It builds on a winner-take-all stereo pipeline [5] and computes the initial cost space using truncated AD (absolute difference). We write this initial cost space as $C(\mathbf{p}, d)$ where $\mathbf{p} = (x, y)$ are the coordinates of a pixel in the left image and d is some disparity hypothesis. For convenience, let $\overline{\mathbf{p}} = (x - d, y)$ be the corresponding pixel in the right image.

The key idea is to aggregate costs over a large support window of 35×35 pixels for each pixel, where each pixel in the support window is weighted according to similarity and proximity to the central pixel. This is motivated by the *Gestalt* theory of perceptual grouping, with the weight between two pixels given by

$$w(\mathbf{p}, \mathbf{q}) = \exp\left(-\frac{\Delta E(\mathbf{p}, \mathbf{q})}{\gamma_c} - \frac{\|\mathbf{p} - \mathbf{q}\|}{\gamma_p} \right), \tag{1}$$

where ΔE is the Euclidean distance between pixel values in the CIELAB colour space, and the parameters γ_c and γ_p control grouping by similarity and proximity, respectively. Yoon and Kweon use default values of $\gamma_c = 5$ and $\gamma_p = 17.5$.

The aggregated cost space C' is now calculated using

$$C'(\mathbf{p}, d) = \frac{1}{k} \cdot \sum_{\mathbf{q} \in N_{\mathbf{p}}} w(\mathbf{p}, \mathbf{q}) \cdot w(\overline{\mathbf{p}}, \overline{\mathbf{q}}) \cdot C(\mathbf{q}, d), \tag{2}$$

where $k = \sum_{\mathbf{q} \in N_{\mathbf{p}}} w(\mathbf{p}, \mathbf{q}) \cdot w(\overline{\mathbf{p}}, \overline{\mathbf{q}})$ is the normalisation quotient and $N_{\mathbf{p}}$ the set of all pixels in the support window. For the winner-take-all stage, we use Yang et al.'s sub-pixel refinement process [6]. We implemented all techniques in this paper using *C for CUDA*, an architecture for general purpose computation on NVIDIA GPUs. We measure run times on an NVIDIA Quadro FX 5800 GPU.

Our straightforward GPU implementation is about $25\times$ faster than reported by Yoon and Kweon and produces comparable results to their publicly-available implementation (on the Middlebury website[2]). However, neither implementation achieves the results reported in the original paper. We believe this to be due to differences in filling in pixels that are invalidated by the left-right consistency check [7]. As we compare different techniques, it is fairest to only compare GPU techniques to other GPU techniques, and also to have all techniques share the same post-processing.

3   Dual-Cross-Bilateral Aggregation

The bilateral filter [8] is a common edge-preserving smoothing filter. One variant, the cross- or joint-bilateral filter [9], smoothes an image with respect to edges in a different image. Yoon and Kweon's technique is another variant that smoothes the cost space while preserving edges in both input images. In the bilateral filtering framework, we call this kind of filter a *dual-cross-bilateral filter* (DCB).

---

[2] http://vision.middlebury.edu/stereo/

We reformulate their approach using Gaussian weights, the *de facto* standard in bilateral filtering. This yields

$$w(\mathbf{p}, \mathbf{q}) = G_{\sigma_r}(\Delta E(\mathbf{p}, \mathbf{q})) \cdot \sqrt{G_{\sigma_s}(\|\mathbf{p} - \mathbf{q}\|)}, \tag{3}$$

where σ_r and σ_s are similarity and proximity parameters, and $G_\sigma(x) = \exp(\frac{-x^2}{2\sigma^2})$ is the unnormalised Gaussian centred on zero, with standard deviation σ. The square root is applied to the second factor, so that $w(\mathbf{p}, \mathbf{q}) \cdot w(\overline{\mathbf{p}}, \overline{\mathbf{q}})$ includes the proximity weight exactly once.

The aggregation remains unchanged from equation 2, resulting in

$$C'(\mathbf{p}, d) = \frac{1}{k} \cdot \sum_{\mathbf{q} \in N_\mathbf{p}} G_{\sigma_r}(\Delta E(\mathbf{p}, \mathbf{q})) \cdot G_{\sigma_r}(\Delta E(\overline{\mathbf{p}}, \overline{\mathbf{q}})) \cdot G_{\sigma_s}(\|\mathbf{p} - \mathbf{q}\|) \cdot C(\mathbf{q}, d), \tag{4}$$

which we compute within a window of 35×35 pixels. We use the parameter values $\sigma_r = 10$ and $\sigma_s = 10$, which we found to produce the best results.

The resulting disparity maps are shown in table 2 and the Middlebury evaluation results in table 3. It is notable that our dual-cross-bilateral aggregation improves on our Yoon and Kweon implementation in the *nonocc* (non-occluded pixels) and *all* pixels categories in almost all cases.

3.1   Bilateral Grid

Full-kernel implementations of the bilateral filter are very slow, so several speedup approaches have been proposed. A separable implementation [11] is too inaccurate for our purposes. Weiss' technique [12] only supports spatial box-filters rather than the Gaussians we use. And Yang *et al.*'s constant-time bilateral filtering [13] does not generalise well to higher dimensions, which we require. We therefore use the bilateral grid [10,14]. It has the interesting property that it runs faster and uses less memory as σ increases.

Consider the example of a greyscale image $I(x, y)$. The bilateral grid embeds it in a 3D space: 2D for spatial coordinates and 1D for pixel values. Each pixel (x, y) is mapped to $(x, y, I(x, y))$ in the bilateral grid Γ. The 1D example in figure 1 illustrates the use of the bilateral grid in three steps.

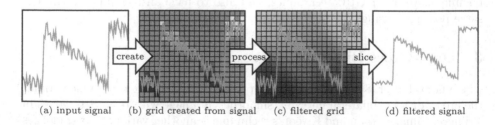

(a) input signal   (b) grid created from signal   (c) filtered grid   (d) filtered signal

Fig. 1. Illustration of 1D bilateral filtering using the bilateral grid: the signal (a) is embedded in the grid (b), which is processed (c) and sliced to obtain the filtered signal (d). See text for details. Adapted from Chen *et al.* [10].

1. Grid Creation All grid voxels (x, y, c) are first zeroed using $\Gamma(x, y, c) = (0, 0)$. Then, for each pixel (x, y),

$$\Gamma\left(\left[\frac{x}{s_s}\right], \left[\frac{y}{s_s}\right], \left[\frac{I(x,y)}{s_r}\right]\right) \mathrel{+}= (I(x, y), 1). \tag{5}$$

where $[\,\cdot\,]$ is the rounding operator, and s_s and s_r are the spatial and range sampling rates, which are set to σ_s and σ_r respectively. Note that the pixel values and the number of pixels are accumulated using homogeneous coordinates, which make it easy to compute weighted averages in the grid slicing stage.

2. Grid Processing The grid is now convolved with a Gaussian filter, of standard deviation σ_s and σ_r along the space and range dimensions. As the previous step has already sub-sampled the data accordingly, we only need to convolve each dimension with a 5-tap 1D kernel with $\sigma = 1$.

3. Grid Slicing The result is now extracted by accessing the grid coordinates $(x/s_s, y/s_s, I(x, y)/s_r)$ using trilinear interpolation, and dividing the homogeneous vector to access the actual data.

The bilateral grid is amenable to real-time GPU implementation, as demonstrated by Chen *et al.* [10].

3.2 Dual-Cross-Bilateral Grid

Chen *et al.* [10] show that the bilateral grid can also be used for cross-bilateral filtering. This is achieved by using an edge image $E(x, y)$ to determine grid coordinates, but storing the pixel values of the image $I(x, y)$ to be filtered:

$$\Gamma\left(\left[\frac{x}{s_s}\right], \left[\frac{y}{s_s}\right], \left[\frac{E(x,y)}{s_r}\right]\right) \mathrel{+}= (I(x, y), 1). \tag{6}$$

The grid processing remains the same, and the slicing stage accesses the grid at $(x/s_s, y/s_s, E(x, y)/s_r)$.

Recall that our *dual-cross-bilateral* cost aggregation smoothes the cost space while preserving edges in the two input images. To implement it, we extend the bilateral grid to take into account both input images as edge images when calculating grid coordinates, and to accumulate cost space values instead of pixel values. We call our extension the dual-cross-bilateral grid, or *DCB grid*.

For a pixel $\mathbf{p}$ at (x, y) in the left image, and its corresponding pixel $\overline{\mathbf{p}}$ at $(x - d, y)$ in the right image, we create the DCB grid using

$$\Gamma\left(\left[\frac{x}{\sigma_s}\right], \left[\frac{y}{\sigma_s}\right], \left[\frac{L_L^\star(\mathbf{p})}{\sigma_r}\right], \left[\frac{L_R^\star(\overline{\mathbf{p}})}{\sigma_r}\right]\right) \mathrel{+}= (C(\mathbf{p}, d), 1). \tag{7}$$

Instead of image intensities, as in Chen *et al.* [10], we use the lightness component L^* of the CIELAB colour space, as it is perceptually more uniform and hence more closely models how we perceive greyscale images. However, this also degrades performance compared to the full-kernel DCB, which uses full-colour images. The subscripts L and R indicate the left and right images, respectively.

The result of slicing the DCB grid is the aggregated cost

$$C'(\mathbf{p}, d) = \Gamma\left(\frac{x}{\sigma_s}, \frac{y}{\sigma_s}, \frac{L_L^*(\mathbf{p})}{\sigma_r}, \frac{L_R^*(\overline{\mathbf{p}})}{\sigma_r}\right). \tag{8}$$

In our implementation, we tile the 4D bilateral grids for all disparities into one large 2D texture. In the slicing stage, we perform the quadrilinear interpolation by using bilinear texture filtering to fetch the values stored at the surrounding four ($[x/\sigma_s], [y/\sigma_s]$) coordinates, and bilinearly interpolate between them.

The run times in table 1 show that the DCB grid runs at 13 *fps* or higher on all data sets, with 70 *fps* on Tsukuba – more than 200× faster than the full-kernel implementation, and more than 165× faster than our GPU implementation of Yoon and Kweon. The disparity maps of all our techniques are shown in table 2 for visual comparison, and evaluated on the Middlebury datasets in table 3.

Table 1. Run time comparison in milliseconds. Our techniques, shown in bold, are benchmarked on an NVIDIA Quadro FX 5800. Asterisks (*) mark run times estimated from reported figures, rounded to one significant digit.

Technique	Tsukuba 384×288×16	Venus 434×383×20	Teddy 450×375×60	Cones 450×375×60
DCB Grid	**14.2**	**25.7**	**75.8**	**75.0**
Real-time GPU [15]	30*	60*	200*	200*
Reliability DP [16]	42	109	300*	300*
Dichromatic DCB Grid	**188**	**354**	**1,070**	**1,070**
Plane-fit BP [17]	200*	400*	1,000*	1,000*
Y&K (our GPU impl.)	**2,350**	**4,480**	**13,700**	**13,700**
Full-kernel DCB	**2,990**	**5,630**	**17,700**	**17,600**
Yoon & Kweon [1]	60,000	100,000*	300,000*	300,000*

3.3   Dichromatic DCB Grid

The dramatic speedup achieved by the DCB grid comes at some loss of quality. This is because the underlying bilateral grid only works on greyscale images and hence does not differentiate colours that have similar greyscale values, as shown in the examples of figure 2b.

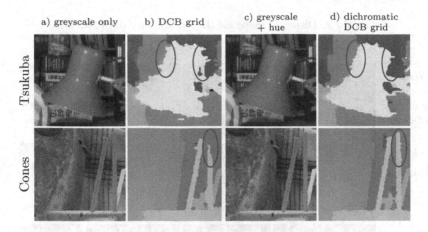

Fig. 2. Comparison of input images (a, c) and disparity maps of the (b) greyscale and (d) dichromatic DCB grids. The input images are displayed as 'seen' by the algorithms. Note that the dichromatic DCB grid (d) visibly improves on (b).

A solution is to add additional colour axes to the grid, to increase its colour discriminability. Unfortunately, the memory requirements of the bilateral grid are exponential in the number of dimensions. The *teddy* and *cones* data sets, for example, each have a total memory footprint of

$$60 \text{ disparities} \times \frac{450}{10} \times \frac{375}{10} \times \left(\frac{100}{10}\right)^k \times 8 \text{ bytes} \qquad (9)$$

when using the standard parameters $\sigma_s = 10$ and $\sigma_r = 10$, k colour dimensions, and two single-precision floating-point numbers per grid cell. For the DCB grid, where $k=2$, this amounts to 78 MB. However, the best results, with full CIELAB colours in both images ($k=6$), would require a prohibitive 764 GB.

The maximum number of colour dimensions that can be afforded on current generation graphics cards is $k=3$ which equates to 783 MB for *teddy*. This allows one additional colour axis in one of the images, in addition to each image's greyscale component. The result is a dichromatic technique which can differentiate colours along two colour axes. This is an interesting trade-off between the common monochromatic (greyscale) and trichromatic (*e.g.* RGB) stereo approaches, that has not previously been explored.

We experimented with several colour dimensions (table 4) and found that CIELAB hue h_{ab} provided the highest discriminability.

The results in tables 1 and 3 show that the dichromatic approach improves on the monochromatic DCB grid in all categories (except run time), achieving results comparable (*tsukuba, teddy*) or superior (*venus*) to our implementation of Yoon and Kweon, at a 13× speedup. The close-ups in figure 2 also show qualitative improvements.

Table 2. Disparity maps for the Middlebury data sets [5]

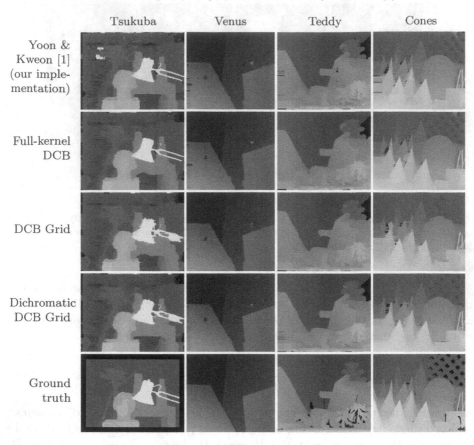

Table 3. Performance comparison of the proposed methods to Yoon & Kweon and selected real-time techniques using the Middlebury stereo benchmark

Technique	Rank	Tsukuba			Venus			Teddy			Cones		
		nonocc	all	disc	nonocc	all	disc	nonocc	all	disc	nonocc	all	disc
Plane-fit BP [17]	19.4	0.97	1.83	5.26	0.17	0.51	1.71	6.65	12.1	14.7	4.17	10.7	10.6
Yoon & Kweon [1]	32.8	1.38	1.85	6.90	0.71	1.19	6.13	7.88	13.3	18.6	3.97	9.79	8.26
Full-kernel DCB	47.7	3.96	4.75	12.9	1.36	2.02	10.4	9.10	15.9	18.4	3.34	9.60	8.26
Y&K (our impl.)	48.2	4.39	5.29	8.10	1.30	2.07	8.31	9.39	16.3	18.4	3.68	9.96	8.42
Dichrom. DCB Grid	52.9	4.28	5.44	14.1	1.20	1.80	9.69	9.52	16.4	19.5	4.05	10.4	10.3
Real-time GPU [15]	56.2	2.05	4.22	10.6	1.92	2.98	20.3	7.23	14.4	17.6	6.41	13.7	16.5
Reliability DP [16]	59.7	1.36	3.39	7.25	2.35	3.48	12.2	9.82	16.9	19.5	12.9	19.9	19.7
DCB Grid	64.9	5.90	7.26	21.0	1.35	1.91	11.2	10.5	17.2	22.2	5.34	11.9	14.9

Table 4. Performance comparison of the dichromatic DCB grid with various colour properties using the Middlebury stereo benchmark. Judging by rank, as computed by the Middlebury website, the best technique is CIELAB hue, h_{ab}.

Technique	Rank	Tsukuba			Venus			Teddy			Cones		
		nonocc	all	disc	nonocc	all	disc	nonocc	all	disc	nonocc	all	disc
$h_{ab} = \mathrm{atan2}(b^*, a^*)$	**48.6**	**4.28**	5.44	14.1	1.20	1.80	9.69	9.52	16.4	19.5	4.05	**10.4**	**10.3**
HSL saturation	49.0	4.44	**5.37**	**12.9**	**1.05**	**1.58**	**8.29**	9.46	16.4	19.4	4.30	10.7	11.3
$C^*_{ab} = \sqrt{a^{*2} + b^{*2}}$	49.9	4.97	5.94	16.7	1.15	1.75	8.65	9.55	16.4	19.9	**4.00**	**10.4**	10.5
$s_{ab} = C^*_{ab}/L^*$	50.0	4.36	5.45	12.9	1.19	1.86	9.32	**9.41**	**16.3**	**19.2**	4.41	10.8	11.6
b^*	50.8	4.79	5.83	16.2	1.25	1.84	10.1	9.53	**16.3**	19.6	4.28	10.7	11.6
a^*	52.0	5.36	6.49	18.3	1.24	1.84	9.13	9.62	16.5	19.9	4.28	10.5	11.3
HSL hue	51.2	4.62	5.85	14.9	1.30	1.87	10.4	9.83	16.6	20.2	4.18	10.7	11.1

3.4 Spatial-Depth Super-Resolution

Yoon and Kweon's method is also used in other contexts such as spatial-depth super-resolution. Yang et al. [6] use it as a central component in their system. Starting from a low-resolution depth map, they iteratively upsample it to the full resolution of the input images using Yoon and Kweon's cost aggregation. We use the same algorithm with our DCB grid and achieve a speedup of more than $100\times$. Figure 3 compares results, run times and errors.

a) Yoon and Kweon [1]   b) Our DCB Grid

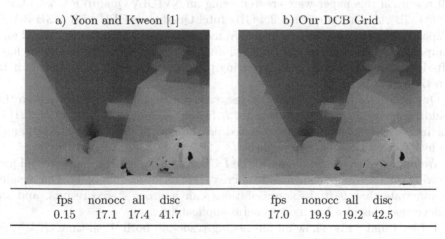

	fps	nonocc	all	disc		fps	nonocc	all	disc
	0.15	17.1	17.4	41.7		17.0	19.9	19.2	42.5

Fig. 3. Comparison of Yoon & Kweon's and our cost aggregation techniques in Yang et al.'s spatial-depth super-resolution on $8\times$ sub-sampled *teddy*. Our technique is more than $100\times$ faster, at only a small loss of quality.

3.5 Temporal DCB Grid

Stereo videos pose different challenges to stereo images: the application of techniques on a per-frame basis is insufficient to achieve flicker-free and temporally coherent disparity maps. Given the success of the DCB grid method, we turned our attention to adding time as an extra dimension, inspired by approaches that aggregate costs over a 3D spatiotemporal support window [18,19]. Our experiments consider a time window of five frames, which we found to work well.

For each frame of the video, the DCB grid is created and processed as described in section 3.2, but the slicing is based on the grids of the last $n = 5$ frames, each weighted by w_i:

$$C'(\mathbf{p}, d) = \sum_{i=0}^{n-1} w_i \cdot \Gamma_i\left(\frac{x}{\sigma_s}, \frac{y}{\sigma_s}, \frac{L_L^\star(\mathbf{p})}{\sigma_r}, \frac{L_R^\star(\overline{\mathbf{p}})}{\sigma_r}\right), \tag{10}$$

where $i = 0$ indicates the current frame, $i = 1$ the previous frame and so on. The original spacetime stereo approaches use constant weights ($w_i = 1$). We use Gaussian weights, $w_i = \exp(-i^2/2\sigma_t^2)$ with $\sigma_t = 2$, which extends the DCB grid into the time dimension. We also tried Paris' adaptive exponential decay [20], but did not see any improvements compared to our simpler technique.

Note that we cannot use the dichromatic and temporal extensions at the same time, as we have insufficient memory to handle 6 dimensions of data (4 GB of GPU memory). Results of qualitative and quantitative nature are discussed next.

4   Results

All results in this paper were created using an NVIDIA Quadro FX 5800 GPU with 4 GB video memory, on a 2.4 GHz Intel Quad Core CPU with 4 GB RAM. Disparity maps created using our per-frame techniques are shown in table 2 and compared to other techniques in tables 1 and 3. Like Yoon and Kweon, we include left-right post-processing when reporting performance figures, but exclude it in run time measurements.

Our DCB grid is currently the fastest stereo correspondence approach on the Middlebury stereo evaluation website. A faster technique by Yang et al. [21] is not listed, as it has not been evaluated on the new Middlebury data sets, and we hence cannot compare to it fairly.

We improved the performance of the DCB grid using a dichromatic technique, drawing on a second colour axis to increase colour discriminability. Our results demonstrate that partial-colour solutions can improve stereo results, and we believe that this idea has more general applicability.

Tables 1 and 3 also show an interesting trade-off: both 'Real-time GPU' [15] and 'Reliability DP' [16] are slower than the DCB grid, but faster than the dichromatic DCB grid, with performance being inversely related: the dichromatic DCB grid outperforms both 'Real-time GPU' and 'Reliability DP' which in turn outperform the DCB grid. Yang et al.'s plane-fit BP [17] outperforms our dichromatic DCB grid at similar run times, but their technique occupies both CPU and GPU, whereas our techniques leave the CPU available for other tasks.

Video frame (red-cyan anaglyph)	Per-frame DCB Grid	Temporal DCB Grid

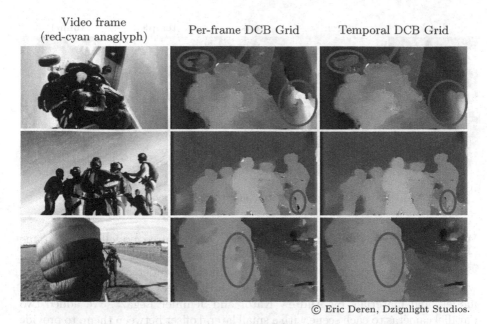

© Eric Deren, Dzignlight Studios.

Fig. 4. Disparity maps for selected frames of the 'skydiving' stereo video. Note that our temporal DCB grid visibly reduces errors (see highlighted regions).

4.1 Stereo Videos

We evaluated the temporal DCB grid qualitatively using real stereo videos and quantitatively on synthetic stereo videos with ground truth disparities, where we also compared it against per-frame techniques.

Qualitative Evaluation. Figure 4 shows frames from the 'skydiving' video[3]. We processed it at a resolution of 480×270 with 40 disparities, without left-right consistency check. On our machine, the per-frame DCB grid runs at 16 *fps* and the temporal DCB grid at 14 *fps*. As can be seen in the supplementary video, the temporal DCB grid visibly reduces flickering compared to the per-frame method.

Stereo Videos with Ground Truth Disparities. The quantitative evaluation of disparity maps from stereo videos is hindered by the general lack of ground truth disparity maps. We created a set of five stereo videos with ground truth disparity maps (see figure 5) and make them available on our project website:

book – turning a page of an old book (41 frames)
street – camera pans across a street view (100 frames)
tanks – camera flies along a grid of tanks (100 frames)
temple – rotating Mayan temple (100 frames)
tunnel – moving through a winding corridor (100 frames)

---

[3] http://www.dzignlight.com/stereo/skydiving.shtml

book   street   tanks   temple   tunnel

Fig. 5. Selected frames and disparity maps from our synthetic stereo videos

We generated the sequences using Blender, an open source modeller. Each frame is 400×300 pixels in size with a disparity range of 64 pixels. The 'book', 'tanks' and 'temple' objects were taken from the Official Blender Model Repository[4], while the *tunnel* scene was our own design. For the 'street' sequence, we combined models and materials by Andrew Kator and Jennifer Legaz[5]. We added two parallel cameras to each scene with a small lateral offset between them, to provide the left and right views, and used the Blender node system to render disparity maps from the point of view of each camera.

Quantitative Evaluation. We compared the temporal DCB grid against per-frame techniques using our synthetic ground truth videos. We processed all video frames by all techniques and used the same left-right consistency post-processing as earlier. Our ground truth stereo videos do not contain any noise, but real videos do. For this reason, we investigated the robustness to noise of per-frame techniques and the temporal DCB grid. We simulate thermal imaging noise by adding zero-centred Gaussian noise to all colour channels of the input frames.

The performance and run times of our implementations are shown in table 5. We summarise the level and variability of errors using the mean and standard deviation of the percentage of bad pixels across frames.

The best results are produced by the temporal DCB grid which significantly outperforms the per-frame techniques on all datasets except *tunnel*, on which it shows the least variation in error. Our per-frame DCB grid techniques come second and third, and our full-kernel implementations are placed last.

We believe that the poor performance of the temporal DCB grid on the *tunnel* video is because it has a lot of texture, so that simple per-frame approaches work well, while our temporal technique tends to over-smooth. Nevertheless, it reduces flickering visibly in all videos, as can be seen in the supplementary videos.

It is also notable that our temporal DCB grid has a run time that is sub-linear in the number of frames: it only takes 76% longer than the per-frame DCB grid to process a five frames window instead of a single frame.

---

[4] http://e2-productions.com/repository/
[5] Licensed under CC-BY 3.0, available at http://www.katorlegaz.com/3d_models/.

Table 5. Performance comparison of the proposed methods on our synthetic stereo videos with additive Gaussian noise ($\sigma = 20$). Shown are the average and standard deviation of the percentage of bad pixels (threshold is 1), and per-frame run times. For most datasets, the temporal DCB grid has the least mean error.

Technique	Time in ms	Book mean stdev		Street mean stdev		Tanks mean stdev		Temple mean stdev		Tunnel mean stdev	
Temporal DCB Grid	90	**44.0**	2.02	**25.9**	**2.00**	**31.4**	6.06	**31.7**	1.82	36.4	**7.88**
DCB Grid	51	52.2	2.04	32.5	2.33	36.0	6.16	39.5	1.91	**25.7**	11.1
Dichromatic DCB Grid	782	58.9	1.83	39.2	2.62	47.8	12.0	43.0	1.73	32.9	12.0
Full-kernel DCB	13,200	65.9	1.45	49.1	3.13	53.5	6.15	52.0	**1.28**	43.0	11.7
Y&K (our impl.)	9,770	84.2	**1.24**	56.1	2.67	87.7	**2.01**	72.8	1.80	58.4	11.7

Plots of the error levels at standard deviations between 0 and 100 (out of 255) are shown in figure 6. The graphs show that the temporal DCB grid improves on the per-frame technique at increased noise levels in all cases. In particular, it is superior for all noise levels in the *street* and *temple* sequences, and starting from noise levels of 5–45 for the other sequences. We assume that it is the integration of temporal evidence across several frames that makes this improvement possible.

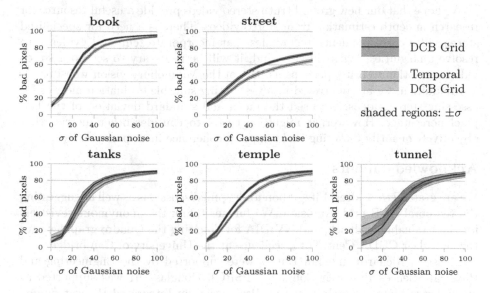

Fig. 6. Error versus noise curves for ground truth stereo videos: the temporal DCB grid performs better than the per-frame DCB grid at higher noise levels. Please also refer to the supplementary videos for a visual comparison.

5 Discussion

Rewriting Yoon and Kweon's adaptive support weights as a dual-cross-bilateral filter with Gaussian weights allows us to use the bilateral grid for acceleration, and to incorporate temporal information into the stereo matching process. Our DCB grid achieves real-time frame-rates through a speedup of more than 200× compared to a full-kernel GPU implementation, at only a small loss of precision. Our DCB grid is currently the fastest method on the Middlebury stereo website. The source code for our techniques, our ground truth stereo videos and further supplementary materials are available from our project website.

The speed of the DCB grid makes it versatile. Techniques building on Yoon and Kweon's method automatically benefit from a large speedup. We showed this by applying it to Yang et al.'s spatial-depth super-resolution, achieving a speedup of 100×, with minimal loss of quality.

Future Work
Using our dichromatic DCB grid, we showed that colour is a useful component in achieving high quality disparity maps. However, the enormous memory requirements of the bilateral grid effectively inhibit filtering in full colour. Recent work by Adams et al. [22] proposes a method with linear memory requirements. They agree that the bilateral grid is currently the fastest bilateral filtering technique for 4 dimensions when using a filter standard deviation of 10, as we do. However, full-colour filtering, using a total of 8 dimensions, would be about four times as fast with their technique, with significantly reduced memory requirements.

We hope that our new ground truth stereo videos provide a useful resource for research in depth estimation from stereo videos. There is a need for specialised stereo video correspondence techniques that incorporate temporal evidence to resolve ambiguities. With this in mind, it will be necessary to set up a stereo video evaluation website, perhaps as part of the Middlebury vision website.

In addition, we are interested in investigating suitable evaluation metrics for assessing stereo videos. We used the mean and standard deviation of the bad pixel percentage. However, it might be useful to consider other metrics that objectively quantify flickering and temporal coherence in disparity videos.

Acknowledgements

We are grateful to Andrew Fitzgibbon for helpful discussions as well as suggesting the temporal DCB grid extension. We further thank the anonymous reviewers for their valuable feedback, and NVIDIA for donating the Quadro graphics card through their CUDA Centre of Excellence at the University of Cambridge.

Christian Richardt and Ian Davies were supported by the Engineering and Physical Sciences Research Council (EPSRC). Douglas Orr was supported as an undergraduate research intern by Presenccia, an Integrated Project funded under the European Sixth Framework Programme (FP6-FET-27731).

References

1. Yoon, K.J., Kweon, I.S.: Adaptive support-weight approach for correspondence search. PAMI 28, 650–656 (2006)
2. Boykov, Y., Veksler, O., Zabih, R.: Fast approximate energy minimization via graph cuts. PAMI 23, 1222–1239 (2001)

3. Felzenszwalb, P.F., Huttenlocher, D.P.: Effcient belief propagation for early vision. IJCV 70, 41–54 (2006)
4. Gong, M., Yang, R., Wang, L., Gong, M.: A performance study on different cost aggregation approaches used in real-time stereo matching. IJCV 75, 283–296 (2007)
5. Scharstein, D., Szeliski, R.: A taxonomy and evaluation of dense two-frame stereo correspondence algorithms. IJCV 42, 7–42 (2002)
6. Yang, Q., Yang, R., Davis, J., Nistér, D.: Spatial-depth super resolution for range images. In: Proc. CVPR (2007)
7. Egnal, G., Wildes, R.P.: Detecting binocular half-occlusions: Empirical comparisons of five approaches. PAMI 24, 1127–1133 (2002)
8. Tomasi, C., Manduchi, R.: Bilateral filtering for gray and color images. In: Proc. ICCV, pp. 839–846 (1998)
9. Paris, S., Kornprobst, P., Tumblin, J., Durand, F.: A gentle introduction to bilateral filtering and its applications. In: SIGGRAPH Classes (2008) Course material available online at http://people.csail.mit.edu/sparis/bf_course
10. Chen, J., Paris, S., Durand, F.: Real-time edge-aware image processing with the bilateral grid. ACM Trans. Graph. 26, 103 (2007)
11. Pham, T., van Vliet, L.: Separable bilateral filtering for fast video preprocessing. In: Proc. ICME (2005)
12. Weiss, B.: Fast median and bilateral filtering. ACM Trans. Graph. 25, 519–526 (2006)
13. Yang, Q., Tan, K.H., Ahuja, N.: Real-time O(1) bilateral filtering. In: Proc. CVPR (2009)
14. Paris, S., Durand, F.: A fast approximation of the bilateral filter using a signal processing approach. IJCV 81, 24–52 (2009)
15. Wang, L., Liao, M., Gong, M., Yang, R., Nistér, D.: High-quality real-time stereo using adaptive cost aggregation and dynamic programming. In: Proc. 3DPVT, pp. 798–805 (2006)
16. Gong, M., Yang, Y.H.: Near real-time reliable stereo matching using programmable graphics hardware. In: Proc. CVPR, pp. 924–931 (2005)
17. Yang, Q., Engels, C., Akbarzadeh, A.: Near real-time stereo for weakly-textured scenes. In: Proc. BMVC (2008)
18. Davis, J., Nehab, D., Ramamoorthi, R., Rusinkiewicz, S.: Spacetime stereo: a unifying framework for depth from triangulation. PAMI 27, 296–302 (2005)
19. Zhang, L., Snavely, N., Curless, B., Seitz, S.M.: Spacetime faces: high resolution capture for modeling and animation. ACM Trans. Graph. 23, 548–558 (2004)
20. Paris, S.: Edge-preserving smoothing and mean-shift segmentation of video streams. In: Forsyth, D., Torr, P., Zisserman, A. (eds.) ECCV 2008, Part II. LNCS, vol. 5303, pp. 460–473. Springer, Heidelberg (2008)
21. Yang, R., Pollefeys, M., Li, S.: Improved real-time stereo on commodity graphics hardware. In: Proc. CVPR Workshops, pp. 36–36 (2004)
22. Adams, A., Baek, J., Davis, A.: Fast high-dimensional filtering using the permutohedral lattice. Comp. Graph. Forum 29, 753–762 (2010)

Fast Multi-labelling for Stereo Matching

Yuhang Zhang[1], Richard Hartley[1,2], and Lei Wang[1]

[1] The Australian National University
[2] NICTA
{yuhang.zhang,richard.hartley,lei.wang}@anu.edu.au

Abstract. We describe a new fast algorithm for multi-labelling problems. In general, a multi-labelling problem is NP-hard. Widely used algorithms like α-expansion can reach a suboptimal result in a time linear in the number of the labels. In this paper, we propose an algorithm which can obtain results of comparable quality polynomially faster. We use the Divide and Conquer paradigm to separate the complexities induced by the label set and the variable set, and deal with each of them respectively. Such a mechanism improves the solution speed without depleting the memory resource, hence it is particularly valuable for applications where the variable set and the label set are both huge. Another merit of the proposed method is that the trade-off between quality and time efficiency can be varied through using different parameters. The advantage of our method is validated by experiments.

1 Introduction

Solving multi-labelling problems by way of Markov random field (MRF) optimization has been a popular research topic in recent years due to its effectiveness. Successful algorithms like α-expansion [1,2] and FastPD [3,4] can already provide high quality solutions in polynomial time. However, most existing work involved images of relatively small size or with a limited number of labels. From the perspective of practical applications, for example large-scale 3D reconstruction based on high resolution images, both the number of variables and the number of labels involved in the optimization will be huge. Therefore, developing an even faster optimization method that is scalable to the size of the Markov random field attracts our attention.

One important attribute of the variables in a Markov random field is that their values (or labels) are generally smooth, whereas violent fluctuation only happens in sparse boundary areas. Based on this assumption, we divide each multi-labelling problem into two smaller multi-labelling problems, which handle the huge variable set and the huge label set respectively. In the first subproblem, we force some of the neighbour variables to share the same labels, so the number of random variables is reduced. In the second problem, we fine tune the result of the first subproblem, so that neighbouring pixels that were forced to share identical labels can now have different labels. During this fine tuning we exclude the possibility of violent variations, so the number of optional labels for each

K. Daniilidis, P. Maragos, N. Paragios (Eds.): ECCV 2010, Part III, LNCS 6313, pp. 524–537, 2010.

variable is largely reduced. Through implementing these two steps recursively, the original problem can be solved in a time sublinear in the number of labels.

High speed and low memory cost is the major contribution of our method. However, rather than exclusively pursuing speed, a trade-off between efficiency and quality can be tuned by varying the parameters in our method. Experiments show that our method possesses strong advantages in efficiency over previous algorithms.

2   Previous Work

Many low level computer vision tasks can be modelled as multi-labelling problems. Examples include stereo matching, image denoising and image segmentation. A multi-labelling problem can be solved by energy minimization. In particular, Markov Random Fields have been popular as a formulation for multi-label energy minimization. The Hammersley-Clifford theorem makes the connection between the probabalistic viewpoint of MRFs and minimization of an abstractly defined cost-functions.

As optimizing a multi-label Markov random field is in general NP-hard [5], all usable algorithms need to sacrifice optimality for time efficiency [1,4,6,7,8] or generality. Among current approaches, α-expansion [1] is one of the most popular algorithms. The divide and conquer paradigm is utilized in α-expansion. Specifically, instead of tackling the intractable full problem directly, α-expansion assumes that the applicability of each label can be checked individually. Therefore, each n-label problem is divided into n 2-label subproblems, each of which determines whether a label α should be applied to variables currently having other labels. Each 2-label problem can be solved with a max-flow algorithm in polynomial time provided the edge costs satisfy a metric [1] or convexity [6] condition. To reach a stationary point, or local minimum, multiple outer iterations are required. One of the most popular max-flow algorithm, Push-relabel, has a time complexity of $O(M^3)$, where M is the number of vertices (variables) in the graph. Assuming the number of variables and the number of labels are independent, and that the number of necessary outer iterations is a constant, the time complexity of α-expansion is linear in the number of labels and the time complexity of its max-flow subroutine, namely $O(M^3N)$, where N is the number of labels.[1] However, in applications like stereo matching, the number of labels is usually proportional to the image resolution. Hence the processing time of α-expansion increases rapidly as the image size grows. A restriction on using α-expansion with max-flow is that the 2-label sub-problems must be submodular; this constrains its applicability to cost functions with metric or convex edge costs. However, there is no need to restrict the method for solving the 2-label problems to max-flow. Other algorithms such as roof-dual (QPBO) [10] or Lazy-Elimination [7] can be used instead. Another method that handles more generic

---

[1] Push-relabel is not the fastest max-flow algorithms. The fastest one so far was proposed in [9] and has a time complexity of $O(\min(M^{2/3}, E^{1/2})E\log(M^2/E+2)\log C)$, where C is the maximum capacity of the network and E is the number of edges.

energy functions is Alphabet Soup [11], which can be viewed as a generalized α-expansion.

FastPD [3] is another very successful multi-labelling algorithm. By relaxing the integrality constraint to a continuous positive constraint, it transforms the original discrete optimization problem into linear programming and then approaches the optimal solution through iteratively applying the primal-dual schema. FastPD can handle quite general types of energy functions and also obtains a convincing suboptimal results very rapidly. However, to pursue high processing speed, the avaliable implementation of FastPD easily exhausts the memory resource even dealing with a middle-sized stereo pair (e.g. 600×500 containing 64 labels). A more comprehensive review of relevant algorithms can be found in [12,13].

Earlier work on enhancing the speed of MRF optimization can be found in [8], where the max-flow problem on a graph is efficiently solved using the known solution for a similar graph. Approaches to accelerating stereo matching were discussed in [14,15], where higher speed (2.8 and 4 times speed-up respectively) is obtained through reducing the search range during matching. Particularly, an idea similar to our work was interpreted as search-range reduction through downscaling, tested and reported to fail in [15]. However, that paper gave only a sketchy description of their algorithm, with insufficient detail for us to distinguish the cause of failure. In contrast, our work shows that through proper construction and implementation, this method can handle MRF optimization with promising quality in a speed significantly faster than the existing algorithms.

3   Dividing the Original Problem

Optimizing a Markov random field containing M variables and N labels can be described as finding the optimal among N^M discrete states. For positive integers M and N both of which are larger than 1, and positive integers m and n which are smaller than M and N respectively:

$$N^{M-m} - 1 \geq n^{M-m}$$
$$\Rightarrow n^m(N^{M-m} - 1) \geq n^M$$
$$\Rightarrow N^m(N^{M-m} - 1) > n^M$$
$$\Rightarrow N^M - N^m > n^M$$
$$\Rightarrow N^M > N^m + n^M$$

Hence the complexity of the original problem can be reduced, if we can divide the original problem, i.e. split M and N into separate subproblems and tackle them respectively.

To construct the first subproblem, we need to reduce the number of random variables. On a 4-connected Markov grid as shown in Figure 1, a minimum cycle is composed of 4 vertices. Each vertex is directly related to 2 out of 3 of the other vertices on the cycle. Hence the values of all vertices on the same cycle should generally be similar. Based on this prior, we favour vertices on the same

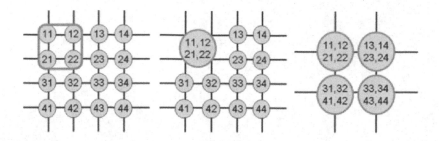

Fig. 1. Left: the original Markov grid; middle: four vertices on the same minimum cycle are merged, their exterior edges are inherited by the super-vertex; right: merging has been implemented with the rest vertices, some duplicate edges connecting the same super-vertices are dropped off.

minimum cycle to share the same value. Note that we cannot force vertices on all the minimum cycles to share the same value, otherwise all the vertices will have identical value. Whereas each vertex participates in 4 minimum cycles, we only force it to share the same value with neighbour vertices in 2 of the cycles. In this way, vertices on the selected minimum cycles are merged into one vertex, which inherits all the exterior edges of its component vertices. By merging all vertices on selected minimum cycles, the number of vertices in the Markov grid is reduced to a quarter of the original. At the same time, the number of edges is also reduced to a quarter of the original. Half of the edges in the original rigid are removed as interior edges, whereas a further quarter are eliminated as duplicate exterior edges. The consequent Markov grid after merging inherits the general structure of the original but loses the local details.

In the second subproblem, we retrieve the details lost due to merging vertices in the first subproblem. Since the general structure of the Markov grid has already been identified, only fine tuning within a small range is necessary for each vertex. That is why we can reduce the number of labels in the second subproblem. The fine tuning range depends on the nature of the problem and the requirement of the user. The proposed method favors problems satisfying the following criterion. Given the labels of surrounding vertices, the possible labels for a vertex can be narrowed down to a subset of all labels. In many practical problems, most of the vertices can be regarded as satisfying the above criterion. In such cases, the loss in optimality is limited. Obviously, the loss in optimality can be reduced through increasing the fine tuning range. The highest quality, as well as the worst time efficiency, is achieved by using all labels in the fine-tuning. In this case, however, the result obtained in the first subproblem is useless, and the problem is solved in its original form in the second subproblem. At the other end of the scale, the best time efficiency is obtained by using as few labels as possible in the fine-tuning step, i.e $\{-1, 0, +1\}$.

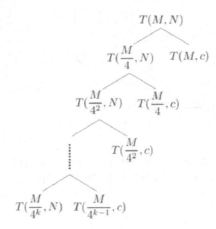

Fig. 2. The original problem as well as its time complexity are divided recursively along the binary tree. The number of variables reduces as the tree branches.

4   Recursion and Solving

Rather than dividing the original problem into two subproblems, our ambition really lies in recursively implementing the division. Theoretically, we can always further divide both the subproblems, as long as they are still large enough. However, in implementation, we generally use a small fine tuning range in the second subproblem for the purpose of time efficiency. Thus the second subproblem usually cannot be further divided. Therefore, the recursive division usually generates a binary tree which only branches on the left children as in Figure 2.

After dividing the original problem according to the binary tree in Figure 2, we solve the subproblems on the leaves and combine them together to generate the solution for the original problem. The time complexity of the proposed algorithm is the sum of the time complexity on all the leaves:

$$T(M, N) = T(\frac{M}{4^k}, N) + \sum_{i=0}^{k-1} T(\frac{M}{4^i}, c) . \tag{1}$$

Among all the leaves, only one of them is the left child of its parent and might have a large number of labels. However, since the number of variables shrinks rapidly as the tree branches, this single left leaf which is on the highest level of the tree contains extremely few variables. The time needed to solve it can be regarded as a small constant. All the other leaves are the right children of their parent, hence have a very small number of labels, which can be solved efficiently using any existing single-scale multi-labelling algorithm. In our work, we adopt α-expansion as the default option. Therefore, (1) can be computed as:

$$T(M, N) = \Theta(1) + \sum_{i=0}^{k-1} O((\frac{M}{4^i})^3 c)$$

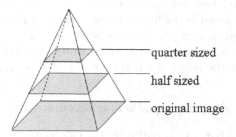

quarter sized

half sized

original image

Fig. 3. The image pyramid generated by the proposed method in stereo matching

$$= \Theta(1) + \sum_{i=0}^{k-1} 64^{-i} O(M^3 c)$$

$$< \Theta(1) + \frac{64}{63} O(M^3 c)$$

$$= O(M^3 c)$$

which shows the time complexity of the proposed method is independent of the number of labels N. As the fine tuning range c can be treated as a small constant independent of the size of the original problem, the time complexity of the proposed method is simply $O(M^3)$. Soon we will see that a dynamic c is even more powerful than a constant c.

Particularly in stereo matching, the above recursive division can be interpreted as depth estimation over a Gaussian-pyramid as shown in Figure 3. The bottom of the pyramid corresponds to the original image. Each division generates a higher level in the pyramid, where the numbers of variables and labels are reduced to a quarter and a half respectively. Optimization starts from the top level, where the number of variables and search range are both the smallest. The solution for the bottom level, namely the original image, is reached through hierarchical fine tuning.

5   Fine Tuning with α-Expansion

As α-expansion calls max-flow algorithms as its subroutine, it is necessary for the binary term in the energy function to be submodular as shown in (2):

$$E(0,0) + E(1,1) \leq E(0,1) + E(1,0) . \tag{2}$$

According to the original design of α-expansion [1], the above requirement is interpreted as

$$E(p,q) + E(\alpha,\alpha) \leq E(p,\alpha) + E(\alpha,q) . \tag{3}$$

In our problem the above interpretation is generalized to a more complex form:

$$E(\hat{p}+p,\hat{q}+q) + E(\hat{p}+\alpha,\hat{q}+\alpha) \leq E(\hat{p}+p,\hat{q}+\alpha) + E(\hat{p}+\alpha,\hat{q}+q) , \tag{4}$$

where $\hat{p}$ and $\hat{q}$ are the labels belonging to the two vertices before the fine tuning, namely the labels obtained in the first subproblem. The original α-expansion can be viewed as a special case in our problem, where $\hat{p} = \hat{q} = 0$. To show what (3) really means, we discuss it in three complementary situations. To simplify the discussion, we assume the range of fine tuning is $\{-1, 0, +1\}$, $\hat{p} - \hat{q} = d$, and that $E(p, q) = f(p - q)$.

- When $\alpha = -1, p = 0, q = 1$, equation (4) is converted to

$$f(d - 1) + f(d) \leq f(d + 1) + f(d - 2) , \tag{5}$$

  requiring the energy function to be convex.
- When $p = -1, \alpha = 0, q = 1$, equation (4) is converted to

$$f(d - 2) + f(d) \leq f(d - 1) + f(d - 1) , \tag{6}$$

  requiring the energy function to be concave.
- When $p = -1, q = 0, \alpha = 1$, equation (4) is converted to (5), requiring the energy function to be convex again.

According to the above discussion, neither concave nor convex functions can fulfill the requirement of submodularity in all situations. However, as has been shown by many previous papers, the Potts model [2] can usually do the job. As we can judge, it does fulfill the requirement of submodularity in all the three conditions when $d = 0$. However, in our case, as d is no longer 0, the Potts model as well as many other energy functions no longer guarantee the submodular requirement.

The solution lies in one particular function:

$$f(x) = |x| , \tag{7}$$

which is globally convex as well as sectionally concave. It is globally convex, hence (5) is naturally met. It is sectionally concave, when all points are sampled from the same side of the origin. Thus (6) can be met as well if we can ensure that the four terms lie on the same side of the origin. Obviously, if the two terms on the left lie on the same side of the origin, the two terms on the right will do so as well. The left two terms, to give their original form in (4), $(m + p) - (n + q)$ and $m - n$, are the label difference between two neighbour variables, before and after the fine tuning. Enforcing $((m + p) - (n + q))(m - n) \geq 0$ indicates that neighbouring variables should not invert their label orders in the fine tuning step. Although such a constraint confines the fine tuning moves, the optimality should not be affected much unless severe mistakes were made earlier, requiring such an inversion in the label orders.

An alternative implementation of α-expansion was proposed in [6], which requires the edge function to be convex in all the 3 situations. With this design, more convex functions can be adopted in our problem. However in practical usage, if we expect the label jumps to happen intensively at narrow edges instead of loosely covering a wide area, concave functions are preferable to convex functions. Thus we use (7) as the smooth term in our method. This is a convex function by definition, but penalizes sharp edges the least among all the convex functions.

Note that α-expansion is not the only option for single-scale MRF optimization. We stick to it in this work because it is widely known. People familiar with other single-scale MRF optimization methods like [3] and [7] can adapt our methods into their work very easily without necessarily restricting to the cost function (7).

6   Experiments

To examine the usefulness of the proposed method, we use it to estimate the disparity between high resolution stereo image pairs. The machine is an average PC, equipped with 2 GB RAM and 2.39 GHz Dual Core CPU. The images are downloaded from the Middlebury stereo dataset [16,17]. All the images are over 1000×1000 in size. The disparity range in each image pair is larger than 100 pixels, requiring more than 100 labels. We will use α-expansion as the subroutine in our method, and compare its performance against the original single-scale α-expansion. Both methods optimize the energy function given by (8), (9), (10), where $I_l(i)$ is the normalized grey value of pixel i in the left image, $I_r(i')$ is the normalized grey value of its corresponding pixel in the right image, and $L(i)$ and $L(j)$ are the labels of pixel i and j respectively. Certainly more sophisticated energy functions can be designed and used instead, which is an important research topic by itself, but not our major concern in this work.

$$E = \sum_i U_i + \frac{1}{100} \sum_{ij} B_{ij} \tag{8}$$

$$U_i = |I_l(i) - I_r(i')| \tag{9}$$

$$B_{ij} = |L(i) - L(j)| \tag{10}$$

We have also implemented our method with FastPD as the subroutine. However, as the single-scale FastPD cannot be executed to solve a problem of this size due to the memory limitation on a normal PC, we cannot conduct detailed comparison with it, but only show our output.

Table 1 shows the processing time, peak memory usage and result quality for the different methods. All values are the average over the 4 image pairs we used in the experiments. We refer to the original single-scale α-expansion as 1-scale in the table. 1-scale* is equivalent to 1-scale except that it is optimized for speed during programming and hence demands a much larger memory space than 1-scale. The other rows in the table correspond to our method implemented over different numbers of hierarchies. The tuning range in the second subproblems is $\{-1, 0, +1\}$ in all cases. Figure 4 shows the left views of the four stereo pairs, the ground truth and the results produced by different methods. The content of the image are chosen to be different and representative. For example, the image in

Table 1. Performance comparison: 1-scale* follows the original α-expansion algorithm, except that it is optimized for speed during programming

Method	Time	Peak Memory	Extra Energy(%)
1-scale	34m03s	270MB	0
1-scale*	17m01s	2.3GB	0
2-scale	2m21s	540MB	4.33
3-scale	37s	540MB	7.63
4-scale	27s	540MB	11.63
5-scale	22s	540MB	18.50

the second column contains many slender objects, which cause frequent and sharp discontinuities in depth value, whereas the image in the last column contains generally smooth surfaces on which depth value varies only mildly.

6.1   Time and Memory Efficiency

The proposed method is absolutely faster than single-scale α-expansion, no matter whether it is optimized for speed or not. The optimized α-expansion uses arrays to store precomputed unary terms. Consequently, it requires 10 times the memory of the original α-expansion. Nevertheless, it only becomes 2 times faster. Moreover, when its memory occupancy exceeds the physical memory limit, virtual memory swapping makes it even slower. That is also why FastPD cannot be used here. On the other hand, the memory requirement of our method is only moderately larger than that of the original α-expansion, but the boost in speed is significant. With FastPD as the subroutine, the peak memory occupancy of our method is 1.4GB, and the algorithm terminates within 15 seconds over 3 levels of hierarchy.

Significant decrease in processing time can be observed between 1-scale and 2-scale, as well as between 2-scale and 3-scale optimization, but as we further increase the number of hierarchies, no further increase is observed. That is because, after merging the vertices once, the size of the first subproblem is still quite huge, whereas after merging twice or three times, the size of the first subproblem is already small enough that further reducing its size will not save much time.

After cutting the problem into small enough pieces, the peak memory occupancy, as well as the processing time of our method is determined by the final fine tuning on the original scale. That is why the peak memory occupancy of our method remains the same irrespective of the number of hierarchy levels. It needs more memory than the original α-expansion because we have pre-computed the unary term. However, since the number of labels in the fine tuning is small, the additionally required memory space does not become a problem for a normal PC. That also suggests that on images of the same size but with increasing number of labels, whereas the running time of α-expansion or the memory occupancy of FastPD will increase accordingly, the cost of our method remains almost the same, because the number of labels needed in the final fine tuning is not changed.

Fig. 4. From the top to the bottom: left views of the stereo pairs, ground truth, result produced by the original α-expansion, the proposed method over 3 levels of hierarchy, using α-expansion and FastPD as subroutines respectively

The time and memory efficiency of single-scale α-expansion and FastPD may vary due to different implementations, however, that will not affect the comparison here, because the proposed method calls them as the subroutine.

Fig. 5. Refinement and convergence of depth values at different levels of resolution. The first row shows depth values. The second row shows which pixels change their labels as resolution is increased during the sequential fine-tuning operation. The pixels colored black are to be decreased in disparity as resolution increases; the pixels colored white are to be increased in disparity, and the pixels colored grey will keep their current disparity.

6.2 Quality

As shown in the second column in Figure 4, our method does not handle slender objects particularly well. Slender objects correspond to a sequence of discontinuities in depth values. This result is not surprising, as our assumption is that neighbouring pixels have similar labels (depth values), and hence can be merged. Such an assumption does not apply to slender objects, where adjacent pixels may possess completely different labels. Merging in these areas leads to severely wrong labelling which cannot be corrected by small range fine tuning. That is why part of the stick is absorbed by the background, and the other part becomes thicker through absorbing background pixels. However, as slender objects are naturally difficult for graph cuts, even the original α-expansion does not perform outstandingly well on them.

Despite the above defects, the proposed method performs quite well with generally smooth surfaces like the cloth image in the last column, and sparse edges like the aloe image on the first column. The extra energy in the MRF due to hierarchical optimization, as shown in Table 1, is minor, as long as we do not use too many hierarchies.

Figure 5 shows how the final result is reached through sequential fine tuning from the coarse estimation. In particular, only the final three levels of recursion are shown here. The total number of recursion levels is 5. The images in the first

Fig. 6. Result produced with different parameters using α-expansion as the subroutine. From left to right: 4 hierarchies, 3 tuning labels; 3 hierarchies, 3 labels; 3 hierarchies, 5 labels.

row show the improvement as the disparity estimate becomes more and more accurate with increasing resolution. The images in the second row reflect the fine tuning operation on different pixels.

6.3   Trade-Off between Efficiency and Quality

Table 1 shows that the trade-off between efficiency and quality can be tuned by changing the number of hierarchy levels of optimization. Another parameter affecting the trade-off is the range of fine tuning. As a rule of thumb, using more labels during fine tuning over all hierarchies will significantly increase the processing time. Consequently, we only increase the range of fine tuning in hierarchies other than the final one. Recall that the processing time of our method is mainly determined by the last fine tuning at the original scale. As long as the problem size of this step remains the same, the time efficiency of the whole algorithm will not be significantly changed.

Table 2 shows how time efficiency and result quality vary as we use different numbers of levels of hierarchy and different tuning ranges. As one would expect, with the same number of levels, the wider the tuning range is, the better the quality will be, and the slower the algorithm will be. However, the opposite results can be found when the tuning range is increased to 7, i.e. $\{-3, -2, -1, 0, +1, +2, +3\}$. Not only the energy in the MRF but also the processing time is reduced. Again, note that the processing time mainly depends on the last fine tuning in the original scale, which is a single-scale α-expansion. The processing time of a single-scale α-expansion algorithm depends not only on the size of the MRF but also on the initial state. The closer the initial state is to the optimal state, the fewer iterations the α-expansion algorithm needs to converge, hence the faster it terminates. Although using a wider tuning range takes more time on the earlier hierarchies, it also generates better initial estimation for the final hierarchy, which is the payoff for previous loss. Figure 6 visually compares the difference in quality due to different combinations of parameters.

Table 2. Efficiency and quality with different combinations of parameters. As expected the quality of the solution is improved by using a larger fine-tuning range. This is done at all levels of hierarchy, except at the finest resolution level. This improvement in quality is also at times accompanied by a decrease in run time. The table also shows that increasing the number of levels can be counter-productive.

Levels	Tuning Range	Time	Extra Energy(%)
3	3	37s	7.63
	5	40s	6.00
4	3	27s	11.63
	5	37s	8.75
	7	35s	7.53
5	3	22s	18.50
	5	37s	10.62
	7	32s	7.98

7   Conclusion

The proposed method provides a mechanism for separating the complexity induced by the variable set and the label set. This mechanism is able to obtain satisfying optimization results in time much shorter than that of the other existing algorithms. This speed opens an opportunity for large scale MRF optimization. The tunable parameters leads to the versatility of our method, which can be applied to different applications through proper parameter selection. For future work, we see the possibility of combining our method with Dynamic Graph Cuts [8], where segmentation in previous frames can be used to guide the formation and fine-tuning in the hierarchy. In another approach, to avoid improperly merging vertices of completely different values, mechanisms like backtracking might be adopted into the proposed method. With these improvements, fast algorithms producing results of even better quality are to be expected.

Acknowledgement

We acknowledge the support of NICTA, which is funded by the Australian Government in part through the Australian Research Council.

References

1. Zabih, R., Veksler, O., Boykov, Y.: Fast approximate energy minimization via graph cuts. In: ICCV 1999, pp. 377–384 (1999)
2. Boykov, Y., Veksler, O., Zabih, R.: Fast approximate energy minimization via graph cuts. IEEE Trans. Pattern Anal. Mach. Intell. 23, 1222–1239 (2001)
3. Komodakis, N., Tziritas, G., Paragios, N.: Performance vs computational efficiency for optimizing single and dynamic mrfs: Setting the state of the art with primal-dual strategies. Comput. Vis. Image Underst. 112, 14–29 (2008)

4. Komodakis, N., Tziritas, G.: Approximate labeling via graph cuts based on linear programming. PAMI 29, 1436–1453 (2007)
5. Boros, E., Hammer, P.L.: Pseudo-boolean optimization. Discrete Applied Mathematics 123, 155–225 (2002)
6. Carr, P., Hartley, R.: Solving multilabel graph cut problems using multilabel swap. In: DICTA, Melbourne, Australia (2009)
7. Carr, P., Hartley, R.: Minimizing energy functions on 4-connected lattices using elimination. In: ICCV, Kyoto, Japan (2009)
8. Kohli, P., Torr, P.: Dynamic graph cuts for efficient inference in markov random fields. PAMI 29, 2079–2088 (2007)
9. Goldberg, A.V., Rao, S.: Beyond the flow decomposition barrier. J. ACM 45, 783–797 (1998)
10. Rother, C., Kolmogorov, V., Lempitsky, V., Szummer, M.: Optimizing binary mrfs via extended roof duality. In: IEEE Conference on Computer Vision and Pattern Recognition, CVPR (2007)
11. Gould, S., Amat, F., Koller, D.: Alphabet SOUP: A framework for approximate energy minimization. In: CVPR (2009)
12. Szeliski, R., Zabih, R., Scharstein, D., Veksler, O., Kolmogorov, V., Agarwala, A., Tappen, M., Rother, C.: A comparative study of energy minimization methods for markov random fields with smoothness-based priors. IEEE Trans. Pattern Anal. Mach. Intell. 30, 1068–1080 (2008)
13. Scharstein, D., Szeliski, R., Zabih, R.: A taxonomy and evaluation of dense two-frame stereo correspondence algorithms. SMBV 2001: Proceedings of the IEEE Workshop on Stereo and Multi-Baseline Vision (SMBV 2001), p. 131 (2001)
14. Wang, L., Jin, H., Yang, R.: Search space reduction for mrf stereo. In: Forsyth, D., Torr, P., Zisserman, A. (eds.) ECCV 2008, Part I. LNCS, vol. 5302, pp. 576–588. Springer, Heidelberg (2008)
15. Veksler, O.: Reducing search space for stereo correspondence with graph cuts. In: BMVC 2006, vol. II, p. 709 (2006)
16. Hirschmuller, H., Scharstein, D.: Evaluation of cost functions for stereo matching. In: CVPR 2007 (2007)
17. Scharstein, D., Pal, C.: Learning conditional random fields for stereo. In: CVPR 2007 (2007)

Anisotropic Minimal Surfaces Integrating Photoconsistency and Normal Information for Multiview Stereo

Kalin Kolev[1], Thomas Pock[2], and Daniel Cremers[1]

[1] Department of Computer Science, TU München, Munich, Germany
[2] Institute for Computer Graphics and Vision, Graz University of Technology

Abstract. In this work the weighted minimal surface model traditionally used in multiview stereo is revisited. We propose to generalize the
classical photoconsistency-weighted minimal surface approach by means
of an anisotropic metric which allows to integrate a specified surface
orientation into the optimization process. In contrast to the conventional isotropic case, where all spatial directions are treated equally, the
anisotropic metric adaptively weights the regularization along different
directions so as to favor certain surface orientations over others. We show
that the proposed generalization preserves all properties and globality
guarantees of continuous convex relaxation methods. We make use of a
recently introduced efficient primal-dual algorithm to solve the arising
saddle point problem. In multiple experiments on real image sequences
we demonstrate that the proposed anisotropic generalization allows to
overcome oversmoothing of small-scale surface details, giving rise to more
precise reconstructions.

1 Introduction

Recovering 3D geometry of the observed scene from multiple calibrated cameras
is one of the fundamental problems in Computer Vision. An established paradigm
for solving this problem – often called *multiview stereo* – is to reconstruct the
spatial structure in a way that maximizes the photoconsistency along the object
surface, i. e. in a way that the projection of surface points into pairs of cameras
gives rise to the same colors or local neighborhood structure. In contrast to other
techniques like shape from shading or shape from silhouettes, multiview stereo
does not require a controlled environment or additional user interaction. It is
applicable to arbitrary Lambertian objects and forms the basis of the currently
most competitive generic reconstruction methods.

However, the viability of the stereo paradigm strongly relies on the success of
the matching process. When objects exhibit low texture or specular reflections
and when the camera calibration is erroneous, this matching process may fail.
In order to suppress the influence of different sources of error, a robust regularization scheme is therefore crucial. Among the pioneering approaches to this
problem are the variational methods introduced by Faugeras and Keriven [1]

K. Daniilidis, P. Maragos, N. Paragios (Eds.): ECCV 2010, Part III, LNCS 6313, pp. 538–551, 2010.

Fig. 1. The figure depicts a challenging test scenario (1 out of 21 images is shown). The input sequence illustrates a bird figurine with a complex geometric structure comprising thin protrusions (e.g. the wings) and fine-scale details (e.g. the feathering). Note that classical photoconsistency is not able to capture the feathering of the wings due to their extremely low thickness. In this paper we propose a new energy minimization approach based on a robust and transparent integration of photoconsistency, silhouette and normal information, capable of accurately recovering such objects. Two views of the reconstructed surface are visualized.

and by Yezzi and Soatto [2]. The key idea in [1] is to specify the 3D geometry as a weighted minimal surface model, where the local metric is defined in terms of a photoconsistency measure reflecting the agreement of projected surface colors among pairs of images. While this approach successfully suppresses noise, it suffers from two important limitations. Firstly, the authors in [1] merely compute suboptimal local minima. In fact, the global minimum is actually the empty set. Secondly, the minimal surface formulation causes oversmoothing effects. As a result, protrusions and surface indentations tend to be suppressed in the reconstructions [3,4].

To overcome these limitations, researchers have devised a variety of strategies. Firstly, one can remove the trivial solution and the related shrinking bias by introducing constant ballooning terms so as to favor shapes of larger volume [5]. As an undesired side effect the resulting expansion force tends to fill in concavities or, respectively, cut off protrusions, depending on the strength of the inflating force. More elaborate methods were presented in [3,4], where the constant ballooning term is replaced by a data-aware volume subdivision. While these procedures help to drastically alleviate the shrinking bias of minimal surface models, they become unreliable in the presence of specular reflections or with very few input images and the reconstruction fails.

An alternative approach to avoid the empty set was recently proposed in [6]. The authors advocate to retain the weighted minimal surface model but restrict the optimization to the set of silhouette-consistent configurations. By imposing that along visual rays, passing silhouette pixels, the voxel occupancy must be at least one, the trivial solution is no longer feasible. Nevertheless, the shrinking bias is still present. Even within the set of silhouette-consistent solutions the obtained reconstruction may suffer from oversmoothing and suppression of indentations that are not captured by the silhouettes.

A different strategy to address the multiview stereo problem was suggested in [7,8,9]. The key idea is to specify additionally to the surface localization in terms of spatial photoconsistency also the local surface orientation. In [9] the gradient of the photoconsistency measure was used to approximate the orientation of the observed shape. [7,8] proposed to estimate the surface orientation directly via an optimization procedure over the local patch distortion. The optimal patch is determined based on the agreement of its projections onto the images, where it is visible. Directionally sensitive anisotropic metrics provide a powerful tool to integrate such shape normal information in the minimization process. Recent advances in this field within the context of discrete optimization [10,11] as well as continuous counterparts [12,13] provide the necessary machinery to compute a globally optimal solution.

Many of the discussed ideas have been developed independently with focus on particular weaknesses of previous methods for multiview reconstruction. For example, the fusion of multiview stereo and silhouettes aims at recovering thin protrusions while retaining concavities. Moreover, the normal information is known to capture high-frequency surface details and enhance reconstructions. This raises the straightforward question of how these different sources of information can be integrated in a unified framework in a robust and transparent manner. The ultimate goal is to combine their advantages and extend the range of applicability of established techniques. In particular, such an approach should be able to reconstruct fine-scale shape details on thin protruding structures, a test scenario for which most of the existing methods fail – see Fig. 1.

The contribution of this paper is to propose an energy minimization framework for multiple view reconstruction that allows to combine multiview photoconsistency, silhouette and normal information. We show that the reconstruction can be efficiently determined as an anisotropic minimal surface which favors not only locations of good photoconsistency but also orientations that are consistent with the specified normal field. By adaptively reducing the smoothing along the predetermined directions, the inherent shrinking bias of traditional minimal surface models is alleviated. Making use of convex relaxation techniques we pose the reconstruction problem as one of minimizing a convex energy functional. We show that globally optimal shapes which best fit the photoconsistency values and the specified normal field are obtained by thresholding the solution of the relaxed problem. In addition, exact silhouette consistency can be imposed by constraining the optimization to the convex set of silhouette consistent surfaces. It should be noted that the proposed approach is a portent of a wide range of applications involving normal field integration including range data fusion [14], shape from shading [15] and photometric stereo [16].

The paper is organized as follows. In the next section we introduce the concept of anisotropic minimal surfaces for multiview stereo. In Section 3 we derive corresponding specific energy functionals to integrate photoconsistency, surface orientation and silhouettes. In Section 4 we provide an efficient primal-dual algorithm for solving the arising saddle point problem. In Section 5 we show experimental results on challenging real data sets. We conclude with a brief summary.

2 Continuous Anisotropic Minimal Surfaces

This section introduces the main concept of anisotropic metrics preferring certain orientation selectivity by generalizing the traditionally used weighted minimal surface model. Similar anisotropic formulations have independently been developed in the context of binocular stereo [12] and image segmentation [13].

We start with some notations. Let $V \subset \mathbb{R}^3$ be a volume which contains the scene of interest and $I_1, \ldots, I_n : \Omega \to \mathbb{R}^3$ a collection of calibrated color images with perspective projections $\pi_1, \ldots, \pi_n$. Let $S_1, \ldots, S_n \subset \Omega$ be the observed silhouettes of the 3D object and $\rho : V \to [0,1]$ be a photoconsistency map measuring the discrepancy among various image projections.

The most photoconsistent shape can be obtained according to the following weighted minimal surface model:

$$E(S) = \int_S \rho(s) \, ds. \tag{1}$$

The model encourages the surface to pass through points with high observation agreement. Its minimization identifies shapes with minimal overall costs according the local isotropic metric induced by ρ. However, the model does not explicitly affect the orientation of the estimated shape. To this end, in case of given surface orientation, a generalization has to be developed. This can be achieved by introducing a family of positive semidefinite anisotropic tensors $D(x) \in \mathbb{R}^{3 \times 3}, x \in V$ tolerating certain directional selectivity. Now, the minimal surface model (1) generalizes to:

$$E(S) = \int_S \sqrt{N_S(s)^T D(s) N_S(s)} \, ds, \tag{2}$$

where $N_S(s) \in S^2 \subset \mathbb{R}^3$ denotes the unit outward surface normal at point s. Obviously, the tensors $D(x)$ can be designed to energetically favor certain shape orientations while suppressing others. Note that D is defined pointwise. However, in the remainder of this section we will omit the argument for the sake of simplicity. The energy model (2) can sill be interpreted as a minimal surface formulation according to the Riemannian metric induced by D (i. e. $\|v\|_D = \sqrt{v^T D v}$). The Euclidean metric, which treats all spatial directions equally, appears as a special case with $D = I$, where $I \in \mathbb{R}^{3 \times 3}$ denotes the identity matrix. Examples of local distance maps in 2D of the Euclidean and the more general Riemannian metric are visualized in Fig. 2. The classical weighted minimal surface model (1) also appears as a special case for $D = \rho^2 I$.

Now, we are confronted with the question of defining the family of anisotropic tensors D appropriately. Let us assume that a vectorfield $F : V \to \mathbb{R}^3$ is provided representing an estimate of the unit outward orientation of the desired shape. In practice, meaningful normal estimates can be computed only for points on the surface of the observed object. For all other points we can set $D = \rho^2 I$, which corresponds to the conventional isotropic case. Thus, in the sequel we will assume $F : V \to S^2 \subset \mathbb{R}^3$, where S^2 denotes the unit sphere. In Section 4 we

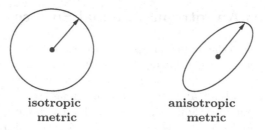

isotropic
metric

anisotropic
metric

Fig. 2. Local distance maps. Examples of local distance maps: $\sqrt{v^T v} = 1$ (isotropic case) and $\sqrt{v^T D v} = 1$ (anisotropic case). While isotropic metrics treat all directions equally, anisotropic metrics possess directional selectivity.

will give more details on how orientation information can be obtained from the input images. Based on this data, we would like to suppress regularization along the corresponding normal and encourage the process along the tangent plane. Moreover, the photoconsistency map ρ should be taken into account. This can be achieved by setting

$$D = \rho^2 \left(\tau F F^T + \frac{3 - \tau}{2} (I - F F^T) \right), \tag{3}$$

where $\tau \in [0, 1]$ is a weighting parameter that controls the distortion of the corresponding metric, i. e. the tolerance of the normal field F. In effect, the formulation in (3) realizes a basis transformation and subsequent scaling. The first term treats the component along F and scales it by τ, whereas the second one affects the tangential components. It is easy to verify that the choice $\tau = 1$ gives the original model (1). On the other hand, $\tau = 0$ will completely turn off smoothing along the vectorfield F. In our experiments we found out $\tau = 0.15$ to be a good compromise.

Next, we will show some favorable properties of the tensor D defined above.

Proposition 1. *For a normalized vector F, $\rho \geq 0$ and $\tau \in [0, 1]$ the matrix D defined in (3) is symmetric and positive semidefinite with $tr(D) = 3\rho^2$.*

Proof. The symmetry of D is obvious.
In order to show that D is positive semidefinite, we observe for $v \in \mathbb{R}^3$

$$v^T D v = \rho^2 \frac{3\tau - 3}{2} \left(v^T F \right)^2 + \rho^2 \frac{3 - \tau}{2} ||v||^2 \geq \rho^2 \tau ||v||^2 \geq 0$$

due to $||F|| = 1$.
Finally, we obtain

$$tr(D) = \rho^2 \left(\frac{3\tau - 3}{2} ||F||^2 + \frac{3(3 - \tau)}{2} \right) = 3\rho^2. \qquad \square$$

The condition that $tr(D)$ does not depend on the choice of the parameter τ assures that the overall smoothing remains fixed.

It should be noted that the inverse of the matrix in (3) as well as its square root can easily be computed as

$$D^{-1} = \frac{1}{\rho^2} \left(\frac{1}{\tau} FF^T + \frac{2}{3-\tau}(I - FF^T) \right)$$

$$D^{1/2} = \rho \left(\sqrt{\tau} FF^T + \sqrt{\frac{3-\tau}{2}}(I - FF^T) \right).$$

(4)

This will be useful for optimization purposes (see Section 4.2).

3   Fusing Photoconsistency, Orientation and Silhouettes

In this section we will formulate specific energy functionals based on the anisotropic minimal surface model (2) which will serve as a data-aware smoothness term.

3.1   Adding Regional Terms

As mentioned previously, an undesired property of minimal surface models of the form (2) is that the empty set always exhibits a global minimum. One way to avoid this trivial solution is to derive additional information from the images, which gives a closer specification of the observed object. This can be achieved by introducing data terms $\rho_{int} : V \to [0, 1]$ and $\rho_{ext} : V \to [0, 1]$ defining costs for each point within the volume for being inside or outside the imaged shape, respectively. Now, we obtain the following energy model:

$$E(S) = \lambda \left(\int_{int(S)} \rho_{int}(x)\, dx + \int_{ext(S)} \rho_{ext}(x)\, dx \right)$$
$$+ \int_S \sqrt{N_S(s)^T D(s) N_S(s)}\, ds,$$

(5)

where $int(S), ext(S) \subset V$ denote the surface interior and exterior, respectively, and $\lambda \in \mathbb{R}_{\geq 0}$ is a weighting parameter.

Next, we are confronted with the optimization of the functional (5). To this end, the first steps are a conversion to an implicit representation $u = 1_{int(S)}$, where $1_{int(S)}$ denotes the characteristic function of $int(S)$, and subsequent relaxation:

$$E(u) = \lambda \int_V (\rho_{int}(x) - \rho_{ext}(x))\, u(x)\, dx + \int_V \sqrt{\nabla u(x)^T D(x) \nabla u(x)}\, dx,$$

(6)

where $u \in C_{rel} := \{ \hat{u} \,|\, \hat{u} : V \to [0, 1] \}$. Note that the "binary" version of (6), i. e. optimization over the set of binary functions $u \in C_{bin} := \{ \hat{u} \,|\, \hat{u} : V \to \{0, 1\} \}$, is equivalent to (5). Fortunately, the optimization of (5) turns out to be as simple as minimizing (6) which exhibits a constrained convex optimization problem. This is stated by the following

Theorem 1. *Let $u^* : V \rightarrow [0,1]$ be a global minimizer of the functional (6). Then the characteristic functions of all upper level sets (i.e. thresholded versions)*

$$\Sigma_{\mu, u^*} = \{ x \in V \mid u^*(x) > \mu \}, \qquad \mu \in (0,1), \tag{7}$$

of u^* are also global minimizers of (6).

Proof. The claim follows directly from the layer cake representation of u^* (see [17]) and the anisotropic coarea formula (see [13] for a detailed derivation). □

The above theorem implies that we can obtain a global minimum of (5) by solving the constrained convex optimization problem (6) and thresholding the result by some $\mu \in (0,1)$.

3.2   Incorporating Silhouette Constraints

In certain practical scenarios obtaining reliable volume subdivision terms may be a challenging task. In such cases a reasonable alternative could be to retain the original minimal surface model (2) but to restrict the domain of feasible shapes in order to exclude the trivial solution. The object silhouettes serve as a useful tool that could provide such constraints:

$$E(S) = \int_S \sqrt{N_S(s)^T D(s) N_S(s)} \, ds, \tag{8}$$

$$\text{s. t.} \qquad \pi_i(S) = S_i \quad \forall i = 1, \dots, n.$$

Note that for $D = \rho^2 I$ the above formulation boils down to the model proposed in [6].

Unfortunately, global optimization of (8) is not a trivial task. Nevertheless, a global minimum can be obtained up to an energetic upper bound. Reverting to an implicit representation and subsequent relaxation yields:

$$E(u) = \int_V \sqrt{\nabla u(x)^T D(x) \nabla u(x)} \, dx,$$

$$\text{s. t.} \qquad u \in [0,1]$$

$$\int_{R_{ij}} u(x) \, dR_{ij} \geq 1 \text{ if } j \in S_i \tag{9}$$

$$\int_{R_{ij}} u(x) \, dR_{ij} = 0 \text{ if } j \notin S_i,$$

where R_{ij} denotes the visual ray through pixel j of image i. It can be verified that (9) exhibits a constrained convex optimization problem for which the global minimum can be obtained. Since we are interested in finding minimizers of the original non-convex problem (8), we threshold the solution of the convex problem u_{min} appropriately:

$$\tilde{u}(x) = \begin{cases} 1, & \text{if } u_{min}(x) \geq \mu \\ 0, & \text{otherwise} \end{cases}, \tag{10}$$

where

$$\mu = \min \left\{ \left(\min_{i \in \{1,\dots,n\}, j \in S_i} \max_{x \in R_{ij}} u_{min}(x) \right), 0.5 \right\}. \tag{11}$$

The threshold is estimated such that the computed binary solution is the closest one that still fulfills exact silhouette consistency. Note that minimizing (8) is equivalent to minimizing the "binarized" version of (9) (where $u \in [0,1]$ is replaced by $u \in \{0,1\}$). Although this approach does not assure finding the global minimum of (8), it entails certain globality guarantees.

Proposition 2. *Let u' be a (global) minimum of the "binary" version of (9), $\tilde{u}$ the computed solution and u_{min} a (global) minimum of (9). Then, a bound $\gamma(u_{min}, \tilde{u})$ exists such that*

$$E(\tilde{u}) - E(u') \leq \gamma(u_{min}, \tilde{u}).$$

Proof. Since the binary functions are a subset of the real-valued functions, we have the relation

$$E(u_{min}) \leq E(u') \leq E(\tilde{u})$$

As a consequence, we obtain the inequality

$$E(\tilde{u}) - E(u') \leq E(\tilde{u}) - E(u_{min}) =: \gamma(u_{min}, \tilde{u}). \qquad \square$$

Generally, we used the energy model in (5) in our experiments, since it does not require silhouette information to be provided, and switched to (8) in cases where computing accurate regional terms was not feasible.

4   Implementation and Numerics

This section will give more details on the particular choice of data terms and the numerical implementation of the proposed approach.

4.1   Data Term Computation

Following the formulation in (3), we need to define multiple data measures: a photoconsistency map ρ, regional subdivision costs ρ_{int}, ρ_{ext} and an outward normal field F.

The photoconsistency estimation that we used in our experiments is based on the voting scheme proposed in [19]. Moreover, we used the propagating approach in [4] to derive volumetric assignment costs for object interior/exterior.

In order to obtain an estimate of a normal field F representing the surface orientation, we assume a sparse oriented point cloud

$$P = \{ p_i \mid p_i \in V \}$$
$$O = \{ v_i \mid v_i \in S^2 \},$$

where S^2 denotes the unit sphere. Such data can be obtained via an optimization procedure over the local photometric consistency (see Fig. 3). In our experiments,

Fig. 3. Surface normal estimation. (a) The orientation of a point in space is obtained, based on a local planar patch. The optimal orientation is given by the maximal photometric agreement of the projections of the patch onto the images, where it is visible. (b) A point cloud for the data set in Fig. 4, generated with the software at [18]. (c) Corresponding color-coded normal vectors.

we used the approach of [7], an implementation of which is publicly available at [18]. See [7] for more details. A sample oriented point cloud for a real image sequence, obtained with the above procedure, is visualized in Fig. 3 (b), (c). Based on this data, we define the vectorfield F as

$$F(x) = \begin{cases} v_i, & \text{if } x = p_i \\ 0, & \text{otherwise} \end{cases}.$$ (12)

In practice, we replace F with a semi-dense blurred version $\tilde{F}$ in order to account for inaccuracies due to image noise.

4.2   Efficient Primal-Dual Optimization

As mentioned previously, the minimization of (6) and (9) poses classical constrained convex optimization problems. Hence, any iterative local optimization procedure will provide the global minimum. However, the particular choice of minimization method will affect the speed of convergence. In the current work, we adopt the primal-dual method proposed in [20].

First, we observe that that the energy functionals in (6) and (9) are both in the form

$$E(u) = \int_V \sqrt{\nabla u^T D \nabla u}\, dx + \int_V fu\, dx,$$ (13)

where $f : V \to \mathbb{R}$ summarizes the constant part not dependent on u. We proceed by splitting D as $D = D^{1/2} D^{1/2}$ and introducing a dual variable $\xi : V \to \mathbb{R}^3$, which allows for the following conversion:

$$
\begin{aligned}
E(u) &= \int_V \sqrt{\nabla u^T D \nabla u}\, dx + \int_V fu\, dx \\
&= \int_V \|D^{1/2} \nabla u\|\, dx + \int_V fu\, dx \\
&= \max_{\|\xi\| \le 1} \int_V \langle \xi, D^{1/2} \nabla u \rangle\, dx + \int_V fu\, dx.
\end{aligned}
$$ (14)

Now, we obtain a new functional

$$E(u, \xi) = \int_V \langle \xi, D^{1/2} \nabla u \rangle \, dx + \int_V f u \, dx, \tag{15}$$

that should be minimized with respect to u and maximized with respect to ξ under the constraint $\|\xi\| \leq 1$. This states a typical saddle point problem that can be solved by a projected gradient descent/ascent strategy. Denoting by $K := \{ \xi \in \mathbb{R}^3 \mid \|\xi\| \leq 1 \}$ the unit ball, our optimization scheme can be described as follows. We choose $(u^0, \xi^0) \in C_{rel} \times K$ and let $\bar{u}^0 = u^0$. We choose two time-steps $\tau, \sigma > 0$. Then, we iterate for $n \geq 0$

$$\begin{aligned}
\xi^{n+1} &= \Pi_K(\xi^n + \sigma(D^{1/2} \nabla \bar{u}^n)) \\
u^{n+1} &= \Pi_{C_{rel}}(u^n + \tau(\operatorname{div}(D^{1/2} \xi^{n+1}) - f)) \\
\bar{u}^{n+1} &= 2u^{n+1} - u^n,
\end{aligned} \tag{16}$$

where Π_K and $\Pi_{C_{rel}}$ denote projections onto the corresponding sets. Both projections are realized by simple normalization and clipping, respectively. For projection onto the set of silhouette-consistent solutions, imposed in (9), we refer to [21]. Note that the matrix square root $D^{1/2}$ can easily be computed according to the construction (see (4)). Note however that $D^{1/2}$ is, in general, spatially varying.

For sufficiently small time-step parameters convergence of the above iterative procedure can be proved [20]. In our experiments we observed stable behavior for $\tau = \sigma = 0.1$.

5   Experiments

To motivate the exploration of anisotropic minimal surface models allowing to integrate normal information, we start with a challenging image sequence illustrated in Fig. 4. Depicted are 3 out of 21 input images and multiple views of the reconstructions with the classical weighted minimal surface model [6] and the proposed anisotropic generalization (8). The data set is quite inconvenient due to the complex geometry of the imaged object comprising multiple thin structures (e.g. the wings or the legs). While the isotropic minimal surface model accurately recovers all elongated structures, it completely fails at small-scale surface details (e.g. the feathering) in contrast to the proposed anisotropic approach which clearly enhances the reconstruction. In Fig. 3 the utilized normal field is illustrated. It should be noted that for very thin geometric structures no meaningful photoconsistency can be derived. In this case the weighted minimal surface model boils down to Euclidean minimal surface model and produces the smoothest silhouette-consistent shape.

Although the Middlebury benchmark [23] is essentially exhausted and no longer provides a major challenge for multiview stereo approaches, it remains one of the most established benchmarks. Fig. 5 shows multiple views of the reconstructions obtained with the model in (5) on the well-known "dinoRing" and

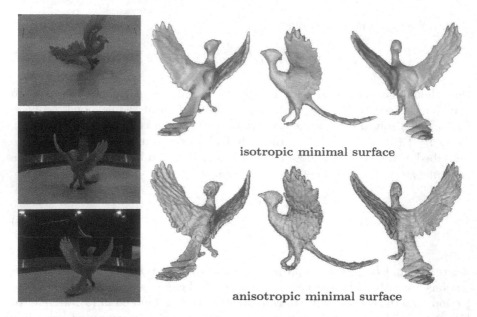

isotropic minimal surface

anisotropic minimal surface

Fig. 4. Bird sequence. 3 out of 21 input images of resolution 1024×768 and multiple views of the reconstructions with the classical isotropic minimal surface model (used for example in [6]) and the proposed anisotropic generalization (8). Note that small-scale structures like the feathering are clearly oversmoothed by the isotropic model in contrast to the proposed anisotropic approach.

Fig. 5. Middlebury data sets. Two of the input images and two views of the reconstructions obtained with the model in (5) on the well-known "dinoRing" (48 images of resolution 640×480) and "templeRing" (47 images of resolution 640×480) data sets. See Table 1 for a quantitative evaluation and [22] for a comparison to other approaches.

"templeRing" data sets. We refer to Table 1 for a quantitative evaluation and a comparison to the results reported in [4] for an isotropic version of (5). Moreover, we refer to [22] for a comparison to alternative approaches. Surprisingly, despite the already very low errors, experiments show that the proposed anisotropic formulation leads to a further reduction of accuracy and completeness scores. It should be recalled that the proposed method operates on a discrete volume grid, which poses a restriction on the precision of the recovered 3D meshes. Additional

Table 1. Quantitative comparison between the anisotropic model in (5) and the isotropic version reported in [4] on the Middlebury data sets (see Fig. 5). The numbers give accuracy (in mm) and completeness (in %). The completeness score measures the percentage of points in the ground truth model that are within $1.25mm$ of the reconstructed model. The accuracy metric shown is the distance d that brings 90% of the reconstructed surface within d from some point on the ground truth.

	isotropic model	anisotropic model
dinoSparseRing	0.53mm / 98.3%	**0.48mm / 98.6%**
dinoRing	0.43mm / 99.4%	**0.42mm / 99.5%**
templeSparseRing	1.04mm / 91.8%	**0.97mm / 92.7%**
templeRing	0.72mm / 97.8%	**0.7mm / 98.3%**

Fig. 6. Niobe sequence. 2 out of 38 input images of resolution 2048 × 3072 and multiple views of the reconstruction obtained by optimizing the energy model in (5). Note the accurate reconstruction of fine-scale surface details.

post-processing refinement of the generated triangle meshes could be included to further increase the scale of accuracy and obtain better evaluation results but this is beyond the scope of the current work.

Finally, we conclude with an experiment on an image sequence capturing a Greek statue (Niobe, reproduction from the 19th century, 2m high). Two of the input images and multiple views of the high-quality reconstruction obtained by optimizing the energy model in (5) are depicted in Fig. 6. Despite the fixed volumetric discretization most of the relevant fine-scale surface details like body parts and creases of the clothing are recovered accurately. Note also the severe brightness variations that make a robust optimization scheme indispensable. It is interesting to mention that the input photographs were acquired by a hand-held camera and calibrated with the Bundler software [24].

All demonstrated reconstructions were computed on volumetric grids consisting of $18-40$ million voxels. On a consumer PC we measured runtimes of up to a couple of hours, whereas most of the time was spent on data term computations.

6 Conclusion

In this paper, we proposed to integrate multiview stereo information and surface orientation estimates by means of anisotropic minimal surfaces. The key idea is that the local photoconsistency enters as the overall weight of the metric, while the additional normal information induces a local anisotropy of the metric which favors discontinuities of the labeling function in directions of the prescribed normal field. We prove that optimal anisotropic minimal surfaces can be computed using convex relaxation and thresholding techniques. In addition, exact silhouette consistency can be imposed by constraining the optimization to the convex set of silhouette-consistent solutions. In experiments on real-world data we demonstrate that stereo-based reconstruction results can be enhanced both qualitatively and quantitatively by incorporating normal information.

Acknowledgments

This research was supported by the German Research Foundation, grant # CR250/1-2 and # CR250/4-1. We thank Svetlana Matiouk for assistance in the image acquisition for the experiment in Fig. 6. We thank the Bundler team for providing their calibration software.

References

1. Faugeras, O., Keriven, R.: Variational principles, surface evolution, PDE's, level set methods, and the stereo problem. IEEE Transactions on Image Processing 7, 336–344 (1998)
2. Yezzi, A., Soatto, S.: Stereoscopic segmentation. International Journal of Computer Vision 53, 31–43 (2003)
3. Hernández, C., Vogiatzis, G., Cipolla, R.: Probabilistic visibility for multi-view stereo. In: Proc. International Conference on Computer Vision and Pattern Recognition, Minneapolis, Minnesota, USA, IEEE Computer Society Press, Los Alamitos (2007)
4. Kolev, K., Klodt, M., Brox, T., Cremers, D.: Continuous global optimization in multiview 3D reconstruction. International Journal of Computer Vision 84, 80–96 (2009)
5. Vogiatzis, G., Torr, P., Cippola, R.: Multi-view stereo via volumetric graph-cuts. In: Proc. International Conference on Computer Vision and Pattern Recognition, pp. 391–399 (2005)
6. Kolev, K., Cremers, D.: Integration of multiview stereo and silhouettes via convex functionals on convex domains. In: Forsyth, D., Torr, P., Zisserman, A. (eds.) ECCV 2008, Part I. LNCS, vol. 5302, pp. 752–765. Springer, Heidelberg (2008)
7. Furukawa, Y., Ponce, J.: Accurate, dense, and robust multi-view stereopsis. In: IEEE Conference on Computer Vision and Pattern Recognition (CVPR), Minneapolis, Minnesota, USA (2007)
8. Habbecke, M., Kobbelt, L.: A surface-growing approach to multi-view stereo reconstruction. In: IEEE Conference on Computer Vision and Pattern Recognition (CVPR), Minneapolis, Minnesota, USA, pp. 1–8 (2007)

9. Boykov, Y., Lempitsky, V.: From photohulls to photoflux optimization. In: Proc. British Machine Vision Conference, vol. 3, pp. 1149–1158 (2006)
10. Kolmogorov, V., Boykov, Y.: What metrics can be approximated by geo-cuts, or global optimization of length/area and flux. In: Proc. International Conference on Computer Vision, Beijing, China, pp. 564–571. IEEE Computer Society, Los Alamitos (2005)
11. Kirsanov, D., Gortler, S.: A discrete global minimization algotithm for continuous variational problems. In: Harvard Computer Science Technical Report: TR-14-04 (2004)
12. Zach, C., Niethammer, M., Frahm, J.M.: Continuous maximal flows and Wulff shapes: Application to MRFs. In: Proc. International Conference on Computer Vision and Pattern Recognition, Miami, FL (2009)
13. Olsson, C., Byröd, M., Overgaard, N.C., Kahl, F.: Extending continuous cuts: Anisotropic metrics and expansion moves. In: International Conference on Computer Vision (2009)
14. Lempitsky, V., Boykov, Y.: Global optimization for shape fitting. In: IEEE Conference on Computer Vision and Pattern Recognition (CVPR), Minneapolis, Minnesota, USA (2007)
15. Horn, B., Brooks, M.: Shape from shading. MIT Press, Cambridge (1989)
16. Woodham, R.J.: Photometric method for determining surface orientation from multiple images. Optical Engineerings 19, 139–144 (1980)
17. Chan, T., Esedoḡlu, S., Nikolova, M.: Algorithms for finding global minimizers of image segmentation and denoising models. SIAM Journal on Applied Mathematics 66, 1632–1648 (2006)
18. PMVS. http://www.cs.washington.edu/homes/furukawa/research/pmvs/
19. Hernandez, C., Schmitt, F.: Silhouette and stereo fusion for 3D object modeling. Computer Vision and Image Understanding 96, 367–392 (2004)
20. Pock, T., Cremers, D., Bischof, H., Chambolle, A.: An algorithm for minimizing the piecewise smooth Mumford-Shah functional. In: IEEE on International Conference,Computer Vision (ICCV), Kyoto, Japan (2009)
21. Dykstra, R.: An algorithm for restricted least squares regression. Journal of the American Statistical Association 78, 837–842 (1983)
22. Middlebury, http://vision.middlebury.edu/mview/
23. Seitz, S., Curless, B., Diebel, J., Scharstein, D., Szeliski, R.: A comparison and evaluation of multi-view stereo reconstruction algorithms. In: Proc. International Conference on Computer Vision and Pattern Recognition, pp. 519–528 (2006)
24. Bundler, http://phototour.cs.washington.edu/bundler/

An Efficient Graph Cut Algorithm
for Computer Vision Problems

Chetan Arora, Subhashis Banerjee, Prem Kalra, and S.N. Maheshwari

Department of Computer Science and Engineering,
Indian Institute of Technology, Delhi, India
{chetan,suban,pkalra,snm}@cse.iitd.ac.in

Abstract. Graph cuts has emerged as a preferred method to solve a class of energy minimization problems in computer vision. It has been shown that graph cut algorithms designed keeping the structure of vision based flow graphs in mind are more efficient than known strongly polynomial time max-flow algorithms based on preflow push or shortest augmenting path paradigms [1]. We present here a new algorithm for graph cuts which not only exploits the structural properties inherent in image based grid graphs but also combines the basic paradigms of max-flow theory in a novel way. The algorithm has a strongly polynomial time bound. It has been bench-marked using samples from Middlebury [2] and UWO [3] database. It runs faster on all 2D samples and is at least two to three times faster on 70% of 2D and 3D samples in comparison to the algorithm reported in [1].

1 Introduction

Many problems in computer vision such as image segmentation [4], stereo [5], texture synthesis [6], multi-view reconstruction [7] have been modelled as label assignment problems involving energy minimization. Label assignment problem is NP hard in general [8]. However, for a number of problems (e.g. texture synthesis, segmentation etc.) the label set has only two labels. It is well known that in the two label case the energy minimization problem can be modelled as determining a minimum capacity cut in a flow graph [9]. Two label case is also important because many multiple labelling algorithms use binary labelling repeatedly to get to an acceptable solution [8,10]. Graph cuts are also used to solve MAP (maximum a *posteriori*) solution for discrete MRFs. Apart from efficient algorithms for determining graph cuts [1,11,12,13], recent research has focussed on mapping computer vision problems on appropriately constructed graphs [6,10,14,15] and characterizing energy functions that can be minimized by graph cuts [8,10].

Finding a minimum cut in a flow graph is equivalent to solving the max-flow in it and [11,12,13] focus on implementing/adapting known polynomial time max-flow algorithms to run on flow graphs obtained from vision problems. Boykov and Kolmogorov [1] have developed a max-flow algorithm specifically with the objective of practical efficiency when run on such flow graphs. They included a study of comparative performance of their algorithm with the standard shortest augmenting path based algorithm [16], and variations of the preflow push algorithm [17,18]. They [1] showed that while

K. Daniilidis, P. Maragos, N. Paragios (Eds.): ECCV 2010, Part III, LNCS 6313, pp. 552–565, 2010.

the provable time bound (for integer capacities) of their algorithm (referred to as BK from now on) was weaker ($O(n^3C)$, where n is the number of nodes and C is the cost of minimum cut in comparison to $O(n^3)$ for the standard algorithms), their algorithm outperformed the others in practice. Goldberg [19] compares experimental performance of BK with some variations of preflow push that have been proposed since [1]. BK continues to out-perform the others on most and particularly the two dimensional data sets.

Contribution: We present in this paper a new flow based graph cut algorithm which is both strongly polynomial and efficient in practice. We show that in comparison to our new algorithm the best known algorithm [1] is slower by a factor of 2 to 3 on most of the BVZ (2D dataset), bone, bunny, babyface and adhead (3D datasets) samples from the UWO database [3]. On the Middlebury database [2] used by [20] to test their GPU implementation, we show that our algorithm is 3 times faster than the time reported for the GPU runs. At a very macro level our algorithm may be viewed as a hybrid of the preflow push strategy with the layered graph approach of augmenting path methods. The algorithm keeps the simplicity and locality of preflow strategies while at same time borrows ideas from layered graph based augmenting path methods to give general directions to flow.

Section 2 describes our algorithm. In Section 3 we present results and comparison with currently known best methods in the field followed by conclusion and discussion in Section 4.

2   Voronoi Based Preflow Push (VPP)

We first review some of the basic terminology we use. We assume that the node set of original grid graph is augmented by two additional vertices s and t called source and sink respectively. The edge set of such graph (called *flow graph* hereinafter) consists of all the neighbourhood edges called n-links, and t-links which connect s and t to all nodes in N (the edges are directed from s to nodes in N, and from nodes in N to t). We assume that between two nodes p and q both directed edges (p, q) and (q, p) exist. Each n-link (p, q), and t-link connecting a node $p \in N$ to s and t has capacity greater than or equal to zero (V_{pq} denotes capacity of edge (p, q)). An (S, T) cut in this flow graph is defined as a partitioning of the nodes into sets S and T such that s is in S and t is in T. Capacity of an (S, T) cut is the sum of the capacities of edges directed from S to T. Flow in a flow graph is a non negative real valued function that associates a value f_{pq} with an edge (p, q) in the flow graph where $f_{pq} \leq V_{pq}$. *Effective flow* in edge (p, q) is, therefore, equal to f_{pq} - f_{qp}. *Residual capacity* of an edge (p, q), denoted by $residue(p, q)$, is a measure of the additional flow that can be sent through it in the presence of some existing flow. An edge with non-zero residual capacity is called a *residual edge*. *In-flow/Out-flow* at node is the sum of the effective flow in all the edges directed into/out of node. A flow is a *preflow* if in-flow is at least as large as out-flow at all nodes other than the source and the sink. *Excess(v)* of a node v is equal to in-flow minus out-flow at node v. Consider a starting configuration in which flow is set equal to the capacity in t-links and equal to zero in n-links. Now if we label the vertices other than s and t by their excesses, it is easy to see that the original max-flow problem is equivalent to finding max-flow in the flow graph in which all t-links have been removed. Source-Sink max-flow problem is solved in the resultant flow graph by treating nodes with positive excesses as sources and those with negative excesses as sinks. From now on we will assume that the max-flow problem is being solved on such a flow graph. It should be noted that in this version of the problem sources and sinks do not have unlimited capacity, rather they have the ability to send or absorb only the amount equal to the excess on them. With every node v of the grid graph we associate label $d(v)$ called *distance label* (or simply *label*) satisfying the following conditions: $d(v) = 0$ for all nodes with negative excesses and for every residual edge (v, w), $d(v) \leq d(w) + 1$. A residual edge (v, w) will be an out-edge/in-edge of v/w if $d(v) = d(w) + 1$.

Broad steps of our algorithm (referred to as *VPP* hereafter) are given in Algorithm 1. Our algorithm differs from standard preflow push based algorithms in some crucial ways.

Algorithm 1. Voronoi Based Preflow Push

1: Create shortest distance based *Voronoi region graphs* around sink clusters;
2: **for** *Voronoi region graphs* with sources **do**
3:     Push flow from the sources towards the sink cluster in each such Voronoi region followed by pushing flow within the sink cluster;
4:     rebuild the *Voronoi region graphs* around remaining sink clusters;
5: **end for**

---

1. Unlike preflow push algorithms we maintain exact distance labels from the sinks. Note that in computer vision problems, sources and sinks are very often *clustered* (collection of source(sink) nodes in which there is a path between any two nodes passing through only nodes in the collection is called a *cluster*). Also such clusters are often interspersed. In *VPP* distance labels are shortest distance to a sink node on a sink cluster boundary. Initially these labels are generated by the standard global labelling procedure of push relabel algorithms and at later iterations by an *incremental relabelling algorithm* developed specifically to control the number of nodes relabelled at each iteration. Assignment of distance labels stops once all the sources are labelled. The subgraphs of nodes and their in and out edges reachable from a sink cluster are called *Voronoi region graph*.
2. Flow is pushed in a push flow iteration by processing the nodes in topological sort order (similar to the *highest label first* heuristic in preflow push algorithms). This ensures that once flow is pushed out of a node flow will not be pushed in it in the current push iteration. There is no local relabelling step at all.
3. Once flow reaches the boundary nodes of a sink cluster the second phase of the push iteration is initiated. This consists of starting from all the boundary nodes of a sink cluster and pushing flow inwards in the sink cluster by processing the cluster nodes in a breadth first manner till either all the excess gets absorbed among the nodes of the cluster or there are no nodes left in the cluster. The first case will result in a smaller sink cluster(s) and in the second the sink cluster will disappear. In push relabel based algorithms when a boundary sink node of a cluster gets saturated, the inside neighbour in the cluster gets exposed. This results in distance labels of

a large set of nodes to be recomputed. Pushing flow within a sink cluster before relabelling contributes to pushing as much flow as possible towards sink clusters between two relabelling steps.

Maintaining exact distance labels and the flow pushing strategy used ensures that flow that gets pushed into a sink cluster originates only from sources that lie on the Voronoi region graphs associated with the sink cluster. Also, because flow pushing to all sink clusters takes place simultaneously between two relabelling iterations, changes in Voronoi boundaries is incremental as long as sink clusters do not disappear. In effect most of the time flow pushing towards a sink cluster takes place within that part of the grid graph that became part of the Voronoi region graph during initialization. Normally only after a cut has been discovered and/or a sink cluster has disappeared will sources change their association and become part of other Voronoi region graphs. Such changes in association contribute significantly to the relabelling cost. Pushing flow within Voronoi regions, therefore, works to control relabelling costs. Preflow push algorithms with local relabelling cannot focus on this issue as implicit Voronoi boundaries can change with every relabel. At the surface level algorithms like HI_PR [18] which use variations of highest level first push strategy with occasional global relabelling (the process of creating exact distance labels) seem to be very similar. However, we show in section 3 that the number of nodes touched in HI_PR in both pushing flow and relabelling phases is an order of magnitude larger than our algorithm. This is primarily due to: (i) there are no wasteful local relabelling steps: flow pushing takes place only within Voronoi region graphs, (ii) repeated relabelling caused by shrinking cluster boundaries is avoided, and (iii) incremental relabelling process, explained in detail in a following section, ensures efficient calculation of exact distance labels.

Details of steps at line number 1, 3, and 4 of Algorithm 1 are provided in the following sections.

2.1 Initialization

We call the process of creating shortest distance based Voronoi region graphs as the initialization phase. This process is similar to the global relabelling phase of a traditional preflow push algorithm starting with initializing all sinks at distance label 0. The Voronoi region graphs with in/out edge lists at every node get created. $Excess(v)$ is initialized to 0 for all nodes v other than sources and sinks. For all source and sink nodes $excess(v)$ is set equal to source capacity if v is a source or equal to negative of sink capacity if v is a sink. Initialization also inserts all sources in structures called Excess List (EL). Excess lists are maintained for each distance label. $EL(d)$ contains source nodes with distance label d. d_{max} is the largest distance label assigned to any node.

2.2 Push Flow

Push flow happens in two phases. First phase (Algorithm 2) takes excess from sources to the boundaries of sink cluster following the highest distance label first strategy. At a node flow is pushed saturating the out edges till the node has no excess left or all out edges of the node get saturated. The saturated out edges are deleted and a node whose

all out-edges are deleted is inserted in a list called *Disconnected List(DL)*. Pushing flow
may also involve inserting the node into which flow is being pushed into an EL and
deleting the node whose excess becomes zero from an EL. DLs are maintained for
each distance label d. Second phase moves the excess that accumulates at boundary
nodes of a sink cluster inside the sink cluster. Second phase (Algorithm 4) starts from
those sink cluster boundary nodes with positive excess on them and pushes the excess
inside the cluster in a breadth first manner.

Algorithm 2. Voronoi Push Flow Phase 1

1: **for** $d = d_{max}..1$ **do**
2:    **for** all v in $EL(d)$ **do**
3:        **while** $excess(v) > 0$ and v has out-edges **do**
4:            pick an out-edge *(v,w)*;
5:            Push_Flow_in_Edge *(v,w)*;
6:            insert w in $EL(d(w))$ if not already inserted;
7:            if $residue(v, w) = 0$, delete edge *(v,w)* from out-edges and in-edges of v and w
                respectively;
8:        **end while**
9:        delete v from $EL(d)$;
10:       if all out-edges of v have been deleted, then insert v in $DL(d)$;
11:   **end for**
12: **end for**

Procedure 3. Push_Flow_in_Edge (v,w)

1: $f \leftarrow min(excess(v), residue(v, w))$;
2: $excess(v) \leftarrow excess(v) - f$;
3: $excess(w) \leftarrow excess(w) + f$;
4: $residue(v, w) \leftarrow residue(v, w) - f$;
5: $residue(w, v) \leftarrow residue(w, v) + f$;

2.3   Rebuilding the Acyclic Voronoi Regions

A node v is labelled disconnected during the Push flow stage because all paths from v
to the sink of a Voronoi region graph have been saturated and there is no remaining path
from v to a sink in the Voronoi region graph on which flow can be pushed. Specifically,
these are nodes put in $DL(d)$ in step 10 of Algorithm 2. It is important to note here
that these nodes are not all the nodes for which there do not exist augmenting paths in
the Voronoi region graphs after the Push flow stage. Other nodes in the Voronoi region
graphs for which all paths to a sink pass through nodes put in $DL(d)$ are also effectively
disconnected. Algorithm 5 identifies all such additional nodes (step 5) and adds them
to the $DL(d)$. Other nodes (i.e. nodes not put in $DL(d)$ in step 10 of Algorithm 2
or step 5 of Algorithm 5) continue to have augmenting paths to sinks in the Voronoi
region graphs and hence have the correct shortest distance label. An augmenting path
from a node v in $DL(d)$ to a sink in the new residual graph will necessarily have to

---

Algorithm 4. Push Flow Phase 2

1: for all sinks v set $BfsLevel(v) = \infty$;
2: **for** all v in EL(0) **do**
3:      **if** $excess(v) \geq 0$ **then**
4:          $BfsLevel(v) = 0$
5:          insert v in *CurrentBfsList*
6:      **end if**
7: **end for**
8: **while** *CurrentBfsList* is not empty **do**
9:      **for** all v in *CurrentBfsList* **do**
10:         **while** any (v,w) with $residue(v,w) > 0$ exists and $excess(v) > 0$ **do**
11:             **if** w is a sink with $BfsLevel(w) > BfsLevel(v)$ **then**
12:                 Push_Flow_in_Edge (v,w);
13:                 if $BfsLevel(w) = \infty$ then $BfsLevel(w) \leftarrow BfsLevel(v) + 1$;
14:                 insert w in *NextBfsList* if not already inserted;
15:             **end if**
16:         **end while**
17:         if $excess(v) \geq 0$ then insert v in $DL(0)$;
18:         delete v from *CurrentBfsList*;
19:     **end for**
20:     swap *CurrentBfsList* and *NextBfsList*;
21: **end while**

---

pass through a node which continues to retain its shortest distance label after a push flow stage. Also, such a path, if it exists, from a node v, whose all out edges have been saturated during push flow, will have to pass through a neighbour w not in its out-edge list as it existed when flow was pushed last. For such a node w, $d(w)$ was greater than or equal to $d(v)$ in the Voronoi region graph in which flow was pushed, and so the new label for v will be larger than its current label. This also implies that the label of all those nodes u, for which augmenting paths to the sink pass through v in the new residual graph, either increase their labels as well or the edge (u,v) be dropped from the Voronoi region graph to retain consistency among distance labels. We give below a two phase incremental relabelling process the first phase of which (Algorithm 5) identifies nodes whose shortest distance labels will increase (the disconnected nodes added to $DL(d)$s) and those which have residual edges pointing to them from a newly discovered disconnected node (inserted in a *Rebuild List (RL)*). In first phase the DL lists are processed in order of increasing distance labels thereby ensuring that at the end of processing nodes in $Dl(d)$, the $DL(d+1)$ and $RL(d)$ lists have been correctly computed. Nodes in $RL(d)$ can provide distance label $d+1$ to disconnected nodes.

To ensure that disconnected nodes get the shortest distance label, second phase (Algorithm 6) starts with the lowest level non empty rebuild list. It can be shown that after $RL(d)$ has been processed all disconnected nodes which are at shortest distance $d+1$ from a sink have been so labelled. Such nodes would necessarily have to have a residual edge directed from them to a node whose shortest distance label is d. The phase one and two ensure that such nodes will be in $RL(d)$. It is possible that in the process of rebuilding, a node shifts from one Voronoi region to another. This will depend upon

Algorithm 5. Rebuild Phase 1

1: **for** $d = 0..d_{max}$ **do**
2:   **for** each v in $DL(d)$ **do**
3:     **for** all edges (w,v) **do**
4:       remove edge (w,v) from out-edges and in-edges of w and v respectively;
5:       if there are no out-edges in w then insert it in $DL(d(w))$;
6:       if w exists in $RL(d(w))$ then delete it from $RL(d(w))$;
7:     **end for**
8:     for all residual edges (v,u), if u has any out-edge, then insert u in RL(d(u)) if not already inserted;
9:     $d(v) \leftarrow \infty$;
10:    delete v from $DL(d)$;
11: **end for**
12: **end for**

---

the Voronoi region to which the node in the rebuild list through which the disconnected node finds a new path to a sink belonged.

Algorithm 6. Rebuild Phase 2

1: **for** $d = 0..d_{max}$ **do**
2:   **for** each v in $RL(d)$ **do**
3:     **for** all edges (w,v) with $residual(w,v) > 0$ **do**
4:       **if** $d(w) = d + 1$ **then**
5:         make (w, v) an out-edge of w and in-edge of v;
6:       **else**
7:         **if** $d(w) = \infty$ **then**
8:           $d(w) \leftarrow d + 1$;
9:           if $d_{max} < d(w)$ then $d_{max} \leftarrow d(w)$;
10:          if $excess(w) > 0$ then insert w in $EL(d(w))$
11:          make (w, v) an out-edge of w and in-edge of v;
12:          insert w in $RL(d(w))$;
13:        **end if**
14:      **end if**
15:    **end for**
16:    delete v from $RL(d)$;
17: **end for**
18: **end for**

Figures 1(a), 1(b), and 1(c) depict the state of the flow graph prior to a push flow iteration, after the push flow iteration, and after the corresponding rebuild phase. In these figures sinks clusters are circles labelled A,B,C, and D. Rest of the circles are source clusters. Figure 1(a) represents a possible scenario prior to a push phase with four Voronoi regions corresponding to the four sink clusters. Directed lines are parts of the shortest paths that exist in the Voronoi region graphs. Flow will get pushed in each of these four Voronoi region graphs starting from the furthest away sources in topological

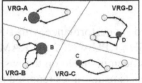
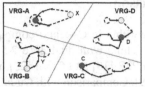
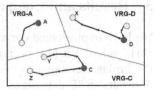

(a) After initialization/rebuild   (b) After Push flow   (c) After rebuilding Voronoi regions

Fig. 1. Flow graph states in VPP

sort order. Figure 1(b) represents the state after the push flow phase. Thick dashed lines indicate saturated edges. Dashed circles show the changes in sources and sink clusters. Note that in region VRG-A the sink cluster has shrunk, in VRG-B the sink cluster has disappeared and a new source created (circle labelled Y). In VRG-C and VRG-D sink clusters have not changed but a few source clusters have disappeared and new ones created. Figure 1(c) represents the state of the flow graph immediately after the rebuild phase. The three Voronoi regions correspond to the remaining sink clusters. Voronoi boundaries have shifted and sources X, Y, and Z are now in different Voronoi regions.

The algorithm finds the value of the max flow and the corresponding minimum energy graph cut. Flow in the graph may be a preflow when the algorithm terminates. The standard phase of converting a preflow into a flow would need to be incorporated to convert the above into a max flow algorithm [18].

Worst case time complexity of the algorithm is easily established. Beyond the initialization phase an iteration of the algorithm involves pushing flow and rebuilding the acyclic Voronoi regions. In a push flow phase, flow is pushed in an edge only once and so the total time taken is bounded by the number of edges in the acyclic Voronoi regions. In grid graphs with bounded degree, number of edges are $O(n)$. Rebuilding the acyclic Voronoi regions requires two passes over the grid graph in which edges and nodes of the graph that are accessed are touched a constant number of times. Rebuild time in each iteration is, therefore, $O(n)$. Shortest distance labels on nodes in the grid graph increase monotonically. Between iterations at least one node in the graph will have its label increased by one. Shortest distance labels can not remain the same between iterations as that would imply no change in the acyclic graph structure between iterations. This is not possible if there are nodes at the end of an iteration with positive excesses. Since there are n nodes in the grid graph the maximum number of iterations possible is $O(n^2)$ (under the assumption that only one node gets its labelled increased in any iteration and that the maximum label any node can have is n). Over all time complexity of the algorithm is, therefore, $O(n^3)$. We would like to mention that the above analysis simply establishes strong polynomial bound and is not necessarily the sharpest bound provable. However, we show experimentally in section 3 that the actual number of iterations on vision grid graphs is much less. Tight analysis of the algorithm on vision grid graphs is an open issue.

3   Results and Comparison

We have implemented our algorithm in C++ and compared its performance with BK [21], and HI_PR [22] on a machine with dual core 2.5 GHz CPU with 2GB RAM. Performance comparison with P2R [19] and CH-n [23] has been included on the basis of results on 3D datasets in [19]. Comparison with CudaCuts is using times reported in [20] on data sets from Middlebury [2]. 2D samples are BVZ and 3D samples are bunny, babyface, adhead and bone from UWO database [3]. For tests that we have conducted we have measured only time taken to run the algorithms after the flow graph has been constructed. Accuracy of the algorithm is verified by matching the flow computed by it to the one given with the database.

Figure 2 tabulates the time taken by our algorithm and CudaCuts time as reported in [20]. Our algorithm is 2 to 3 times faster.

Sample	VPP Time (ms)	CudaCuts Time (ms)
flower	19.81	37
person	20.77	61
sponge	17.74	44

Fig. 2. Time comparison between CudaCuts and VPP

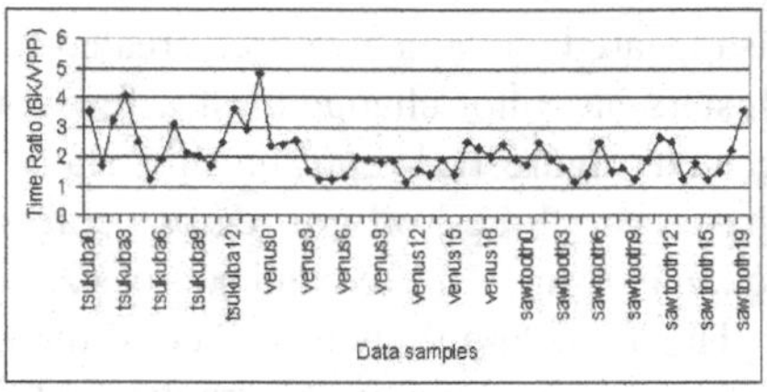

Fig. 3. Graph showing ratio of time for BK Vs VPP algorithms on BVZ test database

Figure 3 plots the ratio of time taken by BK and VPP. Note that BK is slower by at least a factor of 2 on 70% of the samples. Figures 4(a) and 4(b) compare the total number of nodes touched during push flow (expansion/augmentation) and relabelling(adopt orphans) phases in VPP, BK, and HI_PR. In both figures values have been truncated at the upper end. Note that the number of nodes touched during push flow phase in VPP are significantly smaller than those touched in BK and HI_PR. Poor performance of HI_PR is primarily due to use of approximate distance labels and repeated relabelling steps. In BK nodes touched in push flow is large as there is little control over augmenting path lengths and the amount of flow pushed in each path. However, nodes touched in the relabelling phase in BK is comparable to VPP.

It must be pointed out that total relabelling effort in BK is spread over a very large number of flow augmentation iterations. This effort is very small per flow augmentation iteration. This is because source and sink trees maintained by BK undergo very little change per iteration and effort involved (identification of disconnected nodes called orphans and rebuilding of trees by a process called adoption) is limited to searching in a small local neighbourhood in the grid graph. Also, since augmentation is not required to be on shortest paths global nature of the relabelling step in shortest path/distance label based algorithms is avoided. Note, however, that HI_PR which has local and global relabelling performs particularly poorly. This is not only due to the wasteful local relabelling steps but also because global relabelling cannot be made incremental as there is

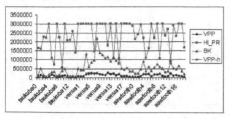

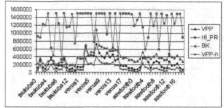

(a) Nodes touched during push flow   (b) Nodes touched during relabel

Fig. 4. Nodes touched

no obvious way to identify nodes whose distance labels will not change between two global relabelling steps in the presence of local relabelling.

We would like to point out that there is further scope for controlling relabelling in VPP. The current incremental relabelling strategy will assign non zero labels to sink cluster nodes at the cluster boundary that were neutralized ($excess(v) = 0$) during a push phase. The impact of this is to increase the number of nodes requiring relabelling in the Voronoi region graph though structurally graph may not have changed much. By carrying out partial labelling first from the shrunk boundary of a sink cluster to the original boundary we can determine the nodes of the original boundary which can still pass flow to the sink cluster nucleus. If we do this, we can effectively retain much of the original boundary of the sink cluster for the purposes of incremental relabelling. We call this the Hybrid VPP algorithm (VPP-h). Note that (Figures 4(a) and 4(b)) while nodes touched in the push phase in both VPP and VPP-h are similar number of nodes touched during relabelling in VPP-h is smaller. This is another instance where focus on the Voronoi subdivision of the grid graph has resulted in a heuristic to control relabelling costs.

Figure 5(a) shows total nodes touched in BK and VPP (sum of numbers in Figures 4(a) and 4(b)). It is interesting to see that time comparison in Figure 5(b) follows the trend showed by touched nodes graph in Figure 5(a). This is intuitive and logical since all the work in max-flow algorithms is concentrated in push and relabel operations.

Figure 6 has cumulative time, flow pushed and the number of nodes touched plotted as function of iteration number for one sample run of VPP algorithm. Note that all

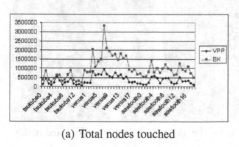

(a) Total nodes touched   (b) Time taken

Fig. 5. Comparing trends of total nodes touched and time taken in VPP and BK

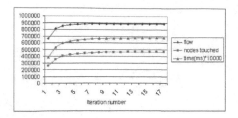

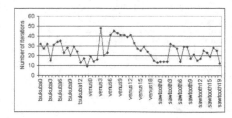

Fig. 6. Per iteration analysis for VPP for sample Sawtooth 9

Fig. 7. Number of iterations on BVZ samples for VPP

the three curves have the same trend. Most of the time is taken as well as most of the flow gets pushed in the first iteration. As iteration number increases both the time taken and amount of flow pushed decrease as do the number of nodes touched. The implication is that Voronoi regions created become progressively smaller as iteration number increases. Also, useful work done per iteration is large in that ratio of the nodes relabelled and nodes involved in pushes in any iteration is high.

The above point gets made even more emphatically in Figure 8(b) and Figure 8(c) which show nodes involved (colored yellow) in a push operation during 1st and 35th iteration respectively when VPP is run on Venus7. It seems as if most of the nodes in the Voronoi region graphs around the sinks were involved in pushing flow from sources to the sinks. Since most of the pushes are saturated, one would expect that flow that reaches the sinks is large. This is indeed so. We have observed that about 90% of flow reaches the sinks in the first few iterations.

The worst case running bound of our algorithm is strongly polynomial compared to $O(n^3 C)$ in case of BK. This is not simply an asymptotic curiosity. Relatively simple tweaks in link capacities can change the edges in such a way that BK slows down by as much as ten times. For the purpose of our experiments we took a sample (Sawtooth 9) from the dataset and scaled the capacities of n-links. Figure 9(a) shows the change in time. The reason for this time degradation is that the number of nodes touched during push flow starts to increase. Figure 9(b) shows the corresponding change in the number of nodes touched in the two algorithms during flow augmentation iterations.

(a) Venus sample image   (b) 1st iteration used nodes   (c) 35th iteration used nodes

Fig. 8. Used nodes (shown in yellow) in one iteration

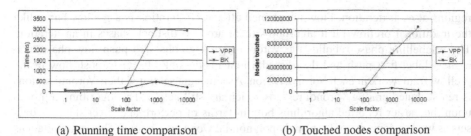

(a) Running time comparison   (b) Touched nodes comparison

Fig. 9. VPP and BK Comparison after scaling n-links in Sawtooth 9

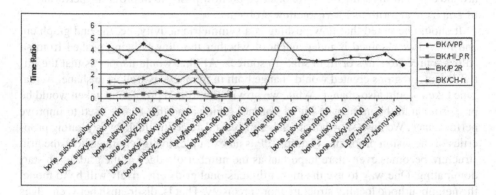

Fig. 10. Performance comparison of BK with VPP, HI_PR, PAR, P2R and CH-n on 3D, 6-connected datasets

Figure 7 shows the number of iterations taken by the VPP algorithm on BVZ samples. One interesting observation is that the upper bound on the number of iterations ($O(n)$) that one can formally prove overestimates the actual observed number significantly.

We have also compared performance of VPP and BK by running the two algorithms on 6 connected 3 dimensional data sets consisting of bone, babyface, bunny and adhead samples [3]. Figure 10 plots the ratio of time taken by BK and VPP, HI_PR, P2R, and CH-n. Ratio of time taken by BK and HI_PR, P2R, and CH-n are as reported in Table 5 in [19]. Note that VPP's performance is comparable to BK's on those samples for which Goldberg's set of algorithms (HI_PR, P2R, CH-n) are slower than BK [19]. On those samples (bone) for which CH-n, P2R are slightly faster than BK, VPP is 3 to 5 times faster.

4 Conclusions

The VPP algorithm presented above uses multiple paths with a single labelling, collects all flow first at a node before pushing, and partitions the grid flow graph in Voronoi regions at each iteration. Flow maintained after each iteration is a preflow but unlike the traditional preflow push algorithms there are two distinct phases in an iteration. The relabelling phase rebuilds the Voronoi region graphs, and push flow phase uses highest label first push and then breadth first inside sink cluster to push flow in the preflow framework in each Voronoi region. As sinks get saturated their Voronoi regions is redistributed among Voronoi regions which are still active. The algorithm improves upon the earlier reported algorithms both in terms of performance over standard data sets as well as demonstrably strongly polynomial worst case bound. This is important as we show cases where performance of algorithms without this property degrades quickly. We would like to re-iterate that our set of algorithms attempts to control the way a sink cluster can hold on to its "Voronoi region". There could be number of other strategies, around this central theme of "Voronoi based preflow push" to improve the performance of graph cut algorithms for vision flow problems.

It should be noted that flow pushing is a symmetric activity, i.e. the end graph cut and max-flow obtained is independent of whether the flow is being pushed from so called sources to sinks or from sinks to sources. All that would happen is that the initial Voronoi regions created would change both in numbers as well as in shape. Actual time taken would also change. While we provide no formal proof, time taken would be proportional to the number of initial Voronoi regions and this can be used to improve performance. We have shown that relabelling costs are controllable by exploiting properties of the vision problems. Hybrid VPP is an example. In higher dimensions the grid structure becomes even more important as the number of edges in the grid graph start dominating. One way to use the higher dimensional grids effectively will be to model the neighbourhood locality structure more precisely. That is, distinguish between edges which are incident on nodes which are grid neighbours and those which are further apart. Preliminary experiments have suggested that in higher dimensions such locality impacts performance of algorithms compared here. How does it do so in higher dimensions is a theme we are exploring.

The authors would like to thank Niloy Mitra and the referees for their comments, inputs and careful reading of the manuscript.

References

1. Boykov, Y., Kolmogorov, V.: An experimental comparison of min-cut/max-flow algorithms for energy minimization in vision. IEEE Trans. Pattern Anal. Mach. Intell. 26, 1124–1137 (2004)
2. http://vision.middlebury.edu/stereo/code/
3. http://vision.csd.uwo.ca/maxflow-data/
4. Boykov, Y., Funka-Lea, G.: Graph cuts and efficient n-d image segmentation. Int. J. Comput. Vision 70, 109–131 (2006)
5. Kolmogorov, V., Zabih, R.: Computing visual correspondence with occlusions using graph cuts. In: Proceedings of the International Conference on Computer Vision, vol. 2, pp. 508–515 (2001)
6. Kwatra, V., Schödl, A., Essa, I., Turk, G., Bobick, A.: Graphcut textures: Image and video synthesis using graph cuts. ACM Transactions on Graphics, SIGGRAPH 22, 277–286 (2003)
7. Lempitsky, V., Boykov, Y., Ivanov, D.: Oriented visibility for multiview reconstruction. In: European Conference on Computer Vision, vol. 3, pp. 226–238 (2006)

8. Kolmogorov, V., Zabih, R.: What energy functions can be minimized via graph cuts? IEEE Transactions on Pattern Analysis and Machine Intelligence 26, 147–159 (2004)
9. Greig, D.M., Porteous, B.T., Seheult, A.H.: Exact maximum a posteriori estimation for binary images. J. R. Statist. Soc. 51, 271–279 (1989)
10. Komodakis, N., Tziritas, G., Paragios, N.: Performance vs computational efficiency for optimizing single and dynamic mrfs: Setting the state of the art with primal-dual strategies. Comput. Vis. Image Underst. 112, 14–29 (2008)
11. Delong, A., Boykov, Y.: A scalable graph-cut algorithm for n-d grids. In: IEEE Conference on Computer Vision and Pattern Recognition, pp. 1–8 (2008)
12. Juan, O., Boykov, Y.: Active graph cuts. In: IEEE Conference on Computer Vision and Pattern Recognition (2006)
13. Juan, O., Boykov, Y.: Capacity scaling for graph cuts in vision. In: Proceedings of the International Conference on Computer Vision, pp. 1–8 (2007)
14. Boykov, Y., Veksler, O., Zabih, R.: Fast approximate energy minimization via graph cuts. IEEE Transactions on Pattern Analysis and Machine Intelligence 23, 1222–1239 (2001)
15. Ishikawa, H.: Exact optimization for markov random fields with convex priors. IEEE Transactions on Pattern Analysis and Machine Intelligence 25, 1333–1336 (2003)
16. Dinic, E.A.: Algorithm for solution of a problem of maximum flow in networks with power estimation. Soviet Math. Dokl. 11, 1277–1280 (1970)
17. Goldberg, A.V., Tarjan, R.E.: A new approach to the maximum-flow problem. Journal of the Association for Computing Machinery 35, 921–940 (1988)
18. Cherkassky, B.V., Goldberg, A.V.: On implementing push-relabel method for the maximum flow problem. Algorithmica 19, 390–410 (1997)
19. Goldberg, A.V.: Two-level push-relabel algorithm for the maximum flow problem. In: Goldberg, A.V., Zhou, Y. (eds.) AAIM 2009. LNCS, vol. 5564, pp. 212–225. Springer, Heidelberg (2009)
20. Vineet, V., Narayanan, P.J.: Cuda cuts: Fast graph cuts on the gpu. In: Computer Vision and Pattern Recognition Workshop, pp. 1–8 (2008)
21. http://www.cs.ucl.ac.uk/staff/V.Kolmogorov/software.html
22. http://www.igsystems.com/hipr/index.html
23. Chandran, B.G., Hochbaum, D.S.: A computational study of the pseudoflow and push-relabel algorithms for the maximum flow problem. Oper. Res. 57, 358–376 (2009)

Non-Local Kernel Regression for Image and Video Restoration

Haichao Zhang[1,2], Jianchao Yang[2], Yanning Zhang[1], and Thomas S. Huang[2]

[1] School of Computer Science, Northwestern Polytechnical University, Xi'an, China
[2] Beckman Institute, University of Illinois at Urbana-Champaign, USA
{hczhang,jyang29,huang}@ifp.uiuc.edu, ynzhang@nwpu.edu.cn

Abstract. This paper presents a non-local kernel regression (NL-KR) method for image and video restoration tasks, which exploits both the non-local self-similarity and local structural regularity in natural images. The non-local self-similarity is based on the observation that image patches tend to repeat themselves in natural images and videos; and the local structural regularity reveals that image patches have regular structures where accurate estimation of pixel values via regression is possible. Explicitly unifying both properties, the proposed non-local kernel regression framework is robust and applicable to various image and video restoration tasks. In this work, we are specifically interested in applying the NL-KR model to image and video super-resolution (SR) reconstruction. Extensive experimental results on both single images and realistic video sequences demonstrate the superiority of the proposed framework for SR tasks over previous works both qualitatively and quantitatively.

1 Introduction

One of the recent trends in image processing is to pursue the low-dimensional models for image representation and manipulation. Examples include the local structure based methods [1], sparse representation methods [2][3], manifold methods [4], etc. The success of such models is guaranteed by the low Degree of Freedom (DOF) of the local structures in natural images, represented as meaningful local structural regularity as well as self-similarity of local patterns.

Many conventional image processing algorithms are based on the assumption of local structural regularity, meaning that there are meaningful structures in the spatial space of natural images. Examples are structure tensor based methods [1][5][6]and bilateral filtering [7]. These methods utilize the local structural patterns to regularize the image processing procedure and are based on the assumption that images are locally smooth except at edges.

Another type of methods exploiting the self-similarity in natural images are recently emerging. The self-similarity property means that higher level patterns (e.g., texton and pixon) will repeat themselves in the image (possibly in different scales). This also indicates the DOF in one image is less than the DOF offered by the pixel-level representation. A representative work is the popular Non-Local Means (NL-Means) [8], which takes advantage of the redundancy of

K. Daniilidis, P. Maragos, N. Paragios (Eds.): ECCV 2010, Part III, LNCS 6313, pp. 566–579, 2010.
© Springer-Verlag Berlin Heidelberg 2010

similar patches existing in the target image for denoising tasks. Later, this idea is generalized to handle multi-frame super-resolution tasks in [9]. Recently, this self-similarity property is thoroughly explored by Glasner *et. al* in [10] for addressing single image super-resolution problems. Gabriel Peyré *et. al* proposed a non-local regularization method for general inverse problems [11].

We propose in this paper a Non-Local Kernel Regression (NL-KR) method for image and video restoration (see Fig. 1 for a graphical illustration of the proposed model). We take advantage of both local structural regularity and non-local similarity in a unified framework for more reliable and robust estimation. The non-local similarity and local structural regularity are intimately related, and are also complimentary in the sense that non-local similar pattern fusion can be regularized by the structural regularity while the redundancy from similar patterns enables more accurate estimation for structural regression.

The rest of the paper is organized as follows. We first review and summarize related works in Section 2, then we propose our NL-KR model and discuss its relations to other algorithms in Section 3. The practical algorithm for SR based on NL-KR is described in Section 4. Experiments are carried out in Section 5 on both synthetic and real image sequences, and extensive comparisons are made with both classical as well as *state-of-the-art* methods. Section 6 provides some discussions and concludes our paper.

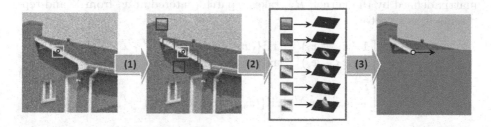

Fig. 1. Non-Local Kernel Regression. (1) Similar patch searching: different colors indicate the similarity (red the highest, green the medium and blue the least); (2) Structural kernel estimation and reweighting: estimate a regression kernel adapted to the structure at each position where the similar patches reside and re-weight them according to similarity; (3) Non-local kernel regression: estimate the value for the query point with both local structural and non-local similar information in raster-scan order.

2   Related Works

In this work, we are interested in image and video restorations where we desire to estimate the pixel value of a given location in the image plane (e.g., image super-resolution, inpainting and denoising). This section presents a brief technical review of local structural regression or filtering method as well as the non-local similarity-based approach.

2.1   Local Structural Regression

Typical image filtering methods usually perform in a local manner, i.e., the value of the estimated image at a query location is influenced only by the pixels within a small neighborhood of that position. They usually take the form of:

$$\hat{z}(\boldsymbol{x}_i) = \arg\min_z \sum_{j \in \mathcal{N}(\boldsymbol{x}_i)} (y_j - z)^2 K_{\boldsymbol{x}_i}(\boldsymbol{x}_j - \boldsymbol{x}_i) \tag{1}$$

where $\mathcal{N}(\boldsymbol{x}_i)$ denotes the neighbors of $\boldsymbol{x}_i$, and $K_{\boldsymbol{x}_i}(\boldsymbol{x}_j - \boldsymbol{x}_i)$ is the spatial kernel at location $\boldsymbol{x}_i$ that assigns larger weights to nearby similar pixels while smaller weights to farther non-similar pixels. Since the local image structure is not isotropic, local structure aware kernels are developed, with representative examples as Orientated Gaussian kernel [1] and Bilateral kernel [7]. To approximate the local structure better, higher order estimation can be used:

$$\hat{\mathbf{a}} = \arg\min_{\mathbf{a}} \| R_{\boldsymbol{x}_i} Y - \varPhi \mathbf{a} \|_{W_{K_{\boldsymbol{x}_i}}}^2 \tag{2}$$

Here $\varPhi$ is the polynomial bases given in Eq. 3 developed from Taylor expansion[1] with $\mathbf{a}$ the corresponding regression coefficients, and $\mathbf{tril}(\cdot)$ extracts the lower triangular part of a matrix and stack it to a column vector. $W_{K_{\boldsymbol{x}_i}} = \mathrm{diag}[K_{\boldsymbol{x}_i}(\boldsymbol{x}_1 - \boldsymbol{x}_i), K_{\boldsymbol{x}_i}(\boldsymbol{x}_2 - \boldsymbol{x}_i), \cdots, K_{\boldsymbol{x}_i}(\boldsymbol{x}_m - \boldsymbol{x}_i)]$ $(m = |\mathcal{N}(\boldsymbol{x}_i)|)$ is the weight matrix defined by the kernel. $R_{\boldsymbol{x}_i}$ takes a patch centered at $\boldsymbol{x}_i$ from Y and represents it as a vector.

$$\varPhi = \begin{bmatrix} 1 & (\boldsymbol{x}_1 - \boldsymbol{x}_i)^T & \mathbf{tril}\{(\boldsymbol{x}_1 - \boldsymbol{x}_i)(\boldsymbol{x}_1 - \boldsymbol{x}_i)^T\}^T & \cdots \\ 1 & (\boldsymbol{x}_2 - \boldsymbol{x}_i)^T & \mathbf{tril}\{(\boldsymbol{x}_2 - \boldsymbol{x}_i)(\boldsymbol{x}_2 - \boldsymbol{x}_i)^T\}^T & \cdots \\ \vdots & \vdots & \vdots & \vdots \\ 1 & (\boldsymbol{x}_m - \boldsymbol{x}_i)^T & \mathbf{tril}\{(\boldsymbol{x}_m - \boldsymbol{x}_i)(\boldsymbol{x}_m - \boldsymbol{x}_i)^T\}^T & \cdots \end{bmatrix} \tag{3}$$

Therefore, the first element of the regression coefficient is the desired pixel value estimation at $\boldsymbol{x}_i$.

$$\hat{z}(\boldsymbol{x}_i) = \mathbf{e}_1^T \left[\varPhi^T W_{K_{\boldsymbol{x}_i}} \varPhi \right]^{-1} \varPhi^T W_{K_{\boldsymbol{x}_i}} R_{\boldsymbol{x}_i} Y \tag{4}$$

where $\mathbf{e}_1$ is a vector with the first element equal to one, and the rest zero.

2.2   Non-Local Similarity-Based Estimation

Local image structures tend to repeat themselves across the image and also the image sequence in videos. This property has been explored in many applications

---

[1] The regression bases do not have to be polynomial, and other choices are open. For more details about deriving the polynomial bases, one can refer to [6], which gives a nice tutorial on kernel regression.

such as texture synthesis [12], image inpainting [13], denoising [8] and super-resolution [9] [14]. This self-similarity property provides the redundancy that is sometimes critical for many ill-posed image processing problems, as similar structures can be regarded as multiple observations from the same underlying ground truth. For instance, the NL-Means algorithm recently introduced by Buades *et al.* in [8] for image denoising has become very popular, due to its effectiveness despite of its simplicity. The algorithm breaks the locality constraints of previous conventional filtering methods, making use of similar patterns found in different locations of the image to denoise the image. Specifically, NL-Means algorithm is a weighted average:

$$z(\boldsymbol{x}_i) = \frac{\sum_{j \in \mathcal{P}(\boldsymbol{x}_i)} w_{ij} y_j}{\sum_{j \in \mathcal{P}(\boldsymbol{x}_i)} w_{ij}} \tag{5}$$

where $\mathcal{P}(\boldsymbol{x}_i)$ denote the index set for similar pixel observations for $\boldsymbol{x}_i$ (includes $\boldsymbol{x}_i$ itself). The weight w_{ij} reflects the similarity between the observations at $\boldsymbol{x}_i$ and $\boldsymbol{x}_j$ [8]. Eq. 5, can be reformulated into an optimization problem:

$$\begin{aligned} \hat{z}(\boldsymbol{x}_i) &= \arg\min_z \sum_{j \in \mathcal{P}(\boldsymbol{x}_i)} \left[y_j - z(\boldsymbol{x}_i) \right]^2 w_{ij} \\ &= \arg\min_z \| \boldsymbol{y} - \boldsymbol{1} z(\boldsymbol{x}_i) \|_{W_{\boldsymbol{x}_i}}^2 \end{aligned} \tag{6}$$

where $\boldsymbol{y}$ denotes the vector consisting of the pixels at the locations in the similar set $\mathcal{P}(\boldsymbol{x}_i)$, $\boldsymbol{1}$ denotes a vector of all ones, and $W_{\boldsymbol{x}_i} = \text{diag}\left[w_{i1}, w_{i2}, ..., w_{im} \right]$ $(m = |\mathcal{P}(\boldsymbol{x}_i)|)$. Compared with Eq. 2, the NL-Means estimation Eq. 6 can be regarded as a zero-order estimation, and the weight matrix is constructed from the similarity measures instead of the spatial kernel as before.

3 Non-Local Kernel Regression Model

3.1 Mathematical Formulation

We derive the Non-Local Kernel Regression (NL-KR) algorithm in this section. The approach makes full use of both cues from *local* structural regularity and *non-local* similarity for image and video restoration. We argue that the proposed approach is more reliable and robust for ill-posed inverse problems: local structural regression regularize the noisy candidates found by non-local similarity search; and non-local similarity provides the redundancy preventing possible overfitting of the local structural regression. Instead of using a *point prediction* model in non-local methods, we use the more reliable *local structure*-based prediction. On the other hand, rather than predicting the value with only one *local patch*, we can try to make use of all the *non-local similar* patches in natural images. Mathematically, the proposed high-order Non-Local Kernel Regression model is formulated as:

$$\hat{\mathbf{a}} = \arg\min_{\mathbf{a}} \frac{1}{2} \overbrace{w_{ii}\|R_{\boldsymbol{x}_i}Y - \varPhi\mathbf{a}\|^2_{W_{K_{\boldsymbol{x}_i}}}}^{local} + \frac{1}{2} \overbrace{\sum_{j\in\mathcal{P}(\boldsymbol{x}_i)\setminus\{i\}} w_{ij}\|R_{\boldsymbol{x}_j}Y - \varPhi\mathbf{a}\|^2_{W_{K_{\boldsymbol{x}_j}}}}^{non-local}$$

$$= \arg\min_{\mathbf{a}} \frac{1}{2} \sum_{j\in\mathcal{P}(\boldsymbol{x}_i)} w_{ij}\|R_{\boldsymbol{x}_j}Y - \varPhi\mathbf{a}\|^2_{W_{K_{\boldsymbol{x}_j}}} \tag{7}$$

$$= \arg\min_{\mathbf{a}} \frac{1}{2} \sum_{j\in\mathcal{P}(\boldsymbol{x}_i)} \|R_{\boldsymbol{x}_j}Y - \varPhi\mathbf{a}\|^2_{\tilde{W}_{\boldsymbol{x}_j}}$$

where $W_{K_{\boldsymbol{x}_j}}$ is the weight matrix constructed from kernel $K_{\boldsymbol{x}_j}$, and $\mathcal{P}(\boldsymbol{x}_i)$ again is the similar index set for $\boldsymbol{x}_i$. w_{ij} is calculated between the location $\boldsymbol{x}_i$ of interest and any position $\boldsymbol{x}_j$ $(j \in \mathcal{P}(\boldsymbol{x}_i))$ by measuring the similarity of their neighborhoods weighted by a Gaussian kernel:

$$w_{ij} = \exp\left(-\frac{\|R_{\boldsymbol{x}_i}Y - R_{\boldsymbol{x}_j}Y\|^2_{W_G}}{2\sigma^2}\right) \tag{8}$$

where W_G is the weight matrix constructed from a Gaussian kernel, which puts larger weights on the centering pixels of the patch. The proposed NL-KR regression model consists of two parts:

1. **Local regression term:** the traditional local regression or filtering term, with w_{ii} set to be 1. This term also contributes as a fidelity loss, as the estimation should be close to the observation.
2. **Non-local regression term:** instead of zero-order point estimation as in Non-Local means, higher-order kernel regression is also used to make full use the structural redundancy in the similar patches.

The effects of these two parts will be more clear with experimental results in Section 5. To get the regression coefficients, differentiate the right hand side of Eq. 7 with respect to $\mathbf{a}$ and set it to zero, we have

$$\hat{\mathbf{a}} = \left[\varPhi^T\left(\sum_{j\in\mathcal{P}(\boldsymbol{x}_i)} w_{ij}W_{K_{\boldsymbol{x}_j}}\right)\varPhi\right]^{-1} \varPhi^T \sum_{j\in\mathcal{P}(\boldsymbol{x}_i)} w_{ij}W_{K_{\boldsymbol{x}_j}}R_{\boldsymbol{x}_j}Y \tag{9}$$

Then $\hat{z}(\boldsymbol{x}_i) = \mathbf{e}_1^T\hat{\mathbf{a}}$. Examination on Eq. 9, we have the following two comments:

– The structural kernel is estimated from contaminated observations, and thus is not robust. Compared with Eq. 4, with non-local redundancy, our estimation is more stable because of the weighted average of kernel weight matrices inside the inverse, and the weighted average of the structural pixel values.
– Compared with Eq. 6, our model can regularize the estimation from the non-local patches by structural higher-order regression, and thus is more robust to outliers.

Therefore, the proposed model make full use of both important cues from local structure and non-local similarity, leading to more reliable and robust estimation, which will be verified by experimental results in Sec. 5.

3.2 Structural Kernel Estimation

It is desirable to use a structure adaptive kernel in estimation. Given the observation Y and a query location $\boldsymbol{x}_i$, we can construct a structure adaptive kernel as:

$$K_{\boldsymbol{x}_i}(\boldsymbol{x} - \boldsymbol{x}_i) = \frac{1}{\sqrt{\det(T)}} \exp\left\{ -\frac{1}{2}(\boldsymbol{x} - \boldsymbol{x}_i)^T T^{-1}(\boldsymbol{x} - \boldsymbol{x}_i) \right\} \quad (10)$$

where T is the diffusion tensor at $\boldsymbol{x}_i$ controlling the spatial structure of the kernel. Given two unit vectors $\mathbf{u}$ and $\mathbf{v}$ defined by the gradient and tangent direction respectively, we can construct $T = f\mathbf{u}\mathbf{u}^T + g\mathbf{v}\mathbf{v}^T$ and adjust f and g according to the underlying structure, so that the induced kernel is isotropic ($f \approx g$) at almost constant regions and aligned along the image contour ($g > f$) otherwise. One possible choice [2] is $f(\alpha, \beta) = \frac{\beta+\gamma}{\alpha+\gamma}$ and $g(\alpha, \beta) = \frac{\alpha+\gamma}{\beta+\gamma}$ ($\gamma \geq 0$), where α and β are the eigen values of the structure tensor [1], reflecting the strength of the gradient along each eigenvector directions. α, β, $\mathbf{u}$ and $\mathbf{v}$ can be calculated from the following relation using singular value decomposition (SVD):

$$\nabla Y_{\boldsymbol{x}_i} \nabla Y_{\boldsymbol{x}_i}^T = \alpha \mathbf{u}\mathbf{u}^T + \beta \mathbf{v}\mathbf{v}^T \quad (11)$$

where $\nabla Y_{\boldsymbol{x}_i}$ is a 2×1 vector, denoting the gradient of Y at $\boldsymbol{x}_i$.

3.3 Relations to Other Works

Tons of works have emerged recently based on non-local redundancy and local regressions for image and video processing. It is worthwhile to talk about the relations of the proposed model to those previously proposed algorithms. The non-local models in [4], [8] and [9] use the redundancy from non-local self-similarity, but do not include the spatial structure explicitly as a regularization. The high order generalization of non-local means in [15] uses the computation of non-local similarity to find the local kernel for regression, which actually violates the philosophy of the non-local model. Local structural regression [1][6][7] explicitly employ the spatial kernel for regularization, but neglect the redundancy of similar local patterns useful for robust estimation. The 3D kernel regression method [16] exploits the local spatial-temporal structure by extending their 2D spatial kernel regression, also discards the non-local self-similarity. Sparse representation for denoising [2] and super-resolution [3] do local regression using bases learned from a training database. They perform estimation on each individual local patch and discard the patch redundancy. The sparse representation model is later generalized in [17] for image denoising by doing simultaneous sparse coding over similar patches found in different locations of the image. However, the non-local redundancy is used in a hard assignment clustering way instead of a soft way. [10] fully explores the self-similarity property for single image super-resolution, but no spatial structural regularization is applied. To summarize, our model is the first work to explicitly unify the self-similarity and local structural regularization into a single model, allowing more robust estimation.

---

[2] One can refer to [1] for other choices of diffusion tensor.

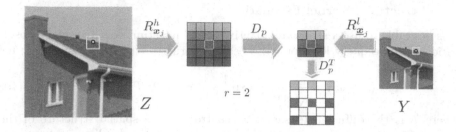

Fig. 2. Operator Illustration. $R^l_{\underline{x}_j} Y$, the patch of the LR image Y at $\underline{x}_j$, is formed by downsampling HR patch $R^h_{x_j} Z$ by factor $r = 2$ as $D_p R^h_{x_j} Z$, keeping the center pixel still in the center. Operator D_p^T up samples a patch with zero padding.

4   Non-Local Kernel Regression for Super-Resolution

The NL-KR model proposed above is a general model that can be applied to many image and video restoration tasks. In this work, we specifically apply the formulation Eq. 7 to image and video super-resolution.

Image super-resolution (SR) aims to estimate a high-resolution image (HR) from a single or a set of low-resolution (LR) observations. Conventional multi-frame SR follows the steps of (1) global motion estimation, (2) image wrapping and (3) data fusion. These methods are limited in the assumed global motion model, and can not be applied to realistic videos that almost certainly contain arbitrary motion patterns. Recently, several multi-frame SR algorithms based on fuzzy motion estimation of local image patches are proposed to process real videos [9][16]. We will show that similarly our model can also be applied to realistic videos, while achieving better results both qualitatively and quantitatively. Besides, due to the self-similarity property of the image, we can also perform single frame SR without additional training, arguing that the motion may not be that critical as in the conventional SR cases for image resolution enhancement. The LR image frames are usually modeled as blurring and downsampling the desired HR image, i.e.:

$$Y_k = D_k H X + \epsilon_k = DZ + \epsilon_k, k = 1, 2, ... \tag{12}$$

where D_k is the downsampling operator, H is the blurring operator and ϵ_k is a noise term, and k is the LR frame index. Therefore, the SR recovery problem can be divided into two steps: LR image fusion and deblurring. In our NL-KR model, we also target recovering Z followed by deblurring. As now we have two different spatial scales, i.e., high- and low-resolution image grids, the following notations are introduced for ease of presentation. We let r denote the zoom factor, x and $\underline{x}$ denote the coordinates on HR and LR grids respectively. R^h and R^l denote the patch extraction and vectorization operator on HR and LR images, where the extracted vectors are of dimension $u^2 \times 1$ and $v^2 \times 1$ respectively, and $u = (v - 1) \times r + 1$ relates the two spatial scales. D_p is a patch downsampling operator which keeps the center pixel of the patch on the LR grid, while D_p^T is a patch upsampling operator with zero-padding (refer to Fig. 2). For a given query position x_i on the HR grid, $\mathcal{P}(x_i)$ can be constructed from the initial HR estimation of the current image or consecutive frames, while keeping only those corresponding to integer positions on the LR grid, i.e., $x_j = (\underline{x}_j - 1) \times r + 1$ ($j \in \mathcal{P}(x_i)$). Then using Eq. 7 and Eq. 12, the NL-KR model tailored for SR tasks is formulated as:

$$\hat{a} = \arg\min_a \frac{1}{2} \sum_{j \in \mathcal{P}(x_i)} \|D_p^T(R_{\underline{x}_j}^l Y - D_p \Phi a)\|_{\tilde{W}_{x_j}}^2$$

$$= \arg\min_a \frac{1}{2} \sum_{j \in \mathcal{P}(x_i)} \|R_{\underline{x}_j}^l Y - D_p \Phi a\|_{\tilde{W}_{x_j}^D}^2 \tag{13}$$

where we denote $\tilde{W}_{x_j} = w_{ij} W_{K_{x_j}}$ to keep the notation uncluttered, Φa is a high order regression for the patch $R_{x_j}^h Z$ centered at query location x_j for the blurred HR image Z, and $\tilde{W}_{x_j}^D = D_p \tilde{W}_{x_j} D_p^T$. Solution of Eq. 13 is straightforward:

$$\hat{a} = \left[\Phi^T \left(\sum_{j \in \mathcal{P}(x_i)} D_p^T \tilde{W}_{x_j}^D D_p\right) \Phi\right]^{-1} \Phi^T \sum_{j \in \mathcal{P}(x_i)} D_p^T \tilde{W}_{x_j}^D R_{\underline{x}_j}^l Y \tag{14}$$

The estimated pixel value at query point x_i is $e_1^T \hat{a}$.

As we can see, the missing pixels in the high resolution grid are filled up by multiple low resolution observations found in a non-local way on the current frame or current sequence. These low resolution observations are further fused with regularization from the local structure. The estimated image is then deblurred with a Total Variation based algorithm [18]. Algorithm 1 describes the practical implementation for the proposed model.

5   Experimental Validation

The proposed NL-KR model can handle both single image and multiple frame SR naturally. In this section, we validate the performance of the proposed method with experiments on single images, synthetic and real video sequences. Performance comparisons are performed with related *state-of-the-art* algorithms. We use both Peak Signal to Noise Ratio (PSNR) and Structural SIMilarity (SSIM) index [19] to evaluate different algorithms objectively.

In all the experiments, we focus on zooming the LR frame(s) by factor of 3. These LR frames are modeled by first blurring the HR frames with a 3×3 uniform PSF and downsampling with decimation factor of 3. Gaussian noise of standard deviation 2 is added to the LR frames to model the real imaging system. In our algorithm, the LR patch size is fixed as 5×5, and the corresponding HR patch size is thus 13×13. The support of the non-local similar patch searching is fixed to be the 10-nearest neighbors. We set $\sigma = 169c$ with $c = 0.06$ for similarity weight calculation and $\gamma = 1$ for diffusion tensor computation. For image deblurring, we use a Total Variation based deblurring algorithm [18].

Algorithm 1. (Non-local kernel regression for image super-resolution).

1: **Input:** a low resolution video sequence $\underline{Y} = [Y_1, Y_2, ..., Y_M]$ and zoom factor r.
2: **Initialize** an enlarged sequence $\underline{\tilde{Y}} = [\tilde{Y}_1, \tilde{Y}_2, ..., \tilde{Y}_M]$ with bicubic interpolation.
3: **For** each pixel location x_i on the high resolution image grid for frame Y_m, do

  − Construct the similar patch index set $\mathcal{P}(x_i)$ with sequence $\underline{\tilde{Y}}$;
  − Estimate the image gradient ∇Y_{x_i};
  − Calculate the diffusion tensor K_{x_i} use Eq. 11 and Eq. 10.

4: **End**
5: **For** each pixel location x_i on the high resolution image grid for frame Y_m, do

  − Construct the spatial weight matrix $\tilde{W}_{x_j}^D$ using estimated K_{x_j} for all $j \in \mathcal{P}(x_i)$;
  − Calculate the regression coefficients with Eq. 14 and update the current estimation of Z_m at x_i with $Z_m(x_i) = e_1^T \hat{a}$.

6: **End**
7: **Perform** deblurring for Z_m: $X_m = \text{TVdeblur}(Z_m)$.
8: **Output:** a high resolution video frame X_m.

5.1   Single Frame Based Super-Resolution

We will first evaluate the proposed method on single image SR. In the first set of experiments, we specifically compare the proposed model with 2D case of Generalized NL-Means (GNL-Means) [9] and Kernel Regression (KR)[6] in order to show that our model is more reliable and robust for estimation. We take one frame from each of the popular test sequences: Foreman, Miss America and Suzie used in [9], degrade it and perform the SR estimation. The PSNR and SSIM results for the three frames are summarized in Table 1, which shows that the proposed method is constantly better than 2D GNL-Means and 2D Kernel Regression. The results of Nearest Neighbor (NN), Bicubic Interpolation (BI) and Sparse Coding (SC) method [3] are also provided as references. Fig. 3 shows the visual quality comparisons on Foreman. As shown, the 2D GNL-Means method is prone to block artifacts due to poor patch matching within a single image and the 2D Kernel Regression method generates ghost effects due to insufficient observation for regularizing the local regression. Our result, however, is free of either of these artifacts. We further make more comparisons with *state-of-the-art* methods on real images, where the input LR image is zoomed by a factor of 4, as shown in Fig. 4 and Fig. 5. Note that these methods are designed specifically to work on single images. In Fig. 4, it can be seen that the proposed method can preserve more details than Fattal's method [20] and is comparable with Kim's method [21] and the more recent work [10]. In Fig. 5, however, our algorithm outperforms both [20] and [10], where our result is free of the *jaggy* artifacts on the edges and the characters generated by our method is more realistic. The improvement comparison could be more impressive if one notices that in [10], multiple scales are used for similar pattern matching while our method only uses one scale.

Fig. 3. Single-frame super resolution (×3, PSNR, SSIM in brackets). Left to right: NN(28.6917, 0.8185), BI(30.9511, 0.8708), GNL-Means(31.9961, 0.8747)[9], KR(32.4479, 0.8862)[6], NL-KR(**32.7558, 0.8918**). GNL-Means generates block effect while KR generates ghost artifacts. Our method does not suffer from these problems.

Fig. 4. Single-frame super resolution for real color images (×4). From left to right: NN, BI, Kim's method [21], Fattal's method [20], Glasner's method [10], NL-KR. Note that our result preserves more details than Fattal's method and is comparable to results from Kim's learning based method and recently proposed method by Glasner.

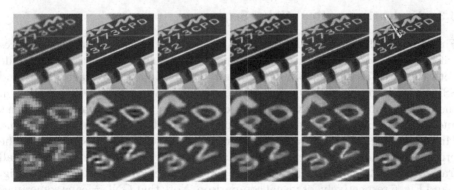

Fig. 5. More results on single-frame SR for real color images (×4). From left to right: NN, GNL-Means [9], KR [6], Fattal's method [20], Glasner's method [10], NL-KR. Note that Fattal's method and Glasner's method generate *jaggy* effects on the edge. Our method is free from the *jaggy* artifacts and preserves better structure.

Table 1. PSNR (Top) and SSIM (Bottom) results for single image super-resolution

Images	NN	BI	GNL-Means [9]	KR [6]	SC [3]	Proposed
Foreman	28.6917	30.9511	31.9961	32.4479	32.5997	**32.7558**
Miss America	31.5765	34.0748	34.4700	34.4419	34.9111	**35.4033**
Suzie	30.0295	31.4660	31.6547	31.8203	31.5208	**32.1033**
Foreman	0.8185	0.8708	0.8747	0.8862	0.8768	**0.8924**
Miss America	0.8403	0.8941	0.9008	0.8990	0.8843	**0.9117**
Suzie	0.7892	0.8286	0.8355	0.8285	0.8334	**0.8449**

Table 2. PSNR (Top) and SSIM (Bottom) results for synthetic test frames

Sequence	NN	BI	GNL-Means [9]	BM3D [22]	Proposed
Foreman	28.8977	30.9493	34.6766	34.9	**35.2041**
Miss America	31.6029	34.0684	36.2508	37.5	**37.8228**
Suzie	30.0307	31.4702	32.9189	33.6	**33.9949**
Foreman	0.8413	0.8709	0.9044	NA	**0.9234**
Miss America	0.8404	0.8928	0.8193	NA	**0.9346**
Suzie	0.7904	0.8290	0.8428	NA	**0.8864**

5.2 Synthetic Experiment for Multi-frame SR

Our second experiment is conducted on synthetic image frames. We generate 9 LR images from one HR image by blurring the HR image with a 3×3 uniform PSF and then decimating the blurred HR image every 3rd row or column with shifts of $\{0, 1, 2\}$ pixels. Gaussian noise with standard deviation of 2 is also added. The PSNR and SSIM results are summarized in Table 2, showing that the proposed method is again constantly better. Note that the results from BM3D is cited directly from [22], which are obtained from noise-free observations.

5.3 Evaluation on Real Video Sequences

Finally, we evaluate the performance of our model on three real image sequences with general motions: Foreman, Miss America and Suzie. Comparisons are made with the GNL-Means [9], BM3D [22], and 3D-KR [16]. The average PSNR and SSIM results on these three test sequences are given in Table 3. As shown, the proposed method achieves better reconstruction accuracy than GNL-Means and BM3D.[3] In Fig. 7, we further show the PSNR results on Foreman and Miss American frame by frame, compared with Bicubic and GNL-Means. The proposed method outperforms GNL-Means method by a notable margin in all frames. The SR results on Miss America and Foreman sequences are given in Fig. 8 and Fig. 6 respectively for visual comparison. Note that GNL-Means sometimes

---

[3] The PSNR results of 3D-KR are not listed, because they are not numerically available in their original papers (plotted in a figure). However, compared with their figure, our method improves over GNL-Means by a larger margin than the 3D-KR method.

Fig. 6. Video super-resolution for Foreman sequence (frame 8, zoom factor 3, PSNR and SSIM in brackets). Left to right: Ground-truth, BI(30.1758, 0.8739), GNL-Means(33.2233, 0.9041), BM3D(33.45, NA), 3D-KR(33.30, NA), NL-KR(**33.7589, 0.9137**). GNL-Means performs well at regular-structured area but generates severe block artifacts where few similar patches can be found; BM3D suffers from *jagged* effects at edges; 3D-KR can not preserve the straight structure well due to the non-robustness of its spatial-temporal kernel and can generate *ghost image*; our method preserves both the larger structure and fine details well and is free of these artifacts.

Table 3. Average PSNR (Top) and SSIM (Bottom) for the three video sequences

Sequence	NN	BI	GNL-Means[9]	BM3D[22]	Proposed
Foreman	28.8444	31.0539	32.8165	33.5	**34.0141**
Miss America	31.6555	34.2424	35.3453	36.3	**36.4377**
Suzie	30.0846	31.4363	32.9725	33.0	**33.0915**
Foreman	0.8207	0.8720	0.9025	NA	**0.9120**
Miss America	0.8426	0.8938	0.9136	NA	**0.9164**
Suzie	0.7857	0.8233	**0.8797**	NA	0.8671

generates severe block artifacts (see the *Mouth* part in Fig. 6 and *Eye* part in Fig. 8). The 3D-KR method, on the other hand, will generate some *ghost* effects, due to overfitting of the regression and inaccurate estimation of the 3D kernel (see the *Mouth* part in Fig. 6). Furthermore, the 3D-KR method has to employ a motion pre-compensation in order for good 3D kernel estimation, while our model does not require this step.

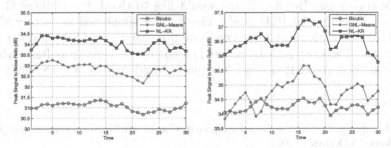

Fig. 7. PSNR plots for Video SR. Left: Foreman and right: Miss America data. The proposed method outperforms other two methods in terms of PSNR in all frames.

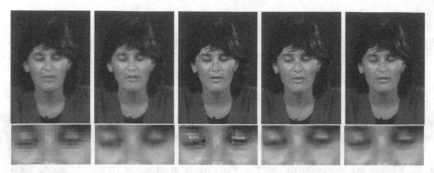

Fig. 8. Video super-resolution for Miss America sequence (frame 8, zoom factor 3, PSNR and SSIM in brackets). Left to right: NN(32.4259, 0.8580), BI(34.5272, 0.8958), GNL-Means(34.7635,0.9132), 3D-KR(35.53, NA), NL-KR(**36.6509, 0.9171**). The GNL-Means method suffers from block effects, while our method is free from artifacts and is comparable to 3D-KR in this case.

6   Conclusions and Future Work

This paper proposes a Non-Local Kernel Regression (NL-KR) model for image and video restoration tasks, which combines the local structural regularity as well as non-local similarity explicitly to ensure a more reliable and robust estimation. The proposed method is a general model that includes many related models as special cases. In this work, we focus on the image and video super-resolution task, and experiments on both single frame and video sequence demonstrate the effectiveness and robustness of our model. Further more, the NL-KR on single image super-resolution may suggest that the image itself contains enough information that SR without training and motion is possible. Also, incorporating more self-similarity information by extending the image into multi-scale space is straightforward under our model. In the current algorithm, the patch matching and spatial kernel calculation are most computationally heavy, which can be speeded up by KD-tree searching and parallel computing respectively. The proposed model can also be applied to other image and video restoration tasks, e.g. inpainting and denoising, and we leave those to be our future work.

Acknowledgement. The authors would like to thank all the reviewers for their valuable comments. Haichao Zhang would like to thank the Chinese Government for supporting his PhD Study. This work is supported in part by NSF of China (No.60872145) and Cultivation Fund from Ministry of Education of China (No.708085). The work is also supported in part by the U.S. Army Research Laboratory and U.S. Army Research Office under grand number W911NF-09-1-0383.

References

1. Tschumperle, D.: PDE's Based Regularization of Multivalued Images and Applications. PhD thesis (2002)
2. Elad, M., Aharon, M.: Image denoising via learned dictionaries and sparse representation. In: CVPR, pp. 17–22 (2006)

3. Yang, J., Wright, J., Huang, T.S., Ma, Y.: Image super-resolution as sparse representation of raw image patches. In: CVPR (2008)
4. Chang, H., Yeung, D.Y., Xiong, Y.: Super-resolution through neighbor embedding. In: CVPR (2004)
5. Li, X.: Video processing via implicit and mixture motion models. IEEE Trans. on Circuits and Systems for Video Technology 17, 953–963 (2007)
6. Takeda, H., Farsiu, S., Milanfar, P.: Kernel regression for image processing and reconstruction. IEEE TIP 16, 349–366 (2007)
7. Tomasi, C.: Bilateral filtering for gray and color images. In: ICCV, pp. 839–846 (1998)
8. Buades, A., Coll, B.: A non-local algorithm for image denoising. In: CVPR (2005)
9. Protter, M., Elad, M., Takeda, H., Milanfar, P.: Generalizing the non-local-means to super-resolution reconstruction. IEEE TIP, 36–51 (2009)
10. Glasner, D., Bagon, S., Irani, M.: Super-resolution from a single image. In: ICCV (2009)
11. Peyre, G., Bougleux, S., Cohen, L.: Non-local regularization of inverse problems. In: Forsyth, D., Torr, P., Zisserman, A. (eds.) ECCV 2008, Part III. LNCS, vol. 5304, pp. 57–68. Springer, Heidelberg (2008)
12. Efros, A., Leung, T.: Texture synthesis by non-parametric sampling. In: ICCV, pp. 1033–1038 (1999)
13. Wong, A., Orchard, J.: A nonlocal-means approach to exemplar-based inpainting. In: ICIP (2002)
14. Protter, M., Elad, M.: Super resolution with probabilistic motion estimation. IEEE TIP, 1899–1904 (2009)
15. Chatterjee, P., Milanfar, P.: A generalization of non-local means via kernel regression. In: SPIE Conf. on Computational Imaging (2008)
16. Takeda, H., Milanfar, P., Protter, M., Elad, M.: Super-resolution without explicit subpixel motion estimation. IEEE TIP (2009)
17. Mairal, J., Bach, F., Ponce, J., Sapiro, G., Zisserman, A.: Non-local sparse models for image restoration. In: ICCV (2009)
18. Getreuer, P.: (2009), http://www.math.ucla.edu/~getreuer/tvreg.html
19. Wang, Z., Bovik, A.C., Sheikh, H.R., Member, S., Simoncelli, E.P., Member, S.: Image quality assessment: From error visibility to structural similarity. IEEE TIP 13, 600–612 (2004)
20. Fattal, R.: Image upsampling via imposed edge statistics. In: SIGGRAPH (2007)
21. Kim, K.I., Kwon, Y.: Example-based learning for single-image super-resolution and jpeg artifact removal. Technical report (2008)
22. Danielyan, A., Foi, A., Katkovnik, V., Egiazarian, K.: Image and video super-resolution via spatially adaptive block-matching filtering. In: Int. Workshop on Local and Non-Local Approx. in Image Process (2008)

A Spherical Harmonics Shape Model
for Level Set Segmentation

Maximilian Baust and Nassir Navab

Computer Aided Medical Procedures (CAMP),
Technische Universität München,
Boltzmannstr. 3, 85748 Garching, Germany
{baust,navab}@in.tum.de
http://campar.in.tum.de

Abstract. We introduce a segmentation framework which combines and shares advantages of both an implicit surface representation and a parametric shape model based on spherical harmonics. Besides the elegant surface representation it also inherits the power and flexibility of variational level set methods with respect to the modeling of data terms. At the same time it provides all advantages of parametric shape models such as a sparse and multiscale shape representation. Additionally, we introduce a regularizer that helps to ensure a unique decomposition into spherical harmonics and thus the comparability of parameter values of multiple segmentations. We demonstrate the benefits of our method on medical and photometric data and present two possible extensions.

Keywords: Segmentation, Level Set Methods, Variational Methods, Shape Models, Spherical Harmonics.

1 Introduction

Level set methods and particularly variational level set methods belong to the most flexible tools for image segmentation as far as the modeling of data terms and the handling of topological changes during the evolution are concerned. However, this topological flexibility may be undesired for two reasons:

- The object boundaries are not clearly defined by strong image gradients or significant changes in the intensity distribution, which occurs especially for many medical applications, where image data often suffers from low tissue contrast or noise. Thus the contour may *leak* into surrounding objects.
- The evolution might get stuck in an undesired local minimum. Thus the segmentation problem needs additional regularization in order to pick out the desired minimum.

In contrast to topologically flexible level set methods, parametrized active contours allow to add the required amount of regularity to such problems as illustrated in Fig. 1. We distinguish three classes of parametrized active contours,

K. Daniilidis, P. Maragos, N. Paragios (Eds.): ECCV 2010, Part III, LNCS 6313, pp. 580–593, 2010.
© Springer-Verlag Berlin Heidelberg 2010

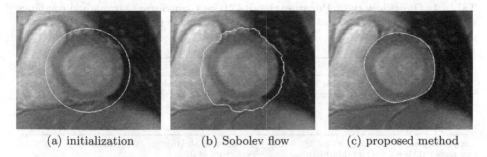

(a) initialization   (b) Sobolev flow   (c) proposed method

Fig. 1. The Benefit of a Parametric Shape Model: The segmentation of the outer wall of the left ventricle acquired with magnetic resonance imaging [1] with a Sobolev gradient flow (cf. Sec. 5) gets stuck in an undesired local minimum (b). In contrast to this, the proposed approach clearly benefits from the employed shape model (c).

no matter whether they use an explicit or implicit surface representation: Methods using a *parametrized surface description*, methods based on *statistical shape models* and methods employing a *parametric shape model*. The first class consists of methods that only have a parametrized surface description, but no model based assumption about the topology of the shape to be segmented. Popular examples are all kinds of topology-adaptive and generalized snakes, which can be subsumed under *deformable models* [2]. The second and the third class are represented by all approaches employing a statistical or a parametric shape model. In both cases the object is represented as a linear combination of basis functions. While for statistical shape models these basis functions are generated from training data and are thus application specific, parametric shape models employ a fixed set of basis functions such as spherical harmonics or wavelets for instance. Of course, many methods based on parametric shape models also use training data in order to adapt the shape model to the specific application by constraining the parameters as it is done in [3], [4], [5], [6], and [7].

However, there are situations where one would like to use a parametric shape model even when no training data is available. The method we propose combines an implicit surface representation with a parametric shape model based on spherical harmonics. Moreover, we propose a regularizer which helps to ensure a unique decomposition into spherical harmonics and thus the comparability of several segmentations, if no training data is available. In detail, our method inherits the following advantages from implicit representations:

- In contrast to explicit surface representations no remeshing of the surface during the evolution is necessary.
- Cost function evaluations, especially for region-based data terms, can be computed very easily using smeared-out versions of the Heaviside function and its derivatives, because the membership of every pixel to fore- or background is automatically given by the level set function.
- The proposed framework inherits the full flexibility of variational level set methods regarding the modeling of region- and surface-based data terms.

Table 1. Overview over Parametrized Active Contours: Our method combines an implicit surface representation with a parametric shape model as well as the advantages from both of them

shape model	none	statistical	parametric
explicit shape representation	Deformable Models (e.g. Terzopoulos in [2])	Active Shape Models (e.g. Cootes et al. [8])	Staib and Duncan [3], Székely et al. [4], Kelemen et al. [5], Nain et al. [6], Yu et al. [7]
implicit shape representation	Huang et al. [9] (MetaMorphs), Morse et al. [10], Ho et al. [11], Slabaugh et al. [12]	Leventon et al. [13], Tsai et al. [14]	our method

Moreover, the presented method also inherits advantages from the employed parametric shape model and the proposed regularizer:

- In contrast to traditional level set methods, the parametrization removes the necessity for the level set function to be a signed distance function in order to avoid numerical problems.
- The spherical harmonics parametrization provides a sparse and multiscale surface description.
- The proposed regularizer helps to ensure a unique decomposition of spherical harmonics, if no training data is available. This makes it possible to compare the parameters of several segmentations, which is helpful for creating an atlas for instance.

Concisely put, the proposed method combines advantages from both implicit surface representations and parametric shape models.

1.1 Related Work

As illustrated in Tab. 1, our method is a missing link in the field of parametrized active contours, because it combines a parametric shape model (based on spherical harmonics) with an implicit surface representation. Related methods have either no parametric shape model, or no level set representation. Note that traditional level set methods are not discussed in this context as they do not feature a parametrization.

Methods Employing no Parametric Shape Model. All methods with a parametrized surface description based on splines or NURBS and an explicit contour representation are referred to as *deformable models* [2]. Besides these methods employing an explicit surface representation, there are several publications on parametrized implicit contours. In 2004 Huang et al. have published their MetaMorphs framework, where a grid of control points is attached to the level set function, which is then deformed via free-from deformations [9]. Level set functions parametrized by radial basis functions have been investigated by Morse et al. [10] and Slabaugh et al. [12] in 2005 and 2007, respectively. Also, in 2005 Ho et al. [11] have suggested to use an unstructured point cloud for discretizing the level set function.

Methods Employing a Statistical Shape Model. As explained above, methods employing a statistical shape model represent the shape using basis functions computed from training data. This makes them very flexible as far as the shape of the object is concerned, but it requires training data for every new application. In 1992 Cootes and Taylor have introduced the so-called *active shape models* or *smart snakes*, characterized by an explicit surface representation (see Cootes et al. [8] for a detailed description). Similar approaches using an implicit contour representation have been developed by Leventon et al. [13] and Tsai et al. [14] in 2000 and 2003, respectively.

Methods Employing a Parametric Shape Model. In 1996 Staib and Duncan have used Fourier surfaces to describe objects with open and closed surface as well as tori and tubes [3]. Also in 1996 Székely et al. have published their framework for segmenting objects with spherical topology [4]. Therefore they discretize the object by a mesh, which is then mapped onto the unit sphere and parametrized by spherical harmonics. Kelemen et al. have used a similar approach in [5] (1999). Recently, these methods have found their counterparts based on spherical wavelets, which have been published by Nain [6] and Yu [7] in 2007. It is important to notice, that all of these methods employ an explicit surface representation and require training data.

1.2 Outline

The remainder of this work is organized as follows. Section 2 describes how the implicit contour representation is combined with the parametric shape model. After that we explain how to use the derived level set framework with exemplary surface- and region-based data terms in section 3. Additionally, we derive a regularizer that helps to ensure a unique decomposition into spherical harmonics while providing the ability to incorporate prior information, if necessary. All necessary information for implementing our method is given in section 4. In section 5 we discuss all performed experiments. Finally, section 6 is dedicated to the conclusion.

2 Level Set Framework

Before explaining how a parametric shape model based on spherical harmonics can be combined with a level set representation, we recap the concept of spherical coordinates. The boundary of any (two- or three-dimensional) *stellar* or *star-shaped* object (see Fig. 2 for explanation) can be described by

$$r(\theta, \varphi) \cdot s(\theta, \varphi), \tag{1}$$

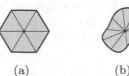

(a)   (b)   (c)   (d)   (e)

Fig. 2. Examples for Star-shaped Objects: *Star-shaped* or *stellar* objects consist of one connected component, with at least one point in the interior from which the whole boundary of the object can bee seen

where $r : [0, \pi] \times [0, 2\pi) \rightarrow [0, +\infty)$ is the radius (function) scaling the corresponding unit vector

$$s(\theta, \varphi) = (\sin(\theta)\cos(\varphi), \sin(\theta)\sin(\varphi), \cos(\theta))^T, \qquad (2)$$

as shown in Fig. 3(a). $\theta \in [0, \pi]$ is called *inclination angle* and $\varphi \in [0, 2\pi)$ is called *azimuth angle*. In the two-dimensional case θ equals $\pi/2$ and we simply write $r(\varphi) = r(\pi/2, \varphi)$.

2.1 Contour Representation

In the following we denote the image domain by $\Omega \subset \mathbb{R}^d$ ($d = 2, 3$) and the embedding function by $\phi : \Omega \rightarrow \mathbb{R}$. First, we consider the case of segmenting a ball $B_r(c)$ with constant radius r and center point $c \in \mathbb{R}^d$. In this case, ϕ can be written as

$$\phi(x) = |x - c| - r \qquad (3)$$

such that the zero level set of ϕ describes the surface of $B_r(c)$. By allowing r to be dependent on $\theta = \theta(x)$ and $\varphi = \varphi(x)$ we can now segment any star-shaped object:

$$\phi(x) = \begin{cases} |x - c| - r(\theta(x), \varphi(x)), & x \neq c, \\ \inf_{x \neq c} \phi(x), & x = c. \end{cases} \qquad (4)$$

In order to keep the notation simple, we will omit the argument x from θ and φ in the following. Before we continue with the parametric shape model, the following two points are important to notice:

- The radius r depends on the position of the center point c as illustrated in Fig. 3(b) and 3(c). Thus, if a unique representation is needed, e.g. in order to compare two segmentations, we need a regularizer that helps to ensure this unique representation. We will discuss this issue in detail in subsection 3.2.
- ϕ has a singularity at $x = 0$. This singularity, however, only affects the vicinity of a few pixels and is thus not an issue for real applications as depicted in Fig. 4. Moreover, traditional level set methods require the embedding function to be a signed distance function in order to avoid shocks causing

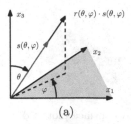
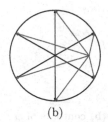
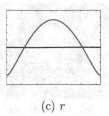

(a) (b) (c) r

Fig. 3. Spherical Coordinates and their Dependency on the Center Point: The radius $r(\theta, \phi)$ (a) depends on the position of the center point (b) as visualized in (c). Thus a regularizer is required, if a unique representation is needed (see Sec. 3.2).

numerical problems during the evolution [15]. Of course, ϕ in the form of (4) is not necessarily a signed distance function (see also Fig. 4), but since ϕ is parametrized via $r(\theta, \varphi)$, there is no need for maintaining this property.

2.2 Parametric Shape Model

The level set representation (4) can now be combined with any parametrization of $r(\theta, \varphi)$, such as double Fourier series, spherical harmonics, or spherical wavelets. However, in contrast to double Fourier series for instance, spherical harmonics have the advantage that no care has to be taken for ensuring correct boundary conditions at the poles. Thus we approximate r with a truncated spherical harmonics expansion [16]:

$$r(\theta, \varphi) \approx \sum_{l=0}^{N} \{r_l^0 \cdot P_l^0(\cos(\theta)) + \sum_{m=1}^{l} [a_l^m \cdot \cos(m\varphi) + b_l^m \cdot \sin(m\varphi)] \cdot P_l^m(\cos(\theta))\}, \quad (5)$$

where P_l^m denotes the associated Legendre Polynomial of degree l and order m. In the two-dimensional case (5) boils down to a Fourier expansion of the form

$$r(\theta, \varphi) \approx r_0^0 + \sum_{l=1}^{N} [a_l^l \cdot \cos(l\varphi) + b_l^l \cdot \sin(l\varphi)], \quad (6)$$

because for $\theta = \pi/2$ we have

$$P_l^m(\cos(\theta)) = P_l^m(0) = \begin{cases} 0, & m < l \\ 1, & m = l \end{cases}. \quad (7)$$

3 Variational Formulation

In this section we show how the level set framework introduced in the last section can be combined with variational level set formulations. Further, we explain how to regularize the level set evolution in order to obtain a unique decomposition into spherical harmonics.

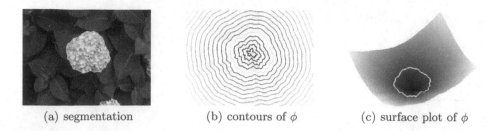

(a) segmentation   (b) contours of ϕ (c) surface plot of ϕ

Fig. 4. A First Example: Segmentation of a flower (a), taken from [17], and a contour plot (b) as well as a surface plot (c) of the embedding function

3.1   Data Terms

The derived level set framework can be combined with arbitrary data terms for variational level set methods. Since the discussion of all possible variational data terms is far beyond the scope of this work, we only consider widely used representatives of surface- and region-based energies.

For the remainder of this work $I : \mathbb{R}^d \to \mathbb{R}$ denotes the image or volume containing the object to be segmented. A well-known surface-based energy is the *geodesic active contour model*

$$\mathcal{G}(\phi) = \int_\Omega \delta(\phi)|\nabla\phi|g \, dx, \tag{8}$$

where g is an *edge-indicator function* such as

$$g(x) = (1 + |\nabla I(x)|^2)^{-1}, \tag{9}$$

which was used by Caselles et al. in [18]. Often, surface-based energies are combined with a region-based ones like the *weighted area term* [15]

$$\mathcal{A}(\phi) = \int_\Omega H(-\phi)g \, dx \tag{10}$$

for forcing the contour either to shrink, or to expand. Another well-known region-based energy is the one proposed by Chan and Vese in [19]

$$\mathcal{P}(\phi) = \int_\Omega H(-\phi)(I - \mu_i)^2 + H(\phi)(I - \mu_o)^2 \, dx, \tag{11}$$

where μ_i and μ_o denote the mean intensity values inside and outside the contour. We denote the linear combination of these three data terms by

$$\mathcal{D}(\phi) = \lambda_G \mathcal{G}(\phi) + \lambda_A \mathcal{A}(\phi) + \lambda_P \mathcal{P}(\phi), \tag{12}$$

where λ_G, λ_A, and λ_P control the influence of each term. While $\lambda_A > 0$ results in a shrinking contour, $\lambda_A < 0$ forces the contour to expand. All these parameters are easy to adjust as shown in Tab. 2.

3.2   Regularization

For many examples a minimization of $\mathcal{D}(\phi)$ using the parametrized embedding function ϕ would already provide us with meaningful segmentation results. However, if we want to use the found coefficients r_l^0, a_l^m, and b_l^m for generating an atlas or if we want to compare them with coefficients of another segmentation, we have to ensure their uniqueness as also illustrated in Fig. 3. Uniqueness of the parameters can be achieved by constraining the radius function. The reason is that any constraint on the radius function is also a constraint on the center and thus a unique decomposition is guaranteed.

At a first glance

$$\frac{1}{2}\left\|\nabla_{(\theta,\varphi)}r\right\|_{L_2}^2 \overset{!}{=} \min \tag{13}$$

might seem to be a reasonable constraint, because smoothness constraints are often used as regularizers. In our case (13) is not a good choice, because r_0^0 is not constrained as $\nabla_{(\theta,\varphi)}r$ does not depend on r_0^0. Instead, by penalizing the L^2-norm of the radius function

$$\frac{1}{2}\|r\|_{L^2}^2 = \frac{1}{2}\int_0^{2\pi}\int_0^{\pi}|r(\theta,\varphi)|^2 \, d\theta \, d\varphi \overset{!}{=} \min \tag{14}$$

we achieve a unique decomposition into spherical harmonics, because applying Parselval's theorem [16] to (14) yields

$$\frac{1}{2}\|r\|_{L^2}^2 = \frac{1}{2}\sum_{l=0}^{N}\{(r_l^0)^2 + \sum_{m=1}^{l}[(a_l^m)^2 + (b_l^m)^2]\} \overset{!}{=} \min. \tag{15}$$

Obviously all coefficients are constrained now. Moreover, (14) allows the following two interpretations.

Let $\bar{x} \in \Omega$ denote the center of mass of the object defined by r. Then

$$\bar{x} = \frac{1}{2\pi^2}\int_0^{2\pi}\int_0^{\pi}c + r(\theta,\varphi)\cdot s(\theta,\varphi) \, d\theta \, d\varphi \tag{16}$$

$$- c + \frac{1}{2\pi^2}\int_0^{2\pi}\int_0^{\pi}r(\theta,\varphi)\cdot s(\theta,\varphi) \, d\theta \, d\varphi \tag{17}$$

From (17) we deduce that

$$\|\bar{x} - c\|_2^2 \leq \frac{1}{2\pi^2}\|r\|_{L^2}^2, \tag{18}$$

which means that (14) has the nice side-effect, that it attracts c towards the center of mass. This can also help to prevent the level set evolution from getting stuck in local minima.

Rewriting (14) as

$$\frac{1}{2}\|r\|_{L^2}^2 = \frac{1}{2}\|r - 0\|_2^2 \tag{19}$$

yields the second interpretation. Obviously (14) forces r to be close to 0 and that is why severe over-regularization might result in a shrinking contour. However,

(a) initialization   (b) Sobolev flow   (c) proposed method

(d) initialization   (e) Sobolev flow   (f) proposed method

Fig. 5. Adding Regularity: If the object of interested is star-shaped, the additional regularity provided by the shape model helps to avoid undesired local minima. Note that the Sobolev flow minimizes the same energy. Both examples are taken from [17].

by replacing 0 with a known radius function $\hat{r}$ prior shape information can be incorporated. Of course, in this case θ and φ have to be replaced by $\theta + \theta_0$ and $\varphi + \varphi_0$, where θ_0 and φ_0 are additional phase angles, that allow us to optimize for rotations as well. An example for this situation is shown in Fig. 6.

3.3   The Complete Model

Combining the data term (12) and the regularizer (14), we obtain the following minimization problem characterizing the optimal configuration of the surface:

$$\min_{\phi, r} \mathcal{E}(\phi, r), \quad \text{where} \quad \mathcal{E}(\phi, r) = \mathcal{D}(\phi) + \frac{\lambda_R}{2} \|r\|_{L_2}^2 . \tag{20}$$

4   Numerical Solution

We minimize (20) using a gradient descent approach, whose details will be described in Sec. 4.1. In Sec. 4.2 we give some details on the implementation and in Sec. 4.3 we discuss the parameter settings and the initialization of the contour.

4.1   Gradient Descent

Let p denote one of the parameters r_l^0, a_l^m, b_l^m, or c_j ($c = (c_1, c_2, c_3)^T$) and ∂_p the partial derivative with respect to p. For every parameter p we perform a fixed number of steepest descent steps $i = 0, 1, 2, \ldots$:

$$p^{i+1} = p^i - \tau \cdot \partial_p \mathcal{E}(\phi, r). \tag{21}$$

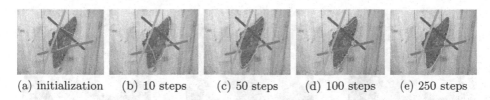

| (a) initialization | (b) 10 steps | (c) 50 steps | (d) 100 steps | (e) 250 steps |

Fig. 6. Incorporating Prior Knowledge: By incorporating prior information into the regularizer we can initialize the level set function arbitrarily and segment the destroyed object successfully

It is important to notice that we perform the steepest descent *simultaneously for all parameters* and that we use the *same* step size τ for all of them. The main reason for this fact is, that r_l^0, a_l^m and b_l^m contribute to the shape of the surface in equal shares. This is not the case when using complex-valued spherical harmonics, where the parameters are the amplitudes and phase shifts, which have not the same units. Further, also the mean values μ_i and μ_o in (11) are updated in every step (cf. [19]).

In order to optimize the phase parameters $p = \theta_0$ and $p = \varphi_0$ (cf. Fig. 6) we recommend to use a modified version of (21):

$$p^{i+1} = p^i - \tau \cdot \text{sign}(\partial_p \mathcal{E}(\phi, r)) \min(|\partial_p \mathcal{E}(\phi, r)|, C), \tag{22}$$

where C is a positive constant restricting the maximal angle change per step to $\tau \cdot C$. In the example of Fig. 6 we set $C = 0.5$ and $\tau = 0.02$.

4.2   Details on the Implementation

In all our experiments we normalized the image intensities to the range $[0, 1]$. Further, we replaced ∇I in (9) by $\nabla(G * I)/\sigma$, where G is a truncated Gaussian kernel with window size 3 and standard deviation 0.5. The only differential operator necessary for computing $\partial_p \mathcal{E}(\phi, r)$ is ∇, which can be approximated using central differences. For computing $\partial_p \mathcal{E}(\psi, r)$ we also require approximations of $H(\phi)$, $\delta(\phi)$, and $\delta'(\phi)$ and we employed their smeared-out versions as suggested by Osher and Fedkiw in [20].

4.3   Initialization and Parameter Choice

The easiest way of initializing the level set evolution consists of defining an initial ball. It is also possible to let the user specify an initial polyhedron which can be easily approximated by spherical harmonics as done in Fig. 6. As far as the choice of the parameters N, λ_G, λ_A, λ_P, λ_R, τ, and σ is concerned we can deduce from Tab. 2 that they do not vary significantly from one experiment to another. The step size τ has to be chosen approximately an order of magnitude smaller when performing segmentations in three dimensions, because the data term $\mathcal{D}(\phi)$ scales with the size of the zero level set.

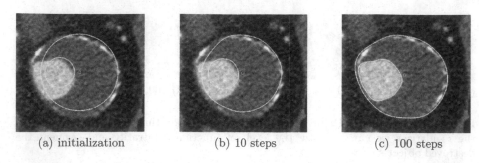

(a) initialization   (b) 10 steps   (c) 100 steps

Fig. 7. Simultaneous Segmentation: We segment the inner and outer wall of an abdominal aortic aneurysm using two level set functions evolved simultaneously by the coupled Chan-Vese model described in Sec. 5.3

5 Experiments

We performed several experiments to demonstrate the potential of our method. The used parameter values can be found in Tab. 2.

5.1 Two Dimensional Experiments

We compared our results with a topological flexible level set method and we used a *Sobolev gradient flow* [21]

$$\phi(x, t + \tau) = \phi(x, t) - \tau \cdot (I - \Delta)^{-1} \nabla \mathcal{D}(\phi), \tag{23}$$

where $\nabla \mathcal{D}(\phi)$ is defined as

$$\frac{d}{dh} \mathcal{D}(\phi + h \cdot \psi) \Big|_{h=0} = \int_{\Omega} \nabla \mathcal{D}(\phi) \psi \, dx. \tag{24}$$

The experiments in Fig. 1 as well as Fig. 5 clearly show that, if the object to be segmented is star-shaped, the parametric shape model and the proposed regularizer add meaningful information to the problem. It is important to notice that *both* methods - the Sobolev flow and our method - minimize the *same* data term.

5.2 Three Dimensional Experiments

The applicability of our method to three dimensional medical applications is presented in Fig. 8. We segmented five abdominal aortic aneurysms (AAAs) from computed tomography angiography (CTA) data. An AAA is a pathological dilation of the lumen in the abdominal part of the aorta, which may rupture, if left untreated. Among others, the maximum diameter is used as an indicator for estimating the rupture risk. Since a segmentation of these AAAs is not only beneficial for diagnosis, but also for treatment planning, this application is of great

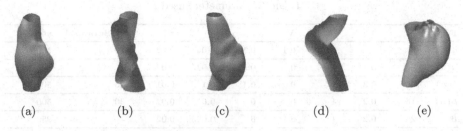

| (a) | (b) | (c) | (d) | (e) |

Fig. 8. 3D Experiments: The segmentation of abdominal aortic aneurysms with our method shows that our method is able to capture the large anatomical variability

relevance. Thanks to the proposed regularizer, the parameter values r_l^0, a_l^m and b_l^m contain meaningful shape information, which could be used for automated diagnosis. As visible in Fig. 8 our method performs well in capturing the large variability of these AAAs.

5.3 Possible Extensions

Fig. 6 shows the incorporation of prior information into the level set evolution by replacing (14) with

$$\frac{1}{2} \|r - \hat{r}\|_{L_2}^2 \overset{!}{=} \min, \tag{25}$$

where $\hat{r}$ is obtained from a segmentation of an unspoilt image. This example shows that our method is not only modular and flexible as far as the choice of data terms is concerned, but also with respect to the employed regularizer. As a suggestion for future research, one could also think of including statistical information about $\hat{r}$.

Another possible extension is shown in Fig. 7, where we minimized the following coupled Chan-Vese model in order to segment the inner and the outer wall of an abdominal aorta acquired by computed tomography angiography:

$$\mathcal{D}(\phi_i) = \int_\Omega H(-\phi_i)[(I - \mu_i)^2 + \lambda H(\phi_o)] + H(\phi_i)H(-\phi_o)(I - \mu_m)^2 \, dx, \tag{26}$$

$$\mathcal{D}(\phi_o) = \int_\Omega H(-\phi_o)H(\phi_i)(I - \mu_m)^2 + H(\phi_o)[(I - \mu_o)^2 + \lambda H(-\phi_i)] \, dx, \tag{27}$$

where ϕ_i is the level set function corresponding to the inner contour and ϕ_o is the level set function corresponding to the outer contour. Consequently μ_i is the mean intensity value inside both contours, μ_m is the mean intensity between both contours, and μ_o is the mean intensity value outside both contours. Thus we are able to segment the lumen as well as the thrombus of an AAA *simultaneously*.

Table 2. Parameters used

Fig.	N	λ_G	λ_P	λ_A	λ_R	σ	τ	τ (Sobolev)	steps
1(a)	5	1	0	0.1	0.1	0.04	0.02	20	100
4(a)	25	0.1	1	0	0.02	0.045	0.02	-	100
5(a)	20	0.3	1	0	0.1	0.1	0.01	20	500
5(d)	15	0.2	1	0	0.1	0.6	0.02	30	500
6	25	0.2	1	0	6	0.023	0.02	-	250
7	8	0	1	0	0.02	-	0.01	-	100
8	12	0.25	1	-0.3	0.1	0.023	0.001	-	500

6   Conclusion

We have introduced a missing link in the field of parametric active contours which
combines advantages of both implicit active contours and parametric shape models. The great flexibility with respect to the choice of data terms and the ability
to work also in three dimensions make the proposed method valuable for many,
especially medical, applications. Another benefit of our method is the proposed
regularizer, which constraints the parameters in a meaningful way and allows to
incorporate prior information very easily. We hope that, due to the presented
extensions and the ability to combine the proposed method also with other shape
models, such as spherical wavelets for instance, our work could serve as a fruitful
basis for further research and applications.

Acknowledgments. The first author is funded by the International Graduate
School of Science and Engineering at Technische Universität München. Moreover,
the authors would like to thank Darko Zikic for many valuable comments.

References

1. Stegmann, M.B.: An annotated dataset of 14 cardiac MR images. Technical report,
   Informatics and Mathematical Modelling, Technical University of Denmark, DTU
   (2002)
2. Osher, S., Paragios, N.: Geometric Level Set Methods in Imaging,Vision,and
   Graphics. Springer, Heidelberg (2003)
3. Staib, L., Duncan, J.: Model-based deformable surface finding for medical images.
   Medical Imaging, IEEE Transactions on 15, 720–731 (1996)
4. Székely, G., Kelemen, A., Brechbühler, C., Gerig, G.: Segmentation of 2-d and 3-d
   objects from mri volume data using constrained elastic deformations of flexible
   fourier contour and surface models. Medical Image Analysis 1, 19–34 (1996)
5. Kelemen, A., Szekely, G., Gerig, G.: Elastic model-based segmentation of 3-d neuro-
   radiological data sets. Medical Imaging, IEEE Transactions on 18, 828–839 (1999)
6. Nain, D., Haker, S., Bobick, A., Tannenbaum, A.: Multiscale 3-d shape representation and segmentation using spherical wavelets. IEEE Transactions on Medical
   Imaging 26, 598–618 (2007)

7. Yu, P., Grant, P., Qi, Y., Han, X., Segonne, F., Pienaar, R., Busa, E., Pacheco, J., Makris, N., Buckner, R., Golland, P., Fischl, B.: Cortical surface shape analysis based on spherical wavelets. IEEE Transactions on Medical Imaging 26, 582–597 (2007)
8. Cootes, T., Taylor, C., Cooper, D., Graham, J.: Active shape models - their training and application. Computer Vision and Image Understanding 61, 38–59 (1995)
9. Huang, X., Metaxas, D., Chen, T.: Metamorphs: Deformable shape and texture models. In: Proceedings of the 2004 IEEE Computer Society Conference on Computer Vision and Pattern Recognition, CVPR 2004, vol. 1, pp. I–496 – I–503 (2004)
10. Morse, B., Liu, W., Yoo, T., Subramanian, K.: Active contours using a constraint-based implicit representation. In: IEEE Computer Society Conference on Computer Vision and Pattern Recognition, CVPR 2005., vol. 1, pp. 285–292 (2005)
11. Ho, H.P., Chen, Y., Liu, H., Shi, P.: Level set active contours on unstructured point cloud. In: IEEE Computer Society Conference on Computer Vision and Pattern Recognition, CVPR 2005., vol. 2, pp. 655–662 (2005)
12. Slabaugh, G., Dinh, Q., Unal, G.: A variational approach to the evolution of radial basis functions for image segmentation, pp. 1 –8 (2007)
13. Leventon, M., Grimson, W., Faugeras, O.: Statistical shape influence in geodesic active contours. In: Proceedings of IEEE Conference on Computer Vision and Pattern Recognition, vol. 1, pp. 316–323 (2000)
14. Tsai, A., Yezzi Jr., A., Wells, W., Tempany, C., Tucker, D., Fan, A., Grimson, W., Willsky, A.: A shape-based approach to the segmentation of medical imagery using level sets. IEEE Transactions on Medical Imaging 22, 137–154 (2003)
15. Li, C., Xu, C., Gui, C., Fox, M.: Level set evolution without re-initialization: a new variational formulation. In: IEEE Computer Society Conference on Computer Vision and Pattern Recognition, CVPR 2005, vol. 1, pp. 430–436 (2005)
16. Groemer, II.: Geometric Applications of Fourier Series and Spherical Harmonics. Cambridge University Press, Cambridge (1996)
17. Alpert, S., Galun, M., Basri, R., Brandt, A.: Image segmentation by probabilistic bottom-up aggregation and cue integration. In: IEEE Conference on Computer Vision and Pattern Recognition, CVPR 2007, pp. 1–8 (2007)
18. Caselles, V., Kimmel, R., Sapiro, G.: Geodesic active contours. Int. J. Comput. Vision 22, 61–79 (1997)
19. Chan, T., Vese, L.: Active contours without edges. IEEE Transactions on Image Processing 10, 266–277 (2001)
20. Osher, S., Fedkiw, R.: Level Set Methods and Dynamic Implicit Surfaces. Springer, Heidelberg (2003)
21. Sundaramoorthi, G., Yezzi, A.J., Mennucci, A.: Sobolev active contours. International Journal of Computer Vision 73, 345–366 (2007)

A Model of Volumetric Shape for the Analysis of Longitudinal Alzheimer's Disease Data[*]

Xinyang Liu[1], Xiuwen Liu[2], Yonggang Shi[3],
Paul Thompson[3], and Washington Mio[1]

[1] Department of Mathematics, Florida State University, Tallahasse, FL 32306
[2] Department of Computer Science, Florida State University, Tallahasse, FL 32306
[3] Laboratory of NeuroImaging, UCLA School of Medicine, Los Angeles, CA 90095

Abstract. We develop a multi-scale model of shape based on a volumetric representation of solids in 3D space. A signed energy function (SEF) derived from the model is designed to quantify the magnitude of regional shape changes that correlate well with local shrinkage and expansion. The methodology is applied to the analysis of longitudinal morphological data representing hippocampal volumes extracted from one-year repeat magnetic resonance scans of the brain of 381 subjects collected by the Alzheimer's Disease Neuroimaging Initiative. We first establish a strong correlation between the SEFs and hippocampal volume loss over a one-year period and then use SEFs to characterize specific regions where hippocampal atrophy over the one-year period differ significantly among groups of normal controls and subjects with mild cognitive impairment and Alzheimer's disease.

Keywords: Shape space, volumetric shape, hippocampal atrophy, Alzheimer's disease, ADNI.

1 Introduction

We construct shape spaces and metrics that provide a framework for the analysis of volumetric morphological data. We use the model to quantify and compare regional and global shape changes in the hippocampus (HC) due to normal aging, tissue loss by conversion to Alzheimer's disease (AD) and progression of the disorder over a one-year period.

AD is the most common form of dementia and afflicted more than 26 million elderly individuals worldwide in 2006; it is projected that, globally, an average of 1 in 85 people will suffer from the disorder by 2050. AD is a neurodegenerative disease and patients experience severe memory loss and progressive decline of various cognitive functions. Studies that track the propagation of neurodegeneration in AD (cf. [1,2]) indicate that the medial temporal lobe structures, including the hippocampus, are among the first to degenerate. As such, the hippocampus

---

[*] This research was supported in part by NSF grants DMS-0713012 and CCF-0514743, and NIH Roadmap for Medical Research grant U54 RR021813.

K. Daniilidis, P. Maragos, N. Paragios (Eds.): ECCV 2010, Part III, LNCS 6313, pp. 594–606, 2010.

has been the focus of many studies of AD, which demonstrate considerable volume loss in the left and right hippocampi as the disease progresses (cf. [3,4] and references therein). Changes in hippocampal shape in AD have also been modeled with large deformation diffeomorphisms (cf. [5]). Although presently there is no cure, mapping the patterns of propagation of tissue loss and advances in early diagnosis will potentially enhance clinical trials that increase our understanding of the disorder and also help in the management of the disease, as symptomatic therapy is likely to be more effective before severe neurodegeneration occurs.

The Alzheimer's Disease Neuroimaging Initiative (ADNI) is a major multi-site study of AD to determine whether brain imaging can help to predict onset and monitor the progression of AD [6,7]. ADNI is a longitudinal MRI (magnetic resonance imaging) and FDG-PET (fluorodeoxyglucose positron emission tomography) study of 800 elderly subjects. One of the main goal of ADNI is data collection for subsequent analysis; existing studies of the hippocampus based on ADNI data include [4,8,9]. The morphological analysis of the hippocampus carried out in this paper employs a subset of the ADNI dataset comprising two scans of each of 381 subjects acquired one year apart. At each scan acquisition, an individual is classified as normal (NL), with mild cognitive impairment (MCI), or with AD. This classification naturally divides the subjects into four groups: NL-NL, MCI-MCI, MCI-AD and AD-AD. Table 1 shows the breakdown of the 381 individuals included in this study for a total of 762 scans. MCI may be viewed as a transitional stage to dementia, even though conversion may not necessarily occur. MCI patients are of particular interest because they exhibit an increased risk of conversion and the MCI-AD group represent the early stages of the disease.

Table 1. Subset of 381 ADNI subjects used in this study

Group	# of Subjects	Group	# of Subjects
NL-NL	118	MCI-MCI	153
MCI-AD	39	AD-AD	71

In this paper, we present a shape model equipped with a multi-scale Sobolev-type metric to quantify volumetric similarity and divergence of solids in 3D Euclidean space. We develop volumetric models of shape because they are potentially more sensitive to morphological changes caused by neurodegeneration than models just based on contour surfaces. The model may be viewed as a continuous extension of classical Procrustes analysis of shapes [10] to solids in 3D space. One major difference, however, is that the metric employed is base not only on the relative positions of points, but also on the first derivatives of parametrizations. First-order metrics are more sensitive to local non-linear deformations such as local contractions or expansions. To suppress the undesirable effect of very small variations or noise, the first-order term is smoothed out with the Riemannian heat operator (cf. [11]). This model provides a framework for the development of a tool, which we refer to as the signed energy function (SEF), to quantify localized shape contrasts in populations. We show that measures derived from SEF correlate well with volume loss in the hippocampus, an important indicator that SEF is sensitive to the morphology of neurodegeneration.

For each subject, the hippocampal volume was segmented from the whole-brain MRI scan using the techniques of [4]. First, triangular meshes were constructed to represent the contour surfaces of all hippocampi. Following a standard procedure, one of the NL meshes was fixed as a reference and all other surfaces were registered with it with the direct mapping method of [12]. Then, the registration of the surfaces was extended to hippocampal volumes using a thin-plate-spline interpolant [13]. For computations, the registered left hippocampal volumes were discretized as "cubical" meshes with 3,908 vertices and 10,533 edges, while the right hippocampus was represented with 3,796 vertices and 10,219 edges. For each subject, the SEF was calculated between the baseline and follow-up scans. For each group, we applied the SEFs to the localization of specific regions with statistically significant shape differences linked with local shrinkage. Moreover, we compared the left hippocampus of the AD-AD group with all other groups, as well as the right hippocampus of the MCI-AD group with the others, since these two groups showed more significant shape changes.

The paper is organized as follows. In Section 2 we present the continuous model of volumetric shape. The signed energy function is discussed in Section 3 and the discretization of the model is sketched in Section 4. Applications of the model to Alzheimer's disease are presented in Section 5.

2   A Multi-scale Model of Shape

2.1   Sobolev Metrics

Let V be a connected solid in 3D space with a smooth contour surface. V will be fixed throughout as a reference domain. A parametric shape will be represented by a mapping $\alpha\colon V \to \mathbb{R}^3$, with coordinates $\alpha(p) = [\alpha_1(p)\ \alpha_2(p)\ \alpha_3(p)]^T$. We impose Neumann boundary conditions $\nabla\alpha_i(p) \cdot \nu(p) = 0$, for every p on the boundary ∂V, where $\nu(p)$ is the outer unit normal at $p \in \partial V$. If we denote the differential of α at p by $d\alpha_p\colon \mathbb{R}^3 \to \mathbb{R}^3$, the usual first-order Sobolev metric on V may be expressed as

$$\langle \alpha, \beta \rangle = \int_V \alpha(p) \cdot \beta(p)\, dp + \int_V \langle d\alpha_p, d\beta_p \rangle\, dp, \tag{1}$$

where $\langle d\alpha_p, d\beta_p \rangle = \mathrm{tr}\,(d\alpha_p \circ d\beta_p^*)$ and $d\beta_p^*$ is the adjoint of $d\beta_p$. This coincides with the usual Euclidean inner product of matrices under the matrix representation of differentials relative to an orthonormal basis.

Since the first-order term can be very sensitive to small deformations and noise, we modify the metric by smoothing it out via the heat kernel. Smoothing of the first-order term also leads to more stable computations. Let $0 = \lambda_0 < \lambda_1 \leq \lambda_2 \leq \cdots \uparrow \infty$ be the eigenvalues of the Laplacian on V subject to Neumann boundary conditions. We denote an associated orthonormal set of eigenfunctions by ϕ_i, $i \geqslant 0$. The heat kernel on V may be expressed as

$$K(p, q, t) = \sum_{i=0}^{\infty} e^{-\lambda_i t} \phi_i(p) \phi_i(q) \,. \tag{2}$$

For each fixed $t > 0$, we obtain a smoothed out version of α via the kernel K given by $\alpha^t(p) = [\, \alpha_1(p; t) \; \alpha_2(p; t) \; \alpha_3(p; t) \,]^T$, where

$$\alpha_i(p; t) = \int_V K(p, q, t) \alpha_i(q) \, dq \,. \tag{3}$$

The Sobolev metric (1) is modified to

$$\langle \alpha, \beta \rangle_t = a \int_V \alpha(p) \cdot \beta(p) \, dp + b \int_V \langle d\alpha_p^t, d\beta_p^t \rangle \, dp \,. \tag{4}$$

We also introduce weights $a, b > 0$ to be able to adjust the contributions of the two terms, as desired, and normalize them to satisfy $a + b = 1$. Note that the smoothing operator is only applied to the derivative term. The associated norm is denoted $\| \cdot \|_t$.

2.2   The Shape Model

As in conventional Procrustes analysis, to obtain a representation of shape that is invariant under translations, we place the centroid of α at 0 by requiring that $\int_V \alpha_i(p) \, dp = 0$, for $1 \leqslant i \leqslant 3$. As in Kendall's formulation [10] and the surface model of [14], we could also normalize size with respect to the proposed metric. However, we shall skip this step since one of our main goals is to use the metric to detect change in shape and size caused by atrophy. Thus, the proposed model is sensitive to scale. We also need to enforce invariance under change of orientation via the action of the group $O(3)$ of 3×3 orthogonal matrices. If $U \in O(3)$, the action of U on α is given by $\alpha \mapsto U\alpha$. Clearly, this is an action by isometries, i.e., $\langle U \circ \alpha, U \circ \beta \rangle_t = \langle \alpha, \beta \rangle_t$. Moreover, if $U, W \in O(3)$,

$$\langle W \circ \alpha, U \circ \beta \rangle_t = \langle \alpha, W^T U \beta \rangle_t = \left\langle \alpha, \tilde{U} \beta \right\rangle_t, \tag{5}$$

where $\tilde{U} = W^T U$. Thus, to calculate the shape distance, one may fix α and only apply orthogonal transformations to β. If s_α, s_β are the shapes represented by α and β, the shape distance is defined as

$$d_t(s_\alpha, s_\beta) = \min_{U \in O(3)} \| \alpha - U \circ \beta \|_t = \| \alpha - \hat{U} \circ \beta \|_t \,, \tag{6}$$

where $\hat{U}$ is the orthogonal transformation that minimizes the distance. To find $\hat{U}$, we extend the classical Procrustes alignment of configurations of landmarks to the present setting. Let $\alpha = [\alpha_1, \alpha_2, \alpha_3]^T$ and $\beta = [\beta_1, \beta_2, \beta_3]^T$. Consider the 3×3 matrix A, whose (i, j)-entry is

$$a_{ij} = \langle \alpha_i, \beta_j \rangle_t = a \int_V \alpha_i(p)\beta_j(p)\, dp + b \int_V \nabla\alpha_i(p;t) \cdot \nabla\beta_j(p;t)\, dp. \qquad (7)$$

If $A = V_1 \Sigma V_2^T$ is an singular value decomposition of A, one can show that $\widehat{U} = V_1 V_2^T$ [15].

3   Signed Energy Function

In practical applications of the model, we are interested not only in the shape metric as a global quantifier of shape dissimilarity, but also in localization tools to detect specific regions where shape divergence is most significant. To design such a tool notice that, although the shape distance (6) has a global nature, the total deformation energy (the square of the shape distance) is an integral of pointwise energies. More precisely, letting $\hat{\beta} = \widehat{U} \circ \beta$, (4) and (6) imply that

$$d_t^2(s_\alpha, s_\beta) = \int_V \left(a\|\alpha(p) - \hat{\beta}(p)\|^2 + b\|d\alpha_p^t - d\hat{\beta}_p^t\|_p^2 \right) dp. \qquad (8)$$

Thus, we define the energy function $E_{\alpha,\beta}^t \colon V \to \mathbb{R}$ by

$$E_{\alpha,\beta}^t(p) = a\|\alpha(p) - \hat{\beta}(p)\|^2 + b\|d\alpha_p^t - d\hat{\beta}_p^t\|_p^2. \qquad (9)$$

The local energy $E_{\alpha,\beta}^t(p)$ quantifies how much the shapes of α and β differ near p from the standpoint of the metric d_t. Note, however, that the energy associated with local shape changes due to local shrinkage and expansion are both non-negative. This raises the question of whether it is possible to modify $E_{\alpha,\beta}^t$ to a signed measurement that can better differentiate these two types of deformation. This is of particular interest in applications to neurodegenerative diseases such as AD. Here, we propose a simple approach to this problem and show in Section 5 that the modified energy function correlates well with total hippocampal volume loss. Assume that α and β are centered and orthogonally aligned. We attribute a '+' sign to $E_{\alpha,\beta}^t(p)$ if $\|\alpha(p)\| \geqslant \|\hat{\beta}(p)\|$ and a negative sign, otherwise. In other words, the sign is positive if the Euclidean distance to the centroid decreases as we change α to β and negative if it increases. Thus, a positive or negative signed energy function (SEF) should indicate local shrinkage or expansion, respectively.

4   The Discrete Model

We briefly sketch the discretization of the model of Section 2. We discretize the reference volume V in 3D space as a regular cubical mesh K with edge length ℓ. Let $\mathcal{V} = \{v_1, v_2, \cdots, v_n\}$ and $\mathcal{E} = \{e_1, e_2, \cdots, e_m\}$ be the vertex and edge sets of K, respectively. We fix an arbitrary orientation for each edge $e_i \in \mathcal{E}$. A discrete parametric shape α is represented by a piecewise linear map $K \to \mathbb{R}^3$, so that α

is completely determined by its values on the vertices of K. Therefore, α can be viewed as a $3 \times n$ matrix, where the jth column represents $\alpha(v_j) \in \mathbb{R}^3$.

We use the discrete exterior derivative to represent the differential of α, which is defined on $\mathcal{E}$. For the oriented edge $e_j \in \mathcal{E}$, we let $d\alpha(e_j) = \left[\alpha(e_j^+) - \alpha(e_j^-)\right]/\ell$, where e_j^+ and e_j^- are the terminal and initial vertices of e_j, respectively. Thus, the derivative can be viewed as a $3 \times m$ matrix, whose jth column represents $d\alpha(e_j) \in \mathbb{R}^3$. To discretize the inner product (4), we first discuss the discrete volume elements. For the first term, it is simply the volume ℓ^3 of the voxels of K. For the second, we use the volume "around" each edge e_j, which is calculated as follows. Each cube σ incident with e_j contributes $\ell^3/12$ to this volume. Thus, for an interior edge, the volume around e_j is $\ell^3/3$.

We use a standard finite-difference discretization of the Laplacian and the eigenvalues and eigenvectors are calculated using the Lanczos subspace method. In computations, we truncate the discrete version of (2) after the first $r + 1$ eigenvalues based on experimental experience. Therefore, for a vertex v, the expression (3) becomes

$$\alpha_i(v;t) = \ell^3 \sum_{k=0}^{r} \sum_{j=1}^{n} e^{-\lambda_k t} \phi_k(v) \phi_k(v_j) \alpha_i(v_j), \tag{10}$$

The Sobolev inner product (4) can now be discretized as

$$\langle \alpha, \beta \rangle_t = a\ell^3 \sum_{i=1}^{n} \alpha(v_i) \cdot \beta(v_i) + \frac{b\ell^3}{3} \sum_{j=1}^{m} d\alpha^t(e_j) \cdot d\beta^t(e_j). \tag{11}$$

Finally, the value of the energy function in (9) at a vertex v is

$$E_{\alpha,\beta}^t(v) = a\|\alpha(v) - \hat{\beta}(v)\|^2 + \frac{b}{6} \sum_{j} \|d\alpha^t(e_j) - d\hat{\beta}^t(e_j)\|^2, \tag{12}$$

where j varies over the indexes of the edges incident with v.

5   Experimental Results

As mentioned in the Introduction, after segmentation of the hippocampal volumes and registration of their contour surfaces, we extended the point correspondences to their entire volumes through a thin-plate-spline interpolant [13]. Using a subset of the baseline scans of normal controls, we construct a hippocampal atlas V as a sample mean shape. We adopted the Fréchet mean shape with respect to the shape metric proposed, that is, the minimizer of the sum of the square shape distances (cf. [8,14]). A regular cubical mesh K was then generated to represent the hippocampal atlas. The atlas reflects the anatomical characteristics shared by the members of a population and provides a common domain for comparison and analysis of different individuals and groups. To obtain compatible meshes, we transferred the cubical mesh K of the atlas via the volume registration to all the other hippocampi. This gives a parametric representation of all shapes over K. We then calculated the shape distance between the baseline and 12-month hippocampal volumes of each subject and their associated SEF. The parameters were set to $a = 0.9$, $b = 0.1$, $t = 0.01$ and $r = 49$. These values were chosen experimentally.

As explained in Section 3, we expect the signed energy functions to reflect shape changes associated with local shrinkage and expansion effectively. Therefore, to make a more convincing case, we first show that our measure of volume loss is consistent with results obtained in other studies and verify that SEFs correlate well with volume loss during the one year period. We then proceed to a finer analysis to detect specific regions where the shape changes in the NL-NL, MCI-MCI, MCI-AD and AD-AD groups differ significantly.

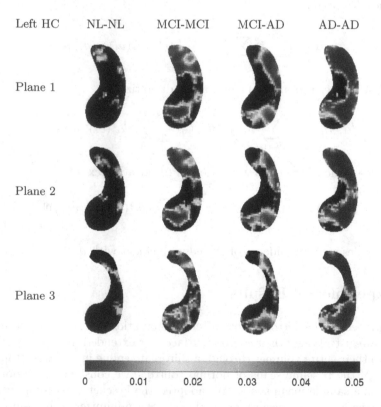

Fig. 1. Volumetric p-value maps of the comparison of the mean SEF with 0 for the left hippocampus

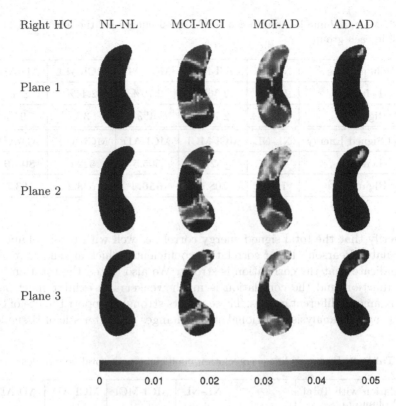

Fig. 2. Volumetric p-value maps of the comparison of the mean SEF with 0 for the right hippocampus

5.1   Correlation with Volume Loss

To simplify the computations, we focus on total volume loss and the sum of the values of each SEF over all vertices of the mesh, which we refer to as the total signed energy. The mean volume loss for the left and right hippocampi in each group is given in Table 2, where MCI-ALL is the combination of both MCI-MCI and MCI-AD. These numbers agree well with the meta-analysis of [3], which includes nine studies from seven centers, with 595 AD and 212 controls. Their study found the annualized hippocampal atrophy rates to be $4.66\%(95\%\,CI\,3.92, 5.40)$ for AD and $1.41\%(0.52, 2.30)$ for controls. Another study [4] also based on the ADNI data showed a similar numerical range, with $5.59\%(95\%\,CI : +/-1.44\%)$ for AD, $3.12\%(+/-0.79\%)$ for MCI and $0.66\%(+/-0.96\%)$ for controls. Two numbers in our calculations that are particularly interesting are the volume loss for the left hippocampus in the AD-AD group and the right hippocampus in the MCI-AD group, which are significantly larger than in the other groups. Table 2 also shows the mean total signed energy of each group. Again, the numbers for the left hippocampus in the AD-AD group and the right hippocampus in the MCI-AD group are relatively high.

Table 2. Mean volume loss and mean total signed energy for the left and right hippocampi in each group

Volume Loss	NL-NL	MCI-MCI	MCI-AD	MCI-ALL	AD-AD
Left HC	1.55%	2.36%	2.79%	2.44%	**5%**
Right HC	0.37%	2.76%	**4%**	3%	3.94%
Total Signed Energy	NL-NL	MCI-MCI	MCI-AD	MCI-ALL	AD-AD
Left HC	333	527	505.5	522.6	**805.9**
Right HC	116.7	508.1	**656.4**	538.2	563.7

To verify that the total signed energy correlates well with total volume loss, we calculated Pearson's linear correlation coefficients, which are shown in Table 3 and indicate that the correlation is strong. We also tested the total unsigned energy function and the correlation is much weaker and exhibit much larger variation among different groups. These results strongly support the use of SEFs for the proposed analysis of regional shape changes characteristic of tissue loss.

Table 3. Pearson's linear correlation coefficient with total volume loss

Correlation with Total Volume Loss		NL-NL	MCI-MCI	MCI-AD	AD-AD
Total Signed Energy	Left HC	0.665	0.741	0.713	0.774
	Right HC	0.742	0.78	0.794	0.793
Total Energy	Left HC	0.016	0.238	0.454	0.554
	Right HC	0.177	0.323	0.564	0.229

5.2   Group Comparison

We are primarily interested in identifying regions that exhibit morphological changes that are characteristic of local shrinkage related to tissue loss due to hippocampal degeneration over a one-year time. According to our sign convention, these regions correspond to positive values of the signed energy functions. Thus, for each of the four groups, we perform a 1-tailed t-test at each vertex to determine whether the mean SEF at that vertex is significantly larger than 0. The corresponding p-value maps for the left and right hippocampi are plotted over the hippocampal atlases and shown in Figs. 1 and 2, respectively. For visualization of these volumetric statistical maps, we sectioned the volumes along 3 planes.

As expected, the AD-AD group in Fig. 1 and MCI-AD group in Fig. 2 show larger "red" areas than the other groups. Somewhat surprising is that there is nothing significant detected for the AD-AD group in Fig. 2. This is very likely due to the high variance for this group. The average value of the variance of SEFs over all vertices is shown in Table 4. We also performed a similar experiment to analyze negative values of the signed energy functions, but nothing noteworthy was detected at comparable significance levels.

Lastly, since the left hippocampus in the AD-AD group and the right hippocampus in the MCI-AD group exhibit the most significant morphological changes, we compare them with the other groups. This time, a 1-tailed t-test at each vertex is performed to examine whether the mean of the SEFs of the

Table 4. Mean of the variance of SEFs over the vertices for the left and right hippocampi

Variance	NL-NL	MCI-MCI	MCI-AD	AD-AD
Left HC	0.39	0.59	0.42	0.72
Right HC	0.6	0.66	0.38	**1.11**

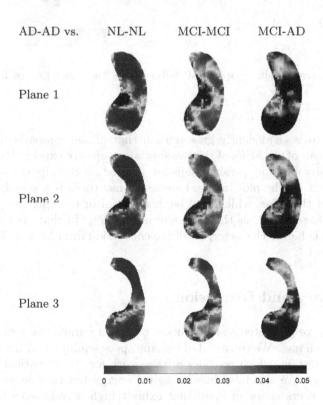

Fig. 3. Volumetric p-value maps of AD-AD versus other groups for the left hippocampus

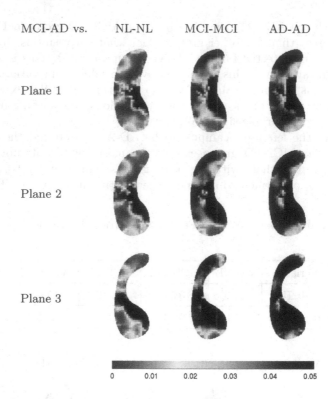

Fig. 4. Volumetric p-value maps of MCI-AD versus the other groups for the right hippocampus

reference group is significantly greater than that of the comparison group. Of course, the mean of the SEFs of the two special groups are expected to be larger. Again, the corresponding p-value maps are plotted on the hippocampal atlases in Figs. 5.2 and 4. The plot in Fig. 4 suggests that there is a specific region at the bottom of the atlas, which may be meaningful in tracking the progression of the early stage of AD, as the change of morphology in that area of the right hippocampus is highly characteristic of the conversion from MCI to AD over the one-year period.

6   Summary and Discussion

In this paper, we presented a shape model based on parametric representations of volumetric shapes. We constructed a shape space equipped with a multi-scale Sobolev-type metric, which provides a framework for the statistical analysis of shape evolution. We also introduced a signed energy function derived from the model that reflects shape changes that exhibit high correlation with regional shape shrinkage and expansion. We applied SEFs to the identification of specific regions of the hippocampus where shape changes related to atrophy differ significantly in normal aging, conversion to Alzheimer's disease and progression of the disorder. This analysis was based on 1-year repeat magnetic resonance scans of the brain of 381 subjects collected by the Alzheimer's Disease Neuroimaging Initiative. The subjects were diagnosed as normal or with mild cognitive impairment (MCI) or Alzheimer's disease (AD) at the time of scan acquisition. Among the results obtained, we identified a region on the right hippocampus in which, according to the model, shape changes differ significantly in the MCI-AD group as compared to groups of subjects whose diagnoses did not progress beyond MCI. We also constructed p-value maps from t-tests of pointwise SEFs to visualize patterns of atrophy that differentiate the normal and pathological groups. In this work, the signs of the energy functions were chosen using a simple criterion to detect localized shrinkage, but other alternatives such as the distance to a medial curve rather the centroid of the hippocampus will be explored in future work.

References

1. Apostolova, L.G., Lu, P.H., Rogers, S., Dutton, R.A., Hayashee, K.M., Toga, A.W., Cummings, J.L., Thompson, P.M.: 3D Mapping of Mini-mental State Examination Performance in Clinical and Preclinical Alzheimer Disease. Alzheimer Disease & Associated Disorders 20, 224–231 (2006)
2. Apostolova, L.G., Dinov, I.D., Dutton, R.A., Hayashee, K.M., Toga, A.W., Cummings, J.L., Thompson, P.M.: 3D Comparison of Hippocampal Atrophy in Amnestic Mild Cognitive Impairment and Alzheimer's Disease. Brain 129, 2867–2873 (2006)
3. Barnes, J., Bartlett, J.W., van de Pol, L.A., Loy, C.T., Scahill, R.I., Frost, C., Thompson, P.M., Fox, N.C.: A Meta-Analysis of Hippocampal Atrophy Rates in Alzheimer's Disease. Neurobiol. Aging 30, 1711–1723 (2009)
4. Morra, J., Tu, Z., Apostolova, L.G., et al.: and the ADNI: Automated Mapping of Hippocampal Atrophy in 1-Year Repeat MRI Data From 490 Subjects with Alzheimer's Disease, Mild Cognitive Impairment, and Elderly Controls. NeuroImage 45(1 Suppl.), 3–15 (2009)
5. Wang, L., Beg, F., Ratnanather, T., Ceritoglu, C., Younes, L., Morris, J.C., Csernansky, J.G., Miller, M.I.: Large Deformation Diffeomorphism and Momentum Based Hippocampal Shape Discrimination in Dementia of the Alzheimer Type. IEEE Trans. Med. Imaging 26(4), 462–470 (2007)
6. Mueller, S.G., Weiner, M.W., Thal, L.J., Petersen, P.C., Jack, C., Jagust, W., Trojanowski, J.Q., Toga, A., Beckett, L.: The Alzheimer's Disease Neuroimaging Initiative. Clin. North Am. 15, 869–877, xi–xii (2005)
7. Mueller, S.G., Weiner, M.W., Thal, L.J., Petersen, P.C., Jack, C., Jagust, W., Trojanowski, J.Q., Toga, A., Beckett, L.: Ways Toward an Early Diagnosis in Alzheimer's Disease: The Alzheimer's Disease Neuroimaging Initiative (ADNI). Alzheimer's Dement. 1, 55–66 (2005)
8. Liu, X., Shi, Y., Morra, J., Liu, X., Thompson, P.M., Mio, W.: Mapping Hippocampal Atrophy with a Multi-Scale Model of Shape. In: 6th IEEE International Symposium on Biomedical Imaging, pp. 879–882. IEEE Press, Boston (2009)

9. Liu, X., Shi, Y., Wang, Y., Thompson, P.M., Mio, W.: A Riemannian Model of Regional Degeneration of the Hippocampus in Alzheimer's Disease. In: 7th IEEE International Symposium on Biomedical Imaging, IEEE Press, Rotterdam (2010)
10. Kendall, D.G.: Shape Manifolds, Prosrustean Metrics and Complex Projective Spaces. Bulletin of London Mathematics Society 16, 81–121 (1984)
11. Rosenberg, S.: The Laplacian on a Riemannian Manifold. Cambridge University Press, New York (1997)
12. Shi, Y., Thompson, P.M., de Zubicaray, G.I., Rose, S.E., Tu, Z., Dinov, I., Toga, A.W.: Direct Mapping of Hippocampal Surfaces with Intrinsic Shape Context. NeuroImage 37(3), 792–807 (2007)
13. Wahba, G.: Spline Models for Obervational Data. SIAM, Philadelphia (1990)
14. Liu, X., Mio, W., Shi, Y., Dinov, I., Liu, X., Lepore, N., Lepore, F., Fortin, M., Voss, P., Lassonde, M., Thompson, P.M.: Models of Normal Variation and Local Contrasts in Hippocampal Anatomy. In: Metaxas, D., Axel, L., Fichtinger, G., Székely, G. (eds.) MICCAI 2008, Part II. LNCS, vol. 5242, pp. 407–415. Springer, Heidelberg (2008)
15. Liu, X.: Shape Spaces, Metrics and Their Applications to Brain Anatomy. Dissertation, Florida State University (2010)

Fast Optimization for Mixture Prior Models

Junzhou Huang, Shaoting Zhang, and Dimitris Metaxas

Division of Computer and Information Sciences, Rutgers University, USA
{jzhuang,shaoting,dnm}@cs.rutgers.edu

Abstract. We consider the minimization of a smooth convex function regularized by the mixture of prior models. This problem is generally difficult to solve even each simpler regularization problem is easy. In this paper, we present two algorithms to effectively solve it. First, the original problem is decomposed into multiple simpler subproblems. Then, these subproblems are efficiently solved by existing techniques in parallel. Finally, the result of the original problem is obtained from the weighted average of solutions of subproblems in an iterative framework. We successfully applied the proposed algorithms to compressed MR image reconstruction and low-rank tensor completion. Numerous experiments demonstrate the superior performance of the proposed algorithm in terms of both the accuracy and computational complexity.

Keywords: Compressive Sensing, MRI Reconstruction, Tensor Completion.

1 Introduction

The mixture of prior models have been used in many fields including sparse learning, computer vision and compressive sensing. For example, in compressive sensing, the linear combination of the total-variation (TV) norm and L1 norm is known as the most powerful regularizer for compressive MR imaging [1,2,3] and widely used in recovering the MR images.

In this paper, we propose two composite splitting algorithms to solve this problem:

$$min\{F(x) \equiv f(x) + \sum_{i=1}^{m} g_i(B_i x), x \in \mathbf{R^p}\} \tag{1}$$

where f is the loss function and $\{g_i\}_{i=1,...,m}$ are the prior models; f and $\{g_i\}_{i=1,...,m}$ are convex functions and $\{B_i\}_{i=1,...,m}$ are orthogonal matrices. If the functions f and $\{g_i\}_{i=1,...,m}$ are well-structured, there are two classes of splitting algorithms to solve this problem: operator splitting and variable splitting algorithms.

The operator-splitting algorithm is to search an x to make the sum of the corresponding maximal-monotone operators equal to zero. Forward-Backward schemes are widely used in operator-splitting algorithms [4,5,6]. These algorithms have been applied in sparse learning [7] and compressive MR imaging [2]. The Iterative Shrinkage-Thresholding Algorithm (ISTA) and Fast ISTA (FISTA) [8] are two important Forward-Backward methods. They have been successfully used in signal processing [8,9], matrix completion [10] and multi-task learning [11].

K. Daniilidis, P. Maragos, N. Paragios (Eds.): ECCV 2010, Part III, LNCS 6313, pp. 607–620, 2010.
© Springer-Verlag Berlin Heidelberg 2010

The variable splitting algorithm is another choice to solve problem (1) based on the combination of alternating direction methods (ADM) under an augmented Lagrangian framework. It was firstly used to solve the numerical PDE problem in [12,13]. Tseng and He et al. extended it to solve variational inequality problems [14,15]. There has been a lot of interests from the field of compressive sensing [16,17], where L1 regularization is a key problem and can be efficiently solved by this type of algorithms [18,19,20]. It also shows the effectiveness for the sparse covariance selection problem in [21]. The Multiple Splitting Algorithm (MSA) and Fast MSA (FaMSA) have been recently proposed to efficiently solve (1), while $\{g_i\}_{i=1,...,m}$ are assumed to be smooth convex functions [22].

However, all these algorithms can not efficiently solve (1) with provable convergence complexity. Moreover, none of them can provide the iteration complexity bounds for their problems, except ISTA/FISTA in [8] and MSA/FaMSA in [22]. Both ISTA and MSA are first order methods. Their complexity bounds are $O(1/\epsilon)$ for ϵ-optimal solutions. Their fast versions, FISTA and FaMSA, have complexity bounds $O(1/\sqrt{\epsilon})$ correspondingly, which are inspired by the seminal results of Nesterov and are optimal according to the conclusions of Nesterov [23,24]. However, Both ISTA and FISTA are designed for simpler regularization problems and can not be applied efficiently to the composite regularization problem in our formulation. While the MSA/FaMSA in [22] are designed to handle the case of $m \geq 1$ in (1), they assume that all $\{g_i\}_{i=1,...,m}$ are smooth convex functions, which make them unable to directly solve the problem (1). Before applying them, we have to smooth the nonsmooth function $\{g_i\}_{i=1,...,m}$ first. Since the smooth parameters are related to ϵ, the FaMSA with complexity bound $O(1/\sqrt{\epsilon})$ requires $O(1/\epsilon)$ iterations to compute an ϵ-optimal solution, which means that it is not optimal for this problem.

In this paper, we propose two splitting algorithms based on the combination of variable and operator splitting techniques. We dexterously decompose the hard composite regularization problem (1) into m simpler regularization subproblems by: 1) splitting the function $f(x)$ into m functions $f_i(x)$ (for example: $f_i(x) = f(x)/m$); 2) splitting variable x into m variables $\{x_i\}_{i=1,...,m}$; 3) performing operator splitting to minimize $h_i(x_i) = f_i(x_i) + g_i(B_ix_i)$ over $\{x_i\}_{i=1,...,m}$ independently and 4) obtaining the solution x by the linear combination of $\{x_i\}_{i=1,...,m}$. This includes both function splitting, variable splitting and operator splitting. We call them Composite Splitting Algorithms (CSA) and fast CSA (FCSA). Compared to ISTA and MSA, CSA is more general as it can efficiently solve composite regularization problems with m ($m \geq 1$) nonsmooth functions. More importantly, our algorithms can effectively decompose the original hard problem into multiple simpler subproblems and efficiently solve them in parallel. Thus, the required CPU time is not longer than the time required to solve the most difficult subproblem using current parallel-processor techniques.

The remainder of the paper is organized as follows. Section 2 briefly reviews the related algorithms. The composite splitting algorithm and its accelerated version are proposed to solve problem (1) in section 3. Numerical experiment results are presented in Section 4. Finally, we provide our conclusions in Section 5.

Algorithm 1. ISTA

 Input: $\rho = 1/L_f, x_0$
 repeat
   for $k = 1$ **to** K **do**
     $x^k = prox_\rho(g)(x^{k-1} - \rho \nabla f(x^{k-1}))$
   end for
 until Stop criterions

---

2 Algorithm Review

2.1 Notations

We provide a brief summary of the notations used throughout this paper.
   Matrix Norm and Trace:

1. Operator norm or 2-norm: $||X||$;
2. L_1 and Total Variation norm: $||X||_1$ and $||X||_{TV}$;
3. Matrix inner product: $\langle X, Y \rangle = trace(X^H Y)$.

   Gradient: $\nabla f(x)$ denotes the gradient of the function f at the point x.
   The proximal map: given a continuous convex function $g(x)$ and any scalar $\rho > 0$, the proximal map associated to function g is defined as follows [9,8]:

$$prox_\rho(g)(x) := \arg \min_u \{g(u) + \frac{1}{2\rho}||u - x||^2\} \qquad (2)$$

   ϵ-optimal Solution: Suppose x^* is an optimal solution to (1). $x \in \mathbf{R}^p$ is called an ϵ-optimal solution to (1) if $F(x) - F(x^*) \leq \epsilon$ holds.

2.2 ISTA and FISTA

The ISTA and FISTA consider the following optimization problem [8]:

$$min\{F(x) \equiv f(x) + g(x), x \in \mathbf{R}^p\} \qquad (3)$$

Here, they make the following assumptions:

1. $g : \mathbf{R}^p \to \mathbf{R}$ is a continuous convex function, which is possibly nonsmooth;
2. $f : \mathbf{R}^p \to \mathbf{R}$ is a smooth convex function of type $C^{1,1}$ and the continuously differential function with Lipschitz constant L_f: $||\nabla f(x_1) - \nabla f(x_2)|| \leq L_f ||x_1 - x_2||$ for every $x_1, x_2 \in \mathbf{R}^p$;
3. Problem (3) is solvable.

Algorithm 1 outlines the ISTA. Beck and Teboulle show that it terminates in $O(1/\epsilon)$ iterations with an ϵ-optimal solution in this case.

Theorem 1. *(Theorem 3.1 in [8]): Suppose $\{x_k\}$ is iteratively obtained by the algorithm of the ISTA, then, we have*

$$F(x^k) - F(x^*) \leq \frac{L_f ||x^0 - x^*||^2}{2k}, \forall x^* \in X_*$$

Algorithm 2. FISTA

Input: $\rho = 1/L_f, r^1 = x^0, t^1 = 1$
repeat
  for $k = 1$ **to** K **do**
    $x^k = prox_\rho(g)(r^k - \rho\nabla f(r^k))$
    $t^{k+1} = \frac{1+\sqrt{1+4(t^k)^2}}{2}$
    $r^{k+1} = x^k + \frac{t^k-1}{t^{k+1}}(x^k - x^{k-1})$
  end for
until Stop criterions

Algorithm 2 outlines the FISTA. Compared with ISTA, the increased computation burdens come from the second step and third step in each iteration, which is almost negligible in large scale applications. Because of these advantages, the key idea of the FISTA is recently widely used in large scale applications, such as compressive sensing [8], image denoising and deblurring [9], matrix completion [10] and multi-task learning [11]. It has been proven that (Theorem 4.1 in [8]), with this acceleration scheme, the algorithm can terminate in $O(1/\sqrt{\epsilon})$ iterations with an ϵ-optimal solution instead of $O(1/\epsilon)$ for those of ISTA.

Theorem 2. *(Theorem 4.1 in [8]): Suppose $\{x^k\}$ and $\{r^k\}$ are iteratively obtained by the FISTA, then, we have*

$$F(x^k) - F(x^*) \le \frac{2L_f\|x^0 - x^*\|^2}{(k+1)^2}, \forall x^* \in X_*$$

The efficiency of the FISTA highly depends on being able to quickly solve their first step $x^k = prox_\rho(g)(x_g)$, where $x_g = r^k - \rho\nabla f(r^k)$. For simpler regularization problems, it is possible, i.e, the FISTA can rapidly solve the $L1$ regularization problem with cost $\mathcal{O}(p\log(p))$ [8] (where n is the dimension of x), since the second step $x^k = prox_\rho(\beta\|\Phi x\|_1)(x_g)$ has a close form solution; It can also quickly solve the TV regularization problem, since the step $x^k = prox_\rho(\alpha\|x\|_{TV})(x_g)$ can be computed with cost $\mathcal{O}(p)$ [9]. However, the FISTA can not efficiently solve the composite regularization problem (1), since no efficient algorithm exists to solve the step

$$x^k = \arg\min_x \frac{1}{2}\|x - x_g\|^2 + \sum_{i=1}^m g_i(B_i x) \qquad (4)$$

To solve (1), the key problem is thus to develop an efficient algorithm to solve (4). In the following section, we will show that a scheme based on composite splitting techniques can be used to do this.

3   Composite Splitting Algorithms

3.1   Problem Definition

We consider the following minimization problem:

$$min\{F(x) \equiv f(x) + \sum_{i=1}^{m} g_i(B_i x), x \in \mathbf{R}^p\} \qquad (5)$$

where we make the following assumptions:

1. $g_i : \mathbf{R}^p \rightarrow \mathbf{R}$ is a continuous convex function for each $i \in \{1, \cdots, m\}$, which is possibly nonsmooth;
2. $f : \mathbf{R}^p \rightarrow \mathbf{R}$ is a smooth convex function of type $C^{1,1}$ and the continuously differential function with Lipschitz constant L_f: $\|\nabla f(x_1) - \nabla f(x_2)\| \le L_f \|x_1 - x_2\|$ for every $x_1, x_2 \in \mathbf{R}^p$;
3. $\{B_i \in \mathbf{R}^{p \times p}\}_{i=1,...,m}$ are orthogonal matrices;
4. Problem (5) is solvable.

If $m = 1$, this problem will degenerate to problem (3) and may be efficiently solved by FISTA. However, it may be very hard to solve by ISTA/FISTA if $m > 1$. For example, we can suppose $m = 2$, $g_1(x) = \|x\|_1$ and $g_2(x) = \|x\|_{TV}$. When $g(x) = g_1(x)$ in the problem (3), the first step in Algorithm 2 has a closed form solution; When $g(x) = g_2(x)$ in the problem (3), the first step in Algorithm 2 can also be solved iteratively in a few iterations [9]. However, if $g(x) = g_1(x) + g_2(x)$ in (3), the first step in Algorithm 2 is not easily solved, which makes the computational complexity of each iteration so high that it is not practical to solve using FISTA.

When all function $\{g_i\}_{i=1,...,m}$ are smooth convex functions, this problem can be efficiently solved by the MSA/FaMSA. However, in our case, the function $\{g_i\}_{i=1,...,m}$ can be nonsmooth. Therefore, the MSA/FaMSA can not be directly applied to solve this problem. Of course, we may smooth these nonsmooth function first and then apply the FaMSA to solve it. However, in this case, the FaMSA with complexity bound $O(1/\sqrt{\epsilon})$ requires $O(1/\epsilon)$ iterations to compute an ϵ-optimal solution. It is obviously not optimal for the first order methods [24].

In the following, we propose our algorithm that overcomes these difficulties. Our algorithm decomposes the original problem (1) into m simpler regularization subproblems, where each of them is more easily solved by the FISTA.

3.2   Building Blocks

From the above introduction, we know that, if we can develop a fast algorithm to solve problem (4), the original composite regularization can then be efficiently solved by the FISTA, which obtains an ϵ-optimal solution in $\mathcal{O}(1/\sqrt{\epsilon})$ iterations. Actually, problem (4) can be considered as a denoising problem. We use composite splitting techniques to solve this problem: 1) splitting variable x into multiple variables $\{x_i\}_{i=1,...,m}$; 2) performing operator splitting over each of $\{x_i\}_{i=1,...,m}$ independently and 3) obtaining the solution x by linear combination of $\{x_i\}_{i=1,...,m}$. We call it Composite Splitting Denoising (CSD) method, which is outlined in Algorithm 3. Its validity is guaranteed by the following theorem:

Theorem 3. *Suppose $\{x^j\}$ the sequence generated by the CSD. If x^* is the true solution of problem (4), x^j will strongly converges to x^*.*

Due to page limitations, the proof for this theorem is given in the supplemental material.

Algorithm 3. CSD

Input: $\rho = 1/L$, α, β, $\{z_i^0\}_{i=1,\ldots,m} = x_g$
for $j = 1$ to J **do**
  for $i = 1$ to m **do**
    $x_i = \arg\min_x \frac{1}{2m}\|x - z_i^{j-1}\|^2 + g_i(B_i x)$
  end for
  $x^j = \frac{1}{m}\sum_{i=1}^{m} x_i$
  for $i = 1$ to m **do**
    $z_i^j = z_i^{j-1} + x^j - x_i$
  end for
end for

3.3 Composite Splitting Algorithm (CSA)

Combining the CSD with ISTA, a new algorithm, CSA, is proposed for composite regularization problem (5). In practice, we found that a small iteration number J in the CSD is enough for the CSA to obtain good reconstruction results. Especially, it is set as 1 in our algorithm. Numerous experimental results in the next section will show that it is good enough for real composite regularization problem.

Algorithm 4 outlines the proposed CSA. In each iteration, Algorithm 4 decomposes the original problem into m subproblems and solve them independently. For many problems in practice, these m subproblems are expected to be far easier to solve than the original joint problem. Another advantage of this algorithm is that the decomposed subproblems can be solved in parallel. Given x^{k-1}, the m subproblems to compute $\{y_i^k\}_{i=1,\cdots,m}$ are solved simultaneously in Algorithm 4.

3.4 Fast Composite Splitting Algorithms

In this section, a fast version of CSA named as FCSA is proposed to solve problem (5), which is outlined in Algorithm 5. FCSA decomposes the difficult composite regularization problem into multiple simpler subproblems and solve them in parallel. Each subproblems can be solved by the FISTA, which requires only $O(1/\sqrt{\epsilon})$ iterations to obtain an ϵ-optimal solution.

In this algorithm, if we remove the acceleration step by setting $t^{k+1} \equiv 1$ in each iteration, we will obtain the CSA. A key feature of the FCSA is its fast convergence performance borrowed from the FISTA. From Theorem 2, we know that the FISTA can obtain an ϵ-optimal solution in $\mathcal{O}(1/\sqrt{\epsilon})$ iterations.

Another key feature of the FCSA is that the cost of each iteration is $\mathcal{O}(mp\log(p))$, as confirmed by the following observations. The step $y_i^k = prox_\rho(g_i)(B_i(r^k - \frac{1}{L}\nabla f_i(r^k)))$ can be computed with the cost $\mathcal{O}(p\log(p))$ for a lot of prior models g_i. The step $x^k =$

Algorithm 4. CSA

Input: $\rho = 1/L$, x^0
repeat
    for $k = 1$ **to** K **do**
        for $i = 1$ **to** m **do**
            $y_i^k = prox_\rho(g_i)(B_i(x^{k-1} - \frac{1}{L}\nabla f_i(x^{k-1})))$
        end for
        $x^k = \frac{1}{m}\sum_{i=1}^m B_i^{-1} y_i^k$
    end for
until Stop criterions

Algorithm 5. FCSA

Input: $\rho = 1/L$, $t^1 = 1$ $x^0 = r^1$
repeat
    for $k = 1$ **to** K **do**
        for $i = 1$ **to** m **do**
            $y_i^k = prox_\rho(g_i)(B_i(r^k - \frac{1}{L}\nabla f_i(r^k)))$
        end for
        $x^k = \frac{1}{m}\sum_{i=1}^m B_i^{-1} y_i^k$
        $t^{k+1} = \frac{1+\sqrt{1+4(t^k)^2}}{2}$
        $r^{k+1} = x^k + \frac{t^k-1}{t^{k+1}}(x^k - x^{k-1})$
    end for
until Stop criterions

$\frac{1}{m}\sum_{i=1}^m B_i^{-1} y_i^k$ can also be computed with the cost of $\mathcal{O}(p\log(p))$. Other steps only involve adding vectors or scalars, thus cost only $\mathcal{O}(p)$ or $\mathcal{O}(1)$. Therefore, the total cost of each iteration in the FCSA is $\mathcal{O}(mp\log(p))$.

With these two key features, the FCSA efficiently solves the composite regularization problem (5) and obtains better results in terms of both the accuracy and computation complexity. The experimental results in the next section demonstrate its superior performance.

4 Experiments

4.1 Application on MR Image Reconstruction

Specifically, we apply the CSA and FCSA to solve the Magnetic Resonance (MR) image recovery problem in compressive sensing [1]:

$$\min_x F(x) \equiv \frac{1}{2}\|Ax - b\|^2 + \alpha\|\Phi^{-1}x\|_{TV} + \beta\|x\|_1 \tag{6}$$

where $A = R\Phi^{-1}$, R is a partial Fourier transform, Φ^{-1} is the wavelet transform, b is the under-sampled Fourier measurements, α and β are two positive parameters.

This model has been shown to be one of the most powerful models for the compressed MR image recovery [1]. However, since the $\|\Phi^{-1}x\|_{TV}$ and $\|x\|_1$ are both nonsmooth in x, this problem is much more difficult to solve than any of those with a single nonsmooth term such as the L1 regularization problem or a total variation regularization problem. In this case, the FISTA can efficiently solve the L1 regularization problem [8], since the first step $x^k = prox_\rho(\|x\|_1)(r^k - \rho \nabla f(r^k))$ has a close form solution in Algorithm 2. The FISTA can also efficiently solve the total variation regularization problem [9], since the first step $x^k = prox_\rho(\|\Phi^{-1}x\|_{TV})(r^k - \rho \nabla f(r^k))$ can be computed quickly in Algorithm 2. However, the FISTA can not efficiently solve the joint L1 and TV regularization problem (6), since $x^k = prox_\rho(\alpha\|\Phi^{-1}x\|_{TV} + \beta\|x\|_1)(r^k - \rho \nabla f(r^k))$ can not be computed in a short time.

The Conjugate Gradient (CG) [1] has been applied to the problem (6) and it converges very slowly. The computational complexity has been the bottleneck that made (6) impractical in the past [1]. To use this model for practical MR image reconstruction, Ma et al. proposed a fast algorithm based on the operator splitting technique [2], which is called TVCMRI. In [3], a variable splitting method (RecPF) was proposed to solve the MR image reconstruction problem. Both of them can replace iterative linear solvers with Fourier domain computations, which can gain substantial time savings. To our knowledge, they are two of the fastest algorithms to solve problem (6) so far. Different from their algorithms, the CSA and FCSA directly attack the joint L1 and total variation norm regularization problem by transferring it to the L1 regularization and TV norm regularization subproblems, which can be efficiently solved. In the following, we compare our CSA and FCSA with their algorithms. The results show that the FCSA is far more efficient than the TVCMRI and RecPF.

Experiment Setup. Suppose a MR image x has n pixels, the partial Fourier transform R in problem (6) consists of m rows of a $n \times n$ matrix corresponding to the full 2D discrete Fourier transform. The m selected rows correspond to the acquired b. The sampling ratio is defined as m/n. The scanning duration is shorter if the sampling ratio is smaller. In MR imaging, we have certain freedom to select rows, which correspond to certain frequencies. In the k-space, we randomly obtain more samples in low frequencies and less samples in higher frequencies. This sample scheme has been widely used for compressed MR image reconstruction [1,2,3]. Practically, the sampling scheme and speed in MR imaging also depend on the physical and physiological limitations [1].

All experiments are conducted on a 2.4GHz PC in Matlab environment. We compare the CSA and FCSA with two of the fastest MR image reconstruction methods, TVCMRI [2] and RecPF [3]. For fair comparisons, we download the codes from their websites and carefully follow their experiment setup. For example, the observation measurement b is synthesized as $b = Rx + \mathbf{n}$, where $\mathbf{n}$ is the Gaussian white noise with standard deviation $\sigma = 0.01$. The regularization parameter α and β are set as 0.001 and 0.035. R and b are given as inputs, and x is the unknown target. For quantitative evaluation, we compute the Signal-to-Noise Ratio (SNR) for each reconstruction result.

Numerical Results. We perform experiments on a full body MR image with size of 924×208. Each algorithm runs 50 iterations. The sample ratio is set to be approximately

25%. To reduce the randomness, we run each experiments 100 times for each parameter setting of each method. Due to page limitations, we include the experimental results and comparisons in the supplemental materials. The examples of the original and recovered images by different algorithms are shown in Figure 1. From there, we can observe that the results obtained by the FCSA are not only visibly better, but also superior in terms of both the SNR and CPU time.

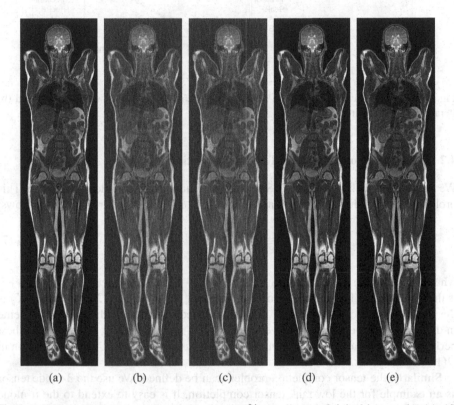

(a)   (b)   (c)   (d)   (e)

Fig. 1. Full Body MR image reconstruction from 25% sampling (a) Original image; (b), (c), (d) and (e) are the reconstructed images by the TVCMRI [2], RecPF [3], CSA and FCSA. Their SNR are 12.56, 13.06, 18.21 and 19.45 (db). Their CPU time are 12.57, 11.14, 10.20 and 10.64 (s).

To further evaluate the reconstruction performance, we use sampling ratio 25% to obtain the measurement b. Different methods are then used to perform reconstruction. To reduce the randomness, we run each experiments 100 times for each parameter setting of each method. The SNR and CPU time are traced in each iteration for each methods. Figure 2 gives the performance comparisons between different methods in terms of the CPU time and SNR. The reconstruction results produced by the FCSA are far better than those produced by the CG, TVCMRI and RecPF. The reconstruction performance of the FCSA is always the best in terms of both the reconstruction accuracy and the computational complexity, which further demonstrate the effectiveness and efficiency of the FCSA for the compressed MR image construction.

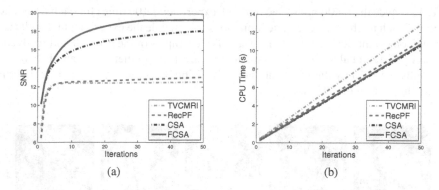

(a)   (b)

Fig. 2. Performance comparisons with sampling ratio 25%: a) Iterations vs. SNR (db) and (b) Iterations vs. CPU Time (s)

4.2   Application on Low-Rank Tensor Completion

We also apply the the proposed FCSA to the low rank tensor completion problem. This problem has gained a lot of attentions recently [25,26,10,27]. It is formulated as follows:

$$\min_{X} F(X) \equiv \frac{1}{2}\|\mathcal{A}(X) - b\|^2 + \alpha\|X\|_* \tag{7}$$

where $X \in \mathbb{R}^{p \times q}$ is a unknown matrix, $\mathcal{A} : \mathbb{R}^{p \times q} \to \mathbb{R}^n$ is the linear map, and $b \in \mathbb{R}^n$ is the observation. The nuclear norm is defined as $\|X\|_* = \sum_i \sigma_i(X)$, where $\sigma_i(X)$ is the singular value of the matrix X. The accelerated proximal gradient (APG) scheme in the FISTA has been used to solve (7) in [10]. In most cases, the APG gains the best performance compared with other methods, since it can obtain an ϵ-optimal solution in $O(1/\sqrt{\epsilon})$ iterations.

Similarly, the tensor completion problem can be defined. We use the 3-mode tensor as an example for the low rank tensor completion. It is easy to extend to the n-mode tensor completion. The 3-mode tensor completion can be formulated as follows [28]:

$$\min_{\mathcal{X}} F(\mathcal{X}) \equiv \frac{1}{2}\|\mathcal{A}(\mathcal{X}) - b\|^2 + \sum_{i=1}^{m} \alpha_i\|B_i\mathcal{X}\|_* \tag{8}$$

where $\mathcal{X} \in \mathbb{R}^{p \times q \times m}$ is the unknown 3-mode tensor, $\mathcal{A} : \mathbb{R}^{p \times q \times m} \to \mathbb{R}^n$ is the linear map, and $b \in \mathbb{R}^n$ is the observation. B_1 is the "unfold" operation along the 1-mode on a tensor $\mathcal{X}$, which is defined as $B_1\mathcal{X} := X_{(1)} \in \mathbb{R}^{p \times qm}$; B_2 is the "unfold" operation along the 2-mode on a tensor $\mathcal{X}$, which is defined as $B_2\mathcal{X} := X_{(2)} \in \mathbb{R}^{q \times pm}$; B_3 is the "unfold" operation along the 3-mode on a tensor $\mathcal{X}$, which is defined as $B_3\mathcal{X} := X_{(3)} \in \mathbb{R}^{m \times pq}$. The opposite operation "fold" is defined as $B_i^T X_i = \mathcal{X}$ where $i = 1, 2, 3$.

Generally, it is far harder to solve the tensor completion problem than the matrix completion because of the composite regularization. The solvers in [10] can not be used to efficiently solve (8). In [28], a relaxation technique is used to separate the dependant

Table 1. Comparisons of the CPU Time and RSE

	CGD-LRTC [28]		APG-LRMC [10]		FCSA-LRTC	
	Time (s)	RSE	Time (s)	RSE	Time (s)	RSE
Window	133.21	0.3843	100.98	0.0962	133.56	0.0563
Cherry	134.39	0.5583	102.43	0.3201	134.65	0.1069
Sheep	134.96	0.5190	101.33	0.1784	131.23	0.1017
Fish	136.29	0.5886	99.89	0.2234	135.31	0.1056

relationships and the block coordinate descent (BCD) method is used to solve the low rank tensor completion problem. As far as we know, it is the best method for the low rank tensor completion so far. However, it converges very slow due to the convergence properties of the BCD. Fortunately, the proposed FCSA can be directly used to efficiently solve 8. Different from the BCD method for LRTC using relaxation techniques [28], the FCSA can directly attack the composite matrix nuclear norm regularization problem by transforming it to multiple matrix nuclear norm regularization subproblems, which can be efficiently solved in parallel. In the following, we compare the proposed FCSA and BCD for the low rank tensor completion. We called them FCSA-LRTC and CBD-LRTC respectively. The results show that the FCSA is far more efficient than the BCD for the LRTC problem.

Experiment Setup. Suppose a color image $\mathcal{X}$ with low rank has the size of $h \times w \times d$, where h, w, d denote its height, width and color channel respectively. When the color values of some pixels are missing in the image, the tensor completion is conducted to recover the missed values. Suppose q pixels miss the color values in the image, the sampling ratio is defined as $(h \times w \times d - q \times d)/(h \times w \times d)$. The known color values in the image are called the samples for tensor completion. We randomly obtain these samples or designate the samples before the tensor completion [28].

All experiments are conducted on a 2.4GHz PC in Matlab environment. We compare the proposed FCSA-LRTC with the CGD-LRTC [28] for the tensor completion problem. To show the advantage of the LRTC over the low rank matrix completion (LRMC), we also compare the proposed FCSA-LRTC with the APG based LRMC method (APG-LRMC)[10]. As introduced in the above section, the APG-LRMC is not able to solve the tensor completion problem (8) directly. For comparisons, we approximately solve (8) by using the APG-LRMC to conduct the LRMC in d color channels independently. For quantitative evaluation, we compute the Relative Square Error (RSE) for each completion result. The RSE is defined as $\|\mathcal{X}_c - \mathcal{X}\|_F / \|\mathcal{X}\|_F$, where $\mathcal{X}_c$ and $\mathcal{X}$ are the completed image and ground-truth image respectively.

Numerical Results. We apply different methods on four 2D color images respectively. To perform fair comparisons, all methods run 50 iterations. Figure 3 shows the visual comparisons of the completion results. In this case, the visual effects obtained by the FCSA-LRTC are also far better than those of the CGD-LRTC [28] and slightly better than those obtained by the APG-LRMC [10]. Table 1 tabulates the RSE and CPU Time by different methods on different color images. The FCSA-LRTC always obtains the

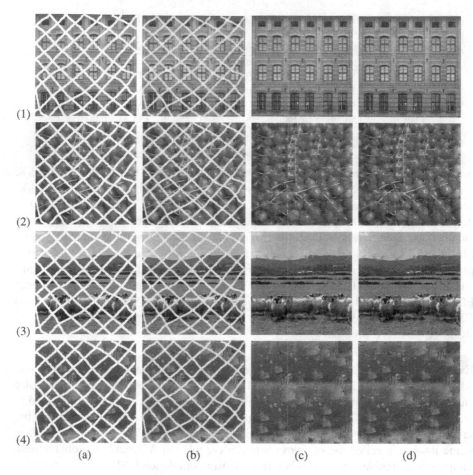

Fig. 3. Comparisons in terms of visual effects. Color images are: (1) Window; (2) Cherry; (3) Sheep and (4) Fish. The column (a), (b), (c) and (d) correspond to the images before completion, the obtained results by the CGD-LRTC [28], APG-LRMC [10] and FCSA-LRTC, respectively.

smallest RSE in all color images, which shows its good performance for the low rank tensor completion.

5 Conclusion

In this paper, we proposed composite splitting algorithms based on splitting techniques and optimal gradient techniques for the mixture prior model optimization. The proposed algorithms decompose a hard composite regularization problem into multiple simpler subproblems and efficiently solve them in parallel. This is very attractive for practical applications involving large-scale data optimization. The computation complexities of the proposed algorithms are very low in each iteration. The promising numerical results on applications of compressed MR image reconstruction and low-rank tensor completion validate the advantages of the proposed algorithms.

References

1. Lustig, M., Pauly, D.L., Donoho, J.M.: Sparse mri: The application of compressed sensing for rapid mr imaging. In: Magnetic Resonance in Medicine (2007)
2. Ma, S., Yin, W., Zhang, Y., Chakraborty, A.: An efficient algorithm for compressed mr imaging using total variation and wavelets. In: Proceedings of CVPR (2008)
3. Yang, J., Zhang, Y., Yin, W.: A fast alternating direction method for tvl1-l2 signal reconstruction from partial fourier data. IEEE Journal of Selected Topics in Signal Processing, Special Issue on Compressive Sensing 4 (2010)
4. Gabay, D.: Applications of the method of multipliers to variational inequalities. In: Augmented Lagrange Methods: Applications to the Solution of Boundary-valued Problems, pp. 299–331. North-Holland, Amsterdam (1983)
5. Combettes, P.L., Wajs, V.R.: Signal recovery by proximal forward-backward splitting. SIAM Journal on Multiscale Modeling and Simulation 19, 1107–1130 (2008)
6. Tseng, P.: A modified forward-backward splitting method for maximal monotone mappings. SIAM Journal on Control and Optimization 38, 431–446 (2000)
7. Hale, E.T., Yin, W., Zhang, Y.: Fixed-point continuation for.1-minimization: Methodology and convergence. SIAM Journal on Optimization 19, 1107–1130 (2008)
8. Beck, A., Teboulle, M.: A fast iterative shrinkage-thresholding algorithm for linear inverse problems. SIAM Journal on Imaging Sciences 2, 183–202 (2009)
9. Beck, A., Teboulle, M.: Fast gradient-based algorithms for constrained total variation image denoising and deblurring problems. IEEE Transaction on Image Processing 18, 2419–2434 (2009)
10. Toh, K., Yun, S.: An accelerated proximal gradient algorithm for nuclear norm regularized least squares problems. Pacific Journal of Optimization (2009)
11. Ji, S., Ye, J.: An accelerated gradient method for trace norm minimization. In: Proceedings of ICML (2009)
12. Gabay, D., Mercier, B.: A dual algorithm for the solution of nonlinear variational problems via finite-element approximations. Computers and Mathematics with Applications 2, 17–40 (1976)
13. Glowinski, R., Tallec, P.L.: Augmented lagrangian and operator-splitting methods in nonlinear mechanics. SIAM, Philadelphia (1989)
14. Tseng, P.: Applications of a splitting algorithm to decomposition in convex programming and variational inequalities. SIAM Journal on Control and Optimization 29, 119–138 (1991)
15. He, B.S., Liao, L.Z., Han, D., Yang, H.: A new inexact alternating direction method for monotone variational inequalities. Mathematical Programming 92, 103–118 (2002)
16. Candes, E.J., Romberg, J., Tao, T.: Robust uncertainty principles: Exact signal reconstruction from highly incomplete frequency information. IEEE Transactions on Information Theory 52, 489–509 (2006)
17. Donoho, D.: Compressed sensing. IEEE Trans. on Information Theory 52, 1289–1306 (2006)
18. Goldstein, T., Osher, S.: The split bregman algorithm for l1 regularized problems. Technical report, UCLA, CAM Report 08-29 (2008)
19. Afonso, M., Bioucas-Dias, J., Figueiredo, M.: Fast image recovery using variable splitting and constrained optimization. IEEE Transactions on Image Processing (2009) (submitted)
20. Yang, J., Zhang, Y.: Alternating direction algorithms for l1-problems in compressive sensing. Technical report, Rice University, TR 09-37 (2009)
21. Yuan, X.: Alternating direction methods for sparse covariance selection (2009) (preprint)
22. Goldfarb, D., Ma, S.: Fast multiple splitting algorithms for convex optimization. Technical report, Department of IEOR, Columbia University, New York (2009)

23. Nesterov, Y.E.: A method for solving the convex programming problem with convergence rate o($1/k^2$). Dokl. Akad. Nauk SSSR 269, 543–547 (1983)
24. Nesterov, Y.E.: Gradient methods for minimizing composite objective function. Technical report (2007), http://www.ecore.beDPs/dp1191313936.pdf
25. Ma, S., Goldfarb, D., Chen, L.: Fixed point and bregman iterative methods for matrix rank minimization. Mathematical Programming (2010)
26. Cai, J.F., Candes, E.J., Shen, Z.: A singular value thresholding algorithm for matrix completion. SIAM Journal on Optimization 20, 1956–1982 (2010)
27. Yang, J., Yuan, X.: An inexact alternating direction method for trace norm regularized least squares problem. In: Preprint (2010)
28. Liu, J., Musialski, P., Wonka, P., Ye, J.: Tensor completion for estimating missing values in visual data. In: Proceedings of ICCV (2009)

3D Point Correspondence by Minimum Description Length in Feature Space

Jiun-Hung Chen[1], Ke Colin Zheng[2], and Linda G. Shapiro[1]

[1] Computer Science and Engineering, University of Washington, Seattle, WA 98195
{jhchen,shapiro}@cs.washington.edu
[2] Microsoft Corporation
cozheng@microsoft.com

Abstract. Finding point correspondences plays an important role in automatically building statistical shape models from a training set of 3D surfaces. For the point correspondence problem, Davies *et al.* [1] proposed a minimum-description-length-based objective function to balance the training errors and generalization ability. A recent evaluation study [2] that compares several well-known 3D point correspondence methods for modeling purposes shows that the MDL-based approach [1] is the best method.

We adapt the MDL-based objective function for a feature space that can exploit nonlinear properties in point correspondences, and propose an efficient optimization method to minimize the objective function directly in the feature space, given that the inner product of any vector pair can be computed in the feature space. We further employ a Mercer kernel [3] to define the feature space implicitly. A key aspect of our proposed framework is the generalization of the MDL-based objective function to kernel principal component analysis (KPCA) [4] spaces and the design of a gradient-descent approach to minimize such an objective function. We compare the generalized MDL objective function on KPCA spaces with the original one and evaluate their abilities in terms of reconstruction errors and specificity. From our experimental results on different sets of 3D shapes of human body organs, the proposed method performs significantly better than the original method.

1 Introduction

Statistical shape models show considerable promise as a basis for understanding and interpreting images and have been widely used in model-based image segmentation and tracking [5]. To automatically build statistical shape models [5] from a training set of shapes, finding point correspondence across images becomes an essential task. In this paper, we focus on establishing dense 3D point correspondences between all 3D surfaces of a training set.

There are as many proposed methods and algorithms in automatically computing point correspondences as in statistical shape modeling itself. These approaches vary in terms of the shape representation and registration procedure [6]. Davies *et al.* [1] assumed the projected coefficients of principal component analysis (PCA) of the data have multivariate Gaussian distributions and derived an objective function for point

K. Daniilidis, P. Maragos, N. Paragios (Eds.): ECCV 2010, Part III, LNCS 6313, pp. 621–634, 2010.

correspondence problems that uses minimum description length (MDL) to balance the training errors and generalization ability. This optimization approach, although slow in convergence, produces high quality matching results. A recent evaluation study [2] compares several well-known 3D point correspondence methods for modeling purposes and shows that the MDL-based approach [1] generates the best results.

Despite all the progress, finding accurate 3D point correspondences has remained a challenging task, largely due to the lack of a well-defined metric for a good correspondence. However, certain properties of a good correspondence can be identified. For example, various nonlinear properties, such as curvature [7] and torsion [8], can not be quantified nor computed by linear combinations of point positions but have been shown not only necessary for modeling shapes but also helpful for finding point correspondences. This suggests that point correspondence algorithms should take nonlinear information into considerations.

Exploiting nonlinear properties in point correspondences to improve results is the main motivation of this paper. Despite being ranked as the state-of-the-art method for finding point correspondences, the MDL-based approach [1] does not capture such knowledge directly, as no local patch information is used. In addition, one key assumption behind the MDL-based approach is that the projected coefficients on principal component analysis have a multivariate Gaussian distribution. Such Gaussian properties are preserved and propagated back via affine transformations (e.g., PCA reconstruction) to all points in the set, which may not reflect reality. In this paper, we propose to overcome this limitation by assuming that the distribution of the projected PCA coefficients of the data in a feature space is a multivariate normal; thus we allow a nonlinear mapping from the input space to the feature space. We further adapt the MDL-based objective function for the feature space, given that the inner product of any vector pair can be computed in the feature space.

Besides presenting a novel objective function, we further propose an efficient optimization method to minimize the objective function directly in the feature space, inspired by the success of applying the gradient descent method proposed by Heimann *et al.* [9][10] on the original MDL-based approach. In order to compute the gradient of the proposed objective function in the feature space, we identify the key condition, which requires the inner product of any vector pair to be computed in the feature space. This requirement is extremely useful for guiding us to a broad set of feature spaces for efficient optimization.

We further employ the Mercer kernel [3] to define the feature space implicitly, given its nice property of supporting pair-wise vector inner product computation. A key aspect of our proposed framework is to generalize the MDL-based objective function to kernel principal component analysis (KPCA) [4] spaces and a gradient descent approach to minimize such an objective function. Although there has been some previous work [11][12] using KPCA in active shape models to model shapes, we are not aware of any previous work that generalizes the MDL-based objective functions to KPCA or shows how to optimize such an objective function. With our generalized framework, the original MDL framework turns out to be a special case where a homogenous polynomial kernel of degree 1 (i.e., an inner product between two vectors) is used.

We compare the generalized MDL objective function on KPCA spaces with the original MDL approach [1] and evaluate their abilities in terms of reconstruction error and specificity. From our experimental results on different sets of 3D shapes of different organs of the body, the proposed method performs significantly better than the original method.

The two main contributions of the paper are summarized below. First, there is a significant theoretical generalization of the MDL-based objective function to feature spaces using gradient descent energy minimization. The original MDL framework, is a special case of this generalization, when an inner product is used. Second, besides the theoretical improvement, the empirical contribution is also substantial. Overcoming the limitation that nonlinear properties are not included in the original MDL framework directly is significant as our proposed KPCA approach yields much better results.

2   Previous Work

The objective functions automatic methods used to quantize the quality of point correspondences can be partitioned into three classes: shape-based, model-based and information-theoretic objective functions [5]. Shape-based objective functions are based on similarity between shapes and the representative examples use Euclidean distances, bending energy, curvatures, shape contexts [13] and SPHARM [14] to measure shape similarity. In contrast model-based objective functions consider the statistics of the dissimilarity among shapes; the determinant of the model covariance is a representative example. Information-theoretic objective functions uses information theoretic measures, such as MDL and mutual information [1][15]. A recent evaluation study [2] that compares several well-known 3D point correspondence methods for modeling purposes shows that an information theoretic objective function, the MDL-based approach [1], is the best method. Because of its superior performance, this class of information theoretic objective functions is the main focus in this paper.

In the following, we first review the MDL-based approach [1] in detail. Then, PCA and KPCA, which play important roles in both MDL-based objective functions and understanding the proposed framework, are reviewed. Assume that we have a training set of N 3D shapes, $\Gamma = \{x_1, x_2, \ldots, x_N\}$, and each shape is represented by M 3D landmarks points. Conventionally, we can represent each such shape by a vector with dimension $3M \times 1$. Note that 3D shapes are used for illustration only and all the methods we will review can be applied to both 2D curves and 3D shapes.

2.1   Correspondence by Minimizing Description Length

Davies *et al.* [1] proposed a MDL-based objective function to quantize the quality of the point correspondences. In this paper, we use the commonly-used version F proposed by Thodberg [16] as defined below.

$$F = \sum_{k=1}^{N} L_k \text{ with } L_k = \begin{cases} 1 + \log(\lambda_k/\lambda_{cut}), & \text{if } \lambda_k \geq \lambda_{cut} \\ \lambda_k/\lambda_{cut}, & \text{otherwise} \end{cases} \tag{1}$$

Given a set of shapes and a set of known point correspondences, PCA is computed on the set of shapes, and the computed eigenvalues, $\{\lambda_k | k = 1, \ldots, N\}$, are used to calculate F in (1). λ_{cut} is a parameter that determines the point where we effectively switch between the determinant-type term (i.e., the if-part in (1)) and the trace-type term (i.e., the otherwise-part in (1)). The determinant-type terms jointly measure the volume of the training set after correspondence in shape space, which favors compactness. The trace-type terms jointly measure similarity of each pair of the training shapes after correspondence via Euclidean distance.

Given the above MDL-based objective function, an efficient method for manipulating point correspondences and an optimization algorithm that minimizes the objective function are required in order to find optimal point correspondences [5][9]. Typically, manipulating point correspondences is treated as parameterizing and then re-parameterizing the surfaces. A parameterization assigns every point on the surface of the mesh to a unique point on the unit sphere, although parameterizations may not exist for arbitrary surfaces. In this paper, we assume that the 3D shapes are closed two-manifolds of genus 0. We use a conformal mapping as a parameterization and a reparameterization that modifies the parameterization based on kernels with strictly local effects, as developed in [9].

We assume that the parameterization of the ith shape is controlled by some parameter vector α_i, for which the individual parameters are given by $\{\alpha_{i,a} | a = 1, \ldots, A\}$. The gradient descent approach is used to minimize F with respect to a parameter vector α_i. The Jacobian matrix for the gradient of the objective function is defined as

$$\frac{\partial F}{\partial \alpha_{i,a}} = \sum_{k=1}^{N} \frac{\partial L_k}{\partial \lambda_k} \frac{\partial \lambda_k}{\partial \alpha_{i,a}} \tag{2}$$

It is easy to compute $\frac{\partial L_k}{\partial \lambda_k}$ (see (1)) and so we focus on $\frac{\partial \lambda_k}{\partial \alpha_{i,a}}$ in the following discussions. $\frac{\partial \lambda_k}{\partial \alpha_{i,a}}$ can be computed by using the following chain rule for derivatives.

$$\frac{\partial \lambda_k}{\partial \alpha_{i,a}} = \frac{\partial \lambda_k}{\partial x_i} \cdot \frac{\partial x_i}{\partial \alpha_{i,a}} \tag{3}$$

While $\frac{\partial x_i}{\partial \alpha_{i,a}}$ is typically computed by using finite differences, the following analytic form for $\frac{\partial \lambda_k}{\partial x_i}$ exists:

$$\frac{\partial \lambda_k}{\partial x_i} = 2(1 - \frac{1}{N})c_{i,k}b_k. \tag{4}$$

where $c_{i,k}$ is the projection coefficient of the i-th shape vector x_i onto the k-th eigenvector b_k.

2.2 PCA and KPCA

PCA. PCA is a common approach to model the shape variations of a given training set of 3D shapes. The total scatter matrix $\mathbf{S}$ is defined as

$$\mathbf{S} = \sum_{i=1}^{N} (x_i - \bar{x})(x_i - \bar{x})^t \tag{5}$$

where $\bar{x}$ is the mean shape vector as defined below.

$$\bar{x} = \frac{\sum_{i=1}^{N} x_i}{N} \tag{6}$$

PCA finds a projection axis b that maximizes $b^t S b$. Intuitively, the total scatter of the projected samples is maximized after the projection of the samples onto b. The optimal Q projection axes $b_q, q = 1, \ldots, Q$ that maximize the above criterion are the eigenvectors of S corresponding to the largest Q eigenvalues, $\{\lambda_q | q = 1, \ldots, Q\}$. The reconstruction $\tilde{x}$ of shape vector x can be used to approximate it.

$$\tilde{x} = \bar{x} + \sum_{q=1}^{Q} c_q b_q \tag{7}$$

where $c_q = (x - \bar{x})^t b_q$.

KPCA. Assume that we have an input space of shapes $\Psi = R^{3M \times 1}$, a feature space Ω, and a mapping $\phi : \Psi \to \Omega$. Instead of performing PCA in the input space Ψ, KPCA performs PCA in the feature space Ω.

The mean of the data points in the feature space, $\hat{x}$, is defined as follows.

$$\hat{x} = \frac{1}{N} \sum_{i=1}^{N} \phi(x_i) \tag{8}$$

The covariance matrix $\mathbf{C}$ can be defined as follows.

$$\mathbf{C} = \sum_{i=1}^{N} (\phi(x_i) - \hat{x})(\phi(x_i) - \hat{x})^t \tag{9}$$

Let β denoting the column vector with entries, $\beta_1, \beta_2, \ldots, \beta_N$, which can be computed by solving the following eigenvalue problem.

$$N\lambda\beta = \tilde{\mathbf{K}}\beta \tag{10}$$

where $\tilde{\mathbf{K}}_{ij} = (\mathbf{K} - 1_N \mathbf{K} - \mathbf{K}1_N + 1_N \mathbf{K}1_N)_{ij}$, $\mathbf{K} = [\mathbf{K}_{ij}]$ is a $N \times N$ Gram matrix, and $\mathbf{K}_{ij} = \phi(x_i) \cdot \phi(x_j)$.

To require e, an eigenvector, to be a unit vector, an additional constraint on β must be posed.

$$1 = \lambda\beta \cdot \beta \tag{11}$$

Let $\{e_q, q = 1, \ldots, Q\}$ be the eigenvectors of $\mathbf{C}$ with the largest Q eigenvalues $\{\lambda_q | q = 1, \ldots, Q\}$. Any eigenvector e_i of $\mathbf{C}$ can be expressed as

$$e_i = \sum_{j}^{N} \beta_{ij} \phi(x_j) \tag{12}$$

The reconstruction $\widetilde{\phi(x)}$ of $\phi(x)$ can be used to approximate it.

$$\widetilde{\phi(x)} = \hat{x} + \sum_{q=1}^{Q} c_q e_q \tag{13}$$

where $c_q = (\phi(x) - \hat{x}) \cdot e_q$.

Instead of using an explicitly defined mapping ϕ, we can use a Mercer kernel [3] that satisfies the following constraint:

$$K(x_i, x_j) = \phi(x_i) \cdot \phi(x_j) \tag{14}$$

Commonly used Mercer kernels include Gaussian radial basis functions (RBFs), inhomogeneous polynomial functions, and sigmoidal functions. Gaussian RBFs are defined as

$$K(x_i, x_j) = \exp(-\frac{||x_i - x_j||^2}{2\sigma^2}) \tag{15}$$

where $\sigma \in R$ is a kernel parameter, and $||x||$ is the Euclidean norm of x. Inhomogeneous polynomial kernels of degree $d \in R$ are defined as

$$K(x_i, x_j) = (x_i \cdot x_j + 1)^d \tag{16}$$

In contrast with inhomogeneous polynomial kernels where the constant one is added in the definition, homogeneous polynomial kernels of degree d are defined as

$$K(x_i, x_j) = (x_i \cdot x_j)^d \tag{17}$$

The common inner product between two vectors x_i and x_j is a special case of a homogenous kernel of degree 1. If such a kernel is used in KPCA, KPCA degenerates to PCA.

3   The Proposed Framework

In the following, we first focus on general feature spaces and then on special feature spaces called Mercer-kernels-induced feature spaces.

3.1   General Feature Spaces

In contrast with [1][16][9] that perform all the work in the input space Ψ, we generalize and perform our work in the feature space Ω. In other words, instead of using the eigenvalues computed by PCA in (1), we propose to use those computed by PCA in the feature space Ω. We propose a gradient descent approach to minimize the objective function based on the ideas in Section 2.2. to compute the Jacobian matrix for the gradient of the objective function.

The Jacobian matrix for the gradient of the objective function is defined as

$$\frac{\partial F}{\partial \alpha_{i,a}} = \sum_{k=1}^{N} \frac{\partial L_k}{\partial \lambda_k} \frac{\partial \lambda_k}{\partial \alpha_{i,a}} \tag{18}$$

As in Section 2.1, it is easy to compute $\frac{\partial L_k}{\partial \lambda_k}$, and so we focus on $\frac{\partial \lambda_k}{\partial \alpha_{i,a}}$ here. $\frac{\partial \lambda_k}{\partial \alpha_{i,a}}$ can be computed by using the following chain rule for derivatives.

$$\frac{\partial \lambda_k}{\partial \alpha_{i,a}} = \frac{\partial \lambda_k}{\partial \phi(x_i)} \cdot \frac{\partial \phi(x_i)}{\partial \alpha_{i,a}} \tag{19}$$

The term, $\frac{\partial \phi(x_i)}{\partial \alpha_{i,a}}$, is typically approximated by using finite differences. For example, we can use a forward difference to approximate $\frac{\partial \phi(x_i)}{\partial \alpha_{i,a}}$ as follows.

$$\frac{\partial \phi(x_i)}{\partial \alpha_{i,a}} \approx \phi(x_i + \triangle \alpha_{i,a}) - \phi(x_i) \tag{20}$$

where $\triangle \alpha_{i,a}$ is a predefined small quantity. In addition to the above forward difference method, it is also possible to use other finite difference methods, such as backward and central differences and high-order difference methods.

In this paper, we focus on a general class of finite difference methods whose calculations can be represented by a weighted linear combination, $\sum_{p=1}^{P} w_p \phi(y_p)$, where $\{w_p | p = 1, \ldots, P\}$ is a given set of weights and $\{y_p | p = 1, \ldots, P\}$ is a given set of shape vectors as shown below.

$$\frac{\partial \phi(x_i)}{\partial \alpha_{i,a}} \approx \sum_{p=1}^{P} w_p \phi(y_p) \tag{21}$$

Note that forward, backward and central differences, as well as high order difference methods, are representative examples in this class.

In contrast with using finite differences to approximate $\frac{\partial \phi(x_i)}{\partial \alpha_{i,a}}$, the following analytic form for $\frac{\partial \lambda_k}{\partial \phi(x_i)}$ exists[1].

$$\frac{\partial \lambda_k}{\partial \phi(x_i)} = 2(1 - \frac{1}{N})c_{i,k}e_k \tag{22}$$

where $c_{i,k}$ is the projection coefficient of the feature vector $\phi(x_i)$ of i-th shape vector x_i onto the k-th eigenvector e_k.

By plugging (21), (22) and (12) into (19),

$$\begin{aligned}
\frac{\partial \lambda_k}{\partial \alpha_{i,a}} &= \frac{\partial \lambda_k}{\partial \phi(x_i)} \cdot \frac{\partial \phi(x_i)}{\partial \alpha_{i,a}} \\
&\approx 2(1 - \frac{1}{N})c_{i,k}e_k \cdot (\sum_{l}^{L} w_l \phi(y_l)) \\
&= 2(1 - \frac{1}{N})c_{i,k}(\sum_{j=1}^{N} \beta_{k,j}\phi(x_j)) \cdot (\sum_{p=1}^{P} w_p \phi(y_p)) \\
&= 2(1 - \frac{1}{N})c_{i,k} \sum_{j=1}^{N} \beta_{k,j} \sum_{p=1}^{P} w_p \phi(x_j) \cdot \phi(y_p) \tag{23}
\end{aligned}$$

---

[1] The full derivations can be found in appendix A.

From (23), a key insight is that the calculation of $\frac{\partial \lambda_k}{\partial \alpha_{i,a}}$ depends on the inner product of two vectors in the feature space ($\phi(x_j) \cdot \phi(y_p)$). If an explicitly defined mapping $\phi(x)$ from Ψ to Ω is used, $\frac{\partial \lambda_k}{\partial \alpha_{i,a}}$ can be computed by (23).

It is easy to see that the previous methods [1][16][9] are special cases of our work when $\phi(x) = x$. In other words, when $\phi(x) = x$ is used in the proposed framework, the objective function degenerates to (1)[1][16], and the above gradient descent optimization approach degenerates to the one in Section 2.2 [9]. In addition, our framework allows nonlinear information easily if we choose $\phi(x)$ as a nonlinear mapping from Ψ to Ω.

3.2   Mercer-Kernel-Induced Feature Spaces

Instead of using an explicitly defined mapping $\phi(x)$ from Ψ to Ω , we can in (23) use a Mercer kernel (14) that implicitly induces a mapping. In other words, (23) can be further simplified as follows by plugging (14) into the right-hand side of the last equation in (23).

$$\frac{\partial \lambda_k}{\partial \alpha_{i,a}} \approx 2(1 - \frac{1}{N})c_{i,k} \sum_{j=1}^{N} \beta_{k,j} \sum_{p=1}^{P} w_p K(x_j, y_p) \tag{24}$$

Although nonlinear mappings are allowed in both (23) and (24), their time complexities can be very different. In contrast with the time complexity of using (23) to compute $\frac{\partial \lambda_k}{\partial \alpha_{i,a}}$ depending on the dimensionality of the feature space, the time complexity of using (24) to compute $\frac{\partial \lambda_k}{\partial \alpha_{i,a}}$ depends on the dimensionality of the input space. If a Mercer kernel is used, our framework can deal with nonlinear mapping functions whose feature spaces with infinite dimensionality (the dimensionality of $\phi(x)$ is infinite) and still keep its time complexity dependent on the dimensionality of the input space and not on the dimensionality of the feature space. Note that although we focus on using a Mercer kernel in the above discussions, the proposed framework naturally allows using multiple Mercer kernels without any modifications.

4   Experiments

We have 3D triangular mesh models of 17 left kidneys, 15 right kidneys, and 18 spleens as shown in Figure 1. All 3D meshes are constructed from CT scans of different patients[2]. After correspondences are found, all the mesh models of the same organ have the same number of vertices (2563) and the same number of faces (5120), and all vertices are used as landmarks to represent the shapes. Two methods, the proposed method and MDL, are compared. The code [10][9] that implements the ideas described in Section 2.1 is used as an implementation of MDL, and the implementation of the proposed method is built on top of it. The same heuristic used in [10][9] is used to select λ_{cut} values for the organ dataset on which the two methods are compared. A weighted forward difference (e.g., a weighted form of (20)) is used in (21).

---

[2] We constructs the shape of an organ from manual segmentation of CT scans of a patient by using marching cubes in ITK-SNAP.

Fig. 1. Some examples of the 3D triangular meshes of different organs used in the experiments. From the top row to the bottom row are left kidneys, right kidneys and spleens, respectively.

We follow a standard procedure extensively used in [1][5][2][9] to compare different point correspondence methods when the ground truth correspondences among different shapes are not available, and two standard evaluation measures, leave-one-out cross validation and specificity, are used. Leave-one-out cross validation is used to determine how accurately an algorithm will be able to predict data that it was not trained on. The evaluation measure for this method is the difference between an unknown shape and its reconstruction. In contrast, given a set of shapes sampled from the probability density function of the training set, the specificity measure computes the average distance from each sampled shape to the nearest element of the training set. In both measures, the Euclidean distance (i.e, the sum of the distances between all pairs of corresponding landmarks) is used to measure the difference between two shapes.

Table 1. The point correspondences found with the compared methods. The columns show different organs. The rows show the results with the proposed method with Gaussian RBF kernels, the results with the proposed method with inhomogeneous polynomial kernels and the results with MDL, respectively. Points that correspond are shown in same colors.

	Left Kidney	Right Kidney	Spleens
MDL+K(G)			
MDL+K(P)			
MDL			

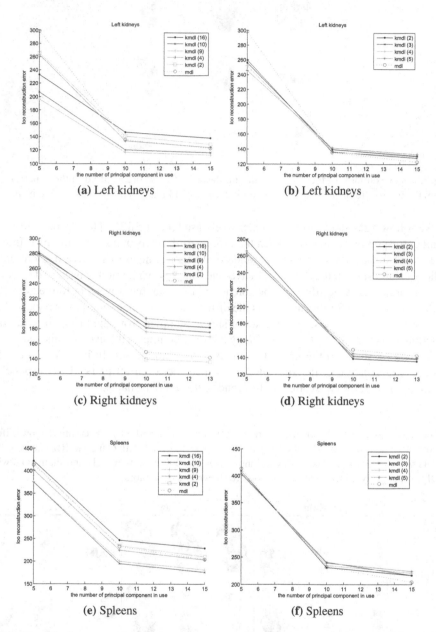

Fig. 2. How the leave-one-out reconstruction errors for different organs change with different kernel parameters and the numbers of principal components in use. The rows show different organs. The first column shows the results with the Gaussian RBF kernels while the second column shows the results with inhomogeneous polynomial kernels.

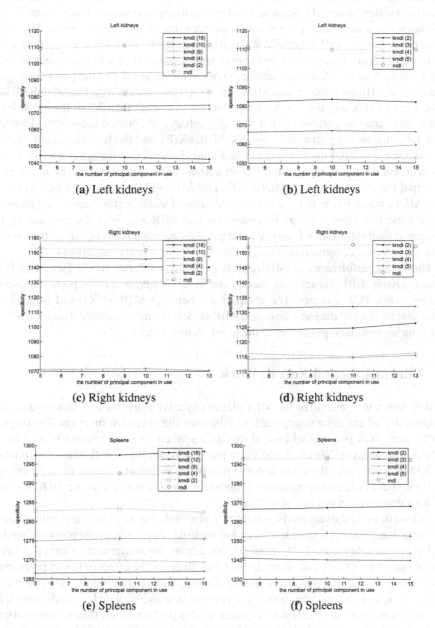

Fig. 3. How the average specificity for different organs change with different kernel parameters and the numbers of principal components in use. The rows show different organs. The first column shows the results with the Gaussian RBF kernels while the second column shows the results with inhomogeneous polynomial kernels.

Figure 2 shows the changes in leave-one-out reconstruction errors for different organs with different kernel parameters and the numbers of principal components in use. The kernel parameters can greatly affect the reconstruction errors; for example, the parameters in Gaussian RBF kernels, 9 and 10, gave significantly lower errors than 2 and 16 in Figure 2(a). In addition, some feature spaces induced by using different parameters in Mercer kernels failed to capture the nonlinear properties in the point correspondences and performed worse than MDL. The proposed method with Gaussian RBF kernels, MDL+K(G), and the best kernel parameters, is better than MDL for left kidneys and spleens and comparable to MDL for right kidneys. In contrast,the proposed method with inhomogeneous polynomial kernels, MDL+K(P), and the best kernel parameters, is comparable to MDL in all the datasets. Figure 3 shows that the specificity measures for different organs change with different kernel parameters and with the numbers of principal components in use. MDL+K(G) and MDL+K(P) have better performances than MDL, which has either the worst or the second worst performance in all datasets. From these two figures, it can be concluded that MDL+K(G) is the best among the compared methods. Table 1 shows point correspondences resulting from the models with the lowest reconstruction errors in Figure 2 in for visual comparisons.

The better performance of MDL+K(G) is mainly attributed to the fact that KPCA with Gaussian RBF kernels can model nonlinear properties in the point correspondences, while PCA can not. The comparisons between MDL+K(G) and MDL+K(P) show that for the test datasets, Gaussian RBF kernels are more suitable than MDL+K(P) in capturing nonlinear properties in the point correspondences.

5   Conclusions and Future Work

In this paper, we generalize the MDL-based objective function to feature spaces and propose a gradient descent approach to minimize the objective function. The original MDL framework is a special case of this theory when an inner product is used in the proposed framework. We empirically compare the generalized MDL objective function on KPCA spaces with the original one. From our experimental results on different sets of 3D shapes of different organs, the proposed method is better than the MDL in terms of the reconstruction errors and specificity.

Instead of using the reconstruction errors and specificity, we plan to use some datasets whose ground truth correspondences are known to directly compare the proposed method with other existing methods. We currently use a brute-force approach to test all possible kernel parameter values and select the best one. Because the effect of kernel parameters can affect the reconstruction errors and specificity greatly, a future study is to investigate how to choose the kernel parameters that perform best and under what conditions on input shapes the proposed framework is guaranteed to perform better than the original one. In the experiments, we only focus on Mercer kernels that can implicitly induce nonlinear feature spaces. However, the induced nonlinear mappings may not be anatomically meaningful. Hence, an interesting future direction is to incorporate priori knowledge into the Mercer kernel, so that an anatomically meaningful feature space can be induced.

Acknowledgment

This work was supported by NSF Grant DBI-0543631 and NIH-NIDCR grant 1U01DE 020050-01.

References

1. Davies, R., Twining, C., Cootes, T., Waterton, J., Taylor, C.: A minimum description length approach to statistical shape modeling. IEEE TMI 21(5), 525–537 (2002)
2. Styner, M., Rajamani, K., Nolte, L.P., Zsemlye, G., Szekely, G., Taylor, C., Davies, R.H.: Evaluation of 3d correspondence methods for model building. In: IPMI, pp. 63–75 (2003)
3. Vapnik, V.: The Nature of Statisticl Learning Theory. Springer, New York (1995)
4. Schölkopf, B., Smola, A., Müller, K.R.: Nonlinear component analysis as a kernel eigenvalue problem. Neural Comput. 10(5), 1299–1319 (1998)
5. Davies, R., Twining, C., Taylor, C.: Statistical Models of Shape: Optimisation and Evaluation. Springer Publishing Company, Heidelberg (2008)
6. Heimann, T., Meinzer, H.P.: Statistical shape models for 3d medical image segmentation: A review. Medical Image Analysis 13(4), 543–563 (2009)
7. Styner, M., Oguz, I., Heimann, T., Gerig, G.: Minimum description length with local geometry. In: ISBI 2008, pp. 1283–1286 (2008)
8. Corouge, I., Gouttard, S., Gerig, G.: Towards a shape model of white matter fiber bundles using diffusion tensor mri. In: ISBI 2004, vol. 1, pp. 344–347 (2004)
9. Heimann, T., Wolf, I., Williams, T.G., Meinzer, H.P.: 3d active shape models using gradient descent optimization of description length. In: IPMI, pp. 566–577 (2005)
10. Heimann, T., Oguz, I., Wolf, I., Styner, M., Meinzer, H.: Implementing the automatic generation of 3d statistical shape models with itk. In: Open Science Workshop at MICCAII (2006)
11. Romdhani, S., Gong, S., Psarrou, R.: A multi-view nonlinear active shape model using kernel pca. In: BMVC, pp. 483–492 (1999)
12. Twining, C.J., Taylor, C.J.: Kernel principal component analysis and the construction of nonlinear active shape models. In: BMVC, pp. 23–32 (2001)
13. Belongie, S., Malik, J., Puzicha, J.: Shape matching and object recognition using shape contexts. PAMI 24, 509–522 (2002)
14. Brechbühler, C., Gerig, G., Kübler, O.: Parametrization of closed surfaces for 3-d shape description. CVIU 61(2), 154–170 (1995)
15. Wang, Y., Chiang, M., Thompson, P.: Mutual informationbased 3d surface matching with applications to face recognition and brain mapping. In: ICCV 2005, vol. 1, pp. 527–534 (2005)
16. Thodberg, H.H.: Minimum description length shape and appearance models. In: IPMI, pp. 51–62 (2003)

Appendix A

In the following, we will derive an analytic form for $\frac{\partial \lambda_k}{\partial \phi(x_i)}$. Assume the k-th eigenvector and eigenvalue of C defined in (9) are e_k and λ_k, respectively. By definition of eigenvalues and eigenvectors of a matrix, we have $Ce_k = \lambda_k e_k$. The inner product of e_k

and $\mathbf{C}e_k$, $e_k^t \mathbf{C} e_k$, is λ_k because $e_k^t \lambda_k e_k = \lambda_k$ and the above relation can be expressed by using the following equation.

$$
\lambda_k = \sum_{i=1}^{N} e_k^t (\phi(x_i) - \hat{x})(\phi(x_i) - \hat{x})^t e_k
$$

$$
= \sum_{i=1}^{N} ((\phi(x_i) - \hat{x})^t e_k)^2 \tag{25}
$$

where the second equality is obtained by substituting $\mathbf{C}$ by its definition in (9). $\frac{\partial \lambda_k}{\partial \phi(x_i)}$ can be obtained by the following chain rules.

$$
\frac{\partial \lambda_k}{\partial \phi(x_i)} = \frac{\partial \lambda_k}{\partial (\phi(x_i) - \hat{x})^t e_k} \frac{\partial (\phi(x_i) - \hat{x})^t e_k}{\partial (\phi(x_i) - \hat{x})} \frac{\partial (\phi(x_i) - \hat{x})}{\partial \phi(x_i)}
$$

$$
= 2(\phi(x_i) - \hat{x})^t e_k e_k^t (1 - \frac{1}{N}) I
$$

$$
= 2(1 - \frac{1}{N})(\phi(x_i) - \hat{x})^t e_k e_k^t \tag{26}
$$

I is an identity matrix both of whose dimensions are the same as e_k. For some nonlinear mapping functions ϕ, the dimensionality of $\phi(x)$ can be infinite. Note that $\frac{\partial \lambda_k}{\partial \phi(x_i)}$ in (26) is treated as a row vector but it is defined as a column vector in the main paper.

Making Action Recognition Robust to Occlusions and Viewpoint Changes

Daniel Weinland[1], Mustafa Özuysal[2,*], and Pascal Fua[2]

[1] Deutsche Telekom Laboratories, TU Berlin, Germany
daniel.weinland@tu-berlin.de
[2] Computer Vision Laboratory, EPFL, Switzerland
{mustafa.oezuysal,pascal.fua}@epfl.ch

Abstract. Most state-of-the-art approaches to action recognition rely on global representations either by concatenating local information in a long descriptor vector or by computing a single location independent histogram. This limits their performance in presence of occlusions and when running on multiple viewpoints. We propose a novel approach to providing robustness to both occlusions and viewpoint changes that yields significant improvements over existing techniques. At its heart is a local partitioning and hierarchical classification of the 3D Histogram of Oriented Gradients (HOG) descriptor to represent sequences of images that have been concatenated into a data volume. We achieve robustness to occlusions and viewpoint changes by combining training data from all viewpoints to train classifiers that estimate action labels independently over sets of HOG blocks. A top level classifier combines these local labels into a global action class decision.

1 Introduction

Action recognition has applications in video surveillance, human computer interaction, and multimedia retrieval, among others. It is also very challenging both because the range of possible human motions is so large and because variations in scene, viewpoint, and clothing add an additional layer of complexity.

Most state-of-the-art approaches compute image-sequence descriptors based on variants of either *sparse interest points* [3,11,17,20,24] or *dense holistic features* [9,13,19,22,23]. They integrate information over space and time into a global representation, *bag of words* or a *space-time volume*, and use a classifier, such as an SVM, to label the resulting representation.

These approaches achieve nearly perfect results on the well-known KTH and Weizmann datasets [20,1]. These, however, are relatively easy because subjects are seen from similar viewpoints and against uniform backgrounds. Furthermore, the motions in the test and training set look very similar, so that test-motions are well explained as small variations of training ones. Most of the above-mentioned publications do not report results on difficult multiview datasets, such as the

---

* This work was funded in part by Swiss National Science Foundation project.

K. Daniilidis, P. Maragos, N. Paragios (Eds.): ECCV 2010, Part III, LNCS 6313, pp. 635–648, 2010.

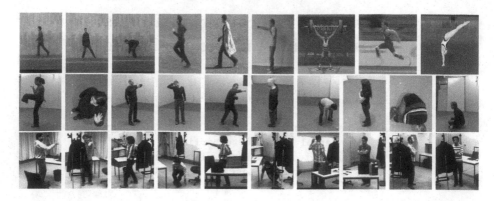

Fig. 1. We evaluate our approach on several datasets. **(Top)** Weizmann, KTH, and UCF datasets. **(Middle)** IXMAS dataset, which contains strong viewpoint changes. **(Bottom)** Finally, to measure robustness to occlusions, we evaluate the models learned from the IXMAS dataset on a new dataset that contains substantial occlusions, cluttered backgrounds, and viewpoint variations.

IXMAS [27] one, which includes subjects seen from arbitrary viewpoints. Nor do they discuss what happens when the subjects are partially occluded so that none of the training samples resembles the observation for the whole body. One must note that some of these approaches have been tested on the even more challenging Hollywood [12] dataset. However, the recognition rates on the Hollywood dataset are much lower, and the action classes contain scene context cues that can be exploited by scene classification techniques. Such discriminative scene context is not always present depending on the set of actions and also for tasks that require action classification in the same scene, such as surveillance or HCI.

To handle occlusions, an alternative to global models is to use part based ones to make independent decisions for individual body parts and to fuse them into a global interpretation [7]. However, robustly tracking body parts remains an open problem, especially in the presence of occlusions. As a result, these methods have not been tested on sequences containing substantial occlusion.

In this paper, we propose a hybrid approach that uses a local partitioning of a dense 3DHOG representation in a hierarchical classifier, which first performs local classification followed by global, to provide robustness to both viewpoint changes and occlusions. Not only can it handle sequences with substantial occlusions such as in Fig. 1, it also yields significant improvements on the IXMAS dataset [27] against recent methods explicitly designed with view-invariance in mind [5,10,27,28]. This is achieved without any performance loss on the Weizmann, KTH, and UCF datasets [1,20,18].

2   Related Work

Early attempts at view independent action recognition [15,16] required individual body parts being detected or feature points being tracked over long sequences. However, in a typical single-camera setup, it is difficult both to track individual limbs and to find feature points in images of people wearing normal clothes. Current approaches proceed differently and can be partitioned into two classes depending on whether they represent the spatio-temporal information densely or sparsely.

Sparse Representations. Many approaches rely on 3D interest points, also known as space-time corners and represent them using SIFT-like 2D descriptors [3,11,17,20,24]. These descriptors are often incorporated into a single histogram to be used for classification purposes using a Bag-of-Words (BoW) approach.

These approaches depend neither on background subtraction nor on exact localization of the person. They perform particularly well with periodic actions, such as walking or running that produce many space-time corners. A major limitation, however, is that all geometric information is lost during the BoW step and we will show that this results in a drop in performance. Furthermore, they are not suitable for action sequences that do not contain enough repeatable space time corners such as aperiodic motions.

Dense Representations. The requirement for space time corners can be eliminated by replacing sparse representations with dense ones, such as those provided by HMAX [21] or HOG [2]. These descriptors can represent 2D gradients, optical flow, or a combination thereof. For instance [22] encodes video sequences into histograms of 2D HOG descriptor and the biologically inspired approaches of [9,19] use 2D Gabor-filter responses combined with optical flow. Such dense representations avoid some of the problems discussed above but require a region of interest (ROI) around the human body, which is usually obtained by using either a separate human body detector or background subtraction followed by blob detection. Nevertheless, they have shown much better performance on the Weizmann [1] and KTH [20] datasets than sparse representations. Interestingly, improved performance on some datasets was obtained using BoW-based representations when the interest point detection was replaced by dense sampling [24].

View Independence. The above described methods have not been designed with view-independence in mind. To achieve it, several avenues have been explored. In [5], the change of silhouettes and optical flow with viewpoint is learned and used to transfer action models from a single *source-view* into novel *target-views*. This requires source and target views that record the same action, which severely limits the applicability of this technique. By contrast, in [10], actions are learned from arbitrary number of views by extracting view-invariant features based on frame-to-frame similarities within a sequence, which yields very stable features under difficult viewing conditions. However, discarding all absolute view information results in a loss of discriminative power. For instance, a moving arm or leg might produce exactly the same self-similarity measures.

Another class of techniques relies on recovering the 3D body orientation from silhouettes. For example, in [27], 3D models are projected onto 2D silhouettes with respect to different viewpoints and, in [28], 2D features are detected and back-projected onto action features based on a 3D visual hull. Such approaches require a search over model parameters to find the best match between the 3D model and the 2D observation, which is both computationally expensive and known to be relatively fragile. As a result, these techniques are usually only deployed in very constrained environments.

Occlusion Handling. The above mentioned approaches for action recognition have not been demonstrated on partially occluded action sequences. Recently, [25] tried to infer occlusion maps from a global HOG-SVM classifier for pedestrian detection by analyzing the individual contribution of each HOG block to the classifier response. However, this approach requires estimation of deterministic local occlusion labels based on a globally trained classifier. By contrast, we directly learn local SVM classifiers, each one tuned to a specific region of the HOG feature and combine the results without the need of hard decisions.

3   Recognition of Action Classes

Our approach is depicted by Fig. 2. It relies on the 3D extension of the HOG descriptor [2] to represent image sequences that have been concatenated into a data volume. The volume is subdivided into equally spaced overlapping blocks and information within each block is represented by a histogram of oriented 3D spatio-temporal gradients [11]. The resulting block descriptors are embedded temporally [26] at each spatial location, providing a discriminative representation that has fixed dimension independent of the duration of a sequence and hence can be easily fed to a classifier. By contrast to HOG and BoW, the feature descriptors are not spatially integrated into a global representation, i.e. by concatenating the blocks into a single vector (HOG) or by computing a location independent histogram of the blocks (BoW). Instead each location is individually encoded using a set of location dependent classifiers. Preserving location dependent information introduces additional discriminative power. Moreover, the local classifiers let us also estimate probabilities for occlusion, which we use to filter out contributions from cluttered and occluded regions when finally combining the local action assignments into a global decision.

   In our experiments, we will demonstrate this additional robustness to occlusion over using the standard HOG and BoW. Moreover, and even though our representation is *not* view-independent, if trained using samples from different viewpoints such as those in the IXMAS dataset [27], our experiments also demonstrate strong robustness to realistic viewpoint variations. Surprisingly, our approach not only outperforms similar learning based approaches, but also those specially designed with view-independence in mind. While our approach can not generalize to view orientations that are significantly far away from all training samples, the performance of our approach does not degrade much trained on the IXMAS data and tested on new recordings acquired in a different setup and with a wide range of different viewpoints depicted by Fig. 1.

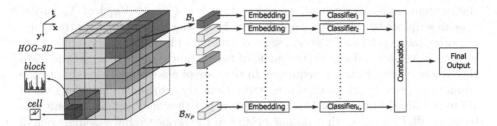

Fig. 2. We use a 3D HOG descriptor to represent a video sequence. Temporal information at each grid location is integrated over time using temporal embedding, and classified using location dependent classifiers. Finally the local results are combined into a global decision.

3.1   3D Histograms of Oriented Gradients

We use the 3DHOG descriptor introduced in [11]. In difference to [11] we compute the descriptor not at previously detected interest locations, but at densely distributed locations within a ROI centered around the person. Computing the descriptor involves the following steps: First, the region to be characterized is partitioned into regular *cells* and a histogram $\mathbf{h}$ of 3D gradient orientations is computed in each one. This compactly represents temporal and spatial texture information and is invariant to local deformations. Histograms for all cells in a small neighborhood are then concatenated into a *block* descriptor $B = L_2\text{-clip}\,([\mathbf{h}_1, \ldots, \mathbf{h}_{N_C}])$, to which SIFT-like L_2 normalization with clipping is applied to increase robustness. Since the *blocks* overlap with each other, this yields a redundant representation, which increases discriminative power because normalization emphasizes different bins in different blocks.

Finally, let

$$\mathcal{B}_p = [B_1, \ldots, B_{N_T}] \quad, \quad p = 1, \ldots, N_P \tag{1}$$

be the sequence of blocks computed at spatial location p along the time axis, where N_T is the number of overlapping blocks that fit within the duration of the sequence, and N_P is the number of blocks that fit within the ROI centered around the subject.

As will be discussed in the following Sections, these blocks are the primitives that we will feed first to the embedding and then to the local classifiers for recognition purposes. Such individual treatment of HOG blocks is what sets us apart from the original HOG and BoW computation that combine all blocks into a global representation, as discussed above. We will show it to be critical for occlusion handling.

3.2   Block Embedding and Classification

In this Section, we present an effective way to compute the probability that a block represents a specific action using information from all subsequences along the temporal axis. To this end, we create a set $V = \{V_1, \ldots, V_{N_V}\}$ of N_V proto-type descriptors by randomly sampling the HOG blocks computed for the training subsequences. Given an action sequence and the block descriptors of Eq.1, we create an N_V-dimensional vector made of the distances of each one of the V_i to the closest block within the sequence. In the case of a sequence belonging to the training set, some of these distances will be exactly zero since some elements of V are contained in its set of block descriptors but they may not be the only one to be small. Prototypes that do not belong to the sequence but resemble one of the blocks will also be assigned a small value. This *Sequence Embedding*, which is inspired by *max-pooling* of action descriptors [9] and *exemplar-based embedding* [26], makes the training and recognition much more effective. We discuss it in more details below.

Let $\mathcal{B}_p$ be a sequence of blocks at spatial location p partitioned into N_T overlapping blocks, as defined in Eq.1. We represent $\mathcal{B}_p$ in terms of minimum-distances to the set V of N_V prototype descriptors introduced above. We take the distance of the sequence to each V_i to be

$$d_i^*(\mathcal{B}_p) = \min_t d(B_t, V_i) \ , \quad B_t \in \mathcal{B}_p \ , \tag{2}$$

where d represents the distance between orientation histograms. We compute it as the χ^2-distance

$$d(B, V) = \frac{1}{2} \sum_k \frac{(h_k - v_k)^2}{h_k + v_k} \ , \tag{3}$$

which we experimentally found to be more suited for our purposes than both the squared-Euclidean-distance and Kullback-Leibler divergence. Fig 3 illustrates the embedding for an action sequence.

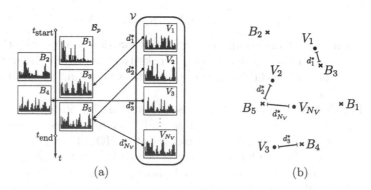

(a)   (b)

Fig. 3. Embedding of HOG block sequence. **(a)** Each exemplar V_i is compared against all blocks extracted from the sequence using the χ^2-distance and the minimum distance d_i^* is stored in a feature vector that we use for classification. The blocks extracted from the HOG descriptors overlap to minimize quantization error. **(b)** Same set of blocks and exemplars visualized in the space of histograms.

We then take the resulting set of d^* distances

$$D_p^* = (d_1^*(\mathcal{B}_p), \ldots, d_{N_V}^*(\mathcal{B}_p))^\top \in \mathbb{R}^{N_V}, \tag{4}$$

as input to a classifier trained for location p.

An alternative is to use a local BoW approach that performs the bagging along the time axis. Each HOG descriptor in the sequence can vote for the closest words in the vocabulary and a histogram over the vocabulary can be input to the SVMs. Since N_V is much larger than N_T in a typical sequence, every descriptor must vote for multiple words in the vocabulary to avoid quantization effects and sparse histograms. This can be facilitated by votes that decay exponentially with the distance between B_t and V_i. Optimizing the rate of decay for each dataset yields comparable performance to the embedding method. However we prefer the embedding method because it is simpler and does not involve adjusting an additional parameter to each dataset.

We pick the exemplars V_i from the training set by random sampling. We experimented with a selection strategy as in [26]. This gave better results with a small number of exemplars, however using a sufficiently large number (500) the performance of both approaches was very close. We therefore report results for random selection since it is simpler.

Finally, we use L2-regularized logistic regression [4] to produce probability estimates $p(c|D_p^*, \Theta_p)$ for each class $c = 1, \ldots, N_C$, where D_p^* is the descriptor of Eq. 4 and Θ_p is the learned logistic regression weights at position p.

3.3   Occlusion Handling

The overall framework that we propose resembles that of a global HOG representation that is well known for being sensitive to occlusions [25]. We have introduced the local partitioning and embedding of the 3DHOG descriptor to preserve the advantages of HOG, while at the same time making it robust to occlusions. This is achieved by individually classifying each embedded block descriptor and then combining the classification responses from all blocks in a final stage as detailed in the next Section.

To further improve occlusion robustness, we learn at each location in addition to the N_c actions a separate class. Thus $p(c = N_C + 1|D_p^*, \Theta_p)$ represents the probability of region p being occluded. If a region is occluded with high probability, and because the probability distribution normalizes to one, the probabilities for all other classes will be reduced. Hence when fusing the results as discussed in the next Section, such a region will carry reduced weight.

To generate a large variety of potential occlusions during training, we artificially hide parts of the training images, as shown in Fig. 4. These occluders are placed so that approximately either the lower part of the body, the right or left side is occluded. We then calculate for each region the amount of overlap with the occluding object; if it is higher than a predefined threshold the corresponding HOG block is labeled as belonging to the *occluded* class during training. In practice, we found that setting the threshold to 90% yields the best results.

Fig. 4. Sample images from artificially occluded training data used to introduce additional robustness against occlusions in learned classifiers

3.4   Classifier Combination

The previously described local classifiers produce action probabilities at uniformly distributed locations of the HOG window. We have evaluated the following strategies to fuse these results into a single decision.

Product Rule. Our classifiers produce probabilities $p(c|D_p^*, \Theta_p)$. Thus if independence can be assumed, the natural choice is to combine these by the product rule $p(c|D_{1:N_P}^*, \Theta_{1:N_P}) = \prod_p p(c|D_p^*, \Theta_p)$. Note that we choose the sigmoid parameters [4] that are used to convert the classifier outputs into probabilities so that the resulting probability estimates are not overly confident.

Sum Rule. It is also possible to compute a score for each class by averaging the probabilities of the individual classifiers, i.e. $f(c) = \sum_p p(c|D_p^*, \Theta_p)$, which can produce better results than the product rules, when the probabilities are not accurately estimated.

Weighted Sum. Not every region of the HOG window carries equally discriminative information for each action. Thus, when summing the individual probabilities from each region they can be weighted accordingly. One way to choose the weights is via conditional error probabilities $p(\tilde{c}|c, p)$, which represent the probability that the true class label is $\tilde{c}$ conditioned on the actual output c of a classifier. Following [8], a weighed sum can then be computed as $p(\tilde{c}|D_{1:N_P}^*, \Theta_{1:N_P}) = \sum_p \sum_c p(c|D_p^*, \Theta_p) p(\tilde{c}|c, p)$. Thus, intuitively, a local classifier that is easily confused between several actions will distribute its vote over all those actions, while a classifier that is very confident in classifying an action will account its vote only to this action. The conditional error probabilities $p(\tilde{c}|c, p)$ are estimated from confusion matrices, i.e. by counting how often an observation is classified as c if the true class label was actually $\tilde{c}$.

Top-Level SVM Classifier. Using a hierarchical classification scheme, we can combine the outputs of all local classifiers into a single feature vector and learn a global SVM classifier on top of this representation.

As shown in Table 2, when there are no occlusions, the product rule combination and the SVM classifier perform best, closely followed by the rest. However, as shown in Table 4, occlusions degrade the performance of the product rule even below that of the sum rule. This was to be expected since we use artificial occlusions in training and real ones in the testing sets and the product rule is the most sensitive one to biases in the learned probabilities. Overall, we therefore prefer the weighted sum and SVM based methods since they result in higher or at least similar classification rates on all datasets.

4   Experiments

We experimented with the well-known Weizmann [1], KTH [20], UCF [18], and IXMAS [27] datasets. Since none of these datasets includes occluded subjects, we also acquired and processed our own video sequences involving the actions in the IXMAS dataset, but with substantial occlusions and cluttered backgrounds.

We implemented two baseline methods to compare our results on this newly acquired multiview dataset with occlusions. Both methods use the same 3DHOG features and training data as the local method that we advocate in this paper. However *global SVM*, the first baseline method, combines the HOG blocks into a single feature vector followed by global embedding along the temporal axis and a linear SVM classifier. This method hence resembles the original global HOG approach [2] combined with the temporal embedding of [26]. *BoW SVM*, the second baseline method, accumulates the HOG blocks into a histogram of 4000 visual words and classifies them using a non-linear SVM with χ^2-kernel. This approach hence resembles the approaches [11,12] and more specifically the dense 3DHOG representations in [24], except that for comparison purposes we sample features *not* at multiple scales, because the local approach and global HOG also use only a single scale, and we use information only within the same ROIs centered around the subjects as for the other methods.

To compute the ROIs around people that our approach requires, we proceed as follows. For KTH, we use the bounding boxes provided by [13]. For UCF we use the bounding boxes available in the dataset. For Weizmann and IXMAS we use the background subtracted silhouettes and fit a bounding box around them.

For our new recordings we interactively determine the bounding box in every first frame of an action, because simple background subtraction can not accurately detect the partially occluded persons. For all datasets, the ROIs are scaled and concatenated to produce $48 \times 64 \times t$ cubes, where t is the number of frames in the sequence.

Unless stated otherwise, we use $16 \times 16 \times 16$ pixel blocks subdivided in $2 \times 2 \times 2$ cells for 3DHOG, which implies an overlap of 8 pixels in all dimensions. We compute histograms using the dodecahedron based quantization [11] with 6 orientation bins. For the embedding we use a set of approximately 500 prototypes.

Also, unless stated otherwise, recognition rates are computed by the leave-one-out method: If K subjects appear in a dataset, we average over K runs, leaving a different person out of the training set each time.

The recognition speed depends on the length of a sequence and on the HOG and embedding dimensions used. With our experimental setting on the IXMAS data, computing the HOG features takes on average 75.5ms per sequence, with our Matlab implementation on a Core i7 CPU. The cost of computing the embedding is on average 34ms per sequence. The hierarchical classification is the fastest step and takes on average 1ms per sequence.

Table 1. Comparison of recognition rates (in %) on Weizmann (left), KTH (middle), and UCF (right) datasets

Method	Weizmann
Local SVM	**100.0**
Local Weighted	**100.0**
Local Product	**100.0**
Local Sum	**100.0**
Global SVM	**100.0**
BoW SVM	**100.0**
Lin [13]	**100.0**
Schindler [19]	**100.0**
Blank [1]	99.6
Jhuang [9]	98.8
Thurau [22]	94.4
Kläser [11]	84.3

Method	KTH
Local SVM	92.2
Local Weighted	92.4
Local Product	92.2
Local Sum	92.0
Global SVM	90.7
BoW SVM	89.3
Gilbert [6]	**94.5**
Lin [13]	93.4
Schindler [19]	92.7
Wang [12]	92.1
Laptev [12]	91.8
Jhuang [9]	91.7
Kläser [11]	91.4
Rodriguez [18]	88.7
Schuldt [20]	71.7

Method	UCF
Local SVM	**90.1**
Local Weighted	89.4
Local Product	87.7
Local Sum	87.7
Global SVM	85.6
BoW SVM	81.2
Wang [24]	85.6
Rodriguez [18]	69.2

4.1   Weizmann, KTH, and UCF Datasets

The Weizmann dataset consists of videos of 9 actors performing 9 actions. Recently, several approaches reported close to perfect recognition rates on this relatively easy dataset. Note that existing approaches use slightly different evaluation methodologies on the data. Some evaluate on the whole sequences, others split sequences into multiple subparts. We report here results for the full sequences, where our method yields perfect recognition rates, that is 100%. In Table 1, we summarize our recognition results and compare them against other approaches.

The KTH dataset consists of 6 actions performed by 25 actors in four different scenarios. We follow the evaluation procedure of the original paper [20] and split the data into training/validation (8+8 people) and testing (9 people) sets, and report results for learning a single model from all scenarios. Note that some of the approaches use slightly different evaluation schemes, e.g. a leave-one-out cross validation, or do not require bounding boxes, etc. Optimizing our parameters on the validation set, we found HOG blocks of size $16 \times 16 \times 2$ subdivided into $2 \times 2 \times 1$ cells, and an icosahedron based quantization to give best results. With this setting, we achieve a recognition rate of 92.4% using the weighted sum based combination, which is among the best results reported for this dataset.

In Table 1, we summarize our recognition results and compare them against other approaches.

We also evaluate our approach on the UCF dataset that consists of 10 actions. Since the publicly available part of the dataset does not contain the videos for *pole vaulting*, we report results using the 9 available ones and achieve a mean recognition rate of 90.1% using the SVM which is the best reported result for this dataset. Note that these are not directly comparable to the reported rate of 69.2% [18], nevertheless, they demonstrate that our approach generalizes well to broadcast action videos.

4.2   IXMAS Dataset

The IXMAS dataset [27] is a multiview action recognition dataset. It consists of videos of 10 actors performing each 3 times 11 actions. Each action was recorded with 5 cameras observing the subjects from very different perspectives and as shown in Fig. 1, the actors freely choose their orientation for each sequence.

We learn single action models from all camera views. Average recognition rates for the different combination strategies are shown in Table 2 evaluated on all cameras. In Table 3 we show individual rates per camera when learning from all views or individual views, and also compare against other methods that used the same evaluation methodology on the full IXMAS dataset. For each camera, we improve upon previously published results.

In summary, we observed that combining training data from multiple viewpoints and using a non-invariant dense representation yields comparable recognition rates than invariant representations. However, performance is adversely affected by local changes in feature statistics. Our local classification step mitigates this problem. As a result, our local approach performs better than competing ones.

Table 2. Average recognition rates (in %) on IXMAS dataset for different combination strategies for our local method compared against the global SVM and BoW SVM baselines

Method	Local SVM	Local Product	Local Sum	Local Weighted	Global SVM	BoW SVM
Rec. Rate	83.4	**83.5**	82.8	82.4	80.6	71.9

4.3   IXMAS Actions with Occlusions

To demonstrate the generalization power of our approach, we recorded our own dataset composed of the IXMAS actions, but performed by different actors, who could be partially occluded. The actions were performed on average 3 times by 6 actors and recorded with 5 cameras. As shown in Fig. 1, actors chose their orientation freely and the occluding objects were rearranged between each take.

We split the data into two subsets: 395 sequences were recorded without occlusions, and 698 sequences contain objects partially occluding the actors. We then evaluate on the two sets by learning from all sequences of the original IXMAS dataset and by testing on either one of these subsets.

Table 3. Recognition rates (in %) on IXMAS dataset for individual cameras. The left half of the table shows the results when all cameras are used for training. The other half shows the results for training using a single camera.

Method	Training with All Cameras						Training with Single Camera				
	all	cam1	cam2	cam3	cam4	cam5	cam1	cam2	cam3	cam4	cam5
Local SVM	83.4	86.7	**89.9**	**86.4**	**87.6**	66.4	84.7	85.8	87.9	**88.5**	72.6
Local Product	**83.5**	**87.0**	88.3	85.6	87.0	**69.7**	**85.8**	**86.4**	**88.0**	88.2	**74.7**
Tran [23]	80.2	—	—	—	—	—	—	—	—	—	—
Liu [14]	—	76.7	73.3	72.0	73.0	—	—	—	—	—	—
Junejo [10]	72.7	74.8	74.5	74.8	70.6	61.2	76.4	77.6	73.6	68.8	66.1
Reddy [17]	72.6	69.6	69.2	62.0	65.1	—	—	—	—	—	—
Yan [28]	—	—	—	—	—	—	72.0	53.0	68.0	63.0	—
Farhadi [5]	58.1	—	—	—	—	—	—	—	—	—	—
Weinland [27]	57.9	65.4	70.0	54.3	66.0	33.6	55.2	63.5	—	60.0	—

Table 4. Average recognition rates (in %) when learning from IXMAS dataset and testing on new *clean* and *occluded* recordings. Results are shown for learning models with (*oc*) and without (*no oc*) the additional *occlusion class*. In all cases our local combination strategy outperforms the baselines.

Method	clean		occluded	
	no oc	oc	no oc	oc
Local SVM	83.5	**86.3**	61.9	**76.7**
Local Weighted	83.3	85.1	61.6	**76.7**
Local Sum	79.0	82.5	54.0	72.8
Local Product	77.7	81.5	44.6	68.9
Global SVM	74.4	76.0	46.1	58.3
BoW SVM	47.1	52.9	18.1	27.8

Results are shown in Fig. 5 and Table 4. Columns *clean* in Table 4 show results on the occlusion free sequences. This is relevant because it still requires that our approach generalizes to new viewpoints and actors not included in the training data. Because the sequences contain no occlusions, also the performance of the global HOG classifier generalizes well to this sequences (74.4%). Interestingly, when introducing the additional occlusion classifier, performance on the dataset improves (86.3% for SVM combination), even though it contains no occlusions. This is because the occlusion classifier also responds to background clutter, reducing its effect on classification. Note, that for columns *oc* the baseline classifiers were trained using all clean as well as all artificially occluded sequences as a single training set.

When evaluating on the sequences with occlusions the effect of the additional occlusion classifier becomes even more evident. We observe the best performance with 76.7% recognition rate for the SVM based combination and also for the weighted sum.

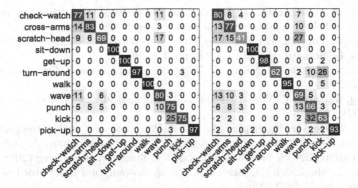

Fig. 5. Confusion matrixes (in %) for the new IXMAS recording. **(Left)** Recordings *without* occlusions with average recognition rate 86.3%. **(Right)** Recordings *with* occlusions with average recognition rate 76.7%.

In all cases, our experiments demonstrates that using local classifiers as well as explicitly introducing occlusions into the training set leads to strong performance improvements for recognition of partially occluded actions.

5   Conclusion

In this paper, we proposed a new approach based on a local 3D HOG descriptor. Our approach is simple, efficient, and combines the benefits of the HOG based dense representation with that of local approaches to achieve occlusion robust action recognition. We demonstrated that our descriptor, when trained from multiple views, can perform action recognition from multiple viewpoints, with highest recognition rates on the difficult IXMAS dataset. Moreover, we showed that these results carry over to new situations, with different backgrounds, subjects, viewpoints, and partial occlusions.

References

1. Blank, M., Gorelick, L., Shechtman, E., Irani, M., Basri, R.: Actions as space-time shapes. In: ICCV, pp. 1395–1402 (2005)
2. Dalal, N., Triggs, B.: Histograms of Oriented Gradients for Human Detection. In: CVPR (2005)
3. Dollar, P., Rabaud, V., Cottrell, G., Belongie, S.: Behavior recognition via sparse spatio-temporal features. In: VS-PETS. pp. 65–72 (2005)
4. Fan, R.E., Chang, K.W., Hsieh, C.J., Wang, X.R., Lin, C.J.: LIBLINEAR: A library for large linear classification. JMLR 9, 1871–1874 (2008)
5. Farhadi, A., Tabrizi, M.K.: Learning to recognize activities from the wrong view point. In: Forsyth, D., Torr, P., Zisserman, A. (eds.) ECCV 2008, Part I. LNCS, vol. 5302, pp. 154–166. Springer, Heidelberg (2008)

6. Gilbert, A., Illingworth, J., Bowden, R.: Fast realistic multi-action recognition using mined dense spatio-temporal features. In: ICCV (2009)
7. Ikizler, N., Forsyth, D.: Searching video for complex activities with finite state models. In: Forsyth, D. (ed.) CVPR, pp. 1–8 (2007)
8. Ivanov, Y., Heisele, B., Serre, T.: Using component features for face recognition. In: FG (2004)
9. Jhuang, H., Serre, T., Wolf, L., Poggio, T.: A biologically inspired system for action. In: ICCV (2007)
10. Junejo, I., Dexter, E., Laptev, I., Pérez, P.: Cross-view action recognition from temporal self-similarities. In: Forsyth, D., Torr, P., Zisserman, A. (eds.) ECCV 2008, Part II. LNCS, vol. 5303, pp. 293–306. Springer, Heidelberg (2008)
11. Kläser, A., Marszałek, M., Schmid, C.: A spatio-temporal descriptor based on 3d-gradients. In: BMVC (2008)
12. Laptev, I., Marszalek, M., Schmid, C., Rozenfeld, B.: Learning realistic human actions from movies. In: CVPR (2008)
13. Lin, Z., Jiang, Z., Davis, L.S.: Recognizing actions by shape-motion prototype trees. In: ICCV (2009)
14. Liu, J., Shah, M.: Learning human actions via information maximization. In: CVPR (2008)
15. Parameswaran, V., Chellappa, R.: View invariants for human action recognition. In: CVPR, vol. 2, pp. II–613–II–19 (2003)
16. Rao, C., Yilmaz, A., Shah, M.: View-invariant representation and recognition of actions. In: IJCV, vol. 50(2), pp. 203–226 (2002)
17. Reddy, K.K., Liu, J., Shah, M.: Incremental action recognition using feature-tree. In: ICCV (2009)
18. Rodriguez, M.D., Ahmed, J., Shah, M.: Action mach a spatio-temporal maximum average correlation height filter for action recognition. In: CVPR, pp. 1–8 (2008)
19. Schindler, K., van Gool, L.: Action snippets: How many frames does human action recognition require? In: CVPR, pp. 1–8 (2008)
20. Schuldt, C., Laptev, I., Caputo, B.: Recognizing human actions: A local svm approach. In: ICPR, pp. 32–36 (2004)
21. Serre, T., Wolf, L., Poggio, T.: Object recognition with features inspired by visual cortex. In: CVPR (2005)
22. Thurau, C., Hlavac, V.: Pose primitive based human action recognition in videos or still images. In: CVPR, pp. 1–8 (2008)
23. Tran, D., Sorokin, A.: Human activity recognition with metric learning. In: Forsyth, D., Torr, P., Zisserman, A. (eds.) ECCV 2008, Part I. LNCS, vol. 5302, pp. 548–561. Springer, Heidelberg (2008)
24. Wang, H., Ullah, M.M., Kläser, A., Laptev, I., Schmid, C.: Evaluation of local spatio-temporal features for action recognition. In: BMVC (2009)
25. Wang, X., Han, T.X., Yan, S.: An hog-lbp human detector with partial occlusion handling. In: ICCV (2009)
26. Weinland, D., Boyer, E.: Action recognition using exemplar-based embedding. In: CVPR (2008)
27. Weinland, D., Boyer, E., Ronfard, R.: Action recognition from arbitrary views using 3d exemplars. In: ICCV (2007)
28. Yan, P., Khan, S.M., Shah, M.: Learning 4d action feature models for arbitrary view action recognition. In: CVPR (2008)

Structured Output Ordinal Regression for Dynamic Facial Emotion Intensity Prediction

Minyoung Kim and Vladimir Pavlovic

Department of Computer Science, Rutgers University
110 Frelinghuysen Road, Piscataway, NJ 08854-8019, USA
{mikim,vladimir}@cs.rutgers.edu
http://seqam.rutgers.edu

Abstract. We consider the task of labeling facial emotion intensities in videos, where the emotion intensities to be predicted have ordinal scales (e.g., low, medium, and high) that change in time. A significant challenge is that the rates of increase and decrease differ substantially across subjects. Moreover, the actual absolute differences of intensity values carry little information, with their relative order being more important. To solve the intensity prediction problem we propose a new dynamic ranking model that models the signal intensity at each time as a label on an ordinal scale and links the temporally proximal labels using dynamic smoothness constraints. This new model extends the successful static ordinal regression to a structured (dynamic) setting by using an analogy with Conditional Random Field (CRF) models in structured classification. We show that, although non-convex, the new model can be accurately learned using efficient gradient search. The predictions resulting from this dynamic ranking model show significant improvements over the regular CRFs, which fail to consider ordinal relationships between predicted labels. We also observe substantial improvements over static ranking models that do not exploit temporal dependencies of ordinal predictions. We demonstrate the benefits of our algorithm on the Cohn-Kanade dataset for the dynamic facial emotion intensity prediction problem and illustrate its performance in a controlled synthetic setting.

Keywords: Video-based Facial Emotion Intensity Analysis, Ordinal Regression, Ranking, Structured Output Prediction.

1 Introduction

A typical task in analyzing video sequences of human emotions (e.g., facial expressions) or hand gestures is to divide the sequence into segments corresponding to different phases or intensities of the displayed artifact. For example, facial emotion signals typically follow envelope-like shapes in time: `neutral`, `increase`, `peak`, and `decrease`, beginning with low intensity, reaching a maximum, then tapering off. A significant challenge in modeling such an envelop is that the rates of increase and decrease differ substantially across subjects (e.g., different

K. Daniilidis, P. Maragos, N. Paragios (Eds.): ECCV 2010, Part III, LNCS 6313, pp. 649–662, 2010.

subjects express the same emotion with substantially different intensities). However, for subsequent recognition of different emotions across subject pools the absolute difference of intensity values is, to a large extent, less significant than the general envelope shape. Qualitative labeling and ranking is also preferred by human annotators, who can more easily judge coarse relative relationships instead of the absolute signal differences. In this work we propose to address these problems by modeling the shape of the emotion intensity envelope using a new structured ordinal regression approach, an extension of ranking to dynamic (structured) sequence domains.

The ordinal regression, often called the preference learning or ranking, is an emerging topic in the machine learning community [1] and has found applications in several traditional ranking problems, such as image classification and collaborative filtering [2,3], or image retrieval [4,5]. In the static setting, we want to predict the label y of an item represented by feature vector $\mathbf{x} \in \mathbb{R}^p$ where the output bears particular meaning of preference or order (e.g., low, medium or high). The ordinal regression is fundamentally different from the standard regression in that the actual absolute difference of output values is nearly meaningless, but only their relative order matters (e.g., low $<$ medium $<$ high). The ordinal regression problems may not be optimally handled by the standard multi-class classification either because of classifier's ignorance of the ordinal scale and independent treatment of different output categories (e.g., low would be equally different from high as it would be from medium).

Despite success in static settings (i.e., vectorial input and a singleton output label), ranking problems are rarely explored in structured output prediction problems, such as the segmentation of emotion signal into regions of neutral, increasing or peak emotion. In this case the ranks or ordinal labels at different time instances should vary smoothly, with temporally proximal instances likely to have similar ranks. One may model this rank envelope by enforcing that the intensity rank at time $t-1$ has to be higher (or lower, depending on which part of the envelope one is on) than the next intensity at time t. Learning a static ranking model individually and independently for each time slice, however, fails to impose the same constraints during the decoding of test sequences.

In this work, we propose an intuitive but principled Conditional Random Field (CRF)-like model that can faithfully represent multiple ranking outputs correlated in a combinatorial structure (e.g., sequence or lattice). The binning modeling strategy adopted by recent static ranking approaches (see (2) in Sec. 2.1) is incorporated into our structured models through graph-based potential functions. This formulation leads to a family of log-nonlinear models that can still be estimated with high accuracy using general gradient-based search approaches. By considering the models that take into account the dynamically changing ranks of different emotion segments instead of their absolute intensity we are able to learn intensity-based segmentation of emotion sequences which is largely invariant to intra- and inter-subject variations.

We formally setup the problem and introduce basic notation below. We then briefly review the static ordinal regression in Sec. 2.1 and the CRF model in

Sec. 2.2, traditionally aimed at non-ordinal scale structured output classification. Our ordinal regression models are described in Sec. 3. After reviewing the related work in Sec. 4, we provide the experimental results in Sec. 5 where the superior prediction performance of the proposed structured output ranking model to the regular CRF model is demonstrated on both synthetic dataset and the real facial emotion intensity prediction problem on the Cohn-Kanade expression database.

1.1 Problem Setup and Notations

In the structured output prediction problems we deal with *multiple* output variables denoted by boldfaced $\mathbf{y}$ for distinction. $\mathbf{y}$ is composed of individual output variables y_r (i.e., $\mathbf{y} = \{y_r\}$) where r is the variable index. Each output variable is assumed to take one of R different categories (i.e., $y_r \in \{1, \ldots, R\}$) which are either nominal (regular classification) or ordinal (ranking or ordinal regression). Although it is fairly straightforward to extend our framework to arbitrary output structures, here we assume that the output variables y_r in $\mathbf{y}$ are correlated in a 1-D temporal structure, with r being the time index. The observation, denoted by $\mathbf{x} = \{\mathbf{x}_r\}$, is structured similarly as the output $\mathbf{y}$, and serves as input covariate for predicting $\mathbf{y}$.

Throughout the paper, we assume a supervised setting: we are given a training set of n data pairs $\mathcal{D} = \{(\mathbf{x}^i, \mathbf{y}^i)\}_{i=1}^n$, which are i.i.d. samples from an underlying but unknown distribution $P_*(\mathbf{x}, \mathbf{y})$.

2 Static Ordinal Regression and Traditional Sequence Segmentation

2.1 Ordinal Regression

The goal of ordinal regression is to predict the label y of an item represented by a feature vector[1] $\mathbf{x} \in \mathbb{R}^p$ where the output indicates the preference or order of this item. Formally, we let $y \in \{1, \ldots, R\}$ for which R is the number of preference grades, and y takes an ordinal scale from the lowest preference $y = 1$ to the highest $y = R$, $y = 1 \prec y = 2 \prec \ldots \prec y = R$.

The most critical aspect that differentiates the ordinal regression approaches from the multi-class classification methods is the modeling strategy. Assuming a linear modeling (straightforwardly extendible to a nonlinear version by kernel tricks), the multi-class classification typically (c.f. [6]) takes the form of

$$y = \arg\max_{c \in \{1, \ldots, R\}} \mathbf{w}_c^\top \mathbf{x} + b_c. \tag{1}$$

For each class c, the hyperplane ($\mathbf{w}_c \in \mathbb{R}^p$, $b_c \in \mathbb{R}$) defines the confidence toward the class c. The class decision is made by selecting the one with the largest

---

[1] We use the notation $\mathbf{x}$ interchangeably for both a sequence observation $\mathbf{x} = \{\mathbf{x}_r\}$ and a vector, which is clearly distinguished by context.

confidence. The model parameters are $\{\{\mathbf{w}_c\}_{c=1}^R, \{b_c\}_{c=1}^R\}$. On the other hand, the recent ordinal regression approaches adopt the following modeling strategy:

$$y = c \text{ iff } \mathbf{w}^\top \mathbf{x} \in (b_{c-1}, b_c], \text{ where } -\infty = b_0 \leq b_1 \leq \cdots \leq b_R = +\infty. \quad (2)$$

The binning parameters $\{b_c\}_{c=0}^R$ form R different bins, where their adjacent placement and the output deciding protocol of (2) naturally enforces the ordinal scale criteria. The parameters of the model become $\{\mathbf{w}, \{b_c\}_{c=0}^R\}$, far fewer than those of the classification models. The state-of-the-art Support Vector Ordinal Regression (SVOR) algorithms [2, 3] conform to this representation while they aim at maximizing margins at the nearby bins in the SVM formulation.

2.2 Conditional Random Fields for Sequence Segmentation

CRF [7, 8] is a log-linear model that represents the conditional distribution $P(\mathbf{y}|\mathbf{x})$ as the Gibbs form clamped on the observation $\mathbf{x}$:

$$P(\mathbf{y}|\mathbf{x}, \boldsymbol{\theta}) = Z(\mathbf{x}; \boldsymbol{\theta})^{-1} e^{s(\mathbf{x}, \mathbf{y}; \boldsymbol{\theta})}. \quad (3)$$

Here $Z(\mathbf{x}; \boldsymbol{\theta}) = \sum_{\mathbf{y} \in \mathcal{Y}} e^{s(\mathbf{x}, \mathbf{y}; \boldsymbol{\theta})}$ is the normalizing partition function ($\mathcal{Y}$ is a set of all possible output configurations), and $\boldsymbol{\theta}$ is the parameters[2] of the *score function* (or the negative energy) that can be written as:

$$s(\mathbf{x}, \mathbf{y}; \boldsymbol{\theta}) = \boldsymbol{\theta}^\top \boldsymbol{\Psi}(\mathbf{x}, \mathbf{y}), \quad (4)$$

where $\boldsymbol{\Psi}(\mathbf{x}, \mathbf{y})$ is the joint feature vector.

The choice of the output graph $G = (V, E)$ and the cliques critically affects model's representational capacity and the inference complexity. For the notational convenience, we further assume that we have either *node* cliques ($r \in V$) or *edge* cliques ($e = (r, s) \in E$). We denote the node features by $\boldsymbol{\Psi}_r^{(V)}(\mathbf{x}, y_r)$ and the edge features by $\boldsymbol{\Psi}_e^{(E)}(\mathbf{x}, y_r, y_s)$. Letting $\boldsymbol{\theta} = \{\mathbf{v}, \mathbf{u}\}$ be the parameters for node and edge features, respectively, the score function can be expressed as:

$$s(\mathbf{x}, \mathbf{y}; \boldsymbol{\theta}) = \sum_{r \in V} \mathbf{v}^\top \boldsymbol{\Psi}_r^{(V)}(\mathbf{x}, y_r) + \sum_{e=(r,s) \in E} \mathbf{u}^\top \boldsymbol{\Psi}_e^{(E)}(\mathbf{x}, y_r, y_s). \quad (5)$$

Although the representation in (5) is so general that it can subsume nearly arbitrary forms of features, in the conventional modeling practice, the node/edge features are often defined as the product of measurement features confined to cliques and the output class indicators. More specifically, denoting the measurement feature vector at node r as $\boldsymbol{\phi}(\mathbf{x}_r)$, the node feature becomes:

$$\boldsymbol{\Psi}_r^{(V)}(\mathbf{x}, y_r) = \left[I(y_r = 1), \cdots, I(y_r = R)\right]^\top \otimes \boldsymbol{\phi}(\mathbf{x}_r), \quad (6)$$

where $I(\cdot)$ is the indicator function that returns 1 (0) if the argument is true (false) and $\otimes$ denotes the Kronecker product. Hence the k-th block ($k = 1, \ldots, R$)

---

[2] For simplicity, we often drop the dependency on $\boldsymbol{\theta}$ in notations.

of $\boldsymbol{\Psi}_r^{(V)}(\mathbf{x}, y_r)$ is $\boldsymbol{\phi}(\mathbf{x}_r)$ if $y_r = k$, and the **0**-vector otherwise. The edge feature is similarly defined where we typically employ the absolute difference between measurement features at adjoining nodes. Thus, $\boldsymbol{\Psi}_e^{(E)}(\mathbf{x}, y_r, y_s)$ is

$$\left[I(y_r = k \ \wedge \ y_s = l)\right]_{R \times R} \otimes |\boldsymbol{\phi}(\mathbf{x}_r) - \boldsymbol{\phi}(\mathbf{x}_s)|. \tag{7}$$

These feature forms are commonly used in CRFs with sequence [7] and lattice outputs [8, 9]. We call the product of parameters and the feature vectors on a clique the *(clique) potential*. For instance, $\mathbf{v}^\top \boldsymbol{\Psi}_r^{(V)}(\mathbf{x}, y_r)$ and $\mathbf{u}^\top \boldsymbol{\Psi}_e^{(E)}(\mathbf{x}, y_r, y_s)$ are the node potential and the edge potential, respectively. Hence the score function is the sum of the potentials over all cliques in the graph.

3   Structured Output Ordinal Regression Model

The above standard CRF modeling aims at *classification*, treating each output category nominally and equally different from all other categories. The consequence is that the model's node potential has a direct analogy to the static multi-class classification model of (1): For $y_r = c$, the node potential equals $\mathbf{v}_c^\top \boldsymbol{\phi}(\mathbf{x}_r)$ where $\mathbf{v}_c$ is the c-th block of $\mathbf{v}$, which corresponds to the c-th hyperplane $\mathbf{w}_c^\top \mathbf{x}_r + b_c$ in (1). The max can be replaced by the *softmax* function. To setup an exact equality, one can let $\boldsymbol{\phi}(\mathbf{x}_r) = [1, \mathbf{x}_r^\top]^\top$.

Conversely, the modeling strategy of the static ordinal regression methods such as (2) can be merged with the CRF through the node potentials to yield a structured output ranking model. The mechanism of doing so is not obvious because of the highly discontinuous nature of (2). We based our approach on the probabilistic model for ranking proposed by [10], which shares the notion of (2).

In [10], the noiseless probabilistic ranking likelihood is defined as

$$P_{ideal}(y = c | f(\mathbf{x})) = \begin{cases} 1 \text{ if } f(\mathbf{x}) \in (b_{c-1}, b_c] \\ 0 \text{ otherwise} \end{cases} \tag{8}$$

Here $f(\mathbf{x})$ is the model to be learned, which could be linear $f(\mathbf{x}) = \mathbf{w}^\top \mathbf{x}$. The effective ranking likelihood is constructed by contaminating the ideal model with noise. Under the Gaussian noise δ and after marginalization, one arrives at the ranking likelihood

$$P(y = c | f(\mathbf{x})) = \int_\delta P_{ideal}(y = c | f(\mathbf{x}) + \delta) \cdot \mathcal{N}(\delta; 0, \sigma^2) d\delta = \Phi\left(\frac{b_c - f}{\sigma}\right) - \Phi\left(\frac{b_{c-1} - f}{\sigma}\right), \tag{9}$$

where $\Phi(\cdot)$ is the standard normal cdf, and σ is the parameter that controls the steepness of the likelihood function.

Now we set the node potential at node r of the CRF to be the log-likelihood of (9), that is,

$$\mathbf{v}^\top \boldsymbol{\Psi}_r^{(V)}(\mathbf{x}, y_r) \longrightarrow \boldsymbol{\Gamma}_r^{(V)}(\mathbf{x}, y_r; \{\mathbf{a}, \mathbf{b}, \sigma\}), \quad \text{where}$$

$$\boldsymbol{\Gamma}_r^{(V)}(\mathbf{x}, y_r) := \sum_{c=1}^R I(y_r = c) \cdot \log\left(\Phi\left(\frac{b_c - \mathbf{a}^\top \boldsymbol{\phi}(\mathbf{x}_r)}{\sigma}\right) - \Phi\left(\frac{b_{c-1} - \mathbf{a}^\top \boldsymbol{\phi}(\mathbf{x}_r)}{\sigma}\right)\right). \tag{10}$$

Here, $\mathbf{a}$ (having the same dimension as $\phi(\mathbf{x}_r)$), $\mathbf{b} = [-\infty = b_0, \ldots, b_R = +\infty]^\top$, and σ are the new parameters, in contrast with the original CRF's node parameters $\mathbf{v}$. Substituting this expression into (5) leads to a new conditional model for structured ranking,

$$P(\mathbf{y}|\mathbf{x}, \Omega) \propto \exp\left(\sum_{r \in V} \Gamma_r^{(V)}(\mathbf{x}, y_r; \{\mathbf{a}, \mathbf{b}, \sigma\}) + \sum_{e=(r,s) \in E} \mathbf{u}^\top \Psi_e^{(E)}(\mathbf{x}, y_r, y_s) \right). \quad (11)$$

We refer to this model as *CORF*, the Conditional Ordinal Random Field. The parameters of the CORF are denoted as $\Omega = \{\mathbf{a}, \mathbf{b}, \sigma, \mathbf{u}\}$, with the ordering constraint $b_i < b_{i+1}, \forall i$. Note that the number of parameters is significantly fewer than that of the regular CRF.

Due to the nonlinear dependency of Γ on $\{\mathbf{a}, \mathbf{b}, \sigma\}$, (11) becomes a *log-nonlinear* model. It should first be noted that the new nonlinear modeling does not impose any additional complexity on the inference task. Since the graph topology remains the same, once the potentials are evaluated, the inference follows exactly the same procedures as that of the standard log-linear CRFs. Second, it is not difficult to see that the node potential $\Gamma_r^{(V)}(\mathbf{x}, y_r)$, although non-linear, remains concave.

Unfortunately, the overall learning of CORF is non-convex because of the log-partition function (*log-sum-exp* of nonlinear concave functions). However, the log-likelihood objective is bounded above by 0, and the quasi-Newton or the stochastic gradient ascent [9] can be used to estimate the model parameters. We briefly describe the learning strategy. Initially, we set the edge parameters $\mathbf{u} = 0$ to form a static ranking model that treats each node independently. After learning the node parameters $\{\mathbf{a}, \mathbf{b}, \sigma\}$, we optimize the model w.r.t. $\mathbf{u}$ by gradient search while fixing the node parameters. The gradient of the log-likelihood w.r.t. $\mathbf{u}$ is (the same as the regular CRF):

$$\frac{\partial \log P(\mathbf{y}|\mathbf{x}, \Omega)}{\partial \mathbf{u}} = \sum_{e=(r,s) \in E} \left(\Psi_e^{(E)}(\mathbf{x}, y_r, y_s) - \mathbb{E}_{P(y_r, y_s|\mathbf{x})}\left[\Psi_e^{(E)}(\mathbf{x}, y_r, y_s) \right] \right). \quad (12)$$

Once we obtain the initial Ω, we can start gradient search simultaneously for the whole parameters. The gradient of the log-likelihood w.r.t. $\mu = \{\mathbf{a}, \mathbf{b}, \sigma\}$ can be derived as:

$$\frac{\partial \log P(\mathbf{y}|\mathbf{x}, \Omega)}{\partial \mu} = \sum_{r \in V} \left(\frac{\partial \Gamma_r^{(V)}(\mathbf{x}, y_r)}{\partial \mu} - \mathbb{E}_{P(y_r|\mathbf{x})}\left[\frac{\partial \Gamma_r^{(V)}(\mathbf{x}, y_r)}{\partial \mu} \right] \right), \quad (13)$$

where the gradient of the node potential can be computed analytically,

$$\frac{\partial \Gamma_r^{(V)}(\mathbf{x}, y_r)}{\partial \mu} = \sum_{c=1}^R I(y_r = c) \cdot \frac{\mathcal{N}(z_0(r,c); 0, 1) \cdot \frac{\partial z_0(r,c)}{\partial \mu} - \mathcal{N}(z_1(r,c); 0, 1) \cdot \frac{\partial z_1(r,c)}{\partial \mu}}{\Phi(z_0(r,c)) - \Phi(z_1(r,c))},$$

$$\text{where } z_k(r, c) = \frac{b_{c-k} - \mathbf{a}^\top \phi(\mathbf{x}_r)}{\sigma} \text{ for } k = 0, 1. \quad (14)$$

3.1   Model Reparameterization for Unconstrained Optimization

The gradient-based learning proposed above has to be accomplished while respecting two sets of constraints: (i) the order constraints on **b**: $\{b_{j-1} \leq b_j$ for $j = 1, \ldots, R\}$, and (ii) the positive scale constraint on σ: $\{\sigma > 0\}$. Instead of general constrained optimization, we introduce a reparameterization that effectively reduces the problem to an unconstrained optimization task.

To deal with the order constraints in the parameters **b**, we introduce the displacement variables δ_k, where $b_j = b_1 + \sum_{k=1}^{j-1} \delta_k^2$ for $j = 2, \ldots, R-1$. So, **b** is replaced by the unconstrained parameters $\{b_1, \delta_1, \ldots, \delta_{R-2}\}$. The positiveness constraint for σ is simply handled by introducing the free parameter σ_0 where $\sigma = \sigma_0^2$. Hence, the unconstrained node parameters are: $\{\mathbf{a}, b_1, \delta_1, \ldots, \delta_{R-2}, \sigma_0\}$. Then the gradients for $\frac{\partial z_k(r,c)}{\partial \mu}$ in (14) then become:

$$\frac{\partial z_k(r,c)}{\partial \mathbf{a}} = -\frac{1}{\sigma_0^2}\phi(\mathbf{x}_r), \quad \frac{\partial z_k(r,c)}{\partial \sigma_0} = -\frac{2\big(b_{c-k} - \mathbf{a}^\top \phi(\mathbf{x}_r)\big)}{\sigma_0^3}, \quad \text{for } k = 0, 1. \quad (15)$$

$$\frac{\partial z_0(r,c)}{\partial b_1} = \begin{cases} 0 & \text{if } c = R \\ \frac{1}{\sigma_0^2} & \text{otherwise} \end{cases}, \quad \frac{\partial z_1(r,c)}{\partial b_1} = \begin{cases} 0 & \text{if } c = 1 \\ \frac{1}{\sigma_0^2} & \text{otherwise} \end{cases}. \quad (16)$$

$$\frac{\partial z_0(r,c)}{\partial \delta_j} = \begin{cases} 0 & \text{if } c \in \{1, \ldots, j, R\} \\ \frac{2\delta_j}{\sigma_0^2} & \text{otherwise} \end{cases}, \quad \frac{\partial z_1(r,c)}{\partial \delta_j} = \begin{cases} 0 & \text{if } c \in \{1, \ldots, j+1\} \\ \frac{2\delta_j}{\sigma_0^2} & \text{otherwise} \end{cases},$$

$$\text{for } j = 1, \ldots, R-2. \quad (17)$$

We additionally employ parameter regularization on the CORF model. For **a** and **u**, we use the typical L2 regularizers $||\mathbf{a}||^2$ and $||\mathbf{u}||^2$. No specific regularization is necessary for the binning parameters b_1 and $\{\delta_j\}_{j=1}^{R-2}$ as they will be automatically adjusted according to the score $\mathbf{a}^\top \phi(\mathbf{x}_r)$. For the scale parameter σ_0 we consider $(\log \sigma_0^2)^2$ as the regularizer, which essentially favors $\sigma_0 \approx 1$ and imposes quadratic penalty in log-scale.

4   Related Work

Developing sequence-based regressors is a recently emerging problem in computer vision. Some related work includes [11] where the problem of dynamic state estimation was tacked by the conditional state space model, an extension of the CRF to the continuous multi-variate output domain. The difficult density integrability constraints were effectively handled by the convex parameter learning. In [12], the joint task of localization and output prediction was considered, aiming at structured prediction and salient input selection at the same time. The approach can be particularly beneficial for un-segmented image/video data.

More closely related to our work, [13] proposes a ranking model based on relations between objects to be ranked, in an document retrieval setting. Unlike our CORF model the proposed continuous CRF model is a general regression model, and unable to impose the ordinal monotonicity constraints. [14] considered the sequence output prediction problem in which the outputs are partially orderable sentiments in a document. Their model is a restricted subset of the CRF. To enforce the monotonicity constraints, they introduced a set of constraints on the CRF parameters based on the strong correlation between specific ordinal states and related binary features, also dependent on the positivity of the sentiment. Hence their approach may be restricted to discrete/binary observations/features and the particular application of the local sentiment flow estimation problem. Unlike these limitations, our approach is applicable to general features and applications since we impose the ordinal constraints on the potential functions.

5   Evaluations

We empirically demonstrate the performance of the proposed CORF model on the sequence labeling problem where each of the output states to be predicted has an ordinal scale. We first consider a synthetic setting, with sequences generated from a model with complex switching dynamics, where the ordinal output states are obtained by discretizing the true system states to emulate an ordinal preference scale. Next, we test the algorithm on the problem of predicting the emotion intensity from the facial image sequence. Each emotion state consists of three different intensity levels, neutral < increasing < apex, which naturally encode the total ordering typically exhibited in dynamic emotion sequences.

In these experiments, we focus on contrasting the performance of our CORF model with the standard CRF which treats the output categories as nominal classes. For both models, the optimization is accomplished using the quasi-Newton limited-BFGS method with a sufficiently large number of iterations to ensure the convergence in the regularized log-likelihood objective within a permissible precision. The balancing tradeoff between the regularization and the log-likelihood terms is estimated by grid search under cross validation. For both models the optimization starts from the zero-valued parameters with the exception of the displacement parameters $\delta_j = 1$ and the scale parameter $\sigma_0 = 1$ for the CORF.

5.1   Synthetic Sequences from Switching Linear Dynamical Systems

Ordinal scales can arise from observing and qualitatively quantizing the states of complex physical processes, while retaining mutual ordering of the quantized states. To simulate a complex physical dynamic processes, we consider the switching linear dynamical system (SLDS) [15]. We then quantize the states of the SLDS using an ordinal scale and seek to infer those dynamic ranks from observations.

In SLDS, the dynamical process can undergo transitions among different switching states over time, which are governed by different linear dynamic models. The overall system can be described using the state-space equations:

$$\mathbf{y}_t = \mathbf{A}(s_{t-1}) \cdot \mathbf{y}_{t-1} + \mathbf{v}_t(s_t), \quad \mathbf{x}_t = \mathbf{C}(s_t) \cdot \mathbf{y}_t + \mathbf{w}_t(s_t), \quad P(s_t = i | s_{t-1} = j) = \mathbf{Q}_{ij},$$

where $\mathbf{y}_t \in \mathbb{R}^d$ is the d-variate system state at time t, $\mathbf{x}_t \in \mathbb{R}^p$ is the p-variate observation features, and s_t is the (discrete) switching state taking K different states ($s_t = 1, \ldots, K$). The system parameters consist of $(\mathbf{A}(j), \mathbf{C}(j)) \in (\mathbb{R}^{d \times d}, \mathbb{R}^{p \times d})$ for each switching state $j = 1, \ldots, K$, and the ($K \times K$) switching transition matrix $\mathbf{Q}$. The model takes into account the white noises $\mathbf{v}_t$ and $\mathbf{w}_t$.

We design the SLDS model with $K = 8$ switching states, $d = 1$-dim system state, and $p = 4$-dim observation features while properly choosing the model parameters and the (Gaussian) white noise variances (i.e., all system dynamics are stable, $|\mathbf{A}(j)| < 1$). We then generate 10 sequences from the SLDS model, where the sequence length T varies as $T \sim \mathcal{N}(500, 30^2)$. For the generated sequences, we regard the system state $\mathbf{y}_t$ as the output to be predicted at time t while $\mathbf{x}_t$ is the input feature vector at time t. To convert the real-valued $\mathbf{y}_t$ to ordinal-scale discrete-valued y_t, we discretize $\mathbf{y}_t$ into $R = 6$ categories, with each category being equally likely. We generate ten pairs of such sequences, one of which ($\mathbf{y}$) is illustrated in Fig. 1 as the blue dotted curve.

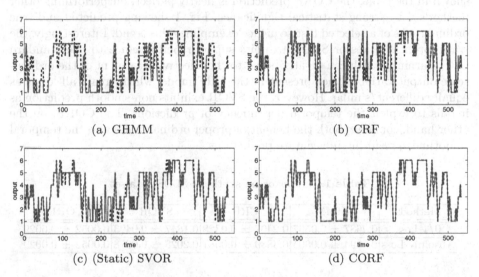

(a) GHMM   (b) CRF

(c) (Static) SVOR   (d) CORF

Fig. 1. Output prediction for synthetic SLDS sequences. The ground truth is depicted as blue dashed line while the predicted outputs are red solid lines.

For this set we perform leave-one-out validation. The average test errors (means and standard deviations) of the competing approaches are shown in Table 1. Here we present both the average 0/1 loss ($\frac{1}{T} \sum_t I(y_t \neq \overline{y}_t)$) and the absolute loss ($\frac{1}{T} \sum_t |y_t - \overline{y}_t|$), where y_t and $\overline{y}_t$ are the predicted and the ground-truth label, respectively.

To see the baseline performance, we first test the Gaussian HMM (denoted by GHMM) where its hidden state at time t represents the ordinal label y_t. Hence the joint likelihood maximization leads to a one-shot learning with no latent variables. The label prediction for a given test sequence can be accomplished using the well-known Viterbi decoding. The next model we contrast with is the regular

CRF. For the measurement features for the CRF, we use the quadratic expansion of $\mathbf{x}_t$ yielding 15-dim node features, which corresponds to the GHMM's Gaussian measurement modeling. The edge features are simply set to 1 to mimic GHMM's transition matrix. Not surprisingly, the CRF's discriminative modeling improves the prediction performance over the generative GHMM models.

We also compare our approach with the *static* ordinal regression approaches, which have been studied considerably in the machine learning community. These approaches are static and unable to handle structured outputs in a principled manner as they treat the time slices $\{(y_t, \mathbf{x}_t)\}_t$ as i.i.d. samples. Here we consider one of the most recent approaches[3], the support vector ordinal regression (SVOR) of [3], which optimizes multiple thresholds to define parallel discriminant hyperplanes for the ordinal scales. We use the method with explicit constraints. The features for the SVOR are the same as the node features of the CRFs. The SVM hyperparameters are selected by 5-fold cross validation.

Our CORF model again uses the same node/edge features as the CRF. As shown in the table, the CORF prediction is nearly perfect, outperforming other methods with strong statistical significance. Fig. 1 showing predicted and true ordinal ranks of a selected test sequence exemplifies this trend. Interestingly, the static ordinal regressor SVOR exhibits superior performance to the standard CRF learning, which can be attributed to the effective treatment of the ordinal-scale output variables, not present in the CRF model which treats all levels as equally different/similar. However, the SVOR exhibits non-smooth prediction as it fails to exploit the temporal dependency of predictions. The CORF, on the other hand, combines both the benefit of proper ordinal scales and the temporal smoothness, resulting in accurate predictions.

Table 1. Test errors in synthetic SLDS data set

Methods	GHMM	CRF	SVOR	CORF
0/1 Loss	0.4687 ± 0.0567	0.2407 ± 0.0328	0.1847 ± 0.0493	0.0052 ± 0.0029
Absolute Loss	0.5894 ± 0.0605	0.3830 ± 0.0581	0.2028 ± 0.0678	0.0052 ± 0.0029

5.2 Dynamic Facial Emotion Intensity Prediction

The next task we consider is the facial emotion intensity prediction. We use the Cohn-Kanade facial expression database [16], which consists of six basic emotions (anger, disgust, fear, happiness, sadness, and surprise) performed by 100 students aged from 18 to 30 years old. In this experiment, we selected image sequences from 96 subjects. We randomly select 66 subjects as the training set, and the rest subjects as the testing set. After detecting faces by the cascaded face detector [17], we normalize them into (64×64) images which are aligned based on the eye locations similar to [18].

---

[3] We also tested the static approach [10], the Gaussian process ordinal regressor (GPOR). However, its test performance on this dataset was far worse than that of the SVOR.

Facial expression recognition is an active research area in computer vision [19, 20, 21, 22]. Unlike the traditional settings (e.g., [21]) where just the ending few peak frames are considered, we use the entire sequences that cover the onset of the expression all the way to the apex in order to conduct the task of dynamic emotion intensity labeling. The sequence lengths are about 20-frame long on average.

The frames in the sequences are manually labeled into three ordinal categories: neutral < increasing < apex. Overall the increasing state takes about $10 \sim 30\%$ of the frames in each sequence, while the other two states occupy the rest roughly equally on average. For the image features, we first extract the Haar-like features, following [22]. To reduce feature dimensionality, we apply PCA on the training frames for each emotion, which gives rise to $20 \sim 30$ dimensional feature vectors corresponding to 95% of the total energy. To normalize the sequence, we subtract the initial-frame feature vector from the subsequent frames, i.e., $\mathbf{x}_t \leftarrow \mathbf{x}_t - \mathbf{x}_1$.

The average per-frame test errors within each emotion class are shown in Table 2. Here we also contrasted with the static ordinal regression approach based on the probabilistic model, called the Gaussian process ordinal regressor (GPOR) [10]. Although the GPOR performs better than the SVOR in this problem, its independent treatment of the frames in sequences yields inferior performance to the dynamic models.

Our CORF consistently performs best for all emotions, exhibiting performance superior to the regular CRF that fails to consider ordering relationships between intensity levels. The static ordinal regressors (SVOR and GPOR) often result in highly biased predictions (e.g., either all neutral frames or all apex), which signifies the importance of capturing the smooth emotion dynamics in this problem. Interestingly, most approaches yield higher errors for "sadness" than other emotions, such as say "surprise". By visually inspecting the videos of these emotions, we have noticed that the intensity variations of "sadness" are far more subtle to discriminate than "surprise". For some selected test sequences, we also depict the decoded intensities by the CRF and the CORF in Fig. 2.

Table 2. Average test errors in facial emotion intensity prediction

(a) Anger

Loss	GHMM	CRF	SVOR	GPOR	CORF
0/1	0.4059	0.2890	0.6103	0.5735	**0.1817**
Abs.	0.4276	0.2951	0.8534	0.7977	**0.2017**

(b) Disgust

Loss	GHMM	CRF	SVOR	GPOR	CORF
0/1	0.1493	0.1154	0.5938	0.5187	**0.0582**
Abs.	0.1493	0.1154	0.9417	0.5662	**0.0582**

(c) Fear

Loss	GHMM	CRF	SVOR	GPOR	CORF
0/1	0.2941	0.2530	0.5733	0.4416	**0.1689**
Abs.	0.2971	0.2564	0.9051	0.6533	**0.1689**

(d) Happiness

Loss	GHMM	CRF	SVOR	GPOR	CORF
0/1	0.2954	0.2341	0.4964	0.4216	**0.1617**
Abs.	0.3035	0.2341	0.7876	0.4515	**0.1617**

(e) Sadness

Loss	GHMM	CRF	SVOR	GPOR	CORF
0/1	0.4598	0.3538	0.6287	0.5561	**0.2760**
Abs.	0.5754	0.4388	0.9836	0.8993	**0.3405**

(f) Surprise

Loss	GHMM	CRF	SVOR	GPOR	CORF
0/1	0.1632	0.1397	0.5855	0.4065	**0.0924**
Abs.	0.1632	0.1397	0.9563	0.5984	**0.0924**

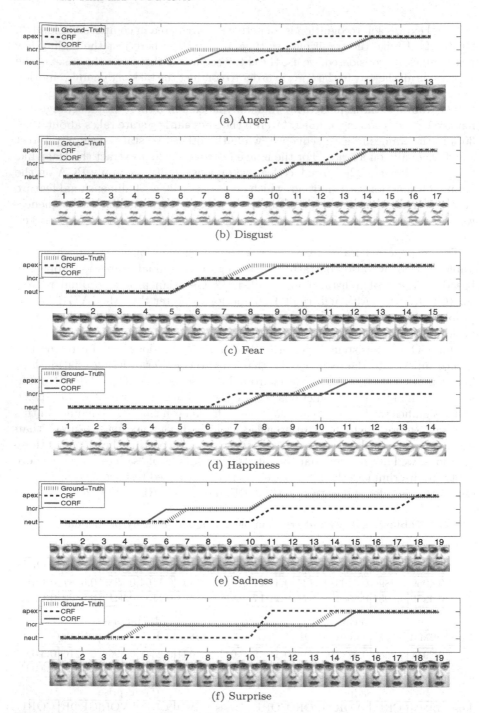

Fig. 2. Facial emotion intensity prediction results for some test sequences. The ground truth is depicted as blue dotted line while the predicted outputs of the regular CRF and the CORF are in black dashed and red solid lines, respectively.

5.3   Discussion and Conclusions

Our approach, much like the similar modeling strategies in static ranking / ordinal regression settings [1,2], treats the ordinal-scale states as intervals on a real line using a binning model. As a consequence, ordering and distinct inter-relationship between different ranks/labels is preserved, which is of essence when modeling ordinal processes. As discussed in [1, 2], the multi-class SVM, and similarly the regular CRF in the dynamic setting, ignore the total ordering of the class labels. These classification-based models fail to model the correlation among the hyperplanes (or potentials in the CRFs) representing the classes, a task necessary for preserving the distinction of relationships among labels.

Another crucial aspect of our CORF model is its ability to preserve the transitivity and asymmetry of the ordinal scale states. As alluded to in [1], learning of preference relations may not be properly treated as a standard classification problem by considering pairs of objects since the properties of transitivity and asymmetry may be violated by traditional approaches due to the problem of stochastic transitivity.

The binning-based node potentials in our model also tend to yield smaller errors as they focus on closest neighboring intervals. That is, when the misclassification occurs, it is more likely to be close to the true class (interval) in the total ordering. On the other hand, in the regular CRF, the class-wise node potentials compete with one another "independently", failing to make use of proximity constraints. As a consequence, the misclassifications away from the true "label" incur higher cost in the ordinal regression compared to the label-distance agnostic classification setting. This all leads to more accurate predictions by CORF on classes of problems where ordinal scales are critical but have been commonly tackled as classification problems.

While this work focuses on the intensity estimation and segmentation of emotion signals as an example of this class of problems, similar approaches can be applied to other instances where dynamically changing ordinal scale is important. Modeling the envelope of hand gesture signals or dynamic qualitative characterizations of video events (e.g., low-to-high-to-low intensity of an explosion) can benefit from this setting.

Acknowledgments. We are grateful to Peng Yang and Dimitris N. Metaxas for their help and discussions throughout the course of this work. This material is based upon work supported by the National Science Foundation under Grant No. IIS-0916812.

References

[1] Herbrich, R., Graepel, T., Obermayer, K.: Large margin rank boundaries for ordinal regression. In: Advances in Large Margin Classifiers, MIT Press, Cambridge (2000)
[2] Shashua, A., Levin, A.: Ranking with large margin principle: Two approaches. In: Neural Information Processing Systems (2003)

[3] Chu, W., Keerthi, S.S.: New approaches to support vector ordinal regression. In: International Conference on Machine Learning (2005)

[4] Hu, Y., Li, M., Yu, N.: Multiple-instance ranking: Learning to rank images for image retrieval. In: Computer Vision and Pattern Recognition (2008)

[5] Jing, Y., Baluja, S.: Pagerank for product image search. In: Proceeding of the 17th International Conference on World Wide Web (2008)

[6] Crammer, K., Singer, Y.: On the algorithmic implementation of multiclass kernel-based vector machines. Journal of Machine Learning Research 2, 265–292 (2001)

[7] Lafferty, J., McCallum, A., Pereira, F.: Conditional Random Fields: Probabilistic models for segmenting and labeling sequence data. In: International Conference on Machine Learning (2001)

[8] Kumar, S., Hebert, M.: Discriminative random fields. International Journal of Computer Vision 68, 179–201 (2006)

[9] Vishwanathan, S., Schraudolph, N., Schmidt, M., Murphy, K.: Accelerated training of conditional random fields with stochastic meta-descent. In: International Conference on Machine Learning (2006)

[10] Chu, W., Ghahramani, Z.: Gaussian processes for ordinal regression. Journal of Machine Learning Research 6, 1019–1041 (2005)

[11] Kim, M., Pavlovic, V.: Discriminative learning for dynamic state prediction. IEEE Transactions on Pattern Analysis and Machine Intelligence 31, 1847–1861 (2009)

[12] Ionescu, C., Bo, L., Sminchisescu, C.: Structural SVM for visual localization and continuous state estimation. In: International Conference on Computer Vision (2009)

[13] Qin, T., Liu, T.Y., Zhang, X.D., Wang, D.S., Li, H.: Global ranking using continuous conditional random fields. In: Neural Information Processing Systems (2008)

[14] Mao, Y., Lebanon, G.: Generalized isotonic conditional random fields. Machine Learning 77, 225–248 (2009)

[15] Pavlovic, V., Rehg, J.M., MacCormick, J.: Learning switching linear models of human motion. In: Neural Information Processing Systems (2000)

[16] Lien, J., Kanade, T., Cohn, J., Li, C.: Detection, tracking, and classification of action units in facial expression. J. Robotics and Autonomous Systems (1999)

[17] Viola, P., Jones, M.: Robust real-time object detection. International Journal of Computer Vision 57, 137–154 (2001)

[18] Tian, Y.: Evaluation of face resolution for expression analysis. In: Computer Vision and Pattern Recognition, Workshop on Face Processing in Video (2004)

[19] Lien, J.J., Cohn, J.F.: Automated facial expression recognition based on FACS action units. In: Int'l Conf. on Automatic Face and Gesture Recognition (1998)

[20] Cohen, I., Sebe, N., Garg, A., Chen, L.S., Huang, T.S.: Facial expression recognition from video sequences: Temporal and static modeling. Computer Vision and Image Understanding 91, 160–187 (2003)

[21] Shan, C., Gong, S., McOwan, P.W.: Conditional mutual information based boosting for facial expression recognition. In: British Machine Vision Conference (2005)

[22] Yang, P., Liu, Q., Metaxas, D.N.: Rankboost with l1 regularization for facial expression recognition and intensity estimation. In: International Conference on Computer Vision (2009)

Critical Nets and Beta-Stable Features for Image Matching

Steve Gu, Ying Zheng, and Carlo Tomasi

Department of Computer Science
Duke University
Durham, North Carolina, USA 27708
{steve,yuanqi,tomasi}@cs.duke.edu

Abstract. We propose new ideas and efficient algorithms towards bridging the gap between bag-of-features and constellation descriptors for image matching. Specifically, we show how to compute connections between local image features in the form of a *critical net* whose construction is repeatable across changes of viewing conditions or scene configuration. Arcs of the net provide a more reliable frame of reference than individual features do for the purpose of invariance. In addition, regions associated with either small stars or loops in the critical net can be used as *parts* for recognition or retrieval, and subgraphs of the critical net that are matched across images exhibit *common structures* shared by different images. We also introduce the notion of *beta-stable features*, a variation on the notion of feature lifetime from the literature of scale space. Our experiments show that arc-based SIFT-like descriptors of beta-stable features are more repeatable and more accurate than competing descriptors. We also provide anecdotal evidence of the usefulness of image parts and of the structures that are found to be common across images.

Keywords: Bag-of-features, constellation, image matching.

1 Introduction

Image matching enables at least tracking, stereo, recognition, and retrieval, and is therefore arguably the most important problem in computer vision.

A fundamental tension exists between the repeatability and distinctiveness of the features used in matching (our terminology is from a recent survey [1]). Features with a small image support can often be made to be repeatable in the sense that they can be found reliably in different views of the same scene. Features with more extended supports are potentially more distinctive in that two large, distinct regions are less likely to look like each other, *ceteris paribus*, than two small ones. Because of this, repeatability reduces false negatives in matching, and distinctiveness reduces false positives. Unfortunately, larger features tend to be less repeatable: They often deform more than smaller features under changes of viewing conditions or scene configuration, and occlusions are more likely to hide different parts of large features in different views.

K. Daniilidis, P. Maragos, N. Paragios (Eds.): ECCV 2010, Part III, LNCS 6313, pp. 663–676, 2010.
© Springer-Verlag Berlin Heidelberg 2010

Two approaches in the literature have shown considerable success in easing this tension. The "constellation" approach [2,3,4] describes both the appearance and the relative positions of small features. The "bag of features" approach [5,6,7,8] foregoes the description of positions, and relies on aggregate statistics of appearance. Constellations subsume bags of features, so the wide use of the latter is justified by considerations of efficiency.

Important steps have been made in recent literature [9,10] to connect local features into more global models efficiently. In this paper, we propose a further step towards practical constellations by defining *repeatable connections between local features*. Specifically, we introduce the notion of a *critical net*, a non-planar but low-average-degree graph that connects extrema of a function of the image intensities. Repeatability is a consequence of the fact that the critical net is invariant to affine deformations of the image domain and a certain wide class of changes in the function values. Our critical nets are a close relative of the Morse-Smale graph [11,12], but can be computed much more reliably and very efficiently on images defined on the integer grid.

We then show how critical nets can be used for matching. First, the primitives being matched are arcs of the net, rather than nodes. Arcs encode relative positions of local features, and are more reliable than individual features in establishing an image-dependent frame of reference to be used as a basis for invariance to geometric image transformation. Second, we use the connectivity induced by the critical net to identify both repeatable image parts and common structures of interest across images. Specifically, *parts* are regions associated with either small stars or loops in the critical net, and *common structures of interest* are the convex hulls of connected components that are matched across two images.

To complement the repeatability of critical nets, we also introduce a notion of *β-stable features* based on a Laplacian scale-space description of the image. We choose the Laplacian for several reasons: this operator has been proven successful in empirical evaluations [13]; the resulting extrema detect image contrast but remain invariant to multiplicative changes or the addition of any harmonic function to the image; and the choice of the Laplacian facilitates comparison with operators like SIFT [14] and its variants (see [1] for a survey). The concept of β-stability is a variation on the theme of a feature's *lifetime* (a.k.a. 'stability' [15] or 'persistence' [11]) familiar to the literature of scale space [16,17,18,19,20], and is built on the notion of *convexity*: rather than selecting features that persist over a wide interval of scales, we compute the features at a scale chosen so that the number of convex and concave regions of the image brightness function remains constant within a scale interval of length β. We show that this shift in selection criterion leads to robustness to high-frequency perturbations of the image, in addition to the invariance advantages deriving from the use of the Laplacian.

For ease of exposition, β-stable features are described first, in section 2, followed by a discussion of the concept of critical net in section 3. Sections 4 and 5 then introduce concepts for – and experiments with – image matching and the definition of image parts and common structures of interest. Section 6 concludes and outlines future work.

2   Beta-Stable Features in Scale Space

One of the most common feature detectors is based on the Laplacian of the Gaussian (LoG, [18,19]). First, the input image $I(x, y)$ is convolved with an Gaussian kernel G_σ multiple times to give a scale space representation $\{I_k\}$:

$$I_k = \underbrace{G_\sigma * G_\sigma \cdots * G_\sigma}_{k} * I = G_{\sqrt{k}\sigma} * I \tag{1}$$

where $*$ is the convolution operator, σ is the smoothing kernel width and k is the index for the scale. Then, the Laplacian operator $\mathcal{L}_k = \nabla^2 I_k$ is well approximated by the Difference of Gaussian (DoG), defined as $\mathcal{L}_k \approx I_{k+1} - I_k$ [14] if $\sigma \cong 1.6$. This value of σ is used throughout this paper. For a fixed scale k, the Laplacian $\mathcal{L}_k$ divides the image domain into regions of convex brightness (positive Laplacian) and concave brightness (negative Laplacian). More precisely:

Definition 1 (Maximally Convex Region). $\mathcal{X} \subseteq \mathbb{R}^2$ *is a convex region at scale k if $\mathcal{X}$ is connected and $\mathcal{L}_k > 0$ in $\mathcal{X}$. The region $\mathcal{X}$ is maximally convex if no convex regions $\mathcal{Y}$ exists such that $\mathcal{X} \subset \mathcal{Y}$.*

Convexity and concavity of image brightness are among the main ingredients for the detection of features in this paper. Figure 1 portrays the evolution of the maximally convex regions of a human face as scale increases. In order to make the maximally convex regions insensitive to moderate variations in scale, we select for image analysis the smallest scale k at which the number of maximally convex regions remains constant within an interval of scales. To this end, we first define the variation speed of the Laplacian:

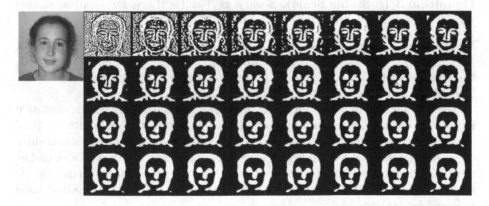

Fig. 1. The maximally convex regions $\mathcal{L}_k > 0$ are shown in white for k ranging from 1 to 100 in approximately equal steps. Image boundaries are handled in standard way: pad images by replication before processing, then remove boundary regions in the results. Unless otherwise indicated, input images in this paper are from Caltech 101 [7].

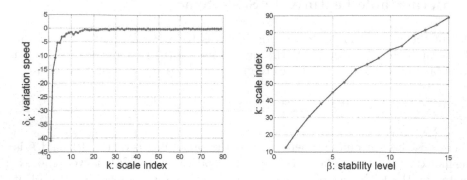

Fig. 2. The left plot shows the speed δ_k versus the scale index k, and the right plot shows the β-stable scale index k for different values of β. Both plots are averages over 48 images from the benchmark data set used in [21].

Definition 2 (Variation Speed of the Laplacian). *Let τ_k be the number of maximally convex regions at scale k. The variation speed δ_k of the Laplacian at scale k is $\delta_k \triangleq \tau_{k+1} - \tau_k$.*

As long as δ_k stays far below zero, we say the Laplacian function is not *stable* in the sense that a small scale change will lead to a substantial structural change that is reflected by the change of the number of maximally convex regions. In contrast, when $\delta_k \approx 0$, we say that the resulting Laplacian function is stable. In the left plot in Figure 2, the absolute value of the speed δ_k is initially very large and quickly approaches zero and stays relatively stable thereafter. Based on this observation, we define the notion of β-stable scale:

Definition 3 (β-Stable Scale). *Scale k is β-stable if k is the smallest integer for which $\delta_\xi = 0$ for all $\xi \in [k - \beta, k)$.*

The right plot in Figure 2 shows the β-stable scale index k for different values of β. This plot is increasing by construction. Figure 3 shows a sample image with the contour plot of its Laplacian at scales $k = 2$ and the 10-stable scale $k = 25$. The 10-stable Laplacian is both smooth and stable.

The advantages of β-stability are threefold: (1) The positive and negative regions of the Laplacian are topologically stable within the scale interval $[k - \beta, k)$. (2) The β-stable Laplacian is robust to high frequency perturbations since these are annihilated by the heavy isotropic smoothing. (3) Since the number of maximally convex regions encodes the richness of details of an image, the β-stable Laplacian balances stability and detail by anchoring to the *smallest* scale required for stability.

We use the extrema of the β-stable Laplacian, *i.e.*, the locally most convex and concave points of the smoothed input image, to define image features:

Definition 4 (β-Stable Features). *The maxima and minima of the β-stable Laplacian of the image intensity function I are called β-stable features of I.*

Figure 4 shows a sample image of a human face overlayed with SIFT features and β-stable features. The β-stable features are better anchored to visually significant parts of the image than SIFT features are. Our experiments in section 4 show that β-stable features are preferable for image matching as well. In addition, and more importantly, section 3 shows how to weave β-stable features into constellations. This connection between features enhances the discriminative power of the β-stable features and helps bridge the gap between bag-of-features and constellation approaches to image matching.

3   The Critical Net

Let f be the β-stable Laplacian function of the intensity image I defined on a grid $\mathcal{G} = \langle \mathcal{V}, \mathcal{E} \rangle$. The vertices in $\mathcal{V}$ group together adjacent pixels with equal values, and the arcs in $\mathcal{E}$ are the remaining arcs induced by pixel neighborhood (4- or 8-connected). By construction of $\mathcal{V}$, $f(a) \neq f(b)$ for all $(a, b) \in \mathcal{E}$. Let Γ_f be the set of the minima of f and Λ_f be the set of the maxima of f. The union $\Gamma_f \cup \Lambda_f$ is the set of β-stable features. In order to construct a constellation model that weaves β-stable features into a graph, we need the notion of *connection*:

Definition 5 (Connection). *For any $a, b \in \mathcal{V}$, there is a connection between a and b on the grid $\mathcal{G}$, denoted as $a \prec b$, if there exists an ascending path from a to b, that is, a sequence $\langle a = p_1, p_2, ..., p_n = b \rangle$ where $(p_i, p_{i+1}) \in \mathcal{E}$ and $f(p_i) < f(p_{i+1})$ for $1 \le i \le n - 1$.*

The connection $\prec$ induces a partial order in $\mathcal{V}$, that is, for any $a, b \in \mathcal{V}$, $a \prec b$, or $b \prec a$, or a, b are not ordered. Transitivity also holds: $\{a \prec b, b \prec c\} \Rightarrow a \prec c$. This connection naturally defines a graph:

Definition 6 (Critical Net). *The critical net of an intensity image I is a directed acyclic graph: $\mathcal{G}_f = \langle \mathcal{V}_f, \mathcal{E}_f \rangle$ where $\mathcal{V}_f = \Gamma_f \cup \Lambda_f$ is the set of β-stable features of I and $\mathcal{E}_f = \{(a, b) \in \Gamma_f \times \Lambda_f \mid a \prec b\}$ is the set of connections in $\mathcal{V}_f$.*

By construction, the arcs of critical nets are associated to local image patches with both convex and concave image brightness patterns. Thus, they encode image content that is rich, local, and stable in a formally well-defined sense.

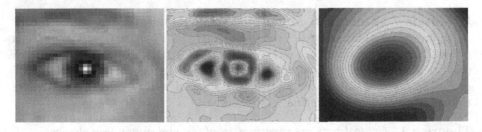

Fig. 3. From left to right: An image patch of a human eye and its Laplacian at scales 2 (middle) and 25 (right). Scale $k = 25$ is 10-stable.

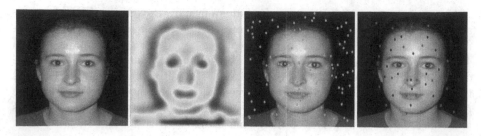

Fig. 4. From left to right: Original image; The 10-stable Laplacian image; SIFT features (green); 10-stable features. Red and blue dots are maxima and minima of $\mathcal{L}_{10}$.

Our critical net is a close relative of the two dimensional Morse-Smale (M-S) graph [11,12], but is both simpler in concept and more reliable in computation. The following three aspects distinguish the critical net from the M-S graph and underscore the computational advantages of the former: (1) Critical nets are well defined for any discrete or continuous function, while M-S graphs requires the extra assumptions that all critical points are non-degenerate and there is no saddle-saddle connection. (2) In critical nets we do not compute saddles, whose identification is usually cumbersome in practice. Instead, saddles are implicitly bounded by the loops formed via pairs of minima and maxima. (3) The M-S graph connects critical points via *integral* paths by following the gradient directions everywhere. In contrast, the critical net connects minima to maxima by *ascending* paths, which require no gradient computation.

Because of these differences, the critical net is much simpler than the M-S graph in both concept and computation. The price paid for these advantages is that the critical net is no longer a planar graph. Nevertheless, the average degree of the critical net is low for real images and resembles a planar graph in efficient computation. Before we present an algorithm for computing the critical net, we analyze its robustness and invariance. Because the critical net is computed on the β-stable Laplacian function, it is insensitive to high frequency perturbations, which are erased by the heavy isotropic smoothing. Moreover, the critical net is invariant to any invertible affine deformation of the image domain and to monotonic changes in the Laplacian function values.

Definition 7 (Affine and Monotonic Changes). *Let $\alpha : \mathbf{x} \rightarrow \mathbf{A}\mathbf{x} + \mathbf{b}$ be an affine transformation of the domain of image I where $\mathbf{x}, \mathbf{b} \in \mathbb{R}^2$ and $\mathbf{A}$ is a 2×2 nonsingular matrix. Let $\lambda : \mathbb{R}^2 \rightarrow \mathbb{R}$ be a function such that for each $(a, b) \in \mathcal{E}, \lambda(a) > \lambda(b)$ if and only if $f(a) > f(b)$ for the β-stable Laplacian f of I. The composition $g = \lambda \circ \alpha^{-1} : \mathbb{R}^2 \rightarrow \mathbb{R}$ is called an affine and monotonic change of the Laplacian f of I.*

Theorem 1. *Critical nets are invariant to affine and monotonic changes.*

Proof. We show that graph $\mathcal{G}_f$ is isomorphic to $\mathcal{G}_g$. First, $\Lambda_f = \Lambda_g$ and $\Gamma_f = \Gamma_g$ since both α and λ preserve the extrema. Second, $\alpha^{-1}(a) \prec \alpha^{-1}(b) \Leftrightarrow a \prec b \Leftrightarrow$

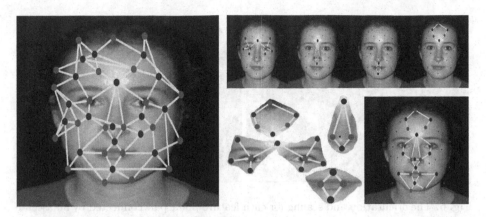

Fig. 5. Left: critical net. Red and blue dots are maxima and minima of $\mathcal{L}_{10}$, respectively, and yellow edges are oriented from blue to red. Middle: Some of the parts overlayed on the image (top) and by themselves (bottom). Eyes are captured by star structures, while nose, mouth and other parts are captured by loops (saddle-like parts). Bottom right: Image parts can be integrated to form objects of interest for high level recognition.

$\exists\,\langle a = p_1, p_2, ..., p_n = b\rangle$ with $f(p_1) < \cdots < f(p_n)$, the latter of which holds if and only if $\lambda(p_1) < \cdots < \lambda(p_n)$.

Algorithm 1 outlines a simple and practically fast algorithm that computes the critical net by starting a breadth-first traversal from each minimum of f. The program takes about 0.1 seconds in Matlab to compute the critical net (after Laplacian computation) for an image of size 200×300 on a regular laptop. The complexity of the algorithm is $O(\lambda n)$ where n is the number of pixels and λ is the average number of the maxima or minima that a single pixel can reach through ascending paths. Although λ could be large under contrived geometrical arrangements, we find that λ is small ($\lambda < 2$) in practice for real images. The left image in Figure 5 shows a sample critical net.

Algorithm 1. Compute the critical net from $\mathcal{G} = <\mathcal{V}, \mathcal{E}>$ and f

---

  for each minimum α of f **do**
    Initialize a queue to be empty and clear all the labels.
    Push α into the queue and mark α as visited.
    while the queue is not empty **do**
      Remove u, the head of the queue.
      Report the minimum-maximum connection $\alpha \prec u$ if u is the maximum.
      Mark all the unvisited vertices $v \in \mathcal{V}$ with $(u,v) \in \mathcal{E}$ and $f(v) > f(u)$ as visited
      and push them into the queue.
    end while
  end for

Fig. 6. The orientation and scaling for each feature point pair connected by an ascending path are uniquely determined through the direction and length of the line segments connecting minima and maxima. Images from [21]

4   Image Matching

4.1   Dual SIFT Descriptor

The success of SIFT descriptors shows the validity of the ideas that underlie their format: Regions around points of interest are divided into small patches, which are then described by the histogram of the local gradient orientations. In this way, both geometric structure and local statistics of image contrast are accounted for. Also, in order to be rotation-invariant, the SIFT descriptor estimates the principal direction of image gradient by looking for the peaks in the histogram of the gradient directions. In cases where peaks are not prominent, multiple directions are assigned in order to handle ambiguity. We incorporate these ideas into the design of our new descriptor called *dual SIFT descriptor*, but make three modifications to enhance discriminative power:

First, we describe arcs connecting minima and maxima by concatenating the SIFT descriptors of the two extrema attached to each arc (minimum followed by maximum). Therefore, the new descriptor ends up with a vector that is twice as long as SIFT, and describes pairs of regions with opposite convexity patterns. This concatenation scheme implicitly enforces that convex patterns can only match convex patterns and the same holds for the concave ones.

Second, by relying on arcs, our descriptor reduces the sensitivity of rotation and scale estimates to noise and modeling errors. To be more specific, given a pair of minimum a and maximum b, the rotation angle for both a and b is determined by the direction of the vector $\overrightarrow{ab}$, which is simpler, longer, and more inherently unique, compared to the SIFT direction. See Figure 6 for an illustration.

Third, SIFT achieves scale invariance by selecting scales at which the DoG is locally an extremum in both scale and space. In contrast, we normalize our descriptor relative to scale by using the distance *between* the arc endpoints a and b, $\|\overrightarrow{ab}\|$. Thus, the support region for the descriptor shrinks when local features cluster together and expands when features are sparsely distributed. We compute the scale of a and b with the sigmoid function: $s(a, b) = \alpha[1 + \exp(-\|\overrightarrow{ab}\|/s)]^{-1}$ where α and s are determined empirically and are not critical (see experiments).

4.2   Matching Criteria and Evaluation

Consider now two images I, J to be matched, and let $\mathcal{G}_f$ and $\mathcal{G}_g$ be two critical nets of their β-stable Laplacians f and g of I and J respectively. Also, let $d(e)$ be the dual SIFT descriptor vector for the arc e. Transferring to arcs the strategy typically used to match SIFT descriptors, arc $e_q \in \mathcal{E}_f$ is matched to arc $e_1 = \arg\min_{e \in \mathcal{E}_g} \|d(e_q) - d(e)\|$ if $\min_{e_2 \in \mathcal{E}_g \setminus e_1} \frac{\|d(e_q) - d(e_2)\|}{\|d(e_q) - d(e_1)\|} > 1.5$ – that is, if the next-best match is at least 50% worse than the best one for e_q. In our experiments, we use *repeatability* and *accuracy* to evaluate the matching quality:

$$\text{Repeatability} = \frac{\text{\# correct matches found in the image pair}}{\min\left\{\text{\# features in image 1}, \text{\# features in image 2}\right\}} \quad (2)$$

$$\text{Accuracy} = \frac{\text{\# correct matches found in the image pair}}{\text{\# total matches found in the image pair}}.$$

Figure 7 shows a first comparison of β-stable features and SIFT features, which illustrates anecdotally the repeatability and accuracy of β-stable features married with the critical net. In the implementation, we use published software [22] with the provided default parameters to produce the dual SIFT descriptors for each arc of the critical net.

We also ran more systematic experiments on a published benchmark data set [21]. This set is composed of 8 image groups, each containing 6 images warped by known homographies relative to each other. We first do the matching using a fixed value $\beta = 10$ for all the images, and find that features based on the critical net already yield better performance than SIFT in both repeatability and accuracy in most of the test image pairs. This is expected, because β-stability promotes more repeatable features by construction.

However, the matching result can further be improved with an automatic selection of β based on the matching of multiple critical nets. Let $F(I)$ be the set of β-stable Laplacian functions of the image I for, say, $\beta \in \{2, 4, 6, 8, 10\}$. Given two input images I and J to match, we select the pair $\mathcal{G}_{\hat{f}}$ and $\mathcal{G}_{\hat{g}}$ such that $(\hat{f}, \hat{g}) = \arg\min_{f \in F(I), g \in F(J)} \rho(\mathcal{G}_f, \mathcal{G}_g)$ where ρ is a criterion to be optimized. We propose two different criteria based on the set $\mathcal{E}_{f,g} \subseteq \mathcal{E}_f \times \mathcal{E}_g$ of matched arcs. The *match count* $\rho_1(\mathcal{G}_f, \mathcal{G}_g) = |\mathcal{E}_{f,g}|$ and the *normalized match count* $\rho_2(\mathcal{G}_f, \mathcal{G}_g) = \frac{|\mathcal{E}_{f,g}|}{\min\{|\mathcal{E}_f|, |\mathcal{E}_g|\}}$. Features obtained by optimizing the match count ρ_1 over $F(I) \times F(J)$ might be preferable in the bag-of-features approach, because their greater number leads to more significant statistics of appearance. In contrast, optimizing the normalized match count ρ_2 leads to sparser graphs of features that can be connected to each other in a more reproducible way by the critical net, and are thereby more in tune with the constellation approach, where geometry matters. Both choices outperform a fixed value of β. Either way, matching based on critical

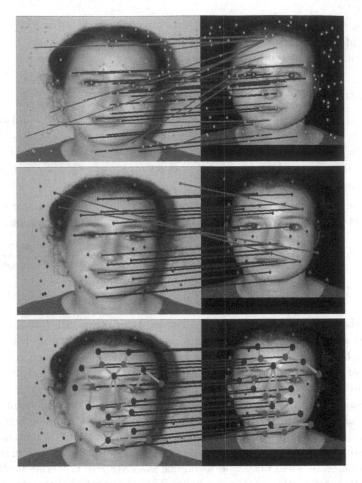

Fig. 7. *Top row:* standard SIFT features and their matching. 164 and 117 features are found respectively in the two images of the pair. Between these, 26 correct matches (marked blue) are found (repeatability = 22.2%), plus 12 wrong ones (marked red; accuracy = 68.43%). *Middle row:* the 10-stable features and the matching result without using the critical net connections; that is, standard SIFT descriptors with fixed scale and rotation are used for individual features. 56 and 41 10-stable feature points are found in the image pair, among which 20 correct and 3 wrong matches are found (repeatability = 48.8%; accuracy = 87.0%). *Bottom row:* same 10-stable features, but with matching based on the critical net where dual SIFT descriptors are used, and rotation and scaling of individual features are determined from the spatial distribution of extrema. All matches are correct (accuracy = 100%) and there are 24 matched feature points (repeatability = 58.54%). If repeatability is computed from the number of arcs instead of the number of points, then 29 correct matches are found among the 117 and 75 critical-net arcs in the image pair (repeatability = 38.7%). Although repeatability based on the critical net vertices is higher, we calculate the repeatability based on the critical net arcs in our experiments, in order to emphasize the importance of connections. Beta-stable features married with the critical net win either way.

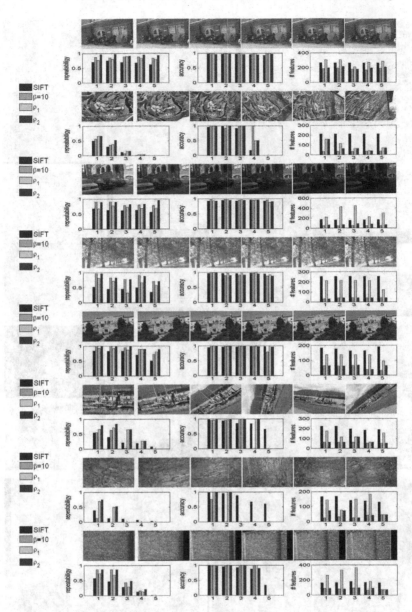

Fig. 8. The first image in each of eight groups is compared to the remaining five (40 image pairs). Images are downsized to 1/3 of original. Default parameters [22] are used for the SIFT features. Critical-net matches use $\beta = 10$ first, and then β selected automatically through ρ_1 or ρ_2. Matches that fall within 5 pixels from truth are considered correct. Matching based on the critical net typically outperforms SIFT in repeatability and accuracy, regardless of how β is chosen. Selection via ρ_2 achieves the highest repeatability in all cases. Selection via ρ_1 produces the largest number of features, comparable to that of the SIFT features.

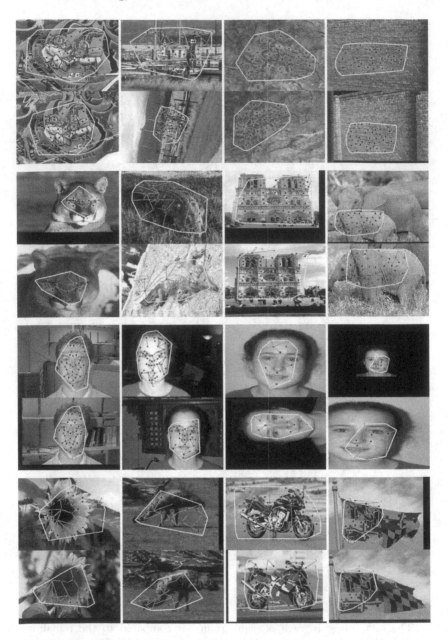

Fig. 9. Common structures of interest for 16 image pairs. In each image pair, we compute and match critical nets. The convex hull (yellow) of the largest connected component of each matched subnet is taken as the common structure across the two images. Matched features that are disconnected from the largest connected subnet are not shown here. Differences in viewpoint, lighting, and scene are often substantial. First 4 pairs from [21], last from [23], Notre Dame through Google Images, others from [7].

nets and with automatic selection of β performs significantly better than SIFT in repeatability and as well or better in accuracy. Results of the matching based on a fixed β or on β selected through either ρ_1 or ρ_2 are shown in Figure 8.

5   Image Parts and Common Structures Across Images

The graph structure of the critical net contains richer information than what the point representation or even the individual arcs are able to capture. Intuitively, there are two types of structures that can serve for the definition of image parts: *star* and *loop*. A star is a minimum of $\mathcal{L}_{k(\beta)}$ together with all its neighboring maxima in the critical net, or a maximum together with all its neighboring minima. A loop is an alternating sequence of minima and maxima that is cyclic. Since saddles are implicitly bounded by loops of minima and maxima, we also call loops 'saddle-like' image parts. These two types of image parts are complementary to each other and Figure 5 shows some examples.

Image parts can further be joined into structures of interest, in the spirit of pictorial structures [10]. In these approaches, the configuration of image parts are represented as deformable models whose parameters are learnt from examples. In contrast, our approach determines the relations among image parts fully via the critical net, one image at a time. In this sense, the critical net can also be considered as a *discriminative constellation model*. Objects of interest can be discovered automatically if these structural relations remain stable across different images. Figure 9 shows some of the matching results together with the extracted *common structures of interest*. These are defined as the convex hull in each image of the largest connected component of matched subnets of the critical nets constructed in each of the two images. These common structures are large and reliable even in the presence of significant changes in scene or viewpoint.

6   Conclusion and Future Work

Beta-stable features are resilient to moderate changes of scale and high-frequency image perturbations. Critical nets are simple graphs that reveal intrinsic connections between features. They are efficiently computed and are invariant to affine geometric distortions and to monotonic changes of the Laplacian values. Critical net arcs provide a more reliable basis for scale and rotation invariance than individual SIFT descriptors do. Stars or loops in the net can be used as parts for recognition and retrieval, and are computed bottom-up from the images, without supervision. The convex hulls of matched subnets across images of the same scene are strikingly reliable indicators of common structures of interest. Again, these are computed from pairs of images, and without supervision. The future work entails the improvement of the feature descriptors so that the critical net structure can handle extreme scale change, significant image deformation and object appearance change. We plan to explore the applications of β-stable features, critical nets, parts, and common structures of interest to video tracking, stereo matching, image recognition, and image and video retrieval.

References

1. Tuytelaars, T., Mikolajczyk, K.: Local invariant feature detectors: A survey. Foundations and Trends in Computer Graphics and Vision 3, 177–280 (2008)
2. Fischler, M.A., Elschlager, R.A.: The representation and matching of pictorial structures. IEEE Transactions on Computers 22, 67–92 (1973)
3. Manjunath, B.S., Chellappa, R., Von der Malsburg, C.: A feature based approach to face recognition. In: CVPR, pp. 373–378 (1992)
4. Burl, M., Weber, M., Perona, P.: A probabilistic approach to object recognition using local photometry and global geometry. In: Burkhardt, H., Neumann, B. (eds.) ECCV 1998. LNCS, vol. 1407, pp. 628–641. Springer, Heidelberg (1998)
5. Sivic, J., Zisserman, A.: Video Google: a text retrieval approach to object matching in videos. In: ICCV, vol. 2, pp. 1470–1477 (2003)
6. Csurka, G., Dance, C.R., Fan, L., Willamowski, J., Bray, C.: Visual categorization with bags of keypoints. In: ECCV Int'l W. on Statistical Learning in Computer Vision (2004)
7. Fei-Fei, L., Perona, P.: A Bayesian hierarchical model for learning natural scene categories. In: CVPR, vol. 2, pp. 524–531 (2005)
8. Grauman, K., Darrell, T.: The pyramid match kernel: Efficient learning with sets of features. J. of Machine Learning Research 8, 725–760 (2007)
9. Lazebnik, S., Schmid, C., Ponce, J.: Semi-local affine parts for object recognition. In: British Machine Vision C, vol. 2, pp. 959–968 (2004)
10. Felzenszwalb, P., Huttenlocher, D.: Pictorial structures for object recognition. IJCV 1, 55–79 (2005)
11. Edelsbrunner, H., Harer, J., Zomorodian, A.: Hierarchical Morse complexes for piecewise linear 2-manifolds. In: Symp. on Computational Geometry, pp. 70–79 (2001)
12. Danovaro, E., De Floriani, L., Vitali, M.: Multi-resolution Morse-Smale complexes for terrain modeling. In: Int'l C. on Image Analysis and Processing, pp. 337–342 (2007)
13. Mikolajczyk, K., Schmid, C.: Indexing based on scale-invariant interest points. In: ICCV, pp. 525–531 (2001)
14. Lowe, D.G.: Object recognition from local scale-invariant features. In: ICCV, pp. 1150–1157 (1999)
15. Matas, J., Chum, O., Urban, M., Pajdla, T.: Robust wide baseline stereo from maximally stable extremal regions. In: BMVC (2002)
16. Koenderink, J.J.: The structure of images. Biol. Cybernetics 50, 363–370 (1984)
17. Witkin, A., Terzopoulos, D., Kass, M.: Signal matching through scale space. Science, 714–719 (1986)
18. Lindeberg, T.: Detecting salient blob-like image structures and their scales with a scale-space primal sketch: A method for focus-of-attention. IJCV 11, 283–318 (1993)
19. Lindeberg, T.: Feature detection with automatic scale selection. IJCV 30, 77–116 (1998)
20. Florack, L.M.J., Kuijper, A.: The topological structure of scale-space images. J. of Mathematical Imaging and Vision 12, 65–79 (2000)
21. Kadir, T., Zisserman, A., Brady, M.: An affine invariant salient region detector. In: ECCV, pp. 228–241 (2004)
22. Vedaldi, A., Fulkerson, B.: VLFeat: An open and portable library of computer vision algorithms (2008), http://www.vlfeat.org/
23. Ling, H., Jacobs, D.: Deformation invariant image matching. In: ICCV, vol. 2, pp. 1466–1473 (2005)

Descriptor Learning for Efficient Retrieval

James Philbin[1], Michael Isard[3], Josef Sivic[2], and Andrew Zisserman[1]

[1] Visual Geometry Group, Department of Engineering Science, University of Oxford
[2] INRIA, WILLOW, Laboratoire d'Informatique de l'Ecole Normale Superieure,
Paris
[3] Microsoft Research, Silicon Valley

Abstract. Many visual search and matching systems represent images using sparse sets of "visual words": descriptors that have been quantized by assignment to the best-matching symbol in a discrete vocabulary. Errors in this quantization procedure propagate throughout the rest of the system, either harming performance or requiring correction using additional storage or processing. This paper aims to reduce these quantization errors *at source*, by learning a projection from descriptor space to a new Euclidean space in which standard clustering techniques are more likely to assign matching descriptors to the same cluster, and non-matching descriptors to different clusters.

To achieve this, we learn a non-linear transformation model by minimizing a novel margin-based cost function, which aims to separate matching descriptors from *two* classes of non-matching descriptors. Training data is generated automatically by leveraging geometric consistency. Scalable, stochastic gradient methods are used for the optimization.

For the case of particular object retrieval, we demonstrate impressive gains in performance on a ground truth dataset: our learnt 32-D descriptor without spatial re-ranking outperforms a baseline method using 128-D SIFT descriptors with spatial re-ranking.

1   Introduction

We are interested in the problem of efficiently retrieving occurrences of a particular object, selected by an image query, in a large unorganized set of images. Typically, methods in particular object retrieval take a text-retrieval approach to the problem in order to achieve fast retrieval at run time [1,2,3,4]. Interest points and descriptors are found in every dataset image and the descriptors are then clustered (usually by k-means or some variant) and quantized to give a visual word representation for each image in the corpus.

Whilst being ostensibly similar to textual words, visual words as generated through clustering suffer from a lot more noise and dropout compared to text. This is caused partly by errors and failures in interest point detection and description, but also by quantization – descriptors that lie close to a Voronoi boundary after clustering being assigned to the "wrong" visual word. Previous work attempted to overcome quantization errors by compensating for mis-clustered descriptors using additional information in the retrieval index, for example by soft-assigning descriptors [5,6,7], or by performing more work at query time [1,8].

K. Daniilidis, P. Maragos, N. Paragios (Eds.): ECCV 2010, Part III, LNCS 6313, pp. 677–691, 2010.

Instead, the goal of this work is to reduce these errors at source, by constructing a projection from the raw descriptor space to a new Euclidean space in which matching descriptors are more likely to land in the same cluster, and non-matching descriptors are more likely to land in different clusters. By removing the initial quantization errors, we keep the indexes small (for example, they become less sparse when soft-assignment is used) and the query times fast. Optionally, our method can also reduce the dimensionality of the projected descriptors resulting in smaller storage requirements for features and increased clustering and quantization speeds during pre-processing.

There have been several recent applications of distance learning to classification problems [9,10,11,12,13,14,15], however these methods assume clean, labelled data indicating pairs of points that belong to the same class and pairs that belong to different classes. In our task, even when the same object appears in two images, the images typically have different backgrounds and there is a non-trivial transformation between the views of a common object, so we cannot simply classify *images* as being matching or non-matching. At the same time the number of individual descriptors per image and the complexity of the correspondence problem between them means that manually labelling the sets of matching and non-matching descriptors would be unacceptably burdensome. Therefore, in this work, we introduce a new method for generating training data from a corpus of unlabelled images using standard techniques from multi-view geometry. In contrast to Hua *et al.* [16], who also generated training pairs from unlabelled image data via patches matched by the Photo Tourism system [17], here we adopt a much cheaper pairwise image measure which doesn't require us to compute a global bundle adjustment over many image pairs. Thus, we can train on patches of objects that appear in as few as two images.

Previous works in distance learning use two categories of point pairs for training: "matching" and "non-matching", typically derived from known class labels. In this work, we show that we can significantly improve performance by forming two "non-matching" categories: random pairs of features; and those which are easily confused by a baseline method. We adopt a margin-based cost function to distinguish these three categories of points, and show that this gives improved performance more than using non-margin-based methods [14,16].

To optimize this cost function, a fast, stochastic, online learning procedure is used that permits the use of millions of training pairs. We will show that non-linear projection methods, previously used for hand-written digit classification [13], perform better than the linear projections previously applied to computer vision distance learning [9,10,11,12].

The next section motivates the distance learning task by showing that retrieval performance is significantly worse using standard quantized descriptors than when a much slower, exhaustive search procedure is applied to the raw SIFT descriptors – this indicates the potential gain achievable from better clustering. After describing in Section 3 how we automatically generate our training data, we set out our learning methods in Section 4 and then conclude with results and a discussion. Improved performance is demonstrated over SIFT descriptors [18] on standard datasets with learnt descriptors as small as 24-D.

2   Datasets and the mAP Performance Gap

To learn and evaluate, we use two publicly available datasets with associated ground truth: (i) the *Oxford Buildings* dataset [19]; and (ii) the *Paris Buildings* dataset [20]. We show that a significant performance gap (the *mAP-gap*) is incurred by using quantized descriptors compared to using the original descriptors. It is this gap that we aim to reduce by learning a descriptor projection.

2.1   Datasets and Performance Measure

Both the Oxford (5.1K images) and Paris (6.3K images) datasets were obtained from Flickr by querying the associated text tags for famous landmarks, and both have an associated ground truth for 55 standard queries: 5 queries for each of 11 landmarks in each city. To evaluate retrieval performance, the Average Precision (AP) is computed as the area under the precision-recall curve for each query. As in [3], an Average Precision score is computed for each of the 5 queries for a landmark. These scores are averaged (over 55 query images in total for each dataset) to obtain an overall mean Average Precision (mAP) score.

Affine-invariant Hessian regions [21] are computed for each image, giving approximately 3,300 features per image (1024×768 pixels). Each affine region is represented by a 128-D SIFT descriptor [18].

2.2   Performance Loss Due to Quantization

To assess the performance loss due to quantization, four retrieval systems (RS) are compared:

The baseline retrieval system (RS1): In this system each image is represented as a "bag of visual words". All image descriptors are clustered using the approximate k-means algorithm [3] into 500K visual words. At indexing and query time each descriptor is associated with its (approximate) nearest cluster centre to form a visual word, and a retrieval ranking score is obtained using tf-idf weighting. No spatial verification is performed. Note that each dataset has its own vocabulary.

Spatial re-ranking to depth 200 (RS2): For this system a spatial verification procedure [3] is adopted, estimating an affine homography from single image correspondences between the query image and each target image. The top 200 images returned from RS1 are re-ranked using the number of inliers found between the query and target images under the computed homography.

Spatial verification to full depth (RS3): The same method is used as in RS2, but here *all* dataset images are ranked using the number of inliers to the computed homography.

Table 1. The mAP performance gap between raw SIFT descriptors and visual words on the Oxford and Paris datasets. In the spatial cases, an affine homography is computed using RANSAC and the data is re-ranked by the number of inliers. Using raw SIFT descriptors coupled with Lowe's second nearest neighbor test [22] gives a 14% retrieval boost over the baseline method for Oxford. (i)-(iii) all use a $K = 500,000$ vocabulary trained on their respective datasets.

Item	Method	Oxford mAP	Paris mAP
i.	RS1: Baseline (visual words, no spatial)	0.613±0.011	0.643±0.002
ii.	RS2: Spatial (visual words, depth=200)	0.647±0.011	0.655±0.002
iii.	RS3: Spatial (visual words, depth=FULL)	0.653±0.012	0.663±0.002
iv.	RS4: Spatial (raw descriptors, depth=FULL)	0.755	0.672

Raw SIFT descriptors with spatial verification (RS4): Putative matches on the raw SIFT descriptors (no quantization) are found between the query and every image in the dataset using Lowe's second nearest neighbour test [18] (threshold = 0.8). Spatial verification as in RS3 is applied to the set of putative matches.

It should be noted that the methods RS3 and RS4 exhaustively match document pairs and so are infeasibly slow for real-time, large scale retrieval. RS3 is ~10 times slower and RS4 is ~100 times slower than RS2 even on the 5.1K Oxford dataset. These run-time gaps increase linearly for larger datasets.

The results for all four methods are shown in table 1. For methods based on visual words, the mean and standard deviation over 3 runs of k-means with different initializations are shown. Going from baseline (i) to baseline plus spatial (ii) gives moderate improvements to both datasets, but reranking significantly more documents gives little appreciable further gain. In contrast, using the raw SIFT descriptors gives a large boost in retrieval performance for both datasets, demonstrating that the *mAP-gap* is principally due to quantization errors. This implies that a lack of visual word matches contributes substantially more to missed retrievals than reranking too few documents at query time. The raw-descriptor matching procedure will be used to generate point pairs for our learning algorithm, so Table 1(iv) gives a rough upper bound to the retrieval improvement we can hope to achieve using any learning algorithm based on those training inputs.

3   Automatic Training Data Generation

In this section, we describe our method to automatically generate training data for the descriptor projection learning procedure. The training data is generated by pair-wise image matching, a much cheaper alternative to the full multi-view reconstruction used in [16,17], allowing us to generate a large number (3M+) of training pairs. In addition to positive (matched) examples, we separately collect "hard" and "easy" negative examples and show later that making this distinction can significantly improve the learnt projections.

We proceed as follows: (i) An image pair is chosen at random from the dataset; (ii) A set of *putative* matches is computed between the image pair. Each putative match consists of a pair of elliptical features, one in each image, that pass Lowe's second nearest neighbour ratio test [18] on their SIFT descriptors; (iii) RANSAC is used to estimate an affine transform between the images together with a number of inliers consistent with that transform. Point pairs are only taken from image matches with greater than 20 verified inliers. The ratio test ensures that putative matches are distinctive for that particular pair of images. This procedure generates three sets of point pairs, shown in Figure 1, that we treat distinctly in the learning algorithm:

1. **Positives:** These are the point pairs found as inliers by RANSAC.
2. **Nearest neighbour negatives (nnN):** These are pairs marked as outliers by RANSAC—they are generally close in descriptor space as they were found to be descriptor-space nearest neighbors between the two images, but are spatially inconsistent with the best-fitting affine transformation found between the images.
3. **Random negatives (ranN):** These are pairs which are not descriptor-space nearest neighbours, i.e. random sets of features generally far apart in the original descriptor space.

A histogram of SIFT distances for the three different sets of point pairs on the Oxford dataset is shown in Figure 2(b). As expected, the original SIFT descriptor easily separates the random negatives from the positive and NN negative point pairs, but strongly confuses the positives and NN negatives. Section 5 will show that the best retrieval performance arises when the positive and NN negative pairs are separated whilst simultaneously keeping the random negative pairs distant. It is important to note that, due to the potential for repeated structure and the limitations of the spatial matching method (only affine planar homographies are considered), some of the nnN point pairs might be incorrectly labelled positives – this can lead to significant noise in the training data. We collect 3M training pairs from the Oxford dataset split equally into positive, NN negative and random negative pairs, and we also have a separate set of 300K pairs used as a validation set to determine regularization parameters.

4 Learning the Descriptor Projection Function

Our objective here is to improve on a baseline distance measure that partially confuses some pairs of points that should be kept apart (the nearest neighbor negatives pairs) with those that should be matched (the positive pairs), as shown in figure 2(b). There is a danger in learning a projection using *only* these training points that are confused in the original descriptor space: although we might learn a function to bring these points closer together, the projection might (especially if it is non-linear) "draw in" other points so that a particular pair of points are no longer nearest neighbours. Being a nearest neighbour explicitly depends on all other points in the space, so great care must be exercised when ignoring other points.

Here, we aim to overcome these problems by incorporating the distances between a large set of random point pairs directly into our cost function. These

Fig. 1. Gathering training point pairs. Three groups of point pairs are shown: (a) inliers to an affine homography found using RANSAC (positives); (b) outliers which are nevertheless nearest neighbors in SIFT space (nnN); and (c) random pairs of points which are usually distant in descriptor space (ranN).

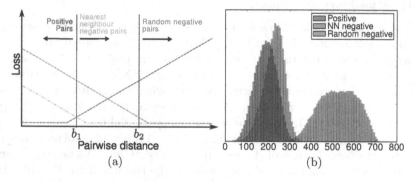

Fig. 2. Multiple margins. (a) Schematic of the multiple margin loss functions. This encourages the ordering on point pairs to be satisfied as per Equation 1. (b) Histograms of the raw 128-D SIFT distances for the three types of point pairs.

are precisely the pairs which can "crowd in" and tend to reduce the precision of clusters during vocabulary building if they are not explicitly considered. This effect has previously been ignored. It will be shown that, if this third set (the random negatives) is not explicitly considered, then a learnt mapping can reduce the confusion between positive and NN negative training pairs, but this simultaneously reduces the distance between random negative point pairs, leading to increased confusion. The solution we propose here is to add an additional loss function to prevent this confusion (and we quantify its benefit in Section 5).

More formally, given a set of positive training pairs **P**, NN negative training pairs **nnN**, and random negatives **ranN**, our aim is to learn a projection function $T : \mathbb{R}^D \rightarrow \mathbb{R}^M$, where D is the dimension of the original descriptor space (e.g. $D = 128$ for SIFT) and M is the dimension of the projected descriptor, such that:

$$d(T(p_i), T(p_j)) < d(T(p_k), T(p_l)) \quad \text{and} \quad d(T(p_i), T(p_j)) \ll d(T(p_m), T(p_n)) \quad (1)$$

for $p_i, p_j \in \mathbf{P}$, $p_k, p_l \in \mathbf{nnN}$ and $p_m, p_n \in \mathbf{ranN}$.

In practice, it is not possible to fully separate these pairwise distances because of noise in the training data and restricted model complexity, so instead a margin based approach will be used which encourages the distance between the three classes of point pairs to separate without enforcing the distance ordering as a hard constraint. The loss function for this situation is illustrated in Figure 2(a). The first margin aims to separate the positive and NN negative point pairs confused by SIFT in the original space. The second margin applies a force to the random negatives to keep them distant from the positive pairs – ideally the overlap in histograms between the positive and random negative point pairs should be small. This motivates learning the projection function by minimizing the cost function:

$$f(\lambda, W) = \sum_{x,y \in P} \mathcal{L}(b_1 - d_W(x,y)) + \sum_{x,y \in nnN} \mathcal{L}(d_W(x,y) - b_1)$$
$$+ \sum_{x,y \in ranN} \mathcal{L}(d_W(x,y) - b_2) + \frac{\lambda}{2}\|W\|^2 \qquad (2)$$

where $\mathcal{L}(z) = \log(1 + \exp(-z))$ is the logistic-loss, a smooth approximation to the hinge loss which is more suitable for learning with gradient-based optimization, $d_W(x,y) = \|T(x;W) - T(y;W)\|_2$ is the standard Euclidean distance between the projected points, and W are the parameters of the projection function T.

The first three terms in (2) give the loss for the three different margins used, and the fourth is a regularization term, controlled by λ, which is used to limit the model complexity and stop over-fitting on the training data. b_1 and b_2 are the positions of the left-hand and right-hand margin biases in projected distance space. $f(\lambda, W)$ can be differentiated w.r.t. W by repeated application of the chain rule provided T is also differentiable. The absolute values of b_1 and b_2 are unimportant due to the scaling freedom in the projection functions – it is the ratio b_1/b_2 which is important.

4.1 Projection Function Models

We consider two different forms for the projection function T: a linear model of the form Wx; and a non-linear form for T based on a deep belief network (DBN). For the linear model, the projection function T is parameterized as $T(x;W) = Wx$, with derivative $\frac{\partial T_i}{\partial W_{ij}} = x_j$, where W is a real valued $D' \times 128$ matrix and so projects x linearly to a D'-dimensional space. This is equivalent to learning a Mahalanobis matrix $M = W^\top W$, therefore the linear model is equivalent in power to that used in [9,10,16]. Because W is real valued, M is positive semi-definite, and by learning W directly one can avoid the complications of adding semi-definiteness constraints into the learning routine. Though the projection function T is linear, the cost function (2) is not convex in W due to the square roots in $d(\cdot)$. However, previous work [13,23] has shown that, in practice, optimizing this cost over W does not lead to serious problems with poor local minima.

For the non-linear model the projection function is based on a DBN [24] using a series of restricted Boltzmann machines (RBM). In this case W contains the projection parameters and biases for all the layers of the DBN. For one hidden layer, the projection function is of the form:

$$T(x; W_1, W_2, W_3, h_0, h_1, h_2) = W_3\sigma(W_2\sigma(W_1\sigma(x + h_0) + h_1) + h_2)$$

where σ is an element-wise logistic sigmoid function, W_i are matrices and h_i are column vectors (the h_i act as per-layer biases for the transformation). For a DBN projecting a 128-D SIFT descriptor to a 32-D descriptor with a single hidden layer of size 384-D, the number of parameters is $= 128 \times 384 + 384 \times 384 + 384 \times 32 + 128 + 384 + 384 = 209,792$. We adopt a DBN architecture because we expect non-linearities to allow the distance function to adapt itself depending on the statistics of the local neighborhood of the features being considered, and so improve the separation in distances between matching and non-matching point pairs. While a kernel method might be thought of as a natural alternative mechanism to introduce non-linearity, this would rule out the direct mapping of descriptors that we seek. DBNs have previously proven successful for distance learning in simple vision tasks, such as handwritten digit classification [13].

One potential problem with DBNs is that again (2) is not a convex function of the parameters W. Nevertheless, with a large amount of training data and good stochastic learning routines (see below), we find solutions which empirically seem to generalize well to unseen data.

4.2 Optimization

The task is to minimize the cost function, $f(\lambda, W)$, w.r.t. to the parameterized weights, W. In this work we use stochastic gradient descent (SGD) methods to optimize the loss function, for two main reasons. First, stochastic gradient methods scale linearly with the number of training points and have constant memory requirements. This makes them attractive in online learning or when the amount of training data is very large as in our case—here we use 3M training pairs, though more could easily be generated. Second, although stochastic gradient methods may require a large number of steps to converge, they often learn models which generalize well to unseen data [25].

SGD incrementally minimizes a cost function f by examining just a few data points at a time. If $f(X, W)$ is the function to minimize, and X is the data, the SGD update is:

$$W_{t+1} = W_t - \Theta_t \nabla_w f(X_{m..n}, W_t)$$

The parameter vector W is updated according to the negative gradient of the cost computed on just a few examples $X_{m..n}$. Θ_t is a learning rate which should decrease over time to ensure convergence. Here, we use "mini-batches" of 200 point pairs (with labels positive, NN negative, and random negative) per parameter update step. In each mini-batch there are about equal numbers of the three types of point pairs. In practice SGD can converge slowly so, to speed up convergence, we use a pseudo second order method known as Stochastic Meta Descent (SMD) [26]. SMD uses a per-parameter learning rate based on an approximation of the local curvature. One difference from the method used in [26] is that here, we estimate the Hessian-vector product using finite-differences: $Hv \approx (\nabla f(W_t + \epsilon v) - \nabla f(W_t))/\epsilon$, rather than using an analytical approach.

4.3   DBN Implementation Details

The weights in the model are initialized using a generative procedure that proceeds layer-by-layer, optimizing weights using contrastive divergence [24]. This performs an initialization that empirically speeds up convergence of the subsequent discriminative training. The generative training is run layer-by-layer for one pass of the training data and takes around 30 minutes on a modern processor.

After this initialization, W is learnt discriminatively by optimizing (2): each point pair of a mini-batch is pushed through the network to give the transformed descriptors. The differentiable cost function (2) is then used to compute the gradient on the output layer based on all the points in the minibatch. Back-propagation is used to compute the gradient for the other layers in the network.

Once the gradient has been computed for all the DBN weights and hidden biases, the parameters W are updated using SMD. This is done once per mini-batch of points for a number of iterations over the dataset. For a DBN with one hidden layer of size 384-D projecting to 32-D, training one iteration of 3M point pairs takes just under 35 minutes on a single core of a modern processor. Training is performed for 50 iterations over the training data – after this we see rapidly diminishing returns.

Table 2. Comparison of several different retrieval methods. The results for the proposed methods are shown under the "Learnt" descriptor. The results for the baseline and raw-matching methods are duplicated from table 1 for completeness. DNF[1]: RS4 is too slow to be run on this dataset.

	Descriptor	Notes	Descriptor size	Dataset	mAP		
					RS1	RS2	RS4
(i)	SIFT		128	Oxford	0.613	0.647	0.755
(ii)	Learnt	Linear	32	Oxford	0.599	0.634	
(iii)	Learnt	Linear	64	Oxford	0.636	0.665	
(iv)	Learnt	Non-linear	24	Oxford	0.606	0.649	
(v)	Learnt	Non-linear	32	Oxford	0.644	0.681	
(vi)	Learnt	Non-linear	64	Oxford	**0.662**	**0.707**	
(vii)	SIFT		128	Paris	0.655	0.669	0.683
(viii)	Learnt	Non-linear	32	Paris	0.669	0.680	
(ix)	Learnt	Non-linear	64	Paris	**0.678**	**0.689**	
(x)	SIFT		128	Oxford-100K	0.490	0.541	DNF[1]
(xi)	Learnt	Non-linear	32	Oxford-100K	0.524	0.592	
(xii)	Learnt	Non-linear	64	Oxford-100K	**0.541**	**0.615**	

5   Results

Our objective is to reduce the *mAP-gap*, and so our principal evaluation measure will be the mAP of the retrieval system. However, as mAP is computed after many steps of processing (and also involves a weighting function, tf-idf, in two of the retrieval systems), in some cases we also show a simpler measure which is the *cluster true positive rate* (CTPR): this is simply the proportion of true positive validation pairs which cluster to the same visual word – for a fixed vocabulary size it is a measure of the recall of each word, and is closer to the informal goal stated in the introduction. In practice the two measures are closely correlated. In the following we learn the projection function on the Oxford dataset. Where results are stated with error bars, these are computed as a standard deviation over 3 vocabularies learnt from different initializations of the k-means clustering, with $k = 500,000$. For the baseline system RS1, CTPR is 0.336 ± 0.005. The regularization parameter, λ, is optimized on the validation set. Other than the generalization experiments, all results are produced on the Oxford dataset.

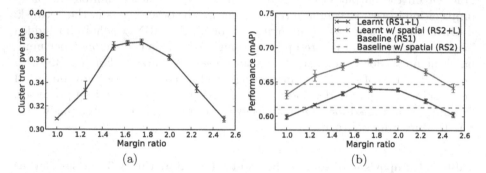

(a)   (b)

Fig. 3. Adjusting the margin ratio. The (a) CTPR, and (b) mAP retrieval performance as a function of the margin ratio, b_2/b_1 (see Equation 2). The hidden layer dimension and final dimension are 384 and 32 respectively. "+L" indicates that a learnt model is used.

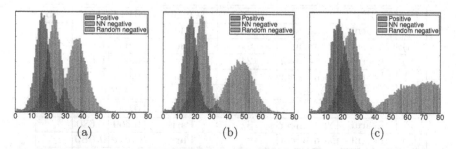

(a)   (b)   (c)

Fig. 4. Histograms of pair distances. The distance histograms of validation pairs after training for (a) $b_2/b_1 = 1.0$ (b) $b_2/b_1 = 1.6$ (c) $b_2/b_1 = 2.5$. The histograms show the positive, NN negative and random negative point pairs.

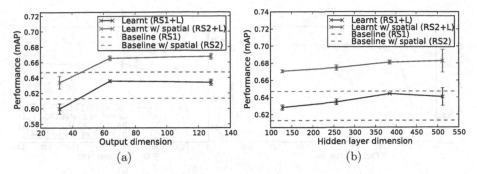

Fig. 5. (a) **Linear model**: mAP performance as the final dimension D' is varied. (b) **Non-linear model**: mAP performance as the hidden layer dimension is varied. The output dimension is fixed to 32.

Choosing the margin ratio: Figure 3 examines the retrieval performance as a function of the margin ratio b_2/b_1 for a non-linear model with one hidden layer of size 384 projecting down to 32-D. This ratio controls the extent to which the random negative pairs should be separated from the positive pairs. At $b_2/b_1 = 1.0$, both margins are the same, which mimics previous methods that use just two types of point pairs: if the ratio is set too low, the random negative pairs start to be clustered with the positive pairs; if it is set too high then the learning algorithm focuses all its attention on separating the random negatives and isn't able to separate the positive and NN negative pairs. Distance histograms for different margin ratios are shown in Figure 4. As the ratio is increased, there is a peak in performance between 1.6 and 1.7. In all subsequent experiments, this ratio is set to 1.6 with $b_1 = 20.0$. These results clearly demonstrate the value of considering both sets of negative point pairs.

Linear model: Results for the linear model are given in Table 2 and are shown in Figure 5(a). Performance increases only up to 64-D and then plateaus. At 64-D the performance without spatial re-ranking is 0.636 ± 0.002, an improvement of 3.4% over RS1. With spatial re-ranking the mAP is 0.665 ± 0.003, an improvement of 1.8% over RS2. Therefore, a learned linear projection leads to a slight but significant performance improvement, and we can reduce the dimensionality of the original descriptors by using this linear projection with no degradation in performance.

We compare to the linear discriminant method of Hua *et al.* [16], using a local implementation of their algorithm on our data. For this method, we used the ranN pairs as the negatives for training (performance was worse when nnN pairs were used as the negatives). Using 1M positive and 1M random negative pairs, reducing the output dimension to 32-D, gives a performance of 0.585 without spatial re-ranking; and 0.625 with spatial re-ranking. This is slightly worse than our linear results which gives an mAP of 0.600 and 0.634 respectively. The difference in performance can be explained by our use of a different margin-based cost function and the consideration of both the nnN and ranN point pairs.

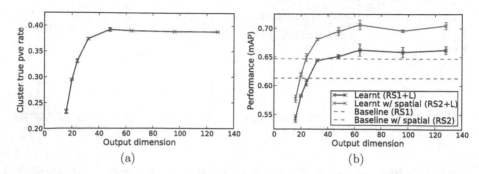

(a)   (b)

Fig. 6. Non-linear model: variation with output dimension for (a) CTPR and (b) mAP performance. The hidden layer dimension is fixed at 384. (a) the CTPR rate increases as the output dimension increases to 48, then flattens. Similarly, (b) shows that at $D = 32$ the projected descriptors without spatial re-ranking (system RS1) achieve performance equal to the original descriptors with spatial re-ranking (system RS2). Performance continues to increase to $D = 64$ and then plateaus. Spatial reranking on the projected descriptors beats RS2 by 5.9% (0.647 to 0.706 mAP).

Non-linear model: Figure 5(b) shows the results of adjusting the dimension of the hidden layer. The hidden layer dimension only affects the time taken to train the model and project the features into the new space and doesn't affect storage requirements or clustering/assignment speed. From the figure, one can see that retrieval performance increases up to around 384-D before leveling off, and for subsequent experiments we fix the hidden layer dimension at 384-D.

Figure 6 and Table 2 show the effect on performance of adjusting the output dimension of the projection function. The learnt descriptor attains the same performance as SIFT at just over 24-D, a saving in storage of over 5 times. At 32-D, but without spatial re-ranking, the learnt descriptor performs as well as using SIFT with spatial re-ranking (RS2). After 32-D, the performance gains start to level off, but still improve up to 64-D. Using a 64-D descriptor with spatial re-ranking beats RS2 by 5.9% (0.647 to 0.706 mAP). Note also that the non-linear model greatly improves performance over the linear model (0.665 to 0.706 mAP). The non-linear model substantially closes the *mAP-gap* and brings the quantized visual word method much closer in performance to the raw SIFT method. This is achieved with no increase in query times or index size.

Generalization: Here we examine the generalization of the learnt descriptor to the held-out Paris dataset. Spatial re-ranking on the raw SIFT descriptors for Paris gave a much lower performance gain than for Oxford, so there is less that our method can do. Nevertheless, we still increase performance over the baseline method. Our 64-D descriptor, learnt on Oxford, gives a score without spatial re-ranking of 0.678 (compared to 0.655) and with spatial re-ranking gives 0.689 (compared to 0.669), slightly exceeding the performance from using the raw descriptors of 0.683. This is principally due to the many non-planar queries present in the Paris dataset which is challenging for the RS4 method.

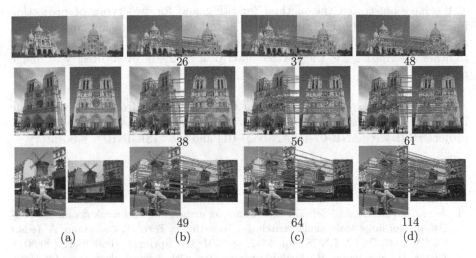

Fig. 7. Qualitative examples on the Paris dataset. Demonstrating the improvements in matching using our quantized learnt descriptor. The number of inliers found are listed beneath each image pair. The four columns are: (a) the original image pair; (b) matches found by the baseline visual words; (c) matches found by our learnt visual words; (d) matches found by the raw SIFT matching method.

In figure 7, we qualitatively examine the spatially verified inliers between some image pairs for the baseline method, our quantized learnt method and the raw descriptor method. The quantized learnt descriptor gives more inliers to the computed homography and closes the gap on the raw matching method.

Table 2(x)-(xii) gives retrieval results for Oxford combined with a large set of 100K images [3]. The additional images do not contain the landmarks and so act as "distractors" for retrieval. Using the quantized learnt descriptor with D=64 and spatial re-ranking gives a substantial boost in performance from 0.541 to 0.615. Again this illustrates that the learnt projection function is able to generalize to other datasets, whilst still boosting retrieval performance.

6   Conclusion

We have shown that, by transforming descriptors prior to clustering, we can boost performance considerably over a baseline retrieval method and can produce results using visual words alone that are as good as the baseline method combined with spatial re-ranking. We have considerably closed the performance gap between the raw SIFT matching method and the much faster quantized retrieval method for both datasets considered here. This performance boost comes at zero runtime cost (though some offline cost) and with reduced data storage.

Since the descriptors are transformed *before* quantization, they can easily be used in conjunction with other recent works that have improved performance over a raw bag of visual words approach, such as [27,28].

We have illustrated the method for SIFT and for two types of projection functions, but clearly the framework of automatically generating training data and learning the projection function through optimization of (2) could be applied to other descriptors, e.g. the DAISY descriptor of [29] or even directly to image patches.

Acknowledgements. We are grateful for financial support from the EPSRC, the Royal Academy of Engineering, Microsoft, ERC grant VisRec no. 228180, ANR project HFIBMR (ANR-07-BLAN-0331-01) and the MSR-INRIA laboratory.

References

1. Jegou, H., Douze, M., Schmid, C.: Hamming embedding and weak geometric consistency for large scale image search. In: Forsyth, D., Torr, P., Zisserman, A. (eds.) ECCV 2008, Part I. LNCS, vol. 5302, pp. 304–317. Springer, Heidelberg (2008)
2. Nister, D., Stewenius, H.: Scalable recognition with a vocabulary tree. In: Proc. CVPR (2006)
3. Philbin, J., Chum, O., Isard, M., Sivic, J., Zisserman, A.: Object retrieval with large vocabularies and fast spatial matching. In: Proc. CVPR (2007)
4. Sivic, J., Zisserman, A.: Video Google: A Text Retrieval Approach to Object Matching in Videos. In: Proc. ICCV (2003)
5. Boiman, O., Shechtman, E., Irani, M.: In defence of nearest-neighbor based image classification. In: Proc. CVPR (2008)
6. Philbin, J., Chum, O., Isard, M., Sivic, J., Zisserman, A.: Lost in quantization: Improving particular object retrieval in large scale image databases. In: Proc. CVPR (2008)
7. van Gemert, J., Geusebroek, J.M., Veenman, C., Smeulders, A.: Kernel codebooks for scene categorization. In: Forsyth, D., Torr, P., Zisserman, A. (eds.) ECCV 2008, Part III. LNCS, vol. 5304, pp. 696–709. Springer, Heidelberg (2008)
8. Chum, O., Philbin, J., Sivic, J., Isard, M., Zisserman, A.: Total recall: Automatic query expansion with a generative feature model for object retrieval. In: Proc. ICCV (2007)
9. Schultz, M., Joachims, T.: Learning a distance metric from relative comparisons. In: NIPS (2003)
10. Weinberger, K., Blitzer, J., Saul, L.: Distance metric learning for large margin nearest neighbor classification. In: NIPS (2005)
11. Kumar, P., Torr, P., Zisserman, A.: An invariant large margin nearest neighbour classifier. In: Proc. ICCV (2007)
12. Frome, A., Singer, Y., Sha, F., Malik, J.: Learning globally-consistent local distance functions for shape-based image retrieval and classification. In: Proc. ICCV (2007)
13. Salakhutdinov, R., Hinton, G.: Learning a nonlinear embedding by preserving class neighbourhood structure. In: AI and statistics (2007)
14. Mikolajczyk, K., Matas, J.: Improving descriptors for fast tree matching by optimal linear projection. In: Proc. ICCV (2007)
15. Ramanan, D., Baker, S.: Local distance functions: A taxonomy, new algorithms, and an evaluation. In: Proc. ICCV (2009)
16. Hua, G., Brown, M., Winder, S.: Discriminant embedding for local image descriptors. In: Proc. ICCV (2007)

17. Snavely, N., Seitz, S., Szeliski, R.: Photo tourism: exploring photo collections in 3D. In: Proc. ACM SIGGRAPH, pp. 835–846 (2006)
18. Lowe, D.: Object recognition from local scale-invariant features. In: Proc. ICCV (1999)
19. http://www.robots.ox.ac.uk/~vgg/data/oxbuildings/
20. http://www.robots.ox.ac.uk/~vgg/data/parisbuildings/
21. Mikolajczyk, K., Schmid, C.: Scale & affine invariant interest point detectors. IJCV 1, 63–86 (2004)
22. Lowe, D.: Distinctive image features from scale-invariant keypoints. IJCV 60, 91–110 (2004)
23. Guillamin, M., Verbeek, J., Schmid, C.: Is that you? Metric learning approaches for face identification. In: Proc. ICCV (2009)
24. Hinton, G.E., Salakhutdinov, R.R.: Reducing the dimensionality of data with neural networks. Science 313, 504–507 (2006)
25. Bottou, L., Bousquet, O.: The tradeoffs of large scale learning. In: NIPS (2007)
26. Bray, M., Koller-Meier, E., Schraudolph, N.N., Van Gool, L.: Stochastic meta-descent for tracking articulated structures. In: Proc. CVPR (2004)
27. Chum, O., Perdoch, M., Matas, J.: Geometric min-hashing: finding a (thick) needle in a haystack. In: Proc. CVPR (2009)
28. Perdoch, M., Chum, O., Matas, J.: Efficient representation of local geometry for large scale object retrieval. In: Proc. CVPR (2009)
29. Winder, S., Hua, G., Brown, M.: Picking the best daisy. In: Proc. CVPR (2009)

Texture Regimes for Entropy-Based Multiscale Image Analysis

Sylvain Boltz[1,2], Frank Nielsen[1], and Stefano Soatto[1]

[1] Laboratoire d'Informatique, École Polytechnique, 91128 Palaiseau Cedex, France
{boltz,nielsen}@lix.polytechnique.fr
[2] UCLA Vision Lab, University of California, Los Angeles; Los Angeles – CA, 90095
soatto@ucla.edu

Abstract. We present an approach to multiscale image analysis. It hinges on an operative definition of texture that involves a "small region", where some (unknown) statistic is aggregated, and a "large region" within which it is stationary. At each point, multiple small and large regions co-exist at multiple scales, as image structures are pooled by the scaling and quantization process to form "textures" and then transitions between textures define again "structures." We present a technique to learn and agglomerate sparse bases at multiple scales. To do so efficiently, we propose an analysis of cluster statistics after a clustering step is performed, and a new clustering method with linear-time performance. In both cases, we can infer all the "small" and "large" regions at multiple scale in one shot.

1 Introduction

Textures represent an important component of image analysis, which in turn is useful to perform visual decision tasks – such as detection, localization, recognition and categorization – efficiently by minimizing decision-time complexity [12]. The goal of image analysis[1] is to compute *statistics* (deterministic functions of the data) that are at the same time insensitive to nuisance factors (*e.g.,* viewpoint, illumination, occlusions, quantization) and useful to the task (*i.e.,* in the context of visual decision tasks, discriminative). Such statistics are often called *features*, or *structures*. Such structures have to satisfy a number of properties to be useful, such as *structural stability, commutativity,* and *proper sampling* [12]. The *dual* of such structures, in a sense made precise by Theorem 5 of [12], are textures, or more precisely *stochastic textures*, defined by spatial stationarity of *some* (a-priori unknown) statistics. *Regular textures,* on the other hand, are defined by cyclo-stationarity (or stationarity with respect to a discrete group) of *some* (a-priori unknown) structure.

---

[1] Image analysis refers to the process of "breaking down the image into pieces," which is *prima facie* un-necessary and even detrimental for data storage and transmission tasks ([11], p. 88), but instead plays a critical role in visual decision tasks [12].

K. Daniilidis, P. Maragos, N. Paragios (Eds.): ECCV 2010, Part III, LNCS 6313, pp. 692–705, 2010.
© Springer-Verlag Berlin Heidelberg 2010

Whether a region of an image is classified as texture or structure *depends on scale*.[2] A region can be a structure at some scale, a texture at a coarser scale, then again a structure at yet a coarser scale and so on (Fig. 1), reflecting the lack of *causality* in two-dimensional scale-space [9]. Therefore, we do not seek for a *single* transition from structure to texture [17,18], but instead seek to represent the entire phase-space of transitions at each location in an image.

To address these issues, in Sect. 2 we introduce a definition of texture that guides the development of efficient schemes for multiscale coding in Sect. 3, where we introduce an algorithm to compute statistics based on three fast clustering algorithms reviewed in Sect. 4.1 and 4.3, and a new variant introduced in Sect. 4.2. These clustering algorithms allow us to perform multiscale analysis in one shot (Sect. 5). The analysis can also be done directly in the clustering process with linear complexity (Sect. 5.2).

Our characterization of textures uses three ingredients: A statistic, ψ, the minimal domain where such a statistic is pooled, ω, and the maximal domain (in the sense of inclusion) where it is stationary, Ω. Therefore, we focus on defining suitable classes of statistics, and on designing efficient algorithms to partition the image into multiple regions. This is done through efficient techniques to create sparse bases (dictionaries), using clustering and dimensionality reduction in high-dimensional non-Euclidean spaces. In particular, we introduce "kNN-Quick Shift," a generalization of [16] modified to handle data distributed in high-dimensional spaces, and to allow different variables, such as scale, as "gap" measures. This enables simultaneous estimation of "small" ω and "big" Ω regions can be performed by alternating Min-Max entropy segmentation in linear time. Our entropy measure exhibits a "staircase-like" behaviour, with each step determining the small regions ω at the lower edge, and the big regions at the upper edge. Note that we achieve this in one-shot, for all scales, without having to match patches or searching for periodic patterns [6].

2   Texture/Structure Multiple Transitions

Image structures are regions of the image that are *salient* (*i.c.*, critical points of some functional, Def. 4 of [12]), *repeatable* (*i.e.*, the functional is structurally stable, Def. 9 of [12]), and *insensitive* to nuisance factors (*i.e.*, the functional is invariant to group nuisances and commutes with respect to non-invertible ones, Def. 6 of [12]). For zero-dimensional structures (attributed points, or *frames*), it has been shown that the attributed Reeb tree (ART) is a complete invariant with respect to viewpoint and contrast away from occlusions [13]. However, *occlusions* of viewpoint and illumination (cast shadows) yield *one-dimensional structures*, such as edges and ridges. The main technical and conceptual problem in encoding

---

[2] Note that scaling alone is not what is critical here. Scaling is a group, so one can always represent any orbit with a single canonical element. What is critical is the composition of scaling with *quantization*, which makes for a *semi-group*. Without quantization we would not need a notion of stochastic texture, since any region would reveal some structure at a sufficiently small scale.

them is that such *critical structures* (extrema and discontinuities) *are not defined in a digital image*. For this reason, we must first *define* a notion of "discrete continuity," lest every pixel boundary is a structure. This is achieved by designing a *detector*, usually an operator defined on a scalable domain, and searching for its extrema at each location in the image, at each scale. In principle one would have to store the response of such detectors at all possible scales. In practice, owing to the statistics of natural images, we can expect the detector functional to have isolated critical loci that can be stored in lieu of the entire scale-space. In between critical scales, structures become part of aggregate statistics that we call *textures*.

To make this more precise, we define a texture as a region $\Omega \subset D$ within which *some* image statistic ψ, aggregated on a subset $\omega \subset \Omega$, is spatially stationary.[3] Thus a texture is defined by two (unknown) regions, *small* ω and *big* Ω, an (unknown) statistic $\psi_\omega(I) \doteq \psi(\{I(y), y \in \omega\})$, under the following conditions of *stationarity* and *non-triviality*:

$$\psi_\omega(I(x+v)) = \psi_\omega(I(x)), \quad \forall v \mid x \in \omega \Rightarrow x + v \in \Omega \tag{1}$$

$$\Omega' \backslash \Omega \neq \emptyset \Rightarrow \psi_{\Omega'}(I) \neq \psi_\Omega(I). \tag{2}$$

The small region ω, that defines the intrinsic scale $s = |\omega|$ (the area of ω), is minimal in the sense of inclusion[4]. Note that, by definition, $\psi_\omega(I) = \psi_\Omega(I)$. A texture segmentation is thus defined, for every quantization scale s, as the solution of the following optimization with respect to the unknowns $\{\Omega_i\}_{i=1}^N, \{\omega_i\}_{i=1}^N, \{\psi_i\}_{i=1}^N$

$$\min \sum_{i=1}^{N(s)} \int_{\Omega_i} d(\psi_{\omega_i}(I(x)), \psi_i) dx + \Gamma(\Omega_i, \omega_i) \tag{3}$$

where Γ denotes a regularization functional and d denotes a distance, for instance ℓ^2, or a nonparametric divergence functional [2,8].

In Sect. 3 we discuss the role of the statistics ψ. In Sect. 4, we discuss about some clustering algorithms, introducing along the way a novel extension of a clustering algorithm that is suited for high-dimensional spaces. Finally we build on these clustering algorithms to derive, in Sect. 5, two methods to automatically compute the set of all regions $\{\omega_i\}$ and $\{\Omega_i\}$.

3   Multiscale Feature Selection and Dictionary Agglomeration

The difficulty in instantiating the definition of texture into an algorithm for image analysis is that neither the regions ω_i, Ω_i, nor the statistics ψ_ω are known

---

[3] Constant-color regions are a particular (trivial) case of texture, where the statistic $\psi(I) = I$ is pooled on the pixel region $\omega = \{x\}$. It is an unfortunate semantic coincidence that such regions are sometimes colloquially referred to as "textureless."

[4] $\{I(x), x \in \omega\}$ is sometimes called a *texton* [7], or *texture generator*. This definition applies to both "periodic" or "stochastic" textures. Regions with homogeneous color or gray-level are a particular case whereby ω is a pixel, and do not need separate treatment.

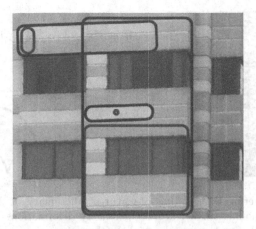

Fig. 1. Left: multiple Texture/Structure Transitions: The same point can be interpreted as either structure or texture depending on scale. Starting from a small red region ω, the green region Ω determines the domain where some statistic computed in ω is stationary (relative some group, which includes cyclo-stationarity when the group is discrete).

a-priori. It is therefore common to define ψ in terms of a class of functions such as a Gabor wavelets or other bases learned directly from the image under sparsity constraints [1]. One can even consider just samples of the image in a window of varying size around each pixel [15]. Whatever representation one chooses for a local neighborhood of the image at a given scale, the fact that all points have to be represented at all scales causes an explosion of complexity. This can be mitigated by clustering the dictionary elements into a codebook, with each dictionary element encoded with an index and representing a mode in the data distribution. Each image region is then then represented by an histogram of these indices. In principle, one could take these to be our statistics ψ, and represent *structures* as locations where the label histogram is surrounded by different ones, and *textures* as locations where the label histogram is surrounded by similar ones.

However, the dictionaries thus learned are usually very large and cumbersome to work with. Therefore, one can reduce the dimensionality of the representation by reducing the number of atoms in the dictionary. However, in order to achieve the *insensitivity* to nuisance factors described in the previous section, clustering cannot just be performed with respect to the standard ℓ_2 distance as the atoms may undergo deformations. Clustering with an histogram-based distance is also ill-advised as the distributions of different classes have significant overlap. Kullback-Leibler's divergence naturally adapts to the supports and the modes of the distributions, and is therefore a natural choice for divergence measure. The feature space is then chosen so as to discount nuisance variability.

We propose clustering in three different feature spaces to agglomerate patches modulo three different types of transformation (Fig. 2): First, we consider $\psi_\omega \doteq \{I(x, y), x, y\}_{(x,y) \in \omega}$ to get rid of small translations. In this feature space one

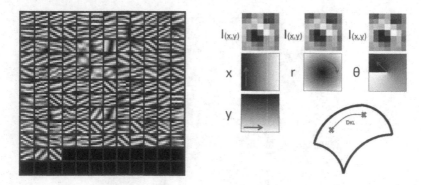

Fig. 2. (left) Clustering with a "bag-of-features" dictionary of 256 image patches. Patches identical modulo small feature / geometry deformations are now agglomerated to one exemplar texture patch. (right) Clustering on sparse representation of images with uncertainty on value and position: the three columns show the different feature spaces, and red arrow shows the direction along which neighbors are preferably searched for. The distance on these feature spaces is the symmetric Kullback-Leibler divergence.

pays a small price to align two similar $I(x, y)$ as long as their (x, y) distance is small. Similarly, polar coordinates $\{I(x, y), r, \epsilon.\theta\}$, with a small weight ϵ on the angle, are insensitive to small rotations and with a small weight on the radius $\{I(x, y), \epsilon.r, \theta\}$ they are insensitive small scalings (Fig. 2).

Now, the last step is the most critical, for it involves clustering in high-dimensional and highly non-Euclidean spaces (Fig. 2). We will describe our approach in the next two sections.

4   Three Fast Clustering Algorithms

In this section we use two existing clustering algorithm, Quick Shift (QS) and Statistical Region Merging (SRM), and introduce a novel one, "kNN Quick Shift," that adapts QS to high-dimensional data.[5] The purpose is to show that the analysis that follows is not dependent on the particular algorithm to arrive at a clustering tree.

4.1   Mode Seeking with Quick Shift

Quick Shift [16] is a modification of Medoid-Shift that retains its benefit of operating on non-Euclidean spaces and still converges in one iteration.

$$y_i(1) = \arg \min_{j:P(j)>P(i)} D_{ij} \tag{4}$$

$$\tau(i) = D_{iy_i(1)} \tag{5}$$

---

[5] Those two families of algorithms were also recently combined in [4].

Its main advantage is simplicity and speed. One clustering with Quick Shift gives a full segmentation tree as all nodes are connected to each other with a different strength τ called the *gap*. Thresholding this gap with different values thus yields different segmentations. The most common use of these clustering algorithms is with the feature space $\{I(x), x, y\}$, yielding compact regions of uniform luminance or color usually called *superpixels*. In practice, the full matrix D_{ij} does not needed to be built, as the feature space often has a geometric component, so physical neighbors are also neighbors in feature space. This limits the search to a small local window. Even if no geometric prior is available, one can still use a window of a certain size h around each datum. When the data distribution is high-dimensional and sparsely distributed, a large h has to be selected, leading to oversmoothing the estimate of the probability density function (PDF), and to a computationally intensive search. In the next section we introduce a modification of this algorithm designed to mitigate this problem, similarly to what [5] has done for Mean Shift.

4.2   kNN Quick Shift

To extend QS to high-dimensional data spaces we replace the Parzen density estimator with a balloon estimator. The analysis of [14] shows that, although baloon estimators underperform Parzen in one dimension, they improve as the dimension of the space increases. We choose the neighborhood of possible connections to be the k-nearest neighbors $\mathcal{N}_k(i)$ of each point.

$$y_i(1) = \arg \min_{j:j \in \mathcal{N}_k(i) \& P_j > P_i} D_{ij} \tag{6}$$

The resulting kNN Quick Shift is made very fast by using approximate nearest neighbors with $(1 + \epsilon)$ tolerance. In practice, this works well if k is low, so we implemented a recursive kNN-Quick Shift algorithm: It first builds a tree connecting pixel values, then unconnected superpixels are connected until every node is linked.

When clustering pixels in an image, D_{ij} is simply the Euclidean distance between two pixel features. When clustering patches for agglomeration of bases modulo some deformations, D_{ij} is the symmetric Kullback-Leibler divergence computed on three different feature spaces (Sec. 3). The parameter k exerts direct control on the cluster size. It can therefore be used as a gap measure to perform a cut of the tree structure provided by QS. This is particularly relevant in the context of texture analysis, where we seek the smallest ω and largest Ω regions where certain statistics are stationary. However, it is inconsistent with a region based energy as defined in eq. (3).

4.3   A Fast Statistical Region Merging (SRM)

SRM is an efficient greedy algorithm [10] for region merging with theoretical guarantees. Every pair of adjacent pixels (both horizontally and vertically) is assigned a strength value, for instance the absolute value of their intensity difference. The list is then sorted, and location labels retained. For each pair of pixels, a test called predicate is run to decide if the regions are to be merged. This runs in linear time as it only goes through all the pixel pairs once ($2N$-complexity). The region merging structure is a union find data structure which allows finding pixel labels with complexity $\mathcal{O}(1)$. In order to build a segmentation tree with this algorithm, the predicate is made to depend on a scalar parameter, and the same algorithm is run repeatedly for increasing values of the parameter and with pairs of adjacent regions instead of pairs of pixels.

5   Recursive Max-Min Entropy for Texture Analysis

From the operational definition of texture (2), we seek to efficiently compute a multiscale representation to simultaneously detect the small ω and large Ω. The basic intuition comes from the observation that aggregating adjacent superpixels yields an increase in the entropy of the aggregate descriptor, up to the point where a minimum stationary region is reached, ω. At that point, aggregating further regions will not change the entropy, because of the stationarity assumption (of course, the complexity of the encoding will decrease, as more and more superpixels are lumped into the same region), up to the point where the boundary of the large region Ω is reached. Aggregating superpixels outside this region will cause the entropy to resume its climb.

The recursive fucntional reads, initializing $\omega_i^{(0)}$ as N different regions of 1 pixel size, where N is the number of pixels in the image,

$$\begin{cases} \Omega_i^{(k)} = \arg\min_{\Omega_i} \sum_{i=1}^{N(s)} \int_{\Omega_i} \mathcal{H}(\psi_{\omega_i^{(k)}}(I(x)))dx + \Gamma(\Omega_i) \\ \omega_i^{(k)} = \arg\max_{\omega_i} \sum_{i=1}^{N(s)} \int_{\omega_i} \mathcal{H}(\psi_{\Omega_i^{(k-1)}}(I(x)))dx - \Gamma(\omega_i) \end{cases} \tag{7}$$

where $\mathcal{H}$ is the Shannon entropy.

We propose two methods to perform this optimization. Building from a segmentation trees e.g. Sec. 4.1, 4.2, or 4.3 Method 1 performs a constrained optimization as a line search in the tree of superpixels. While Method 2 is a free-form optimization in the image domain.

5.1   Method 1: Constrained Solution from a Pre-processed Segmentation Tree

To instantiate this, we use the entropy-based saliency function introduced in [8], followed by entropy-based segmentation, as customary [2].

Using the dictionary features defined in Sect. 3, and the superpixel segmentation map at a given scale, one can compute an entropy $\mathcal{H}$ of features inside the superpixel containing i:

$$\mathcal{H}_i(s) = -\sum_{x=1}^{D} P_i(x, s) \log P_i(x, s) \tag{8}$$

where P_i is the distribution of the reduced dictionary features built on the region defined by i, i.e., the superpixel $\mathcal{S}(i, s)$, D is the size of the dictionary,

$$P_i(x) = \frac{1}{|\mathcal{S}(i, s)|} \sum_{p \in \mathcal{S}(i, s)} \delta(x - d(p)) \tag{9}$$

and δ is Dirac's delta, $d(p)$ is the index of the dictionary at point p. The small scale of a texture is defined as the largest scale at which entropy stops increasing:

$$\begin{cases} \omega(i, s) = \mathcal{S}(i, s') \\ s' = \arg\max_{t>s}\{t \mid \forall v\, s \le v \le t, \frac{\mathrm{d}\mathcal{H}_i(v)}{\mathrm{d}s} > 0\}. \end{cases} \tag{10}$$

The stationary domain of the texture Ω is simply defined as the boundary of the region past which entropy resumes increasing,

$$\begin{cases} \Omega(i, s) = \mathcal{S}(i, s'') \\ s'' = \arg\max_{t>s}\{t \mid \forall v\, s \le v \le t, \frac{\mathrm{d}\mathcal{H}_i(v)}{\mathrm{d}s} \le 0\} \end{cases} \tag{11}$$

Therefore, we perform the final segmentation at the maximum region that preserves stationarity.

While this method can be used with any segmentation tree, the solution will be constrained as unions of preprocessed segmentations. An unconstrained free-form solution can be found by building a segmentation tree that optimizes directly a Min-Max entropy in linear time using the properties of SRM.

5.2   Method 2: SRM with Alternate Min-Max Entropies

We start from an initial segmentation ω_i, e.g., from SRM, to initialize the statistics, then perform SRM again with the ordering of neighboring segments given by sorting the strength between segments $\Gamma = \int_{\partial \Omega_i} \|\nabla I(x)\|^2 \, \mathrm{d}x$ in increasing order. Now the predicate changes to an entropy-increasing or -decreasing test, and regions are merged only if entropy keeps decreasing or is constant. Once a region Ω_i is found, we turn to maximizing the entropy to find the region ω_i. The ordering of Γ neighboring segment is now sorted by decreasing order, and the regions are merged if entropy increases. In this way, one can define an alternating Min-Max entropy exploration of the image with the same complexity, since the neighboring graphs are only processed once. The number of merging tests is again linear in the number of pixels in the image.

5.3   Features Persistence and Stability

If the hypothesis underlying our definition of texture is correct, entropy will have a staircase-like behavior, with flat plateaus bounded below (in the sense of inclusion) by the small region ω, and above by Ω. As the same region can switch back-and-forth from texture to structure, we expect several such plateaus as the scale of inclusion changes. In the next section, we verify this hypothesis empirically on different superpixels from natural images. While this behavior is given *a priori* in the Min-Max entropy clustering, it is not obvious that it will be manifest when using any segmentation tree.

Those entropy profiles at each pixel are now agglomerated into one global histogram of entropies using a voting approach. As a staircase value of entropy appears at one pixel, it sums as a weighted contribution in the histogram of entropies, the weight being simply the length of the step. This histogram thus shows the different stable regimes of entropies appearing in the image. Knowing this histogram, one can deduce simply the local scale at a pixel position by doing mode seeking on this histogram (smoothed as a PDF). The definition of a local scale at one pixel position is the smallest scale where a mode value of the global histogram entropy appears. This allow us to perform stable segmentation and description of the natural scale of the image at a pixel, according to a structural stability criterion where the length of each step measures the *structural stability margin* [12].

6   Experimental Results

6.1   Computational Speed

In this section we explore the complexity and performance of the one dictionary learning and four clustering algorithms discussed. Computational speed is shown in Table 1, measured in seconds on a matlab/C implementation. Three different methods are used to build the dictionaries : (1) Color dictionary using k-means (2) Texture dictionary using k-means (3) Texture dictionary using k-means and agglomerated using a QS with Kullback-Leibler divergence. Based on those three different features, four different segmentation trees have been built: (a) Classical QS as described in Sect. 4.1 (b) kNN QS , with a scale parameter, designed for high dimensional spaces in Sect. 4.2 (c) Classical SRM as described in Sect. 4.3 (d) SRM with alternated min max entropies as described in Sect. 5.2

Table 1. Running times in seconds, (1,2,3) dictionary learning methods (a,b,c,d) segmentation tree methods

Method	(1)	(2)	(3)	(a)	(b)	(c)	(d)
Speed	0.2	4.1	8.1	0.4	0.1	1.5	3.8

6.2   Dictionary Agglomeration

We illustrate agglomeration by clustering a dictionary built on the "Barbara" image to eliminate nuisance variations such as small rotations, translations, and contrast changes. QS does not require a smooth embedding, so it can be used with a non-Euclidean metric, for instance one defined on the quotient space under the nuisance group. We use the symmetrized Kullback-Leibler divergence estimated with an efficient kNN-based estimator [3]. For every atom we build the pairwise distance matrix D_{ij} in (6). The first stage, with feature space $\{I(x,y), x, y\}$, forms a big cluster containing most of the texture elements "stripes" (Fig. 2). This dictionary now contains only one atom representing this texture cluster, or "exemplar."

In order to evaluate the efficiency of this agglomeration we take 32 random images from the Berkeley segmentation dataset. For each one we compare four ways of building a 128-atom dictionary: (i) direct k-means on the patches, (ii) first learning 256 clusters, then reducing QS using either ℓ_2, or (iii) KL clustering on $\{I(x,y)\}$, and finally (iv) KL clustering on $\{I(x,y), x, y\}$. One measure of efficiency of these dictionaries is the spatial coherence of the index of the atoms used. To measure it, one can compute first a color segmentation (in order to be independent of the texture measures) on each image and sum the entropies of each segment. The lower this entropy $\mathcal{H}_{\text{average}}$, the more coherent the index of the atoms.

$$\mathcal{H}_{\text{average}}(\text{feature}) = \frac{1}{32} \sum_{i=1}^{32} \frac{1}{N_S(i)} \sum_{s=1}^{N_S(i)} \mathcal{H}_{(\text{feature})}(i, s) \qquad (12)$$

where $N_S(i)$ is the number of superpixels in image i across all scales, $\mathcal{H}(\text{feature})$ (i, s) is the entropy of a given feature, in image i, inside superpixel s. In this section the feature used is the index of the dictionary. Average entropies shown in Table reveal that one can obtain coherent sparse decompositions in natural images and thus efficient dimensionality reduction.

Table 2. Agglomeration of dictionaries for efficient sparse representation. Sum of entropies over all the superpixels. (a) k-means on 128 elements, (b) (c) (d) k-means with an initial size of 256 reduced to 128 with, (b) ℓ_2 clustering, (c) KL clustering on $\{I(x,y)\}$ (d) KL clustering on $\{I(x,y), x, y\}$.

	(a)	(b)	(c)	(d)
$\mathcal{H}_{\text{average}}(index)$	3.25	3.10	3.17	**2.21**

This method is also computationally tractable as it runs on the space of bases, rather than the space of all image patches as in [2]. However, as the scale of the texture is unknown, it can contain many dictionary elements. A solution is to look for the dictionary dimension that gives uniform regions in the space of coefficients. Another solution is to try to find the natural scale of the textures using region growing algorithms, in our case superpixels aggregating across the tree of possible segmentations.

6.3   Multiscale Region Analysis

An illustration of the multiscale region analysis is shown in Figure 3. From one image, a superpixel map is computed at different scales. Then the dictionary features are computed and agglomerated. Finally, for six randomly select points inside each superpixel, we plot the variations of entropy. It is evident that, as scale increase, entropy increases in steps. The stationary regime corresponds with superpixels merging with others of similar distribution. Structural transitions occur when superpixels merge that have different distributions. The process ends when no new regions are discovered. These phase changes serve to detect ω_i and Ω_i, which are displayed for different superpixels at key scales when the entropy regime changes. In Figure 4, critical scales at successive levels are shown. First on a synthetic image, starting from one pixel, critical scales are: the pixel itself, the dark brown region minimizing entropy, then maximizing entropy, the light brown region to form an "L" , then minimizing entropy again, until the entire image is segmented. The same process is shown for a natural image; a light brick is first selected, then agglomerated with a darker one, then with a window, then with the whole building since all the statistics that describe the building are captured.

Fig. 3. It shows the entropy regime of 6 randomly selected points in the first image, by going through the different scales of the segmentation tree. Staircase is visible and shows the successive entropy regime of superpixels from successive ω regions to Ω regions. The regions are computed with QS trees. Detection of critical scales of textures on two different images. The segmentation scheme is now SRM Min-Max.

6.4   Scale Segmentation

The natural scale of a pixel is then extracted as described in Sect. 5.3. We use the segmentation tree SRM Min-Max with the features based on agglomerated dictionaries. Once the critical scales are computed, one builds a PDF of entropies over all superpixels. The scale at one pixel is defined as the smallest scale at which a mode appears. Those modes show stable regimes of entropies and can be used as a feature for scale segmentation. They also have the property of being accurate at boundaries, since the size of statistics is adaptive.

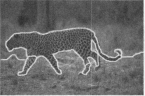

Fig. 4. Scale segmentation results on two images. By computing the statistics at the right scale, one can segment boundaries with pin-point precision, rather than suffering from "fat-boundary effects" common in texture segmentation. Last image shows a result with a standard texture segmentation algorithm [6] suffering from uniform scale selection and "fat-boundary effects"

6.5 Stability

To evaluate stability, again thirty-two images of the Berkeley segmentation dataset are again randomly selected. If the critical scales extracted are correct, there should be some coherence in all the regions extracted across the image (since our definition does not leverage on any matching, this condition is not forced by construction). The measure of stability is then the average entropy over the 32 images over all the superpixels as described in Sect. 6.2 and Equation (12). The features used here are size and color of the superpixels. Such features, if regions are stable and consistent, should have a low entropy across the image. That means that many regions should be similar in size and color in natural images.

Table 3. Stability of critical scales extracted using four different segmentation trees (a,b,c,d) based on three different features (1,2,3). The dictionaries, all of size 128, are: (1) Color (2) Texture (3) Agglomerated Texture using QS with Kullback-Leibler as described in Sect. 3. The segmentation trees are (a) QS described in Sect. 4.1 (b) kNN QS described in Sect. 4.2 (c) SRM described in Sect. 4.3 (d) SRM Min-Max entropy described in Sect. 5.2. The best result for each features and entropy (color or size of the critical scales) is shown in bold. The best overall result is obtained with SRM Min-Max with agglomerated texture dictionary features.

	(a-1)	(a-2)	(a-3)	(b-1)	(b-2)	(b-3)
$\mathcal{H}_{\text{average}}$(color)	3.17	3.01	2.88	3.08	2.97	2.81
$\mathcal{H}_{\text{average}}$(size)	4.87	4.52	4.18	**4.15**	4.12	4.05

	(c-1)	(c-2)	(c-3)	(d-1)	(d-2)	(d-3)
$\mathcal{H}_{\text{average}}$(color)	3.11	3.01	2.95	**2.22**	**2.14**	**2.07**
$\mathcal{H}_{\text{average}}$(size)	4.51	4.21	4.12	4.17	**4.08**	**3.98**

7   Discussion

We have presented an approach to multiscale texture analysis. The operative definition of texture we introduce guides the development of algorithms that efficiently enable the estimation of all the "small regions" (a.k.a. "texton regions"), the "big regions" (a.k.a. "texture segments") and the statistics within. We have introduced a novel clustering algorithm adapted for high-dimensional spaces, and showed how an information-theoretic criterion can be used to define the "gaps" to simultaneously detect small and large regions.

Acknowledgment

Research supported by ONR N00014-08-1-0414 and ARO 56765-CI.

References

1. Aharon, M., Elad, M., Bruckstein, A.M.: The k-svd: An algorithm for designing of overcomplete dictionaries for sparse representation. IEEE Transactions On Signal Processing 54(11), 4311–4322 (2006)
2. Awate, S.P., Tasdizen, T., Whitaker, R.T.: Unsupervised texture segmentation with nonparametric neighborhood statistics. In: European Conference on Computer Vision, Graz, Austria, pp. 494–507 (2006)
3. Boltz, S., Debreuve, E., Barlaud, M.: High-dimensional statistical distance for region-of-interest tracking: Application to combining a soft geometric constraint with radiometry. In: IEEE International Conference on Computer Vision and Pattern Recognition, Minneapolis, USA (2007)
4. Chazal, F., Guibas, L.J., Oudot, S.Y., Skraba, P.: Persistence-based clustering in Riemannian manifolds. Research Report 6968, INRIA (June 2009)
5. Georgescu, B., Shimshoni, I., Meer, P.: Mean shift based clustering in high dimensions: A texture classification example. In: IEEE International Conference on Computer Vision, p. 456 (2003)
6. Hong, B.W., Soatto, S., Ni, K., Chan, T.F.: The scale of a texture and its application to segmentation. In: IEEE International Conference on Computer Vision and Pattern Recognition (2008)
7. Julesz, B.: Textons, the elements of texture perception and their interactions. Nature (1981)
8. Kadir, T., Zisserman, A., Brady, M.: An affine invariant salient region detector. In: European Conference on Computer Vision (2004)
9. Lindeberg, T.: Scale-space theory in computer vision. Kluwer Academic, Dordrecht (1994)
10. Nock, R., Nielsen, F.: Statistical region merging. IEEE Transactions Pattern Analysis Machine Intelligence 26(11), 1452–1458 (2004)
11. Robert, C.P.: The Bayesian Choice. Springer, New York (2001)
12. Soatto, S.: Towards a mathematical theory of visual information (2010) (preprint)
13. Sundaramoorthi, G., Petersen, P., Varadarajan, V.S., Soatto, S.: On the set of images modulo viewpoint and contrast changes. In: Proceedings of the IEEE Conference on Computer Vision and Pattern Recognition (June 2009)

14. Terrell, G.R., Scott, D.W.: Variable kernel density estimation. The Annals of Statistics 20, 1236–1265 (1992)
15. Varma, M., Zisserman, A.: A statistical approach to material classification using image patch exemplars. In: IEEE Transactions Pattern Analysis Machine Intelligence (to appear)
16. Vedaldi, A., Soatto, S.: Quick shift and kernel methods for mode seeking. In: European Conference on Computer Vision, vol. IV, pp. 705–718 (2008)
17. Wu, Y.N., Guo, C., Zhu, S.C.: Perceptual scaling. Applied Bayesian Modeling and Causal Inference from an Incomplete Data Perspective (2004)
18. Zhu, S.C., Wu, Y.N., Mumford, D.: Minimax entropy principle and its application to texture modeling. Neural Computation 9, 1627–1660 (1997)

A High-Quality Video Denoising Algorithm Based on Reliable Motion Estimation

Ce Liu[1] and William T. Freeman[1,2]

[1] Microsoft Research New England
[2] Massachusetts Institute of Technology

Abstract. Although the recent advances in the sparse representations of images have achieved outstanding denosing results, removing real, structured noise in digital videos remains a challenging problem. We show the utility of reliable motion estimation to establish temporal correspondence across frames in order to achieve high-quality video denoising. In this paper, we propose an adaptive video denosing framework that integrates robust optical flow into a non-local means (NLM) framework with noise level estimation. The spatial regularization in optical flow is the key to ensure temporal coherence in removing structured noise. Furthermore, we introduce approximate K-nearest neighbor matching to significantly reduce the complexity of classical NLM methods. Experimental results show that our system is comparable with the state of the art in removing AWGN, and significantly outperforms the state of the art in removing real, structured noise.

Keywords: Video denoising, structured noise, approximate K-nearest neighbors, non-local means, optical flow.

1 Introduction

Image quality enhancement is a long-standing area of research. As low-end imaging devices, such as web-cams and cell phones, become ubiquitous, there is ever more need for reliable digital image and video enhancement technologies to improve their outputs. Noise is dominant factor that degrades image quality.

We focus on video denoising in this paper. Our goal is to achieve an efficient, adaptive and high-quality video denoising algorithm that can effectively remove real, structured noise introduced by low-end camcorders and digital cameras. Unlike synthetic, additive noise, the noise in real cameras can have strong spatial correlations. This structured noise can have many different causes, including the demosaicing process in CCD camera. We find that computer vision analysis and techniques are useful in addressing these noise problems.

For image and video denoising, a key is to exploit the property of *image sparsity* [1, 2, 3]. In the frequency domain, image sparsity can be formulated as high-kurtotic marginal distribution of bandpass filtering, and image coring [4, 5] is a straightforward denoising algorithm that preserves large-magnitude responses while shrinking small-magnitude responses. In the spatial domain, image sparsity arguments imply that for any image patch, there will be similar ones in other locations of the image. The non-local means (NLM) method [6] was introduced to remove noise by averaging pixels in

K. Daniilidis, P. Maragos, N. Paragios (Eds.): ECCV 2010, Part III, LNCS 6313, pp. 706–719, 2010.

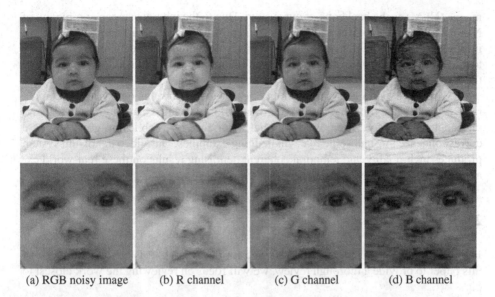

(a) RGB noisy image   (b) R channel   (c) G channel   (d) B channel

Fig. 1. In real video denoising scenarios, images contain structured noise. For this example, the blue channel is heavily contaminated with structured noise that can be mixed with signal. Even the state-of-the-art video denoising algorithm [10] fails to obtain temporally smooth denoising results. On the contrary, the proposed algorithm in this paper is able to remove structured noise and obtain temporally smooth results.

an image weighted by local patch similarities. Recently, these two forms of sparsity are combined in [7] to produce the state of the art in image denoising.

Sparsity also resides in videos. Most videos are temporally consistent; a new frame can be well predicted from previous frames [8, 9]. Indeed, *temporal coherence* can be vital to achieving high quality. Given two noise-free videos that share the same average peak signal-to-noise ratio (PSNR), we may prefer the one with more temporal coherence.

Although the state of the art video denoising algorithms often satisfy the temporal coherence criterion in removing additive white Gaussian noise (AWGN), many real videos contain structured noise that makes it challenging to ensure temporal coherence. As shown in Figure 1, the blue channel of the image contains structured noise that can be misinterpreted as signal by many denoising algorithms. Confused by the jittering blocky noise, block matching techniques (*e.g.* in [10]) may fail to track the true motion of the objects.

Therefore, in contrast with [11], we argue that high-quality video denoising, especially when structured noise is taken into account, indeed needs reliable motion estimation. In theory, estimating motion and noise suffers from a chicken-and-egg problem, since motion should be estimated from the underlying signals after denoising, and denoising relies on the temporal correspondence from motion estimation. In practice, however, we used robust optical flow with spatial regularization to establish reliable temporal correspondence despite noise. Because of its power, we use non-local means (NLM) as the backbone of our system. Due to the inherent search complexity of NLM, searching for similar patches is often constrained to a small neighborhood. We introduce approximate K-nearest neighbor patch matching with much lower complexity to allow for searching over the entire image for similar patches. In addition, we estimate the noise level at each frame for noise-adaptive denoising.

We conduct experiments to test our theories. We first show that our system is comparable with the state of the art [10] in removing additive white Gaussian noise (AWGN) on benchmark videos. Then, we show the importance of establishing good temporal correspondence through some real, challenging examples. Our video denoising system produces high-quality and temporal coherent denoising results on these real-world examples, outperforming the state of the art.

2 Related Work

Image and video denoising has been studied for decades. As it is beyond the scope of this paper to provide a thorough review, we will focus on reviewing the work closest to ours.

Image sparsity can manifest itself in different forms. When images are decomposed into sub-bands, sparsity leads to image coring algorithms on wavelets coefficients [4,5]: large-magnitude coefficients that more likely correspond to true image signal should be retained, whereas small-magnitude coefficients that more likely correspond to noise should be shrunk. When the prior of natural images is incorporated in denoising [12, 13, 14], image sparsity is reflected by the heavy-tailed robust potential functions associated with band-pass filters: pixels in a neighborhood are encouraged to be similar, but occasional dissimilarity is allowed. Other denoising techniques such as PDE's [15] and region-based denoising [16] also implicitly formulate sparsity in their representation.

Unfortunately, wavelet- and natural image prior-based denoising algorithms can introduce unwanted artifacts to denoised images. Recently, image sparsity was formulated as image self similarity, namely patches in an image are similar to one another, which leads to the non-local means (NLM) methods [6]. In NLM, similar patches are aggregated together with weights based on patch similarities. This surprisingly simple algorithm produces high-quality results. NLM was also extended to video denoising [11] by aggregating patches in a space-temporal volume. Because of this, we choose NLM as the framework of our video denoising system.

The frequency and spatial forms of image sparsity are seamlessly integrated in [7], where similar patches are stacked in a 3D array, and both hard and soft shrinkages are performed on a 3D DCT transformed domain. This idea can be easily extended to video denoising, and state of the art video denoising results were reported in [10].

In [17], it was claimed that under the NLM framework "denoising image sequences does not require motion estimation" because the aperture problem, which often causes motion estimation to fail on textureless regions, is indeed beneficial to denoising as redundant patches are available for better denoising. However, we disagree on this point. As shown in Figure 1, structured noise can mislead the search for similar patches and then breaks the temporal coherence criterion in video denoising. We attempt to resolve this issue in this paper.

Patch matching has been widely used for image synthesis and editing, *e.g.* [18]. Recently, random patch matching was proposed to significantly speed up nearest neighbor searching on images [19]. The key ideas are random initialization and improvement, and spatial propagation. We extend this idea to random K-nearest neighbor matching to speed up patching matching under the NLM framework.

3 A Temporally Coherent Video Denoising Framework

For every patch in a video, we want to find a set of supporting patches from this frame and temporal adjacent frames that are similar to this patch. To ensure the nature of spatial and temporal sparsity of videos, we want spatially neighboring pixels and temporally corresponding pixels to share similar structures of supporting patches. This is ensured by approximate K-nearest neighbor matching for a single frame and establishing temporal correspondence using optical flow.

3.1 Approximate K-Nearest Neighbors (AKNN) for a Single Frame

Mathematically, we use notion $\{I_1, I_2, \cdots, I_T\}$ to denote an input noisy sequence that contains T frames. We use $\mathbf{z} = (x, y, t)$ to index the space-time volume, and $P(\mathbf{z})$ (or equivalently $P(x, y, t)$) to denote a patch at location $\mathbf{z}$. In this subsection, we focus on searching for K-nearest neighbors within a single frame, and will extend to multiple frames in next subsection. For notational convenience, we let $\mathbf{q} = (x, y)$ and omit time t from the notation. For each pixel $\mathbf{q}$, we want to obtain a set of *approximate K-nearest neighbors* (AKNN) $\mathcal{N}(\mathbf{q}) = \{P(\mathbf{q}_i)\}_{i=1}^{K}$. Let $\mathbf{v}_i = \mathbf{q}_i - \mathbf{q}$ be the offset of the found patch from the current patch. Searching for $\mathcal{N}(\mathbf{q})$ is equivalent to searching for $\{\mathbf{v}_i\}$.

For efficiency, we used the *priority queue* data structure to store the K-nearest neighbors such that the following increasing order is always maintained for the elements in the priority queue:

$$D\big(P(\mathbf{q}), P(\mathbf{q}_i)\big) \leqslant D\big(P(\mathbf{q}), P(\mathbf{q}_j)\big), \ \forall 1 \leqslant i < j \leqslant K, \tag{1}$$

where $D(\cdot, \cdot)$ is sum of square distance (SSD) over two patches, defined as

$$D\big(P(\mathbf{q}), P(\mathbf{q}_i)\big) = \sum_{\mathbf{u} \in [-s,s] \times [-s,s]} \big(I(\mathbf{q} + \mathbf{u}) - I(\mathbf{q}_i + \mathbf{u})\big)^2. \tag{2}$$

When a new patch is pushed back to this queue, it will be discarded if the distance is greater than the last element of the queue, or will otherwise be added at the appropriate position in the priority queue. A heap implementation of the priority queue has complexity $O(\log K)$.

Suppose there are N pixels in an image, then the complexity of a brute-force K-nearest neighbor search over the entire image is $O(N^2 \log K)$, almost implausible for high-definition (HD) videos. Inspired by the approximate nearest neighbor algorithm in [19], we propose an approximate K-nearest neighbor algorithm that contains three phases, *initialization*, *propagation* and *random search*, which will be explained below.

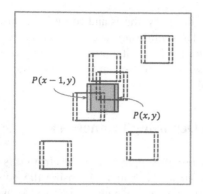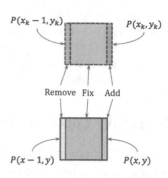

Fig. 2. The approximate K-nearest neighbors (AKNN) of patch $P(x, y)$ (blue) can be improved by propagating AKNN from $P(x-1, y)$ (red). Left: the approximate K-nearest neighbors of $P(x-1, y)$ are shifted one pixel to the right to be pushed to the priority queue of (x, y). Right: we do not need to recompute patch distances with this shift. To compute the distance between $P(x_k, y_k)$ and $P(x, y)$, we can simply take the distance between $P(x_k-1, y_k)$ and $P(x-1, y)$, remove the left column (orange) and add the right column (green).

To ensure the order in Eqn. (1), any new item generated in these phases is pushed back to the priority queue.

Initialization. The K-nearest neighbors are initialized by randomization

$$\mathbf{v}_i = \sigma_s \mathbf{n}_i \qquad (3)$$

where $\mathbf{n}_i$ is a standard 2d normal random variable, and σ_s controls the radius. In this paper we set $\sigma_s = w/3$ where w is the width of an image.

Propagation. After initialization, an iterative process that consists of *propagation* and *random search* is performed in an interleaving manner. The idea is to improve the approximate K-nearest neighbor set based on the fact that neighboring pixels tend to have similar AKNN structures (offsets). The propagation procedure intertwines between scanline order and reverse scanline order [19]. In the scanline order, we attempt to improve AKNN $\{\mathbf{v}_i(x, y)\}$ using neighbor $\{\mathbf{v}_i(x-1, y)\}$ and $\{\mathbf{v}_i(x, y-1)\}$. In the reverse scanline order, we attempt to improve $\{\mathbf{v}_i(x, y)\}$ using neighbor $\{\mathbf{v}_i(x+1, y)\}$ and $\{\mathbf{v}_i(x, y+1)\}$.

As an example, we use the AKNN of patch $P(x-1, y)$ (red, filled square) to improve the AKNN of patch $P(x, y)$ (blue, filled square) as shown in Figure 2. The approximate K-nearest neighbors (red, dashed squares) of $P(x-1, y)$ are shifted one pixel to the right to obtain a *proposal set* (blue, dashed squares), which are pushed back to the priority queue of $P(x, y)$. There is no need of recalculating the patch distance as illustrated in Figure 2. We only need to compute the pixel-distance contributed from the non-overlapping region, as in [19].

This propagation is very similar to the sequential update scheme in belief propagation [20]. Although the (implicit) objective function is independent for neighboring pixels, this propagation scheme makes neighboring patches share similar AKNN structures.

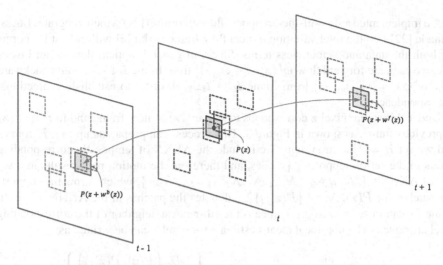

Fig. 3. Illustrations of the supporting patches in spatial-temporal domain for a patch $P(\mathbf{z})$. We use approximate K-nearest neighbor patch matching at frame t to find an initial set of spatially supporting patches $\mathcal{N}(\mathbf{z})$, shown as dashed boxes. Since $\mathbf{z}$ corresponds to $\mathbf{z} + w^f(\mathbf{z})$ in frame $t+1$, the AKNN of $\mathbf{z} + w^f(\mathbf{z})$ is added to the set of supporting patches. Likewise, the AKNN of $\mathbf{z} + w^b(\mathbf{z})$ that $\mathbf{z}$ corresponds to in frame $t-1$ is also added. In fact, we use the AKNN's along the motion path up to $\pm H$ frames to form the entire supporting patches.

Random search. After the propagation step, we allow every patch to randomly match other patches in the image for M times using the following mechanism

$$\mathbf{v}_i = \sigma_s \alpha^i \mathbf{n}_i, \; i = 1, \cdots, M \tag{4}$$

where $\mathbf{n}_i$ is a standard 2d normal random variable, $\alpha = \frac{1}{2}$ and $M = \min(\log_2 \sigma_s, K)$. So the radius of the random search $\sigma_s \alpha^i$ decreases exponentially. Each random guess is again pushed back to the priority queue to maintain the increasing order of the queue.

This approximate K-nearest neighbor patch matching algorithm converges quickly. We found that running more than 4 iterations does not generate more visually pleasing results. Furthermore, in the matching procedure we excluded the patch itself because it has distance zero. In the end, we add patch $P(x, y)$ into $\mathcal{N}(x, y)$.

3.2 Non-local Means with Temporal Coherence

We feel that temporal coherence is vital for denoising. Two algorithms may perform equally well for a single frame, but the one that produces more temporal coherent results is preferred. It was argued in [11] that denoising image sequence does not require motion estimation. But for real sequences, it can be difficult to distinguish high-intensity structured noise from image signal. Therefore, it is important to establish temporal correspondence between adjacent frames and require corresponding pixels to be similar. Instead of formulating this property explicitly, we design a mechanism to satisfy this criterion implicitly.

We implemented a state-of-the-art optical flow algorithm [21] which integrates Lucas-Kanade [22] into the total variation optical flow framework [23] with robust L1 norms for both the data and smoothness terms. Since, in general, optical flow is not invertible, we estimate forward flow $w^f(\mathbf{z}) = [v_x, v_y, 1]$ from frame I_t to I_{t+1}, and backward flow $w^b(\mathbf{z}) = [v_x, v_y, -1]$ from frame I_t to I_{t-1}, in order to establish bidirectional correspondence.

Under this setup, pixel $\mathbf{z}$ corresponds to $\mathbf{z} + w^f(\mathbf{z})$ in next frame and to $z + w^b(\mathbf{z})$ in previous frame, as shown in Figure 3. This process can propagate up to $\pm H$ frames and we set $H = 5$ in our system. We include the AKNN of temporally corresponding pixels to the set of supporting patches, and therefore the motion path results in a series of AKNN's $\{\mathcal{N}_{t-H}, \cdots, \mathcal{N}_{t-1}, \mathcal{N}_t, \mathcal{N}_{t+1}, \cdots, \mathcal{N}_{t+H}\}$, which forms the supporting patches for $P(\mathbf{z})$. $\mathcal{N}_i = \{P(\mathbf{z}_{ij})\}_{j=1}^K$ denotes the patches in the AKNN at the ith frame. Notation $\mathbf{z}_{ij} = (x_{ij}, y_{ij}, i)$ means the jth-nearest neighbor of the corresponding pixel at frame i. The non-local means estimate for pixel $\mathbf{z}$ can be written as:

$$\hat{I}(\mathbf{z}) = \frac{1}{Z} \sum_{i=t-H}^{t+H} \gamma^{|i-t|} \sum_{j=1}^{K} I(\mathbf{z}_{ij}) \exp\left\{ -\frac{D_w\Big(P(\mathbf{z}), P(\mathbf{z}_{ij})\Big)}{2\sigma_t^2} \right\}, \tag{5}$$

where Z is the normalization factor:

$$Z = \sum_{i=t-H}^{t+H} \gamma^{|i-t|} \sum_{j=1}^{K} \exp\left\{ -\frac{D_w\Big(P(\mathbf{z}), P(\mathbf{z}_{ij})\Big)}{2\sigma_t^2} \right\}, \tag{6}$$

and $D_w(\cdot, \cdot)$ is a weighted SSD function, summed over spatial, but not temporal, offsets:

$$D_w\Big(P(\mathbf{z}_1), P(\mathbf{z}_2)\Big) = \frac{1}{Z'} \sum_{\mathbf{u} \in [-s,s] \times [-s,s] \times 0} \Big(P(\mathbf{z}_1 + \mathbf{u}) - P(\mathbf{z}_2 + \mathbf{u})\Big)^2 \exp\left\{ -\frac{\|\mathbf{u}\|^2}{2\sigma_p^2} \right\}, \tag{7}$$

where $\sigma_p = \frac{s}{2}$, and Z' is a normalization constant. We set $\gamma = 0.9$ to control temporal decay. σ_t is related to the noise level in the video sequence, which will be discussed in the next subsection.

For a fixed number of iterations, the complexity of our denoising algorithm for a frame is $O(NHK \log K)$, where N is the number of pixels per frame, H is the temporal window size, and K is the number of approximate K-nearest neighbors. This is a significant reduction compared to $O(N^2)$ of the original NLM algorithm, since $K \ll N$ (typically $K = 10$ and $N = 640 \times 480$). Even if the search space of the original NLM algorithm is reduced to a 3D volume $M \times M \times (2H + 1)$ [11] (typically $M = 40$), the complexity remains as $O(NHM^2)$, still greater than our algorithm, which considers patches over the entire image lattice and $2H+1$ frames.

3.3   Noise Estimation for Adaptive Noise Removal

It is important to set the parameter σ_t appropriately in Eqn (5). Intuitively, when the noise level is low in the original sequence, we should set σ_t small to avoid over-smoothing, and when the noise level is high, we should set σ_t large to smooth out noise. Instead of using a single-frame noise estimator as in [24], we propose a simple noise model based on optical flow.

Theoretically, as we warp frame I_{t+1} back to t according to the forward flow field $w^f(\mathbf{z})$, the difference between the warped frame and I_t should be the difference of independent noise. However, motion estimation can be unreliable especially at textureless regions and the brightness constancy assumption fails for occluded regions. Therefore, we introduce an outlier in noise estimation:

$$I_t(\mathbf{z}) = I_{t+1}(\mathbf{z} + w^f(\mathbf{z})) + \alpha_{\mathbf{z}} n_{\mathbf{z}} + (1 - \alpha_{\mathbf{z}}) u_{\mathbf{z}}. \tag{8}$$

In the above equation, $n_{\mathbf{z}}$ is a pixel-wise Gaussian random variable: $E(n_{\mathbf{z}}) = 0$, $E(n_{\mathbf{z}}^2) = \sigma_n$, and $u_{\mathbf{z}} \sim U[-1,1]$ is a pixel-wise uniform random variable. These two random variables are balanced by weight $\alpha_{\mathbf{z}}$. Let $J_t(\mathbf{z}) = I_t(\mathbf{z}) - I_{t+1}(\mathbf{z} + w^f(\mathbf{z}))$. We use an expectation-maximization (EM) algorithm to estimate parameters:

---

1. Initialize $\sigma_n = 20$. Loop between step 2 and 3 until convergence.

2. (E-step) Evaluate $\alpha_{\mathbf{z}} = \dfrac{\exp\left\{-\dfrac{J_t(\mathbf{z})}{2\sigma_n^2}\right\}}{\exp\left\{-\dfrac{J_t(\mathbf{z})}{2\sigma_n^2}\right\} + \dfrac{1}{2}\sqrt{2\pi}\sigma_n}$.

3. (M-step) Estimate $\sigma_n = \sqrt{\dfrac{\sum_{\mathbf{z}} J_t(\mathbf{z})^2 \alpha_{\mathbf{z}}}{\sum_{\mathbf{z}} \alpha_{\mathbf{z}}}}$.

We perform this estimation for each of R, G and B channels independently.

The relationship between the noise level σ_n and scaling parameter σ_t in Eqn. (5) depends on K and H. Empirically, we have found that when $K = 11$ and $H = 5$ (which means that there are in total $K(2H + 1) = 121$ patches in total for NLM at one pixel), $\sigma_t = \sigma_n$ generates visually pleasing results.

4 Experimental Results

We conducted experiments to examine whether, in the framework we use, video denoising requires reliable motion estimation. In this section, we will first verify that our denoising algorithm is comparable with the state of the art [10] on synthetic sequences. Then, we will show that our algorithm outperforms the state of the art on real video sequences. **Please see denoised videos in the supplementary materials or the authors' websites. Please also use your monitor to view the results in the paper.**

Here are some implementation details of our algorithm. We use 7×7 patches, and $K = 11$ nearest neighbors (including the patch itself), and 11 temporal frames ($H = 5$) in our system. We allow 4 iterations of random K-nearest neighbor matching for each frame. The EM algorithm for noise estimation converges in about 10 iterations. For the optical flow algorithm, we used a coarse to fine scheme on image pyramid (with downsample rate 0.7) to avoid local minimum. The objective function is optimized through

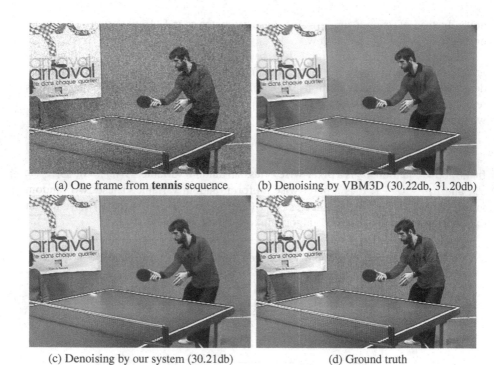

(a) One frame from **tennis** sequence   (b) Denoising by VBM3D (30.22db, 31.20db)

(c) Denoising by our system (30.21db)   (d) Ground truth

Fig. 4. For the **tennis** sequence, although the PSNR of our denoising system is slightly lower, the visual difference is subtle. VBM3D tends to generate smoother regions (but the background is over-smoothed), whereas our system preserves texture better (but the table is under-smoothed).

iterative reweighted least square (IRLS). More details of the flow estimation algorithm can be found in [25], and the source code is available online[1].

We first run our system on the **tennis** sequence with synthetically generated AWGN ($\sigma = 20$) to compare with existing methods. The average peak signal to noise ratio (PSNR) is 30.21db. We also downloaded the code from the BM3D webpage[2] for evaluation. In their MATLAB package, function VBM3D.m is used for gray-scale frames and CVBM3D.m is for color frames. We used VBM3D for the **tennis** sequence and CVBM3D for other sequences, but we will call it VBM3D in general. The first denoising step of VBM3D produces PSNR 30.22db, and the second step boosts it to 31.20db. The gain comes from re-matching patches from the denoising results at the first step and joint Wiener filtering at the second step, which are missing in our model. The backbone of our system is non-local means and therefore performs slightly worse in terms of PSNR. But the visual difference between ours and VBM3D is subtle, as shown in Figure 4.

We move on to a real video sequence named **room** captured by a Canon S90. This is a challenging sequence as the camera moves in between bright and dark rooms. We first examine the importance of regularization in motion estimation by comparing block

---

[1] http://people.csail.mit.edu/celiu/OpticalFlow/
[2] http://www.cs.tut.fi/~foi/GCF-BM3D/index.html

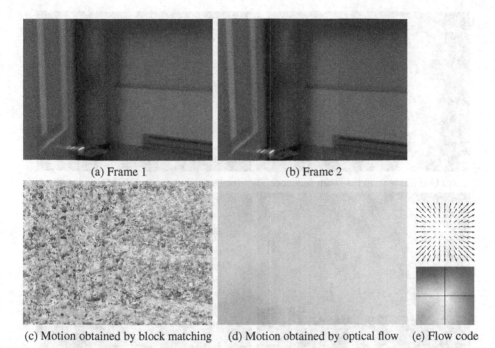

(a) Frame 1   (b) Frame 2

(c) Motion obtained by block matching   (d) Motion obtained by optical flow   (e) Flow code

Fig. 5. The right motion estimation algorithm should be chosen for denoising. For two consecutive frames in the **room** sequence, we apply both block matching [10] and optical flow [21] to estimate motion, shown in (c) and (d), respectively. We used the color scheme in [26] to visualize flow fields (e).

matching to the optical flow algorithm with spatial regularization. The motion estimation of one frame is shown in Figure 5, where motion vectors are visualized by the color scheme proposed in [26]. Clearly, spatially independent block matching in (c) is highly affected by the presence of structured noise. On the contrary, the optical flow with spatial regularization in (d) produces a smooth, discontinuity preserving temporal motion field that corresponds to the human perception of motion, and to the known smooth character of the optical flow induced by a camera moving through this piecewise smooth planar, static scene.

The quality of our motion estimation determines the quality of our video denoising. Because the code we downloaded from VBM3D does not allow input of frame-based noise intensities, we try two parameters $\sigma = 20$ and $\sigma = 40$ to denoise the **room** sequence, with results shown in Figure 6 (b) and (c), respectively. The result of our adaptive denoising system is shown in Figure 6 (d). Although there is no ground truth of this video, it is clear that our system outperforms VBM3D in both smoothing regions and preserving boundaries. The visual difference is more obvious when watching the videos in the supplementary materials.

Average PSNR over the video sequence has been used to measure video denoising qualities, but temporal coherence was not included in the quality assessment. We feel that temporal coherence is indeed vital to evaluate video denoising algorithms. For this

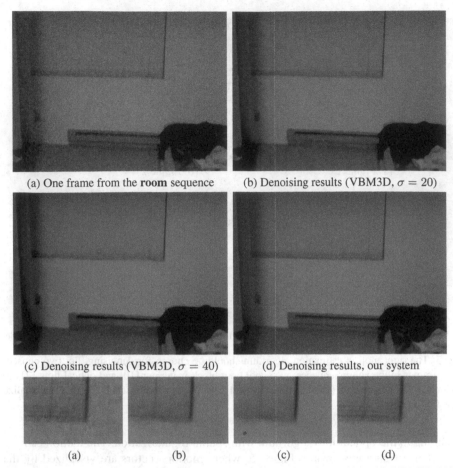

(a) One frame from the **room** sequence   (b) Denoising results (VBM3D, $\sigma = 20$)

(c) Denoising results (VBM3D, $\sigma = 40$)   (d) Denoising results, our system

(a)   (b)   (c)   (d)

Fig. 6. We run our system on the **room** sequence and compare the results with VBM3D [10]. Top: whole frames; bottom: the blowup view of a region. Our system outperforms VBM3D in both smoothing regions and preserving boundaries. **Please view this figure on your monitor.**

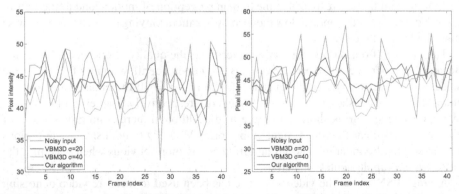

Fig. 7. Temporal smoothness of different denosing algorithms. We measure pixel intensities along motion paths over frames. Two motion paths are shown here. Our system (red curve) has the least amount of temporal fluctuation.

Table 1. The average standard deviation along motion paths is measured for different algorithms at different RGB channels. Our system has overall the least temporal fluctuation.

Std. Dev.	Input data	VBM3D $\sigma = 20$	VBM3D $\sigma = 40$	Our algorithm
Red	4.20	2.22	1.52	1.23
Green	3.81	1.78	1.45	1.13
Blue	9.55	5.77	2.81	2.91

(a)

(b)

Fig. 8. Removing realistic video noise has broad applications. For example, we can turn a noisy HD home video (a) to a high-quality, noise-free video (b), which can be pleasantly played on an HDTV. Please see the **baby** video in the supplementary materials. **Please view this figure on your monitor.**

purpose, we downloaded the human-assisted motion annotation tool [27] to annotate the ground-truth motion of the **room** sequence. Using the annotated motion we can analyze how pixel intensities change over time for different denoising algorithms. Two exemplar motion paths are plotted in Figure 7, and the average standard deviation for each of the RGB channels is listed in Table 1. Clearly, our system has overall the least temporal fluctuation, which we feel is crucial for visual quality.

Lastly, we run our system on another video sequence with real noise, **baby**, a 720P HD video clip captured by SONY HDR-XR150. One input frame and denoised frame are shown in Figure 8. Our video denoising system is able to remove the structured noise and preserve image details without introducing artifacts. This example shows the broad applications for reliable video denoising algorithms.

5   Conclusion

We argue that robust motion estimation is essential for high-quality video denoising, especially in the presence of real, structured noise. Based on the non-local means framework, we introduce an efficient, approximate K-nearest neighbor patch matching algorithm that can search for similar patches in a neighborhood as large as the entire image. This random matching algorithm significantly reduces the complexity of classical NLM methods. A robust optical flow algorithm with spatial regularity was used to estimate temporal correspondence between adjacent frames. The spatial regularity is the key to robust motion estimation in the presence of structured noise. We use the temporal correspondence to enlarge the set of supporting patches over time and to ensure temporal coherence. Experimental results show that our system is comparable with the state of the art in removing AWGN, and significantly outperforms the state of the art in removing real, structured noise. Our system is easy to implement, with broad applications in digital video enhancement.

References

1. Olshausen, B.A., Field, D.J.: Emergence of simple-cell receptive field properties by learning a sparse code for natural images. Nature 381, 607–609 (1996)
2. Mairal, J., Elad, M., Sapiro, G.: Multiscale sparse image representation with learned dictionaries. In: IEEE International Conference on Image Processing, ICIP (2007)
3. Yang, J., Wright, J., Huang, T., Ma, Y.: Image super-resolution as sparse representation of raw image patches. In: IEEE Conference on Computer Vision and Pattern Recognition, CVPR (2008)
4. Simoncelli, E.P., Adelson, E.H.: Noise removal via Bayesian wavelet coring. In: IEEE International Conference on Image Processing (ICIP), vol. I, pp. 379–382 (1996)
5. Portilla, J., Strela, V., Wainwright, M.J., Simoncelli, E.P.: Image denoising using scale mixtures of gaussians in the wavelet domain. IEEE Transactions on Image Processing (TIP) 12, 1338–1351 (2003)
6. Buades, A., Coll, B., Morel, J.M.: A non-local algorithm for image denoising. In: IEEE Conference on Computer Vision and Pattern Recognition, CVPR (2005)
7. Dabov, K., Foi, A., Katkovnik, V., Egiazarian, K.: Image denoising by sparse 3d transform-domain collaborative filtering. IEEE Transactions on Image Processing (TIP) 16 (2007)

8. MPEG: Mpeg-2 video encoding, h.262 (2006),
   http://www.digitalpreservation.gov/formats/fdd/
   fdd000028.shtml
9. Lee, C.U., Pian, D.: Interframe video encoding and decoding system (1996) US Patent 5,576,767
10. Dabov, K., Foi, A., Egiazarian, K.: Video denoising by sparse 3d transform-domain collaborative filtering. In: European Signal Processing Conference, EUSIPCO (2007)
11. Buades, A., Coll, B., Morel, J.M.: Nonlocal image and movie denoising. International Journal of Computer Vision (IJCV) 76, 123–139 (2008)
12. Roth, S., Black, M.J.: Fields of experts: A framework for learning image priors. In: IEEE Conference on Computer Vision and Pattern Recognition, CVPR (2005)
13. Weiss, Y., Freeman, W.: What makes a good model of natural images. In: IEEE Conference on Computer Vision and Pattern Recognition, CVPR (2007)
14. Elad, M., Aharon, M.: Image denoising via learned dictionaries and sparse representation. In: IEEE Conference on Computer Vision and Pattern Recognition, CVPR (2006)
15. Tschumperlé, D.: Fast anisotropic smoothing of multi-valued images using curvature-preserving PDE's. International Journal of Computer Vision (IJCV) 68, 65–82 (2006)
16. Liu, C., Szeliski, R., Kang, S.B., Zitnick, C.L., Freeman, W.T.: Automatic estimation and removal of noise from a single image. IEEE Transactions on Pattern Analysis and Machine Intelligence (TPAMI) 30, 299–314 (2008)
17. Buades, A., Coll, B., Morel, J.M.: Denoising image sequences does not require motion estimation. In: IEEE International Conference on Advanced Video and Signal Based Surveillance (2005)
18. Cho, T., Butman, M., Avidan, S., Freeman, W.: The patch transform and its applications to image editing. In: IEEE Conference on Computer Vision and Pattern Recognition, CVPR (2008)
19. Barnes, C., Shechtman, E., Finkelstein, A., Goldman, D.B.: Patchmatch: A randomized correspondence algorithm for structural image editing. In: Proceedings of ACM SIGGRAPH (2009)
20. Szeliski, R., Zabih, R., Scharstein, D., Veksler, O., Kolmogorov, V., Agarwala, A., Tappen, M., Rother, C.: A comparative study of energy minimization methods for markov random fields with smoothness-based priors. IEEE Transactions on Pattern Analysis and Machine Intelligence (TPAMI) 30, 1068–1080 (2008)
21. Bruhn, A., Weickert, J., Schnörr, C.: Lucas/Kanade meets Horn/Schunk: combining local and global optical flow methods. International Journal of Computer Vision (IJCV) 61, 211–231 (2005)
22. Lucas, B., Kanade, T.: An iterative image registration technique with an application to stereo vision. In: Proceedings of the International Joint Conference on Artificial Intelligence, pp. 674–679 (1981)
23. Horn, B.K.P., Schunck, B.G.: Determing optical flow. Artificial Intelligence 17, 185–203 (1981)
24. Liu, C., Freeman, W.T., Szeliski, R., Kang, S.B.: Noise estimation from a single image. In: IEEE Conference on Computer Vision and Pattern Recognition (CVPR), pp. 901–908 (2006)
25. Liu, C.: Beyond pixels: exploring new representations and applications for motion analysis. PhD thesis, Massachusetts Insitute of Technology (2009)
26. Baker, S., Scharstein, D., Lewis, J.P., Roth, S., Black, M.J., Szeliski, R.: A database and evaluation methodology for optical flow. In: Proc. ICCV (2007)
27. Liu, C., Freeman, W.T., Adelson, E.H., Weiss, Y.: Human-assisted motion annotation. In: IEEE Conference on Computer Vision and Pattern Recognition, CVPR (2008)

An Oriented Flux Symmetry Based Active Contour Model for Three Dimensional Vessel Segmentation

Max W.K. Law and Albert C.S. Chung

Lo Kwee-Seong Medical Image Analysis Laboratory,
Department of Computer Science and Engineering,
The Hong Kong University of Science and Technology, Hong Kong
{maxlawwk,achung}@cse.ust.hk

Abstract. This paper proposes a novel approach to segment three dimensional curvilinear structures, particularly vessels in angiography, by inspecting the symmetry of image gradients. The proposed method stresses the importance of simultaneously considering both the gradient symmetry with respect to the curvilinear structure center, and the gradient antisymmetry with respect to the object boundary. Measuring the image gradient symmetry remarkably suppresses the disturbance introduced by rapid intensity changes along curvilinear structures. Meanwhile, considering the image gradient antisymmetry helps locate the structure boundary. The gradient symmetry and the gradient antisymmetry are evaluated based on the notion of oriented flux. By utilizing the aforementioned gradient symmetry information, an active contour model is tailored to perform segmentation. On the one hand, by exploiting the symmetric image gradient pattern observed at structure centers, the contours expand along curvilinear structures even through there exists intensity fluctuation along the structures. On the other hand, measuring the antisymmetry of the image gradient conveys strong detection responses to precisely drive contours to the structure boundaries, as well as avoiding contour leakages. The proposed method is capable of delivering promising segmentation results. This is validated in the experiments using synthetic data and real vascular images of different modalities, and through the comparison to two well founded and published methods for curvilinear structure segmentation.

1 Introduction

Segmentation of three dimensional curvilinear objects, particularly vascular structures has a wide range of applications. In the past decades, incorporating curvilinear structure-specific image features in active contour models for vessel segmentation has been intensively studied. For instance, Lorigo *et al.* [8] developed the CURVES algorithm based on the geodesic active contour model [1], which aims at driving the active contours to the boundaries where image intensity is rapidly changing. The CURVES algorithm employs the minimal curvature regularization term to prevent the evolving contours from vanishing inside narrow vascular structures. Yan and Kassim refined the geodesic active contour model by introducing the capillary force [14] to encourage contours to propagate into small vessels. The contour dynamics of these segmentation methods are

K. Daniilidis, P. Maragos, N. Paragios (Eds.): ECCV 2010, Part III, LNCS 6313, pp. 720–734, 2010.

governed by the image intensity gradient. It is possibly problematic if the structure intensity fluctuates along and inside structures. The intensity fluctuation can halt the evolving contours inside structures, and such intensity fluctuation commonly exists in some images, such as angiographic images. Furthermore, low contrast structure boundaries cannot exert enough image force to compete against other forces generated from the intensity fluctuations along the structures. The evolving contours can finally stop inside structures instead of at the boundaries of the structures.

To extract reliable image features for segmentation of three dimensional curvilinear structures, the intensity profiles along the structure cross-sectional plane are commonly considered to be symmetric with respect to the structure center. Classic differential operators, such as the second derivatives of Gaussian [6] and the Hessian matrix [10][4], which are based on convolving an image with symmetric filter functions[1], were proposed for the detection of curvilinear structures. The differential operators quantify the difference between the intensity inside a local region defined by a scale parameter and those in the vicinity of that local region. Exploiting the Hessian matrix, Toledo *et al.* [11] developed an active contour model based on the eigenvalues and eigenvectors extracted from the Hessian matrix. In [3], Descoteaux *et al.* fused the Hessian matrix and the flux measure [12] to formulate an active contour model to segment vascular objects. The flux measure was introduced by Vasilevskly and Siddiqi in [12]. It drives the active contours to segment vessels by using a discretized Laplacian operator, which inspects the intensity changes that occur at the boundary of a local sphere with a predefined radius. Analogous to the original Laplacian operator, the discretized version is isotropic and sensitive to symmetric structures. To handle vessels with various widths, these symmetric operators are always incorporated in multiscale frameworks. However, they commonly return faint responses at structure boundaries. It is because the local intensity variations across the structure boundaries are not symmetric with respect to those boundaries. At the boundaries, the active contours driven by the responses of these operators can evolve randomly according to the image noise attached along the object boundaries. It can lead to subsequent contour leakages.

To segment curvilinear objects such as vessels without leakages, this paper proposes a novel approach that inspects the symmetry of image gradients for active contour evolution. The proposed model considers both the image gradient symmetry with respect to the structure center, and the image gradient antisymmetry with respect to the structure boundary. Analyzing both the gradient symmetry and antisymmetry helps devise image features to encourage contour propagation even through there exists intensity fluctuation along structures, and simultaneously avoids contour leakages. In this paper, through the experiments using a noise corrupted synthetic image volume and real vascular image volumes, the proposed method is compared with two well founded published approaches, the flux method [12] and the CURVES algorithm [8]. The ability of the proposed method to correctly segment curvilinear structures, particularly vasculatures without leakages is validated. It consistently delivers promising segmentation results in all cases. It is therefore well suited to perform segmentation of curvilinear structures.

---

[1] The image Hessian matrices can be found by convolving the image with a set of the second derivatives of Gaussian [10].

2 Methodology

Without the loss of generality, we assume that the objects of interest have stronger intensity than image backgrounds. For the detection of curvilinear structures, we first analyze the image gradients at a local spherical region boundary which touches the object boundary. These image gradients are projected along a direction on the object's cross-sectional plane. As shown in Fig. 1a, along the cross-sectional plane of a curvilinear structure, the image gradients point to the structure center and form a symmetric pattern. When the local spherical region centers at the middle of the object, the projected gradients are symmetric (see Fig. 1b). The symmetry of the projected gradients implies that both the magnitudes and the orientations of the projected gradients are symmetric with respect to the spherical region center. When the local spherical region centers at other positions, the projected gradients are aligned in various patterns (see Figs. 1c-e). At the object boundary, the projected gradients at the local spherical region boundary point along the same direction (Fig. 1d). As such, the projected gradient magnitudes are symmetric but the projected gradient orientations are antisymmetric with respect to the spherical region center. This pattern of image gradients is referred to as the antisymmetric pattern (Fig. 1d). In the positions slightly inside or outside the structure, the projected image gradients are similar to the patterns as shown in Figs. 1c and e respectively, in which both the projected gradient magnitudes and orientations are antisymmetric. This pattern of projected gradients is considered as neither symmetric nor antisymmetric. In summary, there are three situations discussed regarding various positions located,

- at the structure centers, the projected gradients are symmetric (the projected gradient magnitudes and orientations are symmetric);
- at object boundaries, the projected gradients are antisymmetric (the projected gradient magnitudes are symmetric but their orientations are antisymmetric); and
- slightly inside or outside the object, the projected gradients are neither symmetric nor antisymmetric.

2.1 Oriented Flux Symmetry

In this section, two measures are devised to analyze the symmetric gradient patterns and the antisymmetric gradient patterns. These two measures jointly quantify the gradient symmetry. They are therefore conveying reliable detection responses to identify the aforementioned three situations. This detection scheme is referred to as *oriented flux symmetry*. In oriented flux symmetry detection scheme, the first measure to help quantify the gradient symmetry is introduced on the basis of a previous work, called *optimally oriented flux* [7]. The oriented flux measure quantifies the amount of image gradient, which is projected on a direction $\hat{\rho}$, flowing into a local spherical region centered at x,

$$f(x; r, \hat{\rho}) = \frac{1}{4\pi r^2} \int_{\partial B_r} \left((v(x + A) \cdot \hat{\rho})\hat{\rho} \right) \cdot \hat{n} dA, \tag{1}$$

where B_r is a local spherical region with radius r, A is the position vector on ∂B_r, $\hat{n}$ is the inward normal of the sphere at A, dA is the infinitesimal area on ∂B_r and v is image gradient. The differentiability of a discrete image can be approximated by

Table 1. The analysis of the response magnitudes of various measures obtained at different positions x. In the second, the third and the fifth columns, $\hat{\rho}$ is given as the direction on the structure cross-sectional plane, pointing from object centers to x. In the second to the fifth columns except the entries with $*$, r is given as the distance from x to the nearest object boundary; in the entries with $*$, r is assumed to be a value smaller than the structure radius.

Location of x, relative to a curvilinear object	$|f(x;r;\hat{\rho})|$	$|s(x;r;\hat{\rho})|$	$|A_{12}(x;r)|$	$Q_{12}(x;r)$	$M(x)$
At the center (Fig. 1b)	$>> 0$	≈ 0	$>> 0$	≈ 0	$>> 0$
At the boundary (Fig. 1d)	$* \approx 0$	$* >> 0$	$* \approx 0$	$* >> 0$	$= 0$
Slightly inside or outside the object (Figs. 1c and e)	> 0	> 0	> 0	> 0	≈ 0

obtaining the image gradient from the image smoothed by a Gaussian filter with the scale factor of 1.

Whereas the authors of [7] focused on finding the optimal projection orientation to maximize the resultant value of the oriented flux measure, we aim at making use of the above equation to help quantify the image gradient symmetry. In this aspect, the oriented flux is regarded as a measure sensitive to the symmetric image gradient pattern. The above oriented flux measure detects curvilinear structures grounded on its high sensitivity to the symmetric gradient pattern, as shown in Fig. 1b. Given that Equation 1 is evaluated when $\hat{\rho}$ is a direction on the structure cross-sectional plane and r is equal to the structure radius, $f(\cdot)$ attains its maximal value at the structure centers. The gradient symmetry decreases with respect to the positions away from the centers and thus, the strength of the oriented flux detection response declines accordingly. To identify the antisymmetric gradient pattern, the second measure is devised as,

$$s(x;r,\hat{\rho}) = \frac{1}{4\pi r^2} \int_{\partial B_r} \left(v(x+A) \cdot \hat{\rho} \right) dA. \tag{2}$$

This measure helps quantify the antisymmetry of the image gradients that contributes to the resultant value of the above oriented flux measure (Equation 1). It is referred to as *oriented flux antisymmetry* (OFA). It is sensitive to antisymmetric gradient patterns occurring at object boundaries. The OFA measure and the oriented flux measure alternatively return strong detection responses at the structure centers and at the structure boundaries (see the second and the third columns of Table 1).

2.2 Quantifying Gradient Symmetry along Structure Cross-Sectional Planes

Developing a measure to indicate the middle of vascular structures is now possible by aggregating the OFA measure and the oriented flux measure. It is achieved by first performing the eigen decomposition on a tensor to obtain the optimal projection axis which maximizes the magnitude of the oriented flux measure [7]. There are three pairs of resultant eigenvalues and eigenvectors, denoted as $\lambda_j(x;r)$ and $\hat{e}_j(x;r)$ respectively, where $j \in [1,2,3], |\lambda_1(\cdot)| \geq |\lambda_2(\cdot)| \geq |\lambda_3(\cdot)|$. To detect curvilinear structures, the amount of the image gradients pointing to the structure center along its cross-sectional plane spanned by $\hat{e}_1(\cdot)$ and $\hat{e}_2(\cdot)$ [7] is evaluated,

$$\Lambda_{12}(\boldsymbol{x};r) = \frac{1}{4\pi r^2} \int_{\partial B_r} \left([\hat{e}_1(\boldsymbol{x};r)\ \hat{e}_2(\boldsymbol{x};r)]^T \boldsymbol{v}(\boldsymbol{x}+\boldsymbol{A}) \right) \cdot \left([\hat{e}_1(\boldsymbol{x};r)\ \hat{e}_2(\boldsymbol{x};r)]^T \hat{n} \right) dA,$$

$$= f(\boldsymbol{x};r,\hat{e}_1(\boldsymbol{x},r)) + f(\boldsymbol{x};r,\hat{e}_2(\boldsymbol{x},r)) = \lambda_1(\boldsymbol{x};r) + \lambda_2(\boldsymbol{x};r). \tag{3}$$

Utilizing Equation 2, an OFA based measure associated with $\hat{e}_1(\cdot)$ and $\hat{e}_2(\cdot)$ is used to inspect the antisymmetry of gradients along structure cross-sectional planes,

$$Q_{12}(\boldsymbol{x};r) = \frac{1}{4\pi r^2} \left| \int_{\partial B_r} \left([\hat{e}_1(\boldsymbol{x};r)\ \hat{e}_2(\boldsymbol{x};r)]^T \boldsymbol{v}(\boldsymbol{x}+\boldsymbol{A}) \right) dA \right|$$

$$= \sqrt{s^2(\boldsymbol{x};r,\hat{e}_1) + s^2(\boldsymbol{x};r,\hat{e}_2)}. \tag{4}$$

The above equation evaluates the magnitude of the sum of the projected image gradients at ∂B_r on the detected structure cross-sectional plane. A moderate or large resultant value signals the situation that $\boldsymbol{x}$ is not located at the structure center (see the fifth column in Table 1). As presented in the second row, the fourth and the fifth columns in Table 1, $\Lambda_{12}(\cdot) >> Q_{12}(\cdot)$ in the middle of a curvilinear structure. Also, both $Q_{12}(\cdot)$ and $\Lambda_{12}(\cdot)$ are robust against the intensity fluctuation along structure because they are evaluated along its cross-sectional planes. Besides, $\Lambda_{12}(\cdot)$ cannot give a very large magnitude outside the middle of structures (see the fourth column in Table 1), including the positions either inside the structures and closed to the structure boundaries, at the boundaries, or slightly outside the structure. It is because the gradients are not symmetric at these positions. Based on $\Lambda_{12}(\cdot)$ and $Q_{12}(\cdot)$, a measure that only reports positive responses in the middle of structure is, $\max\left(0, \Lambda_{12}(\boldsymbol{x};r) - Q_{12}(\boldsymbol{x};r)\right)$. As the target object radius is unknown, the detection response at $\boldsymbol{x}$ is the maximum response among those responses computed in a set of radii. It therefore retrieves the most significant responses induced by the image gradients located at the object boundaries. As such,

$$M(\boldsymbol{x}) = \max_{r \in R} \left(\max\left(0, \Lambda_{12}(\boldsymbol{x};r) - Q_{12}(\boldsymbol{x};r)\right) \right). \tag{5}$$

R is the radius set and is specified to include all possible radii of the target structures.

Regarding the proposed active contour based segmentation algorithm, the measure $M(\boldsymbol{x})$ guides the evolving contours to expand along and inside curvilinear structures, even through there exists intensity fluctuation along them. To illustrate this idea, $M(\boldsymbol{x})$ is evaluated using a noise corrupted synthetic tube with a radius of 4 voxels (Figs. 2a-d). In this example, the radius set for $M(\cdot)$ is specified as $R = \{1, 1.5, 2, ...6\}$ voxels. A sharp intensity drop is observed along the tube. This synthetic tube exaggerates the situation where a sudden intensity change is present along a structure. Many existing active contour approaches [1][8][14] can misidentify sudden intensity drops as parts of object boundaries. On the contrary, the measure $M(\boldsymbol{x})$ can consistently deliver positive detected values in the middle of the synthetic tube despite the intensity drop (Fig. 2e). In each sub-figure of Fig. 2j, it is observed when the detection radius of $M(\boldsymbol{x})$ differs from the structure radius (all cases, except the one with "$R = \{4\}$"), the detection responses are smaller than that with a matched radius (in the case of "$R = \{4\}$"). It is because the symmetric gradient pattern vanishes as the spherical region radius differs from the

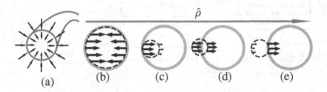

Fig. 1. Illustrations of image gradients which form various patterns. The black arrows and grey solid lines represent image gradients and structure boundaries respectively. (a) Image gradients along a curvilinear structure cross-sectional plane. (b-e) Four examples showing image gradients located at the local spherical region boundaries (black dotted circles), projected along $\hat{\rho}$.

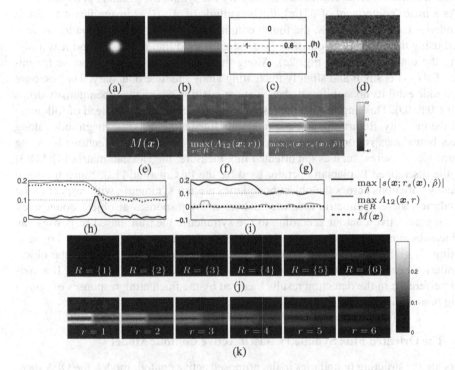

Fig. 2. (a) An xy-plane which shows the cross-section of the synthetic tube with a 4 voxel radius. (b) An xz-plane of the synthetic tube. (c) The numbers represent the intensity of various parts of the image in (b). (d) An xz-plane of the synthetic tube corrupted by additive Gaussian noise with standard deviation 0.1. (e-g) The xz-planes which shows different measures. The black line in (g) showing the boundary where $\max_{\hat{\rho}} |s(\boldsymbol{x}; r_s(\boldsymbol{x}), \hat{\rho})|$ is maximal along the vertical directions from the tube center to the image background. (h-i) The profiles of different measures obtained along the lines shown as dotted lines in (c). (j-k) The values of $M(\boldsymbol{x})$ and $\max_{\hat{\rho}} |s(\boldsymbol{x}; r, \hat{\rho})|$, which are obtained using one radius for each sub-figure.

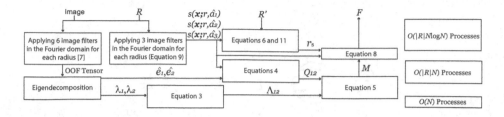

Fig. 3. The flow chart of the efficient algorithm to retrieve the level set evolution speed function $F(x)$ (Equation 8). The block sizes vary according to the complexity of different tasks.

structure radius. Thus, acquiring the maximum response obtained among all radii as in Equation 5 offers a reliable measure to quantify the symmetric gradient patterns.

As a major component of $M(x)$, the magnitude of $\Lambda_{12}(\cdot)$ is insignificant at object boundaries (see the third row, the fourth column in Table 1). This observation is validated using the above synthetic tube (see the grey solid line in Fig. 2i, and it is a plot along the dotted line (i) in Fig. 2c). Along the tube boundary, the response magnitude of $\Lambda_{12}(\cdot)$ is small and slightly fluctuating along the tube boundary. The response magnitude exhibits no significant change at the position where the tube intensity drops from 1.0 to 0.6. This implies that the response fluctuates randomly instead of following the tube intensity. Returning faint and randomly fluctuating response magnitudes along object boundaries is common to the approaches that extract image features by using symmetric measures, such as the oriented flux measure, the Hessian matrix [4][11][3] and the discretized Laplacian operator used by the flux method [12]. Since the local intensity variations across the object boundaries are not symmetric with respect to the boundaries, these symmetric measures deliver noisy responses at object boundaries. Evolving an active contour according to the symmetric measure based responses can lead to subsequent contour leakages. In the proposed method, $M(\cdot)$ is obtained by subtracting $\Lambda_{12}(\cdot)$ from $Q_{12}(\cdot)$. It keeps the resultant values of $M(\cdot)$ zero at the object boundaries (see in the third row, the fourth to the sixth columns in Table 1). It avoids the interference in the detection results incurred by the fluctuating responses of $\Lambda_{12}(\cdot)$ along boundaries.

2.3   The Oriented Flux Symmetry Based Active Contour Model

To locate the structure boundaries in the proposed active contour model, the OFA measure which can capture the antisymmetric gradient patterns occurring at object boundaries is utilized. Suppose that C is a closed contour and $\mathcal{N}$ is the contour inward normal, one of the criteria of finding the desired segmentation solution is to maximize $\int_C s(\mathcal{S}; r, \mathcal{N}) dS$, where $\mathcal{S}$ and dS are the position vector and the infinitesimal area on C respectively. Regarding the value of r, for positions inside curvilinear structures or slightly outside the structures, a proper value is the distance from those positions to the closest object boundary. It ensures that the responses of $s(\cdot)$ computed at the various positions, such as those shown in Figs. 1c and e are significant and produced by the image gradient at the object boundaries. It is illustrated in Fig. 2k, when r is small (1 or 2 voxels), the OFA responses are concentrated in the vicinity of the tube boundary.

As r grows, more OFA responses can be observed in the regions further away from the tube boundary, despite the generally weaker responses than those obtained using smaller values of r. Therefore, large values of r can guide the evolving contours which are located further away from object boundaries. Meanwhile, a small valued r is beneficial to precisely indicate the boundaries. Hence, r is estimated at each location by observing the OFA measure along the direction giving the strongest detection response, which is maximal among a set of radii,

$$r_s(\boldsymbol{x}) = \arg\max_{r \in R'} \left(\max_{\hat{\rho}} |s(\boldsymbol{x}; r, \hat{\rho})| \right) = \arg\max_{r \in R'} \left| \frac{1}{4\pi r^2} \int_{\partial B_r} \boldsymbol{v}(\boldsymbol{x} + \boldsymbol{A}) dA \right|. \quad (6)$$

To recognize structures adjacent to the strong edges of undesired objects, R' can contain only the smallest radius in R discussed in the previous section. This avoids the detection being adversely affected by the strong edges of adjacent objects. For detection of curvilinear structures with complicated geometry (e.g. high curvature vessel or bifurcation) or irregular cross-sections, R' can be defined as the same as R. It ensures that various positions inside or slightly outside the structures can reach the nearest object boundary by those radii in R. In Fig. 2g, the value of $\max_{\hat{\rho}} |s(\boldsymbol{x}; r_s(\boldsymbol{x}), \hat{\rho})|$ is presented. Its profiles along the dotted lines in Fig. 2c are given in Figs. 2h and i. Along the vertical direction in Fig. 2g, from the tube center to the image background regions (in the upper half and in the lower half of Fig. 2g), the locations where $\max_{\hat{\rho}} |s(\boldsymbol{x}; r_s(\boldsymbol{x}), \hat{\rho})|$ attains its maximum are shown as two black lines. These black lines are located along the tube boundaries, which become distinctive in the image of $\max_{\hat{\rho}} |s(\boldsymbol{x}; r_s(\boldsymbol{x}), \hat{\rho})|$. It illustrates that evolving contours according to the OFA measure with the detection radius $r_s(\boldsymbol{x})$ can facilitate the detection of object boundaries.

The OFA measure is not limited to the detection of curvilinear structures unlike the oriented flux measure does. The OFA measure can also highlight the boundaries of various kinds of structures, which deviates from the curvilinear ones. However, this flexibility implies that the OFA measure is sensitive to all intensity changes, including the intensity fluctuation along curvilinear structures. As shown by the black solid line in Fig. 2h, a large value of $\max_{\hat{\rho}} |s(\boldsymbol{x}; r_s(\boldsymbol{x}), \hat{\rho})|$ is observed when the tube intensity drops from 1.0 to 0.6 inside the synthetic tube. Nonetheless, $M(\boldsymbol{x})$ retains a high detection response as compared to $\max_{\hat{\rho}} |s(\boldsymbol{x}; r_s(\boldsymbol{x}), \hat{\rho})|$ (see the black solid line and the black dotted line in Fig. 2h). On the contrary, $\max_{\hat{\rho}} |s(\boldsymbol{x}; r_s(\boldsymbol{x}), \hat{\rho})|$ is large at the tube boundary as compared to $M(\boldsymbol{x})$ (see the black solid line and black dotted line in Fig. 2i). These two measures alternatively deliver higher responses than their counterparts at the structure centers and at the object boundaries (also see the last two columns of Table 1). Hence, the desired resultant contour maximizes the following energy functional,

$$E(\mathcal{C}) = \int_{\text{Inside}(\mathcal{C})} M(\boldsymbol{\mathcal{V}}) dV + \int_{\mathcal{C}} s(\boldsymbol{\mathcal{S}}; r_s(\boldsymbol{\mathcal{S}}), \boldsymbol{\mathcal{N}}) dS, \quad (7)$$

where $\boldsymbol{\mathcal{V}}$ and dV are the position vector and the infinitesimal volume respectively. The evolving contour $\mathcal{C}$ is represented as the zero level of a level set function ϕ [9]. By using the gradient descent approach, the dynamic of the level set function is described as[2] $\phi_t = F|\nabla\phi|$, where F is the first variation of $E(\mathcal{C})$, i.e.

$$F(\boldsymbol{x}) = M(\boldsymbol{x}) - \text{div}\left(\frac{1}{4\pi r_s^2(\boldsymbol{x})}\int_{\partial B r_s(\boldsymbol{x})} v(\boldsymbol{x} + A)dA\right). \tag{8}$$

Considering the large positive responses of $M(\boldsymbol{x})$ in the middle of curvilinear structures, the regions with large values of $M(\boldsymbol{x})$ can be used as the seed positions to initialize the contour evolution. The function $F(\boldsymbol{x})$ is positive inside curvilinear structures to keep the contour expanding. It is negative at the positions slightly outside the structure boundaries. This eventually stops the evolving contour over the structure boundaries.

2.4 Fourier Expressions of the Oriented Flux Measure and the Oriented Flux Antisymmetry Measure

Studying the Fourier expressions helps devise the efficient computation algorithm for the proposed measures. It also reveals the orthogonality of the oriented flux measure and the OFA measure if they are regarded as two types of image filters. Denote FFT be the fast Fourier transform operator, i.e. $FFT^{-1}\{FFT\{I\}\} \equiv I$ and $\boldsymbol{u}$ is the frequency (in cycle per millimeter). The Fourier expression of the OFA measure $s(\boldsymbol{x}; r, \hat{\rho})$ can be found by first rewriting Equation 2 as,

$$s(\boldsymbol{x}; r, \hat{\rho}) = \int_{\text{Image}} D_r(\boldsymbol{V})(\hat{\rho} \cdot (\nabla g) * I)(\boldsymbol{x} + \boldsymbol{V})dV = ((\hat{\rho} \cdot (\nabla g) * D_r)(\boldsymbol{x})) * I(\boldsymbol{x}),$$

where g is the Gaussian filter employed for smoothing the input image as discussed in Section 2.1, and $D_r(\boldsymbol{x})$ is a spherical impulse function which is equal to $(4\pi r^2)^{-1}$ when $||\boldsymbol{x}|| = r$ and 0 elsewhere. By employing the Hankel transform,

$$FFT\{(\hat{\rho} \cdot (\nabla g) * D_r)\} = \sqrt{-1}(r||\boldsymbol{u}||)^{-1}(\hat{\rho} \cdot \boldsymbol{u})e^{-2(\pi||\boldsymbol{u}||)^2}\sin(2\pi r||\boldsymbol{u}||). \tag{9}$$

Besides, as stated in [7], $f(\boldsymbol{x}; r, \hat{\rho})$ can be computed by

$$FFT^{-1}\left\{FFT\{I\}\left(\frac{4\pi r(\hat{\rho}(\boldsymbol{u}^T\boldsymbol{u})\hat{\rho}^T)}{||\boldsymbol{u}||^2 e^{2(\pi||\boldsymbol{u}||\sigma)^2}}\right)\left(\cos(2\pi r||\boldsymbol{u}||) - \frac{\sin(2\pi r||\boldsymbol{u}||)}{2\pi r||\boldsymbol{u}||}\right)\right\}. \tag{10}$$

As such, the computation of the oriented flux measure and the OFA measure are considered as two filtering operations. To facilitate the discussion, we denote $\Phi_{\hat{\rho},r}(\boldsymbol{u}) = FFT\{(\hat{\rho} \cdot (\nabla g) * D_r)\}$, and the non-image terms in Equation 10 (i.e. the terms after $FFT(I)$) as $\Psi_{\hat{\rho},r}(\boldsymbol{u})$. These two functions exhibit the following properties,

$$\Phi_{\hat{\rho},r}(-\boldsymbol{u})\Psi_{\hat{\rho},r}(-\boldsymbol{u}) = -\Phi_{\hat{\rho},r}(\boldsymbol{u})\Psi_{\hat{\rho},r}(\boldsymbol{u}), \lim_{\boldsymbol{u}\to 0}\Phi_{\hat{\rho},r}(\boldsymbol{u}) = \lim_{\boldsymbol{u}\to 0}\Psi_{\hat{\rho},r}(\boldsymbol{u}) = 0, \text{ and thus,}$$

$$\int_{\text{Image}}\left(FFT^{-1}\{\Phi_{\hat{\rho},r}\}(\boldsymbol{x})\right)\left(FFT^{-1}\{\Psi\}^*(\boldsymbol{x})\right)d\boldsymbol{x} = \int_{\text{Image bandwidth}}\Phi_{\hat{\rho},r}(\boldsymbol{u})\Psi_{\hat{\rho},r}(\boldsymbol{u})d\boldsymbol{u} = 0,$$

---

[2] The implementation is based on [13] and a publicly available library, "The Insight Segmentation and Registration Toolkit" (http://www.itk.org). The level set evolution is stopped when the increment of the segmented voxels over 20 iterations is less than 0.01% of them.

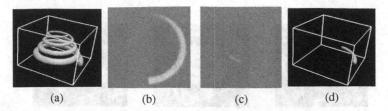

Fig. 4. The $80 \times 80 \times 80$ voxels synthetic image used in the synthetic data experiment. (a) the isosurface of the spiral with the isovalue of 0.5; (b) the 15th slice showing the bottom part of the noise corrupted spiral; (c) the 65th slice showing the top part of the noise corrupted spiral; (d) the initial level set function for the segmentation of the spiral.

where the superscript $*$ is function conjugate. Hence, given the same radius r and orientation $\hat{\rho}$, the oriented flux measure and the OFA measure can be regarded as two orthogonal image filters. They convey two distinct types of information - the gradient symmetry and the gradient antisymmetry. Fusing this information, the measure $M(\boldsymbol{x})$ (Equation 5) judges which type of the information is more significant at a given position. It delivers responses only if that position exhibits a greater degree of gradient symmetry than that of antisymmetry.

On the other hand, the level set evolution speed $F(\boldsymbol{x})$ is independent of the evolving contour. It is therefore evaluated prior to the level set evolution process, in which,

$$[s(\boldsymbol{x};r,\hat{a}_1) \; s(\boldsymbol{x};r,\hat{a}_2) \; s(\boldsymbol{x};r,\hat{a}_3)]^T = \frac{1}{4\pi r^2} \int_{\partial Br} \boldsymbol{v}(\boldsymbol{x}+\boldsymbol{A})dA, \qquad (11)$$

where $\hat{a}_1$, $\hat{a}_1$ and $\hat{a}_3$ are the unit vectors along the x-, y- and z-directions. With the aid of the aforementioned Fourier expressions, $F(\boldsymbol{x})$ is evaluated efficiently, with complexity $O(|R|N \log N)$. This is summarized in Fig. 3. It is noted that, whereas the complicated formulation of $F(\boldsymbol{x})$, its complexity is comparable to that of the FFT-based multiscale Hessian techniques (see [7] for details). Finally, the divergence in Equation 8 is evaluated using the central difference scheme.

3   Experimental Results

The proposed method is compared with two published vascular segmentation techniques, the CURVES algorithm [8] (CURVES) and the flux method [12] (FLUX). Prior to performing segmentation using these methods, the image volumes are smoothed by a Gaussian filter with a scale factor of 1 smallest voxel length, for noise reduction for CURVES and FLUX, and for ensuring differentiability of the discrete image signal for the proposed method. Based on visual assessments of the clinical data, the widths of the target structures are all less than 3mm. The radius set used for FLUX and the proposed method R covers the radii from 1 voxel-length (the physical length depends on the voxel sizes of different images) to 3mm (or 8 voxel-length in the synthetic case). The second radius set for the proposed method R' is the same as R in all tests except the fourth real vascular image case. For CURVES, for each case, we present the structure which reports no leakage and that segmented region has the largest number of segmented voxels among those obtained using different heuristic parameter values used by CURVES.

CURVES   FLUX   The proposed method

Fig. 5. The segmentation results of the noise corrupted synthetic spiral by using CURVES, FLUX and the proposed method

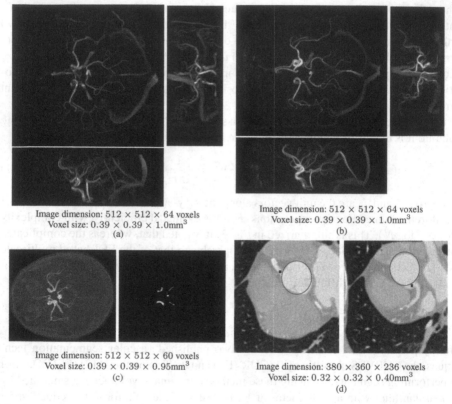

Image dimension: $512 \times 512 \times 64$ voxels
Voxel size: $0.39 \times 0.39 \times 1.0\text{mm}^3$
(a)

Image dimension: $512 \times 512 \times 64$ voxels
Voxel size: $0.39 \times 0.39 \times 1.0\text{mm}^3$
(b)

Image dimension: $512 \times 512 \times 60$ voxels
Voxel size: $0.39 \times 0.39 \times 0.95\text{mm}^3$
(c)

Image dimension: $380 \times 360 \times 236$ voxels
Voxel size: $0.32 \times 0.32 \times 0.40\text{mm}^3$
(d)

Fig. 6. The image volumes used in the real vascular image experiment. (a, b) The perspective maximum intensity projections, along the axial, the sagittal and the coronal directions of two intracranial PC-MRA volumes; (c) the axial perspective maximum intensity projection (left) and the 53th image slice (right) of an intracranial TOF-MRA volume; (d) The 182th (left) and 214th (right) slices of a cardiac CTA volume. The red circles indicate the aorta and the blue dots are the manually placed initial seed points. (Please refer to the electronic version of this paper for better illustration).

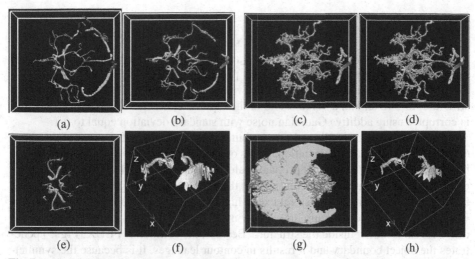

Fig. 7. (a, b, e, f) The segmentation results of the clinical cases shown in Figs. 6a, b, c and d respectively, by using CURVES. (c, d, g, h) The segmentation results of the clinical cases shown in Figs. 6a, b, c and d respectively, by using FLUX.

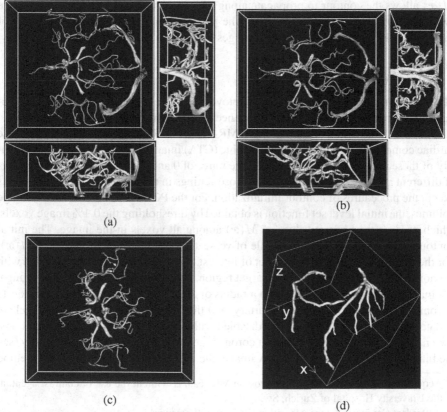

Fig. 8. The segmentation results obtained by using the proposed method from the four angiographic images shown in Figs. 6a-d

3.1 Synthetic Data

Using a noise corrupted synthetic spiral, as shown in Figs. 4a-c, we examine the ability of different approaches to segment an elongated structure, where the intensity is changing along the structure and image noise is present. The inner radius and the intensity of the spiral are gradually reduced from 4 voxels and a value of 1 at the bottom of the structure, to 1 voxel and a value of 0.5 at the top of the structure. This synthetic spiral is corrupted using additive Gaussian noise with standard deviation equal to 0.1.

The active contours of all methods are initialized inside the bottom part of the spiral (Fig. 4d). In Fig. 5, the segmentation results of various approaches are shown. In which, the contour of CURVES cannot propagate along the spiral to reach the top of the structure. As the image intensity declines along the structure, the image gradient generated by the image noise inside the spiral exerts higher image force than that exerted by the weak boundary of the structure having low intensity value. Thus, the evolving contour of CURVES is halted inside the structure. Besides, the contour of FLUX (Fig. 5) penetrates the object boundary and it results in contour leakages. It is because the symmetric discretized Laplacian operator used by FLUX returns faint responses along object boundaries. The contour is randomly evolved at the low contrast spiral boundaries and leaks through these boundaries. On the contrary, for the proposed method, the measure $M(x)$ allows the contour to propagate along structure and the OFA measure stops the evolving contour at object boundaries. The proposed method is therefore capable of segmenting the entire spiral without leakages (see Fig. 5, the proposed method).

3.2 Real Vascular Images

There are four angiographic images employed in this experiment, including two intracranial phrase contrast magnetic resonance angiographic (PC-MRA) images [3] (Figs. 6a and b), one intracranial time-of-flight MRA (TOF-MRA) image [3] (Fig. 6c) and one cardiac computed tomographic angiographic (CTA) image [4] (Fig. 6d). The voxel intensity of these images was scaled to be in the range of 0 and 1. The experimental settings of different approaches are the same as those settings in the synthetic data experiments except the procedures of contour initialization. For the PC-MRA and TOF-MRA image volumes, the initial level set function is obtained by thresholding the 0.1% image voxels, which produce the highest values of $M(x)$ among all voxels in the image. The initial contours are only placed in the middle of vessels with large detected values of $M(x)$. For the CTA image volume, the object of interest - coronary arteries are connected with the aorta, which is not a part of the target region. They share the same intensity range. We manually select two spheres with a radius of 3mm at two positions where the aorta is connected with the left coronary artery, and the right coronary artery. The level set update (i.e. the contour evolution) is disabled within these two spheres for all methods. Two initial seeds are placed in the left coronary artery and the right coronary artery (see the blue dots in Fig. 6d). In this CTA image, the radius set R' of the proposed method

---

[3] Acquired using a Philips 3T ACS Gyroscan MR scanner without the use of contrast agent, at the University Hospital of Zurich, Switzerland.

[4] Rotterdam Coronary Artery Algorithm Evaluation Framework,
http://coronary.bigr.nl/

contains only the smallest radius in R to avoid the disturbance introduced by the edges adjacent to the arteries (see Fig. 6d).

It is noted that the vessel intensity of the flow-sensitive PC-MRA images fluctuates significantly because of the variation of blood flow speeds inside the vessels with different sizes. This intensity fluctuation produces image gradient along vascular structures and stops the evolving contours of CURVES inside the vessels (see Figs. 7a and b). For FLUX, the faint responses detected by the symmetric discretized Laplacian operator cannot precisely position the boundaries of the vessels. The evolving contours leak through the object boundaries and are subsequently guided by image noise as shown in Figs. 7c and d. In TOF-MRA image, the non-vascular tissues can report intensity values similar to those of vascular regions (see Fig 7c, right). It greatly reduces the intensity contrast of the vessel boundaries where a non-vascular structure with similar intensity is nearby. As a result, the weak vessel boundaries cannot exert enough image force to draw the evolving contours of CURVES along the vessels and causes under-segmentation (Fig. 7e). In Fig. 7g, the contour of FLUX expands beyond the weak vessel boundaries and follows the non-vascular structures. In the CTA image, the evolving contours of both CURVES and FLUX (Figs. 7f and h) leak through the arteries and follow the edges of the heart chamber surface. The contour evolution of FLUX and CURVES in this case was manually stopped for contour visualization.

In contrast, the measure $M(x)$ of the proposed method encourages contours to expand along vessels despite the intensity variation of vessels. On the other hand, the OFA based measure, as stated in Equation 7, is capable of halting the evolving contours at the vessel boundaries. It can segment the vessels without leakage (Figs. 8a-c). Based on the visual comparison between the segmented vessels of the proposed method, and the original image volumes shown in Figs. 6a-c, the proposed method is able to deliver faithful segmentation results. It can also withstand the disturbance introduced by the irrelevant edges adjacent to the target structures. Thus, the proposed method successfully segment the coronary arteries as presented in Fig. 8d.

4 Perspective and Conclusion

The proposed active contour model is devised based on various measures which aim at locally quantifying the image gradient symmetry. In our application vascular segmentation, since the tissue intensity can vary spatially due to the presence of multiplicative bias field, the proposed model avoids encapsulating the regional intensity variance information [2][5]. Albeit the three dimensional formulation of the proposed method, it is general to cope with curvilinear structures in two, three or higher dimensions, if any. Also, we are acquiring more data sets and also segmenting ground truth in order to perform quantitative comparison to other approaches.

Besides, analogous to the studies in [8][10], introducing geometric constraints to the proposed active contour model may be beneficial. The major concern is that these geometric constraints require intensive parameter searching. Furthermore, vast numbers of application specific constraints or supplementary information have been proposed recently, for instance, detecting only structures with circular cross sections, regularization based on the curvature of structure centerlines or structure radii, disallowing bifurcation, exploiting training data or interactive segmentation (see [15] for a comprehensive survey). The proposed measures can provide useful features to detect curvilinear structures along with these constraints or supplementary information for particular applications.

Regarding the proposed active contour model, the oriented flux symmetry based formulation expands the evolving contours in the middle of curvilinear structures where the image gradients are symmetric. The contours are eventually driven to the object boundaries, in order to maximize the gradient antisymmetry along the contour inward normal direction. Benefited from the oriented flux antisymmetry measure and the oriented flux measure, the proposed model is capable of segmenting the entire structures without contour leakages, in both the experiments using the synthetic image and the real images of different modalities. It is experimentally demonstrated that the oriented flux symmetry based active contour model achieves promising segmentation results.

References

1. Caselles, V., et al.: Geodesic active contours. IJCV 22(1), 61–79 (1997)
2. Chan, T., Vese, L.: Active contours without edges. TIP 10(2), 266–277 (2001)
3. Descoteaux, M., Collins, L., Siddiqi, K.: Geometric flows for segmenting vasculature in MRI: Theory and validation. In: Barillot, C., Haynor, D.R., Hellier, P. (eds.) MICCAI 2004. LNCS, vol. 3216, pp. 500–507. Springer, Heidelberg (2004)
4. Frangi, A.F., Niessen, W.J., Vincken, K.L., Viergever, M.A.: Multiscale vessel enhancement filtering. In: Wells, W.M., Colchester, A.C.F., Delp, S.L. (eds.) MICCAI 1998. LNCS, vol. 1496, p. 130. Springer, Heidelberg (1998)
5. Gooya, A., Liao, H., Matsumiya, K., Masamune, K., Dohi, T.: Effective statistical edge integration using a flux maximizing scheme for volumetric vascular segmentation in MRA. In: Karssemeijer, N., Lelieveldt, B. (eds.) IPMI 2007. LNCS, vol. 4584, pp. 86–97. Springer, Heidelberg (2007)
6. Koller, T., et al.: Multiscale detection of curvilinear structures in 2-d and 3-d image data. In: ICCV, pp. 864–869 (1995)
7. Law, M., Chung, A.: Three dimensional curvilinear structure detection using optimally oriented flux. In: Forsyth, D., Torr, P., Zisserman, A. (eds.) ECCV 2008, Part IV. LNCS, vol. 5305, pp. 368–382. Springer, Heidelberg (2008)
8. Lorigo, L., et al.: Curves: Curve evolution for vessel segmentation. MedIA 5(3), 195–206 (2001)
9. Osher, S., Sethian, J.: Fronts propagating with curvature dependent speed: Algorithms based on hamilton-jacobi formulations. J. Comp. Phys. 79(1), 12–49 (1988)
10. Sato, Y., et al.: Three-dimensional multi-scale line filter for segmentation and visualization of curvilinear structures in medical images. MedIA 2(2), 143–168 (1998)
11. Toledo, R., et al.: Eigensnakes for vessel segmentation in angiography. In: ICPR, pp. 4340–4343 (2000)
12. Vasilevskiy, A., Siddiqi, K.: Flux maximizing geometric flows. PAMI 24(12), 1565–1578 (2002)
13. Whitaker, R.: A level-set approach to 3d reconstruction from range data. IJCV 29(33), 203–231 (1998)
14. Yan, P., Kassim, A.: Segmentation of volumetric mra images by using capillary active contour. MedIA 10(3), 317–329 (2006)
15. Lesage, D., et al.: A review of 3D vessel lumen segmentation techniques: Models, features and extraction schemes. MedIA 13(6), 819–845 (2009)

MRF Inference by k-Fan Decomposition and Tight Lagrangian Relaxation

Jörg Hendrik Kappes, Stefan Schmidt, and Christoph Schnörr

Image and Pattern Analysis Group & HCI, University of Heidelberg, Germany
{kappes,schmidt,schnoerr}@math.uni-heidelberg.de

Abstract. We present a novel dual decomposition approach to MAP inference with highly connected discrete graphical models. Decompositions into cyclic k-fan structured subproblems are shown to significantly tighten the Lagrangian relaxation relative to the standard local polytope relaxation, while enabling efficient integer programming for solving the subproblems. Additionally, we introduce modified update rules for maximizing the dual function that avoid oscillations and converge faster to an optimum of the relaxed problem, and never get stuck in non-optimal fixed points.

1 Introduction

We focus on the Maximum A Posteriori (MAP) inference problem with discrete Markov Random Field (MRF) models. While applying graph cuts and iterated graph cuts has become standard for inference with exactly solvable submodular models, and for approximate inference with intractable models on sparse grid graphs, respectively [5, 21], recent research has focused on involved higher order models[1] [15, 9, 16], model decomposition and lower bound maximization based on linear programming (LP) duality [10, 12, 11, 17, 8], and tightening the common local polytope relaxation by advanced convex optimization [23, 24, 13, 20].

In this paper, we study the latter two points in connection with a particular class of highly connected graphical models, motivated by applications in computer vision. The models involve k-*fan substructures*[2] as subgraphs of the overall model. As illustrated in Figure 1, the defining property of this sub-structure is that an acyclic graph is obtained if we replace all inner nodes by a single node and merge resulting multiple edges.

Figure 2 illustrates our model for evaluating the HumanEva dataset [19]. Our graphical model detects the human pose in each image based on appearance features inside each view and epipolar-features between the 4 views. The random variables represent model parts (head, elbow, hand ...) defined over a finite set of image positions with a structure shown in Figure 2(b).

---

[1] The order of a model is given by the highest order of a term in the objective.
[2] We use the shorthand $G_{\text{fan}}^{k,n}$ for a fan graph with n nodes and k inner nodes. If n does not matter we just say k-fan.

K. Daniilidis, P. Maragos, N. Paragios (Eds.): ECCV 2010, Part III, LNCS 6313, pp. 735–747, 2010.

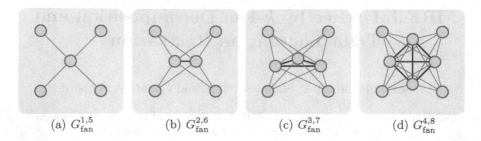

(a) $G_{\text{fan}}^{1,5}$ (b) $G_{\text{fan}}^{2,6}$ (c) $G_{\text{fan}}^{3,7}$ (d) $G_{\text{fan}}^{4,8}$

Fig. 1. Examples for fan graphs. Inner nodes are connected to each other. Outer nodes are connected to all inner nodes, but not among each other.

Exact inference algorithm using this model is not feasible in acceptable time. By decomposing the problem in simple problems involving fan-structures as shown in Figure 2(c), however, high-quality inference becomes feasible by optimizing a bound on the relaxed linear problem via linear programming (LP) duality. We demonstrate below that utilizing fan-structures significantly improves the quality of the bounds obtained by standard LP relaxation.

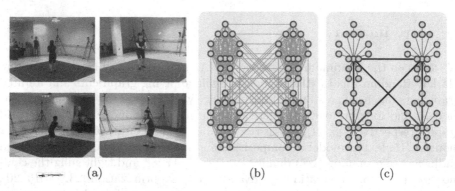

(a)   (b)   (c)

Fig. 2. a) Images from the HumanEva dataset. Detection of human pose is done by processing all four views simultaneously, using the graphical model shown in **b)**. The model enhances a standard representation for each single view by epipolar constraints between views. **c)** shows one of 15 fan-structured subproblems used for tight relaxation.

The primary motivation for the decomposition of graphical models is twofold. Firstly, an approximation to the intractable inference problem can be formulated in terms of a two-level optimization procedure, where at the lower level inference on tractable substructures is carried out, while the master program at the upper level combines these partial solutions via dual variables. Secondly, the resulting objective value at the upper level yields a bound to the original (intractable) objective function, whose optimization through dual variables possibly meets the value of some locally computed optimum, thus providing a certificate that this optimum is indeed a global one. For the general background, we refer to standard textbooks [3, 2], and for sophisticated applications of this principle in computer vision to, e.g. [10, 8, 12, 22].

A major difference to our work presented here is that we do *not* focus on graph decompositions into substructures for which inference can be efficiently done by standard methods, e.g. trees and belief propagation. While trees as substructures are natural for sparse grid graphs (e.g. row/column decomposition [10, 11]), they appear unnatural in connection with highly connected models as sketched above in Figure 2. Rather, we directly focus on more complex cyclic substructures, provided they are embedded into k-fans (Fig. 2(c)). This results in a relaxation of the overall inference problem that is provably tighter than the standard local polytope LP relaxation corresponding to tree structured subproblems. In the literature, cyclic substructures in connection with dual decomposition have been studied for the specific case of planar grid graphs by [11], in a general framework without specific evaluations by [8], and by [20] in terms of iteratively adding higher-order terms for locally improving the local polytope relaxation. Our work differs by focusing on k-fan substructures that can be flexibly applied to a wide range of non-planar, densely connected graphical models.

Another issue concerns the method for optimizing the Lagrangian dual at the upper level. In most work on dual decomposition of graphical models, convergence of the corresponding subgradient-based iteration is not really addressed. Either a "sufficiently small" step size is chosen, or the basic divergent series update rule is applied [7, 14]. In this paper, therefore, we merely raise this issue in the light of more recent pertinent work [18], due to its increasing importance in computer vision, leaving a more comprehensive investigation of this topic for future work.

Contribution. To summarize, our contribution consists in specifying mathematically the novel relaxation and showing both theoretically and empirically the influence of the choice of the subproblems on the relaxation and inference. In particular, we focus on k-fan substructures and general energy functions that are not restricted to any subclass. Furthermore, we improve convergence of the subgradient based optimization of the Lagrangian dual function.

Organization. We describe our problem decomposition and Lagrangian relaxation approach in Section 2 and show that this relaxation is tighter than the standard linear programming relaxation. Optimization of the Lagrangian dual via projected subgradient methods is discussed in Section 3. Finally, we present in Section 4 experimental results for synthetic and real world data.

Notation. Given a graph $G = (V, E)$ we associate to each node $a \in V$ a variable x_a taking values in $\mathcal{X}_a$ and a energy function $J(x) = \sum_{c \in C} f_c(x_c)$ with $C \subset V \cup E$. For $A \subset V$, we define $x_A = (x_a)_{a \in A}$ and $\mathcal{X}_A = \otimes_{a \in A} \mathcal{X}_a$, and as a shorthand $x = x_V$ and $\mathcal{X} = \mathcal{X}_V$. Following [23], we reformulate the problem of determining the optimal configuration x in $\mathcal{X}$,

$$x^* = \arg\min_{x \in \mathcal{X}} \sum_{c \in C} f_c(x_c), \tag{1}$$

in overcomplete form

$$\sum_{c \in C} f_c(x_c) = \langle \theta, \phi(x) \rangle = \sum_{i \in \mathcal{I}(G)} \theta_i \cdot \phi_i(x) \tag{2}$$

with vectors θ and $\phi(x)$ indexed by $\mathcal{I}(G) = \{(c;j)|c \in C, \; j \in \mathcal{X}_c\}$ and $\langle \cdot, \cdot \rangle$ denoting the inner product. Furthermore, given θ according to (2), problem (1) is equivalent to determining μ^* as solution to the LP

$$\mu^* = \underset{\mu \in \mathcal{M}(G)}{\arg \min} \langle \theta, \mu \rangle, \tag{3}$$

where $\mathcal{M}(G)$ denotes the marginal polytope defined as convex hull of all integer configurations with respect to the overcomplete representation. The exponentially large description of the feasible set $\mathcal{M}(G)$ reflects the combinatorial difficulty of the inference problem and necessitates problem approximations for general objective functions.

2   Problem Decomposition and Relaxation

In this section, it will be convenient to distinguish between original parameter vectors $\overline{\theta}, \overline{\theta}^i$ and parameter vectors θ^i defined by the problem decomposition – cf. (6) below. Starting with the convex optimization problem (3),

$$J(\mu^*) = \min_{\mu \in \mathcal{M}(G)} \langle \overline{\theta}, \mu \rangle, \tag{4}$$

we decompose it as follows. Given a set of graphs $\{G^1, \ldots, G^n\}$, with $G^i = (V, E^i)$ such that $E^i \subset E$ and $\bigcup_{i=1}^n E^i = E$, we define $\overline{\theta}^i \in \mathbb{R}^{\mathcal{I}(G)}$:

$$\overline{\theta}^i_{a;j} := \begin{cases} 0 & \text{if } a \notin V \cup E^i, \\ \overline{\theta}_{a;j}/n & \text{if } a \in V, \\ \overline{\theta}_{a;j}/\#a & \text{if } a \in E^i. \end{cases} \tag{5}$$

Here, $\#a$ denotes the number of edge-sets containing a. Note that the decomposition ensures $\overline{\theta} = \sum_i \overline{\theta}^i$. For each subproblem, we define another smaller exponential parameter vector

$$\theta^i := [\overline{\theta}^i]_{\mathcal{I}(G^i)} \tag{6}$$

called the *projection* of $\overline{\theta}^i$ with respect to $\mathcal{I}(G^i)$ and reformulate problem (4):

$$J(\mu^*) = \min_{\mu \in \mathcal{M}(G)} \sum_i \langle \overline{\theta}^i, \mu \rangle \tag{7a}$$

$$= \min_{\substack{\mu \in \mathcal{M}(G) \\ \forall i: \mu^i \in \mathcal{M}(G) \\ \forall i: \mu^i = \mu}} \sum_i \langle \overline{\theta}^i, \mu^i \rangle \overset{\text{eqn. (5)}}{=} \min_{\substack{\mu \in \mathcal{M}(G) \\ \forall i: \mu^i \in \mathcal{M}(G^i) \\ \forall i: \mu^i = [\mu]_{\mathcal{I}(G^i)}}} \sum_i \langle \theta^i, \mu^i \rangle \tag{7b}$$

$$\geq \min_{\substack{\mu \in \mathbb{R}^{\mathcal{I}(G)} \\ \forall i: \mu^i \in \mathcal{M}(G^i) \\ \forall i: \mu^i = [\mu]_{\mathcal{I}(G^i)}}} \sum_i \langle \theta^i, \mu^i \rangle \overset{\text{eqn. (5)}}{=} \min_{\substack{\mu \in \mathbb{R}^{\mathcal{I}(G)} \\ \forall i: [\mu]_{\mathcal{I}(G^i)} \in \mathcal{M}(G^i)}} \langle \overline{\theta}, \mu \rangle \tag{7c}$$

Decomposition (7) has the following properties:

- If all subgraphs are trees the relaxation is equivalent to the standard relaxation over the local polytope [23].
- If the subproblems include cycles, we get tighter relaxations which also take into account higher-order constraints.

In this paper, we focus on the latter option in terms of k-fan structured subproblems and show that this significantly tightens the relaxation and hence improves inference. Because problem (7c) is still difficult to solve, we focus on its dual by adding Lagrangian multipliers for the equality constraints, yielding the dual function

$$g(\lambda^1, \ldots, \lambda^n) := \min_{\substack{\mu \in \mathbb{R}^{\mathcal{I}(G)} \\ \forall i : \mu^i \in \mathcal{M}(G^i)}} \sum_i \langle \theta^i, \mu^i \rangle + \sum_i \sum_{\alpha \in \mathcal{I}(G^i)} \lambda_\alpha^i (\mu_\alpha^i - \mu_\alpha) \quad (8)$$

Since μ is unconstrained, this vector is determined by the corresponding partial derivatives of the right-hand side of (8). This yields the condition

$$(\lambda^1, \ldots, \lambda^n) \in \Lambda := \left\{ (\lambda^1, \ldots, \lambda^n) \; \middle| \; \forall \alpha \in \mathcal{I}(G) : \sum_{i \in \{j | \alpha \in \mathcal{I}(G^j)\}} \lambda_\alpha^i = 0 \right\}, \quad (9)$$

and by insertion into (8) the dual problem of the relaxed LP (7c)

$$\sup_{(\lambda^1, \ldots, \lambda^n) \in \Lambda} \sum_i \min_{\mu^i \in \mathcal{M}(G^i)} \langle (\theta^i + \lambda^i), \mu^i \rangle. \quad (10)$$

Since the feasible set of the primal problem (7c) includes a strict feasible point, Slater's condition [4] holds and guarantees that the duality gap between (7c) and its dual problem (10) is zero, i.e.

$$\sup_{(\lambda^1, \ldots, \lambda^n) \in \Lambda} g(\lambda^i, \ldots, \lambda^n) =: L^* \;\; = \;\; U^* := \min_{\substack{\mu \in \mathbb{R}^{\mathcal{I}(G)} \\ \forall i : [\mu]_{\mathcal{I}(G^i)} \in \mathcal{M}(G^i)}} \langle \overline{\theta}, \mu \rangle. \quad (11)$$

Instead of solving the relaxed primal problem (7c) which is still fairly complex, we can now solve the dual problem (10) by projected sub-gradient descent [3, 18], taking advantage of the problem decomposition into tractable subproblems. To this end, we have to optimize each subproblem

$$\min_{\mu^i \in \mathcal{M}(G^i)} \langle (\theta^i + \lambda^i), \mu^i \rangle \quad (12)$$

for a given λ^i (cf. section 3). Rather than solving the LP in (12) directly, we solve instead the corresponding integer programming problem. This is correct because vertices of the polytopes $\mathcal{M}(G^i)$ correspond to integer configurations. Accordingly, if the decomposition has been chosen properly, these integer problems can be solved very fast. As a by-product, we obtain an upper bound $\overline{U}(t)$ of the original objective function (4) by evaluating[3] in each step t for all subproblems i the solutions $(\mu^i)^t$:

$$\overline{U}(t) = \min_{t'=1,\ldots,t} \min_{i=1,\ldots,n} \langle \overline{\theta}, [(\mu^i)^{t'}]_{\mathcal{I}(G)} \rangle \tag{13}$$

The lower bound, on the other hand, reads

$$L(t) = \max_{t'=1,\ldots,t} \sum_{i=1,\ldots,n} \langle \theta^i + (\lambda^i)^{t'}, (\mu^i)^{t'} \rangle. \tag{14}$$

It crucially depends on the problem decomposition and thus reflects the quality of the relaxation. Figure 3 further explains and illustrates the relation between the different bounds and optima.

3   Solving the Dual Problem

The dual problem (10) is a nonsmooth concave maximization problem with linear constraints. The main difference between most inference algorithm based on dual decomposition [8, 11, 23, 24], besides the decomposition itself, concerns the choice and the computation of updates of λ in each step. A standard solver for such problems is the Projected Sub-Gradient Method (PSGM) [3] that requires to compute a subgradient of g at λ. The set of all subgradients at λ is called the subdifferential at λ and denoted by $\partial g(\lambda)$. We perform inference with respect to all subproblems and select a subgradient from the set

$$\partial g^i(\lambda^i) = \partial \left(\min_{\mu^i \in \mathcal{M}(G^i)} \langle \theta^i + \lambda^i, \mu^i \rangle \right) \tag{15}$$

$$= \left\{ \nabla \langle \theta^i + \lambda^i, \mu^* \rangle \, \middle| \, \mu^* \in \operatorname*{arg\,min}_{\mu^i \in \mathcal{M}(G^i)} g^i(\lambda^i) \right\} \tag{16}$$

$$= \left\{ \mu^* \, \middle| \, \mu^* \in \operatorname*{arg\,min}_{\mu^i \in \mathcal{M}(G^i)} g^i(\lambda^i) \right\}. \tag{17}$$

Concerning the subproblems, inference for a $G_{\text{fan}}^{k,n}$-structured model with L states per variable can be done using the junction tree algorithm [6] with asymptotic complexity $O((n - k) \cdot L^{(k+1)})$. We use an alternative search-based algorithm proposed in [1] having the same asymptotic worst case runtime complexity for fan graphs, but performs faster on average. For the synthetic data in

---

[3] The main trick in (13) is that $(\mu^i)^{t'}$ is integer and both graphs (G and G^i) have the same node set V, consequently the projection $[\cdot]_{\mathcal{I}(G)}$ is well defined.

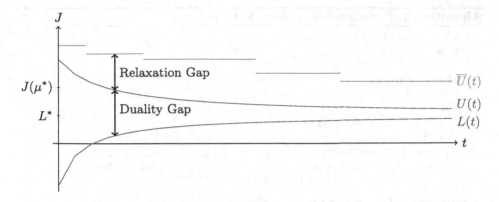

Fig. 3. This figure displays typical progressions of the bounds. Gray lines mark optimal values for the original primal and the relaxed primal/dual problem. Note that $L^* = U^*$ (zero duality gap for the relaxed problems). The blue line shows the current lower bound $L(t)$ of the dual relaxed problem. The red line marks the current upper bound $U(t)$ of the primal relaxed problem whose computation is too complex. Therefore we compute instead an upper bound $\overline{U}$ of the minimum of the original primal problem (marked in red). The observed gap $\overline{U}(t) - L(t)$ includes the current duality gap as well as the current relaxation gap, and we can not infer how they split up the total gap. However, we know that the duality gap will be zero and as a consequence, that after convergence the remaining gap is only due to the relaxation.

section 4 this decreases the dominant term of the average complexity from L^{k+1} to approximately $L^{0.5 \cdot (k+1)}$, which is significant in practise.

Algorithm 1 shows a modified form of the PSGM. This modified version, also known as *heavy ball method*, does not step into the direction of the last subgradient, but rather into the direction of a convex combination of the subgradients observed so far. For $\rho^{(t)} = 1$, we obtain the standard PSGM, and for constant sequence $\rho^{(t)} \in (0,1)$ a 'damped version' of it. We can guarantee that Algorithm 1 converges to an optimum provided that

$$\lim_{t \to \infty} \tau^{(t)} = 0, \qquad \sum_{t=0}^{\infty} \tau^{(t)} = \infty, \qquad \lim_{t \to \infty} \frac{\tau^{(t)}}{\rho^{(t)}} = 0. \qquad (18)$$

For $\tau^{(t)} = \overline{\tau} \frac{1}{1 + \alpha \cdot t}$ conditions (18) is satisfied for any constant sequence $\rho^{(t)}$. The speed of convergence depends highly on good choices of the sequence $\tau^{(t)}$, which we determine offline by grid-search on the parameter space for a particular problem class and the corresponding graphical model. However, a good choice of $\rho^{(t)}$ also depends on the current value of $\tau^{(t)}$. Ruszczynski [18] suggests a damping sequence $\rho^{(t)} = \overline{\rho} \frac{\tau^{(t)}}{\overline{\tau}}$ and shows that for this sequence Algorithm 1 converges for $\overline{\rho} \in (0,1]$, which generalizes the standard conditions (18).

Algorithm 1. Projected Sub-gradient Method

$t = 0, \quad \lambda^{(0)} = 0 \in \Lambda$
repeat
    $s \in \partial g((\lambda)^{(t)})$
    if $t == 0$ **then**
        $\zeta^{(t)} = s$
    else
        $\zeta^{(t)} = \zeta^{(t-1)} + \rho^{(t)}(s - \zeta^{(t-1)})$
    end if
    Compute $\overline{U}(t)$ and $L(t)$
    $(\lambda)^{(t+1)} = \left[(\lambda)^{(t)} + \tau^t \cdot \zeta^{(t)} \right]_{\Lambda}$
    $t = t + 1$
until $\|\overline{U}(t) - L(t)\| \leq \epsilon$ or $t > t_{\max}$

4   Experiments

Dual decomposition with k-fans: computer generated example. We first demonstrate the increasing accuracy achieved by selecting more complex k-fan subproblems, that is by raising k. We generated complete (fully connected) graphs $G = (V, E)$ containing first and second order potentials uniformly sampled between 0 and 1. Next we decomposed the graph into $\lceil |V|/k \rceil$ graphs $G^i = (V, E^i)$, as shown in Figure 4.

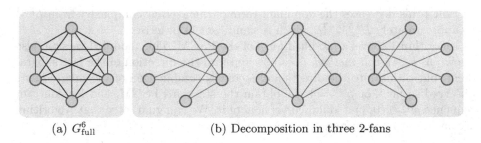

(a) G_{full}^6 (b) Decomposition in three 2-fans

Fig. 4. A decomposition of a full connected graph with 6 nodes in three 2-fan structured graphs

As Figure 5 reveals, we obtain much tighter bounds for decompositions with larger k. Also we achieved better integer solutions and this quite efficiently. Decompositions into cyclic subproblems outperform decompositions with acyclic subproblems (lowest curve). This finding agrees with observations in [11, 8, 20]. Our results show that this property carries over to more complex problems with k-fan graphs as subproblems.

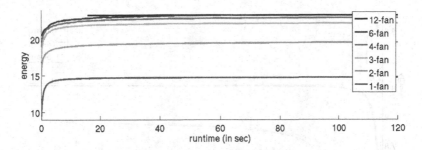

Fig. 5. Lower bounds for different k-fan decompositions as functions of runtime. The original problem involves 12 variables and 10 labels. The second order graph is fully connected, and the potentials were uniformly sampled between 0 and 1. Increasing k leads to tighter (larger) bounds.

Dual decomposition with k-fans: HumanEva dataset. The HumanEva dataset [19] contains 7 calibrated video sequences (4 grayscale and 3 color) that are synchronized together with 3D body poses obtained from a motion capture system. We used the 4 grayscale views and trained a model for images without taking into account temporal context. The graphical structure of our model is shown in Figure 2(b). Random variables take positions in the image domain, and the objective contains unary and pairwise potentials which include information about geometry and appearance. Nodes corresponding to each single view span a fully connected graph. Edges between views represent soft epipolar constraints. For a detailed description of the model, we refer to [1].

As inference for such models is difficult, we use a decomposition of this model into a set of 1-, 4- and 5-fans in order to derive a relaxation of the original problem as described above. The 1-fan corresponds to the approach of Komodakis [12] applied on our non-grid graphs. The 5-fan decomposition consist of 12 subproblems. Inner nodes of the fan of each subproblem correspond to the same single view, as sketched in Figure 7(c). Surprisingly the use of the 5-fans brings no advantage over the 1-fans for this problem. Rather, the decomposition with 1-fans gives even better results (see Table 1). The explanation for this is firstly, that the local relaxation inside a single view seems to be quite tight, and secondly that the computation of a subgradient of the 5-fan decomposition is more expensive than for 1-fans, hence takes more runtime. As we select *some* subgradient of the set $\partial g(\lambda)$, our current implementation does not check the optimality condition $0 \in g(\lambda)$ (Fermat condition), and therefore we additionally impose an upper bound on the runtime for possibly terminating the iteration.

In order to effectively enforce higher order constraints between the same parts in different views, we set up a 4-fan decomposition in which the subproblems contain the clique of variables assigned to the same body-part in all views, as

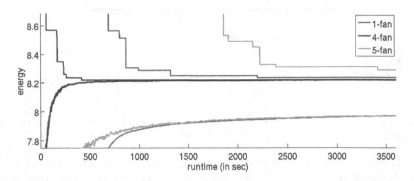

Fig. 6. The plot shows the progression of lower and upper bounds as a function of runtime. While both 1-fan and 5-fan decompositions restricted to single views perform similarly, the 4-fan decomposition enforcing epipolar consistency generates significantly tighter bounds and better integer solutions. The decompositions are sketched in Figure 7.

shown in Figure 7(b). This decomposition gives much better bounds and guarantees a gap which is less than $\epsilon = 10^{-6}$ in nearly 80% of the images and always outperforms the 1-fan decomposition. See Table 1 for more details.

These results show that while our approach can be applied to general graphical models, the overall performance may depend on the choice of a particular decomposition based on application-specific expertise.

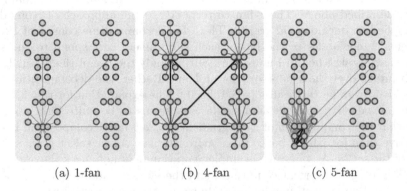

(a) 1-fan   (b) 4-fan   (c) 5-fan

Fig. 7. The three graphs above sketch the structure of subproblems corresponding to three decompositions of the graphical model used for the HumanEva data. The 4-fan subgraphs include all epipolar constraints between single parts. The 5-fan decomposes the 15 nodes in each single view into three 5-fan substructures.

Table 1. We tested 3 different decompositions for 103 images from the HumanEva dataset. We decomposed the original problem into 1-fans, 4-fans and 5-fans as shown in Figure 7. We used a constant as well as a decreasing ρ-sequence (the latter one marked with *) for subgradient ascent with $\epsilon = 10^{-6}$. Choosing 5-fans inside single views does not improve inference while 4-fans between views results in much tighter relaxations. Furthermore, the decreasing ρ-sequence leads to faster convergence. The leftmost two columns specify how often the remaining gap was smaller than ϵ, and how often the best lower bound over all 6 approaches was reached. The 3rd and 4th column specify mean values of the gap and the lower bound. Finally, we compared the runtime for all data where all 6 approaches achieved ϵ-optimality.

	ϵ-gap convergence	best lower bound achieved	mean gap	mean lower bound	mean runtime
1-fan	27.18%	18.45%	0.0165	8.4816	1330 sec
1-fan*	35.92%	24.27%	0.0149	8.4820	1140 sec
4-fan	64.08%	60.19%	0.0011	8.4942	917 sec
4-fan*	78.64%	98.06%	0.0009	8.4943	577 sec
5-fan	11.65%	11.65%	0.0238	8.4760	2422 sec
5-fan*	23.30%	22.33%	0.0178	8.4805	1389 sec

5 Conclusions

We studied the decomposition of complex discrete graphical models into k-fan structured subproblems by Lagrangian relaxation. This enables to take into account more complex constraints as part of the subproblems that can still be solved to optimality within reasonable runtime. We also improved the performance of the subgradient ascent iteration for solving the Lagrangian dual problem, which is relevant not only for our problem but for any dual decomposition approach that are increasingly applied in computer vision research.

Experiments show that just choosing arbitrary decompositions into larger subproblems does not automatically lead to significantly better bounds. With little application-specific expertise, however, decompositions can be chosen that improve inference considerably, at moderate additional costs. The latter becomes immaterial for parallel implementations that are naturally supported by the problem decomposition.

Choosing automatically an optimal set of subproblems remains an open problem for future work, as is the case for automatically determining optimal parameter values for subgradient-based iterative optimization of nonsmooth dual functions.

Acknowledgement. Authors acknowledge partial support by the Research Training Group 1653 (http://graphmod.iwr.uni-heidelberg.de/) funded by the German Research Foundation (DFG).

References

[1] Bergtholdt, M., Kappes, J., Schmidt, S., Schnörr, C.: A study of parts-based object class detection using complete graphs. Int. J. Comp. Vision 87(1-2), 93–117 (2010)

[2] Bertsekas, D.: Nonlinear Programming, 2nd edn. Athena Scientific, Belmont (1999)

[3] Bertsimas, D., Tsitsiklis, J.: Introduction to Linear Optimization. Athena Scientific, Belmont (1997)

[4] Boyd, S., Vandenberghe, L.: Convex Optimization. Cambridge University Press, New York (2004)

[5] Boykov, Y., Veksler, O., Zabih, R.: Fast approximate energy minimization via graph cuts. IEEE Trans. Patt. Anal. Mach. Intell. 23(11), 1222–1239 (2001)

[6] Cowell, R.G., Dawid, A.P., Lauritzen, S.L., Spiegelhalter, D.J.: Probabilistic Networks and Expert Systems: Exact Computational Methods for Bayesian Networks. Springer Publishing Company, Incorporated, Heidelberg (2007)

[7] Ermoliev, Y.: Methods for solving nonlinear extremal problems. Cybernetics 2(4), 1–17 (1966)

[8] Johnson, J.K., Malioutov, D., Willsky, A.S.: Lagrangian relaxation for MAP estimation in graphical models. In: 45th Annual Allerton Conference on Communication, Control and Computing (September 2007)

[9] Kohli, P., Ladický, L., Torr, P.H.: Robust higher order potentials for enforcing label consistency. Int. J. Comput. Vision 82(3), 302–324 (2009)

[10] Kolmogorov, V.: Convergent tree-reweighted message passing for energy minimization. IEEE Trans. Pattern Anal. Mach. Intell. 28(10), 1568–1583 (2006)

[11] Komodakis, N., Paragios, N.: Beyond pairwise energies: Efficient optimization for higher-order MRFs. In: CVPR, pp. 2985–2992. IEEE, Los Alamitos (2009)

[12] Komodakis, N., Paragios, N., Tziritas, G.: MRF optimization via dual decomposition: Message-passing revisited. In: ICCV, pp. 1–8. IEEE, Los Alamitos (2007)

[13] Kumar, M.P., Kolmogorov, V., Torr, P.H.S.: An analysis of convex relaxations for MAP estimation of discrete MRFs. J. Mach. Learn. Res. 10, 71–106 (2009)

[14] Polyak, B.: A general method for solving extremum problems. Soviet Math. 8, 593–597 (1966)

[15] Potetz, B., Lee, T.S.: Efficient belief propagation for higher-order cliques using linear constraint nodes. Comput. Vis. Image Underst. 112(1), 39–54 (2008)

[16] Rother, C., Kohli, P., Feng, W., Jia, J.: Minimizing sparse higher order energy functions of discrete variables. In: CVPR, pp. 1382–1389. IEEE, Los Alamitos (2009)

[17] Rother, C., Kolmogorov, V., Lempitsky, V.S., Szummer, M.: Optimizing binary MRFs via extended roof duality. In: CVPR. IEEE Computer Society, Los Alamitos (2007)

[18] Ruszczynski, A.: A merit function approach to the subgradient method with averaging. Optimization Methods Software 23(1), 161–172 (2008)

[19] Sigal, L., Black, M.: HumanEva: synchronized video and motion capture dataset for evaluation of articulated human motion. Tech. Rep. Technical Report CS-06-08, Brown University (2006)

[20] Sontag, D., Meltzer, T., Globerson, A., Jaakkola, T., Weiss, Y.: Tightening LP relaxations for MAP using message passing. In: McAllester, D.A., Myllymki, P. (eds.) UAI, pp. 503–510. AUAI Press (2008)

[21] Szeliski, R., Zabih, R., Scharstein, D., Veksler, O., Kolmogorov, V., Agarwala, A., Tappen, M., Rother, C.: A comparative study of energy minimization methods for markov random fields with smoothness-based priors. IEEE Trans. Patt. Mach. Intell. 30(6), 1068–1080 (2008)

[22] Vicente, S., Kolmogorov, V., Rother, C.: Joint optimization of segmentation and appearance models. In: Proc. ICCV 2009 (2009)

[23] Wainwright, M.J., Jordan, M.I.: Graphical models, exponential families, and variational inference. Foundations and Trends in Machine Learning 1(1-2), 1–305 (2008)

[24] Werner, T.: Revisiting the decomposition approach to inference in exponential families and graphical models. Tech. rep., Center for Machine Perception, Czech Technical University (May 2009)

Randomized Locality Sensitive Vocabularies for Bag-of-Features Model*

Yadong Mu[1], Ju Sun[1,2], Tony X. Han[3], Loong-Fah Cheong[1,2], and Shuicheng Yan[1]

[1]Electrical and Computer Engineering, National University of Singapore, Singapore
[2]Interactive & Digital Media Institute, National University of Singapore, Singapore
[3]Electrical and Computer Engineering, University of Missouri-Columbia, USA
Email: {elemy, idmsj, eleclf, eleyans}@nus.edu.sg, hantx@missouri.edu

Abstract. Visual vocabulary construction is an integral part of the popular Bag-of-Features (BOF) model. When visual data scale up (in terms of the dimensionality of features or/and the number of samples), most existing algorithms (e.g. k-means) become unfavorable due to the prohibitive time and space requirements. In this paper we propose the *random locality sensitive vocabulary* (RLSV) scheme towards efficient visual vocabulary construction in such scenarios. Integrating ideas from the Locality Sensitive Hashing (LSH) and the Random Forest (RF), RLSV generates and aggregates multiple visual vocabularies based on random projections, without taking clustering or training efforts. This simple scheme demonstrates superior time and space efficiency over prior methods, in both theory and practice, while often achieving comparable or even better performances. Besides, extensions to supervised and kernelized vocabulary constructions are also discussed and experimented with.

1 Introduction

The *bag-of-features* (BOF) model (also known as the *bag-of-words*) has gained much empirical success in producing orderless representations of feature-rich vision data. In this model, in order to obtain uniform representations for feature sets of varying cardinalities, one performs feature quantization for each primitive feature referring to a learnt "visual vocabulary", and then summarizes each set into histograms. Despite its simplicity, the BOF model has shaped the current paradigms towards many high-level vision problems, e.g., object recognition and content-based image retrieval (CBIR). In fact, state-of-the-art approaches to object recognition are to first extract local descriptors such as SIFT [1] from interest points (i.e., local extrema in scale space pyramid) in images, and then devise Mercer kernels such as Pyramid Match Kernels (PMK) or Histogram Intersectional Kernels (HIK) between pairwise feature histograms. Finally, sophisticated classifiers such as the Supporting Vector Machines (SVM) are used for per-sample decision.

* Support of IDMPO Grant R-705-000-018-279 Singapore and NRF/IDM Program under research Grant NRF2008IDMIDM004-029 are gratefully acknowledged.

Visual vocabulary construction is critical to the BOF model. In ideal cases, every visual word in the vocabulary bears concrete meaning, or semantic, inspired from the similar idea of *bag-of-words* models in text analysis. In practice, however, quality of the vocabulary depends on numerous factors associated with the vocabulary creation process, such as the source of samples, the number of visual words specified, and the similarity metric. Hence, a practical criterion for a proper visual vocabulary could be visual features near to the same visual word bear some similarities. This in essence turns the vocabulary construction problem into partitioning the visual feature space according to a few data samples. Numerous methods (as described in Sec-1.1) have been proposed to address this partition problem.

Complications associated with vision data, however, stem from the typical scale issue including huge amount and high dimensionality. For example, the popular SIFT descriptor [1] used for local visual feature description has 128 dimensions, while a typical image at normal resolution can produce 1k $\sim$ 2k such primitive feature descriptors. The complexity quickly explodes for real-world vision databases that usually consist of millions or even billions of such images. Moreover, peculiarities with high dimensionality, such as concentration of distribution [2][3], show up frequently and deserve special investigations. Questing into large-scale problems, most techniques that work nicely in low-dimensional spaces with small amount of data may not healthily scale up. This calls for novel solutions that are efficient and dedicate for large-scale data while producing acceptable levels of performance.

1.1 Prior Work

There are intimate connections between the vocabulary construction and the clustering/space partitioning problem, the latter of which is widely studied in machine learning. Hence various unsupervised clustering methods have been applied to this particular problem, among which k-means clustering[1] is the most popular. Other methods include mean-shift [4], tree-based coding (e.g., tree induced by hierarchical k-means) [5]. On the other hand, for problems where supervision or prior knowledge are available, e.g., labels or segmentations for images, sparsity in representation, supervision is applied to partially guide the unsupervised clustering (e.g., random forest [6] based methods such as ERC-Forest [7]), or to learn informative vocabularies directly (e.g.,[8][9]). Nevertheless, most of the supervised vocabulary learning techniques are very expensive and unlikely to scale up nicely. Hence we will focus on unsupervised clustering techniques (e.g. k-means) and extremely efficient and flexible supervised techniques (e.g. the random forest family).

Sparse coding and its various applications [10] are perhaps the most inviting work into high-dimensional spaces for vision research. In fact for clustering [2] reveals that in high-dimensional spaces, clustering methods such as k-means tend

---

[1] Hereafter we default k-means to the hierarchical k-means algorithm due to its efficiency until otherwise stated.

to return many similar centers to a query, which makes these methods rather unstable. This is partially explained by the concentration of finite number of samples as reported by many authors, e.g. [2][3]. In this case, aggregation of distinct clustering results prove useful to enhancing the stability. This is the underlying principle for the random forest method [6], which also inspires our method.

Randomized algorithms have been widely studied and analyzed in algorithm designs [11]. For large-scale problems, [3] has tried to contrast the random projection with the classic PCA technique. Moreover random vectors sampled from the unit sphere have served as the hashing vectors for one family of LSH [12]. In this vein, there is fruitful research work on LSH theory (e.g.,[13]) and applications (e.g., image database indexing and search[14]). Our method build from the idea of LSH.

1.2 Our Approach

We propose and empirically validate the idea of *randomized locality sensitive vocabulary* (RLSV), which is inspired by both RF and LSH. Instead of building visual vocabularies by optimizing a global objective, our proposed method generates visual words by applying a sequence of random linear bipartitions. Assume all samples are originally embedded in a specific metric space (e.g., Hamming space, ℓ_p-normed space). For any sample pair, theoretic analysis of LSH guarantees that their collision probability in the resulting vocabulary is tightly related to the pairwise similarity or distance. Furthermore, to reduce the inherent randomness, multiple random vocabularies are independently created using the same method, and the final inter-sample distance or similarity is based on the consensus of all vocabularies.

Compared with existing methods, the proposed RLSV has the following merits: 1) No time-consuming training or clustering stage in RLSV. The major computational cost comes from the random hash function generation and histogram binning operations, which can be efficiently handled. 2) Noise resistance and stability by exploiting the ensemble technique. RLSV generates an ensembles of several vocabularies to mitigate the effect of randomness and noise. 3) As stated above, nearest-prototype based methods (e.g., k-means) tend to suffer from the so-called *curse of dimensionality* problem. In contrast, the performance of RLSV is stable for high-dimensional data. 4) Compared to methods such as RF which require supervision, RLSV is unsupervised in nature but can be readily extended to supervised and kernerlized cases.

2   Randomized Locality Sensitive Vocabularies

In this section and the next we elaborate on the proposed vocabulary construction algorithm, and discuss its relationship to existing methods. We provide theoretic analysis on the time and space complexity in contrast with k-means and RF, and also present extensions to the supervised or kernelized cases.

2.1   Preliminaries

A key ingredient to many visual recognition and retrieval applications is to search k-nearest-neighbors (k-NN) for the query (or testing sample). In many cases the performance of the whole system heavily hinges on the efficiency of the k-NN procedure. In practice, exact k-NN is somewhat unnecessary, since in many scenarios approximate nearest neighbors (ANN) results in nearly the same performance. Several efficient algorithms are known for low-dimensional cases (e.g., up to 10 to 20), such as the kd-tree [15] algorithm. However, for high-dimensional cases, these methods often provide little improvement over a linear scan algorithm, which is known to be the phenomenon "the curse of dimensionality". In recent years, various *locality sensitive hashing* (LSH) [16][13] methods are proposed to tackle this problem.

Let $\mathcal{H}$ be an LSH family defined on metric space $\mathbb{R}^d$. For any x, $y \in \mathbb{R}^d$, the following relationship holds[2]:

$$\forall h \in \mathcal{H}, \quad Pr[h(x) = h(y)] = \kappa(x, y), \tag{1}$$

where $\kappa(\cdot, \cdot)$ denotes the similarity measure between samples x and y. In other words, x and y's collision probability (i.e., being mapped to the same hash bucket) is monotonically increasing with their similarity value, which is known as the "locality sensitive" property. Several LSH families have been developed for various distances (or similarities). Here we list some representative work:
Arccos distance: for real-valued feature vectors lying on hypersphere $S^{d-1} = \{x \in \mathbb{R}^d \mid \|x\|_2 = 1\}$, an angle-oriented distance can be defined as $\Theta(x, y) = \arccos\left(\frac{x \cdot y}{\|x\| \|y\|}\right)$. Charikar et al. [12] proposes the following LSH family:

$$h(x) = \begin{cases} 0, & \text{if } \rho^\top x < 0 \\ 1, & \text{if } \rho^\top x \geq 0 \end{cases} \tag{2}$$

where the hashing vector ρ is uniformly sampled from the unit hypersphere S^{d-1}. The collision probability is $Pr[h(x) = h(y)] = 1 - \Theta(x, y)/\pi$.
ℓ_p **distance**: for linear vector spaces equipped with the ℓ_p metric, i.e., $D_{\ell_p}(x, y) = \left(\sum_{i=1}^d |x_i - y_i|^p\right)^{\frac{1}{p}}$, Datar et al. [16] proposes a hashing algorithm based on linear projections onto a 1-dimensional line and chopping the line into equal-length segments, as below:

$$h(x) = \left\lfloor \frac{\rho^\top x + b}{W} \right\rfloor, \tag{3}$$

where the hashing vector $\rho \in \mathbb{R}^d$ is randomly sampled from the *p-stable distribution* and $\lfloor \cdot \rfloor$ is the flooring function for rounding. W is the data-dependent window size and b is sampled from the uniform distribution $U[0, W)$.

---

[2] Note that other definitions of LSH exist, such as the one in [17]. However, they are fundamentally equivalent to the current.

We employ the arccos distance family in the current work, and the locality sensitivity property will be key to ensuring that our hashing vectors properly partition the feature space such that near neighbors are grouped together with high probability.

2.2   Overview

K-means is probably the most popular due to its empirical success. The goal of k-means is to seek K prototypes (or cluster centers) that minimizes a pre-specified functional value. These prototypes constitute a Voronoi diagram per se and each sample is assigned to its nearest prototype according to some specific distance metric. Despite its popularity, for an input feature set of size n, the classic k-means requires $\mathcal{O}(Knd)$ operations per iteration and typically costs tens of iterations before convergence, which is computationally forbidden for massive data source, high dimensional feature spaces and large vocabulary sizes. Tree structured vocabulary [5][7] requires shorter training time compared with k-means, yet consuming exponentially increasing memory space (w.r.t. the tree depth) to store the splitting information (random dimension, threshold etc.) of inner tree nodes.

Compared with these aforementioned structures, the proposed RLSV method is superior in terms of both memory requirement and training time. The major weakness is the inferior discriminant ability of single vocabulary resulting from the intrinsic randomness in visual word generation. To mitigate it, a straight-forward solution is to collect an ensemble of independent random vocabularies, similar to the idea in ERC-Forest [7].

2.3   RLSV Construction

The algorithmic pipeline for RLSV can be described in three consequent steps as follows:

Step-1: visual word generation Assume the similarity between any two samples $p, q \in \mathbb{R}^d$ can be measured by $\kappa(p, q)$. Previous studies (see [18] for a brief survey) reveal the existence of LSH families for many well-known metrics or similarities such as ℓ_p. Formally, let $\mathcal{H}$ be an LSH family such that for any hash function $h \in \mathcal{H} : \mathbb{R}^d \to \{0, 1\}$, the locality-sensitive property holds. Suppose B hash functions are independently generated from $\mathcal{H}$, obtaining $H = \langle h_1, h_2, \ldots, h_B \rangle$ after direct concatenation. We proceed to give a formal definition for "random visual word" as below:

Definition 1. *(random visual word): there is a bi-mapping between any visual word w_i and valid permutation π_i from $\{0, 1\}^B$. Any two samples $p, q \in \mathbb{R}^d$ belong to the same visual word if for any $i \in \{1, \ldots, B\}$, there is $h_i(p) \oplus h_j(q) = 0$, where $\oplus$ denotes the XOR bit operation.*

In ideal case, B hash functions are able to produce at most 2^B unique visual words. However, in practice the evolutionary curve of visual word count seldom demonstrates such an exponentially growing tendency. The phenomena can be geometrically understood, since it is almost impossible for the hyper-plane induced by a hash function intersects with all other polyhedrons produced by other hash functions. Since the relationship between B and the number of valid vocabulary entries cannot be accurately determined, practically we maintain the record of vocabulary sizes and continue adding new hash functions until a pre-defined vocabulary size M is reached.

Step-2: visual word filtering In Fig. 1 we plot the sample counts corresponding to distinct visual words. It can be seen that it roughly follows a power-law

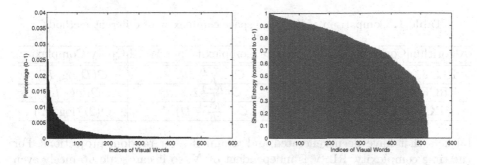

Fig. 1. Illustration of the typical distribution of features (**left**, sorted descendingly) and Shannon entropy of labels (**right**, sorted descendingly) for a 1024 word visual vocabulary in a multi-class problem. Empty words are omitted. Non-informative bins of the vocabulary can be filtered out accordingly by throwing away low-frequency bins.

distribution and thus part of the vocabulary can be trimmed without notable information loss. Moreover, in the supervised (or semi-supervised) settings (discussed in Sec-3.2), we can also abandon the visual words that have weak discriminating power. For multi-class problems, useful statistics can be calculated based on the entropy of class-label distribution for each valid visual word. In Fig. 1 we plot the entropy distribution on the data set of Caltech-101 (vocabulary size M = 1000). In the above two cases, a simple threshold-based visual word filtering will benefit outlier removal and yield more compact representations.

Step-3: histogram binning and normalization In practice, we maintain L independent random vocabularies to ensure the stability and enhance the performance. After vocabulary construction, each feature bag can be transformed into uniform histogram representations by casting its elements into visual words and then perform counting and normalization. For each feature, the binary hash bits $H = \langle h_1, h_2, \ldots, h_B \rangle$ determine a unique decimal value in $[0, 2^B]$. Recall that there are actually no valid visual words corresponding to most decimal values, we maintain a *word-key mapping table* $\mathcal{T} : \{0,1\}^B \to \{1, \ldots, M\}$ for the purpose of efficient binning.

2.4 Complexity Analysis

Here we provide theoretic comparisons amongst RLSV, ERC-Forest (ERCF), and Hierarchical k-means (HK), in terms of the vocabulary construction time complexity, storage requirements, and the query complexity (i.e., a new vector gets assigned to one of the bins in the vocabulary). Table 1 presents these results in Big-$\mathcal{O}$ notation. Here we assume all tree-structures are with splitting factor of 2, and D for feature dimension, N for total number of available samples, K number of desired cluster centers. For simplicity, we further assume $K = 2^d$, where $d + 1$ will be the tree depth for binary splitting trees as we have assumed. Note that c is an undetermined constant in $(1, 2)$, accounting for the empty

Table 1. Comparison of time and space complexity of different methods

Algorithm	Construction Time	Space Complexity per Word	Query Complexity
RLSV	$\mathcal{O}(D \log_c K)$	$\mathcal{O}(\frac{\log_c K}{K} D)$	$\mathcal{O}(D \log_c K)$
ERCF	$\mathcal{O}(\sqrt{D} N \log_2 K)$	$\mathcal{O}(\frac{K-1}{K} D)$	$\mathcal{O}(\log_2 K)$
HK	$\mathcal{O}(2DN \log_2 K)$	$\mathcal{O}(\frac{2(K-1)}{K} D)$	$\mathcal{O}(2D \log_2 K)$

buckets that have been generated and trimmed after random projections. For the time complexity, RLSV is independent of N, so it can scale up nicely even when the data set is huge. For the storage requirement, KLSH approaches 0 for space per word as K goes up, whereas the other two methods remain constant for large K. It is unfortunate that the query complexity of RLSV is not as low as the ERCF, which could be hurt for very high-dimensional data.

3 Extensions

The algorithm presented in subsection 2.3 targets unsupervised cases in finite-dimensional linear feature spaces. However, both kernel tricks and supervision information are ubiquitous in computer vision databases. For the former, the pairwise similarity is gauged via the inner product in *reproducing kernel Hilbert space* (RKHS) [19]. While for the latter, supervision information from manual labeling or annotations is available to regularize the constructed visual words. Both of them are common scenarios in real-world applications. In this section we discuss the extensions to these cases.

3.1 Kernelized RLSV (K-RLSV)

Note that choice of an LSH family in an application depends on the underlying metric in the feature space. Here we focus on ℓ_p distance when $p = 2$ and Arccos distance. Recall that in both cases LSH is feasible based on sampling from standard Gaussian distribution which belongs to the p-stable distribution. Generally, sampling in RKHS is difficult owing to the lack of explicit feature representation. However, we have the following observation (similar to the theoretic results in [14] yet no zero-centered assumption on the Gram matrices here), which reveals that sampling from Gaussian distribution in Hilbert space is feasible:

Theorem 1. *(ℓ_2-keeping projection in RKHS) Denote $\kappa(\cdot, \cdot)$ as the inner product in Hilbert space $\mathcal{K}$. Given an m-cardinality data set $\mathcal{X}$ and corresponding Gram matrix G, the ℓ_2-metric keeping projection can be expressed as $p(x) = \sum_{i=1}^{m} \omega(i)\kappa(x, x_i)$, where $\omega(i)$ only relies on G.*

Proof. Denote the implicit Hilbert mapping function as ψ. The geometric mean can be computed as $\mu_\psi = \frac{1}{m}\sum_{i=1}^{m}\psi(x_i)$. For a t-cardinality subset $\mathcal{S} \subset \{1 \dots m\}$, let $z = \frac{1}{t}\sum_{i \in \mathcal{S}}\psi(x_i)$ and $\tilde{z} = \sqrt{t}(z - \mu_\psi)$. According to the central limit theorem, $\tilde{z}$ is distributed as Gaussian $\Phi(0, \Sigma)$, where Σ is the covariance matrix of $\mathcal{X}$. Further applying a whitening transform, we can obtain the desired hash vector in $\mathcal{K}$, i.e. $r = \Sigma^{1/2}\tilde{z}$. For any datum x, $h(x) = \psi(x)^\top \Sigma^{1/2}\tilde{z}$.

Given Gram matrix $G = \Psi^\top\Psi$, where each column of Ψ corresponds to a feature vector in data set $\mathcal{X}$. It is easily verified that

$$\tilde{z}^\top \Sigma^{1/2}\psi(x) = \tilde{z}^\top(\Psi Q)(QGQ)^{-\frac{1}{2}}(\Psi Q)^\top \psi(x) \tag{4}$$

where $Q = I - \frac{1}{m}ee^\top$. Substituting $\tilde{z} = \sqrt{t}\Psi(\frac{1}{t}\delta_S - \frac{1}{m}e)^\top$, where δ_S is a binary indicator vector for subset $\mathcal{S}$. Finally we get

$$p(x) = \left[\sqrt{t}(\frac{1}{t}\delta_S - \frac{1}{m}e)GQ(QGQ)^{-\frac{1}{2}}Q^\top\right]\Psi^\top\psi(x) \tag{5}$$

Let $\omega \triangleq \left[\sqrt{t}(\frac{1}{t}\delta_S - \frac{1}{m}e)GQ(QGQ)^{-\frac{1}{2}}Q^\top\right]$, thus the conclusion holds. $\square$

The complexity of the above procedure is low since $m \ll n$ where n is the sample count of the whole database (e.g., $m = 200 \sim 1000$ and n is probably on the order of million or billion). From the property of p-stable distribution, for samples x, y, projection difference $|p(x) - p(y)| = \left|\sum_{i=1}^{m}\omega(i)\kappa(x, x_i) - \sum_{i=1}^{m}\omega(i)\kappa(y, x_i)\right|$ sustains their distance in the implicit RKHS induced by $\kappa(\cdot, \cdot)$, which makes the LSH algorithms mentioned in Section 2.1 feasible.

3.2 Discriminative RLSV (D-RLSV)

Denote the ensemble of all feature bags as $\mathcal{B} = \{b_i\}$, where each bag $b_i = \{x_{i_1}, \dots, x_{i_n}\}$. In the supervised case, a unique label y_i is assigned to bag b_i. For tractability, we adopt the same assumption to [7], i.e., assuming all features in a bag share the same label. Recall that the scheme in subsection 2.3 is totally random. A possible improvement is to sequentially select an optimal hashing vectors from a candidate pool according to pre-specified label-oriented criterion, which motivates the Discriminative RLSV (D-RLSV) here. The proposed method works as follows: suppose k hashing vectors have been generated and denote the resulting visual words as $V_k = \{w_i, i = 1 \dots n_k\}$ (n_k is the vocabulary size). To choose the $(k+1)$-th hashing vector, for each candidate $\widetilde{h}$ we calculate a score based on the Shannon entropy as suggested in [20], defined as:

$$S_{k+1}(\widetilde{h}) = \frac{1}{n_k} \sum_{i=1}^{n_k} \frac{2 \cdot I_i(\widetilde{h})}{H_C(\omega_i) + H_S(\widetilde{h}, \omega_i)}, \tag{6}$$

where $H_i^C(\widetilde{h})$ denotes the entropy of the class distribution in the i-th visual word. Note that adopting $\widetilde{h}$ will split each of the existing visual words into two. $H_i^T(\widetilde{h})$ describes the split entropy of the i-th visual word. Formally,

$$H_C(\omega_i) = -\sum_{l \in \mathcal{L}} \frac{n_l}{n} \log_2 \frac{n_l}{n}, \quad \text{and} \quad H_S(\widetilde{h}, \omega_i) = -\sum_{p=1}^{2} \frac{n_p}{n} \log_2 \frac{n_p}{n}. \tag{7}$$

The maximum of $H_i^T(\widetilde{h})$ is reached when the two partitions have equal size. Based on the entropy of a given visual word, the impurity can be calculated by the mutual information of the split, i.e.,

$$I_i(\widetilde{h}) = H_C(\omega_i) - \frac{n_+}{n} H_C(\omega_i^+) - \frac{n_-}{n} H_C(\omega_i^-), \tag{8}$$

where ω_i^+, ω_i^- are the split of ω_i by $\widetilde{h}$, and n_+, n_- denote the number of features belonging to each new visual word respectively. Finally, the optimal hashing vector for the $(k+1)$-th iteration can be determined via $h^* = \arg\max_{\widetilde{h}} S_{k+1}(\widetilde{h})$.

4   Evaluation

In this section, we evaluate the proposed RLSV and its extensions on real-world data sets under three different task settings, i.e., action recognition in video, object recognition, and near-duplicate video detection. Our main concerns include: 1) time used to construct visual vocabularies. 2) memory storage used to keep vocabulary-related information. 3) performance in terms of accuracy. All the experiments are conducted on our common PC with Due-core 3.0Ghz CPU and 8GB physical memory. We choose two representative methods, i.e., Hierarchical K-means and ERC-Forest [7] for comparison. For the former, we adopt a tree branching factor of 2. All statistics are obtained by averaging multiple independent runs.

Experiment-1: KTH Video Database

The KTH video database was developed by Schuldt et al. [21] in 2004 and is one of the popular benchmarks for human action recognition. It contains six different actions captured with appearance variations and mild camera motions such as zooming in and zooming out. The actions are performed by 25 subjects in 4 different scenarios. Each video clips are segmented into 4 sub-clips, resulting in 2400 video sequences in total. See Fig. 2 for the illustration of KTH video clips.

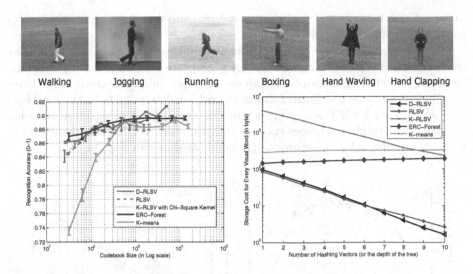

Fig. 2. Top: Example frames from KTH video database. **Bottom Left**: Averaged recognition rates. **Bottom Right**: Storage cost for each visual word. RLSV can consistently achieve comparable performance (with little deviation) with ERC, while consuming less memory. By comparison, k-means is worse in both performance and space efficiency. Please refer to the color pdf for better view.

We use the same dataset splitting as in [21], which contains a training set (8 persons), a validation set (8 persons) and a test set (9 persons). For local feature descriptors, we describe each video segment using Space-time interest points (STIP) as in [21], around which *histogram of gradient* (HOG) and *histogram of flow* (HOF) features are extracted. Both of the counts of independent vocabularies in RLSV or trees in ERC-Forest are set to be 50. Recognition accuracies are presented on the bottom left of Fig. 2. RLSV algorithm family demonstrates comparable discriminating ability to ERC-Forest, but both are obviously better than K-means. D-RLSV reaches a peek performance of 91.4% with around 4000 visual words, which is in sync with the setting and results reported in [22]. In the bottom right of Fig. 2, we illustrate the averaged memory storage for the vocabulary-related information per visual word, which well validates our previous complexity analysis.

Experiment-2: Caltech-101

Caltech-101 is constructed to test object recognition algorithms for semantic categories of images. The data set contains 101 object categories and 1 background category, with 40 to 800 images per category. As pre-processing, the maximum dimension of each image is normalized to be 480-pixel. Most objects contained in the images are of similar scale and orientation. However, considering the large inter-category variation on appearance, lighting and occlusion, the recognition task on Caltech-101 is still challenging and well suitable to testing various local features and visual vocabularies.

For fair comparison between different vocabularies, we guarantee that they share the same type of features, and any post-processing on them. Specifically, we extract 3000 SIFT descriptors from each image. Unlike the traditional dense sampling strategy on a uniform 2-D image grid, we determine both the locations and scales of each SIFT feature in a random way [23], ignoring more complex and effective sampling schemes such as [24]. However, the experimental results for such a simple scheme are amazingly good, as shown in Fig. 3.

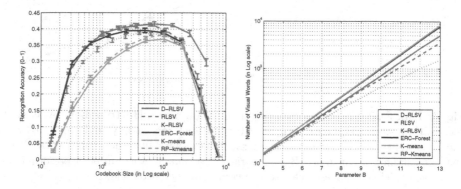

Fig. 3. Left: Performance with 15 training samples per category. Our RLSV family shows consistently (with little deviation) comparable or even better performance than the other methods. **Right**: Vocabulary sizes under varying number of hashing vectors in RLSV or tree depth in ERC-Forest. Please refer to the color pdf for better view.

We test the proposed method in two settings, either with 15 or 30 training samples per category. Here we only present the former due to the space constraint and also the observation that the latter case concurs with the former in terms of algorithmic behaviors as compared to other methods. The peak performance (41.4% for 15 training samples per class) appears with roughly 700 visual words. The performance drastically decreases with extremely smaller or larger vocabularies, which is consistent with previous study in computer vision and our experimental settings. For parameter setting, we use 20 independent visual vocabularies for RLSV and its extensions, and 20 trees for the ERC-Forest. In the classification stage, we regress the histogram feature of the testing sample on the column space spanned by all the training samples in each category, and measure the distance with the regression residue. The overall distance is computed as the summation over individual visual vocabularies or random trees. Classification methods like SVM or NN produce similar yet slightly worse results. As seen in Fig. 3, the accuracies produced by RLSV-related methods and ERC-Forest are comparable, and all are superior to hierarchial K-means. Moreover, it is also observed that the vocabulary sizes roughly linearly increase with respect to the number of hashing vectors in RLSV and tree depth in ERC-Forest or K-means, although the increasing rate of RLSV-related methods are much smaller than others.

An interesting comparison is between k-means and random projection (into a 60-dimensional lower space) followed by k-means (RP-kmeans). The random projection is meant to be a lightweight replacement of the PCA for dimensionality reduction as suggested in [3]. And the simple scheme consistently outperforms the simple k-means for all vocabulary sizes. This can be partially explained by the property of reduced eccentricity exhibited by the random projection discussed in [3]. Nevertheless, there are still significant performance gaps between RP-kmeans and RLSV or ERC-Forest methods. Moreover, there is no fundamental change in the time and space complexity.

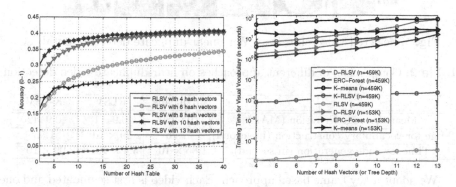

Fig. 4. Left: Performance evolution curve with respect to the number of hash tables in RLSV. **Right**: Time spent to construct visual vocabularies for various approaches.

A random vocabulary as in RLSV or ERC-Forest is very easy to generate, but yet a single one typically performs inferiorly even as compared with k-means in the classification phase. However, we argue that the ensemble of independent "weak" vocabularies significantly outperforms a single elaborately-designed vocabulary, in the same spirit to the bagging algorithm developed in machine learning. We plot the performance evolution curve w.r.t. the number of hashing vectors for RLSV on the left of Fig. 4. As can been seen, the performance of RLSV ensemble hikes rapidly and overruns k-means with only a small number of weak vocabularies.

Fig. 4 (right) also provides an illustration of the time cost for vocabulary construction consumed by various methods. Time spent on vocabulary construction roughly follows a log-linear rule. Among them, RLSV and K-RLSV are order-of-magnitude faster as compared to others.

Experiment-3: Near-Duplicate Video Detection

We also validate the proposed RLSV method for detecting near-duplicate video clips. Being intrinsically unsupervised, ERC-Forest and D-RLSV are not suitable. For such applications, RLSV beats K-means owing to its fast speed and high flexibility. The near duplicate video benchmark is provided by Wu [25]. The benchmark comprises 12876 video clips, divided into 24 sets. The groundtruth of each video set is manually labeled, and the most relevant video is treated as the query video. The task is to distinguish near-duplicate videos to the query among each video set.

Fig. 5. Selected video clips from Wu's near-duplicate detection database

Table 2. Comparison of different approaches on near-duplicate video detection

	K-means	RLSV	K-LSV
Mean Average Precision (MAP)	0.9280	0.9411	0.9442
Time for vocabulary construction (in second)	7.76	2.29×10^{-4}	1.53
Time for code generation (in second)	1.85×10^{-2}	3.4×10^{-3}	2.09×10^{-2}

We adopt a key frame based approach. Each video is first segmented and one key frame is taken from a segment, resulting in 30 key frames per video clip on average. We extract a simple HSV color histogram from each key frame. The 24 dimensional HSV color histogram is concatenated with 18 bins for Hue, 3 bins for Saturation and 3 bins for Value as described in [25]. As seen in Figure 5, the HSV histogram can greatly vary among different key frames, thus the bag-of-feature model well fits this scenario. We test the Mean Average Precision (MAP) over all 24 queries, and together provide a comparison between time spent on vocabulary construction and code generation of each video clip. A K-RLSV method is also included in the experiment, where the Chi-Square kernel is applied. Table 2 indicates RLSV is a good tradeoff between MAP and speed.

5   Conclusion

We have presented a simple yet effective algorithm for visual vocabulary construction combining the idea of LSH and RF. It avoids the severe problems occurring in most existing methods, such as the slow training (e.g., in K-means), or huge storage (e.g., in ERC-Forest). The proposed method strikes a good balance between accuracy and efficacy, and is supposed to be applicable to many real-world applications in computer vision. Moreover, extensions to kernerlized and supervised cases are also presented. We plan to extend the work to on-line settings. Moreover, currently our method is not advantageous in terms of query complexity. This motivates us to investigate the possibility of synergizing construction and query process towards higher efficiency.

References

1. Lowe, D.: Distinctive image features from scale-invariant keypoints. International journal of computer vision 60, 91–110 (2004)
2. Beyer, K.S., Goldstein, J., Ramakrishnan, R., Shaft, U.: When is nearest neigh- bor meaningful? In: Beeri, C., Bruneman, P. (eds.) ICDT 1999. LNCS, vol. 1540, pp. 217–235. Springer, Heidelberg (1998)
3. Dasgupta, S.: Experiments with random projection. In: UAI, pp. 143–151 (2000)
4. Jurie, F., Triggs, B.: Creating efficient codebooks for visual recognition. ICCV, 604–610 (2005)
5. Nistér, D., Stewénius, H.: Scalable recognition with a vocabulary tree. In: CVPR, vol. (2), pp. 2161–2168 (2006)
6. Breiman, L.: Random forests. Machine Learning 45, 5–32 (2001)
7. Moosmann, F., Nowak, E., Jurie, F.: Randomized clustering forests for image classiffcation. IEEE Trans. Pattern Anal. 30, 1632–1646 (2008)
8. Yang, L., Jin, R., Sukthankar, R., Jurie, F.: Unifying discriminative visual code-book generation with classifier training for object category recognition. In: CVPR (2008)
9. Lee, H., Battle, A., Raina, R., Ng, A.: Efficient sparse coding algorithms. In: NIPS, vol. 19, p. 801 (2007)
10. Wright, J., Yang, A., Ganesh, A., Sastry, S., Ma, Y.: Robust face recognition via sparse representation. PAMI, 210–227 (2009)
11. Cormen, T., Leiserson, C., Rivest, R., Stein, C.: Introduction to algorithms. The MIT press, Cambridge (2001)
12. Charikar, M.: Similarity estimation techniques from rounding algorithms. In: STOC, pp. 380–388 (2002)
13. Andoni, A., Indyk, P.: Near-optimal hashing algorithms for approximate nearest neighbor in high dimensions. ACM Commun. 51, 117–122 (2008)
14. Kulis, B., Grauman, K.: Kernelized locality sensitive hashing for scalable image search. In: ICCV (2009)
15. Bentley, J.L.: Multidimensional binary search trees used for associative searching. ACM Commun. 517, 509–517 (1975)
16. Datar, M., Immorlica, N., Indyk, P., Mirrokni, V.: Locality-sensitive hashing scheme based on p-stable distributions. In: SCG, pp. 253–262 (2004)
17. Indyk, P., Motwani, R.: Approximate nearest neighbors: Towards removing the curse of dimensionality. In: STOC, pp. 604–613 (1998)
18. Andoni, A., Indyk, P.: Near-optimal hashing algorithms for approximate nearest neighbor in high dimensions. ACM Commun. 51, 117–122 (2008)
19. Scholkopf, B., Smola, A.J.: Learning with Kernels: Support Vector Machines, Regularization, Optimization, and Beyond. MIT Press, Cambridge (2001)
20. Geurts, P., Ernst, D., Wehenkel, L.: Extremely randomized trees. Machine Learning 63, 3–42 (2006)
21. Schuldt, C., Laptev, I., Caputo, B.: Recognizing human actions: a local SVM approach. In: ICPR (2004)
22. Laptev, I.: Marsza lek, M., Schmid, C., Rozenfeld, B.: Learning realistic human actions from movies (2008)
23. Nowak, E., Jurie, F., Triggs, B.: Sampling strategies for bag-of-features image classification. In: Leonardis, A., Bischof, H., Pinz, A. (eds.) ECCV 2006. LNCS, vol. 3954, pp. 490–503. Springer, Heidelberg (2006)
24. Marée, R., Geurts, P., Piater, J.H., Wehenkel, L.: Random subwindows for robust image classification. In: CVPR, vol. (1), pp. 34–40 (2005)
25. Wu, X., Hauptmann, A.G., Ngo, C.W.: Practical elimination of near-duplicates from web video search. ACM Multimedia, 218–227 (2007)

Image Categorization Using Directed Graphs

Hua Wang, Heng Huang, and Chris Ding

Department of Computer Science and Engineering, University of Texas at Arlington,
Arlington, TX 76019, USA
huawang2007@mavs.uta.edu, heng@uta.edu, chqding@uta.edu

Abstract. Most existing graph-based semi-supervised classification
methods use pairwise similarities as edge weights of an *undirected graph*
with images as the nodes of the graph. Recently several new graph construction methods produce, however, *directed graph* (asymmetric similarity between nodes). A simple symmetrization is often used to convert a
directed graph to an undirected one. This, however, loses important structural information conveyed by asymmetric similarities. In this paper, we
propose a novel symmetric co-linkage similarity which captures the essential relationship among the nodes in the directed graph. We apply this new
co-linkage similarity in two important computer vision tasks for image categorization: object recognition and image annotation. Extensive empirical
studies demonstrate the effectiveness of our method.

Keywords: Directed graph learning, Co-linkage similarity, Multi-label
classification, Object Recognition, Image annotation.

1 Introduction

Many computer vision problems, such as image categorization including object
recognition and image annotation, are often solved by semi-supervised classification algorithms due to the lack of enough labeled training data. Most, if not
all, existing graph-based semi-supervised classification algorithms learn on an
undirected graph [21,20,6,19,16] with images as the nodes and pairwise image
similarities as edge weights. The edge weights of the graph are typically assessed
using traditional graph construction functions, such as Gaussian kernel similarity. Such graph-based semi-supervised classification performance is sensitive
to parameter variances, and there is no reliable way to determine the optimal
parameter value especially when the amount of labeled data is small [20,15,3,18].

In order to tackle this parameter sensitivity problem, several robust graph
construction methods have been proposed recently such as [15,3,18,8]. A common
aspect of these methods, however, is that their immediate output is a *directed
graph* (asymmetric similarity between nodes). In order to make use of existing
graph-base semi-supervised classification algorithms, they convert the directed
graph to an undirected one through a simple symmetrization step. To be more
specific, the weight of an edge on the converted undirected graph is assigned by
the average of the two weights on both directions of the same edge in the original

K. Daniilidis, P. Maragos, N. Paragios (Eds.): ECCV 2010, Part III, LNCS 6313, pp. 762–775, 2010.
© Springer-Verlag Berlin Heidelberg 2010

directed graph. Consequently, the important structural information conveyed by edge directions are simply discarded, and the benefits of these methods are impaired.

In this work, employing four basic second order processes of directed graph, *co-citation*, *co-reference*, and *passage* as shown in Fig. 2, we propose a novel co-linkage similarity (CS) to measure the pairwise similarity between any two vertices in a directed graph, by which the valuable structural information from directed pairwise relationship between vertices is preserved. Besides, motivated by Hypertext Induced Topic Selection (HITS) algorithm [10] and PageRank algorithm [13] but different from them, our CS symmetrically normalizes both in-links and out-links of a directed graph in a balanced manner, such that effective mutual link reinforcement can be achieved. As a result, the pairwise relationships among the vertices are enhanced and the topological structure turns out more lucid, such that the performance of subsequent classifications on the induced undirected graph is improved.

We first show an example that demonstrates the effectiveness of the proposed CS. Fig. 1 shows part of the directed graph generated by the method from [18] using UIUC car data [1]. Vertices e and l are positive training samples, *i.e.*, a car exists in the picture; vertices b and c are negative training samples, *i.e.*, no car exists in the picture; the rest are testing images. The goal is to predict the label of testing image z. Previous methods symmetrize the directed graph to an undirected one. Because the immediate training in-neighbors of z is c, which dominates the label assignment of z, the cars in picture z can not be detected. In our method, the positive co-reference between e and z, together with the positive co-citation between l and z, overwhelms the negative co-reference between b and z, therefore z is correctly assigned with a positive label.

We apply the proposed CS to two important computer vision tasks for image categorization, object recognition and image annotation, using semi-supervised classification algorithms. Promising experimental results demonstrate the effectiveness of our proposed CS.

2 Backgrounds

We first define necessary notations used in the discussions in the sequel.

Semi-supervised learning notations. Suppose we have $n = n_l + n_u$ data points $\{x_i\}_{i=1}^{n}$ corresponding to n images, where the first n_l data points are already labeled by $\{y_i\}_{i=1}^{n_l}$ for K target classes. Here, $x_i \in \mathbb{R}^p$ and $y_i \in \{-1, +1\}^K$, such that $y_i(k) = +1$ if x_i belongs to the k-th class, and -1 otherwise. Our task is to learn the classification $\{y_i\}_{i=n_l+1}^{n}$ for those unlabeled data.

Graph notations. Given the input data as above, we may construct either an undirected graph or a directed graph to capture the pairwise relationships among the data points for succeeding graph-based semi-supervised classification.

Pairwise similarities between data objects are usually described as an undirected graph $\mathcal{G}^u$ with a *symmetric* weight matrix $W \in \mathbb{R}^{n \times n}$.

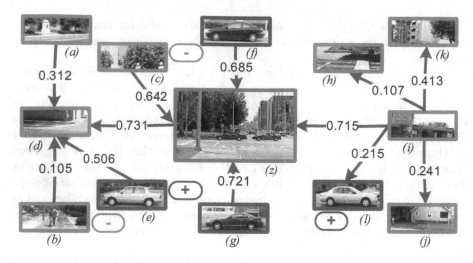

Fig. 1. Part of directed graph generated by L1G method [18]. Vertices e and l are positive training samples, *i.e.*, a car exists in the picture; vertices b and c are negative training samples, *i.e.*, no car exists in the picture; the rest are testing samples. For the test picture z, only our CS measure can correctly detect the existence of the cars.

Suppose $\mathcal{G}^d = (\mathcal{V}, \mathcal{E})$ is an unweighted directed graph with vertex set $\mathcal{V}$ and edge set $\mathcal{E} \subseteq \mathcal{V} \times \mathcal{V}$. $\mathcal{G}^d$ is described by the *asymmetric* adjacency matrix $L = \{0,1\}^{n \times n}$, such that $|\mathcal{V}| = n$, and $L_{ij} = 1$ if there is an edge $i \to j$ from vertex i to vertex j, and $L_{ij} = 0$ otherwise. The edge $i \to j$ is an ordered pair, and we say j is the *out neighbor* of i, or i is the *in-neighbor* of j. The number of out-neighbors of i is the *out-degree* of i, given by $d_i^+ = \sum_k L_{ik}$. Similarly, the number of in-neighbors of j is the *in-degree* of j, given by $d_j^- = \sum_k L_{kj}$. Let D_{out} be a diagonal matrix and $D_{\text{out}}(i,i) = d_i^+$, and D_{in} be a diagonal matrix and $D_{\text{in}}(i,i) = d_i^-$.

A weighted directed graph is described by a weight matrix $R \in \mathbb{R}^{n \times n}$ when there exists a function $r : \mathcal{E} \to \mathbb{R}^+$, which associates a positive value $R_{ij} = r(i,j)$ with every edge $i \to j \in \mathcal{E}$. Here we use R for directed graph to distinguish from W for undirected graph. An unweighted directed graph is a special case of weighted directed graphs when $R = L$. For a weighted directed graph, the out-degree is defined as $d_i^+ = \sum_k R_{ik}$, and the in-degree is defined as $d_i^- = \sum_k R_{kj}$.

When it is clear from context, we use W and $\mathcal{G}^u$ interchangeably, and same for R (or L) and $\mathcal{G}^d$.

2.1   Traditional Undirected Graph for Semi-supervised Learning

Traditional graph construction scheme comprises two steps: adjacency construction and graph weight calculation. For the former, there exist two widely used methods [2]: ϵ ball and K-Nearest Neighbor methods. For the latter, although there exist other methods, Gaussian kernel similarity (GKS) defined as following is the most frequently used one [2]:

$$W_{ij} = \begin{cases} \exp\left(-\|\mathbf{x}_i - \mathbf{x}_j\|^2/\sigma^2\right), & \forall\ (\mathbf{x}_i, \mathbf{x}_j) \in \mathcal{E}, \\ 0, & \text{otherwise}\ . \end{cases} \tag{1}$$

Unfortunately, classification performance using GKS in Eq. (1) heavily depends on the selection of σ, and satisfactory results are not easy to achieve [15].

2.2 Directed Graph for Robust Semi-supervised Learning

Recently, based on sparsity representations, several robust graph construction methods have been proposed [3,18,8]. Graph is a gathering of pairwise relations, while the relation among visual images is essentially an estimation by human cognition system. It has been proved [14] in neural science that the human vision system seeks a sparse coding for the incoming image using a few words in a feature vocabulary. Wright et al. [17] demonstrated that the ℓ_1 linear reconstruction error minimization can naturally lead to a sparse representation for human facial images. In other words, a graph for image data can be naturally constructed in a parameter free way through sparse representation. During the ℓ_1 minimization for the optimal sparse representation, the direction of edges and the graph weights are generated [18].

Sparse representation assumes that [3] any feature vector in a class can be represented as a linear combination of some other feature vectors in the same class. Also, given a feature vector, its sparsest representation is achieved when all the basis feature vectors belong to the same class as the feature vector. Formally, let $\mathcal{X} = \{\mathbf{x}_1, \ldots, \mathbf{x}_n\}$ denote all data vectors (images). For any given $\mathbf{x}_i \in \mathcal{X}$, it can be decomposed as a sparse linear combination of the rest of the feature vectors in $\mathcal{X}$. We denote $F_{\hat{i}} = [\mathbf{x}_1, \ldots, \mathbf{x}_{i-1}, \mathbf{x}_{i+1}, \ldots, \mathbf{x}_n]$, thus the circumflex notation $\hat{i}$ means "not i". Then the linear representation of $\mathbf{x}_i$ can be written as:

$$\mathbf{x}_i = F_{\hat{i}}\mathbf{s}_i\ \in \mathbb{R}^m, \tag{2}$$

where $\mathbf{s}_i \in \mathbb{R}^n$ [1] is a coefficient vector whose nonzero entries are excepted to be as few as possible. Because in image categorization, $m \ll n - 1$, the system equation $\mathbf{x}_i = F_{\hat{i}}\mathbf{s}_i$ is underdetermined, its solution is not unique. Conventionally, this difficulty can resolved by choosing the minimum ℓ_2 norm solution:

$$(P_1) \qquad \underset{\mathbf{s}_i}{\arg\min} \|\mathbf{s}_i\|_{\ell_2}, \quad \text{subject to}\quad \mathbf{x}_i = F_{\hat{i}}\mathbf{s}_i, \tag{3}$$

While this optimization problem can be easily solved (via the pseudo-inverse of $F_{\hat{i}}$), the solution $\mathbf{s}_i$ is not especially informative for categorizing $\mathbf{x}_i$. $\mathbf{s}_i$ obtained by Eq. (3) is generally dense, with large nonzero entries corresponding to many training samples [17]. To tackle this problem, we seek the sparsest solution of $\mathbf{x}_i = F_{\hat{i}}\mathbf{s}_i$ by solving the following optimization problem:

$$(P_1) \qquad \underset{\mathbf{s}_i}{\arg\min} \|\mathbf{s}_i\|_{\ell_0}, \quad \text{subject to}\quad \mathbf{x}_i = F_{\hat{i}}\mathbf{s}_i, \tag{4}$$

where $\|\cdot\|_{\ell_0}$ denotes the ℓ_0 norm, which counts the number of nonzero entries in a vector. Although P_1 is NP-hard and even difficult to approximate, in light of the emerging theory of compressed sensing in signal processing, it can solved as following ℓ_1 minimization problem if $\mathbf{s}_i$ is sparse enough [17]:

$$(P_2) \qquad \arg\min_{\mathbf{s}_i} \|\mathbf{s}_i\|_{\ell_1}, \quad \text{subject to} \quad \mathbf{x}_i = F_i \mathbf{s}_i, \tag{5}$$

where $\|\cdot\|_{\ell_1}$ denotes the ℓ_1 norm. $\mathbf{s}_i$ can be considered as the descriptor of image $\mathbf{x}_i$ using the rest images as basis. Directed graphs can be constructed using two following methods: Sparsity Induced Similarity (SIS) [3] or ℓ_1 graph (L1G) [18]:

$$\text{SIS graph: } R_{ij} = \frac{\max\{\mathbf{s}_i(j), 0\}}{\sum_{k=1, k\neq i}^{N} \max\{\mathbf{s}_i(k), 0\}}, \quad \text{L1G graph: } R_{ij} = |\mathbf{s}_i(j)|. \tag{6}$$

Other directed graph construction methods are also available such as [8,17]. Note that, by the construction in Eq. (6), $R_{ij} \neq R_{ji}$, i.e., a directed graph $\mathcal{G}^d$ is constructed with R as weight matrix. Apparently, R is parameter free.

Besides using sparsity representation, there also exist other mechanisms for robust graph construction, such as linear neighborhood propagation method [15], which also yields a directed graph as immediate output.

In order to work with existing graph-based semi-supervised learning methods, a simple symmetrization step has been used to convert the directed graph R to an undirected graph W [15,3,18] using

$$W_{ij} = (R_{ij} + R_{ji})/2. \tag{7}$$

Obviously, structural information conveyed by edge directions are discarded.

3   Co-linkage Similarity of a Directed Graph

In this section, we will introduce a method to measure similarities in a directed graph. We consider the second order process on a directed graph. We first study the four basic processes and later emphasize the importance of edge weight normalization. This work is motivated by previous works in link analysis [10,13,5,7].

3.1   Co-linkage Similarity from Second Order Random Walk Processes

On a directed graph, we consider the random walk process. If from node i, the random walker has a large probability walks to j, we say there is a large similarity between i, j. We consider the second order process as shown in Fig. 2. There are four type of processes: co-citation, co-reference, passage ($i \rightarrow j$) and passage ($j \rightarrow i$) to as illustrated in Fig. 2. It is sufficient to use these four basic process to describe a directed graph.

Fig. 2. Four fundamental second order processes on a directed graph. 1st figure: vertices i and j are co-cited by vertex k. 2nd figure: vertices i and j co-reference vertex k. 3rd figure: passage from vertices i to j. 4th figure: passage from vertices j to i.

Co-citation. If two vertices i and j are co-cited by many other vertices, such as k in Fig. 2 (1st figure), i and j are likely to be related in some sense. Thus co-citation is a similarity measure, and defined as the number of vertices that co-cite i and j:

$$W_{ij}^{(c)} = \sum_k L_{ki}L_{kj} = \left(L^T L\right)_{ij}. \tag{8}$$

Co-reference. On the other hand, if two vertices i and j co-reference several other vertices, such as k in Fig. 2 (2nd figure), i and j are supposed to have certain commonality. Co-reference also measures similarity between vertices:

$$W_{ij}^{(r)} = \sum_k L_{ik}L_{jk} = (LL^T)_{ij}. \tag{9}$$

Passage. If there is a path between two vertices i and j through a vertex (such as k), i and j can commute each other and have certain similarity. Because the path could have two different directions, there are two types of passage links as shown in 3rd and 4th figures of Fig. 2. Passage($i \rightarrow j$) is computed as

$$W_{i \rightarrow j}^{(p)} = \sum_k L_{ik}L_{kj} = (LL)_{ij} \tag{10}$$

Passage($j \rightarrow i$) is computed as

$$W_{j \rightarrow i}^{(p)} = \sum_k L_{kj}L_{ki} = (L^T L^T)_{ij} \tag{11}$$

All co-citation, co-reference, and passage define the similarity between vertex pairs on a directed graph, therefore we define the co-linkage similarity as following:

$$W = L^T L + LL^T + LL + L^T L^T. \tag{12}$$

where we assume that co-citation and co-reference are equally important.

3.2 Link Normalization

On the web, a vertex/webpage with bigger out-degree has greater influence than another vertex/webpage with smaller out-degree. However, since these out-links can be arbitrarily added by the webpage designer, and the importance of this webpage can be arbitrarily increased.

In PageRank algorithm, every out-going hyperlinks from a vertex is inversely weighted by its out-degree, thereby every vertex has the same total out-going weight. This can be stated as *Internet Democracy* : every web site has a total of one vote.

The hyperlink normalization and its importance are illustrated in Fig. 3. Basically, if a webpage has a large out-degree, the significance/uniqueness of its cocitation is reduced. This points the necessity of out-degree normalization.

Generally speaking, the indegree of a document is not easily manipulated and is therefore a good indicator of the importance of the webpage. But, when counting co-reference between two webpages (see Fig. 3) as similarity between the webpages, in-degree should also be normalized, because a webpage i with large indegree lose the specificity of the those webpages pointing to i.

For the passage between i, j through k, the normalization is also needed. If k has large in-degree and out-degree, then the information flow through k is not *special* or *specific*, because many other pairs also pass through k. In other words, the information flow between any two nodes has a large probability to pass through k. Therefore, the passage through k is not statistically significant as compared to another k' with small in-degree and out-degree. A proper link weight normalization on k will render the mediating power of k constant, independent of the in-degree and out-degree of k.

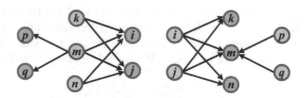

Fig. 3. Importance of hyperlink normalization. Left: vertices i and j are co-cited by vertices k, m and n. However, since vertex m also cites vertices p and q, the co-citation of i and j by m is not as significant as that by either k or n. This fact can be compensated by normalizing the weights on the out-bound links of a vertex, *i.e.*, the co-citation of i and j by m is then $2/4 = 50\%$ as important as that by either k or n. Right: vertices i and j co-reference vertices k, m and n. However, since vertex m is also referenced by p and q, the co-reference of i and j by m is not as significant as that to either k or n. This fact can be similarly compensated by normalizing the in-bound links of a vertex.

With these discussions, the reasonable choices of link normalizations are:

$$L \to D_{\text{out}}^{-1}L, \tag{13}$$

$$L \to L D_{\text{in}}^{-1}, \tag{14}$$

$$L \to D_{\text{out}}^{-1/2} L D_{\text{in}}^{-1/2} \tag{15}$$

Normalization of Eq. (13) uses the out-degree and is used in the PageRank algorithm which is essentially the transition probability of a random walk. Normalization using out-degree is related to the concept of co-citation since co-citation uses out-links from those webpages/nodes pointing to them. Normalization using out-degree will balance the importance of each of these nodes.

Normalization of Eq. (14) uses the in-degree and can be viewed as the transition probability of a random walk on the inverse direction of the directed graph. Normalization using in-degree is related to the concept of co-reference since co-reference uses in-links from those webpages/nodes pointing to them. Normalization using in-degree will balance the importance of each of these nodes.

Normalization of Eq. (15) can be viewed as a compromise between the above two normalization. This is also symmetric among the in-degree and out-degree. Considering the balance of in-degree and out-degree normalization and the balance among co-citation, co-reference, and passage, we adopt this symmetric normalization in our work.

Replacing L with the symmetric normalization, we obtain the **effective similarity** between two nodes on the directed graph

$$W = D_{\text{in}}^{-\frac{1}{2}} L^T D_{\text{out}}^{-1} L D_{\text{in}}^{-\frac{1}{2}} + D_{\text{out}}^{-\frac{1}{2}} L D_{\text{in}}^{-1} L^T D_{\text{out}}^{-\frac{1}{2}}$$
$$+ D_{\text{out}}^{-\frac{1}{2}} L D_{\text{in}}^{-\frac{1}{2}} D_{\text{out}}^{-\frac{1}{2}} L D_{\text{in}}^{-\frac{1}{2}} + D_{\text{in}}^{-\frac{1}{2}} L^T D_{\text{out}}^{-\frac{1}{2}} D_{\text{in}}^{-\frac{1}{2}} L^T D_{\text{out}}^{-\frac{1}{2}} . \tag{16}$$

where the first term is for co-citation the second one is for co-reference and the third and fourth are for the passages. It should be noted that co-citation and co-reference are inherently symmetric as emphasized in [5] and the passages are directional and naturally symmetrized by including both passage($i \rightarrow j$) and passage($j \rightarrow i$). Eq. (16) is the main result of this work, and we call W as co-linkage similarity (CS).

4   Empirical Studies

We apply our proposed co-linkage similarity (CS) defined in Eq. (16) into two important computer vision applications for image categorization, object recognition and image annotation, which are often solved by graph-based semi-supervised classification algorithms.

We evaluate our CS and compare to the following three graph construction schemes. (1) Traditional GKS method as in Eq. (1). This is the most frequently used graph construction method and produces a fully connected undirected graph. In our experiments, σ is fine tuned upon data set to get best performance. (2) Sparsity Induced Similarity (SIS) [3] and (3) ℓ_1 graph (L1G) [18] as in Eq. (6) are two recently published works and have demonstrated better performance than other related methods. The immediate output of these two methods is a directed graph, therefore the original papers used a simple symmetrization in Eq. (7) before classification. For our method, we induce two undirected graphs from the immediate outputs of SIS and L1G methods respectively, which are denoted as CS-SIS and CS-L1G.

4.1   Object Recognition Using Single-Label Classification

Data sets. We use the following three data sets in our evaluations, which are commonly used for semi-supervised learning and object recognition experiments.

Cedar Buffalo binary digit data set [9]. The digits are preprocessed to reduce the size of each image down to a 16×16 by down-sampling and Gaussian smoothing, and the value of each pixel ranges from 0 to 255. Each digit is thus represented by a 256-dimensional vector.

UIUC car training data set [1] consists of 1050 images of cars in side views with resolution of $40(H) \times 100(W)$ pixels. For this data set, we use dense grids of histogram-of-gradient features to represent each image [4], where 20×20 pixel blocks, block stride of 10 pixels, and 8 orientation bins are used to obtain the feature vector of 240 dimensions for each image.

ETH-80 data set [11] contains 8 object categories. In each category there are 10 different objects, and for each object there are 41 different poses. There are $8 \times 10 \times 41 = 3280$ images in total. Here, similar to [11], we use the histogram of the first derivatives $D_x D_y$ with 48 dimensions over 3 different scales to represent each image, and then all features are normalized.

Labeled and unlabeled samples. Similar to [21], for a given class, we randomly pick up samples as labeled data, and the rest are used as unlabeled data.

Classification algorithm. We use the Green's function semi-supervised learning framework [6] for classification, which is a state-of-the-art graph-based semi-supervised classification method and has demonstrated superior performance than several representative competing methods such as [21,20].

Evaluation criterion. We employ recognition accuracy to evaluate the performance of the proposed CS in classification. Each recognition accuracy curve is obtained by averaging the results over 10 different trials. For each trial, again, we randomly select the labeled and unlabeled samples.

Classification performance. We compare the semi-supervised classification performance on the five graphs using the three data sets. We use the same experimental setup as in [3]. For Cedar Buffalo binary digit data set, we use digits "1" and "2" for classification. For UIUC car training data set, two classes, 1050 images of cars and backgrounds, are used in evaluation. These two data sets are used to evaluate binary classification performance. Then we use ETH-80 data set for multi-class classification performance. Three types of objects, apples, pears and tomatoes, are used in our experiments since it is comparatively difficult to distinguish these three categories in this data set [11].

Fgcap 4(a)–4(c) show the classification performance of five compared graph construction methods. The x-axis is the number of labeled samples, and the y-axis is the recognition accuracy. From these figures, we can see that SIS and L1G always have similar performance. This is consistent with the theoretical background as they are derived in a similar way using similar mechanism, $i.e.$, sparsity representation, as detailed in Section 2.2. Both of them are better than GKS

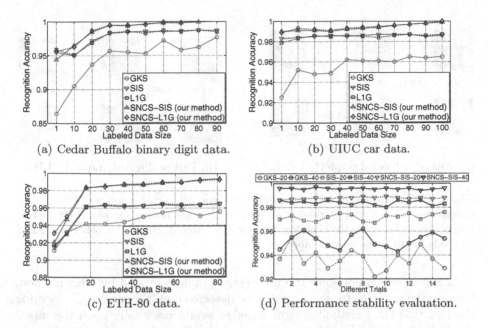

(a) Cedar Buffalo binary digit data.

(b) UIUC car data.

(c) ETH-80 data.

(d) Performance stability evaluation.

Fig. 4. 4(a)–4(c): Recognition accuracy on three data sets. 4(d): The performance stability of different graph construction schemes for different number of labeled samples

method. Our method, as shown by "CS-SIS" and "CS-L1G" in the figures, generally outperforms other methods, sometimes significantly. These results clearly demonstrate the effectiveness of our method.

Effectiveness of directed graph and CS. A careful examination at the classification results show that, many objects can be only correctly detected on our CS induced graph, *e.g.*, the apple of picture z in Fig. 5 for ETH-80 data and the cars of picture z in Fig. 1 for UIUC car training data set. In these figures, the training samples in the same class as the target testing sample (vertex z) are labeled as positive, while other training samples are labeled as negative.

The undirected graph generated by GKS method for a small part of ETH80 data is first shown in Fig. 5(a), where the minor edges (weight less 0.1) are removed for clear illustration. On this graph, picture z can not acquire a positive label by the label propagation algorithm, *i.e.*, the apple can not be detected. In Fig. 5(b), the directed graph generated by L1G method shows that, although the label of vertex z can be correctly inferred from its training neighbors a and c, after the simple symmetrization in Eq. (7), it can only acquire an incorrect negative label. By our CS method, because the co-reference between a and z is stronger than the relationship between c and z due to mutual link reinforcement and link normalization, picture z finally obtains a correct positive label.

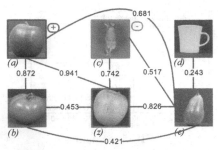

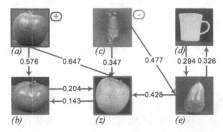

(a) Part of undirected graph (by GKS).   (b) Part of directed graph (by L1G).

Fig. 5. Part of the graphs built from ETH-80 data set. Vertex a is a positive training sample and c is a negative training sample, the rest are testing samples. Test picture z can always be correctly classified on our CS induced graph. All other compared methods fail to assign correct label.

In Fig. 1, we do not show the undirected graph generated by GKS method, because the car in picture z can never be detected on GKS graphs. Considering the fact that GKS method assigns an edge weight essentially upon the image similarity using the Euclidean metric, and the sizes of the cars are relatively small and the picture has a very strong background with trees and buildings, this result is reasonable. For the directed graph generated by L1G method as in Fig. 1, the immediate training in-neighbors of z is c, which dominates the label assignment of z, therefore the cars again can not be detected. However, on our CS induced graph, the positive co-reference between e and z together with the positive co-citation between l and z overwhelm the negative co-reference between b and z, hence z is correctly assigned with a positive label.

Both examples in Fig. 5 and Fig. 1 concretely demonstrate the advantage of our method.

Classification stability. Same as in [15,3], we also study the performance stability when the amount of labeled samples varies. We compare the stability of our CS method to those of GKS method and SIS method. We do not show the stability of L1G method as it is very similar to SIS method theoretically and empirically. We use digits "1" and "2" in Cedar Buffalo binary digit data set for illustration. We compare with two different labeled data size: 20 and 40. We repeat the experiments for 15 times, and the x-axis of Fig. 4(d) is the index of different trials. The curve "GKS-20" denotes the recognition accuracy obtained by classification on GKS graph with 20 labeled samples, similar for the other curves. From Fig. 4(d), we can see that the proposed CS and SIS method have very stable performance for different labeling data sizes, while GKS exhibits relatively large performance fluctuations. Again, these results are consistent with our theoretical analysis.

4.2   Image Annotation Using Multi-label Classification

We also evaluate our proposed CS in image annotation applications. We use standard 5-fold cross validation to evaluate the performance of compared graph construction methods. Because image annotation is a multi-label classification task, we use multi-label correlated Green's function (MCGF) method [16] for classification, which is an extension of the Green's function semi-supervised learning framework [6] to deal with multi-label problems. We set the parameter α in the MCGF method as 0.1, which is same as in the original work.

Data sets. We use the following three benchmark multi-label image data sets in our evaluations.

TRECVID 2005[1] data set contains 61901 images and labeled with 39 concepts (labels). As in most previous works, we randomly sample the data such that each concept has at least 100 images, same as in [16].

MSRC[2] data set is provided by the computer vision group at Microsoft Research Cambridge, which has 591 images annotated by 22 classes.

Barcelona data set[3] contains 139 images with 4 categories, *i.e.*, "building", "flora", "people" and "sky".

In order for a complete evaluation, we first use simple (natural) features of these three image data sets. We divide each image into 64 blocks by a 8×8 grid and compute the first and second moments (mean and variance) of each color band to obtain a 384-dimensional vector as features. In addition, we also evaluate our methods using advanced image features. For MSRC data set and Barcelona data set, 100-dimensional SIFT features (denoted as "SIFT features" in Table 1) are extracted for classification. For TRECVID 2005 data set, SIFT features can not be extracted on typical personal computers due to its big size.

Evaluation criteria. The conventional classification performance metrics in statistical learning, *precision* and *F1 score*, are used to evaluate the compared methods. Precision and F1 score are computed for every class following the standard definition for a binary classification problem. To address multi-label classification, macro average and micro average are used to assess the overall performance across multiple labels [12].

Classification performance. Table 1 presents the classification performance comparison for five methods using 5-fold cross validation on three data sets. From the results, we can see that our method is constantly better than the other compared methods. We achieve about 10.56% improvements on average for TRECVID 2005 data set, about 11.32% improvements on average for MSRC data set and about 6.60% improvements on average for Barcelona data set. Again, these results quantitatively support the theoretical advantages of our proposed method.

---

[1] http://www-nlpir.nist.gov/projects/trecvid
[2] http://research.microsoft.com/en-us/projects/objectclassrecognition/
default.htm
[3] http://mlg.ucd.ie/content/view/61

Table 1. Performance evaluations of compared methods by 5-fold cross validations

Data sets	Evaluation metrics		Compared methods				
			GKS	SIS	L1G	CS-SIS	CS-L1G
TRECVID 2005	Macro average	Precision	0.249	0.258	0.260	0.292	0.293
		F1 score	0.272	0.281	0.283	0.301	0.303
	Micro average	Precision	0.237	0.249	0.248	0.287	0.289
		F1 score	0.270	0.279	0.280	0.295	0.298
MSRC	Macro average	Precision	0.216	0.224	0.221	0.258	0.257
		F1 score	0.285	0.297	0.296	0.322	0.320
	Micro average	Precision	0.214	0.221	0.220	0.254	0.253
		F1 score	0.281	0.296	0.293	0.316	0.315
MSRC (SIFT features)	Macro average	Precision	0.341	0.361	0.360	0.420	0.418
		F1 score	0.391	0.402	0.404	0.457	0.453
	Micro average	Precision	0.324	0.351	0.350	0.424	0.423
		F1 score	0.371	0.406	0.403	0.456	0.455
Barcelona	Macro average	Precision	0.784	0.815	0.813	0.864	0.861
		F1 score	0.724	0.757	0.753	0.811	0.810
	Micro average	Precision	0.781	0.812	0.811	0.859	0.853
		F1 score	0.720	0.751	0.750	0.807	0.806
Barcelona (SIFT features)	Macro average	Precision	0.795	0.836	0.835	0.885	0.883
		F1 score	0.731	0.769	0.768	0.825	0.824
	Micro average	Precision	0.792	0.823	0.823	0.882	0.884
		F1 score	0.730	0.767	0.763	0.827	0.825

5   Conclusions

In this paper, we presented a novel co-linkage similarity (CS) to describe a directed graph in an undirected way. Besides preserving structural directionality information of a directed graph, our CS method also enhances the pairwise relationships among the data objects by taking into account both mutual link reinforcement and symmetric in-links and out-links normalization. As a result, directed graph data can be used in existing graph-based semi-supervised classification algorithms with improved classification performance, which by design can only work with undirected graph data. By applying our proposed CS into two important computer vision problems for image categorization, object recognition for single-label classification and image annotation for multi-label classification, we conducted extensive empirical studies on six benchmark data sets to evaluate various aspects of our method. Clear improvements demonstrated in all experimental results validate the performance of our proposed method.

Acknowledgments. This research is supported by NSF-CCF 0830780, NSF-CCF 0939187, NSF-CCF 0917274, NSF-DMS 0915228, NSF-CNS 0923494.

References

1. Agarwal, S., Roth, D.: Learning a sparse representation for object detection. In: Heyden, A., Sparr, G., Nielsen, M., Johansen, P. (eds.) ECCV 2002. LNCS, vol. 2353, pp. 113–127. Springer, Heidelberg (2002)
2. Belkin, M., Niyogi, P.: Laplacian eigenmaps for dimensionality reduction and data representation. Neural computation 15(6), 1373–1396 (2003)
3. Cheng, H., Liu, Z., Yang, J.: Sparsity Induced Similarity Measure for Label Propagation. In: IEEE ICCV (2009)
4. Dalal, N., Triggs, B.: Histograms of oriented gradients for human detection. In: IEEE CVPR (2005)
5. Ding, C., He, X., Husbands, P., Zha, H., Simon, H.: PageRank, HITS and a unified framework for link analysis. In: ACM SIGIR (2002)
6. Ding, C., Simon, H., Jin, R., Li, T.: A learning framework using Green's function and kernel regularization with application to recommender system. In: ACM SIGKDD (2007)
7. Ding, C., Zha, H., He, X., Husbands, P., Simon, H.: Link analysis: hubs and authorities on the World Wide Web. SIAM Review (2004)
8. Elhamifar, E., Vidal, R.: Sparse subspace clustering. In: IEEE CVPR (2009)
9. Hull, J.: A database for handwritten text recognition research. IEEE TPAMI 16(5), 550–554 (1994)
10. Kleinberg, J.: Authoritative sources in a hyperlinked environment. Journal of the ACM 46(5), 604–632 (1999)
11. Leibe, B., Schiele, B.: Analyzing appearance and contour based methods for object categorization. In: IEEE CVPR (2003)
12. Lewis, D., Yang, Y., Rose, T., Li, F.: Rcv1: A new benchmark collection for text categorization research. Journal of Machine Learning Research 5, 361–397 (2004)
13. Page, L., Brin, S., Motwani, R., Winograd, T.: The pagerank citation ranking: Bringing order to the web. Stanford Digital Library Technologies Project (1998)
14. Rao, R., Olshausen, B., Lewicki, M.: Probabilistic models of the brain: Perception and neural function (2002)
15. Wang, F., Zhang, C.: Label propagation through linear neighborhoods. In: ICML (2006)
16. Wang, H., Huang, H., Ding, C.: Image Annotation Using Multi-label Correlated Greens Function. In: IEEE ICCV (2009)
17. Wright, J., Yang, A., Ganesh, A., Sastry, S., Ma, Y.: Robust face recognition via sparse representation. IEEE TPAMI, 210–227 (2009)
18. Yan, S., Wang, H.: Semi-supervised learning by sparse representation. In: SDM (2009)
19. Yang, W., Zhang, S., Liang, W.: A Graph Based Subspace Semi-supervised Learning Framework for Dimensionality Reduction. In: Forsyth, D., Torr, P., Zisserman, A. (eds.) ECCV 2008, Part II. LNCS, vol. 5303, pp. 664–677. Springer, Heidelberg (2008)
20. Zhou, D., Bousquet, O., Lal, T., Weston, J., Schölkopf, B.: Learning with local and global consistency. In: NIPS (2004)
21. Zhu, X., Ghahramani, Z., Lafferty, J.: Semi-supervised learning using Gaussian fields and harmonic functions. In: ICML (2003)

Robust Multi-View Boosting with Priors*

Amir Saffari, Christian Leistner, Martin Godec, and Horst Bischof

Institute for Computer Graphics and Vision, Graz University of Technology,
Inffeldgasse 16, 8010 Graz, Austria
{saffari,leistner,godec,bischof}@icg.tugraz.at
http://www.icg.tugraz.at

Abstract. Many learning tasks for computer vision problems can be
described by multiple views or multiple features. These views can be
exploited in order to learn from unlabeled data, a.k.a. "multi-view learning". In these methods, usually the classifiers iteratively label each other
a subset of the unlabeled data and ignore the rest. In this work, we propose a new multi-view boosting algorithm that, unlike other approaches,
specifically encodes the uncertainties over the unlabeled samples in terms
of given priors. Instead of ignoring the unlabeled samples during the
training phase of each view, we use the different views to provide an aggregated prior which is then used as a regularization term inside a semi-
supervised boosting method. Since we target multi-class applications, we
first introduce a multi-class boosting algorithm based on maximizing the
mutli-class classification margin. Then, we propose our multi-class semi-
supervised boosting algorithm which is able to use priors as a regularization component over the unlabeled data. Since the priors may contain
a significant amount of noise, we introduce a new loss function for the
unlabeled regularization which is robust to noisy priors. Experimentally,
we show that the multi-class boosting algorithms achieves state-of-the-
art results in machine learning benchmarks. We also show that the new
proposed loss function is more robust compared to other alternatives.
Finally, we demonstrate the advantages of our multi-view boosting approach for object category recognition and visual object tracking tasks,
compared to other multi-view learning methods.

1   Introduction

In recent years, the development and design of classification algorithms has led
to significant progress in various computer vision domains. In most applications
supervised learning algorithms are applied. Usually, these methods require large
amounts of training samples along with their class labels in order to train a
classification function that yields low prediction errors. In practice, the class

---

* This work has been supported by the Austrian FFG project MobiTrick (825840) and
Outlier (820923) under the FIT-IT program.

K. Daniilidis, P. Maragos, N. Paragios (Eds.): ECCV 2010, Part III, LNCS 6313, pp. 776–789, 2010.
© Springer-Verlag Berlin Heidelberg 2010

labels are provided by a human labeler. As the tedious hand labeling cannot take pace with the growing amount of data, *e.g.*, digital images, web sites, research has started to focus on semi-supervised learning (SSL) methods [1,2] that can learn from a small set of labeled data and simultaneously a huge amount of unlabeled data.

This paper deals with a special case of SSL called multi-view learning [3,4]. In multi-view learning (MVL), the data can be expressed by several views or multiple features. For each view a classifier is trained on some labeled data. Then the classifiers iteratively train each other on the unlabeled data. The underlying assumption of MVL is that the unlabeled data can be exploited in a way that enforces the selection of hypotheses that lead to an agreement among the classifiers on the unlabeled data while minimizing the training error on labeled data [5,6]. Overall, this leads to an increased classification margin and thus lower generalization errors. MVL is especially interesting for many computer vision tasks as multiple views are often naturally provided. For instance, in object detection and categorization different features can be considered as different views [7,8]. Multi-view learning can also lead to more stable tracking results [9,10]. Also images collected from the web naturally provide different views, because additional to the visual data text is also frequently provided [11].

Current multi-view methods work by primarily exchanging the information via label predictions on a subset of the unlabeled data. However, this ignores the uncertainty in each estimated label and ignores the information that each view has over the entire set of unlabeled data. In this paper, we propose a novel multi-view boosting algorithm that, on the one hand, performs MVL in the classical sense; *i.e.*, the classifiers provide each other labels for some selected unlabeled samples. On the other hand, however, we regularize each classifier on the rest of the unlabeled samples in a way that it encourages the agreement between the views. In our algorithm, we use an aggregated prior that is set up by the corresponding views; *i.e.*, the iteratively trained classifiers serve each other as priors in order to exploit the rest of the unlabeled samples. However, since the priors can be wrong, we also propose a robust loss function for the semi-supervised regularization which can handle noisy priors. Additionally, most previous MVL methods mainly deal with two-classifier scenarios and are thus mainly co-training variants. Our method is general enough to incorporate not only two, but even an arbitrary number of views.

2   Multi-View Boosting with Priors

In the following sections, we first introduce the concept of multi-view learning with priors. Next, we explain how we can develop multi-class semi-supervised boosting which uses priors provided from multiple views as a regularization term. Finally, we show how robustness can be incorporated into the learning algorithm in terms of proper loss functions.

2.1   Multi-View Learning with Priors

Assume we have a multi-class semi-supervised classification task where the problem domain can be split into V different views [1]. Let $\mathbf{x} = [\mathbf{x}_1^T | \cdots | \mathbf{x}_V^T]^T$ be a data sample which is constructed from V different views, each expressed by D_v-dim feature vector $\mathbf{x}_v \in \mathbb{R}^{D_v}$. In multi-view learning, we train a classifier per view $\mathbf{f}_v(\mathbf{x}_v) : \mathbb{R}^{D_v} \to \mathbb{R}^K$ where K is the number of classes and $\mathcal{F} = \{\mathbf{f}_v\}_{v=1}^V$ is the set of the classifiers. Let $p_v(k|\mathbf{x}_v)$ be the posterior estimate for classifying sample $\mathbf{x}_v$ in k-th class by the v-th learner. The goal of multi-view learning is to produce a set of classifiers which have low mis-classification rates over the labeled samples while having a high consensus over the unlabeled samples. One can express these goals as the following optimization problem

$$\mathcal{F}^* = \arg\min_{\mathcal{F}} \sum_{(\mathbf{x} \in \mathcal{X}_l, y)} \ell(\mathbf{x}, y; \mathcal{F}) + \gamma \sum_{\mathbf{x} \in \mathcal{X}_u} d(\mathbf{x}; \mathcal{F}). \tag{1}$$

The first term expresses the loss $\ell(\cdot)$ for the labeled samples where we have the true class label y, while the last term is a measure of the agreement of views over the unlabeled samples, and γ steers the effect of the unlabeled samples over the entire optimization problem. In this work, we propose to use the posterior estimates for defining the loss over the unlabeled samples. Assume we have a function $\jmath(p\|q)$ for measuring the divergence between two probabilities p and q. Using this divergence measure, we express the unlabeled loss as $d(\mathbf{x}; \mathcal{F}) = \sum_{v=1}^V d_v(\mathbf{x}; \mathcal{F})$ with

$$d_v(\mathbf{x}; \mathcal{F}) = \jmath(p_v(\mathbf{x}_v) \| \frac{1}{V-1} \sum_{s \neq v} p_s(\mathbf{x}_s)), \tag{2}$$

where $p_v(\mathbf{x}_v) = [p_v(1|\mathbf{x}_v), \cdots, p_v(K|\mathbf{x}_v)]^T$. This loss function measures the divergence of the posterior estimates by computing the distance of each view to the average estimate of all other views. For example, if we use $\jmath(p\|q) = \sum_{k=1}^K (p(k|\mathbf{x}) - q(k|\mathbf{x}))^2$ the last term will measure the variance over different views (the proof is omitted due to lack of space). As it will be shown later, we use the *Jensen-Shannon Divergence* as $\jmath(p\|q)$ in our algorithm because of its robustness to noise. We will also refer to

$$q_v(k|\mathbf{x}_v) = \frac{1}{V-1} \sum_{s \neq v} p_s(k|\mathbf{x}_s), \; \forall v \in \{1, \cdots, V\}, k \in \mathcal{Y} \tag{3}$$

as the prior for the v-th view. In order to observe the advantages gained by using this approach over the traditional multi-view learning where the consensus is only encouraged by iterative labeling of the unlabeled data, we propose the following algorithm:

---

[1] For clarity, we always use the co-training settings [3] where the data is represented by different views, while the algorithm can be applied to multiple-learners scenario as well [4].

1. For each view independently, optimize Eq. (1) by using Eq. (2) and using the Eq. (3) as the priors.
2. Label a subset of unlabeled samples and add them to the labeled set.
3. Compute the posteriors and update the priors for each view.
4. If stopping condition is not satisfied, proceed to step 1, otherwise stop.

If we set $\gamma = 0$ in this procedure, then we obtain a classical multi-view learning algorithm, similar to co-training [3]. Therefore, by observing the performance of both of these algorithms, one can see the gain obtained by incorporating the priors. For the second step where we label some unlabeled samples, we use the following approach: 1) Each view proposes the N highest confident samples to be included in the labeled set. 2) If there are disagreements over the label of a sample between some of the views, we let the proposing views to vote with their confidence for the label of this sample, and we select the resulting class which has the highest aggregated confidence. Again, if we would have only two views, this would be equivalent to the original co-training algorithm [3]. In the following sections, we will develop a semi-supervised multi-class boosting algorithm which can be used to solve the first step of this algorithm.

2.2 Multi-class Boosting

Let $\mathcal{X}_l = \{(\mathbf{x}, y) | \mathbf{x} \in \mathbb{R}^D, y \in \{1, \cdots, K\}\}$ to be the set of $i.i.d.$ labeled training examples from an unknown probability distribution $P(y, \mathbf{x})$. Suppose we are given a set of unlabeled samples $\mathcal{X}_u = \{\mathbf{x} | \mathbf{x} \in \mathbb{R}^D\}$ which are also sampled $i.i.d.$ from the marginal distribution $P(\mathbf{x}) = \sum_{y \in \mathcal{Y}} P(y, \mathbf{x})$. With $\mathcal{X}$ we refer to the union of both labeled and unlabeled data samples. The data sample $\mathbf{x}$ is represented as a D-dimensional feature vector and its label for a K-class problem y is coming from the set of labels $\mathcal{Y} = \{1, \ldots, K\}$. Boosting can be considered as a *meta-learning* algorithm, which accepts another learning algorithm (often known as *base* or *weak* learner) and constructs a new function class out of it, *i.e.*, by constructing additive models in form of

$$\mathbf{f}(\mathbf{x}; \boldsymbol{\beta}) = \sum_{t=1}^{T} \alpha_t \, \mathbf{g}(\mathbf{x}; \boldsymbol{\theta}_t), \qquad (4)$$

where $\mathbf{f}(\mathbf{x}) = [f_1(\mathbf{x}), \cdots, f_K(\mathbf{x})]^T$ is the multi-class classifier[2], $\boldsymbol{\beta} = [\boldsymbol{\alpha} | \boldsymbol{\theta}]$ is the collection of model parameters, $\boldsymbol{\alpha}$ are the parameters of boosting algorithm, $\boldsymbol{\theta} = \{\boldsymbol{\theta}_t\}_{t=1}^{T}$, and $\boldsymbol{\theta}_t$ represents the parameters of the t-th base learner $\mathbf{g}(\mathbf{x}; \boldsymbol{\theta}_t) \in \mathcal{G} : \mathbb{R}^D \rightarrow \mathbb{R}^K$. Without loss of generality, we require the following symmetry condition: $\forall \mathbf{x} : \sum_{k \in \mathcal{Y}} f_k(\mathbf{x}) = 0$. Many machine learning algorithms rely on the notion of *margin*, popularized by *support vector machines* (SVMs). For a K-class problem, the multi-class margin can be described as

$$m(\mathbf{x}, y; \mathbf{f}) = f_y(\mathbf{x}) - \max_{k \neq y} f_k(\mathbf{x}). \qquad (5)$$

---

[2] When the context is clear, we interpret $\mathbf{f}(\mathbf{x}; \boldsymbol{\beta})$ and $\mathbf{f}(\mathbf{x})$ as the same representation for a classifier.

Note that for a correct classification via the decision rule $c(\mathbf{x}) = \arg\max_{k \in \mathcal{Y}} f_k(\mathbf{x})$, the margin should be positive $m(\mathbf{x}, y; \mathbf{f}) > 0$. In other words, a negative margin would result in a mis-classification. In this work, we introduce a boosting algorithm which relies on maximizing the true multi-class margin. This is accomplished by minimizing a loss function which uses the multi-class margin. In details, our boosting algorithm minimizes the following *empirical risk*

$$R_{emp}(\boldsymbol{\beta}) = \sum_{(\mathbf{x}, y) \in \mathcal{X}_l} \ell(\mathbf{x}, y; \boldsymbol{\beta}), \tag{6}$$

where $\ell(\cdot)$ is a loss function. Since our learning strategy is based on functional gradient descent technique, it is possible to use a lot of different loss functions here [12]. The usual choices are *Exponential loss* [13], *Logit loss* [14], and *Savage loss* [15]. Figure 1(a) plots the shape of these loss functions with respect to the margin of an example. As it has been shown in previous studies, in the presence of label noise, Savage and Logit loss perform significantly better than exponential loss [14,15]. Since in this work, the multi-view algorithm might introduce noise into the labeled set, we use the Savage loss function for the supervised loss, *i.e.*, $\ell(\mathbf{x}, y; \mathbf{f}) = \frac{1}{(1+e^{2m(\mathbf{x},y;\mathbf{f})})^2}$.

2.3   Semi-supervised Boosting with Robust Loss Functions

We now focus on developing the multi-class semi-supervised boosting algorithms based on the concept of learning from priors [16,17]. Assume we are given a prior probability in form of $q(\cdot|\mathbf{x})$, *e.g.* Eq. (3). We model the posterior estimates of the model by a *multi-nomial logistic regression* model defined as

$$p(k|\mathbf{x}; \boldsymbol{\beta}) = \frac{e^{f_k(\mathbf{x};\boldsymbol{\beta})}}{\sum_{j \in \mathcal{Y}} e^{f_j(\mathbf{x};\boldsymbol{\beta})}}, \tag{7}$$

where $p(k|\mathbf{x}; \boldsymbol{\beta})$ is the posterior probability of assigning sample $\mathbf{x}$ to the k-th class, estimated by a model parameterized by $\boldsymbol{\beta}$.

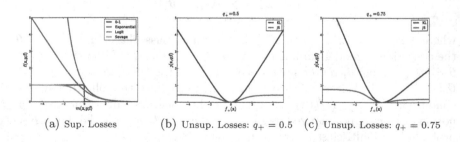

(a) Sup. Losses   (b) Unsup. Losses: $q_+ = 0.5$ (c) Unsup. Losses: $q_+ = 0.75$

Fig. 1. (a) Common loss functions used for supervised boosting methods. (b, c) Divergence measures used for prior regularization with two different priors: (b) $q_+ = 0.5$ and (c) $q_+ = 0.75$.

We formulate the semi-supervised learning as an optimization problem with two goals: 1) the model should attain low mis-classification errors on the labeled data (*e.g.*, by means of maximizing the margin), 2) the model should be able to match the prior probability over the unlabeled training samples. From an *empirical risk minimization* perspective, these goals can be written as the following risk functional

$$R_{emp}(\beta) = \sum_{(\mathbf{x},y) \in \mathcal{X}_l} \ell(\mathbf{x}, y; \beta) + \gamma \sum_{\mathbf{x} \in \mathcal{X}_u} \jmath(\mathbf{x}, q; \beta), \tag{8}$$

where $\jmath$ is a loss function which measures the deviations of the model from prior for a given sample $\mathbf{x}$, and γ tunes the effect of semi-supervised regularization. Since the goal of the regularization in Eq. (8) is to measure the deviations between two probabilities, it is natural to use loss functions which measure the divergence between two given distributions. In this work, we propose the *Jensen-Shannon Divergence* for the regularization term in Eq. (8). The Jensen-Shannon divergence for measuring the deviations of the model from the prior can be expressed as

$$\jmath(\mathbf{x}, q; \beta) = \frac{1}{2}(D_{KL}(q\|m) + D_{KL}(p\|m)), \tag{9}$$

where $D_{KL}(\cdot\|\cdot)$ is the Kullback-Leibler Divergence, $m = \frac{1}{2}(p + q)$. Figure 1(b) plots the shape of the *Kullback-Leibler Divergence* (KL), which has been used previously by Saffari *et al.* [17] for developing a multi-class semi-supervised boosting algorithm, together with the *Jensen-Shannon Divergence* (JS) for a binary problem when the prior is 0.5 for both classes. Figure 1(c) shows the same loss functions when the prior is 0.75 for the positive class. By comparing these loss functions to the supervised loss functions in Figure 1(a), one can see that KL resembles a behavior similar to the Logit loss while JS is very similar to the Savage loss function. Therefore, we could expect the JS loss function to be more robust when faced with noisy priors; *i.e.*, the prior is wrong about the label of an unlabeled sample.

2.4   Learning with Functional Gradient Descent

Given the loss functions from previous sections, the learning process for boosting is defined by the Eq. (8). This requires finding the parameters of the base learners θ together with their weights α. Finding a global solution for this problem is hard, therefore, many boosting algorithms adopt an approximate solution called *stagewise additive modeling* [14]. One of the commonly used techniques is the *functional gradient descent* method [18]. This is a generalization of the traditional gradient descent method to the space of functions. In details, at the t-th iteration of boosting, we find the *steepest descent* direction as $-\nabla R_{emp}(\beta_{t-1})$, where ∇ is the gradient operator. Then the optimization problem for learning t-th weak learner can be written as

$$\theta_t^* = \arg\max_{\theta_t} \langle -\nabla R_{emp}(\beta_{t-1}), \mathbf{g}(.; \theta_t)\rangle, \tag{10}$$

where $\langle , \rangle$ is the inner product operator. Since we have a risk which has labeled and unlabeled samples, we need to compute the gradients for two different loss functions.

Gradients for Labeled Samples. Using the chain rule, we can write the k-th element of the gradient vector $\nabla R_{emp}(\boldsymbol{\beta}_{t-1})$ as [3]

$$\frac{\partial R_{emp}(\boldsymbol{\beta}_{t-1})}{\partial f_k(\mathbf{x})} = \frac{\partial \ell(\mathbf{x}, y; \boldsymbol{\beta}_{t-1})}{\partial m(\mathbf{x}, y; \mathbf{f})} \frac{\partial m(\mathbf{x}, y; \mathbf{f})}{\partial f_k(\mathbf{x})}. \tag{11}$$

Note that the margin term includes a max operator, therefore, the derivatives of the margin can be written as

$$\frac{\partial \max_{j \neq y} f_j(\mathbf{x})}{\partial f_k(\mathbf{x})} = \mathbb{I}(k \neq y) \frac{\mathbb{I}(k \in \mathcal{S}_y(\mathbf{f}(\mathbf{x}))}{|\mathcal{S}_y(\mathbf{f}(\mathbf{x}))|}, \tag{12}$$

where $\mathbb{I}$ is the indicator function, and $\mathcal{S}_y(\mathbf{f}(\mathbf{x})) = \{k | f_k(\mathbf{x}) = \max_{j \neq y} f_j(\mathbf{x})\}$ is the set of classes which are the closest to the target class y. By using these results, we compute the gradients of the margin as

$$\frac{\partial m(\mathbf{x}, y; \mathbf{f})}{\partial f_k(\mathbf{x})} = \mathbb{I}(k = y) - \mathbb{I}(k \neq y) \frac{\mathbb{I}(k \in \mathcal{S}_y(\mathbf{f}(\mathbf{x}))}{|\mathcal{S}(\mathbf{f}(\mathbf{x}))|}. \tag{13}$$

Now we only need to find the derivatives of the loss function with respect to the margin term, which for the Savage loss can be written as

$$\frac{\partial \ell(\mathbf{x}, y; \boldsymbol{\beta}_{t-1})}{\partial m(\mathbf{x}, y; \mathbf{f})} = -\frac{4e^{2m(\mathbf{x}, y; \mathbf{f}_{t-1})}}{(1 + e^{2m(\mathbf{x}, y; \mathbf{f}_{t-1})})^3}. \tag{14}$$

Gradients for Unlabeled Samples. The Jensen-Shannon divergence for semi-supervised part can be written as [4]

$$\jmath(\mathbf{x}, q; \boldsymbol{\beta}) \approx H(p, m) + H(q, m) - H(p) =$$
$$= -2 \sum_{j \in \mathcal{Y}} m(j | \mathbf{x}; \boldsymbol{\beta}) \log m(j | \mathbf{x}; \boldsymbol{\beta}) + \sum_{j \in \mathcal{Y}} p(j | \mathbf{x}; \boldsymbol{\beta}) \log p(j | \mathbf{x}; \boldsymbol{\beta}). \tag{15}$$

where $H(\cdot, \cdot)$ is the cross-entropy between two distributions and $H(\cdot)$ is the entropy. Note that since $H(q)$ is fixed and does not depend on the model, it is dropped from this equations. We will need to compute the gradients of the posterior estimates in this equation, therefore, first we develop this term. We

---

[3] For notational brevity, we simply write $\frac{\partial \ell(\mathbf{x}, y; \mathbf{f})}{\partial f_k(\mathbf{x})}$ instead of the more correct form $\frac{\partial \ell(\mathbf{x}, y; \mathbf{f})}{\partial f_k(\mathbf{x})}|_{\mathbf{f}(\mathbf{x}) = \mathbf{f}_{t-1}(\mathbf{x})}$.

[4] Note that we drop the $\frac{1}{2}$ multiplier of the Eq. (9) as it can be incorporated into γ.

write the gradients of the Eq.(7) as

$$\frac{\partial p(j|\mathbf{x};\boldsymbol{\beta})}{\partial f_k(\mathbf{x})} = \frac{\mathbb{I}(k=j)e^{f_j(\mathbf{x})}\sum_{i=1}^{K}e^{f_i(\mathbf{x})} - e^{f_j(\mathbf{x})}e^{f_k(\mathbf{x})}}{(\sum_{i=1}^{K}e^{f_i(\mathbf{x})})^2} = \qquad (16)$$

$$= \frac{e^{f_j(\mathbf{x})}}{\sum_{i=1}^{K}e^{f_i(\mathbf{x})}}(\mathbb{I}(k=j) - \frac{e^{f_k(\mathbf{x})}}{\sum_{i=1}^{K}e^{f_i(\mathbf{x})}}) = p(j|\mathbf{x};\boldsymbol{\beta})(\mathbb{I}(k=j) - p(k|\mathbf{x};\boldsymbol{\beta})).$$

Using this result, we compute the gradients of the prior regularization term as

$$\frac{\partial \jmath(\mathbf{x},q;\boldsymbol{\beta})}{\partial f_k(\mathbf{x})} = p(k|\mathbf{x};\boldsymbol{\beta})\Big(\log\frac{p(k|\mathbf{x};\boldsymbol{\beta})}{m(k|\mathbf{x};\boldsymbol{\beta})} - \sum_{j\in\mathcal{Y}}p(j|\mathbf{x};\boldsymbol{\beta})\log\frac{p(j|\mathbf{x};\boldsymbol{\beta})}{m(j|\mathbf{x};\boldsymbol{\beta})}\Big)$$

$$= p(k|\mathbf{x};\boldsymbol{\beta})(\log\frac{p(k|\mathbf{x};\boldsymbol{\beta})}{m(k|\mathbf{x};\boldsymbol{\beta})} - D_{KL}(p\|m)). \qquad (17)$$

Learning with Multi-Class Base Classifiers. Given the gradients of the loss functions, the learning process of the t-th base classifier in Eq.(10) can be written as

$$\boldsymbol{\theta}_t^* = \arg\max_{\boldsymbol{\theta}_t} - \sum_{\mathbf{x}\in\mathcal{X}}\sum_{k\in\mathcal{Y}}\frac{\partial R_{emp}(\boldsymbol{\beta}_{t-1})}{\partial f_k(\mathbf{x})}g_k(\mathbf{x};\boldsymbol{\theta}_t). \qquad (18)$$

The solution of this problem will select a base function which has the highest correlation with the steepest descent direction of the risk. Since we want to use multi-class base learners, we have to develop a single label and a single weight for each sample. The following theorem shows the best possible choices for the weights and pseudo-labels.

Theorem 21. *The solution of Eq.(18) using a multi-class classifier $c(\mathbf{x};\boldsymbol{\theta}_t) \in \mathcal{Y}$ can be obtained by solving*

$$\boldsymbol{\theta}_t^* = \arg\min_{\boldsymbol{\theta}_t} \sum_{\mathbf{x}\in\mathcal{X}} w_\mathbf{x}\mathbb{I}(c(\mathbf{x})\neq\hat{y}) \qquad (19)$$

where

$$w_\mathbf{x} = \max_{k\in\mathcal{Y}} -\frac{\partial R_{emp}(\boldsymbol{\beta}_{t-1})}{\partial f_k(\mathbf{x})} \text{ and } \hat{y}_\mathbf{x} = \arg\max_{k\in\mathcal{Y}} -\frac{\partial R_{emp}(\boldsymbol{\beta}_{t-1})}{\partial f_k(\mathbf{x})} \qquad (20)$$

are the weight and the pseudo-label for the sample $\mathbf{x}$, respectively.

Proof. The proof is similar to the one presented by Saffari et al. [17].

The following lemmas show that for labeled and unlabeled samples, the weight is positive or zero and the chosen label for the labeled samples is the true class label. Note that this is an important step in boosting, as the derived weights should always be positive for all the samples.

Lemma 1. *For the labeled samples, the pseudo-label given in Eq.(20) is the true class label and the sample weight is positive.*

Proof. From Eq. (13) and Eq. (14) we have that $\forall k \neq y : -\frac{\partial R_{emp}(\beta_{t-1})}{\partial f_k(\mathbf{x})} < 0$ and only for the target class $-\frac{\partial R_{emp}(\beta_{t-1})}{\partial f_y(\mathbf{x})} > 0$. This also means that the pseudo-label is the true class.

Lemma 2. *For the unlabeled samples, the sample weight given in Eq.(20) is positive or zero.*

Proof. First we show that the sum of the gradients for an unlabeled sample over different classes is always zero. Note that

$$-\sum_{k \in \mathcal{Y}} \frac{\partial R_{emp}(\beta_{t-1})}{\partial f_k(\mathbf{x})} = -\gamma \sum_{k \in \mathcal{Y}} p(k|\mathbf{x};\beta)(\log \frac{p(k|\mathbf{x};\beta)}{m(k|\mathbf{x};\beta)} - D_{KL}(p\|m)) =$$
$$= \gamma(D_{KL}(p\|m) - D_{KL}(p\|m)) = 0. \tag{21}$$

Since the sum of the negative of the gradients is zero, therefore, either all the gradients are equal to zero, or if there are some non-zero gradients, then their maximum over different classes is positive, as it is not possible that the sum of a set of negative terms is zero. Therefore,

$$w_{\mathbf{x}} = \max_{k \in \mathcal{Y}} -\frac{\partial R_{emp}(\beta_{t-1})}{\partial f_k(\mathbf{x})} \geq 0. \tag{22}$$

3   Experiments

3.1   Multi-class Boosting Experiments

We compare the performance of the proposed multi-class boosting algorithm with other state-of-the-art methods on a set of multi-class machine learning benchmark datasets obtained from UCI repository. In these experiments, we compare with the following multi-class classifiers: Random Forests (RF) [19], three multi-class formulations of AdaBoost namely SAMME [20], AdaBoost.ECC [21], and the recent algorithm of AdaBoost.SIP [22][5]. As the last algorithm, we also compare with the multi-class support vector machine algorithm. For Random Forests, we train 250 randomized trees. For the SVM we use the RBF kernel and perform model selection by a grid search for selecting the kernel width σ and capacity parameter C. For our GBoost algorithm, we use 5 extremely randomized trees as weak learners, and set the number of weak learners $T = 50$ and fix the shrinkage factor to $\nu = 0.05$ for all the experiments. We repeat the experiments for 5 times and report the average test error.

The results over *DNA*, *Letter*, *Pendigit*, and *USPS* datasets are shown in Table 1. As it can be seen, our algorithm achieves results comparable to other

---

[5] For these algorithms we report the results presented in [22].

Table 1. Classification error on machine learning benchmark datasets. The bold-face shows the best performing method, while the italic font shows the second best.

Dataset/Method	GBoost	RF	SVM	SAMME [22]	AdaBoost.ECC [22]	AdaBoost.SIP [22]
DNA	0.0582	0.0683	0.0559	0.1071	**0.0506**	*0.0548*
Letter	**0.0265**	0.0468	*0.0298*	0.4938	0.2367	0.1945
Pendigit	*0.0387*	0.0496	**0.0360**	0.3391	0.1029	0.0602
USPS	*0.0524*	0.0610	**0.0424**	N/A	N/A	N/A

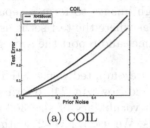

(a) COIL

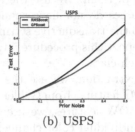

(b) USPS

Fig. 2. Classification error for (a) COIL and (b) USPS dataset with noisy priors

multi-class classifiers. The best performing method is the SVM with RBF kernel. However, our algorithm achieves these results without any need for model selection (we use a fixed setting for all the experiments in this section and the next two sections), and is considerably faster during both training and testing. For example, for the Letter dataset with 15000 training and 4000 samples, our unoptimized Python/C++ implementation[6] finishes the training and testing in 54 seconds, while the training of the SVM using Shogun LibSVM interface [23] takes around 156 seconds.

3.2   Robustness Experiments

In order to show the increased robustness experimentally, we compare our semi-supervised boosting algorithm (GPBoost) with the RMSBoost [17] which uses the Kullback-Leibler divergence. In these experiments, we use the hidden labels of the unlabeled samples in order to produce a prior and then we introduce random label noise into these priors and train both semi-supervised boosting algorithms with the same settings. In order to make the comparison fair, we also change the supervised loss function of the RMSBoost to Savage loss. For these experiments, we choose two semi-supervised learning benchmark datasets [1]. The results averaged over 12 splits provided in the dataset for COIL and USPS datasets are shown in Figure 2. As it can be seen, our algorithm retains lower test errors compared to the RMSBoost. It should be noted that specially for the COIL set which is multi-class dataset, the gap is larger from early on.

---

[6] Code is available at
http://www.ymer.org/amir/software/multi-class-semi-supervised-boosting/

3.3   Object Category Recognition

We evaluate various multi-view semi-supervised boosting algorithms on *Caltech101* object category recognition task. This dataset represent a challenging task for the semi-supervised learners, since the number of classes is large and the number of training samples per class is rather low. For these experiments, we randomly choose up to 80 images from each class and label $\{5, 10, 15, 20, 25, 30\}$ images for each of them. We use the rest of the samples as the test set. Since many of the classes do not have enough images to form a separate unlabeled set, we resort to the transductive settings where the test set is used as the unlabeled set. We repeat this procedure 5 times and report the average classification accuracy per each class.

For feature extraction, we use the precomputed dense SIFT-based bag-of-words and PHOG features from Gehler and Nowozin [24] to form different views. In details, for BOW features, we use a vocabulary of size 300 extracted from gray level and individual color channels. We use a level-2 spatial histogram to represent these 2 views (BOW-grey and BOW-Color). Additionally, we use level-2 PHOG features formed from the oriented (PHOG-360) and unoriented (PHOG-180) gradients. Therefore, in total we have 4 different views for this dataset.

In these experiments, we use the Random Forests (RF), our supervised multi-class boosting algorithm (GBoost), multi-view boosting using GBoost as the basic learners (MV-GBoost), and our multi-view algorithm MV-GPBoost. Additionally, we extended the AgreementBoost algorithm [6] to cope with multi-class problems and report the results for this algorithm as well.

If we set the $\gamma = 0$ in MV-GPBoost, we will end up in exactly the MV-GBoost algorithm. Therefore, the performance gains seen here are totally due to the incorporation of the prior regularization term. The settings for the RFs and our boosting algorithms is exactly the same settings used for machine learning benchmark experiments. For the multi-view algorithms, we iterate the learning process for 10 iterations and label 100 unlabeled samples (1 from each class) in each iteration. Since RFs and GBoost cannot use the views directly, we concatenate the features into a single feature vector.

Figure 3 shows the results for three different settings: (a) only using the two views provided from BOW features, (b) using two views from PHOG features, and (c) using all 4 views. The first observation is that the GBoost algorithm successfully boosts the performance of the random forest and the accuracy gap can be as high as 5%. Comparing the performance of the GBoost and the MV-GBoost, we can see that in general the multi-view learning strategy by labeling a subset of unlabeled samples iteratively, works and there is a clear performance gain between these two algorithms. However, the highest accuracy is obtained by MV-GPBoost which has a considerable gap in classification accuracy compared to the MV-GBoost algorithm. Another observation here is that, as expected, the combination of all 4 views achieves the highest performance, compared to using either two views from BOW or PHOGs. Furthermore, the performance of the

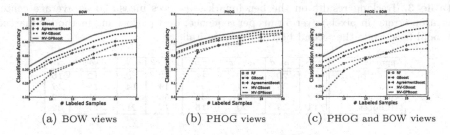

(a) BOW views   (b) PHOG views   (c) PHOG and BOW views

Fig. 3. Caltech101 classification accuracy for: (a) BOW, (b) PHOG, and (c) BOW and PHOG

Table 2. Classification accuracy on Caltech101 with kernel SVMs for 15 and 30 labeled samples per class

Methods - Views	BOW		PHOG		BOW+PHOG	
# Labels	15	30	15	30	15	30
SVM	0.5545	0.6415	0.4612	0.5264	0.6123	0.6888
MV-GPBoost	0.5605	0.6805	0.4745	0.5411	0.6496	0.7158

AgreementBoost which uses the variance of the classifiers over different views to regularize the training process of boosting is not comparable to the performance of other learning methods.

Similar to [24], when we use χ^2 kernels over each of the views and use SVMs as the weak learners of the boosting classifiers, we improve the classification accuracy on this dataset. These results are reported in Table 2.

3.4 Object Tracking

Recently, boosting-based methods have achieved high accurate tracking performances running in real-time [25]. In these methods, usually an appearance-based classifier is trained with a marked object at the first frame versus its local background. The object is then tracked by performing re-detection in the succeeding frames. In order to handle rapid appearance and illumination changes, the classifiers perform on-line self-updating [26]. However, during this self-updating process it is hard to decide where to select the positive and negative updates. If the samples are selected wrongly, slight errors can accumulate over time and cause drifting. Therefore, recent approaches applied on-line extensions of boosting that can handle the uncertainty in the update process, such as CoBoost [9], SemiBoost [27] or MILBoost [28]. The main idea of these approaches is to define a region around the current tracking position and leave it up to the learner which samples to incorporate as positives or negatives in order to stabilize the tracking. In the following, we compare our method to the state-of-the-art.

We use eight publicly available sequences including variations in illumination, pose, scale, rotation and appearance, and partial occlusions. The sequences *Sylvester* and *David* are taken from [29] and *Face Occlusion 1* is taken from [30], respectively. *Face occlusion 2, Girl, Tiger1, Tiger2* and *Coke* are taken from [28].

Table 3. Tracking results on the benchmark sequences measured as average center location errors (in pixels) over 5 runs per sequence. Best performing method is marked in bold face, while the second best is shown in italic.

Approach	*sylv*	*david*	*faceocc2*	*tiger1*	*tiger2*	*coke*	*faceocc1*	*girl*
MV-GPBoost	17	**20**	**10**	**15**	**16**	*20*	**12**	**15**
CoBoost	*15*	33	*11*	22	19	**14**	*13*	*17*
SemiBoost	22	59	43	46	53	85	41	52
MILBoost	**11**	*23*	20	**15**	*17*	21	27	32

All video frames are gray scale and of size 320 × 240. We report the tracking accuracy in terms of average center location error in pixel to the groundtruth.

Since our method is a multi-view approach, it is straight-forward to use different feature information. However, this would make the comparison to other methods that are based on single features unfair. So, in the following we report tracking results only for Haar-features and it should be clear to the reader (also by looking at previous experiments) that further improvement can be achieved by adding additional feature queues. In particular, we use 30 selectors with each 30 weak learners. The different views are generated by random sub-sampling from a large amount of Haar-features. In Table 3 we depict the results for all tracking sequences, *i.e.*, CoBoost [9], SemiBoost [27] and MILBoost [28]. As can be seen, MV-GPBoost performs best on five tracking sequences. The resulting tracking videos can be found in the supplementary material.

4   Conclusions

In this paper, we have introduced a new multi-view boosting algorithm. In contrast to previous approaches that select a subset of the unlabeled data and ignore the rest, we use all unlabeled samples and, we use the different views to provide an aggregated prior which regularizes a semi-supervised loss function. Since priors are noisy, we also propose a novel robust loss function for semi-supervised boosting. Finally, our method is inherently multi-class and can handle more than two views at the same time. We demonstrated the performance of our method on machine learning benchmark sets, Caltech-101 object categorization and object tracking.

References

1. Chapelle, O., Schölkopf, B., Zien, A.: Semi-Supervised Learning, Cambridge, MA (2006)
2. Zhu, X.: Semi-supervised learning literature survey. Technical report (2008)
3. Blum, A., Mitchell, T.: Combining labeled and unlabeled data with co-training. In: COLT, pp. 92–100 (1998)
4. Brefeld, U., Büscher, C., Scheffer, T.: Multi-view discriminative sequential learning. In: Gama, J., Camacho, R., Brazdil, P.B., Jorge, A.M., Torgo, L. (eds.) ECML 2005. LNCS (LNAI), vol. 3720, pp. 60–71. Springer, Heidelberg (2005)

5. Sindhwani, V., Rosenberg, D.S.: An rkhs for multi-view learning and manifold co-regularization. In: ICML, pp. 976–983 (2008)
6. Leskes, B., Torenvliet, L.: The value of agreement a new boosting algorithm. J. Comput. Syst. Sci. 74, 557–586 (2008)
7. Levin, A., Viola, P., Freund, Y.: Unsupervised improvement of visual detectors using co-training. In: ICCV, vol. I, pp. 626–633 (2003)
8. Christoudias, C.M., Urtasun, R., Darrell, T.: Unsupervised distributed feature selection for multi-view object recognition. In: CVPR (2008)
9. Liu, R., Cheng, J., Lu, H.: A robust boosting tracker with minimum error bound in a co-training framework. In: ICCV (2009)
10. Tang, F., Brennan, S., Zhao, Q., Tao, H.: Co-tracking using semi-supervised support vector machines. In: ICCV (2007)
11. Sun, S., Zhang, Q.: Multiple-view multiple-learner semi-supervised learning. Technical report (2007)
12. Leistner, C., Saffari, A., Santner, J., Bischof, H.: Semi-supervised random forests. In: IEEE International Conference on Computer Vision, ICCV (2009)
13. Freund, Y., Schapire, R.: Experiments with a new boosting algorithm. In: ICML, pp. 148–156 (1996)
14. Friedman, J., Hastie, T., Tibshirani, R.: Additive logistic regression: a statistical view of boosting. The Annals of Statistics 38, 337–374 (2000)
15. Shirazi, H.M., Vasconcelos, N.: On the design of loss functions for classification: theory, robustness to outliers, and savageboost. In: NIPS, pp. 1049–1056 (2008)
16. Saffari, A., Grabner, H., Bischof, H.: SERBoost: Semi-supervised boosting with expectation regularization. In: Forsyth, D., Torr, P., Zisserman, A. (eds.) ECCV 2008, Part III. LNCS, vol. 5304, pp. 588–601. Springer, Heidelberg (2008)
17. Saffari, A., Leistner, C., Bischof, H.: Regularized multi-class semi-supervised boosting. In: CVPR (2009)
18. Fricdman, J.: Greedy function approximation: A gradient boosting machine. The Annals of Statistics 29, 1189–1232 (2001)
19. Breiman, L.: Random forests. Machine Learning 45, 5–32 (2001)
20. Zhu, J., Rosset, S., Zou, H., Hastie, T.: Multi-class adaboost. Technical report (2006)
21. Guruswami, V., Sahai, A.: Multiclass learning, boosting, and error-correcting codes. In: COLT (1999)
22. Zhang, B., Ye, G., Wang, Y., Xu, J., Herman, G.: Finding shareable informative patterns and optimal coding matrix for multiclass boosting. In: ICCV (2009)
23. Sonnenburg, S., Rätsch, G., Schäfer, C., Schölkopf, B.: Large scale multiple kernel learning. JMLR 7, 1531–1565 (2006)
24. Gehler, P., Nowozin, S.: On feature combination for multiclass object classification. In: ICCV (2009)
25. Avidan, S.: Ensemble tracking, vol. 2, pp. 494–501 (2005)
26. Grabner, H., Bischof, H.: On-line boosting and vision, vol. 1, pp. 260–267 (2006)
27. Grabner, H., Leistner, C., Bischof, H.: On-line semi-supervised boosting for robust tracking. In: Forsyth, D., Torr, P., Zisserman, A. (eds.) ECCV 2008, Part I. LNCS, vol. 5302, pp. 234–247. Springer, Heidelberg (2008)
28. Babenko, B., Yang, M.H., Belongie, S.: Visual tracking with online multiple instance learning. In: CVPR (2009)
29. Ross, D., Lim, J., Lin, R.S., Yang, M.H.: Incremental learning for robust visual tracking. IJCV (2008)
30. Adam, A., Rivlin, E., Shimshoni, I.: Robust fragments-based tracking using the integral histogram. In: CVPR (2006)

Optimum Subspace Learning and Error Correction for Tensors

Yin Li, Junchi Yan, Yue Zhou*, and Jie Yang

Institute of Image Processing and Pattern Recogntion,
Shanghai Jiaotong University
{happyharry,yanster,zhouyue,jieyang}@sjtu.edu.cn

Abstract. Confronted with the high-dimensional tensor-like visual data, we derive a method for the decomposition of an observed tensor into a low-dimensional structure plus unbounded but sparse irregular patterns. The optimal rank-$(R_1, R_2, ...R_n)$ tensor decomposition model that we propose in this paper, could automatically explore the low-dimensional structure of the tensor data, seeking optimal dimension and basis for each mode and separating the irregular patterns. Consequently, our method accounts for the implicit multi-factor structure of tensor-like visual data in an explicit and concise manner. In addition, the optimal tensor decomposition is formulated as a convex optimization through relaxation technique. We then develop a block coordinate descent (BCD) based algorithm to efficiently solve the problem. In experiments, we show several applications of our method in computer vision and the results are promising.

1 Introduction

As the size of data and the amount of redundancy increase fast with dimensionality, the recent explosion of massive amounts of high-dimensional visual data presents a challenge to computer vision. Most of the existing high-dimensional visual data either has the natural form of tensor (e.g. multi-channel images and videos) or can be grouped into the form of tensor (e.g. tensor face [1]). On one side, one may seek a compact and concise low-dimensional representation of the data, such as dimension reduction [2–4] or image compression [5]. On the other side, one may seek to detect the irregular patterns of the data, such as saliency detection [6] or foreground segmentation [7]. As a consequence, it is desirable to develop tools that can find and exploit the low-dimensional structure in a high-dimensional tensor-like visual data.

In the two-dimensional case, i.e. the matrix case, the "rank" plays an important part in capturing the global information of visual data. One simple and useful assumption is that the data lie near certain low-dimensional subspace,

---

* The work is supported by National Science Foundation of China (Grant No.60772097); Open Projects Program of National Laboratory of Pattern Recognition, Institute of Automation, Chinese Academy of Science.

K. Daniilidis, P. Maragos, N. Paragios (Eds.): ECCV 2010, Part III, LNCS 6313, pp. 790–803, 2010.

Fig. 1. Result of our method on a color facade (left). The method automatically seek a low dimensional representation (middle) and separate the sparse irregular patterns (right). Better viewed in color and zoom in for details.

which is closely related to the notation of rank. Although the "rank" itself is nonconvex, it can be approximated by its convex envelop, namely the trace norm. The validation of this approximation is justified in theory [8]. Among all the trace norm minimization problems, matrix completion may be a well-known one [8, 9]. Recently, [10] extends the matrix completion problem to the tensor case and develops an efficient solution.

The "sparsity" is also a useful tool for visual data analysis. One common observation is that the irregular patterns often occupy a small portion of the data. This sparse prior has demonstrated a wide range of applications including image denoising [11], error correction [12] and face recognition [13]. It was not until very recently that had much attention been focused on the rank-sparsity problem for matrix [14, 15], namely the Principal Component Pursuit (PCP) or the Robust Principal Component Analysis (RPCA). These work seek to directly decompose a matrix into a low-rank part plus a sparse part. Theoretic analysis [15] shows that under rather weak assumptions, the problem can be solved by the joint minimization of trace norm and l_1 norm.

We consider the decomposition of an observed tensor data into a low dimensional structure and an additive (sparse) irregular pattern. Analogy to the PCP problem in the matrix case, the optimal rank-$(R_1, R_2, ...R_n)$ tensor decomposition model that we propose in the paper, could automatically explore the low-dimensional structure of the tensor data, seeking optimal dimension and basis for each mode and separating the irregular patterns (See Fig.1 for an example and the core idea). Our method is an multilinear extension of the PCP problem and subsumes the matrix PCP problem as a special case. The optimal tensor decomposition is formulated as a convex optimization through relaxation technique. In addition, we develop a efficient block coordinate descent (BCD) based solution. We show several applications of our method in computer vision and the results are promising.

The rest of the paper is organized as follows: Section 2 briefly reviews related work. Section 3 provides the foundations of tensor algebra that are relevant to our approach. Section 4 formulates our proposed optimal rank-$(R_1, R_2, ..., R_n)$ tensor decomposition model together with its solution. Section 5 reports experimental results of our algorithm for several computer vision tasks. Finally, Section 6 concludes the paper.

2   Related Work

Prior research on subspace analysis is abundant, including Principal Component Analysis (PCA) [2], Linear Discriminant Analysis (LDA) [3], Locality Preserving Projection (LPP) [4], etc. These models are widely adopted in computer vision problems. They usually treat an image as a vector and consider only one factor of the problem (e.g. only the face identity is considered in face recognition task). Various researchers have attempted to overcome the shortcomings of these methods by considering the image as a 2-mode tensor (i.e. matrix), including 2DPCA [7], tensor subspace analysis (tensor LPP) [16], tensor LDA [17], etc.

Much effort has been focused on the tensor representation and analysis of visual data. Vasilescu and Terzopoulos [1] introduce a multilinear tensor framework to the analysis of face ensembles that explicitly accounts for each of the multiple factors implicit in image formation. Possible applications of the multilinear approach cover face recognition [18–20], facial expression decomposition [20, 21] and face super-resolution [22]. These methods are based on the higher order singular value decomposition [23], i.e. the Tucker decomposition, leading to best rank-$(R_1, R_2, ...R_n)$ approximations of higher-order tensors (See Section 2 for details).

Shashua and Levin [24] propose 3-way tensor decomposition for the images as a 3D cube. They develop compression algorithms for images and video, that take advantage of spatial and temporal redundancies. The method is further extended to non-negative 3D tensor factorization [22] for the purpose of establishing a local parts feature decomposition from an object class of images. The non-negative tensor factorization is also applied to hypergraph clustering [25] to study a series of vision problems including 3D multi-body segmentation and illumination-based face clustering. These methods are based on the PARAFAC decomposition [26], leading to best (non-negative) rank-R approximations of higher-order tensors.

The optimal rank-$(R_1, R_2, ...R_n)$ tensor decomposition model that we propose in the paper seeks a best n-rank condition for the tensor data, yielding a rather different approach from previous work. Our model could simultaneously find the optimal dimension and basis for each mode and separate the irregular patterns in an automatic manner. As a result, by rather weak prior, our method can account for the implicit multi-factor structure of tensor-like visual data in an explicit and concise manner.

3   Tensor Basics

A tensor, or n-way array, is a higher-order generalization of matrix. We use lower case letters ($a, b,...$) for scalars, bold lower case letters ($\boldsymbol{a}, \boldsymbol{b},...$) for vectors, upper case letters ($A, B,...$) for matrix, and calligraphic upper case letters ($\mathcal{A}, \mathcal{B},...$) for higher order tensors. Formally, a n-mode tensor is defined as $\mathcal{A} \in R^{I_1 \times I_2 \times \cdots \times I_n}$, with its elements $a_{i_1} \ldots a_{i_k} \ldots a_{i_n} \in R$. Therefore, a vector can be seen as a 1-mode tensor and a matrix can be seen as a 2-mode tensor.

It is often convenient to flatten a tensor into a matrix, also called matricizing or unfolding. The "unfold" operation along the kth mode on a tensor $\mathcal{A}$ is defined as $unfold(\mathcal{A}, k) := \mathcal{A}_{(k)} \in R^{I_k \times (I_1 \cdots I_{k-1} I_{k+1} \cdots I_n)}$. Accordingly, its inverse operator $fold$ can be defined as $fold(\mathcal{A}_{(k)}, k) := A$. Moreover, the k-rank of tensor $\mathcal{A}$, denoted by r_k, is defined as the rank of the matrix $\mathcal{A}_{(k)}$:

$$r_k = rank_k(\mathcal{A}) = rank(\mathcal{A}_{(k)}) \tag{1}$$

The Frobenius norm of a tensor is defined as $\|\mathcal{A}\|_F := (\sum_{i_1, i_2, \ldots i_n} |a_{i_1} a_{i_2} \ldots a_{i_n}|^2)^{\frac{1}{2}}$. Besides, denote the l_0 norm $\|\mathcal{A}\|_0$ as the number of non-zero entities in $\mathcal{A}$ and the l_1 norm $\|\mathcal{A}\|_1 := \sum_{i_1, i_2, \ldots i_n} |a_{i_1} a_{i_2} \ldots a_{i_n}|$ respectively. Then, we have $\|\mathcal{A}\|_F = \|A_{(k)}\|_F$, $\|\mathcal{A}\|_0 = \|A_{(k)}\|_0$ and $\|\mathcal{A}\|_1 = \|A_{(k)}\|_1$ for any $1 \leq k \leq n$.

A generalization of the product of two matrix is the product of a tensor and a matrix. The mode-k product of a tensor $\mathcal{A} \in R^{I_1 \times I_2 \times \cdots \times I_n}$ by a matrix $M \in R^{J_k \times I_k}$, denoted by $\mathcal{A} \times_k M$, is a tensor $\mathcal{B} \in R^{I_1 \times \cdots I_{k-1} \times J_k \times I_{k+1} \times \cdots \times I_n}$ with its elements given by

$$b_{i_1 \times \cdots i_{k-1} \times j_k \times i_{k+1} \times \cdots \times i_n} = \sum_{i_k} a_{i_1 \times \cdots i_{k-1} \times i_k \times i_{k+1} \times \cdots \times i_n} m_{j_k i_k} \tag{2}$$

The mode-k product can be expressed in tensor notation, or in terms of flattened matrix:

$$\mathcal{B} = \mathcal{A} \times_k M = fold(M A_{(k)}, k) \tag{3}$$

The notion of rank for tensors with order greater than two is subtle. There are two types of higher-order tensor decompositions, but neither of them has all the nice properties of the matrix SVD. The PARAFAC decomposition [26] represents the n-mode tensor $\mathcal{A} \in R^{I_1 \times I_2 \times \cdots \times I_n}$ as the outer product of vectors $u_k^j \in R^{I_k}$ (Fig.2).

$$A = \sum_{j=1}^{R} \lambda_j u_1^j \circ u_2^j \circ \ldots \circ u_n^j \tag{4}$$

where u_k^j are unit length vectors. Under mild conditions, the rank-R decomposition is essentially unique [26]. The $rank$ of a n-mode tensor $\mathcal{A}$, is the minimal number of R, indicating the optimal rank-R decomposition. It is a natural extension of the matrix rank-R decomposition, but it does not compute the orthonormal subspace associated with each mode.

The Tucker decomposition, in the other hand, does not reveal the rank of the tensor, but it naturally generalizes the orthonormal subspaces corresponding to the left/right singular matrix computed by the matrix SVD [23]. The n-mode tensor $\mathcal{A} \in R^{I_1 \times I_2 \times \cdots \times I_n}$ can be decomposed as

$$\mathcal{A} = \mathcal{Z} \times_1 U_1 \times_2 U_2, \ldots \times_k U_k \ldots \times_n U_n \tag{5}$$

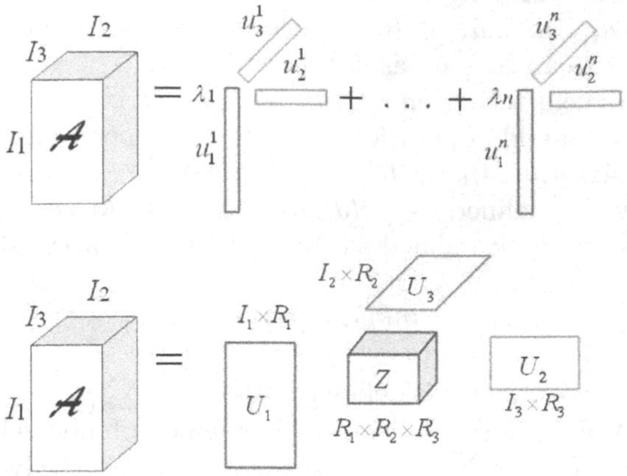

Fig. 2. Comparison of different decomposition for 3D tensor; Top: Rank-R decomposition. Bottom: Rank-$(R_1, R_2, \ldots R_N)$.

where $U_i \in R^{I_i \times R_i}$ are n orthogonal matrix. U_i spans the R_i dimensional subspace of the original R^{I_i} space, with its orthonormal columns as the basis. U_i accounts for the implicit factor of the ith-mode dimension of tensor $\mathcal{A}$. $\mathcal{Z}$ is the (dense) core tensor associating each of the n subspace (Fig.2).

4   Optimum Rank-$(R_1, R_2, \ldots R_N)$ Tensor Decomposition

4.1   The Model

To begin with, we give a brief introduction to the best Rank-$(R_1, R_2, \ldots R_N)$ approximation (decomposition) problem in [17, 20, 23]. Consider a real n-mode tensor $\mathcal{A} \in R^{I_1 \times I_2 \times \cdots \times I_n}$, the best rank-$(R_1, R_2, \ldots R_N)$ approximation is to find a tensor $\tilde{\mathcal{A}} \in R^{I_1 \times I_2 \times \cdots \times I_n}$ with pre-specified $rank_k(\tilde{A}) = R_k$, that minimizes the least-squares cost function:

$$\min_{\tilde{\mathcal{A}}} \quad f(\tilde{\mathcal{A}}) = \|\mathcal{A} - \tilde{\mathcal{A}}\|_F^2$$
$$s.t. \quad rank_i(\tilde{\mathcal{A}}) = R_i \quad \forall i \tag{6}$$

The n-rank conditions imply that $\tilde{\mathcal{A}}$ should have the Tucker decomposition as (5): $\tilde{\mathcal{A}} = \mathcal{Z} \times_1 U_1 \times_2 U_2, \ldots \times_k U_k \ldots \times_n U_n$. The decomposition is discussed in [23] and Higher Order Orthogonal Iteration (HOOI) has been proposed to solve the problem.

HOOI requires strong prior knowledge of the tensor $\mathcal{A} \in R^{I_1 \times I_2 \times \cdots \times I_n}$, namely $rank_i(A) = R_i$, to find the (local) minimum solution. However, for visual data in real applications (e.g. a video clip or CT data), such prior knowledge is hardly available. Problem arises that if only weak prior knowledge is known (e.g. the configuration of the tensor data), can one design a method that could automatically find the optimal n-rank condition of the given tensor $\mathcal{A}$. To simplify the problem, we consider a ideal model that the corruption is produced by additive irregular patterns $\mathcal{S}$.

$$\mathcal{A} = \mathcal{L} + \mathcal{S} \tag{7}$$

where $\mathcal{A}$, $\mathcal{L}$ and $\mathcal{S}$ are n-mode tensors with identical size in each mode. $\mathcal{A}$ is the observed data tensor. $\mathcal{L}$ and $\mathcal{S}$ represent the correspondent structured part and irregular part, respectively.

The underlining assumption of (7) is that the tensor data $\mathcal{A}$ is generated by a highly structured tensor $\mathcal{L}$, and then corrupted by an additive irregular patterns $\mathcal{S}$. One straightforward assumption may be that the n-rank of $\mathcal{L}$ should be small and the corruption $\mathcal{S}$ is bounded, leading to the formulation:

$$\min_{\mathcal{L}} \quad \sum_i \lambda_i \ rank_i(\mathcal{L})$$
$$s.t. \quad \|\mathcal{L} - \mathcal{A}\|_F^2 \le \varepsilon^2 \tag{8}$$

where $U_i \in R^{I_i \times rank_i(\mathcal{L})}$. Intuitively, the weights λ_i indicates the preference towards different "unfold" operation, i.e. the configuration of the tensor. For example, we would prefer to explain the tensor representation of a video as the collection of frames.

(8) imposes constraints on the least square errors, suggesting that the corruption of the irregular patterns $\mathcal{S}$ is bounded. The constraint could be the case in certain situations. However, the irregular patterns in real world visual data is unknown and unbounded in general. A reasonable observation is that the irregular patterns $\mathcal{S}$ usually occupy only a small portion of the data. Therefore, we could impose l_0 norm penalization on $\mathcal{S}$ and form the problem as follows:

$$\min_{\mathcal{L},\mathcal{S}} \quad \sum_i \lambda_i \ rank_i(\mathcal{L}) + \eta\|\mathcal{S}\|_0$$
$$s.t. \quad \|\mathcal{L} + \mathcal{S} - \mathcal{A}\|_F^2 \le \varepsilon^2 \tag{9}$$

The constant η balances between the low-dimensional structure and sparse irregularity. In addition, it is easy to check that (7) is a special case of (9) if we force $\mathcal{S} = 0$. Thus, we will focus on problem (9) in the rest of the paper.

When the optimal $\mathcal{L}$ is achieved, similar to the Tucker Decomposition, the core tensor $\mathcal{Z}$ can be computed by [23]

$$\mathcal{Z} = \mathcal{L} \times_1 U_1^T \times_2 U_2^T \dots \times_n U_n^T \tag{10}$$

where U_i is the left singular matrix of $\mathcal{L}_i$. Accordingly, we can get the rank-$(R_1, R_2, \dots R_N)$ decomposition of $\mathcal{L} = \mathcal{Z} \times_1 U_1 \times_2 U_2, \dots \times_i U_i \dots \times_n U_n$. We call the correspondent decomposition in (11)

$$\mathcal{A} \sim \mathcal{Z} \times_1 U_1 \times_2 U_2, \dots \times_i U_i \dots \times_n U_n \tag{11}$$

to be **the optimal rank-$(R_1, R_2, \ldots R_N)$ decomposition of tensor** $\mathcal{A}$ under the sense of l_1 norm . The term **"optimal"** means that the model could automatically exploit the low-dimensional structure of the n-mode tensor $\mathcal{A}$, finding optimal dimension and basis for each mode and separating the sparse irregular patterns. The unknown support of the errors makes the problem more difficult than the tensor completion problem that has been recently much studied [10]. In the next section, we discuss the solution toward the optimization problem and propose the rank sparsity tensor decomposition (RSTD) algorithm.

4.2 Simplified Formulation

Equation (9) provides a promise for simultaneously exploring the low-dimensional structure and separating the irregular patterns of given tensor data $\mathcal{A} \in R^{I_1 \times I_2 \times \ldots \times I_n}$. However, (9) as the combination of two NP hard problem (matrix rank and l_0 norm), is highly nonconvex optimization. Given the fact that the trace norm $\|\mathcal{L}_{(i)}\|_{tr}$ and l_1 norm $\|\mathcal{S}\|_1$ are the tightest convex approximation of $rank_i(L)$ and $\|\mathcal{S}\|_0$ respectively, one can relax $rank_i(\mathcal{L})$ and $\|\mathcal{S}\|_0$ by $\|\mathcal{L}_{(i)}\|_{tr}$ and $\|\mathcal{S}\|_1$. Therefore, we could obtain a tractable optimization problem:

$$\min_{\mathcal{L},\mathcal{S}} \quad \sum_i \lambda_i \|\mathcal{L}_{(i)}\|_{tr} + \eta\|\mathcal{S}\|_1$$
$$s.t. \quad \|\mathcal{L}+\mathcal{S}-\mathcal{A}\|_F^2 \le \varepsilon^2 \tag{12}$$

where the trace norm, or the nuclear norm of matrix $\mathcal{L}_{(i)}$ is defined as the sum of its singular values σ_j, i.e. $\|\mathcal{L}_{(i)}\|_{tr} = \sum_j \sigma_j(\mathcal{L}_{(i)})$. If $rank_i\mathcal{L} \ll I_i$ and $\|\mathcal{S}\|_0 \ll \Pi_{i=1}^n I_i$, i.e. tensor $\mathcal{L}$ is highly structured and tensor $\mathcal{S}$ is sparse enough, under rather mild conditions, the approximation can be highly accurate [8, 15]. Empirically, for general visual data with high redundancy, the approximation produces good results.

Problem (12) is still hard to solve due to the interdependent trace norm and l_1 norm constraint. To simplify the problem, we introduce additional auxiliary matrix $M_i = \mathcal{L}_{(i)}$ and $N_i = \mathcal{S}_{(i)}$. Thus, we obtain the equivalent formulation:

$$\min_{\mathcal{L},\mathcal{S},M_i,N_i} \quad \frac{1}{n}\sum_{i=1}^n \lambda_i\|M_i\|_{tr} + \frac{\eta}{n}\sum_{i=1}^n \|N_i\|_1$$
$$s.t. \quad M_i = \mathcal{L}_{(i)} \qquad N_i = \mathcal{S}_{(i)} \qquad \forall i$$
$$\|M_i + N_i - \mathcal{A}_{(i)}\|_F^2 \le \varepsilon^2 \qquad \forall i \tag{13}$$

In (13), the constrains $M_i = \mathcal{L}_{(i)}$ and $N_i = \mathcal{S}_{(i)}$ still enforce the consistency of all M_i and N_i. Thus, we further relax the equality constrains $M_i = \mathcal{L}_{(i)}$ and $N_i = \mathcal{S}_{(i)}$ by $\|M_i - \mathcal{L}_{(i)}\|_F \le \varepsilon_1$ and $\|N_i - \mathcal{S}_{(i)}\|_F \le \varepsilon_2$. Then, it is easy to check that the dense noise term by $\|M_i + N_i - \mathcal{A}_{(i)}\|_F \le \varepsilon_3$ corresponds to the stable Principle Component Pursuit(sPCP) in the matrix case [27]. Then, we get the relaxed form:

$$\min_{\mathcal{L},\mathcal{S},M_i,N_i} \quad \frac{1}{n}\sum_{i=1}^{n}\lambda_i\|M_i\|_{tr} + \frac{\eta}{n}\sum_{i=1}^{n}\|N_i\|_1$$

$$\text{s.t.} \quad \|M_i - \mathcal{L}_{(i)}\|_F^2 \le \varepsilon_1^2 \qquad \|N_i - \mathcal{S}_{(i)}\|_F^2 \le \varepsilon_2^2 \qquad \forall i$$

$$\|M_i + N_i - \mathcal{A}_{(i)}\|_F^2 \le \varepsilon_3^2 \qquad \forall i \tag{14}$$

For certain α_i, β_i and γ_i, (14) can be converted to its equivalent form by Lagrange multiplier.

$$\min_{\mathcal{L},\mathcal{S},M_i,N_i} \quad F(\mathcal{L},\mathcal{S},M_i,N_i) = \frac{1}{2n}\sum_{i=1}^{n}\alpha_i\|M_i - \mathcal{L}_{(i)}\|_F^2 + \frac{1}{2n}\sum_{i=1}^{n}\beta_i\|N_i - \mathcal{S}_{(i)}\|_F^2$$

$$+ \frac{1}{2n}\sum_{i=1}^{n}\gamma_i\|M_i + N_i - \mathcal{A}_{(i)}\|_F^2 + \frac{1}{n}\sum_{i=1}^{n}\lambda_i\|M_i\|_{tr} + \frac{\eta}{n}\sum_{i=1}^{n}\|N_i\|_1 \tag{15}$$

Intuitively, the weights α_i, β_i and γ_i indicate the preference towards different "unfold" operation similar to λ_i. The optimization problem in (15) is convex but nondifferentiable. Next, we show how to solve this problem.

4.3 The Proposed Algorithm

We propose to employ the alternating direction method (ADM) for the optimization (15), leading to an block coordinate descent (BCD) algorithm. The core idea of the BCD is to optimize a group of variables while fixing the other groups. The variables in the optimization are $N_1,..., N_n$, $M_1,..., M_n$, $\mathcal{L}$, $\mathcal{S}$, which can be divided into $2n + 2$ blocks. To achieve the optimal solution, we estimate N_i, M_i, $\mathcal{L}$ and $\mathcal{S}$ sequentially, followed by certain refinement in each iteration. For clarity, we first define the "shrinkage" operator $D_\tau(x)$ with $\tau > 0$ by

$$D_\tau(x) = \begin{cases} x - \tau & \text{if } x > \tau \\ \tau - x & \text{if } x < -\tau \\ 0 & \text{otherwise} \end{cases} \tag{16}$$

The operator can be extended to the matrix or tensor case by performing the shrinkage operator towards each element. Then, we introduce the solution towards each subproblem.

Computing N_i: The optimal N_i with all other variables fixed is the solution to the following subproblem

$$\min_{N_i} \quad \frac{\beta_i}{2}\|N_i - \mathcal{S}_{(i)}\|_F^2 + \frac{\gamma_i}{2}\|N_i + M_i - \mathcal{A}_{(i)}\|_F^2 + \eta\|N_i\|_1 \tag{17}$$

By the well-known l_1 minimization [28], the global minimum of the optimization problem in (17) is given by

$$N_i^* = D_{\frac{\eta}{\beta_i+\gamma_i}}\left(\frac{\beta_i \mathcal{S}_{(i)} + \gamma_i(A_{(i)} - M_i)}{\beta_i + \gamma_i}\right) \tag{18}$$

where D_τ is the "shrinkage" operation.

Computing M_i: The optimal M_i with all other variables fixed is the solution to the following subproblem:

$$\min_{M_i} \quad \frac{\alpha_i}{2}\|M_i - \mathcal{L}_{(i)}\|_F^2 + \frac{\gamma_i}{2}\|M_i + N_i - \mathcal{A}_{(i)}\|_F^2 + \lambda_i\|M_i\|_{tr} \tag{19}$$

As shown in [9], the global minimum of the optimization problem in (19) is given by

$$M_i^* = U_i D_{\frac{\lambda_i}{\alpha_i+\gamma_i}}(\Lambda)V_i^T \tag{20}$$

where $U_i \Lambda V_i^T$ is the singular value decomposition given by

$$U_i \Lambda V_i^T = \frac{\alpha_i L_{(i)} + \gamma_i(\mathcal{A}_{(i)} - N_i)}{\alpha_i + \gamma_i} \tag{21}$$

Computing $\mathcal{S}_i$: The optimal $\mathcal{S}$ with all other variables fixed is the solution to the following subproblem

$$\min_{\mathcal{S}} \quad \frac{1}{2}\sum_{i=1}^n \beta_i\|N_i - \mathcal{S}_{(i)}\|_F^2 \tag{22}$$

It is easy to show that the solution to (22) is given by

$$\hat{\mathcal{S}}^* = \frac{\sum_{i=1}^n \beta_i fold(N_i, i)}{\sum_{i=1}^n \beta_i} \tag{23}$$

Computing $\mathcal{L}_i$: The optimal $\mathcal{L}$ with all other variables fixed is the solution to the following subproblem

$$\min_{\mathcal{L}} \quad \frac{1}{2}\sum_{i=1}^n \alpha_i\|M_i - \mathcal{L}_{(i)}\|_F^2 \tag{24}$$

Similar to (22), the solution to (24) is given by

$$\hat{\mathcal{L}}^* = \frac{\sum_{i=1}^n \alpha_i fold(M_i, i)}{\sum_{i=1}^n \alpha_i} \tag{25}$$

We choose the difference of L and S in successive iterations against a certain tolerance as the stopping criterion. N_i^*, M_i^*, $\mathcal{L}^*$ and $\mathcal{S}^*$ are estimated iteratively until the convergence. We call the proposed algorithm Rank Sparsity Tensor Decomposition (RSTD). The pseudo-code of RSTD is summarized in Algorithm 1. We can further show that accelerated BCD for RSTD is guaranteed to reach the global optimum of (15), since the first three terms in (15) are differentiable and the last two terms are separable [29].

Algorithm 1. RSTD for Optimum Rank-$(R_1...R_N)$ Tensor Approximation

---

Input : n-mode tensor $\mathcal{A}$

Parameters : α, β, γ, λ, η

Output : n-mode tensor $\mathcal{L}$, $\mathcal{S}$, $\mathcal{Z}$, matrix U_i from 1 to n

1. Set $\mathcal{L}^{(0)} = \mathcal{A}$, $\mathcal{S}^{(0)} = 0$, $M_i = \mathcal{L}_{(i)}$, $N_i = 0$, $k = 1$, $t^{(0)} = 1$

2. **while** no convergence

3.   **for** $i = 1$ to n

4. $N_i{}^* = D_{\frac{\eta}{\beta_i + \gamma_i}}\left(\frac{\beta_i S_{(i)} + \gamma_i(A_{(i)} - M_i)}{\beta_i + \gamma_i}\right)$

5. $M_i{}^* = U_i D_{\frac{\lambda_i}{\alpha_i + \gamma_i}}(\Lambda)V_i^T$ *where* $U_i \Lambda V_i^T = \frac{\alpha_i L_{(i)} + \gamma_i(A_{(i)} - N_i)}{\alpha_i + \gamma_i}$

6.   **end for**

7. $\mathcal{S}^* = \frac{\sum_{i=1}^{n} \beta_i fold(N_i, i)}{\sum_{i=1}^{n} \beta_i}$

8. $\mathcal{L}^* = \frac{\sum_{i=1}^{n} \alpha_i fold(M_i, i)}{\sum_{i=1}^{n} \alpha_i}$

9. **end while**

10. $\mathcal{Z} = \mathcal{L} \times_1 U_1^T \times_2 U_2^T ... \times_n U_n^T$

---

5 Experiments

5.1 Implementation Details

In the implementation, we adopt the Lanczos bidiagonalization algorithm with partial reorthogonalization [30] to obtain a few singular values and vectors during each iteration. The prediction rule for the dimension of the principal singular space is the same as [15]. A major challenge of our method is the selection of parameters. As the redundancy usually grows with the dimension, we simply set $\alpha = \beta = \gamma = [I_1/I_{max}, I_2/I_{max}, ..., I_n/I_{max}]^T$ for all experiments, where $I_{max} = max\{I_i\}$. Similarly, we set $\lambda = [sv_1/sv_{max}, sv_2/sv_{max}, ..., sv_n/sv_{max}]$, where sv_i is the 95% singular value of $A_{(i)}$ and $sv_{max} = max\{sv_i\}$. Finally, we choose $\eta = 1/\sqrt{I_{max}}$ as suggested in [15]. During the experiments, we observe that for most of the samples our implementation is able to converge in less than 100 iterations with a tolerance equal to 10^{-6}.

5.2 Image Restoration

As shown in Fig.1, our algorithm can be used to separate unbounded sparse noise in visual data. One straightforward application of our method is the image restoration. However, we must point out that our algorithm assumes the tensor be well structured. This assumption would not be reasonable for some natural images, but it should be applicable for many visual data such as structured object (e.g. the facade), CT/fMRI data, multi-spectral image, etc. Therefore, we apply our algorithm on a set of MRI data including 181 brain images, which is also used in [10]. We add different percent of unbounded random noise to the image and demonstrate some of the results produced by our method in Fig.3.

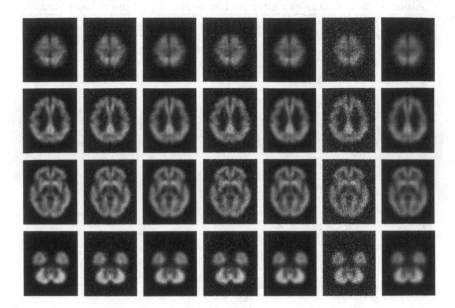

Fig. 3. Demonstration of the results produced by our algorithm (from left to right): original image, 5% corrupted image, recovered image from 5% corrupted noise; 10% corrupted image, recovered image from 10% noise; 30% corrupted image, recovered image from 30% corrupted noise

Our algorithm is able to find the structured data and separate the noise without the location of the corruption (about 30 percent of the data). Table.1 further provides quantitative results of our algorithm.

Table 1. Error correction for the brain MRI data

Percentage of Corruption	5%	10%	15%	20%	30%
Average PSNR (dB)	37.41	34.41	30.70	28.95	20.35

5.3   Background Subtraction

Another possible application of our algorithm is the background subtraction problem. Background substraction establishes a background model (the structured part) and segments the foreground object (sparse irregular pattern). For most of the video clip, redundancy is abundant. We conduct experiments on several video clips. Fig.4 demonstrates some of our results in one of the highly dynamic scenes. The results are comparable to the-state-of-art background subtraction algorithms.

Fig. 4. Background subtraction by our method (no filter is performed on the results)

5.4   Face Representation and Recognition

By the TensorFace in [1], we test our algorithm on the CMU PIE dataset, which contains 68 person under various viewpoints, expressions and illuminations. We use the same data set as [16] with the resolution at 64×64. For simplicity, only the five near frontal view under 21 different illuminations (105 images) of one person are used as training and the rest (65 images including the expressions) is for testing. Thus, we get a $5 \times 21 \times 68 \times 64 \times 64$ tensor. Then, the method learns a $5 \times 5 \times 68 \times 23 \times 22$ core tensor. Fig.5 compares the reconstructed faces with the original ones. We can see that the shadows have been removed. As a consequence, we achieve a competitive 94.3% accuracy by the recognition method in [19].

Fig. 5. Original Face (left) v.s. Reconstructed Face (right): the shadow caused by different illumination has been removed

6   Conclusion and Future Work

In this paper, we propose the optimal rank-$(R_1, R_2, ...R_n)$ tensor decomposition model. The model could automatically explore the low-dimensional structure of the tensor data seeking optimal dimension and basis for each mode and separating the irregular patterns. We are currently working on parameters and the optimization method of our model (e.g the proximal gradient), which may lead to better efficiency. We would also like to further explore additional applications and to investigate the theoretic side of our method in the future work.

References

1. Vasilescu, M.A.O., Terzopoulos, D.: Multilinear analysis of image ensembles: Tensorfaces. In: Heyden, A., Sparr, G., Nielsen, M., Johansen, P. (eds.) ECCV 2002. LNCS, vol. 2350, pp. 447–460. Springer, Heidelberg (2002)
2. Turk, M., Pentland, A.: Eigenfaces for recognition. J. Cognitive Neuroscience 3, 71–86 (1991)
3. Belhumeur, P.N., Hespanha, J.P., Kriegman, D.J.: Eigenfaces vs. fisherfaces: Recognition using class specific linear projection. IEEE Transactions on Pattern Analysis and Machine Intelligence 19, 711–720 (1997)
4. He, X., Niyogi, P.: Locality preserving projections. In: Neural Information Processing Systems, NIPS (2004)
5. Lewis, A., Knowles, G.: Image compression using the 2-d wavelet transform. IEEE Transactions on Image Processing 1, 244–250 (1992)
6. Itti, L., Koch, C., Niebur, E.: A model of saliency-based visual attention for rapid scene analysis. IEEE Transactions on Pattern Analysis and Machine Intelligence 20, 1254–1259 (1998)
7. Sheikh, Y., Shah, M.: Bayesian modeling of dynamic scenes for object detection. IEEE Transactions on Pattern Analysis and Machine Intelligence 27, 1778–1792 (2005)
8. Candès, E.J., Recht, B.: Exact matrix completion via convex optimization. Found. of Comput. Math. 9, 717–772 (2008)
9. Cai, J.F., Candes, E.J., Shen, Z.: A singular value thresholding algorithm for matrix completion (2008) (preprint)
10. Liu, J., Musialski, P., Wonka, P., Ye, J.: Tensor completion for estimating missing values in visual data. In: International Conference on Computer Vision, ICCV (2009)
11. Elad, M., Aharon, M.: Image denoising via sparse and redundant representations over learned dictionaries. IEEE Transactions on Image Processing 15, 3736–3745 (2006)
12. Wright, J., Ma, Y.: Dense error correction via ℓ^1-minimization (2008) (preprint), http://perception.csl.uiuc.edu/~jnwright/
13. Wright, J., Yang, A., Ganesh, A., Sastry, S., Ma, Y.: Robust face recognition via sparse representation. IEEE Transactions on Pattern Analysis and Machine Intelligence 31, 210–227 (2009)
14. Wright, J., Ganesh, A., Rao, S., Peng, Y., Ma, Y.: Robust principal component analysis: Exact recovery of corrupted low-rank matrices via convex optimization. In: Neural Information Processing Systems, NIPS (2009)
15. Cands, E., Li, X., Ma, Y., Wright, J.: Robust principal component analysis? (2009) (preprint)
16. He, X., Cai, D., Niyogi, P.: Tensor subspace analysis. In: Neural Information Processing Systems, NIPS (2005)
17. Xu, D., Yan, S., Zhang, L., Zhang, H.J., Liu, Z., Shum, H.Y.: Concurrent subspaces analysis. In: IEEE Conference on Computer Vision and Pattern Recognition (CVPR), vol. 2, pp. 203–208 (2005)

18. Vasilescu, M., Terzopoulos, D.: Multilinear subspace analysis of image ensembles. In: IEEE Conference on Computer Vision and Pattern Recognition (CVPR), vol. 2, pp. II – 93–II –9 (2003)
19. Vasilescu, M., Terzopoulos, D.: Multilinear projection for appearance-based recognition in the tensor framework. In: International Conference on Computer Vision (ICCV), pp. 1–8 (2007)
20. Wang, H., Ahuja, N.: A tensor approximation approach to? dimensionality reduction. International Journal of Computer Vision 76, 217–229 (2008)
21. Wang, H., Ahuja, N.: Facial expression decomposition. In: International Conference on Computer Vision (ICCV), vol. 2, pp. 958–965 (2003)
22. Jia, K., Gong, S.: Multi-modal tensor face for simultaneous super-resolution and recognition. In: International Conference on Computer Vision (ICCV), vol. 2, pp. 1683–1690 (2005)
23. Lathauwer, L.D., Moor, B.D., Vandewalle, J.: On the best rank-1 and rank-(r1,r2,.,rn) approximation of higher-order tensors. SIAM J. Matrix Anal. Appl. 21, 1324–1342 (2000)
24. Shashua, A., Levin, A.: Linear image coding for regression and classification using the tensor-rank principle. In: IEEE Conference on Computer Vision and Pattern Recognition (CVPR), vol. 1, pp. I–42–I–49 (2001)
25. Shashua, A., Zass, R., Hazan, T.: Multi-way clustering using super-symmetric non-negative tensor factorization. In: Leonardis, A., Bischof, H., Pinz, A. (eds.) ECCV 2006. LNCS, vol. 3954, pp. 595–608. Springer, Heidelberg (2006)
26. Kruskal, J.B.: Three-way arrays: rank and uniqueness of trilinear decompositions, with application to arithmetic complexity and statistics. Linear Algebra and its Applications 18, 95–138 (1977)
27. Zhou, Z., Li, X., Wright, J., Candes, E., Ma, Y.: Stable principal component pursuit. In: International Symposium on Information Theory (2010)
28. Hale, E.T., Yin, W., Zhang, Y.: Fixed-point continuation for l1-minimization: Methodology and convergence. SIAM Journal on Optim. 19, 1107–1130 (2008)
29. Tseng, P.: Convergence of a block coordinate descent method for nondifferentiable minimization. J. Optim. Theory Appl. 109, 475–494 (2001)
30. Simon, H.D.: The lanczos algorithm with partial reorthogonalization. Math. Comp. 42, 115–142 (1984)

Author Index

Printed in the United States
by Bookmasters

Printed in the United States
By Bookmasters